# SOCIAL
# PSYCHOLOGY

## second edition

# SOCIAL
## PSYCHOLOGY

second edition

David Myers, Jackie Abell and Fabio Sani

Mc
Graw
Hill
Education

London   Boston   Burr Ridge, IL   Dubuque, IA   Madison, WI   New York   San Francisco
St. Louis   Bangkok   Bogotá   Caracas   Kuala Lumpur   Lisbon   Madrid   Mexico City
Milan   Montreal   New Delhi   Santiago   Seoul   Singapore   Sydney   Taipei   Toronto

*Social Psychology, Second Edition*
David Myers, Jackie Abell, Fabio Sani
ISBN-13 9780077152352
ISBN-10 0077152352

Published by McGraw-Hill Education
Shoppenhangers Road
Maidenhead
Berkshire
SL6 2QL
Telephone: 44 (0) 1628 502 500
Fax: 44 (0) 1628 770 224
Website: www.mcgraw-hill.co.uk

**British Library Cataloguing in Publication Data**
A catalogue record for this book is available from the British Library

**Library of Congress Cataloguing in Publication Data**
The Library of Congress data for this book has been applied for from the Library of Congress

Executive Editor: Natalie Jacobs
Development Editor: Alexander Krause
Senior Production Editor: James Bishop
Marketing Manager: Geeta Kumar

Text Design by S R Nova Pvt Ltd, India
Cover design by Adam Renvoize
Printed and bound in the UK by Ashford Colour Press Ltd

First edition published in 2010 by McGraw-Hill Education

ISBN-13 9780077152352
ISBN-10 0077152352

# brief table of contents

# detailed table of contents

## 12 Social Categorization and Social Identity 483

## 13 Prejudice, Intergroup Relations and Conflict 523

# about the authors

## PROFESSOR DAVID MYERS

David Myers is the John Dirk Werkman Professor of Psychology at Michigan's Hope College, where students have voted him 'Outstanding Professor'. His love for teaching psychology is manifest in his writings for the lay public. His articles have appeared in two dozen magazines, and he has authored or co-authored a dozen books, including *The Pursuit of Happiness* (Avon, 1993) and *Intuition: Its Powers and Perils* (Yale University Press, 2002). Also an award-winning researcher, he received the Gordon Allport Prize from Division 9 of the American Psychological Association for his work on group polarization. His scientific articles have appeared in more than two dozen journals, including *Science, American Scientist, Psychological Science* and *The American Psychologist*. He has served his discipline as consulting editor to the *Journal of Experimental Social Psychology* and the *Journal of Personality and Social Psychology*. In his spare time he has chaired his city's Human Relations Commission, helped found a community action agency that assists impoverished families, and spoken to dozens of collegiate and religious groups.

## DR JACKIE ABELL

Dr Jackie Abell is a Reader in Social Psychology at Conventry University, UK. She is also the Director of Research for the African Lion & Environmental Research Trust. Jackie was involved in the five-year longitudinal qualitative research project 'Nationals & Migrants: Constitutional Change and Identity' (funded by the Leverhulme Trust), which examined the impact devolution in the UK had on British, English and Scottish national identity. Her current areas of interest include the application of social psychology to conservation and environmental issues, national identity and football support, place and identity, and social inclusion.

## PROFESSOR FABIO SANI

Professor Fabio Sani holds a Chair in Social Psychology at the University of Dundee. His general research interest concerns group processes and social identity, with special emphasis on the cognitive, affective, behavioural, and health implications of group identification. At present he is leading 'Health in Groups', a cross-national and longitudinal research projects on the health implications of group life, funded by the UK-based Economic and Social Research Council. His scientific articles are regularly published in international journals such as *Personality & Social Psychology Bulletin, Journal of Experimental Social Psychology*, and *Developmental Psychology*. He has also co-authored *Experimental Design and Statistics for Psychology* (Blackwell, 2006), co-edited *The Development of the Social Self* (Psychology Press, 2004), and edited *Self-Continuity: Individual and Collective Perspectives* (Psychology Press, 2008). He has served his discipline as consulting editor to the *European Journal of Social Psychology, British Journal of Social Psychology, British Journal of Developmental Psychology*, and *Social and Personality Psychology Compass*.

# preface

If you've ever wondered, 'Why does that person behave differently when they're on their own, compared to when they're with a group?' or, 'Why are some people much more aggressive than others?' or even, 'What factors have led to me being attracted to my partner?' then you've come to the right place. These are the types of questions that social psychology, and hence this book, seeks to address and while much of human behaviour and relationships remains a mystery, the research conducted in this discipline thus far can at least provide us with some partial answers to these questions.

The first edition was a solid foundation and using invaluable reviewer feedback, we have built upon this in a number of ways in order to create a book which we feel will be factually rigorous, yet an accessible and compelling read. First, we have included up-to-date references to international research throughout, so that it provides a global overview of the discipline and also closely matches European teaching.

Second: we introduced a lot of new material in the first edition, including models and theories that the US edition hadn't covered. For this edition we have made sure that these models and theories are explained in depth, to facilitate a greater understanding of their importance to the relevant topics. We have also added others, such as the Broken Window Theory and Door-in-the-Face Technique, where needed. Third: the social world is changing rapidly, thanks in no small part to the likes of social media. To reflect this, we have added coverage of the impact that the internet and social media are having on the discipline of social psychology, and we have also included social neuroscience material where appropriate, as this field is gaining prominence.

Finally, as the issues of the validity of published research and the ability to replicate experiments have affected the field of social psychology and of science in general, we have decided to address this in the book, by taking a more critical approach to the content and including opposing theories and viewpoints where possible. We want students to think deeply about the content and constantly question theories and models to see if they are valid or can be improved, thus ultimately helping to drive forward the field of social psychology.

## Organization and Hallmark Features

The second edition has undergone a number of structural changes, following reviewer feedback, in order to help the book offer more flexibility and fluidity with its coverage. Although the structure remains largely intact from the previous edition, we have removed the 'parts' sections, which governed this structure. We felt that some of the chapters were wedged into parts topics that didn't wholly reflect the full scope of these chapters. Removing these, we feel, will allow a greater flexibility for the teaching and learning of these topics and will aid the narrative of the story of social psychology.

As a result, we have moved the chapter on Persuasion, so that it now follows Attitudes and Behaviour, and comes before Conformity and Obedience. Persuasion and Attitudes are frequently treated in conjunction with one another, so it thus makes sense for them to sit together.

The effect of Genes, Culture and Gender can often be felt within the topics of the other chapters, so we moved this chapter to the end of the book, where we can use it to draw together the key themes presented and act as a treatise on the genes (nature) versus culture (nurture) debate, with gender serving as the active example for the two different sides.

Finally, we have moved chapter 15 on Applied Social Psychology to the website. While it is very useful, we feel that it is more important to include applications of social psychology throughout each individual chapter, so that topics are easier to understand and have real-world context. Consequently, we have looked at the pedagogy of the previous edition and have revised or included new features in order to provide a better fit for this remit.

**Research Close-Up:** This feature has been substantially altered from the first edition, so that it now follows the layout of published journal articles. We are aware that research articles, when first encountered, can be pretty daunting to read due to their length and complexity. Our Research Close-Ups help ease the transition into a heavier focus on article-based learning by detailing the scientific explorations and research methods used by social psychologists succinctly, making them an accessible version of published papers.

**Focus On:** Fully revised from the first edition, this feature has been standardised across the book and now looks at controversial research, opposing viewpoints or alternative approaches to topics presented in each chapter. By doing this we offer a more critical outlook on these topics and with the aid of a couple of questions, encourage deeper, more judicious thinking.

**Recommended Reading:** Brand new to this edition, each chapter now has a number of further readings, which can be used as a springboard for further consideration of the topics discussed. We have split these up into 'Classic' and 'Contemporary' readings so that pertinent developments in the subject over the years can easily be seen.

**Critical Questions:** Updated from the previous edition, the book now contains more holistic questions at the end of each chapter about the subjects covered, prompting a deeper, critical reflection on the issues raised.

**Summing Up:** In the previous edition a summary was presented at the end of each section of a chapter. These have now been collated and appear at the end of the chapter which has enabled the book to have a better narrative flow to it. The summary remains to be broken up by section heading, making it easy to go back to sections that need reading through again.

## Updates to the Second Edition

### CHAPTER 1: INTRODUCING SOCIAL PSYCHOLOGY

- ☐ We've added more in this chapter to explain why the book mainly focuses on findings produced by experiments, and
- ☐ We have also added a small introduction to the intra- and inter-group relations chapters (11, 12 and 13).

### CHAPTER 2: RESEARCH METHODS IN SOCIAL PSYCHOLOGY

- ☐ This chapter has been revised to show the relevance of quantitative and qualitative research methods to the subject of social psychology in particular, before delving deeper into what the various methods are and how they can be used for real life research projects.
- ☐ New Focus On: The Importance of Replication.

### CHAPTER 3: THE SELF

- ☐ This chapter has been revised to include more recent research throughout, as well as additional content on self-presentation online. There is also an introduction to Social Identity, which is covered in more depth in chapter 12.
- ☐ The sections on self-presentation, self-handicapping and impression management have been re-ordered and revised to provide a more logical flow to the topics.

- [ ] A new section on The Self and its Brain investigates the underlying social cognitive neuroscience that affects one's sense of self.

- [ ] New Focus On: Are We Witnessing an Epidemic of Narcissism among Younger Generations?

## CHAPTER 4: SOCIAL BELIEFS AND JUDGEMENTS

- [ ] This chapter has been updated to include more recent research throughout and we have added coverage of social cognition, as this is an increasingly prominent field.

- [ ] Inclusion of a new section on social encoding, which includes Solomon Asch's studies of person perception.

- [ ] Expanded section on social judgements to cover the impact of social neuroscience in this area.

- [ ] More content on attribution and attribution theories has been added throughout.

- [ ] New Research Close-Up: Can the Way We Retrieve Information from Memory Affect how We Judge Other People?

- [ ] Focus On: How Do We Know if We are Poor Judges of Social Reality or Highly Efficient at these Judgements? has been revised and expanded upon.

## CHAPTER 5: ATTITUDES AND BEHAVIOUR

- [ ] We have updated this chapter to provide greater depth of some of the topics we covered in the first edition. As such, Formation of Attitudes and Function of Attitudes have been separated into their own sections and have been expanded upon. An expanded introduction also goes into more depth on the ABC model.

- [ ] Implicit attitudes and the implicit association test are gone into in greater detail.

- [ ] Expanded coverage of instrumental learning.

- [ ] Expanded coverage of the theory of planned behaviour.

- [ ] New Research Close-Up: Development and Validation of a Scale Measuring Attitudes towards Non-Drinkers.

- [ ] New Focus On: Do Attitudes to Conservation and the Environment Predict Protective Behaviours towards Wildlife?

## CHAPTER 6: PERSUASION

- [ ] This chapter was already strong in terms of its coverage, but it has been updated to include more recent research in the area and a few more theories.

- [ ] New coverage of the Sleeper Effect.

- [ ] New coverage of the Door-in-the-Face Technique.

- [ ] New coverage of the Broken Window Theory.

- [ ] New Research Close-Up: I Know I Like This Brand but Did I Like the Ad?

- [ ] New Research Close-Up: Adult Perceptions of Neighbourhood Safety.

- [ ] New Focus On: The Lucifer Effect: Bad Apples or Bad Barrels?

## CHAPTER 7: CONFORMITY AND OBEDIENCE

- [ ] We have added a discussion about the ecological validity of laboratory experiments on conformity and obedience, as well as adding new references.

- ☐ Expanded coverage of minority influence.

- ☐ New coverage of social impact theory.

- ☐ New section on Conformity as Entertainment, which includes UK/European replications of the Milgram experiment.

- ☐ New Research Close-Up: Judging our Own and Others' Behaviour.

- ☐ New Focus On: The Ordinary Monster.

## CHAPTER 8: AGGRESSION

- ☐ This chapter was already a good match to current teaching, but we have added coverage on non-intentional aggression and direct/indirect aggression to balance out the intentional side.

- ☐ Expanded coverage on gender, gene, hormone and neural influences on aggression.

- ☐ New analysis of hate crimes.

- ☐ New Research Close-Up: Harassment Online.

- ☐ New Focus On: Teaching Them a Lesson: Motivations for Driver Aggression.

## CHAPTER 9: ATTRACTION AND INTIMACY

- ☐ There's no denying the impact that the internet has had on attraction and intimacy, and as a result, this chapter has a new section on internet dating, with up-to-date references. We have also acknowledged the imbalance of coverage with respect to LGBT individuals, compared to their heterosexual counterparts, and have tried to address this throughout.

- ☐ New sections on similarity and liking; passionate love and neuroscience; Rusbelt and commitment; and forgiveness.

- ☐ Expanded coverage of attachments.

- ☐ Expanded coverage of why relationships flourish and fail.

- ☐ New Research Close-Up: Does Love Mean Never Having to Say You're Sorry?

- ☐ New Focus On: Sexuality and Attraction, Are There Real Differences?

## CHAPTER 10: HELPING

- ☐ The act of helping doesn't just occur in emergency situations and thus we have added examples of helping in other contexts throughout and our new Research Close-Up reflects this added coverage. We have also updated references and noted the difference between the bystander effect and political inaction.

- ☐ Expanded coverage of helping on the internet.

- ☐ Expanded coverage of the effect of guilt on helping.

- ☐ New Research Close-Up: Young Children Are Intrinsically Motivated to see Others Helped.

- ☐ Revised Research Close-Up: Identity and Emergency Intervention.

## CHAPTER 11: SMALL GROUP PROCESSES

- ☐ This chapter now contains the topic of sports psychology and we have consolidated the coverage on leadership, which used to be split across several chapters, into this one.

- ☐ New section on the structure and composition of groups.

☐ New coverage on the negative power minorities may hold over the majority.

☐ New Research Close-Up: An Experiment on the Social Facilitation of Gambling Behaviour.

☐ New Research Close-Up: The Relationship between Group Cohesion, Groups Norms and Perceived Social Loafing in Soccer Teams.

☐ New Focus On: Have Small Group Processes such as Risky Shift and Groupthink Contributed to Cyber-Bullying?

## CHAPTER 12: SOCIAL CATEGORIZATION AND SOCIAL IDENTITY

☐ We have included a new, large section on Social Identity and Health, which explores the ways in which the two topics are connected and influence each other.

☐ Expanded Social Identity and Help section, with a cross link to chapter 10.

☐ New Research Close-Up: Laughing: The Influence of the In-Group.

## CHAPTER 13: PREJUDICE, INTERGROUP RELATIONS AND CONFLICT

☐ This chapter has been revised, with the topic of prejudice coming first, followed by intergroup conflict and then intergroup harmony. This has been done to create a more logical flow to the chapter, making it easier to understand prejudicial behaviours and conflicts and the methods that can be used to combat these. This has also facilitated more discussion of individual prejudice before moving on to a discussion of group prejudice.

☐ Social Identity Theory and Self-Categorization Theory section has been expanded to include 'basking in reflected glory' and 'cutting off reflected failure'.

☐ New coverage of the linguistic intergroup bias.

☐ New section on 'dual identities', covering the idea that minority group members may hold superordinate and subordinate identities.

☐ New Focus On: Is Prejudice all in our Heads?

## CHAPTER 14: GENES, CULTURE AND GENDER

☐ A new introduction draws together all of the chapters and uses gender as an example to further explore the complexities of the topics discussed throughout the book.

☐ Gender and Culture: Doing as the Culture Says? section has been expanded.

☐ New Research Close-Up: Gender Wording in Job Advertisements Leads to Gender Inequality.

☐ New Focus On: Mind The Gap: From Sexed Brains to Gendered Behaviour.

We hope that you enjoy studying social psychology, or find this book useful for teaching the subject. Any feedback that you may have on the second edition would be very welcome. Happy reading!

Jackie Abell and Fabio Sani

# acknowledgements

## Authors' acknowledgements

We would like to thank friends, colleagues and anonymous reviewers who suggested material and offered advice in revising the chapters. We would also like to thank our editors, Natalie Jacobs and Alexander Krause, for their involved and continued support.

Jackie Abell gives particular thanks to her colleagues and peers in social psychology for helpful discussions that have helped shape this book.

Fabio Sani is particularly grateful to his colleagues in the Development and Identity Group at Dundee University, School of Psychology, for useful discussions; and would like to extend special thanks to his wife, Lorella, and his son, Leonardo, for their support and patience during the project.

## Publisher's acknowledgements

Our special thanks go to Lin Bailey at Southampton Solent University and Emma Vine at Sheffield Hallam University for their contributions to the book.

Our thanks go to the following reviewers for their comments at various stages in the text's development:

Nazar Akrami, Uppsala University

Alison Attril, De Montfort University

Lucy Betts, Nottingham Trent University

Richard Cooke, Aston University

Ute Gabriel, Norwegian University of Science and Technology

Ilka Gleibs, University of Surrey

Tobias Greitemeyer, Universitat Innsbruck

Johan Karremans, Radboud Nijmegen University

John Kremer, Queen's University Belfast

Ingela Lundin Kvalem, University of Oslo

Silas Makhubela, University of Pretoria

Robert Nash, University of Surrey

Johan Naslund, Linköping

Mzikazi Ndunda, University of the Witwatersrand

Calum Neill, Napier University

Sture Njord, Karlstad University

Paddy O'Donnell, University of Glasgow

Georgina Randsley de Maura, University of Kent

Afsane Riazi, Royal Holloway, University of London

Ron Roberts, Kingston University

Gerhard Schwar, University of Johannesburg

Sana Sheikh, University of St Andrews

Shaun Speed, University of Manchester

Chris Stiff, Keele University

Ian Tucker, University of East London

Joop van der Plight, University of Amsterdam

Jan Willem van Prooijen, Vrije Universiteit Amsterdam

We would also like to thank all the reviewers who commented and advised on the first edition.

We would like to thank the following for their contributions to our digital support materials:

Gary Huggs, Lancaster University
Kirsty Miller, University of Dundee

We would like to thank the following for permission to reprint images:

Alamy Images

Corbis Images

Dreamstime

Getty Images

iStock Images

Liberty

# guided tour

## Research Close-Up

Research Close-Up boxes introduce you to the format of real research in social psychology. Each box summarizes an important research paper, explaining the methods the authors used, the results they obtained and a discussion to help you think critically about the significance of the study.

## Focus On

These boxes focus on opposing viewpoints or controversial topics and research that are related to each chapter. They are supported by questions to help you think critically about the topic and challenge preconceptions.

## Key Terms

These are highlighted and defined in the margins. An ideal tool for last-minute revision or to check definitions as you read.

## Summing Up

Use this section at the end of the chapter to check your understanding of the core theories and concepts.

## Critical Questions

Each chapter concludes with a set of questions that have been designed to help students critically reflect on the topics and discussions raised in the chapter.

## Recommended Reading

Use the recommended reading section at the end of each chapter as a starting point for further research.

## www.mcgraw-hill.co.uk/textbooks/myers

Students- Helping you to Connect, Learn and Succeed

Take advantage of study tools offered to reinforce the material you have read in the text and to develop your knowledge of social psychology in a fun way.

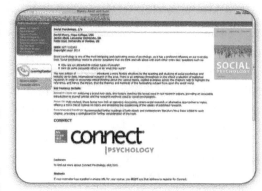

*Self-test questions* to prepare you for mid-term tests and exams

*Glossary* of key terms to revise core concepts

*Web links* to online sources of information to help you prepare for class

Lecturer support- Helping you to help your students

The Online Learning Centre also offers lecturers adopting this book a range of resources designed to support teaching and help you deliver your course:

☐ *Lecturer's Manual* to support your module preparation, with case notes, guide answers, teaching tips and more

☐ *PowerPoint presentations* to use in lecture presentations

☐ *Image library* of artwork from the textbook

☐ *Seminar suggestions* to support interactive and engaging seminars and workshops

To request your password to access these resources, contact your McGraw-Hill Education representative or visit www.mcgraw-hill.co.uk/textbooks/myers

## Test Bank available in McGraw-Hill EZ Test Online

A test bank of hundreds of questions is available to lecturers adopting this book for their module through the EZ Test online website. For each chapter you will find:

☐ A range of multiple choice, true or false, short answer or essay questions

☐ Questions identified by type, difficulty, and topic to help you to select questions that best suit your needs

McGraw-Hill EZ Test Online is:

☐ **Accessible** anywhere with an internet connection – your unique login provides you access to all your tests and material in any location

☐ **Simple** to set up and easy to use

☐ **Flexible,** offering a choice from question banks associated with your adopted textbook or allowing you to create your own questions

☐ **Comprehensive,** with access to hundreds of banks and thousands of questions created for other McGraw-Hill titles

☐ **Compatible** with Blackboard and other course management systems enabling you to deploy tests seamlessly through your VLE

☐ **Time-saving-** students' tests can be immediately marked and results and feedback delivered directly to your students to help them to monitor their progress.

To register for this FREE resource, visit www.eztestonline.com

# connect®
## PSYCHOLOGY

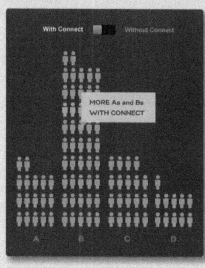

McGraw-Hill Connect Psychology is a learning and teaching environment that improves student performance and outcomes whilst promoting engagement and comprehension of content.

You can utilize publisher-provided materials, or add your own content to design a complete course to help your students achieve higher outcomes.

PROVEN EFFECTIVE

## INSTRUCTORS

### With McGraw-Hill Connect Psychology, instructors get:

- ☐ Simple **assignment management,** allowing you to spend more time teaching.

- ☐ **Auto-graded** assignments, quizzes and tests, including video material and interactive excercises.

- ☐ **Detailed visual reporting** where students and section results can be viewed and analysed.

- ☐ Sophisticated **online testing** capability.

- ☐ A **filtering and reporting** function that allows you to easily assign and report on materials that are correlated to learning outcomes, topics, level of difficulty, and more. Reports can be accessed for individual students or the whole class, as well as offering the ability to drill into individual assignments, questions or categories.

- ☐ **Instructor materials** to help supplement your course.

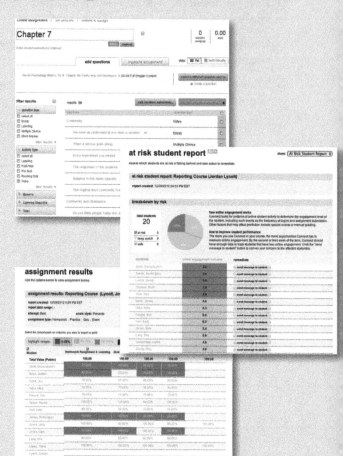

# Get Connected. Get Results.

## STUDENTS

**With McGraw-Hill Connect psychology, students get:**

**Assigned content**

- ☐ Easy **online access** to homework, tests and quizzes.

- ☐ **Immediate feedback** and 24-hour tech support.

## MATERIALS

### Social Sense Videos

Video clips help to bring social psychology topics to life; they offer a range of coverage including footage of classic experiments. The videos are supported by questions which help ensure the key concepts have been understood.

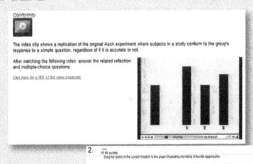

### Interactive Activities

Interactive Activities are designed to reinforce textbook concepts and aim at a higher level of understanding and application. The activities provided feature seamless assignability and automatic grading capabilities, and a variety of assessment types including click-and-drag and multiple choice.

### Pre- and Post-test Quizzes

These quizzes help to test the concepts and theories from each chapter to ensure that students understand and learn the key components from the chapter coverage. They take a multiple choice format so that they can be automatically marked and students can receive immediate feedback if desired.

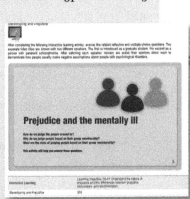

## Let us help make our content your solution

At McGraw-Hill Education our aim is to help lecturers to find the most suitable content for their needs delivered to their students in the most appropriate way. Our **custom publishing solutions** offer the ideal combination of content delivered in the way which best suits lecturer and students.

Our custom publishing programme offers lecturers the opportunity to select just the chapters or sections of material they wish to deliver to their students from a database called CREATE™ at

### www.mcgrawhillcreate.co.uk

CREATE™ contains over two million pages of content from:

☐ textbooks

☐ professional books

☐ case books – Harvard Articles, Insead, Ivey, Darden, Thunderbird and BusinessWeek

☐ Taking Sides – debate materials

Across the following imprints:

☐ McGraw-Hill Education

☐ Open University Press

☐ Harvard Business Publishing

☐ US and European material

There is also the option to include additional material authored by lecturers in the custom product – this does not necessarily have to be in English.

We will take care of everything from start to finish in the process of developing and delivering a custom product to ensure that lecturers and students receive exactly the material needed in the most suitable way.

With a Custom Publishing Solution, students enjoy the best selection of material deemed to be the most suitable for learning everything they need for their courses – something of real value to support their learning. Teachers are able to use exactly the material they want, in the way they want, to support their teaching on the course.

Please contact your local McGraw-Hill Education representative with any questions or alternatively contact Warren Eelse: **warren.eels@mheducation.com**.

"Man is by nature a social animal."

Aristotle, 350 BC

# INTRODUCING SOCIAL PSYCHOLOGY

## WHAT IS SOCIAL PSYCHOLOGY?

To begin a textbook on social psychology we need first to define what we mean by social psychology. So, what is it about?

**social psychology** *the scientific study of how people think about, relate to, and influence one another, either interpersonally or within groups*

Social psychology is interested in the way people think about and subjectively experience themselves and their social world, as well as in the way people influence and relate to one another in either interpersonal exchanges or group settings. More specifically, we can say that social psychology deals with both *'within skins'* issues (the 'thinking' and experiential aspect of our social existence, which includes self-concept, perceptions, emotions, motivation, values and attitudes) and *'between skins'* issues (the relational dimension of social life, which includes interaction, communication and mutual influence among individuals and groups). (See Figure 1.1 for a schematic illustration of what social psychology is about).

Because it is interested in a vast and diverse range of phenomena, social psychology intersects with various other disciplines. Social psychologists share interests in common with sociologists, anthropologists, philosophers, linguists, biologists and neuroscientists. In addition, social psychological research and theory may have implications for other branches of psychology, including cognitive, neurological, organizational, personality, developmental, clinical and health psychology (see Figure 1.1).

The structure of this textbook is based around some of the main areas which social psychologists have studied and researched to understand human social behaviour.

Most of us are interested in social behaviour, or at least some aspects of it. You probably wouldn't be studying or reading about social psychology if you weren't. However, there are important differences between lay people and social psychologists' way of looking at people's social relationships and behaviour. You may have a hunch about why someone has behaved in the way they have in a particular set of circumstances, but social psychologists try to investigate *how*

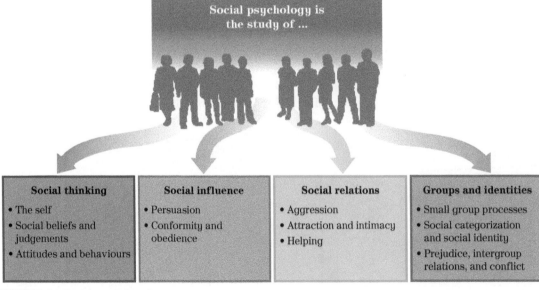

**FIGURE 1.1** Social psychology is...

and *why* that behaviour has occurred. This requires established methods to collect evidence of the behaviour and systematically analyse it, comparing it to existing research and social psychological theory. Sometimes the conclusions reached by lay people and social psychologists are very different, which can make social psychological discoveries surprising and intriguing. But, of course, there are times when social psychology confirms what we already thought.

As we shall see throughout this textbook, how social psychologists go about studying these aspects of humans' social and cultural life are varied. They don't always agree. Yet, taken together, these studies offer us a comprehensive investigation of human social behaviour and food for thought as we develop our knowledge.

## A BRIEF HISTORY OF SOCIAL PSYCHOLOGY

To begin to understand how these diverse perspectives came to exist in their current form let us briefly explore the history of social psychology and some of its early influences (see Table 1.1 for a summary).

At a first glance it can appear that social psychology is fairly modern. The first social psychology experiments were reported barely more than a century ago (1898), and the first social psychology texts did not appear until just before and after 1900, in France, Italy, the USA and Germany (Smith, 2005). In the 1930s social psychology took on its current form, and after the Second World War it emerged as the vibrant field it is today.

But an interest in social psychological issues has a much longer history than this.

In the eighteenth century, important contributions to social psychological theorizing were given by both European and North American scholars. For instance, the British philosopher David Hume wrote the *Treatise on Human Nature* (1739), which dealt with *passions* or strong emotions, sympathy and the relation between self and others. He thought sympathy contributed to social conformity and is the basis of our attachment to society. In 1742 he also wrote an essay about the cause and content of national characters, stating that there are differences in frequencies of national traits. This was a forerunner for the notable American social psychologist Gordon Allport's later classic work *The Nature of Prejudice* (1954). Another British thinker, the economist Adam Smith, considered the formation of the 'self'. In his book *The Theory of Moral Sentiments* (1759), he reasoned that the person we become is largely shaped by interactions with other people. Adam Smith used metaphors like the 'mirror' and the 'looking glass self', which were later adopted by Charles H. Cooley and George Herbert Mead, who made important theoretical contributions to how the self develops (see Chapter 3 for a more detailed description).

Social psychological theorizing was also evident in Germany in the eighteenth century. The philosopher Immanuel Kant concerned himself with psychological topics such as knowledge, feeling, the self, how people manipulate each other, the inclination for power, and characters of people. He argued that the study of humans should involve a study of the 'whole mind' to understand human experience of the world. Kant's 'holistic' ideas informed gestalt psychology, which emphasizes how the mind constructs reality and perceptually orders the world (see Figure 1.2 for

*gestalt psychology a German school of psychology advocating a holistic theory of mind and brain, focusing on how these actively structure our perceptions and impressions. It emphasizes that one needs to look at the comprehensive situation to fully understand the human conscious experience, asserting 'the whole is more than the sum of its parts'*

**TABLE 1.1** Summary of some prominent figures and their contribution to social psychology

| Name | Dates | Country of origin | Examples of their contribution to social psychology |
|---|---|---|---|
| David Hume | 1711–76 | Scotland | 'Of national characters' (1742) influenced later work on prejudice (such as Gordon Allport) that emphasizes trait explanations for behaviour |
| Adam Smith | 1723–90 | Scotland | *The Theory of Moral Sentiments* (1759) influences some modern-day thinking on the self |
| Immanuel Kant | 1724–1804 | Germany | Theorizing on the mind influenced the subsequent rise of gestalt psychology |
| Johann Friedrich Herbart | 1776–1841 | Germany | Emphasizes the social aspects of the self. These ideas shaped the later development of *Völkerpsychologie* (mass psychology) |
| Auguste Comte | 1798–1857 | France | Argues that the methods used in the natural sciences could be used in the social sciences. The principle of positivism subsequently enters social psychology |
| Wilhelm Wundt | 1832–1920 | Germany | Develops *Völkerpsychologie*. Advocates the use of laboratories to study human mental processes. Known as the founding father of experimental psychology |
| Gustave Le Bon | 1841–1931 | France | *La psychologie des foules* (1895) influenced modern-day psychology of the crowd, intergroup relations and aggression |
| William James | 1842–1910 | USA | The founder of American psychology. Produces the book *Principles of Psychology* (1890). Around this time social psychology becomes a discipline in its own right |
| Emile Durkheim | 1858–1917 | France | Distinguishes between individual and collective thought. His ideas contributed to theorizing on language, social interactions and 'Social Representations Theory' |
| George Herbert Mead | 1863–1931 | USA | Lectures and publications on self and society influence modern theorizing on language and communication |
| Edward Alsworth Ross | 1866–1951 | USA | Produces American textbook *Social Psychology* (1908) |
| William McDougall | 1871–1938 | England | Writes textbook *An Introduction to Social Psychology* (1908) |
| Kurt Lewin | 1890–1947 | Germany | Gestalt psychologist. His theorizing on prejudice, intergroup relations, leadership and decision making contributes to present-day social psychology |
| Floyd Allport | 1890–1978 | USA | Publishes social psychology textbook (1924), emphasizing individual processes in understanding human behaviour |
| Gordon Allport | 1897–1967 | USA | Focuses on the role of personality traits to understand social psychological topics such as prejudice |

**FIGURE 1.2** Two faces or a vase? Gestalt psychologists have used visual illusions such as Rubin's Goblet to illustrate the point that the mind creatively constructs reality.

an example). The social psychologist Kurt Lewin (1930s) took a gestaltic approach to the analysis of social interaction and group behaviour, which implied an examination of the whole situation rather than some isolated elements of it. Lewin's 'action research' tried to understand and tackle prejudice, and foster positive intergroup relations. His research remains influential in social psychology today.

Johann Friedrich Herbart stressed the inextricable link between individual and society, by contending that the 'human being is nothing outside society'. Many believe that Herbart is the founder of social psychology as his ideas were taken up in Central Europe and later influenced social psychological work in England, the USA and the rest of the world, either directly or indirectly.

Herbart inspired German scholars who first formulated *Völkerpsychologie*, a German word for mass psychology or the psychology of the people, which was established in 1879. *Völkerpsychologie* is typically associated with the work of Wilhelm Wundt, who saw it as concerning 'those mental products which are created by a community of human life and are, therefore, inexplicable in terms merely of individual consciousness since they presuppose the reciprocal action of many' (1916, p. 3). However, Wundt did not dismiss individual mental functions as irrelevant, and advocated the use of laboratories to investigate perception, mental disorders and abnormal behaviour. As a consequence, he is often referred to as the 'father of experimental psychology'.

*Völkerpsychologie sometimes called mass psychology, folk psychology or 'the psychology of the people'. It claims that people who belong to the same social group(s) tend to think in the same way, holding collective beliefs, norms and values*

Topics studied in social psychology today were also analysed by scholars in nineteenth-century France, for instance, by the philosopher Auguste Comte (1798–1857), who is regarded by many as one of the founding fathers of social psychology. He certainly had an influence on the methods social psychologists use to study behaviour. Comte is best known for his claim that social phenomena can be studied by the same methods as those used in natural science since there are general laws existing in all sciences, and the aim for the researchers is to reveal them by 'positivistic' methods (positivism). As we shall see, this claim has gained increasing popularity over the years.

positivism *an approach to science that claims true knowledge can be achieved only through sense perception and empirical investigation*

Towards the end of the nineteenth century the work of Gustave Le Bon, captured in his book *Psychologie des foules* (*The Crowd*) (1895) had an enormous impact, and continues to do so, in modern social psychology (see Chapter 13). Gordon Allport declared it 'Perhaps the most influential book ever written in social psychology' (Allport, 1954, p. 35). Émile Durkheim was another influential French social scientist in this period making important contributions to social psychology, noting a distinction between individual thought and collective thought. He suggested that collective thought was social ideas and values which exist independently of individuals but at the same time have great influence on individual ways of thinking. Durkheim's work shaped the later theorizing of Serge Moscovici who produced 'social representations theory', a flourishing field in European social psychology in recent years (see Chapter 4), which emphasizes the role of language and shared social understandings of the world in guiding our behaviour.

Perhaps controversially, Norman Triplett (1898) is often credited with carrying out the first social psychology experiment provoked by his observation that people's behaviour is often facilitated by the presence of other people. He had noticed that cyclists rode their bikes quicker when racing someone else than they did when racing themselves against the clock. To test this he asked girls and boys aged 8–17 to wind in fishing rods. The 'experiment' had two conditions. In one condition the young people competed against one another. In the other condition, they wound in the rods as fast as they could alone, and against the clock. He found that in the first condition the fishing rods were wound up much quicker. So, the presence of others did seem to facilitate some behaviour. Despite disagreements concerning whether it was truly an experiment or not, this study is an important stepping stone in what became social psychology's fascination with laboratory experiments in its quest for facts about human social behaviour. It also became important in social psychology's sought-after status as a 'science'. In Chapter 2 we consider in

Johann Friedrich Herbart (1776–1841), thought by many to be the founding father of social psychology.

SOURCE: © Getty Images

Wilhelm Wundt (1832–1920), the father of experimental psychology.
SOURCE: © Getty Images

The presence of others can facilitate our behaviour. Athletes often produce their 'personal best' performance when competing against others.
SOURCE: © P_Wei/iStock

William James (1842–1910), the founder of North American psychology.
SOURCE: © Getty Images

more detail the principles and practices of experiments in our exploration of the many methods social psychologists use. Throughout this textbook we examine many laboratory and field experiments and scientific studies of various aspects of human social behaviour.

In the second half of the nineteenth century social psychology was given its name and became a discipline in its own right. Ways of thinking about social relationships had emigrated to the USA and continents outside Europe, including colonies in Africa, Asia and Australia. Social psychology soon became a well-known discipline in many places in the world. Not least in the New World, in the United States of America.

William James is generally regarded as the founder of North American psychology and, in his renowned *Principles of Psychology* (1890), he deals with what he calls the 'social self', meaning 'the recognition [a man] gets from his mates'. He went on to say that '*a man has as many social selves as there are individuals who recognize him* and carry an image of him in their mind' (James, 1890, vol. 1, pp. 293–4, emphasis in original).

George Herbert Mead also became a famous name in (sociological) social psychology, especially his analysis of the self (see Chapter 3). His works were published posthumously in the 1930s but he was formulating his ideas about social psychology at the turn of the nineteenth century. From 1901 he gave an annual course in social psychology at the University of Michigan. His lectures were later published under the title *Mind, Self and Society; from the Standpoint of a Social Behaviourist* (Mead, 1934). Mead was an original thinker combining Darwinism with other scientific issues including communication. This was one of his most important contributions to social psychology.

### 1908: A CRUCIAL YEAR?

The year 1908 has been said to be crucial in social psychology since two textbooks with social psychology in the title were published. The two textbooks were both looking more backwards than forwards. In England, William McDougall's book *An Introduction to Social Psychology* (1908) was heavily influenced by evolutionary theory and the work of Charles Darwin. McDougall had the idea that instinctive dispositions were part of our evolutionary heritage and that these instincts made human social life possible. Evolutionary psychology remains part of modern-day social psychology. The other book published in 1908 was Edward Alsworth Ross's *Social Psychology*. Ross was an American sociologist who had originally trained as an economist. Unlike McDougall, Ross did not take Darwinism as his point of departure but focused on the relationship between individuals and their group, discussing topics like social influence, crowds and control. His book was very successful on first publication and the issues presented in it are still relevant in social psychology.

*evolutionary psychology a field of study that looks at the role of evolutionary processes and principles of natural selection in shaping cognition and behaviour*

These two textbooks managed to put the name 'social psychology' more generally on the map. However, from our journey so far you can see that social psychology did not start that year; the phrase 'social psychology' had been used several times before by other scholars and social scientists.

At the time these two textbooks were published, social psychology became established in the USA. Social psychology in the USA became an empirical and even experimental social science. In fact by the 1940s and 1950s, the USA characterized much of social psychology. Large research centres were founded and developed for social psychological research.

However, a social psychology that was dominated by the USA reflected the history and ideological values of individualism which characterized the USA. Floyd Allport had published a famous textbook on social psychology in 1924 that focused more on the individual than on the social or the group. For Allport there was nothing about the group or social relations that couldn't be explained as a function of the individuals concerned.

"There is no psychology of groups which is not essentially and entirely a psychology of individuals."
   Allport, 1924

So, if we quickly summarize, the first 'social psychologists' were scholars engaged in analytical reflection, intellectual and logical thinking. However, from the eighteenth century there began a search for empirical methods to better understand the topic studied: man and his social relationships. With the advance of the scientific method in the natural sciences, social psychology departed even further from its philosophical roots and became increasingly concerned with scientific empiricism in its quest for knowledge about human social behaviour.

## THE 'CRISIS' IN SOCIAL PSYCHOLOGY

With its increasing emphasis on individual psychology some social psychologists became concerned that social psychology was beginning to lose its 'social' aspect. In the late 1960s and early 1970s, some serious questions were being asked about the direction of the discipline. In particular, there were concerns about over-reliance on experimental methods at the expense of more naturalistic approaches such as observation and interviewing, and about excessive emphasis on individuals *as individuals* rather than as parts of more complex social, historical, cultural and political contexts.

Dissatisfied social psychologists – some American, but mostly European – came together in meetings and conferences to plan a new direction for a European social psychology. We see the fruits of this movement reflected in the abundance of European journals and conferences today. It emphasizes the study of human behaviour in terms of the individual but also their relationships with others, the social groups they belong to, and the cultural norms and ideological values that form their everyday social world. In other words, to understand human beings, we need different 'levels of explanation'.

**levels of explanation** *human behaviour can be understood and interpreted at different levels: the personal, interpersonal, group and ideological*

At the time of the crisis, two main figures were prominent in redirecting European social psychology. They were Henri Tajfel and Serge Moscovici. Both were committed to putting the 'social' back into social psychology. Tajfel used experiments to investigate how identity and behaviour are influenced by the social groups to which one belongs, in his social identity theory (see Chapters 12 and 13). Moscovici started with the exploration of the mechanisms that allow minorities to influence majorities, using laboratory experiments as method (see Chapter 11). Subsequently, he emphasized the importance of studying how everyday language shapes 'social representations' – that is, shared understandings of aspects of reality – encouraging the use of an array of non-experimental methods, such as the analysis of interview data and media communications (see Chapter 4). As we shall see, these theories remain influential in modern social psychology, particularly – although not only – in Europe.

After the second European conference the European Planning Committee (Gustav Jahoda, Serge Moscovici, Mauk Mulder, Jozef Nuttin and Henri Tajfel) was elected with the role of developing research links and the profile of European social psychology. This is the basis of the current European Association of Social Psychology (EASP).
SOURCE: © European Association of Social Psychology

It is important to consider that, while promoting a more 'social' and less individualistic social psychology, from a methodological perspective many representatives of this European movement did not object to the use of experimentation. In fact, experiments remained a major methodological approach among these social psychologists, to the extent that the first name of the association that they created was the European Association of *Experimental* Social Psychology. The word 'experimental' has been dropped only recently, following a far from unanimous decision.

Experiments (and other forms of investigations based on the collection of quantitative data) remain the predominant research methodology in North American social psychology, and a very important methodology in Europe and other continents. This may be due to various reasons, but the most important is probably that social psychologists are trained in psychology departments, where experimenting is traditionally considered the most rigorous method for the investigation of mental processes (see Chapter 2 for the specific features of the experimental approach to research). As a consequence, the bulk of this book is based on findings produced by experiments and other quantitative approaches. Having said that, we do not refrain from reporting studies based on qualitative approaches (see Chapter 2 for a detailed discussion of this methodological perspective) when they have contributed to a better understanding of the phenomena and issues under scrutiny.

Critical Social Psychology

The 'crisis' drew attention to the role of human values in social psychological research and the context of human social behaviour. These claims have led to the rise of critical social psychology. This movement has embraced the influence of social constructionism (e.g. Gergen, 1973, 1999), and to some extent includes forms of discursive psychology, phenomenological psychology, and the promotion of qualitative and non-experimental methods. For example, at the time of writing, the Qualitative Section of the British Psychological Society is the largest section in terms of membership. Critical social psychology defines a diverse array of social psychologists dedicated to examining the social (and ideological) context in which human behaviour occurs and the role of the researcher in producing the knowledge s/he discovers, and promoting social psychology's role in social reform and change. For example, discursive social psychologists have examined how racism and prejudice are embedded within discourse as speakers construct differences between race groups (e.g. Wetherell and Potter, 1992; also see Chapter 13 for more examples). Critical discourse analysts note that people are often not free to behave in any way they wish, but are positioned in relations of power to one another within a particular society. These power relationships require analytical attention (e.g. Parker, 1989, 2002). Phenomenological psychologists examine conscious experience of the social world and how this shapes our feelings and sense of self within it (e.g. Langdridge, 2007, 2008). For example, Ian Burkitt (1999) has considered how understandings of the 'self' are tied to embodiment and cultural definitions of our bodies.

## SOCIAL PSYCHOLOGY AND HUMAN VALUES

*Social psychologists' values penetrate their work in ways both obvious and subtle. What are these ways?*

The crisis in social psychology flagged how human values shape research. Social psychology is less a collection of findings than a set of strategies for answering questions. In science, as in courts of law, personal opinions are inadmissible. When ideas are put on trial, evidence determines the verdict. But are social psychologists really that objective? Because they are human beings, don't their *values* – their personal convictions about what is desirable and how people ought to behave – seep into their work? If so, can social psychology really be scientific?

As we've already noted, the extent to which social psychology can be considered a science, and the usefulness of examining human social behaviour using experiments, is a matter of discussion. Jack Martin and Jeff Sugarman (2009) outline the debate between the philosophers Charles Taylor and Thomas Kuhn. Taylor argues that because social psychology relies on human social beings (social psychologists) studying other human social beings, it cannot possibly produce objective knowledge that remains independent from the human beings who study it. This is a feature of social psychology that sets it apart from the natural sciences whose subject matter is not human. But not everyone agrees that this is peculiar to social psychology. Thomas Kuhn proposes that as all science involves human scientists, then none of it can ever be objective in a true sense as it all relies on a degree of human interpretation. However, this particular debate

*critical social psychology a movement promoting a social psychology that (i) recognizes its own political, social, historical situatedness, and that of its researchers and participants, and that (ii) pursues social change and reform*

*social constructionism an approach to how our understanding of reality is formed and structured, which argues that all cognitive functions originate in social interaction, and must therefore be explained as products of social interactions*

*discursive psychology proposes a view of language as 'social action' as speakers construct the social world and their position within it through talk and text. It examines how cognitive entities and psychological phenomena are constructed in discourse*

*phenomenological psychology influenced by phenomenological philosophy, this form of psychology argues that subjective conscious experience and a sense of 'being-in-the-world' are fundamental in understanding human social behaviour*

The relationship between a scientist and the aspects of reality he/she studies can be compared with the relationship between the boy and the print he is observing. The boy is looking at a print that is apparently an object external to him, but in fact includes him. So, the boy is part of the reality he is observing.

SOURCE: M.C. Escher's 'Print Gallery' © 2013. The M. C. Escher Company – The Netherlands. All Rights Reserved.

is academic for the present purposes. What matters is the concern over social psychology's claim to be a 'science', and to study human social behaviour using scientific principles and practices.

## OBVIOUS WAYS VALUES ENTER PSYCHOLOGY

Values enter the picture when social psychologists *choose research topics*. It was no accident that the study of prejudice flourished during the 1940s as fascism raged in Europe; that the 1950s, a time of look-alike fashions and intolerance of differing views, gave us studies of conformity; that the 1960s saw interest in aggression increase with riots and rising crime rates; that the feminist movement of the 1970s helped stimulate a wave of research on gender and sexism; that the 1980s offered a resurgence of attention to psychological aspects of the arms race; and that the 1990s and the early twenty-first century were marked by heightened interest in how people respond to diversity in culture, race and sexual orientation. Social psychology reflects contemporary society.

Values differ not only across time but also across cultures. In Europe, as well as in the rest of the world, people take pride in their nationalities. But this is not to the same degree in all nations, and occurs in some historical periods more than in others. Social psychologists in Europe have been concerned about this phenomenon of belonging and pride in social groups, and as a result have given us major theories of 'social identity' and 'social categorization' (see Chapters 12 and 13). On the other hand, American social psychologists have typically focused more on individuals and independence – but also on how one person thinks about others, is influenced by them and relates to them (Fiske, 2004; Tajfel, 1981; Turner, 1984).

Values obviously enter the picture as the *object* of social psychological analysis. Social psychologists investigate how values form, why they change, and how they influence attitudes and actions. None of that, however, tells us which values are 'right'. But it can teach us to be tolerant towards many values, including those different from the ones at the top of our personal value hierarchy.

## NOT-SO-OBVIOUS WAYS VALUES ENTER PSYCHOLOGY

Modern-day social psychology reflects our social world.

SOURCE: © Sean Locke/iStock

We less often recognize the subtler ways in which value commitments masquerade as objective truth. Consider the not-so-obvious ways values enter psychology.

"Science does not simply describe and explain nature; it is part of the interplay between nature and ourselves; it describes nature as exposed to our method of questioning."
Heisenberg, 1958

## THE SUBJECTIVE ASPECTS OF SCIENCE

Scientists and philosophers now agree: science is not purely objective. Scientists do not simply read the book of nature. Rather, they interpret or construct nature and the social world, using their own mental categories. In our daily lives, too, we view the world through the lens of our preconceptions. Pause a moment: what do you see in Figure 1.3? Can you see a young girl or an old lady? Once your mind grasps the concept, it informs your interpretation of the picture – so much so that it becomes difficult *not* to see the one or the other.

This is the way our minds work. While reading these words, you have been unaware that you are also looking at your nose. Your mind blocks from awareness something that is there, if only you were predisposed to perceive it. This tendency to prejudge reality based on our expectations is a basic fact about the human mind.

**FIGURE 1.3** What do you see?

SOURCE: © Ian Paterson/Alamy Stock Photo

Because scholars at work in any given area often share a common viewpoint or come from the same culture, their assumptions may go unchallenged. What we take for granted – the shared beliefs, or our social representations (Moscovici, 1988) – are often our most important yet most unexamined convictions (see Chapter 4). Sometimes, however, someone from outside the camp will call attention to those assumptions. During the 1980s feminists and Marxists exposed some of social psychology's unexamined assumptions. Feminist critics called attention to subtle biases – for example, the political conservatism of some scientists who favoured a biological interpretation of gender differences in social behaviour (Unger, 1985). Some feminist critics have also challenged one of the most accepted traditions in social psychology, *the bystander effect*, for not taking into consideration the gender aspect of what initiated that tradition: the murder of Kitty Genovese (see Chapter 10). Marxist critics called attention to competitive, individualist biases – for example, the assumption that conformity is bad and that individual rewards are good. This critique has been expressed not only by Marxists. Today most social psychologists accept that conformity also reveals social identity and solidarity (Chapter 7). Marxists and feminists, of course, make their own assumptions, as critics of academic 'political correctness' are fond of noting. Social psychologist Lee Jussim (2005), for example, argues that progressive social psychologists sometimes feel compelled to deny group differences and to assume that stereotypes of group difference are never rooted in reality but always in racism.

culture *the enduring behaviours, ideas, attitudes and traditions shared by a large group of people and transmitted from one generation to the next*

social representations *socially shared beliefs – widely held ideas and values, including our assumptions and cultural ideologies. Our social representations help us to make sense of our world*

In Chapter 4 we will see more ways in which our preconceptions guide our interpretations. As research in social psychology reminds us, what guides our behaviour is less the situation-as-it-is than the situation-as-we-construe-it.

## PSYCHOLOGICAL CONCEPTS CONTAIN HIDDEN VALUES

Implicit in our understanding that psychology is not objective is the realization that psychologists' own values may play an important part in the theories and judgements they support. Psychologists may refer to people as mature or immature, as well adjusted or poorly adjusted, as mentally healthy or mentally disordered, as normal or abnormal, and cultures as developed or underdeveloped.

They may talk as if they were stating facts, when they are really making *value judgements*. Here are some examples.

### Defining the Good Life

Values influence our idea of the best way to live our lives. The personality psychologist Abraham Maslow, for example, was known for his descriptions of 'self-actualized' people – people who, with their needs for survival, safety, belonging and self-esteem satisfied, go on to fulfil their human potential. Few readers noticed that Maslow himself, guided by his own values, selected the sample of self-actualized people he described. The resulting description of self-actualized personalities – as spontaneous, autonomous, mystical and so forth – reflected Maslow's personal values. Had he begun with someone else's heroes – say, Napoleon, Alexander the Great and Margaret Thatcher – his resulting description of self-actualization would have differed (Smith, 1978). This hierarchy of values also expresses the values of the Western individualistic culture in which it was formed. To develop in Western culture means to be more individualistic and independent, and to realize your personal self, rather than uphold collectivistic values or be able to create harmony with others. What characterizes well-functioning and modern humans in other cultures is sometimes the opposite: the ability to control and reduce your individuality in the name of harmony and solidarity.

### Professional Advice

Psychological advice also reflects the advice-giver's personal values. When mental health professionals advise us how to get along with our spouse or our co-workers, when child-rearing experts tell us how to handle our children, and when some psychologists advocate living free of concern for others' expectations, they are expressing their own personal and cultural values. (In Western cultures, those values usually will be individualistic – encouraging what feels best for 'me'. Non-Western cultures more often encourage what's best for 'us'.) Many people, unaware of those hidden values, defer to the 'professional'. But professional psychologists cannot answer questions of ultimate moral obligation, of purpose and direction, and of life's meaning.

Tell me your problems? In offering advice, we display our personal and cultural values.

SOURCE: © Lisafx/iStock

### Forming Concepts

Hidden values even seep into psychology's research-based *concepts*. Pretend you have taken a personality test and the psychologist, after scoring your answers, announces: 'You scored high in self-esteem. You are low in anxiety. And you have exceptional ego-strength.' 'Ah,' you think, 'I suspected as much, but it feels good to know that.' Now another psychologist gives you a similar test. For some peculiar reason, this test asks some of the same questions. Afterwards, the psychologist informs you that you seem defensive, for you scored high in 'repressiveness'. 'How could this be?' you wonder. 'The other psychologist said such nice things about me.' It could be because all these labels describe the same set of responses (a tendency to say nice things about oneself and not to acknowledge problems). Shall we call it high self-esteem or defensiveness? The label reflects the judgement.

### Labelling

Value judgements, then, are often hidden within our social psychological language – but that is also true of everyday language. Whether we label someone engaged in guerrilla warfare a 'terrorist' or a 'freedom fighter' depends on our view of the cause. Whether we view wartime civilian deaths as 'the loss of innocent lives' or as 'collateral damage' affects our acceptance of such. Whether we call public assistance 'welfare' or 'aid to the needy' reflects our political views. When 'they' exalt their country and people, it's ethnocentrism; that is, the belief that my ethnic group are better than others. Whether someone involved in an extramarital affair is practising 'open marriage' or 'adultery' depends on one's personal values and if we want to condemn or accept. We select concepts that justify the intention. Language is never neutral. 'Brainwashing' is social influence we do not approve of. 'Perversions' are sex acts we do not practise. Remarks about 'ambitious' men and 'aggressive' women convey a hidden message.

As these examples indicate, values lie hidden within the language and the concepts we use. They influence our cultural definitions of mental health, our psychological advice for living and our psychological scientific labels. Throughout this book we will call your attention to additional examples of hidden values. The point is never that the implicit values are necessarily bad. The point is that scientific interpretation, even at the level of labelling phenomena, is a human activity. It is therefore natural and inevitable that prior beliefs and values will influence what social psychologists think and write.

Should we dismiss science because it has its subjective side? Quite the contrary: the realization that human thinking always involves interpretation is precisely why we need researchers with varying biases to undertake scientific analysis. By constantly checking our beliefs against the facts, as best we know them, we check and restrain our biases. Systematic observation, empirical data and experimentation help us clean the lens through which we see our research object.

## SOCIAL PSYCHOLOGY'S KEY IDEAS

The historical journey of social psychology from its early philosophical beginnings to the present day reveals a diverse discipline, containing a wealth of knowledge and debate about human social behaviour and how we should study it. So, what are its big lessons – its overarching themes, debates and questions? In many academic fields, the results of tens of thousands of studies, the conclusions of thousands of investigators, and the insights of hundreds of theorists can be boiled down to a few central ideas. Biology offers us principles such as natural selection and adaptation. Sociology builds on concepts such as social structure and organization. Music harnesses our ideas of rhythm, melody and harmony.

What concepts are on social psychology's shortlist of key ideas? What are some of the crucial questions that social psychologists dedicate their time and resources to answering? What themes or fundamental principles will be worth remembering long after you have forgotten most of the details? Let us consider some of the candidates (see Figure 1.4).

### WE CONSTRUCT OUR SOCIAL REALITY

We humans have an irresistible urge to explain behaviour, to attribute it to some cause, and therefore to make it seem orderly, predictable and controllable. We may react differently to similar situations because we 'think' and 'feel' differently from one another. We may also describe and 'construct' that situation very differently.

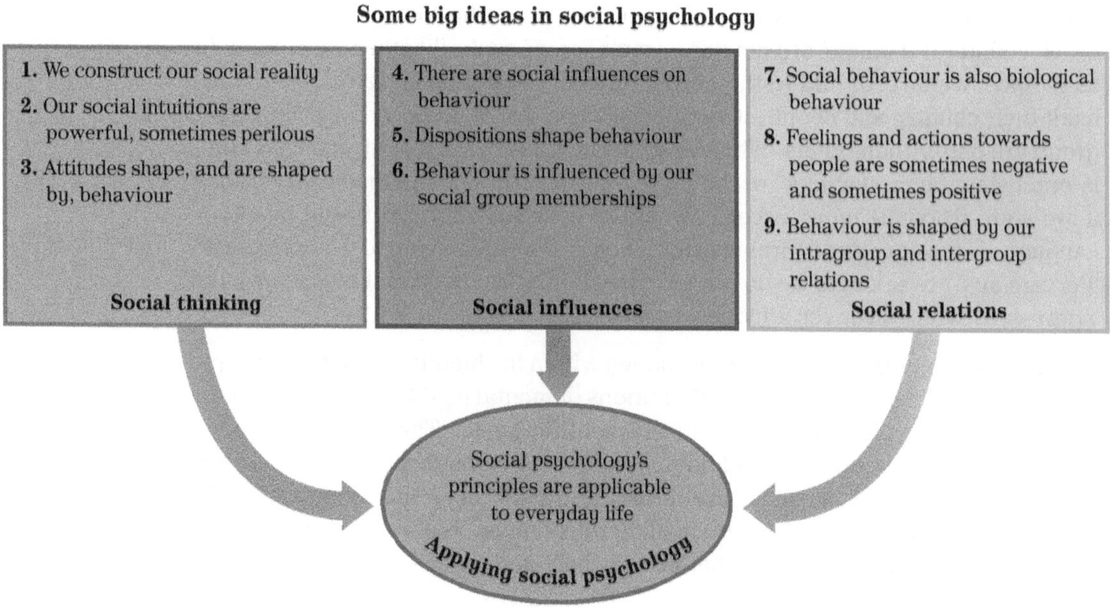

**Some big ideas in social psychology**

1. We construct our social reality
2. Our social intuitions are powerful, sometimes perilous
3. Attitudes shape, and are shaped by, behaviour

**Social thinking**

4. There are social influences on behaviour
5. Dispositions shape behaviour
6. Behaviour is influenced by our social group memberships

**Social influences**

7. Social behaviour is also biological behaviour
8. Feelings and actions towards people are sometimes negative and sometimes positive
9. Behaviour is shaped by our intragroup and intergroup relations

**Social relations**

Social psychology's principles are applicable to everyday life

*Applying social psychology*

**FIGURE 1.4**  Some key ideas in social psychology

The same event can be described and evaluated very differently by two people. They may not pay attention to the same features of that event, but actively select aspects to describe. Sometimes people see what they want to see, and they explain or evaluate an event in a way that is in accordance with their expectations, or serves us in some way. In this way we construct social events, people and social 'facts' so it suits our interests and what we want to perceive and convey to others.

Let us consider an example. A football match in 1951 between university teams at Princeton and Dartmouth Universities provided a classic example of how we construct reality in a way that suits our own interests (Hastorf & Cantril, 1954; see also Loy & Andrews, 1981). The game lived up to its billing as a grudge match; it turned out to be one of the roughest and dirtiest games in the history of either university. Fist-fights erupted and there were injuries on both sides. Not long afterwards, two psychologists, one from each university, showed films of the game to students on each campus. The students played the role of scientist-observer, noting each hostile incident as they watched and who was responsible for it. But they could not set aside their loyalties. The Princeton students saw twice as many Dartmouth violations as the Dartmouth students saw. The conclusion: we grasp reality in a subjective way. We construct it through the lens of our own interests, values, expectations and beliefs. *Cognitive social psychologists*, for example, have examined how the demands and limits of our mental abilities (such as the need to categorize) result in biases that influence how we construct the world around us. In constructing it in particular ways, we also simplify it.

Our beliefs about ourselves also matter. Do we have an optimistic outlook on life? Do we see ourselves as in control of things? Do we view ourselves as relatively inferior or superior to others? Our answers influence our emotions and actions. Of course, the way we view ourselves is influenced by the context of our culture and the society in which we are socialized. We internalize a culture's beliefs and values and they form part of our own. Much of the time we are unaware of this influence and often assume that the way we see ourselves and others is how others see them too. We will consider this in some detail in Chapter 3, when we examine the self. This is an accusation that has been levelled at social psychology. As we've noted earlier, cultural values enter social psychological research in subtle and obvious ways. The explanations social psychologists have arrived at to explain human social behaviour may reflect the social and cultural context of the theorist. However, what social psychologists have focused on is how people construct the social world around them.

## SOCIAL INTUITIONS ARE POWERFUL BUT CAN BE PERILOUS!

Our instant intuitions shape our fears (is flying dangerous?), impressions (can I trust him?) and relationships (does she like me?). Intuitions influence governments in times of crisis, gamblers at the roulette table, jurors in their assessments of guilt, employers when interviewing prospective employees. We rely on our intuitions in our everyday lives.

This intuition is our everyday wisdom in making decisions and judgements. However, as well as it being a powerful aspect of our decisions, it can also be perilous. For example, we cruise through our life mostly on automatic pilot. We intuitively judge the likelihood of something happening by how easily it comes to mind. When boarding the plane for a holiday we can easily bring to mind plane crashes. Yet, as we get into the car to go to the supermarket, car crashes tend not to figure in our imagination. This perhaps explains why people fear flying more than driving. Actually, we are about three dozen times safer (per mile travelled) in a commercial plane than in a motor vehicle.

Even our intuitions about ourselves often err. We intuitively trust our memories more than we should. We misread our own minds; in experiments we deny being affected by things that do influence us. We mispredict our own feelings – how bad we'll feel a year from now if we lose our job or our romance breaks up, if we fail our examinations, and how good we'll feel a year from now if we win the lottery. And we often mispredict our own future.

By reminding us of intuition's gifts and alerting us to its pitfalls, social psychologists aim to fortify our thinking. In most situations, 'fast and frugal' snap judgements serve us well enough. But in others, where accuracy matters – as when needing to fear the right things and spend our resources accordingly – we had best restrain our impulsive intuitions with critical thinking. So our intuitions are powerful resources in navigating us through our daily lives, but they carry an element of danger and can be perilous.

## SOCIAL INFLUENCES SHAPE OUR BEHAVIOUR

We are, as Aristotle long ago observed, social animals. We speak and think in words and ways we learned from others (such as parents and friends), and from the society and culture into which we're socialized. Parents and guardians are sometimes considered to be the 'agents of culture' as they shape our psychological functions in accordance with social norms, values and ways of thinking. Part of the socialization process is to be an integrated and valuable member of a society. Some of the norms and values we share with other members of our culture, while others are individual to us. We long to connect, to belong and to be thought well of. Throughout this textbook we present examples of how a sense of 'we-ness' and membership of a social group shapes our behaviour, thinking and our sense of self.

As social creatures, we respond to our immediate contexts. Sometimes the power of a social situation leads us to act in ways that depart from beliefs, values and behaviour in other situations. Indeed, powerful situations sometimes overwhelm good intentions, inducing people to agree with falsehoods or comply with cruelty. For example, behaviourist theory which dominated social psychology in the 1950s, concerned itself precisely with the role of the situation in eliciting social behaviour (Skinner, 1963). Behaviourism considers how behaviour is related to reinforcement and positive and negative outcomes. So, for example, we may engage in aggressive behaviour if we are positively reinforced and receive positive outcomes from others (e.g. enhanced reputation and status) for doing so (see Chapter 8). We have to wonder what situational factors played a role in eliciting certain negative behaviours throughout our history. For example, in the USA, many Americans accepted Negro slavery for decades. During apartheid in South Africa, many white Europeans approved of the system, particularly those living in South Africa. The colonialism in Africa was not questioned at the time by many in Europe. Under Nazi influence, many decent-seeming people supported the Nazi regime. But, of course, other situations can elicit great generosity and compassion. After the tsunami catastrophe in Asia, in December 2004, victims were overwhelmed with donations of food, money, clothing and help from eager volunteers from all over the world.

behaviourism *a school of psychology that emphasizes the effects of learning, reinforcement and situational factors on the facilitation or inhibition of behaviour. The theory claims psychology should be a study of observable behaviour, since thoughts, motives and feelings are unavailable for research*

More generally, our cultures help define the situation in which we find ourselves, and guide behaviour. For example:

☐ whether you define social justice as equality (everyone receives the same) or as equity (those who earn more receive more) depends on whether your ideology has been shaped more by socialism or capitalism

☐ whether you tend to be expressive or reserved, casual or formal, hinges partly on your culture

☐ whether you focus primarily on yourself – your personal needs, desire and morality – or on your family, clan and communal groups depends on how much you are a product of Western individualism.

Social psychologist Hazel Markus (2005) sums it up: 'People are above all, malleable.' Said differently, we do not just adapt to our culture and society, but we actively engage in forming it.

### GENETIC HERITAGE AND INDIVIDUAL DISPOSITIONS INFLUENCE BEHAVIOUR

Our genetic heritage and individual dispositions affect and create our individual psychological functions and behaviour. We are not passive tumbleweeds merely blown this way and that by the social and cultural winds. Our values and attitudes acquired during socialization will influence behaviour. For example, our political attitudes influence voting behaviour. Our attitudes to smoking influence our susceptibility to peer pressure to smoke. Our attitudes towards the poor influence our willingness to help. As we shall see in Chapter 5, our attitudes also follow our behaviour, which leads us to believe in those things we have committed ourselves to, or suffered for. Temperament and personality dispositions also affect behaviour. Facing the same situation, different people may react differently. For example, while one person responds to an argument with aggression, another simply walks away. Emerging from years of political imprisonment, one person exudes bitterness. Another, such as South Africa's Nelson Mandela, seeks reconciliation and unity with former enemies.

## BEHAVIOUR IS SHAPED BY INTRAGROUP AND INTERGROUP RELATIONS

The way we define and experience ourselves is not always in terms of our individual and unique characteristics. In many contexts the self is defined and experienced in terms of group membership ('I am French'; 'I am a woman'; 'I am black'; 'I am a student'). The groups and social categories to which we belong and which define who we are, are at the basis of many of our behaviours. We may drink heavily in order to feel accepted by a group of friends that matter to us; we can make an effort to attend a given lecture, even though we dread the idea, because this is what a committed student is expected to do; we may go on strike to defend the rights of our professional category; and so on. What is more, when we are acutely aware of being part of a group, we are likely to make an effort to be cooperative and supportive with other members of our group, and if our group is competing with another for scarce resources, we may develop forms of bias and prejudice toward the members of the other group.

Social psychologists have always been interested in collective behaviour, and have produced important findings and insight about a number of processes both within and between groups. As we will discover in Chapters 11, 12 and 13, some of the most celebrated studies in the history of modern social psychology have concerned group related phenomena.

## SOCIAL PSYCHOLOGICAL PROCESSES ARE BIOLOGICALLY ROOTED

Since the end of the twentieth century, there has been an ever-growing focus on behaviour's biological foundations. The 1990s was introduced as the 'decade of the brain' and it was heavily researched for its role in guiding behaviour. With the development of imaging techniques such as computed axial tomography (CAT), magnetic resonance imaging (MRI), and nuclear magnetic resonance imaging (NMRI) our understanding of the structure and functions of the brain has advanced rapidly. With these imaging techniques we can consider in detail the localization of neuropsychological functions and processes.

If every psychological event (every thought, every emotion and every behaviour) is simultaneously a biological event, then we can also examine the neurobiology that underlies social behaviour. What brain areas enable our experiences of love and contempt, helping and aggression, perception and belief? How do brain, mind and behaviour function together as one co-ordinated system? What does the timing of brain events reveal about how we process information? Such questions are asked by those in social neuroscience (e.g. Heatherton et al., 2004; Ochsner & Lieberman, 2001). For example, social neuroscience has observed that mirror neurons, located in the premotor cortex, become active when a person watches someone perform an action and when that person then performs the action for him/herself. Interestingly, the more expert s/he is at the action the stronger the activation in the brain (e.g. Calvo-Merino et al., 2005; Fiske and Taylor, 2007).

We'll discuss more about the individual differences in aggression in Chapter 8 and how biology, circumstances and environment influence aggressive behaviour.

social neuroscience *seeks to understand how physiology, in particular the brain, influences behaviour*

Chapter 9 discusses how women look for a mate who can protect and provide for them, while men's decisions are based on a potential mate's nurturing abilities to care for their potential offspring.

But to know where something is processed in the brain does not tell us why it happens. With an ever-increasing focus on the brain, the relationship between mind, brain and the social world becomes a topic for discussion and research. The forces of biology and the social act on each other. But how they are related remains a scientific and social psychological challenge. *Evolutionary psychologists* argue our inherited human nature predisposes us to behave in ways that helped our ancestors survive and reproduce. We carry the genes of those whose traits enabled them to survive and reproduce (whose children did the same). Evolutionary psychologists ask how natural selection might predispose our actions and reactions when dating and mating, hurting and hating, caring and sharing. For example, April Bleske-Rechek and David Buss (2001) suggest that men and women have different goals in heterosexual relationships.

*Social neuroscientists* do not reduce complex social behaviours, such as helping and hurting, to simple neural or molecular mechanisms. Their point is this: to understand social behaviour, we must consider both under-the-skin (biological) and between-skins (social) influences. Mind and body are one grand system. Stress hormones affect how we feel and act. Social ostracism elevates blood pressure; social support strengthens the disease-fighting immune system. We are bio-psycho-social organisms. We reflect the interplay of our biological, psychological and social influences. And this is why today's psychologists study behaviour from these different levels of analysis.

## SOCIAL PSYCHOLOGY'S PRINCIPLES ARE APPLICABLE IN EVERYDAY LIFE

Social psychology has the potential to illuminate your life, to make visible the subtle influences that guide your thinking and acting. And, as we will see, it offers many ideas about how to know ourselves better, how to win friends and influence people, how to transform closed fists into open arms.

Scholars are also applying social psychological insights. Principles of social thinking, social influence and social relations have implications for human health and well-being, for war and peace, for performance and relationships in organizations and the workplace, and for the encouragement of behaviours that will enable an environmentally sustainable human future.

As but one perspective on human existence, psychological science does not seek to engage life's ultimate questions: what is the meaning of human life? What should be our purpose? What is our ultimate destiny? But social psychology does give us a method for asking and answering some exceedingly interesting and important questions. *Social psychology is all about life – your life: your beliefs, your attitudes, your relationships.*

## SUMMING UP: INTRODUCING SOCIAL PSYCHOLOGY

### WHAT IS SOCIAL PSYCHOLOGY?

☐ Social psychology is the scientific study of how people think about, influence and relate to one another.

☐ Social psychology's central themes concern (1) how we think about the self, others, and social issues (social thinking), (2) what shapes people's minds and behaviour (social influence), (3) the mechanisms underlying aggression, intimacy and helping (social relations), and (4) processes within and between groups (people in groups).

## A BRIEF HISTORY OF SOCIAL PSYCHOLOGY

☐ Social psychological topics and issues have been debated in Europe for centuries by philosophers and other scholars and thinkers, long before social psychology became a discipline in its own right. Much of this early thought formed the basis for present-day social psychology.

☐ Its history of debates about the underlying assumptions and methods social psychologists use to examine human social behaviour remains a feature of modern-day social psychology, giving us a rich and diverse discipline.

## SOCIAL PSYCHOLOGY AND HUMAN VALUES

☐ Social psychologists' values penetrate their work in obvious ways, such as their choice of research topics and the types of people who are attracted to various fields of study.

☐ They also do this in more subtle ways, such as their hidden assumptions when forming concepts, choosing labels and giving advice.

☐ This penetration of values into science is not a reason to fault social psychology or any other science. That human thinking is seldom dispassionate is precisely why we need systematic observation and experimentation if we are to check our cherished ideas against reality.

## SOCIAL PSYCHOLOGY'S KEY IDEAS

☐ Social psychology's central themes concern (1) how we construct and construe our social worlds, (2) how our everyday thinking, habits and social intuitions guide and sometimes deceive us, (3) how our psychological functions are shaped by biology, temperament, culture and other people, and (4) how social psychology's principles apply to our everyday lives and to various other fields of study.

## CRITICAL QUESTIONS

**1** How strong do you think is the link between pre-modern and modern-day social psychology?

**2** Should social psychology try to model itself on the harder sciences (e.g., physics, biology)?

**3** Social psychology is to some extent driven by current social concerns and problems. What modern-day examples can you think of that have received social psychological attention?

**4** What role do you think social psychology should play in addressing social problems? Should we be engaged in social reform and change?

## RECOMMENDED READING

Farr, R. M. (1996). *The Roots of Modern Social Psychology*. Oxford: Blackwell.

Jahoda, G. (2007). *A History of Social Psychology: From the Eighteenth-century Enlightenment to the Second World War*. Cambridge: Cambridge University Press.

*Two excellent books about the way social psychology took its modern form.*

**2**

Communications House Cam 1
Eng 211

Communications Ho
Eng 212

0410206

0410207

Victory House Eng Eng 231

Clydesdale bank Eng

*"The application of philosophical ideas to social research must not lose touch with the practices and aims of social researchers."*

*Alan Bryman, 1988*

# RESEARCH METHODS IN SOCIAL PSYCHOLOGY

In Chapter 1 we've considered some intriguing questions that social psychologists seek to answer. Now let's consider the ways, or 'methods', that are typically used to address those questions.

Research methods are extremely important. To find something out about human behaviour we need to examine it. But this isn't always terribly easy. Human beings are complex. How do we decide which aspects of behaviour to focus on? How should we collect evidence of that behaviour? How should we then interpret and evaluate it? What is the status of the knowledge we discover? Have we discovered universal and stable 'facts' about human beings, or have we discovered socially and historically contingent 'facts', which are prone to change? And how does social psychology differ from common sense? Social psychologists have developed a variety of methods for the study of human behaviour, and this chapter considers what these are.

## I KNEW IT ALL ALONG: IS SOCIAL PSYCHOLOGY SIMPLY COMMON SENSE?

*We've already mentioned how social psychology can produce findings that surprise us. Yet, there are those other times when social psychology simply seems to confirm what we already knew. So does social psychology provide new insights into the human condition? Or does it only describe the obvious?*

In Chapter 1, our historical journey into social psychology alerted us to the fact that social behaviour has been a topic for discussion and scrutiny by scholars and thinkers for centuries. But, it is also a topic that everyday human beings feel they know something about. After all, it's *our* social behaviour that is the focus of interest. So does that mean social psychology is just common sense in fancy words? Do we need a rigorous study of human beings' social behaviour at all if, in fact, we knew it all along?

Of course, one problem with common sense is that we invoke it after we know the facts. Events are far more 'obvious' and predictable in hindsight than beforehand. Experiments reveal that when people learn the outcome of an experiment, that outcome suddenly seems unsurprising – certainly less surprising than it is to people who are simply told about the experimental procedure and the possible outcomes (Slovic & Fischhoff, 1977). Even when research finds the opposite of common sense, ordinary people often adjust their attitudes to what is believed to be a scientific fact, as if they should never have been thinking something else.

In everyday life we often do not expect something to happen until it does. *Then* we suddenly see clearly the forces that brought about the event and feel unsurprised. After elections, most commentators find the turn of events unsurprising. After the recession in the world economy from the end of 2008, it seemed obvious that economists and political commentators (and social psychologists?) should have anticipated the crisis in the financial sector due to rotten loan financing and extreme profit in the financial sector of the economy. As the Danish philosopher-theologian Søren Kierkegaard put it: 'Life is lived forwards, but understood backwards.'

If this hindsight bias (also called the *I-knew-it-all-along phenomenon*) is pervasive, you may now be feeling that you already knew about this phenomenon. Indeed, almost any conceivable result of a social psychological study can seem like common sense – *after* you know the result.

hindsight bias *the tendency to exaggerate, after learning an outcome, one's ability to have foreseen how something turned out. Also known as the 'I-knew-it-all-along' phenomenon*

You can demonstrate the phenomenon yourself. Take a group of people and tell half of them one psychological finding and the other half the opposite result. For example, tell half as follows:

Social psychologists have found that, whether choosing friends or falling in love, we are most attracted to people whose traits are different from our own. There seems to be wisdom in the old saying 'Opposites attract'.

Tell the other half:

Social psychologists have found that, whether choosing friends or falling in love, we are most attracted to people whose traits are similar to our own. There seems to be wisdom in the old saying 'Birds of a feather flock together'.

Ask the people first to explain the result. Then ask them to say whether it is 'surprising' or 'not surprising'. Virtually all will find a good explanation for whichever result they were given and will say it is 'not surprising'.

The beauty of hindsight! Did we anticipate the global recession?
SOURCE: © pidjoe/iStock

Indeed, we can draw on our stockpile of proverbs to make almost any result seem to make sense. If a social psychologist reports that separation intensifies romantic attraction, John Q. Public responds, 'You get paid for this? Everybody knows that "absence makes the heart grow fonder".' Should it turn out that separation *weakens* attraction, John will say, 'My grandmother could have told you, "Out of sight, out of mind".'

The Norwegian social psychologist Karl Halvor Teigen (1986) must have had a few chuckles when he asked University of Leicester (England) students to evaluate actual proverbs and their opposites. When given the proverb 'Fear is stronger than love', most rated it as true. But so did students who were given its reversed form, 'Love is stronger than fear'. Likewise, the genuine proverb 'He that is fallen cannot help him who is down' was rated highly, but so too was 'He that is fallen can help him who is down'. Our favourites, however, were two highly rated proverbs: 'Wise men make proverbs and fools repeat them' (authentic) and its made-up counterpart, 'Fools make proverbs and wise men repeat them'.

The hindsight bias creates a problem for many psychology students. Sometimes results are genuinely surprising (for example, that Olympic *bronze* medallists take more joy in their achievement than do silver medallists). More often, when you read the results of research in your textbooks, the material seems easy, even obvious. When you later take a multiple-choice test on which you must choose among several plausible conclusions, the task may become surprisingly difficult. 'I don't know what happened,' the befuddled student later moans. 'I thought I knew the material.'

The I-knew-it-all-along phenomenon can have unfortunate consequences. It is conducive to arrogance – an overestimation of our own intellectual powers.

Moreover, because outcomes seem as if they should have been foreseeable, we are more likely to blame decision makers for what are in retrospect 'obvious' bad choices than to praise them for good choices, which also seem 'obvious'.

Likewise, we sometimes blame ourselves for 'stupid mistakes' – perhaps for not having handled a person or a situation better. Looking back, we see how we should have handled it. 'I should have known how busy I would be at the term's end and started that paper earlier.' But sometimes we are too hard on ourselves. We forget that what is obvious to us *now* was not nearly so obvious at the time.

What do we conclude – that common sense is usually wrong? Sometimes it is. At other times, conventional wisdom is right – or it falls on both sides of an issue: does happiness come from knowing the truth or preserving illusions? From being with others or living in peaceful solitude? Opinions are numerous and commonplace; no matter what we find, there will be someone who foresaw it. But which of the many competing ideas best fit reality? And what is actually the 'reality', if it is constructed? Research can specify the circumstances under which a common-sense truism is valid, but never reach absolute truth.

'Everything important has been said before.'
  Philosopher Alfred North Whitehead (1861–1947)

The point is not that common sense is predictably wrong. Rather, common sense usually is right – *after the fact*. We therefore easily deceive ourselves into thinking that we know and knew more than we do and did. And that is precisely why we need science to help us sift reality from illusion and genuine predictions from easy hindsight. There are other causes as well, however, why research is necessary if we want to understand and explain human behaviour and relationships.

## APPROACHES TO DOING RESEARCH

quantitative research *approach to research aimed at studying the relationships between variables. Variables are expressed numerically, and their relationships are explored via statistical analyses*

variable *a thing that can vary in quantity and quality. Of particular relevance to social psychology are variables such as self-esteem, aggression, attraction, etc. Their level will vary from person to person, situation to situation*

Although there are several methods and techniques that can be used to investigate social psychological phenomena, it is possible to distinguish between two general approaches: the quantitative and the qualitative approach. Social psychologists tend to have a predilection for either one or the other, although some researchers are perfectly happy to use both.

### QUANTITATIVE SOCIAL PSYCHOLOGY

Social psychologists adopting a quantitative research approach see the social psychological world in terms of variables. For quantitative researchers things such as gender and nationality, but also anxiety, self-esteem, life satisfaction, physical attraction to one's partner, empathy, academic performance, attachment to a social group, attitude toward immigrants, commitment to work, willingness to help a person in a crisis, motivation to achieve a goal, and so on are first and foremost variables. That means that a variable may concern any conceivable characteristic – demographics, feelings, cognitions, behaviours – that can vary in some way. Gender may obviously vary in that one is either male or female (although one might want to consider other possible categories), self-esteem may vary from being very low to very high, commitment to work may range from being tenuous to very strong, and so on. People are stable on some variables (gender and nationality tend to remain the same across the lifespan), but may easily change over time on other variables (one may be unsatisfied with life when young but become increasingly more satisfied while ageing) and across situations (one may feel anxious in the company of strangers but totally at ease with close friends).

Quantitative social psychologists are interested in studying the interplay between variables. For example, they may want to discover whether, in general, students who perform well have greater self-esteem than students whose performance is not so good. Or they could decide to investigate whether a relaxed leadership style leads to greater group productivity than an authoritarian style. Obviously, social psychologists can also consider physical variables (e.g., temperature in a room, level of noise, etc.) in their research, insofar as these may impact upon social psychological phenomena. For instance, does heat make people more aggressive? Does noise facilitate cohesion in a football crowd?

In order to conduct these sorts of investigation, researchers need to *measure* the variables under scrutiny. For instance, self-esteem may be measured by using a set of questions that will produce a total score ranging from 0 (total lack of self-esteem) to 10 (very high self-esteem), and mathematical performance could be expressed in terms of number of problems in a test that have been resolved. Subsequently, researchers must perform some statistical calculations – which may have various degrees of complexity – aimed at establishing whether and how strongly the variables are linked to one another. The term quantitative approach derives from the fact that variables and their connections are expressed numerically, that is, in terms of *quantities*.

## QUALITATIVE SOCIAL PSYCHOLOGY

Social psychologists endorsing a qualitative research approach tend to be sceptical about the possibility of reducing people's social psychological life in terms of discrete, neatly identified variables. As eloquently put by Stuart Wilson and Rory MacLean, 'our minds, our inner life and our experiences exist within a network of influencing factors that is large and does not lend itself to being easily packaged into discrete boxes' (2011, p. 186). In addition, these social psychologists believe that representing psychological states and experiences through numerical scales does not say much about what people's true states and experiences really are like. For instance, what do people really mean when they say that, on a 7-point scale where 1 = not at all satisfied and 7 = totally satisfied, their satisfaction with life equals 5? People's inner life is much more complex and textured than that. Also, qualitative social psychologists feel uncomfortable with the idea that human social psychology can be understood by studying people in artificial situations such as the laboratory experiment – which is what many quantitative psychologists do. The real situations that people have to face in everyday life cannot easily be reproduced in the lab.

qualitative research *approach to research based on the interpretation of qualitative data, not statistical analysis of numerical data (contrasted with quantitative research)*

As a result, qualitative social psychologists prefer to use methods that capture the richness and complexity of human psychology. This may involve, for example, studying the meanings attached to specific experiences (e.g., being the target of prejudice, living with a chronic illness, participating in a rally). The data used for these studies may involve texts obtained via the transcription of recorded interviews (that tend to be in-depth and unstructured) or field-notes taken by the researcher during specific events. Normally, the researcher will try to collect the data in contexts and/or ways that are as natural as possible. In general, qualitative researchers are happy to accept the idea that their findings concern socially contingent phenomena, rather than 'stable', universal facts. In other words, these social psychologists believe that, while laws of nature are fixed (e.g., protons will always be positively charged), human social behaviour depends on a whole array of things, such as the immediate context in which it occurs and broader cultural values. Kenneth Gergen (1973) makes the point that while the natural scientist receives no argument from his or her subject about the findings s/he produces, the social psychologist has no such luxury. Our subjects talk back. And, as we've seen, can dismiss our findings as common sense (remember the hindsight bias and the I-knew-it-all-along phenomenon) or untrue. Gergen argues that the better able a theory is to predict human behaviour the more likely it is the population will then change its behaviour to invalidate it. Human beings react to revelations about their own behaviour.

## SOME GENERAL OBSERVATIONS ON THE TWO APPROACHES

Are the two approaches to research irreconcilable? Well, not necessarily. They may be so for some social psychologists who believe that these approaches stem from completely different conceptions of what human psychology and its study are about (i.e., different epistemologies). In particular, some qualitative researchers actively resist quantitative methods in the belief that they are not the appropriate way to research human beings. These debates over method reflect those we considered in Chapter 1 concerning *if*, and *to what extent*, social psychology is a 'science' capable of producing objective 'facts' about human beings and their social behaviour. Some social psychologists, however, are more flexible, and are happy to use whatever method appears to be ideal and suitable for the specific research question at stake. This attitude has produced an increasing body of mixed-methods research in social psychology. That is, there are researchers who like to run projects involving both quantitative and qualitative methodologies.

In the next section we will discuss in some detail what each type of approach to research involves in practice. To anticipate briefly we can say that, at the broadest level, the main features of the quantitative approach are a high degree of control exerted by the researcher on the research setting, the rigorous measurement of behaviour, and an analysis of data based on statistical procedures. On the contrary, the main characteristics of the qualitative approach are the use of naturalistic research settings, the observation of spontaneous behaviour and the facilitation of subjective experience unconstrained by rigid protocols, and the interpretative analysis of behaviours and language in terms of their intrinsic meaning. Consider, however, that most of what you will learn about social psychological methods will come from your reading of the next chapters as we consider specific topics in social psychology. Here we will glimpse behind the scenes so you can get some insight into how social psychologists do their research, and this should help in appreciating and evaluating the studies considered throughout the rest of this textbook.

data *notes, information, registered observations, statistical measurements or responses, collected together for scientific analysis or interpretation, and then to inform knowledge*

We summarize the main differences between quantitative and qualitative research methodologies in Table 2.1.

**TABLE 2.1**  Some of the main differences between quantitative and qualitative approach to research

| Quantitative approach | Qualitative approach |
|---|---|
| Pursue the systematic measurement of phenomena, often in controlled laboratory settings | Focus on the interpretation of phenomena as emerged in naturalistic, unconstrained situations |
| Make predictions about the outcome of research | Are open to new, surprising and previously unthought-of findings |
| Aim at establishing general laws and principles about types of phenomena | Aim at providing a thorough description and understanding of the specific phenomena under investigation |

## QUANTITATIVE RESEARCH

Social psychologists conducting quantitative research tend to adhere to a standard process involving a number of stages. All investigations start with a research question. For instance, do young people who have low self-esteem tend to engage in risky behaviour (such as smoking and alcohol consumption) more than those with high self-esteem? Do people who feel excluded from a group exaggerate their conformity to group norms in order to be accepted? Do people with many friends feel happier than more solitary people? It is to address questions such as these that social psychologists undertake research.

> research question *a question that guides the focus of current research*

But how are research questions generated? A research question may stem from existing theory in social psychology. Theories consist of a set of assumptions and propositions that organize findings from previous research into a coherent story. However, theories also contribute to generate new research questions to be investigated. For instance, suppose that there exists a theory stating that people find uncertainty aversive. Then suppose that, according to such a theory, when people facing an uncertain situation experience anxiety they, as a consequence, become especially dependent on significant others such as a friend or spouse. Now, you might decide that this is a plausible and convincing theory but that, at the same time, there are aspects that the theory overlooks. For instance, you may wonder whether people facing uncertainty may also become more prone to join groups holding firm and clear views on reality, and decide that this is a worthwhile research question to be addressed.

> theory *an interrelated set of principles that guide what should be studied, and explain and predict the observed relationship between variables*

A specific research question may also be triggered by events currently going on in the world. In Chapter 1, we considered how many of social psychology's studies were driven by world events and concerns. For example, there is a recent spurt in social psychological work on climate change and the sustainability of the planet as a response to contemporary concerns (Kazdin, 2009).

Finally, the decision to address a certain question may be based on your everyday experience and life. You might want to understand the reasons underlying some of your behaviours. For instance, you may have observed that when you must play a competitive game and believe you will lose, you tend to do things that will actually increase the probabilities of being defeated, such as using a bad racket in a tennis game. You may therefore wonder why you behave that way, and whether this is a common phenomenon.

> Blaming your equipment is a phenomenon known as 'self-handicapping'; Chapter 3 discusses this in more detail.

hypothesis *a testable proposition that describes a relationship that may exist between variables*

Once a research question has been established, social psychologists formulate a hypothesis. This means that, when asking a research question, social psychologists normally have an answer in mind. For instance, you could hypothesize that the reason people may handicap themselves when playing a competitive game is to have a ready-made excuse for defeat, thereby protecting self-esteem. The important feature of hypotheses is that of being testable. That is, it has to be possible to test a hypothesis in order to see if it is correct. Like research questions, hypotheses are often derived from theories. What is more, when a hypothesis is based on a theory, testing the hypothesis implies testing the theory too (Sani & Todman, 2006). If the hypothesis is proved incorrect, then some aspects of the theory may need revision, or the theory may even be rejected altogether. If, on the other hand, the hypothesis is confirmed, the theory will increase its credibility. That will not imply, however, that the theory is true once and for all, but rather that for the time being the theory cannot be said to be false. This general approach to research derives from the work of a philosopher of science, Karl Popper. In a widely acclaimed book titled *Conjectures and Refutations* (Popper, 1963), he contended that the objective of scientific research should be that of disproving, rather than proving, theories. A theory can be considered a plausible account of the phenomenon at stake as long as researchers fail to disprove the theory. Building on this idea, philosophers and researchers taking a positivistic stance believe that, to be considered 'scientific', a theory must be *falsifiable*.

Once a testable hypothesis has been formulated, social psychologists must decide which specific method they want to use. In general, the chosen method depends on the nature of the hypothesis. If this is concerned with the association (or correlation) between variables, the researcher will likely opt for a survey study. But if the hypothesis concerns the possibility that changes in one variable cause changes in another variable, then the researcher will be more likely to conduct an experiment. (See Table 2.2 for a summary of the different stages in the quantitative approach.)

## CORRELATIONAL RESEARCH: EXPLORING ASSOCIATIONS

Today's psychologists relate personal and social factors to human health. Among the researchers have been Douglas Carroll at Glasgow Caledonian University and his colleagues, George Davey Smith and Paul Bennett (1994). In search of possible links between socio-economic status and health, the researchers ventured into Glasgow's old graveyards. As a measure of health, they noted from grave markers

**TABLE 2.2** A summary of the main stages in the quantitative approach to research

| Stage | Meaning |
| --- | --- |
| Research question | A broad or narrow question to be addressed by the research |
| Theory | A set of interrelated assumptions and propositions used to define and/or explain a specific phenomenon or a set of phenomena |
| Hypothesis | A testable proposition |
| Method | A specific research procedure used to test the hypothesis |

the life spans of 843 individuals. As an indication of status, they measured the height of the pillars over the graves, reasoning that height reflected cost and therefore affluence. As Figure 2.1 shows, taller grave markers were related to longer lives, for both men and women.

Commemorative markers in Glasgow Cathedral graveyard.

SOURCE: © nonimatge/iStock

Carroll and his colleagues explain how other researchers, using contemporary data, have confirmed the status–longevity association. Scottish postal-code regions having the least overcrowding and unemployment also have the greatest longevity. In today's Britain, occupational status varies with longevity. One study followed 17 350 British civil service workers over 10 years. Compared with top-grade administrators, those at the professional-executive grade were 1.6 times more likely to have died. Clerical workers were 2.2 times and labourers 2.7 times more likely to have died (Adler et al., 1993, 1994). So it seems that across times and places, there does exist a reliable association between social status and health. One seems to vary with the other.

The research conducted by Carroll and colleagues made use of information that did not need to be produced because it was already available. However, in many cases researchers have to devise ways of producing the information they need. To obtain data that allow assessing the degree of association between variables, researchers commonly design a questionnaire and ask people to complete it. The questionnaire will obviously include items tapping upon the variables of interest. For instance, if you decided to investigate the relationship between social status and health by means of a questionnaire, your questionnaire should include questions aimed at measuring one's social status (e.g., employment, educational attainments, salary earned) as well as questions that are able to produce a measure of the respondent's health status (e.g., whether they suffer from a chronic illness, whether they are under medication, number of working days

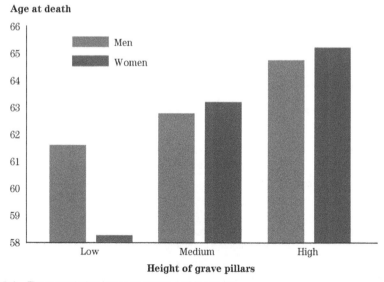

**FIGURE 2.1** The association between status and longevity
Tall grave pillars commemorated people who also tended to live longer.

missed because of illness, etc.). Questionnaires can be administered in various way, for instance by telephone, online or more simply by handing respondents a pencil and a paper copy of the questionnaire.

When designing a questionnaire we must take into consideration five important aspects.

**1** **Nature of sample.** Is it important that the sample is representative of a given population? It might not. But if it is important then we must ensure that we use an appropriate sampling strategy (see Table 2.3).

**2** **Order of questions.** The order in which we ask questions may produce biased responses. For instance, people's support for civil unions of gays and lesbians rises if they are first asked their opinion of gay marriage, compared with which civil unions apparently seem a more moderate alternative (Moore, 2004). Therefore, we need to give careful consideration to the way we order the questions.

**3** **Response options.** Consider the dramatic effects of the response options. When Joop van der Plight and his co-workers (1987) asked English voters what percentage of Britain's energy they wished came from nuclear power, the average preference was 41 per cent. They asked other voters what percentage they wished came from (1) nuclear, (2) coal, and (3) other sources. The average preference for nuclear power among these respondents was 21 per cent.

**4** **Wording of questions.** The precise wording of questions may also influence answers. For example, one poll found that most people favour cutting 'foreign aid' and *increasing* spending 'to help hungry people in other nations' (Simon, 1996). How questions are asked in a questionnaire is a very delicate matter. Even subtle changes in the tone of a question can have marked effects (Krosnick & Schuman, 1988; Schuman & Kalton, 1985). Even when people say

**TABLE 2.3** Sampling strategies in correlational research

| Type of sampling strategy | Main features |
| --- | --- |
| Random sampling | Where everyone in the population under study has an equal chance of being represented in the sample |
| Systematic sampling | Where members are drawn from a population at fixed intervals (e.g. every fifth person) |
| Stratified sampling | Aims to ensure all features of a population are represented in the sample |
| Cluster sampling | When the population is organized into groups (or clusters) and some 'clusters' feature in the sample |
| Opportunity/convenience sampling | A pragmatic form of sampling, where those who form the sample are those we have the best access to – or are the most 'convenient' (e.g. due to limited time and resources) |
| Snowball sampling | When the researcher 'snowballs' further participants from one respondent (e.g. their family and friends) |
| Theoretical/principled/ purposive sampling | When participants are chosen for inclusion in research on 'principled' reasons for their inclusion. Does not seek representativeness |

they feel strongly about an issue, a question's form and wording may affect their answer.

**5** **Validity and reliability of measures.** Questionnaire items are used to measure variables. For these measures to produce meaningful results, they must be valid and reliable. For instance, suppose we measure 'academic self-esteem' using the following two items: 'I regard myself as a competent student', 'I have good studying skills'. What we need to ensure in this case is that the items (i) are valid indicators of the construct they are meant to assess, that is self-esteem (validity issue), and that (ii) they jointly contribute to measure self-esteem and would produce the same results under similar conditions (reliability issue).

### Association and Causation

The status–longevity question illustrates the most irresistible thinking error made by both amateur and professional social psychologists: when two factors such as status and health go together, it is terribly tempting to conclude that one is causing the other. Status, we might presume, somehow protects a person from health risks. But might it be the other way around? Could it be that health promotes vigour and success? Perhaps people who live longer simply have more time to accumulate wealth (enabling them to have more expensive grave markers). So associations indicate a relationship, but to establish what causes what is not straightforward. In other words, research that detects associations cannot necessarily tell us whether changing one variable (such as social status) will *cause* changes in another (such as health). The association–causation confusion is behind much muddled thinking in popular psychology.

The investigation of these associations in social psychology is called correlational research. Consider a very real correlation – between self-esteem and academic achievement. Children with high self-esteem tend also to have high academic achievement. (As with any correlation, we can also state this the other way around: high achievers tend to have high self-esteem.) Why do you suppose that is (Figure 2.2)?

correlational research *the study of the naturally occurring relationships among variables*

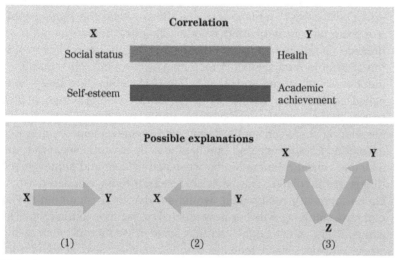

**FIGURE 2.2**   Correlation and causations

Some people believe a 'healthy self-concept' contributes to achievement. Thus, boosting a child's self-image may also boost school achievement But when two variables correlate, any combination of three explanations is possible. Either one may cause the other, or both may be affected by an underlying 'third factor'. It is not surprising, therefore, that alternative accounts of the association between self-esteem and academic achievement among children have been proposed.

William Damon (1995), Robyn Dawes (1994), Mark Leary (1999), Martin Seligman (1994, 2002) and Roy Baumeister and colleagues (2003), doubt that self-esteem is really 'the armour that protects kids' from underachievement (or drug abuse and delinquency). Perhaps it is the other way around: Perhaps problems and failures cause low self-esteem. Perhaps self-esteem often reflects the reality of how things are going for us. Perhaps self-esteem grows from hard-won achievements. Do well and you will feel good about yourself; skive off and fail and you will feel like a bit of an idiot! A study of 635 Norwegian schoolchildren showed that a (legitimately earned) string of gold stars by one's name on the spelling chart and accompanying praise from the admiring teacher can boost a child's self-esteem (Skaalvik & Hagtvet, 1990). Or perhaps, as in a recent study of nearly 6000 German seventh-graders, the traffic between self-esteem and academic achievements runs both ways (Trautwein & Lüdtke, 2006).

One way of quantifying correlations is by using the coefficient known as Pearson's $r$, which is a measure of the degree of relationship between two factors. Scores on this coefficient may range from –1.0 (as one factor score goes up, the other goes down) through 0 to +1.0 (the two factors' scores rise and fall together). Scores on self-esteem and depression tests have a negative correlation (about –.6). Identical twins' intelligence scores have a positive correlation (above +.8). The great strength of correlational research is that it tends to occur in real-world settings where we can examine factors such as race, gender and social status (factors that we cannot manipulate in the laboratory). See Figure 2.3 for a graph representation of a positive and a negative correlation.

Advanced correlational research and techniques *can* suggest cause–effect relations. *Time-lagged* correlations reveal the *sequence* of events (for example, by indicating whether changed achievements more often precede or follow changed self-esteem). Recall our earlier mention of a third variable, such as diet, which may have an influence on the apparent association of status and health. Third variables like these, sometimes called 'confounding' variables, can be removed using statistical techniques to see if the association between status and health still survives. The correlation between self-esteem and achievement evaporated after extracting intelligence and family status. So it would seem that there isn't a simple causal relationship between self-esteem and achievement. Other things are involved. The Scottish research team wondered whether the status–longevity relationship would survive their removing the effect of cigarette smoking, which is now much less common among those higher in status. It did, which suggested that some other factors, such as increased stress and decreased feelings of control, may also account for poorer people's earlier mortality.

**negative correlation** *when one variable increases as the other decreases*

**positive correlation** *when two variables both increase, or both decrease*

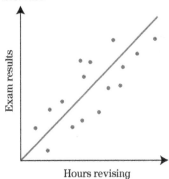

**Positive correlation**

- People who do more revision get higher exam results.
- Revising increases success.

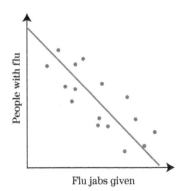

**Negative correlation**

- When more jabs are given the number of people with flu falls.
- Flu jabs prevent flu.

**FIGURE 2.3** Examples of a positive correlation and a negative correlation

SOURCE: http://scienceaid.co.uk/psychology/approaches/images/correlation.jpg

A study that is based on a questionnaire is often called a *survey study*. Bear in mind, however, that survey studies are very often employed to gather fairly straightforward descriptive information about people, with no ambition to assess correlations between complex dimensions. For instance, surveys may be used to assess the percentage of people in a given region or country who intend to vote for a specific political candidate. In this case, researchers want to make predictions about what could be expected to happen in a whole population. Therefore they may obtain a *representative* group by taking a random sample – *one in which every person in the population being studied has an equal chance of inclusion* (see Table 2.4 for a range of sampling

Even exit polls require a random (and therefore representative) sample of voters.

SOURCE: © asiseeit/iStock

techniques survey researchers might use). With this procedure any subgroup of people – blondes, joggers, liberals – will tend to be represented in the survey to the extent that they are represented in the total population. It is an amazing fact that whether we survey people in a city or in a whole country, 1200 randomly selected participants will enable us to be 95 per cent confident of describing the entire population with an error margin of 3 percentage points or fewer. Imagine a huge jar filled with beans, 50 per cent red and 50 per cent white. Randomly sample 1200 of these, and you will be 95 per cent certain to draw out between 47 per cent and 53 per cent red beans – regardless of whether the jar contains 10 000 beans or 100 million beans. If we think of the red beans as supporters of one political candidate and the white beans as supporters of the other candidate, we can understand why, since 1950, the Gallup polls taken just before national political elections have diverged from election results by an average of less than 2 per cent. As a few drops of blood can speak for the whole body, so can a random sample speak for a population.

**random sample** *survey procedure in which every person in the population being studied has an equal chance of inclusion*

**TABLE 2.4**  Recognizing correlational and experimental research

|  | Can participants be randomly assigned to condition? | Independent variable | Dependent variable |
|---|---|---|---|
| Are early-maturing children more confident? | No → Correlational | | |
| Do students learn more in online or classroom courses? | Yes → Experimental | Take class online or in classroom | Learning |
| Do school grades predict vocational success? | No → Correlational | | |
| Does playing violent video games increase aggressiveness? | Yes → Experimental | Play violent or non-violent game | Aggressiveness |
| Do people find comedy funnier when alone or with others? | (you answer) | | |
| Do higher-income people have higher self-esteem? | (you answer) | | |

## EXPERIMENTAL RESEARCH: SEARCHING FOR CAUSE AND EFFECT

The difficulty of discerning cause and effect among naturally correlated events prompts many social psychologists to create laboratory simulations of everyday processes whenever this is feasible and ethical.

### Control: Manipulating Variables

Social psychologists experiment by constructing social situations that simulate important features of our daily lives. By varying just one or two factors at a time – called independent variables – the experimenter pinpoints their influence. The experiment enables the social psychologist to discover principles of social thinking, social influence and social relations (the following chapters will offer many research-based insights, a few of which will be highlighted in 'Research Close-Up' boxes that describe a sample study in depth).

independent variables *the experimental factors that a researcher manipulates*

To illustrate the laboratory experiment, consider two experiments that typify research from upcoming chapters on prejudice and aggression. Each suggests possible cause–effect explanations of correlational findings.

### Correlational and Experimental Studies of Prejudice Against the Obese

The first experiment concerns prejudice against people who are obese. People often perceive the obese as slow, lazy and sloppy (Ryckman et al., 1989). Do such attitudes spawn discrimination? In the hope of finding out, Steven Gortmaker and his colleagues (1993) studied 370 obese 16- to 24-year-old women. When they re-studied them seven years later, two-thirds of the women were still obese and were less likely to be married and earning high salaries than a comparison group of some 5000 other women. Even after correcting for any differences in aptitude test scores, race and parental income, the obese women's incomes were well below the national average.

Correcting for certain other factors makes it look as though discrimination might explain the correlation between obesity and lower status. But we can't be sure. (Can you think of other possibilities?) Enter social psychologists Mark Snyder and Julie Haugen (1994, 1995). They asked 76 male students to get acquainted with a female student over the telephone. Unknown to the women, each man was shown a photograph he believed to be of his conversational partner. Half were shown an obese woman (not the actual partner); the other half a normal-weight woman. Later analysis of just the women's side of the conversation revealed that *they spoke less warmly and happily if they were presumed obese.* Clearly, something in the men's tone of voice and conversational content induced the supposedly obese women to speak in a way that confirmed the idea that obese women are undesirable. Prejudice and discrimination were having an effect.

Does viewing violence on television or in other media lead to imitation, especially among children? Experiments suggest that it does.

SOURCE: © paparazzit/iStock

### Correlational and Experimental Studies of Television Violence Viewing

As a second example of how experiments clarify causation, consider the correlation between television viewing and children's behaviour. Some research seems to show that when children watch violent television they also display aggressive behaviour. So are children learning and re-enacting what they see on the screen? As we hope you now recognize, this is a correlational finding. Figure 2.2 reminds us that there are two other cause–effect interpretations. (What are they?)

Social psychologists have therefore brought television viewing into the laboratory, where they control the amount of violence the children see. By exposing children to violent and non-violent programmes, researchers can observe how the amount of violence affects behaviour. Chris Boyatzis and his colleagues (1995) showed some primary school children, but not others, an episode of the 1990s' most popular – and violent – children's television programme, *Power Rangers*. Immediately after viewing the episode, the viewers committed seven times as many aggressive acts per two-minute interval as the non-viewers. The observed aggressive acts we call the dependent variable. Such experiments indicate that television can be one cause of children's aggressive behaviour.

So far we have seen that the logic of experimentation is simple: by creating and controlling a miniature reality, we can vary one factor and then another and discover how those factors, separately or in combination, affect people. Now let's go a little deeper and see how an experiment is done.

Every social psychological experiment has two essential ingredients. We have just considered one – *control*. We manipulate one or more independent variables while trying to hold everything else constant. The other ingredient is *random assignment*.

### Random Assignment: The Great Equalizer
Recall that we were reluctant, on the basis of a correlation, to assume that obesity *caused* lower status (via discrimination) or that violence viewing *caused* aggressiveness (see Table 2.4 for more examples). A survey researcher might measure and remove other factors that might be responsible for the association and see if the correlations survive. But one can never control for all the factors that might distinguish obese from non-obese, and viewers of violence from non-viewers. Maybe violence viewers differ in education, culture, intelligence – or in dozens of ways the researcher hasn't considered.

In one fell swoop, random assignment (not to be confused with the concept of random *sampling* in surveys) eliminates all such extraneous factors. With random assignment, each person has an equal chance of viewing the violence or the non-violence. Thus, the people in both groups would, in every conceivable way – family status, intelligence, education, initial aggressiveness – average about the same. Highly intelligent people, for example, are equally likely to appear in both groups. Because random assignment creates equivalent groups, any later aggression difference between the two groups will almost surely have something to do with the only way they differ – whether or not they viewed violence (Figure 2.4).

### Quasi-Experiments
Sometimes social psychological research cannot be conducted in a laboratory, yet the principles of experimental research are still required. In these circumstances researchers may adopt a quasi-experiment design. There are two basic types.

#### Natural Experiments
These are experiments in which the researcher does not directly manipulate the independent variable (IV). This may be for practical reasons or for research reasons. For example, you might want to see how long male shoppers spend in the

**dependent variable** *the variable expected to be dependent on the manipulation or change in the independent variable(s)*

**random assignment** *the process of assigning participants to the conditions of an experiment such that all persons have the same chance of being in a given condition*

**experimental research** *studies that seek to understand cause–effect relationships by manipulating one or more factors (independent variables) while controlling others (holding them constant)*

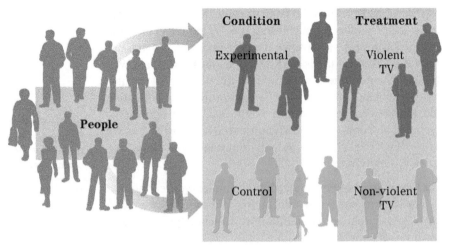

**FIGURE 2.4**  Random assignment

Experiments randomly assign people either to a condition that receives the experimental treatment or to a control condition that does not. This gives the researcher confidence that any later difference is somehow caused by the treatment.

ecological validity *the extent to which findings observed in a study reflect what actually occurs in natural settings. Psychological laboratory research has been criticized for its low ecological validity*

confounding variables *in an experiment, these are uncontrolled variables that interact with the independent variable, which affect the outcome of the research. The researcher can then not determine which variable (or which combination of variables) is responsible for the observed results*

supermarket shopping for groceries as compared to female shoppers. You cannot directly control the IV (gender), but you can match the number of respondents in each group (e.g. 20 male shoppers and 20 female shoppers), and you can still measure the effect the IV has on the dependent variable (amount of time shopping). There are some strengths in doing research in this way. As they do not rely on any intervention from the researcher, they have high ecological validity. However, there are some limitations also. As they occur in a natural setting you have no control over other variables (confounding variables). For example, we don't know if our sample are doing their weekly shop or just a daily shop. We can't control if they meet people they know in the supermarket and start talking to them.

*Field Experiments*

Unlike natural experiments, field experiments do offer the researcher the opportunity to control the IV, but they take place 'in the field'. This means the researcher has directly intervened with the research in some way. For example, a researcher might want to see if women are more helpful than men in a particular situation. To test this, the researcher might conduct the field experiment in a busy shopping centre and 'drop' bags of shopping in front of men and women to see if they help him or her to pick them up. Will women be more likely than men to go chasing after the researcher's fallen apples and oranges as they roll across the precinct floor? These kinds of experiments also have their advantages. As they take place in a natural environment (in the field) they have high ecological validity. However, they also have their problems. Taken out of the confines of the laboratory, the researcher has much less control over the experiment and cannot foresee all the confounding variables. For example, whether a shopper helps may not be due to their gender but whether they are capable of helping (e.g. what if s/he has an unobservable back problem?).

Both of our examples here are of an 'observation study', which we consider in more detail later in this chapter.

Generalizing from Laboratory to Life

As the research on children, television and violence illustrates, social psychology mixes everyday experience with experimental designs. Hunches gained from everyday experience often inspire experiments, which deepens our understanding of our experience.

This interplay appears in the children's television experiment. What people saw in everyday life suggested correlational research, which led to experimental research. Network and government policy makers, those with the power to make changes, are now aware of the results. The consistency of findings on television's effects – in the laboratory and in the field – is true of research in many other areas, including studies of helping, leadership style, depression and self-efficacy. The effects one finds in the laboratory have been mirrored by effects in the field. 'The psychology laboratory has generally produced psychological truths rather than trivialities', note Craig Anderson and his colleagues (1999).

We need to be cautious, however, in generalizing from laboratory to life. Although the laboratory uncovers basic dynamics of human existence, it is still a simplified, controlled reality. It tells us what effect to expect of variable $X$, all other things being equal – which in real life they never are! Moreover, as you will see, the participants in many experiments are university students. Although that may help you identify with them, college students are hardly a random sample of all humanity. Would we get similar results with people of different ages, educational levels and cultures? That is always an open question.

Nevertheless, we can distinguish between the *content* of people's thinking and acting (their attitudes, for example) and the *process* by which they think and act (for example, *how* attitudes affect actions and vice versa). The content varies more from culture to culture than does the process. People from various cultures may hold different opinions yet form them in similar ways.

Although our behaviours may differ, we are influenced by the same social forces. Beneath our surface diversity, we are more alike than different.

'There are lies, damned lies, and statistics.'
  Mark Twain

## QUALITATIVE RESEARCH

As with quantitative research, social psychologists taking a qualitative approach start with a research question they wish to address. However, such a research question does not concern the interplay between variables, and is not meant to produce hypotheses to be tested. Instead, the question is framed in a way that allows a free exploration of the issue at stake, with no specific expectations about what is to be found. For instance, a qualitative researcher could ask: 'How do foreign students experience their first year at university?' or 'How do Western people define happiness?' This type of question implies a focus on the meaning of experiences and the understanding of situations and issues. The findings of qualitative research can be interpreted as representing 'facts' (or testimony) about human experience (essentialist), or as 'socially constructed' (or versions). Most qualitative research is open to either interpretation. While essentialist interpretations try to reveal psychological properties of people and between people (e.g. emotions, memory, personality), social constructionists regard what people say and/or do as embedded within the context of its production. The concerns over accuracy of data (sometimes the honesty of the participant in relaying their experiences) which trouble the essentialist are not a concern to the social constructionist. For the social constructionist, what is of interest is 'why this version now?'

Qualitative research differs from quantitative research in other important ways. First of all, sampling is typically not as random as that found in quantitative studies, but is purposive (sometimes called 'principled' or 'theoretical' sampling – see Table 2.1). As the concern is not necessarily with generalization but with people's experiences, samples do not always need to be representative. Indeed, a study may involve only one person (a case study), chosen because s/he is interesting in some way. People can be selected for inclusion in a qualitative study for all kinds of reasons. They may typify what we've already seen and heard among our sample. For example, in a sample of left-wing voters perhaps we've noticed that they all explain homelessness as the fault of the government. We may seek more left-wing voters to warrant this further, or we might try to find someone who may say something different. What might a right-wing voter say about homelessness? Or a liberal voter? So participants are selected for inclusion in a study for *principled* reasons.

Another important difference between qualitative and quantitative research concerns the role of the researcher. While quantitative researchers see themselves as interchangeable and almost like neutral elements that are external to the phenomena that are investigated, qualitative researchers see themselves as enmeshed in what they are studying. They are fully aware that, by virtue of being present, they may change, alter or influence in some way the behaviour of research participants. So, qualitative researchers feel compelled to reflect on their role in the research process and make this clear in the analysis. This is usually referred to as 'reflexivity' and denotes the influence of the researcher, as well as the immediate and wider social context, upon the research process.

**reflexivity** *to recognize the role of the researcher in the production of the research findings*

## COLLECTING DATA IN QUALITATIVE RESEARCH

Qualitative researchers have a vast array of methods that they can use, some of which may be similar to the methods used by quantitative researchers. Interviewing is perhaps the most commonly used method. The researcher may follow a schedule, but this is unlikely to include structured questions, that is, questions to be answered with pre-formatted response options. Interviews used by qualitative researchers tend to have minimal structure. The researcher may either have some questions to ask, to which the participant will give personal and usually lengthy responses, or opt for a conversational approach where the only constraint is to adhere to the research question. (See Table 2.5 for the different styles of interviewing.)

**interviewing** *a strategy to obtain qualitative data based on talking with and asking questions of a research participants; questions may be asked either directly or indirectly, and responses are given in an open format*

Researchers normally record the interviews and transcribe them either partially or fully, so that the text can be carefully analysed and interpreted. However, interviewing does not need to be done on an individual basis. In fact, some

**TABLE 2.5**  Different styles of interviewing

| Type of interview | Main features of interview | Limitations of interview style |
|---|---|---|
| Structured | Fixed questions asked in the same order. These are typically answered using a predefined set of response options. Because response options tend to correspond to quantities, this type of interview is more commonly used in a quantitative approach | Can lack validity as the questions may not reflect participants' experiences or understandings |
| Semi-structured | Contains key questions to maintain relevance. Flexible order in which questions are phrased and presented during interview to suit the experiences of the participant. Can build good rapport with interviewee. Useful for studying sensitive topics and issues | Lacks reliability. Poor researcher control for directing what is discussed in the interview and how it is discussed |
| Conversational/ unstructured | Contains key topic(s). Very flexible wording and presentation of questions. Participant-driven to capture their experience and understanding of the phenomena under investigation. Can build good rapport with interviewee. Useful for studying sensitive topics and issues | Very poor reliability. Researcher has very little control over the interview. Interview may not reflect interests or concerns of the research |

research questions are better investigated with small groups of people, known as focus groups. When running a focus group, the role of the researcher is to facilitate the discussion of the topic under investigation (i.e., act as moderator). Focus groups have typically been used in market research, but can be used to investigate all sorts of issues, including health education and promotion (Basch, 1987).

*focus group a strategy to obtain qualitative data based on a small group discussion about the issue of interest facilitated by the researcher*

Qualitative researchers may also use observational methods. This will often involve the direct participation of the researcher in the event or situation studied, in which case we talk of participant observation. By using direct involvement and full immersion in the context examined, the researcher tries to see the world through the eyes of the individuals and groups being studied. This is meant to provide the researcher with deep knowledge and understanding.

Other ways of obtaining data for qualitative research include the recording of naturally occurring conversations (e.g. interactions between a doctor and patient), and the collection of texts available from various sources including newspaper articles, diaries, letters, political transcripts, pamphlets, leaflets, booklets and the Internet (e.g., forums, blogs, dating sites).

*participant observation a research strategy in which the researcher spends time in close contact with the people studied (tribe, group, community, team) for a prolonged period of time in order to gain a deep understanding of their perspectives and practices*

## QUALITATIVE DATA ANALYSIS

The aim of qualitative data analysis is to capture 'meaning'. This requires researchers to carefully code data, and discern themes, patterns and deviances present within their sample. Researchers have developed particular ways of doing this. Let's consider some of the main traditions of qualitative analysis.

### Grounded Theory

Grounded theory (GT) was founded by Barney Glaser and Anselm Strauss (1967), who developed the technique to challenge the grand theories that imposed a priori ways of collecting and analysing data. Working as sociologists involved in research with hospital patients, they had become frustrated with research techniques that understood their experiences in relation to pre-existing grand theories. These are outlined in their earlier work *Awareness of Dying* (1965). So, in grounded theory,

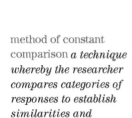

method of constant comparison *a technique whereby the researcher compares categories of responses to establish similarities and differences in meaning*

rather than beginning by developing a hypothesis based on existing research and theory, data collection is the first step. From the data collected, concepts are developed and from these concepts categories are formed, which, using the method of constant comparison, are the basis for the creation of a theory. 'In discovering theory, one generates conceptual categories or their properties from evidence, then the evidence from which the category emerged is used to illustrate the concept' (Glaser & Strauss, 1967, p. 23).

Grounded theory does not aim for the 'truth' but seeks to develop a theory which accounts for every single piece of data, to explain what's going on in the data. So it remains humble in its claims. It doesn't seek to generalize this theory beyond the data, thus resulting in another 'grand theory'. However, researchers may check their findings against similar studies for the validity and robustness of their claims. In a way GT resembles what many researchers do when retrospectively formulating new hypotheses to fit data. However, in GT the researcher does not claim to have formulated the hypotheses in advance since this is not allowed (Glaser & Strauss, 1967).

Grounded theory can be used on most kinds of data. Fieldnotes can come from informal interviews, lectures, seminars, expert group meetings, newspaper articles, Internet mail lists, even television shows, conversations with friends, etc. It is even possible, and sometimes a good idea, for a researcher with much knowledge in the studied area to interview him/herself, treating that interview like any other data, coding and comparing it to other data and generating concepts from it.

### Discourse Analysis

Discourse analysis (DA) has a long history in the social sciences, but is typically credited with being brought into social psychology by Jonathan Potter and Margaret Wetherell. Their book *Discourse and Social Psychology: Beyond Attitudes and Behaviour* (1987) applied the principles of DA to social psychological phenomena. Discourse analysts argue that 'talk' and 'text' should be the principal concerns of social psychology. Potter (1996) argues that language is not simply a mirror neutrally reflecting how we see the world and ourselves but is the construction yard in which social (and psychological) life is constructed (see also Edwards, 1997; Edwards and Potter, 2005). In other words, through language we create the world around us and our position within it, and in a way that is appropriate at the time. Discourse analysis typically studies language obtained from interviews, focus groups, natural conversations and forms of text (such as diaries and newspaper articles). For example, people's responses to questions asked in interviews or questionnaires, or their thoughts, feelings, memories and experiences reported in a focus group or interview, or even written down in a diary, should be evaluated, interpreted and put into the context in which they were produced before it is possible to conclude what is actually being communicated. The analytical tool of DA is the '*interpretative repertoire*', which is used to refer to the linguistic resources people have available to them in understanding aspects of their social world.

A good example of findings produced through a discourse analytic method is research conducted by Carlo Perrotta (2006). He was interested in how Italian psychologists define what it means to become a psychologist. Therefore he randomly selected 20 discussions among young Italian psychologists from some online forum. The analysis identified three interpretative repertoires.

**1** Professional boundaries – this repertoire established clear boundaries between psychologists and others who used psychology but were not actually 'psychologists'. For example, Michele said: 'We will carry on fighting anyway but sometimes I have the feeling that I am trying to empty the sea with a teaspoon, because besides counsellors there are others who are trying to invade our field.'

**2** A disempowered psychology – this repertoire concerned the lack of respect psychology receives in comparison to other professions. For example, from Eowyn: 'What really bothers me is that basically there is no room for the psychologist because the public recognizes all the following professions: psychiatrists, nurses, educators, social workers. But the psychologist is ABSOLUTELY MARGINAL in the health system.'

**3** Psychology and health – this repertoire emphasized the importance of psychology in the health profession. For example, Danielita wrote: 'This is my experience: doctors often do what we should be doing; they don't value our contribution for diagnostic purposes . . . Furthermore, they can become therapists themselves, and this feeds even more their all-powerful attitude, and reduces drastically our job opportunities.'

Perrotta concluded that these interpretative repertoires are ways of understanding the profession of 'psychology' and reflect its troubled history for credibility among the other sciences (such as biology). This troubled history forms the socially constructed identity of 'psychologist' among these young professionals.

Some discourse analysts (sometimes called critical discourse analysts) have argued that the form of DA presented by Potter and Wetherell tends to assume people are free to use language in whatever way they choose (e.g. Parker, 1992). They point out that this isn't always the case. They are influenced by the work of the philosopher Michel Foucault, who emphasized the role of power in shaping language (e.g. Wodak, 2009; Wodak & Meyer, 2009). Foucault remarked that people are positioned in society in relation of power to one another. The most powerful make decisions about what is appropriate social behaviour, and what can be said and what can't. For example, in history, ruling governments and leaders have decreed homosexuality as deviant and even an illness. This has shaped how sexuality is talked about and people's own behaviour. It has defined what can be said and what cannot. The point is that we are not always free to construct the world in precisely the way we'd like.

Discourse analysis has become widespread and popular among social psychologists, especially in Europe and Australia. For example, studies of prejudice or racism often benefit from a more detailed analysis of the language in which they are produced, warranted and justified as acceptable or deviant ways of seeing the world (see Chapter 13 for more detailed studies).

### Interpretative Phenomenological Analysis

Interpretative phenomenological analysis (IPA) is based on the philosophy of phenomenology. Phenomenologists emphasize the inextricable relationship between the mind and the outside world (sometimes referred to as 'lifeworld').

Michel Foucault (1926–84).
SOURCE: © INTERFOTO/Alamy

They consider how our conscious experience of being-in-the-world is constituted by our feelings, embodiment, relationships, and sense of time and space, with the outside world. Founded by Jonathan Smith, IPA adopts an idiographic approach to focus on the subjective conscious experience of individuals. Drawing on data obtained from interviews or focus groups, sometimes letters and reports, IPA encourages the researcher to obtain as much description and knowledge of the participant's lifeworld as possible. In analysing the data, IPA engages with the meaning conveyed by participants in their described experiences. It tries to identify themes that occur and reoccur in the description of the participant, and if appropriate group, and organize the themes hierarchically. Does the participant prioritize the importance of some things over others? The production of a summary of themes for each participant then enables the researcher to look for comparisons in data obtained from other individual participants. Are any experiences common across all the data?

For example, in their IPA study Matthew Knight, Til Wykes and Peter Hayward (2003) conducted semi-structured interviews with six outpatients who had a diagnosis of schizophrenia. Present in their experiences were superordinate themes of judgement, comparison and personal understanding of the issue. Subsumed under judgement were themes of being judged in terms of negative attitudes, prejudice and discrimination by society and others. Themes within comparison concerned how respondents compared their lives before and after the diagnosis of schizophrenia. Embedded within these narratives were experiences of inclusion and exclusion from social circles. Their personal understanding of the issue focused on themes of health and coping. Participants considered whether they regarded themselves as 'ill' and what mechanisms they had in place to cope with their condition. Knight et al. argue that these descriptions of experiences reflect the public and personal stigma surrounding schizophrenia.

## RESEARCH ETHICS

Some may now feel that Milgram's classic experiment, where people thought they were inflicting pain on others, is an example of the end not justifying the means. See Chapter 7 for a full explanation of the experiment and its replications.

Researchers often walk a tightrope in designing experiments and research that will be involving yet ethical. To believe that you are hurting someone, or to be subjected to strong social pressure, may be temporarily uncomfortable. Even the simple fact of being deceived about the real purpose of a study – which is what happens to participants in a substantial number of cases (Korn & Nicks, 1993; Vitelli, 1988) – may be an unpleasant experience. Such research raises the age-old question of whether the ends justify the means. Do the insights gained justify deceiving and sometimes distressing people?

Clearly, since social psychological research usually involves human beings, we have to be extra careful in how we treat them. That means that, however we conduct research, whatever methods we use, they all raise ethical issues. University ethics committees review social psychological research to ensure that it will treat people humanely. Ethical principles developed by the British Psychological Society (2000), American Psychological Association (2002) and the Canadian Psychological Association (2000) mandate investigators to do the following:

- ☐ Tell potential participants enough about the experiment to enable their informed consent.

- ☐ Be truthful. Use deception only if essential and justified by a significant purpose and not 'about aspects that would affect their willingness to participate'.

- ☐ Protect participants (and bystanders, if any) from harm and significant discomfort.

- ☐ Treat information about the individual participants confidentially.

- ☐ Debrief participants. Fully explain the experiment afterward, including any deception.

The only exception to this rule is when the feedback would be distressing, such as by making participants realize they have been stupid or cruel.

The experimenter should be sufficiently informative *and* considerate that people leave feeling at least as good about themselves as when they came in. Or, in other words, people should leave your research unaffected by it. Better yet, the participants should be compensated by having learned something. When treated respectfully, few participants mind being deceived (Epley & Huff, 1998; Kimmel, 1998). Indeed, say social psychology's advocates, professors provoke far greater anxiety and distress by giving and returning course examinations than researchers provoke in their experiments!

## ETHICS IN ONLINE RESEARCH

There are additional ethical considerations if social psychological research is conducted online. As the researcher is not in direct contact with the participant this poses particular problems. For example, the detection of a distressed or troubled participant is more difficult online. Verifying the identity of your participants and ensuring informed consent become hurdles that require extra thought. The public nature of information provided on the Internet means that privacy and confidentiality of data may not be possible. Professional psychology bodies offer advice and guidance on the kinds of ethical issues a psychologist needs to be aware of if s/he chooses to collect data online. For example, see Table 2.6 for a summary of ethical issues identified by the British Psychological Society in online research.

**informed consent** *an ethical principle requiring that research participants be told enough to enable them to choose whether they wish to participate*

**deception** *in research, an effect by which participants are misinformed or misled about the study's methods and purposes*

**debrief** *in social psychology, the post-experimental explanation of a study to its participants. Debriefing usually discloses any deception and often questions participants regarding their understandings and feelings*

**TABLE 2.6**  Types of online research and ethical issues

| Participants | Identifiable | Anonymous |
|---|---|---|
| Recruited | Verifying identity | Levels of control |
| | Informed consent | Monitoring the consequences of research |
| | Withdrawal | Protecting participants and researchers |
| | Data protection | |
| Unaware | Deception | Understanding of public and private space |
| | | Debriefing |

SOURCE: The British Psychological Society Working Party Guidelines on Conducting Research Online. Reprinted with permission.

## focus on

### THE IMPORTANCE OF REPLICATION

A prominent North American social psychologist, Daryl Bem, recently conducted a very unusual study. He recruited a sample of students and showed them 48 words, one at a time, asking to visualize the referent of each word (e.g., if the word was *tree*, they were to visualize a tree). Then, students were given a (surprise) free recall test that involved typing all the words they could recall in any order. Subsequently participants were instructed to scan the full list of 48 words and click on six specific words that the computer had randomly selected, as a way to practise. Then the list of 48 words was rescrambled and the task of clicking on the 6 words was repeated. This specific task was performed a total of four times. Data analysis produced some bewildering results. In the recall task, students were more likely to write those words that were subsequently used in the practice task. Basically, students appeared to know in advance which words they would eventually practise. This provided evidence that a well-known psychological phenomenon – the effect of practice on recall — had been time-reversed. In sum, Bem seemed to have demonstrated the existence of precognition and psychic power! This study, together with eight other similar studies, was included in a paper titled 'Feeling the Future' published in the prestigious *Journal of Personality and Social Psychology* (Bem, 2011).

Needless to say, the paper was received with a great deal of scepticism, which has grown even stronger after two independent research teams failed to replicate Bem's findings (Galak et al., 2012; Ritchie et al., 2012). As well as casting serious doubts on the veracity of the phenomenon allegedly proved by Bem, these failed attempts at replicating his findings started a debate about the validity of the results that are regularly published in social psychology journals. To what extent can we trust those results? Are the processes and phenomena reported by social psychologists real or just fiction?

For sure, the problem is not specific to social psychology. For instance, epidemiologist John Ioannidis, currently at the Stanford School of Medicine, claimed that most published research findings in medicine are false (Ioannidis, 2005). In line with that, Glem Begley, vice president of research at Amgen, a prominent bio-technology firm based in California, admitted that they are very often unable to reproduce findings published by researchers in bio-medical journals (Naik, 2011).

Many scientists, including social psychologists, are now insisting that authors of studies that produce interesting results should make an effort to reproduce these results, especially if they are surprising and counter-intuitive, before publishing them. This would prevent non-existing effects and processes from being published in journals and from being accepted by many as established *facts*. This sounds like a simple recipe, but there is a problem: Researchers are often in a hurry to publish for career reasons, and so they are unwilling to spend time conducting replications after some interesting results have been obtained. But then, shouldn't researchers at least try to replicate their results after their first set of studies have been published? Or indeed, shouldn't researchers try to replicate published studies more generally, regardless of who the author of the original article was? The consensus is that, ideally, they definitely should! The problem in this case is that there are no incentives to do so. Attempts to replicate previously published studies are generally not welcome by academic journals. This is especially the case when an attempt at replication fails to reproduce the original results, because journals prefer to publish studies with *positive* results, that is, studies that successfully demonstrate the hypothesized existence of processes, mechanisms and phenomena. Daniele Fanelli (2011), a social scientist based at Edinburgh University, found that the proportion of positive results published in scientific journals is on the rise, and this is especially the case with psychology and psychiatry journals (see Figure 2.5).

Some argue that, actually, scientists are already sending replication studies to journals, as testified by the fact that many published studies actually replicate previous studies using different methods (e.g., different ways of measuring the variables under scrutiny, different participants, etc.). But although *conceptual replications* – as psychologists like to call these types of replications – are important because they show the generalizability of the results (Nussbaum, 2012), many researchers still believe that what is needed is *direct replications*, that is, exact copies of the studies to be replicated. Brian Nosek, a social psychologist from the University of Virginia, put it plainly: 'To show that "A" is true you don't do "B". You do "A"

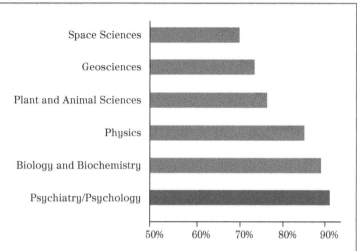

**FIGURE 2.5** Percentage of published studies reporting positive findings (i.e. those that support the tested hypotheses) across disciplines.

SOURCE: Adapted from Fanelli, 2011.

again' (Yong, 2012). One of the reasons for preferring direct over conceptual replications is that, as demonstrated by Joseph Simmons and his colleagues (2011), flexibility in the way we try to reproduce previous studies enhances the chances of confirming the existence of the phenomenon.

The necessity of conducting direct replications and finding out what is true and what is actually not true has recently prompted interesting initiatives among psychologists. The prestigious journal *Perspectives in Psychological Science* is now publishing 'registered replication reports'. These are replications of important psychology experiments based on shared and vetted protocols that are commented upon by the authors of the original studies. Also, Brian Nosek has launched the *reproducibility project*, where a group of psychologists will replicate a large number of papers recently published in some selected journals, including the *Journal of Personality and Social Psychology*.

In sum, while we may legitimately worry that some psychological phenomena we assume to be true may actually not be so, it is encouraging to see that psychologists, including social psychologists, have boldly started a process of self-correction. Hopefully, in the future we will feel more confident in the results produced by our research community.

## QUESTIONS

**1** Why do you think that many published studies fail to replicate?

**2** Can you think of any other initiative, beyond those mentioned above, that could contribute to increase our confidence in published results?

## SUMMING UP: RESEARCH METHODS IN SOCIAL PSYCHOLOGY

### I KNEW IT ALL ALONG: IS SOCIAL PSYCHOLOGY SIMPLY COMMON SENSE?

☐ Social psychology is criticized for being trivial because it documents things that seem obvious.

☐ Systematic research methods, however, reveal that 'outcomes' are more 'obvious' after the facts are known.

☐ This hindsight bias (the 'I-knew-it-all-along' phenomenon) often makes people overconfident about the validity of their judgements and predictions.

## APPROACHES TO DOING RESEARCH

☐ There are two broad approaches to doing research in social psychology: the quantitative and the qualitative approach.

☐ Researchers using a quantitative approach focus on the relationship between variables. With this aim in mind, the researcher will set up studies where the variables of interest can be measured, and then he/she will perform statistical analysis on the data.

☐ Researchers adopting a qualitative approach are interested in the experiential dimension of social psychological phenomena. Data are normally collected in naturalistic (not artificial) settings, and the data analysis focuses on the interpretation of meanings.

## QUANTITATIVE RESEARCH

☐ Quantitative researchers start by formulating a research question and deriving testable hypotheses. Then, the researcher must decide upon a method to be used for hypothesis testing, with correlational and experimental methods being the two common procedures.

☐ Correlational methods are used to explore the relationship between variables, such as between amount of education and amount of income. Knowing two things are related is valuable information, and represent what often happens in and between humans: the variables interact and there is a multicausality in real life.

☐ The experimental method is based on the construction of a miniature reality that is under the control of the experimenter. We randomly assign participants to an experimental condition, which receives the experimental treatment, or to a control condition, which does not. We can then attribute any resulting difference between the two conditions to the independent variable. This is the essence of experimentation in social psychology.

☐ Quasi-experimental designs offer less (or no) control than laboratory designs over variables, but are also concerned with relationships between variables.

## QUALITATIVE RESEARCH

☐ Qualitative methods of data collection and analysis seek to consider social behaviour in the context in which it occurs, and focus on how people construct, understand and give meaning to their own experience of the social world.

☐ In qualitative research, data can be collected using a number of strategies, the most common being interviewing, focus groups and participant observation.

☐ The analysis of qualitative data can be conducted in accordance with different traditions. Three important traditions are grounded theory, discourse analysis and interpretative phenomenological analysis. (1) Grounded theorists use the data in order to create a theory about the phenomena under scrutiny. (2) Discourse analysts are interested in the way people actively construe the world though language. (3) Researchers using interpretative phenomenological analysis are interested in finding out how a person will experience and frame facts or life such as marriage or illness.

## RESEARCH ETHICS

☐ In doing research, social psychologists sometimes stage situations that engage people's emotions, or observe them in their everyday lives. In doing so, they are obliged to follow professional ethical guidelines, such as obtaining people's informed consent, protecting them from harm, and fully disclosing afterwards any temporary deceptions.

## CRITICAL QUESTIONS

**1** Does social psychology really differ from common sense? If so, how?

**2** In your opinion, are the two general approaches to doing research in social psychology radically different, or are they complementary?

**3** Do you think that establishing cause-effect relationships between psychological variables is more important than establishing a correlation? What is the difference between correlation and causation?

**4** How strict should researchers be concerning ethical issues? Might exaggerated concerns limit researchers' ability to make progress?

## RECOMMENDED READING

Wilson, S. and MacLean, R. (2011). *Research Methods and Data Analysis for Psychology*. London: McGraw-Hill.

*Though not specifically devoted to social psychology, this is an excellent resource for social psychology students. It covers both quantitative and qualitative approaches in a balanced and unbiased fashion.*

# 3

"*There are three things extremely hard, Steel, a Diamond, and to know one's self.*"

Benjamin Franklin

# THE SELF

self *a complex web of psychological entities (e.g., cognitions, emotions) and processes (e.g., monitoring, evaluating) concerning one's own person*

At the centre of our worlds, more fundamental for us than anything else, is our self. As we journey through our daily lives, our sense of self over and again engages with the world. We have more information about our self than anybody else has. We know our self better than we know any other person and than any other person knows our self. Or perhaps not? Sometimes we doubt. We start thinking 'Who am I really?' In the play *Peer Gynt* Henrik Ibsen tells the story of a man searching for his real self, but he does not find it. It is like peeling an onion: you can take away layer after layer but there is no hard substance there at the end. Similarly, we may be unsure about our own value. Sometimes we may feel fairly happy about ourselves, while other times we are unsatisfied, we feel insecure. This links to our preoccupations for the impression we make on others. We may wonder whether we are behaving appropriately, whether others like or despise our conduct. In sum, we cannot escape thinking about who we are, how much we are worth, how we should behave, and what others think of us. We cannot escape ourselves! To some extent – as Mark Leary (2004) has noted – our self-centredness and egocentric preoccupations may be a curse, becoming an impediment to a satisfying life. This is what some forms of meditation practices seek to prune, by quieting the self, reducing its attachments to material pleasures and redirecting it. 'Mysticism,' adds fellow psychologist Jonathan Haidt (2006), 'everywhere and always, is about losing the self, transcending the self, and merging with something larger than the self.' In many ways this is what the Eastern self is about, an attachment to others and having the feeling that I am something larger than a single individual and that I have to behave accordingly. However, having a sense of self – particularly a sense of a temporally extended self – allows us to take our past into account, to assess our present, and to plan our future. In this respect the self does not make our existence more miserable; on the contrary, it improves it by enhancing the control we have on our life.

*In this chapter, we explore all these aspects of the self. We discuss how the self-concept is formed and organized, and how we perceive, evaluate, protect and strategically present ourselves, pointing to the burden that the self may represent, as well as to its adaptive functions.* But first of all, let's highlight the centrality of the self in our daily life by discussing the tendency to overestimate our own prominence in the social situations.

## SPOTLIGHTS AND ILLUSIONS

spotlight effect *the belief that others are paying more attention to one's appearance and behaviour than they really are*

Humans, especially those raised and living in Western cultures, tend to overestimate their conspicuousness. This spotlight effect means that we tend to see ourselves at centre stage, and so intuitively overestimate the extent to which others' attention is aimed at us.

Thomas Gilovich, Victoria Medvec and Kenneth Savitsky (2000) explored the spotlight effect by having individual students wear embarrassing Barry Manilow (an American singer-songwriter) T-shirts before entering a room with other students. The self-conscious T-shirt wearers guessed that nearly half their peers would notice the shirt. Actually, only 23 per cent did. What's true of our geeky clothes, bad hair and glasses is also true of our emotions: our

## research close-up

ON BEING NERVOUS ABOUT LOOKING NERVOUS

*Source: Savitsky, K., & Gilovich, T. (2003) The illusion of transparency and the alleviation of speech anxiety.* Journal of Experimental Social Psychology, *39, 618–625.*

### Introduction

Have you ever felt self-conscious when approaching someone you felt attracted to, and worried that your nervousness was obvious? Or have you felt yourself trembling while speaking before an audience, and presumed that everyone was noticing?

Many people who find themselves having to speak in public report being not only nervous but also anxious that they will seem so. And if they then feel their knees shaking and hands trembling as they present, their presumption that others are noticing may compound and perpetuate their anxiety. This is rather like fretting about not falling asleep, which further impedes one's falling asleep, or like one's anxiety about stuttering worsening one's stuttering. In sum, people speaking in public overestimate the extent to which their internal states 'leak out', and this makes them especially nervous. This study sought evidence for this 'illusion of transparency' among inexperienced public speakers, and investigated whether such perception disrupts performance.

### Study 1

*Method*

Forty university students went to the laboratory in pairs. One person was asked to stand at a podium with the other seated, and speak for 3 minutes about 'The Best and Worst Things about Life Today'. Then the two switched positions and the other person gave a 3-minute impromptu talk on a different topic. Afterwards, they each rated how nervous they thought they appeared while speaking (from 0, *not at all*, to 10, *very*) and how nervous the other person seemed.

*Results*

People rated themselves as appearing more nervous (6.65, on average) than they seemed to their partner (5.25), a difference great enough to be statistically significant (meaning that a difference this great, for this sample of people, is very unlikely to have been due to chance variation). Twenty-seven of the 40 participants (68 per cent) believed that they appeared more nervous than did their partner.

Might informing speakers that their nervousness isn't so obvious help them relax and perform better? A further study was run in order to assess this possibility.

### Study 2

*Method*

Seventy-seven students were asked to give a 3-minute videotaped speech on race relations at their university. Those in one group – the *control condition* – were given no further instructions. To those in two experimental groups, the experimenter acknowledged that 'I realize you might be anxious. It's perfectly natural ...', and explained how people may feel anxious both about their performance and about appearing nervous. To half – those in the *reassured condition* – he added, 'You shouldn't worry much about what other people think ... With this in mind you should just relax and try to do your best. Know that if you become nervous, you probably shouldn't worry about it.' To the other half – those in the *informed condition* – he explained the illusion of transparency: 'Research has found that audiences can't pick up on your anxiety as well as you might expect ... Those speaking feel that their nervousness is transparent, but in reality their feelings are not so apparent ... With this in mind, you should just relax and try to do your best. Know that if you become nervous, you'll probably be the only one to know.'

After the speeches, the speakers rated their speech quality and their perceived nervousness (this time using a 7-point scale), and were also rated by the observers.

### Results

As Table 3.1 shows, those informed about the illusion-of-transparency phenomenon felt better about their speech and their appearance than did those in the control and reassurance conditions. What's more, the observers confirmed the speakers' self-assessments.

**TABLE 3.1**  Average ratings of speeches by speakers and observers, on a 1 (low) to 7 (high) scale for perceived nervousness

| Type of rating | Control condition | Reassured condition | Informed condition |
|---|---|---|---|
| *Speakers' self-ratings* | | | |
| Speech quality | 3.04 | 2.83 | 3.50* |
| Relaxed appearance | 3.35 | 2.69 | 4.20* |
| *Observers' ratings* | | | |
| Speech quality | 3.50 | 3.62 | 4.23* |
| Composed appearance | 3.90 | 3.94 | 4.65* |

* Each of these results differs by a statistically significant margin from those of the control and reassured condition.

### DISCUSSION

When one feels nervous about looking nervous, pausing to remember that the sense of being transparent is an illusion, and that other people are noticing less than one might suppose, may reduce anxiety and improve performance. Might the technique used in this research – telling people about the illusion of transparency – be useful for clinical psychologists and psychotherapists treating speech anxiety? To the extent that one's speech anxiety is due to fear of looking nervous, and not to other factors, this technique should be effective. However, consider that participants in study 2 were informed about the illusion of transparency shortly before their speech delivery. Perhaps a larger time lag between the information and the speech would have reduced, or even eliminated, the beneficial effects of the information. Clearly, if the effects did not endure beyond the limits of the experimental session, the technique could not be used as a form of therapeutic intervention. It is for future research to shed light on this aspect.

**illusion of transparency** *the illusion that our concealed emotions leak out and can be easily read by others*

anxiety, irritation, disgust, deceit or attraction (Gilovich et al., 1998). Fewer people notice than we presume. Keenly aware of our own emotions, we often suffer an illusion of transparency. If we're happy and we know it, then our face will surely show it. And others, we presume, will notice. Actually, we can be more opaque than we realize. (See Research Close-Up: On Being Nervous about Looking Nervous.)

We also overestimate the visibility of our social blunders and public mental slips. When we trigger the library alarm or are the only guest who shows up for the dinner without a gift for the host, we may be mortified ('everyone thinks I'm a jerk'). But research shows that what we agonize over, others may hardly notice and soon forget (Savitsky et al., 2001).

The spotlight effect and the related illusion of transparency are only two of many examples of the interplay between our sense of self and our social worlds. Here are more examples:

☐ *Social surroundings affect our self-awareness.* As members of a specific culture, race, gender or social class, we may notice how we differ and how others are reacting to our difference. Being a white European in a rural village in Africa, an upper class person walking through a deprived suburb of a large city, or a woman being exceptionally invited to visit a men-only golf club in Scotland, would certainly raise self-consciousness!

☐ *Self-concern motivates our social behaviour.* In the hope of making a positive impression, we agonize about our appearance. (In fact, as we will see, even if our clothes and little imperfections are noticed less than we suppose, one's overall attractiveness does have effects.) Like shrewd politicians, we also monitor others' behaviour and expectations, and adjust our behaviour accordingly.

☐ *Social relationships help define our self.* In our varied relationships, we have varying selves, note Susan Andersen and Serena Chen (2002). We may be one self with Mum, another with friends and then another with teachers. How we think of ourselves is linked to whom we are in relationship with at the moment. This is even more typical for interdependent and collectivistic cultures where people are more engaged in creating harmony and balance in a group of people. To be a mature person in such cultures means to know how to fit in and change yourself accordingly.

Bad hair day? Fewer people notice our flaws than we think.
SOURCE © VikaValter/iStock

'No topic is more interesting to people than people. For most people, moreover, the most interesting person is the self.'
   Roy F. Baumeister, *The Self in Social Psychology*, 1999

## SELF-CONCEPT: WHO AM I?

*What determines the concept we have of ourselves? And how accurately do we actually know ourselves?*

As a unique and complex creature, you have many ways to complete the sentence 'I am _____.' (What five answers might you give?) Taken together, your answers define your self-concept.

self-concept *a person's answers to the question 'Who am I?'*

This simple but effective way to elicit one's self-concept – known as the Twenty Statements Test (TST) – was developed by Manfred Kuhn, one of the founders of the Iowa School of Social Psychology, and his collaborator Thomas McPartland (Kuhn & McPartland, 1954).

### OUR SENSE OF SELF

Self-schemas

The elements of your self-concept are your self-schemas (Markus & Wurf, 1987). *Schemas* are mental templates by which we organize our world, which obviously

self-schemas *beliefs about self that organize and guide the processing of self-relevant information*

We will discuss schemes, and their role in guiding us around the social world, in more detail in Chapter 4.

includes ourselves. Our self-schemas – our perceiving ourselves as athletic, overweight, smart or whatever – powerfully affect how we perceive, remember and evaluate other people and ourselves. If athletics is central to your self-concept then you will tend to notice others' bodies and skills. You will quickly recall sports-related experiences. And you will welcome information that is consistent with your self-schema (Kihlstrom & Cantor, 1984).

### Self-reference

**self-reference effect** *the tendency to process efficiently and remember well information related to oneself*

The self-concept has implications for information processing and memory. Consider the phenomenon known as the self-reference effect: when information is relevant to our self-concepts, *we process it quickly and remember it well* (Higgins & Bargh, 1987; Kuiper & Rogers, 1979; Symons & Johnson, 1997). Nicholas Kuiper's ground-breaking studies in the 1970s and 1980s asked students to rate adjectives (e.g. 'energetic', 'prudent') to describe themselves and other people. For the self-referent task, adjectives independently assessed as being extremely like or unlike the self had significantly faster rating times than adjectives only moderately self-descriptive. This has been called the 'inverted-U Rating Time effect' (Kuiper, 1981).

If asked whether a specific word, such as 'outgoing' or 'caring', describes us, we later remember that word better than if asked whether it describes someone else. If asked to compare ourselves with a short-story character, we remember that character better. Two days after a conversation with someone, our recall is best for what the person said about us (Kahan & Johnson, 1992). When we think about something in relation to ourselves, we remember it better. Interestingly, Kuiper and colleagues also found that people with depression focused on self-referent negative attributes, distinctive from most other people (Swallow & Kuiper, 1987).

The self-reference effect illustrates a basic fact of life, at least in Western cultures: our own self is the centre of gravity of our world. Not only do people tend to see themselves at centre stage, overestimating the extent to which they are noticed by others, as we saw when discussing the spotlight effect, but when judging someone else's performance or behaviour we often spontaneously compare it with our own (Dunning & Hayes, 1996). And if, while talking to one person, we overhear our name spoken by another in the room, our auditory radar instantly shifts our attention. If the self-reference effect is an expression of focusing on the personal self we would expect it to occur less in collectivistic cultures, where people do not want to stand out and be exceptional, than in individualistic cultures.

### Possible Selves

**possible selves** *images of what we dream of or dread becoming in the future*

The self-concept does not just concern who we think we are in the present but also who we think we might become in the future – the possible selves. Hazel Markus and her colleagues (Inglehart et al., 1989; Markus & Nurius, 1986) note that the possible selves include the visions of the self we dream of becoming – the helping self, the wise self, the passionately loved and loving self. They also include the self we fear becoming – the underemployed self, the unloved self, the academically failed self. Such possible selves motivate us with a vision of the life we long for.

### Self-discrepancy Theory

Our various self-perceptions may not be consistent with one another, thereby creating discrepancies that may produce psychological discomfort. This idea is elaborated by Edward Higgins (1987) in his self-discrepancy theory. This theory identifies three types of self-representation:

1. the *actual* self, regarding features that people believe they possess;

2. the *ideal* self, which includes characteristics that people wish or hope to possess; and

3. the *ought* self, concerning attributes that people believe they have a responsibility to possess.

The theory postulates that a discrepancy between the actual and the ideal self leads to dejection-related emotions (disappointment, dissatisfaction, sadness), and that a discrepancy between the actual and ought self generates agitation-related emotions (fear, threat, restlessness). Because of the negative mental states deriving from self-discrepancies, people strive to match their actual self with both their ideal and their ought self. Interestingly, Bizman and Yinon (2002) extended self-discrepancy theory to social identity (one's sense of self derived from membership in a social group). These authors studied a sample of Israelis and found that a discrepancy between actual and ideal Israeli identity produced dejection-related emotions while a discrepancy between actual and ought Israeli identity prompted agitation-related emotions.

It should be kept in mind, however, that a motivation to maintain a sense of consistency between different self-perceptions may be more marked in Western than in Eastern cultures. In fact, in East Asian cultures people tend to accept inconsistency and even antagonism in their self. They also accept that sometimes there will be differences between their aspirations and their actual behaviours.

### The Self and its Brain

Researchers in the field of social cognitive neuroscience (Lieberman, 2007) are investigating the brain activity that underlies different aspects of the self. To start with, they have asked themselves where our constant sense of being oneself arises. Some studies suggest an important role for the right hemisphere. Put yours to sleep (with an anaesthetic to your right carotid artery) and you likely will have trouble recognizing your own face. One patient with right hemisphere damage failed to recognize that he owned and was controlling his left hand (Decety & Sommerville, 2003). The 'medial prefrontal cortex', a neuron path located in the cleft between your brain hemispheres just behind your eyes, seemingly helps stitch together your sense of self. It becomes more active when you think about yourself (Zimmer, 2005). Consistent with that, studies have found that thinking about our own personality traits leads to greater activation of the medial prefrontal cortex, but also the medial parietal cortex, than thinking about someone else's personality characteristics (D'Argenbeau et al., 2005; Kjaer et al., 2002).

Intriguingly, social cognitive neuroscientists have also observed significant activations of the medial prefrontal cortex when people think about the personality traits and mental states of their mother (Ruby & Decety, 2004), a close friend (Ochsner et al., 2005), or someone considered as similar to self (Mitchell et al., 2005). The fact that thinking about oneself and thinking about others who are somehow associated with oneself activate similar areas of the brain, suggests that others may be experienced as in some way enmeshed with oneself.

The Social Construction of the Self

Researchers taking a constructionist perspective to the self, such as Kenneth Gergen (1991, 1994) or Margaret Wetherell (Wetherell & Maybin, 1996), contend that considering self-conceptions as enclosed and private, as residing into one's own head, gives an incomplete and misleading description of the human self. My thoughts and feelings about myself may seem to be locked inside my head, to be properties of my mind, but actually they are part of an always changing, fluid, dynamic system of social relationships in which I am involved. 'Who I am' is not just in my mind, but it is recounted in the stories I tell other people, the diaries I may write, and the letters I exchange. People who listen to us and read what we write form ideas about us, and relate to us on the basis of their own version of who we are, which in turn impacts upon our sense of self. As a consequence, the self is better described as *distributed* rather than localized, as embedded into a web of social relationships rather than as an entity under the skull (Bruner, 1990). This perspective also emphasizes that the self finds expression in our daily social encounters and interactions, which should be seen as *joint actions* within which the self emerges (Shotter, 1993). Clearly, if the self emerges in conversations and interactions, then it is largely contextual rather than singular and unitary.

## DEVELOPMENT OF THE SOCIAL SELF

The self-concept has become a major social psychological focus because it helps organize our thinking and guide our social behaviour (Figure 3.1). But what determines our self-concepts? Culture and social experience play, according to George Herbert Mead and many social psychologists today, an important part (e.g. Heine, 2005; Heine et al., 1999; Markus and Kitayama, 1991, 1994; Oyserman et al., 2002). Among these influences are the following:

☐ the roles we play

☐ the social identities we form

☐ the comparisons we make with others

☐ our successes and failures

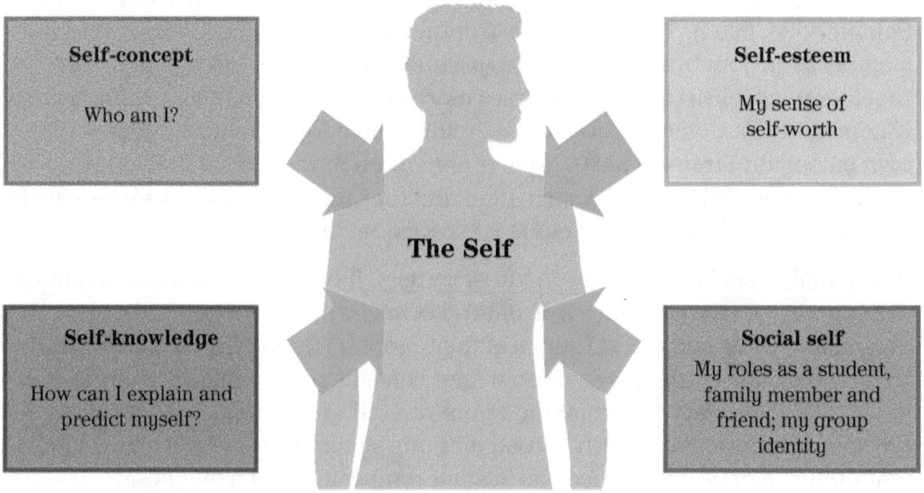

**Self-concept**

Who am I?

**Self-esteem**

My sense of self-worth

**The Self**

**Self-knowledge**

How can I explain and predict myself?

**Social self**

My roles as a student, family member and friend; my group identity

**FIGURE 3.1** The self

☐ how other people judge us

☐ the surrounding culture.

### The Roles We Play

When we take on a new role – college student, parent, salesperson – we initially feel self-conscious. Gradually, however, what begins as play-acting in the theatre of life is absorbed into our sense of self. For example, while playing our roles we may support something we haven't really thought much about. Having made a pitch on behalf of our organization, we then justify our words by believing more strongly in it. Role playing becomes reality (see Chapter 5).

*theatre*

### Social Identity

Following the pioneering work of Henri Tajfel (1981), social psychologists make a distinction between a personal and a social identity. Personal identity concerns our unique, idiosyncratic attributes, such as being hardworking (or laid back), and extrovert (or introvert). Social identity is the sense of who we are, derived from our membership in groups and collectives of various sorts. Being female, Spanish, Muslim, African American, a psychology student, socialist, a teacher, or a Real Madrid supporter are all aspects that may confer on one a social identity; that is, an identity that is shared in common with other people. The extent to which we are aware of any specific social identity depends, however, on the nature of the context. For instance, when we're part of a small group surrounded by a larger group, we are often conscious of our social identity; when our social group is the majority, we think less about it. As a solo female in a group of men, or as a solo Japanese in a group of Europeans, we are more conscious of our unique social identity or belongingness (Oakes et al., 1994).

**social identity** *one's sense of self and identity based on membership in social groups*

> Chapter 12 discusses Tajfel's work and the distinction between personal and social identity in more detail.

### Social Comparisons

People are generally eager to compare themselves with other individuals. They want to know if they are richer, smarter or taller than others, to make social comparisons (Festinger, 1954). As we shall see throughout this book, comparing ourselves with others has a huge impact on how we think and act. Others around us help to define the standard by which we define ourselves as rich or poor, smart or dumb, tall or short: we compare ourselves with them and consider how we differ. Social comparison explains why students tend to have a higher academic self-concept if they attend a school with few exceptionally capable students (Marsh et al., 2000), and how that self-concept can be threatened when a student who excelled in an average high school goes on to an academically selective university. The 'big fish' is no longer in a small pond.

**social comparison** *evaluating one's abilities and opinions by comparing oneself with others*

Much of life revolves around social comparisons. We feel handsome when others seem plain, smart when others seem dull, caring when others seem callous. When we witness a peer's performance, we cannot resist implicitly comparing ourselves (Gilbert et al., 1995). In a competitive society we may, therefore, privately take some pleasure in a peer's failure, especially when it happens to someone we envy and when we don't feel vulnerable to such misfortune ourselves (Lockwood, 2002; Smith et al., 1996). But social comparison does not just concern our personal identity, but also the in-groups that are part of our social identity. That is, people may compare their in-group with relevant out-groups in order to ascertain the status and prestige of the in-group (Tajfel, 1981). Intriguingly, taking pleasure at the misfortunes of others may imply taking malicious pleasure at the suffering of another group which we normally compare to our own group. This phenomenon, known as 'schadenfreude', has been studied in detail by Russell Spears and Colin Wayne Leach (Spears & Leach, 2004; Leach & Spears, 2009). These social psychologists have found that the stronger drive for the experience of schadenfreude is the pain of in-group inferiority and the anger based on this pain (Leach & Spears, 2008).

Social comparisons can also diminish our satisfaction. When we experience an increase in affluence, status or achievement, we 'compare upwards' – we raise the standards by which we evaluate our attainments. When climbing the ladder of success, we tend to look up, not down; we compare ourselves with others doing even better (Gruder, 1977; Suls & Tesch, 1978; Wheeler et al., 1982). When facing competition, we often protect our shaky self-concept by perceiving the competitor as advantaged (for example, in one study of collegiate swimmers (Shepperd & Taylor, 1999) as having better coaching and more practice time).

### Success and Failure

Self-concept is fed not only by our roles, our social identity and our comparisons but also by our daily experiences. To undertake challenging yet realistic tasks and to succeed is to feel more competent. After mastering the physical skills needed to repel a sexual assault, women feel less vulnerable, less anxious and more in control (Ozer & Bandura, 1990). After experiencing academic success, students develop higher appraisals of their academic ability, which often stimulate them to work harder and achieve more (Felson, 1984; Marsh & Young, 1997).

The success-feeds-self-esteem principle has led several research psychologists to question efforts to boost achievement by raising self-esteem with positive messages ('You are somebody! You're special!'). Self-esteem comes not so much from telling children how wonderful they are – which according to Twenge (2006) has actually damaged a generation of young Americans – but from hard-earned achievements. Feelings follow reality.

Low self-esteem does sometimes cause problems. Compared with those with low self-esteem, people with a sense of self-worth are happier, less neurotic, less troubled by insomnia, less prone to drug and alcohol addictions, and more persistent after failure (Brockner & Hulton, 1978; Brown, 1991; Tafarodi & Vu, 1997). But, as we will see, critics argue that it's at least as true the other way around: problems and failures can cause low self-esteem.

## SELF AND CULTURE

individualism or independence *a cultural orientation where the individual is more important than the group. People in such cultures commonly give priority to one's own goals over group goals, and define one's identity in terms of personal attributes rather than group identifications (compare to* collectivism*)*

How did you complete the 'I am _____' statement on page 55? Did you give information about your personal traits, such as 'I am honest', 'I am tall' or 'I am outgoing'? Or did you also describe your social identity, such as 'I am a Pisces', 'I am a MacDonald' or 'I am a Muslim'?

For some people, especially those in industrialized Western cultures, individualism or independence prevails. Identity is pretty much self-contained. Adolescence is a time of separating from parents, becoming self-reliant and defining one's personal, *independent self*. Uprooted and placed in a foreign land, one's identity – as a unique individual with particular abilities, traits, values and dreams – would remain intact.

The psychology of Western cultures assumes that your life will be enriched by defining your possible selves and believing in your power of personal control. Western literature, from the *Iliad* to *The Adventures of Huckleberry Finn*, celebrates the self-reliant individual. Movie plots feature rugged heroes who buck the establishment. Songs have proclaimed 'I Gotta Be Me' and revered 'The Greatest Love of All', which were about loving oneself (Schoeneman, 1994). Individualism flourishes when people experience affluence, mobility, urbanism and mass media (Freeman, 1997; Marshall, 1997; Triandis, 1994).

Many cultures native to Asia, Africa and Central and South America place a greater value on collectivism. They nurture what Shinobu Kitayama and Hazel Markus (1995) call the interdependent self. People are more self-critical and have less need for positive individual self-regard (Heine et al., 1999). Malaysians, Indians, Japanese and traditional Kenyans such as the Maasai, for example, are much more likely than Australians, Americans and the British to complete the 'I am' statement with their group identities (Kanagawa et al., 2001; Ma & Schoeneman, 1997). When speaking, people using the languages of collectivist countries say 'I' less often (Kashima & Kashima, 1998, 2003). A person might say 'Went to the cinema' rather than 'I went to the cinema.'

However, researchers should resist the temptation to oversimplify the picture. As a matter of fact, most cultures have a combination of individualism and collectivism qualities. A categorization of cultures as either individualistic or collectivistic fails to reflect the cultural diversity in most modern societies, for instance in Europe (Lu, 2003; Lu & Yang, 2006). There are individualist Chinese and collectivist Americans, and most of us sometimes behave communally, sometimes individualistically. Cultures can also change over time, and many seem to be growing more individualistic. Chinese citizens under 25 are more likely than those over 25 to agree with individualistic statements such as 'make a name for yourself' and 'live a life that suits your tastes' (Arora, 2005). Growing individualism in the United States shows in the names that parents give to their children. While nearly 20 per cent of boys born in 1990 received one of the ten most common names, only 9 per cent received such a common name by 2007 (Twenge et al., 2008). Today, an American child does not need to be the child of a celebrity to get a name as unique as Knox or Apple.

In his book *The Geography of Thought* (2003), social psychologist Richard Nisbett proposes that interdependence is not only evident in social relations but is also apparent in ways of thinking. For example, consider: which two – of a panda, a monkey and a banana – go together? Perhaps a monkey and a panda, because they both fit the category 'animal'? Asians more often than Americans see relationships: monkey eats banana. When shown an animated underwater scene (Figure 3.2), Japanese participants spontaneously recalled 60 per cent more background features than American participants, and they spoke of more relationships (the frog beside the plant). Americans, as confirmed in a follow-up eye-tracking study, attend more to the focal object, such as a single big fish, and attend less to the surroundings (Chua et al., 2005a; Nisbett, 2003). These results have been duplicated

collectivism *a cultural orientation where the group is more important than the individual. People in such cultures commonly give priority to the goals of their group and define their identity accordingly (the opposite of* individualism*)*

interdependent self *construing one's identity in relation to others*

FIGURE 3.2 Asian and Western thinking. When shown an underwater scene, Asians often describe the environment and the relationships among the fish. Americans attend more to a single big fish.

SOURCE: Photo by Stephen Ausmus, USDA-ARS

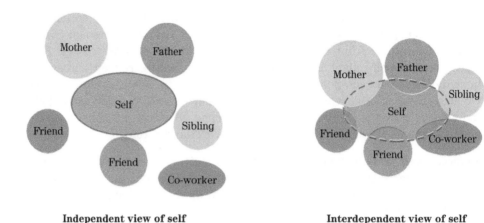

Independent view of self          Interdependent view of self

**FIGURE 3.3** Self-construal as independent or interdependent
The independent self acknowledges relationships with others, but the interdependent self is more deeply embedded in others (Markus & Kitayama, 1991).

in studies examining activation in different areas of the brain (Goh et al., 2007; Lewis et al., 2008), leading to the conclusion that a person's socio-cultural context is likely to shape the neural mechanisms that underlie cognition (Han & Northoff, 2008). Nisbett and Masuda (2003) conclude from such studies that East Asians think more holistically – perceiving and thinking about objects and people in relationship to one another and to their environment.

With an interdependent self, one has a greater sense of belonging. Uprooted and cut off from family, colleagues and loyal friends, interdependent people would lose the social connections that define who they are. As Figure 3.3 and Table 3.2 suggest, the interdependent self is embedded in group memberships. Conversation is less direct and more polite (Holtgraves, 1997). The goal of social life is not so much to enhance one's individual self as to harmonize with and support one's communities. The individualized latte – 'decaf, single shot, skinny, extra hot' – that seems just right at a North American espresso shop would seem strange in Seoul, note Heejung Kim and Hazel Markus (1999). In Korea, people place less value on expressing their uniqueness and more on tradition and shared practices (Choi & Choi, 2002, and Figure 3.4) Korean advertisements tend to feature people together; they seldom highlight personal choice or freedom (Markus, 2001).

**FIGURE 3.4** Which pen would you choose?

When Heejung Kim and Hazel Markus (1999) invited people to choose one of the pens (Figure 3.4), 77 per cent of Americans but only 31 per cent of Asians chose the uncommon colour (regardless of whether it was purple, as here, or green). This result illustrates differing cultural preferences for uniqueness and conformity, noted Kim and Markus.

Self-esteem is influenced by cultural context too. For instance, in collectivist cultures self-esteem correlates closely with 'what others think of me and my group'. Also, for those in individualistic cultures, self-esteem is more personal and less relational and contextual. Threaten our *personal* identity and we'll feel angrier and gloomier than

**TABLE 3.2** Self-concept: independent or interdependent?

|  | Independent | Interdependent |
|---|---|---|
| Identity is | Personal, defined by individual traits and goals | Social, defined by connections with others |
| What matters | Me – personal achievement and fulfilment; my rights and liberties | We – group goals and solidarity; our social responsibilities and relationships |
| Disapproves of | Conformity | Egotism |
| Illustrative motto | 'To thine own self be true' | 'No one is an island' |
| Cultures that support | Individualistic Western | Collectivistic Asian and 'Third World' |

when someone threatens our collective identity (Gaertner et al., 1999). Unlike the Japanese, who persist more on tasks when they are failing (wanting not to fall short of others' expectations), people in individualistic countries persist more when succeeding, because success elevates self-esteem (Heine et al., 2001). Western individualists like to make comparisons with others that boost their self-esteem. Asian collectivists make comparisons (often upwards, with those doing better) in ways that facilitate self-improvement (White & Lehman, 2005).

So when, do you suppose, are university students in collectivist Japan and individualist USA most likely to report positive emotions such as happiness and elation? For Japanese students, report Kitayama and Markus (2000), happiness comes with positive social engagement – with feeling close, friendly and respectful. For American students, it more often comes with disengaged emotions – with feeling effective, superior and proud. Conflict in collectivist cultures often is between groups; individualist cultures breed more conflict (and crime and divorce) between individuals (Triandis, 2000).

When Kitayama (1999), after ten years of teaching and researching in America, visited his Japanese alma mater, Kyoto University, graduate students were 'astounded' when he explained the Western idea of the independent self: 'I persisted in explaining this Western notion of self-concept – one that my American students understood intuitively – and finally began to persuade them that, indeed, many Americans do have such a disconnected notion of self. Still, one of them, sighing deeply, said at the end, "Could this *really* be true?".'

When East meets West – as happens, for example, thanks to Western influences in urban Japan and to Japanese exchange students visiting Western countries – does the self-concept become more individualized? Are the Japanese influenced when exposed to Western promotions based on individual achievement, with admonitions to 'believe in one's own possibilities', and with movies in which the heroic individual police officer catches the crook *despite* others' interference? They seem to be, report Steven Heine and his co-researchers (1999). Personal self-esteem increased among Japanese exchange students after spending seven months at the University of British Columbia. In Canada individual self-esteem is also higher among long-term Asian immigrants than among more recent immigrants (and than among those living in Asia).

## SELF-KNOWLEDGE

'Know thyself', admonished an Ancient Greek oracle. We certainly try. We readily form beliefs about ourselves, and we don't hesitate to explain why we feel and act as we do. According to Mead (1934), self-knowledge comes mainly from feedback we receive from other people. We may rely either on what particular individuals have to say about us, or on the picture offered by a combination of other people (what Mead called the 'generalized other'). But how well do we actually know ourselves?

'There is one thing, and only one in the whole universe which we know more about than we could learn from external observation' noted C. S. Lewis (1952, pp. 18–19). 'That one thing is [ourselves]. We have, so to speak, inside information; we are in the know.' Indeed. Yet sometimes we *think* we know, but our inside information is wrong. Or to put it in a less dramatic way: my understanding and perception of myself is different from how other people understand and perceive me. That is the unavoidable conclusion of some fascinating research.

### Explaining our Behaviour

Why did you choose your university? Why did you lash out at your room-mate? Why did you support just that football team? Why did you fall in love with that special person? Sometimes we know. Sometimes we don't. Asked why we have felt or acted as we have, we produce plausible answers. Yet, when causes are subtle, our self-explanations are often wrong. We may dismiss factors that matter and inflate others that don't. In studies, people have misattributed their rainy-day gloom to life's emptiness, and their excitement while crossing a suspension footbridge to their attraction to a good-looking bystander (Dutton & Aron, 1974; Schwarz & Clore, 1983) (see Chapter 9). And people routinely deny being influenced by the media, which, they acknowledge, affects *others*.

Acting together: following the 2009 earthquake in Indonesia, people helped each other.

SOURCE: © AFP/Getty Images

Richard Nisbett and Stanley Schachter (1966) demonstrated people's misreading of their own minds after asking Columbia University students to endure a series of electric shocks of steadily increasing intensity. Beforehand, some students took a fake pill that, they were told, would produce heart palpitations, breathing irregularities and butterflies in the stomach – the typical reactions to being shocked. Nisbett and Schachter anticipated that people would attribute the shock symptoms to the pill and thus tolerate more shock than people not given the pill. Indeed, the effect was enormous. People given the fake pill took four times as much shock. When asked why they withstood so much shock, they didn't mention the fake pill. When told the predicted pill effect, they granted that *others* might be influenced but denied its influence on themselves. 'I didn't even think about the pill' was a typical reply.

Also thought provoking are studies in which people recorded their moods every day for two or three months (Stone et al., 1985; Weiss & Brown, 1976; Wilson et al., 1982). They also recorded factors that might affect their mood: the day of the week, the weather, the amount they slept and so forth. At the end of each study, the people judged how much each factor had affected their moods. Remarkably (given that their attention was being drawn to their daily moods), there was little relationship between their perceptions of how well a factor predicted their mood and how well it actually did. Those findings raise a disconcerting question: how much insight do we really have into what makes us happy or unhappy?

### Predicting our Behaviour

People also err when predicting their behaviour. If asked whether they would obey demands to deliver severe electric shocks or would hesitate to help a victim if several other people were present, people overwhelmingly deny their vulnerability to such influences. But as we will see, experiments have shown that many of us are vulnerable. Moreover, consider what Sidney Shrauger (1983) discovered when he had college students predict the likelihood that they would experience dozens of

Does the weather really affect our mood as much as we might suppose?
SOURCE: © Borut Trdina/iStock

different events during the ensuing two months (becoming romantically involved, being sick and so forth): their self-predictions were hardly more accurate than predictions based on the average person's experience.

People also frequently err when predicting the fate of their relationships. Dating couples tend to predict the longevity of their relationships through rose-tinted glasses. Their friends and family often know better, report Tara MacDonald and Michael Ross (1997) from studies with University of Waterloo students. (Many a parent, having seen his or her child lunge confidently into an ill-fated relationship against all advice, nods yes.) In fact, the people who know you can probably predict your behaviour in a variety of situations better than you can – for example, how nervous and chatty you will be when meeting someone new (Kenny, 1994). So, how can you improve your self-predictions? The best advice is to consider your past behaviour in similar situations (Osberg & Shrauger, 1986, 1990). To predict your future, consider your past.

In Chapter 7 you can read about yawning as something contagious. Generally humans have a tendency to react with congruent facial expressions when looking at an emotional face. This phenomenon is called *facial mimicry*. It appears to be an automatic and unconscious reaction, without awareness or conscious control, and it cannot be completely suppressed (Dimberg et al., 2002). Our 'self' therefore accomplishes activities with consequences for our relationship to others without being able to fully control it.

### Predicting our Feelings

Many of life's big decisions involve predicting our future feelings. Would marrying this person lead to lifelong contentment? Would entering this profession make for satisfying work? Would going on this vacation produce a happy experience? Or would the likelier results be divorce, job burnout and holiday disappointment?

Sometimes we know how we will feel – if we fail that examination, win that big game or soothe our tensions with a half-hour jog. We know what exhilarates us, and what makes us anxious or bored. Other times we may mispredict our responses. Asked how they would feel if asked sexually harassing questions on a job interview, most women studied by Julie Woodzicka and Marianne LaFrance (2001) said they would feel angry. When actually asked such questions, however, women more often experienced fear.

## research close-up

### AN ILLUSION OF CONSCIOUS WILL

*Source*: Wegner, D. M., Sparrow, B., & Winerman, L. (2004). *Vicarious agency: Experiencing control over the movements of others. Journal of Personality and Social Psychology, 86, 838–848.*

### Introduction

In everyday life, we routinely will actions, such as raising our hand. We will an act. It happens. And, witnessing the sequence, we understandably infer that we caused it. Sometimes, however, we experience what psychologist Daniel Wegner (2002) calls an 'illusion of conscious will'. People whose hand is jointly controlling a computer mouse will perceive that they caused it to stop on a square that actually was predetermined by their partner (an experimenter's accomplice). Could people also be induced to sense themselves raising someone else's hand?

### Method

In one condition of the experiment participants watched themselves in a mirror while another behind them placed their hands where the participants' hands would normally appear (see Figure 3.5). So, the participants knew those arms weren't their own; they didn't perceive the arms as looking or feeling like their own. Then, participants were requested hand movements, such as 'make the A-OK sign'. That enabled the participant to anticipate the observed hand movements. There was also a baseline condition, in which the same hand movements occurred without any instruction (and thus no mental anticipation).

### Results

When participants could anticipate the hand movement, they reported feeling some degree of control, as if they were willing the hands to move (Figure 3.6). In the baseline condition, however, participants felt little sense of control. It was when the participants visualized an action and it promptly happened that they felt some responsibility.

**FIGURE 3.5** Vicarious agency.
The photo at left shows a participant seen as she would have seen herself in the mirror. The photo at right shows the participant and a research assistant.

SOURCE: Wegner, D. M., Sparrow, B., & Winerman, L. (2004). Vicarious agency: Experiencing control over the movements of others. Journal of Personality and Social Psychology, 86, 838–848, APA, reprinted with permission.

### Discussion

This study shows that when our thoughts are consistent with someone else's action, we may feel that we have caused the action. These findings relate to our ability to empathize with other people's actions, in our daily life. We often experience an empathic extension of self to movie characters, imaginary people from books, or people who are close and important to us (spouse, child, friend). This experience might be a form of the vicarious agency observed in this study: Our ability to anticipate another person's actions prompts a sense that those actions are ours, which in turn enhances our emotional connection with that person.

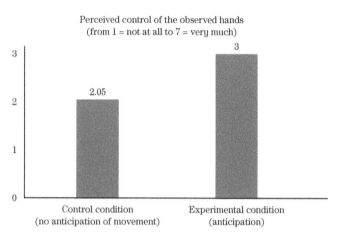

Perceived control of the observed hands
(from 1 = not at all to 7 = very much)

**FIGURE 3.6**   An illusion of willpower
When watching themselves in a mirror and witnessing a simulation of their own hand movements, people who anticipated the movement felt increased control over it.

Moreover, we are especially prone to impact bias after *negative* events. When people being tested for HIV predict how they will feel five weeks after getting the results, they expect to be feeling misery over bad news and elation over good news. Yet, five weeks later, the bad news recipients are less distraught and the good news recipients are less elated than they anticipated (Sieff et al., 1999). And when Daniel Gilbert and his colleagues (1998) asked assistant professors to predict their happiness a few years after achieving permanent job security (tenure) or not, most believed a favourable outcome was important for their future happiness. 'Losing my job would crush my life's ambitions. It would be terrible.' Yet when surveyed several years after the event, those denied tenure were about as happy as those who received it. Impact bias is important, say Timothy Wilson and Daniel Gilbert (2005), because people's 'affective forecasts' – their predictions of their future emotions – influence their decisions. If people overestimate the intensity and the duration of the pleasure they will gain from purchasing a new car or undergoing cosmetic surgery, then they may make ill-advised investments in that new Mercedes or extreme makeover.

Let's make this personal. Gilbert and Wilson invite us to imagine how we might feel a year after losing our non-dominant hands. Compared with today, how happy would you be?

Thinking about that, you perhaps focused on what the calamity would mean: no clapping, no shoe tying, no competitive tennis, no speedy keyboarding. Although it is likely that you would forever regret the loss, your general happiness some time after the event would be influenced by 'two things: (a) the event, and (b) everything else' (Gilbert & Wilson, 2000). In focusing on the

Predicting behaviour, even one's own, is no easy matter, which may be why this visitor goes to a tarot card reader in hope of help.

SOURCE: © Greg Nicholas/iStock

negative event, we discount the importance of everything else that contributes to happiness and so overpredict our enduring misery. 'Nothing that you focus on will make as much difference as you think,' concur researchers David Schkade and Daniel Kahneman (1998).

### The Wisdom and Illusions of Self-analysis

To a striking extent, then, our intuitions are often wrong about what has influenced us and what we will feel and do. But let's not overstate the case. When the causes of our behaviour are conspicuous and the correct explanation fits our intuition, our self-perceptions will be accurate (Gavanski & Hoffman, 1987). When the causes of behaviour are obvious to an observer, they are usually obvious to us as well.

As Chapter 4 explores further, we are unaware of much that goes on in our minds. Perception and memory studies show that we are more aware of the *results* of our thinking than of its process. For example, we experience the results of our mind's unconscious workings when we set a mental clock to record the passage of time or to awaken us at an appointed hour, or when we somehow achieve a spontaneous creative insight after a problem has unconsciously 'incubated'. Similarly, creative scientists and artists often cannot report the thought processes that produced their insights, although they have superb knowledge of the results.

Timothy Wilson (1985, 2002) offers a bold idea: the mental processes that *control* our social behaviour are distinct from the mental processes through which we *explain* our behaviour. Our rational explanations may therefore omit the unconscious attitudes that actually guide our behaviour. In nine studies, Wilson and his co-workers (1989) found that the attitudes people consciously expressed towards things or people usually predicted their subsequent behaviour reasonably well. Their attitude reports became useless, however, if the participants were first asked to *analyse* their feelings. For example, dating couples' level of happiness with their relationship accurately predicted whether they would still be dating several months later. But other participants first listed all the *reasons* they could think of why their relationship was good or bad before rating their happiness. These participants' happiness ratings were useless in predicting the future of the relationship! Apparently, the process of dissecting the relationship drew attention to easily verbalized factors that were actually not as important as harder-to-verbalize aspects of the relationship. We are often 'strangers to ourselves', Wilson concluded (2002).

Murray Millar and Abraham Tesser (1992) believe that Wilson overstates our ignorance of self. Their research suggests that, yes, drawing people's attention to *reasons* diminishes the usefulness of attitude reports in predicting behaviours that are driven by *feelings*. They argue that if, instead of having people analyse their romantic relationships, Wilson had first asked them to get more in touch with their feelings ('How do you feel when you are with and apart from your partner?'), the attitude reports might have been more insightful. Other behaviour domains – say, choosing which university to attend based on considerations of cost, career advancement and so forth – seem more cognitively driven. For these, an analysis of reasons rather than feelings may be most useful. Although the heart has its reasons, sometimes the mind's own reasons are decisive.

# SELF-ESTEEM

*People desire self-esteem, which they are motivated to enhance. But inflated self-esteem also has a dark side.*

Is self-esteem – our overall self-evaluation – the sum of all our self-schemas and possible selves? If we see ourselves as attractive, athletic, clever and destined to be rich and loved, will we have high self-esteem? Yes, say Jennifer Crocker and Connie Wolfe (2001), when we feel good about the domains (looks, abilities or whatever) important to our self-esteem. 'One person may have self-esteem that is highly contingent on doing well in school and being physically attractive, whereas another may have self-esteem that is contingent on being loved by God and adhering to moral standards.' Thus, the first person will feel high self-esteem when made to feel clever and good looking, the second person when made to feel moral.

self-esteem *a person's overall negative or positive self-evaluation or sense of self-worth*

But Jonathon Brown and Keith Dutton (1994) argue that this 'bottom-up' view of self-esteem is not the whole story. The causal arrow, they believe, also goes the other way. People who value themselves in a general way – those with high self-esteem – are more likely to value their looks, abilities and so forth. They are like new parents who, loving their infant, delight in its fingers, toes and hair: the parents do not first evaluate their infant's fingers or toes and then decide how much to value the whole baby.

Specific self-perceptions do have some influence, however. If you think you are good at maths, you will be more likely to do well at maths. Although general self-esteem does not predict academic performance very well, academic self-concept – whether you think you are good in school – does predict performance (Marsh & O'Mara, 2008). Of course, each causes the other: Doing well at maths makes you think you are good at maths, which then motivates you to do even better. So if you want to encourage someone (or yourself!), it's better if your praise is specific ('you are good at maths') instead of general ('you are great') and if your kind words reflect true abilities and performance ('you really improved on your last test') rather than unrealistic optimism ('you can do anything'). Feedback is best when it is true and specific (Swann et al., 2006).

## SELF-ESTEEM MOTIVATION

Abraham Tesser (1988) reported that a 'self-esteem maintenance' motive predicts a variety of interesting findings, even friction among brothers and sisters. Do you have a sibling of the same gender who is close to you in age? If so, people probably compared the two of you as you grew up. Tesser presumes that people's perceiving one of you as more capable than the other will motivate the less able one to act in ways that maintain self-esteem. (Tesser thinks the threat to self-esteem is greatest for an older child with a highly capable younger sibling.) Men with a brother with markedly different ability typically recall not getting along well with him; men with a similarly able brother are more likely to recall very little friction.

Self-esteem threats occur among friends, whose success can be more threatening than that of strangers (Zuckerman & Jost, 2001). And it can occur among married partners, too. Although shared interests are healthy, *identical* career goals may produce tension or jealousy (Clark & Bennett, 1992). When a partner outperforms us in a domain important to both our identities, we may reduce the threat by affirming our relationship, saying, 'My capable partner, with whom I'm very close, is part of who I am' (Lockwood et al., 2004).

What underlies the motive to maintain or enhance self-esteem? Mark Leary (1998, 2003) believes that our self-esteem feelings are like a fuel gauge. Relationships enable surviving and thriving. Thus, the self-esteem gauge alerts us to threatened social rejection, motivating us to act with greater sensitivity to others' expectations. Studies confirm that social rejection lowers our self-esteem and makes us more eager for approval. Spurned or jilted, we feel unattractive or inadequate. Like a blinking dashboard light, this pain can motivate action – self-improvement and a search for acceptance and inclusion elsewhere (also see Chapter 9).

## THE 'DARK SIDE' OF SELF-ESTEEM

Among sibling relationships, the threat to self-esteem is greatest for an older child with a highly capable younger brother or sister.

SOURCE: © Izmabel/iStock

Does low self-esteem lead to greater aggression, anti-social behaviour and delinquency? Although researchers have tried to address this important issue for decades, they haven't reached agreement (Boulton et al., 2010; Ostrowsky, 2010). While some researchers have produced evidence confirming the hypothesis (e.g., Donnellan et al., 2005b), others have actually found that low self-esteem is associated with higher levels of aggression (Bushman et al., 2009). However, what research is revealing with sufficient clarity is that people finding their favourable self-esteem threatened often react by putting others down, sometimes with violence. A youth who develops a big ego, which then is threatened or deflated by social rejection, is potentially dangerous. In one experiment, Todd Heatherton and Kathleen Vohs (2000) measured the self-esteem of undergraduate men. They then threatened those in the experimental condition with a failure experience on an aptitude test. In response to the failure, only high-self-esteem men became considerably more antagonistic (Figure 3.7).

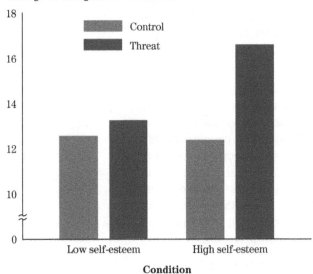

**Ratings of antagonistic behaviour**

FIGURE 3.7 When big egos are challenged
When feeling threatened, only high-self-esteem people became significantly more antagonistic – arrogant, rude and unfriendly.
SOURCE: Heatherton & Vohs, 2000.

In another study, Brad Bushman and Roy Baumeister (1998) had 540 undergraduate volunteers write a paragraph, in response to which another supposed student gave them either praise ('great essay!') or stinging criticism ('one of the worst essays I have read!'). Then each essay writer played a reaction time game against his or her evaluator. When the evaluator would lose, the writer could assault him or her with noise of any intensity and for any duration. After receiving criticism, the writers with the biggest egos – those who had agreed with 'narcissistic' statements such as 'I am more capable than other people' – were 'exceptionally aggressive'. They delivered three times the auditory torture of those with normal self-esteem. Wounded pride can motivate retaliation. A more recent study has found that students with high self-esteem receiving poor feedback from a professor were more likely to evaluate the professor using aggressive language such as 'hope that I never find you!', than students with lower self-esteem (Vaillancourt, 2012).

So perhaps self-esteem is not so good for us. 'The enthusiastic claims of the self-esteem movement mostly range from fantasy to hogwash,' says Baumeister (1996). High-self-esteem people, he reports, are more likely to be obnoxious, to interrupt, and to talk at people rather than with them (in contrast to the more shy, modest, self-effacing folks with low self-esteem). He concludes: 'I'm sorry to say, my recommendation is this: Forget about self-esteem and concentrate more on self-control and self-discipline' (Baumeister, 2005a).

## SELF-LOVE

Sometimes people become extremely focused on themselves and even start to love themselves more than anybody else. This egocentric loving attitude has got a particular name: *narcissism*, used by Greek writers and philosophers thousands of years ago. According to Ancient Greek mythology, a young man named Narcissus wandered the countryside in search of love. Thirsty from his travels, he stopped to drink from a pool of water where he became entranced by his own reflection. This self-love and self-preoccupation eventually caused Narcissus to die of thirst as he could not disturb the image of himself.

Narcissism is an uncontrolled, compulsive self-love. Narcissus has given name to a psychiatric disorder characterized by a pervasive pattern of grandiosity (in fantasy or behaviour), need for admiration, lack of empathy, excessive self-love and selfishness, disregard for others and the use of people for one's self gain, according to the DSM-IV definition (Millon, 1996). More recent studies indicate that narcissists maintain low views of others, express mistrust, hostility and Machiavellianism (Sedikides et al., 2004). We would expect that high self-esteem is typical for narcissists, that self-esteem and narcissism are positively correlated, and that this has an impact on psychological health. And indeed this is what has been demonstrated (e.g. Sedikides et al., 2004).

**Machiavellianism** *manipulative behaviour aimed at obtaining an advantage for the self, without any moral concern and regard for the dignity of others. The term derives from the name of the Italian Renaissance writer Niccolò Machiavelli, who described this behaviour in the work* The Prince

Certainly the goals of most narcissistic actions serve to bolster high self-esteem. Narcissism and high self-esteem, though, are not synonymous. Narcissists and individuals with high self-esteem both hold favourable self-views and may even see themselves as better than average. However, the distinction between the two rests on their differing interpersonal implications. Narcissism is a detriment to interpersonal relationships because narcissists feel a strong sense of superiority and entitlement. When their high personal opinions are challenged or questioned, narcissists tend to respond aggressively towards the specific individuals providing the threat (Bushman & Baumeister, 1998). The self-serving bias offers some explanation why narcissists engage in such behaviour (e.g. Sedikides et al., 2004). High self-esteem, on the other hand, is beneficial to interpersonal relationships as it confers confidence (not egotism) necessary for forming successful communal bonds (Campbell et al., 2002).

Bullies exhibit a defensive, self-aggrandizing form of self-esteem, report Christina Salmivalli and her University of Turku (Finland) colleagues (1999). Those with 'genuine self-esteem' – who feel secure self-worth without seeking to be the centre of attention or being angered by criticism – are more often

*Narcissus* by Caravaggio.
SOURCE: © INTERFOTO/Alamy

Secure positive self-esteem is based on feeling good about who you are.

SOURCE: © Anton Hlushchenko/iStock

found defending the victims of bullying. When we feel securely good about ourselves, we are less defensive (Epstein & Feist, 1988; Jordan et al., 2003). We are also less thin-skinned and judgemental – less likely to inflate those who like us and berate those who don't (Baumgardner et al., 1989).

So secure self-esteem – one rooted more in feeling good about who one is than in grades, looks, money or others' approval – is conducive to long-term well-being (Kernis, 2003; Schimel et al., 2001). Jennifer Crocker (2002) and her colleagues (Crocker & Knight, 2005; Crocker & Luhtanen, 2003; Crocker & Park, 2004) confirmed this in studies with students. Those whose self-worth was most fragile – most contingent on external sources – experienced more stress, anger, relationship problems, drug and alcohol use, and eating disorders than did those whose worth was rooted more in internal sources, such as personal virtues.

## PERCEIVED SELF-CONTROL

*Several lines of research point to the significance of our perceived self-control. What concepts emerge from this research?*

So far we have considered what a self-concept is, how it develops and how well (or poorly) we know ourselves. Now let's see why our self-concepts matter, by viewing the self in action.

The self's capacity for action has limits, note Roy Baumeister and his colleagues (2000; Muraven et al., 1998). For instance:

☐ People who exert self-control – by forcing themselves to eat radishes rather than chocolates, or by suppressing forbidden thoughts – subsequently quit faster when given unresolvable puzzles.

☐ People who have tried to control their emotional responses to an upsetting movie exhibit decreased physical stamina.

☐ People who have spent their willpower on tasks such as controlling their emotions during an upsetting film lately become more aggressive and more likely to fight with their partners (deWall et al., 2007; Finkel & Campbell, 2001). They also become less restrained in their sexual thoughts and behaviours. In one study, students who depleted their willpower by focusing their attention on a difficult task were later, when asked to express a comfortable level of intimacy with their partner, more likely to make out and even remove some clothing (Gailliot & Baumeister, 2007).

Effortful self-control depletes our limited willpower reserves. Our brain (especially in the prefrontal areas of the frontal lobe) consumes available blood sugar when engaged in self-control (Gailliot, 2008). Self-control therefore operates similarly to muscular strength, conclude Baumeister and Julia Exline (2000): Both are weaker after exertion, replenished with rest, and strengthened by exercise.

Although the self's energy can be temporarily depleted, our self-concept does influence our behaviour (Graziano et al., 1997). Given challenging tasks, people who imagine themselves as hardworking and successful outperform those who imagine themselves as failures (Ruvolo & Markus, 1992). Envision your positive possibilities and you become more likely to plan and enact a successful strategy. Stanford psychologist Albert Bandura (1997, 2000) captured the power of positive thinking in his research and theorizing about self-efficacy (how competent we feel on a task). Believing in our own competence and effectiveness pays dividends (Bandura et al., 1999; Maddux & Gosselin, 2003). Children and adults with strong feelings of self-efficacy are more persistent, less anxious and less depressed. They also live healthier lives and are more academically successful.

However, anticipating possible negative outcomes (negative thinking) may help very anxious people coping with situations that present the possibility for failure and threat to self-esteem. Spencer and Norem (1996) found that, when performing a dart throwing task, anxious people did much better after imagining what could go wrong than after relaxation imagery.

## LOCUS OF CONTROL

'I have no social life,' complained a 40-something single man to student therapist Jerry Phares. At Phares's urging, the patient went to a dance, where several women danced with him. 'I was just lucky,' he later reported. 'It would never happen again.' When Phares reported this to his mentor, Julian Rotter, it crystallized an idea he had been forming. In Rotter's experiments and in his clinical practice, some people seemed to persistently 'feel that what happens to them is governed by external forces of one kind or another, while others feel that what happens to them is governed largely by their own efforts and skills' (quoted by Hunt, 1993, p. 334).

What do you think about your own life? Are you more often in charge of your destiny, or a victim of circumstance? Rotter called this dimension locus of control. With Phares, he developed 29 paired statements to measure a person's locus of control. Imagine yourself taking this test (Table 3.3). Which do you more strongly believe?

If your answers to these questions (from Rotter, 1973) were mostly 'a', you probably believe you control your own destiny (*internal* locus of control). If your answers were mostly 'b', you probably feel chance or outside forces determine your fate (*external* locus of control). Those who see themselves as *internally* controlled are more likely to do well in school, successfully stop smoking, wear seat belts, deal with marital problems directly and delay instant gratification to achieve long-term goals (Findley & Cooper, 1983; Lefcourt, 1982).

*self-efficacy one's sense of competence and ability to handle different situations, and produce an intended result: distinguished from self-esteem, which is one's sense of self-worth. A bombardier, for instance, might feel high self-efficacy and low self-esteem*

*locus of control a person's belief about who or what is responsible for what happens. Can either be internal (I control my life) or external (the environment, a higher power or other people control my life)*

**TABLE 3.3** The extent to which people perceive outcomes as internally controllable by their own efforts and actions, or as externally controlled by chance or outside forces

| a | | b |
|---|---|---|
| In the long run, people get the respect they deserve in this world | or | Unfortunately, people's worth passes unrecognized no matter how hard they try |
| What happens to me is my own doing | or | Sometimes I feel that I don't have enough control over the situation |
| The average person can have an influence in government decisions | or | This world is run by the few in power and there is not much the little guy can do about it |

How much control we feel is related to how we explain setbacks. Perhaps you have known students who view themselves as victims – who blame poor grades on things beyond their control, such as their feelings of stupidity or their 'poor' teachers, texts or tests. If such students are coached to adopt a more hopeful attitude – to believe that effort, good study habits and self-discipline can make a difference – their academic performance tends to go up (Noel et al., 1987; Peterson & Barrett, 1987).

## LEARNED HELPLESSNESS VERSUS SELF-DETERMINATION

The benefits of feelings of control also appear in animal research. Dogs confined in a cage and taught that they cannot escape shocks will learn a sense of helplessness. Later, these dogs cower passively in other situations when they *could* escape punishment. Dogs that learn personal control (by successfully escaping their first shocks) adapt easily to a new situation. Researcher Martin Seligman (1975, 1991) noted similarities to this learned helplessness in human situations. Depressed or oppressed people, for example, become passive because they believe their efforts have no effect. Helpless dogs and depressed people both suffer paralysis of the will, passive resignation, even motionless apathy (Figure 3.8).

**learned helplessness** *the hopelessness and resignation learned when a human or an animal perceives no control over repeated bad events; this commonly leads to depressive symptoms*

On the other hand, people benefit by training their self-control 'muscles'. That is the conclusion of studies by Megan Oaten and Ken Cheng (2006). For example, students who were engaged in practising self-control by daily exercise, regular study and time management became more capable of self-control in other settings, both in the laboratory and when taking exams.

Studies confirm that systems of governing or managing people that promote personal control will indeed promote health and happiness (Deci & Ryan, 1987). Here are some examples:

☐ Prisoners given some control over their environments – by being able to move chairs, control television sets and operate the lights – experience less stress, exhibit fewer health problems and commit less vandalism (Ruback et al., 1986; Wener et al., 1987).

☐ Workers given leeway in carrying out tasks and making decisions experience improved morale (Miller & Monge, 1986).

☐ Institutionalized residents allowed choice in matters such as what to eat for breakfast, when to go to a movie, whether to sleep late or get up early, may live longer and certainly are happier (Timko & Moos, 1989).

☐ Homeless shelter residents who perceive little choice in when to eat and sleep, and little control over their privacy, are more likely to have a passive, helpless attitude regarding finding housing and work (Burn, 1992).

Personal control: inmates of Spain's modern Valencia prison have, with work and appropriate behaviour, gained access to classes, sports facilities, cultural opportunities and money in an account that can be charged for snacks.

SOURCE: © Marc DEVILLE/Gamma-Rapho via Getty Images

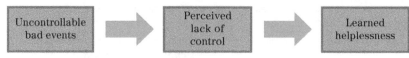

**FIGURE 3.8** Learned helplessness
When animals and people experience uncontrollable bad events, they learn to feel helpless and resigned.

The Costs of Excess Choice

Can there ever be too much of a good thing such as freedom and self-determination? Swarthmore College psychologist Barry Schwartz (2000, 2004) contends that individualistic modern cultures indeed have 'an excess of freedom', causing decreased life satisfaction and increased clinical depression. Too many choices can lead to paralysis, or what Schwartz calls 'the tyranny of freedom'. After choosing from among 30 kinds of jams or chocolates, people express less satisfaction with their choices than those choosing from among six options (Iyengar & Lepper, 2000). With more choice comes information overload and more opportunities for regret. Another study, conducted by Daniel Gilbert and Daniel Ebert (2002), has revealed that people are more satisfied with irrevocable choices (such as those made in 'all purchases final' sale) than with reversible ones (as when allowing refunds or exchanges). This is somewhat ironic, given that people like and will pay for the freedom to reverse their choices. The fact is that, as noted by Gilbert and Ebert, that same freedom 'can inhibit the psychological processes that manufacture satisfaction'.

Christopher Hsee and Reid Hastie (2006) illustrate how choice may enhance regret. Give employees a free trip to either Paris or Hawaii and they will be happy. But give them a choice between the two and they may be less happy. People who choose Paris may regret that it lacks the warmth and the ocean. Those who choose Hawaii may regret the lack of great museums.

It is important to note, however, that whether or not any negative psychological consequence of having too much choice will occur may depend on the extent to which 'too much choice' increases the complexity of the choice. Rainer Greifeneder, Benjamin Scheibehenne and Nina Kleber (2010) found that consumers who had to choose from a vast array of products, felt dissatisfied when the products were differentiated by many attributes, but not when the differences concerned a small number of attributes. For instance, participants who had to choose the one coloured pen they liked best from a set of six different pens, felt more satisfied with their choice when the pens differed only by colour than when they differed on a number of additional attributes such as design, pen width and duration of use.

## SELF-SERVING BIAS

*As we process self-relevant information, a potent bias intrudes. We readily excuse our failures, accept credit for our successes, and in many ways see ourselves as better than average. Such self-enhancing perceptions enable most people to enjoy the bright side of high self-esteem, while occasionally suffering the dark side.*

One of social psychology's most provocative yet firmly established conclusions concerns the potency of self-serving bias, which influences how we account for our behaviour and that of other people (also see Chapter 4).

**self-serving bias** *the tendency to perceive oneself favourably*

### EXPLAINING POSITIVE AND NEGATIVE EVENTS

Many dozens of experiments have found that people accept credit when told they have succeeded. They attribute the success to their ability and effort, but they attribute failure to external factors such as bad luck or the problem's

**self-serving attributions** *a form of self-serving bias; the tendency to attribute positive outcomes to oneself and negative outcomes to other factors*

inherent 'impossibility' (Campbell & Sedikides, 1999). Similarly, in explaining their victories, athletes commonly credit themselves, but they attribute losses to something else: bad breaks, bad referee calls, or the other team's super effort or dirty play (Grove et al., 1991; Lalonde, 1992; Mullen & Riordan, 1988). This phenomenon of self-serving attributions (attributing positive outcomes to oneself and negative outcomes to something else) is one of the most potent of human biases (Mezulis et al., 2004).

## CAN WE ALL BE BETTER THAN AVERAGE?

Self-serving bias appears when people compare themselves with others. There are cultural differences, however, and in Eastern cultures there has been a tradition for being modest and not standing out. The sixth-century BC Chinese philosopher Lao-tzu expressed this attitude when he stated that 'at no time in the world will a man who is sane over-reach himself, over-spend himself, overrate himself'. In the individualistic West most people see themselves as better than the average person on *subjective* and *socially desirable* dimensions. Compared with people in general, most people see themselves as more ethical, more competent at their job, friendlier, more intelligent, better looking, less prejudiced, healthier, and even more insightful and less biased in their self-assessments. A meta-analysis of 266 studies conducted by Amy Mezulis and her colleagues (2004) confirmed the existence of a substantial cross-cultural variation in self-serving bias, with Asians displaying much smaller biases than Westerners.

The French social psychologist, Jean-Paul Codol, found evidence of self-serving bias in group life. He conducted a large number of experiments demonstrating that an individual group member considers him/herself as being more respectful of group norms and values than the average member (Codol, 1975). Yun-Suk Lee and Linda Waite (2005) observed a marital version of self-serving bias, in a study involving 265 US married couples with children. Husbands estimated they did 42 per cent of the housework, while the wives estimated their husbands did 33 per cent. When researchers tracked actual housework (by sampling participants' activity at random times using beepers), they found husbands actually carrying 39 per cent of the domestic workload.

People display one other ironic bias: they see themselves as freer from bias than most people (Ehrlinger et al., 2005; Pronin et al., 2002). Indeed, people even see themselves as less vulnerable to self-serving bias! They will admit to some bias in the abstract, and they see others as biased. But when asked about specific traits and behaviours, such as when rating their own ethics or likeability, they judge their self-assessments as untainted.

## UNREALISTIC OPTIMISM

Neil Weinstein (1980, 1982) at Rutgers University developed the idea of unrealistic optimism about future life events. Optimism predisposes a positive approach to life and many of us have this ability to look towards a happy and successful future. Partly because of their relative pessimism about others' fates, students perceive themselves as far more likely than their classmates to get a good job, draw a good salary and own a home. They also see themselves as far *less* likely to experience negative events, such as developing a drinking problem, having a heart attack before age 40, or being fired (Shepperd, 2003).

Those who cheerfully shun seat belts, deny the effects of smoking and stumble into ill-fated relationships remind us that blind optimism, like pride, may go before a fall. When gambling, optimists more than pessimists persist even when piling up losses (Gibson & Sanbonmatsu, 2004). If those who deal in the stock market or in real estate perceive their business intuition superior to that of their competitors, they, too, may be in for disappointment. Even the seventeenth-century economist Adam Smith, a defender of human economic rationality, foresaw that people would overestimate their chances of gain. This 'absurd presumption in their own good fortune', he said, arises from 'the overweening conceit, which the greater part of men have of their own abilities' (Spiegel, 1971, p. 243).

Optimism definitely beats pessimism in promoting self-efficacy, health and well-being (Armor & Taylor, 1996; Segerstrom, 2001). Being natural optimists, most people believe they will be happier with their lives in the future – a belief that surely helps create happiness in the present (Robinson & Ryff, 1999).

Yet a dash of realism – or what Julie Norem (2000) calls defensive pessimism – can save us from the perils of unrealistic optimism by anticipating problems and motivating effective coping. Students who are overconfident tend to underprepare, whereas their equally able but less confident peers study harder and get higher grades (Goodhart, 1986; Norem & Cantor, 1986; Showers & Ruben, 1987). There is a power to negative as well as positive thinking. The moral: success in school and beyond requires enough optimism to sustain hope and enough pessimism to motivate concern.

**defensive pessimism** *the adaptive value of anticipating problems and harnessing one's anxiety to motivate effective action*

### FALSE CONSENSUS AND UNIQUENESS

We have a curious tendency to enhance our self-images by overestimating or underestimating the extent to which others think and act as we do. On matters of *opinion*, we find support for our positions by overestimating the extent to which others agree – a phenomenon called the false consensus effect (Krueger & Clement, 1994; Marks & Miller, 1987; Mullen & Goethals, 1990).

**false consensus effect** *the tendency to overestimate the commonality of one's opinions and one's undesirable or unsuccessful behaviours*

When we behave badly or fail in a task, we reassure ourselves by thinking that such lapses also are common. If we cheat on our income taxes, or smoke, we are likely to overestimate the number of other people who do likewise. If we feel sexual desire towards another, we may overestimate the other's reciprocal desire. Four recent studies illustrate this.

1. People who sneak a shower during a shower ban believe (more than non-bathers) that lots of others are doing the same (Monin & Norton, 2003).

2. Those thirsty after hard exercise imagine that lost hikers would become more bothered by thirst than by hunger. That's what 88 per cent of thirsty post-exercisers guessed in a study by Leaf Van Boven and George Lowenstein (2003), compared with 57 per cent of people who were about to exercise.

3. As people's own lives change, they see the world changing. Protective new parents come to see the world as a more dangerous place. People who go on a diet judge food ads to be more prevalent (Eibach et al., 2003).

4. People who harbour negative ideas about another racial group presume that many others also have negative stereotypes (Krueger, 1996). Thus, our perceptions of others' stereotypes may reveal something of our own.

'Everybody says I'm plastic from head to toe. Can't stand next to a radiator or I'll melt. I had [breast] implants, but so has every single person in LA.'
    Actress Pamela Lee Anderson (quoted by Talbert, 1997)

'We don't see things as they are,' says the Talmud. 'We see things as we are.'

Dawes (1990) proposes that this false consensus may occur because we generalize from a limited sample, which prominently includes ourselves. Lacking other information, why not 'project' ourselves; why not impute our own knowledge to others and use our responses as a clue to their likely responses? Most people are in the majority; so when people assume they are in the majority they are usually right. Also, we're more likely to spend time with people who share our attitudes and behaviours and, consequently, to judge the world from the people we know.

false uniqueness effect *the tendency to underestimate the commonality of one's abilities and one's desirable or successful behaviour*

On matters of *ability* or when we behave well or successfully, however, a false uniqueness effect more often occurs (Goethals et al., 1991). We serve our self-image by seeing our talents and moral behaviours as relatively unusual. For example, those who use marijuana but use seat belts will *overestimate* (false consensus) the number of other marijuana users and *underestimate* (false uniqueness) the number of other seat belt users (Suls et al., 1988). Thus, we may see our failings as relatively normal and our virtues as relatively exceptional.

To sum up, self-serving bias appears as self-serving attributions, self-congratulatory comparisons, illusory optimism, and false consensus for one's failings (Figure 3.9).

### REFLECTIONS ON SELF-ESTEEM AND SELF-SERVING BIAS

If you are like some readers, by now you are finding the self-serving bias either depressing or contrary to your own occasional feelings of inadequacy. Even the people who exhibit the self-serving bias may feel inferior – to specific individuals, especially those who are a step or two higher on the ladder of success, attractiveness or skill. Moreover, not everyone operates with a self-serving bias. Some people *do* suffer from low self-esteem. Positive self-esteem does have some benefits.

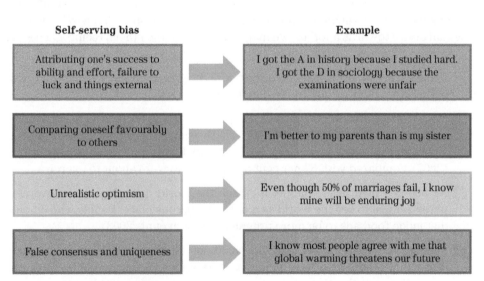

| Self-serving bias | Example |
|---|---|
| Attributing one's success to ability and effort, failure to luck and things external | I got the A in history because I studied hard. I got the D in sociology because the examinations were unfair |
| Comparing oneself favourably to others | I'm better to my parents than is my sister |
| Unrealistic optimism | Even though 50% of marriages fail, I know mine will be enduring joy |
| False consensus and uniqueness | I know most people agree with me that global warming threatens our future |

**FIGURE 3.9**  How self-serving bias works

### The Self-serving Bias as Adaptive

Self-esteem has its dark side, but also its bright side. When good things happen, high more than low-self-esteem people tend to savour and sustain the good feelings (Wood et al., 2003). 'Believing one has more talents and positive qualities than one's peers allows one to feel good about oneself and to enter the stressful circumstances of daily life with the resources conferred by a positive sense of self,' note Shelley Taylor and her co-researchers (2003). Self-serving bias and its accompanying excuses also help protect people from depression (Snyder & Higgins, 1988; Taylor et al., 2003). Non-depressed people usually exhibit self-serving bias. They excuse their failures on laboratory tasks or perceive themselves as being more in control than they are. Depressed people's self-appraisals and their appraisals of how others really view them are not inflated.

In their 'terror management theory', Jeff Greenberg, Sheldon Solomon and Tom Pyszczynski (1997) propose another reason why positive self-esteem is adaptive: it buffers anxiety, including anxiety related to our certain death. In childhood we learn that when we meet the standards taught us by our parents, we are loved and protected; when we don't, love and protection may be withdrawn. We therefore come to associate viewing ourselves as good with feeling secure. Greenberg and colleagues argue that positive self-esteem even protects us from feeling terror over our eventual death. Their research shows that reminding people of their mortality (say, by writing a short essay on dying) motivates them to affirm their self-worth. When facing such threats, self-esteem buffers anxiety.

> Terror management theory proposes a basic psychological conflict resulting from having a desire to live but realizing that death is inevitable; TMT is discussed in more detail in Chapter 13.

### The Self-serving Bias as Maladaptive

Although self-serving pride may help protect us from feeling sad and useless, it can also be maladaptive. People who blame others for their social difficulties are often unhappier than people who can acknowledge their mistakes (Anderson et al., 1983; Newman & Langer, 1981; Peterson et al., 1981).

Research by Barry Schlenker (1976; Schlenker & Miller, 1977a, 1977b) has shown how self-serving perceptions can poison a group. As a rock band guitarist during his college days, Schlenker noted that 'rock band members typically overestimated their contributions to a group's success and underestimated their contributions to failure. I saw many good bands disintegrate from the problems caused by these self-glorifying tendencies'. In his later life as a social psychologist, Schlenker explored group members' self-serving perceptions. In nine experiments, he had people work together on some task. He then falsely informed them that their group had done either well or poorly. In every one of those studies, the members of successful groups claimed more responsibility for their group's performance than did members of groups that supposedly failed at the task.

'Other men's sins are before our eyes; our own are behind our back.'
Seneca, *De Ira*, AD43

## IMPRESSION MANAGEMENT

*Humans seem motivated not only to perceive themselves in self-enhancing ways but also to present themselves favourably to others. We engage in 'impression management'.*

Perhaps you have wondered: are self-enhancing expressions always sincere? Do people have the same feelings privately as they express publicly? Or are they just putting on a positive face even while living with self-doubt?

## FALSE MODESTY

There is indeed evidence that people sometimes present a different self than they feel. The clearest example, however, is not false pride but false modesty. Perhaps you have by now recalled times when someone was not self-praising but self-disparaging. Such put-downs can be subtly self-serving, for often they elicit reassurance. 'I felt like a fool' may trigger a friend to say 'You did fine!'

There is another reason people disparage themselves and praise others. Understating one's own ability serves to reduce performance pressure and lower the baseline for evaluating performance (Gibson & Sachau, 2000). Think of the coaches who, before the big game, extol the opponent's strength and point out weaknesses that their own team 'needs to work on'. Is the coach utterly sincere? When exalting their opponents, coaches convey an image of modesty and good sportsmanship, and set the stage for a favourable evaluation no matter what the outcome. A win becomes a praiseworthy achievement, a loss attributable to the opponent's 'great defence'. Modesty, said the seventeenth-century philosopher Francis Bacon, is but one of the 'arts of ostentation'.

Anita Pomerantz (1978) was the first researcher to study how people respond to compliments in everyday conversation. She found that people experienced something of a dilemma when they were complimented. On the one hand they did not want to reject the compliment, but on the other they did not want to look immodest.

Let us consider some of her examples of displays of modesty to overcome this dilemma:

A: You have lost so much weight
P: Uhh hmhh uhh hmhh well, not *that* much
   (Pomerantz, 1978, p. 98)

Here we can see that the person receiving the compliment does not disagree with the compliment, but instead plays down the significance of it.

People can also avoid a compliment by locating the praise elsewhere. For example:

R: You're a good rower, Honey
I: These are very easy to row. Very light
   (Pomerantz, 1978, p. 102)

Here the recipient deflects the praise by pointing out the type of boat she is (easily) rowing.

Robert Gould, Paul Brounstein and Harold Sigall (1977) found that, in a laboratory contest, their students similarly aggrandized their anticipated opponent, but only when the assessment was made publicly. Anonymously, they credited their future opponent with much less ability.

False modesty appears in people's autobiographical accounts of their achievements. At awards ceremonies, recipients of honours graciously thank others for their support. Upon receiving an Academy Award, Maureen Stapleton thanked 'my family, my children, my friends, and everyone I have ever met in my entire life'. Does such sharing of credit contradict the common finding that people readily attribute success to their own effort and competence?

To find out, Roy Baumeister and Stacey Ilko (1995) invited students to write a description of 'an important success experience'. They asked some students to sign their names and to anticipate reading their story to others; these students often acknowledged the help or emotional support they had received. Those who wrote anonymously rarely made such mentions; rather, they portrayed themselves achieving their successes on their own. To Baumeister and Ilko, these results suggest 'shallow gratitude' – superficial gratitude that *appears* humble, whereas 'in the privacy of their own minds' the students credited themselves.

Shallow gratitude may surface when, like Maureen Stapleton, we outperform others around us and feel uneasy about other people's feelings towards us. If we think our success will make others feel envious or resentful – a phenomenon that Julia Exline and Marci Lobel (1999) call 'the perils of out-performance' – we may downplay our achievements and display gratitude. For super-achievers, modest self-presentations come naturally.

## SELF-HANDICAPPING

Sometimes people sabotage their chances for success by creating impediments that make success less likely (self-handicapping). Far from being deliberately self-destructive, such behaviours typically have a self-protective aim (Arkin et al., 1986; Baumeister & Scher, 1988; Rhodewalt, 1987): 'I'm really not a failure – I would have done well except for this problem.'

self-handicapping
*protecting one's self-image with behaviours that create a handy excuse for later failure*

Why would people handicap themselves with self-defeating behaviour? Recall that we eagerly protect our self-images by attributing failures to external factors. Can you see why, *fearing failure*, people might handicap themselves by partying half the night before a job interview or playing video games instead of studying before a big examination? When self-image is tied up with performance, it can be more self-deflating to try hard and fail than to procrastinate and have a ready excuse. If we fail while handicapped in some way, we can cling to a sense of competence; if we succeed under such conditions, it can only boost our self-image. Handicaps protect both self-esteem and public image by allowing us to attribute failures to something temporary or external ('I was feeling sick'; 'I was out too late the night before') rather than to lack of talent or ability.

'With no attempt there can be no failure; with no failure no humiliation.'
  William James, *Principles of Psychology*, 1890

Steven Berglas and Edward Jones (1978) confirmed this analysis of *self-handicapping*. One experiment was announced as concerning 'drugs and intellectual performance'. Imagine yourself in the position of their Duke University participants. You guess answers to some difficult aptitude questions and then are told, 'Yours was one of the best scores seen to date!' Feeling incredibly lucky, you are then offered a choice between two drugs before answering more of these items. One drug will aid intellectual performance and the other will inhibit it. Which drug do you want? Most students wanted the drug that would supposedly disrupt their thinking, thus providing a handy excuse for anticipated poorer performance.

Researchers have documented other ways people self-handicap. Fearing failure, people will:

☐ reduce their preparation for important individual athletic events (Rhodewalt et al., 1984)

☐ give their opponent an advantage (Shepperd & Arkin, 1991)

☐ perform poorly at the beginning of a task in order not to create unreachable expectations (Baumgardner & Brownlee, 1987)

☐ not try as hard as they could during a tough, ego-involving task (Hormuth, 1986; Pyszczynski & Greenberg, 1987; Riggs, 1992; Turner & Pratkanis, 1993).

### SELF-PRESENTATION

Erving Goffman, a sociologist and social psychologist born in Canada, collected the material for his book *The Presentation of Self in Everyday Life* on the Shetland Islands in the North Sea, in 1950 (Goffman, 1959). His account of social life was based on a symbolic interactionist perspective (see Chapter 1), and was modelled on the theatre. Goffman saw people as actors, executing different performances in front of various audiences. He also claimed that when in public (front stage), people strive to comply with societal norms and expectations. When not in public (behind stage), these social rules do not need to be followed.

self-presentation *the act of expressing oneself and behaving in ways designed to create a favourable impression or an impression that corresponds to one's ideals*

Goffman pioneered the study of self-presentation, which refers to our wanting to present a desired image both to an external audience (other people) and to an internal audience (ourselves). We work at managing the impressions we create. We excuse, justify or apologize as necessary to shore up our self-esteem and verify our self-images (Schlenker & Weigold, 1992). In familiar situations, this happens without conscious effort. In unfamiliar situations, perhaps at a party with people we would like to impress or in conversation with someone we have romantic interest in, we are acutely self-conscious of the impressions we are creating and we are therefore less modest than when among friends who know us well (Leary et al., 1994; Tice et al., 1995).

But of course not all of our interactions are face to face. Online social networking (OSN) sites such as MySpace and Facebook provide a new and sometimes intense venue for self-presentation. They are, says communications professor Joseph Walther, 'like impression management on steroids' (Rosenbloom, 2008). Users make careful decisions about which pictures, activities and interests to highlight in their profiles. Some even think about how their friends will affect the impression they make on others; one study found that those with more attractive friends were perceived as more attractive themselves (Walther et al., 2008).

Do people use OSN sites to portray idealized versions of themselves, or do people consider OSN sites just as an extended social context for the expression of the actual self? Researchers appear to disagree on this (Back et al., 2010). Proponents of the *idealized virtual-identity hypothesis* believe that people use the internet to display idealized selves that do not match actual personality characteristics (Manago et al., 2008). On the contrary, some researcher's endorse an *extended real-life hypothesis*, according to which the personal information that people include on OSN sites mirrors their real thoughts, feelings, interests and physical appearance (Vazire & Gosling, 2004). Although the question is still open, a study conducted by Back and his colleagues in which the two hypotheses were compared indicates that the *extended real-life hypothesis* might be a better account of the way in which people tend to use OSN sites. These researchers assessed both the actual and ideal personality of 236 OSN users from either the US or Germany, and then compared these with personality ratings made by some external judges, based on the information about participants that was available on OSN sites. It was found that observers' impressions of participants matched participants' actual, but not ideal personality. Nonetheless, there is no doubt that, as proposed by Katelyn McKenna and John Bargh (2000), the Internet offers a 'blank slate, the individual is then free to construct him or herself in any number of ways' (p. 63). Aren't people really capitalizing on this opportunity to present a different self? It seems that people may do so, but not necessarily in order to present a faked, more desirable self, but rather to present their 'true', most genuine self. Some theorists point out that in face-to-face interactions, who we present ourselves to be is limited by the roles we fulfil, who our friends and family believe us to be, and sometimes because aspects of our 'true self' are controversial (e.g. Bargh et al., 2002; McKenna and Bargh, 2000). So there are aspects of our self which we consider important, which we would like recognized, but which we are not comfortable with expressing. This has received empirical support. For example, in a series of experiments, John Bargh, Katelyn McKenna and Grainne Fitzsimons (2002) found that New York students were not only more aware of their true selves in online interactions with strangers, but were also more likely to present them online than face to face. We consider the influence of the Internet and computer-mediated interaction on our friendships and romantic relationships in more detail in Chapter 9.

After losing to some younger rivals, tennis great Martina Navratilova confessed that she was 'afraid to play my best ... I was scared to find out if they could beat me when I'm playing my best because if they can, then I am finished' (Frankel & Snyder, 1987).
SOURCE: © Sbukley/ Dreamstime.com

Are there particular sorts of people who are more likely to use social media for self-presentation purposes? Probably, you will not be surprised to hear that people high in narcissistic traits thrive on Facebook, tallying up more friends and choosing more attractive pictures of themselves. Laura Buffardi and Keith Campbell (2008) believe that narcissists are particularly willing to join online communities for two reasons. First, 'narcissists function well in the context of shallow (as opposed to emotionally deep and committed) relationships' (p. 1304). Second, by creating their own web pages narcissists get a perfect opportunity to present themselves in a self-promoting fashion.

For some people, conscious self-presentation is a way of life. They continually monitor their own behaviour and note how others react, then adjust their social performance to gain a desired effect. Those who score high on a scale of self-monitoring tendency (who, for example, agree that 'I tend to be what people expect me to be') act like social chameleons – they adjust their behaviour in response to external situations (Gangestad & Snyder, 2000; Snyder, 1987). Having attuned their behaviour to the situation, they are more likely to espouse attitudes they don't really hold (Zanna & Olson, 1982). Being conscious of others, they are less likely to act on their own attitudes. As Mark Leary (2007) observed, the self they know often differs from the self they show.

self-monitoring *letting situational cues guide the way one presents oneself in social situations, and adjusting one's performance to create the desired impression, rather than acting on own needs or values*

Those who score low in self-monitoring care less about what others think. They are more internally guided and thus more likely to talk and act as they feel and believe (McCann & Hancock, 1983). For example, if asked to list their thoughts about gay couples, they simply express what they think, regardless of the attitudes of their anticipated audience (Klein et al., 2004). As you might imagine, someone who is extremely low in self-monitoring could come across as an insensitive boor, whereas extremely high self-monitoring could result in dishonest behaviour worthy of a con artist. Most of us fall somewhere between those two extremes.

Presenting oneself in ways that create a desired impression is a delicate balancing act. People want to be seen as able but also as modest and honest (Carlston & Shovar, 1983). In most social situations, modesty creates a good impression. Hence the false modesty phenomenon: we often display lower self-esteem than we privately feel (Miller & Schlenker, 1985). But when we have obviously done extremely well, the insincerity of a disclaimer ('I did well, but it's no big deal') may be evident. To make good impressions – as modest yet competent – requires social skill.

In Asian countries, self-presentation is restrained. Children learn to share credit for success with other group members.

SOURCE: Imagemore/Glow Images

Self-presented modesty is greatest in cultures that value self-restraint and self-improvement, such as those of China and Japan (Heine, 2005; Mezulis et al., 2004). Japanese children learn to share credit for success and to accept responsibility for failures. 'When I fail, it's my fault, not my group's' is a typical Japanese attitude (Anderson, 1999).

## focus on

### ARE WE WITNESSING AN EPIDEMIC OF NARCISSISM AMONG YOUNGER GENERATIONS?

It is fairly common to hear older people complaining about younger generations, which are depicted as self-centred, arrogant and disrespectful, and are said to dismiss traditions and good old habits. This popular view of younger people is echoed by the writings of scholars from across the social science spectrum, particularly in North America. Over the last two or three decades – it is argued – Western societies in general, and the US in particular, have embraced an individualistic ethos, whereby all attentions and preoccupations revolve around the self at the expense of civic engagement, empathy, solidarity and societal concerns. For instance, Robert Putnam (2000) lamented the gradual disintegration of communities and social networks, and Robert Lane (2000) stressed how a focus on individual success is replacing appreciation of companionship. In line with that, Robert Frank (1999) argued that our obsessive desire to enhance the self has led to a 'luxury fever', a tendency to consume self-promoting luxury goods that is forcing people to spend more time at work while neglecting family and friends. In sum, we are said to be living in an era of self-centredness or, as the sociologist Christopher Lash (1979) foresaw, in a 'culture of narcissism'.

But is this truly the case? Are we really witnessing a fast-growing tendency toward self-absorption and egotism? The social psychologist Jean Twenge and her colleagues believe so, and have characterized the current climate as an 'epidemic of narcissism' (Twenge & Campbell, 2009). Twenge agrees that cultural and pedagogic trends are largely responsible for such an epidemic. In particular, she blames American parents for wanting to make their children feel 'special' regardless of their real skills and abilities. In order to put this thesis under test, Twenge and her colleagues (2008) decided to investigate

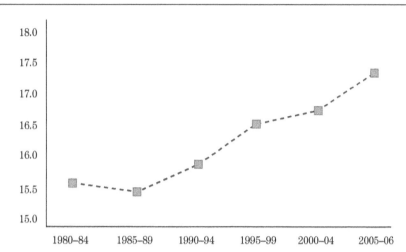

**FIGURE 3.10** American college students' scores on narcissism by time period

SOURCE: Adapted from Twenge et al., 2008, p. 883.

changes in levels of narcissism among different generations of college students in the US. These researchers amassed 85 studies conducted between 1982 and 2006, in which the degree of narcissism of over 16,000 college students had been assessed using the Narcissistic Personality Inventory (NPI). The NPI is based on 40 forced-choice dyads. For each dyad the person taking the test may choose either a narcissistic response (e.g., 'I really like to be the centre of attention') or a non-narcissistic response ('It makes me uncomfortable to be the centre of attention'). Each narcissistic response counts as 1 in the overall score, which therefore may range between 0 and 40. The analysis of these data revealed that more recent generations have higher levels of narcissism. More precisely, NPI scores have gradually increased over the years, moving from an initial average score of 15.06 in 1982 to an average score of 17.29 in 2006 (see Figure 3.10).

Twenge considers these results as consistent with cultural trends and indicators. For instance, the lyrics of the more popular songs are more individualistic than ever (DeWall et al., 2011), the rates for plastic surgery are constantly increasing (Twenge & Campbell, 2009), and being rich and famous is increasingly judged as important in pools. According to Twenge, these are all signs that people want to feel special, they want to stand out rather than fit in.

Some researchers, however, believe that the claims made by researchers like Twenge are grossly exaggerated, and that there is no epidemic of narcissism in contemporary society. For instance, Jeffrey Jensen Arnett (2010) contends that, rather than selfish, younger people are self-focused as they need to explore their identities and options for future life. Arnett also thinks that, rather than grandiose, younger people are optimistic because their dreams have not yet been tested by the reality of adult life. Along similar lines, Brent Roberts, Grant Edmonds and Emily Grijalva (2010) re-analysed the data previously used by Twenge using alternative statistical procedures, and did not find significant generational changes in narcissism. What they found, instead, was evidence that every generation of younger people is more narcissistic than their elders. But perhaps the sharpest attack on Twenge's thesis comes from US-based social psychologists Kali Trzesniewski and Brent Donnellan (2009, 2010). First, these authors stress the fact that Twenge's data stem from college students, whose characteristics cannot be generalized to the whole American youth. In addition, Trzesniewski and Donnellan noted that the trend for increasing narcissism in Twenge's data is much more pronounced for women than for men. Therefore, rather than unveiling a general epidemic of narcissism, Twenge's results might simply indicate that the last generation of women have become more assertive and confident than previous generations. Finally, Trzesniewski and Donnellan question the relevance of the increase in narcissism found by Twenge. Is a change of slightly more than 2 scale points on the NPI a meaningful change? Does it have any practical implications? They suspect that such change should not be of concern, and that it does not justify an alarm about today's youth. On the other hand, Twenge and Campbell believe that a change of 2 points on the NPI deserves to be taken seriously (Twenge & Campbell, 2010). If the average level of narcissism has increased even by a small amount, they argue, then there must be many more young people than before having extreme scores on NPI. Having thousands more people out there with a very strong sense of entitlement and low empathy – Twenge and Campbell believe – may have noticeably negative consequences for society.

The debate is still open and heated. More data and studies, and perhaps new analyses of existing data are required to resolve it. For sure, it is an issue that deserves attention. If the epidemic of narcissism was found to be a myth, it would be important to acknowledge that younger generations are not more self-absorbed than previous ones, and to avoid fuelling a negative stereotype of today's young people. On the other hand, if the epidemic of narcissism was confirmed, then the negative consequences of our contemporary culture and ethos should be taken very seriously by politicians, intellectuals and general public alike.

## QUESTIONS

**1** Can you see any evidence of an epidemic of narcissism in the country where you live? If so, how worrying do you think that is?

**2** Would you agree that younger people, regardless of their generation, tend to be more self-centred than older people? If so, why do you think that is the case?

## SUMMING UP: THE SELF

### SPOTLIGHTS AND ILLUSIONS

☐ Concerned with the impression we make on others, we tend to believe that others are paying more attention to us than they are (the spotlight effect).

☐ We also tend to believe that our emotions are more obvious than they are (the illusion of transparency).

### SELF-CONCEPT: WHO AM I?

☐ Our sense of self helps organize our thoughts and actions. When we process information with reference to ourselves, we remember it well (the *self-reference effect*). *Self-concept* consists of two elements: the *self-schemas* that guide our processing of self-relevant information, and the possible selves that we dream of or dread.

☐ *Self-esteem* is the overall sense of self-worth we use to appraise our traits and abilities. Our self-concepts are determined by multiple influences, including the roles we play, the comparisons we make, our social identities, how we perceive others appraising us, and our experiences of success and failure.

☐ Cultures shape the self, too. Many people in individualistic Western cultures assume an independent self. Others, often in collectivistic cultures, assume a more interdependent self. As Chapter 14 further explains, these contrasting ideas contribute to cultural differences in social behaviour.

☐ Our self-knowledge is curiously flawed. We often do not know why we behave the way we do. When influences upon our behaviour are not conspicuous enough for any observer to see, we, too, can miss them. The unconscious, implicit processes that control our behaviour may differ from our conscious, explicit explanations of it. We also tend to mispredict our emotions.

## SELF-ESTEEM

☐ Self-esteem motivation influences our cognitive processes: facing failure, high-self-esteem people sustain their self-worth by perceiving other people as failing too, and by exaggerating their superiority over others.

☐ Although high self-esteem is generally more beneficial than low, researchers have found that a variety of social offenders tend towards *higher*-than-average self-esteem. Someone with a big ego, which then is threatened or deflated by social rejection, is potentially aggressive.

## PERCEIVED SELF-CONTROL

☐ Several lines of research show the benefits of a sense of *self-efficacy* and feelings of control. People who believe in their own competence and effectiveness, and who have an *internal locus of control*, cope better and achieve more than others.

☐ *Learned helplessness* often occurs when attempts to improve a situation have proven fruitless; *self-determination*, in contrast, is bolstered by experiences of successfully exercising control and improving one's situation.

☐ When people are given too many choices, they may be less satisfied with what they have than when offered a smaller range of choices.

## SELF-SERVING BIAS

☐ Research has consistently found that many people exhibit a *self-serving bias*. In experiments and everyday life, we often take credit for our successes while blaming failures on the situation. In addition, people often rate themselves as better than average on subjective, desirable traits and abilities, and can exhibit unrealistic optimism about their futures. Also, we overestimate the commonality of our opinions and foibles (*false consensus*) while underestimating the commonality of our abilities and virtues (*false uniqueness*).

☐ Such perceptions arise partly from a motive to maintain and enhance self-esteem, a motive that protects people from depression but contributes to misjudgement and group conflict.

☐ Self-serving bias can be adaptive in that it allows us to savour the good things that happen in our lives. When bad things happen, however, self-serving bias can have the maladaptive effect of causing us to blame others or feel cheated out of something we 'deserved'.

## IMPRESSION MANAGEMENT

☐ As social beings, we adjust our words and actions to suit our audiences. To varying degrees, we note our performance and adjust it to create the impressions we desire.

☐ Such tactics explain examples of false modesty, in which people put themselves down, extol future competitors, or publicly credit others when privately they credit themselves.

☐ Sometimes people will even self-handicap with self-defeating behaviours that protect self-esteem by providing excuses for failure.

☐ Self-presentation refers to our wanting to present a favourable image both to an external audience (other people) and to an internal audience (ourselves). Many people these days make use of online social networking sites for self-presentation purposes. With regard to an external audience, those who score high on a scale of self-monitoring adjust their behaviour to each situation, whereas those low in self-monitoring may do so little adjusting that they seem insensitive.

## CRITICAL QUESTIONS

**1** To what extent, in your opinion, does one's sense of self depend on culture?

**2** Should we help people with low self-esteem to increase it?

**3** How would you rate your self-knowledge in terms of accuracy?

**4** Do you think narcissistic people are more attractive than non-narcissistic ones? If so, why?

**5** Is conscious self-monitoring a good or a bad thing?

## RECOMMENDED READINGS

### Classic Works

Goffman, E. (1959). *The Presentation of Self in Everyday Life*. London: Penguin Books.

*A highly readable and fascinating account of the many strategies and concerns underlying the public presentation of self.*

Higgins, E. T. (1987). Self-discrepancy: A theory relating self and affect. *Psychological Review,* **94**, 319–340.

*A very influential paper presenting a theory about the emotional consequences of specific discrepancies between the self as it is, the self as one would like it to be, and the self as one thinks it is expected to be.*

Lash, C. (1979). *The Culture of Narcissism: American Life in an Age of Diminishing Expectations*. New York: Norton & Company.

*The first book denouncing the narcissistic turn in American society.*

### Contemporary Works

Dufner, M., Rauthmann, J. F., Czarna, A. Z., and Denissen, J. J. A. (2013). Are narcissists sexy? Zeroing in on the effect of narcissism on short-term mate appeal. *Personality and Social Psychology Bulletin,* **39**, 870–882.

*An intriguing paper using various methodological approaches showing that narcissistic individuals are especially appealing as short-term romantic or sexual partners.*

Leach, C. W., & Spears, R. (2008). 'A vengefulness of the impotent': The pain of in-group inferiority and schadenfreude toward successful out-groups. *Journal of Personality and Social Psychology,* **95**, 1383–1396.

*A fascinating paper schowing that 'schadenfreude' (taking pleasure at the misfortune of an out-group) is especially driven by the pain of in-group inferiority and the anger associated with this pain.*

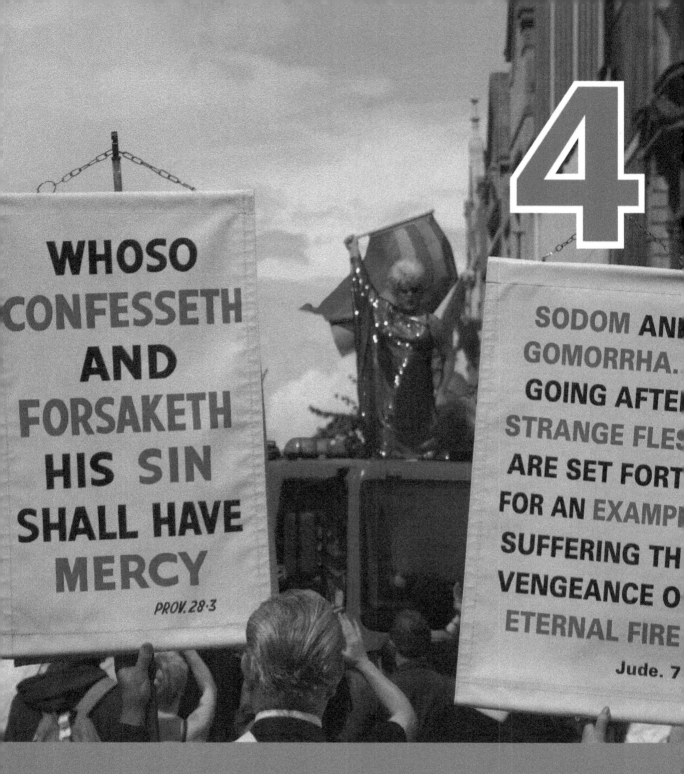

**4**

WHOSO
CONFESSETH
AND
FORSAKETH
HIS SIN
SHALL HAVE
MERCY

PROV. 28·3

SODOM AN[
GOMORRHA.
GOING AFTE[
STRANGE FLES[
ARE SET FORT[
FOR AN EXAMP[
SUFFERING TH[
VENGEANCE O[
ETERNAL FIRE

Jude. 7

*"Most of the mistakes in thinking are inadequacies of perception rather than mistakes of logic."*

Edward De Bono

# SOCIAL BELIEFS
# AND JUDGEMENTS

The earthquake that struck the Italian city of L'Aquila on 9 April 2009 killed hundreds of people and left many more injured and homeless. Many of us witnessed the scale of the devastation through the media as journalists recorded the images of victims and rubble left in its wake. Very soon afterwards people started to ask 'Why?' Why had this occurred? Was someone or something to blame? Could this have been avoided? The earthquake exposed poor building standards that had been used in the construction of modern buildings, such as hospitals and schools, which crumbled alongside the historic churches and old housing. So who was to blame for the destruction and devastation that ensued? Was the disaster an act of God which we could not have foreseen? Or was it a natural disaster that, with our advanced scientific knowledge and instruments of technology, we could have predicted, warned people about and saved thousands of lives? While that is an incredibly tricky question to answer, what it does highlight is that the human response to any scale of disaster is to try to explain it. From the tsunami in 2004, to the floods in the UK of 2007, to the earthquake in Italy in 2009, people try to work out how they were caused and how they could be prevented. Social influences such as the media and our discussions with each other shape the variety of beliefs we hold to explain why an event occurs.

Such social beliefs emerge as we:

☐ *perceive* and recall events through the filters of our own culturally influenced assumptions

☐ *judge* events, informed by our intuition, by implicit rules that guide our snap judgements, and by our moods

☐ *explain* events by attributing them to the situation or to the person

☐ therefore *expect* certain events, which sometimes helps bring them about.

This chapter therefore explores how we perceive, judge and explain our social worlds, and how – and how much – our expectations influence others. Because this chapter is about social thinking and thought processes involved in social judgements, the focus is broadly on social cognition and therefore on experimental social psychology. Other perspectives, such as the psychodynamic approach and social learning are not included in the scope of the chapter. However, we would still encourage you to also consider alternative explanations and influences with regard to perceiving, judging, explaining and expectations, especially cultural differences, the social context, social interactions and personality and individual differences.

## PERCEIVING OUR SOCIAL WORLD

*Striking research reveals the extent to which our assumptions and prejudgements guide our perceptions, interpretations and recall.*

Chapter 1 noted an important fact: that our cultural preconceptions guide how we perceive and interpret information. We construe the world through cultural-tinted glasses. 'Sure, preconceptions matter', people will agree; yet, they fail to realize how great the effect is.

Let us consider some provocative experiments. The first group of experiments examines how *predispositions* and *pre*judgements affect how we perceive and interpret information. The second group plants a judgement in people's minds *after* they have been given information to see how after-the-fact ideas bias recall. The overarching point: *we respond not to reality as it is but to reality as we construe it.*

## PRIMING

Even before we attend to the world around us, unattended stimuli can subtly predispose how we will interpret and recall events. Imagine yourself, during an experiment, wearing earphones and concentrating on ambiguous spoken sentences such as 'We stood by the bank'. When a pertinent word (*river* or *money*) is simultaneously sent to your other ear, you do not consciously hear it. Yet the word 'primes' your interpretation of the sentence (Baars & McGovern, 1996).

Our memory system is a web of associations, and priming is the awakening or activating of certain associations. Priming experiments reveal how one thought, even without awareness, can influence another thought, or even an action. In an experiment, John Bargh and his colleagues (1996a) asked people to complete a sentence containing words such as 'old', 'wise' and 'retired'. Shortly afterwards, they observed these people walking more slowly to the elevator than those not primed with ageing-related words. Furthermore, the slow walkers had no awareness of their walking speed or of having just viewed words that primed ageing.

priming *activating particular associations in memory*

Often our thinking and acting are primed by events of which we are unaware. Rob Holland and his colleagues (2005) observed that Dutch students exposed to the scent of an all-purpose cleaner were quicker to identify cleaning-related words. In follow-up experiments, other students exposed to a cleaning scent recalled more cleaning-related activities when describing their day's activities and even kept their desk cleaner while eating a crumbly cookie. Moreover, all these effects occurred without the participants' conscious awareness of the scent and its influence.

Priming experiments have their counterparts in everyday life.

- ☐ Watching a scary movie alone at home can prime our thinking, by activating emotions that, without our realizing it, cause us to interpret furnace noises as a possible intruder.

- ☐ Depressed moods, as this chapter explains later, prime negative associations. But put people in a *good* mood and suddenly their past seems more wonderful, their future brighter.

- ☐ Watching violence primes people to interpret ambiguous actions (being pushed by a passer-by) and words ('punch') as aggressive.

- ☐ For many psychology students, reading about psychological disorders primes how they interpret their own anxieties and gloomy moods. Reading about disease symptoms similarly primes medical students to worry about their congestion, fever or headache.

In a host of studies, priming effects surface even when the stimuli are presented subliminally – too briefly to be perceived consciously. What is out of sight may not be completely out of mind. An electric shock that is too slight to be felt may increase the perceived intensity of a later shock. An imperceptibly flashed word, 'bread', may prime people to detect a related word such as 'butter' more quickly than an unrelated word such as 'bottle' or 'bubble'. A subliminal colour name facilitates speedier identification when the colour appears on the computer screen, whereas an unseen wrong name delays colour identification (Epley et al., 1999; Merikle et al., 2001). In each case, an invisible image or word primes a response to a later task.

## CATEGORICAL THINKING

Priming effects can lead us to perceive people as members of social groups. Categorical thinking describes this process of perceiving a person in terms of cues that indicate their social group membership. Interestingly, theorists have found that group stereotypes can be triggered simply through the presence of a category-relevant feature. 'How useful!' you may exclaim. Such a mechanism certainly saves us a lot of time and effort working out who someone is. As Neil Macrae and Douglas Martin (2007, p. 793) state, 'categorical thinking economises the process of person understanding'. However, while this might have benefits, it comes with costs such as negative stereotyping, discrimination and prejudice simply on the basis of a visual feature. So, for example, you might see someone's hairstyle and on the basis of that assume them to be a member of a social group (e.g. goths, punks, emos), which may lead you to behave towards them favourably or unfavourably, depending on how you feel about the group. In fact, Macrae and Martin found that simply perceiving the visual cue of long or short hair caused the activation of sex stereotypes (i.e. if long hair was primed then the person was assumed to be female). John Bargh, Mark Chen and Lara Burrows (1996b) reported that participants' behaviour changed in accordance with the stereotypical information they had been primed with. For example, when primed with the stereotype of African-American, participants behaved in a more hostile manner to provocative questions from the experimenter. The researchers drew on the notion of a racial stereotype held by white Americans towards black Americans which they propose influences perceptions of black Americans' hostility. They argue that this perception of black Americans' hostility produces a tendency towards hostile behaviour in the perceiver when primed with this stereotype. So it seems categorical thinking influences how we perceive and behave towards people. We consider this again in Chapter 12 when we examine how categorical thinking shapes the identities we ascribe to ourselves and other people, and in Chapter 13 to see how perceptions of social group membership and stereotypes can lead to discrimination and prejudice.

However, we need to be a little cautious here. It isn't simply the case that we will always engage in stereotypical categorical thinking. Neil Macrae and Galen Bodenhausen (2000), and Luigi Castelli, Neil Macrae, Cristina Zogmaister and Luciano Arcuri (2004) have suggested that stereotyping occurs when:

☐ it is relevant to the perceiver's information-processing goals

☐ the perceiver holds prejudiced beliefs about such groups

☐ the perceiver has sufficient attentional resources to engage in this kind of information processing

☐ the cues are easy to process and are presented to the perceiver for a period of time.

> The way we categorise within our social world has implications for stereotyping, the production of prejudice and discriminatory behaviour. See Chapter 13 for an overview of prejudice.

We make assumptions about people on the basis of their physical appearance. How might categorical thinking influence your perceptions and behaviour?
SOURCE: © ShyMan/iStock

Studies of how implanted ideas and images can prime our interpretations and recall illustrate one of this book's take-home lessons from twenty-first-century social psychology: *much of our social information processing is automatic.* It is unintentional, out of sight and without awareness.

## PERCEIVING AND INTERPRETING EVENTS

Despite some startling and often confirmed biases and logical flaws in how we perceive and understand one another, we're mostly accurate (Jussim, 2005). The better we know people, the more accurately we feel we can read their minds and feelings. But on occasion our prejudgements err. The effects of prejudgements and expectations are standard fare for psychology's introductory course. Recall the Dalmatian photo in Chapter 1. Or consider this phrase:

A

BIRD

IN THE

THE HAND

Did you notice anything wrong with it? There is more to perception than meets the eye. The same is true of social perception. As social perceptions are very much in the eye of the beholder, even a simple stimulus may strike two people quite differently. Saying Britain's Tony Blair was 'an OK prime minister' may sound like a put-down to one of his ardent admirers and like praise to someone who regards him with contempt. When social information is subject to multiple interpretations, preconceptions matter (Hilton & von Hippel, 1990).

An experiment by Robert Vallone, Lee Ross and Mark Lepper (1985) reveals just how powerful preconceptions can be. They showed pro-Israeli and pro-Arab students six network news segments describing the 1982 killing of civilian refugees at two camps in Lebanon. As Figure 4.1 illustrates, each group perceived the networks as hostile to its side.

The phenomenon is commonplace: sports fans perceive referees as partial to the other side. Political candidates and their supporters nearly always view the news media as unsympathetic to their cause. But it's not just fans and politicians. People everywhere perceive mediators and media as biased against their position. 'There is no subject about which people are less objective than objectivity', noted one media commentator (Poniewozik, 2003). Indeed, people's perceptions of bias can be used to assess their attitudes (Saucier & Miller, 2003). Tell me where you see bias, and you will signal your attitudes.

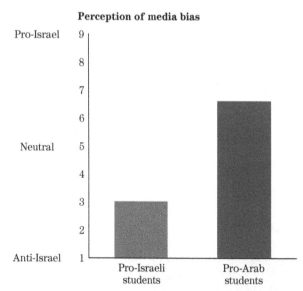

**FIGURE 4.1** Perception of media bias
Pro-Israeli and pro-Arab students who viewed network news descriptions of the 'Beirut massacre' believed the coverage was biased against their point of view.
SOURCE: Data from Vallone et al., 1985.

'Once you have a belief, it influences how you perceive all other relevant information. Once you see a country as hostile, you are likely to interpret ambiguous actions on their part as signifying their hostility.'

Political scientist Robert Jervis (1985)

Our assumptions about the world can even make contradictory evidence seem supportive. For example, Ross and Lepper assisted Charles Lord (1979) in asking two groups of students to evaluate the results of two supposedly new research studies. Half the students favoured capital punishment and half opposed it. Of the studies they evaluated, one confirmed and the other disconfirmed the students' beliefs about the deterrent effect of the death penalty. The results: both proponents and opponents of capital punishment readily accepted evidence that confirmed their belief but were sharply critical of disconfirming evidence. Showing the two sides an *identical* body of mixed evidence had not lessened their disagreement but *increased* it.

Researchers have manipulated people's preconceptions – with astonishing effects upon their interpretations and recollections.

Myron Rothbart and Pamela Birrell (1977) had university students assess the facial expression of a man (Figure 4.2). Those told he was a Gestapo leader responsible for barbaric medical experiments on concentration camp inmates during the Second World War intuitively judged his expression as cruel. (Can you see that barely suppressed sneer?) Those told he was a leader in the anti-Nazi underground movement whose courage saved thousands of Jewish lives judged his facial expression as warm and kind. (Just look at those caring eyes and that almost-smiling mouth.)

Film-makers can control people's perceptions of emotion by manipulating the setting in which they see a face. They call this the 'Kulechov effect', after a Russian film director who would skilfully guide viewers' inferences by manipulating their assumptions. Kulechov demonstrated the phenomenon by creating three short films that presented identical footage of the face of an actor with a neutral expression after viewers had first been shown one of three different scenes: a dead woman, a dish of soup or a girl playing. As a result, in the first film the actor seemed sad, in the second thoughtful and in the third happy.

Construal processes also colour others' perceptions of us. When we say something good or bad about another, people spontaneously tend to associate that trait with us, report Lynda Mae, Donal Carlston and John Skowronski (1999; Carlston & Skowronski, 2005) – a phenomenon they call *spontaneous trait inference*. If we go around talking about others being gossipy, people may then unconsciously associate 'gossip' with us. Call someone a fool and people may later construe *you* as one. Describe someone as sensitive, loving and compassionate, and you may seem more so. There is, it appears, intuitive wisdom in the childhood taunt, 'I'm rubber, you're glue; what you say bounces off me and sticks to you.'

**FIGURE 4.2**   Judge for yourself: is this person's expression cruel or kind? If told he was a Nazi, would your reading of his face differ?

SOURCE: © Constantinis/iStock

The bottom line: we view our social worlds through the spectacles of our beliefs, attitudes and values. These are shaped by the normative framework of the culture, society and community in which we live. That is one reason our beliefs are so important: they shape our interpretation of everything else.

## BELIEF PERSEVERANCE

Imagine a grandparent who decides, during an evening with a crying infant, that bottle-feeding produces colicky babies: 'Come to think of it, cow's milk obviously suits calves better than babies.' If the infant turns out to be suffering a high fever, will the sitter nevertheless persist in believing that bottle-feeding causes colic (Ross & Anderson, 1982)? To find out, Lee Ross, Craig Anderson and their colleagues planted a falsehood in people's minds and then tried to discredit it.

Their research reveals that it is surprisingly difficult to demolish a falsehood, once the person conjures up a rationale for it. Each experiment first *implanted a belief*, either by proclaiming it to be true or by showing the participants some anecdotal evidence. Then the participants were asked to *explain why* it is true. Finally, the researchers totally *discredited* the initial information by telling the participants the truth: the information was manufactured for the experiment, and half the participants in the experiment had received opposite information. Nevertheless, the new belief survived about 75 per cent intact. Therefore, only a quarter of the implanted belief was lost when the researchers discredited it. This is presumably because the participants still retained their invented explanations for the belief. This phenomenon, called belief perseverance, shows that beliefs can grow their own legs and survive the discrediting of the evidence that inspired them.

In another example of belief perseverance, Anderson, Lepper and Ross (1980) asked participants to decide whether individuals who take risks make good or bad firefighters. One group considered a risk-prone person who was a successful firefighter and a cautious person who was an unsuccessful one. The other group considered cases suggesting the opposite conclusion. After forming their theory that risk-prone people make better or worse firefighters, the participants wrote explanations for it – for example, that risk-prone people are brave or that cautious people have fewer accidents. Once each explanation was formed, it could exist independently of the information that initially created the belief. When that information was discredited, the participants still held their self-generated explanations and therefore continued to believe that risk-prone people really do make better or worse firefighters.

These experiments also suggest that the more we examine our theories and explain how they *might* be true, the more closed we become to information that challenges our beliefs. Once we consider why an accused person might be guilty, why an offending stranger acts that way, or why a favoured stock might rise in value, our explanations may survive challenging evidence to the contrary (Davies, 1997; Jelalian & Miller, 1984).

The evidence is compelling: our beliefs and expectations powerfully affect how we mentally construct events. Usually, we benefit from our preconceptions, just as scientists benefit from creating theories that guide them in noticing and interpreting events. But the benefits sometimes entail a cost: we become prisoners of our own thought patterns. Thus, the supposed Martian 'canals' that twentieth-century astronomers delighted in spotting turned out to be the product of intelligent life – an intelligence on Earth's side of the telescope. As another example, Germans, who widely believed that the introduction of the euro currency led to increased prices, overestimated such price increases when comparing actual restaurant menus – the prior menu with German mark prices and a new one with

**belief perseverance** *persistence of one's initial conceptions, as when the basis for one's belief is discredited but an explanation of why the belief might be true survives*

euro prices (Traut-Mattausch et al., 2004). As an old Chinese proverb says, 'Two-thirds of what we see is behind our eyes.'

Belief perseverance may have important consequences, as Stephan Lewandowsky and his international collaborators (2005) discovered when they explored implanted and discredited information about the Iraq war that began in 2003. As the war unfolded, the Western media reported and repeated several claims – for example, that Iraqi forces executed coalition prisoners of war – that later were shown to be false and were retracted. Alas, having accepted the information, which fitted their pre-existing assumptions, Americans tended to retain the belief (unlike Germans and Australians, who tended to be more predisposed to question the war's rationale).

Is there a remedy for belief perseverance? There is: *explain the opposite*. Charles Lord, Mark Lepper and Elizabeth Preston (1984) repeated the capital punishment study described earlier and added two variations. First, they asked some of their participants when evaluating the evidence to be 'as *objective* and *unbiased* as possible'. That instruction accomplished nothing; whether for or against capital punishment, those who received the plea made evaluations as biased as those who did not.

> 'No one denies that new evidence can change people's beliefs. Children do eventually renounce their belief in Santa Claus. Our contention is simply that such changes generally occur slowly, and that more compelling evidence is often required to alter a belief than to create it.'
>
> Lee Ross & Mark Lepper, 1980

The researchers asked a third group of individuals to consider the opposite – to ask themselves 'whether you would have made the same high or low evaluations had exactly the same study produced results on the *other* side of the issue'. After imagining an opposite finding, these people were much less biased in their evaluations of the evidence for and against their views. In his experiments, Craig Anderson (1982; Anderson & Sechler, 1986) consistently found that explaining *why* an opposite theory might be true – why a cautious rather than a risk-taking person might be a better firefighter – reduces or eliminates belief perseverance. Indeed, explaining any alternative outcome, not just the opposite, drives people to ponder various possibilities (Hirt & Markman, 1995).

## CONSTRUCTING MEMORIES OF OURSELVES AND OUR WORLDS

Do you agree or disagree with the following statement?

> Memory can be likened to a storage chest in the brain into which we deposit material and from which we can withdraw it later if needed. Occasionally, something is lost from the 'chest', and then we say we have forgotten.

About 85 per cent of college students said they agreed (Lamal, 1979). As one magazine advertisement put it: 'Science has proven the accumulated experience of a lifetime is preserved perfectly in your mind.'

Actually, psychological research has proved the opposite. Our memories are not exact copies of experiences that remain on deposit in a memory bank. Rather, we construct memories at the time of withdrawal, as well as when we store experiences. Like a palaeontologist inferring the appearance of a dinosaur from bone fragments, we reconstruct our distant past by using our current feelings and expectations to combine information fragments. Thus, we can easily (though unconsciously) revise our memories to suit our current knowledge. But there has to be something stored in the memory to be used when constructing what happened.

When an experimenter or a therapist manipulates people's presumptions about their past, a sizeable percentage of people will construct false memories. Asked to imagine vividly a made-up childhood experience in which they ran, tripped, fell and stuck their hand through a window, or knocked over a punch bowl at a wedding, about a quarter will later recall the fictitious event as something that actually happened (Loftus & Bernstein, 2005). In its search for truth, the mind sometimes constructs a falsehood.

In experiments involving more than 20 000 people, Elizabeth Loftus (2003) and her collaborators have explored our mind's tendency to construct memories. In the typical experiment, people witness an event, receive misleading information about it (or not), and then take a memory test. The repeated finding is the misinformation effect. People incorporate the misinformation into their memories: they recall a give way sign as a stop sign, hammers as screwdrivers, *Vogue* magazine as *Mademoiselle*, Dr Henderson as Dr Davidson, breakfast cereal as eggs, and a clean-shaven man as a fellow with a moustache. However, of greater concern, analyses of hundreds of cases in which patients were led to falsely believe that they were abducted by aliens or molested in satanic rituals reveal that suggestion is a key factor in these beliefs. This shows that suggested misinformation may even produce false memories of supposed child sexual abuse, argues Loftus. These false memories can have severe consequences for the individual.

misinformation effect *incorporating 'misinformation' into one's memory of the event, after witnessing an event and receiving misleading information about it*

Furthermore, suggestion has important implications for criminal investigations that rely on memory in order to track down a perpetrator or work out a motive. Suspects and witnesses who are subject to suggestive police interviews can confuse suggestions made in the interview for memories of the actual event. So merely imagining the occurrence of the suggested event can lead to the development of false memories for the event (e.g. Garry et al., 1996; Lindsay et al., 2004). Sarah Drivdahl, Maria Zaragoza and Dianne Learned (2009) observed that when participants were asked to emotionally elaborate on a suggested event, it not only increased false memories for the event having actually happened, but also false beliefs in its authenticity.

This process affects our recall of social as well as physical events. Jack Croxton and his colleagues (1984) had students spend 15 minutes talking with someone. Those who were later informed that this person liked them recalled the person's behaviour as relaxed, comfortable and happy. Those informed that the person disliked them recalled the person as nervous, uncomfortable and not so happy.

Researchers have also used qualitative methods to focus on the content of constructed memories as they occur in language. Derek Edwards and David Middleton (1987) argue that memories are better understood as rhetorical strategies that produce a version of an event that is appropriate for the context in which it is produced. This sidelines an analysis of whether memories are an accurate representation of what happened, and instead looks at why and how they are created in language and for what purposes. For example, Abigail Locke and Derek Edwards (2003) considered how ex-US President Bill Clinton recalled his relationship with his intern Monica Lewinsky under cross-examination from the Grand Jury. His memory of the relationship centres on a constructed memory of Monica as a problematic young woman with irrational emotions and a troubled character. Clinton claims his own caring disposition led him to befriend the young woman. Locke and Edwards point to how such a memory involves a particular representation of emotions and personality that reduce Clinton's own culpability in the affair and diminish the sexual aspects of the relationship. He was simply helping a troubled young woman, which resulted in 'inappropriate contact'. So, in this kind of research memory is not studied as an accurate reflection of what actually happened, but is considered a *version* of what happened, rhetorically designed to attend to the demands of the context in which it is produced.

### Reconstructing our Past Attitudes

Five years ago, how did you feel about nuclear power? About your country's president or prime minister? About your parents? If your attitudes have changed, what do you think is the extent of the change?

Researchers have explored such questions, and the results have been unnerving. People whose attitudes have changed often insist that they have always felt much as they now feel. Daryl Bem and Keith McConnell (1970) conducted a survey among university students. Buried in it was a question concerning student control over the university curriculum. A week later the students agreed to write an essay opposing student control. After doing so, their attitudes shifted towards greater opposition to student control. When asked to recall how they had answered the question before writing the essay, the students 'remembered' holding the opinion that they *now* held and denied that the experiment had affected them.

After observing students similarly denying their former attitudes, researchers D. R. Wixon and James Laird (1976) commented, 'The speed, magnitude, and certainty' with which the students revised their own histories 'was striking'. As George Vaillant (1977) noted after following adults through time, 'It is all too common for caterpillars to become butterflies and then to maintain that in their youth they had been little butterflies. Maturation makes liars of us all.'

The construction of positive memories brightens our recollections. Terence Mitchell, Leigh Thompson (1994) and their colleagues (1997) report that people often exhibit *rosy retrospection* – they recall mildly pleasant events more favourably than they experienced them. College students on a three-week bike trip, older adults on a guided tour of Austria, and undergraduates on vacation all reported enjoying their experiences as they were having them. But they later recalled such experiences even more fondly, minimizing the unpleasant or boring aspects and remembering the high points.

Cathy McFarland and Michael Ross (1985) found that, as our relationships change, we also revise our recollections of other people. They had university students rate their steady dating partners. Two months later, they rated them again. Students who were more in love than ever had a tendency to recall love at first sight. Those who had broken up were more likely to recall having recognized the partner as somewhat selfish and bad-tempered.

Diane Holmberg and John Holmes (1994) discovered the phenomenon also operating among 373 newlywed couples, most of whom reported being very happy. When resurveyed two years later, those whose marriages had soured recalled that things had always been bad. The results are 'frightening', say Holmberg and Holmes. 'Such biases can lead to a dangerous downward spiral. The worse your current view of your partner is, the worse your memories are, which only further confirms your negative attitudes.'

It's not that we are totally unaware of how we used to feel, just that when memories are hazy, current feelings guide our recall. Parents of every generation bemoan the values of the next generation, partly because they misrecall their youthful values as being closer to their current values. And teens of every generation recall their parents as – depending on their current mood – wonderful or woeful (Bornstein et al., 1991).

### Reconstructing our Past Behaviour

Memory construction enables us to revise our own histories. The hindsight bias involves memory revision. Hartmut Blank and his colleagues (2003) showed this when inviting University of Leipzig students, after a surprising German election outcome, to recall their voting predictions from two months previously. The students misrecalled their predictions as closer to the actual results.

Our memories reconstruct other sorts of past behaviours as well. Michael Ross, Cathy McFarland and Garth Fletcher (1981) exposed some University of Waterloo students to a message convincing them of the desirability of toothbrushing. Later, in a supposedly different experiment, these students recalled brushing their teeth more often during the preceding two weeks than did students who had not heard the message. Likewise, projecting from surveys, people report smoking many fewer cigarettes than are actually sold (Hall, 1985). And they recall casting more votes than were actually recorded (Bureau of the Census, 1993).

Social psychologist Anthony Greenwald (1980) noted the similarity of such findings to happenings in George Orwell's novel *Nineteen Eighty-Four* – in which it was 'necessary to remember that events happened in the desired manner'. Indeed, argued Greenwald, we all have 'totalitarian egos' that revise the past to suit our present views. Thus, we under-report bad behaviour and over-report good behaviour.

Sometimes our present view is that we've improved – in which case we may mis-recall our past as more unlike the present than it actually was. This tendency resolves a puzzling pair of consistent findings: those who participate in psychotherapy and self-improvement programmes for weight control, anti-smoking and exercise show only modest improvement on average. Yet they often claim considerable benefit (Myers, 2004). Michael Conway and Michael Ross (1986) explain why: having expended so much time, effort and money on self-improvement, people may think, 'I may not be perfect now, but I was worse before; this did me a lot of good.' We all selectively notice, interpret and recall events in ways that sustain our ideas. Our social judgements are a mix of observation and expectation, reason and passion.

So far we have seen that there can be many influences on our perceptions and also that perceiving our social world can become distorted. This has a knock-on effect on our social judgements too. These judgements can also occur very quickly as we will see when we turn to a consideration of social judgements in the following section.

## JUDGING OUR SOCIAL WORLD

*As we have already noted, our cognitive mechanisms are efficient and adaptive, yet occasionally error-prone. Usually they serve us well. But sometimes clinicians misjudge patients, employers misjudge employees, people of one race misjudge people of another, and spouses misjudge their mates. The results can be misdiagnoses, labour strife, prejudices and divorces. So, how – and how well – do we make intuitive social judgements?*

By drawing on advances in cognitive psychology – in how people perceive, represent and remember events – social psychologists have shed welcome light on how we form judgements. Let us look at what that research reveals of the marvels and mistakes of our social intuition.

### INTUITIVE JUDGEMENTS

What are our powers of intuition – of immediately knowing something without reasoning or analysis? Advocates of 'intuitive management' believe we should tune in to our hunches. When judging others, they say, we should plug in to the non-logical smarts of our 'right brain'. When hiring, firing and investing, we should listen to our premonitions. In making judgements, we should follow the example of *Star Wars'* Luke Skywalker by switching off our computer guidance systems and trusting the force within.

Are the intuitionists right that important information is immediately available apart from our conscious analysis? Or are the sceptics correct in saying that intuition is 'our knowing we are right, whether we are or not'?

Priming research suggests that the unconscious indeed controls much of our behaviour. As John Bargh and Tanya Chartrand (1999) explain, 'Most of a person's everyday life is determined not by their conscious intentions and deliberate choices but by mental processes that are put into motion by features of the environment and that operate outside of conscious awareness and guidance.' When the light turns red, we react and hit the brake before consciously deciding to do so. Indeed, reflect Neil Macrae and Lucy Johnston (1998), 'to be able to do just about anything at all (e.g., driving, dating, dancing), action initiation needs to be decoupled from the inefficient (i.e., slow, serial, resource consuming) workings of the conscious mind, otherwise inaction inevitably would prevail'.

However, a word of caution is perhaps needed here. Although conscious decisions are slower than automatic processes this does not mean that they are less important. They characterize human beings. Behaviour that has become automated has previously been deliberate and conscious. For example, if you are a driver, you once consciously thought through all the steps of driving, but now it is a fairly automatic process. Riding a bike involved learning to ride, yet once this is accomplished not much conscious thought is needed to balance the bike and to cycle.

#### The Powers of Intuition

'The heart has its reasons which reason does not know,' observed seventeenth-century philosopher-mathematician Blaise Pascal. Three centuries later, scientists have proved Pascal correct. We know more than we know we know. Studies of our unconscious information processing confirm our limited access to what's going on in our minds (Bargh & Ferguson, 2000; Greenwald et al., 2003a; Greenwald & Banaji, 1995; Perkins et al., 2008; Strack & Deutsch, 2004). Our thinking is partly controlled processing (reflective, deliberate and conscious) and – more than psychologists once supposed – partly automatic processing (impulsive, effortless and without our awareness). Automatic, intuitive thinking occurs not 'on-screen' but off-screen, out of sight, where reason does not go. But we should remember that humans are not born with some preferred knowledge or behaviour. What is automatic today has been acquired and learned by conscious training.

Social judgements have a profound influence upon our behaviour. So can what we already know influence our social judgements and bring about automatic behaviour change? Researchers argue that for these automatic processes to occur we need to be able to activate pre-existing knowledge (Amodio and Ratner, 2011; Bertram and Bodenhausen, 2005). To test whether the presence of situational cues will bring about automatic behaviour change, John Bargh, Mark Chen and Lara Burrows (1996b) primed participants with the task of unscrambling scrambled sentences. There were three conditions. Either the scrambled sentences contained rude words or polite words or neutral words. After this, participants were told to approach the experimenter to ask what their next task would be. However, to place the participants in a situation that would lead to social judgements the experimenters had set up a fake situation where the experimenter was supposedly engaged in conversation and did not acknowledge the presence of the participant. If you were in this situation would you think the experimenter was rude? Would you interrupt the experimenter and if so how long do you think you would wait before interrupting? In the study, 60 per cent of those who had taken part in the rude words condition interrupted within ten minutes while less than 40 per cent of participants in the neutral condition interrupted during this time and less than 20 per cent interrupted if they were in the polite condition. The researchers argue that the participants' behaviour was driven by the environmental stimuli – rude words or polite words and that this was preconscious and automatic. Because we need to have some idea about what is rude and polite and what these mean we need to draw on what we have already learned – what we already know. Therefore, Bargh et al. (1996b) also point out the implications of implicit rather than explicit cognition with regard to making judgements and stereotyping. After two further experiments were carried out that activated stereotypes automatically, Bargh et al. (1996b) argued that this indicates people can behave in negative ways towards stereotyped groups without even realizing it! This clearly shows that we know more than we know we know and it also demonstrates the more negative implication of our automatic behaviour.

Amodio and Ratner (2011) propose that there are different memory systems for different patterns of learning and behaviour. Exploring memory systems can therefore help us to understand more about the processes involved in making social judgements that appear to be intuitive. Spunt and Lieberman (2013) argue for a dual process model of the brain system: one process when we automatically identify a person's behaviour and one process when we make judgements about a person's behaviour. Spunt and Lieberman propose that when we are making judgements these are controlled rather than spontaneous because we are 'weighing up' the

**controlled processing** *mental activities that require conscious, deliberate and reflective thinking*

**automatic processing** *mental activities happening with little or no conscious awareness. This is both effortless and habitual*

causes of someone's behaviour in an effort to understand this behaviour. They also point out that it would be impossible to function in the social world if all our social cognition was controlled. Imagine how huge the effort would be for making sense of people and engaging in social interactions if it was all down to conscious awareness and control.

Amodio and Ratner's (2011) and Spunt and Lieberman's (2013) work is within social neuroscience. Social neuroscience is a fast growing discipline in social psychology. What appears to be intuitive may actually involve complex processing and social neuroscience can explore this further. Social neuroscientists argue that our biology helps shape our social environments. As outlined in Chapter 1, social neuroscience is concerned with understanding the structure and functions of the brain that underlie our behaviour and enable our emotional experiences and how we process information. This discipline is therefore currently making important contributions in furthering our understanding of how we make social judgements.

Social neuroscience brings together multi-levels of analysis and is concerned with the biological, psychological and the social. John Cacioppo and Gary Berntson (1992) argue that research in social psychology and social neuroscience is important in two main ways: to investigate how neurochemical events influence social processes and to investigate how social processes influence neurochemical events. They therefore argue that social psychological theories should also consider physiological factors and mechanisms.

Three methods of neuroimaging are frequently used in social neuroscience. Functional magnetic resonance imaging (fMRI) and event-related potentials (ERPs) are both non-invasive methods that provide images of brain activity. ERPs are derived from averages of EEG activity in response to certain stimuli (Cacioppo et al., 1994). Both are correlational techniques. fMRI provides exploration of brain regions that are active when engaged in specific mental operations and ERPs provide exploration of rapid changes in brain activity. The third method, transcranial magnetic stimulation (TMS), stimulates brain cells and allows exploration into what causes particular brain regions to become activated for specific mental operations.

The networks in the brain region that are involved in making social judgements may not function in the same way for everybody. Neuroimaging has also been applied to understanding impairments in social judgements of people diagnosed with schizophrenia or with autistic spectrum disorders (ASD). For example, Hall, Whalley, McKirdy, Sprengelmeyer, Santos, Donaldson et al. (2010) used fMRI to investigate the neural systems activated when people make social decisions. They found that there is a common network of brain regions activated when people without any history of psychiatric disorders make social judgements about approachability or intelligence based on faces. They therefore propose that it is the dysfunction of this network that could contribute to a broad range of deficits in social functioning seen in people diagnosed with schizophrenia and ASD. Later in the chapter we shall consider how social neuroscience can help us further understand the way we explain our social world.

## SOCIAL SCHEMA THEORY

We began to consider the concept of 'schemas' in Chapter 3 when we discussed how people understand their sense of 'self'. Schema is a construct social psychologists use to illustrate how we store information about the world, people, roles and how to behave in particular situations. Schemas serve many functions including guiding our memory, predicting what will happen, informing us how to behave appropriately and enabling us to work out what to do when it's not obvious from a situation. Susan Fiske and Shelley Taylor (1991) define the four main schema types that we have as follows:

1. **Self schemas** – the most complex. This is the information we hold about ourselves in terms of our traits, our values, our mannerisms and so on. They define 'who I am'. See also Chapter 3 for more detail on the implications they have for presentations of our 'self' and our sense of well-being.

2. **Person schemas** – these include personality traits so we can categorize people when we first meet them on the basis of their perceived personality, and specific traits related to a particular person (e.g. your mother or your best friend).

3. **Role schemas** – these contain information about what behaviour and norms to expect of someone holding a particular role in society (e.g. doctor, mother, politician, lecturer).

4. **Event schemas** – these hold information about appropriate behaviour for events (e.g. going to a football match, attending a funeral).

Before a schema is activated and made available, we must first categorize the event, person or object appropriately. This is largely an automatic process. Eleanor Rosch (1975) argued that we hold prototypes for each category so we can compare new instances to see if it belongs there. So imagine visiting the fine dining restaurant, Michel Roux Junior's 'Le Gavroche', for the first time. We need to make use of our event schemas to work out how to behave appropriately. Is this an example of the category 'restaurant', or is it something else? To make such a judgement you compare it against a prototype of restaurant (which may be a specific instance or an amalgamation of several instances). This will then inform you how to behave in Le Gavroche. Should you leave a tip? Will someone clear the table for you when you've finished your meal?

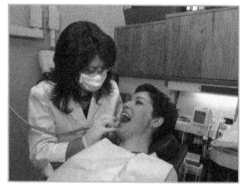

Our knowledge of the role of the dentist (role schema) and the event of a visit to the dentist (event schema) help us to anticipate what will happen and how we should behave. Without this knowledge a trip to the dentist would prove very confusing!

SOURCE: © David H. Lewis/iStock

Clearly schemas serve many advantageous functions. They enable us to categorize a complex social world quickly and efficiently, guiding us around it. However, as we shall see, they can malfunction!

### The Limits of Intuition

We have seen how automatic, intuitive thinking can 'make us smart' (Gigerenzer & Todd, 1999) or at least process information faster and repeatedly. Elizabeth Loftus and Mark Klinger (1992) nevertheless speak for other cognitive scientists in having doubts about the brilliance of intuition. They report 'a general consensus that the unconscious may not be as smart as previously believed'.

Social psychologists have explored not only our error-prone hindsight judgements but also our capacity for illusion – for perceptual misinterpretations, fantasies and constructed beliefs. If we return to social schema theory, we can

Should you tip the waiter? Our schemas help guide our actions.

SOURCE: © webphotographer/iStock

imagine the problems if we select the wrong schema in a particular situation. Imagine a young employee, someone who walks in to his regular place of work and alight upon a young woman he's never seen before. He may assume this is an office assistant and ask her to do some photocopying for him. Now suppose it turns out this woman is actually his new manager! Suddenly his behaviour is inappropriate. As we categorize people, events and objects in order to work out how to behave towards them these can lead to stereotypical judgements. Such generalizations may not be accurate, and may lead to inappropriate behaviour.

While schemas have become established within social psychology as the fundamental processes involved in social thought and attitude, Mark Landau, Brian Meier and Lucas Keefer (2010) propose that people use schemas to structure their social environment in a straightforward way but use conceptual metaphors to make sense of the world. Conceptual metaphors are unique cognitive mechanisms that shape social thought and attitudes. They liken social concepts to superficially dissimilar things and rely on taken-for-granted shared knowledge. For example, we know what somebody means if they describe a person as 'shallow' but the literal meaning of this word is actually quite different. Therefore, conceptual metaphors complement the schema view in social psychology through the way people use them to infer personal attributes and also to interpret and evaluate abstract social concepts. We will next consider how we encode information about people and make judgements about them.

In the following section on social encoding we will consider Solomon Asch's (1946) studies of person perception and see how the words warm or cold were highly influential in creating an image of a person when added to a list of personal character traits. This gives an indication of conceptual metaphors in action because warm and cold can describe physical properties but when applied to configuring a person they take on particular meanings and facilitate images of particular persons and in turn are involved in forming attitudes towards them.

### SOCIAL ENCODING

social encoding
*the process of getting social information into memory. It comprises initially attending to and perceiving social information, understanding it and making connections with information already in memory. Our previous social experiences are a very important part of the process*

Social encoding occurs within social cognition. E. Tory Higgins and John Bargh (1987) refer to social cognition as 'the knowing of people'. Social cognition refers to the way we perceive our social world and also our beliefs about people, their behaviour and the causes of social events.

Social encoding involves how we think about ourselves and other people. It is about how we select, interpret, remember and use social information to make judgements and decisions. Processing of the social world involves:

☐ Preattentive analysis – the unconscious and automatic taking in of information

☐ Focusing of attention – identifying, and categorizing information

☐ Comprehension – giving meaning to information

☐ Elaborative reasoning – linking information together and elaborating information.

Social information is ambiguous so when we encode information about a person, relevant person-related information is activated which helps us to make sense of the new information. Encoding and interpretation of a person or person's behaviour are in part a function of easily accessible mental representations and stereotypes, especially if aspects of the person or their behaviour are salient. This means that if these particular aspects are distinctive and different they will stand out and capture the attention of the person encoding the information. This also means that we remember a more clear and consistent impression of salient people and salient behaviour. If, for example, somebody was talking loudly on their mobile phone in a library and everyone else was quietly choosing books and reading, this behaviour would stand out for being different as well as for not fitting in with expectations. If you witnessed this behaviour you might find yourself making immediate judgements about the type of person the mobile phone user is. When people memorize information about a person based on their behaviour at the same time as they encode this information they base personality judgements by drawing on the most memorable aspects of this behaviour.

When we meet someone at a party and spend time talking with them, how do we decide what we think of our new acquaintance? Are we seeing them through the way we perceive their personality traits to be or are we thinking about them in a much more holistic way and forming an impression of their whole personality?

Solomon Asch (1946) argues that people appear to configure impressions of people holistically rather than simply as a collection of various independent traits. Asch's (1946) configural model is a model of person perception that argues that central traits have a stronger influence on configuring an impression of others than peripheral traits. Asch noted that the process of person perception appears to happen so fast it seems to be automatic. He also noted that once we have formed an impression of a person this impression appears to be long lasting and difficult to change.

Asch (1946) recruited psychology undergraduates for his study of person perception. A series of 10 experiments were conducted. In one experiment two different groups of participants were read identical lists of traits except for the inclusion of one different word for each group. For example, both groups were read the following list: intelligent—skilful—industrious—determined—practical—cautious but Group A's list had the word warm within their list of characteristics and Group B had the word cold within their list. Cold and warm are central traits while the other words on the list were peripheral traits. Participants were then asked to describe the impression they had formed of the person based on their list of traits and were able to give quite detailed descriptions of an overall type of person from lists of traits. They were then asked to select from a list of pairs of characteristics the characteristic that most agreed with the impression they had formed.

Here are some examples of the pairs of traits Asch used for the experiment. Most of the pairs Asch constructed were opposites:

Shrewd—wise

Irritable—good-natured

Sociable—unsociable

Unreliable—reliable

Persistent—unstable

Imaginative—hard-headed

Participants in Group A – the warm condition – were more positive about the person they described and selected the more positive characteristic from the list of paired characteristics whereas Group B – the cold condition – were not as positive as Group A about the person they described and selected the more negative characteristic from the list of pairs. Just changing one word in a list of characteristics led participants to form very different overall impressions. Therefore, the characteristics warm and cold as central traits had a greater influence on the way people form impressions of others than the peripheral traits intelligent, skilful, industrious, determined, practical and cautious. Asch (1946) also proposed that the value of a particular trait can change. For example, a trait seen as central in one person may not be seen as a central trait in another person. This may be involved with the way in which people configure an overall impression of a person. However, the way we conceive people as a whole was not explored fully. Asch addressed this further by seeing what would happen if participants were given traits that did not fit with each other (Asch and Zukier, 1984). If these contradictory traits provided obstacles to configuring an overall impression of a person, the way participants attempted to overcome this would indicate the processes involved when configuring a person as unified.

Solomon Asch and Henri Zuckier compiled a list of pairs that also included some pairs of non-contradictory characteristics. Psychology students were asked to describe a person after being given a pair of characteristics selected from the list. For example:

Sociable—lonely

Cheerful—gloomy

Warm—humorous

Shy—courageous

Strict—kind

Do you think a person is a unified whole or a multiplicity of characteristics? Can we only be one thing but not another – that is, have certain characteristics without their opposites? Furthermore, are we consistent as a person or are we a multiplicity of malleable characteristics?

Asch and Zukier (1984) found that the processes participants engaged in seemed to be an attempt to reconcile inconsistencies in order to configure the person as a whole. When participants were given pairs of contradictory traits, one of the traits would become dominant and this was usually the positive one. Participants also described the less dominant trait as temporary and also dependent on the context. This meant that focusing on the positive trait as dominant was less complicated when describing a person. For example, with the pair sociable—lonely it was easier to attribute loneliness to a temporary situation when configuring the person as sociable. Yet when loneliness was conceived of as the dominant trait, this was interpreted more deeply such as imagining the person puts on a façade to hide their loneliness. It appears that we do a lot of cognitive work when we organize and put into order the way we configure a coherent image of a person and as Asch and Zukier showed, this can all be on very little initial information too. They argue that we strive for unity when configuring an image of a person so we do more than try to resolve discrepancies; we try to assimilate these inconsistencies within a comprehensive image.

Further studies have also shown that if people are primed with particular traits before they encode information about a target person this will affect how people will judge the target person. However, Lerouge and Smeesters (2008) found that when people are primed with behavioural traits after encoding particular aspects of behavioural information, this can lead to assimilating an image of a person and making a social judgement post-encoding. This suggests that the initial social encoding is malleable in certain conditions and also that new trait information works together with already encoded person information to construct a unified image of that person.

In Lerouge and Smeesters' (2008) study participants first memorized behavioural descriptions about a target person related to kindness and unkindness. They were then primed with either kind or unkindness concepts. Participants were far more likely to judge a person as kind if kind-related concepts were activated after the initial encoding process or unkind if unkind-related concepts were activated after the encoding process. They were able to assimilate an overall image of a target person from thinking about kind concepts or unkind concepts and drawing on the relevant information they had initially encoded. The researchers argue that this demonstrates ease of accessibility of the encoded behavioural traits when later information about behavioural traits fitted in with the information that had been encoded. This shows that if trait concepts are accessible they can have an assimilation effect after the encoding stage. When participants are asked to think of a concept such as kindness to make a person judgement, this concept could activate kindness-related concepts in memory such as caring and helping and this would increase the accessibility of the information related to kindness that they had encoded about the target person.

How much difference do you think it makes in studies that investigate the social encoding of traits when the traits themselves have been selected by the researchers?

Higgins and McCann (1984) propose that the way we encode social information is 'context-driven' and this process also interacts with personal goals, person perception and interpersonal communication. They point out that interpersonal communication provides a situation where social encoding frequently occurs and that the way we perceive that other people in the social context view a person will influence our own judgement of that person. This influence will be higher the more we are motivated to make a favourable impression upon these others. This is an important consideration in experimental studies on social encoding because in everyday situations we are influenced by others around us and we also have differences in motivation depending on individual differences and the context. A criticism of social encoding studies is the way they tend to rely on giving participants lists of words and verbal/written descriptions. Fieldler, Schenk, Watling and Menges (2005) argue that picture presentations, especially moving pictures such as film clips, can evoke behaviour information far more than verbal descriptions. Actually seeing behaviour enhances relevance and external validity as well as facilitates rich inferences.

It is not just behaviour that facilitates the way in which we encode information about a person. Physical appearance is also very important and is perhaps the first thing that we notice. Andrew Engell, James Haxby and Alexander Todorov (2007) found that judgements about a person's trustworthiness were extremely rapid when looking at faces. The researchers used fMIR to investigate this and propose that the amygdala automatically categorizes faces in terms of facial features that are commonly perceived as signifying untrustworthiness. Furthermore, the extent to which a person is perceived as physically attractive can have a profound effect on our social judgements. Back in 1972, Karen Dion, Ellen Berscheid and Elaine Walster argued that there is a 'What is beautiful is good' stereotype. In their study American students were told that they were taking part in a study on person perception accuracy. The photographs used for this study had been rated in a previous study for varying levels of physical attractiveness. The participants assumed that the physically attractive people in the photographs were more likely to be successful and happy and were more likely to possess socially desirable personalities. The 'What is beautiful is good' stereotype was supported by Stuart McKelvie (1993). Higher positive trait evaluations were given to faces rated pleasant than were given to faces rated unpleasant. These studies indicate that with no other knowledge about a person except their physical appearance, people make all kinds of assumptions about the type of person someone is and even make assumptions about their future life.

## OVERCONFIDENCE

So far we have seen that our cognitive systems process a vast amount of information efficiently and automatically. But our efficiency has a trade-off; as we interpret our experiences and construct memories, our automatic intuitions sometimes err. Usually, we are unaware of our flaws. The 'intellectual conceit' evident in judgements of past knowledge ('I knew it all along') extends to estimates of current knowledge and predictions of future behaviour. Although we know we've messed up in the past, we have more positive expectations for our future performance in meeting deadlines, managing relationships, following an exercise routine and so forth (Ross & Newby-Clark, 1998).

overconfidence phenomenon *the tendency to be more confident than correct – to overestimate the accuracy of one's beliefs*

To explore this overconfidence phenomenon, Daniel Kahneman and Amos Tversky (1979) gave people factual questions and asked them to fill in the blanks, as in the following: 'I feel 98 per cent certain that the air distance between New Delhi and Beijing is more than _____ miles but less than _____ miles.' Most individuals were overconfident: about 30 per cent of the time the correct answers lay outside the range they felt 98 per cent confident about.

The air distance between New Delhi and Beijing is 2500 miles.

To find out whether overconfidence extends to social judgements, David Dunning and his associates (1990) created a little game show. They asked students to guess a stranger's answers to a series of questions, such as 'Would you prepare for a difficult exam alone or with others?' and 'Would you rate your lecture notes as neat or messy?' Knowing the type of question but not the actual questions, the participants first interviewed their target person about background, hobbies, academic interests, aspirations, astrological sign – anything they thought might be helpful. Then, while the targets privately answered 20 of the two-choice questions, the interviewers predicted their target's answers and rated their own confidence in the predictions.

The interviewers guessed right 63 per cent of the time, beating chance by 13 per cent. But, on average, they *felt* 75 per cent sure of their predictions. When guessing their own room-mates' responses, they were 68 per cent correct and 78 per cent confident. Moreover, the most confident people were most likely to be overconfident. People also are markedly overconfident when judging whether someone is telling the truth or when estimating things such as the sexual history of their dating partner or the activity preferences of their room-mates (DePaulo et al., 1997; Swann & Gill, 1997).

Interestingly, brain imaging studies have revealed that confidence in the recollection of a memory is located in different places of the brain depending on whether it was a real event or an illusory one. Hongkeun Kim and Roberto Cabeza (2007) found that while high confidence for real events was indicated by brain activity in the medial temporal lobe, high confidence for false memory was reflected in brain activity in the frontoparietal regions.

Ironically, incompetence feeds overconfidence. It takes competence to recognize what competence is, note Justin Kruger and David Dunning (1999). Students who score at the bottom on tests of grammar, humour and logic are most prone to overestimating their gifts at such. Those who don't know what good logic or grammar is are often unaware that they lack it. If you make a list of all the words you can form out of the letters in 'psychology', you may feel brilliant – but then stupid when a friend starts naming the ones you missed. Deanna Caputo and David Dunning (2005) re-created this phenomenon in experiments, confirming that our ignorance of our ignorance sustains our self-confidence. Follow-up studies indicate that this 'ignorance of one's incompetence' occurs mostly on relatively easy-seeming tasks, such as forming words out of 'psychology'. On really hard tasks, poor performers more often appreciate their lack of skill (Burson et al., 2006).

Are people better at predicting their own *behaviour*? To find out, Robert Vallone and his colleagues (1990) had college students predict in September whether they would drop a course, declare a major, elect to live off campus next year, and so forth. Although the students felt, on average, 84 per cent sure of those self-predictions, they were wrong nearly twice as often as they expected to be. Even when feeling 100 per cent sure of their predictions, they erred 15 per cent of the time.

In estimating their chances of success on a task, such as a major examination, people's confidence runs highest when removed in time from the moment of truth. By examination day, the possibility of failure looms larger and confidence typically drops (Gilovich et al., 1993; Shepperd et al., 2005). Roger Buehler and his colleagues (1994, 2002; Buehler & Griffin, 2003) report that most students also confidently underestimate how long it will take them to complete papers and other major assignments.

What produces overconfidence? Why doesn't experience lead us to a more realistic self-appraisal? For one thing, people tend to recall their mistaken judgements as times when they were *almost* right. Phillip Tetlock (1998, 1999) observed this after inviting various academic and government experts to project – from their viewpoint in the late 1980s – the future governance of the Soviet Union, South Africa and Canada. Five years later communism collapsed, South Africa had become a multiracial democracy, and Canada's French-speaking minority had not seceded. Experts who had felt more than 80 per cent confident were right in predicting these turns of events less than 40 per cent of the time. Yet, reflecting on their judgements, those who erred believed they were still basically right. I was 'almost right', said many. 'The hardliners almost succeeded in their coup attempt against Gorbachev.' 'The Quebecois separatists almost won the secessionist referendum.' 'But for the coincidence of de Klerk and Mandela, there would have been a lot bloodier transition to black majority rule in South Africa.' Among political experts – and stock market forecasters, mental health workers and sports prognosticators – overconfidence is hard to dislodge.

'When you know a thing, to hold that you know it; and when you do not know a thing, to allow that you do not know it; this is knowledge.'

Confucius, *Analects*

### Confirmation Bias

People also tend not to seek information that might disprove what they believe. P. C. Wason (1960) demonstrated this, as you can, by giving participants a sequence of three numbers – 2, 4, 6 – that conformed to a rule he had in mind. (The rule was simply *any three ascending numbers*.) To enable the participants to discover the rule, Wason invited each person to generate additional sets of three numbers. Each time, Wason told the person whether or not the set conformed to his rule. As soon as participants were sure they had discovered the rule, they were to stop and announce it.

The result? Seldom right but never in doubt: 23 of the 29 participants convinced themselves of a wrong rule. They typically formed some erroneous belief about the rule (for example, counting by twos) and then searched for *confirming* evidence (for example, by testing 8, 10, 12) rather than attempting to *disconfirm* their hunches. We are eager to verify our beliefs but less inclined to seek evidence that might disprove them, a phenomenon called the confirmation bias (Nickerson, 1998).

**confirmation bias** *a tendency to search for information that confirms one's preconceptions, rather than considering opposing information*

The confirmation bias helps explain why our self-images are so remarkably stable. In experiments at the University of Texas at Austin, William Swann and Stephen Read (1981; Swann et al., 1992a, 1992b) discovered that students seek, elicit and recall feedback that confirms their beliefs about themselves. People seek as friends and spouses those who bolster their own self-views – even if they think poorly of themselves (Swann et al., 1991, 2003).

### Remedies for Overconfidence

What lessons can we draw from research on overconfidence? One lesson is to be wary of other people's dogmatic statements. Even when people are sure they are right, they may be wrong. Confidence and competence need not coincide.

Three techniques have successfully reduced the overconfidence bias. One is prompt feedback (Lichtenstein & Fischhoff, 1980). In everyday life, weather forecasters and those who set the odds in horse racing both receive clear, daily feedback. And experts in both groups do quite well at estimating their probable accuracy (Fischhoff, 1982).

To reduce 'planning fallacy' overconfidence, people can be asked to 'unpack' a task – to break it down into its subcomponents – and estimate the time required for each. Justin Kruger and Matt Evans (2004) report that doing so leads to more realistic estimates of completion time. When people think about why an idea *might* be true, it begins to seem true. Thus, a third way to reduce overconfidence is to get people to think of one good reason why their judgements might be wrong; that is, force them to consider disconfirming information (Koriat et al., 1980), in the same way Karl Popper (see Chapter 2) is arguing for falsification rather than verification of theories. Managers might foster more realistic judgements by insisting that all proposals and recommendations include reasons why they might *not* work.

Still, we should be careful not to undermine people's reasonable self-confidence or to destroy their decisiveness. In times when their wisdom is needed, those lacking self-confidence may shrink from speaking up or making tough decisions. Overconfidence can cost us, but realistic self-confidence is adaptive.

## HEURISTICS: MENTAL SHORTCUTS

People interpret others' behaviour by making inferences based on other people's intentions, thoughts and personality. Social inference can involve two processes: top-down, which relies on stored information in memory such as schemas and stereotypes; and bottom-up which relies on specific events. With precious little time to process so much information, our cognitive system is fast and frugal. It specializes in mental shortcuts. With remarkable ease, we form impressions, make judgements and invent explanations. We do so by using heuristics – simple, efficient and fast thinking strategies. In some situations, however, haste makes error. When we make errors in social judgements these are often prone to biases.

*heuristic a thinking strategy and problem-solving method that enables quick and easy judgements and search procedures*

### The Representativeness Heuristic

The representative heuristic is a cognitive shortcut that we use to place people into categories based on deciding that they resemble this category through having the relevant traits or characteristics. Categorization requires knowing a good deal of information and also requires a lot of information processing to do this effectively. Unfortunately when we do this with people we tend to take a shortcut based on very little information about the person or people and this is where errors can occur. For example, errors can occur when we ignore base rates when making cognitive shortcuts to categorize people. A base rate is factual information about people and categories. So rather than weighing up and considering factual information when making a social categorical decision, we ignore this to make our assumptions as quickly as possible.

University students were told that a panel of psychologists interviewed a sample of 30 engineers and 70 lawyers, and summarized their impressions in thumbnail descriptions. The following description, they were told, was drawn at random from the sample of 30 engineers and 70 lawyers:

> Twice divorced, Frank spends most of his free time hanging around the country club. His clubhouse bar conversations often centre around his regrets at having tried to follow his esteemed father's footsteps. The long hours he had spent at academic drudgery would have been better invested in learning how to be less quarrelsome in his relations with other people.

*Question*: What is the probability that Frank is a lawyer rather than an engineer?

Asked to guess Frank's occupation, more than 80 per cent of the students surmised he was one of the lawyers (Fischhoff & Bar-Hillel, 1984). Fair enough. But how do you suppose those estimates changed when the sample description was given to another group of students, modified to say that 70 per cent were engineers? Not in the slightest. The students took no account of the base rate of engineers and lawyers; in their minds Frank was more *representative* of lawyers, and that was all that seemed to matter.

representativeness heuristic *the tendency to presume, sometimes despite contrary odds, that someone or something belongs to a particular group if resembling (representing) a typical member*

To judge something by intuitively comparing it to our mental representation of a category is to use the representativeness heuristic. Representativeness (typicalness) usually is a reasonable guide to reality. But, as we saw with 'Frank' above, it does not always work. Consider Linda, who is 31, single, outspoken and very bright. She majored in philosophy in college. As a student she was deeply concerned with discrimination and other social issues, and she participated in anti-nuclear demonstrations. Based on that description, would you say it is more likely that:

**1** Linda is a bank teller

**2** Linda is a bank teller and active in the feminist movement.

Most people think *2* is more likely, partly because Linda better *represents* their image of feminists (Mellers et al., 2001). But ask yourself: is there a better chance that Linda is *both* a bank teller *and* a feminist than that she's a bank teller (whether feminist or not)? As Amos Tversky and Daniel Kahneman (1983) remind us, the conjunction of two events cannot be more likely than either one of the events alone.

### The Availability Heuristic

The availability heuristic is a cognitive shortcut based on whatever information is most readily available. This can be from what we already 'know' and on what is going on around us at the time and how we interpret all this. It is therefore rather a 'lazy' way to make inferences and judgements and is also open to errors. When we use the availability heuristic we draw on whatever comes to mind so we are likely to ignore important information.

We use heuristics to quickly make social inferences. As outlined above heuristics can be prone to biases but they can sometimes be accurate and efficient. This can give the impression that they rely on intuition. However, one of the problems is the way we rely on schemas to make inferences. Schemas can have quite powerful influences on our judgements and can also lead us to pay attention to misleading

availability heuristic *a rule of thumb that judges the likelihood of things based on their availability in memory. If something comes readily to mind, we presume it to be commonplace*

information.

Consider the following question: Do more people live in Iraq or in Tanzania? (See page 116.)

You probably answered according to how readily Iraqis and Tanzanians come to mind. If examples are readily *available* in our memory – as Iraqis tend to be – then we presume that other such examples are commonplace. Usually this is true, so we are often well served by the availability heuristic (Table 4.1).

**TABLE 4.1**  Fast and frugal heuristics

| Heuristic | Definition | Example | But may lead to |
|---|---|---|---|
| Representativeness | Snap judgements of whether someone or something fits a category | Deciding that Carlos is a librarian rather than a trucker because he better represents one's image of librarians | Discounting other important information |
| Availability | Quick judgements of the likelihood of events (how available in memory) | Estimating teenager violence after school shootings | Overweighting vivid instances and, for example, fearing the wrong things |

But sometimes the rule deludes us. If people hear a list of famous people of one sex (Jennifer Lopez, Venus Williams, Margaret Thatcher) intermixed with an equal-size list of unfamous people of the other sex (Donald Scarr, William Wood, Mel Jasper), the famous names will later be more cognitively available. Most people will subsequently recall having heard more (in this instance) women's names (McKelvie, 1995, 1997; Tversky & Kahneman, 1973). The publicizing of lottery winners, pools winners, or even the audible sound of coins falling into the payout tray of a fruit machine indicating a 'win', can lead people to think that wins are commonplace, encouraging gambling behaviour (Griffiths, 1994). Vivid, easy-to-imagine events, such as shark attacks or diseases with easy-to-picture symptoms, may likewise seem more likely to occur than harder-to-picture events (MacLeod & Campbell, 1992; Sherman et al., 1985). Even fictional happenings in novels, on television and in movies leave images that later penetrate our judgements (Gerrig & Prentice, 1991; Green et al., 2002). The more absorbed and 'transported' the reader ('I could easily picture the events'), the more the story affects the reader's later beliefs (Diekman et al., 2000). Readers who are captivated by romance novels, for example, may gain readily available sexual scripts that influence their own sexual attitudes and behaviours.

Our use of the availability heuristic highlights a basic principle of social thinking: people are slow to deduce particular instances from a general truth, but they are remarkably quick to infer general truth from a vivid instance. No wonder that, after hearing and reading stories of rapes, robberies and beatings, 9 out of 10 Canadians overestimate – usually by a considerable margin – the percentage of crimes that involve violence (Doob & Roberts, 1988). And no wonder that South Africans, after a series of headline-grabbing gangland robberies and slayings, estimated that violent crime had almost doubled between 1998 and 2004, when actually it had decreased substantially (Wines, 2005).

The availability heuristic explains why powerful anecdotes can nevertheless be more compelling than statistical information and why perceived risk is therefore often badly out of joint with real risks (Allison et al., 1992). As news footage of aeroplane crashes is a readily available memory for most of us we often suppose we are more at risk travelling in commercial airplanes than in cars. A plane crash in Madrid (in August 2008) resulted in the death of 153 passengers. However, travelling by aeroplane remains one of the safest forms of travel. For most air travellers, the most dangerous part of the journey is the drive to the airport.

By now it is clear that our naive statistical intuitions, and our resulting fears, are driven not by calculation and reason but by emotions attuned to the availability heuristic. After this book is published, there is likely to be another dramatic natural or terrorist event, which will again propel our fears, vigilance and resources in a new direction. Terrorists, aided by the media, may again achieve their objective of capturing our attention, draining our resources and distracting us from the mundane, undramatic, insidious risks that, over time, devastate lives, such as the rotavirus that each day claims the equivalent of four 747 aeroplanes filled with children (Glass, 2004). But then again, dramatic events can also serve to awaken us to real risks.

*Answer to question on page 114: Tanzania's 37 million people greatly outnumber Iraq's 26 million. Many people, having more vivid images of Iraqis, guess wrong.*

### Counterfactual Thinking

Easily imagined (cognitively available) events also influence our experiences of guilt, regret, frustration and relief. If our team loses (or wins) a big game by one point, we can easily imagine how the game might have gone the other way, and thus we feel greater regret (or relief). Imagining worse alternatives helps us feel better. Imagining better alternatives, and pondering what we might do differently next time, helps us prepare to do better in the future (Boninger et al., 1994; Roese, 1994, 1997).

counterfactual thinking
*imagining alternative scenarios and outcomes that might have happened, but did not*

In Olympic competition, athletes' emotions after an event reflect mostly how they did relative to expectations, but also, in one analysis, counterfactual thinking – *mentally simulating what might have been* (McGraw et al., 2005; Medvec et al., 1995). Bronze medallists (for whom an easily imagined alternative was finishing without a medal) exhibited more joy than silver medallists (who could more easily imagine having won the gold). Similarly, the higher a student's score within a grade category (such as B+), the *worse* they feel (Medvec & Savitsky, 1997). The B+ student who misses an A– by a point feels worse than the B+ student who actually did worse and just made a B+ by a point.

Such counterfactual thinking occurs when we can easily picture an alternative outcome (Kahneman & Miller, 1986; Markman & McMullen, 2003), as in the following examples:

☐ If we barely miss a plane or a bus, we imagine making it *if only* we had left at our usual time, taken our usual route, not paused to talk.

☐ If we miss our connection by a half hour or after taking our usual route, it is harder to simulate a different outcome, so we feel less frustration.

☐ If we change an examination answer, then get it wrong, we will inevitably think 'If only . . .' and will vow next time to trust our immediate intuition – although, contrary to student lore, answer changes are more often from incorrect to correct (Kruger et al., 2005).

☐ The team or the political candidate that barely loses will simulate over and over how they could have won (Sanna et al., 2003).

Counterfactual thinking underlies our feelings of luck. When we have barely escaped a bad event – avoiding defeat with a last-minute goal or standing nearest a falling icicle – we easily imagine a negative counterfactual (losing, being hit) and therefore feel 'good luck' (Teigen et al., 1999). 'Bad luck', on the other hand, refers to bad events that did happen but easily might not have.

The more significant the event, the more intense the counterfactual thinking (Roese & Hur, 1997). Bereaved people who have lost a spouse or a child in a vehicle accident, or a child to sudden infant death syndrome, commonly report replaying and undoing the event (Davis et al., 1995, 1996).

Across Asian and Western cultures most people, however, live with less regret over things done than over things they failed to do, such as, 'I wish I had been more serious in college' or 'I should have told my father I loved him before he died' (Gilovich & Medvec, 1994; Gilovich et al., 1993; Savitsky et al., 1997). In one survey of adults, the most common regret was not taking their education more seriously (Kinnier & Metha, 1989). Would we live with less regret if we dared more often to reach beyond our comfort zone – to venture out, risking failure, but at least having tried?

### Anchoring and Adjustment

When people make an inference, they often begin from a starting point – an anchor (Tversky & Kahneman, 1974). The anchoring and adjustment heuristic is a cognitive shortcut influenced by initial knowledge and information. This provides a starting point to make inferences and judgements and we use these initial impressions as an anchor. We tend to stick with our initial impression but may make adjustments based on later information. Therefore, this later information would not make much change to our (anchored) initial impression.

*anchoring and adjustment when inferences are based on an initial starting point (standard) and adjusted accordingly*

We can think of everyday examples of this. In negotiating the value of a house, the initial figure given serves as an anchor for further discussion. When negotiating the price of a car, the price on the windscreen serves as the starting point for debate. How far we stray from this anchor is called 'adjustment'. Chris Janiszewski and Dan Uy (2008) give us a further anecdotal example. If you are asked 'Is the freezing point of water 32°F (0°C)'? and then 'What is the freezing point of vodka?', the initial 32°F serves as the anchor for your judgement. You know 32°F is the freezing point for water therefore it can't be the same for vodka. Yet, this figure serves as a diagnostic tool for adjusting downwards in your educated guess at the answer. The influence and real effects of anchoring and adjustment have also been demonstrated in the medical field. Susan Michie, Kathryn Lester, Julia Pinto and Theresa Marteau (2005) found that medical patients respond very differently to how medical information is presented. If an illness is described as of 'moderate risk' then while patient response might be more positive, the seriousness with which they treat it may be inadequate in terms of seeking sufficient help. They may adjust their perception away from the dangers of the illness and not regard medical intervention and lifestyle changes as necessary. If, on the other hand, an illness is presented as reducing life expectancy to 60 per cent, it will be treated much more seriously and encourage less adjustment away from the original diagnosis.

How far we adjust from the anchor depends on how much confidence we have in the anchor. If we perceive the asking price for a house to be a fair reflection of its value we will probably adjust downwards only slightly. If we feel it is a trick to get us to pay more than its value, we will adjust much more severely downwards.

We make social inferences through using different types of heuristics but do we use different social inferences at the same time? Studies have shown that multiple social inferences can occur simultaneously and automatically about other people's traits and social situations based on their behaviour. Fieldler, Schenk, Watling and Menges (2005) found that multiple simultaneous inferences regarding traits of different target persons were evident using complex ambiguous film clips as an experimental stimulus. In Todd, Molden, Ham and Vonk's (2011) study participants activated both trait and situational inferences about a person's behaviour within similar times despite reporting no intention or awareness of this. Even when researchers manipulated the goal for inference – and participants deliberately pursued a trait inference or deliberately pursued a situational inference, they still activated both inferences at the same time and reported they were not aware of doing this.

Our social inferences may also have different levels of importance as they occur. Malle and Holbrook (2012) propose that there is a hierarchy of social inferences. They argue that even though making inferences can occur simultaneously, researchers often study inferences one at a time. They point out that by studying inferences one at a time we don't know how inferences relate to each other or if one inference is more important than another. Malle and Holbrook (2012) investigated the speed of forming inferences. They also investigated whether inferences occur simultaneously and whether some inferences have greater priority. They found that inferences about intentionality and desire both had greater priority because they were both more likely to be inferred and both were formed quicker than inferences about belief and personality. The slowest and least likely to be inferred from these four inferences was personality. Therefore, a hierarchy was demonstrated and the most important inferences in this hierarchy were formed more quickly.

It is interesting that personality inferences were at the bottom of this hierarchy. As already discussed, many studies investigate how we make judgements about a person and form an overall image of that person. However, Malle and Holbrook (2012) point out that these studies have investigated person perception using traits. The researchers included sentences about people's behaviours and also video clips of people's behaviours in naturalistic settings. They argue that asking participants to infer traits from stimuli designed especially to bring to mind certain traits in tightly controlled experimental conditions will increase people's tendency to make personality inferences. However, they propose that this is less likely in a more naturalistic context such as those used in their study. This is an important consideration because it is in everyday settings that we encounter people's behaviours and make inferences about them. It suggests that there may be a lot of other information in everyday contexts influencing our thinking about personality.

## ILLUSORY THINKING

Another influence on everyday thinking is our search for order in random events, a tendency that can lead us down all sorts of wrong paths.

### Illusory Correlation

illusory correlation
*perception of a relationship where none exists or perception of a stronger relationship than actually exists*

It's easy to see a correlation where none exists. When we expect to find significant relationships, we easily associate random events, perceiving an illusory correlation. William Ward and Herbert Jenkins (1965) showed people the results of a hypothetical 50-day cloud-seeding experiment. Cloud seeding is where clouds are sprayed with chemicals in the attempt to induce rain. They told participants which of the 50 days the clouds had been seeded and which days it rained. That information was nothing more than a random mix of results: sometimes it rained after seeding; sometimes it didn't. Participants nevertheless became convinced – in conformity with their ideas about the effects of cloud seeding – that they really had observed a relationship between cloud seeding and rain. Of course this can have real-world consequences. Michael Smith and Geoffrey Alpert (2007) note how Hispanics and Blacks are consistently stopped more times by the police and searched than any other ethnic or racial group. They claim that it is such illusory correlations that explain the overestimation of negative behaviours with minority groups by the police in the USA. Jane Risen, Thomas Gilovich and David Dunning (2007) have observed how the occurrence of a behaviour displayed by a rarely encountered group is quickly attributed to the entire group, forming a group stereotype. They call this the 'one-shot illusory correlation'.

Other experiments confirm that people easily misperceive random events as confirming their beliefs (Crocker, 1981; Jennings et al., 1982; Trolier & Hamilton, 1986). If we believe a correlation exists, we are more likely to notice and recall confirming instances. If we believe that premonitions correlate with events, we notice and remember the joint occurrence of the premonition and the event's later occurrence. We seldom notice or remember all the times unusual events do not coincide. If, after we think about a friend, the friend calls us, we notice and remember that coincidence. We don't notice all the times we think of a friend without any ensuing call or receive a call from a friend about whom we've not been thinking.

### Illusion of Control

Our tendency to perceive random events as related feeds an illusion of control – the idea that *chance events are subject to our influence*. This keeps gamblers going and makes the rest of us do all sorts of unlikely things.

*illusion of control perception of uncontrollable events as subject to one's control or as more controllable than they are*

#### Gambling

Ellen Langer (1977) demonstrated the illusion of control with experiments on gambling, as people expect a rate of success more than random chance would predict. Compared with those given an assigned lottery number, people who chose their own number demanded four times as much money when asked if they would sell their ticket. When playing a game of chance against an awkward and nervous person, they bet significantly more than when playing against a dapper, confident opponent. Throwing the dice or spinning the wheel increases people's confidence (Wohl & Enzle, 2002). In these and other ways, more than 50 experiments have consistently found people acting as if they can predict or control chance events (Presson & Benassi, 1996; Thompson et al., 1998).

Observations of real-life gamblers confirm these experimental findings. Dice players may throw softly for low numbers and hard for high numbers (Henslin, 1967). The specialist features on a fruit machine ('nudge', 'hold') may lead regular fruit machine gamblers to believe more skill is involved than there actually is, encouraging continuous play as s/he becomes familiar with the machine and develops their 'skills' (Griffiths, 1994). The gambling industry thrives on gamblers' illusions. Gamblers attribute wins to their skill and foresight. Losses become 'near misses' or 'flukes', or for the sports gambler, a bad call by the referee or a freakish bounce of the ball (Gilovich & Douglas, 1986).

## research close-up

### HEURISTICS AND ILLUSIONS OF CONTROL IN SLOT MACHINE GAMBLERS

**Source**: *Parke, J., Griffiths, M. D., & Parke, A. (2007). Positive thinking among slot machine gamblers: A case of maladaptive coping?* International Journal of Mental Health Addiction, 5, 39–52.

### Introduction

People engage in particular cognitive processes to compensate for a negative emotional state. An exaggerated sense of optimism and overestimating personal control has also been found to be key responses to extremely bad news (Taylor, 1983, 1989; Taylor and Brown, 1988). Gambling carries a high risk towards negative emotional states because regular gamblers lose money regularly. Therefore, regular gamblers engage in certain cognitive strategies to avoid the negative emotions of losing money. According to Wagenaar (1988), gamblers selectively use a variety of heuristics and cognitive biases and hence gamblers are motivated by their way of reasoning, not some personality defect. Regular gamblers appear to engage in an 'illusion of control'. The present study aims to investigate the strategies that gamblers use to evoke positive thinking to compensate and reduce negative emotions from experiencing a loss.

### Method

Eighty-seven regular slot machine gamblers in the UK aged between 12 and 64 years took part in 104-item semi-structured interview schedules. These were administered in places they frequent to use slot machines. Recruiting participants and administering the interview schedules to them in their natural environments aimed to aid the ecological validity of the study. The interview schedule investigated motivation, demographic information, physiological experiences, thought processes, emotions, personality and the existence of other potentially addictive behaviours. The questionnaire yielded qualitative data from the semi-structured questions as this enabled participants to express their view. In addition, the questionnaire used a 10-point scale labelled at the endpoints – Never (1) and Always (10). Thus, participants had 10 options to choose when reporting how much they agreed or disagreed with a statement. Seven areas were assessed: leisure time availability; risk taking; responsibility; negative affect; environmental preferences; competitiveness; enterprise. The qualitative data was categorized into 9 types of positive thinking.

### Results

The 9 types of positive thinking by gamblers were categorized as: *Comparative thinking; Prophylactic thinking; Biased frequency thinking; Chasing validation; Responsibility avoidance; Prioritization: Resourcefulness; Thoughtfulness; Fear reduction.* The findings indicated that regular slot machine gamblers use cognitive biases to sustain their gambling and to alleviate feelings of guilt when they inevitably lose. For example, Comparative thinking consisted of at least two comparative evaluations. One was thinking that at least the money was spent with the chance of winning some money in comparison to other ways of spending money. Another was comparing gambling more favourably than other types of addiction such as drinking alcohol/drug use and smoking. Prophylactic thinking consisted of perceiving large losses of money as a way to prevent gambling in the future. Chasing validation involves thinking that persistence in trying to win back losses is rewarded in the long run. Fear reduction assumed personal improvement and increases in self-esteem as a result of risk taking ability.

## Discussion

The results demonstrate the way in which gamblers seek to reduce negative feelings caused by guilt as these negative feelings can be attributed to the gambler themselves whereas anger, frustration and feeling cheated can be attributed to a third party such as the machine manufacturers. Persistence and imagining one has control are usually seen as psychologically healthy. However, positive thinking strategies are maladaptive in the context of gambling. Within the context of gambling, believing that one will win eventually is an example of the representative bias where information that is contradictory to winning is ignored and illusory thinking is engaged in. The cognitive mechanisms used by gamblers assist in compensating them from feelings of loss and guilt and constrain gamblers from accepting that gambling has a negative impact on their life, therefore preventing the gambler from stopping his or her gambling behaviour. Future research should investigate which type of gambler uses which type of positive thinking and whether or not they employ a number of these thinking styles.

Stock traders also like the 'feeling of empowerment' that comes from being able to choose and control their own stock trades, as if their being in control can enable them to outperform the market average. One advertisement declared that online investing 'is about control'. Alas, the illusion of control breeds overconfidence, and frequent losses after stock market trading costs are subtracted (Barber & Odean, 2001).

### Regression towards the Average

Amos Tversky and Daniel Kahneman (1974) noted another way by which an illusion of control may arise: we fail to recognize the statistical phenomenon of regression towards the average. Because examination scores fluctuate partly by chance, most students who get extremely high scores on an examination will get lower scores on the next examination. Because their first score is at the ceiling, their second score is more likely to fall back ('regress') towards their own average than to push the ceiling even higher. That is why a student who does consistently good work, even if never the best, will sometimes end a course at the top of the class. Conversely, the lowest-scoring students on the first examination are likely to improve. If those who scored lowest go for tutoring after the first examination, the tutors are likely to feel effective when the student improves, even if the tutoring had no effect.

**regression towards the average** *the statistical tendency for extreme scores or extreme behaviour to return towards one's average*

Indeed, when things reach a low point, we will try anything, and whatever we try – going to a psychotherapist, starting a new diet and exercise plan, reading a self-help book – is more likely to be followed by improvement than by further deterioration. Sometimes we recognize that events are not likely to continue at an unusually good or bad extreme. Experience has taught us that when everything is going great, something will go wrong, and that when life is dealing us terrible blows, we can usually look forward to things getting better. Often, though, we fail to recognize this regression effect. We puzzle at why Formula 1's rookie of the year often has a more ordinary second year – did he become overconfident? Self-conscious? We forget that exceptional performance tends to regress towards normality.

By simulating the consequences of using praise and punishment, Paul Schaffner (1985) showed how the illusion of control might infiltrate human relations. He invited Bowdoin College students to train an imaginary fourth-grade boy, 'Harold', to come to school by 8.30 each morning. For each school day of a three-week period, a computer displayed Harold's arrival time, which was always between 8.20 and 8.40. The students would then select a response to Harold, ranging from strong praise to strong reprimand. As you might expect, they usually praised Harold when he arrived before 8.30 and reprimanded him when he arrived after 8.30. Because Schaffner had programmed the computer to display a random sequence of arrival times, Harold's arrival time tended to improve (to regress towards 8.30) after he was reprimanded. For example, if Harold arrived at 8.39, he was almost sure to be reprimanded, and his randomly selected next-day arrival time was likely to be earlier than 8.39. Thus, *even though their reprimands were having no effect*, most students ended the experiment believing that their reprimands had been effective.

Table 4.2 provides examples of biases, heuristics and illusions along with strategies and definitions.

## MOODS AND JUDGEMENTS

Social judgement involves efficient, though fallible, information processing. It also involves our feelings: our moods infuse our judgements. We are not cool

**TABLE 4.2**  A summary of biases, heuristics and illusions

| Strategy | Examples | Definition |
|---|---|---|
| Bias: when our assumptions and prejudgements guide our perceptions and interpretations of the social world | Priming | The activation of learned or experienced associations in memory |
| | Belief perseverance | The persistence of one's initial conceptions |
| | Misinformation effect | The incorporation of false information into memory, guided by assumed relevance and appropriateness |
| | Intuition | When past learning and repeated experience cause us to process information automatically |
| | Overconfidence | To overestimate the accuracy of one's beliefs, memory or account of some aspect of social reality |
| | Confirmation bias | To search for information that confirms one's preconceptions (and ignore disconfirming information) |
| Heuristics: thinking strategies that enable quick and efficient judgements | Representative heuristic | The tendency to assume something is an instance of a group or category based on its perceived similarity to typical members |
| | Availability heuristic | The assumption that what comes to mind most easily is more commonplace |
| | Recognition heuristic | To assume that what is easily recognized is important |
| | Anchoring and adjustment | When inferences are guided by an initial starting point and adjusted accordingly |
| | Counterfactual thinking | Imagining counter scenarios and outcomes that didn't actually happen |
| Illusory thinking: to search for order in otherwise random events | Illusory correlations | The perception that a relationship exists between things where one doesn't exist |
| | Illusion of control | The perception that uncontrollable events are under one's own control |

computing machines; we are emotional creatures. The extent to which feeling infuses cognition appears in new studies comparing happy and sad individuals (Myers, 1993). Unhappy people – especially those bereaved or depressed – tend to be more self-focused and brooding. A depressed mood motivates intense thinking – a search for information that makes one's environment more understandable and controllable (Weary & Edwards, 1994).

Happy people, by contrast, are more trusting, more loving, more responsive. If people are made temporarily happy by receiving a small gift while shopping, they will report, a few moments later on an unrelated survey, that their cars and television sets are working beautifully – better, if you took their word for it, than those belonging to folks who replied after not receiving gifts.

Moods pervade our thinking. To West Germans enjoying their team's World Cup football victory (Schwarz et al., 1987) and to Australians emerging from a heartwarming movie (Forgas & Moylan, 1987), people seem good-hearted, life seems wonderful. When we are in a happy mood, the world seems friendlier, decisions are easier, good news more readily comes to mind (Isen & Means, 1983; Johnson & Tversky, 1983; Stone & Glass, 1986). Let a mood turn gloomy, however, and thoughts switch onto a different track. Off come the rose-tinted glasses; on come the dark glasses. Now the bad mood primes our recollections of negative events (Bower, 1987; Johnson & Magaro, 1987). Our relationships seem to sour. Our self-images take a dive. Our hopes for the future dim. Other people's behaviour seems more sinister (Brown & Taylor, 1986; Mayer & Salovey, 1987).

The social psychologist Joseph Forgas (1999) had often been struck by how moody people's 'memories and judgements change with the colour of their mood'. To understand this 'mood infusion' he began to experiment. Imagine yourself in one such study. Using hypnosis, Forgas and his colleagues (1984) put you in a good or a bad mood and then have you watch a videotape (made the day before) of yourself talking with someone. If made to feel happy, you feel pleased with what you see, and you are able to detect many instances of your poise, interest and social skill. If you've been put in a bad mood, viewing the same tape seems to reveal a quite different you – one who is stiff, nervous and inarticulate (Figure 4.3). Given how your mood colours your judgements, you feel relieved at how things brighten when the experimenter switches you to a happy mood before leaving the experiment. Curiously, note Michael Ross and Garth Fletcher (1985), we don't attribute our changing perceptions to our mood shifts. Rather, the world really seems different.

Regression to the average. When we are at an extremely low point, anything we try will often seem effective. 'Maybe a yoga class will improve my life.' Events seldom continue at an abnormal low.

SOURCE: © webphotographer/iStock

Our moods colour how we judge our worlds partly by bringing to mind past experiences associated with the mood. In a bad mood, we have more depressing thoughts. Mood-related thoughts may distract us from complex thinking about something else. Thus, when emotionally aroused – when angry or even in a very good mood – we become more likely to make snap judgements and evaluate others based on stereotypes (Bodenhausen et al., 1994; Paulhus & Lim, 1994).

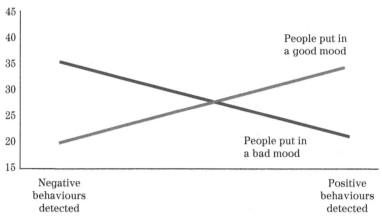

**Per cent perceived behaviours**

**FIGURE 4.3**  Percentage of perceived behaviours
A temporary good or bad mood strongly influenced people's ratings of their videotaped behaviour. Those in a bad mood detected far fewer positive behaviours.
SOURCE: Forgas et al., 1984.

Now that we have considered ways that people make social judgements about people and situations we next turn to the way we understand our social world in order to attempt to explain it.

## EXPLAINING OUR SOCIAL WORLD

*People make it their business to explain other people, and social psychologists make it their business to explain people's explanations. So, how do people explain others' behaviour? Attribution theory suggests some answers.*

Our judgements of people depend on how we explain their behaviour. How we explain their behaviour is influenced by cultural norms and assumptions. Depending on our explanation, we may judge killing as murder, manslaughter, self-defence or heroism. Depending on our explanation, we may view a homeless person as lacking initiative or as victimized by job and welfare cutbacks. Depending on our explanation, we may interpret someone's friendly behaviour as genuine warmth or as ingratiation. How we explain something has real-world consequences.

### ATTRIBUTING CAUSALITY: TO THE PERSON OR THE SITUATION

We endlessly analyse and discuss why things happen as they do, especially when we experience something negative or unexpected (Bohner et al., 1988; Weiner, 1985). In particular we tend to explain why things happen in terms of internal attributions, which place the cause within the individual (e.g. the personality, traits or dispositions) and external explanations, which locate the reason in the environment.

So as an employer, if worker productivity declines, do we assume the workers are getting lazier? Or has their workplace become less efficient? A teacher trying to work out why a young boy hits his classmates wonders if he has a hostile personality or is responding to relentless teasing? Amy Holtzworth-Munroe and

Neil Jacobson (1985; Holtzworth & Jacobson, 1988) report that married people often analyse their partners' behaviours, especially their negative behaviours. Cold hostility, more than a warm hug, is likely to leave the partner wondering *why?*

Spouses' answers correlate with their marriage satisfaction. Those in unhappy relationships typically offer distress-maintaining internal explanations for negative acts ('she was late because she doesn't care about me'). Happy couples more often externalize ('she was late because of heavy traffic'). With positive partner behaviour, their explanations similarly work either to maintain distress ('he brought me flowers because he wants sex') or to enhance the relationship ('he brought me flowers to show he loves me') (Hewstone & Fincham, 1996; Weiner, 1995).

How we attribute cause for the problems in our relationship indicates the quality of it and its likelihood of success.

SOURCE: © UygarGeographic/iStock

Antonia Abbey (1987, 1991) and her colleagues (1998) have repeatedly found that men are more likely than women to attribute a woman's friendliness to mild sexual interest. That misreading of warmth as a sexual come-on – an example of misattribution – can contribute to behaviour that women regard as sexual harassment (Johnson et al., 1991; Pryor et al., 1997; Saal et al., 1989).

misattribution
*mistakenly attributing a behaviour to the wrong source*

Some research suggests men and women have quite different attributional styles. For example, Susan Assouline, Nicholas Colangelo, Daniel Ihrig and Leslie Forstadt (2006) found that gifted female students tended to account for success in some subjects, such as mathematics and science, using external attributions (e.g. I worked hard), whereas boys tended to use internal attributions (I am smart). In a study done by Kimberly Smirles (2004), male and female students read an account of an employer who sexually harasses an employee. She found that if participants didn't know the gender of the victim, men tended to hold the victim more responsible, whereas women thought the perpetrator was more accountable. Smirles suggests this occurs because these women were displaying defensive attribution. They minimized blame towards those people they most readily identified with.

Such misattributions help explain the greater sexual assertiveness exhibited by men across the world and the greater tendency of men in various cultures, from Boston to Bombay, to justify rape by arguing that the victim consented or implied consent (Kanekar & Nazareth, 1988; Muehlenhard, 1988; Shotland, 1989). Women more often judge forcible sex as meriting conviction and a stiff sentence (Schutte & Hosch, 1997).

How we attribute cause for behaviour can actually have an effect on our health. Christopher Peterson (1988) studied the attributional style of ex-soldiers who had served during the Second World War. He found that those who talked about their experiences during the war using an optimistic attributional style, such as emphasizing the close sense of community during wartime, were in much better health than those who adopted a more pessimistic attributional style.

Friendly interest or something more? Some research suggests that men often wrongly recognize the display of friendliness by a woman as a sexual come-on.

SOURCE: © aldomurillo/iStock

attribution theory *the theory of how people explain others' behaviour; for example, by attributing it either to internal dispositions (enduring traits, motives and attitudes) or to external situations*

### Attribution Theory

Attribution theory was developed to examine these patterns of internal and external explanations, and why they occur. The theory arose out of three theoretical foundations:

1 Fritz Heider's (1958) 'theory of naïve psychology'

2 Jones and Davis's (1965) 'theory of correspondent inference'

3 Harold Kelley's (1973) 'covariation model'.

The early pioneer of attribution theory, Fritz Heider (1958), formed his 'theory of naïve psychology' to account for how people explain everyday events. Heider noted that we tend to assume people's behaviour is not random, but is motivated and intentional. While sometimes we will attribute someone's behaviour to *internal* causes (dispositional attribution), at other times it will be explained as having an external cause (situational attribution). Some people are more inclined to attribute behaviour to stable personality; others tend more to prefer to attribute behaviour to situations (Bastian & Haslam, 2006; Robins et al., 2004). However, Heider maintained that, on the whole, people have a preference for applying internal attributions, as personality characteristics tend to be regarded as stable. But Heider's conclusions tend to come from experiences and studies in individualistic cultures, where people tend to focus on the individual and their own responsibility for their behaviour. In collective or interdependent cultures people in general seem to pay more attention to the context and the situation when explaining behaviour.

dispositional attribution *attributing behaviour to the person's disposition and traits*

situational attribution *attributing behaviour to the environment*

### Inferring Traits

Edward Jones and Keith Davis (1965) noted that we often infer that other people's actions are indicative of their intentions and dispositions. If I observe Rick making a sarcastic comment to Linda, I infer that Rick is a hostile person. Jones and Davis's 'theory of correspondent inferences' specified the conditions under which people infer traits. For example, normal or expected behaviour tells us less about the person than does unusual behaviour. If Samantha is sarcastic in a job interview, where a person would normally be pleasant, that tells us more about Samantha than if she is sarcastic with her siblings.

To what should we attribute a student's sleepiness? To lack of sleep? To boredom? Whether we make internal or external attributions depends on whether we notice him consistently sleeping in this and other classes, and on whether other students react as he does to this particular class.

SOURCE: © Juanmonino/iStock

In experiments it has been found that the ease with which we infer traits is remarkable. In James Uleman's (1989) experiment students were given statements to remember, such as 'The librarian carries the old woman's groceries across the street.' The students would instantly, unintentionally and unconsciously infer a trait. When later they were helped to recall the sentence, the most valuable clue word was not 'books' (to cue librarian) or 'bags' (to cue groceries) but 'helpful' – the inferred trait that we suspect you, too, spontaneously attributed to the librarian.

Although Heider had noted people's preference for internal attributions, it was the work of

Edward Jones with Keith Davis (1965), and later Harold Kelley (1973), that aimed to explain how we choose between internal and external explanations for behaviour.

### Common-sense Attributions

Jones and Davis (1965) suggested that we use five different sources of information to judge whether a behaviour should be given an internal or external explanation. These are as follows:

1. Was it freely chosen behaviour or prescribed by someone else? If it was freely chosen then we are likely to give an internal attribution.

2. Was the behaviour unusual? If so, then we are likely to give an internal explanation.

3. Was it socially desirable behaviour? Socially desirable behaviour actually tells us very little about a person as they are simply behaving as they should. So when behaviour is socially deviant, then we are likely to give an internal explanation for it.

4. Does it serve the interests of the person doing the behaviour (i.e. is it hedonistic)? If so, then we are likely to give an internal explanation.

5. Does it have a high impact on us personally? If so, then an internal explanation is likely.

As Heider, Jones and Davis claim, we have a preference for internal attributions as they make people appear more predictable to us, owing to stable traits and dispositions. However, as we shall see later in this chapter, it's important to note that these theories have some drawbacks. The preference for internal attributions seems to be prevalent in some cultures but not all. In cultures less focused on stable personality traits and consistency – for example, China – people do not expect individuals to be predictable and they therefore pay more attention to the context when explaining behaviour.

So far our reading of the foundations of attribution theory has focused on intentional behaviour. But what about those behaviours that are not intentional? This has been examined in more recent reformulations of attribution theory.

The attribution theorist Harold Kelley (1973) described how we use information about 'consistency', 'distinctiveness' and 'consensus', often called CCD information (Figure 4.4). When explaining why Edgar is having trouble with his computer, most people use information concerning *consistency* (Is Edgar usually unable to get his computer to work?), *distinctiveness* (Does Edgar have trouble with other computers, or only this one?) and *consensus* (Do other people have similar problems with this make of computer?). If we learn that Edgar alone consistently has trouble with this and other computers, we likely will attribute the troubles to Edgar, not to defects in this computer. Note how this allows us to take into account unintentional behaviour by making a judgement based on consistency of behaviour across time and space.

Three factors – consistency, distinctiveness and consensus – influence whether we attribute someone's behaviour to internal or external causes. Try creating your own examples, such as: if Mary and many others criticize Steve (with consensus),

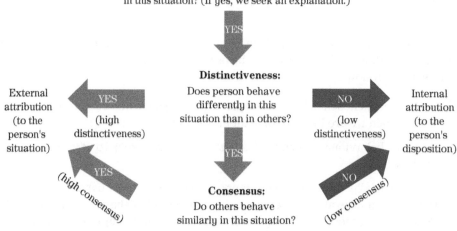

**FIGURE 4.4** Harold Kelley's theory of attributions

and if Mary isn't critical of others (high distinctiveness), then we make an external attribution (it's something about Steve). If Mary alone (low consensus) criticizes Steve, and if she criticizes many other people, too (low distinctiveness), then we are drawn to an internal attribution (it's something about Mary).

*Consistency:* How consistent is the person's behaviour in this situation?
*Distinctiveness:* How specific is the person's behaviour to this particular situation?
*Consensus:* To what extent do others in this situation behave similarly?

So our common-sense psychology often explains behaviour logically. But Kelley also found that people often discount a contributing cause of behaviour if other plausible causes are already known. If we can specify one or two sufficient reasons a student might have done poorly on an exam, we often ignore or discount alternative possibilities (McClure, 1998).

As well as making attributions about others we make attributions about ourselves. This is a way to understand ourselves. As we shall see later, perceived self-knowledge also appears to be highly influential to our attributions about others. Self-perception theory (Bem, 1972) proposes that self-knowledge comes about through making self-attributions. Thus, we observe our own behaviour, examine our thoughts and feelings and attribute these to the type of person we think we are by making assumptions about ourselves. Bernard Weiner's (1986) attributional theory proposes that the attributions made for our experiences of success and failure are based on three areas: locus (can be internal or external), stability (whether the internal or external cause is stable or changes over time) and controllability (the extent to which something is under the individual's control). This theory includes an emotional aspect. Positive or negative emotions are experienced depending on whether the individual has succeeded or failed and in turn individuals make attributions about success or failure which then produce more specific emotions. This theory brings us onto the next self-attribution theory – Schachter's emotional lability. This theory proposes that the experience of emotion depends on attributions made about those feelings.

*self-perception theory proposes that attitudes are inferred from observations of one's own behaviour*

According to Stanley Schachter (1964) emotions have two distinct components: a physiological component which leads to arousal and a cognitive component which labels the arousal and establishes the emotion that is being experienced. Taken together, we therefore make attributions to understand the type of person we are, our abilities and our feelings. When we make self-attributions these tend to lead to the idea that we are fairly stable and consistent and this occurs when we make attributions about others.

Self-perception theory is discussed further in Chapter 5 in relation to our own attitudes and behaviours and how we view ourselves.

Even though people sometimes behave in ways that are inconsistent and unpredictable, we form very stable impressions of what people are like. This is despite encountering new information which might not fit with our initial impressions. Jennifer Croker, Darlene Hannah and Renee Weber (1983) were interested in how the recall of information affected the impression we formed of a person. To investigate this, participants were shown 12 slides with initial information that related to the friendliness of a target person John. This was followed by four slides that depicted John's neutral behaviour. The last slide showed one of two behaviours. Either John's behaviour fitted in with friendliness such as 'He gave up his seat on the subway to an elderly man' or John's behaviour did not fit with friendliness such as 'He cut in line in front of three people at the bank'. If participants were told that these behaviours were due to the situation such as John was sitting in a seat reserved for elderly people or John's behaviour at the bank was because he had just been paged for an emergency, the initial information about John's friendliness didn't make a difference to the behaviour they recalled (friendly and unfriendly) within this specific situation. However, when participants were told that these behaviours were due to John's disposition, for example John did this because he was courteous (when he gave up his seat) or John did this because he did not care about what others thought (when he pushed in front of people in the bank queue), they were most likely to only recall behaviour that did not fit with the initial information about John's friendliness. Croker et al. (1983) propose this indicates that recall is related to impression formation in certain situations such as when people infer or are told that behaviour reflects a person's dispositional character rather than situational pressures. If people are told a person's behaviour occurs because of their disposition and this behaviour does not fit with initial information about that person, then this dissimilar behaviour will be recalled and it will influence overall impression formation. It also seems that we are drawn to internal explanations of behaviour rather than situational explanations. However, as we shall see in the next section, this can often lead to errors of judgement.

Neuroscience has made important contributions to exploring social beliefs about causal attributions. For example, a study in Germany used fMRI to explore self-attributions and external attributions for social events. Eva-Maria Seidel, Simon Eickhoff, Thilo Kellermann, Frank Schneider, Ruben Gur, Ute Habel and Birgit Derntl (2010) found that different regions of the brain are more active when participants are attributing blame on the self towards a social event than when they are attributing external blame towards a social event. The right temporaparietal junction (TPJ) was activated for self-attributions and Seidel et al. (2010) propose that this contributes to previous evidence that the right TPJ is involved with self-representation and agency and this region has a fundamental role in shaping the self-concept. Attributing external blame towards a social event revealed activation in the left region of the TPJ. This region could be where we differentiate between self and others. The fMRI scan also revealed that the activations for self-attributions were clustered with quicker reaction times but the activations for external attributions were more extended. The researchers propose that this indicates self-attributions may be automatic whereas external attributions require more work.

### THE FUNDAMENTAL ATTRIBUTION ERROR

Social psychology's most important lesson concerns the influence of our social environment. At any moment, our internal state, and therefore what we say and do, depends on the situation as well as on what we bring to the situation.

What theories of attribution agree on is that people in individualistic cultures have a preference for internal explanations for behaviour. When explaining someone's behaviour, we in the West often underestimate the impact of the situation and overestimate the extent to which it reflects the individual's traits and attitudes.

fundamental attribution error *the tendency for observers to underestimate situational influences and overestimate dispositional influences upon others' behaviour. (Also called* correspondence bias, *because we so often see behaviour as corresponding to a disposition)*

This discounting of the situation, dubbed by Lee Ross (1977) the fundamental attribution error, appears in many experiments. In the first such study, Edward Jones and Victor Harris (1967) had university students read debaters' speeches supporting or attacking Cuba's leader, Fidel Castro. When told that the debater chose which position to take, the students logically enough assumed it reflected the person's own attitude. But what happened when the students were told that the debate coach had assigned the position? People who are merely feigning a position write more forceful statements than you'd expect (Allison et al., 1993; Miller et al., 1990). Thus, even knowing that the debater had been told to take a pro-Castro position did not prevent students from inferring that the debater in fact had some pro-Castro leanings (Figure 4.5). People seemed to think, 'Yeah, I know he was assigned that position, but, you know, I think he really believes it.'

The error is so irresistible that even when people know they are *causing* someone else's behaviour, they still underestimate external influences. If individuals dictate

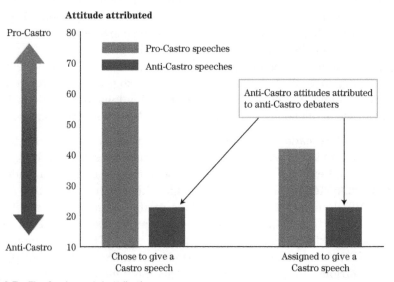

**FIGURE 4.5** The fundamental attribution error

When people read a debate speech supporting or attacking Fidel Castro, they attributed corresponding attitudes to the speechwriter, even when the debate coach assigned the writer's position.

SOURCE: Data from Jones & Harris, 1967.

an opinion that someone else must then express, they still tend to see the person as actually holding that opinion (Gilbert & Jones, 1986). If people are asked to be either self-enhancing or self-deprecating during an interview, they are very aware of why they are acting so. But they are *un*aware of their effect on another person. If Juan acts modestly, his naive partner Bob is likely to exhibit modesty as well. Juan will easily understand his own behaviour, but he will think that poor Bob suffers low self-esteem (Baumeister and Scher, 1988). In short, we tend to presume that others *are* the way they act. Observing Cinderella cowering in her oppressive home, people (ignoring the situation) infer that she is meek; dancing with her at the ball, the prince sees a suave and glamorous person.

When viewing a movie actor playing a 'good-guy' or a 'bad-guy' role, we find it difficult to escape the illusion that the scripted behaviour reflects an inner disposition. Perhaps that is why Leonard Nimoy, who played Mr Spock in the original *Star Trek*, titled one of his books *I Am Not Spock*.

SOURCE: © Frazer Harrison/Getty Images

The discounting of social constraints was evident in an experiment by Lee Ross and his collaborators (1977). The experiment re-created Ross's first-hand experience of moving from graduate student to professor. His doctoral oral examination had proved a humbling experience as his apparently brilliant professors quizzed him on topics they specialized in. Six months later, Dr Ross was himself an examiner, now able to ask penetrating questions on *his* favourite topics. Ross's hapless student later confessed to feeling exactly as Ross had a half-year before – dissatisfied with his ignorance and impressed with the apparent brilliance of the examiners.

In the experiment, with Teresa Amabile and Julia Steinmetz, Ross set up a simulated quiz game. He randomly assigned some Stanford University students to play the role of questioner, some to play the role of contestant, and others to observe. The researchers invited the questioners to make up difficult questions that would demonstrate their wealth of knowledge. Any one of us can imagine such questions using one's own domain of competence: 'Where is Bainbridge Island?' 'How did Mary, Queen of Scots, die?' 'Which has the longer coastline, Europe or Africa?' If even those few questions have you feeling a little uninformed, then you will appreciate the results of this experiment.*

Everyone had to know that the questioner would have the advantage. Yet both contestants and observers (but not the questioners) came to the erroneous conclusion that the questioners *really were* more knowledgeable than the contestants (Figure 4.6). Follow-up research shows that these misimpressions are hardly a reflection

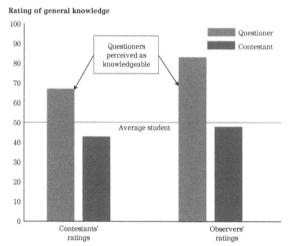

**FIGURE 4.6** Rating of general knowledge
Both contestants and observers of a simulated quiz game assumed that a person who had been randomly assigned the role of questioner was far more knowledgeable than the contestant. Actually the assigned roles of questioner and contestant simply made the questioner seem more knowledgeable. The failure to appreciate this illustrates the fundamental attribution error.

SOURCE: Data from Ross et al., 1977.

* Bainbridge Island is across Puget Sound from Seattle. Mary was ordered to be beheaded by her cousin Queen Elizabeth I. Although the African continent is more than double the area of Europe, Europe's coastline is longer. (It is more convoluted, with lots of harbours and inlets, a geographical fact that contributed to its role in the history of maritime trade.)

of low social intelligence. If anything, intelligent and socially competent people are *more* likely to make the attribution error and the correspondence bias (Block & Funder, 1986).

In real life, those with social power usually initiate and control conversations, which often leads underlings to overestimate their knowledge and intelligence. Medical doctors, for example, are often presumed to be experts on all sorts of questions unrelated to medicine. Similarly, students often overestimate the brilliance of their teachers. (As in the experiment, teachers are questioners on subjects of their special expertise.) When some of these students later become teachers, they are usually amazed to discover that teachers are not so brilliant after all.

To illustrate the fundamental attribution error, most of us need look no further than our own experiences. Determined to make some new friends, Ann plasters a smile on her face and anxiously plunges into a party. Everyone else seems quite relaxed and happy as they laugh and talk with one another. Ann wonders to herself, 'Why is everyone always so at ease in groups like this while I'm feeling shy and tense?' Actually, everyone else is feeling nervous, too, and making the same attribution error in assuming that Ann and the others *are* as they *appear* – confidently convivial.

### Why Do We Make the Attribution Error?

So far we have seen a bias in the way we, and especially people in the Western individualistic cultures, explain other people's behaviour: we often ignore powerful situational determinants. However, this is not true when attributing cause for our own behaviour. As Richard Nisbett, Craig Caputo, Patricia Legant and Jeanne Marecek (1973) have observed, when participants are asked to describe their friends' behaviour they tick the dispositional items provided on a checklist. However, when asked to describe their own behaviour, they tick the situational items. So why do we tend to underestimate the situational determinants of others' behaviour but not of our own? Some of the explanations are outlined below.

#### Perspective and Situational Awareness

*Actor–Observer Difference* Attribution theorists point out that we observe others from a different perspective than we observe ourselves (Jones, 1976; Jones & Nisbett, 1971). When we act, the *environment* commands our attention. When we watch another person act, that *person* occupies the centre of our attention and the environment becomes relatively invisible. However, this is not the case in East Asian cultures, as Hannah Faye Chua and colleagues (2005b) have revealed. People in Japan, China and Korea, for instance, focus and notice the context and environment in their visual perception. They do not concentrate so much on the 'figure', but pay much more attention to the 'background'. This cultural difference, due to the importance of the single individual compared to the group or collective and the corresponding shift in visual focus, has an impact on causal attribution.

To most observers in the West, another person grabs our attention and seems to cause whatever happens. As actors, we're inclined to attribute our own behaviour to the situation to which we're attending. If that is true, what might we expect if the perspectives were reversed? What if we could see ourselves as others see us and if we saw the world through their eyes? Shouldn't that eliminate or reverse the typical attribution error?

See if you can predict the result of a clever experiment conducted by Michael Storms (1973). Picture yourself as a participant in Storms' experiment. You are seated facing another student, with whom you are to talk for a few minutes. Beside you is a television camera that shares your view of the other student. Facing you from alongside the other student are an observer and another television camera. Afterwards, both you and the observer judge whether your behaviour was caused more by your personal characteristics or by the situation.

Question: Which of you – participant or observer – will attribute less importance to the situation? Storms found it was the observer (another demonstration of the fundamental attribution tendency). What if we reverse points of view by having you and the observer each watch the videotape recorded from the other's perspective? (You now view yourself, and the observer views what you were seeing while you were being videotaped.) This reverses the attributions: the observer now attributes your behaviour mostly to the situation you faced, and you now attribute it to your person. *Remembering* an experience from an observer's perspective – by 'seeing' oneself from the outside – has the same effect (Frank & Gilovich, 1989).

From his analysis of 173 studies, Bertram Malle (2006) concludes that the actor–observer difference is often minimal. People typically exhibit empathy when they observe someone after explaining their own behaviour in the same situation. It's when one person misbehaves while another observes that the two will offer strikingly different attributions.

*The Camera Perspective Bias* In some experiments, people have viewed a videotape of a suspect confessing during a police interview. If they viewed the confession through a camera focused on the suspect, they perceived the confession as genuine. If they viewed it through a camera focused on the detective, they perceived it as more coerced (Lassiter & Irvine, 1986; Lassiter et al., 2005). The camera perspective influenced people's guilt judgements even when the judge instructed them not to allow it to (Lassiter et al., 2002).

In law courts, most confession videotapes focus on the confessor. As we might expect, noted Daniel Lassiter and Kimberly Dudley (1991), such tapes yield a nearly 100 per cent conviction rate when played by prosecutors. Aware of this research, reports Lassiter, New Zealand has made it a national policy that police interrogations be filmed with equal focus on the officer and the suspect, such as by filming them with side profiles of both.

*The False Consensus Effect* (McArthur, 1972) If we think back to Kelley's CCD model of attribution, we'll recall that a feature we attend to when deciding how to attribute cause to someone's behaviour is consensus – that is, what other people would do in a similar situation. However, when assuming what the 'consensus' is, we tend to assume everyone behaves as we (and our friends and acquaintances) do! Recall in Chapter 3 that we noted that people tend to assume they are just like everyone else. We typically assume our behaviour is 'typical', or 'normal'. People seek people who are similar to themselves, so deviances from our consensus are regarded as 'atypical'. For example, Laurie Chassin, Clark Presson and Steven Sherman (1984), who examined smoking among schoolchildren, found that those who smoked had lots of friends who also smoked and sought out even more smoking friends. When someone behaves in a way that doesn't match what 'we' would do, we may explain their actions as reflections of their odd traits or deviant personality disposition.

*The Self-serving Bias* Often people make attributions that are designed to enhance their own image in the eyes of others and themselves. This means we deny our failures and take credit for our successes. As Martha Augoustinos, Iain Walker and Ngaire Donaghue (2006) have noticed, athletes often give internal explanations for winning an event (e.g. level of fitness, being 'in the zone'), but blame their failures on external circumstances (e.g. weather, being pushed by another athlete). Mary Wiley, Kathleen Crittenden and Laura Birg (1979) found that academics display similar attribution patterns when explaining why a research paper was accepted or rejected for publication. They suggest that 'self-esteem is preserved by seeing failure as more external than success' (p. 220).

> Self-serving attributions also raise our image in the eyes of others; see Chapter 3 for further discussion of this.

*Self-knowledge* It may simply be the case that, because we know ourselves better than we know anyone else, we are able to make more external attributions for our negative behaviour than for other people's. If I omit to say 'Thank you' to the host of a party, it isn't because I'm rude but because the host was unpleasant. I know that I am, by and large, a nice person. However, if someone else doesn't say thank you to the host, without such knowledge of their usual behaviour, I may make an internal attribution of their being a hostile and ungrateful person by nature.

*Perspectives Change with Time* As the once-visible person recedes in their memory, observers often give more and more credit to the situation. As we saw above in the ground-breaking attribution error experiment by Edward Jones and Victor Harris (1967), immediately after hearing someone argue an assigned position, people assume that's how the person really felt. The day after a presidential election, Burger and Pavelich (1994) asked voters why the election turned out as it did. Most attributed the outcome to the candidates' personal traits and positions (the winner from the incumbent party was likeable). When they asked other voters the same question a year later, only a third attributed the verdict to the candidates. More people now credited circumstances, such as the country's good mood and the robust economy.

*Self-awareness* Circumstances can also shift our perspective on ourselves. Seeing ourselves on television redirects our attention to ourselves. Seeing ourselves in a mirror, hearing our tape-recorded voices, having our pictures taken, or filling out biographical questionnaires, similarly focuses our attention inwards, making us *self*-conscious instead of *situation*-conscious. Looking back on ill-fated relationships that once seemed like the unsinkable *Titanic*, people can more easily see the icebergs (Berscheid, 1999).

**self-awareness** *a self-conscious state in which attention focuses on oneself. It makes people more sensitive to their own attitudes and dispositions*

Robert Wicklund, Shelley Duval and their collaborators have explored the effects of self-awareness (Duval & Wicklund, 1972; Silvia & Duval, 2001). When our attention focuses upon ourselves, we often attribute responsibility to ourselves. Allan Fenigstein and Charles Carver (1978) demonstrated this by having students imagine themselves in hypothetical situations. Some students were made self-aware by thinking they were hearing their own heartbeats while pondering the situation. Compared with those who thought they were just hearing extraneous noises, the self-aware students saw themselves as more responsible for the imagined outcome.

Some people are typically quite self-conscious. In experiments, people who report themselves as privately self-conscious (who agree with statements such as 'I'm generally attentive to my inner feelings') behave similarly to people whose attention has been self-focused with a mirror (Carver & Scheier, 1978). Thus, people whose attention focuses on themselves – either briefly during an experiment or because they are self-conscious persons – view themselves more as observers typically do; they attribute their behaviour more to internal factors and less to the situation.

All these experiments point to a reason for the attribution error: *we find causes where we look for them.* To see this in your own experience, consider: would you say your social psychology tutor is a quiet or a talkative person?

Our guess is you inferred that he or she is fairly outgoing. But consider: your attention focuses on your tutor while he or she behaves in a public context that demands speaking. The tutor also observes their own behaviour in many different situations – in the classroom, in meetings, at home. 'Me talkative?' your tutor might say. 'Well, it all depends on the situation. When I'm in class or with good friends, I'm rather outgoing. But at conventions and in unfamiliar situations I feel and act rather shy.' Because we are acutely aware of how our behaviour varies with the situation, we see ourselves as more variable than other people (Baxter & Goldberg, 1987; Kammer, 1982; Sande et al., 1988). 'Nigel is uptight, Fiona is relaxed. With me it varies.'

*The Just World Hypothesis* Melvin Lerner (1980) claims that we tend to hold a common-sense belief that 'people get what they deserve'. This is a general notion that we live in a 'just' world where good things happen to good people, and bad things happen to the bad. This can mean that we assume people are responsible for their own misfortunes. This can lead to such things as blaming poverty on laziness, rape as a woman's own fault, the depressed for wallowing in self-pity, and so on. In their study of articles that appeared over a six-month period on the life experiences of African Americans, N. Caplan and S. D. Nelson (1973) found that 82 per cent attributed their social problems to personal shortcomings of the group. As Brian Nosek and colleagues (2009) point out, 'just world hypotheses' serve important political functions as they detract from the government's responsibility in resolving social problems by placing blame upon the victims. What is worrying about such hypotheses is that victims can falsely believe they are responsible for their misfortunes. To consider yourself to be personally responsible can be a way of regaining control of the problem. The idea that negative things happen to people in a random fashion, subject to the whims of a complex social world, renders that world as uncontrollable, unpredictable and a very disorientating place to be.

The just world hypothesis seems to have a powerful influence on the judgements we make about others but do we all draw on this belief in the same way and across all contexts? Melvin Lerner and Dale Miller (1978) argue that individuals may adopt cognitive strategies such as blaming victims for their misfortune and derogation towards them in order to minimise the injustices they perceive are happening to others. They reviewed a number of studies that investigated the just world hypothesis and argue that the just world hypothesis is far from a simple process. Lerner and Miller (1978) propose that people's concern over injustices depends on a number of factors. For example, it depends on whether upsetting events are close to home. If people directly witness an event such as a car accident or if they were survivors of a disaster such as the earthquake outlined at the beginning of the chapter, they will have a much greater need to explain and make sense of what has happened. In these close-to-home situations, people will be far more likely to believe in a just world and blame the victims for what happened to them.

Empathy is another factor that can have an impact on people's belief in a just world. How much empathy people feel for victims also has an influence on victim derogation and whether we blame people for their misfortunes. We are far less likely to blame a victim we empathize with and we see this as reducing the likelihood that we would be blamed if we found ourselves in the same situation. Lerner and Miller (1978) also note that individual differences are involved with the belief in a just world. They argue that this is evident from the way not all participants in experiments investigating the just world hypothesis blame the victim. Uwe Wolfradt and Claudia Dalbert (2003) investigated the relationship between individual differences and the belief in a generally just world. They found that those who endorsed the belief in a generally just world also valued security and conformity and were conscientious. In addition, those with an internal locus of control appear to have higher beliefs in a just world than those with an external locus of control. It would seem that people who believe that they have control over their own lives tend to blame the victim more than people who believe that the external world influences our fate. Adrian Furnham (2003) points out that this is a challenging notion to social psychology because the locus of self-control is conceived as a psychologically healthy individual difference variable making it difficult to reconcile with victim derogation and blame because these behaviours can have detrimental consequences.

The threat to an individual's belief in a just world may be increased if the victim shares a common identity with the observer and may also be affected by how much the observer endorses the belief in a just world. Isabel Correia, Helder Alves, Robbie Sutton, Miguel Ramos, Maria Gouveia-Pereira and Jorge Vala (2012) found that high believers in a just world are more likely to engage in victim derogation and blame an innocent victim who shares a common identity with them than an innocent victim who they do not identify with. If the observers are low believers in a just world, the degree of victim derogation is not affected by whether observers identify with the innocent victim or not. Correia et al. (2012) propose that when a victim shares a common identity with an observer, the observer perceives a threat of interchangeability with the victim so attempts to create as much distance to the victim as possible. This threat is more apparent when the observer has a high belief in a just world because this belief also becomes threatened. Individuals can then believe that the same misfortune will not happen to them because they are different in certain ways to the victim and they can also restore their belief in a just world by blaming and devaluing the victim without perceiving threats to their own identity.

The just world hypothesis is highly influential in social psychology and can be applied to understanding a range of issues such as prejudice and the extent that people are likely to help others. However, to date studies investigating individuals' belief in a just world tend to use correlations which cannot determine cause and effect and often use questionnaires with scales for participants to complete in response to artificial situations. Ethically, artificial situations must be used in studies that investigate individuals' responses to victims as real victims should not be created in studies! Nevertheless, the just world hypothesis provides a way to further our understanding of victim derogation and victim blaming over a range of important real-life issues. For example, the just world hypothesis has been applied to traumatic events such as understanding people's judgements about rape victims and perpetrators (Strömwall et al., 2012). Many studies have been conducted to understand judgements on people with different diseases such as AIDs (Furnham, 2003). The just world hypothesis has also been applied to understanding stigmatization such as stigma towards eating disorders (Ebneter et al., 2011) and discrimination such as gender discrimination in the workplace (Bastounis and Minibas-Poussard, 2012).

### Cultural Differences

But how 'fundamental' is the fundamental attribution error? Many researchers have noted its absence in collectivist cultures. You may remember the experiences of Hazel Markus and Shinobu Kitayama (outlined in Chapter 3), who observed cultural differences in understandings and explanations for self-behaviour. Markus and Kitayama (1991) argue that the fundamental attribution error exists only in cultures where this is an independent understanding of 'the self'. As children grow up in Western culture, they learn to explain behaviour in terms of the other's personal characteristics (Rholes et al., 1990; Ross, 1981).

So cultures influence how we attribute cause and the attribution error (Ickes, 1980; Krull et al., 1999; Watson, 1982). A Western worldview predisposes people to assume that people, not situations, cause events. Internal explanations are more socially approved (Jellison & Green, 1981). 'You can do it!' we are assured by the pop psychology of positive-thinking Western culture. You get what you deserve and deserve what you get. Yet people in Eastern Asian cultures are somewhat more sensitive to the importance of situations. Thus, when aware of the social context, they are less inclined to assume that others' behaviour corresponds to their traits (Choi et al., 1999; Farwell & Weiner, 2000; Masuda & Kitayama, 2004).

Some languages promote external attributions. Instead of 'I was late', Spanish idiom allows one to say, 'The clock caused me to be late.' In collectivist cultures, people less often perceive others in terms of personal dispositions (Lee et al., 1996; Zebrowitz-McArthur, 1988). They are less likely to spontaneously interpret a behaviour as reflecting an inner trait (Newman, 1993).

The fundamental attribution error is *fundamental* because it colours our explanations in basic and important ways. Researchers in Britain, India, Australia and the USA have found that people's attributions predict their attitudes towards the poor and the unemployed (Furnham, 1982; Pandey et al., 1982; Skitka, 1999; Wagstaff, 1983; Zucker & Weiner, 1993). Those who attribute poverty and unemployment to personal dispositions ('They're just lazy and undeserving') tend to adopt political positions unsympathetic to such people (Figure 4.7). This *dispositional attribution* ascribes behaviour to the person's disposition and traits. Those who make *situational attributions* ('If you or I were to live with the same overcrowding, poor education and discrimination, would we be any better off?') tend to adopt political positions that offer more direct support to the poor.

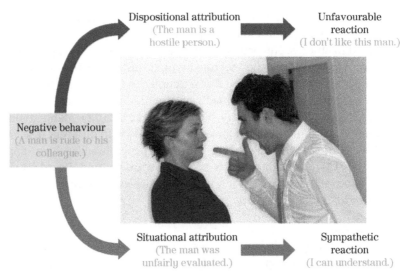

**FIGURE 4.7** Attributions and reactions
How we explain someone's negative behaviour determines how we feel about it.
SOURCE: Ingram Publishing

## INTERGROUP ATTRIBUTION

As we noted earlier in this chapter we often perceive people as members of social groups (e.g. students, Spaniards, nurses, Muslims) and may therefore explain their behaviour in accordance with what we know and feel about that group. This includes our fellow ingroup members (e.g. other students) as well as outgroup members. As we shall see in Chapters 12 and 13, people feel affiliated or as though they psychologically belong to various social groups, and often behave according to what is expected of a group member. So explanations for behaviours do not just occur at an individual level, but also at an intragroup (within group) and intergroup (between groups) level.

To explain a social group's behaviour we make inferences about that social group and classify the group. Daniel Ames (2004) proposes that when we make inferences about social groups these inferences rely on both the self – individual differences in social projection – and on stereotypes – prevalence of stereotyping. Social projection is a simple heuristic and occurs when people project their attitudes onto another group. This means that people will greatly estimate that attributes they see in themselves are also present in members of a particular group. Social projection can therefore be related to wanting to be liked as well as having our attributes validated by others.

Ames (2004) also proposes that the more a person perceives themselves to be similar to a particular group, the less they will stereotype this group. Instead, they will project their own attributes and values onto the group, estimating that the group also shares a high level of the same attributes and values as them. However, the opposite will happen if a person perceives themselves to be dissimilar to a group. They will then search their memory for stereotyped information to make sense of a dissimilar group. The implications of perceived similarity are important because getting people to focus on similarities with another social group can contribute towards reducing stereotyping, especially as Ames (2004) found that perceived similarity wasn't related to actual similarity. It is simply the thinking that one is similar to a social group that reduces stereotyping regardless of how similar a person really is to this group.

As mentioned at the beginning of this chapter, classifying people into social groups is a fundamental part of stereotyping and forms a process of social categorization. We categorize people into social groups and then judge them on the basis of how similar we perceive them to be to us. This process is therefore based on our self-knowledge. Stereotyping is a powerful influence towards making attributions about people's behaviour and is involved with how different we perceive social groups from ourselves. Theresa DiDonato, Johannes Ullrich and Joachim Krueger (2011) propose that self-knowledge is highly important within the process of social categorization and that social categorization has an effect on social projection. They also propose that social categorization occurs at a fairly early stage when forming social inferences. In their study, social projection was high for ingroups (groups participants perceived themselves belonging to) and low for outgroups (groups that participants clearly did not perceive themselves to belong to). Social projection towards a mixed ingroup/outgroup was lower than towards an ingroup and higher than towards an outgroup. DiDonato et al. (2011) found that self-judgements related to ingroup judgements were faster. They argue that this suggests people project self-judgements to the ingroup rather than drawing on perceived inferences about the ingroup to make self-judgements. Most people have a positive self-image and most strongly project this positive image to ingroups rather than outgroups. The more that is known about a person's self-image the easier it is to understand how they make attributions about social groups.

These attributions follow very similar patterns to those we considered at an individual level. Intergroup attributions are often characterized by self-serving biases and ethnocentrism. We give internal explanations for 'our' group's positive behaviour, and explain away our negative behaviour by pointing to situational factors. On the contrary, we explain 'their' positive behaviour as having an external cause, but regard their negative behaviour as driven by the internal characteristics of members of that group. 'How predictable!' you may exclaim, when members of another group behave badly. Thomas Pettigrew (1979) termed this the 'ultimate attribution error'. We see examples of this in our everyday lives. If our favourite football team wins, it's because it is made up of very good players. If it loses, the referee was biased and the pitch was in a poor condition. If our rival team wins, it got lucky, or perhaps it cheated. If it lost, it's because we know its players are not very good and have a bad attitude. Of course examples of the ultimate attribution error can be much more serious than this. We only need to pick up a newspaper to see how a rise in crime may be attributed to the criminal tendencies of an incoming national, racial or ethnic group. This has been demonstrated many times in empirical work. For example, in R. Barry Ruback and Purnima Singh's (2007) study, they drew upon a history of Muslim–Hindu riots that had accounted for many deaths in five states of India. In an experimental design, they asked Muslim and Hindu participants to read descriptions of riots that had been instigated by either Muslims or Hindus. The task of the participant was to attribute blame for the deaths that occurred as a result. What they found was ingroup bias. Blame

ultimate attribution error *a bias in which positive actions of one's own group are perceived as normative, and negative acts are seen as unusual or exceptional. Conversely, negative actions carried out by a member of an outgroup are seen as normative for that group, and positive acts are regarded as unusual*

for the riots was placed upon the opposite group from the participant (so if the participant was Hindu the blame was placed upon Muslims) and their perceptions of that group became even more negative than previously. Such attributions serve to reinforce stereotypes held at the time about particular groups. They also enable 'us' to compare ourselves favourably in comparison to 'them'. As we shall see in Chapters 12 and 13, we belong to social groups to the extent that they give us positive self-esteem. To maintain this we engage in a process of social comparison in which 'we' are better than 'them'.

A growing number of studies investigate how we make attributions about others through social neuroscience. These judgements may occur, for example, when we are weighing up another person in terms of personality traits, mental states and behavioural dispositions (Cacioppo and Decety, 2011). As we have seen, the decisions we make about people we don't really know in terms of personality and behaviour involve judgements related to person perception and person categorization and can lead to attributions influenced by stereotyping. But what processes are involved in accessing stereotypical knowledge?

Susanne Quadflieg and Neil Macrae (2011) have reviewed recent social neuroscience studies exploring stereotyping and point out that fMRI data indicate that the retrieval of stereotypic knowledge activates brain regions such as the medial prefrontal cortex, the posterior cingulated and the anterior temporal lobe. The important thing about these brain regions is that they are all considered to be involved in social cognition. However, Quadflieg and Macrae (2011) argue that it is possible stereotypic person knowledge is more widely distributed across brain regions because we draw on different aspects of the person when making stereotypes. For example, stereotyping a person's behaviour may be involved in an action stereotype and could be activated in different regions in the left hemisphere of the brain known to be involved with action knowledge. On the other hand, stereotyping a person's appearance could be activated in regions of the brain known to be involved with visual knowledge such as the ventral occipital and the temporal region.

Can social neuroscience contribute to reducing stereotyping? A study in Australia using undergraduate students explored this in relation to implicit gender stereotypes (Wong et al., 2012). Participants were assigned to either an inhibitory repetitive transcranial magnetic stimulation (rTMS) of the anterior temporal lobe (ANL) or a pretend stimulation of the ANL. Both groups took part in a gender implicit test association (IAT). IATs are designed to measure prejudice that people either try to hide or may be unaware of, so in this study the researchers were measuring gender stereotyping that participants may either try to hide or gender stereotyping they may be unaware of. Cara Wong et al. (2012) found that there was a reduction in the IAT scores for implicit gender stereotyping in those participants who had received rTMS to the ANL. Manipulating this brain region and reducing the IAT scores also provides evidence that the ANL region of the brain is involved with some aspect of stereotypical processes. This has important implications for understanding the neural networks in the ANL that are involved in implicit stereotypes and prejudice. Gary Berntson and John Cacioppo (2000) point out that social neuroscience can show how people may hold both prejudiced and non-prejudiced beliefs. Looking at prejudice in this two-sided way suggests that people may believe that they do not hold prejudice views but they may act in a discriminatory manner because this discriminatory behaviour may be unintentional. This can have considerable contributions towards our understanding of the processes involved in prejudice. On the other hand, it may also point towards prejudice being an inevitable attitude.

Studies in social neuroscience are often criticized for lacking ecological validity. Quadflieg and Macrae (2011) argue that social neuroscience is no less ecologically valid than traditional social cognitive studies. Participants do very similar tasks to those in many traditional social psychology experiments, such as investigations into social judgements. Quadflieg and Macrae also defend the use of brain scanners and say in everyday life people do lie down in darkened rooms at times. They also point out that neuroscience is a fairly new discipline and has a great deal of scope for development; exploring general rules of brain function can enable specific psychological constructs to be further explored and redefined. Neuroscientists argue that a main strength of this discipline and its contribution to social psychology is the way that multi-levels of analysis are explored without reducing the exploration to brain mechanisms alone. However, see the Focus On Box at the end of this chapter to consider these arguments further.

While Quadflieg and Macrae argue that social neuroscience is no less ecologically valid than social cognitive studies, this not only leaves open to question how ecologically valid social cognitive studies are but brings into question how 'social' they are. Social attributions occur in everyday life within rich social environments and appear to be influenced by the people around us. Our attributions are also highly influenced by our personal experiences and our personal histories as well as our cultural experiences. Therefore, it is important to emphasize here that how attributions are made depends on the relations that exist at that time between groups in a particular cultural, social, political and historical context. They are shaped by the cultural and societal norms that we live by.

## COMMUNICATING OUR SOCIAL WORLD: SOCIAL REPRESENTATIONS THEORY AND A THINKING SOCIETY

Some social psychologists have argued that cognitive theories of social beliefs and judgements have underplayed the importance of social factors in shaping these processes. This was a particular concern of social psychologist Serge Moscovici. He felt social psychology had offered theories about processes within the individual's mind (e.g. schemas, illusory correlations, attribution processes) without really exploring how they got there. You may recall his criticism of experimental social psychology, which he claimed had become 'asocial' (see Chapters 1 and 2). His primary aim, therefore, was to reintroduce a 'social' focus into the discipline by emphasizing how society, ideology and cultural norms shaped how we perceive, think about and judge our social world. In other words he wanted to stress the importance of language in communicating social reality, as people discuss their ideas, values and beliefs with each other in everyday life. As we live as members of a collective, Moscovici reasoned that this must influence how we see the world. We are a 'thinking society' capable of shaping society as we share and discuss our thoughts and ideas with one another.

The sociologist Emile Durkheim had already defined collective social thought – that is, those thoughts that are shared by members of a group (e.g. common sense, traditions, legends, myths, and so on). Moscovici redefined these as

## research close-up

CAN THE WAY WE RETRIEVE INFORMATION FROM MEMORY AFFECT HOW WE JUDGE OTHER PEOPLE?

*Source:* Bertram, G., & Bodenhausen, G. V. (2005). *Accessibility effects on implicit social cognition: The role of knowledge activation and retrieval experiences.* Journal of Personality and Social Psychology, *89, 672–685.*

### Introduction

Techniques to measure implicit attitudes, stereotypes, self-esteem and self-concept have made a considerable contribution to social cognition (e.g. De Houwer, 2003; Nosek and Banaji, 2001). These techniques use indirect measurements to measure psychological attributes such as the attitudes and beliefs we are either not aware of or try to conceal. Therefore the tests used are also designed to minimize the tendency for individuals to conceal their underlying attitudes. Techniques often investigate implicit measures through the speed of responses when individuals make connections to concepts or sort them into categories and also by examining the strength of an individual's automatic associations between a concept and an attribute. The experiment in the present study aims to investigate the different influences of an individual's knowledge activation and subjective experiences of retrieval on implicit measures of gender stereotyping.

### Method

Participants were 48 female and 22 male undergraduates in America. They were randomly assigned to four conditions in a between-subjects design. There was an 'easy' or 'difficult' condition for a retrieval task and there was a *stimulus* compatibility condition and a *response* compatibility condition for a priming task. For the retrieval task, participants were asked to generate lists of counter-stereotypical women. In the 'easy' condition participants were asked to provide a list of three women who were 'strong'; in the 'difficult' condition participants were asked to generate a list of ten women who were 'strong'. It may be that if participants feel that they struggle to identify counter-stereotypical women (i.e. identify ten women who were 'strong') they may implicitly believe that they hold stereotypical views of women. Immediately afterwards participants performed a priming task. Early in this task the word male or female appeared on a computer screen for 15 milliseconds. After this, letter sequences from a set of stereotypically female target words such as dainty or fragile, and from stereotypically male target words such as powerful or assertive, and letter sequences from non-words, appeared on the screen. Participants in the stimulus compatibility condition were asked to make a lexical decision about whether the letter sequences made up words or non-words. Participants in the response compatibility condition were asked to think about whether the letter sequences made them think about strength or weakness. In the response compatibility condition participants were additionally told that they might see non-words included in the letter sequences but to respond to these with their first inclinations anyway. Participants therefore took part in one of four combinations: 'easy' plus *stimulus* compatibility; 'difficult' plus *stimulus* compatibility; 'easy' plus *response* compatibility; or 'difficult' plus *response* compatibility. The quantitative data was analysed by a between-subjects ANOVA.

### Results

Participants in the stimulus compatibility condition (where they had to identify gender stereotypical words that had missing letters) showed a lower level of implicit gender stereotyping if they had been in the 'difficult' condition (where they had to try to generate a high number of counter-stereotypical women). In contrast to this, participants in the response compatibility condition (where they had to evaluate whether the target word sequences made them think about strength or weakness) showed a higher level of implicit gender stereotyping if they had been in the 'difficult' condition.

## Discussion

The results demonstrate higher implicit gender stereotyping when participants are asked to make evaluative judgements. This effect appears to be from the nature of the two tasks (evaluative judgements in the response compatibility task or lexical decisions in the stimulus compatibility task) because the initial task (the difference in generating lists of low or high numbers of counter-stereotypical women – 'easy' or 'difficult') did not have an overall influence on these results. The findings suggest that implicit attitudes based on evaluative judgements are influenced by the ease of retrieving relevant information from memory. However, implicit attitudes that are based on making lexical decisions are influenced by direct knowledge activation in associated memory. When more effort is put into retrieval such as making decisions by activating knowledge, the influence upon attitudes is not as great as when retrieval of information is easier. By investigating the underlying mechanisms of implicit gender stereotyping the present study goes beyond demonstrating the influence of externally provided context stimuli on implicit measures. Furthermore, the findings from the present study may indicate that subjective experiences and feelings translate into overt responses and may not just influence responses in response compatibility tasks but may also influence spontaneous responses in social interactions. In contrast, implicit measures in the stimulus compatibility task may represent a conceptual cognitive component rather than represent subjective feelings. Overall, the present study demonstrates that the way information is retrieved from memory influences different types of implicit measures. Future research could investigate the underlying mechanisms of other kinds of context effects to not only gain an understanding of the influence of different contexts but to also develop an understanding of implicit measures in general.

'social representations', which are the knowledge, images, thoughts and ideas members of a collectivity share and communicate with one another through language. For example, in Western society there is a social representation that people are autonomous agents, responsible for their own actions, which goes some way to explaining why we see the fundamental attribution error occur in such societies.

But where do these social representations come from? Moscovici thought people turn the unfamiliar into the familiar through two processes.

1. *Anchoring:* we compare the unfamiliar with our existing stock of knowledge and anchor it onto what we already know. So, by giving something a name we are not only able to now recognize it, but we also give it meaning. This reveals something about our society, culture, and group norms and values. We can view it positively or negatively. Treat it as normative or deviant.

2. *Objectification:* the process in which an unfamiliar idea, notion or image is transformed into a concrete object. Consider Freud's concept of 'neurosis'. What do you see when you think of the concept? Is it represented in a concrete image of a person?

Moscovici was particularly interested in the popularization of scientific concepts by the mass media, noting how they become shared social representations that we discuss in our everyday lives. This gives us a population of amateur scientists. The television phenomenon of *Big Brother* has turned many people into lay psychologists as they analyse the behaviour of the housemates. Thanks to the mass media, ordinary people can have a discussion about the greenhouse effect, give relationship advice, and even diagnose medical conditions and suggest treatment. We hold social representations about scientific issues through communicating our perceptions and judgements about them in our talking and thinking society.

More recently Mai Doan Anh Thi and others (2008) have considered how people with HIV and AIDS are evaluated in Ho Chi Minh City in Vietnam (with over 260 000 people suffering from HIV). Focus groups conducted with people who have HIV and/or AIDS, revealed how social representations present in the media and everyday understandings of the condition included misperceptions about how it was contracted (e.g. through casual contact) and how people should be treated. The representation of HIV and AIDS as a 'social evil' means people with the condition are perceived as socially deviant, and are marginalized and discriminated against in all areas of their lives.

### Studying Social Representations

Are people who live in the countryside less likely to suffer ill health than those who live in the city? In a classic study Claudine Herzlich (1973) set out to examine the social representations people in France held of health and illness, in terms of how to explain them. Using open-ended interviews with 80 middle-class Parisians, Herzlich concluded that there exists a social representation that city life is responsible for illness. Those who live in the city were perceived to be unhealthy on the basis of poor diet, contaminated water, stress and pollution. City life was thought to be responsible for heart attacks, cancer and fatigue. On the other hand, those who live in the country were thought to be much healthier. Indeed it was believed that a move to the country could improve your health! The countryside was associated with a slower pace of life, clean water, fresh food and clean air. So being ill or healthy was not attributed to the individual, but to the environment in which they lived.

Is living in the countryside of France really better for your health than living in the city?

SOURCE: (L) © lillis Photography/iStock; (R) © rusm/iStock

When it comes to explaining people's behaviour in our social world, we use attributions and these can be prone to error. However, as we have seen culture makes an important difference to our attributions, especially the fundamental attribution error. So we need to carefully consider the social when thinking about how we explain people's behaviour. Social representation theory does take more account of the social and incorporates the values held in a particular culture, the common sense beliefs and norms. In the final section, we turn to how important our social beliefs are.

# EXPECTATIONS OF OUR SOCIAL WORLD

*Having considered how we explain and judge others – efficiently, adaptively, but sometimes erroneously – we conclude this chapter by pondering the effects of our social judgements. Do our social beliefs matter? Do they change reality?*

Our social beliefs and judgements do matter. They influence how we feel and act, and by so doing may help generate their own reality. When our ideas lead us to act in ways that produce their apparent confirmation, they have become what sociologist Robert Merton (1948) termed self-fulfilling prophecies – beliefs that lead to their own fulfilment. If led to believe that their bank is about to crash, customers will race to withdraw their money and their false perceptions may create reality, noted Merton. This is exactly what happened in the UK during 2007 when the Northern Rock bank was reported to be suffering from funding problems. In response, existing customers formed long queues outside a local branch with the intention of withdrawing their savings.

*self-fulfilling prophecy occurs when people's expectations lead to the occurrence of the expected behaviour or outcome. A girl or a teacher's belief that girls are never good at sciences could thus lead to its own fulfilment*

In his well-known studies of *experimenter bias*, Robert Rosenthal (1985) found that research participants sometimes live up to what they believe experimenters expect of them. In one study, experimenters asked individuals to judge the success of people in various photographs. The experimenters read the same instructions to all their participants and showed them the same photos. Nevertheless, experimenters who expected their participants to see the photographed people as successful obtained higher ratings than did those who expected their participants to see the people as failures. Even more startling – and controversial – are reports that teachers' beliefs about their students similarly serve as self-fulfilling prophecies. If a teacher believes a student is good at mathematics, will the student do well in the class? Let's examine this.

## TEACHER EXPECTATIONS AND STUDENT PERFORMANCE

Teachers do have higher expectations for some students than for others. Perhaps you have detected this after having a brother or sister precede you in school, or after receiving a label such as 'gifted' or 'learning disabled', or after being tracked with 'high-ability' or 'average-ability' students. Perhaps conversation in the staff room sent your reputation ahead of you. Or perhaps your new teacher scrutinized your school file or discovered your family's social status. It is clear that teachers' evaluations correlate with student achievement: teachers think well of students who do well. That's mostly because teachers accurately perceive their students' abilities and achievements (Jussim, 2005).

But are teachers' evaluations ever a *cause* as well as a consequence of student performance? One correlational study of 4300 British schoolchildren by William Crano and Phyllis Mellon (1978) suggested yes. Not only is high performance followed by higher teacher evaluations, but the reverse is true as well.

Could we test this 'teacher-expectations effect' experimentally? Pretend we gave a teacher the impression that Dana, Sally, Todd and Manuel – four randomly selected students – are unusually capable. Will the teacher give special treatment to these four and elicit superior performance from them? In a famous experiment, Robert Rosenthal and Lenore Jacobson (1968) reported precisely that. Randomly selected children in a San Francisco elementary school who were said (on the basis of a fictitious test) to be on the verge of a dramatic intellectual spurt did then spurt ahead in IQ score.

That dramatic result seemed to suggest that the school problems of 'disadvantaged' children might reflect their teachers' low expectations. The findings were soon publicized in the national media as well as in many college textbooks in psychology and education. However, further analysis – which was not as highly publicized – revealed the teacher-expectations effect to be not as powerful and reliable as this initial study had led many people to believe (Spitz, 1999). By Rosenthal's own count, in only about 4 in 10 of the nearly 500 published experiments did expectations significantly affect performance (Rosenthal, 1991, 2002). Low expectations do not doom a capable child, nor do high expectations magically transform a slow learner into a valedictorian. Human nature is not so pliable.

High expectations do seem to boost low achievers, for whom a teacher's positive attitude may be a hope-giving breath of fresh air (Madon et al., 1997). How are such expectations transmitted? Rosenthal and other investigators report that teachers look, smile and nod more at 'high-potential students'. Teachers also may teach more to their 'gifted' students, set higher goals for them, call on them more, and give them more time to answer (Cooper, 1983; Harris & Rosenthal, 1985, 1986; Jussim, 1986).

In one study, Elisha Babad, Frank Bernieri and Robert Rosenthal (1991) videotaped teachers talking to, or about, unseen students for whom they held high or low expectations. A random 10-second clip of either the teacher's voice or the teacher's face was enough to tell viewers – both children and adults – whether this was a good or a poor student and how much the teacher liked the student. (You read that right: 10 seconds.) Although teachers may think they can conceal their feelings and behave impartially towards the class, students are acutely sensitive to teachers' facial expressions and body movements (Figure 4.8).

Reading the experiments on teacher expectations makes us wonder about the effect of *students'* expectations upon their teachers. You no doubt begin many of your courses having heard 'Professor Smith is interesting' and 'Professor Jones is a bore'. Robert Feldman and Thomas Prohaska (1979; Feldman & Theiss, 1982) found that such expectations can affect both student and teacher. Students in a learning experiment who expected to be taught by an excellent teacher perceived their

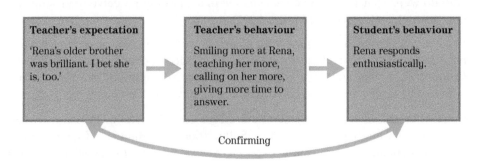

**FIGURE 4.8**  Self-fulfilling prophecies
Teacher expectations can become self-fulfilling prophecies. But, for the most part, teachers' expectations accurately reflect reality (Jussim & Harber, 2005).

teacher (who was unaware of their expectations) as more competent and interesting than did students with low expectations. Furthermore, the students actually learned more. In a follow-up experiment, Feldman and Prohaska videotaped teachers and had observers rate their performances. Teachers were judged most capable when assigned a student who non-verbally conveyed positive expectations.

To see whether such effects might also occur in actual classrooms, a research team led by David Jamieson (Jamieson et al., 1987) experimented with four high school classes taught by a newly transferred teacher. During individual interviews, they told students in two of the classes that both other students and the research team rated the teacher very highly. Compared with the control classes, the students given positive expectations paid better attention during class. At the end of the teaching unit, they also got better grades and rated the teacher as clearer in her teaching. The attitudes that a class has towards its teacher are as important, it seems, as the teacher's attitude towards the students.

## GETTING FROM OTHERS WHAT WE EXPECT

So the expectations of experimenters and teachers, though usually reasonably accurate assessments, occasionally act as self-fulfilling prophecies. How widespread are self-fulfilling prophecies? Do we get from others what we expect of them? Studies show that self-fulfilling prophecies also operate in work settings (with managers who have high or low expectations), in law courts (as judges instruct juries), and in simulated police contexts (as interrogators with guilty or innocent expectations interrogate and pressure suspects) (Kassin et al., 2003; Rosenthal, 2003).

Do self-fulfilling prophecies colour our personal relationships? There are times when negative expectations of someone lead us to be extra nice to that person, which induces him or her to be nice in return – thus *dis*confirming our expectations. But a more common finding in studies of social interaction is that, yes, we do to some extent get what we expect (Olson et al., 1996).

In laboratory games, hostility nearly always begets hostility: people who perceive their opponents as non-cooperative will readily induce them to be non-cooperative (Kelley & Stahelski, 1970). Each party's perception of the other as aggressive, resentful and vindictive induces the other to display those behaviours in self-defence, thus creating a vicious self-perpetuating circle.

So, do intimate relationships prosper when partners idealize each other? Are positive illusions of the other's virtues self-fulfilling? Or are they more often self-defeating, by creating high expectations that can't be met? Among university dating couples followed by Sandra Murray and her associates (1996a, 2000), positive ideals of one's partner were good omens. Idealization helped buffer conflict, bolster satisfaction, and turn self-perceived frogs into princes or princesses. When someone loves and admires us, it helps us become more the person he or she imagines us to be.

Among married couples, too, those who worry that their partner doesn't love and accept them interpret slight hurts as rejections, which motivate them to devalue the partner and distance themselves. Those who presume their partner's love and acceptance respond less defensively, read less into stressful events, and treat the partner better (Murray et al., 2003). Love helps create its presumed reality.

Several experiments conducted by Mark Snyder (1984) show how, once formed, erroneous beliefs about the social world can induce others to confirm those beliefs, a phenomenon called behavioural confirmation. In a now-classic study, Snyder, Elizabeth Tanke and Ellen Berscheid (1977) had men students talk on the telephone with women they thought (from having been shown a picture) were either attractive or unattractive. Analysis of just the women's comments during the conversations revealed that the supposedly attractive women spoke more warmly than the supposedly unattractive women. The men's erroneous beliefs had become a self-fulfilling prophecy by leading them to act in a way that influenced the women to fulfil the men's stereotype that beautiful people are desirable people.

*behavioural confirmation a type of self-fulfilling prophecy whereby people's social expectations lead them to behave in ways that cause others to confirm their expectations*

Behavioural confirmation also occurs as people interact with partners holding mistaken beliefs. People who are believed lonely behave less sociably (Rotenberg et al., 2002). Men who are believed sexist behave less favourably towards women (Pinel, 2002). Job interviewees who are believed to be warm behave more warmly.

Imagine yourself as one of the 60 young men or 60 young women in an experiment by Robert Ridge and Jeffrey Reber (2002). Each man is to interview one of the women to assess her suitability for a teaching assistant position. Before doing so, he is told either that she feels attracted to him (based on his answers to a biographical questionnaire) or not attracted. The result was behavioural confirmation: applicants believed to feel an attraction exhibited more flirtatiousness (and without being aware of doing so). Ridge and Reber believe that this process may be one of the roots of sexual harassment. If a woman's behaviour seems to confirm a man's beliefs, he may then escalate his overtures until they become sufficiently overt for the woman to recognize and interpret them as inappropriate or harassing.

Behavioural confirmation. The image above shows English fans in France for a football match for Euro 2016. When England football fans came to France for the 1998 World Cup, they were expected to live up to their reputation as aggressive 'hooligans' (e.g. Stott et al., 2001). Local French youth and police, expecting hooligan behaviour, reportedly displayed hostility towards the English, who retaliated, thus confirming the expectation (Klein & Snyder, 2003).

SOURCE: © Mike_Sheridan/iStock

Expectations influence children's behaviour, too. After observing the amount of litter in three classrooms, Richard Miller and his colleagues (1975) had the teacher and others repeatedly tell one class that they should be neat and tidy. This persuasion increased the amount of litter placed in waste baskets from 15 to 45 per cent, but only temporarily. Another class, which also had been placing only 15 per cent of its litter in waste baskets, was repeatedly congratulated for being so neat and tidy. After eight days of hearing this, and still two weeks later, these children were fulfilling the expectation by putting more than 80 per cent of their litter in waste baskets. Tell children they are hard-working and kind (rather than lazy and mean), and they may live up to their labels.

Told that someone we are about to meet is intelligent and attractive, we may come away impressed with just how intelligent and attractive he or she is. These experiments help us understand how social beliefs, such as stereotypes about people with disabilities or about people of a particular race or sex, may be self-confirming. How others treat us reflects how we and others have treated them.

As with every social phenomenon, the tendency to confirm others' expectations has its limits. Expectations often predict behaviour simply because they are accurate (Jussim, 2005).

'The more he treated her as though she were really very nice, the more Lotty expanded and became really very nice, and the more he, affected in his turn, became really very nice himself; so that they went round and round, not in a vicious but in a highly virtuous circle.'
  Elizabeth von Arnim, *The Enchanted April*, 1922

## CONCLUSIONS

*Social psychology studies reveal that our information-processing powers are impressive for their efficiency and adaptiveness ('in apprehension how like a god!' exclaimed Shakespeare's Hamlet), yet vulnerable to predictable errors and misjudgements ('headpiece filled with straw', said T. S. Eliot). How we perceive, judge and explain our social experiences is guided by the norms and values that exist within society. What practical lessons, and what insights into human nature, can we take home from this research?*

We have reviewed some reasons why people sometimes come to believe what may be untrue. We cannot easily dismiss these studies; most of their participants were intelligent people, often students at leading universities. Moreover, these predictable distortions and biases occurred even when payment for right answers motivated people to think optimally. As one researcher concluded, the illusions 'have a persistent quality not unlike that of perceptual illusions' (Slovic, 1972).

Research in cognitive social psychology thus mirrors the mixed review given humanity in literature, philosophy and religion. Many research psychologists have spent lifetimes exploring the awesome capacities of the human mind. We are smart enough to have cracked our own genetic code, to have invented talking computers, to have sent people to the moon. Three cheers for human reason.

Well, two cheers – because the mind's premium on efficient judgement makes our intuition more vulnerable to misjudgement than we suspect. With remarkable ease, we form and sustain false beliefs. Led by our preconceptions, overconfident, persuaded by vivid anecdotes, and perceiving correlations and control even where none may exist, we construct our social beliefs and then influence others to confirm them. 'The naked intellect', observed novelist Madeleine L'Engle, 'is an extraordinarily inaccurate instrument.'

But have these studies just been intellectual tricks played on hapless participants, thus making them look worse than they are? Richard Nisbett and Lee Ross (1980) contended that, if anything, they overestimate our intuitive powers. The experiments usually present people with clear evidence and warn them that their reasoning ability is being tested. Seldom does real life say to us: 'Here is some evidence. Now put on your intellectual Sunday best and answer these questions.'

Often our everyday failings are inconsequential, but not always so. False impressions, interpretations and beliefs can produce serious consequences. Even small biases can have profound social effects when we are making important social judgements: why are so many people homeless? Unhappy? Homicidal? Does my friend love me or my money? Cognitive biases even creep into sophisticated scientific thinking.

Is this too cynical? Leonard Martin and Ralph Erber (2005) invite us to imagine that an intelligent being swooped down just for a moment and begged for information that would help it understand the human species. When you hand it this social psychology text, the alien says 'thank you' and zooms back off into space. After resolving your remorse over giving up this book, how would you feel about having offered social psychology's analysis? Joachim Krueger and David Funder (2004a, 2004b) wouldn't feel too good. Social psychology's preoccupation with human foibles needs balancing with 'a more positive view of human nature', they argue.

Fellow social psychologist Lee Jussim (2005) agrees, adding, 'Despite the oft-demonstrated existence of a slew of logical flaws and systematic biases in lay judgement and social perception, such as the fundamental attribution error, false consensus, over-reliance on imperfect heuristics, self-serving biases, etc., people's perceptions of one another are surprisingly (though rarely perfectly) accurate.' The elegant analyses of the imperfections of our thinking are themselves a tribute to human wisdom. Were one to argue that all human thought is illusory, the assertion would be self-refuting, for it, too, would be but an illusion. It would be logically equivalent to contending 'All generalizations are false, including this one.'

Nobel laureate psychologist Herbert Simon (1957) was among the modern researchers who first described the bounds of human reason. Simon contends that to cope with reality, we simplify it. Consider the complexity of a chess game: the number of possible games is greater than the number of particles in the universe. How do we cope? We adopt some simplifying rules – heuristics. These heuristics sometimes lead us to defeat. But they do enable us to make efficient snap judgements.

## focus on

### HOW DO WE KNOW IF WE ARE POOR JUDGES OF SOCIAL REALITY OR HIGHLY EFFICIENT AT THESE JUDGEMENTS?

Are human beings inaccurate judges of social reality? The research on heuristics, biases and mental shortcuts suggests that we are. However, Gerd Gigerenzer and Daniel Goldstein (1996; Goldstein and Gigerenzer, 2002) argue that these cognitive processes are not 'errors' but are illustrations of our creative and complex human mind. With the cognitive revolution of the 1960s in psychology computers were used to model the human brain. This led to a rethinking of the mind, and what they call 'the mind as computer'. But whereas the computer could perform calculations and solve problems perfectly every time, the human brain was fallible. But are people really deficient thinkers? Or is this a sign of our intelligence? Gigerenzer and Goldstein invite their reader to consider the recognition heuristic as an example. The recognition heuristic proposes that if one of two objects is recognized then it can be inferred that the recognized object is of higher value. They now ask their reader to imagine three Parisian sisters who are told they will take a test on the 100 largest German cities. The test will comprise pairs of cities, and they must decide which is the larger. Before the test the older sister studies the cities of Germany so she can find out the 100 largest ones. She will recognize all the cities presented in the test. The middle sister has heard of some of the cities of Germany and will recognize about half of those presented in the test. The youngest sister has never heard of any of the cities in Germany, nor has she done any studying. So who will perform the best? The eldest sister relies on her knowledge and gets more than half of them correct. The youngest sister can only guess throughout the test. The middle sister does the best. Why? She's the only one using the recognition heuristic. She recognizes half of the cities and assumes that the reason she's heard of them is because they're large. So she chooses them. She doesn't have to sort through all the cities, like the eldest sister does, nor does she have to completely guess, like the youngest sister.

As Gigerenzer and Goldstein observe, we learn to associate recognition with quality, power and importance. To be able to recognize important things has distinct advantages for us. It enables us to distinguish things that will be of benefit to us, from those that are of no value or may even be harmful. So far from being deficient processors of social reality, the use of heuristics is 'a capacity that evolution has shaped over millions of years that allows organisms to benefit from their own ignorance' (Goldstein & Gigerenzer, 2002, p. 88). As they conclude, in a complex social world, heuristics may be evidence of the unique intelligence of human beings to exploit information to make creative, accurate and efficient judgements. But to what extent can this research be applied to our ability to use quick judgements about others? And how do we know if we are efficient at social judgements or poor judges of social reality?

Alexander Todorov, Lasana Harris and Susan Fiske (2006) propose that social neuroscience is ideal for studying the efficiency and spontaneity of social judgements. We have seen in this chapter the contribution social neuroscience is making towards understanding activities in our brains when we are making inferences and making sense of social information. This approach assumes that brain mechanisms and structures guide our judgements and shape the way we behave. Social neuroscientists propose that studying brain activity can aid our understanding about how we make apparently spontaneous judgements such as through the use of heuristics and inferences. Todorov et al. (2006) argue that research in social neuroscience demonstrates that person inferences are highly efficient and that this has significant consequences for our social judgements and behaviour. Cacioppo and Berntson (1992) see exploring the brain as a gateway to the mind.

Gigerenzer and Goldstein refer to the human mind as a computer, not just able to efficiently distinguish important information in our social world but also able to think logically and scientifically. This distinction between efficient logical scientific thinking and faulty irrational thinking has been established in the social cognition studies on inferences and attributions outlined in this chapter. However, critical social psychologists such as Brendan Gough, Majella McFadden and Mathew McDonald (2013) argue that the human mind is not completely 'scientific' or 'logical'. Furthermore, they argue methods of research within social cognition treat individuals and their minds as objects separate from the social environment to be investigated in carefully controlled experimental conditions. Not only this, they also argue that social neuroscience tends to reduce people to the effects of psycho-biological processes. Taken together, the concern to critical social psychologists is just how 'social' are both social neuroscience and social cognition? How much can studies in social neuroscience and social cognition tell us about people's everyday experiences in understanding our social world and how we view ourselves and others? Not only this, what can these studies tell us about where we get our ideas of reality in the first place?

Methods adopted within social cognition and social neuroscience aim to tightly control variables in order to carefully measure the ways people make social judgements. Social phenomena in the form of lists of words or lists of specific traits contrived by the researchers are typically used in these experimental tasks and cognitive processes or brain activities are inferred from the results. Increasingly photographs are used in experimental tasks such as implicit association tests (IAT) and film clips are used depicting people's behaviour. These are closer to everyday situations but still not the same as experiencing real everyday situations and may not enable us to fully understand how and why people make social judgements in their real-life social situations.

Research within social neuroscience and social cognition often aims to address social issues such as stereotyping and prejudice by seeking to understand how we form these judgements and engage in negative behaviour towards certain others. Therefore, whether we efficiently make social inferences or are prone to make errors of judgement through cognitive shortcuts can lead to crucial assumptions about the way individuals engage in negative judgements and behaviour towards others. Critical social psychologists are particularly concerned with the way that social cognition and social neuroscience make assumptions that these types of thinking and the ensuing behaviour are innate processes that are not only universal but are also inevitable. From the point of view of social cognition, the individual is a contained information processor who will engage in stereotyping as the most efficient way to make sense of their self and others even though the stereotypes may have very little to do with an accurate picture of those who are stereotyped. This can appear to paint a gloomy deterministic picture rather than addressing how stereotyping and prejudice may be reduced. To explore how prejudice may be reduced, critical social psychologists look to how people draw on cultural values and the taken-for-granted ways of talking about people in their society to make assumptions about others. Some critical social psychologists explore how these taken-for granted ideas about people become constructed, reinforced and maintained through language. (See 'The Language of Prejudice' in Chapter 13.)

A key criticism by critical social psychologists of social neuroscience and research into social cognition is that these approaches fail to take account of a person's personal history or their experiences within their social environment and culture. As pointed out earlier in this chapter, a person's culture has a considerable influence upon their social judgements and understanding their social world. Furthermore we cannot assume that everyone in the same culture has the same social experiences.

## QUESTIONS

**1** How far do you think people's social judgements are influenced by their individual characteristics, cognitions and brain mechanisms?

**2** What other factors could be involved in the way people make social judgements in real-life situations and in experimental tasks?

**3** Discuss the 'social' in social neuroscience and social cognition.

## SUMMING UP: SOCIAL BELIEFS AND JUDGEMENTS

### PERCEIVING OUR SOCIAL WORLD

☐ Our preconceptions strongly influence how we interpret and remember events. In a phenomenon called *priming*, people's prejudgements have striking effects on how they perceive and interpret information.

☐ Experiments have planted judgements or false ideas in people's minds *after* they have been given information. These experiments reveal that as *before-the-fact judgements* bias our perceptions and interpretations, so *after-the-fact judgements* bias our recall.

☐ *Belief perseverance* is the phenomenon in which people cling to their initial beliefs and the reasons why a belief might be true, even when the basis for the belief is discredited.

☐ Far from being a repository for facts about the past, our memories are actually formed when we construct them in language, and are subject to strong influence by the attitudes and feelings we hold at the time, and the demands of the context in which they are produced.

## JUDGING OUR SOCIAL WORLD

☐ We have an enormous capacity for automatic, efficient, intuitive thinking. We quickly assimilate information to judge types of persons. Our cognitive efficiency, though generally adaptive, comes at the price of occasional error. Since we are generally unaware of those errors entering our thinking, it is useful to identify ways in which we form and sustain false beliefs.

☐ First, we often overestimate our judgements. This *overconfidence phenomenon* stems partly from the much greater ease with which we can imagine why we might be right than why we might be wrong. Moreover, people are much more likely to search for information that can confirm their beliefs than for information that can disconfirm them.

☐ Second, when given compelling anecdotes or even useless information, we often ignore useful base-rate information. This is partly due to the later ease of recall of vivid information (the *availability heuristic*).

☐ Third, we are often swayed by illusions of correlation and personal control. It is tempting to perceive correlations where none exists (*illusory correlation*), and to think we can predict or control chance events (the *illusion of control*).

☐ Finally, moods infuse judgements. Good and bad moods trigger memories of experiences associated with those moods. Moods colour our interpretations of current experiences. And, by distracting us, moods can also influence how deeply or superficially we think when making judgements.

## EXPLAINING OUR SOCIAL WORLD

☐ Attribution theory involves how we explain people's behaviour.

☐ Although we usually make reasonable attributions, we often commit the *fundamental attribution error* (also called *correspondence bias*) when explaining other people's behaviour. This is more common in Western, individualistic cultures than in Eastern interdependent or collective cultures. We attribute their behaviour so much to their inner traits and attitudes that we discount situational constraints, even when those are obvious. Social categorization and stereotyping also influence our attributions. We expect people from certain social groups to behave in particular ways and this is based on very little actual information about them, therefore prone to error. We make this attribution error partly because when we watch someone act, that *person* is the focus of our attention and the situation is relatively invisible. When *we* act, our attention is usually on what we are reacting to – the situation is more visible.

☐ Social representations are the common-sense beliefs, values, theories and norms we hold about social phenomena. They are communicated and shared between people and are discussed by a 'thinking society' that shapes how we experience the world around us.

## EXPECTATIONS OF OUR SOCIAL WORLD

☐ Our beliefs sometimes take on lives of their own. Usually, our beliefs about others have a basis in reality. But studies of experimenter bias and teacher expectations show that an erroneous belief that certain people are unusually capable (or incapable) can lead teachers and researchers to give those people special treatment. This may elicit superior (or inferior) performance and, therefore, seem to confirm an assumption that is actually false.

☐ Similarly, in everyday life we often get *behavioural confirmation* of what we expect.

## CONCLUSIONS

☐ Research on social beliefs and judgements reveals how we form and sustain beliefs that usually serve us well but sometimes lead us astray. A balanced social psychology will therefore appreciate both the powers and the perils of social thinking.

---

## CRITICAL QUESTIONS

**1** What cognitive biases have social psychologists identified in how we perceive, understand and evaluate the world around us? Think further about what may influence these biases.

**2** When might it be useful to use mental shortcuts?

**3** Are these biases a symptom of flaws in human thinking, or evidence of our intelligence? And how 'social' are these biases?

**4** Under what conditions is the fundamental attribution error likely to occur?

**5** To what extent does social representation theory offer a more 'social' view of how we perceive, understand and evaluate the world around us?

---

## RECOMMENDED READINGS

Here are some recommended classic and contemporary readings on social judgements and how they have been understood and investigated in social psychology.

### Classic Papers

Kraut, R. E., & Lewis, S. H. (1982). Person perception and self-awareness: Knowledge of influences on one's own judgments. *Journal of Personality and Social Psychology*, **42**, 448–460.

*This paper presents interesting findings of people's awareness of their social cognitive processes when making social judgements.*

Kulik, J. A. (1983). Confirmatory attributions and the perpetuation of social beliefs. *Journal of Personality and Social Psychology*, **44**, 1171–1181.

*A carefully designed experiment to measure causal attributions about a target person's behaviour in particular situations after participants were led to believe the target person was either an extrovert or an introvert.*

Lerner, M. J., & Miller, D. T. (1978). Just world research and the attribution process: Looking back and ahead. *Psychological Bulletin*, **85**, 1030–1051.

*A comprehensive review of the early experimental research investigating the just world hypothesis. The paper also includes a clear explanation of the just world hypothesis and notes research that has led to its conceptualization.*

**Contemporary Papers**

Blanchard-Fields, F., Hertzog, C., & Horhotta, M. (2012). Violate my beliefs? Then you're to blame! Belief content as an explanation for causal attribution biases. *Psychology and Aging*, **27**, 324–337.

*This paper explores age differences in dispositional inferences when making blame attributions for negative outcomes in relationship situations. Both cognitive demand and personal relevant schemas are considered alongside the variation of social situations, social beliefs and values.*

Rubie-Davies, C. M. (2010). Teacher expectations and perceptions of student attributes: Is there a relationship? *British Journal of Educational Psychology*, **80**, 121–135.

*Rather than investigating teacher expectations at the individual level, this study takes it further by investigating teacher expectations of whole classes, including their perceptions of students' attributes and how these relate to academic achievement.*

Shane, J., & Heckhausen, J. (2013). University students' causal perceptions about social mobility: Diverging pathways for believers in personal merit and luck. *Journal of Vocational Behaviour*, **82**, 10–19.

*This paper investigates differences in contemporary ethically and economically diverse students' beliefs in causal factors for their future socioeconomic status attainment. In today's uncertain economic climate do students in the USA still endorse the American dream or endorse luck-oriented causal conceptions?*

**5**

"*Better contraceptives will control population only if people will use them.*"

*B. F. Skinner, Beyond Freedom and Dignity, 1971*

# ATTITUDES AND BEHAVIOUR

Gordon Allport declared 'attitudes' and attitude research as the most fundamental and important area of social psychology. Rather a grand statement. Why? Well, this is because attitudes may answer the question 'Why do people do what they do?' Philosophers, theologians and educators have long speculated about the connections between attitude and action, character and conduct, private word and public deed. Underlying much teaching, counselling and child rearing is an assumption that our private beliefs and feelings determine our public behaviour. So if we want to change someone's behaviour, we need to change their attitudes. This goes some way to explaining why our attitudes are under so much exploitation from the mass media, advertisers, politicians, policy-makers, and so on. We often see, for example, media coverage of Parliament or Presidential elections in most countries, and witness the direct appeals to the population's attitudes by politicians in order to win votes.

Although there are lots of different ways of defining attitudes, social psychologists are agreed that they involve evaluations (McGuire, 1985; Zanna & Rempel, 1988). These can be evaluations of anything. Darwin, religion, chocolate, exercise, Spain, war, even cabbage! When social psychologists talk about someone's attitude, they refer to beliefs and feelings related to a person, object or an event. Taken together, favourable or unfavourable evaluative reactions towards something – often rooted in beliefs and exhibited in feelings, and inclinations to act – define

**attitude** *a favourable or unfavourable evaluative reaction towards something or someone, rooted in one's beliefs, and exhibited in one's feelings and inclinations to act*

a person's attitude (Eagly & Chaiken, 2005). So a person may have a negative attitude towards coffee, a neutral attitude towards the French and a positive attitude towards their next-door neighbour. Attitudes provide an efficient way to size up the world. When we have to respond quickly to something, the way we feel about it can guide how we react. For example, a person who *believes* a particular ethnic group is lazy and aggressive may *feel* dislike for such people and therefore intend to *act* in a discriminatory manner. Yale University researchers proposed the ABC model of attitudes to define these three kinds of responses someone can have towards an 'attitude-object' (such as coffee, fox-hunters or cabbage). These are affective emotional responses, behavioural responses (verbal and non-verbal) and cognitive responses (our knowledge and beliefs). Or in other words, the ABC model proposes that attitudes are made up of feeling (A), doing (B) and thinking (C). See Figure 5.1 for the ABC representation of these three dimensions of attitudes.

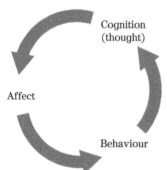

**FIGURE 5.1** The ABCs of attitudes: Affect (feelings), Behaviour tendency and Cognition (thoughts)

These three components of attitudes are thought to be responsible for our overall evaluation of an attitude-object. Social psychologists have sought to measure each of these components in assessing their contribution to an overall attitude. Affect can be measured physiologically (e.g. heart rate) or through self-report: 'Tell me how you feel about X.' Behaviour can be investigated through observations, or asking people to self-report on their past and present behaviour and their future intentions. Cognition requires information from the participant about their knowledge, beliefs and perceptions of whatever the attitude-object is being studied. But are all three always involved in the formation of an attitude? Do they all equally contribute? Consider Kristina Hood and Natalie Shook's (2013) finding that women's attitudes towards, and intentions to use, condoms was related to feelings (A) and beliefs (C) about them, but less so to past behaviour (B). The women in their study often expressed negative feelings about using them but had very positive beliefs and knowledge about why they should be used. The authors recommend that information such as this can aid researchers and health practitioners in encouraging people to practise safe sex. So an attitude may contain a mix of these components to a greater or lesser degree.

This ABC-model has a fairly long history in social psychology, having been around since the 1960s. It is not without its critics. This model contains within it some underlying assumptions about the nature of attitudes and their role. First, this model assumes that attitudes are enduring across time and space. As we shall see later in this chapter, not all social psychologists agree. Many argue that attitudes are constructed in the moment and are tailored for a specific context (see 'Attitudes as Social Actions'). Second, this model assumes that attitudes are linked to behaviour. But are they? As we shall see throughout this chapter, this is a major point of debate. If, and to what extent, attitudes are linked to behaviour is an argument that has exercised social psychologists for decades!

Where do these attitudes reside? Some social psychologists consider attitudes to be underlying cognitive entities within individuals that are fairly stable and enduring features of people. So, the reason why people tend to behave consistently is in some part due to their underlying stable and consistent attitudes. However, attitudes are also a part of our everyday interactions with other people. We offer our attitudes about various aspects of the world, and we listen to other people's. On the one hand they seem to have a cognitive aspect to them and on the other they also have a communicative component as we express and discuss our attitudes about things with one another in our everyday lives.

Our attitudes position and label us within the societies and communities where we live. If you hold negative attitudes towards eating meat, you may be labelled a vegetarian, which not only affects your own behaviour but also how other people evaluate and behave towards you. Attitudes define cultural and societal ideologies. Attitudes also explain our behaviour towards certain people and objects. If we hold negative attitudes about the poor (remember the 'just world hypothesis' from Chapter 4) this might explain why we do not give money to people who beg on the streets. There appears to be a link between attitude and behaviour.

In the beginning, social psychologists agreed: to know people's attitudes is to predict their actions. As demonstrated by the Nazi genocide, extreme attitudes can produce extreme behaviour. But some scepticism on the link had already been cast. The American sociologist Richard LaPiere (1934) demonstrated that attitudes do not necessarily predict behaviour. In a famous study, LaPiere travelled with a Chinese couple along the US west coast, staying overnight at guest houses and campsites. It is important to bear in mind that this study took place at a time when there was much anti-Chinese feeling throughout the USA. Despite this, only once were the Chinese couple denied accommodation during their travels. But when LaPiere later wrote to all the guest houses and campsites asking if they would accept Chinese guests, over 90 per cent said 'No'. So here we seem to have a difference in behaviour and attitudes towards the Chinese couple. Why? Perhaps the respectable middle-class Chinese couple simply didn't fit the stereotype the guest-house and campsite managers held of Chinese people. Or maybe the relationship between attitudes and behaviour is more complex.

Further problems with the attitude–behaviour relationship were found by Leon Festinger. In 1964 Festinger concluded that the evidence showed that *changing* people's attitudes hardly affects their behaviour at all (see Recommended Readings). Rather, Festinger believed the attitude–behaviour relation works the other way around. As Robert Abelson (1972) put it, we are 'very well trained and very good at finding reasons for what we do, but not very good at doing what we find reasons for'.

So, the topic of attitudes is a rich and complex one in social psychology. In this chapter we will consider both cognitive and communicative understandings of attitude, and explore this complex interplay of attitudes and behaviour.

## ORGANIZATION OF ATTITUDES

### FORMATION OF ATTITUDES

*How are our attitudes formed? Where do we get them from? Social psychologists have offered some explanations.*

The behavioural approach (or behaviourism) proposes that most attitudes are the result of direct experience with an object. Whether that experience is positive or negative will influence the formation of our attitudes towards it. A disastrous experience at the hairdresser as a child may well give you negative attitudes towards hairdressers for the rest of your life. S.J. Addison and Susan Thorpe (2004) found that people who had direct positive experiences with those who are mentally ill had formed positive attitudes to mental illness. Robert Zajonc (1968) suggested that simply being repeatedly presented with an object, or what he terms 'mere exposure', would invoke and influence an evaluation of it (see Chapter 9 on how exposure makes something more attractive).

**classical conditioning**
*a learned response which results from the repeated pairing of a neutral stimulus with a conditioned stimulus*

*Within the behaviourist approach* classical conditioning has also been suggested as an explanation for the formation of attitudes. This occurs when an attitude object is regularly paired with another stimulus that can be positive or negative. So, the presentation of an object in a pleasant environment increases our positive attitudes towards that object. For example, the child who is given crisps on a visit to the dentist may well form more positive attitudes about dentists as a consequence. The attitude object (the dentist) has been paired with a positive stimulus (crisps). Irving Janis et al. (1965) found that those participants who read a message while drinking a pleasant soft drink found it much more persuasive than those who did not. But are we seeing the formation of an attitude in these studies, or is it simply participants correctly guessing what the experimenter wants to hear? After all, it isn't too difficult to work out the hypothesis of the study. Michael Olson and Russell Fazio (2001) checked by hiding pairings of stimuli (e.g. a Pokemon character and the word 'excellent') amongst hundreds of other paired images which were presented very quickly to participants on a computer screen. Participants were instructed to hit a response key as soon as one of the target images appeared. A subsequent test revealed attitudes had been formed of the target images which were consistent with the positive or negative stimuli they had been paired with. Olson and Fazio concluded that in the real world, human beings unconsciously detect environmental

Do you give? Our attitudes towards homelessness go some way to predicting our actions.
SOURCE: © JerryPDX / iStock

co-occurences, and this is the basis of attitude formation. See Recommended Readings for a paper by Anthony Greenwald and his team outlining their thoughts on implicit measures of attitudes. Instrumental learning (sometimes called operant conditioning) suggests that positive or negative consequences that follow behaviour will inform positive or negative attitudes towards it. Many parents have told their children that if they behave in the doctor's waiting room, they will receive some sweets afterwards. This form of learning can have a large influence on children's attitudes. Recent neuroscience work has demonstrated that instrumental learning can be accomplished subconsciously. Mathias Pessiglione and his colleagues (2008) note the ability of pro-gamblers to subconsciously associate winning with behavioural cues from their opponents: the gamblers tell. The player isn't consciously aware of what it is that s/he perceives about the opponent, but is able to subconsciously detect the likelihood of winning. Pessiglione and colleagues report that even when participants are consciously unaware that instrumental learning is taking place, activity occurs in a specific area of the brain (ventral striatum) which demonstrates it is. This activity corresponds to participants when performing well on a task which requires subconscious instrumental learning to obtain rewards. In other words, participants have learned to associate consciously undetectable cues with rewards, but they don't know how they've done it. Advances in neuroscience now allow us to see where this subconscious learning has taken place. Both classical conditioning and instrumental learning focus on the role of positive and negative enforcers in forming attitudes towards an object.

*instrumental learning when behaviour is modified on the basis of consequences*

Parental and peer influence are also responsible for the formation of some of our attitudes. Tuuli Anna Mähöen and her colleagues (2011) considered the development of attitudes to other ethnic groups among young people aged 13-16 years. They found that for girls, their family's positive attitudes to other ethnic groups is sufficient to ensure they are also favourable. However, for boys, family influence is not enough. Boys also require direct positive personal experience with members of other ethnic groups. Interestingly for both boys and girls, family influence outweighs peer influence in the formation of attitudes.

From *social learning theory*, the concept of modelling describes the acquisition of behaviour through direct observation of other people (models) performing it and the subsequent positive or negative consequences (Bandura, 1973). Observing good consequences may well dispose us to form positive attitudes towards an object or behaviour. So attitudes are often formed on observations of behaviour rather than what we are told they should be. The instruction, 'Do as I say, not as I do' is familiar to many of us, yet we may focus on actions rather than words.

*modelling the acquisition of behaviour on the basis of observing that of others (models)*

We base our attitudes on those of other people when it is unclear what they objectively should be. Engaging in a process of *social comparison*, we check the legitimacy of our views. Leon Festinger argues that we tend to compare ourselves to other people we consider to be similar to ourselves in some way. Michael O'Fallon and Kenneth Butterfield (2012) note how this tendency can lead to unethical attitudes in the workplace. If our colleagues are perceived to be adopting unethical attitudes in order to get ahead, we are likely to join them. Sharing attitudes with colleagues, no matter how dubious they may be, gives the individual a shared sense of identity with their fellow workmates as well as a means of getting ahead.

We will return to social learning theory and the role of modelling in Chapter 8 on aggression; this concept is important when considering if aggression is a learned social behaviour rather than an innate one.

Daryl Bem's 'self-perception theory' suggests that actually, when it comes to forming attitudes, we perhaps don't put much thought into it at all. Instead we look at our own behaviour and from that deduce what our attitudes must be. We will consider self-perception theory in more detail later in this chapter.

*Cognitive theories* emphasize the role of cognitive development in the formation of attitudes. As we acquire experience of objects in the social world we develop attitudes about them. These attitudes require something of a balancing act as we build more and more associative connections between them. For example, Fritz Heider's balance theory considers the objects that are cognitively represented within the mind of the individual. Balance theory proposes that individuals are motivated to maintain balance between all the attitudes held about these various objects. We have a preference for agreement or accordance. In the absence of information to the contrary we tend to assume people see the world in the same way we do. Heider's theory suggests that because we have a preference to maintain balance in our attitudes, we will do whatever costs least effort to retain it.

*balance theory proposes that people will avoid having contradicting attitudes and evaluations of one object. If such inconsistency occurs, people are likely to adjust this*

The issue of cognitive consistency is the cornerstone of Leon Festinger's *Theory of Cognitive Dissonance* (1957), which asserts that people are motivated to keep their attitudes, beliefs and behaviour consistent. When they get out of line, people will reduce feelings of dissonance by changing their attitudes, beliefs or behaviour or may even justify having them to rationalize the discrepancy. We will return to this theory later in our discussion of the link between attitudes and behaviour.

For the moment it is worth us observing that all of these approaches emphasize the role of experience in the formation of attitudes, and alert us to the influence our network of social relationships, interactions and methods of communication (e.g. mass media) have on them.

## FUNCTION OF ATTITUDES

Attitudes of course, also have functions. They 'do' things. Perhaps most importantly, they immediately provide us with information about how to respond to an attitude-object. As we saw in Chapter 4, human beings have developed a range of cognitive strategies to help them navigate their way around a complex world. Having attitudes about things focuses our attention, enabling us to filter out unnecessary or unimportant features of our environment. They also aid our memory, free up cognitive space to deal with other things, help us make decisions, and categorise the world in meaningful ways. For example, knowing that we have positive or negative attitudes towards fox-hunting helps us work out how to respond when confronted by a fox-hunting parade that goes through our village. Some researchers have proposed that the main function of attitudes also includes serving our psychological needs. The work of M. Brewster Smith and Daniel Katz has been at the forefront of developing a functional approach to the study of attitudes. Daniel Katz (1960) has suggested that attitudes have four main functions.

1 A knowledge function – they provide a sense of structure and order, helping us to explain and understand the world based on our knowledge of objects and our evaluations of them.

2 An instrumental function – they allow us to maximize our chances of receiving rewards and minimizing the likelihood of negative outcomes due to our

evaluation of objects as 'good' or 'bad' for us. We will change our attitudes if it is likely to result in favourable rewards.

**3** An ego defensive function – they protect threats to our sense of self by projecting insecurities about our self onto others. Attitudes can serve as a defence mechanism against anxiety.

**4** A value-expressive function – they allow us to express and reinforce our sense of self and identity by displaying those attitudes we consider important.

Katz maintains that attitudes may serve one or more of these functions at any one time (see Recommended Readings). Which ones they will fulfil depends upon the context in which it is presented. Katz further suggests that we will change our attitudes towards something when they no longer serve our psychological needs. So it isn't so much that our perception of the attitude-object which changes, but our psychological requirements.

Social psychological work has tended to focus upon the structure of attitudes rather than their content and function. Thankfully, there have been some recent attempts to empirically demonstrate Katz's functional approach. Scott Vollum and Jacqueline Buffington-Vollum (2010) observed that people's support for the death penalty served a value-expressive function. It enabled those individuals to portray a particular self-image to the world, which is so important that she or he will hold on to that attitude even when presented with information that points out some of the problems of having a death penalty. Rajdeep Grewal and colleagues (2000) point out that understanding the value-expressive functions of attitudes can assist companies in targeting products at consumers. Owning products helps people achieve a particular identity and status, therefore they have positive attitudes towards them. Knowing what identity someone wants to achieve can help in targeting a particular product at them. Maria Knight Lapinski and Franklin Boster (2001) note that attitude objects which threaten our sense of self, serve an ego-defensive function, projecting our own insecurities onto it.

Attitudes can also help or hinder us in coping during times of trouble. Barbara Felton and colleagues (1980) found that women who had non-traditional sex-role attitudes coped much better during periods of marital disruption than those who held traditional attitudes towards the role of men and women. Having particular attitudes to how men and women should behave in a marriage can serve a knowledge function, helping or hindering us when dealing with marital strife. Indeed it seems once formed, attitudes are extremely resistant to change as Rune Lines (2005) found out when changes were proposed within the workplace. Employees developed attitudes towards the change very quickly. These functioned to filter employees' attention to the detail (e.g. only focusing on perceived threats to jobs), bias memory for that detail, and create resistance to information which challenges the attitude in any way (e.g. that there won't be any job losses).

More recently attitude theorists have revised Katz's original functions, adding to the list. Gregory Herek (1987) identifies an *experiential schematic* function based on experience and stereotypes that help guide our reactions to objects. For example, Brian Griffiths and Anne Pedersen (2009) found that experience helped explain positive reactions to Muslim and indigenous Australians by residents in Perth. Those who had negative reactions towards these groups lacked direct

People often display their attitudes publicly to express their sense of self-identity.

SOURCE: Reproduced with kind permission of Liberty. www.liberty-human-rights.org.uk

positive experiences and instead were influenced by stereotypes. Similar findings are reported by Safiyya Khan and Anne Pedersen (2010) who observed the importance of value-expressive and experiential-schematic functions of attitudes in accepting Black African immigrants to Australia, and *indirect experiential schematic* (reliance on stereotypes) in rejecting them. Attitudes only change when they no longer serve their function. It is important to remember that attitudes not only perform a function for the individual that holds them, but also social functions in establishing meaning in social interaction. We shall consider these social aspects of attitudes more closely later in this chapter.

## MEASURING ATTITUDES

So far we've noted the complex definitions, organization and functions of attitudes. We've already begun to see some of the problems in trying to capture them. They are organized in complex associative networks and are prone to change depending on the context in which they are produced. There are some attitudes we're not even consciously aware of. So how can the social psychologist begin to measure them? It's not easy!

One of the earliest methods for studying attitudes was to simply ask people what they were. The *case method* asks people what their, or their friends', attitudes are towards something. These kinds of studies can require participants to verbally describe the attitudes (sometimes called the informal case method) or to write them down essay style (formal case method). For example, Emory S. Bogardus (1925) asked Americans to outline their attitudes to Filipinos in this way. D. D. Droba (1932) points out that while case studies provide us with some understanding of the development and depth of someone's attitudes, such descriptions cannot easily be subject to any kind of statistical analyses. Consequently, while different methods have been put forward, many social psychologists agree that the best way to study attitudes is quantitatively. Droba outlines some of the historical development of quantitative measures for studying attitudes in social psychology. For example, the *method of absolute ranking* requires participants to read a statement such as: 'Jews will try to get the best of a bargain even if they have to cheat to do so', and then indicate their attitude by choosing one of five options: 'All', 'Most', 'Many', 'Few', 'No'. Quick to administer but they have drawbacks. First, participants are given very few choices to reflect their attitude. Second, how can we be sure that the choices have the same meaning for everyone who takes the test? What one participant takes 'Most' to mean, may be very different from another's definition. Third, how do we know the distance between 'All' and 'Most' is equivalent to that between 'Most' and 'Many'? The alternative *method of relative ranking* requires participants to rank either attitude-objects in order of preference (e.g. nationalities) or attitude statements about an object. However, once again we have the problem of analyzing such responses. How do we know that what one participant has ranked as number 1 (e.g. the French) is equivalent to someone else's number 1 rank? Does this reflect the same positive attitude? The *graphic rating scale* is the indication of an attitude along a line. There are steps plotted along the line which may be represented by words, statements or numbers. Somewhere along the line the participant notes his or her attitude towards some object or idea. These could be

**Method of Absolute Ranking**

Choose the response which best reflects your attitude to the following statement:

'Jews will try to get the best of a bargain even if they have to cheat to do so'

All

Most

Many

Few

No

*(from Droba, D.D. (1932). Methods for measuring attitudes. Psychological Bulletin, 29(5), 309–323.)*

**Method of Relative Ranking**

Arrange the following list of occupations in order of their social standing according to your own judgment:

Banker

Carpenter

Engineer

Clergyman

Professor

Factory Manager

Insurance Agent

Machinist

Man of Leisure

Soldier

*(from Anderson, W.A. (1927). The occupational attitudes and choices of a group of college men, Part I. Social Forces, 6(2), 278–283.)*

**Graphic Rating Scale**

Indicate using an 'X', your own general political attitude:

/            /            /            /

Radicalism      Liberalism      Conservatism      Reactionaryism

*(from Rice, S.A. (1926). Differential changes of political preference under campaign stimulation. Journal of Abnormal and Social Psychology, 21(3), 297–303.)*

**Method of Paired Comparisons**

Underline the one nationality of the pair, that would you rather associate with:

Japanese – Italian

*(from Thurstone, L.L. (1928). An experimental study of nationality preferences. Journal of General Psychology, 1, 405–425.)*

FIGURE 5.2   Early methods for measuring attitudes

completed to reflect the participant's own attitude or those of friends and family. People want to be seen in a positive light. The *method of paired comparisons*, first used by Louis Leon Thurstone (1928b) presented participants with a pair of words or statements, from which s/he must choose which one of the pair best reflected her or his attitude. Thurstone used this method to measure attitudes to different nationalities and races. It is from these early attempts to quantitatively measure attitudes that different attitude scales have been developed.

Let's consider some of the types of attitude scales currently used in social psychology.

### The Thurstone Scale

Developed by Louis Leon Thurstone (1928a) it comprises a questionnaire containing 22 independent statements about a particular issue. The participant was asked to rate their feelings towards each of the items on a scale of 1–11, indicating whether they had favourable or unfavourable feelings towards it. This method of measuring attitudes was based on a one-component model of feelings towards an object. Those items that reflected a positive attitude were given higher numerical scores than those that were negative. The statements could then be statistically analysed.

A recent example comes from James Guffey and colleagues (2007) who used the Thurstone scale to examine attitudes towards the police by serving police officers and police agencies. On a scale of 1–11, participants rated how favourable each of the 27 statements presented to them was in evaluating police officers. 1 reflected extremely unfavourable, and 11 extremely favourable. The statements included: 'He/She possesses excellent judgement' and 'He/She possesses excellent moral character'.

### The Likert Scale

This bipolar scaling method was developed to simplify the Thurstone questionnaire in terms of scoring as it is fairly cumbersome! Rensis Likert (1932) produced a scale that contained statements (similar to the Thurstone scale); for example, 'A university education makes people more selfish', but this scale allowed for five response categories:

1 = Strongly disagree

2 = Disagree

3 = Neither disagree or agree

4 = Agree

5 = Strongly agree

For each item the participant ticks which numbered response best reflects their attitude to the statement presented. On completion of the scale the participant's scores are calculated and used as a measure of his or her attitudes towards a particular issue. In developing the attitude measurement instrument the researcher ensures that all the statements used are good indicators of attitudes (i.e. they provoke scores of 1–2 or 4–5), and any ambiguous ones, or those that simply do not provoke an attitude (regularly getting a score of 3), are removed (a process sometimes referred to as 'item analysis'). The Likert scale remains a very popular measuring tool for attitudes in social psychology. For example, Shelley

## research close-up

DEVELOPMENT AND VALIDATION OF A SCALE MEASURING ATTITUDES TOWARD NON-DRINKERS

*Source: Regan, D. & Morrison, T.G. (2011). Development and validation of a scale measuring attitudes toward non-drinkers.* Substance Use & Misuse, *46, 580–590.*

### Introduction

Is binge-drinking a way of fitting in? Do we engage in excessive alcohol consumption to avoid the social embarrassment of being a non-alcohol-drinker? Daniel Regan and Todd Morrison decided to find out. Research was conducted in Ireland, a country that has one of the highest rates of binge-drinking in Europe. Social Identity Theory (SIT) proposes that individuals are motivated to identify with groups that they feel they belong to, and to evaluate those groups positively. In countries such as Ireland, where drinking alcohol is the 'norm', might non-drinkers constitute an outgroup that many people are motivated to avoid being identified with? Is this expressed in the form of negative attitudes towards non-drinkers, and excessive consumption of alcohol?

### Method

Three studies aimed to find out whether attitudes towards non-drinkers motivated the quantity and frequency of alcohol consumption and binge-drinking. Whilst the first study tested the robustness of the Regan Attitudes towards Non-Drinkers Scale (RANDS), studies 2 and 3 assessed how well it predicted drinking behaviour. The RANDS contains 74 items such as: 'I would not see there being a problem socially, with myself being a non-drinker' and 'I would hate to be a non-drinker'.

In study 2, 148 undergraduate students of a university in Western Ireland, between the ages of 19 and 21 took part. They were given two questionnaires. The first asked them to estimate the amount of alcohol they drank, and how frequently they engaged in binge-drinking. The second was the RANDS. RANDS is an 11-item scale about attitudes towards non-drinkers. Attitudes are assessed using a 5-point Likert scale, where a high score indicates negative attitudes to non-drinkers.

In study 3, 236 individuals comprising students and non-students, with an age range of 17–63, took part. They were given six questionnaires. As in study 1, they were given a measure of the quantity and frequency of their alcohol consumption, and the RANDS. In addition they were also given a 5-point Likert scale to measure their *sensation-seeking behaviour*, with a high score denoting high levels of this behaviour. Participants were also given a 5-point Likert scale to measure their *fear of being negatively evaluated*. A high score denoted a greater fear of being negatively evaluated. They were also tested for their *need to belong*. This 5-point scale was scored such that a high score denoted high need to fit in with others. Finally, participants were given a *social-desirability* scale to check they were giving answers that reflected their actual behaviour and attitudes rather than reporting socially desirable ones.

### Results

In both studies 2 and 3, attitudes on RANDS predicted the amount of alcohol participants consumed and the frequency in which they indulged in binge-drinking. The more negative their attitudes towards non-drinkers, the more likely they were to drink alcohol.

In study 3, participants under the age of 21 years reported higher quantities and frequencies of drinking alcohol than older participants. This younger age group also indicated a stronger need to belong, greater levels of sensation-seeking behaviour, and higher negative attitudes towards non-drinkers than those participants over the age of 21 years. However, scores on RANDS show no relationship with those on the fear of negative evaluation scale. For those over the age of 21 years, scores on RANDS correlate with sensation-seeking behaviour (but not for those under 21 years old). So, for the older age group, the more you engage in sensation-seeking behaviour, the more negative your attitudes are towards non-drinkers.

## Discussion

Those people who express negative attitudes towards non-drinkers (as identified on RANDS) consume more alcohol, engage in binge-drinking, and have a stronger need to belong. However, attitudes towards non-drinkers are not related to a fear of negative evaluation, and for those under 21 years of age, it doesn't have any relationship with sensation-seeking either.

So it seems peer pressure and the desire to identify positively with 'normative' behaviour can involve excessive alcohol-drinking to avoid the risk of social exclusion as a non-drinker. Group boundaries between drinkers (normative) and non-drinkers (deviant) are marked in terms of behaviour (alcohol consumption) and attitudes. However, the authors note that their study concerned predominantly university students, so further research is needed into attitudes towards non-drinkers from a broader population.

Long and colleagues (2012) examined predominantly female students' attitudes towards sex-workers, using the Hostility Towards Women Likert scale as part of their investigation. This scale includes 10 statements such as 'Sex workers are unattractive' and 'Sex workers are responsible for sexually transmitted infections'. Participants rate on a scale of 1–7 how much they disagree (1 – strongly disagree) or agree (7 – strongly agree) with each item. They found that those who held more hostile attitudes towards women held negative stereotypical attitudes towards sex-workers.

### Osgood's Semantic Differential Scale

Unlike Thurstone and Likert scales, Charles Osgood's semantic differential scale does not use statements, but instead asks participants to rate their feelings on a topic on a bipolar scale of opposing adjectives. So, for example:

| Government's policy on tackling economic recession | | | | | | | | |
|---|---|---|---|---|---|---|---|---|
| Good | 1 | 2 | 3 | 4 | 5 | 6 | 7 | Bad |
| Strong | | | | | | | | Weak |
| Nice | | | | | | | | Evil |
| Informed | | | | | | | | Misguided |

On a series of seven points (with a midway point) ranging from one adjective to its opposing other, the participant rates their feelings about the issue in question. Osgood makes the case that attitudes contain emotional meaning (connotative) reflected in our use of adjectives to describe how we feel about something (e.g. good/bad, nice/evil). Osgood proposed that there are essentially three evaluative dimensions which people use in attitudes: activity, evaluation and potency.

Ana Cazáres (2010) used the Osgood semantic differential scale to examine psychology students' attitudes towards the use of technology in their classes. The scale consisted of 28 bipolar adjectives (i.e. Necessary – Not Necessary) presented on a scale of 1–7. What she discovered was that attitudes towards the use of technology in the classroom did not predict proficiency at using it.

The development of attitude scales has proved popular. They are extremely quick to construct and convenient to administer and score. But, they do suffer from some problems such as restricting people's responses to a narrow range of options and inducing what is sometimes called acquiescence biases (just saying yes/agreeing to everything!). One obvious problem with attitude scales such as these is that of social desirability. Might people be simply giving us socially desirable attitude expressions rather than their true attitudes? If so, how accurate can our measures be? As we shall see, this becomes an issue when trying to study people's prejudicial attitudes. Will someone self-report that they hold prejudiced attitudes to old people, homosexuals, women? Unlikely. We also know that people are often unaware of their attitudes. They hold implicit attitudes. How can they inform us about attitudes of which they are unaware?

The quantitative measures outlined so far rely on people being able to self-report on their attitudes accurately. Thankfully, there are some ways around this. One way is to use *symbolic attitude measures*. These present statements that are more subtle in their approach. Consider this example from Kurt Boniecki (1998) '*Black students receive too much financial assistance from the university*'. But there are problems here too. Whilst this may ensure a less monitored response, it may also rely on knowledge rather than attitudes towards Black students. Another way is to obtain physiological measures of attitudes, e.g. heart rate, skin resistance, pupil dilation. These are not usually under our conscious control and can be measured without the participant realizing it's their attitudes that are being studied. However, the problem with these kinds of measures is that it is difficult to relate a physiological response to an attitude (Cacioppo & Petty, 1981). Physiological responses happen in response to all kinds of environmental features (e.g. the heating, the lighting, the presence of someone in the room). Can we be sure it's in response to the attitude we're interested in? Another method that's been used is observational techniques. These are really only useful when the person being observed is unaware that they are the subject of an observation. Awareness of being observed can lead to changes in behaviour, which may reflect social desirability responses (as in self-reports). Watching people can tell us a lot about their attitudes. You may have witnessed the non-verbal behaviour of a group of friends sitting down for a meal. Who they choose to sit next to, and who they avoid, tells us a lot about their attitudes towards certain people. Emory S. Bogardus' social distance scale (1925) has been developed and used in the study of attitudes towards ethnic and racial groups. Those we hold positive attitudes towards tend to be further into our personal space than those we maintain social distance from. Nishra Dogra and colleagues (2012) used the social distance scale to examine the attitudes of Nigerian children towards people with mental illness. They found that these children held very negative attitudes towards people who are mentally ill, which was reflected in their social and physical distance from them. Alternatively, tracing the display of attitudes in texts over time (e.g. reports about binge drinking in men and women in national newspapers) can tell us something about how they change.

social distance scale *measures people's willingness to have close social contact with people from diverse social groups*

Another way to get around the problems associated with measures of explicitly expressed attitudes is to measure those attitudes we hold unconsciously. Anthony

implicit association
test (IAT) *an implicit*
*method of measuring*
*attitudes based on*
*automatic associations*
*that exist between*
*objects and concepts*

Greenwald, Debbie McGhee and Jordan Schwartz (1998), wanted to study implicit attitudes and the influence they have on behaviour. To do so, they developed the implicit association test (IAT). The most prevalent IATs measure race bias (see Chapter 13 on prejudice) measuring associations between the presentation of black faces and negative words, but they have also been used to look at other kinds of prejudices such as ageism (e.g. Hummert et al., 2002) and sexism (Rudman & Glick, 2008). Implicit associations affect the way we perceive the world and evaluate it. IATs have become increasingly popular as they appear to avoid the tricky problems faced by explicit measures such as faking responses in attending to concerns with social desirability. As attitudes exist in associative networks, it is thought that these associations should be quickly recognized. In an IAT, participants are faced with four sets of stimuli comprising two types of attitude objects (e.g. old people and young people), and two types of words based on 'valence' (attractiveness and aversiveness). During the test, the participant is presented with pairs of the attitude object (e.g. a picture of a young face) with a valence word (e.g. attractive). The task of the respondent is simply to decide as quickly as they can whether the valence word is Good or Bad indicating their decision by hitting a computer response key. If we associate some things together (e.g. young people as attractive) we should be very quick to recognize that the valence word is Good. However, if the attitude object is paired with a valence word we wouldn't normally associate them with (e.g. a young face and the word 'slow') we should be much slower to recognize that this is a Bad word. For example, Ralf Brand and his colleagues (2011) measured athletes' attitudes towards illegal doping using an IAT. Athletes were given words to indicate two types of attitude object: those relating to illegal doping substances (e.g. 'peptide hormones', 'amphetamines') and those relating to tea (e.g. 'herbal', 'hibiscus flowers'). These words were then paired with valence words (e.g. 'joy', 'agony'). The speed at which they recognized the valence word as Good or Bad was measured. What Brand found was that his athletes were much quicker to recognize Bad words when they were paired with doping substances than when paired with tea words. He concludes that athletes hold negative attitudes towards doping substances. Kathleen Schmidt and Brian Nosek (2010) used IATs to reveal that since Barack Obama has been the president of the US there has been no change in attitudes towards black people as a result. Attitudes still remain as negative as they were prior to his presidency.

Champions of IAT tests argue they rely solely on automatic processes and as participants have no conscious control over them they are robust tests of attitudes. But they have come under scrutiny from other researchers. One criticism concerns the construct validity of these tests. Are they actually a measure of attitudes, or of something else? Eric Siegel (Siegel et al., 2012) is sceptical. He argues there is a lack of consistency on these tests by individuals over time. The context in which these tests take place seems to have some effect on people's responses. Participants may be responding to cues in the environment in which the test takes place, be that the physical environment and/or the researcher conducting the experiment, which affects how quickly they respond to the IAT. Siegel also suggests that these tests may be a measure of processing speed rather than attitudes. You may simply be very quick to respond to these kinds of tasks. If we compare younger people with older people we may find older people are slower to respond. Is this because they hold different attitudes or because their processing speed is slower? Questions also concern the predictive validity of IATs. Do they actually predict our future behaviour? The results of IAT tests have real-world implications if we take them seriously. Greenwald and colleagues (2009) suggest that we should use both explicit and implicit attitude measures. The debate over the usefulness of implicit association tests is by no means resolved.

As we move to consider the relationship between attitudes and behaviour, we shall come across many empirical examples of studies using various methods for measuring attitudes (and behaviour). On our journey we can ponder their relative strengths and weaknesses in providing social psychologists with an understanding of the nature and expression of attitudes and their role in the performance of behaviour.

Observing people's seating arrangements and non-verbal behaviour can sometimes offer some interesting insights into their attitudes towards each other.

SOURCE: © nullplus/iStock

## HOW WELL DO OUR ATTITUDES PREDICT OUR BEHAVIOUR?

*To what extent, and under what conditions, do the attitudes of the heart drive our outward actions? Why were social psychologists at first surprised by a seemingly small connection between attitudes and actions?*

A blow to the supposed power of attitudes came when social psychologist Allan Wicker (1969) reviewed several dozen research studies covering a wide variety of people, attitudes and behaviours. Wicker offered a shocking conclusion: people's expressed attitudes hardly predicted their varying behaviours.

- ☐ Student attitudes towards cheating bore little relation to the likelihood of their actually cheating.

- ☐ Attitudes towards the church were only modestly linked with church attendance on any given Sunday.

- ☐ Self-described racial attitudes provided little clue to behaviours in actual situations.

An example of the disjuncture between attitudes and actions is what Daniel Batson and his colleagues (1997a, 2002; Batson & Thompson, 2001) call 'moral hypocrisy' (appearing moral while avoiding the costs of being so). Their studies presented people with an appealing task (where the participant could earn raffle tickets towards a cash prize) and a dull task with no positive consequences. The participants had to assign themselves to one of the tasks and a supposed second participant to the other. Only 1 in 20 believed that assigning the positive task to themselves was the more moral thing to do, yet 80 per cent did so. In follow-up experiments on moral hypocrisy, participants were given coins they could flip privately if they wished. Even if they chose to flip, 90 per cent assigned themselves to the positive task! (Was that because they could specify the consequences of heads and tails after the coin toss?) In yet another experiment, Batson put a sticker on each side of the coin, indicating what the flip outcome would signify. Still, 24 of 28 people who made the toss assigned themselves to the positive task. When morality and greed were put on a collision course, greed won.

If people don't walk the same line that they talk, it's little wonder that attempts to change behaviour by changing attitudes often fail. Warnings about the dangers of smoking affect only minimally those who already smoke if used as the only means. Increasing public awareness of the desensitizing and brutalizing effects of television violence has stimulated many people to voice a desire for less violent programming – yet they still watch media murder as much as ever. Sex education programmes have often influenced *attitudes* towards abstinence and condom use without affecting long-term abstinence and condom use *behaviours*. Shelley Aikman and colleagues (2006) found that having positive attitudes towards healthy foods did not predict eating them. Rather, taste and having eaten food in the past was a better predictor of current eating habits. We are, it seems, a population of hypocrites.

All in all, the developing picture of what controls behaviour emphasized external social influences, such as others' behaviour and expectations, and played down internal factors, such as attitudes and personality. The original thesis that attitudes determine actions was countered during the 1960s by the antithesis that attitudes determine virtually nothing.

Thesis. Antithesis. Is there a synthesis? The surprising finding that what people *say* often differs from what they *do* sent social psychologists scurrying to find out why. Surely, we reasoned, convictions and feelings must sometimes make a difference.

## WHEN ATTITUDES PREDICT BEHAVIOUR

The reason – now obvious – why our behaviour and our expressed attitudes differ is that both are subject to other influences. Many other influences. One social psychologist counted 40 factors that complicate their relationship (Triandis, 1982; see also Kraus, 1995). But if we could just neutralize the other influences on behaviour – make all other things equal – might attitudes accurately predict behaviours?

## WHEN SOCIAL INFLUENCES ON WHAT WE SAY ARE MINIMAL

Unlike a physician measuring heart rate, social psychologists never get a direct reading on attitudes. Rather, we measure *expressed* attitudes. Like other behaviours, expressions are subject to outside influences. Sometimes, for example, we say what we think others want to hear.

Today's social psychologists have some clever means at their disposal for minimizing social influences on people's attitude reports. One method offers a 'bogus pipeline' to the heart. It wires people to a fake lie detector, which the participants are told is real. The researchers show them how well it displays their (previously obtained) attitudes, and then ask them new questions. In one study, students admitted more prejudice when hooked up (Sigall & Page, 1971). No wonder people who are first persuaded that lie detectors work may then admit the truth – in which case, the lie detector has worked! (Note the irony of deceiving people to elicit their truthfulness.) Also, across 126 studies, implicit attitudes measured by the Implicit Association Test (IAT) have correlated, on average, a modest .24 with explicit self-reported attitudes (Hofmann et al., 2005).

## WHEN OTHER INFLUENCES ON BEHAVIOUR ARE MINIMAL

On any occasion, it's not only our inner attitudes that guide us but also the situation we face. Social influences can be enormous – enormous enough to induce people to violate their deepest convictions. So, would *averaging* many occasions enable us to detect more clearly the impact of our attitudes?

To use a research example, people's general attitude towards religion poorly predicts whether they will go to worship during the coming week (because attendance is also influenced by the weather, the worship leader, how one is feeling, and so forth). But religious attitudes predict quite well the total quantity of religious behaviours over time (Fishbein & Ajzen, 1974; Kahle & Berman, 1979). The findings define a *principle of aggregation*: the effects of an attitude become more apparent when we look at a person's aggregate or average behaviour rather than at isolated acts. We also need to take into account if people actually can engage in the behaviour they have an attitude towards. For example, someone may have very positive attitudes towards vigorous exercise yet not be able to engage in such exercise for health reasons.

## WHEN ATTITUDES SPECIFIC TO THE BEHAVIOUR ARE EXAMINED

Icek Ajzen and Martin Fishbein (1977, 2005) point out that when the measured attitude is a general one – say, an attitude towards Asians – and the behaviour is very specific – say, a decision whether to help a particular Asian in a particular situation – we should not expect a close correspondence between words and actions. Indeed, report Fishbein and Ajzen, in 26 out of 27 such research studies, attitudes did not predict behaviour. But self-reported attitudes did predict self-reports of behaviour in all 26 studies they could find in which the measured attitude was directly pertinent to the situation. Thus, attitudes towards the general concept of 'health fitness' poorly predict specific exercise and dietary practices, but an individual's attitudes about the costs and benefits of jogging are a fairly strong predictor of whether he or she jogs regularly. Ajzen and Fishbein's theory of reasoned action (TRA) offers us a model for explaining the relationship between attitude and behaviour.

*theory of reasoned action (TRA) that a person's intended behaviour is contingent upon their attitude about that behaviour and subjective norms*

### The Theory of Reasoned Action

To predict behavioural intention we need to know four things about a person:

1. their expectation of important or significant others – i.e. how they will view your behaviour (subjective norms)

2. their attitudes towards the behaviour (positive or negative)

3. their behavioural intention

4. their actual behaviour.

What is immediately striking about this approach is that it goes beyond simply a consideration of attitude and behaviour. It also includes an understanding of subjective norms (what other people think about the behaviour) and intentions for behaviour. This theory has received much empirical support. Four dozen experimental tests confirm that inducing new intentions induces new behaviour (Webb & Sheeran, 2006).

However, this theory has one quite serious limitation. It can only be applied to those behaviours we have conscious control of (volitional control). What about those behaviours we have less, or no, control of? How can those be understood in relation to attitudes?

### The Theory of Planned Behaviour

In light of this criticism, Icek Ajzen revisited the theory to include an additional element, that of 'perceived behavioural control'. This new element refers to how much control someone believes they have in doing a behaviour. Ajzen thought this was probably a crucial part in working out whether they would perform it or not. So the renamed theory of planned behaviour (TPB) now accounted for those behaviours we have less control of (see Figure 5.3).

The theory of planned behaviour has also received a lot of empirical support. For example, Joshua Smith and his colleagues (2008) found that men are less likely to seek psychological help (or therapy) than women. Using the TPB the authors found that men hold negative attitudes about psychological help, worried how they will be viewed by others and society if they seek such services. Eun-Seok Cha, Kevin Kim and Thelma Patrick (2008) found that the theory of planned behaviour could explain gender differences in condom use among Korean students. While peer norms (i.e. what significant others will think) were important for men in predicting condom use, it wasn't important for women. The authors suggest this reflects a cultural norm which dictates that men can discuss sexual activities with others, but for women this is taboo. Richard Wood and Mark Griffiths (2004) have used the TPB to explain the relationship between young people's attitudes

*theory of planned behaviour (TPB) as TRA, but with the addition that people's behaviour is shaped by their confidence in being able to perform it, or having it under their control*

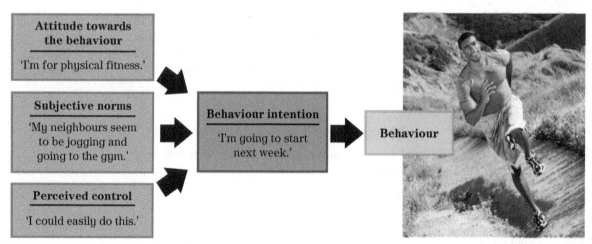

**FIGURE 5.3** The theory of planned behaviour

Icek Ajzen, working with Martin Fishbein, has shown that one's (a) attitudes, (b) perceived social norms, and (c) feelings of control together determine one's intentions, which guide behaviour.

Compared with their general attitudes towards a healthy lifestyle, people's specific attitudes regarding jogging predict their jogging behaviour much better.

SOURCE: © Tom Young/iStock

to gambling and playing the National Lottery and scratchcards in the UK. They discovered a range of factors to explain why young people engage in such behaviour, including the positive reinforcement of such activity from parents, friends and society, and that it's often not recognized as gambling. Of particular interest is the role of perceived behavioural control in this study. Wood and Griffiths found that when they asked participants about the likelihood of winning, many participants thought they had a good chance of doing so. The authors point to the availability heuristic we mentioned in Chapter 4, which suggests that in the absence of detailed information, people make assumptions on the basis of the limited information they do have (for example, the publicity afforded to winners).

The TPB has been used extensively in health research to investigate the relationship between attitudes and healthy eating behaviour. In the Netherlands, Gert-Jan de Bruijn, Willemieke Kroeze, Anke Oenema and Johannes Brug (2008) have found that the TPB is a good predictor of the amount of saturated fat an adult consumes. Their Dutch participants were asked how often they ate food high in saturated fat, what they believed others would think of them eating such food, what kinds of food they usually eat, their attitudes towards such food, and how much control they believed they had in choosing their diet. While their participants often held negative attitudes towards fatty food, their perceived lack of control over their diet (e.g. choosing convenient food due to a busy lifestyle) and their past eating habits were good predictors of what food they would continue to eat now and in the future. In a qualitative approach to the TPB, Kirsten Dunn, Philip Mohr, Carlene Wilson and Gary Wittert (2008) interviewed Australian adults about their beliefs and attitudes towards fast food. They also found that while participants held very negative attitudes towards fast food, and even noted how other people would think badly of them for eating fast food, it was their perceived lack of behavioural control over their diet that led to the consumption of fast food.

So we can see that the relationship between attitudes and behaviour is complicated by a range of other factors.

The TPB has been modified slightly to include 'identity'. Melanie Giles and her colleagues (2004) used the TPB to predict whether students at the University of Ulster would give blood when the blood donation service arrived, on the basis of the answers they'd given on a questionnaire prior to its arrival. As well as asking students about their attitudes towards blood donation, what other people would think if they donated blood and their ability to give blood, they also included an item about their self-identity (e.g. 'To give blood is an important part of who I am'). They found a correlation between having blood donation as part of one's self-identity and actual blood donation.

Although the Theory of Planned Behaviour has received considerable empirical support, and is very popular in applied areas such as health research, it has been subject to some criticism. Russell Fazio and Michael Olson (2003) think that the theory requires too specific a definition of the attitude for it to be linked to behaviour. As they suggest, discovering the attitude towards 'eating chocolate on the counter within the next two minutes' leads to subsequently eating it, would not be very surprising. Perhaps in its efforts to pin down the detailed relationship between specific attitude and specific behaviour, the TPB has lost sight of relating more general enduring attitudes to behaviour? Fazio and Olson's biggest criticism though, of the TPB, is that it only considers intentional behaviour. The TPB tends to assume that we cogitate and deliberate over whether we want to, can do, and what others will think about us if we do, behave in a particular way. Considering the automaticity of attitudes in helping us to navigate our way around our environment, it seems likely then that we often just behave accordingly but thoughtlessly. We do not always ruminate over our behaviour before we do it. We don't worry what our parents will think, whether the behaviour fits in with our image of ourselves, or whether we can actually succeed. Behaviour can be spontaneous rather than carefully thought through.

So far we have seen two conditions under which attitudes will predict behaviour:

**1** when we minimize other influences upon our attitude statements and on our behaviour, and

**2** when the attitude is specifically relevant to the observed behaviour.

There is a third condition: an attitude predicts behaviour better when the attitude is potent.

## WHEN ATTITUDES ARE POTENT

Much of our behaviour is automatic. We act out familiar cultural scripts without reflecting on what we're doing. We respond to people we meet in the hall with an automatic 'Hi'. We answer the restaurant cashier's question 'How was your meal?' by saying, 'Fine', even if we found it tasteless.

Such mindlessness is adaptive. It frees our minds to work on other things. For habitual behaviours – seat belt use, coffee consumption, class attendance – conscious intentions hardly are activated (Ouellette & Wood, 1998). As the philosopher Alfred North Whitehead argued, 'Civilization advances by extending the number of operations which we can perform without thinking about them.'

In novel situations, where our behaviour is less automatic, attitudes become more potent. Lacking a script, we think before we act. So, if prompted to think about our attitudes before acting, would we be truer to ourselves? Mark Snyder and William Swann (1976) wanted to find out. Two weeks after 120 of their University of Minnesota students indicated their attitudes towards affirmative-action employment policies, Snyder and Swann invited them to act as jurors in a sex discrimination court case. They found that the participants' attitudes predicted verdicts only for those who were first induced to remember their attitudes – by giving them 'a few minutes to organize your thoughts and views on the affirmative-action issue'. Our attitudes become potent *if* we think about them.

'Thinking is easy, acting difficult, and to put one's thoughts into action, the most difficult thing in the world'.
Goethe, 1749–1832

Self-conscious people usually are in touch with their attitudes (Miller & Grush, 1986). That suggests another way to induce people to focus on their inner convictions: *make them self-aware*, perhaps by having them act in front of a mirror (Carver & Scheier, 1981). Maybe you, too, can recall suddenly being acutely aware of yourself upon entering a room with a large mirror. Other researchers have found similar results: making people self-aware in this way promotes consistency between words and deeds (Froming et al., 1982; Gibbons, 1978).

YOU'VE NOT GOT MAIL: PREJUDICIAL ATTITUDES PREDICT DISCRIMINATORY BEHAVIOUR

**Source:** *Bushman, B.J., & Bonacci, A.M. (2004). You've got mail: Using e-mail to examine the effect of prejudiced attitudes on discrimination against Arabs.* Journal of Experimental Social Psychology, *40, 753–759.*

Introduction

We have seen that strongly held attitudes predict specific actions, especially when the actions are unconstrained by social pressures. University of Michigan social psychologist Brad Bushman and his co-researcher Angelica Bonacci (2004) wondered how strongly attitudes towards Arab Americans might influence unconstrained *behaviour* towards them. To explore that, they wanted to assess the race-relevant attitudes of university students and then, some time later, to correlate their expressed attitudes with their natural behaviour in a situation offering anonymity.

Method

Eleven attitude statements about Arab Americans were embedded in a set of questionnaires administered to nearly 1000 introductory psychology students early in their spring 2002 semester. Using a 1 ('strongly disagree') to 10 ('strongly agree') scale, the students responded to statements such as these:

☐ 'A major fault of Arab Americans is their conceit, their overbearing pride and their idea that they are a chosen ethnic group.'

☐ 'If there are too many Arab Americans in America, our country will be less safe.'

☐ 'If I knew I had been assigned to live in a dorm room with an Arab American, I would ask to change rooms.'

Among the many other questions the students answered was one asking if they would be willing to participate later in an 'unsolicited e-mail study'. With their attitudes now measured, and their informed consent granted, more than 500 of these students (all European American) would, two weeks later, unwittingly participate in a clever experiment. Each person received an e-mail addressed to an individual with an Arabic name (Mohammed Hameed for male participants and Hassan Hameed for female participants) or to a European name (Peter Brice or Jullianna Brice). Half the students received an e-mail stating that the intended recipient had received a prestigious scholarship that required acceptance within 48 hours:

> Thank you for applying for a Glassner Foundation Scholarship. These scholarships are highly competitive and are given only to a few select individuals. They cover tuition for four years ... Because of the large number of applicants, this year we are late in sending out these notices ... We are happy to inform you that you have been selected to receive a Glassner Foundation Scholarship. Congratulations! ... We ask that you respond to this e-mail within 48 hours to inform us whether you will formally accept our scholarship offer. [If not] we would like to extend offers to other students on our waiting list ...

The other half were told the bad news: they did not receive the scholarship (but were welcome to respond if they wanted to be on the waiting list).

Had you received such a misdirected e-mail, without knowing you were actually participating in an experiment, would you have returned the e-mail to the sender, noting the error so that it could be re-sent? Some 26 per cent of women but only 16 per cent of men did so. And did it matter who the intended recipient was?

## Results

As Figure 5.4 shows, it did indeed matter who the intended recipient was. The participants (who generally expressed stronger feelings of prejudice towards Arab Americans than towards African Americans, Asian Americans, or Hispanic Americans) were less likely to reconvey the good news of the scholarship award to intended recipients with Arabic names. This discriminatory behaviour was most strikingly evident among those students who had earlier expressed higher-than-average prejudice towards Arab Americans. Moreover, as Figure 5.5 shows, the students with highly prejudicial attitudes also were *more* willing than were those low in prejudice to reconvey *bad* news to Arabs. Thus, in the months after 9/11, prejudicial attitudes did indeed predict subtle but relevant discriminatory behaviour.

## Discussion

Remember Batson's studies of moral hypocrisy described on page 171? In a later experiment, Batson and his colleagues (1999b) found that mirrors did bring behaviour into line with espoused moral attitudes. When people flipped a coin while facing a mirror, the coin flip became scrupulously fair. Exactly half of the self-conscious participants assigned the other person to the positive task.

To summarize, it is now plain that, depending on the circumstances, the relationship between expressed attitudes and behaviour can range from no relationship to a strong one (Kraus, 1995). Our attitudes predict our actions if:

☐ other influences are minimal

☐ the attitude is specific to the action

☐ the attitude is potent, as when we are reminded of it or made self-conscious.

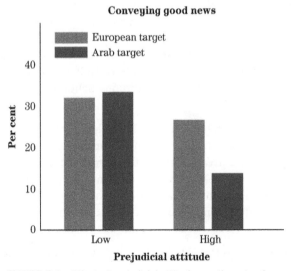

**FIGURE 5.4** Effect of prejudicial attitudes on the rate of reconveying good news to those with European and Arabic names

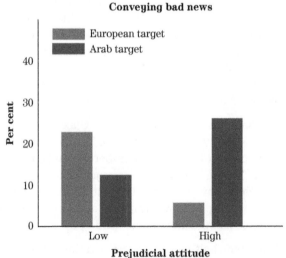

**FIGURE 5.5** Effect of prejudicial attitudes on the rate of reconveying bad news to those with European and Arabic names

Edward Diener and Mark Wallbom (1976) noted that nearly all college students say that cheating is morally wrong. But will they follow the advice of Shakespeare's Polonius, 'To thine own self be true'? Diener and Wallbom set University of Washington students to work on an anagram-solving task (which, they were told, was to predict IQ) and told them to stop when a bell in the room sounded. Left alone, 71 per cent cheated by working past the bell. Among students made self-aware – by working in front of a mirror while hearing their own tape-recorded voices – only 7 per cent cheated. It makes one wonder: would eye-level mirrors in stores make people more self-conscious of their attitudes about stealing?

'It is easier to preach virtue than to practice it'.
La Rochefoucauld, *Maxims*, 1665

## WHEN DOES OUR BEHAVIOUR AFFECT OUR ATTITUDES?

*If social psychology has taught us anything during the last 25 years, it is that we are likely not only to think ourselves into a way of acting but also to act ourselves into a way of thinking. What evidence supports that assertion?*

Now we turn to the more startling idea that behaviour determines attitudes. It's true that we sometimes stand up for what we believe. But it's also true that we come to believe in what we stand up for. Social psychological theories inspired much of the research that underlies that conclusion.

Consider the following incidents.

☐ Sarah is hypnotized and told to take off her shoes when a book drops on the floor. Fifteen minutes later a book drops, and Sarah quietly slips out of her loafers. 'Sarah,' asks the hypnotist, 'why did you take off your shoes?' 'Well … my feet are hot and tired,' Sarah replies. 'It has been a long day.' The act produces the idea.

☐ George has electrodes temporarily implanted in the brain region that controls his head movements. When neurosurgeon José Delgado (1973) stimulates the electrodes by remote control, George always turns his head. Unaware of the remote stimulation, he offers a reasonable explanation for his head turning: 'I'm looking for my slipper.' 'I heard a noise.' 'I'm restless.' 'I was looking under the bed.'

☐ Carol's severe seizures were relieved by surgically separating her two brain hemispheres. Now, in an experiment, psychologist Michael Gazzaniga (1985) flashes a picture of a nude woman to the left half of Carol's field of vision and thus to her non-verbal right brain hemisphere. A sheepish smile spreads over her face, and she begins chuckling. Asked why, she invents – and apparently believes – a plausible explanation: 'Oh – that funny machine.' Frank, another split-brain patient, has the word 'smile' flashed to his non-verbal right hemisphere. He obliges and forces a smile. Asked why, he explains, 'This experiment is very funny.'

The mental after-effects of our behaviour also appear in many social psychological phenomena. The following examples illustrate such self-persuasion – attitudes following behaviour.

## ROLE PLAYING

**role** *a set of norms that defines how people in a given social position ought to behave*

The word role is borrowed from the theatre and, as in the theatre, refers to actions expected of those who occupy a particular social position. In Chapter 3 we considered how the roles we perform shape our sense of self. When enacting new social roles, we may at first feel phony. But our unease seldom lasts.

Think of a time when you stepped into some new role – perhaps your first days on a job or at college. That first week on campus, for example, you may have been supersensitive to your new social situation and tried valiantly to act mature and suppress your high school behaviour. At such times you may have felt self-conscious. You observed your new speech and actions because they weren't natural to you. Then one day something amazing happened: your pseudo-intellectual talk no longer felt forced. The role began to fit as comfortably as your old jeans and T-shirt.

Frederick Douglass, a former slave, recalls his new owner's transformation as she absorbed her role:

> My new mistress proved to be all she appeared when I first met her at the door – a woman of the kindest heart and finest feelings ... I was utterly astonished at her goodness. I scarcely knew how to behave towards her. She was entirely unlike any other white woman I had ever seen ... The meanest slave was put fully at ease in her presence, and none left without feeling better for having seen her. Her face was made of heavenly smiles, and her voice of tranquil music. But, alas! this kind heart had but a short time to remain such. The fatal poison of irresponsible power was already in her hands, and soon commenced its infernal work. That cheerful eye, under the influence of slavery, soon became red with rage; that voice, made all of sweet accord, changed to one of harsh and horrid discord; and that angelic face gave place to that of a demon.

(Douglass, 1845, pp. 57–58)

## WHEN SAYING BECOMES BELIEVING

People often adapt what they say to please their listeners. They are quicker to tell people good news than bad, and they adjust their message towards their listener's position (Manis et al., 1974; Tesser et al., 1972; Tetlock, 1983). When induced to give spoken or written support to something they doubt, people will often feel bad about their deceit. Nevertheless, they begin to believe what they are saying – *provided* they weren't bribed or coerced into doing so. When there is no compelling external explanation for one's words, saying becomes believing (Klaas, 1978).

Tory Higgins and his colleagues (Higgins & McCann, 1984; Higgins & Rholes, 1978) illustrated how saying becomes believing. They had university students read a personality description of someone and then summarize it for someone else, who was believed either to like or to dislike that person. The students wrote a more positive description when the recipient liked the person. Having said positive things, they also then liked the person more themselves. Asked to recall what they had read, they remembered the description as more positive than it was. In short, people tend to adjust their messages to their listeners, and, having done so, believe the altered message.

## EVIL AND MORAL ACTS

The attitudes-follow-behaviour principle works with immoral acts as well. Evil sometimes results from gradually escalating commitments. A trifling evil act can whittle down one's moral sensitivity, making it easier to perform a worse act. To paraphrase La Rochefoucauld's *Maxims* (1665), it is not as difficult to find a person who has never succumbed to a given temptation as to find a person who has succumbed only once. After telling a 'white lie' and thinking, 'Well, that wasn't so bad', the person may go on to tell a bigger lie.

In Chapters 7 and 13 we will consider a field experiment conducted by Philip Zimbardo, that provides a classic demonstration of how behaving can influence attitudes, and how both are shaped by the situation an individual finds him or herself in. In his Stanford Prison Experiment, participants randomly assigned to the role of prisoners or guards not only behaved according to these roles, but also formed consistent attitudes. Behaving as the situation required, acts and attitudes rapidly became increasingly extreme with demonstrations of brutality by the guards towards the prisoners. Zimbardo later termed this the 'Lucifer Effect' (2007) to describe what happens when the social situation overwhelms someone, causing a shift in behaviour from good to evil.

Another way in which evil acts influence attitudes is the paradoxical fact that we tend not only to hurt those we dislike but also to dislike those we hurt. Several studies (Berscheid et al., 1968; Davis & Jones, 1960; Glass, 1964) found that harming an innocent victim – by uttering hurtful comments or delivering electric shocks – typically leads aggressors to disparage their victims, thus helping them justify their cruel behaviour. This is especially so when we are coaxed into it, not coerced. When we agree to a deed voluntarily, we take more responsibility for it.

The phenomenon appears in wartime. Prisoner-of-war camp guards would sometimes display good manners to captives in their first days on the job, but not for long. Soldiers ordered to kill may initially react with revulsion to the point of sickness over their act. But not for long (Waller, 2002). Often they will denigrate their enemies with dehumanizing nicknames.

Attitudes also follow behaviour in peacetime. A group that holds another in slavery is likely to come to perceive the slaves as having traits that justify their oppression. Prison staff who participate in executions experience 'moral disengagement' by coming to believe (more strongly than do other prison staff) that their victims deserve their fate (Osofsky et al., 2005). Actions and attitudes feed each other, sometimes to the point of moral numbness. The more one harms another and adjusts one's attitudes, the easier harm-doing becomes. Conscience is corroded.

Evil acts shape the self, but so, thankfully, do moral acts. Our character is reflected in what we do when we think no one is looking. Researchers have tested character by giving children temptations when it seems no one is watching. Consider what happens when children resist the temptation. In a dramatic experiment, Jonathan Freedman (1965) introduced elementary school children to an enticing battery-controlled robot, instructing them not to play with it while he was out of the room. Freedman used a severe threat with half the children and a mild threat with the others. Both were sufficient to deter the children.

Cruel acts, such as the 1994 Rwandan genocide, tend to breed even crueller and more hate-filled attitudes.

SOURCE: © RollingEarth/iStock

Several weeks later a different researcher, with no apparent relation to the earlier events, left each child to play in the same room with the same toys. Of the 18 children who had been given the severe threat, 14 now freely played with the robot; but two-thirds of those who had been given the mild deterrent still resisted playing with it. Apparently, the deterrent was strong enough to elicit the desired behaviour yet mild enough to leave them with a sense of choice. Having earlier chosen consciously *not* to play with the toy, the mildly deterred children apparently internalized their decisions. Moral action, especially when chosen rather than coerced, affects moral thinking.

Moreover, positive behaviour fosters liking for the person. Doing a favour for an experimenter or another participant, or tutoring a student, usually increases liking of the person helped (Blanchard & Cook, 1976). It is a lesson worth remembering: If you wish to love someone more, act as if you do.

'We become just by the practice of just actions, self-controlled by exercising self-control, and courageous by performing acts of courage'.
    Aristotle

## WHY DOES OUR BEHAVIOUR AFFECT OUR ATTITUDES?

*What theories help explain the attitudes-follow-behaviour phenomenon? How does the contest between these competing theories illustrate the process of scientific explanation?*

We have seen that several streams of evidence merge to form a river: the effect of actions on attitudes. Do these observations contain any clues to *why* action affects attitude? Social psychology's detectives suspect three possible sources. *Self-presentation theory* assumes that for strategic reasons we express attitudes that make us appear consistent. *Cognitive dissonance theory* assumes that to reduce discomfort, we justify our actions to ourselves. *Self-perception theory* assumes that our actions are self-revealing (when uncertain about our feelings or beliefs, we look to our behaviour, much as anyone else would). Let's examine each.

### PRESENTING CONSISTENCY

In Western cultures especially, appearing inconsistent is undesirable. To avoid seeming so, we express attitudes that match our actions. To appear consistent, we may pretend those attitudes. Even if that means displaying a little insincerity or hypocrisy, it can pay off in managing the impression of consistency we are displaying. Two theories explain how people manage a concern with consistency.

### SELF-JUSTIFICATION: COGNITIVE DISSONANCE

One theory is that our attitudes change because we are motivated to maintain consistency among our cognitions. That is the implication of Leon Festinger's (1957) cognitive dissonance theory. The theory is simple, but its range of application is enormous, making 'cognitive dissonance' part of the vocabulary of today's educated people. It assumes that we feel tension, or a lack of harmony ('dissonance'), when two simultaneously accessible thoughts or beliefs ('cognitions') are psychologically inconsistent – as when we decide to say or do something we have mixed feelings about. Festinger argued that to reduce this unpleasant arousal, we often adjust our thinking. This simple idea, and some surprising predictions derived from it, have spawned more than 2000 studies (Cooper, 1999).

Dissonance theory pertains mostly to discrepancies between behaviour and attitudes. We are aware of both. Thus, if we sense some inconsistency, perhaps some hypocrisy, we feel pressure for change. That helps explain why, in a British survey, half of cigarette smokers disagreed with non-smokers, who nearly all believed that smoking is 'really as dangerous as people say' (Eiser et al., 1979). In the USA, too, 40 per cent of smokers – but only 13 per cent of non-smokers – judge smoking as not very harmful (Saad, 2002).

Cognitive dissonance theory offers an explanation for self-persuasion, and it offers several surprising predictions.

### INSUFFICIENT JUSTIFICATION

Imagine you are a participant in an experiment staged by Festinger and his student J. Merrill Carlsmith (1959). For an hour, you are required to perform dull tasks, such as turning wooden knobs again and again. After you finish, the experimenter (Carlsmith) explains that the study concerns how expectations affect performance. The next participant, waiting outside, must be led to expect an *interesting* experiment. The seemingly upset experimenter, whom Festinger had spent hours coaching until he became extremely convincing, explains that the assistant who usually creates this expectation couldn't make this session. Wringing his hands, he pleads, 'Could you fill in and do this?'

It's for science and you are being paid, so you agree to tell the next participant (who is actually the experimenter's accomplice) what a delightful experience you have just had. 'Really?' responds the supposed participant. 'A friend of mine was in this experiment a week ago, and she said it was boring.' 'Oh, no,' you respond, 'it's really very interesting. You get good exercise while turning some knobs. I'm sure you'll enjoy it.' Finally, someone else who is studying how people react to experiments has you complete a questionnaire that asks how much you actually enjoyed your knob-turning experience.

Now for the prediction: under which condition are you most likely to believe your little lie and say that the experiment was indeed interesting? When paid $1 for fibbing, as some of the participants were? Or when paid a then-lavish $20, as others were? Contrary to the common notion that big rewards produce big effects, Festinger and Carlsmith made an outrageous prediction: those paid just $1 (hardly sufficient justification for a lie) would be most likely to adjust their attitudes to their actions. Having insufficient justification for their actions, they would experience more discomfort (dissonance) and thus be more motivated to believe in what they had done. Those paid $20 had sufficient justification for what

**cognitive dissonance** *tension that arises when one is simultaneously aware of two inconsistent cognitions. For example, dissonance may occur when we realize that we have, with little justification, acted contrary to our attitudes. This inconsistency is unpleasant, and people use different methods to combat the dissonance. Concept coined by Leon Festinger (1957)*

**insufficient justification effect** *reduction of dissonance by internally justifying one's behaviour when external justification is 'insufficient'*

183

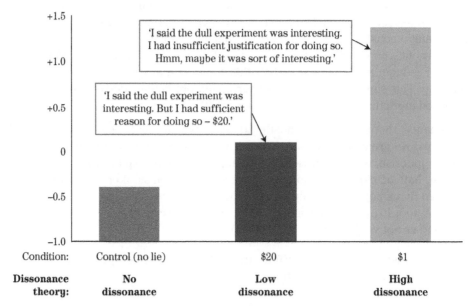

'How much I enjoyed the experiment' (–5 to +5)

'I said the dull experiment was interesting. I had insufficient justification for doing so. Hmm, maybe it was sort of interesting.'

'I said the dull experiment was interesting. But I had sufficient reason for doing so – $20.'

| Condition: | Control (no lie) | $20 | $1 |
|---|---|---|---|
| **Dissonance theory:** | **No dissonance** | **Low dissonance** | **High dissonance** |

**FIGURE 5.6** Insufficient justification
Dissonance theory predicts that when our actions are not fully explained by external rewards or coercion, we will experience dissonance, which we can reduce by believing in what we have done.
SOURCE: Data from Festinger & Carlsmith, 1959.

they had done and hence should have experienced less dissonance. As Figure 5.6 shows, the results fit this intriguing prediction.*

In dozens of later experiments, this attitudes-follow-behaviour effect was strongest when people felt some choice and when their actions had foreseeable consequences. One experiment had people read disparaging lawyer jokes into a recorder (for example, 'How can you tell when a lawyer is lying? His lips are moving'). The reading produced more negative attitudes towards lawyers when it was a chosen rather than a coerced activity (Hobden & Olson, 1994). Other experiments have engaged people to write essays for a measly sum of money. When the essay argues something they don't believe in – say, a tuition increase – the underpaid writers begin to feel somewhat greater sympathy with the policy. Pretence becomes reality.

Earlier we noted how the insufficient justification principle works with punishments. Children were more likely to internalize a request not to play with an attractive toy if they were given a mild threat that insufficiently justified their compliance. When a parent says, 'Clean up your room, Joshua, or else expect a hard spanking', Joshua won't need to internally justify cleaning his room. The severe threat is justification enough.

Note that cognitive dissonance theory focuses not on the relative effectiveness of rewards and punishments administered after the act but on what induces a desired action. It aims to have Joshua say, 'I am cleaning up my room because I want a clean

---

* There is a seldom reported final aspect of this 1950s experiment. Imagine yourself finally back with the experimenter, who is truthfully explaining the whole study. Not only do you learn that you've been duped, but also the experimenter asks for the $20 back. Do you comply? Festinger and Carlsmith note that all their Stanford student participants willingly reached into their pockets and gave back the money. This is a foretaste of some quite amazing observations on compliance and conformity discussed in Chapter 7. As we will see, when the social situation makes clear demands, people usually respond accordingly.

room', rather than, 'I am cleaning up my room because my parents will shout at me if I don't'. Students who perceive their required community service as something they would have chosen to do are more likely to anticipate future volunteering than those who feel coerced (Stukas et al., 1999). The principle: *attitudes follow behaviours for which we feel some responsibility.*

Authoritarian management will be effective, the theory predicts, only when the authority is present – because people are unlikely to internalize forced behaviour. Bree, a formerly enslaved talking horse in C. S. Lewis's *The Horse and his Boy* (1974), observes, 'One of the worst results of being a slave and being forced to do things is that when there is no one to force you any more you find you have almost lost the power of forcing yourself' (p. 193). Dissonance theory insists that encouragement and inducement should be enough to elicit the desired action (so that attitudes may follow the behaviour). But it suggests that managers, teachers and parents should use only enough incentive to elicit the desired behaviour.

Dissonance theory suggests that parents should aim to elicit desired behaviour non-coercively, thus motivating children to internalize the appropriate attitudes.

SOURCE: © Maica / iStock

## DISSONANCE AFTER DECISIONS

The emphasis on perceived choice and responsibility implies that decisions produce dissonance. When faced with an important decision – what college to attend, whom to date, which job to accept – we are sometimes torn between two equally attractive alternatives. Perhaps you can recall a time when, having committed yourself, you became painfully aware of dissonant cognitions – the desirable features of what you had rejected and the undesirable features of what you had chosen. If you decided to live on campus or in a student town, you may have realized you were giving up the spaciousness and freedom of an apartment in favour of cramped, noisy dorm quarters. If you elected to live outside a student house, you may have realized that your decision meant physical separation from campus and friends, and having to cook and clean for yourself.

After making important decisions, we usually reduce dissonance by upgrading the chosen alternative and downgrading the unchosen option. In the first published dissonance experiment (1956), Jack Brehm asked women to rate eight products, such as a toaster, a radio and a hairdryer. Brehm then showed the women two objects they had rated closely and told them they could have whichever they chose. Later, when re-rating the eight objects, the women increased their evaluations of the item they had chosen and decreased their evaluations of the rejected item. It seems that after we have made our choices, the grass does not then grow greener on the other side of the fence.

Festinger notes that it matters whether we feel coerced into acting in a particular way. If we feel as though we've been forced into acting in a way that is inconsistent with our attitudes we are much less likely to shift our attitudes to match the behaviour than if we feel we've acted with freedom of choice.

With simple decisions, this deciding-becomes-believing effect can breed overconfidence (Blanton et al., 2001): 'What I've decided must be right.' The effect can occur very quickly. Robert Knox and James Inkster (1968) found that racetrack betters who had just put down their money felt more optimistic about their bets than did those who were about to bet. In the few moments that intervened between standing in line and walking away from the betting window, nothing had changed – except the decisive action and the person's feelings about it. There may sometimes be but a slight difference between two options, as I can recall in helping make faculty tenure decisions. The competence of one faculty member who barely makes it and that of another who barely loses seem not very different – until after you make and announce the decision.

Once made, decisions grow their own self-justifying legs of support. Often, these new legs are strong enough that when one leg is pulled away – perhaps the original one – the decision does not collapse.

## DISSONANCE AND GROUP IDENTITY

Recent research in social psychology has suggested that the groups to which we psychologically belong and feel attached also have an influence on how we deal with feelings of cognitive dissonance. Social groups, such as being a university student, guide our behaviour and often also our broader moral, social and political values. However, if those groups adopt behaviour or attitudes that differ from those we personally believe, then we should experience feelings of dissonance. In such circumstances Festinger predicts we should feel motivated to reduce such dissonance.

Big decisions can produce big dissonance when one later ponders the negative aspects of what is chosen and the positive aspects of what was not chosen.
SOURCE: © ZoneCreative/iStock

Demis Glasford, Felicia Pratto and John Dovidio (2008) wondered how American citizens would respond when confronted with ingroup values about basic health care that conflicted with their own. To find out, they first established how strongly each participant identified with the national ingroup (American) and what their personal beliefs were towards health care. Some of the participants were then presented with a scenario in which health care was strongly endorsed by America, and others given a report in which American values were opposed to basic health care. The most discomfort was felt by those participants who strongly identified with the national ingroup (American) and held strong personal beliefs about basic health care, and were presented with a scenario which described America as being against basic health care for its citizens. When participants were later asked how much they identified with the national group, their levels of identification had reduced. A strategy for dealing with their discomfort was to distance themselves from the national group. But could dissonance motivate them to change the group itself? In a follow-up study participants were given one of two scenarios in which the USA was seen to be upholding the value of self-reliance, or flouting it. Again the researchers found that the most discomfort was experienced by those participants who strongly identified with the national ingroup, held positive values for self-reliance and had read a scenario in which their national ingroup had flouted this value. However, this time participants were also asked about their willingness to actively engage in changing the values of the group. They found that those who had displayed the most discomfort were also those who were most willing to engage in behaviour to redress the group's value of self-reliance.

What Glasford and his colleagues had observed was that group identity had an influence on feelings of cognitive dissonance experienced by people, and also influenced their strategies for reducing it – either by psychologically distancing themselves from the group or attempting to change the behaviour of the group. This has some important real-world implications. When a group behaves in a way that differs from the values of individual members (e.g. in the case of displays of extreme prejudice), what may happen is that those more tolerant members leave and the bias within the group continues. But, on the other hand there are times when a group member may try to tackle the group norms.

However, before we get swept away by this wealth of evidence on the effects of dissonance, it's worth drawing breath for a quick word of caution here. We should be aware that the motivation to reduce feelings of dissonance may be a Western phenomenon. In parts of East Asia, to experience contradictions within oneself is what makes you human, and it actually is not desirable to resolve them (e.g. Heine & Lehman, 1997; Hoshino-Browne et al., 2004). So while the research tells us something extremely interesting about behaviour in certain cultures, it would be a folly to generalize this as a feature of human beings per se.

## SELF-PERCEPTION

Although dissonance theory has inspired much research, an even simpler theory also explains its phenomena. Consider how we make inferences about other people's attitudes. We see how a person acts in a particular situation, and then we attribute the behaviour either to the person's traits and attitudes or to environmental forces (remember our discussion of attribution theory in Chapter 4?). If we see parents coercing 10-year-old Brett into saying, 'I'm sorry', we attribute Brett's apology to the situation, not to his personal regret. If we see Brett apologizing with no apparent inducement, we attribute the apology to Brett himself (Figure 5.7).

Self-perception theory (proposed by Daryl Bem, 1972) assumes that we make similar inferences when we observe our own behaviour. When our attitudes are weak or ambiguous, we are in the position of someone observing us from the outside. Hearing myself talk informs me of my attitudes; seeing my actions provides clues to how strong my beliefs are. This is especially so when I can't easily attribute my behaviour to external constraints. The acts we freely commit are self-revealing.

**self-perception theory**
*the theory that when we are unsure of our attitudes, we infer them much as would someone observing us, by looking at our behaviour and the circumstances under which it occurs*

**Why do actions affect attitudes?**

**FIGURE 5.7** Attitudes follow behaviour.

SOURCE: © pecaphoto77/iStock

The pioneering psychologist William James (see Chapter 1) proposed a similar explanation for emotion a century ago. We infer our emotions, he suggested, by observing our bodies and our behaviours. A stimulus such as a growling bear confronts a woman in the forest. She tenses, her heartbeat increases, adrenaline flows and she runs away. Observing all this, she then experiences fear. When James's brother, Henry, died, he was deeply depressed but persuaded himself to act as if life were manageable; it soon became so.

'Self-knowledge is best learned, not by contemplation, but action.'
    Goethe, 1749–1832

Do people who observe themselves agreeing to a small request indeed come to perceive themselves as the helpful sort of person who responds positively to requests for help? Yes, report Jerry Burger and David Caldwell (2003). Behaviour can modify self-concept.

### EXPRESSIONS AND ATTITUDE

When James Laird (1974, 1984) induced college students to frown while attaching electrodes to their faces – 'contract these muscles', 'pull your brows together' – they reported feeling angry. It's more fun to try out Laird's other finding: those induced to make a smiling face felt happier and found cartoons more humorous. Those induced to repeatedly practise happy (versus sad or angry) expressions may recall more happy memories and find the happy mood lingering (Schnall & Laird, 2003). Viewing one's expressions in a mirror magnifies the self-perception effect (Kleinke et al., 1998).

We have all experienced this phenomenon. We're feeling crabby, but then the phone rings or someone comes to the door and elicits from us warm, polite behaviour. 'How's everything?' 'Just fine, thanks. How are things with you?' 'Oh, not bad...'. If our feelings are not intense, this warm behaviour may change our whole attitude. It's tough to smile and feel grouchy.

Even your gait can affect how you feel. When you get up from reading this chapter, walk for a minute taking short, shuffling steps, with eyes downcast. It's a great way to feel depressed. 'Sit all day in a moping posture, sigh, and reply to everything with a dismal voice, and your melancholy lingers,' noted William James (1890, p. 463). Want to feel better? Walk for a minute taking long strides with your arms swinging and your eyes straight ahead.

Our facial expressions also influence our attitudes. In a clever experiment, Gary Wells and Richard Petty (1980) had University of Alberta students 'test headphone sets' by making either vertical or horizontal head movements while listening to a radio editorial. Who most agreed with the editorial? Those who had been nodding their heads up and down. Why? Wells and Petty surmised that positive thoughts are compatible with vertical nodding and incompatible with horizontal motion within Western cultures. Try it yourself when listening to someone: do you feel more agreeable when nodding rather than shaking your head?

### OVERJUSTIFICATION AND INTRINSIC MOTIVATIONS

Recall the insufficient justification effect – the smallest incentive that will get people to do something is usually the most effective in getting them to like the activity and keep on doing it. Cognitive dissonance theory offers one explanation for this: when external inducements are insufficient to justify our behaviour, we reduce dissonance by justifying the behaviour internally.

Self-perception theory offers a different explanation: people explain their behaviour by noting the conditions under which it occurs. Imagine hearing someone proclaim the wisdom of a tuition increase after being paid to do so. Surely the statement would seem less sincere than if you thought the person was expressing those opinions for no pay. Perhaps we make similar inferences when observing ourselves. We observe our uncoerced action and infer our attitude.

According to German psychologist Fritz Strack and colleagues (1988), people find cartoons funnier while holding a pen with their teeth (using a smiling muscle) than while holding it with their lips (using muscles incompatible with smiling).

Self-perception theory goes a step further. Contrary to the notion that rewards always increase motivation, it suggests that unnecessary rewards can have a hidden cost. Rewarding people for doing what they already enjoy may lead them to attribute their action to the reward, thus undermining their self-perception that they do it because they like it. Experiments by Edward Deci and Richard Ryan (1991, 1997) at the University of Rochester, by Mark Lepper and David Greene (1979) at Stanford, and by Ann Boggiano and her colleagues (1985, 1987) at the University of Colorado have confirmed this overjustification effect. Pay people for playing with puzzles, and they will later play with the puzzles less than those who play for no pay. Promise children a reward for doing what they intrinsically enjoy (for example, playing with Magic Markers), and you will turn their play into work (Figure 5.8).

overjustification effect *the result of bribing people to do what they already like doing; they may then see their actions as externally controlled rather than intrinsically appealing*

A folk tale illustrates the overjustification effect. An old man lived alone on a street where boys played noisily every afternoon. The din annoyed him, so one day he called the boys to his door. He told them he loved the cheerful sound of children's voices and promised them each 50 cents if they would return the next day. Next afternoon the youngsters raced back and played more lustily than ever. The old man paid them and promised another reward the next day. Again they returned, whooping it up, and the man again paid them; this time 25 cents. The following day they got only 15 cents, and the man explained that his meagre resources were being exhausted. 'Please, though, would you come to play for 10 cents tomorrow?' The disappointed boys told the man they would not be back. It wasn't worth the effort, they said, to play all afternoon at his house for only 10 cents.

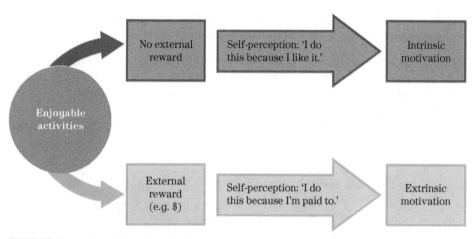

**FIGURE 5.8** Intrinsic and extrinsic motivation
When people do something they enjoy, without reward or coercion, they attribute their behaviour to their love of the activity. External rewards undermine intrinsic motivation by leading people to attribute their behaviour to the incentive.

As self-perception theory implies, an unanticipated reward does not diminish intrinsic interest, because people can still attribute their actions to their own motivation (Bradley & Mannell, 1984; Tang & Hall, 1995). (It's like the heroine who, having fallen in love with the woodcutter, now learns that he's really a prince.) And if compliments for a good job make us feel more competent and successful, this can actually increase our intrinsic motivation. When rightly administered, rewards may also boost creativity (Eisenberger et al., 1999; Eisenberger & Rhoades, 2001; Eisenberger & Shanock, 2003).

The overjustification effect occurs when someone offers an unnecessary reward beforehand in an obvious effort to control behaviour. What matters is what a reward implies: rewards and praise that inform people of their achievements – that make them feel, 'I'm very good at this' – boost intrinsic motivation. Rewards that seek to control people and lead them to believe it was the reward that caused their effort – 'I did it for the money' – diminish the intrinsic appeal of an enjoyable task (Rosenfeld et al., 1980; Sansone, 1986).

How then can we cultivate people's enjoyment of initially unappealing tasks? Maria may find her first piano lessons frustrating. Toshi may not have an intrinsic love of ninth-grade science. DeShawn may embark on a career not looking forward to making those first sales calls. In such cases, the parent, the teacher or the manager should probably use some incentives to coax the desired behaviour (Boggiano & Ruble, 1985; Workman & Williams, 1980). After the person complies, suggest an intrinsic reason for doing so: 'I'm not surprised that sales call went well, because you are so good at making a first impression.'

All Nippon Airways employees, biting wooden chopsticks, beam during a smile training session.
SOURCE: © Sipa Asia/REX/Shutterstock

If we provide students with just enough justification to perform a learning task, and use rewards and labels to help them feel competent, we may enhance their enjoyment and their eagerness to pursue the subject on their own. When there is too much justification – as happens in classrooms where teachers dictate behaviour and use rewards to control the children – student-driven learning may diminish (Deci & Ryan, 1985, 1991).

## COMPARING THE THEORIES

We have seen one explanation of why our actions might only *seem* to affect our attitudes (self-presentation theory). And we have seen two explanations of why our actions genuinely affect our attitudes: (1) the dissonance-theory assumption that we justify our behaviour to reduce our internal discomfort; and (2) the self-perception-theory assumption that we observe our behaviour and make reasonable inferences about our attitudes, much as we observe other people and infer *their* attitudes.

The last two explanations seem to contradict each other. Which is right? It's difficult to find a definitive test. In most instances they make the same predictions, and we can bend each theory to accommodate most of the findings we have considered (Greenwald, 1975). Self-perception theorist Daryl Bem (1972) even suggested it boils down to a matter of personal loyalties and preferences. This illustrates the human element in scientific theorizing (see Chapter 1). Neither dissonance theory nor self-perception theory has been handed to us by nature. Both are products of human imagination – creative attempts to simplify and explain what we've observed.

It is not unusual in science to find that a principle, such as 'attitudes follow behaviour', is predictable from more than one theory. Physicist Richard Feynman (1967) marvelled that 'one of the amazing characteristics of nature' is the 'wide range of beautiful ways' in which we can describe it: 'I do not understand the reason why it is that the correct laws of physics seem to be expressible in such a tremendous variety of ways.' Like different roads leading to the same place, different sets of assumptions can lead to the same principle. If anything, this strengthens our confidence in the principle. It becomes credible not only because of the data supporting it but also because it rests on more than one theoretical pillar.

### Dissonance as Arousal

On one key point, strong support has emerged for dissonance theory. Recall that dissonance is, by definition, an aroused state of uncomfortable tension. To reduce that tension, we supposedly change our attitudes. Self-perception theory says nothing about tension being aroused when our actions and attitudes are not in harmony. It assumes merely that when our attitudes are weak to begin with, we will use our behaviour and its circumstances as a clue to those attitudes (like the person who said, 'How do I tell what I think till I see what I say?' (Forster, 1976)).

Are conditions that supposedly produce dissonance (for example, making decisions or acting contrary to one's attitudes) indeed uncomfortably arousing? Clearly yes, providing that the behaviour has unwanted consequences for which the person feels responsible (Cooper, 1999). If, in the privacy of your closet, you say something you don't believe, dissonance will be minimal. It will be much greater if there are unpleasant results – if someone hears and believes you, if the statement causes harm and the negative effects are irrevocable, and if the person harmed is someone you like. If, moreover, you feel responsible for those consequences – if you can't easily excuse your act because you freely agreed to it and if you were able to foresee its consequences – then uncomfortable dissonance will be aroused. Moreover, the arousal will be detectable as increased perspiration and heart rate (Cacioppo & Petty, 1986; Croyle & Cooper, 1983; Losch & Cacioppo, 1990).

Why is 'volunteering' to say or do undesirable things so arousing? Because, suggests Claude Steele's (1988) self-affirmation theory, such acts are embarrassing. They make us feel foolish. They threaten our sense of personal competence and goodness. Justifying our actions and decisions is therefore *self-affirming*; it protects and supports our sense of integrity and self-worth.

**self-affirmation theory**
*a theory that (a) people often experience a self-image threat, after engaging in an undesirable behaviour; and (b) they can compensate by affirming another aspect of the self. Threaten people's self-concept in one domain, and they will compensate either by refocusing or by doing good deeds in some other domain*

What do you suppose happens, then, if we offer people who have committed self-contradictory acts a way to reaffirm their self-worth, such as doing good deeds? In several experiments Steele found that, with their self-concepts restored, people felt much less need to justify their acts (Steele et al., 1993). People with high and secure self-esteem also engage in less self-justification (Holland et al., 2002).

So dissonance conditions do indeed arouse tension, especially when they threaten positive feelings of self-worth. But is this arousal necessary for the attitudes-follow-behaviour effect? Steele and his colleagues (1981) believe the answer is yes. When drinking alcohol reduces dissonance-produced arousal, the attitudes-follow-behaviour effect disappears. In one of their experiments, they induced University of Washington students to write essays favouring a big tuition increase. The students reduced their resulting dissonance by softening their anti-tuition attitudes – *unless* after writing the unpleasant essays they drank alcohol, supposedly as part of a beer- or vodka-tasting experiment.

### Self-perceiving When Not Self-contradicting

Dissonance procedures are uncomfortably arousing. That makes for self-persuasion after acting contrary to one's attitudes. But dissonance theory cannot explain attitude changes that occur without dissonance. When people argue a position that is in line with their opinion, although a step or two beyond it, procedures that eliminate arousal do not eliminate attitude change (Fazio et al., 1977, 1979). Dissonance theory also does not explain the overjustification effect, since being paid to do what you like to do should not arouse great tension. And what about situations where the action does not contradict any attitude – when, for example, people are induced to smile or grimace? Here, too, there should be no dissonance. For these cases, self-perception theory has a ready explanation.

In short, it appears that dissonance theory explains what happens when we act contrary to clearly defined attitudes: we feel tension, so we adjust our attitudes to reduce it. Dissonance theory, then, explains attitude change in Western cultures. In situations where our attitudes are not well formed, self-perception theory explains attitude *formation*. As we act and reflect, we develop more readily accessible attitudes to guide our future behaviour (Fazio, 1987; Roese & Olson, 1994).

## ATTITUDES AS SOCIAL ACTIONS

*So far we have considered the complex relationship between attitudes and behaviour. What this work has illustrated is that how these attitudes are expressed and their relationship to behaviour is dependent on the context. It is this dependency on the context that has led some social psychologists to question whether attitudes have any cognitive basis at all.*

Jonathan Potter and Margaret Wetherell (1987) in their book *Discourse and Social Psychology: Beyond Attitudes and Behaviour* boldly questioned some of the claims and assumptions made by social psychologists in their hunt for attitudes.

These included the following:

☐ *Attitudes as cognitive entities*: Potter and Wetherell argue that if attitudes do have a stable cognitive component then they should be more consistent than they actually are. Instead, they point to how attitudes tend to be highly variable and are often contradictory. The same person can express different attitudes about an event, person, object or idea over the course of a conversation. The authors suggest that this points to their communicative aspects and context dependence. So rather than thinking of attitudes as evaluations that exist pre-communication, Potter and Wetherell argue they are actually produced during communication. Or as social psychologist Michael Billig (1989) puts it, attitudes are a form of argumentative thinking done in dialogue with others.

☐ *Attitudes predict behaviour*: if attitudes are produced in language as we interact with other people, Potter and Wetherell propose that attitudes don't lead to behaviour, but actually *are* the behaviour (or social action). We use them all the time to perform social actions (for example justifying, blaming, excusing, explaining).

☐ *Attitudes can be measured quantitatively*: attitudes are often measured using rating scales (such as Likert scales), which require participants to rate their attitude towards something on a pre-labelled scale. Potter and Wetherell warn that this data shouldn't be relied upon too heavily or treated as accurate reflections of cognitive processes. They argue that when confronted with a rating scale, the participant gives attitudes that best fit the current context (e.g. what they think the researcher wants, the labels on the rating scale, or monitoring their self-presentation).

☐ *Attitudes are formed towards pre-defined objects in the environment: what we have attitudes about is a rhetorical construction.* How we describe a person, an event, an object or idea is an achievement of language. So in evaluating something, we produce the thing we have attitudes about.

Let's consider some examples.

We have already seen in this chapter how attitudes to certain food are related to their consumption. Sally Wiggins has considered this relationship from a discursive standpoint in a series of studies. In her work she examines the discussions that surround meal times and in doing so considers how the food is argued over and evaluated (and consumed, or not!). In one of her examples of a family meal she observes how a discussion about 'pasta tuna' between a father who is trying to encourage his daughter to eat it revolves around whether it is pasta with tuna (the father), or tuna with pasta (the daughter). The daughter's negative evaluation of the meal is based on her description of it, which she refuses to eat (Wiggins et al., 2001).

This work highlights how the thing to be evaluated (in this case food) is subject to discussion and argumentation in terms of how it is defined.

Margaret Wetherell and Jonathon Potter's (1992) own study of white middle-class New Zealanders talking about immigrants is a classic example. Potter and Wetherell interviewed them about their views on New Zealand as a place to live. What they found was that their participants produced an array of attitudes towards this society. Interestingly this included attitudes towards Polynesian immigrants who live in New Zealand. The researchers found that negative attitudes were expressed when Polynesian immigrants were represented as uneducated or a threat to employment opportunities for other New Zealanders. Such negative evaluations of the group were presented as reasonable, perhaps even 'justifiable'. Participants would clearly define themselves as not being prejudiced but realistic ('I'm not prejudiced but . . .') considering the circumstances. However, the participants could also present very positive attitudes towards immigrants when they talked about the need for unskilled workers in New Zealand, or spoke about how they contribute to the rich tapestry of cultural life in New Zealand.

See Chapter 13 for further discussion on the use of disclaimers and prejudice; disclaimers and an expression of cultural tolerance can inoculate against the prejudice which follows.

For Potter and Wetherell the basic point of such a study is this: how the Polynesian immigrants are evaluated depends on how the group (or attitude–object) is constructed (as a threat, unskilled, uneducated, willing to contribute to society, etc.), and these evaluations perform social actions (such as blaming) for the speaker. If we were to ask these New Zealanders to fill out an attitude scale to measure their evaluations of Polynesian immigrants, we most certainly would not obtain these highly varied 'attitudes' and would gain little sense of how they are related to the context in which they are produced.

The topic of attitudes provokes debates and tensions in social psychology about how we ought to study them, and what we consider their role to be in the prediction of behaviour. Despite these ongoing debates, what social psychologists do agree on is that attitudes are evaluations and that they are sensitive to the context in which they are produced.

## focus on

DO ATTITUDES TO CONSERVATION AND THE ENVIRONMENT PREDICT PROTECTIVE BEHAVIOURS TOWARDS WILDLIFE?

The accelerated global loss in biodiversity has led to increased social scientific study of the psychological, cultural and social factors that contribute to it (Bekoff & Bexell, 2010). What are the barriers that prevent people from engaging in pro-environmental behaviours? Under what conditions will we act in environmentally sustainable ways that could ensure a future for us all? What role do our attitudes towards other animals and the environment play in conservation behaviour?

Riley E. Dunlap and Kent D. Van Liere (1978) devised the New Environmental Paradigm (NEP) Scale to measure environmental attitudes. Since its original development, the NEP has been revised and adapted, and become the world's most used measure of environmental attitudes. For example, it has been used to show that individuals who engaged in outdoor activities as a child have more pro-environmental attitudes (Ewert, Place & Sibthorp, 2005). The NEP has also been used to explore whether pro-environmental attitudes predict pro-environmental behaviours (for example, Poortinga, Steg & Vlek, 2004). However, as Wouter Poortinga et al. (2004) discovered, and many other researchers besides, a simple mapping of environmental attitudes onto environmental-friendly behaviours is fraught with difficulties. There are many different kinds of pro-environmental behaviours, some of which we can choose to do (e.g. recycle glass), but some which may simply not be possible for us to do (e.g. buy an eco-friendly car), despite our pro-environmental attitudes.

Riley Dunlap (2008) points out that the NEP was never intended as a predictor of specific pro-environmental behaviours, and other factors may need to be considered. Furthermore, a measure like the NEP may not

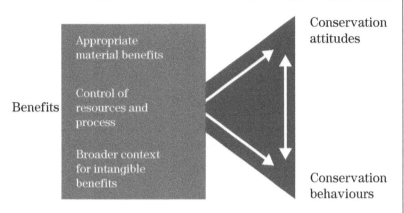

FIGURE 5.9  The framework for understanding the relationship between benefits, attitudes and behaviours to conservation

be applicable beyond the Western cultural context in which it was developed. The 'anti-environmental' attitudes it measures (e.g. 'Plants and animals exist primarily to be used by humans') may not translate as necessarily negative cross-culturally, and can, as we shall see, under certain conditions, facilitate conservation behaviour.

Lauren Scanlon and Christian Kull (2009) wanted to know how well attitudes predicted conservation behaviours amongst poor southern African communities, where conservation may be a luxury they can ill afford. They point out that attitudes are only part of a complex story. People will only act in environmentally sustainable ways, and conserve wildlife, if there are benefits and incentives for doing so. Scanlon and Kull focused their efforts specifically on the Torra Conservancy in northwest Namibia, a community-based natural resource management (CBNRM) initiative. Here, Conservancy residents benefit from protecting wildlife in terms of employment (eco-tourism), meat (sustainable hunting), and selling crafts. Here attitudes and behaviours towards conserving wildlife have changed rapidly in response to the CBNRM initiative. From a series of interviews and attitude scales, Scanlon and Kull proposed a three-way relationship between attitudes, benefits and behaviours (Figure 5.9).

Scanlon and Kull found that 80 per cent of Conservancy members had positive attitudes towards the environment and conservation when they were in receipt of benefits (e.g. 'Now that I have received benefits, I support conservation because I can see that it brings me benefits like money and meat'). Furthermore, these benefits also fostered conservation behaviours ('We get the benefits because we protect the wildlife and don't hunt anymore'). However, Scanlon and Kull thought that although attitudes do influence behaviour, it was the conservation behaviour that was most influential in shaping attitudes ('Through my involvement I have learned about conservation and now I'm much more interested in conservation'). Remember Leon Festinger's Cognitive Dissonance Theory? Festinger claimed that the stronger influence was behaviour over attitudes rather than the other way around. Importantly, what Scanlon and Kull found by mixing qualitative (interviews) with quantitative (attitude scales), was that the conditions under which attitudes and behaviours are linked is complex and mediated, in this case, by appropriate benefits (such as meat and employment) to this community.

So, general attitude measures, like the NEP, can be problematic once we try to apply them beyond the context in which they were devised. What we might consider to be a positive or negative attitude, might not be recognised as such cross-culturally. Furthermore, the link between attitudes and behaviour is not as clear-cut as we might hope.

The debate continues about the importance of measuring attitudes and the usefulness of developing attitude scales such as the NEP, in understanding if and when people behave in particular ways.

QUESTIONS

**1** To what extent do you think negative attitudes towards the environment are responsible for disengagement with environmentally responsible behaviours?

**2** How useful are attitude scales?

## SUMMING UP: ATTITUDES AND BEHAVIOUR

### ORGANIZATION OF ATTITUDES

☐ Social psychologists have offered various explanations for how attitudes are formed. These include direct experience with objects and living things, classical and operant conditioning, parental and peer influence and modelling.

☐ Attitudes are useful as they enable us to 'do' certain things. They have particular functions such as providing us with knowledge about the world, facilitating us to receive positive outcomes and avoid negative ones, enabling us to protect our sense of self, and expressing and reinforcing our sense of identity. Our attitudes can help us through a crisis but they can also hinder us, depending on what our attitudes are towards something.

☐ Social psychologists have developed an array of methods for measuring people's attitudes. These have included case studies and rating scales. The most well-known attitudes scales in social psychology include those by Thurstone, Likert and Osgood. These explicit measures of attitudes have been subject to criticism as participants may express those attitudes which are socially desirable rather than those they actually hold.

☐ More subtle and implicit measures of attitudes have recently been developed to avoid social desirability biases which can hamper explicit measures such as rating scales. These have included the Implicit Association Test (IAT) and rely on reaction times rather than explicit declarations of attitudes. However, IATs have also been criticized for their validity. The extent to which they measure attitudes, rather than processing speed, has been questioned.

### HOW WELL DO OUR ATTITUDES PREDICT OUR BEHAVIOUR?

☐ How do our inner attitudes (evaluative reactions towards some object or person, often rooted in beliefs) relate to our external behaviour? Although popular wisdom stresses the impact of attitudes on behaviour, in fact, attitudes are often poor predictors of behaviours. Moreover, changing people's attitudes typically fails to produce much change in their behaviour. These findings sent social psychologists scurrying to find out why we so often fail to play the game we talk.

☐ Our expressions of attitudes and our behaviours are each subject to many influences. Our attitudes will predict our behaviour (1) if these 'other influences' are minimized, (2) if the attitude corresponds very closely to the predicted behaviour (as in voting studies), and (3) if the attitude is potent (because something reminds us of it, or because we acquired it by direct experience). Thus there is, under these conditions, a connection between what we think and feel and what we do.

## WHEN DOES OUR BEHAVIOUR AFFECT OUR ATTITUDES?

The attitude–action relation also works in the reverse direction: we are likely not only to think ourselves into action but also to act ourselves into a way of thinking. When we act, we amplify the idea underlying what we have done, especially when we feel responsible for it. Many streams of evidence converge on this principle. The actions prescribed by social roles mould the attitudes of the role players.

- ☐ Similarly, what we say or write can strongly influence attitudes that we subsequently hold.

- ☐ Actions also affect our moral attitudes: that which we have done, even if it is evil, we tend to justify as right.

## WHY DOES OUR BEHAVIOUR AFFECT OUR ATTITUDES?

- ☐ Three competing theories explain why our actions affect our attitude reports. *Self-presentation theory* assumes that people, especially those who self-monitor their behaviour hoping to create good impressions, will adapt their attitude reports to appear consistent with their actions. The available evidence confirms that people do adjust their attitude statements out of concern for what other people will think. But it also shows that some genuine attitude change occurs.

- ☐ Two theories propose that our actions trigger genuine attitude change. *Dissonance theory* explains this attitude change by assuming that we feel tension after acting contrary to our attitudes or making difficult decisions. To reduce that arousal, we internally justify our behaviour. Dissonance theory further proposes that the less external justification we have for our undesirable actions, the more we feel responsible for them, and thus the more dissonance arises and the more attitudes change.

- ☐ *Self-perception theory* assumes that when our attitudes are weak, we simply observe our behaviour and its circumstances, then infer our attitudes. One interesting implication of self-perception theory is the 'overjustification effect': rewarding people to do what they like doing anyway can turn their pleasure into drudgery (if the reward leads them to attribute their behaviour to the reward).

- ☐ Evidence supports predictions from both theories, suggesting that each describes what happens under certain conditions.

## ATTITUDES AS SOCIAL ACTIONS

- ☐ Some social psychologists (usually discursive) have argued that attitudes do not predict behaviour, but *are* a form of social action.

- ☐ They suggest that attitudes are constructed in interaction between people, and are shaped according to the context in which they are produced. This means attitudes can be highly variable.

- ☐ They also argue that what we have attitudes about (attitude–objects) do not pre-exist the evaluation but are themselves constructed in language as part of that evaluation.

- ☐ Discursive psychologists argue that we should study attitudes qualitatively and examine how they are formed, and what they are used for, in language.

---

## CRITICAL QUESTIONS

**1** What definitions have social psychologists offered to describe 'attitudes'?

**2** Do IATs offer a truer reflection of people's attitudes than other methods?

▶

**3** How well can attitudes predict behaviour?

**4** What social psychological theories have been proposed to explain attitude change?

**5** Where do attitudes reside?

**6** Are attitudes just talk?

## RECOMMENDED READINGS

Here are some recommended classic and contemporary readings on attitudes and how they have been understood and measured in social psychology.

### Classic Papers

Festinger, L. (1964). Behavioral support for opinion change. *Public Opinion Quarterly*, **28**(3), 404–417.

*This paper outlines different approaches to measuring attitudes, as outlined in this chapter.*

Katz, D. (1960). The functional approach to the study of attitudes. *Public Opinion Quarterly*, **24**(2), 163–204.

*A classic paper that considers what we have attitudes for and how they help (or hinder!) us in our daily lives.*

### Contemporary Papers

Fazio, R.H., & Olson, M. A. (2003). Implicit measures in social cognition research: Their meaning and use. *Annual Review of Psychology*, **54**(1), 297–327.

*Examines how our environment, and what we experience on a day-to-day basis, unconsciously shapes our attitudes.*

Greenwald, A., McGhee, D. E., and Schwartz, J. L. K. (1998). Measuring individual differences in implicit cognition: The implicit association test. *Journal of Personality and Social Psychology*, **74**(6), 1464–1480.

*Provides an overview of the IAT, including an evaluation of the benefits of implicit measures of attitudes over explicit ones.*

Poobalan, A. S., Aucott, L. S., Clarke, A., Smith, W., & Cairns, S. (2012). Physical activity attitudes, intentions and behaviours among 18–25 year olds: A mixed methods study. *BMC Public Health*, **12**(1), 640–649.

*A good empirical example of an application of the Theory of Planned Behaviour in the health field. Offers a critical evaluation of TPB, adopting qualitative and quantitative approaches to assess the relationship between attitudes and physical exercise.*

"Character may almost be called the most effective means of persuasion."

*Aristotle, Rhetoric*

# PERSUASION

The Ancient Greek philosopher Aristotle (384–322 BC) wrote extensively on the art of persuasion. In his classic work *Rhetoric* he stated that persuasion involves the manipulation of the audience's mind through emotion or reasoned argument. But, when rhetoric is coupled with scientific certainty ('logic') and reasoned informed debate ('dialect') people can be persuaded and educated on the basis of knowledge rather than emotion. As history teaches us, when it's achieved, the consequences of successful persuasion can range from revolution to catastrophy.

Joseph Goebbels, Germany's Minister for National Enlightenment and Propaganda from 1933 to 1945, certainly understood the power of persuasion. Given control of publications, radio programmes, motion pictures and the arts, he undertook to persuade Germans to accept Nazi ideology in general and anti-Semitism in particular. His colleague Julius Streicher published a weekly anti-Semitic newspaper, *Der Stürmer*, which boasted a circulation of 500 000 and was the only paper read cover to cover by Adolf Hitler. Streicher also published anti-Semitic children's books and, with Goebbels, spoke at the mass rallies that became part of the Nazi propaganda machine. Hitler himself, however, hardly mentioned the Jews from the moment he took power in 1933 until the outbreak of the war (Koonz, 2003, from Reicher et al., 2008; also see Chapter 7). In his propaganda speeches Hitler focused on the virtues of (ethnic) Germans as moral, pure, selfless and loyal. Hitler pledged to defend these qualities and promised to create a new society in which they could flourish (Reicher et al., 2008). This was a propaganda most Germans acknowledged even if they did not want to be anti-Semitic, anti-homosexual or against the mentally challenged. The Nazis persuaded many Germans by emphasizing ingroup virtue, and paved the way for outgroup hatred towards the groups that blocked the realization of the Third Reich.

How effective were Goebbels, Streicher and other Nazi propagandists? Did they, as the Allies alleged at Streicher's Nuremberg trial, 'inject poison into the minds of millions and millions' (Bytwerk, 1976)?

Most Germans were not persuaded to express raging hatred for the Jews. But some were. Others became sympathetic to measures such as firing Jewish university professors, boycotting Jewish-owned businesses and, eventually, sending Jews to concentration camps. Most other Germans became either sufficiently uncertain or sufficiently intimidated to condone the regime's massive genocidal programme, or at least to allow it to happen. Without the complicity of millions of people, there would have been no Holocaust (Goldhagen, 1996).

persuasion *the process by which a message induces change in beliefs, attitudes or behaviours*

The powers of persuasion were partly apparent in what a Pew survey (2003) called the 'rift between Americans and Western Europeans' over the Iraq war. Surveys shortly before the war revealed that Americans favoured military action against Iraq by about two to one, while Europeans were opposing it by the same margin (Burkholder, 2003; Moore, 2003; Pew, 2003). Once the war began, Americans' support for the war rose, for a time, to more than three to one (Newport et al., 2003). Except for Israel, people surveyed in all other countries were opposed to the attack.

'Speech has power. Words do not fade. What starts as a sound ends in a deed.'
    Rabbi Abraham Heschel, 1961

The huge rift between Americans and the citizens of other countries is partly a sign of persuasion at work. What persuaded most Americans to favour the war? What persuaded most people elsewhere to oppose it?

Attitudes were being shaped, at least in part, by persuasive messages in the US media that led half of Americans to believe that Saddam Hussein was directly involved in the 9/11 attacks and four in five to falsely believe that weapons of mass destruction would be found (Duffy, 2003; Newport et al., 2003). Sociologist James Davison Hunter (2002) notes that culture-shaping usually occurs top-down, as cultural elites control the dissemination of information and ideas. Thus, Americans, and people elsewhere, learned about and watched two different wars (della Cava, 2003; Friedman, 2003a; Goldsmith, 2003; Krugman, 2003; Tomorrow, 2003). Depending on the country where you lived and the media available to you, you may have heard about 'America's liberation of Iraq' or 'America's invasion of Iraq'.

In the view of many Americans, the other nations' media combined a pervasive anti-American bias with a blindness to the threat posed by Saddam. To many people elsewhere, the 'embedded' American media were biased in favour of the military. Regardless of where bias lay or whose perspective was better informed, this much seems clear: depending on where they lived, people were given (and discussed and believed) somewhat differing information. So the written and spoken word, and the cultural and societal context of norms and values upon which they are based, are a crucial component in understanding persuasion. Moreover, persuasion really matters.

Persuasive forces have also been harnessed to promote healthier living. Thanks partly to health-promotion campaigns, smoking among UK adults has dropped from 45 per cent of the population in 1974, to 20 per cent in 2011. Surveys also show that there has been a decline in the number of men who drink alcohol at least 5 days a week from 22 per cent in 2005 to 16 per cent in 2011 (General Lifestyle Survey, ONS, 2011). More than at any time in recent decades, health-and safety-conscious educated adults are shunning cigarettes and beer. So in contemporary society we see 'rhetoric', 'logic' and 'dialect' combine, influencing the way we conduct our everyday lives.

As these examples show, efforts to persuade are sometimes diabolical, sometimes controversial and sometimes beneficial. Persuasion is neither inherently good nor bad. It is a message's purpose, form and content that elicits judgements of good or bad. The bad we call 'propaganda'. The good we call 'education' or 'information'. Education is less coercive than propaganda. Yet generally we call it 'education' when we believe it, 'propaganda' when we don't (Lumsden et al., 1980). In the last decade, support for gay rights and gay civil unions or marriage has significantly increased across the USA and Europe (e.g. Myers & Scanzoni, 2005). Some people view such attitude changes as reflecting 'education', others as reflecting 'propaganda'. Our opinions have to come from somewhere. Persuasion – whether it be education or propaganda – is therefore inevitable. Indeed, persuasion is everywhere – at the heart of politics, marketing, courtship, parenting, negotiation, evangelism and courtroom decision making.

However, persuasion doesn't just describe the practices of these large-scale campaigns designed to influence our attitudes and opinions about wars, healthy living and political policies, but is part of our everyday lives – what we might call 'mundane persuasion'. When we engage in dialogue with one another we are involved in rhetorical discourse, whether it be explaining events that happened in a nightclub or on holiday, or justifying our actions towards a friend. We are trying to persuade someone else of our version of events. As we saw in Chapter 5, some social psychologists (such as discursive psychologists) have argued that persuasion is part and parcel of our everyday attitudes and our daily lives. So the kinds of questions about persuasion and rhetoric that the Ancient Greek philosophers sought to address are the same as those social psychologists are still trying to answer today. The act of persuasion crosses time and space.

*mundane persuasion we are involved in acts of persuasion in our everyday lives*

However, social psychologists differ in how they study the act of persuasion. Experimental social psychologists seek to understand what leads to effective, long-lasting attitude change. What factors affect persuasion? And how, as persuaders, can we most effectively 'educate' others? Other, more discursive social psychologists have focused primarily on language to examine how messages are put together in rhetorical ways that present versions of social reality as 'facts', either on a grand scale or at a mundane level. In all cases, the 'art' of persuasion has become a 'science' of identifying how and what works. To begin to consider these things, it's useful to distinguish between the 'form' and 'content' of a message in understanding how they achieve influence.

'A fanatic is one who can't change his mind and won't change the subject.'
  Winston Churchill, 1954

Michael Billig (1996) argues that social psychologists tend to study persuasion in the way some geologists study erosion – by observing the effects of various factors in brief, controlled experiments. The effects are small and are most potent on weak attitudes that don't touch our values (Johnson & Eagly, 1989; Petty & Krosnick, 1995). Yet they enable us to understand how, given enough time, such factors could produce big effects. However, such experiments have frequently focused on the 'form' of a message – what aspects of its style, structure and delivery can be noted as being 'successful' in persuading an audience. There have been fewer experimental studies of the 'content' of messages in ensuring persuasive influence. What we shall consider here are some of the general features of persuasion that have been suggested in social psychology, using experiments. However, persuasion is inextricably linked to local and broader social context (e.g. cultural ideology, our social networks, the narrative course of a conversation, societal norms and values) and as this varies across time and space, from individual to individual, group to group, it is impossible to provide an abstract generalizable list of factors of persuasion as you will always come across the exception to the rule (Billig, 1996). What 'works' in one case may not work in another. So in examining the factors of persuasion that have been confirmed in experimentation, we should also bear in mind that these should be understood as 'working' within a specific social context at a particular time.

Social psychology does not always fully understand or is able to explain all forms of persuasion. This chapter does not aim to suggest otherwise. That said, social psychology has made some extremely useful inroads into understanding and explaining some aspects of the phenomenon. To begin, let's first consider the main cognitive routes to persuasion that have been identified using controlled experiments.

## WHAT PATHS LEAD TO PERSUASION?

*What two paths lead to influence? What type of cognitive processing does each involve – and with what effects?*

One of the earliest and most comprehensive contributions to the social psychology of persuasion came from the work of Carl Hovland in his attempts to understand the effectiveness of propaganda. While serving as chief psychologist for the US War Department during the Second World War, Yale professor Carl Hovland and his colleagues (1949) helped the war effort by studying persuasion. Hoping to boost soldier morale, Hovland and his colleagues systematically studied the effects of training films and historical documentaries on new recruits' attitudes towards the war. Back at Yale after the war, they continued studying what makes a message persuasive. Their research found varied factors related to the communicator, the content of the message, the channel of communication and the audience. They summarized the goal of their research as the study of 'the formula of who says what to whom with what effect' (Hovland et al., 1953, p. 12).

Hovland's work resulted in a categorization of factors that characterized successful persuasion. As shown in Figure 6.1, persuasion entails clearing several hurdles. Any factors that help people clear the hurdles in the persuasion process increase the likelihood of persuasion. For example, if an attractive source increases your attention to a message, then the message should have a better chance of persuading you. The Yale group's approach to studying persuasion provides us with a good understanding of *when* persuasion is likely to occur.

Researchers at Ohio State University then suggested that people's thoughts in response to persuasive messages also matter. If a message is clear but unconvincing, then you will easily counter-argue the message and won't be

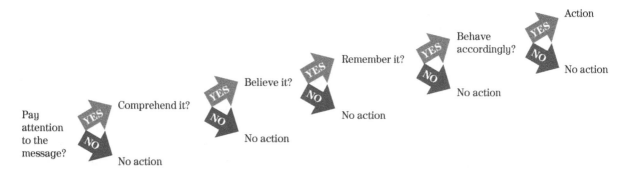

**FIGURE 6.1** The hurdles of the persuasion process

To elicit action, a persuasive message must clear several hurdles. What is crucial, however, is not so much remembering the message itself as remembering one's own thoughts in response.

SOURCE: Adapted from W. J. McGuire. 'An Information-Processing Model of Advertising Effectiveness', in *Behavioural and Management Sciences in Marketing*, H. L. Davis & A. J. Silk, eds. Copyright © 1978. Reprinted by permission of John Wiley & Sons, Inc.

persuaded. If the message offers convincing arguments, then your thoughts will be more favourable and you will most likely be persuaded. This 'cognitive response' approach helps us understand why persuasion occurs more in some situations than in others.

## THE CENTRAL ROUTE

central route to persuasion *occurs when after careful consideration of the content of a message people find the argument persuasive (the opposite of the peripheral route to persuasion)*

Currently the dominant approach to persuasion in social psychology, Richard Petty and John Cacioppo (1986; Petty & Wegener, 1999) and Alice Eagly and Shelly Chaiken (1993, 1998) theorized that persuasion is likely to occur via one of two routes. Petty and Cacioppo developed the *Elaboration-likelihood model* of persuasion (ELM), which proposes that when people are motivated and able to think about an issue, they are likely to engage with the content of a message and as such take the central route to persuasion – focusing on the arguments. If those arguments are strong and compelling, persuasion is likely. People scrutinize the information embedded within a message and relate it to the information they already have stored in memory about an issue. They evaluate and may modify their existing attitudes about the issue accordingly (see Chapter 5). If the message offers only weak arguments, thoughtful people will notice that the arguments aren't very compelling and will counter-argue.

## THE PERIPHERAL ROUTE

peripheral route to persuasion *occurs when people are influenced by incidental cues (such as the speaker's attractiveness) and, due to this, find the argument persuasive, rather than by careful consideration of the argument's validity (the opposite of the central route to persuasion)*

But sometimes the strength of the arguments doesn't matter. It's the form that counts. Petty and Cacioppo suggest that this happens when people do not think too much about an issue. So if we're distracted, uninvolved, or just plain busy, we may not take the time to reflect on the message's content. Rather than noticing whether the arguments are particularly compelling, we might follow the peripheral route to persuasion – focusing on cues that trigger acceptance without much thinking. So an attractively packaged message will be better received than one that has compelling arguments. In these situations, easily understood familiar statements are more persuasive than novel statements with the same meaning.

So if we consider central and peripheral routes to persuasion, Michael Billig (1996) argues that what we have here are 'the two competing demands of experience: one whispers seductively that people can be fooled and the other warns that the audience can argue back. For any given situation, orators must use their judgement to decide between these two voices of theirs' (p. 109). Smart advertisers adapt advertisements to their consumers' thinking. They do so for good reason, given how much of consumer behaviour – such as one's spontaneous decision, while shopping, to pick up some ice cream of a particular brand – is made unthinkingly (Dijksterhuis et al., 2005). Something as minor as German music may lead customers to buy German wine, whereas others, hearing French music, reach for French wine (North et al., 1997). Billboards and television commercials – media that consumers are able to take in for only brief amounts of time – therefore use the peripheral route, by using visual images as peripheral cues. Instead of providing arguments in favour of smoking, cigarette advertisements associate the product with images of beauty and pleasure. So do soft-drink advertisements that promote 'the real thing' with images of youth, vitality and happy polar bears. On the other hand, magazine computer advertisements (which interested, logical consumers may pore over for some time) seldom feature movie stars or great athletes. Instead they offer customers information on competitive features and prices. Government campaigns that ask us to recycle our rubbish and decrease our dependence on plastic carrier bags may well decide to engage their audience with the central arguments on the virtues of greener ways of living.

## DIFFERENT ROUTES FOR DIFFERENT PURPOSES

The ultimate goal of the advertiser, the preacher, and even the teacher, is not just to have people pay attention to the message and move on. Typically, the goal also involves some sort of behaviour change (buying a product, loving one's neighbour, or studying more effectively). Are the two routes to persuasion equally likely to fulfil that goal? Petty and his colleagues (1995) note how central route processing can lead to more enduring change than does the peripheral route. When people are thinking carefully and mentally elaborating on issues, they rely not just on the strength of persuasive appeals but on their own thoughts in response as well. It's not so much the arguments that are persuasive as the way they get people thinking. And when people think deeply rather than superficially, any changed attitude will more likely persist, resist attack and influence behaviour (Petty et al., 1995; Verplanken, 1991).

Thus, the central route is more likely to lead to attitude and behaviour changes that 'stick', whereas the peripheral route may lead merely to superficial and temporary attitude change. As sex educators know, changing attitudes is easier than changing behaviour. Studies assessing the effectiveness of abstinence education find some increase in attitudes supporting abstinence but little long-term impact on sexual behaviour (Hauser, 2005). Likewise, HIV-prevention education tends to have more effect on attitudes towards condoms than on condom use (Albarracin et al., 2003). In both cases, changing behaviour as well as attitudes seems to require people's actively processing and rehearsing their own convictions.

None of us has the time to thoughtfully analyse all issues. Often we take the peripheral route, by using simple rule-of-thumb heuristics, such as 'trust the experts' or 'long messages are credible'.

Shelly Chaiken (1980) developed the 'heuristic-systematic model' (HSM) to describe the differences between heuristic processing and systematic processing. It has much in common with the ELM. Both were developed in the 1980s, and both propose that there are different persuasion processes which can occur depending on the situation. However, the HSM distinguishes between systematic processing and heuristic processing. Whereas systematic processing involves a thorough cognitive engagement with the arguments within a message (similar to the central processing of ELM), heuristic processing is a way of dealing with information quickly taking mental short-cuts (not too dissimilar from the peripheral processing of ELM). We all make snap judgements using such heuristics: if a speaker is articulate and appealing, has apparently good motives, and has several arguments (or, better, if the different arguments come from different sources), we usually take the easy peripheral route and accept the message without much thought (Figure 6.2). Richard Petty and Duane Wegener (1998) suggest that we will use the heuristic route to the extent that we can remain confident in our decisions on the basis of this method of dealing with a message.

Where this confidence comes from may be in part down to our social networks and what attitudes already exist among the people around us. Our social networks are

> Recall the discussion of heuristics in social thinking and judgement from Chapter 4; snap judgements based on heuristics are common in everyday life.

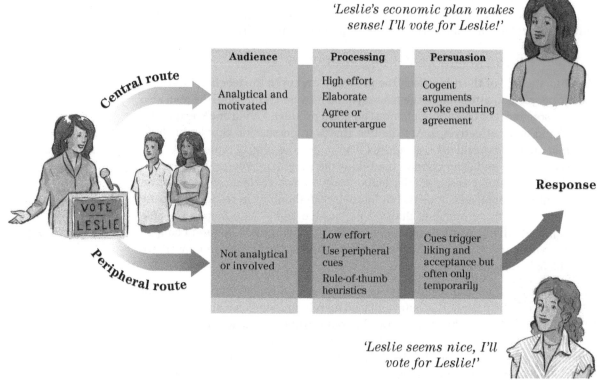

*'Leslie's economic plan makes sense! I'll vote for Leslie!'*

| Audience | Processing | Persuasion |
|---|---|---|
| Analytical and motivated | High effort / Elaborate / Agree or counter-argue | Cogent arguments evoke enduring agreement |
| Not analytical or involved | Low effort / Use peripheral cues / Rule-of-thumb heuristics | Cues trigger liking and acceptance but often only temporarily |

Central route

Peripheral route

Response

*'Leslie seems nice, I'll vote for Leslie!'*

**FIGURE 6.2** The central and peripheral routes to persuasion

Computer advertisements typically take the central route, by assuming their audience wants to systematically compare features and prices. Soft-drink advertisements usually take the peripheral route, by merely associating their product with glamour, pleasure and good moods. Central route processing more often produces enduring attitude change.

made up of the people with whom we have personal and professional relationships. Lindsey Levitan and Penny Visser (2007) have found that the amount of variability there is in the attitudes of your social network affects how likely you are to be persuaded, and which route to persuasion you are likely to take. In their study of 353 US participants who favoured capital punishment, those who came from attitudinally diverse social networks were much more likely to be persuaded against it than those from fairly homogenous social networks. Furthermore, they were persuaded by the presentation of strong arguments rather than weak ones, therefore using the central (or systematic) methods for processing the information. Those participants from more attitudinally homogeneous networks did not distinguish between strong and weak arguments, and were much more resistant to persuasion. Levitan and Visser argue that when we are surrounded by like-minded people, we are not motivated to change our attitudes and beliefs about things. Indeed, to do so might risk ridicule and even ostracism within the social network or ingroup. However, when we are within diverse social networks we are motivated to examine information carefully, working out our own attitudes.

## JUST ONE ROUTE TO PERSUASION?

Some social psychologists have been critical of these two route models of persuasion, and have suggested that really there's just one route to persuasion.

Arie Kruglanski and Erik Thompson (1999) argue that the 'central' and 'peripheral' routes of the ELM, and the 'systematic' and 'heuristic' paths of the HSM, are really just one path, and can be integrated into a *unimodel* of persuasion. They propose that the distinction between 'central' processing of a message's content, and peripheral processing based on cues, is actually a feature of the information presented rather than a description of the persuasion process we go through. In other words, they are all types of persuasive evidence. Kruglanski and Thompson suggest that, in the real world, messages contain a variety of content and cues in order to achieve their rhetorical effects. Both the content and the cues of the message are working to persuade you of its truth.

However, whatever social psychologists consider to be the route of persuasion, they are all interested in how messages convince you of their truth.

## THE ELEMENTS OF PERSUASION AND THEIR RELATIONSHIP TO SOCIAL NORMS

The classification of the elements of persuasion developed partly from Harold D. Laswell's (1948) claim that it was about 'Who says what in what channel to whom with what effect?' As such, among the primary ingredients of persuasion explored by social psychologists are these four: (1) the communicator; (2) the message; (3) how the message is communicated; and (4) the audience. In other words, who says what by what means to whom? Using experimental methods some social psychologists have examined how each of these factors affects the likelihood that we will take either the central or the peripheral route to persuasion, as well as their overall success in achieving influence. As we have already seen, some of this experimental work acknowledges the role of the situation and the broader social context in which the individual is embedded in the effectiveness of social influence. Using qualitative methods some social psychologists have sought to investigate this relationship between persuasion and social context. So, in this section we will consider the four main elements from a range of experimental and qualitative studies and ideas (see Figure 6.9 for a summary of these four elements).

### WHO SAYS? THE COMMUNICATOR

'It is simplicity that makes the uneducated more effective than the educated when addressing popular audiences.'
   Aristotle, *Rhetoric*

Social psychologists have found that who speaks affects how an audience receives a message. In one experiment, when the Socialist and Liberal leaders in the Dutch parliament argued identical positions using the same words, each was most effective with members of his own party (Wiegman, 1985). It's not just the message that matters, but also who says it. Does s/he belong to the ingroup or the outgroup? What, then, makes one communicator more persuasive than another?

### Credibility

Many of us would find a statement about the benefits of exercise more believable if it came from the Royal Society or National Academy of Sciences rather than from a tabloid newspaper. But the effects of source credibility (perceived expertise and trustworthiness) diminish after a month or so. If a credible person's message is

credibility *believability; a credible communicator is perceived as both expert and trustworthy*

persuasive, its impact may fade as its source is forgotten or dissociated from the message. And the impact of a non-credible person may correspondingly increase over time if people remember the message better than the reason for discounting it (Cook & Flay, 1978; Gruder et al., 1978; Pratkanis et al., 1988).

However, of course what, or who, is perceived as a credible source depends on the context in which it is presented.

### Perceived Expertise

How does one become an authoritative 'expert'? One way is to begin by saying things the audience agrees with, which makes one seem smart. Another is to be introduced as someone who is *knowledgeable* on the topic.

A message about tooth-brushing from 'Dr James Rundle of the Canadian Dental Association' is probably much more convincing than the same message from 'Jim Rundle, a local high school student who did a project with some of his classmates on dental hygiene' (Olson & Cal, 1984). After spending more than a decade studying high school marijuana use, researchers concluded that scare messages from unreliable sources did not affect marijuana use during the 1960s and 1970s.

The findings from experiments can tell us a lot about how people respond to sources they consider to be 'experts'. However, producing a credible source in terms of expertise relies on shared cultural understandings that some individuals, or categories of people, are experts in some social contexts. The sociologist Harvey Sacks (1992) explains that within each culture there is shared knowledge and understandings about the roles people occupy and the social categories to which they belong. These categories carry with them implicit knowledge about what such people know (category entitlements) and how they 'ought' to behave in accordance with their category membership (category bound activities). So in the above example we 'know' dentists are experts with respect to certain kinds of knowledge (oral health) and we have a shared understanding of how they 'ought' to behave. So there are clear limits to their expertise. As we share this knowledge people can populate their accounts of social life with references to such 'experts' rhetorically bolstering the persuasiveness of the message they are trying to convey.

Jason Clark and his research collaborators point out that we tend to scrutinize messages more when they are delivered by an expert than by a non-expert. We give them greater cognitive attention. Consequently, recent research evidence has suggested that the effectiveness of an expert depends on whether the expert is arguing from a position that we agree with, or one we do not (Clark et al., 2012). When an expert tries to convince us about something for which we are already convinced, we do not really scrutinize what they say. When you're preaching to the converted, it doesn't matter who's doing the preaching. But when the message is one we do not already agree with, this is when an expert might prove more effective. A credible expert and message can force us to engage with the message at a deeper level than previously, and shift our attitudes from an unfavourable stance to a favourable one.

Another way to appear credible is to *speak confidently*. Bonnie Erickson and her collaborators (1978) had students evaluate courtroom testimony given in a straightforward manner or in a more hesitant manner. For example:

*Question:* Approximately how long did you stay there before the ambulance arrived?

*Answer:* *[Straightforward]* Twenty minutes. Long enough to help get Mrs. David straightened out.

*[Hesitating]* Oh, it seems like it was about uh, twenty minutes. Just long enough to help my friend Mrs. David, you know, get straightened out.

The students found the straightforward witnesses much more competent and credible.

### Perceived Trustworthiness

Speech style also affects a speaker's apparent trustworthiness. Gordon Hemsley and Anthony Doob (1978) found that if, while testifying, videotaped witnesses looked their questioner *straight in the eye* instead of gazing downwards, they impressed people as more believable.

Trustworthiness is also higher if the audience believes the communicator is *not trying to persuade* them. In an experimental version of what later became the 'hidden camera' method of television advertising, Elaine Hatfield and Leon Festinger (Walster & Festinger, 1962) had some undergraduates eavesdrop on graduate students' conversations. (What they actually heard was a tape recording.) When the conversational topic was relevant to the eavesdroppers (having to do with campus regulations), the speakers had more influence if the listeners presumed the speakers were unaware of the eavesdropping. After all, if people think no one is listening, why would they be less than fully honest? There also seems to be some cross-cultural evidence to suggest that perceptions of trustworthiness are important in persuasion in both the USA and Korea (Yoon et al., 1998).

As millions of us now surf the Internet looking for advice and guidance, how do we know what information to trust? This was exactly the question Pam Briggs and her colleagues (2002) asked. They found that, first, people trust an online source of information when it appears as though the source is credible, knowledgeable and impartial. Second, people need to feel the information is personal to them. Finally, people tend to trust websites that offer the advice they expected. In a study of how women in England choose and use online health advice about hormone replacement therapy (HRT) Elizabeth Sillience, Pam Briggs and their colleagues (2007) noticed how women began the selection process by sifting through sites simply on the basis of their appearance. Websites that were attractive to the user were then examined for the quality and credibility of their information. However, the researchers are quick to point out the limited role the Internet has in shaping behaviour. We don't blindly follow. While it influences our decisions, the women in Sillience's study still tested it against advice from friends and family, and fundamentally trusted their own doctor as the prime source of help and advice.

We also perceive as sincere those who *argue against their own self-interest*. Alice Eagly, Wendy Wood and Shelly Chaiken (1978) presented students with a speech attacking a company's pollution of a river. When they said the speech was given by a political candidate with a business background or to an audience of company supporters, it seemed unbiased and was persuasive. When the same anti-business speech was supposedly given to environmentalists by a pro-environment politician, listeners could attribute the politician's arguments to personal bias or to the audience. Being willing to suffer for one's beliefs – which Gandhi, Martin Luther King, Jr, Nelson Mandela and other great leaders have done – also helps convince people of one's sincerity (Knight & Weiss, 1980).

**dilemma of stake and interest** *the management of self-interest in language*

Discursive social psychologists have termed this the 'dilemma of stake and interest' (Edwards, 1997; Potter, 1996). This means that if people are seen to have an 'axe to grind' in presenting a particular message, or having a personal interest or motivation in persuading people, they may not be regarded as trustworthy or credible. The canvassing politician seeking your vote, who tries to convince you that your taxes will not be raised should they be elected into power, is likely to be accused of having an interest in the version they present of their intended policies, and may not be believed. The man accused of assault in a bar-room brawl, who later tries to convince a jury that he was not responsible, can have his protestations dismissed on the grounds of 'Well, you would say that, wouldn't you!' G. Nigel Gilbert and Michael Mulkay (1984) found that when biochemists were asked to account for the trustworthiness of their scientific findings they emphasized the objectivity of science, the data-driven nature of the findings, free from human intervention. They called this an 'empiricist repertoire': one that managed their own stake in their findings to present accurate and trustworthy results. However, when asked to explain how other biochemists had achieved contradictory results to their own, they switched to a 'contingent repertoire', which emphasized how personal motives can drive scientific research contaminating the accuracy of the findings. So, to present your case as that of a disinterested and unmotivated communicator is often a very real concern in persuading people of the credibility and the trustworthiness of you and the message you convey.

Norman Miller and his colleagues (1976) found that trustworthiness and credibility also increase when people *talk fast*. People who listened to tape-recorded messages rated fast speakers (about 190 words per minute) as more objective, intelligent and knowledgeable than slow speakers (about 110 words per minute). They also found the more rapid speakers more persuasive. John F. Kennedy, an exceptionally effective public speaker, sometimes spoke in bursts approaching 300 words per minute.

Some television advertisements are obviously constructed to make the communicator appear both expert and trustworthy. A drug company may peddle its pain reliever using a speaker in a white laboratory coat, who declares confidently that most doctors recommend their key ingredient (which is merely aspirin). Given such peripheral cues, people who don't care enough to analyse the evidence may automatically infer that the product is special without questioning the expertise of the speaker in the white coat. Other advertisements seem not to use the credibility principle. It's not primarily for his expertise about sports apparel that Adidas paid David Beckham huge sums of money to appear in its advertisements.

**attractiveness** *having qualities that are pleasing or appealing to others. Also refers to a person being physically attractive or sexually alluring*

### Attractiveness and Liking

Most of us deny that endorsements by star athletes and entertainers affect us. We know that stars are seldom knowledgeable about the products they endorse. Besides, we know the intent is to persuade us; we don't just accidentally eavesdrop on Jennifer Lopez discussing clothes or fragrances. Such advertisements are based on another characteristic of an effective communicator: attractiveness.

We may think we are not influenced by attractiveness or likeability, but researchers have found otherwise. We're more likely to respond to those we like, a phenomenon well known to those organizing charitable solicitations, sweet sales and Tupperware parties. Marketing experts have discovered an attractive presenter for an unattractive product can contribute to persuading the public to buy the product (Praxmarer and Rossiter, 2011). Even a mere fleeting conversation with someone is enough to increase our liking for that person, and our responsiveness to his or her influence (Burger et al., 2001). Our liking may open us up to the communicator's arguments (central route persuasion), or it may trigger positive associations when we see the product later (peripheral route persuasion). As with credibility, the liking-begets-persuasion principle suggests applications (see Table 6.1).

Attractiveness varies in several ways. *Physical appeal* is one. Arguments, especially emotional ones, are often more influential when they come from people we consider beautiful (Chaiken, 1979; Dion & Stein, 1978; Pallak et al., 1983).

*Similarity* is another. As Chapter 9 emphasizes, we tend to like people who are like us. We also are influenced by them, a fact that has been harnessed by a successful anti-smoking campaign that features youth appealing to other youth through advertisements that challenge the tobacco industry about its destructiveness and its marketing practices (Krisberg, 2004). People who *act* as we do, subtly mimicking our postures, are likewise more influential. Furthermore, it seems this similarity effect also extends to our names. Daniel Howard and Roger Kerin (2011) found that participants exposed to advertised products with brand names similar to their own, were more favourably disposed to them than when the same product was given a generic name. So cranberry juice branded as V. Zack (participants first name initial, and full surname) was considered to be more desirable and beneficial than the same cranberry juice that was given a name dissimilar from their own. Why? Howard and Kerin suggest that the presence of a familiar name causes participants to engage in a more elaborate cognitive assessment of the product. And, it appears, we like things that are like us!

**TABLE 6.1**   Six persuasion principles

| Principle | Application |
| --- | --- |
| *Authority: People defer to credible experts* | Establish your expertise; identify problems you have solved and people you have served |
| *Liking: People respond more affirmatively to those they like* | Win friends and influence people. Create bonds based on similar interests, praise freely |
| *Social proof: People allow the example of others to validate how to think, feel and act* | Use 'peer power' – have respected others lead the way |
| *Reciprocity: People feel obliged to repay in kind what they've received* | Be generous with your time and resources. What goes around, comes around |
| *Consistency: People tend to honour their public commitments* | Have others write or voice their intentions. Don't say 'Please do this by …'. Instead, elicit a 'yes' by asking |
| *Scarcity: People prize what's scarce* | Highlight genuinely exclusive information or opportunities |

SOURCE: In his book *Influence: Science and Practice*, persuasion researcher Robert Cialdini (2001) illustrates six principles that underlie human relationships and human influence. (This chapter describes the first two.)

Theodore Dembroski, Thomas Lasater and Albert Ramirez (1978) gave African American junior high students an audiotaped appeal for proper dental care. When a dentist assessed the cleanliness of their teeth the next day, those who heard the appeal from an African American dentist (whose face they were shown) had cleaner teeth. As a general rule, people respond better to a message that comes from someone in their group (Van Knippenberg & Wilke, 1992; Wilder, 1990). As we outline in Chapters 12 and 13, social identity theory and self-categorization theory would explain this as illustrative of ingroup favouritism. People discriminate in favour of their own group at the expense of other perceptually relevant outgroups. As such, we are much more likely to be persuaded by someone we consider one of 'us' on some socially relevant dimension, than someone we consider one of 'them'.

Often our desire to fit in and be accepted by our peers influences our behaviour.

SOURCE: © monkeybusinessimages/iStock

Similarity can also be achieved through the content of a message. In an examination of the BBC *Panorama* interview the late Princess Diana gave in November 1997, Jackie Abell and Elizabeth Stokoe (2001) analysed how she presented herself as occupying roles that the audience could readily identify with. Referring to herself as a 'mother', 'wife' and 'woman', Diana presented herself as someone who understood the pressures everyday people were under to fulfil. Beneath the title and the nice palace, she was just an ordinary woman trying to deal with the same issues they do. Drawing on her ordinariness, Diana detailed the cause of her depression, eating disorders, self-harming behaviour and her love affairs. As a princess, she may not have won the sympathy of her audience for her behaviour. As an ordinary woman, juggling the roles of wife and mother, experiencing the stresses of everyday life, as well as those of royal duties, she achieved an increase in popularity among her 21.1 million audience and a nation, who felt they understood.

But is similarity more important than credibility? Well it seems to depend on the situation as the answer is sometimes yes and sometimes no! Timothy Brock (1965) found paint store customers more influenced by the testimony of an ordinary person who had recently bought the same amount of paint they planned to buy than by an expert who had recently purchased 20 times as much. On the other hand, recall that when discussing dental hygiene, a leading dentist (a dissimilar but expert source) was more persuasive than a student (a similar but inexpert source).

Such seemingly contradictory findings often bring out the detective in the scientist. Possibly an undiscovered factor is at work – that similarity is more important given the presence of factor X, and credibility is more important given the absence of factor X. Factor X, as George Goethals and Erick Nelson (1973) suggest, is whether the topic is more one of *subjective preference* or *objective reality*. When the choice concerns matters of personal value, taste or way of life, *similar* communicators have the most influence. But on judgements of fact – Does Sydney have less rainfall than London? – confirmation of belief by a *dissimilar* person does more to boost confidence. A dissimilar person provides a more independent judgement.

## WHAT IS SAID? THE MESSAGE CONTENT

It matters not only who says something but also *what* that person says. If you were to help organize an appeal to get people to vote for school taxes or to give money to world hunger relief, you might wonder how to concoct a recipe for central route persuasion. Common sense could lead you to either side of these questions:

☐ Is a purely logical message more persuasive – or one that arouses emotion?

☐ Will you get more opinion change by advocating a position only slightly discrepant from the listeners' existing opinions or by advocating an extreme point of view?

☐ Should the message express your side only, or should it acknowledge and refute the opposing views?

☐ If people are to present both sides – say, in successive talks at a community meeting or in a political debate – is there an advantage to going first or last?

Let's take these questions one at a time.

### Reason versus Emotion

Remember at the start of this chapter we noted Aristotle's distinction between rhetoric (manipulation of the emotions), logic (scientific certainty) and dialect (reasoned debate). Suppose you were campaigning in support of world hunger relief. Which of these might you best rely on to convey your message? Would you best itemize your arguments and cite an array of impressive statistics? Or would you be more effective presenting an emotional approach – perhaps the compelling story of one starving child? Of course, an argument can be both reasonable and emotional. You can marry rhetoric, dialect and logic. Still, which is *more* influential – reason or emotion? Was Shakespeare's Lysander right: 'The will of man is by his reason sway'd'? Or was Lord Chesterfield's advice wiser: 'Address yourself generally to the senses, to the heart, and to the weaknesses of mankind, but rarely to their reason'?

The answer: it depends on the audience. Well-educated or analytical people are often more responsive to rational appeals than are less educated or less analytical people (Cacioppo et al., 1983, 1996; Hovland et al., 1949). Jane McKay-Nesbitt and her colleagues (2011) found that younger adults (18–36 years) recalled negative emotional messages better than rational ones, and considered them to be more persuasive. However, older adults (48–89 years) showed the same levels of recall for rational and emotional messages. But, these older adults preferred rational and positive emotional messages and found them to be more persuasive than negative ones. So age seems to matter in how we receive persuasive rational and emotional messages.

Thoughtful, involved audiences often travel the central route; they are more responsive to reasoned arguments. Uninterested audiences more often travel the peripheral route; they are more affected by how much they like the communicator (Chaiken, 1980; Petty et al., 1981).

### The Effect of Good Feelings

Messages also become more persuasive through association with good feelings. Irving Janis and his colleagues (1965; Dabbs & Janis, 1965) found that students were more convinced by persuasive messages if they were allowed to enjoy peanuts and Pepsi while reading the messages (Figure 6.3). Similarly, Mark Galizio and Clyde Hendrick (1972) found that their students were more persuaded by folk-song lyrics accompanied by pleasant guitar music than they were by unaccompanied lyrics. Those who like conducting business over sumptuous lunches with soft background music can celebrate those results.

Good feelings often enhance persuasion, partly by enhancing positive thinking – if people are motivated to think – and partly by linking good feelings with the message (Petty et al., 1993). As noted in Chapter 4, in a good mood, people view the world through rose-tinted glasses. But they also make faster, more impulsive decisions; they rely more on peripheral cues (Bodenhausen, 1993; Braverman, 2005; Schwarz et al., 1991). Unhappy people ruminate more before reacting, so they are less easily swayed by weak arguments. Thus, if you can't make a strong case, you might want to put your audience in a good mood and hope they'll feel good about your message without thinking too much about it.

Feeling 'right' about a message is a key part in achieving persuasion. Joseph Cesario and Tony Higgins (2008) argue that the effect of non-verbal behaviour in making a recipient of a message feel right are extremely important in persuasion. In their study of 90 US students, they found that those who were 'promotion-focused' were more persuaded by a message that was delivered by an animated and eager schoolteacher, advocating a new after-school assistance programme for children. Those who were identified as 'prevention-focused' were more persuaded when the teacher delivered the information in a cautious manner. Cesario and Higgins conclude that for a message to be persuasive the non-verbal cues must match the orientations of the participant such that the message 'feels right'.

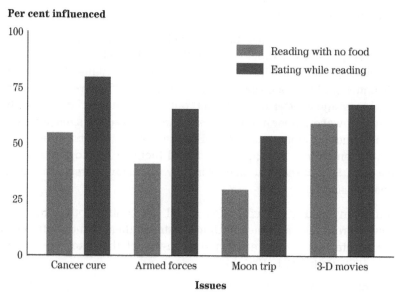

**FIGURE 6.3**   People who snacked as they read were more persuaded than those who read without snacking

SOURCE: Data from Janis et al., 1965.

Therefore, the style and manners of your lecturer in social psychology will not be assessed in the same way by all students. Some prefer to be entertained, to have a teacher who makes jokes and performs like an actor. Other students appreciate the presentation of complex theories and research results in a factual manner. Some enjoy lectures presenting subjective viewpoints, while others dislike those who do not present material in an objective manner. The saying 'you can please some of the people some of the time, but never all of the people all of the time', would seem to be very appropriate here!

### The Effect of Arousing Fear

Messages can also be effective by evoking negative emotions. When one is trying to persuade people to brush their teeth more often, get a tetanus shot or drive carefully, a fear-arousing message can be potent (Muller & Johnson, 1990). Mary Dodge (2006) has noted how the police may persuade young informants to provide information about the criminal activities of their peers and social networks using a variety of incentives (e.g. money, promises of leniency), but also by instilling fear. But how much fear should you arouse? Should you evoke just a little fear, lest people become so frightened that they tune out your painful message? Or should you try to scare the daylights out of them? Experiments by Howard Leventhal (1970) and his collaborators and by Ronald Rogers and his collaborators (Robberson & Rogers, 1988) show that, often, the more frightened people are, the more they respond. Research shows that women who are exposed to Flemish crime dramas are more fearful of becoming a victim of sexual violence in real life, than those women who are not (Custers and van den Bulck, 2013). Verolien Cauberghe and colleagues (2009) found that evoking fear in a sample of 18- to 28-year-old Belgian young people, fostered anti-speeding attitudes and behavioural intentions.

Fear-arousing communications have been used to increase people's detection behaviours, such as getting mammograms, doing breast or testicular self-examinations, and checking for signs of skin cancer. Sara Banks, Peter Salovey and their colleagues (1995) had women aged 40–66 who had not obtained mammograms view an educational video on mammography. Of those who received a positively framed message (emphasizing that getting a mammogram can save your life through early detection), only half got a mammogram within 12 months. Of those who received a fear-framed message (emphasizing that not getting a mammogram can cost you your life), two-thirds got a mammogram within 12 months. Anxiety-creating health messages about, say, the risks of high cholesterol can increase people's intentions to eat a low-fat, low-cholesterol diet (Millar & Millar, 1996). To have one's fears aroused is to become more intensely interested in information about a disease, and in ways to prevent it (Das et al., 2003; Ruiter et al., 2001). For example, John B. F. De Wit, Enny Das and Raymond Vet (2008) have found that how fear and risk are presented to someone affects how they will respond to it. In their study of men who have sex with other men, the risk of contracting the Hepatitis B virus was presented to them in the form of either narrative evidence, statistics, a mere assertion of increased risk, or no risk information was given. Their results showed that when the risk was presented to the men as a narrative of evidence they were much more likely to respond with the intention to have a vaccination against the virus. Fear-framed messages work better when trying to prevent a bad outcome (such as cancer) than when trying to promote a good outcome (such as fitness) (Lee & Aaker, 2004).

Playing on fear won't always make a message more potent, though. For example, it has been found that fear arousal in promoting driver safety has little effect on actual behaviour (Lewis et al., 2007). When the fear pertains to a pleasurable activity, notes Elliot Aronson (1997), the result often is not behavioural change but denial. For that reason, fear-arousing messages are more effective if they lead people not only to fear the severity and likelihood of a threatened event but also to perceive a solution and feel capable of implementing it (Devos-Comby & Salovey, 2002; Maddux & Rogers, 1983; Ruiter et al., 2001). Many advertisements designed to reduce sexual risks will aim both to arouse fear – 'AIDS kills' – and to offer a protective strategy: abstain, or wear a condom, or save sex for a committed relationship.

### Discrepancy

Some social psychologists propose that disagreement produces discomfort, and discomfort prompts people to change their opinions. This is central to Cognitive Dissonance Theory which we discussed in Chapter 5 (recall from Chapter 5 the effects of dissonance). So perhaps greater disagreement will produce more change. Then again, a communicator who proclaims an uncomfortable message may be discredited. People who disagree with conclusions drawn by a newscaster rate the newscaster as more biased, inaccurate and untrustworthy. People are more open to conclusions within their range of acceptability (Liberman & Chaiken, 1992; Zanna, 1993). So, perhaps greater disagreement will produce less change.

Based on the concepts of cognitive consistency and cognitive dissonance *social judgement theory* (SJT) proposes that how persuasive a person finds a message depends on how they evaluate the position or conclusions of that message. Does it fall within their own range of views and beliefs? The latitude of acceptance concerns all those attitudes that someone would find acceptable, whereas the latitude of rejection covers those they would find unacceptable. The latitude of non-commitment defines those attitudes that someone has no feelings about either way. So, for a message to be persuasive it should fall within the latitude of acceptance, or possibly non-commitment for it to work. The influence of SJT has been particularly highlighted in clinical research when prescribing treatment for mental disorders (e.g. Smith et al., 2003) and campaigns to reduce binge-drinking among university students (e.g. Smith et al., 2006).

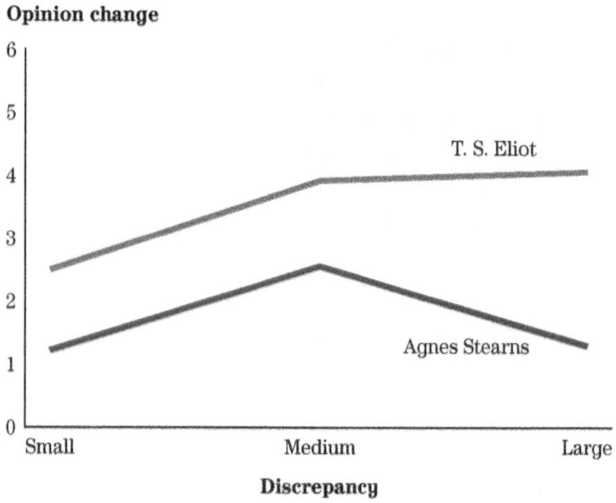

But, this isn't to say messages which are discrepant from the receiver's own beliefs and values are necessarily doomed. Elliot Aronson, Judith Turner and Merrill Carlsmith (1963) reasoned that a *credible source* – one hard to discount – would elicit the most opinion change when advocating a position *greatly discrepant* from the recipient's. Sure enough, when credible T. S. Eliot was said to have highly praised a disliked poem, people changed their opinion more than when he gave it faint praise. But when 'Agnes Stearns, a student at Mississippi State Teachers College', evaluated a disliked poem, high praise was no more persuasive than faint praise. Thus, as Figure 6.4 shows, discrepancy and credibility

**Opinion change**

T. S. Eliot

Agnes Stearns

Small    Medium    Large

**Discrepancy**

**FIGURE 6.4** Discrepancy interacts with communicator credibility
Only a highly credible communicator maintains effectiveness when arguing an extreme position.
SOURCE: Data from Aronson et al., 1963.

*interact*: the effect of a large versus small discrepancy depends on whether the communicator is credible.

Deeply involved people tend to accept only a narrow range of views. To them, a moderately discrepant message may seem foolishly radical, especially if the message argues an opposing view rather than being a more extreme version of a view with which they already agree (Pallak et al., 1972; Petty & Cacioppo, 1979; Rhine & Severance, 1970).

### One-sided versus Two-sided Appeals

Persuaders face another practical issue: how to deal with opposing arguments. Once again, common sense offers no clear answer. Acknowledging the opposing arguments might confuse the audience and weaken the case. On the other hand, a message might seem fairer and be more disarming if it recognizes the opposition's arguments.

Carol Werner and her colleagues (2002) showed the disarming power of a simple two-sided message in experimental messages that promoted aluminium-can recycling. Signs added to wastebaskets in a university classroom building said, for example, 'No Aluminum Cans Please!!!!! Use the Recycler Located on the First Floor, Near the Entrance'. When a final persuasive message acknowledged and responded to the main counterargument – 'It May Be Inconvenient. But It Is Important!!!!!!!!!!!' – recycling reached 80 per cent (double the rate before any message, and more than in other message conditions).

After Germany's defeat in the Second World War, the US Army did not want soldiers to relax and think that the still-ongoing war with Japan would become easy. Social psychologist Carl Hovland (whom we mentioned earlier in this chapter) and his colleagues (1949) in the Army's Information and Education Division designed two radio broadcasts arguing that the war in the Pacific would last at least two more years. One broadcast was one-sided; it did not acknowledge the existence of contradictory arguments, such as the advantage of fighting only one enemy instead of two. The other broadcast was two-sided; it mentioned and responded to the opposing arguments. As Figure 6.5 illustrates, the effectiveness of the message depended on the listener. A one-sided appeal was most effective with those who already agreed. An appeal that acknowledged opposing arguments worked better with those who disagreed.

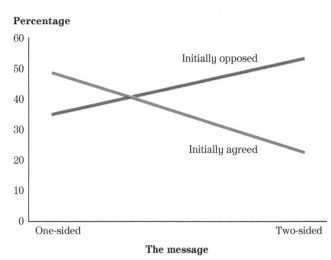

**FIGURE 6.5** The interaction of initial opinion with one-versus two-sidedness

After Germany's defeat in the Second World War, American soldiers sceptical of a message suggesting Japan's strength were more persuaded by a two-sided communication. Soldiers initially agreeing with the message were strengthened more by a one-sided message.

SOURCE: Data from Hovland et al., 1949.

Experiments also reveal that a two-sided presentation is more persuasive and enduring if people are (or will be) aware of opposing arguments (Jones & Brehm, 1970; Lumsdaine & Janis, 1953). In simulated trials, a defence case becomes more credible when the defence brings up damaging evidence before the prosecution does (Williams et al., 1993). Apparently, a one-sided message stimulates an informed audience to think of counter-arguments and to view the communicator as biased. Thus, a political candidate speaking to a politically informed group would indeed be wise to respond to the opposition. So, *if your audience will be exposed to opposing views, offer a two-sided appeal.*

### Primacy versus Recency

People often pay more attention to what comes first. Then again, people remember recent things better. So how might we seek to persuade someone? Speak first or last?

The primacy effect: information presented early is most persuasive. First impressions are important. For example, can you sense a difference between these two descriptions?

☐ John is intelligent, industrious, impulsive, critical, stubborn and envious.

☐ John is envious, stubborn, critical, impulsive, industrious and intelligent.

> **primacy effect** *other things being equal, information presented first usually has the most influence*

When Solomon Asch (1946) gave these sentences to college students, those who read the adjectives in the intelligent-to-envious order rated the person more positively than did those given the envious-to-intelligent order. The earlier information seemed to colour their interpretation of the later information, producing the primacy effect.

A similar effect occurs in experiments where people succeed on a guessing task 50 per cent of the time. Those whose successes come early seem more capable than those whose successes come after early failures (Jones et al., 1968; Langer & Roth, 1975; McAndrew, 1981). A curious primacy effect also appears in political polls and in primary election voting: candidates benefit from being listed first on the ballot (Moore, 2004). As another example, Norman Miller and Donald Campbell (1959) gave university students a condensed transcript from an actual civil trial. They placed the plaintiff 's testimony and arguments in one block, those for the defence in another. The students read both blocks. When they returned a week later to declare their opinions, most sided with the information they had read first.

> **recency effect** *information presented last sometimes has the most influence. Recency effects are less common than primacy effects*

What about the opposite possibility? Would our better memory of the most recent information we've received ever create a recency effect? We have all experienced what the book of Proverbs observed: 'The one who first states a case seems right, until the other comes and cross-examines.' We know from our experience (as well as from memory experiments) that today's events can temporarily outweigh significant past events. To test this, Miller and Campbell gave another group of students one block of testimony to read. A week later the researchers had them read the second block and then immediately state their opinions. The results were the reverse of the other condition – a recency effect. Apparently the first block of arguments, being a week old, had largely faded from memory.

Forgetting creates the recency effect (1) when enough time separates the two messages *and* (2) when the audience commits itself soon after the second message. When the two messages are back to back, followed by a time gap, it is the primacy effect that usually occurs (Figure 6.6). This is especially so when the first message stimulates thinking (Haugtvedt & Wegener, 1994).

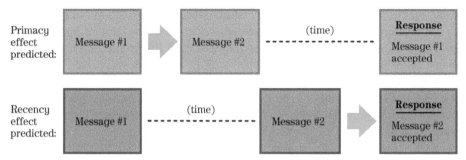

**FIGURE 6.6** Primacy effect versus recency effect
When two persuasive messages are back to back and the audience then responds at some later time, the first message has the advantage (primacy effect). When the two messages are separated in time and the audience responds soon after the second message, the second message has the advantage (recency effect).

## HOW IS IT SAID? THE CHANNEL OF COMMUNICATION

For persuasion to occur, there must be communication. And for communication to occur, there must be a channel of communication: a face-to-face appeal, a written sign or document, a television or radio advertisement.

Common-sense psychology places faith in the power of written words. How do we try to get people out to a campus event? We post notices. How do we get drivers to slow down and keep their eyes on the road? We put 'Drive Carefully' messages on billboards. How do we discourage students from dropping litter on campus? We post anti-litter messages on campus bulletin boards and in mailboxes.

*channel of communication the way the message is delivered – whether face to face, in writing, on film or in some other way*

### Active Experience or Passive Reception?

Are spoken appeals more persuasive? Not necessarily. Those of us who speak publicly, as teachers or persuaders, become so enamoured of our spoken words that we are tempted to overestimate their power. Ask college students what aspect of their college experience has been most valuable or what they remember from their first year, and few, sad to say, recall the brilliant lectures that we remember giving!

Thomas Crawford (1974) and his associates tested the impact of the spoken word by going to the homes of people from 12 churches shortly before and after they heard sermons opposing racial bigotry and injustice. When asked during the second interview whether they had heard or read anything about racial prejudice or discrimination since the previous interview, only 10 per cent recalled the sermons spontaneously. When the remaining 90 per cent were asked directly whether their priest had 'talked about prejudice or discrimination in the last couple of weeks', more than 30 per cent denied hearing such a sermon. The end result: the sermons left racial attitudes unaffected.

When you stop to think about it, an effective preacher has many hurdles to surmount. As Figure 6.1 showed, a persuasive speaker must deliver a message that not only gets attention but also is understandable, convincing, memorable and compelling. A carefully thought-out appeal must consider each of those steps in the persuasion process.

Consider another well-intentioned effort. At Scripps College in California, a week-long anti-litter campaign urged students to 'Keep Scripps' campus beautiful', 'Let's clean up our trash' and so forth. Such slogans were placed in students' mailboxes each morning and displayed on prominent posters across the campus. The day before the campaign began, social psychologist Raymond Paloutzian (1979) placed litter near a rubbish bin along a well-travelled sidewalk. Then he stepped back to record the behaviour of 180 passers-by. No one picked up anything. On the last day of the campaign, he repeated the test with 180 more passers-by. Did the pedestrians now race one another in their zeal to comply with the appeals? Hardly. Only two of the 180 picked up the litter.

*sleeper effect when a highly persuasive message is paired with a discounting, or low-credibility cue, leading to increased persuasiveness of the message over time*

The aptly named sleeper effect describes how a message can become more persuasive over time when paired with information that discredits its validity (Hovland et al., 1949). For example, imagine you are given a vivid and informative leaflet about the degraded state of the environment that asks you to use eco-friendly household products, such as washing powder. Initially you may find the message extremely persuasive and resolve to act accordingly. Unfortunately, over time this persuasive influence decays and we continue to purchase our usual non-environmentally friendly brands. However, suppose that message about the state of the environment is sponsored by a well-known eco-friendly brand of washing powder. Their name is visible on the leaflet. Now we might be suspicious. Is the state of the environment really that bad, or is this company simply trying to sell us more of their product? Our attitude towards the environment and the need to use certain products may be unchanged. However, what experiments have shown is that over time that message becomes persuasive. In fact we may see a delayed attitude change towards the topic (environmental degradation), and even a trip to the shops to buy the product. Why? There have been two main hypotheses put forward (Kumkale & Albarracín, 2004). The first suggests we simply forget the discounting information, so all we remember is the leaflet about the state of the environment, and forget about the company that sponsored it. The second suggests that rather than forgetting the discounting information, we simply dissociate it from the message. So we can recall both the message (the environment is in a terrible state) and the product (eco washing powder) but we do not associate them with one another. However, evidence for the sleeper effect is mixed, with some studies finding no proof that it exists at all. As an example, see Research Close-Up: I Know this Brand, But Did I Like the Ad?

Advertising power. Cigarette advertising campaigns have correlated with teen smoking increases among the targeted gender (Pierce & Gilpin, 1995; Pierce et al., 1994). This photo shows models practising the 'correct' pucker and blow technique for a 1950s television advertisement.

SOURCE: © Time Life Pictures/Getty Images

With such power, can the media help a wealthy political candidate buy an election? In presidential primaries those who spend the most usually get the most votes (Grush, 1980; Open Secrets, 2005). Advertising exposure helps make an unfamiliar candidate into a familiar one. As we will see in Chapter 9 on attraction, mere exposure to unfamiliar stimuli breeds liking. Moreover, *mere repetition* can make things believable. People rate trivial statements such as 'Mercury has a higher boiling point than copper' as more truthful if they read and rated them a week before.

Researcher Hal Arkes (1990) calls such findings 'scary'. As political manipulators know, believable lies can displace hard truths. Repeated clichés can cover complex realities. Even repeatedly saying that a consumer claim ('Shark cartilage is good for arthritis') is *false* can, when the discounting is presented amid other true and false claims, lead older adults later to misremember it as *true* (Skurnik et al., 2005). As they forget the discounting, their lingering familiarity with the claim can make it seem believable.

Mere repetition of a statement also serves to increase its fluency – the ease with which it spills off our tongue – which increases believability (McGlone & Tofighbakhsh, 2000). Wesley Moons and his colleagues (2009) found that regardless of whether a message was weak or strong, mere repetition increased its persuasiveness to participants. Other factors, such as rhyming, also increase fluency and believability. 'Haste makes waste' may say essentially the same thing as 'rushing causes mistakes', but it seems more true. Whatever makes for fluency (familiarity, rhyming) also makes for credibility.

The persuasive techniques of foot-in-the-door, door-in-the-face, and low-balling cause behavioural changes which then lead to shifts in attitudes. These are discussed in relation to the persuasive power of cults later in this chapter.

Because passively received appeals are sometimes effective and sometimes not, can we specify in advance the topics on which a persuasive appeal will be successful? There is a simple rule: persuasion *decreases* as the significance and familiarity of the issue *increase*. On minor issues, such as which brand of aspirin to buy, it's easy to demonstrate the media's power. On more familiar and important issues, such as attitudes about a lengthy and controversial war, persuading people is like trying to push a piano uphill. It is not impossible, but one shove won't do it.

As we saw in Chapter 5, 'Attitudes and Behaviour', active experience also strengthens attitudes. When we act, we amplify the idea behind what we've done, especially when we feel responsible. What is more, attitudes more often endure and influence our behaviour when rooted in our own experience. Compared with attitudes formed passively, experience-based attitudes are more confident, more stable and less vulnerable to attack. These principles are evident in many studies which show that the most effective HIV-prevention interventions not only give people information but also give them behavioural training, such as by practising assertiveness in refusing sex and using protection (Albarracin et al., 2005).

### Personal versus Media Influence

Persuasion studies often demonstrate that the major influence on us is not the media but our contact with people. Modern selling strategies seek to harness the power of word-of-mouth personal influence through 'viral marketing', 'creating a buzz' and 'seeding' sales (Walker, 2004). The Harry Potter series of books was not expected to be a best seller (*Harry Potter and the Philosopher's Stone* had a first printing of 500 copies) until kids talking to other kids made it so.

'You do realize, you will never make a fortune out of writing children's books?'
    J. K. Rowling's literary agent before release of *Harry Potter and the Philosopher's Stone*

Two classic field experiments illustrate the strength of personal influence. Some years ago, Samuel Eldersveld and Richard Dodge (1954) studied political persuasion in Ann Arbor, Michigan. They divided citizens intending not to vote for a revision of the city charter into three groups. Among those exposed only to

## research close-up

I KNOW THIS BRAND, BUT DID I LIKE THE AD?

**Source:** *Pashupati, K. (2003). 'I know this brand, but did I like the ad?' An investigation of the familiarity-based sleeper effect.* Psychology & Marketing, *20 (11), 1017–1043.*

### Introduction

Existing research suggests that there are certain factors that increase the influence of an advertisement. We have better recall for advertisements that have emotional content than we do for advertisements that are neutral. But how long does this recall last? Can we increase its retention in memory, and if we do, will this make the advertisement more persuasive? Repeated exposure to an advertisement can also aid recall for it and increase its influential power. But is it possible to repeat something too much? Can influence turn to boredom? Does it enhance or diminish our evaluation of it?

Research also suggests that how we evaluate the advertisement will influence our attitudes towards the brand being promoted. However, the familiarity-brand-sleeper effect predicts that those advertisements that evoke strong positive or negative evaluations will result in positive attitudes towards the brand after a delay (see the sleeper effect earlier in the chapter). Put simply, this effect predicts that emotive advertisements (good and bad) are better recalled than neutral ones. Furthermore, we are good at recalling familiar brands and we tend to like them more than unfamiliar ones. So, even after a delay, we should be able to remember the brand quite well. A memorable advertisement (positive or negative) and a memorable brand (familiar, positively evaluated) should result in delayed positive evaluation of the brand. Advertisements that are neutral will be quickly forgotten, as will the brand they promoted.

Based on existing research, seven hypotheses were generated to examine the extent to which each of these factors matters in the persuasiveness of advertisements. The hypotheses were as follows:

H1: Affective (positive and negative) advertisements will be recalled better than neutral advertisements, both immediately after exposure and 7 days later.

H2: Regardless of content, recall for all advertisements will diminish after 7 days. However, there will be a greater decline in recall for the neutral advertisements than the positive and negative affective ones.

H3: Advertisements that are negatively evaluated will result in the most negative attitudes towards the brand. Those advertisements that are evaluated the most positive will lead to the most positive attitudes towards the brand. Those advertisements evaluated as neutral will result in intermediate evaluations of the brand.

H4: Advertisements evaluated positively or negatively will lead to positive evaluations of the brand after a 7-day delay (sleeper effect).

H5: Repeated exposure to advertisements will result in more positive evaluations of the advertisement, regardless of its content, than advertisements just seen once.

H6: Repeated exposure to an advertisement, regardless of content, will result in more positive evaluations of the brand, than for advertisements just seen once.

H7: Participants will have better recall for advertisements seen three times, than those seen once.

## Method

### Participants

A total of 211 undergraduate students were recruited, of which 87 were male and 124 were female. Age range was 17–53 years, with a mean age of 24 years.

### Stimuli

The advertisements were TV commercials shown during a 30-minute documentary programme. To mimic real life as much as possible, the target advert was embedded amongst eight filler advertisements.

### Independent Variables

Advertisement type: Three types to evoke positive (Instant Chicken), negative (Potato Chips) or neutral (Bread) evaluations of the advertisement.

Repetition of the advertisement: Participants either saw the target advertisement once, or three times.

Delay: Participants were either tested immediately after seeing the advert, or 7 days later.

### Dependent Variables

Participants were asked a series of questions in relation to the hypotheses.

Attitude to Brand – assessed on a 7-point Likert scale (1 = very negative, 7 = very positive), participants were asked to rate how favourable they were to the brand being advertised.

Purchase Intention – assessed on a bipolar scale (e.g. likely – unlikely, probably – improbably), participants were asked if they would intend buying the product if they were in the market for one. (See Chapter 5 for discussion on Likert and bipolar attitudinal scales.)

Advertisement Recall – participants were asked to recall what brand was advertised. This was divided into an Aided condition (presented with a list of brand names and asked to indicate which they had seen), and Unaided condition (simply list the brand names you remember seeing).

### Procedure

Participants were asked if they would like to take part in a study on TV viewing habits and purchasing behaviour. Upon acquiring consent, they were then led to the testing room. They watched the TV programme, including the advertisements. Which target advert they saw depended on the condition they were in (positive, negative or neutral). Participants either saw the target advert once, or three times during the course of their TV viewing. Participants in the delay condition were thanked and asked to return in 7 days' time, whereupon they would be given the dependent measures. Participants in the immediate response condition were then given a post-test questionnaire that consisted of a recall test (aided or unaided) for the adverts and brands seen during the testing phase, and the Attitude to Brand and Purchase Intention scales. They were also asked for evaluations of each commercial for the target advertisement as a manipulation check to ensure that those adverts considered to be positive (Instant Chicken), negative (Potato Chips) and neutral (Bread) by the experimenters were also rated this way by the participants. This was done on a 7-point Likert scale (1 = very negative, 7 = very positive).

## Results

The manipulation check showed that participants did rate the adverts in the same way as the experimenters. The Potato Chip advert was considered most negative (Mean 3.35). the Bread advert was evaluated more positively (3.90), and the Instant Chicken advertisement was considered the most positive (5.31).

To test H1, the percentage of accurate overall recall for the adverts (aided and unaided, immediate and after 7 days) was calculated. The highest overall recall was for the negative advert (Potato Chips) (unaided 60.9 per cent, unaided 92.6 per cent). The next highest recall was for the neutral advert (Bread) (unaided 51 per cent, aided 80 per cent). The lowest recall was for the positive advertisement (Instant Chicken) (unaided 35.3 per cent, aided 56.4 per cent). So H1 was partially rejected as the neutral advert produced higher recall than the positive advertisement.

H2 predicted that those advertisements that were positively and negatively evaluated (Chicken, Potato Chips) would be better remembered after 7 days than the neutral advertisement (Bread). The negative advert had the highest level of recall (63 per cent), the positive had the lowest (25.8 per cent) and the neutral had an intermediate recall rate (37 per cent). So H2 is partially supported as while the negative advert had the highest level of recall after 7 days, the positive one had the lowest.

H3 and H4 both took into account the sleeper-effect. For the no-delay group, negative attitudes towards the advertisement resulted in negative attitudes towards the brand (mean score 3.85). Likewise, advertisements that were evaluated as neutral produced slightly higher evaluations of the product (4.30), and positive adverts gave rise to the most positively evaluated products (4.39). H3 was therefore supported. However, consistent with the sleeper-effect, H4 predicted that these results would be somewhat different for the 7-day delay group. For this group, both the positive and negatively evaluated advertisements should produce more positive evaluations of the product than the neutral advertisement. This was not the case. Although the negative advertisement produced a more positive evaluation of the product after the 7-day delay than the no-delay group (mean = 4.08), the evaluations of the products from the positive and neutrally evaluated advertisements remained the same as the no-delay group. See Table 6.2.

A $t$-test revealed no significant differences in scores between the Delay (immediate, 7-day) groups in Product Attitude scores according to advertisement type (positive, negative, neutral).

H5, H6 and H7 concerned the effects of repetition on brand evaluation. H5 predicted that participants who were exposed to the target advertisement three times would be more positive towards it than those who had only seen it once. H6 predicted that this repetition effect would also lead to more positive evaluation of the brand being advertised. Both of these hypotheses were supported. An inspection of the means shows that evaluations of the advertisement and the product were more positive when participants saw them three times, regardless of the type of advert (positive, negative, neutral). See Table 6.3.

**TABLE 6.2** Mean attitude towards brand scores by ad type, and delay condition

| Ad type | Attitude to product | |
| --- | --- | --- |
| | No delay | 7-day delay |
| Negative | 3.85 | 4.08 |
| Neutral | 4.30 | 4.31 |
| Positive | 4.39 | 4.27 |

Despite this increase in means for positive evaluation when exposed to an advertisement three times, this increase was only statistically significant when the advertisement was a negative one (Potato Chips).

H7 predicted that the advertisement would be better recalled when seen three times than when seen only once. This was supported as 69 per cent of participants who saw the advertisement three times, recalled it. This compares with only 38.2 per cent of participants who recalled an advertisement when only seen once.

**TABLE 6.3**  Mean attitude scores to advertisement and product according to repetition

| Ad type | Advertisement | | Product | |
|---|---|---|---|---|
| | Single exposure | Three exposures | Single exposure | Three exposures |
| All ads | 3.60 | 4.40 | 3.89 | 4.34 |
| Negative | 2.83 | 3.83 | 3.55 | 4.36 |
| Neutral | 3.36 | 4.23 | 4.18 | 4.35 |
| Positive | 4.99 | 5.65 | 4.22 | 4.28 |

## Discussion

This study only offers partial support for some of the experimental hypotheses. It seems we recall negative advertisements better than positive or neutral ones (H1, H2). However, this does not lead to increased liking over time for the product being advertised as no support was found for the sleeper-effect (H3, H4). Repetition increases positive evaluations of advertisements and brands regardless of the type of advert (H5, H6). However, this is only statistically significant for negative advertisements. So perhaps being exposed to a negative advert means we become more tolerant of it over time. We also remember better those advertisements we see more often.

Overall, this study failed to find support for the sleeper-effect. However, there are some criticisms that could be made of the study. The TV commercials may not have been extreme enough in terms of their positive and negative content. Furthermore, there was only one example of each type of advertisement. Perhaps more examples might have produced different results. The sample consisted of undergraduate students. Might a more heterogeneous population have behaved in a different way? Finally, the study did not check how familiar participants were with each of the brands being advertised. Any effect brand familiarity may have upon evaluations of it, need to be investigated. Trying to pin down the factors which make advertisements persuasive and encourage us to buy products, is extremely complex.

what they saw and heard in the mass media, 19 per cent changed their minds and voted in favour of the revision on election day. Of a second group, who received four mailings in support of the revision, 45 per cent voted for it. Among people in a third group, who were visited personally and given the appeal face to face, 75 per cent cast their votes for the revision.

In another field experiment, a research team led by John Farquhar and Nathan Maccoby (Farquhar et al., 1977; Maccoby, 1980; Maccoby & Alexander, 1980) tried to reduce the frequency of heart disease among middle-aged adults in three small California cities. To check the relative effectiveness of personal and media influence, they interviewed and medically examined 1200 participants before the project began and at the end of each of the following three years. Residents of Tracy, California, received no persuasive appeals other than those occurring in their regular media. In Gilroy, California, a two-year multimedia campaign used television, radio, newspapers and direct mail to teach people about coronary risk and what they could do to reduce it. In Watsonville, California, this media campaign was supplemented by personal contacts with two-thirds of those participants whose blood pressure, weight and age put them in a high-risk group. Using behaviour-modification principles, the researchers helped the Watsonville participants set specific goals and reinforced their successes.

As Figure 6.7 shows, after one, two and three years, the high-risk participants in Tracy (the control town) were at about as much risk as before. High-risk participants in Gilroy, which was deluged with media appeals, improved their health habits and decreased their risk somewhat. Those in Watsonville, who received personal contacts as well as the media campaign, changed most.

Do you recognize the potency of personal influence in your own experience? Most college students say in retrospect that they have learned more from their friends and other students than from contact with books or professors. Educational researchers have confirmed the students' intuition: out-of-class personal relationships powerfully influence how students mature (Astin, 1972; Wilson et al., 1975).

**broken window theory** *states that visible displays of disorder set norms for crime and anti-social behaviour*

And it seems we aren't just persuaded by our peers and family about how the world is. We are also influenced by our environment. The controversial broken window theory (Wilson & Kelling, 1982) has been adopted by police and social scientists, to explain how certain features in an environment, such as noisy neighbours, graffiti, gangs and derelict buildings, can lead to high crime rates in the area. Proponents of this theory argue that visible cues of apparent disorder create norms for crime. Consequently, it has been argued that one way to tackle crime is to tidy up an area and bring it in visible order. See Research Close-Up: Adult Residents' Perceptions of Neighbourhood Safety for an empirical example of how well broken-window theory explains perceptions of crime amongst older adults.

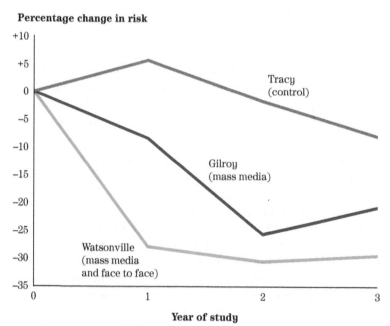

**FIGURE 6.7** Percentage change from baseline (0) in coronary risk after one, two or three years of health education

SOURCE: Data from Maccoby, 1980.

### Media Influence

Although face-to-face influence is usually greater than media influence, we should not underestimate the media's power. Those who personally influence our opinions must get their ideas from some source, and often their sources are the media. In a qualitative study of the language of televised political press conferences surrounding the meeting of the former Chinese President Jiang Zemin and the US president George W. Bush, Aditi Bhatia (2008) observes how what might appear a spontaneous discussion and airing of views is actually a carefully controlled piece of discourse. Bhatia notes how the media's influence over their discussion enables two ideologically opposed speakers to disguise their fundamental differences and appear to be in mutual agreement. The media becomes a powerful tool for persuading its audience that political similarity exists.

Elihu Katz (1957) observed that many of the media's effects operate in a two-step flow of communication: from media to opinion leaders to the rank and file. In any large group, it is these *opinion leaders* and trendsetters – 'the influentials' – that marketers and politicians seek to woo (Keller & Berry, 2003). Opinion leaders are individuals perceived as experts. They may include talk show hosts and editorial columnists; doctors, teachers and scientists; and people in all walks of life who have made it their business to absorb information and to inform their friends and family. If I want to evaluate computer equipment, I defer to the opinions of my sons, who get many of their ideas from the printed page. Sell them and you will sell me.

two-step flow of communication *the process by which media influence often occurs through opinion leaders, who in turn influence others*

The two-step flow model reminds us that media influences penetrate the culture in subtle ways. Even if the media had little direct effect on people's attitudes, they could still have a big indirect effect. Those rare children who grow up without watching television do not grow up beyond television's influence. Unless they live as hermits, they will join in television-imitative play on the school ground. They will ask their parents for the television-related toys their friends have. They will beg or demand to watch their friends' favourite programmes, and will do so when visiting friends' homes. Parents can just say no, but they cannot switch off television's influence.

### Comparing Media

Lumping together all media, from mass mailings to television to podcasting, oversimplifies. Studies comparing different media find that the more lifelike the medium, the more persuasive its message. Thus, the order of persuasiveness seems to be: live (face to face), videotaped, audiotaped and written. To add to the complexity, messages are best comprehended and recalled when written. Comprehension is one of the first steps in the persuasion process (recall Figure 6.1). So Shelly Chaiken and Alice Eagly (1976) reasoned that if a message is difficult to comprehend, persuasion should be greatest when the message is written, because readers will be able to work through the message at their own pace. The researchers gave university students easy or difficult messages in writing, on audiotape or on videotape. Figure 6.8 displays their results: difficult messages were indeed most persuasive when written; easy messages, when videotaped. The television medium takes control of the pacing of the message away from the recipients. By drawing attention to the communicator and away from the message itself, television also encourages people to focus on peripheral cues, such as the communicator's attractiveness (Chaiken & Eagly, 1983).

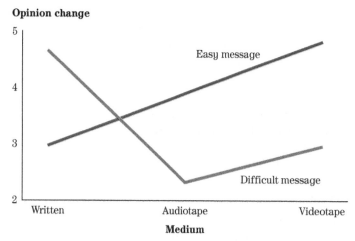

**Opinion change**

**FIGURE 6.8** Easy-to-understand messages are most persuasive when videotaped. Difficult messages are most persuasive when written. Thus, the difficulty of the message interacts with the medium to determine persuasiveness.

SOURCE: Data from Chaiken & Eagly, 1976.

## TO WHOM IS IT SAID? THE AUDIENCE

As we will see in Chapter 7, people's traits often don't predict their responses to social influence. A particular trait may enhance one step in the persuasion process (Figure 6.1) but work against another. Take self-esteem. People with low self-esteem are often slow to comprehend a message and therefore hard to persuade. Those with high self-esteem may comprehend yet remain confident of their own opinions. The conclusion: people with moderate self-esteem are the easiest to influence (Rhodes & Wood, 1992).

Let's also consider two other characteristics of those who receive a message: age and thoughtfulness.

### HOW OLD ARE THEY?

People tend to have different social and political attitudes depending on their age. Social psychologists give two explanations for the difference, and these explanations seem to contradict each other. One is a *life-cycle explanation*: attitudes change (for example, become more conservative) as people grow older. The other is a *generational explanation*: attitudes do *not* change; older people largely hold on to the attitudes they adopted when they were young. Because these attitudes are different from those being adopted by young people today as society's norms and values change, a generation gap develops. There are differences between *cohorts* (those born in the same decade, for example) and not only differences due to age.

The evidence mostly supports the generational or cohort explanation. In surveys and resurveys of groups of younger and older people over several years, the attitudes of older people usually show less change than do those of young people. As David Sears (1979, 1986) puts it, researchers have 'almost invariably found generational rather than life cycle effects'.

The teens and early twenties are important formative years (Krosnick & Alwin, 1989). Attitudes are changeable during that time and the attitudes formed then tend to stabilize through middle adulthood. Young people might therefore be advised to choose their social influences – the groups they join, the media they imbibe, the roles they adopt – carefully. In analysing National Opinion Research Center archives, James Davis (2004) discovered, for example, that Americans reaching age 16 during the 1960s have, ever since, been more politically liberal than average. Much as tree rings can, years later, reveal the telltale marks laid down by a drought, so attitudes decades later may reveal the events, such as the Vietnam War and civil rights era of the 1960s, that shaped the adolescent and early-twenties mind. For many people, these years are a critical period for the formation of attitudes and values.

## research close-up

### ADULT RESIDENTS' PERCEPTIONS OF NEIGHBOURHOOD SAFETY

**Source:** *Pitner, R. O., Yu, M., & Brown, E. (2011). Exploring the dynamics of middle-aged and older adult residents' perceptions of neighborhood safety.* Journal of Gerontological Social Work, *54, 511–527.*

### Introduction

Generally speaking, we all prefer to live in places where we feel safe. Middle-aged and older adults especially value this in their neighbourhood. It is important not only for well-being and happiness, but also retaining our independence and ability to remain in our own home as we get older. So what factors can make people feel unsafe in their neighbourhoods? What leads to feelings of vulnerability?

The broken window hypothesis states that we feel unsafe when there are visible cues of disorder in the environment. These include apparent physical incivilities (e.g. derelict buildings, graffiti) and social incivilities (noisy neighbours, sex-workers on the street). Broken window theory goes even further than this and argues that features such as these in our neighbourhoods directly contribute to a high crime rate as seemingly appropriate norms for crime and disorder emerge as a consequence. Others have pointed towards community cohesion and attachment to an area in explaining why we may feel unsafe. Collective efficacy describes high levels of community cohesion, offering a safe (and monitored) environment for people to live. Where this doesn't exist, people may feel isolated and vulnerable. There is a lack of vigilance in ensuring the safety of residents.

This current study tested four hypotheses to see which of these theories best explains middle-aged and older adults' perceptions of crime in their neighbourhood:

H1 Community care and vigilance is a predictor of middle-aged and older adults' perceptions of neighbourhood crime.

H2 Perceptions of physical and social incivilities is the main predictor of perceptions of neighbourhood crime.

H3 The actual level of crime (as measured by police reports) predicts fears of safety, and this differs depending on whether they are crimes against the person or property.

H4 Actual incivilities are the strongest predictor of perceptions of crime.

### Method

Eighty-five participants took part, of which 81 per cent were women and 19 per cent were men. Of this sample, 37 per cent were White residents, 63 per cent were African-American. Their average age was 61.4 years. There were 49 per cent middle-aged adults, aged 40–64, and 51 per cent older adults, aged 65 and above. They came from a large urban city in a Midwestern area in the US, which was divided into 9 police districts. A stratified sampling procedure was used to recruit participants from each of the 9 districts. They had lived in their neighbourhoods for a mean length of 19.7 years.

Participants were sent a postal survey to complete, which they returned, or were telephoned to complete it. Police crime data for all 9 districts was collected.

Participants completed a 22-item survey. The survey asked questions about their safety concerns in their neighbourhood (2 questions: e.g. 'How safe is your neighbourhood for children?'), their perception of community cohesion and vigilance (6 questions: e.g. 'My neighbourhood feels like a community'), physical incivilities (6 questions: e.g. the presence of graffiti), social incivilities (4 questions: e.g. the presence of nuisance neighbours). All items were rated on a 5-point Likert scale (1 = strongly disagree, 5 = strongly agree). They were also asked demographic questions (race, gender, annual income, length of residency).

The data were analysed using chi-square and independent $t$-tests, to see whether demographic variables (e.g. gender), perceived crime variables (incivilities, neighbourhood cohesion) and safety concerns, differed between middle-aged and older adults. Univariate analyses and correlations were conducted to assess the extent to which the crime variables (community cohesion, incivilities) and demographic variables (e.g. gender) predicted safety concerns.

### Results

Ninety-six per cent of participants reported at least one example of incivility that made their neighbourhood feel less safe. Middle-aged participants noted more social incivilities than older adults. Middle-aged adults lived in areas with a higher crime rate than older adults ($t = 2.96$, $p = 0.004$). No other differences were found between the two age groups.

Feelings of neighbourhood safety were associated with perceptions of physical and social incivilities, low levels of community cohesion and vigilance, and actual high crime rates against the person and property. The strongest predictor of feelings of neighbourhood safety were perceptions of physical incivility ($t = 10$, $p = 0.002$). Actual crimes against property were the next highest predictor ($t = 7.33$, $p = 0.008$), and then community cohesion and vigilance ($t = 5.38$, $p = 0.023$).

### Discussion

Support was found for H1, H3 and H4. Community care and vigilance does predict feeling unsafe in a neighbourhood. Furthermore, actual crime rates against property was also a strong predictor of feeling unsafe. So the visibility of derelict buildings and graffiti matter in how safe people felt in their homes. H2 was only partially supported as it was only physical incivilities (and not social incivilities) that featured in people's concerns about safety in their neighbourhoods.

From this research it can be concluded that a sense of community, and taking pride in maintaining the physical aspects of it, really matter in making a place feel safe. Social incivilities, such as neighbours arguing in the street, do not affect how safe these people feel in their residential areas. So while the theory that community cohesion and attachment really matter in perceptions of neighbourhood safety, the broken window theory is only partially supported in this study.

This study has limitations, however. Response biases (who comes forward to take part), perceptions of safety and incivilities, and a small sample size from just 9 areas could contribute to results that are not as valid or representative as might be hoped. But, there are valuable lessons to be learned from these results. If councils, police forces and residents are to improve safety in their neighbourhoods, the formation of community groups, repairing visible displays of disorder (such as cleaning up graffiti) and instilling a sense of pride and attachment to a place can make a lot of difference to increasing perceptions and actual safety there.

Adolescent and early-adult experiences are formative partly because they make deep and lasting impressions. When Howard Schuman and Jacqueline Scott (1989) asked people to name the one or two most important national or world events of the previous half-century, most recalled events from their teens or early twenties. For those Americans who experienced the Great Depression or the Second World

War as 16- to 24-year olds, those events overshadowed the civil rights movement and the Kennedy assassination of the early 1960s, the Vietnam War and moon landing of the late 1960s, and the women's movement of the 1970s – all of which were imprinted on the minds of younger people who experienced them as 16- to 24-year olds. We may therefore expect that today's young adults will include events such as the invasion of Iraq, the controversial election of Robert Mugabe in Zimbabwe, and the Dalai Lama and his campaign to separate Tibet from China as memorable turning points.

That is not to say that older adults are inflexible. Studies conducted by Norval Glenn in 1980 and 1981 found that most people in their fifties and sixties had more liberal sexual and racial attitudes than they had in their thirties and forties. Given the 'sexual revolution' that began in the 1960s and became mainstream in the 1970s, these middle-aged people had apparently changed with the times. Most of us are influenced by changing cultural norms. In fact social norms shape many of our attitudes and thoughts about things. Moreover, research by Penny Visser and Jon Krosnick (1998) suggests that elderly adults, near the end of the life cycle, may again become more susceptible to attitude change, possibly because of a decline in the strength of their attitudes.

### What Are They Thinking?

The crucial aspect of central route persuasion is not the message but the responses it evokes in a person's mind. Our minds are not sponges that soak up whatever pours over them. If the message summons favourable thoughts, it persuades us. If it provokes us to think of contrary arguments, we remain unpersuaded.

#### Forewarned Is Forearmed – If You Care Enough to Counter-argue

What circumstances breed counter-argument? One is knowing that someone is going to try to persuade you. If you had to tell your family that you wanted to drop out of school, you would probably anticipate their pleading with you to stay. So you might develop a list of arguments to counter every conceivable argument they might make and in making your case adopt what Jonathan Potter (1996) calls 'defensive rhetoric'. This style of language is designed to resist and undermine potential counter-arguments. 'Offensive rhetoric' is adopted when a speaker or writer attacks an alternative account to their own.

defensive rhetoric *when a speaker or writer develops arguments to counter being undermined by other points*

Jonathan Freedman and David Sears (1965) demonstrated the difficulty of trying to persuade people who had already been forewarned of the attempt to persuade them. They warned one group of California high schoolers that they were going to hear a talk: 'Why Teenagers Should Not Be Allowed to Drive'. Those forewarned did not budge in their opinions. Others, not forewarned, did budge. In law courts, too, defence attorneys sometimes forewarn juries about prosecution evidence to come. With mock juries, such 'stealing thunder' neutralizes its impact (Dolnik et al., 2003).

offensive rhetoric *when a speaker or writer attacks an alternative account to their own*

#### Distraction Disarms Counter-arguing

Verbal persuasion is also enhanced by distracting people with something that attracts their attention just enough to inhibit counter-arguing (Festinger & Maccoby, 1964; Keating & Brock, 1974; Osterhouse & Brock, 1970). Political advertisements often use this technique. The words promote the candidate, and the visual images keep us occupied so we don't analyse the words. Distraction is especially effective when the message is simple (Harkins & Petty, 1981; Regan & Cheng, 1973). Sometimes, though, distraction precludes our processing an advertisement. That perhaps helps explain why advertisements viewed during violent or sexual television programmes are sometimes unremembered and ineffective (Bushman, 2005; Bushman & Bonacci, 2002).

*Uninvolved Audiences Use Peripheral Cues*

Recall the two routes to persuasion – the central route of systematic thinking and the peripheral route of heuristic cues. Like a road that winds through a small town, the central route has starts and stops as the mind analyses arguments and formulates responses. Like the freeway that bypasses the town, the peripheral route speeds people to their destination. Analytical people – those with a high need for cognition – enjoy thinking carefully and prefer central routes (Cacioppo et al., 1996). People who like to conserve their mental resources – those with a low need for cognition – are quicker to respond to such peripheral cues as the communicator's attractiveness and the pleasantness of the surroundings.

**need for cognition** *the motivation to think and analyse. Assessed by agreement with items such as 'The notion of thinking abstractly is appealing to me' and disagreement with items such as 'I only think as hard as I have to'*

This simple theory – that *what we think in response to a message is crucial,* especially if we are motivated and able to think about it – has generated many predictions, most of which have been confirmed by Petty, Cacioppo and others (Axsom et al., 1987; Harkins & Petty, 1987; Leippe & Elkin, 1987). Many experiments have explored ways to stimulate people's thinking:

- ☐ by using rhetorical questions
- ☐ by presenting *multiple speakers* (for example, having each of three speakers give one argument instead of one speaker giving three)
- ☐ by making people *feel responsible* for evaluating or passing along the message, by using *relaxed postures* rather than standing ones
- ☐ by *repeating* the message
- ☐ by getting people's *undistracted attention.*

The consistent finding with each of these techniques: stimulating thinking makes strong messages more persuasive and (because of counter-arguing) weak messages less persuasive.

'Things can only get better.' A carefully chosen song and catchphrase helped Tony Blair and the Labour Party to election victory in 1997, ending 22 years of Conservative government in the UK.

SOURCE: © Mark Waters/Dreamstime.com

The theory also has practical implications. Effective communicators care not only about their images and their messages but also about how their audience is likely to react. The best teachers tend to get students to think actively. They ask rhetorical questions, provide intriguing examples, and challenge students with difficult problems. All these techniques are likely to foster a process that moves information through the central route to persuasion. In classes where the instruction is less engaging, you can provide your own central processing. If you think about the material and elaborate on the arguments, you are likely to do better in the course.

## EXTREME PERSUASION: HOW DO CULTS INDOCTRINATE?

*What persuasion and group influence principles are harnessed by new religious movements ('cults')?*

On 22 March 1997, Marshall Herff Applewhite and 37 of his disciples decided the time had come to shed their bodies – mere 'containers' – and be whisked up to a UFO (unidentified flying object) trailing the Hale-Bopp Comet, en route to Heaven's Gate. So they put themselves to sleep by mixing phenobarbital into pudding or apple sauce, washing it down with vodka, and then fixing plastic bags over their heads so they would suffocate in their slumber. On that same day, a cottage in the French Canadian village of St Casimir exploded in an inferno, consuming five people – the latest of 74 members of the Order of the Solar Temple to have committed suicide in Canada, Switzerland and France. All were hoping to be transported to the star Sirius, nine light years away.

The question on many minds: what persuades people to join these gangs? Shall we attribute their strange behaviours to strange personalities? Or do their experiences illustrate the common dynamics of social influence and persuasion? As we shall see, everyday strategies of persuasion are used. But social psychology cannot explain everything about the influence of cults. Their powers of persuasion go beyond the everyday.

Bear two things in mind. First, this is hindsight analysis. It uses persuasion principles as categories for explaining, after the fact, a troubling social phenomenon. Second, explaining *why* people believe something says nothing about the *truth* of their beliefs. That is a logically separate issue. A psychology of religion might tell us *why* a theist believes in God and an atheist disbelieves, but it cannot tell us who is right. Explaining either belief does nothing to change its validity. Remember that when someone tries to discount your beliefs by saying, 'You just believe that because ...'. You might recall Archbishop William Temple's reply to a questioner who challenged: 'Well, of course, Archbishop, the point is that you believe what you believe because of the way you were brought up.' To which the archbishop replied: 'That is as it may be. But the fact remains that you believe I believe what I believe because of the way I was brought up, because of the way you were brought up.'

What is perceived to be a 'cult' changes with time and place. Broadly speaking a cult is a group of people who share beliefs and practices that operate outside the mainstream way of doing things. Of course, what is considered to be 'mainstream' is different from culture to culture, society to society, and across time. In recent decades, several cults have been defined – which some social scientists prefer to call new religious movements – and have gained much publicity: Opus Dei, Zhushen Jiao (Religion of the primary deity), Order of the Solar Temple, Jim Jones's People's Temple, Charles Manson's Manson Family, and Marshall Applewhite's Heaven's Gate.

Sun Myung Moon's mixture of Christianity, anti-communism and glorification of Moon himself as a new messiah attracted a worldwide following. In response to Moon's declaration, 'What I wish must be your wish', many people committed themselves and their incomes to the Unification Church.

In 1978 in Guyana, 914 disciples of Jim Jones, who had followed him there from San Francisco, shocked the world when they died by following his order to down a suicidal grape drink laced with tranquillizers, painkillers and a lethal dose of cyanide.

In 1993, high-school dropout David Koresh used his talent for memorizing scripture and mesmerizing people to seize control of a faction of a sect called the Branch Davidians. Over time, members were gradually relieved of the contents of their bank accounts and their possessions. Koresh also persuaded the men to live celibately while he slept with their wives and daughters, and he convinced his 19

cult (also called new religious movement) *a group typically characterized by (1) distinctive ritual and beliefs related to its devotion to a god or a person, (2) isolation from the surrounding 'evil' culture, and (3) a charismatic leader. (A sect, by contrast, is a spinoff from a major religion)*

'wives' that they should bear his children. Under siege after a shootout that killed six members and four federal agents, Koresh told his followers they would soon die and go with him straight to heaven. Federal agents rammed the compound with tanks, hoping to inject tear gas, but by the end of the assault, 86 people were consumed in a fire that engulfed the compound.

Marshall Applewhite was not similarly tempted to command sexual favours. Having been fired from two music teaching jobs for affairs with students, he sought sexless devotion by castration, as had seven of the other 17 Heaven's Gate men who died with him (Chua-Eoan, 1997; Gardner, 1997). While in a psychiatric hospital in 1971, Applewhite had linked up with nurse and astrology dabbler Bonnie Lu Nettles, who gave the intense and charismatic Applewhite a cosmological vision of a route to 'the next level'. Preaching with passion, he persuaded his followers to renounce families, sex, drugs and personal money with promises of a spaceship voyage to salvation.

How could these things happen? What persuaded these people to give such total allegiance? Shall we make dispositional explanations – by blaming the victims? Shall we dismiss them as gullible or unbalanced? Or can familiar principles of conformity, compliance, dissonance, persuasion and group influence explain their behaviour to some extent – putting them on common ground with the rest of us who in our own ways are shaped by such forces?

## ATTITUDES FOLLOW BEHAVIOUR

As Chapter 5 showed over and again, people usually internalize commitments made voluntarily, publicly and repeatedly. Cult leaders seem to know this.

### Compliance Breeds Acceptance

New converts soon learn that membership is no trivial matter. They are quickly made active members of the team. Behavioural rituals, public recruitment and fund-raising strengthen the initiates' identities as members. As those in social psychological experiments come to believe in what they bear witness to (Aronson & Mills, 1959; Gerard & Mathewson, 1966), so cult initiates become committed advocates. The greater the personal commitment, the more the need to justify it.

### The Foot-in-the-door Phenomenon

How are people induced to make a commitment to such a drastic life change? Seldom by an abrupt, conscious decision. One does not just decide, 'I'm through with mainstream religion. I'm gonna find a cult.' Nor do cult recruiters approach people on the street with, 'Hi. I'm a Moonie. Care to join us?' Rather, the recruitment strategy exploits the foot-in-the-door phenomenon (Fern et al., 1986). This works simply on the principle that if someone can be persuaded to comply with a small request, then they can be persuaded by increasingly larger requests. Unification Church recruiters, for example, would invite people to a dinner and then to a weekend of warm fellowship and discussions of philosophies of life. At the weekend retreat, they would encourage the attenders to join them in songs, activities and discussion. Potential converts were then urged to sign up for longer training retreats. The pattern in cults is for the activities to become gradually more arduous, culminating in having recruits solicit contributions and attempt to convert others.

**foot-in-the-door phenomenon**
*manipulation technique in which getting people to first agree to a small request increases the chances that they will later comply with a larger request*

Once into the cult, converts find that monetary offerings are at first voluntary, then mandatory. Jim Jones eventually inaugurated a required contribution of 10 per cent of income, which soon increased to 25 per cent. Finally, he ordered members to turn over to him everything they owned. Workloads also became progressively more demanding. Former cult member Grace Stoen recalls the gradual progress:

> Nothing was ever done drastically. That's how Jim Jones got away with so much. You slowly gave up things and slowly had to put up with more, but it was always done very gradually. It was amazing, because you would sit up sometimes and say, wow, I really have given up a lot. I really am putting up with a lot. But he did it so slowly that you figured, I've made it this far, what the hell is the difference?

(Conway & Siegelman, 1979, p. 236)

### The Door-in-the-face Technique

The door-in-the-face technique (DITF) has been used to great effect in persuading people to a request they had previously rejected (Cialdini et al., 1975). This rather risky strategy involves asking someone to comply with a very large request that will almost certainly be refused. On receiving the almost inevitable rejection, a second less demanding request is then made. In the context of the large request, this second one doesn't seem so bad. The theory goes that this second request therefore has a much better chance of being accepted in this context than if it was presented on its own. So you get what you wanted all along. And there's a lot of evidence to show that the strategy does indeed work. For example, Nicolas Guéguen and his colleagues (2011) found that if a waitress asked customers if they wanted tea or coffee immediately after offering them dessert (which they declined), they tended to say Yes. If the waitress left a 3-minute delay between asking for dessert orders and tea/coffee orders, both requests were typically declined. This strategy can be, and has been, used in many areas of social life such as health, charity, retail and hapless researchers trying to encourage people to take part in their studies!

*door-in-the-face*
*technique (DITF)*
*facilitating the*
*likelihood of a second*
*less-demanding request*
*being accepted by*
*presenting a more*
*demanding request first*

> The door-in-the-face technique is also of interest in considering helping, in Chapter 10. Research indicates that more people agree to help when the door-in-the-face technique is employed.

### Low-balling

Low-balling works by getting someone to agree to an attractive, often cheap, deal, and then raising the charge for it. You may recognize this technique in the pitch of various financial sellers as they try to entice customers to accept their offers. Advertisements for cheap insurance sometimes offer to insure your car or home for a very cheap price. Attracted by the offer you give them a call. During the course of the phone call you may be told why it will be a bit more expensive to insure your car or home. Having already committed yourself to the idea of taking up their insurance, you find yourself agreeing to the newer, more expensive, deal. You reason that it will be more convenient to accept the offer here and now rather than chase around more insurance companies. But why do we allow this low-balling technique to work? In Chapter 5 we noted how people like to maintain consistency in their attitudes and behaviour. Having already formed a positive attitude towards the insurance company, you now behave accordingly and accept the offer.

A classic social psychological demonstration of this strategy comes from Robert Cialdini, John Cacioppo, Rodney Bassett and John Miller (1978), who invited students to take part in a study. On receiving a 'Yes' response, they were then told the study would begin at 7 a.m. and could withdraw if they now chose, owing to the unsociable hour. Almost all the students turned up for the study. Compare this with the students who were told the early starting time of the study at the time they were asked to take part. Only 24 per cent agreed.

## PERSUASIVE ELEMENTS

We can also analyse cult persuasion using the factors discussed in this chapter (and summarized in Figure 6.9): *who* (the communicator) said *what* (the message) to *whom* (the audience)?

### The Communicator

Successful cults typically have a charismatic leader – someone who attracts and directs the members. We know a credible communicator is someone the audience perceives as expert and trustworthy – for example, as 'Father' Moon.

Jim Jones used 'psychic readings' to establish his credibility. Newcomers were asked to identify themselves as they entered the church before services. Then one of his aides would quickly call the person's home and say, 'Hi. We're doing a survey, and we'd like to ask you some questions.' During the service, one ex-member recalled, Jones would call out the person's name and say

> Have you ever seen me before? Well, you live in such and such a place, your phone number is such and such, and in your living room you've got this, that, and the other, and on your sofa you've got such and such a pillow … Now do you remember me ever being in your house?

(Conway & Siegelman, 1979, p. 234)

Trust is another aspect of credibility. Cult researcher Margaret Singer (1979) noted that middle-class Caucasian youths are more vulnerable to recruitment because they are more trusting. They lack the 'street knowledge' of lower-class youths (who know how to resist a hustle) and the wariness of upper-class youths (who have been warned of kidnappers since childhood). Many cult members have been recruited by friends or relatives, people they trust (Stark & Bainbridge, 1980).

### The Message

The vivid, emotional messages and the warmth and acceptance with which the group showers lonely or depressed people can be strikingly appealing: trust the master, join the family; we have the answer, the 'one way'. The message echoes through channels as varied as lectures, small-group discussions and direct social pressure.

### The Audience

Recruits are often young people under 25, still at that comparatively open age before attitudes and values stabilize. Some, such as the followers of Jim Jones, are less educated people who like the simplicity of the message and find it difficult to counter-argue. Lack of education and aspirations has been understood as a factor

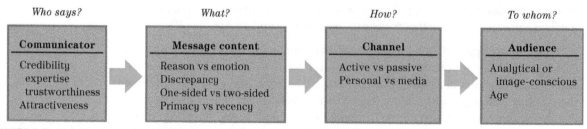

**FIGURE 6.9** Variables known to affect the impact of persuasive communications
In real life, these variables may interact; the effect of one may depend on the level of another.

in the UK in the recruitment of young working-class men at football grounds into right-wing political groups and hooligan gangs, and has received much social psychological attention (Burke and Sunley, 1998). But most are educated, middle-class people who, taken by the ideals, overlook the contradictions in those who profess selflessness and practise greed, who pretend concern and behave indifferently.

Potential converts are often at turning points in their lives, facing personal crises, or vacationing or living away from home. They have needs; the cult offers them an answer (Lofland & Stark, 1965; Singer, 1979). Gail Maeder joined Heaven's Gate after her T-shirt shop had failed. David Moore joined when he was 19, just out of high school, and searching for direction. Times of social and economic upheaval are especially conducive to someone who can make apparent simple sense out of the confusion (O'Dea, 1968; Sales, 1972).

Most of those who have carried out suicide bombings in the Middle East (and other places such as Bali, Madrid and London) were, likewise, young men at the transition between adolescence and adult maturity. Like cult recruits, they come under the influence of authoritative, sometimes religiously orientated communicators who indoctrinate them into seeing themselves as 'living martyrs' whose fleeting moment of self-destruction will be their portal into bliss and heroism. To help ensure their overcoming the will to survive, each candidate makes public commitments – creating a will, writing goodbye letters, making a farewell video – that create a psychological point of no return (Kruglanski & Grolec de Zavala, 2005). All this typically transpires in the relative isolation of small cells, with group influences that fan hatred for the enemy.

## GROUP EFFECTS

Cults also illustrate the next chapter's theme: the power of a group to shape members' views and behaviour. The cult typically separates members from their previous social support systems and isolates them with other cultists. There may then occur what Rodney Stark and William Bainbridge (1980) call a 'social implosion': external ties weaken until the group collapses inwards socially, each person engaging only with other group members. Cut off from families and former friends, they lose access to counter-arguments. The group now offers collective identity and defines reality. Because the cult frowns on or punishes disagreements, the apparent consensus helps eliminate any lingering doubts. Moreover, stress and emotional arousal narrow attention, making people 'more susceptible to poorly supported arguments, social pressure, and the temptation to derogate nongroup members' (Baron, 2000).

Marshall Applewhite and Bonnie Nettles at first formed their own group of two, reinforcing each other's aberrant thinking – a phenomenon that psychiatrists call *folie à deux* (French for 'insanity of two'). As others joined them, the group's social isolation facilitated more peculiar thinking. As Internet conspiracy theory discussion groups illustrate (Heaven's Gate was skilled in Internet recruiting), virtual groups can likewise foster paranoia.

These techniques – increasing behavioural commitments, persuasion and group isolation – do not, however, have unlimited power. The Unification Church has successfully recruited fewer than 1 in 10 people who attend its workshops

(Ennis & Verrilli, 1989). Most who joined Heaven's Gate had left before that fateful day. David Koresh ruled with a mix of persuasion, intimidation and violence. As Jim Jones made his demands more extreme, he, too, increasingly had to control people with intimidation. He used threats of harm to those who fled the community, beatings for non-compliance, and drugs to neutralize disagreeable members. By the end, he was as much an arm-twister as a mind-bender.

Some of these cult influence techniques bear similarities to techniques used by more benign, widely accepted groups. Buddhist and Catholic monasteries, for example, have cloistered adherents with their kindred spirits. And fraternity and sorority members have reported that the initial 'love bombing' of potential cult recruits is not unlike their own 'rush' period. Members lavish prospective pledges with attention and make them feel special. During the pledge period, new members are somewhat isolated, cut off from old friends who did not pledge. They spend time studying the history and rules of their new group. They suffer and commit time on its behalf. They are expected to comply with all its demands. The result is usually a committed new member.

Much the same is true of some therapeutic communities for recovering drug and alcohol abusers. Zealous self-help groups form a cohesive 'social cocoon', have intense beliefs and exert a profound influence on members' behaviour (Galanter, 1989, 1990).

Group processes similar but not identical to what has been demonstrated above in cults, have also been found in the most respected layers of society – for instance, the Masonic Lodge. The secret meetings and rituals going on in this kind of brotherhood among the wealthiest and most influential people in society, create unity and protect members from other influences and counter-arguments. Even in the highest political circles, among the members of the President's Administration or the Prime Minister's government, there are examples of cohesive ingroup processes where the desire for concurrence between group members overrides realistic appraisals. This phenomenon is called 'groupthink'.

> Groupthink is explained further in Chapter 11 when we consider small group influence.

A constructive use of persuasion is in counselling and psychotherapy, which social-counselling psychologist Stanley Strong views 'as a branch of applied social psychology' (1978, p. 101). Like Strong, psychiatrist Jerome Frank (1974, 1982) recognized years ago that it takes persuasion to change self-defeating attitudes and behaviours. Frank noted that the psychotherapy setting, like cults and zealous self-help groups, provides (1) a supportive, confiding social relationship, (2) an offer of expertise and hope, (3) a special rationale or myth that explains one's difficulties and offers a new perspective, and (4) a set of rituals and learning experiences that promises a new sense of peace and happiness.

Military training creates cohesion and commitment through some of the same tactics used by leaders of new religious movements, fraternities and therapeutic communities.

SOURCE: Glow Images

These examples of fraternities, sororities, self-help groups and psychotherapy help to illustrate three concluding observations. First, if we attribute new religious movements to the leader's mystical force or to the followers' peculiar weaknesses, we may delude ourselves into thinking we are immune to social control techniques. In truth, our own groups – and countless political leaders, educators and other persuaders – successfully use many of these same tactics on us. Between education and indoctrination, enlightenment and propaganda, conversion and coercion, therapy and mind control, there is but a blurry line.

Second, the fact that Jim Jones and other cult leaders abused the power of persuasion does not mean persuasion is intrinsically bad. Nuclear power enables us to light up homes or wipe out cities. Sexual power enables us to express and celebrate committed love or exploit people for selfish gratification. Similarly, persuasive power enables us to enlighten or deceive, to promote health or to sell addictive drugs, to advance peace or stir up hatred. Knowing that these powers can be harnessed for evil purposes should alert us, as scientists and citizens, to guard against their immoral use. But the powers themselves are neither inherently evil nor inherently good; it is how we use them that determines whether their effect is destructive or constructive. Condemning persuasion because of deceit is like condemning eating because of gluttony.

Third, persuasion pervades our everyday lives. Whenever we interact with one another we are involved in some degree of persuasion through our language. We are persuading someone to accept our version of events, our portrayal of someone's behaviour, or perhaps just how we think things ought to be. Persuasion is not simply the weapon of the cult leader or the advertiser, it is a fundamental aspect of our social interactions with others.

## HOW CAN PERSUASION BE RESISTED?

*How might we prepare people to resist unwanted persuasion?*

Martial arts trainers devote as much time to teaching defensive blocks, deflections and parries as they do to teaching attack. 'On the social influence battlefield,' note Brad Sagarin and his colleagues (2002), researchers have focused more on persuasive attack than on defence. Being persuaded comes naturally, Daniel Gilbert and his colleagues (1990, 1993) report. It is easier to accept persuasive messages than to doubt them. To *understand* an assertion (say, that lead pencils are a health hazard) is to *believe* it – at least temporarily, until one actively undoes the initial, automatic acceptance. If a distracting event prevents the undoing, the acceptance lingers.

Still, blessed with logic, information and motivation, we do resist falsehoods. If the credible-seeming repair person's uniform and the doctor's title have intimidated us into unthinking agreement, we can rethink our habitual responses to authority. We can seek more information before committing time or money. We can question what we don't understand.

### STRENGTHENING PERSONAL COMMITMENT

Chapter 7 presents another way to resist: before encountering others' judgements, make a public commitment to your position. Having stood up for your convictions, you will become less susceptible (or, should we say, less 'open') to what others have to say. As we saw in the Asch experiment, when participants were invited to declare which of the lines matched each other before anyone else, they gave the correct answer. When asked if they would like to change their mind having heard the confederates give a consistently incorrect answer, the participants rarely did so. So prior personal and public commitment to a position reduces the effectiveness of persuasion. In mock civil trials, straw polls of jurors can foster a hardening of expressed positions, leading to more deadlocks (Davis et al., 1993).

### Confident Beliefs

The self-validation hypothesis proposes that the confidence we have in our own beliefs is subject to many different factors. The more confidence we have in what we believe, the less likely our attitudes are to change. Confidence can be increased by simply nodding your head when voicing your beliefs about something (Brinol & Petty, 2003), or by reminding yourself of a time when your beliefs helped you achieve a desired goal (Petty et al., 2002), or even writing them down (Brinol & Petty, 2003). As we have seen in this chapter, strong arguments tend to be more persuasive than weaker ones. So the likelihood of having our beliefs and attitudes changed by strong arguments is higher. However, Brinol & Petty (2003) found that even when confronted by strong arguments, participants who shook their head to indicate their rejection of them were much less likely to accept the argument or consider it to be credible.

### Challenging Beliefs

How might we stimulate people to commit themselves? From his experiments, Charles Kiesler (1971) offered one possible way: mildly attack their position using *offensive rhetoric*. Kiesler found that when committed people were attacked strongly enough to cause them to react, but not so strongly as to overwhelm them, they became even more committed. Kiesler explained: 'When you attack committed people and your attack is of inadequate strength, you drive them to even more extreme behaviours in defense of their previous commitment' (p. 88). Perhaps you can recall a time when that happened in an argument, as those involved escalated their *defensive rhetoric*, committing themselves to increasingly extreme positions.

### Developing Counter-arguments

There is a second reason a mild attack might build resistance. Like inoculations against disease, even weak arguments will prompt counter-arguments, which are then available for a stronger attack. William McGuire (1964) documented this in a series of experiments. McGuire wondered: Could we inoculate people against persuasion much as we inoculate them against a virus? Is there such a thing as attitude inoculation? Could we take people raised in a 'germ-free ideological environment' – people who hold some unquestioned belief – and stimulate their mental defences? And would subjecting them to a small dose of belief-threatening material inoculate them against later persuasion?

attitude inoculation *exposing people to weak attacks upon their attitudes so that when stronger attacks come, they will have refutations available*

That is what McGuire did. First, he found some cultural truisms, such as 'It's a good idea to brush your teeth after every meal if at all possible'. He then showed that people were vulnerable to a powerful, credible assault upon those truisms (for example, prestigious authorities were said to have discovered that too much tooth-brushing can damage one's gums). If, however, before having their belief attacked, they were 'immunized' by first receiving a small challenge to their belief, *and* if they read or wrote an essay in refutation of this mild attack, then they were better able to resist the powerful attack.

Robert Cialdini and his colleagues (2003) agree that appropriate counter-arguments are a great way to resist persuasion, but wondered how to bring them to mind in response to an opponent's ads, especially when the opponent (like most political incumbents) has a huge spending advantage. The answer, they suggest, is a 'poison parasite' defence – one that combines a poison (strong counter-arguments) with a parasite (retrieval cues that bring those arguments to mind when seeing the opponent's advertisements). In their studies, participants who viewed a familiar political ad were least persuaded by it when they had earlier seen counter-arguments overlaid on a replica of the advertisement. Seeing the advertisement again thus also brought to mind the puncturing counter-arguments. Anti-smoking ads have effectively done this, for example by re-creating a 'Marlboro Man' commercial set in the rugged outdoors but now showing a coughing, decrepit cowboy.

## REAL-LIFE APPLICATIONS: INOCULATION PROGRAMMES

Could attitude inoculation work outside the laboratory by preparing people to resist unwanted persuasion? Applied research on smoking prevention and consumer education offers encouraging answers.

### Inoculating Children against Peer Pressure to Smoke

In a demonstration of how laboratory research findings can lead to practical applications, a research team led by Alfred McAlister (1980) had high school students 'inoculate' seventh graders against peer pressures to smoke. The seventh graders were taught to respond to advertisements implying that liberated women smoke by saying, 'She's not really liberated if she is hooked on tobacco'. They also acted in role plays in which, after being called 'chicken' for not taking a cigarette, they answered with statements such as 'I'd be a real chicken if I smoked just to impress you'. After several of these sessions during the seventh and eighth grades, the inoculated students were half as likely to begin smoking as were uninoculated students at another junior high school that had an identical parental smoking rate (Figure 6.10).

Anti-smoking and drug education programmes apply other persuasion principles, too. They use attractive peers to communicate information. They trigger the students' own cognitive processing ('Here's something you might want to think about'). They get the students to make a public commitment (by making a rational decision about smoking and then announcing it, along with their reasoning, to their classmates). Some of these smoking-prevention programmes require only 2 to 6 hours of class, using prepared printed materials or DVDs. Today any school district or teacher wishing to use the social psychological approach to smoking prevention can do so easily, inexpensively, and with the hope of significant reductions in future smoking rates and associated health costs.

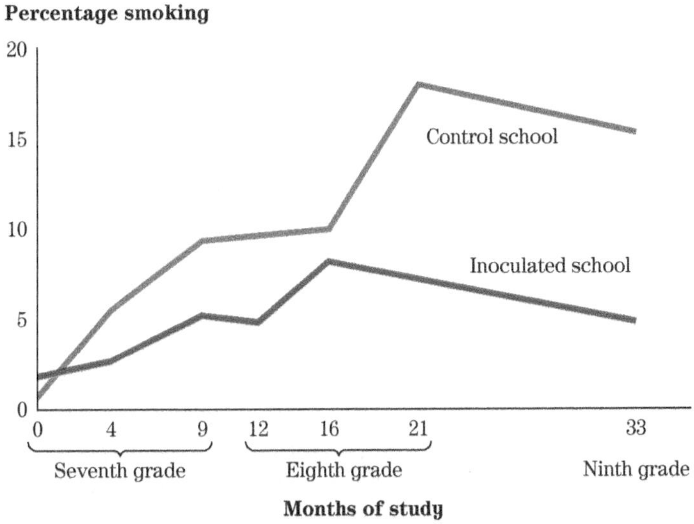

### Inoculating Children against the Influence of Advertising

Belgium, Denmark, Greece, Ireland, Italy, Norway and Sweden all restrict advertising that targets children, and other European

**FIGURE 6.10** The percentage of cigarette smokers at an 'inoculated' junior high school was much less than at a matched control school using a more typical smoking education programme.

SOURCE: Data from McAlister et al., 1980; Telch et al., 1981.

countries have been discussing doing the same (McGuire, 2002). In England, the 2004 National Health Service survey of 9715 children aged 11–15 reports an increase in the consumption of alcopops by girls, and beer, cider and lager by boys. Most alarmingly they found that 45 per cent of 15 year olds surveyed reported having consumed an alcoholic drink within the last week. In 2006, the Advertising Standards Agency banned a series of alcopop advertisements on the grounds that they were too attractive to adolescents and young people, contributing to national trends in binge and underage drinking.

Hoping to restrain advertising's influence, researchers have studied how to immunize young children against the effects of television commercials. Their research was prompted partly by studies showing that children, especially those under 8 years old, (1) have trouble distinguishing commercials from programmes and fail to grasp their persuasive intent, (2) trust television advertising rather indiscriminately, and (3) desire and badger their parents for advertised products (Adler et al., 1980; Feshbach, 1980; Palmer & Dorr, 1980). Children, it seems, are an advertiser's dream: gullible, vulnerable and an easy sell. Armed with this data, citizens' groups have campaigned against the advertisers of such products (Moody, 1983).

'When it comes to targeting kid consumers, we at General Mills follow the Procter and Gamble model of 'cradle to grave.' ... We believe in getting them early and having them for life.'

   Wayne Chilicki, General Mills (quoted by Motherhood Project, 2001)

On the other side are the commercial interests. They claim that advertisements allow parents to teach their children consumer skills and, more important, finance children's television programmes. In the USA, for example, the Federal Trade Commission has been in the middle, pushed by research findings and political pressures while trying to decide whether to place new constraints on television advertisements for unhealthy foods and for R-rated (restricted to over 17 year olds unless accompanied by an adult) movies aimed at underage youth.

Consumer advocates worry that inoculation may be insufficient. Better to clean the air than to wear gas masks. It is no surprise, then, that parents resent it when advertisers market products to children, then place them on lower store shelves where kids will see them, pick them up, and nag and whine until sometimes wearing the parent down. For that reason, urges the 'Mothers' Code for Advertisers', there should be no advertising in schools, no targeting children under 8, no product placements in movies and programmes targeting children and adolescents, and no advertisements directed at children and adolescents 'that promote an ethic of selfishness and a focus on instant gratification' (Motherhood Project, 2001).

## IMPLICATIONS OF ATTITUDE INOCULATION

The best way to build resistance to brainwashing probably isn't stronger indoctrination into one's current beliefs. If parents are worried that their children might become members of a cult, they might better teach their children about the various cults and prepare them to counter persuasive appeals.

For the same reason, religious educators should be wary of creating a 'germfree ideological environment' in their churches and schools. An attack, if refuted, is more likely to solidify one's position than to undermine it, particularly if the threatening material can be examined with like-minded others (Visser & Mirabile,

2004). Cults apply this principle by forewarning members of how families and friends will attack the cult's beliefs. When the expected challenge comes, the member is armed with counter-arguments.

Another implication is that, for the persuader, an ineffective appeal can be worse than none. Can you see why? Those who reject an appeal are inoculated against further appeals. Consider an experiment in which Susan Darley and Joel Cooper (1972) invited students to write essays advocating a strict dress code. Because that was against the students' own positions and the essays were to be published, all chose *not* to write the essay – even those offered money to do so. After turning down the money, they became even more extreme and confident in their anti-dress-code opinions. Having made an overt decision against the dress code, they became even more resistant to it. Those who have rejected initial appeals to quit smoking may likewise become immune to further appeals. Ineffective persuasion, by stimulating the listener's defences, may be counterproductive. It may 'harden the heart' against later appeals.

## focus on

### THE LUCIFER EFFECT: BAD APPLES OR BAD BARRELS?

In Philip Zimbardo's classic Stanford Prison experiment (see Chapter 5) we saw how attitudes can shift to match the roles we carry out. In the case of the Stanford prison study, when asked to act as prisoner or guard, participants not only behaved accordingly but internalized those roles, with shocking consequences for their acts towards one another. So shocking, the study was abandoned after only a few days as the guards' brutality towards the prisoners intensified. And it wasn't only the prisoners and guards who found their behaviour affected by the situation they were in. Zimbardo notes his own complicity in colluding with the guards, covering up the extent of deterioration in the prisoner-guard relationship, so as not to upset the prisoners' families. Zimbardo called this the Lucifer Effect. It explains how good people can become evil. Key to this effect is the power of the situation. Morality breaks down, as vulnerable humans allow the situation to overwhelm them. Norms of what is appropriate behaviour in that situation arise, and people adhere to them. It isn't simply a few bad apples turning the rest rotten, but a situation that turns everyone bad. Don't look at the apples, warns Zimbardo, look at the barrel which turned them bad. We might want to lay the blame at the door of a few dysfunctional people, states Zimbardo, but actually it's the situation they're in which requires analysis. The fundamental attribution error (Chapter 4) might hold a clue as to why there is a tendency to blame a few 'evil' people, rather than look to the context which everyone is in.

This effect could be used to explain what persuades people to evil acts throughout history – genocide, holocausts, the Abu Ghraib atrocities in Iraq. However, it begs a question about responsibility. If the situation is to blame, to what extent should people be held responsible for their actions?

### QUESTIONS

**1** To what extent can we hold people responsible for their actions?

**2** Do you think Zimbardo's account of why good people turn evil is correct?

**3** Social psychologists have tended to focus on when persuasion is a negative force. When might it be a force for good?

# SUMMING UP: PERSUASION

## WHAT PATHS LEAD TO PERSUASION?

☐ Sometimes persuasion occurs as people focus on arguments and respond with favourable thoughts. Such systematic, or 'central route', persuasion occurs when people are naturally analytical or involved in the issue.

☐ When issues don't engage systematic thinking, persuasion may occur through a faster, 'peripheral route', as people use heuristics or incidental cues to make snap judgements.

☐ Central route persuasion, being more thoughtful and less superficial, is more durable and more likely to influence behaviour.

☐ Unimodels of persuasion propose that there is just one route to persuasion, but messages contain a variety of kinds of persuasive evidence in convincing their readers/hearers of their truth.

☐ Whether we are convinced may be subject to wider social factors such as the attitudes and beliefs of people within our social networks.

## THE ELEMENTS OF PERSUASION AND THEIR RELATIONSHIP TO SOCIAL NORMS

☐ What makes persuasion effective? Researchers have explored four factors: the communicator (who says it), the message (what is said), the channel (how it is said) and the audience (to whom it is said).

☐ Credible communicators have the best success in persuading. People who speak unhesitatingly, who talk fast and who look listeners straight in the eye seem more credible. So are people who argue against their own self-interest and manage their 'dilemma of stake or interest'. An attractive communicator also is effective on matters of taste and personal values.

☐ The message itself persuades; associating it with good feelings makes it more convincing. People often make quicker, less reflective judgements while in good moods. Fear-arousing messages can also be effective, especially if the recipients can take protective action.

☐ How discrepant a message should be from an audience's existing opinions depends on the communicator's credibility. And whether a one- or two-sided message is more persuasive depends on whether the audience already agrees with the message, is unaware of opposing arguments and is unlikely later to consider the opposition.

☐ When two sides of an issue are included, the primacy effect results in the first message being more persuasive. If a time gap separates the presentations, the result is likely to be a recency effect in which the second message prevails.

☐ Another important consideration is how the message is communicated. Usually, face-to-face appeals work best. Print media can be effective for complex messages. And the mass media can be effective when the issue is minor or unfamiliar, using rhetorical strategies for persuasion.

☐ Finally, it matters who receives the message. The age of the audience makes a difference: young people's attitudes are arguably more subject to change. What does the audience think while receiving a message? Do they think favourable thoughts? Do they counter-argue? Were they forewarned?

## EXTREME PERSUASION: HOW DO CULTS INDOCTRINATE?

The successes of religious cults provide an opportunity to see powerful persuasion processes at work. It appears that their success has resulted from four general techniques:

☐ eliciting behavioural commitments (as described in Chapter 4)

☐ applying principles of effective persuasion (this chapter)

- ☐ isolating members in like-minded groups (to be discussed in Chapter 11)

- ☐ forming a collective identity which group members conform to (see Chapters 12 and 13).

- ☐ How do people resist persuasion? A *prior public commitment* to one's own position, stimulated perhaps by a mild attack on the position, breeds resistance to later persuasion.

- ☐ A mild attack can also serve as an *inoculation*, stimulating one to develop counter-arguments that will then be available if and when a strong attack comes.

- ☐ This implies, paradoxically, that one way to strengthen existing attitudes is to challenge them, though the challenge must not be so strong as to overwhelm them.

## CRITICAL QUESTIONS

**1** What are the main aspects of persuasion that social psychologists have identified and studied?

**2** Are some people more likely to be persuaded than others?

**3** How can social psychology help to understand why some people join gangs and cults?

**4** What strategies can we use to resist persuasion?

**5** Should we always try to resist being persuaded?

## RECOMMENDED READINGS

### Classic Readings

Billig, M. (1987). *Arguing and Thinking: A Rhetorical Approach to Social Psychology.* Cambridge: Cambridge University Press.

*Offers a rhetorical approach to understanding persuasive language and the importance of argumentation.*

Cialdini, R. (2001). *Influence: Science and practice.* Needham Heights, MA: Allyn & Bacon.

*A complete description of the 6 norms of influence, as identified by Cialdini.*

Hovland, C. I., Janis, I. L., & Kelley, H. H. (1953). *Communication and Persuasion: Psychological Studies of Opinion Change.* New Haven: Yale University Press.

*Describes various techniques used in communicating a message persuasively.*

Petty, R. E., & Cacioppo, J. T. (1986). *Communication and Persuasion: Central and Peripheral Routes to Persuasion.* New York: Springer-Verlag.

*Outlines the Elaboration Likelihood Model, denoting the two routes to persuasion.*

### Contemporary Readings

Briscoe, C., & Aboud, F. (2012). Behaviour change communication targeting four health behaviours in developing countries: A review of change techniques. *Social Science & Medicine*, **75**(4), 612–621.

*Reviews a range of communicated intervention programmes for promoting child health in developing countries. Notes the importance of matching the style and content of the communication to the target audience for such messages to be effective.*

Clark, J. K., Wegener, D. T., Habashi, M. M., & Evans, A. T. (2012). Source expertise and persuasion: The effects of perceived opposition or support on message scrutiny. *Personality and Social Psychology Bulletin*, **38**(1), 90–100.

*An example of recent research that considers the effectiveness of expertise as a persuasive technique. Reviews past research in the area.*

Kruglanski, A. W., & Thompson, E. P. (1999). Persuasion by a single route: A view from the unimodel. *Psychological Inquiry*, **10**(2), 83–109.

*Offers a critique of the Elaboration Likelihood Model, and outlines a one-route model to persuasion.*

Zimbardo, P. (2007). *The Lucifer Effect: Understanding How Good People Turn Evil.* New York: Random House.

*A complete explanation of the Lucifer Effect based on the Stanford Prison Experiment, and applied to more recent events including Abu Ghraib.*

**7**

"It is striking how often those involved in the greatest brutality are those who expend great efforts to extol ingroup virtue."

*Reicher, Haslam and Rath (2008)*

# CONFORMITY AND OBEDIENCE

You have surely experienced the phenomenon: as a controversial speaker or music concert finishes, the adoring fans near the front leap to their feet, applauding. The approving folks just behind them follow their example and join the standing ovation. Now the wave of people standing reaches people who, unprompted, would merely be giving polite applause from their comfortable seats. Seated among them, part of you wants to stay seated ('this speaker doesn't represent my views at all'). But as the wave of standing people sweeps by, will you alone stay seated? It's not easy, being a minority of one. Unless you heartily dislike what you've just heard, you will probably rise to your feet, at least briefly.

Such scenes of conformity raise this chapter's questions:

- ☐ Why, given the diversity of individuals in large groups, do they so often behave as social clones?

- ☐ Under what circumstances do people conform?

- ☐ Are certain people more likely than others to conform?

- ☐ Who resists the pressure to conform?

- ☐ Is conformity as bad as the image of a docile 'herd' implies? Should we instead be describing their 'group solidarity', 'interdependence' and 'social sensitivity'?

## WHAT IS CONFORMITY?

Let us take the last question first. Is conformity good or bad? That is a question that has no scientific answer. Assuming the values most of us share, we can say that conformity is at times bad (when it leads someone to drive drunk or to join in racist behaviour), at times good (when it inhibits people from cutting into a theatre queue), and at times inconsequential (when it disposes men to wear a tie).

In Western individualistic cultures, where submitting to peer pressure is not admired, the word 'conformity' tends to carry a negative value judgement. How would you feel if you overheard someone describing you as a 'real conformist'? We suspect you would feel hurt. Hence, North American and European social psychologists, reflecting their individualistic cultures, give social influence negative labels (conformity, submission, compliance) rather than positive ones (communal sensitivity, responsiveness, co-operative team play).

In Japan, going along with others is a sign not of weakness but of tolerance, self-control and maturity (Markus & Kitayama, 1994). 'Everywhere in Japan,' observed Lance Morrow (1983), 'one senses an intricate serenity that comes to a people who know exactly what to expect from each other'.

The moral: we choose labels to suit our values and judgements. Labels both describe and evaluate, and they are inescapable. We cannot discuss the topics of this chapter without labels. So let us be clear on the meanings of the following labels: conformity, obedience, compliance, acceptance.

conformity *a change in behaviour or belief as the result of real or imagined group pressure*

Conformity is not just acting as other people act; it is also being affected by how they act. It is acting or thinking differently from the way you would act and think if you were alone. Thus, conformity is a change in behaviour or belief to accord with others or be affected by others against one's own beliefs. When, as part of a crowd, you rise to cheer a game-winning goal, are you conforming? When, along with millions of others, you drink milk or coffee, are you conforming? When you and everyone else agree that women look better with longer hair than with crewcuts, are you conforming? Maybe, maybe not. The key is whether your behaviour and beliefs would be the same apart from the group. Would you rise to cheer the goal if you were the only fan in the stands?

Conformity has to do with implicit social influence. Sometimes we conform to an expectation or a request without really believing in what we are doing. We put on the tie or the dress, though we dislike doing so. Or we find it unpleasant not to agree with the majority. This insincere, outward conformity is compliance. We comply primarily to reap a reward or avoid a punishment.

*compliance conformity that involves publicly acting in accord with an implied or explicit request even if privately disagreeing*

If our compliant behaviour is a result of explicit social influence, for instance an explicit command, we call it obedience.

*obedience acting in accord with a direct order or command*

Sometimes we genuinely believe in what the group has persuaded us to do. We may join millions of others in exercising because we all have been told that exercise is healthy and we accept that as true. This sincere, inward conformity is called acceptance. Acceptance sometimes follows compliance; we may come to inwardly believe something we initially questioned. As Chapter 5 emphasized, attitudes follow behaviour. Unless we feel no responsibility for our behaviour, we usually become sympathetic to what we have stood up for.

*acceptance conformity that involves both acting and believing in accord with social pressure*

## WHAT ARE THE CLASSIC CONFORMITY AND OBEDIENCE STUDIES?

*How have social psychologists studied conformity in the laboratory? What do their findings reveal about the potency of social forces, the power of the situation and in particular the nature of evil?*

Experimental researchers who study conformity and obedience construct miniature social worlds – laboratory micro-cultures that simplify and simulate important features of everyday social influence. Other researchers study conformity using the method of naturalistic observation and even analyse historical events. Some of the laboratory studies revealed such startling findings that they have been widely replicated and widely reported by other researchers, earning them the name of 'classic' experiments. We will consider three studies, each of which provides a method for studying conformity – and plenty of food for thought.

### SHERIF'S STUDIES OF NORM FORMATION

The first of the three classics bridges Chapter 14's focus on culture's power to create and perpetuate norms and this chapter's focus on conformity. Muzafer Sherif (1935, 1937) wondered whether it was possible to observe the emergence of a social norm in the laboratory. Like biologists seeking to isolate a virus so they can then experiment with it, Sherif wanted to isolate and then experiment with norm formation.

As a participant in one of Sherif's studies, you might have found yourself seated in a dark room. Fifteen feet in front of you a pinpoint of light appears. At first, nothing happens. Then for a few seconds it moves erratically and finally disappears. Now you must guess how far it moved. The dark room gives you no way to judge distance, so you offer an uncertain '6 inches'. The experimenter repeats the procedure. This time you say, '10 inches'. With further repetitions, your estimates continue to average about 8 inches.

The next day you return to the darkened room, joined by two other participants who had the same experience the day before. When the light goes off for the first time, the other two people offer their best guesses from the day before. 'One inch,' says one. 'Two inches,' says the other. A bit taken aback, you nevertheless say, 'Six inches.' With successive repetitions of this group experience, both on this day and for the next two days, will your responses change? The Columbia University men whom Sherif tested changed their estimates markedly. As Figure 7.1 illustrates, a group norm typically emerged. In actual fact the norm was false. Why? The light never moved! Sherif had taken advantage of an optical illusion called the autokinetic phenomenon.

**autokinetic phenomenon** *self (auto) motion (kinetic). The apparent movement of a stationary point of light in the dark*

Sherif and others have used this technique to answer questions about people's suggestibility. When people were retested alone a year later, would their estimates again diverge or would they continue to follow the group norm? Remarkably, they continued to support the group norm (Rohrer et al., 1954). (Does that suggest compliance or acceptance?)

Struck by culture's seeming power to perpetuate false beliefs, Robert Jacobs and Donald Campbell (1961) studied the transmission of false beliefs in their laboratory. Using the autokinetic phenomenon, they had a confederate give an inflated estimate of how far the light moved. The confederate then left the experiment and was replaced by another real participant. The newcomer conformed to the inflated estimate, and the inflated illusion persisted (although diminishing) in successive exchange of single participants, at least for five generations. These people had become 'unwitting conspirators in perpetuating a cultural fraud'. The lesson of these experiments: our views of reality are not ours alone.

In everyday life the results of suggestibility are sometimes amusing. One person coughs, laughs or yawns, and others are soon doing the same. (See Research Close-Up: Contagious Yawning.) Comedy-show laugh tracks capitalize on our suggestibility. Laugh tracks work especially well when we presume that the laughing audience is people like us – 'recorded here at La Trobe University' in one study by Michael Platow and

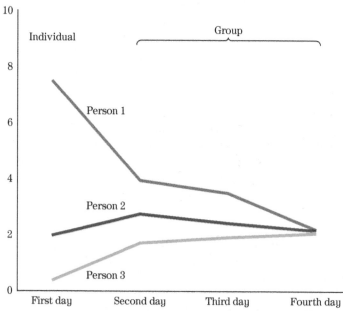

**Estimated movement, inches**

**FIGURE 7.1** A sample group from Sherif's study of norm formation
Three individuals converge as they give repeated estimates of the apparent movement of a point of light.

SOURCE: Data from Sherif & Sherif, 1969, p. 209.

colleagues (2005) – rather than a group that's unlike us. Just being around happy people can help us feel happier, a phenomenon that Peter Totterdell and his colleagues (1998) call 'mood linkage'. In their studies of British nurses and accountants, people within the same work groups tended to share up and down moods.

'Why doth one man's yawning make another yawn?'
   Robert Burton, *Anatomy of Melancholy*, 1621

Another form of social contagion is what Tanya Chartrand and John Bargh (1999) call 'the chameleon effect'. Picture yourself in one of their experiments, working alongside a confederate who occasionally either rubbed her face or shook her foot. Would you – like their participants – be more likely to rub your face when with a face-rubbing person and shake your foot when with a foot-shaking person? If so, it would quite likely be an automatic behaviour done without any conscious intention to conform. And, because our behaviour influences our attitudes and emotions, it would incline you to feel what the other feels (Neumann & Strack, 2000). An experiment in the Netherlands by Rick van Baaren and his colleagues (2004) indicates that your mimicry would also incline the other to like you and be helpful to you and to others. People become more likely to help pick up dropped pens for someone whose behaviour has mimicked their own. Being mimicked seems to enhance social bonds, which even leads to actions like donating more money to a charity.

Fashion is another example of conformity and common norm formation, even if we vehemently deny we are victims of the trends set by others. We may confidently declare that we do not follow trends in clothing, hairstyles and the kind of coffee we prefer simply because everybody else does. We may be convinced that we are following our own taste, our personal aesthetic preferences and what kind of coffee we personally like, even if five years later when the fashions have changed, we dress differently and drink another kind of coffee. Similarly, how many students would you expect to order a glass of lemonade when the rest of the regular gang is ordering a beer? There are specific norms to follow and conform to as a student as well, and that is of course not necessarily a bad thing. It lubricates social relations and improves feelings of togetherness.

Suggestibility and social influence are not always harmless. Hijackings, UFO (unidentified flying object) sightings, and even suicides tend to come in waves. Shortly after the 1774 publication of *The Sorrows of Young Werther*, Johann Wolfgang von Goethe's first novel, young European men started dressing in yellow trousers and blue jackets, as had Goethe's protagonist, a young man named Werther. Although the fashion epidemic triggered by the book was amusing, another apparent effect was less amusing and led to the book's banning in several areas. In the novel, Werther commits suicide with a pistol after being rejected by the woman whose heart he failed to win; after the book's publication, reports began accumulating of young men imitating Werther's desperate act.

Two centuries later, sociologist David Phillips confirmed such imitative suicidal behaviour and described it as 'the Werther effect'. Phillips and his colleagues (Phillips, 1985; Phillips et al., 1989) discovered that suicides, as well as fatal automobile accidents and private airplane crashes (which sometimes disguise

## research close-up

### CONTAGIOUS YAWNING

*Source: Provine, R. (2005). Yawning.* American Scientist, *93, 532–539.*

#### Introduction

Yawning is a behaviour common to most vertebrates. Yawning appears to be a primal activity and can even be seen in babies in the womb. Robert Provine (2005) has studied a number of commonplace human behaviours, including yawning and laughing. Provine is particularly interested when we yawn and the potential social aspect of such a behaviour.

Provine describes yawning as a 'fixed action pattern' that lasts about 6 seconds, with a long inward breath and shorter climactic (and pleasurable) exhalation. It often comes in bouts, with just over a minute between yawns. And it is equally common among men and women. Even patients who are totally paralysed and unable to move their body voluntarily may yawn normally, indicating that this is automatic behaviour.

In addition to the apparently physiological reasons behind yawning, we also appear to yawn as a social response to seeing others yawn. Provine conducted a series of experiments in order to determine how common contagious yawning is, using video footage of a man yawning as a stimulus.

#### Method

Participants were divided into two conditions. In the experiential condition, the participants were shown a 5-minute video of 30 repetitions of a man yawning. In the control condition, the video was of a man smiling. The experiment was also carried out with alterations to the experimental condition that altered the yawning video stimulus, masking part of the face, changing the video from colour to black and white, as well as using still images of yawns. To see what parts of the yawning face were most potent, Provine had viewers watch a whole face, a face with the mouth masked, a mouth with the face masked, or (as a control condition) a non-yawning smiling face.

Robert Provine (2005) invited four groups of 30 people each to watch 5-minute videotapes of a smiling adult, or a yawning adult, parts of whose face were masked for two of the groups. A yawning mouth triggered some yawns, but yawning eyes and head motion triggered even more.

### Results

In the yawning condition, 55 per cent of viewers yawned, as compared to only 21 per cent of those viewing a video of smiles. The changes in the presentation of the video – changing the colour or altering the position of the picture – did not alter the participants' yawning responses. The results support Provine's argument that a yawning face acts as a stimulus that activates a yawn's fixed action pattern, even if the yawn is presented in black and white, upside down, or as a mid-yawn still image.

### Discussion

Provine's experiments show that we are triggered to yawn when we see someone else yawning, even if we only see a yawning mouth, or the rest of the yawning face without the mouth. The discovery of brain 'mirror neurons' – neurons that rehearse or mimic witnessed actions – suggests a biological mechanism that explains why our yawns so often mirror others' yawns. These 'mirror neurons' could explain why we seem to find ourselves mimicking the actions of others, so when other people smile at us, we are very likely to smile back. This is probably why people around us who are happy and smiling seem to make us smile more, and so lift our own mood. Their cheerfulness seems to make us cheerful.

Thus, covering your mouth when yawning probably won't suppress yawn contagion. This totally unconscious response to others is an example of a neurologically programmed social behaviour. Thus, Provine argues, the unconsciously controlled human behaviour opens the discussion of human behaviour to a much wider scope of study.

Just thinking about yawning usually produces yawns, reports Provine – a phenomenon you may have noticed while reading this box. And maybe it made you feel a little drowsy as well? Influenced by the yawning your brain believes you are tired.

suicides), increase after a highly publicized suicide. For example, following Marilyn Monroe's suicide on 6 August 1962, there were 200 more August suicides in the USA than normal. Moreover, the increase happens only in places where the suicide story is publicized. The more publicity, the greater the increase in later fatalities.

Although not all studies have found the copycat suicide phenomenon, it has surfaced in Germany; in a London psychiatric unit that experienced 14 patient suicides in one year; and in one high school that, within 18 days after one student committed suicide, suffered two suicides, seven suicide attempts, and 23 students reporting suicidal thoughts (Joiner, 1999; Jonas, 1992). In both Germany and the USA, suicide rates rise slightly following fictional suicides on soap operas and, ironically, even after serious dramas that focus on the suicide problem (Gould & Shaffer, 1986; Hafner & Schmidtke, 1989; Phillips, 1982). Phillips reports that teenagers are most susceptible, a finding that would help explain the occasional clusters of teen copycat suicides. In a baffling set of cases, Bridgend, a small community in Wales, has seen at least 24 suicides of young people between 2007 and 2012, far above the expected number of suicides. There was a lot of speculation about why there were so many cases in such a small area. One of the things raised as possibly being part of the cause was the use of social media. It was speculated that the suicide victims' social media activity was a contribution to the trend, as well as tribute sites set up after each case where people left messages of remembrance and support. However, the police looked into this and they stated that although some of the people who committed suicide knew each other, they could find no concrete link between them all. The police also asked the media to stop reporting on suicides in the town to stop it potentially influencing other young people.

## ASCH'S STUDIES OF GROUP PRESSURE

Participants in Sherif's darkened-room autokinetic experiments faced an ambiguous reality. Consider a less ambiguous perceptual problem faced by a young boy named Solomon Asch (1907–96). While attending the traditional Jewish Seder at Passover, Asch recalled:

> I asked my uncle, who was sitting next to me, why the door was being opened. He replied, 'The prophet Elijah visits this evening every Jewish home and takes a sip of wine from the cup reserved for him.'

> I was amazed at this news and repeated, 'Does he really come? Does he really take a sip?'

> My uncle said, 'If you watch very closely, when the door is opened you will see – you watch the cup – you will see that the wine will go down a little.'

> And that's what happened. My eyes were riveted upon the cup of wine. I was determined to see whether there would be a change. And to me it seemed . . . that indeed something was happening at the rim of the cup, and the wine did go down a little.

(Aron & Aron, 1989, p. 27)

Years later, social psychologist Asch re-created his boyhood experience in his laboratory. Imagine yourself as one of Asch's volunteer subjects. You are seated sixth in a row of seven people. The experimenter explains that you will be taking part in a study of perceptual judgements, and then asks you to say which of the three lines in Figure 7.2 matches the standard line. You can easily see that it's line 2. So it's no surprise when the five people responding before you all say, 'Line 2'.

The participants judged which of three comparison lines matched the standard.

The next comparison proves as easy, and you settle in for what seems a simple test. But the third trial startles you. Although the correct answer seems just as clear-cut, the first person gives a wrong answer. When the second person gives the same wrong answer, you sit up in your chair and stare at the cards. The third person agrees with the first two. Your jaw drops; you start to perspire. 'What is this?' you ask yourself. 'Are they blind? Or am I?' The fourth and fifth people agree with the others. Then the experimenter looks at you. Now you are experiencing an epistemological dilemma: 'What is true? Is it what my peers tell me or what my eyes tell me?'

Dozens of college students experienced that conflict as participants in Asch's experiments. Those in a control condition who answered alone were correct more than 99 per cent of the time. Asch wondered: if several others (confederates coached by the experimenter) gave identical wrong answers, would people declare what they would otherwise have denied? Although some people never conformed, three-quarters did so at least

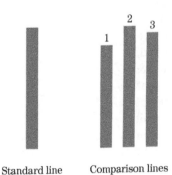

Standard line    Comparison lines

**FIGURE 7.2** Sample comparison from Solomon Asch's conformity procedure

once. All told, 37 per cent of the responses were conforming (or should we say '*trusting* of others'). Of course, that means 63 per cent of the time people did *not* conform. The experiments show that most people 'tell the truth even when others do not', note Bert Hodges and Anne Geyer (2006). Despite the independence shown by many of his participants, Asch's (1955) feelings about the conformity were as clear as the correct answers to his questions: 'That reasonably intelligent and well-meaning young people are willing to call white black is a matter of concern. It raises questions about our ways of education and about the values that guide our conduct.'

The Sherif and Asch results are startling because they involved no obvious pressure to conform – there were no rewards for 'team play', no punishments for individuality. The Sherif and Asch experiments are also interesting because they show how quickly people will change their answers in the face of conflicting information from others. In the Sherif experiment the ambiguity of the autokinetic effect seems to provide a task that you might easily reassess your answer on. Without anything to measure the movement against, maybe you are wrong and it really *did* move that far. In the Asch experiment, the task is far less ambiguous and the difference in the lengths of lines is much clearer; you are more in a position to give an answer that you *know* is wrong in order to agree with others. These experiments replicate the day-to-day social influence that leads us to agree with others or go along with other people to appear socially acceptable or compliant. It is often much easier to agree with others in public, just for a quiet life and avoid conflict.

Asch's experiments are also influential from a group perspective and are further considered in Chapters 11 and 12.

If people are that conforming in response to such minimal pressure, how compliant will they be if they are directly coerced? Could someone force the average American or European citizen to perform cruel acts? We would have guessed not: their humane, democratic, individualistic values would make them resist such pressure. Besides, the easy verbal pronouncements of those experiments are a giant step away from actually harming someone; you and I would never yield to coercion to hurt another. Or would we? History tells us otherwise. In Africa, Asia and Australia, American and European people have performed cruel acts against others often without being ordered or forced to. Think about the American treatment of their indigenous population. Or the British killing of the Australian aborigines and the destruction of the cultures in the Pacific. Or the German treatment of Jews, Gypsies, homosexuals and disabled people during the Second World War, and the European and Israeli dealing of the Palestinian refugees for more than 60 years.

Social psychologist Stanley Milgram wondered if direct coercion and compliance to perform cruel acts could be reproduced in the laboratory. His work about obedience to authority started and was funded in USA at a time when conformity was regarded exclusively as a 'bad thing' as it came on the back of the Second World War. The Western world was horrified by the obedience and its consequences in the Third Reich. To conform (to a Nazi regime and propaganda) was regarded as antithetical to Western values of individualism (although there's a conundrum here about how if everyone conforms to individualism this is an act of conformity in itself!). Governments and people in general wanted to know what caused it so they could prevent it. The topics of obedience, authoritarianism and 'mass psychology' were studied extensively by social researchers, psychologists and psychiatrists after the Second World War. In Germany the social psychoanalyst Wilhelm Reich wrote about the mass psychology of fascism, and in the USA German and American sociologists, social psychologists and psychoanalysts under the lead of Theodor Adorno published in 1950 the influential book *The Authoritarian Personality* (referred to in Chapter 13). These and many other research programmes and studies illustrate how social psychology is 'situated' in the times. Conformity was regarded as a bad thing after the Second World War and Stanley Milgram has been the most influential social psychologist in carrying this spirit of obedience as something evil into science and examining it in the laboratory.

## MILGRAM'S STUDIES OF OBEDIENCE

Milgram (1965, 1974) tested what happens when the demands of authority clash with the demands of conscience. These have become social psychology's most famous and controversial laboratory studies. 'Perhaps more than any other empirical contributions in the history of social science', notes Lee Ross (1988), 'they have become part of our society's shared intellectual legacy – that small body of historical incidents, biblical parables, and classic literature that serious thinkers feel free to draw on when they debate about human nature or contemplate human history'. Although you may therefore recall a mention of this research in a prior course, let's go backstage and examine the studies in depth. Although the studies take place in a laboratory, Milgram's empirical work is more properly described as a series of demonstrations, rather than as an experiment (Burger, 2009).

Here is the scene staged by Milgram, a creative artist who wrote stories and stage plays: two men come to Yale University's psychology laboratory to participate in a study of learning and memory. A stern experimenter in a laboratory coat explains that this is a pioneering study of the effect of punishment on learning. The experiment requires one of them to teach a list of word pairs to the other and to punish errors by delivering shocks of increasing intensity. To assign the roles, they draw slips out of a hat. One of the men (a mild-mannered, 47-year-old accountant who is actually the experimenter's confederate) says that his slip says 'learner' and is ushered into an adjacent room. The other man (a volunteer who has come in response to a newspaper advertisement) is assigned to the role of 'teacher'. He takes a mild sample shock and then looks on as the experimenter straps the learner into a chair and attaches an electrode to his wrist.

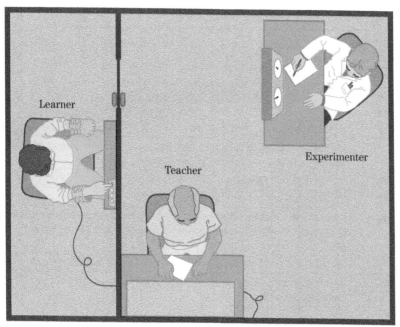

**FIGURE 7.3** Milgram's obedience experiment
SOURCE: Milgram, 1974.

Teacher and experimenter then return to the main room (see Figure 7.3), where the teacher takes his place before a 'shock generator' with switches ranging from 15 to 450 volts in 15-volt increments. The switches are labelled 'Slight Shock', 'Very Strong Shock', 'Danger: Severe Shock', and so forth. Under the 435- and 450-volt switches appears 'XXX'. The experimenter tells the teacher to 'move one level higher on the shock generator' each time the learner gives a wrong answer. With each flick of a switch, lights flash, relay switches click and an electric buzz sounds.

If the participant complies with the experimenter's requests, he hears the learner grunt at 75, 90 and 105 volts. At 120 volts the learner shouts that the shocks are painful. And at 150 volts he cries out, 'Experimenter, get me out of here! I won't be in the experiment any more! I refuse to go on!' By 270 volts his protests have become screams of agony, and he continues to insist to be let out. At 300 and 315 volts, he screams his refusal to answer. After 330 volts he falls silent (Table 7.1). In answer to the teacher's inquiries and pleas to end the experiment, the experimenter states that the non-responses should be treated as wrong answers. To keep the participant going, he uses four verbal prods:

Prod 1: Please continue (or Please go on).
Prod 2: The experiment requires that you continue.
Prod 3: It is absolutely essential that you continue.
Prod 4: You have no other choice; you must go on.

How far would you go? Milgram described the experiment to 110 psychiatrists, college students and middle-class adults. People in all three groups guessed that they would disobey by about 135 volts; none expected to go beyond 300 volts. Recognizing that self-estimates may reflect self-serving bias, Milgram asked them how far they thought *other* people would go. Virtually no one expected anyone

TABLE 7.1   The learner's schedule of protests in milgram's 'heart disturbance' experiments

| 75 volts | Ugh! |
|---|---|
| 90 volts | Ugh! |
| 105 volts | Ugh! (Louder) |
| 120 volts | Ugh! Hey, this really hurts. |
| 135 volts | Ugh!! |
| 150 volts | Ugh!!! Experimenter! That's all. Get me out of here. I told you I had heart trouble. |
| | My heart's starting to bother me now. Get me out of here, please. My heart's starting to bother me. I refuse to go on. Let me out |
| 165 volts | Ugh! Let me out! (Shouting) |
| 180 volts | Ugh! I can't stand the pain. Let me out of here! (Shouting) |
| 195 volts | Ugh! Let me out of here. Let me out of here. My heart's bothering me. Let me out of here! You have no right to keep me here! Let me out! Let me out of here! Let me out! |
| | Let me out of here! My heart's bothering me. Let me out! Let me out! |
| 210 volts | Ugh! Experimenter! Get me out of here. I've had enough. I won't be in the experiment any more. |
| 225 volts | Ugh! |
| 240 volts | Ugh! |
| 255 volts | Ugh! Get me out of here. |
| 270 volts | (Agonized scream) Let me out of here. Let me out of here. Let me out of here. Let me out. Do you hear? Let me out of here. |
| 285 volts | (Agonized scream) |
| 300 volts | (Agonized scream) I absolutely refuse to answer any more. Get me out of here. You can't hold me here. Get me out. Get me out of here. |
| 315 volts | (Intensely agonized scream) I told you I refuse to answer. I'm no longer part of this experiment. |
| 330 volts | (Intense and prolonged agonized scream) Let me out of here. Let me out of here. My heart's bothering me. Let me out, I tell you. (Hysterically) Let me out of here. Let me out of here. You have no right to hold me here. Let me out! Let me out! Let me out! Let me out of here! Let me out! Let me out! |

SOURCE: From Stanley Milgram, *Obedience to Authority*. New York: Harper & Row, 1974, pp. 56–57.

to proceed to XXX on the shock panel. (The psychiatrists guessed about one in a thousand.)

But when Milgram conducted the experiment with 40 men – a vocational mix of 20 to 50 year olds – 26 of them (65 per cent) progressed all the way to 450 volts. In fact, all who reached 450 volts complied with a command to *continue* the procedure until, after two further trials, the experimenter called a halt.

Having expected a low rate of obedience, and with plans to replicate the study in Germany and assess the culture difference, Milgram was disturbed (Milgram, 2000). So instead of going to Germany, Milgram next made the learner's protests even more compelling. As the learner was strapped into the chair, the teacher heard him mention his 'slight heart condition' and heard the experimenter's reassurance that 'although the shocks may be painful, they cause no permanent tissue damage'. The learner's anguished protests were to little avail; of 40 new

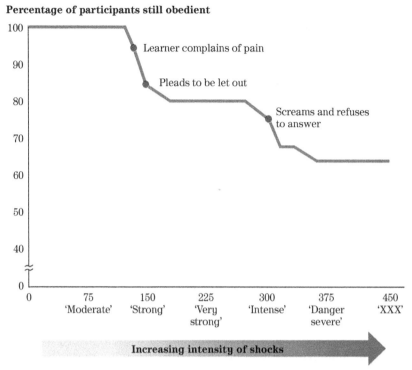

**Percentage of participants still obedient**

**FIGURE 7.4** The Milgram obedience experiment
Percentage of participants complying despite the learner's cries of protest and failure to respond.
SOURCE: Adapted from Milgram, 1965.

men in this experiment, 25 (63 per cent) fully complied with the experimenter's demands (Figure 7.4).

### The Ethics of Milgram's Experiments

The obedience of the participants disturbed Milgram. The procedures he used disturbed many social psychologists (Miller, 1986). The 'learner' in these experiments actually received no shock (he disengaged himself from the electric chair and turned on a tape recorder that delivered the protests). Nevertheless, some critics said that Milgram did to his participants what they presumed they were doing to their victims: he stressed them against their will. Indeed, many of the 'teachers' did experience agony. They sweated, trembled, stuttered, bit their lips, groaned, or even broke into uncontrollable nervous laughter. A *New York Times* reviewer complained that the cruelty inflicted by the experiments 'upon their unwitting subjects is surpassed only by the cruelty that they elicit from them' (Marcus, 1974).

Critics also argued that the participants' self-concepts may have been altered. One participant's wife told him, 'You can call yourself Eichmann' (referring to Nazi death camp administrator Adolf Eichmann). CBS television depicted the results and the controversy in a two-hour dramatization. 'A world of evil so terrifying no one dares penetrate its secret. Until Now!' declared a *TV Guide* advertisement for the programme (Elms, 1995).

In his own defence, Milgram pointed to the important lessons taught by his nearly two dozen studies with a diverse sample of more than 1000 participants. He also reminded critics of the support he received from the participants after the deception was revealed and the purpose explained. When surveyed afterwards, 84 per cent said they were glad to have participated; only 1 per cent regretted volunteering. A year later, a psychiatrist interviewed 40 of those who had suffered most and concluded that, despite the temporary stress, none was harmed.

The ethical controversy was 'terribly overblown', Milgram believed:

> There is less consequence to subjects in this experiment from the standpoint of effects on self-esteem, than to university students who take ordinary course examinations, and who do not get the grades they want. . . . It seems that [in giving exams] we are quite prepared to accept stress, tension, and consequences for self-esteem. But in regard to the process of generating new knowledge, how little tolerance we show.

(quoted by Blass, 1996)

If we consider Milgram's original experiments in relation to current ethical guidelines, it can be argued that there was nothing in the experiments that actually breaches the guidelines. We are still able to use deception in very specific and exceptional cases, where the ends are felt to justify the means and provided we fully debrief afterwards. Possibly the thing that disturbs us most about the Milgram experiment is not the nature of the experiment, but the insight it gives us into the capacity for ordinary people to do horrible things with little provocation.

## WHAT BREEDS OBEDIENCE?

Milgram did more than reveal the extent to which people will obey an authority; he also examined the conditions that breed obedience. When he varied the conditions, compliance ranged from 0 to 93 per cent fully obedient. Four factors that determined obedience were (1) the victim's distance, (2) the authority's closeness and legitimacy, (3) whether or not the authority was part of a respected institution, and (4) the liberating effects of a disobedient fellow participant.

### The Victim's Distance

Milgram's participants acted with greatest obedience and least compassion when the 'learners' could not be seen (and could not see them). When the victim was remote and the 'teachers' heard no complaints, nearly all obeyed calmly to the end.

That situation minimized the learner's influence relative to the experimenter's. But what if we made the learner's pleas and the experimenter's instructions more equally visible? When the learner was in the same room, 'only' 40 per cent obeyed to 450 volts. Full compliance dropped to a still-astonishing 30 per cent when teachers were required to force the learner's hand into contact with a shock plate.

In everyday life, too, it is easiest to abuse someone who is distant or depersonalized. People who might never be cruel to someone in person may be downright nasty when posting comments aimed at anonymous people on Internet discussion boards. Throughout history, executioners have often depersonalized those being executed by placing hoods over their heads. The ethics of war allow one to bomb a helpless village from 40 000 feet but not to shoot an equally helpless villager or a wedding party when watching it close.

As the Holocaust began, some Germans, under orders, used machine guns or rifles to kill men, women and children standing before them. But others could not bring themselves to do so, and some who did were left shaken by the experience of face-to-face killing. That led Heinrich Himmler, the Nazi 'architect of genocide', to devise a killing, more 'humane' for the executioners, one that would visually separate the killers and their victims and was highly 'efficient'. The solution was the construction of concrete gas chambers, where the killers would not see or hear the human consequences of their horror (Russell & Gregory, 2005).

On the positive side, people act most compassionately towards those who are personalized and need care. That is why appeals for the disabled, for the hungry or for animal rights are nearly always personalized with a compelling photograph or description. Perhaps even more compelling is an ultrasound picture of one's own developing foetus. When queried by researchers John Lydon and Christine Dunkel-Schetter (1994), expectant women expressed more commitment to their pregnancies if they had seen ultrasound pictures of their foetuses that clearly displayed body parts.

## Closeness and Legitimacy of the Authority

The physical presence of the experimenter also affected obedience. When Milgram's experimenter gave the commands by telephone, full obedience dropped to 21 per cent (although many lied and said they were obeying). Other studies confirm that when the one making the command is physically close, compliance increases. Given a light touch on the arm, people are more likely to lend a dime, sign a petition, or sample a new pizza (Kleinke, 1977; Smith et al., 1982; Willis & Hamm, 1980).

The authority, however, must be perceived as legitimate. In another twist on the basic experiment, the experimenter received a rigged telephone call that required him to leave the laboratory. He said that since the equipment recorded data automatically, the 'teacher' should just go ahead. After the experimenter left, another person, who had been assigned a clerical role (actually a second confederate), assumed command. The clerk 'decided' that the shock should be increased one level for each wrong answer and instructed the teacher accordingly. Now 80 per cent of the teachers refused to comply fully. The confederate, feigning disgust at this defiance, sat down in front of the shock generator and tried to take over the teacher's role. At that point most of the defiant participants protested. Some tried to unplug the generator. One large man lifted the zealous confederate from his chair and threw him across the room. This rebellion against an illegitimate authority contrasted sharply with the deferential politeness usually shown the experimenter.

It also contrasts with the behaviour of hospital nurses who in one study were called by an unknown physician and ordered to administer an obvious drug overdose (Hofling et al., 1966). The researchers told one group of nurses and nursing students about the experiment and asked how they would react. Nearly all said they would not have followed the order. One said she would have replied, 'I'm sorry, sir, but I am not authorized to give any medication without a written order, especially one so large over the usual dose and one that I'm unfamiliar with. If it were possible, I would be glad to do it, but this is against hospital policy and my own ethical standards.' Nevertheless, when 22 other nurses were actually given the phoned-in overdose order, all but one obeyed without delay (until being intercepted on their way to the patient). Although not all nurses are so compliant (Krackow & Blass, 1995; Rank & Jacobson, 1977), these nurses were following a familiar script: doctor (a legitimate authority) orders; nurse obeys.

### Institutional Authority

If the prestige of the authority is that important, then perhaps the institutional prestige of Yale University legitimized the Milgram experiment commands. In post-experimental interviews, many participants said that had it not been for Yale's reputation, they would not have obeyed. To see whether that was true, Milgram moved the experiment to less prestigious Bridgeport, Connecticut. He set himself up in a modest commercial building as the 'Research Associates of Bridgeport'. When the 'learner-has-a-heart-condition' experiment was run with the same personnel, what percentage of the men do you suppose fully obeyed? Although the obedience rate (48 per cent) was still remarkably high, it was significantly lower than the 65 per cent rate at Yale.

In 1962 Martin Orne carried out a series of experiments looking at the demand characteristics of laboratory experiments. He argued that asking participants to act 'normally' in such an artificial setting simply didn't work, participants are driven by demand characteristics, wanting to give the experimenter what they think they want. As an example, participants were given unrealistically huge tasks to complete; one was a maths task, asking participants to add two numbers – there were 244 of these on each page, and participants were given a stack of 2000 pages. Once the participants were given the task and the instructions, they were told that the experimenter had to leave but that they would return 'eventually'. One participant carried on for so long that after over five hours the experimenter gave up and stopped them. Participants were given tasks that were clearly pointless and repetitive, yet they continued them for hours at a time. Orne's position is that the very 'scientific' nature of laboratory experiments is one of the flaws, that they lack ecological validity. We might do things in a laboratory experiment that we would never do in our everyday lives.

In everyday life, too, authorities backed by institutions wield social power. Robert Ornstein (1991) tells of a psychiatrist friend who was called to the edge of a cliff above San Mateo, California, where one of his patients, Alfred, was threatening to jump. When the psychiatrist's reasoned reassurance failed to dislodge Alfred, the psychiatrist could only hope that a police crisis expert would soon arrive.

Although no expert came, another police officer, unaware of the drama, happened onto the scene, took out his power bullhorn, and yelled at the assembled cliffside group: 'Who's the ass who left that Pontiac station wagon double-parked out there in the middle of the road? I almost hit it. Move it *now*, whoever you are.' Hearing the message, Alfred obediently got down at once, moved the car, and then without a word got into the police cruiser for a trip to the nearby hospital.

Agentic State Theory

The evidence is solidly supportive of Milgram's view that the power of authority, rather than aggressive tendencies, was the primary determinant of the punishing behaviour in his studies. Milgram (1974) argued that obedience involves denial of responsibility of one's actions and a willingness to hand it over to authority. A person comes to view him or herself as an instrument for carrying out another person's wishes, and therefore no longer sees him or herself as responsible for their own actions. Milgram referred to this process as a shift from a state of autonomy to an *agentic state*. The evidence is not very supportive, however, since the theory cannot explain the different levels of obedience obtained in variants of the baseline study (varying from 65 per cent when participants only hear the reactions of the 'learner' to 30 per cent where they have to force his hand down onto an 'electric contact plate' and down to 10 per cent where there is a dissenting confederate teacher). Film and transcript of the studies also show that, far from becoming morally disengaged and passive, participants were profoundly troubled by what they were doing and initiated long debates about the justification for continuing the study. Subsequent studies do not find a relationship between the amount of responsibility attributed to the experimenter and levels of obedience. In short, the '*agentic state*' theory does not give the complete explanation (Blass, 2004). Our tendency to be obedient in specific situations has a more complex causality than people giving up their autonomy.

## REFLECTIONS ON THE CLASSIC STUDIES

The common response to Milgram's results is to note their counterparts in recent history: the 'I was only following orders' defences of Adolf Eichmann in Nazi Germany; of American Lieutenant William Calley, who in 1968 directed the unprovoked slaughter of hundreds of Vietnamese in the village of My Lai; the American soldiers, among them Lynndie England, who humiliated Islamic war-prisoners in Abu Ghraib prison and British soldiers who did the same in Basra; and of the 'ethnic cleansing' occurring in Iraq, Rwanda, Bosnia and Kosovo.

Soldiers were trained to obey superiors even if the orders were illegal and would result in atrocities. Thus, one participant in the My Lai massacre recalled:

> [Lieutenant Calley] told me to start shooting. So I started shooting, I poured about four clips into the group. . . . They were begging and saying, 'No, no.' And the mothers were hugging their children and . . . . Well, we kept right on firing. They was waving their arms and begging.

> (Wallace, 1969)

The Structural Atrocities

These examples of humiliation and atrocities focus on individuals as perpetrators. But sometimes a whole system or society is responsible for the misdeeds, killings and maltreatment of the enemies of the state. The slaughter becomes natural and the rule rather than the exception. Some social structures have an inbuilt injustice. The people in power and their followers have their benefits and protect the status quo by any means. Apartheid in South Africa was such a system for more than a hundred years. The atrocities could not be personified, the social structure was the main perpetrator and many white South Africans looked at themselves as good patriots when they killed and humiliated black enemies. The apartheid system developed gradually over many years. In the second half of the eighteenth century, the colonists – mainly of Dutch, German and French stock – had begun to lose their sense of identification with Europe and looked at themselves as the masters and owners of South Africa, including the black people. The separation of the blacks and whites (the apartheid system) became official government ideology from 1948 when the Nationalist Party gained power. The 1950s brought more and more repressive laws against black South Africans, which naturally created growing resistance. This set the stage for the even more polarized 1960s, when the suppression, violence and cruelty towards the black South Africans increased.

Many white South Africans were born and socialized into a society where hostility towards the black majority was looked upon as natural and necessary, and many conformed and participated in the cruelties during the apartheid period. One of the most high profile of these was Eugene de Kock, nicknamed 'Prime Evil', apartheid's chief murderer. He was later sentenced to 212 years for crimes against humanity. However, Pumla Goboda-Madikizela, a black female psychologist at the University of Cape Town, tried to understand the person behind these crimes and claimed to find a human being worthy of pardon and freedom. She published a remarkable book about her conversations with de Kock, entitled, *A Human Being Died that Night: A South African Story of Forgiveness* (Goboda-Madikizela, 2003). Her conclusion was that even the Prime Evil is a human being and was a victim of conformity to a suppressing and cruel system more than a man of absolute malignity.

According to the Nuremberg trial after the Second World War it became illegal for soldiers to obey inappropriate, unlawful orders. It is no excuse that they 'only followed orders'.

The 'safe' scientific contexts of the obedience experiments differ from the wartime contexts. Moreover, much of the mockery and brutality of war and genocide goes beyond obedience (Miller, 2004). Some of those who implemented the Holocaust were 'willing executioners' who hardly needed to be commanded to kill (Goldhagen, 1996). Many of them were proud to participate in the new Third Reich by being obedient and trustworthy. Few were aggressive or emotional and unable to control their temper when they dealt with the victims of the Nazi ideology. They conformed to the vision of building a new Germany – a new 'magnificent World', and as such, believed that all those considered unworthy or unfit for this ideal had to be exterminated. See Focus On: The Ordinary Monster.

The obedience studies differ from the conformity experiments in the strength of the social pressure: obedience is explicitly commanded. Without the coercion, people did not act cruelly. Yet both the Asch and the Milgram experiments share certain commonalities. They showed how compliance can take precedence over moral sense. They did more than teach an academic lesson; they sensitized us to moral conflicts in our own lives. And they illustrated and affirmed some familiar social psychological principles: the link between behaviour and attitudes, the power of the situation, and the strength of the fundamental attribution error.

Step by Step towards Insensibility

In Chapter 5 we noted that attitudes fail to determine behaviour when external influences override inner convictions. These experiments vividly illustrate that principle. When responding alone, Asch's participants nearly always gave the correct answer. It was another matter when they stood alone against a group.

In the obedience experiments, a powerful social pressure (the experimenter's commands) overcame a weaker one (the remote victim's pleas). Torn between the pleas of the victim and the orders of the experimenter, between the desire to avoid doing harm and the desire to be a good participant, a surprising number of people chose to obey.

Why were the participants unable to disengage themselves? Imagine yourself as the teacher in yet another version of Milgram's experiment (one he never conducted). Assume that when the learner gives the first wrong answer, the experimenter asks you to zap him with 330 volts. After flicking the switch, you hear the learner scream, complain of a heart disturbance and plead for mercy. Do you continue?

We think not. Recall the step-by-step entrapment of the foot-in-the-door phenomenon (Chapter 6) as we compare this hypothetical experiment to what Milgram's participants experienced. Their first commitment was mild – 15 volts – and it elicited no protest. By the time they delivered 75 volts and heard the learner's first groan, they already had complied five times, and the next request was to deliver only slightly more. By the time they delivered 330 volts, the participants had complied 22 times and reduced some of their dissonance. They were therefore in a different psychological state from that of someone beginning the experiment at that point. This method of gradually increasing shocks, starting from something harmless and moving slowly towards more and more severe punishment, is sometimes overlooked as an important contribution to obedience. Milgram has been criticized for not taking this aspect of sequentialization into account in his obedience experiments. Jerry Burger (2009) has made a comment on this in his replication of Milgram's demonstration of obedience (see p. 260 in this chapter). If people are obedient to authority per se, then surely Milgram could have started at, for example, 330 volts and people would have delivered the fatal electric shock. But he didn't. Instead he crept along an incremental sequence of shocks in order to get the effect by the help of the foot-in-the-door phenomenon.

So it is in our everyday lives: the drift towards evil usually comes in small increments, without any conscious intent to do evil. Procrastination involves a similar unintended drift, towards self-harm (Sabini & Silver, 1982).

### Blame-the-Victim

As we saw in Chapter 5, external behaviour, attitudes and internal disposition can feed each other, sometimes in an escalating spiral. Thus:

> Many subjects harshly devalue the victim as a consequence of acting against him. Such comments as, 'He was so stupid and stubborn he deserved to get shocked,' were common. Once having acted against the victim, these subjects found it necessary to view him as an unworthy individual, whose punishment was made inevitable by his own deficiencies of intellect and character.

(Milgram, 1974, p. 10)

During the early 1970s, Greece's military junta used this 'blame-the-victim' process to train torturers (Haritos-Fatouros, 1988, 2002; Staub, 1989, 2003). The military selected candidates based on their respect for and submission to authority. But such tendencies alone do not a torturer make. Thus, they would first assign the trainee to guard prisoners, then to participate in arrest squads, then to hit prisoners, then to observe torture, and only then to practise it. Step by step, an obedient but otherwise decent person evolved into an agent of cruelty. Compliance bred acceptance.

As a Holocaust survivor, University of Massachusetts social psychologist Ervin Staub knows too well the forces that can transform citizens into agents of death. From his study of human genocide across the world, Staub (2003) shows where gradually increasing aggression can lead. Too often criticism produces contempt, which licenses cruelty, which, when justified, leads to brutality, then killing, then systematic killing. Evolving attitudes both follow and justify actions. Staub's disturbing conclusion: 'Human beings have the capacity to come to experience killing other people as nothing extraordinary' (1989, p. 13).

But individuals and groups also have capacity for heroism. During the Nazi Holocaust, the French village of Le Chambon sheltered 5000 Jews and other refugees destined for deportation to Germany. The villagers were mostly Protestants whose own authorities, their pastors, had taught them to 'resist whenever our adversaries will demand of us obedience contrary to the orders of the Gospel' (Rochat, 1993; Rochat & Modigliani, 1995). Ordered to divulge the locations of sheltered Jews, the head pastor modelled disobedience: 'I don't know of Jews, I only know of human beings'. Without knowing how terrible the war would be, the resisters, beginning in 1940, made an initial commitment and then – supported by their beliefs, by their own authorities and by one another – remained defiant until the village's liberation in 1944. Here and elsewhere, the ultimate response to Nazi occupation came early. Initial helping heightened commitment, leading to more helping. Even within the concentration camps there was resistance and Hermann Langbein (1994) makes the point that resistance was only possible at a collective level. Those who were most effective in fighting back (and in surviving) were those that had most solidarity and most cohesion: the communists among the political prisoners, the Zionists among the Jews, the Russians and the Spaniards among nations.

Sometimes social psychologists have given the impression that groups or crowds necessarily lead to destructive and antisocial behaviour (Le Bon, 1895). Steven Reicher and his colleagues reject such a view and give historical examples of self-sacrifice on behalf of others:

> It is certainly true, for example, that, in the Soviet Union, many millions were imprisoned or starved simply for being designated a 'kulak' or a member of some other pathologized category. But it is equally true that, without collective solidarity, this and other dictatorships would not have been toppled. The Romanian revolution, for instance, began in Timisoara where large crowds challenged Ceausescu's notorious Securitate police force. Many demonstrators were killed. Still, the numbers of demonstrators grew . . . the fate of the Romanian people was more important than life itself.
> (Reicher et al., 2008)

## The Power of the Social Context

In Chapter 14 you will be introduced to the very important role that culture and context take in influencing our lives. Although we like to think of ourselves as entirely independent in our thinking and actions, we are influenced by external factors. The situational forces that influence us are very powerful. Where we are, who we are with, what we are doing and the social context we are in make a huge impact on our behaviour. To feel this for yourself, imagine violating some minor norms: standing up in the middle of a class; singing out loud in a restaurant; playing golf in a suit. In trying to break with social norms and constraints, we suddenly realize how strong they are.

Milgram's experiments also offer a lesson about evil. According to what we see in horror movies and suspense novels, evil results from a few bad apples, a few depraved killers. In real life we similarly think of Hitler's extermination of Jews, of Saddam Hussein's extermination of Kurds, of Osama Bin Laden's plotting terror. Evil also results from social forces, from heat, humidity and disease that help make a whole barrel of apples go bad (see the Lucifer Effect noted in Chapter 6). The American military police, whose abuse of Iraqi prisoners at Abu Ghraib prison horrified the world, were under stress, taunted by many of those they had come to 'save', angered by comrades' deaths, overdue to return home and under lax supervision – an evil situation that produced evil behaviour (Fiske et al., 2004). Situations can induce ordinary people to capitulate to cruelty.

This is especially true when, as happens often in complex societies, the most terrible evil evolves from a sequence of small evils. German civil servants surprised Nazi leaders with their willingness to handle the paperwork of the Holocaust. They were not killing Jews, of course; they were merely pushing paper (Silver & Geller, 1978). When fragmented, evil becomes easier. Milgram studied this compartmentalization of evil by involving yet another 40 men more indirectly. With someone else triggering the shock, they had only to administer the learning test. Now, 37 of the 40 fully complied.

Even in an individualistic culture, few of us desire to challenge our culture's clearest norms, as did Stephen Gough while walking the length of Britain naked (apart from hat, socks, boots and a rucksack). Starting in June 2003, he made it from Land's End, England's most southerly point, to John O'Groats, Scotland's most northerly mainland point. During his seven-month 847-mile trek he was arrested 15 times and spent about five months behind bars. 'My naked activism is firstly and most importantly about me standing up for myself, a declaration of myself as a beautiful human being', Gough (2003) declared from his website.

SOURCE: © Jeff J Mitchell/Getty Images

'History, despite its wrenching pain, cannot be unlived, and if faced with courage, need not be lived again.'

   Maya Angelou, *Presidential Inaugural Poem*, 20 January 1993

### The Fundamental Attribution Error

Why do the results of these classic experiments so often startle people? Is it because we expect people to act in accord with their dispositions? Recall that the fundamental attribution error is the tendency to interpret others' actions as expressing their dispositions rather than the situation they are in (see Chapter 4). It doesn't surprise us when a surly person is nasty, but we expect those with pleasant dispositions to be kind. Bad people, we assume, do bad things; good people do good things.

The 'senseless' 9/11 horror was perpetrated, we heard over and over again in the media, by 'madmen', by 'evil cowards', by 'demonic monsters'. Today, some still hold these opinions, but we now also know that the perpetrators did have their own logic for the attacks on the USA. The aim was not only to kill innocent people (though by creating 'terror' in this way, Al Qaeda drew attention to its cause), but also to attack the symbols (the World Trade Center and the Pentagon) of Western capitalist society, which is itself seen by some as an unfair, immoral and repressive system, responsible for widespread human suffering all over the world. To conquer the enemy it is always a good idea to try to understand their motives and ways of thinking, as opposed to demonizing them as mad monsters without any human qualities. If we know why people behave in the way they do, then we can argue against their thinking rather than just react senselessly to their behaviour.

When you read about Milgram's experiments, what impressions did you form of the obedient participants? Most people, when told about one or two of the obedient persons, judge them to be aggressive, cold and unappealing – even after learning that their behaviour was typical (Miller et al., 1973). Cruelty, we presume, is inflicted by the cruel at heart.

Günter Bierbrauer (1979) tried to eliminate this underestimation of social forces (the fundamental attribution error). He had university students observe a vivid re-enactment of the experiment or play the role of obedient teacher themselves. They still predicted that, in a repeat of Milgram's experiment, their friends would be only minimally compliant. Bierbrauer concluded that although social scientists accumulate evidence that our behaviour is a product of our social histories and current environments, most people continue to believe that people's inner qualities reveal themselves – that good people do good and that evil people do evil.

It is tempting to assume that Eichmann and the Auschwitz death camp commanders were uncivilized monsters. Indeed, their evil was fuelled by virulent anti-Semitism. And the social situation alone does not explain why, in the same neighbourhood or death camp, some personalities displayed vicious cruelty and others heroic kindness. Still, the commanders would not have stood out to us as monsters. After a hard day's work, they would relax by listening to Beethoven and Schubert. Of the 14 men who formulated the Final Solution leading to the Nazi Holocaust, eight had European university doctorates (Patterson, 1996). Like most other Nazis, Eichmann himself was outwardly indistinguishable from common people with ordinary jobs (Arendt, 1963; Zillmer et al., 1995). Mohamed Atta, the leader of the 9/11 attacks, reportedly had been a 'good boy' and an excellent student from a healthy family. Zacarias Moussaoui, the would-be twentieth 9/11 attacker, had been very polite when applying for flight lessons and buying knives. He called women 'ma'am'. The pilot of the second plane to hit the World Trade Center was said to be an amiable, 'laid-back' fellow, much like the 'intelligent, friendly, and "very courteous"' pilot of the plane that dove into the Pentagon. Osama Bin Laden also has a reputation for being a warm and caring person, paying much attention to those suffering from an unjust world. If these men had lived next door to us, they would hardly have fitted our image of evil monsters. They were 'unexceptional' people (McDermott, 2005).

Hijackers Nawaf al-Hazmi and Salem al-Hazmi were normal-looking, normal-acting passengers as they went through Dulles Airport security on 11 September 2001, an example of performance or presentation of normality more than proof that the hijackers were run-of-the-mill, everyday individuals.
SOURCE: Aaron Roeth Photography

'I would say, on the basis of having observed a thousand people . . . that if a system of death camps were set up in the United States of the

sort we had seen in Nazi Germany, one would be able to find sufficient personnel for those camps in any medium-sized American town.'
    Stanley Milgram, on CBS's *60 Minutes, 1979*

As Milgram noted (1974, p. 6), 'The most fundamental lesson of our study is that ordinary people, simply doing their jobs, and without any particular hostility on their part, can become agents in a terrible destructive process.' Under the sway of evil forces, even nice people are sometimes corrupted as they construct moral rationalizations for immoral behaviour (Tsang, 2002). So it is that ordinary soldiers may, in the end, follow orders to shoot defenceless civilians; admired political leaders may lead their citizens into ill-fated wars; ordinary employees may follow instructions to produce and distribute harmful, degrading products; and ordinary group members may heed commands to brutally haze initiates.

So, does a situational analysis of harm-doing exonerate harm-doers? Does it absolve them of responsibility? In laypeople's minds, the answer is to some extent yes, notes Arthur Miller (2006). But the psychologists who study the roots of evil insist otherwise. To explain is not to excuse. To understand is not to forgive. You can forgive someone whose behaviour you don't understand, and you can understand someone whom you do not forgive. Moreover, adds James Waller (2002), 'When we understand the ordinariness of extraordinary evil, we will be less surprised by evil, less likely to be unwitting contributors to evil, and perhaps better equipped to forestall evil.'

Social psychologists from the University of St Andrews and the University of Exeter in England have re-examined the historical and psychological case for 'the banality of evil' – the idea that people commit extreme acts of inhumanity in a state where they lack awareness or control over what they are doing. Steve Reicher, Alex Haslam and Rakshi Rath (2008) argue instead that those who commit great wrongs, for instance genocides, knowingly choose to act as they do because they believe that what they are doing is right. The British social psychologists present a five-step social identity model explaining why inhumane acts against other groups can come to be celebrated as right.

## BANALITY OF EVIL OR CELEBRATION OF VIRTUE?

After the Second World War many people were left asking the question of how apparently normal, ordinary people could do such terrible things. Once the men and women who were responsible for the Holocaust were captured, these people did not look evil, they were just like everyone else. Hannah Arendt coined the phrase 'banality of evil' in her book on the trial of Eichmann. She was struck by his unassuming appearance, so counter to the assumption that the people who took part in the Holocaust must been monsters (see Focus On: The Ordinary Monster at the end of the chapter for more on this). The idea of 'the banality of evil' explanation was fuelled by many studies in social psychology, according to Reicher et al. (2008). Muzafer Sherif (1966) created hostility between ordinary friends simply by dividing them into two competing groups, and made nice boys into wicked, disturbed and vicious individuals (see Chapter 13). The conformity studies by Asch (1952) are also remembered by most people as illustrations of how group processes can lead innocent people into wrongdoing.

Milgram's 'obedience' studies are also directly associated with the 'banality of evil' perspective, conducted when Eichmann's trial was in progress. According to Reicher and his colleagues, Milgram demonstrated that ordinary Americans, no less than ordinary Germans, are capable of cruelty through unthinking conformity. People simply focus on how well they can serve an authority. The ordinary person who shocked a stranger did so out of a sense of obligation, not from any peculiarly aggressive tendencies (Milgram, 1974, pp. 23, 24).

Zimbardo's Stanford Prison Experiment (SPE) also explains nasty and abusive behaviour in terms of conformity to roles. The situation alone is sufficient to produce immoral acts since the role players lose the ability to make moral choices. The prison guard's aggression was 'emitted simply as a "natural" consequence of being in the uniform of a "guard" and asserting the power inherent in that role' (Haney et al., 1973, p. 12).

We will revisit Zimbardo's study in Chapter 13 when we examine intergroup relationships and prejudice.

Reicher and his colleagues, who re-examined the classical social psychological studies and the 'banality of evil' explanation, did not accept that inhumanity is thoughtless. Rather, people *believe* that what they are doing is right. They manage to make a virtue out of evil (Staub, 1989). The purpose of Reicher and his colleagues' attempt is to understand from a social identity approach how this is made possible.

First, the issues are to do with collective phenomena and collective identities. Genocides are perpetrated against others not because of what they have done but because of the groups they belong to. Second, there is nothing inherent about ingroup processes that tends to be either ill or good. The same underlying psychological processes can lead to both good and evil acts. Third, there are five steps in the definition of social identities that allow for acts of extreme inhumanity. These are: (1) the creation of a cohesive ingroup through shared social identification; (2) the exclusion of specific populations from the ingroup; (3) the constitution of the outgroup as a danger to the existence of the ingroup; (4) the representation of the ingroup as uniquely virtuous; and (5) the celebration of outgroup annihilation as the defence of (ingroup) virtue. Let's consider each of these in more detail.

☐ *Step 1: The creation of a cohesive ingroup through shared social identification.* The definition of the ingroup is *as* crucial, if not *more* crucial, than definitions of outgroups in generating hatred. The very notion of 'them' is contingent upon how we determine the criteria that define 'us'. One cannot understand how people can do ill in the name of their group unless one also acknowledges the good that they derive from group membership. According to the social identity tradition, and to self-categorization theory in particular, a shared sense of category membership (i.e. of social identity) is the psychological basis of group action. It is only to the extent that we think of ourselves as Catholics, Fascists, Germans, or whatever, that we can act together as Catholics, Fascists or Germans. Groups, especially cohesive and powerful collectivities, are essential to our social presence and our social being. That is why people are so attached to and so passionate about their group memberships. That is why they can kill and are even prepared to die for their group.

☐ *Step 2: Exclusion – placing targets outside the ingroup.* How we define ingroup and outgroups or the category boundaries is critical between 'us' and 'them'. It is impossible to explain the appeal of Nazism without understanding how it was presented as a *moral* project – a project of cleansing and renewal in a world of decay and chaos. Above all, it was about rediscovering community and solidarity: creating bonds to others and putting service above self. As Goebbels put it: 'What is the first Commandment of every National Socialist? . . . Love Germany above all else and your ethnic comrade [*Volksgenosse*] as your self' (quoted in Koonz, 2003, p. 7). The German ingroup is defined in an exclusive way that excludes Jewish people, Gypsies and others. All the love and support and service are reserved for the ethnic ingroup, and the ethnic outgroup can have no hope of their solidarity (Reicher et al., 2008).

☐ *Step 3: Threat – the outgroup represents a danger to the existence of the ingroup.* There are many groups who are not 'us', but this fact does not necessarily make them 'against us'. The problems come when the problems in the ingroup are seen as the fault of outgroups: their stupidity, their aggressiveness, their deviousness, or whatever. It becomes possible to see the destruction of the outgroup as an act of self-defence rather than an act of aggression. However, although self-defence may be a legitimate act and one that makes aggression something that is acceptable to the ingroup (and even to wider communities beyond the group), it is still not sufficient to make attacks on others into something noble and something to be celebrated. For this to be possible, one further step is needed.

☐ *Step 4: Virtue – representing the ingroup as (uniquely) good.* Despite Hitler's candid anti-Semitism in *Mein Kampf*, Claudia Koonz notes that, from the moment he took power in 1933 until the outbreak of war, he hardly ever made mention of Jews. Instead, he devoted his efforts to extolling the distinctive virtues of (ethnic) Germans. The German *Volk*, he argued, were moral and pure and selfless and loyal. They were humble and they were just and they were devout. His watchword was, 'Cleanliness everywhere, cleanliness of our Government, cleanliness in public life, and also this cleanliness in our culture' (quoted in Koonz, 2003, p. 22). When 'we' are held to be virtuous, the more serious the outgroup threat becomes and the more it becomes acceptable to 'defend ourselves' by eliminating this outgroup threat – even if this means eliminating the outgroup itself.

☐ *Step 5: Celebration – eulogizing inhumanity as the defence of virtue.* Once all the pieces are in place, it becomes easy to see how genocide can be made something to celebrate. Where 'they' are defined as not being one of 'us' but as being against 'us', and where we create a view of the world in which we represent good and they represent evil, extreme violence towards other groups is possible.

It is frightening to think how easily we could be persuaded to abandon our ethical and moral objection to harming others. If we look at conflicts like Rwanda or Yugoslavia, we can see the group identities shifting to allow for the attempted destruction of the outgroup. The people who carried out crimes against humanity in these conflicts were as ordinary as the German war criminals were; they had come to think that they were defending the honour or purity of their ingroup.

## INFRAHUMANIZATION

This tacitly held belief that one's ingroup is more human than the outgroup is also called *infrahumanization*, a term proposed by the Belgian Jacques-Philippe Leyens and colleagues at Université Catholique de Louvain (UCL). Infrahumanization arises when people view their ingroup and outgroup as essentially different and accordingly reserve the 'human essence' for the ingroup and deny it to outgroups. It has been studied by looking at what kind of emotions people believe ingroup and outgroup members possess (Leyens et al., 2000). In a series of studies Leyens and colleagues showed that people attribute uniquely human emotions (e.g. love, regret, nostalgia) to the ingroup, but not the outgroup, reflecting the tacit belief that they are less human than the ingroup. Interestingly, although the ingroup regards the outgroup negatively, potential negative traits of the ingroup may be treated as evidence of human nature. They are, after all, 'only human'. Thus, the trait being judged is not viewed objectively, but subjectively, in the context of the group membership (Koval et al., 2012).

Evidence of infrahumanization can be seen in conflicts, including the Nazi treatment of the Jews – describing them as 'rats', and the description of Hutus as 'cockroaches' during the Rwandan genocide (Kellow & Steeves, 1998). Clearly, by reducing the outgroup to less than human, it becomes easier to justify treating them in a less than human manner (Lammers & Stapel, 2011). It is, after all, easier to justify killing a cockroach than a human. Nick Haslam and his colleagues Steve Loughnan and Pamela Sun (2011) analysed animal metaphors used in dehumanization of outgroups. In their analysis they found that the most offensive metaphors were those of disliked animals, such as rats or snakes. These metaphors appear not to carry the meaning that the outgroup are actually rats or snakes, but that they provoke moral disgust. The metaphors that most dehumanize the outgroup were metaphors such as dog or ape. These were found to be more dehumanizing, equating the outgroup with the animal metaphor.

Infrahumanization can have practical consequences, such as unwillingness to offer help at a time of crisis. Studying helping in the aftermath of Hurricane Katrina, which devastated New Orleans in the USA in 2005, Amy Cuddy, Mindi Rock and Michael Norton (2007) found that people were less likely to help people they perceived to be members of an outgroup. How helping behaviour is influenced by our membership of social groups will be considered in more detail in Chapter 10.

If infrahumanization impacts how we view outgroup members and their behaviour, this has implications for judgement of our own behaviour. As already mentioned, we are more likely to judge our own transgressions as evidence of 'being human', although those of the outgroup are more likely to be judged as reinforcement of their negativity and failure. By forgiving our own transgressions of social and moral codes, while condemning the transgressions of others, we are viewing these social and moral codes through a lens of our own bias.

## LABORATORY AND EVERYDAY LIFE

Finally, a comment on the laboratory studies used in conformity research (see synopsis, Table 7.2): conformity situations in the laboratory differ from those in everyday life. How often are we asked to judge line lengths or administer shock? Erich Fromm argued that the Milgram experiments, and others like them, are flawed. The very nature of the experimental model leads the participants into a specific set of responses. He stated 'I do not think that this experiment permits a conclusion with regard to most situations in real life. The psychologist was not

## research close-up

### JUDGING OUR OWN AND OTHERS' MISDEEDS*

**Source**: *Lammers, J., Stapel, D.A., & Galinksy, A.D. (2010). Power increases hypocrisy: moralizing in reasoning, immorality in behaviour.* Psychological Science, *21, 5, 737–744.*

### Introduction

We would like to believe that the judgement of behaviour depends solely on whether that behaviour is good or bad. However, it certainly appears that our judgement involves other factors including whether we feel in a position to judge (Yzerbyt et al., 1994: Lammers et al., 2009). It has been argued that the powerful are more self-interested than the powerless, and are therefore more focused on the potential rewards of a behaviour than the judgement of it (Keltner et al., 2003). There are regularly stories in the news about politicians who abuse their position of power, while at the same time they condemn the actions of others. This hypocrisy is infuriating! If they are telling us how to behave, why don't they follow their own guidance? Financial institutions have requested multi-billion dollar loans to support their organizations from bankruptcy, whilst awarding themselves massive bonuses (Kanagaretnam et al., 2008). Joris Lammers, Diederik Stapel and Adam Galinsky (2010) set out to investigate if there is a link between power and moral hypocrisy. They proposed a hypothesis that states that the powerful are less likely to practise what they preach than the powerless.

### Experiment 1

#### Method

Sixty-one students were randomly assigned to two conditions – high power and low power. Participants had a sense of power induced using an experiential power prime. An experiential power prime uses experiences that participants have had that made them feel either more powerful or less powerful. In the high power condition participants were asked to recall a high power experience, for example winning a prize in sport. In the low power participants were asked to recall a low power one such as getting a really bad mark in an exam. Participants were placed in private cubicles to complete the tasks in the experiment.

Half of the participants in both conditions were told that they would be financially compensated for their participation. Their financial reward would be determined by lottery and the more lottery tickets the better chance they had of winning a larger amount. They were provided with a pair of 10-sided dice to determine their number of lottery tickets. The participants were told that they should roll the dice once and the numbers that they rolled would be multiplied together to give the number of lottery tickets that they would receive. They rolled the dice in private without the researcher watching. They were then asked what numbers they rolled, without the researcher verifying it. This procedure provided the participants ample opportunity to cheat and increase their number of lottery tickets. As the range of numbers they could get was theoretically between 0 and 99, the mean number of tickets should have been 50. If the recorded mean was significantly higher than this it would show that participants had cheated in reporting the results of their dice rolls.

The other half of the participants were not involved in the lottery, but were asked to judge whether it is morally acceptable to cheat travelling expenses on a 9-point scale.

---

* In September 2011, Diederik Stapel was suspended from his professorship duties, after it was suspected that he used fake data for his research publications. In October 2011 the Levelt Committee was entrusted with investigating the extent of Stapel's fraud. The article on which this Research Close-Up is based has been cleared by the Levelt Committee, as their investigation has found no evidence of fraudulent data or practice. See: http://pss.sagepub.com/content/23/7/828

*Results*

Lammers et al. standardized responses to both conditions. They were then analysed on a 2 (power: high vs. low) × 2 (judgement vs. behaviour) analysis of variance and found that high power participants were stricter in their judgement of cheating than low power participants. However, high power participants claimed a larger number of lottery tickets than the low power participants. While this finding is interesting, there is the potential flaw that the measures of honesty and hypocrisy are different. For example, if you score quite low on an honesty scale, then if you were to act in a dishonest way, then you wouldn't be hypocritical. However, if you were to score highly on an honesty scale, and then you were dishonest, this would be hypocritical. Following on from this experiment, Lammers et al. carried out another three experiments that further investigated their hypothesis addressing this flaw.

Experiments 2, 3 and 4

*Method*

A total of 172 different students were again randomly assigned to high or low power conditions. In experiment 2, 42 participants were primed for their power status by placing them in a simulated bureaucratic environment with some in prime ministerial roles and others in civil servant roles. The 88 participants in experiment 3 used the same experience recall power priming as in experiment 1. In experiment 4, 42 participants were given a power priming word search (Chen et al., 2001). In all experiments, participants were also assigned to one of two conditions; in the low power condition they were judging themselves, and in the high power condition they were judging the behaviour of others.

Participants in the experiments were presented with a variety of moral dilemmas; in experiment 2 they were given one about speeding offences, in experiment 3 it was tax evasion, and in experiment 4 they were presented with one about keeping apparently stolen property. Participants in the high power condition were given gender neutral names of hypothetical others such as Chris. They were asked how acceptable it would be for that hypothetical person to engage in the described behaviour. In the low power condition, participants were asked how acceptable it would be if they engaged in the described behaviour.

*Results*

The data in these experiments were analysed using a *t* test, and all three experiments showed the same results in the same direction, that the powerful were more likely to engage in moral hypocrisy than the powerless. In all three experiments, the interaction between the power of the participant and the target of that participant's judgement was found to be significant.

Discussion

Throughout their experiments, only the participants in the powerful condition showed hypocrisy. Indeed, it seems that the powerless were more likely to be lenient in judging others' behaviour in comparison with their own. Lammers et al. refer to this phenomenon as '*hypercrisy*': being overly critical of one's own actions.

These experiments highlight some fascinating aspects of the way that power imbalances in societies allow the misbehaviour of the powerful while maintaining the conformity of the powerless to the social norms of that society. It certainly implies that those with less power are more likely to self-police, while those in power are more likely to justify their own transgressions of the social code.

Lammers et al. describe this as 'the powerless collaborate in reproducing social inequality', thus the powerful impose social rules on the powerless, but are themselves more likely to break their own rules. Conformity is not maintained by the knowledge or fear of the law's reach (Arendt, 1951), but instead by the apparent acceptance of social inequality, and the individual's belief in their own power status.

**TABLE 7.2** Summary of classic studies

| Topic | Researcher | Method | Real-life example |
|---|---|---|---|
| Norm formation | Sherif | Assessing suggestibility regarding seeming movement of light | Interpreting events differently after hearing from others; appreciating a tasty food that others love |
| Conformity | Asch | Agreement with others' obviously wrong perceptual judgements | Doing as others do; fads such as tattoos |
| Obedience | Milgram | Complying with commands to shock another | Soldiers or employees following questionable orders |

only an authority to whom one owes obedience but as a representative of science and on one of the most prestigious institutions of higher education in the United States' (1973, p. 74). By creating an experiment of conformity in the laboratory, the experience of conformity is removed from the real world and placed in the artificiality of the research lab, with its unfamiliar equipment and personnel. But as combustion is similar for a burning match and a forest fire, so we assume that psychological processes in the laboratory and in everyday life are similar (Milgram, 1974). We must be careful in generalizing from the simplicity of a burning match to the complexity of a forest fire, yet experiments on burning matches can give us insights into combustion that we cannot gain by observing forest fires. So, too, the social psychological laboratory studies offer insights into behaviour not readily revealed in everyday life. The situation is unique, but so is every social situation. By testing with a variety of unique tasks, and by repeating the studies in different times and places, researchers probe for the common principles that lie beneath the surface diversity.

The classic demonstrations of core items in social psychology answered some questions but raised others: (1) sometimes people conform or obey; sometimes they do not. *When* do they conform or obey? (2) *Why* do people conform or obey? Why don't they ignore the group and 'to their own selves be true'? (3) Is there a type of *person* who is likely to conform or obey? In the next section we will take these questions one at a time.

## WHAT PREDICTS CONFORMITY?

*Some situations trigger much conformity, others little conformity. If you wanted to produce maximum conformity, what conditions would you choose?*

Social psychologists wondered: if even Asch's non-coercive, unambiguous situation could elicit a 37 per cent conformity rate, would other settings produce even more? Researchers soon discovered that conformity did grow if the judgements were difficult or if the participants felt incompetent. The more insecure we are about our judgements, the more influenced we are by others.

Group attributes also matter. Conformity is highest when the group has three or more people and is unanimous, cohesive and high in status. Conformity is also highest when the response is public and made without prior commitment. Let's look at each of these conditions.

### GROUP SIZE

In laboratory experiments, a small group can have a large effect. Asch and other researchers found that three to five people will elicit much more conformity than just one or two. Increasing the number of people beyond five yields diminishing returns (Gerard et al., 1968; Rosenberg, 1961). In a field experiment, Milgram and his colleagues (1969) had 1, 2, 3, 5, 10 or 15 people pause on a busy New York City sidewalk and look up. As Figure 7.5 shows, the percentage of passers-by who also looked up increased as the number looking up increased. However, the effect of increasing the number of persons looking up slowed down considerably in this study when the crowd had reached five people. Campbell and Fairey (1989) have suggested that whether the growth in conformity with group size is linear or not depends on the type of task.

The influence of a minority on the responses of a majority was first demonstrated in laboratory studies on colour perception tasks carried out in France in the 1960s (Moscovici et al., 1969). Serge Moscovici and his colleagues identified three main determinants of a minority being able to influence a majority: consistency, self-confidence and defection (Moscovici, 1985). Angelica Mucchi-Faina and Stefano Pagliaro (2008) observed how the presence of a minority produces ambivalence among the majority. Presented with a minority who consistently argue a counter position, the members of the majority group start to experience ambivalence or dissonance as unpleasant (as discussed in Chapter 5). Accepting the views of the minority can reduce the uncomfortable feeling. Moscovici (1985) believed that it

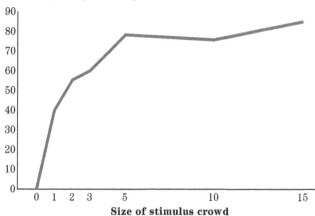

**FIGURE 7.5**  Group size and conformity

The percentage of passers-by who imitated a group looking upwards increased as group size increased to five persons.

SOURCE: Data from Milgram et al., 1969.

SOURCE: © Cimmerian / iStock

was the power of consistency and persistency of minority members that caused a majority to rethink their ideas and be influenced. Consistency and persistence convey self-confidence, and Charlan Nemeth and Joel Wachtler (1974) reported that any behaviour by a minority that communicates self-confidence – taking the head seat at the table, for instance – tends to raise self-doubts among the majority. Russell D. Clark (1995) used the play 'Twelve Angry Men' as the basis of an experiment examining minority influence. Participants were asked to make a decision as if they were in a jury evaluating the guilt or innocence of a young man on a charge of murdering his father. At first it appeared that the accused was clearly guilty, but there was also a minority argument that he was not guilty as the evidence was not as persuasive as it seemed. Clark found that participants were more likely to move to the minority position if the argument made was persuasive and informed. They were also more likely to move if the minority consisted of more than one. It should be remembered that all new influences are minority until they are taken up by the majority. By being firm and forceful, the minority's self-confidence may prompt the majority to reconsider its position. Most often, however, the majority influences minorities. People prefer not to stand out, but to conform.

> Minority influence and the way that the minority can sway the majority to change their way of thinking links closely to persuasion (Chapter 6). The Clark (1995) study shows what features are required for the minority to be influential; these have similar characteristics to how persuasive a message is in persuasion studies.

## UNANIMITY

Imagine yourself in a conformity experiment in which all but one of the people responding before you give the same wrong answer. Would the example of this one non-conforming confederate be as liberating as it was for the individuals in Milgram's obedience experiment? Several experiments reveal that someone who punctures a group's unanimity deflates its social power (Allen & Levine, 1969; Asch, 1955; Morris & Miller, 1975). As Figure 7.6 illustrates, people will usually voice their own convictions if just one other person has also differed from the majority. The participants in such experiments often later say they felt warm towards and

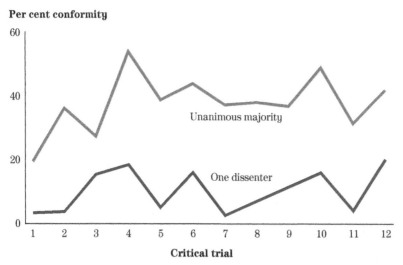

FIGURE 7.6 The effect of unanimity on conformity
When someone giving correct answers punctures the group's unanimity, individuals conform only one-fourth as often.
SOURCE: from Asch, 1955.

close to their non-conforming ally. Yet they deny that the ally influenced them: 'I would have answered just the same if he weren't there.'

It is easier to stand up for something if you can find someone else to stand up with you. Many religious groups recognize this. Following the example of Jesus, who sent his disciples out in pairs, the Mormons send two missionaries into a neighbourhood together. The support of the one comrade greatly increases a person's social courage.

Observing someone else's dissent – even when it is wrong – can increase our own independence. Charlan Nemeth and Cynthia Chiles (1988) discovered this after having people observe a lone individual in a group of four misjudge blue stimuli as green. Although the dissenter was wrong, once they had observed him the observers were more likely to exhibit their own form of independence: 76 per cent of the time they correctly labelled red slides 'red' even when everyone else was incorrectly calling them 'orange'. Participants who had no opportunity to observe the 'green' dissenter conformed 70 per cent of the time.

### COHESION

cohesiveness *a 'we feeling'; the extent to which members of a group are bound together, such as by attraction for one another*

A minority opinion from someone outside the groups we identify with – from someone at another university or of a different religion – sways us less than the same minority opinion from someone within our group as a result of cohesiveness (Clark & Maass, 1988). A heterosexual arguing for gay rights would sway heterosexuals more effectively than a homosexual would. People even comply more readily with requests from those said to share their birthday, their first name or features of their fingerprint (Burger et al., 2004; Silvia, 2005). We will consider the importance of feeling connected to something bigger than you and the significance of social identity in Chapter 12.

### SOCIAL IMPACT THEORY

Conformity does not occur simply because we slavishly seek to copy others. Instead, there appear to be specific factors that are required for the environment to be ideal for conformity to occur. Bibb Latané (1981) devised Social Impact Theory, a mathematical theory of social influence. Latané expresses this as Influence = f(SIN). This means that the amount of influence that an individual experiences is a result of the combination of the strengths of the sources of influence (S), the immediacy or proximity of these sources (I), and the number of sources of influence (N). This combination is not the factors added together, but instead these factors are multiplied together to produce their influence.

We have already discussed the question of group size and conformity and that although group size is important in influence, it is the first few people who have the most significant influence on us. Latané also suggests that it is the nature of the people who potentially have influence over us that has a large effect on the influence they exert. Those who are most likely to influence us tend to have a higher status, such as age or socio-economic, and prior relationship with, or future power over, us. Therefore *who* influences us is as important as the *number* of people who are influencing us. We are more likely to be influenced by those who are important to us – who we admire or value – than those whose opinion is of low importance to us. Think about how much easier it is not to conform to a group if we are away from it than when we are in it. So when we are with a group and they are doing something that we may not want to go along with, if that group is something we want to be a part of, we are more likely to go along with them. It also explains how people in a position of power or status can have a disproportionate influence over us, persuading us to conform even when it is against our own norms.

Eric Pedersen, Joseph LaBrie and Andrew Lac (2008) carried out a study into the perceived drinking norms of American college students. They investigated how individuals respond in different contexts when asked about their drinking behaviours and attitudes, as well as the drinking behaviours and attitudes of relevant groups to the individual. These groups include the fraternities and sororities that are so important in American universities. Participants were questioned in both isolated online conditions as well as with their salient group. Pedersen et al. found that individual drinking behaviour and group specific behaviours differ when assessed in individual conditions as opposed to being in a group of peers of the salient group. The participants' perception of the groups' drinking behaviour and attitudes were significantly higher in the group condition than the individual condition.

What this study highlights is that the context of self-report studies has an influence on the participants' response. They suggest that this may be because participants in groups have other members to refer to in devising their own answers, whereas in the individualized condition, they consider only their own behaviour. The discrepancy between responses from the same participant in different conditions seems to support Latané's theory that immediacy and strength are significant factors in social influence.

We will see in Chapter 9 on attraction that we tend to like others who are similar to ourselves. We discussed in Chapter 6 that people are persuaded by others they consider to be similar to themselves (either on an individual or group basis). So, as we might expect, people tend to align their opinions with members of their 'we' group. For example, they express more favourable opinions towards a piece of music after observing the liking of someone akin to themselves. And they express more negative opinions when the music is liked by someone unlike themselves (Hilmert et al., 2006).

## STATUS

As you might suspect, higher-status people tend to have more impact (Driskell & Mullen, 1990). Junior group members – even junior social psychologists – acknowledge more conformity to their group than do senior group members (Jetten et al., 2006). Milgram (1974) reported that in his obedience experiments, people of lower status accepted the experimenter's commands more readily than people of higher status. After delivering 450 volts, a 37-year-old welder turned to the higher-status experimenter and deferentially asked, 'Where do we go from here, Professor?' (p. 46). Another participant, a divinity school professor who disobeyed at 150 volts, said 'I don't understand why the experiment is placed above this person's life' and plied the experimenter with questions about 'the ethics of this thing' (p. 48).

### PUBLIC RESPONSE

One of the first questions researchers sought to answer was this: would people conform more in their public responses than in their private opinions? Or would they wobble more in their private opinions but be unwilling to conform publicly, lest they appear wishy-washy? The answer is now clear: in experiments, people conform more when they must respond in front of others rather than writing their answers privately. Asch's participants, after hearing others respond, were less influenced by group pressure if they could write answers that only the experimenter would see. It is much easier to stand up for what we believe in the privacy of the voting booth than before a group.

### NO PRIOR COMMITMENT

People almost never back down. Once having made a public commitment, they stick to it. At most, they will change their judgements in later situations (Saltzstein & Sandberg, 1979). We may therefore expect that judges of ski-jumping or gymnastic competitions, for example, will seldom change their ratings after seeing the other judges' ratings, although they might adjust their later performance ratings.

Prior commitments restrain persuasion, too. Making a public commitment makes people hesitant to back down. Smart persuaders know this. Salespeople ask questions that prompt us to make statements for, rather than against, what they are marketing. Environmentalists ask people to commit themselves to recycling, energy conservation or bus riding – and find that behaviour then changes more than when environmental appeals are heard without inviting a commitment (Katzev & Wang, 1994). Teens aged 14 to 17 who make a public virginity-til-marriage pledge reportedly become somewhat more likely to remain sexually abstinent, or to delay intercourse, than similar teens who don't make the pledge (Bearman & Brückner, 2001; Brückner & Bearman, 2005). (If they violate their pledge they are, however, somewhat less likely to use a condom.)

## WHY CONFORM?

*'Do you see yonder cloud that's almost in the shape of a camel?' asks Shakespeare's Hamlet of Polonius. "Tis like a camel indeed,' replies Polonius. 'Methinks it is a weasel,' says Hamlet a moment later. 'It is backed like a weasel,' acknowledges Polonius. 'Or like a whale?' wonders Hamlet. 'Very like a whale,' agrees Polonius. Question: why does Polonius so readily agree every time Hamlet changes his mind?*

**normative influence** *conformity based on a person's desire to fulfil others' expectations, often to gain acceptance*

**informational influence** *conformity occurring when people accept evidence about reality provided by other people*

What prompted this conformity? Why did Polonius so readily echo Hamlet's words? And why do we generally like to tune in to 'our' group? There are three possibilities: a person may fit in and follow the group (a) to create a harmonious and pleasant atmosphere, (b) to be accepted and avoid rejection, or (c) because others are an important source of information. The first solution is frequent in collectivistic or interdependent cultures. Individuals in these cultures seek compromise to create harmony. They are more interested in understanding the other than promoting themselves and do not stick to their own but to the group. Morton Deutsch and Harold Gerard (1955) studied why Westerners bow to the group in individualistic cultures and named the two possibilities normative influence and informational influence.

The first springs from our desire to be liked and is demonstrated in Asch conformity studies, and the second from our desire to be right, the reason individuals attuned to the group in Sherif's demonstrations.

Normative influence is 'going along with the crowd' to avoid rejection, to stay in people's good grace, or to gain their approval. Perhaps the subordinate Polonius was willing to change his mind and agree with Hamlet, the higher-status Prince of Denmark, to curry favour. Studies in the laboratory and in everyday life in the West have revealed that groups often reject those who consistently deviate (Miller & Anderson, 1979; Schachter, 1951). This is especially so when dissent is not just 'within the family' but when one's group is engaged with another group (Matheson et al., 2003). It's socially permissible for members of a parliament or of Congress to disagree with their country's war plans during the internal debate before a war. But once the conflict has begun, everyone is expected to 'support our troops'. In some Eastern, collectivistic and hierarchical cultures it is more common to agree even during the planning and accept the 'wise leader's' decisions.

As most of us know, social rejection is painful; when we deviate from group norms, we often pay an emotional price. Gerard (1999) recalls that in one of his conformity experiments an initially friendly participant became upset, asked to leave the room and

> returned looking sick and visibly shaken. I became worried and suggested that we discontinue the session. He absolutely refused to stop and continued through all 36 trials, not yielding to the others on a single trial. After the experiment was over and I explained the subterfuge to him, his entire body relaxed and he sighed with relief. Color returned to his face. I asked him why he had left the room. 'To vomit,' he said. He did not yield, but at what a price! He wanted so much to be accepted and liked by the others and was afraid he would not be because he had stood his ground against them. There you have normative pressure operating with a vengeance.

Sometimes the high price of deviation compels people to support what they do not believe in, or at least to suppress their disagreement. Fearing a court martial for disobedience, some of the soldiers at My Lai participated in the massacre. Normative influence leads to compliance especially for people who have recently seen others ridiculed, or who are seeking to climb a status ladder (Hollander, 1958; Janes & Olson, 2000). Informational influence, on the other hand, leads people to privately accept others' influence. Polonius may actually see what Hamlet helps him see. When reality is ambiguous, as it was for participants in the autokinetic situation, other people can be a valuable source of information. The individual may reason, 'I can't tell how far the light is moving. But this guy seems to know.'

It has been argued that conformity has an adaptive function. Julie Coultas (2004) argued that conformity has an evolutionary basis. She carried out a series of experiments around conformity to a fairly inconsequential behaviour – where to put the keyboard cover while working on a PC. If the majority of people in the room put the keyboard cover on the top of their monitor then participants were more likely to copy that. Coultas states that we have a predisposition to imitate common behaviours. By observing the behaviour of others and copying that, we learn how to behave in new situations. She calls this the 'when in Rome, do as Romans do' shortcut.

In many Eastern and more interdependent cultures the reason for changing attitudes due to others' opinion is also a result of dialectical, holistic and more complex thinking. Everything can be seen in different and even opposite ways, from different angles, and most things contain opposite and different qualities at the same time: good and bad, cold and warm. The cloud can look like a camel or a whale, depending on the context and the person perceiving. The truth is not absolute, and the person seeing a cloud as something other than what I see, may be right. I may have to adjust my own perception. Two opposing standpoints may both be true, and by compromise an in-between or even a contradictory standpoint for everything can always be found. This is a typical Eastern way of thinking, far from the either-or thinking in the West where it is a virtue to hold attitudes and opinions independent of the context and the group you are communicating with. To change attitudes due to social pressure has many negative connotations in the West: indecisiveness – 'a wind vane', a weak ego, non-integration. To be an 'integrated' person in the West means not to be contradictory, incongruous, inconsistent or able to change depending on the context. In the East these are not preferable abilities or traits, and they are not encouraged during socialization. The opposite, to fall in with the other, is looked upon as more mature for a human being.

Concern for *social image* produces *normative influence*. The desire to be *correct* produces *informational influence*. In day-to-day life, normative and informational influence often occur together.

Conformity experiments have sometimes isolated either normative or informational influence. Conformity is greater when people respond publicly before a group; this surely reflects normative influence (because people receive the same information whether they respond publicly or privately). On the other hand, conformity is greater when participants feel incompetent, when the task is difficult, and when the individuals care about being right – all signs of informational influence.

In many Eastern cultures the concern for the image (not 'losing face') and to do the right thing has a long tradition founded in philosophy and education. To find and accept their place in a hierarchy and obey the rulers – the father in the family and the eldest son among the siblings – has been natural for East Asian people for centuries. The right to govern, however, is not absolute but dependent on the moral qualities of the ruler (the Mandate of Heaven). This way of thinking and relating to each other was introduced in China 2500 years ago by Confucius (551–479 BC). His teachings gained pre-eminence and since then China has been a hierarchical family-orientated and interdependent society.

## CULTURE

Cultural background also influences why people conform and prefer to agree in a group, and how obedient they are towards authorities. In some Eastern, collectivistic cultures, not to fit in to the group is looked upon as childish and as a sign of being unable to behave as a responsible grown-up. To seek harmony, compromise and balance in relationships is considered more mature.

An example is the traditional Chinese culture, which exhibits the very essence of Confucian collectivism, emphasizing the precedence of social relationships and group welfare over individual needs and desires. As a result, behaviours, relative to the actions of people in the West, are more likely to strongly reflect social norms and obligations. Personal desires are still a determinant of behaviour, but play a secondary role. Co-operation and harmony in the group are given priority over individual interests (Triandis et al., 1988; Waterman, 1984). Effort and contribution are directed towards the collective good rather than towards personal benefits and self-recognition (Hui & Tan, 1996).

James Whittaker and Robert Meade (1967) repeated Asch's conformity experiment in several countries and found similar conformity rates in most – 31 per cent in Lebanon, 32 per cent in Hong Kong, 34 per cent in Brazil – but 51 per cent among the Bantu of Zimbabwe, a tribe with strong sanctions for non-conformity. An analysis by Rod Bond and Peter Smith (1996) of 133 studies in 17 countries showed how cultural values influence conformity. Compared with people in individualistic countries, those in collectivist countries (where harmony is prized and connections help define the self) are more responsive to others' influence.

When researchers in Australia, Austria, Germany, Italy, Jordan, South Africa and Spain repeated the obedience experiments, how do you think the results compared with those of American participants? The obedience rates were similar, or even higher: over 90 per cent in Spain and Holland – 85 per cent in Munich (Blass, 2000).

Confucius (551–479 BC) was a Chinese thinker and social philosopher, whose teachings have deeply influenced Chinese, Korean, Japanese, Taiwanese and Vietnamese thought and life. His philosophy emphasized personal and governmental morality, correctness of social relationships, justice and sincerity.

SOURCE: © nashvilledino2/iStock

Stanley Milgram (1961) conducted a cross-cultural study of conformity in Norway and France prior to his obedience research. Volunteers were asked to judge which of two sounds lasted longer. The participants wore headphones and heard the two tones followed by the judgement of five other people who always agreed but on just over half the trials gave an incorrect answer. In actual fact these other judges' responses were taped and only the one volunteer and the experimenter were present in the laboratory. Quite consistently, the Norwegians conformed more to the 'group' judgements (62 per cent of the time) than the French (50 per cent of the time) in the basic experiment. Overall, 12 per cent of Norwegian volunteers conformed completely to the group, but only 1 per cent of French volunteers; 25 per cent of the Norwegians showed 'strong independence', compared with 41 per cent of the French. Milgram suggests a relationship between these results and the 'highly cohesive' Norwegian society, orientated towards social responsibility and group identification, versus the politically unstable, low-consensus French society, with a 'tradition of dissent and critical argument'. That is to say that conformity is not necessarily something negative or bad, but is an expression of national unity and cultural cohesion.

However, cultures, values and norms may change over time. Replications of Asch's experiment with university students in Britain, Canada and the USA sometimes trigger less conformity than Asch observed two or three decades earlier (Lalancette & Standing, 1990; Larsen, 1974, 1990; Nicholson et al., 1985; Perrin & Spencer, 1981). Conformity and obedience are universal phenomena, yet the prevalence varies across cultures and eras depending on cultural norms and values – as well as the situation.

The influence and importance of cultural norms on conformity are also revealed in subcultures and small groups. In a qualitative study based on interviews with adolescent children from 11 to 14 years old in Northern Ireland, Barbara

J. Stewart-Knox of the University of Ulster and her co-workers (2005) demonstrated how starting to smoke could be explained by conformity to group norms. They found that starting smoking rarely occurred as a result of direct peer pressure, but it did happen as adolescents sought to fit in with the group, conforming to its norms and values.

The findings are consistent with social identity theory and self-categorization theory in that smoking activity appears to provide a means through which to visibly display membership of a social group.

## WHO CONFORMS?

*Conformity varies not only with situations and cultures but also with people. How much so? And in what social contexts do personality traits shine through?*

Are some people generally more susceptible (or should we say, more open and sensible) to social influence? Among your friends, can you identify some who are 'conformists' and others who are 'independent' and even egoistic? In their search for the conformer, researchers have focused on personality and social roles.

### PERSONALITY

During the late 1960s and 1970s, researchers observed only weak connections between personal characteristics and social behaviours such as conformity (Mischel, 1968). In contrast to the demonstrable power of situational factors, personality scores were poor predictors of individuals' behaviour. If you wanted to know how conforming or aggressive or helpful someone was going to be, it seemed you were better off knowing about the situation than the person's psychological test scores. As Milgram (1974) concluded: 'I am certain that there is a complex personality basis to obedience and disobedience. But I know we have not found it' (p. 205). One reason could be that Milgram's obedience experiments created 'strong' situations; their clear-cut demands made it difficult for personality differences to operate since personality predicts behaviour better when social influences are weak.

Personality effects loom larger when we note people's differing reactions to the same situation, as when one person reacts with terror and another with delight to a roller-coaster ride.

SOURCE: © Image Source/SuperStock

Even so, Milgram's participants differed widely in how obedient they were, and there is good reason to suspect that sometimes his participants' hostility, respect for authority and concern for meeting expectations affected their obedience (Blass, 1990, 1991). And in 'weaker' situations – as when two strangers sit in a waiting room with no cues to guide their behaviour – individual personalities are free to shine (Ickes et al., 1982; Monson et al., 1982).

But even in strong situations, individuals differ. An Army report on the Abu Ghraib prison abuse praised three men who, despite threats of ridicule and court martial, stood apart from their comrades (O'Connor, 2004). Lieutenant David Sutton terminated one incident and alerted his commanders. 'I don't want to judge, but yes, I witnessed something inappropriate and I reported it,' said Sutton. Navy dog handler William Kimbro resisted 'significant pressure' to participate in 'improper interrogations'. And Specialist Joseph Darby blew the whistle, giving military police the evidence that raised the alarm. Darby, called a 'rat' by some, received death threats for his dissent and was given military protection. But, back home, his mother joined others in applauding: 'Honey, I'm so proud of you because you did the good thing and good always triumphs over evil, and the truth will always set you free' (ABC News, 2004).

It is interesting how the pendulum of professional opinion swings. Without discounting the undeniable power of the social forces recognized in the 1960s and 1970s, the pendulum has swung back towards an appreciation of individual personality and its genetic predispositions. Personality researchers are clarifying and reaffirming the connection between who we are and what we do, and most social psychologists agree with pioneering theorist Kurt Lewin's (1936) dictum: 'Every psychological event depends upon the state of the person and at the same time on the environment, although their relative importance is different in different cases' (p. 12) – socialization and situation.

## WOULD PEOPLE STILL OBEY TODAY?

Perhaps you have wondered if people are as obedient today as they were in the 1960s when Milgram conducted his studies? You are not the only one. Many students learning about Milgram's (1963, 1965, 1974) obedience studies often ask whether similar results would be found today. Some people have argued that individuals these days are more aware of the dangers of blindly following authority than they were in the early 1960s and therefore the obedience rates are lower. The Hungarian social psychologist Thomas Blass performed a meta-analysis on the results of studies up to the year 2000. He found that the percentage of participants who are prepared to inflict fatal voltages remains remarkably constant, 61–66 per cent, regardless of time or place, and he found no evidence for a change in obedience over time (Blass, 2004).

Jerry Burger of Santa Clara University also wondered, and has recently conducted a partial replication of Milgram's studies (Burger, 2009). As you hopefully have grasped by now the obedience studies are arguably the most well-known social psychological research inside and outside the field. They are mentioned in most introductory textbooks in psychology, and references to the studies continue to appear in popular media, including movies and songs (Blass, 2004). Jerry Burger therefore had to select his respondents more carefully than in the 1960s. He had to be sure that the participants did not know anything about the study. When he did so he found obedience rates in the USA only slightly lower than those Milgram found 45 years earlier (Burger, 2009).

Due to critics of the ethical standards of Milgram's original study, the detailed procedure had to be changed in consecutive studies. In Burger's study the participants were stopped when giving a 150-volt shock and the percentage who would have given a 450-volt shock was calculated using probability measures. This could have had some impact on the results. But we have to conclude that there has been no dramatic change in people's willingness to harm another person if the situation makes it difficult to refuse, and if an authority gives orders and apparently takes the responsibility. The obedience studies therefore are a dramatic demonstration of how individuals typically underestimate the power of situational forces when explaining a person's behaviour.

## CONFORMITY AS ENTERTAINMENT?

Although the ethics of the Milgram experiment make it difficult to replicate in the laboratory, there have been some interesting replications of conformity studies made as television programmes. In 2006 Derren Brown replicated the Milgram experiment in a larger experiment for Channel 4, billed as 'The Heist'. This scenario was that of a motivational seminar and documentary with 13 participants. He attempted to select and persuade four people to carry out an armed robbery, stealing £100 000. During the process of selecting participants to carry this out, there was a replication of the Milgram experiment, with the participants carrying out the same role as the 'teacher' in the original experiment. The results of the replications reflected Milgram's original results, with over half of participants continuing to administer shocks to the 'learner' up to 450v.

In 2010 a French-Swiss documentary *Le Jeu de la Mort* replicated the Milgram experiment in the guise of a reality/game show format. Participants were given €40 and told that they would not win any money from the game as it was only a pilot. Again, the majority of participants continued up to 450v, with only 16 of 80 refusing to go all the way!

## GENDER DIFFERENCES IN CONFORMITY?

Milgram relied almost exclusively on male participants in his obedience studies. The one exception was a replication of the basic procedure in which women were used as participants. The women complied fully with the experimenter's commands 65 per cent of the time, a rate identical with men as participants. Blass (2000) found no evidence of a gender difference in eight out of nine conceptual replications of Milgram's studies he reviewed. Also in Burger's recent study there was little difference in obedience rates between men and women (Burger, 2009). He did not find any effect for education, age or ethnicity either. The situation created in the laboratory seems to dilute all precaution.

The state of affairs today seems to be the same as nearly 50 years ago and Milgram's conclusion in his article from 1974 deserves to be repeated:

> I set up a simple experiment at Yale University to test how much pain an ordinary citizen would inflict on another person simply because he was ordered to by an experimental scientist. Stark authority was pitted against the subjects' strongest moral imperatives against hurting others, and, with the subjects' ears ringing with the screams of the victims, authority won more often than not. The extreme willingness of adults to go to almost any lengths on the command of an authority constitutes the chief finding of the study and the fact most urgently demanding explanation.

(Milgram, 1974)

As we can learn from this quote, Milgram's obedience study was about harming another human being if ordered to.

## research close-up

### A VIRTUAL REPLICATION OF MILGRAM'S OBEDIENCE STUDY

**Source:** Slater, M., Antley, M., Davison, A., Swapp, D., Guger, C., Barker, C., Pistrang, N., & Sanchez-Vives, M. V. (2006). A virtual reprise of the Stanley Milgram experiment. PLoS ONE, 1(1), e39. doi:10.1371/journal.pone.00000329 (open access).

### Introduction

It is increasingly difficult to replicate the Milgram obedience experiments, given the serious ethical implications of the original study. While carrying out a study on a live participant would be ethically problematic, there are other ways of replicating the study, particularly with the use of virtual reality. By using virtual reality, the participant can be involved in an experiment that allows for conditions that would not be available in real life. Mel Slater, Angus Antley, Adam Davison, David Swapp, Christoph Guger, Chris Barker, Nancy Pistrang and Maria Sanchez-Vives (2006) created a virtual reality version of the Milgram study. Their main aim was not to test for obedience, but to measure if participants would respond in an emotional and psychological manner to a virtual person, as if they were responding to a real person. Studies have shown that participants respond to virtual environments in a realistic way (Bailenson & Yee, 2006). This suggests that the use of virtual reality may enable the study of potentially problematic psychological scenarios. Slater et al. (2006) created a study in which participants were required to give 'electric shocks' to a virtual woman character. All subjects knew that the subject of the experiment was not a real human being, but did this knowledge eliminate the discomfort by hurting another human being?

### Method

Thirty-four participants were recruited from the staff and students of University College London. They were divided into two groups: (1) Visual Condition (VC) where the virtual woman was visible ($n = 23$); and (2) Hidden Condition (HC) where the virtual woman was not visible for the participants ($n = 11$). The volunteers in the VC condition could see the virtual woman (see Figure 7.7). As you can see, the virtual woman had a quite realistic face; she could move her eyes and had facial expressions; she visibly breathed, spoke and appeared to respond with pain to the 'electric shocks'. She also seemed to be aware of the presence of the participant by gazing at him or her, and even protesting ('I don't want to continue – don't listen to him!'). Participants in the HC condition interacted only with text.

The procedure of the 'learning experiment' was the same as the original Milgram experiment, with 32 sets of 5 word learning trials. The participant was placed in front of an 'electric shock machine', and was instructed that they were to increase the voltage and shock the learner every time that she gave an incorrect answer.

In addition to the standard experiment, the participants in both conditions were given the Autonomic Perceptions Questionnaire (AQM) that had 24 questions designed to give a subjective measure of the participants' self-awareness of physiological indicators of stress. They were also monitored for their electrodermal activity (EDA), recording the participants' sympathetic arousal. EDA measures reactions that are beyond our control, our biological reactions to our environment. In stressful situations, our heart rate increases and we sweat more. The EDA measures several physiological responses, the skin conductance

**FIGURE 7.7** The virtual woman who was the victim in the study.

level (SCL), the skin conductance response (SCR), the heart rate and heart rate variability. These are symptoms of our sympathetic arousal and by measuring them we can see how stressed we are in a more objective way than giving a verbal report of how stressed we feel, for example on a scale of 1 to 10. Using both the AQM and EDA monitoring, the stress of shocking the virtual woman was measured both subjectively and objectively.

### Results

Slater and his colleagues found that participants who could not see the female character were more likely to administer shocks of maximum voltage than those who could see her.

The various data-gathering measures were analysed separately to determine the stress that participants felt giving shocks to the virtual woman in both the visual and hidden conditions. The AQM scores showed that the median stress score after the experiment had been raised from the score before the experiment; in the visual conditions, this rise was significant, but not for the hidden condition.

Analysing the data from the EDA, it was found that all of the factors measured were significant in showing increased stress for the visual condition, where participants could see the virtual woman, in comparison to the hidden condition, where the participants could not.

### Discussion

The findings of this experiment reflect the findings of the original Milgram experiment. As the results show that stress is significantly higher for the participants who could see the virtual woman, it appears that the emotional brain of the human volunteers didn't quite get the message that this was only virtual reality.

Slater et al. (2006) argue that participants were displaying obedience, as participants were willing to put up with their own discomfort for the sake of honouring their agreement to be a participant in the experiment. Similar arguments have been made in relation to the original experiments by Milgram.

The line of research opened up by Milgram stopped 40 years ago due to ethical concerns, especially the problem of major deception. But with advances in technology, virtual environments can provide an alternative methodology for pursuing laboratory-based experimental research even in an extreme social situation. The problem of major deception was avoided in this study since every participant knew for certain that the victim was a virtual character. The virtual environment studies could therefore open a new door to direct empirical studies of obedience in extreme social situations.

However, although no pain was inflicted, the participants were still stressed by the situation, and certainly more so when they interacted directly with a visible victim rather than only through a text interface with a hidden victim. If virtual reality became so realistic as to be indistinguishable from reality, then its use in such experiments may raise the same ethical questions as Milgram's work did.

## DO WE EVER WANT TO BE DIFFERENT?

*Will people ever actively resist social pressure? When compelled to do A, will they instead do Z? What would motivate such anticonformity?*

This chapter emphasizes the power of social forces. It is therefore fitting that we conclude by again reminding ourselves of the power of the person. We are not just billiard balls moving where pushed. We may act according to social and private values, independently of the immediate situational forces that push upon us. Knowing that someone is trying to coerce us may even prompt us to react in the *opposite* direction.

## REACTANCE

Individuals in Western cultures value personal freedom, independence and self-efficacy. When social pressure becomes so blatant that it threatens their sense of freedom, they often rebel. Think of Romeo and Juliet, whose love was intensified by their families' opposition. Or think of children asserting their freedom and independence by doing the opposite of what their parents ask. Shrewd parents therefore offer their children choices instead of commands: 'It's time to clean up: do you want a bath or a shower?' In Eastern, interdependent cultures individual freedom is traditionally not looked upon as the ultimate or even a very important goal, and children therefore listen to and obey their parents and even other adults to a higher degree.

The theory of psychological reactance – that people in the independent West act to protect their sense of freedom – is supported by experiments showing that attempts to restrict a person's freedom often produce an anticonformity 'boomerang effect' (Brehm & Brehm, 1981; Nail et al., 2000). After today's Western university women give thought to how traditional culture expects women to behave, they become less – not more – likely to exhibit traditional feminine modesty (Cialdini et al., 1998).

reactance *a motive to protect or restore one's sense of freedom. Reactance arises when someone threatens our freedom of action*

## ASSERTING UNIQUENESS

People feel uncomfortable when they appear too different from others. But in individualist Western cultures they also feel uncomfortable when they appear exactly like everyone else. It appears that our identity is bound up with how we view ourselves as either confirming the majority, or as being unique and therefore non-conformist. The way in which we identify ourselves, and the groups that we identify with, will therefore have an influence of the norms that we adhere to. As experiments by C. R. Snyder and Howard Fromkin (1980) have shown, people feel better when they see themselves as moderately unique. Moreover, they act in ways that will assert their individuality. In one experiment, Snyder (1980) led Purdue University students to believe that their '10 most important attitudes' were either distinct from or nearly identical to the attitudes of 10 000 other students. When they next participated in a conformity experiment, those deprived of their feeling of uniqueness were the ones most likely to assert their individuality by non-conformity.

Sometimes the desire to be unique may mean that we may be actively not conforming to the majority group, but instead we are conforming to the minority non-conformist group. If you look at groups like youth sub-cultures you can see that while these people stand out in a group of majority conformists, when they are within their own sub-culture they are very much conforming to their own group's non-conformist position.

For those of us in Western cultures, our distinctiveness is central to our identity (Vignoles et al., 2000). This is not the case in all cultures. In the traditional interdependent cultures in the East people do not like to push themselves forward or to be unique and different. They are more modest in groups and do not have the urge to be something extraordinary, but rather try to fit in and create a balance between each other where everybody can contribute with strengths and weaknesses.

People in industrialized Western cultures are more likely to demonstrate an independent self, defining their identity in terms of their personal attributes rather than part of their social groups (see Chapter 3).

In the West, seeing oneself as unique also appears in people's 'spontaneous self-concepts'. William McGuire and his colleagues (McGuire & Padawer-Singer, 1978; McGuire et al., 1979) report that when children are invited to 'tell us about yourself', they are most likely to mention their distinctive attributes. Foreign-born children are more likely than others to mention their birthplace. Redheads are more likely than black- and brown-haired children to volunteer their hair colour. Light and heavy children are the most likely to refer to their body weight. Minority children are the most likely to mention their race.

Asserting our uniqueness. Though not wishing to be greatly deviant, most of us express our distinctiveness through our personal styles and dress.
SOURCE: © CREATISTA / iStock

Likewise, we become more keenly aware of our gender when we are with people of the other gender (Cota & Dion, 1986). The principle, says McGuire, is that 'one is conscious of oneself insofar as, and in the ways that, one is different'. Thus, 'If I am a Black woman in a group of White women, I tend to think of myself as a Black; if I move to a group of Black men, my blackness loses salience and I become more conscious of being a woman' (McGuire et al., 1979). This insight helps us understand why White people who grow up amid non-White people tend to have a strong White identity, and why any minority group tends to be conscious of its distinctiveness and how the surrounding culture relates to it (Knowles & Peng, 2005). The majority group, being less conscious of race, may see the minority group as hypersensitive.

When the people of two cultures are nearly identical, they still will notice their differences, however small. Even trivial distinctions may provoke scorn and conflict. Jonathan Swift satirized the phenomenon in *Gulliver's Travels* with the story of the Little-Endians' war against the Big-Endians. Their difference: the Little-Endians preferred to break their eggs on the small end, the Big-Endians on the large end. On a world scale, the differences may not seem great between Serbs and Croatians, Hutus and Tutsis, or Catholic and Protestant Northern Irish, and even between the Christians, the Muslims and the Jews. They all believe in the same God, though He has different 'faces'. But anyone who reads the news knows that these small differences mean big conflicts (Rothbart & Taylor, 1992). Rivalry is often most intense when the other group closely resembles you.

## focus on

THE ORDINARY MONSTER

One of the phenomena in the twentieth century that has caused a flurry of research and comments is why so many supported the Nazi movement. How was the Nazi Holocaust possible? What kind of situation was created that made it feasible for so many Europeans to take part in the extermination of Jews, Gypsies, homosexuals, and people with mental disabilities and disorders? We have already discussed the phenomena of obedience and conformity, and in Chapter 14 we will consider Theodor Adorno and his colleagues' (1950) survey on anti-Semitism, ethnocentrism and racism trying to reveal some other mechanisms behind victimization and discrimination.

But there are other explanations, and three social psychologists from the University of St Andrews in Scotland and the University of Exeter in England have questioned the most influential explanation given for the participation in the Nazi Holocaust: Milgram's 'The obedience to authority' study. While Milgram studied the phenomenon in the laboratory there have been numerous books and papers analysing what happened in real life. Hannah Arendt, who wrote a book about Adolf Eichmann, an organizer of the Holocaust, tries to understand how Eichmann could be so barbarous. She wrote her book after her presence at the Eichmann trial in Jerusalem. There is a picture from the trial which also has become famous and embodies our understanding of the Holocaust participants; a picture of Eichmann, an ordinary man, somewhat slight and balding. He did not look like a monster able to do monstrous acts. His very ordinariness was profoundly shocking. Hannah Arendt caught and immortalized it in her book *Eichmann in Jerusalem* (Arendt, 1963/1994). According to Arendt, Eichmann looked like a typical bureaucrat, carrying out orders, making things work, doing his job efficiently. The fact that the job involved mass murder seemed almost incidental. The message to be drawn from this was: 'the lesson of the fearsome, word-and-thought defying *banality of evil*' (1963/1994, p. 252, emphasis in original). The term 'banality of evil', although it occurs only in the last sentence of her 250-page book, has become an explanatory concept also for many social psychologists dealing with evil-doing and monstrous behaviour: everybody will obey if the situation demands it since people lack awareness or control over what they are doing.

However, Reicher, Haslam and Rath (2008) reject this explanation. From a social identity approach (see Chapter 12 for further discussion of this theory) they re-examined the historical and psychological case for '*the banality of evil*', and suggested it consisted of three core elements.

The first was that Eichmann and his ilk did not represent a 'psychological type' distinct from the rest of us. The second was that Arendt suggested that the acts of Nazis arose out of commonplace motives that most people share: the desire to be valued and accepted by others, to do one's job well, to advance in one's career, and not simply because we *wanted* to conform or obey. These two arguments constitute the idea that 'anyone can do it'. This view is bolstered by a wealth of recent research arguing that the killers could be described as 'ordinary men'. Arendt's third argument deals with the psychological processes that permit ordinary men (and they almost always are men) to commit mass slaughter. They become obsessed with doing their jobs and how well they fulfil the demands put upon them. As Arendt puts it, Eichmann 'had no motives at all. He *merely*, to put the matter colloquially, "*never realized what he was doing*"' (Arendt, 1994, p. 287, emphasis added).

The concept of 'banality of evil' is further challenged by Cesarani (2004) who suggested that, as Arendt had only attended part of Eichmann's trial, specifically his own defence period, she gathered only a very carefully presented version of Eichmann. Eichmann had able defence lawyers who sought to present him as a mild-mannered man, not a sadistic monster. Cesarani argues that Arendt's representation of Eichmann as 'merely thoughtless' shows that she was taken in by his self-presentation. Acts of genocide, such as those of the Holocaust, as well as in many conflicts since then do not occur in a social and political vacuum. The reduction of the outgroup to 'sub-human' is an important step on the way to justifying the destruction of them, as well as maintaining the superiority of ourselves as ingroup.

Reicher et al. (2008) sought to show that the picture of Eichmann as a man obeying and not knowing what he did has misled researchers by taking them down the wrong path when seeking to understand the psychology of genocide. They argue that killing does not derive from inattention. Rather, killing becomes acceptable (or 'natural') only when it can be celebrated as *the right thing to do*.

Another lesson is that the way we define ourselves may often be more relevant to genocide than the way we define others. It is our social identity and the protection of our values that counts, not our lack of awareness and desire to conform and be obedient in a particular situation. These phenomena are further dealt with in Chapters 13 and 14.

What is notable in Reicher et al.'s critique of both the Milgram study and the concept of '*the banality of evil*' is that it brings into question the idea that we are blindly obedient. Instead, we do obey, but only within specific limits. We need to identify ourselves and those we obey, as being within our specific ingroup. This raises questions about conformity and obedience; we are not blind or thoughtless in our conformity, we have agency and choice. Our context influences us, but we also have other factors that must be in play in order for us to conform. It is too simple to view the Milgram experiments and assume that they provide a comprehensive answer to the question of why people obey.

### QUESTIONS

1 To what extent do you think conformity explains crimes against humanity?

2 Can we ever understand conformity in such extreme situations as crimes against humanity without understanding the wider socio-political context they occur in?

## SUMMING UP: CONFORMITY AND OBEDIENCE

### WHAT IS CONFORMITY?

☐ *Conformity* – changing one's behaviour or belief as a result of group pressure – comes in two forms. *Compliance* is outwardly going along with the group while inwardly disagreeing. *Acceptance* is believing as well as acting in accord with social pressure.

### WHAT ARE THE CLASSIC CONFORMITY AND OBEDIENCE STUDIES?

Three classic sets of studies illustrate how researchers have studied conformity.

☐ Muzafer Sherif observed that others' judgements influenced people's estimates of the movement of a point of light that actually did not move. Norms for 'proper' answers emerged and survived both over long periods of time and through succeeding generations of research participants.

☐ Solomon Asch had people listen to others' judgements of which of three comparison lines was equal to a standard line and then make the same judgement themselves. When the others unanimously gave a wrong answer, the participants conformed 37 per cent of the time.

☐ Stanley Milgram's obedience studies elicited an extreme form of compliance. Under optimum conditions – a legitimate, close-at-hand commander, a remote victim and no one else to exemplify disobedience – 65 per cent of his adult male participants fully obeyed instructions to deliver what were supposedly traumatizing electric shocks to a screaming innocent victim in an adjacent room.

☐ These classic laboratory studies expose the potency of several phenomena. Behaviour and attitudes are mutually reinforcing, enabling a small act of evil to foster the attitude that leads to a bigger evil act. The power of the situation is seen when good people, faced with dire circumstances, commit reprehensible acts (although dire situations may produce heroism in others). The fundamental attribution error leads us to think that evil is committed by people who are bad and that good is done by good people, and to discount situational forces and social categorization that induce people to conform to falsehoods or capitulate to cruelty.

## WHAT PREDICTS CONFORMITY?

- ☐ Using conformity testing procedures, experimenters have explored the circumstances that produce conformity. Certain situations appear to be especially powerful. For example, conformity is affected by the characteristics of the group: People conform most when three or more people, or groups, model the behaviour or belief.

- ☐ Conformity is reduced if the modelled behaviour or belief is not unanimous.

- ☐ Conformity is enhanced by group cohesion.

- ☐ The higher the status of those modelling the behaviour or belief, the greater likelihood of conformity.

- ☐ People also conform most when their responses are public (in the presence of the group).

- ☐ A prior commitment to a certain behaviour or belief increases the likelihood that a person will stick with that commitment rather than conform.

## WHY CONFORM?

- ☐ *Normative influence* results from a person's desire for acceptance: we want to be liked. The tendency to conform more when responding publicly reflects normative influence.

- ☐ *Informational influence* results from others' providing evidence about reality. The tendency to conform more on difficult decision-making tasks reflects informational influence: we want to be right.

- ☐ *Cultural influence* results from norms and values acquired during socialization. In some cultures it is more important to fit in, seek harmony and adjust to others.

## WHO CONFORMS?

- ☐ The question 'Who conforms?' has produced few definitive answers. Global personality scores are poor predictors of specific acts of conformity but better predictors of average conformity. Trait effects are strongest in 'weak' situations where social forces do not overwhelm individual differences.

- ☐ Although conformity and obedience are universal, different cultures socialize people to be more or less socially responsive, independent or interdependent.

- ☐ Recent replications of classic conformity and obedience studies have shown that people do still allow themselves to be influenced in these kinds of situations.

## DO WE EVER WANT TO BE DIFFERENT?

- ☐ Social psychology's emphasis on the power of social pressure must be joined by a complementary emphasis on the power of the person. We are not puppets. When social coercion becomes blatant, people often experience *reactance* – a motivation to defy the coercion in order to maintain their sense of freedom.

- ☐ We are not comfortable being too different from a group, but neither do we want to appear the same as everyone else. Most people, especially in the West, act in ways that preserve their sense of uniqueness and individuality.

## CRITICAL QUESTIONS

**1** What is meant by 'the copycat suicide phenomenon'? Are we seeing higher numbers of suicide because the rate has increased or because we are looking for them?

**2** Is the Milgram experiment disturbing because of the ethics involved or because of what it reveals about the capacity of ordinary people to inflict harm?

**3** Can the classic conformity studies of Asch, Sherif and Milgram be applied to real-life situations? Try to give an example for each study as well as thinking about the limitations for these studies in real-life study.

**4** Define and provide examples of both normative influence and informational influence.

**5** 'Without conformity, there would be social chaos'. Do you agree? Why or why not?

## RECOMMENDED READINGS

### Classic Papers

Asch, S. E. (1955). Opinions and social pressure. *Scientific American*, November, 31–35.

*This looks at conformity with a group, and how pressure from others can make us conform.*

Milgram, S. (1974). *Obedience to Authority: An Experimental View*. New York: Harper & Row.

*The great classic of conformity studies. Milgram's groundbreaking work continues to inspire research today.*

Sherif, M. (1935). A study of some social factors in perception. *Archives of Psychology*, 187.

*The earliest of the conformity studies, this is still a fascinating study that examines how we come to a group consensus and conform to that.*

### Contemporary Studies

Lammers, J., & Stapel, D. A. (2011). Power increases dehumanization. *Group Processes and Intergroup Relations*, **14**, 1–14.

*Lammers and Stapel argue convincingly in this paper that the more powerful our ingroup becomes, the less powerful and human the outgroup becomes. They look at this in the light of genocidal civil war, and how easily neighbours can become enemies.*

Pedersen, E. R., LaBrie, J. W., & Lac, A. (2008). Assessment of perceived and actual alcohol norms in varying contexts: Exploring social impact theory among college students. *Addictive Behaviours*, **33**, 552–564.

*This paper argues that even in something as individual as a self-report task, the group we are in influences us.*

Reicher, S. D., Haslam, S. A., & Smith, J. R. (2012). Working toward the experimenter: Reconceptualizing obedience within the Milgram paradigm as identification-based followership. *Perspectives on Psychological Science*, **7**, 315–324.

*This is a fascinating paper; the authors question the 'naturalness' of conformity, and argue that our conformity is more about doing what the group thinks is 'right' than us going along with something we feel is 'wrong'.*

**8**

"Our behaviour toward each other is the strangest, most unpredictable, and most unaccountable of all the phenomena with which we are obliged to live. In all of nature, there is nothing so threatening to humanity as humanity itself."

*Lewis Thomas, 1981*

# AGGRESSION

What do we mean by the term 'aggression'? Broadly speaking, aggression defines behaviour that is destructive in some way, causing harm or injury. This can be towards other people, but may also include damage to inanimate objects (e.g. furniture or property), or animals. Of course, some examples of aggressive behaviour are very easily recognized when they accompany intentional violence towards others (e.g. in the time of war). However, not all aggression is so obvious. Aggression can take other more subtle forms such as the verbal aggression displayed in an argument, the occurrence of bullying in the school or workplace, or a scuffle in the street, and as such may be witnessed in our everyday lives. So aggression has many faces, and how social psychologists define it has implications for what they treat as evidence of it, how they measure it, explain it, and the solutions offered for reducing or preventing it. In this chapter we consider some empirical studies, theories and influences on aggression, and examine the diverse range of definitions and methodologies for studying this phenomenon.

In doing so we ask four more-specific questions:

1 Is aggression biologically predisposed, or do we learn it?

2 What circumstances prompt hostile outbursts?

3 Do the media influence aggression?

4 How might we reduce aggression?

First, however, we need to clarify the term 'aggression'.

## WHAT IS AGGRESSION?

The lack of consistency in defining aggression in everyday language is reflected in social psychology. How aggression is defined often depends on the theoretical perspective and the methods used. If we define aggression in its most direct form, as physical acts, then we can only collect evidence of physical behaviour. However, if we define aggression in a more indirect form, perhaps as a subtle feature of language (e.g. spreading malicious gossip), then we would attend to what people say and perhaps how they say it. Some social psychologists/theorists have settled on a compromised definition of aggression as physical or verbal behaviour intended to cause harm, and this has been reflected in textbooks (e.g. Baron and Byrne, 2000; Carlson et al., 1989). However, this definition excludes unintentional harm such as collisions in the street, or the accidental spilling of a hot drink onto someone else; it also excludes actions that may involve pain as an unavoidable side effect of helping someone, such as dental treatments or – in the extreme – assisted suicide. It does include kicks and slaps, threats and insults, even gossip or snide 'digs'; and decisions, during experiments, about how much to hurt someone, such as how much of an electric shock to impose. It also includes destroying property, lying and other behaviour whose aim is to cause mental or physical hurt. However, even this compromise of 'intentional' aggression is not without its problems. Not all aggression is intentional. Some aggressive acts are caused accidentally, with no intention to cause harm. For example, over-exuberance at a music concert can result in harm to others if we accidentally hit or push them as we express our excitement. Unintentional aggression can also describe behaviour that harms others, but the individual causing that harm cannot be held responsible for that action. Children and adults with ADHD (Attention Deficit/Hyperactivity Disorder) may behave aggressively as a consequence of their disorder rather than intention to harm someone (Nigg, 2003).

Aggression can be indirect as well as direct. Consider Dan Olweus's work (1993) on bullying behaviour. Olweus defines bullying as negative behaviour that occurs to a victim 'repeatedly and over time' involving acts of direct physical aggression and indirect aggression. From his study of Norwegian schoolchildren he found that boys tended to conduct most of the bullying. As we shall see in this chapter, this finding is consistent with a lot of aggression research that suggests men are more aggressive than women. Biology, and the presence of hormones such as testosterone and cortisol, are a major contributing factor. But, as we shall also see in this chapter, it is possible to learn aggressive behaviour. So surely it is possible that women are as capable as men of aggression (Bjorkqvist, 1994). This raises issues surrounding the definition and methods used for capturing aggressive behaviour for the social psychologist. Larry Owens, Rosalyn Shute and Phillip Slee (2000a, 2000b) found from their interviews and focus groups with Australian teenage girls, that they use fairly subtle and indirect ways to bully other girls. This bullying can take the form of excluding girls from peer groups. Girls seem to value friendship groups more than boys, so excluding girls from their friends can be a very effective method of bullying. Teenage girls also report using other strategies such as verbal bullying (e.g. spreading malicious gossip), and non-verbal bullying (e.g. hostile staring), which can leave their marginalized victims feeling miserable. These indirect forms of aggression can be more difficult for the social psychologist to capture. Consequently how we define aggression may boil down to what we can see, capture and analyse.

## SOME THEORIES OF AGGRESSION

In analysing the causes of aggression, social psychologists have focused on three main explanations: (1) aggression is the result of a biologically based aggressive drive; (2) aggression is a response to frustration; and (3) aggressive behaviour is learned. Here we shall focus on some key theories in social psychology, which have taken these explanations as their starting point for understanding aggression. Those theories outlined here are not exhaustive of social psychology's engagement with aggression (there are many others!), but they do offer some important insights for the discipline.

### AGGRESSION AS A BIOLOGICAL PHENOMENON

Philosophers have debated whether our human nature is fundamentally that of a benign, contented, 'noble savage' or that of a brute. The first view, argued by the eighteenth-century French philosopher Jean-Jacques Rousseau (1712–78), blames society, not human nature, for social evils. His famous quote, 'Man is born free but everywhere he is in chains', summarizes his opinion that the natural state of man was good, but it was society that corrupted him. On the other hand, the second idea, associated with the English philosopher Thomas Hobbes (1588–1679), credits society for restraining the human brute. In the twentieth century, the 'brutish' view – that aggressive drive is inborn and thus inevitable – was argued by Sigmund Freud in Vienna and Konrad Lorenz in Germany.

### Instinct Theory and Evolutionary Psychology

Freud speculated that human aggression springs from a self-destructive impulse. It redirects towards others the energy of a primitive death urge (the 'death instinct', sometimes called Thanatos in post-Freudian theory). Lorenz, an animal behaviour expert, saw aggression as adaptive rather than self-destructive. The two agreed that aggressive energy is instinctual (unlearned and universal), that is, causes instinctive behaviour. If not discharged, it supposedly builds up until it explodes or until an appropriate stimulus 'releases' it, like a mouse releasing a mousetrap.

The idea that aggression is an instinct collapsed as the list of supposed human instincts grew to include nearly every conceivable human behaviour. Nearly 6000 supposed instincts were enumerated in one 1924 survey of social science books (Barash, 1979). The social scientists had tried to *explain* social behaviour by *naming* it. It's tempting to play this rather circular explaining-by-naming game: 'Why do sheep stay together?' 'Because of their herd instinct.' 'How do you know they have a herd instinct?' 'Just look at them: they're always together!'

Instinct theory also fails to account for the variations in aggressiveness from person to person, culture to culture and across time and space. How would a shared human instinct for aggression explain the difference between the peaceful Iroquois before White invaders came and the hostile Iroquois after the invasion (Hornstein, 1976)? Although aggression may be biologically influenced, the human propensity to aggress does not qualify as instinctive behaviour.

Our distant ancestors nevertheless sometimes found aggression adaptive, according to evolutionary psychologists David Buss and Todd Shackelford (1997). Aggressive behaviour was a strategy for gaining resources, defending against attack, intimidating or eliminating male rivals for females, and deterring mates from sexual infidelity. In some preindustrial societies, being a good warrior made for higher status and reproductive opportunities (Roach, 1998). The adaptive value of aggression, Buss and Shackelford believe, helps explain the relatively high levels of male–male aggression across human history: 'This does not imply … that men have an "aggression instinct" in the sense of some pent-up energy that must be released. Rather, men have learned from their successful ancestors psychological mechanisms' that improve their odds of contributing their genes to future generations.

### Genetic Influences

Heredity influences the neural system's sensitivity to aggressive cues. For example, animals can be bred for aggressiveness. Sometimes this is done for practical purposes (the breeding of fighting cocks or dogs). Sometimes breeding is done for research. Finnish psychologist Kirsti Lagerspetz (1979) took normal albino mice and bred the most aggressive ones together; she did the same with the least aggressive ones. After repeating the procedure for 26 generations, she had one set of fierce mice and one set of placid mice. Chapter 14 discusses the impact of genes on our behaviour more holistically as well as in relation to gender differences.

Aggressiveness varies among primates and humans (Asher, 1987; Olweus, 1979). Our temperaments – how intense and reactive we are – are partly brought with us into the world, influenced by our sympathetic nervous system's reactivity (Kagan, 1989). A person's temperament, observed in infancy, usually endures (Larsen &

---

**instinctive behaviour**
*an innate, unlearned behaviour pattern exhibited by all members of a species*

Chapter 14 discusses the impact of genes on our behaviour more holistically as well as in relation to gender differences.

Diener, 1987; Wilson & Matheny, 1986). A child who is non-aggressive at age 8 will very likely still be a non-aggressive person at age 48 (Huesmann et al., 2003). But it is not easy to say if this is due to genetic inheritance or social learning or socialization, or to tease these two things apart. Identical twins, when asked separately, are more likely than fraternal twins to agree on whether they have 'a violent temper' or have got into fights (Rowe et al., 1999; Rushton et al., 1986).

Do genes predispose the pit bull's aggressiveness?

SOURCE: © dageldog/iStock

Long-term studies following several hundred New Zealand children reveal that a recipe for aggressive behaviour combines a gene, called monoamine oxidase-A (MAOA), that alters neurotransmitter balance with childhood maltreatment (Caspi et al., 2002; Moffitt et al., 2003). Avshalom Caspi and colleagues found that 12 per cent of males in their study had low levels of MAOA and had been subjected to abuse as children between the ages of 3 and 11 years old. Of this group, 85 per cent of them had engaged in antisocial behaviour, which in some cases led to convictions for violent conduct. Consequently, MAOA has been termed the 'warrior gene' (Gibbons, 2004) due to the effect it seems to have upon behaviour. The warrior gene has also been used successfully as a form of mitigating circumstances in murder convictions. In Italy, Abdelmalek Bayout, who confessed to murdering Walter Perez, had his sentence reduced on the grounds of having low levels of MAOA (Levitt, 2013). However, genes alone do not explain aggressive behaviour. Nature and nurture interact. Rose McDermott and her colleagues (2009) found that participants with low activity of MAOA would be aggressive to opponents in an experimental study, but only when they had been severely provoked. So it appears that biology interacts with the environment in producing aggressive responses.

### Biochemical Influences

Blood chemistry also influences neural sensitivity to aggressive stimulation.

### Alcohol

Both laboratory experiments and police data indicate that alcohol unleashes aggression when people are provoked (Bushman, 1993; Taylor & Chermack, 1993; Testa, 2002). Consider:

> In experiments, when asked to think back on relationship conflicts, intoxicated people administer stronger shocks and feel angrier than do sober people.
>
> (MacDonald et al., 2000)

In Britain, a Home Office Study (Richardson & Budd, 2003) using survey and interview methods, conducted between 1998 and 2002 with young people aged 18–24 years, found that those who drank heavily at least once a week were five and a half more times likely to have committed a violent offence than those who got drunk less than once a month.

However, there is a question about the direction of causality here. In a study of young people aged 11–15

Alcohol and aggressive behaviour. Laboratory experiments and police data indicates that alcohol unleashes aggression when people are provoked.

SOURCE: © mediaphotos/iStock

years in the west of Scotland, Robert Young, Helen Sweeting and Patrick West (2007) found that antisocial behaviour can predict long-term alcohol (mis)use. The 'susceptibility hypothesis' suggests that people who are already engaging in antisocial behaviour, or who are likely to do so, are much more 'susceptible' to abuse alcohol in the short or long term. So here we have an example where the causal order is reversed (antisocial behaviour causing alcohol misuse). But, whatever the direction of the relationship between alcohol and aggression, what is clear is that alcohol enhances aggressiveness by lowering people's self-awareness and their thresholds for antisocial behaviour due to reduced control from social and cultural norms, by reducing their ability to consider consequences, and by people's mentally associating alcohol with aggression (Bartholow & Heinz, 2006; Ito et al., 1996; Steele & Southwick, 1985).

### Testosterone

Hormonal influences appear to be much stronger in lower animals than in humans. But human aggressiveness does appear to correlate to some extent with the male sex hormone, testosterone. Consider:

Drugs that diminish testosterone levels in violent human males can subdue their aggressive tendencies.

Among the normal range of teen boys and adult men, those with high testosterone levels have been found to be prone to delinquency, hard drug use and aggressive responses to provocation (Archer, 1991; Dabbs & Morris, 1990; Olweus et al., 1988). After handling a gun, people's testosterone levels rise, and the more their testosterone rises the more aggression they will impose on another (Klinesmith et al., 2006). Shawn Geniole and his colleagues (2011) discovered that higher testosterone levels were associated with reactive aggression in men. Interestingly, Kimberly Cote and her research team (2013) found that sleep deprivation lowered testosterone levels and reactive aggression in men.

But we need to be careful here. Taken at face value this would lead us to the assumption that men must be more aggressive than women. As we shall see later in this chapter, this is not always the case. You may remember one of the lessons from Chapter 2: correlation does not mean causation. Winning a rugby match might cause a brief increase in testosterone levels among the players. Does this mean they will then behave aggressively? Most probably not.

### Serotonin

Low levels of serotonin have been linked to heightened aggression (Birger et al., 2003; de Almeida et al., 2005).

Those studies which propose a link between aggression and serotonin include the dietary manipulation of tryptophan, which is an amino acid used in the production of serotonin. In one study by Gerard Moeller and his team (1996) participants were put on a low tryptophan diet for 24 hours to reduce the levels of serotonin produced. These participants were also asked to take part in a maths task that involved being provoked by a researcher. What the researchers discovered was that aggressive responses started to increase from 5 hours of being on the diet. Furthermore, when a low tryptophan diet is mixed with alcohol consumption serotonin levels drop even further, and aggressive behaviours are displayed in an experimental context (LeMarquand et al., 1998).

susceptibility hypothesis *when features of someone's environment make him/her more susceptible to particular kinds of behaviour as a consequence*

Studies such as these directly manipulate serotonin levels through diet. Yet these studies show us that our environment may interact with our biology. For example, those individuals who find themselves of low social status often have low levels of serotonin (Manuck et al., 2004). Deficiencies in this neurotransmitter are associated with risky and impulsive behaviour (Moeller et al., 1996). So is it the biology that determines the risky behaviour, or the social standing? Most probably, it's an interaction of both.

### Neural Influences

Exerting self-control in a situation where we feel angry can be extremely difficult. And, as neuroimaging studies show, it can be more difficult for some people than others.

Reactive aggression defines a response to being provoked. We may want to respond to being threatened, frustrated or angry at someone's actions or a set of circumstances. Perhaps you've been insulted, tricked, embarrassed or put in a dangerous position. How do you react?

reactive aggression *an aggressive response to being provoked*

Denson and his colleagues (2012) outline 'I-Theory', which states that there are three processes behind aggression: instigation (being provoked), impellance (dispositional and situational factors which prepare you for an aggressive response) and inhibition (self-control). So your ability to avoid an aggressive reaction is based on the relative strength of your self-control (inhibition) over provocation (instigation) and impellance (preparedness to be aggressive). And it seems that processes within the brain have some influence over our ability to exercise self-control. Prefrontal cortex regions are involved in regulating our emotions and help us to maintain self-control. Damage to these regions is often linked to violent behaviour. But they can be temporarily impeded too by alcohol consumption (as we'll see later in this chapter) and depletion from feeling overwhelmed. The good news is that practice makes perfect, as we control our urge to react aggressively to provocation. Another tastier method of controlling our aggressive urges seems to be consuming sugar, which has been shown to improve those neural processes involved in self-control (Denson et al., 2010).

But not all aggression is reactive. Instrumental aggression defines behaviour that is aggressive in order to acquire a desired reward. For example, a son who murders his father for the inheritance would be an act of instrumental aggression. Instrumental aggression requires a lack of empathy with the victim. Research suggests that this lack of empathy is related to poor functioning of the amygdala. This is particularly evident in psychopathic populations, where personality is characterized by a lack of guilt for their actions. Dennis Reidy and his colleagues (2011) report examples of studies which have shown instrumental aggressive acts are much more likely to be conducted by psychopaths than non-psychopaths. It seems the amygdala, responsible for feelings of empathy and shame, plays a key role in instrumental aggression.

instrumental aggression *a behaviour which requires aggression in order to obtain a desired (often material) reward*

### Biology and Behaviour Interact

It is important to remember that the traffic between hormonal influences, brain structure, alcohol, drugs and behaviour flows both ways. Testosterone, for example, may facilitate dominance and aggressiveness, but dominating or defeating behaviour also boosts testosterone levels (Mazur & Booth, 1998).

After a World Cup football match or a big basketball game between arch-rivals, testosterone levels rise in the winning fans and fall in the losing fans (Bernhardt et al., 1998). That, plus celebration-related drinking, probably explains the finding of Cardiff University researchers that fans of *winning* rather than losing football and rugby teams commit more postgame assaults (Sivarajasingam et al., 2005). The more athletic competitions women enter, the more their levels of testosterone and cortisol rise (Edwards & Casto, 2013). As Thomas Denson and his colleagues discovered (2013), women with high levels of testosterone and cortisol reacted much more aggressively when insulted than women who had average or low levels of these hormones.

So, instinctive, genetic, neural and biochemical influences may predispose some people to react aggressively to conflict and provocation. But perhaps we need to be careful in interpreting these data, and not to assume that such features are solely responsible for aggressive behaviour.

Many of the tried and tested methods for treating and changing deviant behaviour do not involve biological intervention but concern adjustment of people's social environment and ways of thinking about themselves. Cognitive behavioural therapy (CBT) tackles the way in which people think about themselves, others and the world at large in order to alter their cognition and behaviour. So a complex array of factors is involved, and we need to think about 'what' we define as aggression and what we treat as evidence of it.

Some early social psychological theories of the causes of aggression focused on particular types: those aggressive acts which occurred as a result of frustration, and those that occurred as a consequence of relative deprivation. Let's consider each of these in turn.

### AGGRESSION AS A RESPONSE TO FRUSTRATION

**frustration-aggression theory** *the theory that frustration triggers a readiness to aggress*

**frustration** *the blocking of goal-directed behaviour*

One of the first psychological theories of aggression, frustration-aggression theory, argues 'Frustration always leads to some form of aggression' (John Dollard and his colleagues, 1939). Frustration is anything that blocks our attaining a goal. Barker et al. (1941) found that young children who were shown a room full of attractive toys but prevented from playing with them displayed much more aggressive behaviour towards those toys, compared to other children who had been allowed to play with them immediately, when finally allowed to enter the room.

When Rupert Brown and his colleagues (2001) surveyed British ferry passengers heading to France, they found much higher than normal aggressive attitudes on a day when French fishing boats blockaded the port, preventing their travel. Blocked from obtaining their goal, the passengers became more likely (in responding to various vignettes) to agree with an insult towards a French person who had spilled coffee. In her study of queue-jumpers, Mary Harris (1974) found that when people were pushed in front of in a supermarket queue, the closer they were to the checkout when the incident occurred was related to the level of aggression they displayed. The nearer they were to the goal, the more intense the expression of aggression displayed became.

As Figure 8.1 suggests, the aggressive energy need not explode directly against its source. We learn to inhibit direct retaliation, especially when others might disapprove or punish; instead, we *displace* our hostilities to safer targets.

Displacement occurs in an old anecdote about a man who, humiliated by his boss, berates his wife, who yells at their son, who kicks the dog, which bites the mail-carrier (who goes home and berates his wife ...). In experiments and in real life, displaced aggression is most likely when the target shares some similarity to the instigator and does some minor irritating act that unleashes the displaced aggression (Marcus-Newhall et al., 2000; Miller et al., 2003; Pedersen et al., 2000). When a person is harbouring anger from a prior provocation, even a trivial offence – one that would normally produce no response – may elicit an explosive overreaction (as you may realize if you have ever yelled at your room-mate after losing money in a malfunctioning vending machine).

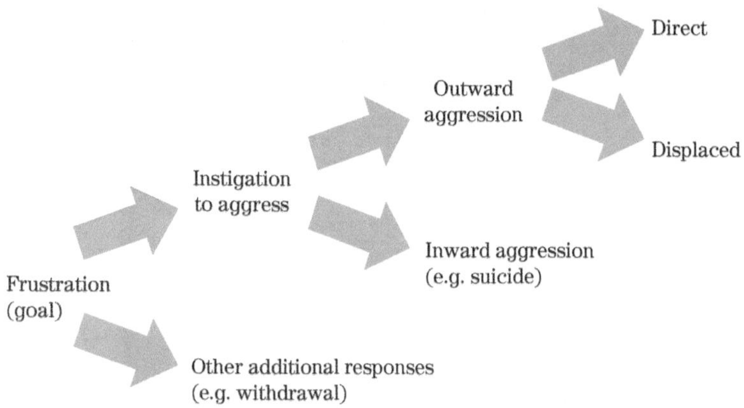

**FIGURE 8.1** The classic frustration-aggression theory
Frustration creates a motive to aggress. Fear of punishment or disapproval for aggressing against the source of frustration may cause the aggressive drive to be displaced against some other target or even redirected against oneself.
SOURCE: Based on Dollard et al., 1939; Miller, 1941.

displacement *the redirection of aggression to a target other than the source of the frustration. Generally, the new target is a safer or more socially acceptable target*

However, it is important to remember that frustration as well as aggression is culture dependent. In some cultures people do not have the same individual expectations as most people have in other cultures and they therefore do not feel frustrated for not reaching the individual goals. This also reduces the consequences of frustration and the prevalence of aggression.

A different approach to the aggression-frustration model is based in the work of Dolf Zillman (1979) and his excitation-transfer model. Zillman suggests that when we are physiologically aroused from a particular event or situation, this state of arousal does not simply disappear but can have effects on other situations we find ourselves in. Under such conditions a person may transfer feelings of frustration to a different situation and act aggressively.

excitation-transfer model *when a state of physiological arousal is transferred from one situation to another, resulting in heightened expressive behaviour*

Various commentators have observed that the intense American anger over 9/11 contributed to the eagerness to attack Iraq. Americans were looking for an outlet for their rage and found one in an evil tyrant, Saddam Hussein, who was once their ally. 'The "real reason" for this war', noted Thomas Friedman (2003b), 'was that after 9/11 America needed to hit someone in the Arab-Muslim world ... We hit Saddam for one simple reason: because we could, and because he deserved it, and because he was right in the heart of that world.' One of the war's advocates, Vice-President Richard Cheney (2003), seemed to concur. When asked why most others in the world disagreed with America's launching war, he replied, 'They didn't experience 9/11.'

### Frustration-Aggression Theory Revised

Laboratory tests of the frustration-aggression theory have produced mixed results: sometimes frustration increased aggressiveness but sometimes not. For example, if the frustration was understandable – if, as in one experiment, a confederate disrupted a group's problem solving because his hearing aid malfunctioned (rather than just because he wasn't paying attention) – then

Frustrated as the referee allows an own goal to stand, Patrice Eura of Manchester United begins to argue with him over his decision.

SOURCE: © Getty Images

**FIGURE 8.2** A simplified synopsis of Leonard Berkowitz's revised frustration-aggression theory

frustration led to irritation, not aggression (Burnstein & Worchel, 1962).

Leonard Berkowitz (1978, 1989) realized that the original theory overstated the frustration-aggression connection, so he revised it. Berkowitz theorized that frustration produces *anger*, an emotional readiness to aggress. Anger arises when someone who frustrates us could have chosen to act otherwise (Averill, 1983; Weiner, 1981). A frustrated person is especially likely to lash out when aggressive cues pull the cork, releasing bottled-up anger (Figure 8.2). Sometimes the cork will blow without such cues. But, as we will see, cues associated with aggression amplify aggression (Carlson et al., 1990).

Frustration may be unrelated to deprivation. The most sexually frustrated people are probably not celibate. The most economically frustrated people are probably not the impoverished residents of African shanty towns. Likewise, Palestinian suicide bombers have not been the most deprived of Palestinians. Like Northern Ireland's IRA, Italy's Red Brigades and Germany's Bader-Meinhof gang, they are mostly middle class (Krueger & Maleckova, 2003; Pettigrew, 2003). So, too, were the 9/11 terrorists, who were professionally trained and world travelled.

### Relative Deprivation

Frustration is often compounded when we compare ourselves with others. Workers' feelings of well-being depend on whether their compensation compares favourably with that of others in their line of work (Yuchtman, 1976). A raise in salary for a city's police officers, while temporarily lifting their morale, may deflate that of the firefighters.

relative deprivation *the perception that one is less well off than others with whom one compares oneself*

Such feelings are called relative deprivation. This goes some way to explaining why East Germans revolted against their communist regime: they had a higher standard of living than some Western European countries, but a frustratingly lower one than their West German neighbours (Baron et al., 1992).

One possible source of such frustration today is the affluence depicted in television programmes and commercials. In cultures where television is a universal appliance, it helps turn absolute deprivation (lacking what others have) into relative deprivation (feeling deprived). Karen Hennigan and her co-workers (1982) analysed crime rates in American cities around the time television was introduced. In 34 cities where television ownership became widespread in 1951, the 1951 larceny theft rate (for crimes such as shoplifting and bicycle stealing) took an observable jump. In 34 other cities, where a government freeze had delayed the introduction of television until 1955, a similar jump in the theft rate occurred – in 1955.

But of course, to claim that all aggression is simply the result of frustration and/ or relative deprivation is simply untrue. So social psychologists have examined other causes and explanations for aggressive behaviour.

## AGGRESSION AS LEARNED SOCIAL BEHAVIOUR

Theories of aggression based on instinct and frustration assume that aggression arises from hostile urges which erupt from within the individual, which naturally 'push' aggression out into the social world from forces within. However, some social psychologists contend that the source of aggression may be located within the social world.

### The Rewards of Aggression

By experience and by observing others, we learn that aggression often pays. People can learn the rewards of aggression. A child whose aggressive acts successfully intimidate other children is likely to become increasingly aggressive (Patterson et al., 1967). Aggressive hockey players – those sent most often to the penalty box for rough play – score more goals than non-aggressive players (McCarthy & Kelly, 1978a, 1978b). Canadian teenage hockey players whose fathers applaud physically aggressive play show the most aggressive attitudes and style of play (Ennis & Zanna, 1991). In these cases, aggression is instrumental in achieving certain rewards.

The same is true of terrorist acts, which enable powerless people to garner widespread attention. 'The primary targets of suicide-bombing attacks are not those who are injured but those who are made to witness it through media coverage,' note Paul Marsden and Sharon Attia (2005). Terrorism's purpose is, with the help of media amplification, to terrorize. Deprived of what Margaret Thatcher called 'the oxygen of publicity', terrorism would surely diminish, concluded Jeffrey Rubin (1986). It's like the 1970s incidents of naked spectators 'streaking' onto football fields for a few seconds of television exposure. Once the networks decided to ignore the incidents, the phenomenon ended.

### Observational Learning

Albert Bandura (1997) proposed a social learning theory of aggression. He believes that we learn aggression not only by experiencing its rewards but also by observing others (also see Chapter 5). As with many social behaviours, we acquire aggression by watching others act and noting the consequences.

**social learning theory** *Bandura's theory that we learn social behaviour by observing and imitating others, and then by self-regulating our own behaviour accordingly*

In one of Bandura's experiments (Bandura et al., 1961) a pre-school child is put to work on an interesting art activity. An adult is in another part of the room, where there are Tinker Toys, a mallet and a big, inflated, Bobo doll. After a minute of working with the Tinker Toys, the adult gets up and for almost 10 minutes attacks the inflated doll. She pounds it with the mallet, kicks it and throws it, while yelling, 'Sock him in the nose ... Knock him down ... Kick him'.

After observing this outburst, the child is taken to a different room with many very attractive toys. But after 2 minutes the experimenter interrupts, saying these are her best toys and she must 'save them for the other children'. The frustrated child now goes into yet another room with various toys designed for aggressive and non-aggressive play, two of which are a Bobo doll and a mallet.

Children who were not exposed to the aggressive adult model did not display any aggressive play or talk. Although frustrated, they nevertheless played calmly. However, those who had observed the aggressive adult were more likely to pick up the mallet and lash out at the doll. Watching the adult's aggressive behaviour lowered their inhibitions. Furthermore, the children often reproduced the model's specific acts and said her words. Observing aggressive behaviour had both lowered their inhibitions and taught them ways to aggress. Bandura argued that modelling this behaviour was enough for a child to acquire and perform aggressive behaviour.

In a later study Bandura tested whether the consequences of aggressive actions had any effect on children's modelling behaviour. He found that if children witnessed the adult being punished as a consequence of their negative actions towards the Bobo doll, the children did not mimic their actions. However, if they saw the adult rewarded, then their behaviour was re-enacted by the child towards the doll.

Since Bandura's studies there have been some questions raised over his claims. For example, Steve Hayes, Arnold Rincover and Diane Volosin (1980) replicated Bandura's study, and examined the levels of aggression children displayed to a free-moving Bobo doll as compared to one with limited movement. They found that when the Bobo doll was free-moving, providing the child with a lot of visual stimulation, this produced and maintained high levels of aggression. Athena Drewes (2008) reviews some further concerns that surround Bandura's studies, including the observation that Bobo dolls are 'meant to be hit', so it's unclear to what degree these are demonstrations of aggression. She also asks if behaviours that are allowed in a study are fair reflections of acts of aggression that occur in real life. That said, Drewes does not dispute that Bandura's work gives us some of the strongest evidence about how aggressive behaviour is acquired and performed.

Bandura (1979) believes that everyday life exposes us to three main aggressive models: the family, one's subculture and, as we will see, the mass media.

### The Family
The role the family plays in the acquisition, maintenance and extinguishing of aggressive behaviour in children has been well documented within the research. While many children engage in physical aggression between the ages of 1 and 3 years, its subsequent decline is attributed to prosocial parenting and socialization

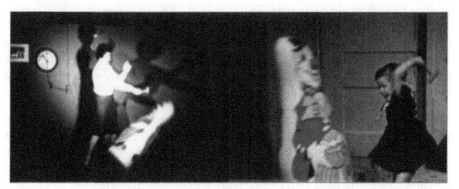

In Bandura's famous experiment, children exposed to an adult's aggression against a Bobo doll became likely to reproduce the observed aggression.
SOURCE: © Albert Bandura

by peers and teachers into non-violent ways of behaving. Jasmina Burdzovic Andreas and Malcolm Watson (2009) suggest that it is when children believe aggression is a justifiable and valuable tool in social interactions that they develop the habit of aggression. However, optimal family environments which exhibit low conflict and high levels of cohesion can reduce aggression in children. Anne Borge and colleagues (2004) found aggression was more common in children looked after at home in 'high-risk' families than those in daycare. She concluded that high physical aggression in children was associated with low maternal education, high number of siblings, low socio-economic status and very poor family functioning.

Sadly, not all family environments are havens of peace. Physically aggressive children often have had physically punitive parents, who disciplined them with screaming, slapping and beating (Patterson et al., 1982). These parents are likely to have parents who were themselves physically punitive (Bandura & Walters, 1959; Straus & Gelles, 1980). In Diane English and her colleagues' study (2009) with a non-clinical US sample, they found that children's outcomes were better when they came from homes that had never experienced domestic violence, neglect or maltreatment. But they also observed that much of the aggression reported was verbal rather than physical.

The presence of a violent parent or guardian within the family has received particular attention from psychologists. Timothy Ireland and Carolyn Smith (2009) reported a relationship between violent partner and homes during adolescence and adolescent conduct problems. The absence of a parent or guardian has also been studied for its role in aggression. A British study that followed more than 10 000 individuals for 33 years since their birth in 1958 found that a parental breakup during childhood had negative consequences for their mental health as adults (Chase-Lansdale et al., 1995). The point raised by these studies is not that children from single-parent homes are doomed to become delinquent, dysfunctional or violent, but rather, nurtured by a caring parent or guardian and extended family, most children thrive.

It is often thought that deprived neighbourhoods can be a harmful place for children and adolescents to grow up in. Yet, Candice Odgers and colleagues (2009) found quite the reverse. In deprived neighbourhoods with high social cohension and a willingness to intervene in family situations where it was thought to be for the greater good, these local communities with 'collective efficacy' were capable of reducing youth aggression and protecting children.

In fact it would seem that a complex array of factors inside and outside the family contribute to aggression in children. What this array of diverse research does alert us to is how difficult it is to produce simple cause-and-effect relationships to explain the role of the family in aggression. As Gayla Margolin and colleagues (2009) observed from their longitudinal study of children and adolescents, different forms of violence tend to co-occur within the lifetime of an individual. These can include marital aggression, parent–child abuse and community violence. To understand aggression and violence we need to look further than just the family, and to the broader social context in which it occurs.

### The Culture

The social environment outside the home also provides models and societal norms. In communities where 'macho' images are admired, aggression is readily transmitted to new generations (Cartwright, 1975; Short, 1969). The violent subculture of teenage gangs, for instance, provides its junior members with aggressive models. Among Chicago adolescents who are otherwise equally at risk for violence, those who have observed gun violence are at doubled risk for violent behaviour (Bingenheimer et al., 2005).

Henri Tajfel (1974) pointed out that explanations of aggression must also consider the broader cultural context in which the individual is placed. For example, Conor McGuckin and Christopher Lewis (2003, 2008) have found that the prevalence of bullying in schools in Northern Ireland, where violent conflict between political and religious groups has been rife, is much higher than incidences found in Wales, England, Scotland and Ireland. In China and Japan, where the crime rates are low, children are thought not to be aggressive from an early age. Aggressiveness is looked upon as childish and a sign of being immature. In East Asian interdependent cultures the feeling of shame is also important in contributing to the low crime rates. To violate the law is to bring shame on oneself and the whole family, and to be caught means that the family is 'losing face'. These cultural norms reduce offending in East Asian shame cultures.

Richard Nisbett (1990, 1993) and Dov Cohen (1996, 1998) have explored the subculture effect within the USA. The sober, co-operative White folk who settled in New England and the Middle Atlantic region produced a different culture from that of the swashbuckling, honour-preserving White folk who settled much of the South. The former were farmer-artisans; the latter, more aggressive hunters and herders. To the present day, American cities and areas populated by southerners have much higher white homicide rates than those populated by northerners.

In their study of antigay aggression, Wilson Vincent and his colleagues (2011) note cultural influence in the development of heterosexual masculinity. Culture brings with it traditional expectations about how men 'ought' to behave, think and feel, and what the values and norms of men 'should' be. These cultural influences may underlie antigay aggression. Feeling insecure in one's own heterosexual masculine identity, or what Vincent and his colleagues call 'masculine gender-role stress', can express itself in antigay anger and aggression. It is the fear of being excluded from heterosexual groups and mainstream values that may motivate some reportedly straight men to be aggressive towards gay men, as an explicit reaffirmation of their heterosexual masculine identity.

Stanley Schachter's two-factor theory of emotion (1959) suggests that emotions, such as anger and frustration, are rooted in the physiology of the individual but also in how people interpret the situation and what is considered to be culturally appropriate behaviour. For example, Joe Vandello and Dov Cohen (2003) note how the cultural scripts in Brazil surrounding matters of 'honour' mean that under certain circumstances domestic violence is an acceptable way of punishing female infidelity and restoring a male's honour. Patricia Rodriguez Mosquera, Anthony Manstead and Agneta Fischer (2002) found differences in responses of Spanish and Dutch participants when confronted with threats and insults. Whereas Dutch participants became angered when the insults were directed towards their autonomy and individual achievements, Spanish participants displayed anger when their family honour was challenged. The researchers argue that these different patterns of responses mark the contrasting significance of

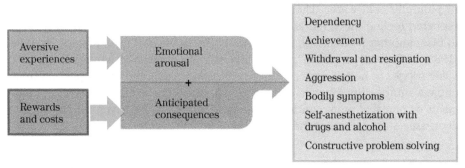

**FIGURE 8.3** The social learning view of aggression
The emotional arousal stemming from an aversive experience motivates aggression. Whether aggression or some other response actually occurs depends on what consequences we have learned to expect.

SOURCE: Based on Bandura, 1979, 1997.

concepts of individualism (in the Netherlands) and honour (in Spain) provoking aggression when they are challenged or undermined. So, there are cultural scripts that influence what is regarded as an appropriate emotion to have under certain circumstances and what is an acceptable expression of it.

But when will aggressive responses actually occur? Bandura (1979) contended that aggressive acts are motivated by a variety of aversive experiences – frustration, pain, insults (Figure 8.3). Such experiences arouse us emotionally. But whether we act aggressively depends on the consequences we anticipate. Aggression is most likely when we are aroused, and it seems safe, appropriate and rewarding to aggress.

## SOME INFLUENCES ON AGGRESSION

Under what conditions do we aggress? Here we examine some specific influences: aversive incidents, arousal, the media, hate and collective identity.

### AVERSIVE INCIDENTS

Recipes for aggression often include some type of aversive experience: pain, uncomfortable heat, an attack or overcrowding.

Pain
Researcher Nathan Azrin (1967) was doing experiments with laboratory rats in a cage wired to deliver electric shocks to the animals' feet. Azrin wanted to know if switching off the shocks would reinforce two rats' positive interactions with each other. He planned to turn on the shock and then, once the rats approached each other, cut off the pain. To his great surprise, the experiment proved impossible. As soon as the rats felt pain, they attacked each other, before the experimenter could switch off the shock. The greater the shock (and pain) the more violent the attack. Of course today's ethical guidelines restrict researchers' use of painful stimuli.

Pain heightens aggressiveness in humans, too. Many of us can recall such a reaction after stubbing a toe or suffering a headache. Leonard Berkowitz and his associates demonstrated this by having students hold one hand in either lukewarm water or painfully cold water. Those whose hands were submerged in the cold water reported feeling more irritable and more annoyed, and they were more willing to blast another person with unpleasant noise. In view of such results, Berkowitz (1983, 1989, 1998) proposed that aversive stimulation rather than frustration is the basic trigger of hostile aggression. Frustration is certainly one important type of unpleasantness. But any aversive event, whether a dashed expectation, a personal insult or physical pain, can incite an emotional outburst. Even the torment of a depressed state increases the likelihood of hostile, aggressive behaviour.

### Heat

People have theorized for centuries about the effect of climate on human action. Hippocrates (c. 460–377 BC) compared the civilized Greece of his day with the savagery in the region further north (what is now Germany and Switzerland) and decided that northern Europe's harsh climate was to blame. More than a millennium later, the English attributed their 'superior' culture to England's ideal climate. French thinkers proclaimed the same for France. Because climate remains relatively steady while cultural traits change over time, the climate theory of culture obviously has limited validity.

Pain attack. Frustrated after losing the first two rounds of his 1997 heavyweight championship fight with Evander Holyfield, and feeling pain from an accidental head butt, Mike Tyson reacts by biting off part of Holyfield's ear.
SOURCE: JEFF HAYNES/Getty Images

Temporary climate variations can, however, affect behaviour. Offensive odours, cigarette smoke and air pollution have all been linked with aggressive behaviour (Rotton & Frey, 1985). But the most studied environmental irritant is heat. William Griffitt (1970; Griffitt & Veitch, 1971) found that compared with students who answered questionnaires in a room with a normal temperature, those who did so in an uncomfortably hot room (over 90°F) reported feeling more tired and aggressive, and expressed more hostility towards a stranger. Follow-up experiments revealed that heat also triggers retaliative actions (Bell, 1980; Rule et al., 1987).

Does uncomfortable heat increase aggression in the real world as well as in the laboratory? Consider:

In heat-stricken Phoenix, Arizona, drivers without air-conditioning have been more likely to display road rage (Kenrick & MacFarlane, 1986).

The riots that broke out in 79 US cities between 1967 and 1971 occurred on hotter rather than cool days; none of them happened in winter.

In 2007/08 violent crimes against the person fell considerably in London during the winter months.

'I pray thee, good Mercutio, let's retire; The day is hot, the Capulets abroad, And, if we meet, we shall not 'scape a brawl, For now, these hot days, is the mad blood stirring.'
Shakespeare, *Romeo and Juliet*

Do these real-world findings show that heat discomfort directly fuels aggressiveness? Although the conclusion appears plausible, these *correlations* between temperature and aggression don't prove it. People certainly could be more irritable in hot, sticky weather. And in the laboratory, hot temperatures do increase arousal and hostile thoughts and feelings (Anderson et al., 1999). There may be other contributing factors, though. Maybe hot summer evenings drive people into the streets. There, other group influence factors may well take over as group interactions increase. Then again (researchers are debating this), maybe there comes a point where stifling heat suppresses violence (Bell, 2005; Bushman et al., 2005b, 2005c; Cohn & Rotton, 2005).

### Attacks

Being attacked or insulted by another is especially conducive to aggression. The reciprocity principle means we tend to react to a direct attack, which can of course lead to an escalation of violence. Several experiments, including one at Osaka University by Kennichi Ohbuchi and Toshihiro Kambara (1985), confirm that intentional attacks breed retaliatory attacks. In most of these experiments, one person competes with another in a reaction-time contest. After each test trial,

Road rage has been found to be more likely in humid conditions.

SOURCE: © Carlofranco/iStock

the winner chooses how much shock to give the loser. Actually, each person is playing a programmed opponent, who steadily escalates the amount of shock. Do the real participants respond charitably? Hardly. Extracting 'an eye for an eye' is the more likely response.

**reciprocity principle** *asserts that we should treat like with like. So responses to a positive action should be positive, whereas those to a negative action should be negative*

## INTERPRETING AROUSAL

So far we have seen that various aversive stimulations can arouse anger. Do other types of arousal, such as those that accompany exercise or sexual excitement, have a similar effect? Imagine that Lourdes, having just finished a stimulating short run, comes home to discover that her date for the evening has called and left word that he has made other plans. Will Lourdes more likely explode in fury after her run than if she discovered the same message after awakening from a nap? Or, since she has just exercised, will her aggressive tendencies be exorcised? To discover the answer, consider how we interpret and label our bodily states.

In a famous experiment, Stanley Schachter and Jerome Singer (1962) found we can experience an aroused bodily state in different ways. They aroused University of Minnesota men by injecting adrenaline. The drug produced body flushing, heart palpitation and more rapid breathing. When forewarned that the drug would produce those effects, the men felt little emotion, even when waiting with either a hostile or a euphoric person. Of course, they could readily attribute their bodily sensations to the drug. Schachter and Singer led another group of men to believe the drug produced no such side effects. Then they, too, were placed in the company of a hostile or a euphoric person. How did they feel and act? They were angered when with the hostile person, amused when with the person who was euphoric. The principle seemed to be: *a given state of bodily arousal feeds one emotion or another, depending on how the person interprets and labels the arousal.*

Other experiments indicate that arousal is not as emotionally undifferentiated as Schachter believed. Yet being physically stirred up does intensify just about any emotion (Reisenzein, 1983). For example, Paul Biner (1991) reports that people find radio static unpleasant, *especially* when they are aroused by bright lighting. And Dolf Zillmann (1988), Jennings Bryant and their collaborators found that

## research close-up

### HARASSMENT ONLINE

*Source: Workman, M. (2010). A behaviourist perspective on corporate harassment online: Validation of a theoretical model of psychological motives.* Computers and Security, *29, 831–839.*

#### Introduction

Why do some people take to insulting and abusing others online? The phenomenon known as 'trolling' is receiving social psychological attention as its occurrence increases with the rise in our Internet use. So what motivates such cyber aggression? Perpetrators do not just abuse individuals, but also victimize companies. Cyber harassment can be dismissed as irritating, but at its worst can lead to considerable distress and in some cases suicide of their targeted victim. Corporate companies and their employees can be the targets of abuse, but also their employees can be the perpetrators. So what advice can be offered to businesses to prevent their employees from engaging in it?

This research draws on the findings of the Honeynet Project (2004; http://www.honeynet.org.uk), which identified six motives underlying individual attacks on computer systems. These included a need for entertainment, status-seeking, to promote a cause or ideology, a need for social acceptance, uncontrollable impulses and economic motives. Could motives such as these be behind cyber-attacks on individuals and corporations? The following six hypotheses were developed to predict who is likely to engage in trolling behaviour.

H1: People who are self-indulgent will be more likely to commit cyber harassment that people who are less self-indulgent.

H2: People who are more narcissistic will be more likely to commit cyber harassment than people who are less narcissistic.

H3: People who are more idealistic will be more likely to commit cyber harassment than people who are less idealistic.

H4: People who have a greater need for acceptance will be more likely to commit cyber harassment than people who have less need for acceptance.

H5: People who are less emotionally stable will be more likely to commit cyber harassment than people who are more emotionally stable.

H6: People who are more exploitative will be more likely to commit cyber harassment than people who are less exploitative.

#### Method

Of the 112 surveys given out to randomly sampled college students (mean age = 24 years), 54 were returned completed. The surveys consisted of a personality questionnaire to measure the characteristics of self-indulgence, narcissism, idealism, need for social acceptance, emotional stability and exploitation. This was a 7-point Likert scale that asked people how much they agreed with statements such as, 'My values are more important to me than offending people' (measure of idealism) and 'I seek to come out ahead no matter what' (a measure of exploitation). Participants were also asked whether they had ever written critical comments or something negative about people and companies on social media, which they knew was not true.

## Results

A structured equation model was carried out. This provided correlations on the different personality measures (such as narcissism and self-indulgence) and having engaged in cyber harassment.

Statistical significance was found for all six hypotheses, and in the direction predicted by the research.

H1: People who are more self-indulgent are more likely to commit cyber harassment than people who are less self-indulgent ($\beta = -.55, p < .01$).

H2: People who are more narcissistic are more likely to commit cyber harassment than those who are less narcissistic ($\beta = -.33, p < .05$).

H3: People who are idealistic are more likely to commit cyber harassment than those who are less narcissistic ($\beta = -.25, p < .05$).

H4: People who have a greater need for acceptance are more likely to commit cyber harassment than those who have less need for acceptance ($\beta = -.46, p < .01$).

H5: People who are less emotionally stable are more likely to commit cyber harassment than those who are more emotionally stable ($\beta = -.27, p < .05$)

H6: People who are more exploitative are more likely to commit cyber harassment than people who are less exploitative ($\beta = .40, p < .01$).

## Discussion

People who are more self-indulgent, narcissistic, idealistic, have high need for acceptance, emotionally unstable, and exploitative in their relationships with others are more likely to attack people and companies via social media, than those who are not strong on these personality characteristics.

So, what can companies do to discourage and prevent employees from getting involved in trolling, and protect themselves from becoming the victim of one? On a practical level companies can take out legal protection against incidences such as these happening. Software can be purchased that can trawl the Internet to detect any negative comments that have been posted up about a company. However, there are also things you can do to tackle perpetrators. These include ignoring the attacker in the hope that this will extinguish the behaviour. From a behaviourist perspective, this lack of reinforcement may be enough to stop the negative behaviour being continued. Alternatively, a company may wish to try and reason with an attacker to help him/her see the consequences of their behaviour. Finally, a company can punish the attacker either through corporate measures (such as dismissal) or via legal channels.

There are some limitations with this study. The truthfulness of participants' accounts may be compromised considering the sensitive and undesirable nature of the topic. The sample is also small in number (54) and young in age. This makes generalization to the wider population difficult. Moreover, these motives may not on their own explain trolling behaviour. There may be other attitudes involved, such as those about the legal system and fairness, which moderate trolling behaviour. We also have some potential discrepancy between individuals about what constitutes negative and critical comments. Furthermore, a study such as this does not consider any social factors involved in cyber-harassment including the context in which it is done. It assumes cyber-harassment is done by individuals.

Perhaps personality characteristics go some way to explaining cyber-harassment and targeted attacks on individuals and companies, but arguably other more social factors are involved.

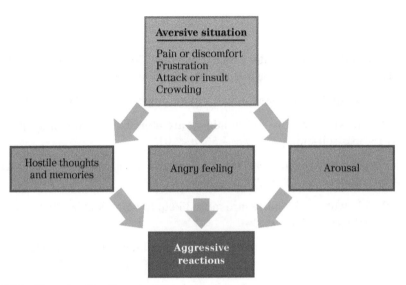

**FIGURE 8.4** Elements of hostile aggression
An aversive situation can trigger aggression by provoking hostile cognitions, hostile feelings and arousal. These reactions make us more likely to perceive harmful intent and to react aggressively.
SOURCE: Simplified from Anderson et al., 1995.

people who have just pumped an exercise bike or watched a film of a Beatles rock concert find it easy to misattribute their arousal to a provocation. They then retaliate with heightened aggression.

Although common sense might lead us to assume that Lourdes's run would have drained her aggressive tensions, enabling her to accept bad news calmly, these studies show that *arousal feeds emotions*.

Sexual arousal and other forms of arousal, such as anger, can therefore amplify one another (Zillmann, 1989b). Love is never so passionate as after a fight or a fright. In the laboratory, erotic stimuli are more arousing to people who have just been frightened. Similarly, the arousal of a roller-coaster ride may spill over into romantic feeling for one's partner.

A frustrating, hot or insulting situation heightens arousal. When it does, the arousal, combined with hostile thoughts and feelings, may form a recipe for aggressive behaviour (Figure 8.4).

### AGGRESSION CUES: THE INFLUENCE OF THE ENVIRONMENT

As we noted when considering the frustration-aggression hypothesis, violence is more likely when aggressive cues in the environment release pent-up anger. Leonard Berkowitz (1968, 1981, 1995) and others have found that the sight of a weapon is such a cue. In one experiment, children who had just played with toy guns became more willing to knock down another child's blocks. In another, angered University of Wisconsin men gave more electric shocks to their tormenter when a rifle and a revolver (supposedly left over from a previous experiment) were nearby than when badminton rackets had been left behind (Berkowitz & LePage, 1967). Guns prime hostile thoughts and punitive judgements (Anderson et al., 1998; Dienstbier et al., 1998). What's within sight is within mind. This is especially so when a weapon is perceived as an instrument of violence rather than a recreational item. So the labels and evaluative meanings we give people and objects influence our behaviour. For hunters, for example, seeing a hunting rifle does not prime aggressive thoughts, though it does for non-hunters (Bartholow et al., 2004).

Berkowitz notes how in the USA, a country with some 200 million privately owned guns, half of all murders are committed with handguns, or that handguns in homes are far more likely to kill household members than intruders. 'Guns not only permit violence,' he reported, 'they can stimulate it as well. The finger pulls the trigger, but the trigger may also be pulling the finger.' Perhaps this is echoed in the UK independent charity Crimestoppers report, that between 2007/08 and 2009, there was a rise in attempted murder with the use of knives.

Berkowitz also draws attention towards the fact that countries that ban handguns have lower murder rates. Compared with the USA, Britain has one-fourth as many people and one-sixteenth as many murders. The USA has 10 000 handgun homicides a year; Australia has about a dozen, Britain two dozen and Canada 100. When Washington, DC, adopted a law restricting handgun possession, the numbers of gun-related murders and suicides each abruptly dropped about 25 per cent. No changes occurred in other methods of murder and suicide, nor did adjacent areas outside the reach of this law experience any such declines (Loftin et al., 1991).

Researchers have also examined risks of violence in homes with and without guns. This is controversial research, because such homes may differ in many ways. One study sponsored by the Centers for Disease Control compared gun owners and non-owners of the same gender, race, age and neighbourhood. The ironic and tragic result was that those who kept a gun in the home (often for protection) were 2.7 times as likely to be murdered – nearly always by a family member or a close acquaintance (Kellermann et al., 1993; Kellermann, 1997). Another study found that the risk of suicide in homes with guns was five times as high as in homes without them (Taubes, 1992). A newer national study found a slightly weaker, but still significant, link between guns and homicide or suicide. Compared with others of the same gender, age and race, people with guns at home were 41 per cent as likely to be homicide victims and 3.4 times as likely to die of suicide (Wiebe, 2003).

However, once again we need to be careful about correlation not necessarily meaning causation. In his 2002 film documentary *Bowling for Columbine*, Michael Moore concluded that there is no direct cause between gun ownership and gun violence. Comparing the number of gun-related deaths and gun-ownership in Canada and the USA, he noted that of Canada's 7 million gun-owners there are very few gun-related deaths, compared to the USA. Moore suggests that what is responsible is a 'fear culture' created by the government, media and gun-making companies, which not only leads

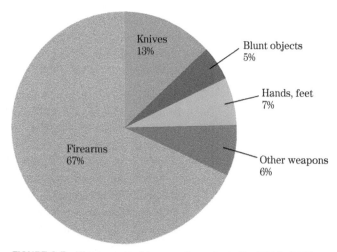

**FIGURE 8.5** Weapons used to commit murder in the USA in 2002
SOURCE: FBI Uniform Crime Reports.

Americans to arm themselves, but also makes them trigger-happy. So the cues in the environment may not simply be the presence of the gun but can extend to the social context in which we live.

Guns can not only serve as aggression cues but also put psychological distance between aggressor and victim. As Milgram's obedience studies taught us, remoteness from the victim facilitates cruelty. A knife can kill someone, but a knife attack requires a great deal more personal contact than pulling a trigger from a distance (Figure 8.5).

## MEDIA INFLUENCES: PORNOGRAPHY AND SEXUAL VIOLENCE

As we've already seen, Bandura makes the claim that the mass media is an influential model for aggressive behaviour. Berkowitz's study, and the work of Schachter, illustrates how we may take cues from the environment in interpreting states of arousal, and express our behaviour in a way that seems appropriate.

Sadly, aggression in the form of violent crime seems to be on the rise. As the numbers of arrests for violent crime have increased across Europe and the USA since the 1960s, we may attribute some of this to better techniques of detection, but we might also wonder what has prompted such increases in aggressive behaviour. What social forces caused the mushrooming violence? Might the answer partially lie in the media's increasing modelling of unrestrained sexuality and violence, such that these acts become acceptable, and the individual becomes desensitized to their effects?

Increased rates of criminal violence, including sexual coercion, coincided with the increased availability of violent and sexual material in the media that started during the 'sexual revolution' of the 1960s. Is the historical correlation a coincidence? To find out, researchers have explored the social consequences of pornography (which *Webster's* defines as erotic depictions intended to excite sexual arousal) and the effects of modelling violence in movies and on television.

In many countries pornography has become a big business thanks to the billions a year spent on the industry's cable and satellite networks, on its theatres and pay-per-view movies, on in-room hotel movies, phone sex and sex magazines, and on for-profit websites (National Research Council, 2002; Rich, 2001; Schlosser, 2003). Gender differences in the reported use of Internet sex sites have been widely suggested. In a survey of 1845 Chinese college students, Yan Hong, Li Xiaoming, Mao Rong and Bonita Stanton (2007) found that 10 per cent of men claimed to have visited sex websites, while less than 1 per cent of women did so.

Social psychological research on pornography has focused mostly on depictions of sexual violence. A typical sexually violent episode finds a man forcing himself upon a woman. She at first resists and tries to fight off her attacker. Gradually she becomes sexually aroused, and her resistance melts. By the end she is in ecstasy, pleading for more. We have all viewed or read non-pornographic versions of this sequence: she resists, he persists. Dashing man grabs and forcibly kisses protesting woman. Within moments, the arms that were pushing him away are clutching him tight, her resistance overwhelmed by her unleashed passion. In *Gone with the Wind*, Scarlett O'Hara is carried to bed protesting and kicking, and wakes up singing.

Social psychologists report that viewing such fictional scenes of a man overpowering and arousing a woman can distort one's perceptions of how women actually respond to sexual coercion and increase men's aggression against women, at least in laboratory settings.

### Distorted Perceptions of Sexual Reality

Does viewing sexual violence reinforce the 'rape myth' – that some women would welcome sexual assault – that 'no doesn't really mean no'? To find out, Neil Malamuth and James Check (1981) showed University of Manitoba men either two non-sexual movies or two movies depicting a man sexually overcoming a woman. A week later, when surveyed by a different experimenter, those who saw the films with mild sexual violence were more accepting of violence against women.

Other studies confirm that exposure to pornography increases acceptance of the rape myth (Oddone-Paolucci et al., 2000). For example, while spending three evenings watching sexually violent movies, male viewers in an experiment by Charles Mullin and Daniel Linz (1995) also became progressively less bothered by the raping and slashing. Compared with others not exposed to the films, three days later they expressed less sympathy for domestic violence victims, and they rated the victims' injuries as less severe. In fact, said researchers Edward Donnerstein, Daniel Linz and Steven Penrod (1987), what better way for an evil character to get people to react calmly to the torture and mutilation of women than to show a gradually escalating series of such films?

Note that the sexual message (that many women enjoy being 'taken') was subtle and unlikely to elicit counter-arguing. Given frequent media images of women's resistance melting in the arms of a forceful man, we shouldn't be surprised that even women often believe that some *other* women might enjoy being sexually overpowered – though virtually none think it of themselves (Malamuth et al., 1980).

'Pornography that portrays sexual aggression as pleasurable for the victim increases the acceptance of the use of coercion in sexual relations.'
>  Social science consensus at Surgeon General's Workshop on Pornography and Public Health (Koop, 1987)

You may recall our discussion from Chapter 2 about the ecological validity such experiments have. What do they tell us about the real world? The extent to which these can be translated into explanations of how and why sexual violence occurs remains a topic of debate within social psychology.

### Aggression against Women

Although limited to the sorts of short-term behaviours that can be studied in the laboratory, controlled experiments reveal what correlational studies cannot: cause and effect. A consensus statement by 21 leading social scientists summed up the results: 'Exposure to violent pornography increases punitive behaviour toward women' (Koop, 1987). One of those social scientists, Edward Donnerstein (1980), had shown 120 University of Wisconsin men a neutral, an erotic or an aggressive-erotic (rape) film. Then the men, supposedly as part of another experiment, 'taught' a male or female confederate some nonsense syllables by choosing how much shock to administer for incorrect answers. The men who had

Did Ted Bundy's (1989) comments on the eve of his execution for a series of rape-murders acknowledge pornography's toll or make it a handy excuse? 'The most damaging kinds of pornography [involve] sexual violence. Like an addiction, you keep craving something that is harder, harder, something which, which gives you a greater sense of excitement. Until you reach a point where the pornography only goes so far, you reach that jumping off point where you begin to wonder if maybe actually doing it would give you that which is beyond just reading it or looking at it.'

SOURCE: © Bettman/Corbis Images

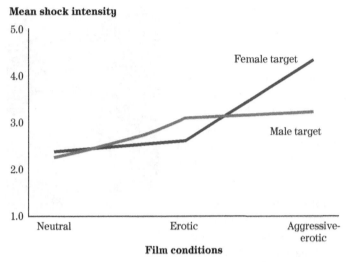

**Mean shock intensity**

5.0

4.0

3.0

2.0

1.0

Female target

Male target

Neutral       Erotic       Aggressive-
erotic

**Film conditions**

**FIGURE 8.6** After viewing an aggressive-erotic film, college men delivered stronger shocks than before, especially to a woman.

SOURCE: Data from Donnerstein, 1980.

watched the rape film administered markedly stronger shocks (Figure 8.6), especially when angered and with a female victim.

The ethical implications of such experiments are very serious considering the controversial and powerful experience they are giving participants. Only after giving their knowing consent do people participate, and they are free to withdraw from such studies at any time. Moreover, after the experiment, researchers effectively debunk any myths the films communicated (Check & Malamuth, 1984). Justification for this experimentation is not only scientific but also addresses real-world concerns:

☐ According to the Worldwide Sexual Assault Statistics, one in three women worldwide has experienced rape or sexual assault (2001; http://www.nsvrc.org/publications/fact.sheets/worldwide-sexual-assault-statistics).

☐ From a sample of 198 850 women in North America, 40 per cent reported having been raped (2003).

☐ In a random study of 1200 young girls in Geneva, Switzerland, 20 per cent revealed they had been the victim of some form of sexual assault (2002).

☐ Between 10 and 12 per cent of women in Peru, Samoa and Tanzania have suffered sexual violence by someone who is not their partner, by the time they reach 15 years of age.

☐ In Canada, 12 per cent of women, and in New Zealand and Australia up to 20 per cent of women, report some form of sexual assault from non-partners during their lifetime (World Health Organization, 2005).

☐ Surveys in industrialized countries offer similar results (Table 8.1). Three in four stranger rapes and nearly all acquaintance rapes went unreported to police. Thus, the official rape rate greatly underestimates the actual rape rate.

Repeated exposure to erotic films featuring quick, uncommitted sex also tends to:

☐ decrease attraction for one's partner

☐ increase acceptance of extramarital sex and of women's sexual submission to men

☐ increase men's perceiving women in sexual terms (see D. G. Myers, 2000).

### MEDIA INFLUENCES: TELEVISION

We have seen that watching an aggressive model attack a Bobo doll can unleash children's aggressive urges and teach them new ways to aggress. And we have seen that, after viewing movies depicting sexual violence, many angry men will

**TABLE 8.1**  Percentage of women in five countries reporting rape experiences

| Country | Sample of women | Completed and attempted rape |
|---|---|---|
| Canada | Student sample at 95 colleges and universities | 23% rape or sexual assault |
| Germany | Berlin late adolescents | 17% criminal sexual violence |
| New Zealand | Sample of psychology students | 25% |
| United Kingdom | Student sample at 22 universities | 19% |
| United States | Representative sample at 32 colleges and universities | 28% |
| Seoul, Korea | Adult women | 22% |

SOURCE: Studies reported by Koss et al. (1994) and Krahé (1998).

act more violently towards women. Does everyday television viewing have any similar effects?

Although very recent data are scarce (funding for media monitoring waned after the early 1990s), these facts about television watching remain: today, in much of the industrialized world, nearly all households (99.2 per cent in Australia, for example) have a television set, more than have telephones (Trewin, 2001). Most homes have more than one set, which helps explain why parents' reports of what their children watch correlate minimally with children's reports of what they watch (Donnerstein, 1998). With MTV in 140 countries and CNN spanning the globe, television is creating a global culture (Gundersen, 2001).

Women watch more television than men, pre-schoolers and retired people more than those in school or working, and the less educated more than the highly educated (Comstock & Scharrer, 1999). For the most part, these facts characterize the viewing habits of Americans, Europeans, Australians and Japanese (Murray & Kippax, 1979).

During all those hours, what social behaviours are modelled? From 1994 to 1997, bleary-eyed employees of the National Television Violence Study (1997) analysed some 10 000 programmes from the major networks and cable channels. They found 6 in 10 programmes contained violence ('physically compelling action that threatens to hurt or kill, or actual hurting or killing'). During fistfights, people who went down usually shook it off and came back stronger – unlike most real fistfights that last one punch (often resulting in a broken jaw or hand). In 73 per cent of violent scenes, the aggressors went unpunished. In 58 per cent, the victim was not shown to experience pain. In children's programmes, only 5 per cent of violence was shown to have any long-term consequences; two-thirds depicted violence as funny. By the end of elementary school, the average child has witnessed some 8000 television murders and 100 000 other violent acts (Huston et al., 1992). Reflecting on his 22 years of cruelty-counting, media researcher George Gerbner (1994) lamented: 'Humankind has had more bloodthirsty eras but none as filled with *images* of violence as the present. We are awash in a tide of violent representations the world has never seen ... drenching every home with graphic scenes of expertly choreographed brutality.' Sally Black and Alice Hausman's (2008) study of gun-carrying behaviour among adolescents from high-violence communities, points to the role the media plays in displays of 'flossing'. Flossing describes copying gunplay as seen in the media which can involve shooting the gun into the air. The authors note how this often results in self-inflicted injuries. They suggest that this behaviour isn't just showing off, but also serves as a release of aggressive excitement.

Does prime-time crime stimulate the behaviour it depicts? Or, as viewers vicariously participate in aggressive acts, do the shows drain off aggressive energy? The latter idea, a variation on the catharsis hypothesis, maintains that watching violent drama enables people to release their pent-up hostilities. For example, Seymour Feshbach and Robert Singer (1971) in their study of 9- to 15-year-old boys from underprivileged backgrounds and boarding schools, found that those who observed a diet of aggressive television displayed fewer acts of hostility (e.g. arguments and fights) than those who had watched non-aggressive programmes such as comedy shows. Defenders of the media cite this theory frequently and remind us that violence pre-dates television.

> 'One of television's great contributions is that it brought murder back into the home where it belongs. Seeing a murder on television can be good therapy. It can help work off one's antagonisms.'
>
> Alfred Hitchcock

### Television's Effects on Behaviour
#### Correlating Television Viewing and Behaviour

Researchers often use correlational and experimental studies to examine the effects of viewing violence. One technique, commonly used with schoolchildren, correlates their television watching with their aggressiveness. The frequent result: the more violent the content of the child's television viewing, the more aggressive the child (Eron, 1987; Turner et al., 1986). The relationship is modest but consistently found in North America, Europe and Australia. The finding also extends to 'indirect aggression', which has recently attracted psychological attention. This includes behaviour such as gossiping, manipulating others, spreading malicious gossip, and social exclusion. Sarah Coyne and John Archer (2004) found that in a content-analytic study of over 200 hours of television programmes watched by British adolescents, 92 per cent of these programmes contained indirect aggression. Moreover, the indirect aggressor was most likely to be an attractive female who was rewarded in some way for her actions. They discovered that, of 347 British female teenagers studied, those who engaged in indirect aggression were more likely to watch television that contained indirect aggressive acts than their non-aggressive counterparts.

However, because these are often correlational studies, the cause–effect relation could also work in the opposite direction. Maybe aggressive children prefer aggressive programmes. Or maybe some underlying third factor, such as lower intelligence, predisposes some children to prefer both aggressive programmes and aggressive behaviour.

Researchers have developed two ways to test these alternative explanations. They test the 'hidden third factor' explanation by statistically pulling out the influence of some of these possible factors. For example, William Belson (1978; Muson, 1978) studied 1565 London boys. Compared with those who watched little violence, those who watched a great deal (especially realistic rather than

*catharsis emotional cleansing. In psychodynamic theory this is the process of expressing repressed emotions, so these no longer cause neurotic problems*

cartoon violence) admitted to 50 per cent more violent acts during the preceding six months (for example, vandalizing a public telephone). Belson also examined 22 likely third factors, such as family size. The 'heavy violence' and 'light violence' viewers still differed after the researchers equated them with respect to potential third factors. So Belson surmised that the heavy viewers were indeed more violent *because* of their television exposure.

Similarly, Leonard Eron and Rowell Huesmann (1980, 1985) found that violence viewing among 875 children aged 8 correlated with aggressiveness even after statistically pulling out several obvious possible third factors. Moreover, when they re-studied those individuals as 19 year olds, they discovered that viewing violence at age 8 modestly predicted aggressiveness at age 19, but that aggressiveness at age 8 did *not* predict viewing violence at age 19. Aggression followed viewing, not the reverse. Moreover, by age 30, those who had watched the most violence in childhood were more likely than others to have been convicted of a crime (Figure 8.7).

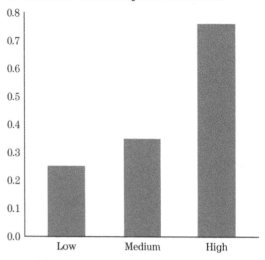

**Mean number of criminal justice convictions**

**Frequency of television viewing at age 8**

**FIGURE 8.7** Children's television viewing and later criminal activity
Violence viewing at age 8 was a predictor of a serious criminal offence by age 30.
SOURCE: Data from Eron & Huesmann, 1984.

Follow-up studies have confirmed these findings in various ways, including:

☐ correlating 8 year olds' violence viewing with their later likelihood of adult spouse abuse (Huesmann et al., 1984, 2003)

☐ correlating adolescents' violence viewing with their later likelihood of assault, robbery and threats of injury (Johnson et al., 2002)

☐ correlating elementary schoolchildren's violent media exposure with how often they got into fights when re-studied two to six months later (Gentile et al., 2004).

In all these studies, the investigators were careful to adjust for likely 'third factors' such as pre-existing lower intelligence or hostility.

Also it seems to be the case that where television goes, increased violence follows. Even murder rates increase when and where television comes. In Canada and the USA, the homicide rate doubled between 1957 and 1974 as violent television spread. In census regions where television came later, the homicide rate jumped later, too. And in a closely studied rural Canadian town where television came late, playground aggression doubled soon after (Williams, 1986).

Notice that these studies illustrate how researchers are now using correlational findings to *suggest* cause and effect. Yet an infinite number of possible third factors could be creating a merely coincidental relation between viewing violence and aggression.

*Television Viewing Experiments*

The Bobo doll experiments by Albert Bandura and Richard Walters (1963) sometimes had young children view the adult pounding the inflated doll on film instead of observing it live – with much the same effect. Then Leonard Berkowitz and Russell Geen (1966) found that angered college students who viewed a violent film acted more aggressively than did similarly angered students who viewed non-aggressive films. These laboratory experiments, coupled with growing public concern, seemed to confirm that viewing violence amplifies aggression (C. A. Anderson et al., 2003).

For example, research teams led by Ross Parke (1977) in the USA and Jacques Leyens (1975) in Belgium showed institutionalized American and Belgian delinquent boys a series of either aggressive or non-aggressive commercial films. Their consistent finding: 'Exposure to movie violence ... led to an increase in viewer aggression.' Compared with the week preceding the film series, physical attacks increased sharply in cottages where boys were viewing violent films. Dolf Zillmann and James Weaver (1999) similarly exposed men and women, on four consecutive days, to violent or non-violent feature films. When participating in a different project on the fifth day, those exposed to the violent films were more hostile to the research assistant. Likewise, Jennifer Linder and Douglas Gentile (2009) found that teachers reported higher levels of aggression in students who had watched televised physical and verbal aggression than those who had not. Furthermore, they found that the television industry's age-based rating system for the coding of material was not a valid reflection of its aggressive content.

The aggression provoked in these experiments is not assault and battery; it's more on the scale of a shove in the lunch queue, a cruel comment, a threatening gesture. Nevertheless, the convergence of evidence is striking. 'The irrefutable conclusion,' said a 1993 American Psychological Association youth violence commission, is 'that viewing violence increases violence'. This is especially so among people with aggressive tendencies, and when an attractive person commits justified, realistic violence that goes unpunished and that shows no pain or harm (Bushman, 1995; Donnerstein, 1998).

All in all, conclude researchers Brad Bushman and Craig Anderson (2001), violence viewing's effect on aggression surpasses the effect of passive smoking on lung cancer, calcium intake on bone mass, and homework on academic achievement. As with smoking and cancer, not everyone shows the effect – other factors matter as well. Media executives have discounted the evidence. But the evidence is now 'overwhelming', say Bushman and Anderson: 'Exposure to media violence causes significant increases in aggression.' The research base is large, the methods diverse and the overall findings consistent, echoes a National Institute of Mental Health task force of leading media violence researchers (C. A. Anderson et al., 2003): 'Our in-depth review ... reveals unequivocal evidence that exposure to media violence can increase the likelihood of aggressive and violent behaviour in both immediate and long-term contexts.'

### *Why Does Television Viewing Affect Behaviour?*

Given the convergence of correlational and experimental evidence, researchers have explored *why* viewing violence has this effect. Consider three possibilities (Geen & Thomas, 1986). One is that it is not the violent content that causes social violence but the *arousal* it produces (Mueller et al., 1983; Zillmann, 1989a). As we noted earlier, arousal tends to spill over: one type of arousal energizes other behaviours.

Other research shows that viewing violence *disinhibits*. In Bandura's experiment, the adult's punching of the Bobo doll seemed to make those outbursts legitimate and to lower the children's inhibitions. Viewing violence primes the viewer for aggressive behaviour by activating violence-related thoughts (Berkowitz, 1984; Bushman & Geen, 1990; Josephson, 1987). Listening to music with sexually violent lyrics seems to have a similar effect (Barongan & Hall, 1995; Johnson et al., 1995; Pritchard, 1998).

Media portrayals also evoke *imitation*. The children in Bandura's experiments re-enacted the specific behaviours they had witnessed. The commercial television industry is hard-pressed to dispute that television leads viewers to imitate what they have seen: its advertisers model consumption. Are media executives right, however, to argue that television merely holds a mirror to a violent society? Actually, on television programmes, acts of assault have outnumbered affectionate acts four to one. In other ways as well, television models an unreal world.

But there is good news here, too. If the ways of relating and problem solving modelled on television do trigger imitation, especially among young viewers, then television modelling of prosocial behaviour should be socially beneficial.

**prosocial behaviour**
*positive, constructive, helpful social behaviour; the opposite of antisocial behaviour*

### Television's Effects on Thinking

We have focused on television's effect on behaviour, but researchers have also examined the cognitive effects of viewing violence: does prolonged viewing desensitize us to cruelty? Does it give us mental scripts for how to act? Does it distort our perceptions of reality? Does it prime aggressive thoughts?

#### *Desensitization*

Repeat an emotion-arousing stimulus, such as an obscene word, over and over and the emotional response will 'extinguish'. After witnessing thousands of acts of cruelty, there is good reason to expect a similar emotional numbing. Victor Cline and his colleagues (1973) observed when they measured the physiological arousal of 121 Utah boys who watched a brutal boxing match. Compared with boys who watched little television, the responses of those who watched habitually were more a shrug than a concern.

Of course, these boys might differ in ways other than television viewing. But in experiments on the effects of viewing sexual violence, similar desensitization – a sort of psychic numbness – occurs among young men who view 'slasher' films. Moreover, experiments by Ronald Drabman and Margaret Thomas (1974, 1975, 1976) confirmed that such viewing breeds a more blasé reaction when later viewing a brawl or observing two children fighting. In one survey of 5456 middle-school students, exposure to movies with brutality was widespread (Sargent et al., 2002). Two-thirds had seen *Scream*. Such viewing patterns help explain why, despite the portrayals of extreme violence (or, should we say, *because* of it), Gallup youth surveys show that the percentage of 13 to 17 year olds feeling there was too much movie violence has declined, from 42 per cent in 1977 to 27 per cent in 2003.

Today's teens 'appear to have become considerably more desensitized to graphic depictions of violence and sex than their parents were at their age', concludes Gallup researcher Josephine Mazzuca (2002).

### Social Scripts and Social Representations

social scripts *culturally provided mental instructions for how to act in various situations*

When we find ourselves in new situations, uncertain how to act, we rely on social scripts ('schemas'), or what Serge Moscovici termed 'social representations' (see Chapter 4) – which are culturally provided mental instructions for how to act. These are acquired through experience of the social world and in interactions with others. In the case of television viewing of so many action films, youngsters may acquire a script that is played when they face real-life conflicts. Challenged, they may 'act like a man' by intimidating or eliminating the threat. Likewise, after viewing multiple sexual innuendoes and acts in most prime-time television hours – mostly involving impulsive or short-term relationships – youths may acquire sexual scripts they later enact in real-life relationships (Kunkel et al., 2001; Sapolsky & Tabarlet, 1991). Thus, the more sexual content that adolescents view (even when controlling for other predictors of early sexual activity), the more likely they are to perceive their peers as sexually active, to develop sexually permissive attitudes, and to experience early intercourse (Escobar-Chaves et al., 2005; Martino et al., 2005).

### Altered Perceptions

Does television's fictional world also mould our conceptions of the real world? George Gerbner and his associates (1979; Gerbner, 1994) suspected that this is television's most potent effect. Their surveys of both adolescents and adults showed that heavy viewers (four hours a day or more) are more likely than light viewers (two hours or fewer) to exaggerate the frequency of violence in the world around them and to fear being personally assaulted. Similar feelings of vulnerability have been expressed by South African women after viewing violence against women (Reid & Finchilescu, 1995). For those who watch much television, the world becomes a scary place.

### Cognitive Priming

Some evidence also reveals that watching violent videos primes networks of aggressive-related ideas (Bushman, 1998). After viewing violence, people offer more hostile explanations for others' behaviour (was the shove intentional?). They interpret spoken homonyms with the more aggressive meaning (interpreting 'punch' as a hit rather than a drink). And they recognize aggressive words more quickly.

Perhaps television's biggest effect relates not to its quality but to its quantity. Compared with more active recreation, television watching sucks people's energy and dampens their mood (Kubey & Csikszentmihalyi, 2002). Moreover, television annually replaces in people's lives a thousand or more hours of other activities. If, like most others, you have spent a thousand-plus hours per year watching television, think how you might have used that time if there were no television. What difference would that have made in who you are today? In seeking to explain the post-1960 decline in civic activities and organizational memberships, Robert Putnam (2000) reported that every added hour a day spent watching television competes with civic participation. Television steals time from club meetings, volunteering, congregational activities and political engagement.

## MEDIA INFLUENCES: VIDEO GAMES

Researchers have shifted their attention to video games, which have exploded in popularity and are exploding with increasing brutality. In 2007 the video-game industry celebrated its thirty-fifth birthday. Since the first video game in 1972, we have moved from electronic ping-pong to splatter games (Anderson, 2004; Gentile & Anderson, 2003). Today's mass-murder simulators are not obscure games.

As Lillian Bensley and Juliet van Eenwyk (2001) have observed, society's attitudes on the impact video games have on individuals is mixed. It perhaps shouldn't surprise us then that social psychology's view of their potential harm or educational benefits is also mixed. While many argue the kind of aggression displayed in playing video games is fundamentally different to that shown in real life (as no one gets hurt in gamespace), others argue they can foster violent thoughts, feelings and actions (e.g. Sherry, 2001).

However, educational research shows that there are many benefits from video games. Gentile and Anderson (2003) argue that 'video games are excellent teaching tools', but 'If health video games can successfully teach health behaviours, and flight simulator video games can teach people how to fly, then what should we expect violent murder-simulating games to teach?'

### The Games Children Play

In one survey of fourth-graders in the USA, 59 per cent of girls and 73 per cent of boys reported their favourite games as violent ones (Anderson, 2003, 2004). Games rated '18' are supposedly intended for sale only to those 18 and older but often are marketed to those younger.

'We had an internal rule that we wouldn't allow violence against people.'
   Nolan Bushnell, Atari founder

In the popular *Grand Theft Auto: San Andreas*, youth are invited to play a psychopath, notes Gentile (2004). 'You can run down pedestrians with the car, you can do car-jackings, you can do drive-by shootings, you can run down to the red-light district, pick up a prostitute, have sex with her in your car, and then kill her to get your money back.' In effective three-dimensional graphics, you can knock people over, stomp on them until they cough up blood, and watch them die. And as research by Susan Persky and James Blascovich (2005) demonstrates, virtual-reality games promise even more realism, engagement and impact.

### Effects of the Games Children Play

'There is absolutely no evidence, none, that playing a violent game leads to aggressive behaviour', contended Doug Lowenstein (2000), president of the Interactive Digital Software Association. Gentile and Anderson (2003) nevertheless offer some reasons why violent game playing *might* have a more toxic effect than watching violent television. With game playing, players:

☐ identify with, and play the role of, a violent character

☐ actively rehearse violence, not just passively watch it

☐ engage in the whole sequence of enacting violence – selecting victims, acquiring weapons and ammunition, stalking the victim, aiming the weapon, pulling the trigger

☐ are engaged with continual violence and threats of attack

☐ repeat violent behaviours over and over

☐ are rewarded for effective aggression.

For such reasons, military organizations often prepare soldiers to fire in combat (which many in the Second World War reportedly were hesitant to do) by engaging them with attack-simulation games. Craig Anderson (2003, 2004; Anderson et al., 2004) offers statistical digests of three dozen available studies that reveal five consistent effects. Playing violent video games, more than playing non-violent games:

1 *increases arousal.* Heart rate and blood pressure rise.

2 *increases aggressive thinking.* For example, Brad Bushman and Anderson (2002) found that after playing games such as *Duke Nukem* and *Mortal Kombat*, university students became more likely to guess that a man whose car was just rear-ended would respond aggressively, by using abusive language, kicking out a window or starting a fight.

3 *increases aggressive feelings.* Frustration levels rise, as does expressed hostility.

4 *increases aggressive behaviours.* After violent game play, children and youth play more aggressively with their peers, get into more arguments with their teachers, and participate in more fights. The effect occurs inside and outside the laboratory, across self-reports, teacher reports and parent reports, and for reasons illustrated in Figure 8.8. Is this merely because naturally hostile kids are drawn to such games? No, even when controlling for personality and temperament, exposure to video-game violence desensitizes people to cruelty and increases aggressive behaviour (Fraser et al., 2012). Moreover, observed Douglas Gentile and his co-researchers (2004) from a study of young adolescents, even among those who scored low in hostility, the percentage of heavy violent gamers who got into fights was ten times the 4 per cent involved in fights among their non-gaming counterparts. And after they start playing the violent games, previously non-hostile kids become more likely to have

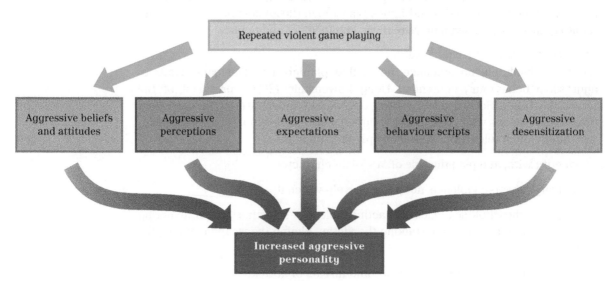

**FIGURE 8.8** Violent video-game influences on aggressive tendencies

SOURCE: Adapted from Bushman & Anderson, 2001.

fights. Playing violent video-games has a negative impact on our ability to empathize with others, and this lack of empathy may be responsible for behaviours such as cyber-bullying (Ang and Goh, 2010) and vandalism (Carrasco et al., 2006).

5 *decreases prosocial behaviours*. After violent video-game playing, people become slower to help a person whimpering in the hallway outside and slower to offer help to peers. On a later monetary decision-making task, they become more likely to exploit rather than to trust and co-operate with a partner (Sheese & Graziano, 2005). They also, as revealed by decreased brain activity associated with emotion, become desensitized to violence (Bartholow et al., 2006).

Does playing violent video games lead to aggressive behaviour?

SOURCE: © R-J-Seymour/iStock

Moreover, the more violent the games played, the bigger the effects. Video games *have* become more violent, which helps explain why newer studies find the biggest effects. Although much remains to be learned, these studies indicate that, contrary to the catharsis hypothesis, practising violence breeds rather than releases violence.

Anderson (2003, 2004) therefore encourages parents to discover what their kids are ingesting and to ensure that their media diet, at least in their own home, is healthy. Parents may not be able to control what their child watches, plays and eats in someone else's home. Nor can they control the media's effect on their children's peer culture. But parents can oversee consumption in their own home and provide increased time for alternative activities. Networking with other parents can build a child-friendly neighbourhood. And schools can help by providing media awareness education.

However, we may need to question whether what's being observed reflects real aggression or 'play' aggression. In their study of aggressive play and aggressive behaviour Joel Cooper and Diane Mackie (1986), concluded that violent video games affect the former and not the latter. Mark Griffiths (1997) found that while partaking in violent video games increases aggression in young children, it had no effect on teenagers. The discrepancy in these figures may reflect either that video games do not have the same effect on older children as they do on younger children, or that what is being defined as evidence of aggressive behaviour is present only in the younger sample. Interestingly, recent research suggests that violent video games do have an effect on older children and adults, but on lowering prosocial behaviour rather than directly heightening aggression. In their study of 780 young adults (mean age 19.60 years), Ashley Fraser and his colleagues (2012) found that playing violent video games lowers empathy levels which results in decreased prosocial behaviour towards strangers. So although displays of aggression may be absent from studies with older children and adults, what is more apparent are reductions in helping behaviour.

> Observation of aggression can heighten aggression; the same can be said for helping with prosocial models promoting altruism. See Chapter 10 for further discussion of prosocial behaviour, specifically helping.

## GENDER AND AGGRESSION

The research on bullying alerts us to something of a stereotype within common sense and social psychological understandings of aggression: that men are more aggressive than women. On the face of it, this might seem to be a sensible assumption as official crime statistics repeatedly show that men are much more likely to appear as perpetrators of aggressive crimes. Academic work notes gender differences across cultures and situations. For example, Eleanor Maccoby and Carol Jacklin (1974) report a gender difference in the display of aggression from 2 years of age.

Within social psychology, it's often assumed that women are not as aggressive as men for socio-biological reasons. First, there is the argument that claims men are more aggressive than women due to the presence of higher testosterone levels. We noted earlier in this chapter the link between hormones and violent behaviour in human beings, and men in particular. The second argument is evolutionary, documenting that women nurture their young. Conversely it is the role of men to protect women and their children from threats, which may mean using aggression to do so. Reinforcing these socio-biological arguments are processes of socialization into specific gender roles, such that while young boys might be rewarded for behaving aggressively, young girls may be punished.

However, there have been some studies that have examined the onset of physical aggression in girls. In a 15-year longitudinal study of 6- to 12-year-old girls, Nathalie Fontaine and colleagues (2008) found that those with high levels of hyperactivity and high physical aggression were also more likely to report nicotine addiction, low educational attainment, physical aggression in intimate relationships, and early pregnancy. Fontaine concludes that targeted intensive prevention programmes would be useful in tackling these problems.

Jacquelyn White and Robin Kowalski (1994) make the point that aggressive women tend to be seen as social deviants and even mentally ill. Media attention on 'ladettes' has pointed to this stigmatization of women who do not present normative gender-role behaviour. Reidy et al. (2009) found that hyper-masculine men were more likely to be aggressive towards women who violated feminine gender-role behaviour.

White and Kowalski consider crime statistics that report a difference in men and women as perpetrators of aggressive crimes. They note a number of factors that might account for this, including the following.

☐ Willingness of a victim to report a crime. Men who are subject to domestic violence from their female partners may be less willing to report the crime for fear of being stigmatized.

☐ The act must be regarded as being 'serious' for it to be reported. This may be less likely where women are the perpetrators.

☐ Women may be treated much more leniently by the criminal justice system than men, and as such may not show up in the official crime statistics.

In a culture where the norm, or the stereotype, is of the 'unaggressive woman', recognizing aggressive behaviour may prove tricky. As men are predominantly used in social psychology studies of aggression, White and Kowalski argue that the definition and understanding of 'what' aggression is, comes from a male perspective. They suggest that if researchers examine female aggression in situations that are congruent with their gender role, such as family settings, and extend the definition of aggression to include non-physical acts as well as just physical ones, then the evidence points to women being as, if not more, aggressive than men under such circumstances.

As well as the difficulties in defining aggression, we also have the problem of collecting evidence. If we rely on a method of collecting self-reports, which many of these studies do, then what we might be seeing are differences between men and women in terms of what *they* define as aggression rather than accurate reflections of its occurrence. In Penny Tinkler and Carolyn Jackson's (2007) study of 'ladettes' in the media, they consider how aggression is defined in particular ways to stigmatize young women. This is interesting when you consider Steven Muncer and his colleagues' (2001) report that, for the young women themselves, there is no correlation between holding laddish attitudes and engaging in aggressive behaviour.

The point? There is no simple explanation or definition of aggression. Nor is there any simple way of collecting evidence of it. As we've seen throughout this chapter, there is a tendency to study examples of aggression which can be easily identified and measured in some way. This can mean an over-reliance on evidence of physical violence to represent aggression. We noted at the start of this chapter that aggression comes in many guises, but this complexity is arguably not reflected in social psychological studies of the topic. Indeed, it might be the attempt to simplify the behaviour that is partly responsible for the generalization that women are not as aggressive as men. Is this true? In Chapter 14 we discuss the relationship between gender and behaviour in terms of biological influences and cultural socialization.

### Collective Identity

Behaviour is seldom random and is often organized around a shared sense of social identity which provides the group with norms about what is, and what is not, appropriate behaviour. Youths sharing antisocial tendencies and lacking close family bonds and expectations of academic success may find social identity in a gang (Staub, 1996). Members give themselves over to the group, often feeling a satisfying oneness with the others.

Social identity theory argues that crowds will be violent to the extent that violent actions are consistent with the group's identity. Where this does turn into acts of aggression they do not occur randomly but are aimed at very specific targets who represent a meaningful outgroup.

Hate crimes can occur when someone is attacked on the basis of being a member of a group. We have already seen in this chapter that individuals identified as members of a minority group, such as homosexuals, may be the victims of verbal and physical aggression. Often this is because these people represent deviance away from cultural norms and values. Prejudice towards the group they represent underlies these attacks. Rebecca Stotzer and Emily Hossellman (2012) consider how the increased presence of US students from ethnic and racial minority groups in higher education can lead to greater harmony between them, or aggravate tensions between them leading to heightened prevalence of hate crime on university campuses. On the one hand, increased contact between students of different racial and ethnic groups can lead to racial tolerance. We shall consider Gordon Allport's 'contact hypothesis' in Chapter 13, which suggests that when certain optimal conditions are in place (most notably equal status of

Membership of a gang can give individuals a sense of social identity which shapes its activities.

SOURCE: © monkeybusinessimages/iStock

all groups), increasing contact between groups can lead to reduced prejudice. On the other, increased contact can intensify racial and ethnic tensions leading to the occurrence of hate crimes. Stotzer and Hossellman note that which way things go partly depends on the communication of values from the academic institution to its students, but also the values of the students themselves and how the white majority perceive the legitimacy of ethnic diversity in higher education.

In Chapters 4 and 13 we consider how behavioural expectations shape perception. There we have examples from the extensive research on football hooligans that has shown how the presence and perception of the police, opposing fans, and their actions, influences the levels of aggression displayed by the supporters (Drury et al., 2003; Reicher et al., 2004; Stott et al., 2001). Where opposing team supporters are perceived to be engaging in illegitimate acts of violence towards the ingroup, that group will respond by asserting its own identity in 'legitimate' violent ways towards the outgroup. We will discuss these ideas in more detail in Chapter 13 when we consider intergroup relations.

The twentieth-century massacres that claimed over 150 million lives were 'not the sums of individual actions', notes Robert Zajonc (2000). '*Genocide is not the plural of homicide.*' Massacres are *social* phenomena fed by 'moral imperatives' – a collective mentality (including images, rhetoric and ideology) that mobilizes a group or a culture for extraordinary actions. The massacres of Rwanda's Tutsis, of Europe's Jews and of America's native population were collective phenomena requiring widespread support, organization and participation. Before launching the genocidal initiative, Rwanda's Hutu government and business leaders bought and distributed 2 million machetes.

Experiments in Israel by Yoram Jaffe and Yoel Yinon (1983) confirm that groups can amplify aggressive tendencies. In one, university men angered by a supposed fellow participant retaliated with decisions to give much stronger shocks when in groups than when alone. In another experiment (Jaffe et al., 1981), people decided, either alone or in groups, how much punishing shock to give someone for incorrect answers on a task. As Figure 8.9 shows, individuals gave progressively more of the assumed shock as the experiment proceeded, and group decision making magnified this individual tendency. When circumstances provoke an individual's aggressive reaction, the addition of group interaction will often amplify it (see Research Close-Up: When Provoked, Are Groups More Aggressive than Individuals?).

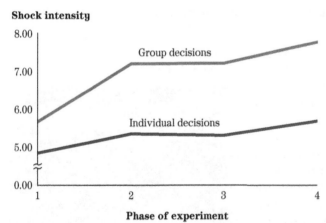

**Shock intensity**

**FIGURE 8.9** Group-enhanced aggression
When individuals chose how much shock to administer as punishment for wrong answers, they escalated the shock level as the experiment proceeded. Group decision making further polarized this tendency.

SOURCE: Data from Jaffe et al., 1981.

Aggression studies provide an apt opportunity to ask how well social psychology's laboratory findings generalize to everyday life. Do the circumstances that trigger someone to deliver electric shock or allocate hot sauce really tell us anything about the circumstances that trigger verbal abuse or a punch in the face? Craig Anderson and Brad Bushman (1997; Bushman & Anderson, 1998) note that social psychologists have studied aggression in both the laboratory and everyday worlds, and the findings are strikingly consistent. In *both* contexts, increased aggression is predicted by the following:

- [ ] male actors
- [ ] aggressive or Type A personalities
- [ ] alcohol use
- [ ] violence viewing
- [ ] anonymity
- [ ] provocation
- [ ] the presence of weapons
- [ ] group interaction.

The laboratory allows us to test and revise theories under controlled conditions. Real-world events inspire ideas and provide the venue for applying our theories. Aggression research illustrates how the interplay between studies in the controlled laboratory and the complex real world advances psychology's contribution to human welfare. Hunches gained from everyday experience inspire theories, which stimulate laboratory research, which then deepens our understanding and our ability to apply psychology to real problems.

## CAN AGGRESSION BE REDUCED?

We have examined instinct, frustration-aggression and social learning theories of aggression, and we have scrutinized biological and social influences on aggression. How, then, can we reduce aggression?

Theory and research suggest that aggression can be tackled at the level of the individual, the group and society. For example, we can try to implement measures to control alcohol abuse, improve relationships within families, educate people about the effects of war and genocide, and enable groups in society to learn about one another, thus promoting shared understanding. For example, the role of society in educating young people has been highlighted in Sally Black and Alice Hausman's study of gun-carrying behaviour among adolescents (2008). They suggest that, 'Primary prevention starts by producing meaningful roles and economic opportunities for youth in inner cities and providing culturally competent prevention education. Generally, adolescents need safe opportunities for independence and the resources to build identity' (p. 606). However all of these measures are complex to implement due to the multifaceted nature of aggression, but that is not to say we shouldn't try. There are some key factors that have been outlined in this chapter that are worth bearing in mind.

### CATHARSIS?

'Youngsters should be taught to vent their anger.' So advised Ann Landers (1969). If a person 'bottles up his rage, we have to find an outlet. We have to give him an opportunity of letting off steam'. So asserted the once prominent psychiatrist Fritz Perls (1973). 'Some expression of prejudice . . . lets off steam . . . it can siphon

## research close-up

WHEN PROVOKED, ARE GROUPS MORE AGGRESSIVE THAN INDIVIDUALS?

*Source: Meier, B. P., and Hinsz, V. B. (2004). A comparison of human aggression committed by groups and individuals: An interindividual-intergroup discontinuity.* Journal of Experimental Social Psychology, 40, 551–559.

### Introduction

At the time of writing their study Brian Meier and Verlin Hinsz point out that despite some classic examples, such as Sherif and Sherif's Robber's Cave Study (see Chapter 13), there is very little social psychological study into aggression that is carried out by groups. In our social world we are faced with lots of incidences of groups aggressing against others, yet we seem to have little study on why this occurs. The social psychological literature tells us that groups tend to be more competitive towards one another than individuals. A famous example is the Prisoners' Dilemma where if both parties are groups, they choose competition to obtain rewards rather than co-operation. Why? Chester Insko and his colleagues (2001) suggest that group situations provide people with anonymity and a diffusion of responsibility (see Chapters 11 and 13), which may explain their behaviour. This is known as the interindividual-intergroup discontinuity effect. So if a sense of competition is heightened in a group context, can we anticipate that people will behave more aggressively towards one another in these circumstances than they would do if they were in an individual context?

Aggression researchers are noted for their creative methods for measuring aggression, which in various experiments has involved such tactics as administering shock, blasting sound and hurting people's feelings. Holly McGregor and her colleagues (1998) took their cue from a cook's arrest for assault after lacing two police officers' food with tabasco sauce, and from child abuse cases in which parents have force-fed hot sauce to their children. This inspired the idea of measuring aggression by having people decide how much hot sauce someone else must consume.

That is what Gettysburg College psychologist Bruce Meier and North Dakota State University psychologist Verlin Hinsz (2004) did when comparing aggressive behaviour by groups and individuals.

### Method

The researchers told participants, either as individuals or in groups of three, that they were studying the relationship between personality and food preferences, and that they would be tasting and rating hot sauce. The experimenter explained that he needed the participants to choose the size of the portion given to the rest of the participants (either individuals or groups of three). After having the participants sample the intense hot sauce using a wooden stick, the experimenter left to collect the amount of hot sauce that the individuals or groups had selected. In reality he actually ignored the amount they had decided to give the other participants, and handed everyone a cup filled with 48 grams of the sauce, which each participant expected later to consume. Now was the chance for revenge! Once the second set of participants had been given the hot sauce, chosen for them by the first set of participants, to consume, they could now return the favour! This second set of participants were now to spoon as much or as little hot sauce as they wished into a cup for the supposed other people to consume. (In reality, no participant was forced to consume anything.)

**TABLE 8.2** Mean amount of hot sauce dished out (GRAMS)

| Source | Target | |
|---|---|---|
| | Individual | Group |
| **Individual** | 58.2 | 71.0 |
| **Group** | 71.1 | 92.9 |

SOURCE: Meier & Hinsz, 2004.

---

### Results

The striking result, seen in Table 8.2, was that groups retaliated by dishing out 24 per cent more hot sauce than individuals did. So groups were more aggressive than individuals in dishing out the hot stuff! Furthermore, they were dishing it out to other groups! In fact groups received 24 per cent more hot sauce than individuals. Thus, given toxic circumstances, interaction with a group (as a source or target) amplifies individual aggressive tendencies. This finding was particularly evident in the intergroup condition. Group members, after each receiving a nasty 48 grams of hot sauce, retaliated by dishing out 93 grams of hot sauce for each member of the group that had given them hot sauce. Apparently, surmised Meier and Hinsz, groups not only respond more aggressively to provocation but also perceive more hostility from other groups than they do from individuals.

### Discussion

What Meier and Hinsz's study had shown was that more hot sauce (the measure of aggression) was allocated in intergroup contexts than interindividual interactions. Groups allocate hot sauce to other groups. However, groups are also more likely to receive hot sauce from individuals, than other individuals are. So groups influence aggressive behaviour either when they are the cause of the aggression or on the receiving end.

Why? The researchers suggest that what may be going on is group polarization (see Chapter 11). Individuals' attitudes strengthen within a group context. If a dominant response of individuals within a group is towards aggression anyway this becomes intensified in a group situation. Chester Insko wonders if trust may also be an issue here. Groups are considered less trustworthy than individuals. So increased competition and feelings of aggression may become heightened in the context of people we distrust.

As entertaining as this study might appear, it has limitations as well as strengths. While it tells us something about the context in which aggression is more likely to occur, we may want to question the measure of aggression. Hot sauce. Is this the same as physical or verbal aggression which can have long-lasting consequences for all concerned? How generalizable are studies such as this to the real-world? Does it have ecological validity?

---

off conflict through words, rather than actions.' So argued Andrew Sullivan in a *New York Times Magazine* article on hate crimes (1999).

The concept of catharsis is usually credited to Western thinking, especially to Aristotle. Although Aristotle actually said nothing about aggression, he did argue that we can purge emotions by experiencing them, and that viewing the classic tragedies therefore enabled a catharsis (purging) of pity and fear. To have an emotion excited, he believed, is to have that emotion released (Butcher, 1951). The catharsis hypothesis has been extended to include the emotional release supposedly obtained not only by observing drama but also through our recalling and reliving past events, through our expressing emotions, and through our actions.

Assuming that aggressive action or fantasy drains pent-up aggression, some therapists and group leaders have encouraged people to ventilate suppressed aggression by acting it out – by whopping one another with foam bats or beating a bed with a tennis racket while screaming. If led to believe that catharsis effectively vents emotions, people will react more aggressively to an insult as a way to improve their mood (Bushman et al., 2001). Some psychologists, believing that catharsis is therapeutic, advise parents to encourage children's release of emotional tension through aggressive play.

Many laypeople have also bought the catharsis idea, as reflected in their nearly two-to-one agreement with the statement 'Sexual materials provide an outlet for bottled-up impulses' (Niemi et al., 1989). But then, other national surveys reveal that most Americans also agree, 'Sexual materials lead people to commit rape'. So is the catharsis approach valid or not?

Actually, notes researcher Brad Bushman (2002), 'Venting to reduce anger is like using gasoline to put out a fire'. Consider: if viewing erotica provides an outlet for sexual impulses, places with high consumption of sex magazines should have low rape rates. After viewing erotica people should experience diminished sexual desire and men should be less likely to view and treat women as sexual objects. But studies show the opposites are true (Kelley et al., 1989; McKenzie-Mohr & Zanna, 1990).

The near consensus among social psychologists is that – contrary to what Freud, Lorenz and their followers supposed – viewing or participating in violence fails to produce catharsis (Geen & Quanty, 1977). For example, Robert Arms and his associates report that Canadian and American spectators of football, wrestling and hockey games exhibit *more* hostility after viewing the event than before (Arms et al., 1979; Goldstein & Arms, 1971; Russell, 1983). Not even war seems to purge aggressive feelings. After a war, a nation's murder rate has tended to jump (Archer & Gartner, 1976).

In laboratory tests of catharsis, Brad Bushman (2002) invited angered participants to hit a punching bag while either ruminating about the person who angered them or thinking about becoming physically fit. A third group did not hit the punching bag. Then, when given a chance to administer loud blasts of noise to the person who angered them, people in the punching bag plus rumination condition felt angrier and were most aggressive. Moreover, doing nothing at all more effectively reduced aggression than did 'letting off steam' by hitting the bag.

In some real-life experiments, too, aggressing has led to heightened aggression. Ebbe Ebbesen and his co-researchers (1975) interviewed 100 engineers and technicians shortly after they were angered by layoff notices. Some were asked questions that gave them an opportunity to express hostility against their employer or supervisors – for example, 'What instances can you think of where the company has not been fair with you?' Afterwards, they answered a questionnaire assessing attitudes towards the company and the supervisors. Did the previous opportunity to 'vent' or 'drain off ' their hostility reduce it? On the contrary, their hostility increased. Expressing hostility bred more hostility.

'He who gives way to violent gestures will increase his rage.'
Charles Darwin, *The Expression of Emotion in Man and Animals*, 1872

Recall as we noted in analysing Stanley Milgram's obedience experiments (see Chapter 7), little aggressive acts can breed their own justification. People derogate their victims, rationalizing further aggression.

Retaliation may, in the short run, reduce tension and even provide pleasure (Ramirez et al., 2005). But in the long run it fuels more negative feelings. Should we therefore bottle up anger and aggressive urges? Silent sulking is hardly more effective, because it allows us to continue reciting our grievances as we conduct conversations in our head. Brad Bushman and his colleagues (2005a) experimented with the toxic effect of such rumination. After being provoked by an obnoxious experimenter with insults such as 'Can't you follow directions? Speak louder!' half were given a distraction (by being asked to write an essay about their campus landscape) and half were induced to ruminate (by writing an essay about their experiences as a research participant). Next, they were mildly insulted by a supposed fellow participant (actually a confederate), to whom they responded by prescribing a hot sauce dose this person would have to consume. The distracted participants, their anger now abated, prescribed only a mild dose, but the still-seething ruminators displaced their aggressive urge and prescribed twice as much.

Fortunately, there are non-aggressive ways to express our feelings and to inform others how their behaviour affects us. Across cultures, those who reframe accusatory 'you' messages as 'I' messages – 'I feel angry about what you said' or 'I get irritated when you leave dirty dishes' – communicate their feelings in a way that better enables the other person to make a positive response (Kubany et al., 1995). We can be assertive without being aggressive.

## A SOCIAL LEARNING APPROACH

If aggressive behaviour is learned, then there is hope for its control. Aversive experiences such as frustrated expectations and personal attacks predispose hostile aggression. So it is wise to refrain from planting false, unreachable expectations in people's minds. Anticipated rewards and costs influence instrumental aggression. This suggests that we should reward co-operative, non-aggressive behaviour.

In experiments, children become less aggressive when caregivers ignore their aggressive behaviour and reinforce their non-aggressive behaviour (Hamblin et al., 1969). Punishing the aggressor is less consistently effective. Threatened punishment deters aggression only under ideal conditions when the punishment is strong, prompt and sure; when it is combined with reward for the desired behaviour; and when the recipient is not angry (Baron, 1977).

Moreover, there are limits to punishment's effectiveness. Most homicide is impulsive, hot aggression – the result of an argument, an insult or an attack. If mortal aggression were cool and instrumental, we could hope that waiting until it happens and severely punishing the criminal afterwards would deter such acts. In that world, states that impose the death penalty might have a lower murder rate than states without the death penalty. But in our world of hot homicide, that is not so (Costanzo, 1998). Thus, we must *prevent* aggression before it happens. We must teach non-aggressive conflict-resolution strategies.

Physical punishment can also have negative side effects. Punishment is aversive stimulation; it models the behaviour it seeks to prevent. And it is coercive (recall that we seldom internalize actions coerced with strong external justifications). These are reasons why violent teenagers and child-abusing parents so often come from homes where discipline took the form of harsh physical punishment.

To foster a gentler world, we could model and reward sensitivity and co-operation from an early age, perhaps by training parents how to discipline without violence. Training programmes encourage parents to reinforce desirable behaviours and to frame statements positively ('When you finish cleaning your room, you can go play', rather than, 'If you don't clean your room, you're grounded'). One 'aggression-replacement programme' has reduced re-arrest rates of juvenile offenders and gang members by teaching the youths and their parents communication skills, training them to control anger, and raising their level of moral reasoning (Goldstein et al., 1998).

If observing aggressive models lowers inhibitions and elicits imitation, then we might also reduce brutal, dehumanizing portrayals in films and on television – steps comparable to those already taken to reduce racist and sexist portrayals. We can also inoculate children against the effects of media violence. Wondering if the television networks would ever 'face the facts and change their programming', Eron and Huesmann (1984) taught 170 Oak Park, Illinois, children that television portrays the world unrealistically, that aggression is less common and less effective than television suggests, and that aggressive behaviour is undesirable. (Drawing upon attitude research, Eron and Huesmann encouraged children to draw these inferences themselves and to attribute their expressed criticisms of television to their own convictions.) When re-studied two years later these children were less influenced by television violence than were untrained children. In a more recent study, Stanford University used 18 classroom lessons to persuade children to simply reduce their television watching and video-game playing (Robinson et al., 2001). They reduced their television viewing by a third – and the children's aggressive behaviour at school dropped 25 per cent compared with children in a control school.

Aggressive stimuli also trigger aggression. This suggests reducing the availability of weapons such as handguns. In 1974 Jamaica implemented a sweeping anti-crime programme that included strict gun control and censorship of gun scenes from television and movies (Diener & Crandall, 1979).

Suggestions such as these can help us minimize aggression, but we should be aware that this isn't as simple as flicking a magic wand. Given the complexity of aggression's causes and the difficulty of controlling them, who can feel the optimism expressed by Andrew Carnegie's forecast that in the twentieth century, 'To kill a man will be considered as disgusting as we in this day consider it disgusting to eat one.' Since Carnegie uttered those words in 1900, some 200 million human beings have been killed. It is a sad irony that although today we understand human aggression better than ever before, humanity's inhumanity endures. Nevertheless, cultures can change.

## focus on

### TEACHING THEM A LESSON: MOTIVATIONS FOR DRIVER AGGRESSION

Road rage is increasing in those countries where we rely heavily on vehicles to take us from A to B. Many of us have been subject at some point to actions such as someone honking their horn at us, sharply swerving in front of the car you're in, making obscene hand gestures, or driving far too close to the rear of the car. Statistics show that the majority of drivers in the UK, US and Australia have been on the receiving end of these behaviours. We're a little less willing to admit that we've been the person doing these behaviours to other motorists, however. But why does road rage happen? Are we stressed out? Are other drivers so bad that they deserve these actions? Do we enjoy the danger? Do we think we're invincible once we're behind the wheel of a car? Is it mostly young men who get road rage? All of these factors, and more besides, have been found to play a role in explaining road rage (Lennon & Watson, 2011). However, what is less clear is, do people who commit road rage intend on harming the recipient of their aggressive behaviour?

In their qualitative study of motorists, Alexia Lennon and Barry Watson found they explained their mildly aggressive acts (such as horn-honking and light-flashing) as points of information to let another driver know s/he was driving badly. The potential negative impact upon the other driver was denied or mitigated. So whilst these motorists recognized their behaviour as mildly aggressive, there was no intention to actually harm the other motorist. However, if the motorist perceived other drivers as intending on harming them then they regarded their subsequent actions towards them as 'justified retaliation'. Such people needed to be 'taught a lesson'. What Lennon and Watson found was that despite aggression being a socially undesirable behaviour, motorists were fairly open about admitting to it when they felt their actions had been deserved. However, many drivers downplayed the potential consequences of their actions leading to harm to the other driver. So whilst the aggression may be seen as justified, the intention to cause harm is denied.

So the distinction between intentional and unintentional aggression may not be quite so clear-cut. As we can see from this example, aggressors may admit their behaviour but deny the intent. Does this make the act any more palatable? Is it still aggression?

### QUESTIONS

1 Who should define what counts as aggressive behaviour? The social psychologist? The person who commits the act?

2 Should we treat unintentional aggression with the same seriousness as intentional aggression?

3 If you were to design a study into aggression, what behaviours would you focus on? How would you collect evidence of them and analyse them?

## SUMMING UP: AGGRESSION

### WHAT IS AGGRESSION?

☐ Aggression has been defined in various ways by social psychologists. Broadly speaking its definition can include direct and/or indirect physical and verbal acts. It can refer to intentional and/or unintentional behaviour.

☐ How we define aggression has implications for what we treat as evidence of it and the conclusions we reach about its presence in human society.

### SOME THEORIES OF AGGRESSION

We have considered three broad theories of aggression.

☐ The *instinct* view, most commonly associated with Sigmund Freud and Konrad Lorenz, contended that aggressive energy will accumulate from within, like water accumulating behind a dam. Although the available evidence offers little support for that view, aggression is biologically influenced by heredity, blood chemistry and the brain.

☐ According to the second view, *frustration* causes anger and hostility. Given aggressive cues in the environment may provoke aggression. Frustration stems not from deprivation itself but from the gap between expectations and achievements.

☐ The *social learning* view presents aggression as learned behaviour. By experience and by observing others' success, we sometimes learn that aggression pays. Social learning enables family, cultural and subcultural influences on aggression, as well as media influences (which we will discuss in the next section). In some cultures children are taught not to be aggressive since it is an immature reaction.

## SOME INFLUENCES ON AGGRESSION

☐ Many factors exert influence on aggression. One factor is aversive experiences, which include not only frustrations but also discomfort, pain and personal attacks, both physical and verbal.

☐ Arousal from almost any source, even physical exercise or sexual stimulation, can be transformed into anger.

☐ Aggression cues in the environment, such as the presence of a gun, increase the likelihood of aggressive behaviour.

☐ Viewing violence (1) breeds a modest increase in *aggressive behaviour*, especially in people who are provoked, and (2) *desensitizes* viewers to aggression and alters their *perceptions* of reality. These two findings parallel the results of research on the effects of viewing violent pornography, which can increase men's aggression against women and distort their perceptions of women's responses to sexual coercion.

☐ Television permeates the daily life of millions of people and portrays considerable violence. Correlational and experimental studies converge on the conclusion that heavy exposure to televised violence correlates with aggressive behaviour.

☐ Repeatedly playing violent video games may increase aggressive thinking, feelings and behaviour even more than television or movies do, as the experience involves much more active participation than those other media.

☐ A special kind of aggression is committed by groups. Circumstances that provoke individuals may also provoke groups. By diffusing responsibility and polarizing actions, group situations amplify aggressive reactions.

## CAN AGGRESSION BE REDUCED?

☐ How can we minimize aggression? Contrary to the catharsis hypothesis, expressing aggression by catharsis tends to breed further aggression, not reduce it.

☐ The social learning approach suggests controlling aggression by counteracting the factors that provoke it: by reducing aversive stimulation, by rewarding and modelling non-aggression, and by eliciting reactions incompatible with aggression.

---

## CRITICAL QUESTIONS

**1** How have social psychologists defined aggression?

**2** What implications does the definition of aggression have for research on its occurrence?

**3** What are some of the causes social psychologists have identified for aggression?

**4** Why does aggression occur?

**5** What can we do to reduce aggression?

## RECOMMENDED READINGS

Below are some recommended classic and contemporary readings within social psychology on aggression.

### Classic Books and Papers

Dollard, J., Doob, L., Miller, N., Mowrer, O. & Sears, R. (1939). *Frustration and Aggression*. New Haven, CT: Yale University Press.

*This book outlines John Dollard and his colleagues' frustration-aggression hypothesis.*

Berkowitz, L. (1989). Frustration-aggression hypothesis: Examination and reformulation. *Psychological Bulletin*, **106**(1), 59–73.

*A revision of John Dollard's frustration-aggression hypothesis that includes the conditions under which frustration leads to aggression.*

Bandura, A., Ross, D., & Ross, S.A. (1961). Transmission of aggression through imitation of aggressive models. *Journal of Abnormal and Social Psychology*, **63**, 575–582.

*Classic social learning demonstration which shows how children learn aggressive behaviour through observation.*

Zillmann, D., & Bryant, J. (1974). Effect of residual excitation on the emotional response to provocation and delayed aggressive behavior. *Journal of Personality and Social Psychology*, **30**(6), 782–791.

*Offers a good explanation and demonstration of Dolf Zillman's excitation-transfer model.*

### Contemporary Papers

Hayes, S.C., Rincover, A., & Volosin, D. (1980). Variables influencing the acquisition and maintenance of aggressive behavior: Modelling versus sensory reinforcement. *Journal of Abnormal Psychology*, **89**(2), 254–262.

*Discusses Bandura's social learning experiments (Bobo doll studies), and argues that there may be other facilitatory sensory factors involved in aggressive behaviour, which have been previously ignored.*

Workman, M. (2010). A behaviourist perspective on corporate harassment online: Validation of a theoretical model of psychological motives. *Computers & Security*, **29**, 831–839.

*A qualitative study that investigates how cultural norms shape aggressive and prejudiced behaviour, such as antigay violence.*

q

"Love cures people – both the ones who give it and the ones who receive it."

Psychiatrist Karl Meninger, 1893–1990

# ATTRACTION AND INTIMACY

© patty_c/iStock

Our lifelong dependence on one another puts relationships at the core of our existence. We cannot survive as individuals without relationships with others, and we cannot survive as a species without sexual intercourse with other human beings. Social relationships, to care and be cared for is essential to human life. Aristotle called humans 'a social animal'. Indeed, we have what today's social psychologists call a need to belong – to connect with others in close relationships.

**need to belong** *a motivation to bond with others in relationships that provide ongoing, positive interactions*

Interconnection, attachment and intimate relationships are, however, not only instruments for survival; they result in great pleasure and have important qualities in themselves, by making people feel happier, more able, and improving health and well-being.

Underlying our social relationships is a feeling of attraction and a need for intimacy. In this chapter we'll explore how social psychologists have theorized and researched not only how we form intimate relationships with other people, but the principles behind attraction.

Social psychologists Roy Baumeister and Mark Leary (1995) illustrate the power of social attractions bred by our necessity to belong and relate to others.

☐ For our ancestors, mutual attachments enabled group survival. When hunting game or erecting shelter, 10 hands were better than 2. Today we still experience the benefits of working together and sharing.

☐ For children and their caregivers, social attachments make life easier and more pleasant, and enhance survival. Unexplainably separated from each other, caregiver and toddler may both panic until reunited in a tight embrace.

☐ Feeling accepted and belonging to a primary group, such as a family, make us stronger, more safe and relaxed. This is especially true of Eastern cultures where the family ties are still very strong and parents and offspring prove a particular attraction, love and responsibility towards each other.

☐ For university students, relationships consume much of life. How much of your waking life is spent talking with people? One sampling of 10 000 tape recordings of half-minute slices of students' waking hours (using belt-worn recorders) found them talking to someone 28 per cent of the time – and that doesn't count the time they spent listening to someone (Mehl & Pennebaker, 2003).

☐ For people everywhere (no matter what their sexual orientation), actual and hoped-for close relationships can dominate thinking and emotions. Finding a supportive soul mate in who we can confide, we feel accepted and prized. Falling in love, we feel irrepressible joy. Even seemingly dismissive people relish being accepted (Carvallo & Gabriel, 2006).

☐ Exiled, imprisoned or in solitary confinement, people ache for their own people and places. Rejected, we are at risk of sadness and depression (Nolan et al., 2003). Time goes more slowly and life seems less meaningful (Twenge et al., 2003).

☐ For the jilted, the widowed and the sojourner in a strange place, the loss of social bonds triggers pain, loneliness or withdrawal. Losing a soul-mate relationship, adults feel jealous, distraught or bereaved, as well as more mindful of death and the fragility of life.

☐ Reminders of death in turn heighten our need to belong, to be with others and hold close those we love (Mikulincer et al., 2003; Wisman & Koole, 2003). The shocking death of a classmate, a co-worker or a family member brings people together, their differences no longer mattering.

We are, indeed, social animals. When we do belong – when we feel supported by close, intimate relationships – we tend to be healthier and happier.

## WHAT LEADS TO FRIENDSHIP AND ATTRACTION?

*What factors nurture liking and loving? Let's start with those that help initiate attraction: proximity, physical attractiveness, similarity and feeling liked.*

What predisposes one person to like, or to love, another? Few questions about human nature arouse greater interest. The ways affections flourish and fade form the stuff and fluff of soap operas, popular music, novels, and much of our everyday conversation.

So much has been written about liking and loving that almost every conceivable explanation – and its opposite – has already been proposed. For most people – and for you – what factors nurture liking and loving?

☐ Does absence make the heart grow fonder? Or is someone who is out of sight also out of mind?

☐ Is it likes that attract? Or opposites?

☐ How much do good looks matter?

☐ What has fostered your close relationships?

Let's start with those factors that help a friendship begin, and then consider those that sustain and deepen a relationship, thus satisfying our need to belong.

### WHERE DO YOU FIND YOUR PARTNER?

You have decided after long deliberation that the single life is not for you. You have concluded that you should look for a partner. You know the type of person you would like to meet. You know what kinds of activities you enjoy, the kind of people you like and what turns you on. Now comes the hard part: where can you find him or her?

Going to university not only helps you to get an interesting career after years of improving your knowledge, it also sets you in a circle of friends and acquaintances among whom may be your life partner. Or do you have to go somewhere else to meet the right one? What about evening classes, holiday locations, beaches, hotels, gyms, swimming, walking and climbing? Perhaps you'll meet him or her at the theatre, opera, at an art exhibition, a music festival, even a funeral or birthday celebration. You can meet someone who is right for you everywhere of course, and often accidentally, without even planning for it.

Close relationships with friends and family contribute to health and happiness.

SOURCE: © technotr/iStock

349

Though it may seem trivial to those pondering the mysterious origins of romantic love, sociologists long ago found that most people marry someone who lives in the same neighbourhood, or works at the same company or job, or sits in the same class, or visits the same favourite place (Bossard, 1932; Burr, 1973; Clarke, 1952; McPherson et al., 2001). Proximity predicts liking. In a Pew survey (2006) of people married or in long-term relationships, 38 per cent met at work or at school, and some of the rest met when their paths crossed in their neighbourhood, church or gym, or while growing up.

There have been, however, some interesting cultural differences. The French researched the issue and concluded that where you meet your spouse depends on who you are and which social class you belong to (Bozon and Héran, 1989). Michel Bozon and Francois Héran divided the meeting places into three categories: public places, private places and semi-private places. They found that the choice of partner is not random, and neither is the place where the first meeting occurs. Men in lower social categories often meet their partner in a public place, open to everyone. Semi-private places, where people meet with others 'of their kind', are frequented mainly by groups ranked among the higher social categories, in particular the intellectual professions. These are places with restricted access where strict rules of behaviour apply (e.g. a psychology conference). Private-sector executives, company directors and professionals appear to be more at home in purely private places, with friends or family (e.g. at a birthday celebration). Consider, for example, that 16 per cent of French farmers met their partners in a private place, 18 per cent in a semi-private place and 66 per cent in a public place. Richard Lampard (2007) used these categories developed by Bozon and Héran to examine couples' places of meeting in the second half of the twentieth century in Great Britain. He found that many people tended to meet their partner in the workplace or education, rather than in public places such as pubs, restaurants and parties. Lampard concluded that this reflected changes in the importance of places, particularly among the middle classes. But, for the working classes there was still a high likelihood of meeting your partner in a public space.

proximity *geographical nearness. Proximity (more precisely, 'functional distance') powerfully predicts liking*

Due to increased migration, the Internet, travelling and moving around, most people in Western societies do not live in the same place all their life. They change universities, jobs and home. So the possibility of meeting somebody living far away when travelling to another country or around the world (which many students do), and falling in love with somebody who represents different and even mysterious qualities, is more prevalent than before. The 'rules' governing mate selection have become more complicated. The increasing use of the Internet has challenged traditional social psychological theories' assumptions about the importance of proximity in forming and maintaining relationships. Rather it seems to be the case that accessibility is more important than geography. We do not have to choose the girl next door or the boy on the farm across the valley. The importance of physical proximity for relationships remains important but other factors are becoming more influential.

### Interaction

More significant than geographical distance is therefore functional distance and interaction – how often people's paths cross. We frequently become friends with those who are in the same study groups or who use the same recreation areas as us. Interaction enables people to explore their similarities, to sense one another's liking, and to perceive themselves as a social unit (Arkin & Burger, 1980).

The chance nature of such contacts helps explain a surprising finding. Consider: if you had an identical twin who became engaged to someone, wouldn't you (being in so many ways similar to your twin) expect to share your twin's attraction to that person? Not according to researchers David Lykken and Auke Tellegen (1993), who found that only half of identical twins recall really liking their twin's selection, and only 5 per cent said, 'I could have fallen for my twin's fiancé'. Romantic love is often rather like ducklings' imprinting, surmised Lykken and Tellegen. With repeated exposure to and interaction with someone, our infatuation may fix on almost anyone who has roughly similar characteristics and who reciprocates our affection. (Later research has shown that identical twins' spouses do, however, tend to have fairly similar personalities – Rushton & Bons, 2005.)

Why does proximity breed liking? One factor is availability; obviously there are fewer opportunities to get to know someone who attends a different university or lives in another town. But there is more to it than that. Those close by are potential enemies as well as friends. So why does proximity encourage affection more often than animosity?

### Anticipation of Interaction

Not only does proximity enable people to discover commonalities and exchange rewards, but also merely *anticipating* interaction boosts liking. John Darley and Ellen Berscheid (1967) discovered this when they gave female students ambiguous information about two other women, one of whom they expected to talk with intimately. Asked how much they liked each one, the women preferred the person they expected to meet. Expecting to date someone similarly boosts liking (Berscheid et al., 1976). Even voters on the losing side of an election will find their opinions of the winning candidate – whom they are now stuck with – rising (Gilbert et al., 1998).

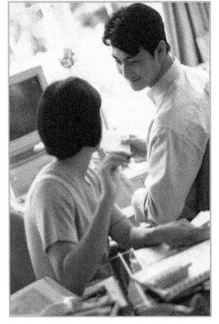

The phenomenon is adaptive. Anticipatory liking – expecting that someone will be pleasant and compatible – increases the chance of forming a rewarding relationship (Klein & Kunda, 1992; Knight & Vallacher, 1981; Miller & Marks, 1982). It's a good thing that we are biased to like those we often see, for our lives are filled with relationships with people whom we may not have chosen but with whom we need to have continuing interactions – room-mates, siblings, grandparents, teachers, classmates, co-workers. Liking such people is surely conducive to better relationships with them, which in turn makes for happier, more productive living.

### Mere Exposure

Proximity leads to liking not only because it enables interaction and anticipatory liking but also for another reason: more than 200 studies reveal that, contrary to an old proverb, familiarity does not breed contempt. Rather, it fosters fondness (Bornstein, 1989, 1999).

Feeling close to those close by. People often become attached to, and sometimes fall in love with, familiar co-workers and co-students.

SOURCE: © Kwame Zikomo/Purestock/SuperStock

The social psychologist Robert B. Zajonc made important contributions to the mere exposure effect more than 40 years ago (also see Chapter 5). In 1968 he conducted three studies showing that the more people were exposed to all sorts of stimuli, the more they liked them. This effect even occurs in animals and birds (Zajonc et al., 1973). In 2004 he concluded that the mere-exposure effect is 'a robust phenomenon. These effects are valid across cultures, species, and diverse stimulus domains' (Zajonc, 2004).

**mere-exposure effect** *the tendency for novel stimuli to be liked more or rated more positively after the rater has been repeatedly exposed to them*

Do the supposed Turkish words *nansoma, saricik* and *afworbu* mean something better or something worse than the words *iktitaf, biwojni* and *kadirga*? Students tested by Zajonc (1968, 1970) preferred whichever of these words they had seen most frequently. The more times they had seen a meaningless word or a Chinese ideograph, the more likely they were to say it meant something good (Figure 9.1).

Consider: what are your favourite letters of the alphabet? People of differing nationalities, languages, and ages prefer the letters that frequently appear in their own languages and especially in their own names (Hoorens et al., 1990; Hoorens & Nuttin, 1993; Kitayama & Karasawa, 1997; Nuttin, 1987). French students rate capital W, the least frequent letter in French, as their least favourite letter. Japanese students prefer not only letters from their names but also numbers corresponding to their birth dates. This 'name-letter and birthday-number effect' reflects more than mere exposure, however.

The mere-exposure effect violates the common-sense prediction of boredom – *decreased* interest – regarding repeatedly beautiful scenery, heard music or tasted foods (Kahneman & Snell, 1992). Unless the repetitions are incessant ('Even the best song becomes tiresome if heard too often', says a Korean proverb), familiarity

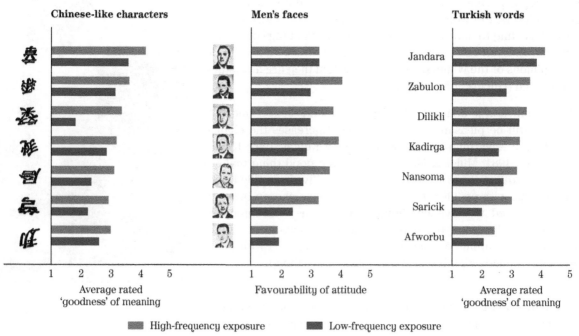

**FIGURE 9.1** The mere-exposure effect

Students rated stimuli – a sample of which is shown here – more positively after being shown them repeatedly.

SOURCE: Zajonc, 1968.

usually doesn't breed contempt, it increases liking (Green, 2007; Hansen & Wänke, 2009; Zebrowitz et al., 2008). When completed in 1889, the Eiffel Tower in Paris was mocked as grotesque (Harrison, 1977). Today it is the beloved symbol of Paris. At its premiere in 1913, Stravinsky's *Rite of Spring* was vehemently condemned by critics and the public alike; today it is a classic admired the world over.

So, do visitors to the Louvre in Paris really adore the *Mona Lisa* for the artistry it displays, or are they simply delighted to find a familiar face? It might be both: to know her is to like her. Eddie Harmon-Jones and John Allen (2001) explored this phenomenon experimentally. When they showed people a woman's face, their cheek (smiling) muscle typically became more active with repeated viewings. Mere exposure breeds pleasant feelings.

Leonardo Da Vinci's *Mona Lisa*. A pretty face or just a familiar one?

SOURCE: © Andrew_Howe/iStock

Zajonc and his co-workers William Kunst-Wilson and Richard Moreland reported that even exposure without awareness leads to liking (Kunst-Wilson & Zajonc, 1980; Moreland & Zajonc, 1977; Wilson, 1979). Joachim Hansen and Michaela Wänke at the University of Basel have recently confirmed that repeated exposure affects attitude formation independently of conscious recognition, stressing the role of unconscious familiarity (Hansen & Wänke, 2009). In fact, mere exposure has, according to Robert Bornstein and Paul D'Agostino (1992), an even stronger effect when people receive stimuli without awareness. In one experiment, women students using headphones listened in one ear to a prose passage. They also repeated the words out loud and compared them with a written version to check for errors. Meanwhile, brief, novel melodies played in the other ear. This procedure focused attention on the verbal material and away from the tunes. Later, when the women heard the tunes interspersed among similar ones not previously played, they did not recognize them. Nevertheless, they *liked best* the tunes they had previously heard (Bornstein & D'Agostino, 1992). But, not everybody agrees with the findings of Bornstein and Agostino. Ben Newell and David Shanks (2007) found in their study of faces that a mere-exposure effect was found only when recognition performance was at a high level, that is, conscious or 'supraliminal' (Newell & Shanks, 2007).

Note that conscious judgements about the stimuli in Zajonc's experiments provided fewer clues to what people had heard or seen than did their instant feelings. You can probably recall immediately and intuitively liking or disliking something or someone without consciously knowing why. Zajonc (1980) argues that *emotions are often more instantaneous than thinking*. Zajonc's rather astonishing idea – that emotions are semi-independent of thinking ('affect may precede cognition') – has found support in recent brain research. However, there are also emotional reactions and evaluations tied to cognition and conscious evaluation of sense impressions. The immediate emotional reaction is sometimes overruled by later reflections and cognitions. The mere-exposure effect has 'enormous adaptive significance', notes Zajonc (1998). It is a 'hardwired' phenomenon that predisposes our attractions and attachments. It helps us to categorize things and people as either familiar and safe, or unfamiliar and possibly dangerous. The mere-exposure effect colours our evaluations of others: we like familiar people (Swap, 1977). It works the other way around, too: people we like (for example, smiling rather than unsmiling strangers) seem more familiar (Garcia-Marques et al., 2004). Mere exposure to something or somebody breeds liking since we are less afraid or suspicious towards things with which we are familiar. It also reduces stereotyping since we see individual traits and distinctiveness more.

The phenomenon's negative side is our wariness of the unfamiliar – which may explain the automatic, unconscious prejudice people often feel when confronting those who are different (as we will see in Chapter 13). Fearful or prejudicial feelings are not always expressions of stereotyped beliefs; sometimes the beliefs arise later as justifications for intuitive feelings. Or they are enforced by a combination of emotions and cognitions of the unfamiliar. For example, increased familiarity with faces of a different race from our own increases liking for them (Zebrowitz et al., 2008). So mere exposure can also reduce prejudice.

We even like ourselves better when we are the way we're used to seeing ourselves. In a delightful experiment, Theodore Mita, Marshall Dermer and Jeffrey Knight (1977) photographed women students and later showed each one her actual picture along with a mirror image of it. Asked which picture they liked better, most preferred the mirror image – the image they were used to seeing. (No wonder our photographs never look quite right.) When close friends of the women were shown the same two pictures, they preferred the true picture – the image *they* were used to seeing.

Advertisers and politicians exploit this phenomenon. When people have no strong feelings about a product or a candidate, repetition alone can increase sales or votes (McCullough & Ostrom, 1974; Winter, 1973). After endless repetition of a commercial, shoppers often have an unthinking, automatic, favourable response to the product (also see Chapter 6 on peripheral routes to persuasion). If candidates are relatively unknown, those with the most media exposure usually win (Patterson, 1980; Schaffner et al., 1981). Political strategists who understand the mere-exposure effect have replaced reasoned argument with brief advertisements that hammer home a candidate's picture, name and sound-bite message.

The mere-exposure effect. If she is like most of us, German Chancellor Angela Merkel may prefer her familiar mirror-image (left), which she sees each morning while brushing her teeth, to her actual image (right).
SOURCE: © Ulrich Baumgarten/Getty Images

### INTERNET DATING

As a place for meeting romantic partners, the Internet has become a major environment. From tiny beginnings, Internet dating has become a huge source for contacting people and chatting with them. You might be looking on a broad basis on sites like PlentyOfFish, an apparently 'scientifically selecting' site like eHarmony, or have a very specific interest like VampireLovers. It is claimed that Internet dating sites have revolutionized the way that we now find our romantic partners, and that they offer a way to meet far more people than we would in our normal day-to-day lives. Many sites use mathematical algorithms to match us against compatible people and this apparently weeds out the people that we don't share anything in common with (Finkel et al., 2012). Dating sites are also useful for those people who may not have access to the groups that they find attractive, or who would otherwise have problems finding a romantic partner. For LGBT individuals in small communities where they feel isolated, Internet dating opens a much wider range of potential partners. After all, if you live in a small town, and there really isn't anyone around who is sexually compatible, the Internet can provide a means of meeting a partner. Katelyn McKenna, Amie Green and Marci Gleason (2002) suggest that the Internet has provided a safer environment in which people who are socially anxious and lonely can form relationships, revealing aspects of themselves they would find difficult to articulate in face-to-face interactions.

Monica Whitty has examined why people use the Internet to form friendships and romantic relationships. She points out that virtual reality offers people a space to be creative and construct their identity in forming relationships with others. Of course the relationships people form online can reach across into their offline lives as well.

Whitty (2008) found that the importance of physical appearance was more of a live issue for women than for men, and that women were also more likely to list their personal interests. Perhaps the finding that users should pay particular heed to is that both men and women admitted to stretching the truth in constructing their identity online in their efforts to attract a mate. But of course there are no guarantees that a relationship that works well online will also work well offline. As the real and virtual worlds meet, our illusions can be shattered. In a study, Rosanna Guadagno, Bradley Okdie and Sara Kruse (2011) found that male participants were more likely to be deceptive in their self-presentation in online dating than female participants. Also, men are more likely to lie about their social or economic status, while women are more likely to lie about their weight (Hitsch et al., 2010). This seems to reflect people's understanding of sexual mate selection, that men are said to seek women who are physically attractive and fertile, while women seek men who are resource rich.

## PHYSICAL ATTRACTIVENESS

What do (or did) you look for in a potential date? Sincerity? Character? Humour? Conversational ability? Good looks? Sophisticated, intelligent people are unconcerned with such superficial qualities as good looks; they know 'beauty is only skin deep' and 'you can't judge a book by its cover'. At least, they know that's how they *ought* to feel. As Cicero counselled, 'Resist appearance.'

'We should look to the mind, and not to the outward appearances.'
   Aesop, *Fables*

The belief that looks are unimportant may be another instance of how we deny real influences upon us, for there is now a filing cabinet full of research studies showing that appearance *does* matter. The consistency and pervasiveness of this effect is astonishing. Good looks are a great asset, even if it is sometimes socially unacceptable to accept it.

**implicit measures**
*implicit measures aim to assess attitudes that respondents may not be willing to report directly, or of which they may not even be aware*

The methodological innovation of implicit measures (see Chapters 5 and 13) has been useful for research on attraction, love and preferences. Results from surveys and experimental studies are often biased by social desirability. When asked in a survey, college students rated the romantic attractiveness of opposite-sex peers as equal, regardless of the presence or absence of a physical disability. However, using the *implicit association test* revealed a clear preference for physical health over physical disabilities. The discrepancy between the explicit attractiveness ratings and the implicit attitudes towards physical disabilities suggests that the former were biased by social desirability (Rojahn et al., 2008).

### Attractiveness and Dating

Like it or not, a young woman's physical attractiveness is a moderately good predictor of how popular she is and a young man's attractiveness is a modestly good predictor of how popular he is (Berscheid et al., 1971; Krebs & Adinolfi, 1975; Reis et al., 1980, 1982; Walster et al., 1966). Moreover, women more than men say they would prefer a mate who's homely and warm over one who's attractive and cold (Fletcher et al., 2004b). Does this imply, as many have surmised, that women are better at following Cicero's advice? Or that nothing has changed since 1930, when the English philosopher Bertrand Russell (1930, p. 139) wrote, 'On the whole women tend to love men for their character while men tend to love women for their appearance'? Or does it merely reflect the fact that men more often do the inviting (at least this has been the tradition)? If women were to indicate their preferences among various men, would looks be as important to them as to men?

To see whether men are indeed more influenced by looks, researchers have provided male and female students with information about someone of the other sex, including the person's picture. Or they have briefly introduced a man and a woman and later asked each about their interest in dating the other. In such studies, men do put somewhat more value on opposite-sex physical attractiveness than women do (Figure 9.2) (Feingold, 1990; Sprecher et al., 1994a). But women, too, respond to a man's looks.

### The Matching Phenomenon

Not everyone can end up paired with someone stunningly attractive. So how do people pair off? Judging from research by Bernard Murstein (1986) and others, they get real. They pair off with people who are about as attractive as they are. Several studies have found a strong correspondence between the rated attractiveness of husbands and wives, of dating partners, and even of those within particular fraternities (Feingold, 1988).

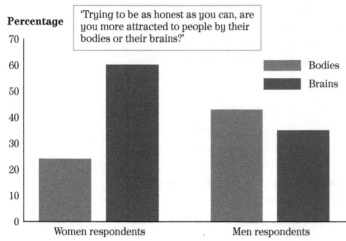

**FIGURE 9.2** What American women and men report finding most attractive

SOURCE: Fox News/Opinion Dynamics Poll of registered voters, 1999.

People tend to select as friends, and especially to marry, those who are a 'good match' not only to their level of intelligence but also to their level of attractiveness.

'If you would marry wisely, marry your equal.'
   Ovid, 43 BC–AD 17

Experiments confirm this matching phenomenon. When choosing whom to approach, knowing the other is free to say yes or no, people often approach someone whose attractiveness roughly matches (or not too greatly exceeds) their own (Berscheid et al., 1971; Stroebe et al., 1971). They seek out someone who seems desirable, but are mindful of the limits of their own desirability. Good physical matches may be conducive to good relationships, reported Gregory White (1980) from a study of student dating couples. Those who were most similar in physical attractiveness were most likely, nine months later, to have fallen more deeply in love.

*matching phenomenon the tendency for men and women to choose as partners those who are a 'good match' in attractiveness and other traits*

Perhaps this research prompts you to think of happy couples who are not equally attractive. In such cases, the less attractive person often has compensating qualities. Each partner brings assets to the social marketplace, and the value of the respective assets creates an equitable match. Personal advertisements exhibit this exchange of assets (Cicerello & Sheehan, 1995; Koestner & Wheeler, 1988; Rajecki et al., 1991). Men typically offer wealth or status and seek youth and attractiveness; women more often do the reverse: 'Attractive, bright woman, 26, slender, seeks warm, professional male.' You can test this hypothesis yourself: check 100 personal dating advertisements placed by men and women in a magazine, newspaper or on the Internet.

Angelina Jolie and Brad Pitt: a perfect match?
SOURCE: © Filmspiegel/Dreamstime.com

But does this work? Donald Strasberg and Stephen Holty did not limit their research to a content analysis of personal advertisements. They placed four 'female seeking male' advertisements on two large Internet bulletin boards which specialized in such advertisements, to study which ones received most responses. The most popular advertisement was, contrary to prior research, one in which the woman described herself as 'financially independent, successful [and] ambitious', producing over 50 per cent more responses than the next most popular advertisement, one in which the woman described herself as 'lovely . . . very attractive and slim'. So perhaps there is some gender stereotyping going on here: men don't seem to rely solely on a woman's physical appearance when deciding whether to answer a personal advertisement (Strassberg and Holty, 2003).

Some research suggests that what women want and offer seems to differ by sexual orientation. Bisexual women offer the most physical descriptors and also request more physical attributes than do lesbians and heterosexual women (Smith & Stillman, 2002).

Asset matching. High-status Rolling Stones guitarist Keith Richards has been married to supermodel Patti Hansen, 19 years his junior, since 1983.
SOURCE: © Xinhua/Alamy Stock Photo

### Similarity and Liking

As we have already seen, we humans love to feel good about ourselves. Not only are we prone to self-serving bias, we also exhibit what Brett Pelham, Matthew Mirenberg and John Jones (2002) call *implicit egotism*: we like what we associate with ourselves.

That includes the letters of our name, our date of birth, the people, places, careers and things that we unconsciously connect with ourselves (Jones et al., 2002; Koole et al., 2001). If a stranger's face is morphed to include features of our own, we like the new face better (DeBruine, 2004). We are also more attracted to people whose arbitrary experimental code number resembles our birth date, and we are even disproportionately likely to marry someone whose first or last name resembles our own, such as by starting with the same letter (Jones et al., 2004). Weirder still (and we are not making this up!) people seem to prefer careers related to their names. There are 2.5 times as many dentists named Denise in the USA as there are with the equally popular name Beverly or Tammy. People named George or Geoffrey are overrepresented among geoscientists (geologists and geophysicists). And even more bizarrely: in academic institutions that use letter grades, students with names beginning with 'A' tend to do better in their assessed pieces of work than students whose names begin with 'D'.

Psychologists Frederik Anseel and Wouter Duyck from Ghent University, Belgium, were interested in testing the extent of the name-letter effect and if it was potent enough to affect where we choose to work. The psychologists analysed a database containing information about Belgian employees and looked at the employees' name and how often their first initial matched the first letter of their company's name. The researchers estimated the expected number of these matches (using a probability calculation) and compared this to what they actually observed. The results? They found that there is indeed a name-letter effect between employee names and the company they work for. There were 12 per cent more matches than was expected based on the probability estimate. The researchers noted that for about one in nine people whose initials matched their company's initial, their choice of employer seems to have been influenced by the fact that the letters matched. In addition, when they looked across all letters, they found that this effect occurred with every letter of the alphabet. The authors concluded that they 'have demonstrated that people are more likely to work for companies with initials matching their own than to work for companies with other initials' (Anseel & Duyck, 2009).

Perhaps you are sceptical of the results? You are not alone. The statistical validity of some studies of this phenomenon have been disputed. Marcello Gallucci (2002) carried out a meta-analysis on data from Pelham et al. (2002) studies in this area and found that the data are unreliable. Gallucci criticized the studies, and found that the original data did not support the concept that implicit egotism influences us in our major decisions. However, Gallucci did acknowledge that it might be possible to show that implicit egotism did influence our decisions, but only if far greater and more reliable studies are carried out.

### The Physical-attractiveness Stereotype

What is more, we assume that beautiful people possess certain desirable traits. Other things being equal, we guess beautiful people are happier, sexually warmer, and more outgoing, intelligent and successful – though not more honest or concerned for others (Eagly et al., 1991; Feingold, 1992b; Jackson et al., 1995).

> Attribution of success to internal factors and failures to external factors is a common phenomenon. Self-serving bias is covered more explicitly in Chapters 3 (the self) and 4 (social beliefs and judgements).

The findings define a physical-attractiveness stereotype: what is beautiful is good. Children learn the stereotype quite early – and one of the ways they learn it is through stories told to them by adults. Snow White and Cinderella are beautiful – and kind. The witch and the stepsisters are ugly – and wicked. 'If you want to be loved by somebody who isn't already in your family, it doesn't hurt to be beautiful', surmised one 8-year-old girl. Or as one kindergarten girl put it when asked what it means to be pretty, 'It's like to be a princess. Everybody loves you' (Dion, 1979).

And we continue to believe in the beautiful-is-good assertions, even as students. Regan Gurung and Kristin Vespia (2007) wondered if the appearance of instructors influenced students' evaluation of them as well as their grades and learning. It did. They found in a study with 861 undergraduate students that likeable, good-looking and well-dressed teachers had students who said they learned more, had higher grades and liked the class better (Gurung & Vespia, 2007).

*physical-attractiveness stereotype the presumption that physically attractive people possess other socially desirable traits as well: what is beautiful is good*

### First Impressions

To say that attractiveness is important, other things being equal, is not to say that physical appearance always outranks other qualities. Some people more than others judge people by their looks (Livingston, 2001). Moreover, attractiveness probably most affects first impressions. But first impressions are important – and are becoming more so as societies become increasingly mobile and urbanized, and as contacts with people become more fleeting (Berscheid, 1981).

Leslie Zebrowitz and Joann Montepare have reviewed studies on first impressions to see if there is a tendency to generalize what someone is like from a quick glance at their physical appearance. And there is! Even if we are warned not to form impressions about people's abilities and qualities based on their looks, we often still do just that (Zebrowitz & Montepare, 2008).

Though interviewers may deny it, attractiveness and grooming affect first impressions in job interviews (Mack & Rainey, 1990). This helps explain why attractive people and tall people have more prestigious jobs and make more money (Engemann & Owyang, 2003; Persico et al., 2004). Patricia Roszell and her colleagues (1990) looked at the incomes of a national sample of Canadians whom interviewers had rated on a 1 (homely)-to-5 (strikingly attractive) scale. They found that for each additional scale unit of rated attractiveness, people earned, on average, an additional $1988 annually. Irene Hanson Frieze and her associates (1991) did the same analysis with 737 graduates after rating them on a similar 1-to-5 scale using student yearbook photos. For each additional scale unit of rated attractiveness, men earned an added $2600 and women an added $2150.

Research has shown that people tend to look longer at attractive than at unattractive faces (Sui & Liu, 2009). But, people should not be too stunningly beautiful, at least not women. When the effect of advertising using highly physically attractive models on male and female adolescents was investigated, the findings suggested that these highly attractive models were less effective (persuasive) than those models who were 'normally' attractive (Tsai & Chang, 2007).

The speed with which first impressions form, and their influence on thinking and attitudes, helps explain why pretty prospers. Even a .013-second exposure – too brief to discern a face – is enough to enable people to guess a face's attractiveness (Olson & Marshuetz, 2005). Moreover, when categorizing subsequent words as either good or bad, an attractive face predisposes people to categorize good words faster. Pretty is perceived promptly and primes positive processing.

### Is the 'Beautiful Is Good' Stereotype Accurate?

Do beautiful people indeed have desirable traits? For centuries, those who considered themselves serious scientists thought so when they sought to identify physical traits (shifty eyes, a weak chin) that would predict criminal behaviour. Or, on the other hand, was Leo Tolstoy correct when he wrote that it's 'a strange illusion ... to suppose that beauty is goodness'? There is some truth to the stereotype. Attractive children and young adults are somewhat more relaxed, outgoing and socially polished (Feingold, 1992b; Langlois et al., 2000). William Goldman and Philip Lewis (1977) demonstrated this by having 60 male students call and talk for five minutes with each of three female students. Afterwards the men and women rated the most attractive of their unseen telephone partners as somewhat more socially skilful and likeable. Physically attractive individuals tend also to be more popular, more outgoing and more gender typed – more traditionally masculine if male, more feminine if female (Langlois et al., 1996).

These small average differences between attractive and unattractive people probably result from self-fulfilling prophecies. Attractive people are valued and favoured, and so many develop more social self-confidence (see Chapter 3). By that analysis, what's crucial to your social skill is not how you look but how people treat you and how you feel about yourself – whether you accept yourself, like yourself and feel comfortable with yourself.

Some evolutionary psychologists have argued differently. Although most researchers dismiss that physically attractive people are more intelligent, Satoshi Kanazawa and Jody Kovar contend that beautiful people indeed are more intelligent. They argue that: (1) men who are more intelligent are more likely to attain higher status than men who are less intelligent; (2) higher-status men are more likely to mate with more beautiful women than lower-status men; (3) intelligence is heritable; and (4) beauty is heritable (Kanazawa & Kovar, 2004). As often with claims from evolutionary psychologists, this kind of 'logical truth' is not easy to verify empirically.

### Bad Is Stronger than Good

Dissimilar attitudes, we have noted, turn us off to others more than similar attitudes turn us on. And others' criticism captures our attention and affects our emotion more than does their praise. Roy Baumeister, Ellen Bratslavsky, Catrin Finkenauer and Kathleen Vohs (2001) say this is just the tip of an iceberg: 'In everyday life, bad events have stronger and more lasting consequences than comparable good events.'

The power of the bad prepares us to deal with threats, and protects us from death and disability. For survival, bad can be worse than good is good. The importance of the bad is one likely reason why the first century of psychology focused so much more on the bad than on the good. Since 1887 *Psychological Abstracts* (a guide to psychology's literature) had included over 13 062 articles mentioning anger, 83 345 mentioning anxiety and 105 281 mentioning depression. There were 17 articles on these topics for every one dealing with the positive emotions of joy (1476), life satisfaction (5357) or happiness (4826). Similarly, 'fear' (26 651 articles) has triumphed over 'courage' (1158). But the strength of the bad is 'perhaps the best reason for a positive psychology movement', Baumeister and his colleagues surmise. To overcome the strength of individual bad events, 'human life needs far more good than bad'.

## Who Is Attractive?

We have described attractiveness as if it were an objective quality like height, which some people have more of, some less. Strictly speaking, attractiveness is whatever the people of any given place and time find attractive. This, of course, varies. The beauty standards by which Miss World is judged hardly apply even to the whole planet. People in various places and times have pierced noses, lengthened necks, dyed hair, painted skin, gorged themselves to become voluptuous, starved to become thin, and bound themselves with leather corsets to make their breasts seem small – or used silicone and padded bras to make them seem big. For cultures with scarce resources and for poor or hungry people, plumpness seems attractive; for cultures and individuals with abundant resources, beauty more often equals slimness (Nelson & Morrison, 2005). In Europe, the use of size-zero models has proved controversial in promoting a particular image of beauty.

Standards of beauty differ from culture to culture. Yet some people are considered attractive throughout most of the world.
SOURCE: (1) © tunart/iStock; (2) © Kevin Landwer-Johan/iStock; (3) © kimeveruss/iStock; (4) © Andresr/iStock

### Evolution and Attraction

Psychologists working from the evolutionary perspective often explain the human preference for attractive partners in terms of reproductive strategy (see Chapter 14). They assume that beauty signals biologically important information: health, youth and fertility. Over time, men who preferred fertile-looking women had more children than those who were as happy to mate with post-menopausal females. They also assume evolution predisposes women to favour male traits that signify an ability to provide and protect resources. That, David Buss (1989) believes, explains why the males he studied in 37 cultures – from Australia to Zambia – did indeed prefer youthful female characteristics that signify reproductive capacity. It perhaps also explains why physically attractive females tend to marry high-status males, and why men compete with such determination to display status by achieving fame and fortune.

But both 'beauty' and 'high status' could also be explained by social norms. There is no logic, for example, that a slim beautiful woman is more fertile or more able to give birth and raise a child, than a less attractive physically strong woman with lots of muscles who is able to lift 80 kg. In screening potential mates, report Norman Li and his fellow evolutionary psychologists (2002), men require a modicum of physical attractiveness, women require status and resources, and both welcome kindness and intelligence. But again, this could be a product of social norms in terms of what is considered to be desirable.

Anthony Little at the University of Stirling has done a lot of pertinent work on the evolutionary aspects of attraction. In a recent study with colleagues at the University of Aberdeen and McMaster University in Canada, he examined preferences for symmetry, masculinity and femininity in features, using computer-manipulated faces. Both males and females preferred symmetric faces more when judging the opposite sex than when judging same-sex faces. Women preferred more masculine male faces than men did and also showed stronger preference for femininity in female faces than men reported. This actually reveals that women are more concerned with female femininity than are men (Little et al., 2008).

Evolutionary psychologists have also explored men and women's response to other cues to reproductive success. Judging from glamour models and beauty pageant winners, men everywhere have felt most attracted to women whose waists are 30 per cent narrower than their hips – a shape associated with peak sexual fertility (Singh, 1993; Singh & Young, 1995; Streeter & McBurney, 2003). Circumstances that reduce a woman's fertility – malnutrition, pregnancy, menopause – also change her shape. But peak fertility does not say too much about ability to take care of, and raise, children. This waist and hip proportion seems more adequate for selecting a prestigious partner than an able mother.

According to evolutionary psychologists, when judging males as potential marriage partners, women also prefer a male waist-to-hip ratio suggesting health and vigour, and during ovulation they show heightened preference for men with masculinized features (Gangestad et al., 2004; Macrae et al., 2002). This makes evolutionary sense, notes Jared Diamond (1996): a muscular hunk was more likely than a scrawny fellow to gather food, build houses and defeat rivals. But today's women prefer men with high incomes even more (Singh & Young, 1995). It seems that what is attractive is in the eye of the beholder, and the norms of a culture.

Much of the data used in studies of the female waist-to-hip ratio is problematic, coming from very small and non-representative samples. In one study, the body measurements used were from the Miss America contest winners between 1927 and 1987 (Bivans, 1991), and another, Playboy centrefolds (Garner et al., 1980). These were presented as historically evidenced 'proof' of the evolutionary psychology theory of female waist-to-hip ratio.

In most industrialized cultures today the beauty business is big and growing. Asians, Britons, Germans and Americans are all seeking cosmetic surgery in rapidly increasing numbers (Wall, 2002). In the USA, for example, 10.3 million surgical and non-surgical cosmetic procedures such as liposuction, breast augmentation and Botox injections were performed in 2008, as reported by the American Society for Aesthetic Plastic Surgery (ASAPS). The global market for cosmetic surgery services was $31.7 billion in 2008, a figure that is expected to reach $40.1 billion in 2013. Beverly Hills has twice as many plastic surgeons as paediatricians (*People*, 2003). Modern, affluent people who have cracked or discoloured teeth fix them. More and more, so do people with wrinkles and flab.

In her 1995 book *Reshaping the Female Body,* Kathy Davis at Utrecht University, reports her research on the increasing use of cosmetic surgery in the Netherlands. She argues that cosmetic surgery cannot be understood as a matter of individual choice; nor is it an artefact of consumer culture which, in principle, affects us all. Rather, the shift to cosmetic surgery has to be understood in the context of how gender and power are exercised in modern Western culture. Cosmetic surgery belongs to a broad regime of technologies, practices and discourses, which define the female body as deficient and in need of constant transformation (Davis, 2002).

### The Attractiveness of Those We Love

Let's conclude our discussion of attractiveness on an upbeat note. First, a 17-year-old girl's facial attractiveness is a surprisingly weak predictor of her attractiveness at ages 30 and 50. Sometimes an average-looking adolescent, especially one with a warm, attractive personality, becomes a quite attractive middle-aged adult (Zebrowitz et al., 1993, 1998).

Second, not only do we perceive attractive people as likeable, we also perceive likeable people as attractive. The beautiful-is-good stereotype also works the other way round: information about somebody's personality influences the perceptions of their physical attributes and beauty. Some personality characteristics are more important than others. Sampo Paunonen (2006) informed students about the intelligence, independence and honesty of a person shown on a picture and asked the students to rate him or her on several physical characteristics. The person described as honest was seen as being in better health and as having a face that looked more kind, attractive and even feminine. It is not easy to accept that a nice and honest person is ugly or that a beautiful person is bad. We prefer consistency and try to get rid of cognitive and emotional dissonance (see Chapter 5). Alan Gross and Christine Crofton (1977) had students view someone's photograph after reading a favourable or an unfavourable description of the person's personality. Those portrayed as warm, helpful and considerate also *looked* more attractive. It may be true, then, that 'handsome is as handsome does'.

Perhaps you can recall individuals who, as you grew to like them, became more attractive. Their physical imperfections were no longer so noticeable. Discovering someone's similarities to us also makes the person seem more attractive (Beaman & Klentz, 1983; Klentz et al., 1987).

Moreover, love sees loveliness: the more in love a woman is with a man, the more physically attractive she finds him (Price et al., 1974). And the more in love people are, the less attractive they find all others of the opposite sex (Johnson & Rusbult, 1989; Simpson et al., 1990). These studies were all carried out with heterosexual couples, so it would be interesting to see if research looking at gay and lesbian couples comes to the same conclusions. It does seem, however, that being in love makes us view our partner as the most attractive, even if there are alternatives available. 'The grass may be greener on the other side,' note Rowland Miller and Jeffry Simpson (1990), 'but happy gardeners are less likely to notice.' Beauty really *is*, to some extent, in the eye of the beholder.

## SIMILARITY VERSUS COMPLEMENTARITY

From our discussion so far, one might surmise Leo Tolstoy was entirely correct: 'Love depends ... on frequent meetings, and on the style in which the hair is

Henry James's description of novelist George Eliot (the pen name of Mary Ann Evans): 'She is magnificently ugly – deliciously hideous. She has a low forehead, a dull grey eye, a vast pendulous nose, a huge mouth, full of uneven teeth, and a chin and jawbone qui n'en finissent pas ... now in this vast ugliness resides a most powerful beauty which, in a very few minutes, steals forth and charms the mind, so that you end as I ended, in falling in love with her.'
SOURCE: © Pictorial Press Ltd/Alamy Stock Photo

done up, and on the colour and cut of the dress.' As people get to know one another, however, other factors influence whether acquaintance develops into friendship.

### Do Birds of a Feather Flock Together?

Of this much we may be sure: birds that flock together are of a feather. Friends, engaged couples and spouses are far more likely than randomly paired people to share common attitudes, beliefs and values. Furthermore, the greater the similarity between husband and wife, the happier they are and the less likely they are to divorce (Byrne, 1971; Caspi & Herbener, 1990). Such correlational findings are intriguing. But cause and effect remain an enigma. Does similarity lead to liking? Or does liking lead to similarity?

*Likeness Begets Liking*

To discern cause and effect, we experiment. Imagine that at a campus party Lakesha gets involved in a long discussion of politics, religion, and personal likes and dislikes with Les and Lon. She and Les discover they agree on almost everything, she and Lon on few things. Afterwards, she reflects: 'Les is really intelligent ... and so likeable. I hope we meet again.' When others think as we do, we not only appreciate their attitudes but also make positive inferences about their character (Montoya & Horton, 2004). In experiments, Donn Byrne (1971) and his colleagues captured the essence of Lakesha's experience. Over and over again, they found that the more similar someone's attitudes are to your own, the more likeable you will find the person. Likeness produces liking not only for college students but also for children and the elderly, and for people of various occupations. There may be some cultural and gender differences. Joanna Schug, Masaki Yuki, Hiroki Horikawa and Kosuke Takemura (2009) found that the preference for similarity between friends is higher in the West than in East Asian countries. Maarten Selfhout, Susan Branje and Wim Meeus (2007) found from their study of 267 Dutch adolescents that similarity in general played a larger role in mutual best friendships between girls than between boys.

Whether there is love at first sight or if love develops more gradually also seem to matter: in a sample of 137 married or cohabiting couples, it was found that partners who fell in love at first sight became romantically involved more quickly, and showed more dissimilar personalities with regard to levels of extraversion, emotional stability and autonomy (Barelds & Barelds-Dijkstra, 2007).

The likeness-leads-to-liking effect has been tested in real-life situations by noting who comes to like whom.

☐ At two of Hong Kong's universities, Royce Lee and Michael Bond (1996) found that room-mate friendships flourished over a six-month period when room-mates shared values and personality traits, but more so when they perceived their room-mates as similar. As so often happens, reality matters, but perception matters more.

☐ People like not only those who think as they do but also those who act as they do. Subtle mimicry fosters fondness. Have you noticed that when someone nods their head as you do and echoes your thoughts, you feel a certain rapport and liking? That's a common experience, report Rick van Baaren and his colleagues (2003a, 2003b), and one result is higher tips for Dutch restaurant servers who mimic their customers by merely repeating their order. Natural mimicry increases rapport, note Jessica Lakin and Tanya Chartrand (2003), and desire for rapport increases mimicry.

☐ In a study of 63 female Canadian adolescents, it was found that they had a more favourable rating of their friends when they perceived similarity on autonomy, prosociality and caregiving (Linden-Andersen et al., 2009).

☐ University students in the Netherlands rated their perceived similarity with friends during the acquaintanceship process in a naturalistic setting. The undergraduates' personality data were also gathered. While perceived similarity in personality was associated with more friendship, actual similarity in personality was not. What counts is in the eye of the beholder (Selfhout et al., 2009).

☐ When Peter Buston and Stephen Emlen (2003) surveyed nearly 1000 college-age people, they found that the desire for similar mates far outweighed the desire for beautiful mates. Attractive people sought attractive mates. Wealthy people wanted mates with money. Family-orientated people desired family-orientated mates.

☐ Studies of newlyweds reveal that similar attitudes and values help bring couples together and predict their satisfaction (Luo & Klohnen, 2005). That reality is the basis of one psychologist-founded Internet dating site, which claims to match singles using the similarities that mark happy couples (Carter & Snow, 2004; Warren, 2005).

So similarity breeds content. Birds of a feather *do* flock together. Surely you have noticed this upon discovering a special someone who shares your ideas, values and desires, a soul mate who likes the same music, the same activities, even the same foods you do.

*Dissimilarity Breeds Dislike*

We have a bias – the false consensus bias (see Chapter 4) – towards assuming that others share our attitudes. When we discover that someone has dissimilar attitudes, we may dislike the person. If those dissimilar attitudes pertain to our strong moral convictions, we dislike and distance ourselves from them all the more (Skitka et al., 2005). People in one political party often are not so much fond of fellow party members as they are disdainful of the opposition (Hoyle, 1993; Rosenbaum, 1986).

In general, dissimilar attitudes depress liking more than similar attitudes enhance it (Singh and Teoh, 1999; Singh and Ho, 2000). Within their own groups, where they expect similarity, people find it especially hard to like someone with dissimilar views (Chen & Kenrick, 2002). That perhaps explains why dating partners and room-mates become more similar over time in their emotional responses to events and in their attitudes (C. Anderson et al., 2003; Davis & Rusbult, 2001). 'Attitude alignment' helps promote and sustain close relationships, a phenomenon that can lead partners to overestimate their attitude similarities (Kenny & Acitelli, 2001; Murray et al., 2002).

Whether people perceive those of another race as similar or dissimilar influences their racial attitudes. Wherever one group of people regards another as 'other' – as

See Chapters 12 and 13 for further discussion of inter- and intra-group relations and the conflict that results in relation to attitudes, perceptions and behaviours.

creatures who speak differently, live differently, think differently – the potential for conflict is high. In fact, except for intimate relationships such as dating, the perception of like minds seems more important for attraction than like skins or genes. Most Whites have expressed more liking for, and willingness to work with, a like-minded Black than a dissimilarly minded White (Insko et al., 1983; Rokeach, 1968). The more that Whites presume that Blacks support their values, the more positive their racial attitudes (Biernat et al., 1996).

'Cultural racism' persists, argues social psychologist James Jones (1988, 2003, 2004), because cultural differences are a fact of life. Black culture tends to be present orientated, spontaneously expressive, spiritual and emotionally driven. White culture tends to be more future orientated, materialistic and achievement driven. Rather than trying to eliminate such differences, says Jones, we might better appreciate what they 'contribute to the cultural fabric of a multicultural society'. There are situations in which expressiveness is advantageous and situations in which future orientation is advantageous. Each culture has much to learn from the other. In most Western European countries, where migration and differing birthrates make for growing diversity, educating people to respect and enjoy those who differ is a major challenge. Given increasing cultural diversity and given our natural wariness of differences, this may in fact be the major social challenge of our time.

### Do Opposites Attract?

Are we not also attracted to people who in some ways *differ* from ourselves, in ways that complement our own characteristics? Researchers have explored that question by comparing not only friends' and spouses' attitudes and beliefs, but also their ages, religions, race, smoking behaviour, economic levels, education, height, intelligence and appearance. In all these ways and more, similarity still prevails (Buss, 1985; Kandel, 1978). Smart birds flock together. So do rich birds, Protestant birds, tall birds, pretty birds.

Still we resist: are we not attracted to people whose needs and personalities complement our own? Would a sadist and a masochist find true love? Sociologist Robert Winch (1958) reasoned that the needs of an outgoing and domineering person would naturally complement those of someone who is shy and submissive. The logic seems compelling, and most of us can think of couples who view their differences as complementary: 'My husband and I are perfect for each other. I'm Aquarius – a decisive person. He's Libra – can't make decisions. But he's always happy to go along with arrangements I make.'

Given the idea's persuasiveness, the inability of researchers to confirm it is astonishing. For example, most people feel attracted to expressive, outgoing people (Friedman et al., 1988). Would this be especially so when one is down in the dumps? Do depressed people seek those whose gaiety will cheer them up? On the contrary, it is non-depressed people who most prefer the company of happy people (Locke & Horowitz, 1990; Rosenblatt & Greenberg, 1988, 1991; Wenzlaff & Prohaska, 1989). When you're feeling blue, another's bubbly personality can be aggravating. The contrast effect that makes average people feel homely in the company of beautiful people also makes sad people more conscious of their misery in the company of cheerful people.

Some complementarity may evolve as a relationship progresses (even a relationship between identical twins). Yet people seem slightly more prone to like and to marry those whose needs and personalities are *similar* (Botwin et al., 1997; Buss, 1984; Fishbein & Thelen, 1981a, 1981b; Nias, 1979). Perhaps one day we will discover some ways (other than heterosexuality) in which differences commonly breed liking.

complementarity *the popularly supposed tendency, in a relationship between two people, for each to complete what is missing in the other*

## LIKING THOSE WHO LIKE US

Liking is usually mutual. Proximity and attractiveness influence our initial attraction to someone, and similarity influences longer-term attraction as well. If we have a deep need to belong and to feel liked and accepted, would we not also take a liking to those who like us? Are the best friendships mutual admiration societies? Indeed, one person's liking for another does predict the other's liking in return (Kenny & Nasby, 1980).

But does one person's liking another *cause* the other to return the appreciation? People's reports of how they fell in love suggest so (Aron et al., 1989). Discovering someone you like really likes you seems to awaken romantic feelings. Studies confirm it. For example, Susan Sprecher (1998) found reciprocal liking to be one of the major determinants of interpersonal attraction, and Andrew Lehr and Glenn Geher (2006) found the reciprocity principle to be a stronger force for attraction than shared attitudes.

reciprocity principle *the human tendency to want to give something back when something is received. Respond to a positive action with another positive action, and to a negative action with a negative one*

However, people with low and high self-esteem respond differently. People with high self-esteem base their liking for others less strongly on whether other people like them, than do people with low self-esteem.

And consider this finding by Ellen Berscheid and her colleagues (1969): students like another student who says eight positive things about them better than one who says nine positive things and one negative thing. We are sensitive to the slightest hint of criticism. Writer Larry L. King (1986) speaks for many in noting, 'I have discovered over the years that good reviews strangely fail to make the author feel as good as bad reviews make him feel bad.'

Whether we are judging ourselves or others, negative information carries more weight because, being less usual, it grabs more attention (Yzerbyt & Leyens, 1991). Skowronski & Carlston (1987) demonstrated consequently that negative information about other people was better recalled than positive information.

People's votes are more influenced by their impressions of politicians' weaknesses than by their impressions of strengths (Klein, 1991), a phenomenon that has not been lost on those who design negative campaigns. It's a general rule of life, noted Roy Baumeister and his colleagues (2001): bad is stronger than good.

Our liking for those we perceive as liking us was recognized long ago. Observers from the ancient philosopher Hecato ('If you wish to be loved, love') to Ralph Waldo Emerson ('The only way to have a friend is to be one') to Dale Carnegie ('Dole out praise lavishly') anticipated the findings. What they did not anticipate was the precise conditions under which the principle works.

### Attribution

As we've seen, flattery *will* get you somewhere. But not everywhere. If praise clearly violates what we know is true – if someone says, 'Your hair looks great', when we haven't washed it in three days – we may lose respect for the flatterer and wonder whether the compliment springs from ulterior motives (Shrauger, 1975). Thus, we often perceive criticism to be more sincere than praise (Coleman et al., 1987). In fact, when someone prefaces a statement with 'To be honest', we know we are about to hear a criticism.

'If 60 000 people tell me they loved a show, then one walks past and says it sucked, that's the comment I'll hear.'
  Musician Dave Matthews, 2000

ingratiation *the use of strategies, such as flattery, by which people seek to gain another's favour*

Laboratory studies reveal something we've noted in previous chapters: our reactions depend on our attributions. Do we attribute the flattery to ingratiation – to a self-serving strategy? Is the person trying to get us to buy something, to acquiesce sexually, to do a favour? If so, both the flatterer and the praise lose appeal (Gordon, 1996; Jones, 1964). But if there is no apparent ulterior motive, then we warmly receive both flattery and flatterer.

### 'Licking Upward–Kicking Downward'

You may have disliked, or distrusted, a friend or colleague because their behaviour towards superiors seemed unusually flattering, too supportive or a little bit too interested. Most likely, we have to admit that we too have engaged in some fawning on occasion. It goes on every day and everywhere simply because it is often in our best interests to establish a favourable impression with those that can potentially affect our future – for instance, the university lecturer deciding on a student's marks.

Roos Vonk at Leiden University in the Netherlands has studied the ingratiating phenomenon in the laboratory, observing that people who are 'licking upward–kicking downward' are usually judged as extremely dislikeable and highly 'slimey' (Vonk, 1998). The student participants who read a series of behaviour descriptions of a person who behaved in likeable or dislikeable ways towards superiors and subordinates did not even need to see the kicking downwards before they concluded on the basis of licking upwards that this person was slimey.

### Gender Differences

In Vonk's laboratory study the actor was always a man and this could be responsible for the *slime effect*. According to gender stereotypes, men are (a) less likely to be supportive, interested and flattering; (b) more ambitious; and (c) more likely to ingratiate themselves in this rather blatant, unsubtle manner (Vonk, 1998). However, when the actor's sex has been varied in further studies Roos Vonk found no gender difference. Licking upwards is considered an undesirable behaviour regardless of whether it is a man or a woman doing it.

### Cultural Variations

Vonk's study was carried out in the Netherlands, and in Western culture there is virtue in not ingratiating oneself with the people in power, to obey or to 'bootlick' them. But in some other cultures there are other traditions and perceptions of what is courteous and correct behaviour. To lick upwards and kick downwards can be looked upon as acceptable and well-adapted behaviour.

### Self-esteem and Attraction

Elaine Hatfield (Walster, 1965) wondered if another's approval is especially rewarding after we have been deprived of approval, much as eating is most rewarding when we're hungry. To test that idea, she gave some female students either very favourable or very unfavourable analyses of their personalities, affirming some and wounding others. Then she asked them to evaluate several people, including an attractive male confederate who just before the experiment had struck up a warm conversation with each woman and had asked each for a date. (Not one turned him down.) Which women do you suppose most liked the man? It was those whose self-esteem had been temporarily shattered and who were presumably hungry for social approval. (After this experiment Hatfield spent almost an hour talking with each woman and explaining the experiment. She reports that, in the end, none remained disturbed by the temporary ego blow or the broken date.)

This helps explain why people sometimes fall passionately in love on the rebound, after an ego-bruising rejection. Unfortunately, however, low-self-esteem individuals tend to underestimate how much their partner appreciates them. They also have less generous views of their partner and therefore feel less happy with the relationship (Murray et al., 2000). If you feel down about yourself, you are likely to feel pessimistic about your relationships. Feel good about yourself and you're more likely to feel confident of your dating partner or spouse's regard.

### Gaining Another's Esteem

If approval that comes after disapproval is powerfully rewarding, then would we most like someone who liked us after initially disliking us? Or would we most like someone who liked us from the start (and therefore gave us more total approval)? Ray is in a small discussion class with his room-mate's cousin, Sophia. After the first week of classes, Ray learns via his 'pipeline' that Sophia thinks him rather shallow. As the semester progresses, he learns that Sophia's opinion of him is steadily rising; gradually she comes to view him as bright, thoughtful and charming. Would Ray like Sophia more if she had thought well of him from the beginning? If Ray is simply counting the number of approving comments he receives, then the answer will be yes. But if, after her initial disapproval, Sophia's rewards become more potent, Ray then might like her better than if she had been consistently affirming.

To see which is more often true, Elliot Aronson and Darwyn Linder (1965) captured the essence of Ray's experience in a clever experiment. They 'allowed' 80 female students to overhear a sequence of evaluations of themselves by another woman. Some women heard consistently positive things about themselves, some consistently negative. Others heard evaluations that changed either from negative to positive (like Sophia's evaluations of Ray) or from positive to negative. In this and other experiments, the target person was especially well liked when the individual experienced a gain in the other's esteem, especially when the gain occurred gradually and reversed the earlier criticism (Aronson & Mettee, 1974; Clore et al., 1975). Perhaps Sophia's nice words have more credibility coming after her not-so-nice words. Or perhaps after being withheld, they are especially gratifying.

It seems we tend to like others who grow to like us (the loss–gain hypothesis) and really dislike those who initially like us and then cool off on us (the gain–loss hypothesis). Inderjeet Kaur and Vandana Sharma found that the loss–gain liking sequence was associated more closely to interpersonal attraction than the gain–loss hypothesis. They also revealed that the most powerful determinant of interpersonal attraction is an indication that one is liked; and the best liked person is often the one whose comments are initially negative but become increasingly positive (Sharma & Kaur, 1996).

Aronson speculated that constant approval can lose value. When a husband says for the five-hundredth time, 'Wow, honey, you look great', the words carry far less impact than were he now to say, 'Oh, honey, you look awful in that dress'. A loved one you've doted on is hard to reward but easy to hurt. This suggests that an open, honest relationship – one where people enjoy one another's esteem and acceptance yet are honest – is more likely to offer continuing rewards than one dulled by the suppression of unpleasant emotions, one in which people try only, as Dale Carnegie advised, to 'lavish praise'. Aronson (1980) put it this way:

> As a relationship ripens toward greater intimacy, what becomes increasingly important is authenticity – our ability to give up trying to make a good impression and begin to reveal things about ourselves that are honest even if unsavory … If two people are genuinely fond of each other, they will have a more satisfying and exciting relationship over a longer period of time if they are able to express both positive and negative feelings than if they are completely 'nice' to each other at all times. (p. 323)

Someone who really loves us will be honest with us but will also tend to see us through rose-tinted glasses. When Sandra Murray and her co-workers (1996b; Murray & Holmes, 1997) studied dating and married couples, they found that the happiest (and those who became happier with time) were those who idealized each other, who even saw their partners more positively than their partners saw themselves. When we're in love, we're biased to find those we love not only physically attractive but socially attractive as well. Moreover, the most satisfied married couples tend to approach problems without immediately criticizing their partners and finding fault (Karney & Bradbury, 1997). Honesty has its place in a good relationship, but so does a presumption of the other's basic goodness.

## EVALUATIVE CONDITIONING

*Why do we like or prefer something at all? People often have little insight into the reasons behind their preferences and even why they like a particular activity.*

**evaluative conditioning** *how we can come to like or dislike something through an association with something we already like or dislike*

Empirical evidence suggests that the majority of likes and dislikes are learned rather than innate, as the mere exposure phenomenon illustrates. Until recently, however, the nature of the underlying mechanism and processes behind the development of likes and dislikes has been relatively neglected. Sara Thomas at the University of Southampton in England, and Jan De Houwer and Frank Baeyens at the University of Leuven in Belgium have investigated this topic and in their research they have related the acquisition of liking through associative learning or conditioning. This is commonly referred to as evaluative conditioning (EC). We like those we associate with good feelings. According to Donn Byrne and Gerald Clore (1970), Albert Lott and Bernice Lott (1974), and Jan De Houwer and colleagues (2001), conditioning creates positive feelings towards things and people linked with other stimuli we already regard as positive, pleasant or beautiful. When, after a strenuous week, we relax in front of a fire, enjoying good food, drink and music, we are likely to feel a special warmth towards those around us. We are not likely to take a liking to someone we meet while suffering a splitting headache.

Evaluative conditioning effects have been obtained using a large variety of stimuli and procedures. In the so-called 'luncheon technique', participants were initially asked to rate a range of stimulus materials including music, photographs, paintings and political slogans. Next, participants were presented with the photographs a second time, either in the context of a positive stimulation or while exposed to unpleasant odours. The researchers found that the photographs paired with the pleasant experience were subsequently rated more positively than those associated with the aversive odours. It has also been demonstrated that nonsense words paired with either positive or negative words acquired the same affective value of the word with which they were paired.

The EC research has also contributed to understanding how preferences and liking can be changed. Merely presenting a stimulus in isolation appears to have little effect on the acquired valence of that stimulus. To change preferences, it seems to be more effective to pair the stimulus with another stimulus of the opposite valence (De Houwer et al., 2001). If you want to like a person who does not turn you on you should invite her or him to join you in something you already are fond of. Elaine Hatfield, William Walster and E. Berscheid (1978) found a practical tip in these research studies: 'Romantic dinners, trips to the theatre, evenings at home together, and vacations never stop being important … If your relationship is to survive, it's important that you *both* continue to associate your relationship with good things.'

Other experiments confirm this phenomenon of liking – and disliking – by association. In one, college students who evaluated strangers in a pleasant room liked them better than those who evaluated them in an uncomfortably hot room (Griffitt, 1970). In another, people evaluated photographs of other people while in either an elegant, sumptuously furnished room or a shabby, dirty room (Maslow & Mintz, 1956). Again, the good feelings evoked by the elegant surroundings transferred to the people being rated.

This simple theory of attraction – we like those who reward us and those we associate with rewards – helps us understand why people everywhere feel attracted to those who are warm, trustworthy and responsive (Fletcher et al., 1999; Regan, 1998; Wojciszke et al., 1998). The reward theory also helps explain some of the influences on attraction.

- ☐ *Proximity* is rewarding. It costs less time and effort to receive friendship's benefits with someone who lives or works close by, or who we have easy access to (such as in online relationships).

- ☐ We like *attractive* people because we perceive that they offer other desirable traits and because we benefit by associating with them.

- ☐ If others have *similar* opinions, we feel rewarded because we presume that they like us in return. Moreover, those who share our views help validate them. We especially like people if we have successfully converted them to our way of thinking (Lombardo et al., 1972; Riordan, 1980; Sigall, 1970).

- ☐ We like to be liked and love to be loved. Thus, liking is usually *mutual*. We like those who like us.

## WHAT IS LOVE?

*What is this thing called 'love'? Can passionate love endure? If not, what can replace it?*

Loving is more complex than liking and thus more difficult to measure, more perplexing to study. People yearn for it, live for it, die for it. Yet only in the last couple of decades has loving become a serious topic in social psychology.

'Love is nature's way of giving a reason to be living.'
Paul Webster, 'Love Is a Many Splendored Thing'

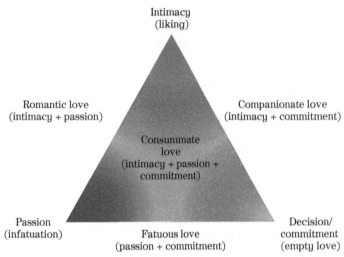

FIGURE 9.3   Robert Sternberg's (1988) conception of kinds of loving as combinations of three basic components of love

Most attraction researchers have studied what is most easily studied – responses during brief encounters between strangers. The influences on our initial liking of another – proximity, attractiveness, similarity, being liked, and other rewarding traits – also influence our long-term, close relationships (Hendrick & Hendrick, 2008). The impressions that dating couples quickly form of each other therefore provide a clue to their long-term future (Berg, 1984; Berg & McQuinn, 1986). Even if first impressions are important, long-term loving is not merely an intensification of initial liking. To understand why couples stay together, social psychologists study not only the attraction experienced during first encounters but also enduring, close relationships.

### PASSIONATE LOVE

The first step in scientifically studying romantic love, as in studying any variable, is to decide how to define and measure it. We have ways to measure aggression, altruism, prejudice and liking – but how do we measure love?

'How do I love thee? Let me count the ways,' wrote Elizabeth Barrett Browning. Social scientists have counted various ways. Psychologist Robert Sternberg (1998, 2004, 2006) views love as a triangle consisting of three components: passion, intimacy and commitment (Figure 9.3). Drawing from ancient philosophy and literature, sociologist John Alan Lee (1998) suggests romantic love stems from twelfth-century France and is a consequence of a capitalistic society. He concludes that love has become a consumer good in postmodern society. However, not everybody agrees. Elaine Hatfield and Richard Rapson (2006) argue that passionate love has always existed between humans. But, culture has a profound impact on how people experience love, and on the way they think, feel and behave in romantic settings. According to Hatfield and her colleagues people's love lives are written in their cultural and personal history, as well as in their genes (Hatfield et al., 2007).

*positive psychology the study of the strengths and virtues of individuals founded on the belief that people want to cultivate what is best within themselves, and to enhance their experiences of love, work and play*

Recently, studies of love and relationships have become an important part of positive psychology (Hendrick & Hendrick, 2009). This new branch of psychology focuses on a pleasant, good and meaningful life. It examines the 'life of enjoyment', studying how people experience the positive feelings that are part of normal and healthy living (e.g. relationships and romantic love). It also studies the extraordinary 'flow', which can be juxtaposed with falling in love, the feeling of being optimally engaged with somebody or something.

Some elements are common to all loving relationships: mutual understanding, giving and receiving support, enjoying the loved one's company. Some elements are distinctive. If we experience passionate love, we express it physically, we expect the relationship to be exclusive and we are intensely fascinated with our partner.

Passionate love is emotional, exciting, intense. Elaine Hatfield (1988) defined it as *'a state of intense longing for union with another'* (p. 193). If reciprocated, one feels fulfilled and joyous; if not, one feels empty or despairing. Passionate love therefore contributes to positive as well as negative emotions (Kim & Hatfield, 2004). Like other forms of emotional excitement, passionate love involves a roller-coaster of elation and gloom, tingling exhilaration and dejected misery. 'We are never so defenceless against suffering as when we love,' observed Freud. Passionate love preoccupies the lover with thoughts of the other – as Robert Graves put it in his poem 'Symptoms of Love', 'Listening for a knock; waiting for a sign'.

Researchers report that sustained eye contact, nodding and smiling are indicators of passionate love.

SOURCE: © emre ogan / iStock

passionate love *a form of love characterized by intense love and longing for the other. Passionate lovers are absorbed in each other, feel ecstatic at attaining their partner's love, and are disconsolate on losing it*

### Social Neuroscience and Passionate Love

Passionate love may seem to many people to be an ephemeral concept, so difficult to force into being or pin down and describe. Yet there are clearly some neurological processes in action when we are in love, and as technology has developed, we have developed a clearer picture of the processes involved.

To explain passionate love, Hatfield notes that a given state of arousal can be steered into any of several emotions, depending on how we attribute the arousal. An emotion involves both body and mind – both arousal and the way we interpret and label that arousal. Imagine yourself with pounding heart and trembling hands: are you experiencing fear, anxiety, joy? Physiologically, one emotion is quite similar to another. You may therefore experience the arousal as joy if you are in a euphoric situation, anger if your environment is hostile and passionate love if the situation is romantic. In this view, passionate love is the psychological experience of being biologically aroused by someone we find attractive.

If indeed passion is a heightened state that's labelled 'love', then whatever causes this state should intensify feelings of love. In several experiments, college men aroused sexually by reading or viewing erotic materials had a heightened response to a woman – for example, by scoring much higher on a love scale when describing their girlfriend (Carducci et al., 1978; Dermer & Pyszczynski, 1978; Stephan et al., 1971). Proponents of the two-factor theory of emotion (see Chapter 8), developed by Stanley Schachter and Jerome Singer (1962), argue that when the men who had been aroused responded to a woman, they easily misattributed some of their own arousal as due to her.

According to this theory, being aroused by *any* source should intensify passionate feelings – providing the mind is free to attribute some of the arousal to a romantic stimulus. In a dramatic demonstration of this phenomenon,

two-factor theory of emotion *Schachter's theory that the perception of our emotions is based on two different cues: our evaluation of the environment tells us which emotion we are experiencing, while the intensity of the psychological arousal tells us how strong our emotion is*

Donald Dutton and Arthur Aron (1974) asked an attractive young woman to approach individual young men as they crossed a narrow, wobbly, 450-foot-long suspension walkway hanging 230 feet above British Columbia's rocky Capilano River. The woman asked each man to help her fill out a class questionnaire. When he had finished, she scribbled her name and phone number and invited him to call if he wanted to hear more about the project. Most accepted the phone number, and half who did so called. By contrast, men approached by the woman on a low, solid bridge, and men approached on the high bridge by a *male* interviewer, rarely called. Once again, physical arousal accentuated romantic responses.

Scary movies, roller-coaster rides and physical exercise have the same effect, especially to those we find attractive (Foster et al., 1998; White & Kight, 1984). Those who do exciting things together often report the best relationships. And after doing an arousing rather than a mundane laboratory task (roughly the equivalent of a three-legged race on their hands and knees), couples also reported higher satisfaction with their overall relationship (Aron et al., 2000). Adrenaline makes the heart grow fonder. As this suggests, passionate love is a biological as well as a psychological phenomenon.

Social neuroscience is a growing field that seeks to use neuroscience research techniques to examine the social aspects of human life. John Cacioppo and Stephanie Ortigue (2011) describe social neuroscience as being a move on from cognitive neuroscience. They say that if cognitive neuroscience regards the human brain as a computer, social neuroscience regards it more as a computer connected to the Internet. They argue that our brain function and structure do not exist in isolation from our social selves, but are instead closely interconnected

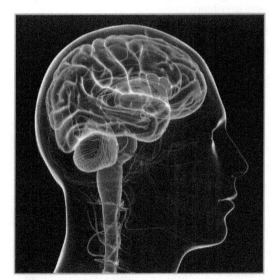

**FIGURE 9.4** Love is in the brain
MRI scans from young adults intensely in love revealed areas, such as the caudate nucleus, which became more active when gazing at the loved one's photograph (but not when gazing at the photograph of another acquaintance).
SOURCE: © Science Photo Library/Alamy Stock Photo

with it. By imaging the brain of people in love, we can gain a far wider understanding of how passionate love influences us through our cognitive mechanisms.

Research by social psychologist Arthur Aron and his colleagues (2005) indicates that passionate love engages dopamine-rich brain areas associated with reward (see Figure 9.4). This is a good example of a general social psychological idea: mind states influence brain states. As we will see in Chapter 14, psychological functions, emotions and cognitions, have an impact on the activity in the brain. The structure of the brain is not hardware, but software, changing with emotional and cognitive input.

Andreas Bartels and Semir Zeki (2000, 2004) carried out fMRI studies on people who described themselves as 'truly, deeply, and madly in love'. The researchers gave nineteen participants two colour photographs as stimulus, one of the person that they loved as the research stimuli and one of a friend as a control measure. When looking at the picture of their beloved, the imaging results from all the participants showed increased brain activity associated with euphoria-inducing drugs. This seems to explain the 'blissed-out' feeling of being passionately in love.

So if love makes our brains react with such euphoria, what happens when our relationships break down? Helen Fisher (2004) conducted fMRI studies on people who had been rejected in love and were still feeling heartbroken. In these studies the areas of the brain associated with anxiety, pain and attempts to control anger were activated. This supports our understanding of relationship breakdown as painful and psychologically distressing. Just as the overwhelming feelings of falling in love are beyond our control, it would seem that the misery of being rejected is also outside our control.

### Variations in Love: Culture and Gender

There is always a temptation to assume that most others share our feelings and ideas. We assume, for example, that love is a precondition for marriage. Most cultures – 89 per cent in one analysis of 166 cultures – do have a concept of romantic love, as reflected in flirtation or couples running off together (Jankowiak & Fischer, 1992). We often take for granted that we have to love before we marry or cohabit. But this is not a universal way of thinking. In many cultures outside of Europe and North America the parents or another family member make suggestions and sometimes even the decision on who their children should marry. Sometimes it is better not to prioritize passionate love. In cultures that practise arranged marriages, love tends to follow rather than to precede marriage (see Figure 9.5).

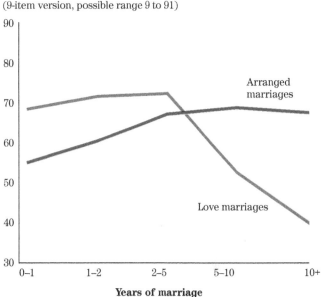

**Scores on Rubin's love scale**
(9-item version, possible range 9 to 91)

**Years of marriage**

**FIGURE 9.5** Romantic love between partners in arranged or love marriages in Jaipur, India

SOURCE: Data from Gupta & Singh, 1982.

Do males and females differ in how they experience passionate love? Studies of men and women falling in and out of love reveal some surprises. Most people, including the writer of the following letter to a newspaper advice columnist, suppose that women fall in love more readily:

> Dear Dr. Brothers:
>
> Do you think it's effeminate for a 19-year-old guy to fall in love so hard it's like the whole world's turned around? I think I'm really crazy because this has happened several times now and love just seems to hit me on the head from nowhere ... My father says this is the way girls fall in love and that it doesn't happen this way with guys – at least it's not supposed to. I can't change how I am in this way but it kind of worries me. – P. T.
>
> (quoted by Dion & Dion, 1985)

P. T. would be reassured by the repeated finding that it is actually men who tend to fall more readily in love (Dion & Dion, 1985; Peplau & Gordon, 1985). Men also seem to fall out of love more slowly and are less likely than women to break up a premarital romance. Once in love, however, women are typically as emotionally involved as their partners, or more so. They are more likely to report feeling euphoric and 'giddy and carefree', as if they were 'floating on a cloud'. Women are also somewhat more likely than men to focus on the intimacy of the friendship and on their concern for their partner. Men are more likely than women to think about the playful and physical aspects of the relationship (Hendrick & Hendrick, 1995).

### COMPANIONATE LOVE

**companionate love** *an affectionate relationship, where one is dedicated and devoted to the partner and his or her happiness (commonly contrasted with passionate love)*

Although passionate love burns hot, it inevitably simmers down. The longer a relationship endures, the fewer its emotional ups and downs (Berscheid et al., 1989). The high of romance may be sustained for a few months, even a couple of years. But no high lasts forever. 'When you're in love it's the most glorious two-and-a-half days of your life,' jests comedian Richard Lewis. The novelty, the intense absorption in the other, the thrill of the romance, the giddy 'floating on a cloud' feeling often fades. After two years of marriage, spouses express affection about half as often as when they were newlyweds (Huston & Chorost, 1994). About four years after marriage, the divorce rate peaks (H. Fisher, 1994). If a close relationship is to endure, it will settle to a steadier but still warm afterglow that Hatfield calls companionate love.

Unlike the wild emotions of passionate love, companionate love is lower key; it's a deep, affectionate attachment. It activates different parts of the brain (Aron et al., 2005). And it is just as real. Nisa, a !Kung San woman of the African Kalahari Desert, explains: 'When two people are first together, their hearts are on fire and their passion is very great. After a while, the fire cools and that's how it stays. They continue to love each other, but it's in a different way – warm and dependable' (Shostak, 1981).

Unlike passionate love, companionate love can last a lifetime.

SOURCE: © ManoAfrica / iStock

It won't surprise those who know the rock song 'Addicted to Love' to find out that the flow and ebb of romantic love follows the pattern of addictions to coffee, alcohol and other drugs. At first, a drug gives a big kick, perhaps a high. With repetition, opponent emotions gain strength and tolerance develops. An amount that once was highly stimulating no longer gives a thrill. Stopping the substance, however, does not return you to where you started. Rather, it triggers withdrawal symptoms such as malaise and depression. The same often happens in love. The passionate high is fated to become lukewarm. The no-longer-romantic relationship becomes taken for granted – until it ends. Then the jilted lover, the widower, the divorcé, are surprised at how empty life now seems without the person they long ago stopped feeling passionately attached to. Having focused on what was not working, they stopped noticing what was (Carlson & Hatfield, 1992).

'When two people are under the influence of the most violent, most insane, most delusive, and most transient of passions, they are required to swear that they will remain in that excited, abnormal, and exhausting condition continuously until death do them part.'
George Bernard Shaw, 'Getting Married', 1908

The cooling of passionate love over time and the growing importance of other factors, such as shared values, can be seen in the feelings of those who enter arranged versus love-based marriages in India. Usha Gupta and Pushpa Singh (1982) asked 50 couples in Jaipur, India, to complete a love scale. They found that those who married for love reported diminishing feelings of love after a five-year newlywed period. By contrast, those in arranged marriages reported *more* love if their marriage was five or more years old (Figure 9.5).

The cooling of intense romantic love often triggers a period of disillusion, especially among those who regard that feeling of romantic love as essential both for a marriage and for its continuation. Compared with North Americans, Asians tend to focus less on personal feelings and more on the practical aspects of social attachments (Dion & Dion, 1988; Sprecher et al., 1994b; Sprecher & Toro-Morn, 2002). Thus, they are less vulnerable to disillusionment. Asians are also less prone to the self-focused individualism that in the long run can undermine a relationship and lead to divorce (Dion & Dion, 1991, 1996; Triandis et al., 1988). They also feel more obliged to stay married and it is considered shameful to divorce. Therefore the divorce rate in most Asian countries is much lower than in the West. But the rate of divorce is increasing in Asia partly due to the strong cultural influence from the West.

The result of passionate love frequently is children, whose survival is aided by the parents' waning obsession with each other (Kenrick & Trost, 1987). Nevertheless, for those married more than 20 years, some of the lost romantic feeling is often renewed as the family nest empties and the parents are once again free to focus their attention on each other (Hatfield & Sprecher, 1986; White & Edwards, 1990). 'No man or woman really knows what love is until they have been married a quarter of a century,' said Mark Twain. If the relationship has been intimate and mutually rewarding, companionate love rooted in a rich history of shared experiences deepens.

## WHAT ENABLES CLOSE RELATIONSHIPS?

*What factors influence the ups and downs of our close relationships? Let's consider commitment and some factors associated with it: attachment styles, equity and self-disclosure. We will also look at the role of apology and forgiveness in resolving relationship problems.*

### COMMITMENT

Commitment can be defined as the intention to maintain a relationship as well as feelings of psychological attachment to the other (Rusbult et al., 1998). It would be obvious to say that it would be automatic for a person to commit to a relationship if they care for the other person, but this would be a far too simplistic model of human relationships. We know that some people stay in apparently unsatisfactory relationships, as well as others who leave satisfactory relationships for another relationship. Caryl Rusbult's (1980; Rusbult et al., 1998) Investment Model (IM) of relationships puts forward a more nuanced approach to relationships and commitment and why some couples stay together and others split. The Investment Model is based on Kelley & Thibault's (1978) interdependence theory, positing that people are generally motivated to maximize the rewards of a relationship while at the same time minimizing the cost of that relationship. IM states that the more satisfied you are with a relationship the more you are desirous of maintaining it, and that increased satisfaction also reflects an increase in relationship rewards and a decrease in relationship costs. Commitment not only is affected

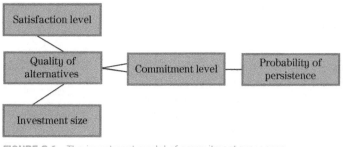

**FIGURE 9.6** The investment model of commitment processes
SOURCE: Rusbult et al., 1998.

by the positive outcomes of the current relationship and the negative outcomes of the alternative to being in that relationship, but also reflects the amount of investment the individual has put into the relationship. Therefore, the more a couple have invested to make a relationship work, the more likely they are to maintain that relationship. As the commitment factors interact, they predict the likely outcome of the relationship (Figure 9.6.)

The investment in our relationships can be extrinsic or intrinsic. Extrinsic relationship investments are things like the family home or children that a couple have together. These represent a physical or financial tie to the other person that would make leaving them more difficult and complicated. Where extrinsic investments exist in a relationship, the partners are less likely to leave the relationship. Intrinsic relationship investment represents things like the time and emotional effort that the partners put into the relationship. Rusbult states that both the extrinsic and intrinsic investments are non-portable, and that if the person leaves the relationship they cannot take these with them in that form – they are exclusive to that relationship. So although some ties, such as children, may continue once the relationship is over, the format of those ties is altered by the break-up – so the children may see much less of one parent after their parents separate than they did while their parents were still together.

In a study examining heterosexual, gay and lesbian relationships using IM it was found that commitment and investment predicted relationship satisfaction and durability. Interestingly, it was found that all women, both heterosexual and lesbian, reported higher investment than all male participants (Duffy & Rusbult, 1986). This raises some interesting questions about possible gender differences in relationship commitment and maintenance.

Commitment in relationships, maintaining the stability and supportive nature of the couple, allows the people involved greater overall satisfaction. As well as commitment, other factors affect the level of satisfaction in a relationship. Factors such as: the feeling of 'belonging' that we share with our partner (Baumeister & Leary, 1995); the gratitude we have for them (Kubacka et al., 2011); the sharing of emotional burdens and the intimacy we enjoy (Wieselquist, Rusbult, Foster & Agnew, 1999), all come together as investments in the relationship and its continuance. By investing in the relationship it becomes more valuable and stable for both parties.

### ATTACHMENT

The relationships and attachments we have to other people vary from the distant and formal to the very close and intimate. We start our lives being attached to our parents and our immediate family. We learn from necessity to relate to other people, and we find pleasure in this. For the rest of our lives most of us strive to be attached and integrated, to be accepted and appreciated by others. The family attachment plays a particular role in most people's lives. We never forget the intimate and caring relationship to our closest family and we carry this experience with us for the rest of our lives. In some cultures the interdependence on the family is stronger than in other cultures. In traditional Eastern cultures there are very close connections between grandparents, parents and offspring. They often live in the same house, share everything, and have a practical and emotional interrelationship. In modern Western civilization the generations do not relate in the same manner. The immediate family consists of parent(s) and children up to about 20 years of age. Then the children leave the parents and establish their own family. But the influence from the parents never disappears. The experience and longing for close connections to other people has been acquired from a very early age.

Our infant dependency strengthens our human bonds. Soon after birth we exhibit various social responses – love, fear, anger. But the first and greatest of these is love. As babies, we almost immediately prefer familiar faces and voices. We coo and smile when our caregivers give us attention.

Deprived of familiar attachments, sometimes under conditions of extreme neglect, children may become withdrawn, frightened, silent. After studying the mental health of homeless children for the World Health Organization, the British psychiatrist John Bowlby (1980, p. 442) reflected: 'Intimate attachments to other human beings are the hub around which a person's life revolves … From these intimate attachments [people draw] strength and enjoyment of life.'

Researchers have compared the nature of attachment and love in various close relationships – between parents and children, between friends, and between spouses or lovers (Davis, 1985; Maxwell, 1985; Sternberg & Grajek, 1984). Some elements are common to all loving attachments: mutual understanding, giving and receiving support, valuing and enjoying being with the loved one. Passionate love is, however, spiced with some added features: physical affection, an expectation of exclusiveness and an intense fascination with the loved one.

Passionate love is not just for lovers. The intense love of care givers and infant for each other qualifies as a form of passionate love, even to the point of engaging brain areas akin to those enabling passionate romantic love. Phillip Shaver and his co-workers (1988) note that 1-year-old infants, like young adult lovers, welcome physical affection, feel distress when separated, express intense affection when reunited, and take great pleasure in the significant other's attention and approval. Knowing that infants vary in their styles of relating to caregivers, Shaver and Cindy Hazan (1993, 1994) wondered whether infant attachment styles might carry over to adult relationships.

### Attachment Styles

John Bowlby declared that the attachments young children develop with their caregiver(s) are the foundation for their later emotional development, and 'The propensity to make strong emotional bonds to particular individuals [is] a basic component of human nature' (1988). Most infants and adults exhibit secure attachment (Baldwin et al., 1996; Bowlby, 1980, 1999; Jones & Cunningham, 1996; Mickelson et al., 1997). When infants in the USA and the Western world are placed in a strange situation (usually a laboratory playroom), they play comfortably in their mother's presence, happily exploring this strange environment. If she leaves, they become distressed; when she returns, they run to her, hold her, then relax and return to exploring and playing (Ainsworth, 1973, 1979). This trusting attachment style, many researchers believe, forms a working model of intimacy – a blueprint for one's adult intimate relationships, in which underlying trust sustains

secure attachment
*attachments rooted in trust and marked by intimacy*

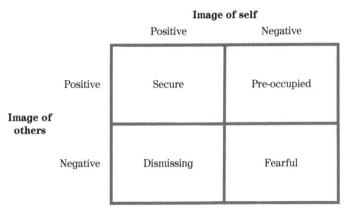

**Image of self**

| | Positive | Negative |
|---|---|---|
| Positive | Secure | Pre-occupied |
| Negative | Dismissing | Fearful |

**Image of others**

**FIGURE 9.7** Attachment styles
Kim Bartholomew and Leonard Horowitz (1991) proposed four distinct attachment styles based on a person's ideas of self and of others.

relationships through times of conflict (Miller & Rempel, 2004). Secure adults find it easy to get close to others and don't fret about getting too dependent or being abandoned. As lovers, they enjoy sexuality within the context of a secure, committed relationship. And their relationships tend to be satisfying and enduring (Feeney, 1996; Feeney & Noller, 1990; Simpson et al., 1992).

Kim Bartholomew and Leonard Horowitz (1991) proposed an influential attachment model that classifies people's attachment styles according to their images of self (positive or negative) and of others (positive or negative). Secure people have a positive image of both self and others (Figure 9.7). They sense their own worth and lovability, and expect that others will accept and respond to their love.

**preoccupied attachment** *attachments marked by a sense of one's own unworthiness and anxiety, ambivalence and possessiveness*

People with the preoccupied attachment style (also called *anxious-ambivalent*) have positive expectations of others but a sense of their own unworthiness. In the strange situation, anxious-ambivalent infants are more likely to cling tightly to their mother. If she leaves, they cry; when she returns, they may be indifferent or hostile. As adults, anxious-ambivalent individuals are less trusting, and therefore more possessive and jealous. They may break up repeatedly with the same person. When discussing conflicts, they get emotional and often angry (Cassidy, 2000; Simpson et al., 1996). By contrast, friends who support each other's freedom and acknowledge each other's perspectives usually have a satisfying relationship (Deci et al., 2006).

**dismissing attachment** *an avoidant relationship style marked by distrust of others*

**fearful attachment** *an avoidant relationship style marked by fear of rejection*

People with negative views of others exhibit either the dismissing or the fearful attachment style; the two styles share the characteristic of *avoidance*. Although internally aroused, avoidant infants reveal little distress during separation or clinging upon reunion. As adults, avoidant people tend to be less invested in relationships and more likely to leave them. They also are more likely to engage in one-night stands of sex without love. Examples of the two styles might be 'I want to keep my options open' (dismissing) and 'I am uncomfortable getting close to others' (fearful).

Some researchers attribute these varying attachment styles, which have been studied across 62 cultures (Schmitt et al., 2004), to parental responsiveness and social inheritance. Cindy Hazan and colleagues (2004) sum up the idea: 'Early attachment experiences form the basis of *internal working models* or characteristic ways of thinking about relationships.' Thus, sensitive, responsive mothers – mothers who engender a sense of basic trust in the world's reliability – typically have securely attached infants, observed Mary Ainsworth (1979) and Erik Erikson (1963). In fact, one study of 100 Israeli grandmother–daughter–granddaughter threesomes found intergenerational consistency of attachment styles (Besser & Priel, 2005).

An interesting development in the discussion of attachment styles and adult relationships is that it appears that adult relationships echo the child–caregiver relationship of childhood. Brooke Feeney and Roxanne Van Vleet (2010) argue that attachment security has an influence on the exploratory behaviour of the adult; those who feel secure and supported in their relationship have a foundation for exploring new ideas and goals, safe in the knowledge that they have a strong relationship to support them through both success and failure. Also, a degree of dependence on the other partner in the relationship allows for greater self-confidence and autonomy.

Attachment, especially to caregivers, is a powerful survival impulse.

SOURCE: © Studio1One / iStock

Attachment style seems to have an influence on how we deal with threats to our relationship. Gurit Birnbaum, Yanna Weisberg and Jeffry Simpson (2010) state that sexual intimacy is commonly used as a means of repairing a relationship, returning to the intimacy of our close attachment. They found that avoidantly attached individuals were the most likely to avoid intimacy with their partner, showing less desire and using distancing strategies in the face of relationship threats. Anxiously attached individuals were (unsurprisingly) the most anxious, and were the least likely to have hedonistic motivations in relation to intimacy.

The style of care giving by the other partner seems to have an effect on the person. In a longitudinal study of newly married couples, Brooke Feeney and Meredith Thrush (2010) found that partners who were intrusive and interfered in their spouses' lives in the first year of marriage had a clear impact. A year after marriage, for those with intrusive spouses, women showed less exploration and autonomy, and men had lower self-esteem and self-efficacy. What is important is that we consider not just the attachment style of the individual, but also the care-giving style they exhibit.

Today most researchers agree that fathers and other caregivers are just as important as mothers (e.g. Day et al., 2005; Lewis & Lamb, 2006). And youths who have experienced nurturant and involved parenting tend later to have warm and supportive relationships with their romantic partners (Conger et al., 2000). Other researchers believe attachment styles may reflect inherited temperament (Harris, 1998). Teens who are prone to anger and anxiety tend to have, as young adults, more fragile relationships (Donnellan et al., 2005a). For better or for worse, early attachment styles do seem to lay a foundation for future relationships.

### Friends with Benefits

The number of people (and not the least students) who engage in one-night stands of sex without love has become more prevalent. It seems, however, to be more of a fashionable lifestyle in some subcultures than a result of a particular attachment style in childhood.

'Friends with benefits' (FWB) is a phrase expressing sex in a non-romantic friendship where the benefit of the relationship is primarily sexual. Analysis of survey data from over 1000 undergraduates at a large university in the USA revealed that over half reported experience in a FWB relationship. Those engaged in FWB were characterized as non-romantic hedonists who have a pragmatic view of relationships (Puentes et al., 2008). They were more likely to be males, and women and men differed significantly in their understanding of the FWB relationship. Women tended to view the relationship as more involved and emotional, with the emphasis on friends, while men tended to view the relationship as more casual with an emphasis on benefits (sexual pleasure) (McGinty et al., 2007).

The 'friends with benefits' participants have no illusion that they are with their one true love (indeed they reject such a notion) and they make it clear that they are cashing in on their friendships by adding sex. While some may argue that adding sex to a friendship may strengthen the friendship, others suggest that it complicates the friendship and compromises its stability.

## EQUITY

If each partner pursues his or her personal desires willy-nilly, the relationship will die. Therefore, our society teaches us to exchange rewards by what Elaine Hatfield, William Walster and Ellen Berscheid (1978) have called an equity principle of attraction: what you and your partner get out of a relationship should be proportional to what you each put into it. If two people receive equal outcomes, they should contribute equally; otherwise one or the other will feel it is unfair. If both feel their outcomes correspond to the assets and efforts each contributes, then both perceive equity.

equity *a condition in which the outcomes people receive from a relationship are proportional to what they contribute to it. Note: Equitable outcomes needn't always be equal outcomes*

Strangers and casual acquaintances maintain equity by exchanging benefits: you lend me your class notes; later, I'll lend you mine. I invite you to my party; you invite me to yours. Those in an enduring relationship, including room-mates and those in love, do not feel bound to trade similar benefits – notes for notes, parties for parties (Berg, 1984). They feel freer to maintain equity by exchanging a variety of benefits ('When you drop by to lend me your notes, why don't you stay for dinner?') and eventually to stop keeping track of who owes whom.

### Long-term Equity

Is it crass to suppose that friendship and love are rooted in an equitable exchange of rewards? Don't we sometimes give in response to a loved one's need, without expecting any sort of return? Indeed, those involved in an equitable, long-term relationship are unconcerned with short-term equity. Margaret Clark and Judson Mills (1979, 1993; Clark, 1984, 1986) have argued that people even take pains to *avoid* calculating any exchange benefits. When we help a good friend, we do not want instant repayment. If someone invites us for dinner, we wait before reciprocating, lest the person attribute the motive for our return invitation to be merely paying off a social debt. True friends tune in to one another's needs even when reciprocation is impossible (Clark et al., 1986, 1989). Similarly, happily married people tend not to keep score of how much they are giving and getting (Buunk & Van Yperen, 1991). As people observe their partners being self-giving, their sense of trust grows (Wieselquist et al., 1999). No one says, and few even think, 'I'll trade you my good looks for your big income'. But in relationships that last, equity is the rule.

### Perceived Equity and Satisfaction

Those in an equitable relationship are more content (Fletcher et al., 1987; Hatfield et al., 1985; Van Yperen & Buunk, 1990). Those who perceive their relationship as inequitable feel discomfort: the one who has the better deal may feel guilty and the one who senses a raw deal may feel strong irritation. (Given the self-serving bias – most husbands perceive themselves as contributing more housework than their wives credit them for – the person who is 'overbenefited' is less sensitive to the inequity.)

Researchers have found that women tend to do more housework and childcare than men, even if they are in full-time employment. What is really interesting is that this unequal division of domestic labour may not be seen as unfair by the couple themselves. Rather, to take on certain household tasks (or not!) may reflect what society expects of the gender roles in the distribution of domestic labour (see also Chapter 14). As John Dixon and Margaret Wetherell (2004) found out from their research with couples, what is 'fair' in a relationship is a matter of moral evaluations that are culturally contingent. The 'normalizing' of these unfair arrangements is apparent in people's everyday language. During the honeymoon and empty-nest stages, spouses are more likely to perceive equity and to feel satisfaction with their marriages (Feeney et al., 1994). When both partners freely give and receive, and make decisions together, the odds of sustained, satisfying love are good.

Perceived inequity triggers marital distress, agree Nancy Grote and Margaret Clark (2001) from their tracking of married couples over time. But they also report that the traffic between inequity and distress runs both ways: marital distress exacerbates the perception of unfairness (Figure 9.8).

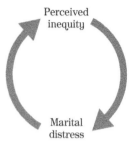

**FIGURE 9.8** Perceived inequities trigger marital distress, which fosters the perception of inequities

SOURCE: Adapted from Grote & Clark, 2001.

## SELF-DISCLOSURE

Deep, companionate relationships are intimate. They enable us to be known as we truly are and to feel accepted. We discover this delicious experience in a good marriage or a close friendship – a relationship where trust displaces anxiety and where we are free to open ourselves without fear of losing the other's affection (Holmes & Rempel, 1989). Such relationships are characterized by what the late Sidney Jourard called self-disclosure (Derlega et al., 1993). As a relationship grows, self-disclosing partners reveal more and more of themselves to each other; their knowledge of each other penetrates to deeper and deeper levels. Irwin Altman & Dalmas Taylor (1973) developed social penetration theory to explain how over time relationships move to deeper levels of intimacy in terms of breadth and depth of self-disclosure.

**self-disclosure** *revealing intimate aspects of oneself to others*

**social penetration theory** *states that closeness between people develops as a result of gradual self-disclosure*

Research studies find that most of us enjoy this intimacy. We feel pleased when a normally reserved person says that something about us 'made me feel like opening up' and shares confidential information (Archer & Cook, 1986; Taylor et al., 1981). It's gratifying to be singled out for another's disclosure. Not only do we like those who disclose, we also disclose to those whom we like. And after disclosing to them, we like them more (Collins & Miller, 1994). Lacking opportunities for intimacy, we experience the pain of loneliness (Berg & Peplau, 1982; Solano et al., 1982).

Experiments have probed both the *causes* and the *effects* of self-disclosure. When are people most willing to disclose intimate information concerning 'what you like and don't like about yourself' or 'what you're most ashamed and most proud of?' And what effects do such revelations have on those who reveal and receive them?

**disclosure reciprocity**
*the tendency for one person's intimacy of self-disclosure to match that of a conversational partner*

The most reliable finding is the disclosure reciprocity effect: disclosure begets disclosure (Berg, 1987; Miller, 1990; Reis & Shaver, 1988). We reveal more to those who have been open with us. But intimacy is seldom instant. (If it is, the person may seem indiscreet and unstable.) Appropriate intimacy progresses like a dance: I reveal a little, you reveal a little – but not too much. You then reveal more, and I reciprocate.

For those in love, deepening intimacy is exciting. 'Rising intimacy will create a strong sense of passion', note Roy Baumeister and Ellen Bratslavsky (1999). This helps explain why those who remarry after the loss of a spouse tend to begin the new marriage with an increased frequency of sex, and why passion often rides highest when intimacy is restored following severe conflict.

Some people – most of them women – are especially skilled 'openers'; they easily elicit intimate disclosures from others, even from those who normally don't reveal very much of themselves (Miller et al., 1983; Pegalis et al., 1994; Shaffer et al., 1996). Such people tend to be good listeners. During conversation they maintain attentive facial expressions and appear to be comfortably enjoying themselves (Purvis et al., 1984). They may also express interest by uttering supportive phrases while their conversational partner is speaking. They are what psychologist Carl Rogers (1980) called 'growth-promoting' listeners – people who are genuine in revealing their own feelings, who are accepting of others' feelings, and who are empathic, sensitive, reflective listeners.

What are the effects of such self-disclosure? Humanistic psychologist Sidney Jourard (1964) argued that dropping our masks, letting ourselves be known as we are, nurtures love. He presumed that it is gratifying to open up to another and then to receive the trust another implies by being open with us. For example, having an intimate friend with whom we can discuss threats to our self-image seems to help us survive such stresses (Swann & Predmore, 1985). A true friendship is a special relationship that helps us cope with our other relationships. 'When I am with my friend,' reflected the Roman playwright Seneca, 'methinks I am alone, and as much at liberty to speak anything as to think it.' At its best, marriage is such a friendship, sealed by commitment.

Children in a family also need openness and sincerity from parents. Self-disclosure is important in parent–child interaction and has impact on how adolescents develop, according to research by Håkan Stattin and Margaret Kerr at Örebro University, Sweden. The parent who most actively seeks information about the child may not in fact be the one who is best informed. Being informed may rest on the child being forthcoming rather than on the parent actively seeking information (Fletcher et al., 2004a). When researchers have considered both child self-disclosure and elicitation by parents in having knowledge of the child's whereabouts and companions, child-disclosure was far more predictive of accurate knowledge than parental control or solicitation (Stattin & Kerr, 2000).

Child self-disclosure appears to be important in predicting child outcomes as well, with those disclosing more showing less delinquency and depression, fewer deviant peer connections, and better school performance (Kerr & Stattin, 2000; Stattin & Kerr, 2000).

Intimate self-disclosure is also one of companionate love's delights. Dating and married couples who most reveal themselves to each other, express most satisfaction with their relationship and are more likely to endure in it (Berg & McQuinn, 1986; Hendrick et al., 1988; Sprecher, 1987). In a study of newlywed couples that were all equally in love, those who most deeply and accurately knew each other were most likely to enjoy enduring love (Neff & Karney, 2005). Married partners who mostly strongly agree that 'I try to share my most intimate thoughts and feelings with my partner' tend to have the most satisfying marriages (Sanderson & Cantor, 2001).

Researchers have also found that women are often more willing to disclose their fears and weaknesses than are men (Cunningham, 1981). As feminist writer Kate Millett (1975) put it, 'Women express, men repress'. Nevertheless, men today, particularly men with egalitarian gender-role attitudes, seem increasingly willing to reveal intimate feelings and to enjoy the satisfactions that accompany a relationship of mutual trust and self-disclosure. And that, say Arthur Aron and Elaine Aron (1996), is the essence of love – two selves connecting, disclosing and identifying with each other; two selves, each retaining their individuality, yet sharing activities, delighting in similarities and mutually supporting (Figure 9.9).

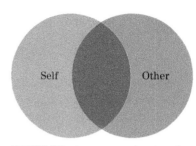

**FIGURE 9.9** Love: an overlapping of selves – you become part of me, I part of you

SOURCE: A. L. Weber and J. Harvey, *Perspective on Close Relationships*. Published by Allyn & Bacon, Boston, MA. Copyright © 1994 by Pearson Education. Reprinted by permission of the publisher.

That being so, might we cultivate closeness by experiences that mirror the escalating closeness of budding friendships? The Arons and their collaborators (1997) wondered. So they paired volunteer students who were strangers to each other for 45 minutes. For the first 15 minutes, they shared thoughts on a list of personal but low-intimacy topics such as 'When did you last sing to yourself?' The next 15 minutes were spent on more intimate topics such as 'What is your most treasured memory?' The last 15 minutes invited even more self-disclosure, with questions such as 'Complete this sentence: "I wish I had someone with whom I could share …" ' and 'When did you last cry in front of another person? By yourself?'

Compared with control participants who spent the 45 minutes in small-talk ('What was your high school like?' 'What is your favourite holiday?'), those who experienced the escalating self-disclosure ended the hour feeling remarkably close to their conversation partners – in fact, 'closer than the closest relationship in the lives of 30 per cent of similar students', reported the researchers. These relationships surely were not yet marked by the loyalty and commitment of true friendship. Nevertheless, the experiment provides a striking demonstration of how readily a sense of closeness to others can grow, given open self-disclosure – which can also occur via the Internet.

Sometimes self-disclosure is easier on the Internet where you do not meet people face to face. You can reveal things about yourself in a fairly anonymous situation. The people that you are revealing your inner secrets to may not even know your name. Researchers have found that the process of self-disclosure is much quicker in online relationships as the environment is a much safer one to reveal private aspects of our selves (e.g. Whitty, 2008). This possibility of self-disclosure has been used in therapy and psychological counselling on the Internet. Those using these services sometimes find it easier or more convenient to talk about their problems and situations where nobody is watching them face to face. When you open up in cyberspace you have more control. You can stop whenever you feel like it, and turn off your computer.

Your behaviour on the Internet versus face-to-face contact can differ due to the security of anonymity; a wider discussion of individual behaviour and differences between virtual and physical behaviour can be found in Chapter 3.

## research close-up

### DOES LOVE MEAN NEVER HAVING TO SAY YOU'RE SORRY?

*Source*: *Schumann, K. (2012). Does love mean never having to say you're sorry? Associations between relationship satisfaction, perceived apology sincerity, and forgiveness.* Journal of Social and Personal Relationships, *29(7), 997–1010.*

### Introduction

Researchers have often stated that apologies can heal relationships that are damaged and can be used in the resolution of conflict (Gibney et al., 2008; Lazare, 2004). An apology can increase a person's likelihood of forgiving the transgressor. This study argues that many studies of forgiveness have used hypothetical examples or apologies for minor offences against strangers. In order to gain a more 'real-world' understanding of forgiveness it is important to examine real relationships and forgiveness, rather than artificially created scenarios that have no real emotional context for the participants. Mathias Allemand, Irina Amberg, Daniel Zimprich and Frank Fincham (2007) suggest that people in romantic relationships with high levels of satisfaction are more likely to forgive their partner for transgressions. However, what remains to be examined is the connection between apology and forgiveness in romantic relationships. Some apologies are more likely to evoke forgiveness. Certainly, the sincerity of an apology is important in forgiveness – the more sincere the apology is judged, the more likely a person is to forgive (Risen & Gilovich, 2007). This study sets out to examine cohabiting partners and determine if apologies were more strongly associated with forgiveness among participants who rate their relationship as high satisfaction than those who rate their relationship as low satisfaction, as well as the effects of the sincerity of the apology on the forgiveness by the other partner.

### Method

A total of 120 participants (60 male and 60 female) were recruited. All were in some form of cohabiting romantic relationship. The mean relationship length was 4.93 years (sd = 2.89 years). Participants were asked to complete a four-item measure of relationship satisfaction, and the four items were combined to create a reliable satisfaction score.

Participants were then given a username and password and were asked to complete an online diary every night for seven consecutive nights. Participants were asked to keep their diary entry confidential, even from their partner. Each time they logged into their diary they were asked to report anything their partner had done that day to them that they felt was negative. They were then asked how severe they felt that transgression was, if they had forgiven their partner, and to what extent the issue was resolved. They were also asked if there had been an apology. For those participants who said there had been an apology, they were asked how sincere they felt the apology to be, and to report the apology verbatim. Apologies and transgression were coded into groups for quantitative analysis.

### Results

Overall, the relationship satisfaction of the participants was reported as high. Of the 120 participants, the overall completion of the diary was high, with the average completion being 6.67 of the 7 days; 104 participants reported at least 1 transgression over the 7 days, and the mean number of transgressions for these participants was 2.23 over the week. Participants received an apology in 30.84 per cent of cases. The apologies given included some frequent elements, the most frequent element was remorse, and this was in 91.86 per cent of the reported apologies. The other elements that occurred in the apologies were an explanation (36.05 per cent), and acceptance of responsibility (27.91 per cent), admission of wrongdoing (6.98 per cent), an offer of reparation (5.81 per cent), forbearance or patience (5.82 per cent) and acknowledgement of harm (1.16 per cent). Interestingly, none of the apologies included a request for forgiveness. Participants' relationship satisfaction was strongly correlated with forgiveness. Also, one's willingness to forgive one's partner transgression depended on the interplay between relationship satisfaction and whether or not there was an apology. Specifically participants' ratings of apology, forgiveness and the resolution of the dispute were highly correlated ($r = .71$, $p < .001$). The level of satisfaction in the relationship was also positively associated with forgiveness (parameter estimate $= .35$ (SE $= .13$), $t(79.49) = 2.74$, $p = .008$).

## Discussion

These results support the idea that an apology is important in resolving conflicts in romantic relationships. But more interestingly, it seems that it is the state of the relationship as well as the presence of an apology, and the level of satisfaction felt, that is an indicator for forgiveness.

Interestingly, when there was no apology given, participants who reported high relationship satisfaction were more likely to forgive their partner than participants with low satisfaction even when they had received an apology. What also emerges from the analysis is that participants who felt more satisfied in their relationship, were more likely to report the apology as sincere. This seems to indicate that disputes in highly satisfying relationship are more likely to be resolved, making them more secure. However, disputes in less satisfying relationships are less likely to be resolved, making those relationships less stable. This would explain why couples who are involved in mutually satisfying, happy relationships seem to be able to cope with problems that occur and maintain their relationship, while those in less stable relationships seem to have serious problems over things that other couples cope with.

As the mean level of relationship satisfaction was reported as high, this does bring into question what the results would be with a mean level of satisfaction that was lower. Also, the reporting took place every evening, giving participants a chance to cool off from the initial hurt or anger at the transgression. It would therefore be interesting to have a reporting method that allowed participants to give their feelings closer to the event. All participants in this study were heterosexual, so it would be useful to have gay or lesbian participants included in order to be more representative of wider romantic relationships.

This study would seem to suggest further investigation into the relationship between forgiveness, apology, and nature of the relationship between the victim and transgressor.

## Forgiveness

As happy and fulfilling as relationships can be, there are almost inevitably going to be problems. Arguments, hurting the other's feelings, and betrayal can all cause bumps in the road of a relationship. In order to maintain the relationship, we need to forgive the other. While this is easy to say, it can be more difficult to do. When our partner hurts us, whether purposively or not, in order for the relationship to be maintained and continue, we need to forgive them. Apology is important. We are far more likely to forgive someone who apologizes to us than if they don't. Relationships in which transgressions are apologized for, and where forgiveness takes place are likely to be more satisfactory than those where the apology/forgiveness process is not present (Hannon et al., 2010).

Single. A social failure or a social success?

SOURCE: © Jonathon Ross/Dreamstime.com

### Being Single

As many societies place a high value on being in a close romantic relationship and marriage, it is unsurprising that those of us who find ourselves single, without a partner, can feel on the margins of society and something of a social failure. At a time with high divorce rates and falling marriage rates, being single is not an uncommon experience. In their interview study of young single women (aged 20–48 years), Anna Sandfield and Carol Percy (2003) found that they treated their single status as both problematic and temporary. In their qualitative study of single women, Jill Reynolds and Margaret Wetherell (2003) noted that they can find themselves in a dilemma. On the one hand, single women can consider themselves a social failure. They have not met society's standards of a successful partnership. However, on the other hand, as a single woman they have achieved independence and exercised personal choice and self-actualization. It is perhaps notable that the research literature on single men is somewhat more scant!

## HOW DO RELATIONSHIPS END?

*Often love dies. What factors predict marital dissolution? How do couples typically detach or renew their relationships?*

In 1971 a man wrote a love poem to his bride, slipped it into a bottle, and dropped it into the Pacific Ocean between Seattle and Hawaii. A decade later, a jogger found it on a Guam beach:

> If, by the time this letter reaches you, I am old and gray, I know that our love will be as fresh as it is today.

> It may take a week or it may take years for this note to find you … If this should never reach you, it will still be written in my heart that I will go to extreme means to prove my love for you. Your husband, Bob.

The woman to whom the love note was addressed was reached by phone. When the note was read to her she burst out laughing. And the more she heard, the harder she laughed. 'We're divorced,' she finally said, and slammed down the phone.

So it often goes. Comparing their unsatisfying relationship with the support and affection they imagine are available elsewhere, people are divorcing more often all over the world. The differences in divorce rates between countries are however huge and culturally dependent. Enduring relationships are rooted in enduring love and satisfaction, but also in inattention to possible alternative partners, fear of the termination cost, and a sense of moral obligation (Adams & Jones, 1997; Miller, 1997). As economic and social barriers to divorce weakened during the 1960s and 1970s, thanks partly to women's increasing employment, divorce rates rose. 'We are living longer, but loving more briefly,' quipped Os Guiness (1993, p. 309).

When a marriage is 'very happy', life as a whole usually seems 'very happy' (see Figure 9.10).

When relationships suffer, those without better alternatives or who feel invested in a relationship (through time, energy, mutual friends, possessions and, perhaps, children) will seek alternatives to exiting the relationship. Caryl Rusbult and her colleagues (1986, 1987, 1998) have explored three ways of coping with a failing relationship (Table 9.1). Some people exhibit *loyalty* – by waiting for conditions to improve. The problems are too painful to confront and the risks of separation are too great, so the loyal partner perseveres, hoping the good old days will return. Others (especially men) exhibit *neglect*; they ignore the partner and allow the relationship to deteriorate. With painful dissatisfactions ignored, an insidious emotional uncoupling ensues as the partners talk less and begin redefining their lives without each other. Still others will *voice* their concerns and take active steps to improve the relationship by discussing problems, seeking advice and attempting to change.

Study after study – in fact, 115 studies of 45 000 couples – reveal that unhappy couples disagree, command, criticize and put down. Happy couples more often agree, approve, assent and laugh (Karney & Bradbury, 1995; Noller & Fitzpatrick, 1990). After observing 2000 couples, John Gottman (1994, 1998) noted that healthy marriages were not necessarily devoid of conflict. Rather, they were marked by an ability to reconcile differences and to overbalance criticism with affection. In successful marriages, positive interactions (smiling, touching, complimenting, laughing) outnumbered negative interactions (sarcasm, disapproval, insults) by at least a five-to-one ratio.

It's not distress and arguments that predict divorce, add Ted Huston and colleagues (2001) from their following of newlyweds through time. (Most newlyweds experience conflict.) Rather, it's coldness, disillusionment and hopelessness that predict a dim marital future. This is especially so, observed William Swann and his associates (2003, 2006), when inhibited men are coupled with critical women.

Why do some relationships flourish while others fail? While it is difficult to be exact, some of the aspects of commitment we looked at earlier in the chapter seem to be important. In addition, there seem to be other factors at play as well. Edward Deci and Richard Ryan (1985; Ryan and Deci, 2000) devised the self-determination theory, in which the autonomy of the individual is central to understanding how people approach the resolution of conflict in relationships, and thus their continuance. Autonomy refers to the sense of control the individual has over their actions, behaviours or choices. They found that people who show autonomy in their romantic relationships and who are autonomously invested in those relationships will be less defensive in their

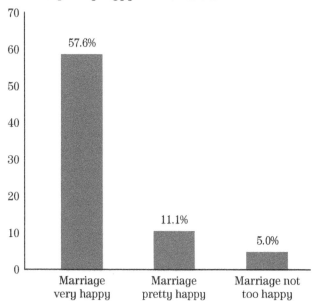

**Percentage very happy with life as whole**

FIGURE 9.10 National Opinion Research Center surveys of 23 076 married Americans, 1972–2004

TABLE 9.1 Responses to relationship distress

|  | Passive | Active |
|---|---|---|
| **Constructive** | *Loyalty: Await improvement* | *Voice: Seek to improve relationships* |
| **Destructive** | *Neglect: Ignore the partner* | *Exit: End the relationship* |

SOURCE: Rusbult et al., 1986, 1987, 1998, 2001.

response to relationship conflict. These people are likely to remain more satisfied in the relationship. So people who are in satisfying relationships where they have a sense of control over the relationship will tend to be open to resolving conflicts in that relationship. Raymond Knee, Cynthia Lonsbary, Amy Canevello and Heather Patrick (2005) argue that the autonomy of one partner may help the other partner to feel unconditionally supported. This unconditional support is then related to a less defensive response by the partners to conflict within the relationship, making it more likely that conflicts will be resolved and the relationship will continue.

There are also individual differences to threats to the romantic relationship. Sandra Murray, John Holmes and Nancy Collins (2006) discussed how risk regulation theory examines the interaction of self-esteem and the security the individual feels in their relationship. Risk regulation theory states that those with low self-esteem often have high levels of anxiety about how much their partner loves and accepts them. In the face of threats to their relationship, even if that threat is very minor, they will tend to react with exaggerated self-protection, and distance themselves from their partner. As a result, this can often be a self-fulfilling prophesy, with the partner of the person with low self-esteem eventually withdrawing from the relationship in which their partner has distanced themselves from them in reaction to a threat. One strategy that can address this is the use of self-affirmation strategies to increase the self-esteem. By increasing the individual's self-esteem this should help to stop them from distancing themselves from their partner when a threat to a relationship occurs. This should then reduce the distancing which can lead to the break-up of the relationship (Jaremka et al., 2011).

Successful couples have learned, sometimes aided by communication training, to restrain the poisonous put-downs and gut-level reactions, to fight fairly (by stating feelings without insulting), and to depersonalize conflict with comments such as 'I know it's not your fault' (Markman et al., 1988; Notarius & Markman, 1993; Yovetich & Rusbult, 1994). Would unhappy relationships get better if the partners agreed to *act* more as happy couples do – by complaining and criticizing less, by affirming and agreeing more, by setting aside times to voice their concerns, by praying or playing together daily? As attitudes trail behaviours, do affections trail actions?

Joan Kellerman, James Lewis and James Laird (1989) wondered. They knew that among couples passionately in love, eye gazing is typically prolonged and mutual (Rubin, 1973). Would intimate eye gazing similarly stir feelings between those not in love (much as 45 minutes of escalating self-disclosure evoked feelings of closeness among those unacquainted students)? To find out, they asked unacquainted male–female pairs to gaze intently for 2 minutes either at each other's hands or into each other's eyes. When they separated, the eye gazers reported a tingle of attraction and affection towards each other. Simulating love had begun to stir it.

By enacting and expressing love, researcher Robert Sternberg (1988) believes the passion of initial romance can evolve into enduring love:

> 'Living happily ever after' need not be a myth, but if it is to be a reality, the happiness must be based upon different configurations of mutual feelings at various times in a relationship. Couples who expect their passion to last forever, or their intimacy to remain unchallenged, are in for disappointment ... We must constantly work at understanding, building, and rebuilding our loving

relationships. Relationships are constructions, and they decay over time if they are not maintained and improved. We cannot expect a relationship simply to take care of itself, any more than we can expect that of a building. Rather, we must take responsibility for making our relationships the best they can be.

What is evident is that in order for relationships to flourish there must be commitment, investment and effort from both parties. The greater the effort, the more rewarding the relationship ultimately is.

### focus on

SEXUALITY AND ATTRACTION: ARE THERE REAL DIFFERENCES?

Much of the research in the area of sexual mate attraction is focused solely on heterosexual couples. This leaves an important question open: is there a difference in the role of physical attraction for people who are gay and lesbian in contrast to people who are heterosexual? Do gay men and lesbian women have different priorities around physical attraction from their heterosexual counterparts? Some perspectives on sexual mate selection don't seem to have answers to the question of what do people who find the same sex attractive find attractive about them. The evolutionary perspective focuses on heterosexual attraction, and views the attraction traits as evidence of their theory of biological imperative; the core goal of reproduction in heterosexual relationships. If attraction isn't heterosexual, do the traits valued by heterosexual individuals have the same desirability?

Richard Lippa (2007) analysed data from a BBC Internet survey that attracted 119 733 male and 98 462 female participants from around the world, looking at the traits that they found attractive in a partner. Participants were asked to list the three traits that they found most important from a list of 23. Lippa found that there were predictable results for heterosexual men and women, with men valuing intelligence, good looks and humour as the most important and women valuing humour, intelligence and honesty as the most important traits in a mate. Interestingly, the traits that gay and lesbian participants identified were closely matched to their heterosexual counterparts, although the overall results for gay men did place slightly more emphasis on physical attractiveness than for heterosexual men. Lippa argues that the patterns of trait attractiveness is more of a function of your desired partners' gender than your own.

Thao Ha, Judith van den Berg, Rutger Engels and Anna Lichtwarch-Ashoff (2012) carried out a study examining partner preference in heterosexual male and female, gay and lesbian participants. Participants were shown hypothetical profiles of the gender that they were attracted to. These profiles included details of the person's status and ambition. The participants were also asked to complete self-reported ratings of the traits that they found most important in the desirability of a mate. They found that it was the heterosexual men that valued physical attractiveness the most, followed by homosexual men. Heterosexual women valued physical attractiveness slightly less than gay men, and homosexual women valued physical attractiveness least of all. In terms of status, heterosexual women rated social status as most important, followed by homosexual men, then heterosexual men, with lesbian women placed the lowest importance on status in a potential partner.

These studies seem to indicate that, while there are some differences between sexualities, the things that we find attractive are very similar, and that instead of looking at this question in terms of what do particular sexualities find attractive, it has more to do with the gender of the person we find attractive than our own gender. The major flaw of any study that examines what we find attractive is that the nuances and individualities of our own desires are lost in the mass of data. Human desire is complex and often surprising; just look around at the people you know, sometimes the people we would least predict as a couple come together in mutual desire.

QUESTIONS

**1** How could the evolutionary perspective on sexual mate selection explain non-heterosexual desire?

**2** If research shows that men and women both value similar traits in sexual mate selection, how useful is it to examine human desire divided by gender?

## SUMMING UP: ATTRACTION AND INTIMACY

### WHAT LEADS TO FRIENDSHIP AND ATTRACTION?

☐ The best predictor of whether any two people are friends is their proximity or availability to each other. These are conducive to repeated exposure and interaction, which enables us to discover similarities and to feel each other's liking.

☐ An important determinant of initial attraction is physical attractiveness. Both in laboratory studies and in field experiments involving blind dates, college students tend to prefer attractive people. In everyday life, however, people often choose someone whose attractiveness roughly matches their own (or who, if less attractive, has other compensating qualities). Positive attributions about attractive people define a physical-attractiveness stereotype – an assumption that what is beautiful is good.

☐ Liking is greatly aided by similarity of attitudes, beliefs and values. Likeness leads to liking; opposites rarely attract.

☐ We are conditioned to like somebody or something placed in a context we already enjoy.

### WHAT IS LOVE?

☐ Researchers have characterized love as having components of friendship, passion and uncommitted game playing. Passionate love is experienced as a bewildering confusion of ecstasy and anxiety, elation and pain. The two-factor theory of emotion suggests that in a romantic context, arousal from any source, even painful experiences, can be steered into passion.

☐ In the best of relationships, the initial passionate high settles to a steadier, more affectionate relationship called companionate love.

### WHAT ENABLES CLOSE RELATIONSHIPS?

☐ From infancy to old age, attachments are central to human life. Secure attachments, as in an enduring marriage or partnership, mark happy lives.

☐ Companionate love is most likely to endure when both partners feel the partnership is equitable, with both perceiving themselves receiving from the relationship in proportion to what they contribute to it.

☐ One reward of companionate love is the opportunity for intimate self-disclosure, a state achieved gradually as each partner reciprocates the other's increasing openness.

### HOW DO RELATIONSHIPS END?

☐ Often love does not endure and researchers have discerned predictors of marital dissolution. One predictor is an individualistic culture that values feelings over commitment; other factors include the couple's age, education, values and similarity.

☐ Researchers are also identifying the process through which couples either detach or rebuild their relationships. And they are identifying the positive and non-defensive communication styles that mark healthy, stable marriages.

## CRITICAL QUESTIONS

**1** How can the mere-exposure effect be explained?

**2** Why do we like things associated with ourselves?

**3** How does Internet dating differ from the more traditional spaces for meeting a partner? If we start to use Internet dating more to find a partner, will this have an impact on the scope of people we are exposed to?

**4** Critically evaluate the concept that beauty is a good predictor of character.

**5** Could you become a human being without interacting with others? Explain.

## RECOMMENDED READINGS

### Classic Papers

Buss, D. M. (1989). Sex differences in human mate preferences: Evolutionary hypotheses tested in 37 cultures. *Brain and Behavioural Sciences*, **12**, 1–49.

*One of the classic examinations of the evolutionary basis for sexual mate selection. Particularly useful for the cross-cultural basis for the data.*

Sternberg, R. J., & Grajek, S. (1984). The nature of love. *Journal of Personality and Social Psychology*, **47**(2), 312–329.

*This looks at the structure of love and the bonds that maintain it.*

### Contemporary papers

Castro, F. N., & de Araujo Lopes, F. (2011). Romantic preferences in Brazilian undergraduate students: From the short term to the long term. *Journal of Sex Research*, **48**(5), 479–485.

*This examines the shift in what male and female participants value in a relationship depending on whether the relationship is short or long term.*

Finkel, E. J., Eastwick, P. W., Karney, B. R., Reis, H. T., & Sprecher, S. (2012). Online dating: A critical analysis from the perspective of psychological science. *Psychological Science in the Public Interest*, **13**(1), 3–66.

*An interesting examination of an expanding space for meeting a partner.*

**10**

"*Doing nothing for others is the undoing of ourselves.*"

Horace Mann, 1796–1859

# HELPING

© AFP/Getty Images

The statue of Buddha at Wat Mahathat, Sukhothai (Thailand). The teachings of Buddhism are based on compassion and helping.

SOURCE: © Dibrova/iStock

The de Long expedition, with their boat *Jeannette*, searched in vain from 1879 to 1881 for the Swedish polar explorer Nordenskj ld and his boat *Vega*. *Jeanette* became trapped in the ice in the Arctic Sea and, after one year, she went down in the ice and was abandoned by de Long and his crew. They had to walk across the ice towards Siberia and civilization. One of the crew, a Dane called Eriksen, got frostbitten legs and could not walk. They faced a dilemma. Should they leave him on the ice and hasten towards food and shelter, or should they reduce their speed, risking their own lives, but try to save Eriksen? The group of polar explorers chose the second option. Many of them, including Eriksen, did not survive. This situation has been a dilemma for many explorers and polar expeditions. De Long and his crew had demonstrated altruistic behaviour (De Long, 1883).

Hearing the rumble of an approaching New York subway train, Everett Sanderson leapt down onto the tracks and raced towards the approaching headlights to rescue Michelle De Jesus, a 4 year old who had fallen from the platform. Three seconds before the train would have run her over, Sanderson flung Michelle into the crowd above. As the train roared in, he himself failed in his first effort to jump back to the platform. At the last instant, bystanders pulled him to safety (Young, 1977).

Less dramatic acts of comforting, caring and compassion abound every day. Without asking anything in return, people offer directions, donate money, give blood, volunteer time.

☐ Why, and when, will people help?

☐ Who will help?

☐ What can be done to lessen indifference and increase helping?

These are this chapter's primary questions.

We focus primarily on how and why individuals react towards others in need of help more than on how societies support those in need. Some cultures and societies emphasize helping more than others, by redistributing wealth and resources by their infrastructure (for example, taxation to pay for national healthcare). The welfare states in Europe practise what could be called 'prosocial politics'. Collectivistic cultures also offer help, but this tends to be done through family solidarity.

## ALTRUISM AND HELPING

**altruism** *a motive to increase another's welfare without conscious regard for one's self-interests*

Altruism is selfishness in reverse. An altruistic person is concerned and helpful even when no benefits are offered or expected in return. In Christianity, Jesus' parable of the Good Samaritan provides the classic illustration:

A man was going down from Jerusalem to Jericho, and fell into the hands of robbers, who stripped him, beat him, and went away, leaving him half dead. Now by chance a priest was going down that road; and when he saw him, he passed by on the other side. So likewise a Levite, when he came to the place and saw him, passed by on the other side. But a Samaritan while travelling came near him; and when he saw him, he was moved with pity. He went to him and bandaged his wounds, having poured oil and wine on them. Then he put him on his own animal, brought him to an inn, and took care of him. The next day he took out two denarii, gave them to the innkeeper, and said, 'Take care of him; and when I come back, I will repay you whatever more you spend.'

(Luke 10:30–35, NRSV)

The Samaritan illustrates altruism. Filled with compassion, he is motivated to give a stranger time, energy and money while expecting neither repayment nor appreciation.

Other religions also encourage altruism through stories of selfless acts. In Islam, the narration from the Prophet Muhammad 'None of you truly believes until he loves for his brother what he loves for himself' is a depiction of altruism, and one of the five pillars of Islam is *zakat* or almsgiving. Important principles of Buddhism include *Sila*, which requires people to treat others as they would prefer to be treated themselves, and *Dãna*, which loosely translates as 'generosity'. Buddha also proclaimed 'right action' (or altruism) as one of the eight steps on the path to enlightenment. The neopagan religion Wicca, has teachings in morality which are based on the Wiccan Rede, stating 'an it harm none, do what ye will'. Put simply, you are free to act as you wish, but you must take responsibility for your own actions and the consequences they have for others.

There are many examples of altruism outside of religion. On 15 April 1989, one of the worst tragedies in football occurred: the Hillsborough disaster. Ninety-six Liverpool fans lost their lives while watching an FA cup semi-final match between their team and Nottingham Forest at the Hillsborough stadium in Sheffield. While the tragedy was unfolding, fans, some badly injured themselves, tried to help rescue others from the crush that was occurring in one of the stands and in the direct aftermath local residents, who had no ties with those involved, freely offered their support in the form of the use of their phones, hot food and drink, lifts back home and sometimes even a place to stay for the evening.

## WHY DO WE HELP?

*To study helping acts, social psychologists identify circumstances in which people perform such deeds. Before looking at what the research reveals, let's consider what might motivate helping.*

### SOCIAL EXCHANGE AND SOCIAL NORMS

Suppose the blood donation service turns up at your university campus and you're asked to participate. Might you not weigh the *costs* of donating (needle prick, time, fatigue) against those of not donating (guilt, disapproval)? Might you not also weigh the *benefits* of donating (feeling good about helping someone, free refreshments) against those of not donating (saving the time, discomfort and anxiety)? According to social-exchange theory – supported by studies of blood donors by Jane Allyn Piliavin (2003) and her research team (1982) – such subtle calculations precede decisions to help or not. This pro and contra calculation characterizes adults' decision making generally, not just with regard to helpful actions or deeds.

Several theories of helping agree that, in the long run, helping behaviour benefits the giver as well as the receiver. Most cultures do not only exchange material goods and money but also social goods – love, services, information, status (Fisek & Hysom, 2008; Foa & Foa, 1975). Social-exchange theory does not declare that we *consciously* monitor costs and rewards of every single social transaction, but that such considerations influence our behaviour.

social-exchange theory *the theory that human interactions are most accurately described as social transactions between people, where people exchange rewards and costs*

### Rewards

Rewards that motivate helping may be external or internal. When businesses donate money to improve their corporate image or when someone offers another a ride hoping to receive appreciation or friendship, the reward is external. We give to get. Thus, we are most eager to help someone attractive to us, someone whose approval we desire (Krebs, 1970; Unger, 1979). External rewards from somebody else tell us that they appreciate our helpful behaviour. This acknowledgement is important for our status and reputation and we are eager to please. Helping is used as a tool for achieving something, such as honour, respect or money. External rewards could, however, reduce spontaneous motivation to help – altruistic behaviour.

Felix Warneken and Michael Tomasello found helping behaviour among infants 20 months of age. They concluded that external rewards undermine altruistic tendencies, 'even the earliest helping behaviours of young children are intrinsically motivated and socialization practices involving extrinsic rewards can undermine this tendency' (Warneken & Tomasello, 2008).

If helping is used as a tool for achieving money, could money be used to get help? And what kind of help would that be? Felix Oberholzer-Gee wondered if people would be more willing to allow an apparently busy and harassed stranger to jump the queue if they offered money as compensation. He found that money does encourage helping behaviour, but the exchange of favours is no ordinary market transaction. Money does not reliably trigger greater assistance on every occasion. Once helpers understand that a stranger wilfully employs incentives to encourage assistance, these incentives prove ineffective (Oberholzer-Gee, 2007).

Rewards may also be internal and personal when they increase our sense of self-worth. Nearly all blood donors in Jane Piliavin's research agreed that giving blood 'makes you feel good about yourself' and 'gives you a feeling of self-satisfaction'. Indeed, 'Give blood', advises an old Red Cross poster. 'All you'll feel is good'. This helps explain why people far from home will do kindnesses to strangers whom they will never see again.

The positive effect of helping on feelings of self-worth is one explanation for why so many people feel good after doing good. One month-long study of 85 couples found that giving emotional support to one's partner was positive for the giver; giving support boosted the giver's mood (Gleason et al., 2003). Carolyn Schwartz, Penelope Keyl, John Marcum and Rita Bode (2009) report that teenagers who engage in altruistic behaviours experience better mental health and have lower mortality rates than non-altruistic adults. They also found that altruism was positively associated with health for females and with well-being for both young males and females. Piliavin (2003) and Susan Andersen (1998) point to dozens of studies showing that youth engaged in community service projects, school-based 'service learning' or tutoring children, develop social skills and positive social values. They are at markedly less risk for delinquency and school dropout, and are more likely to become engaged citizens. Volunteering likewise benefits the morale and even the health of adults. Those who do good tend to do well.

This cost–benefit analysis can seem demeaning. In defence of the theory, however, is it not a credit to humanity that helping can be inherently rewarding, that much of our behaviour is not antisocial but 'prosocial', that we can find fulfilment in the giving of love? How much worse if we gained pleasure only by serving ourselves.

'Men do not value a good deed unless it brings a reward.'
   Ovid, *Epistulae ex Ponto*

'True,' some readers may reply. 'Still, reward theories imply that a helpful act is never truly altruistic – that we merely call it "altruistic" when its rewards are inconspicuous. If we help the screaming woman so we can gain social approval, relieve our distress, prevent guilt or boost our self-image, is it really altruistic?'

This has been hotly debated for a long time and concerns to some extent how we define altruism. Most social psychologists today will say that helping behaviour makes the helper feel good, but this is not the only motivation. Egoism – the idea that self-interest motivates all behaviour – has fallen into disrepute. By focusing on rewards within the individual it ignores the social aspects of a person – that they might actually want to help others.

**egoism** *a motive (supposedly underlying all behaviour) to increase one's own welfare. The opposite of altruism, which aims to increase another's welfare*

### Internal Rewards

The benefits of helping include internal self-rewards. Near someone in distress, we may feel distress. You feel hurt when innocent people are beaten or seen starving. You take care of your dog when it needs help because you feel bad leaving it alone. A woman's scream outside your window arouses and distresses you. If you cannot reduce your arousal by interpreting the scream as a playful shriek, then you may investigate or give aid, thereby reducing your distress (Piliavin & Piliavin, 1973). Altruism researcher Dennis Krebs (1975) found that male students whose physiological responses and self-reports revealed the most arousal in response to another's distress also gave the most help to the person. Also Eric Stocks, David Lishner and Stephanie Decker (2009) found that higher rates of helping were observed among empathically aroused participants. The main reason, however, was not egoistical, to reduce one's own distress, but to help somebody else 'as empathy evokes an altruistic motive to reduce the victim's suffering rather than an egoistic aversive-arousal motive'.

### Guilt

Distress is not the only negative emotion we act to reduce. Throughout recorded history, guilt has been a painful emotion, so painful that we will act in ways that avoid guilt feelings. As Everett Sanderson remarked after saving the child who fell from the subway platform, 'If I hadn't tried to save that little girl, if I had just stood there like the others, I would have died inside. I would have been no good to myself from then on.'

Cultures and institutions, for instance the church, have institutionalized ways to relieve guilt: animal and human sacrifices, offerings of grain and money, penitent behaviour, confession, denial. In ancient Israel, the sins of the people were periodically laid on a 'scapegoat' animal that was then led into the wilderness to carry away the people's guilt.

## research close-up

### YOUNG CHILDREN ARE INTRINSICALLY MOTIVATED TO SEE OTHERS HELPED

**Source:** *Hepach, R., Vaish, A., & Tomasello, M. (2012). Young children are intrinsically motivated to see others helped.* Psychological Science, *23(9), 967–972.*

### Introduction

Psychological research has shown that young children, from about 12 months old, start to help others. By the time they are 2 years old, they will offer help to someone else at a cost to themselves. But why? Where does this intrinsic motivation to help come from? Is it because the infant benefits in some way, or is it because even at a young age humans can be motivated by a genuine desire to help someone in need? Robert Hepach, Amrisha Vaish and Michael Tomasello set out to investigate. Their measure was a physiological one: pupil dilation. The pupil of the eye is connected to our sympathetic arousal system. In other words, when we feel sympathy for someone, it should be reflected in pupil dilation.

### Method

The 36 participants were 2 year olds, of which 18 were boys and 18 girls. A construction resembling a 'house' was placed in the lab, and each child in turn was placed on their parent's lap, seated facing the window of the house. At the window was a monitor screen. Every child watched a short video of an adult putting a toy cuddly dolphin to bed. During this stage, the child's pupil diameter was measured using an eye-tracking device. Children were then randomly assigned to one of three conditions.

Condition 1 was a 'help' condition. Children in this condition were carried away from the window and allowed to move freely inside the house for 15 seconds. In the house was the adult they had seen in the video, putting the toy dolphin to bed. Children were then carried back to the window and their pupil diameter was measured once again.

These children were then shown two further videos at the window. One video was of the adult reaching for the final can to complete a stacking tower. The other video showed an adult reaching for a crayon to complete a drawing. After each video, the child was carried into the house, allowed to move freely within 2 metres of the adult seen in the video, and given the opportunity to retrieve the object (crayon and can) the adult had been reaching for in the video, and hand it to the adult personally. Ten out of 12 children did so on both trials. The diameter of their pupil was re-measured once the child was carried back to the seat in front of the window.

Condition 2 was a 'no-help' condition. This followed the same procedure as for the 'help' condition, with one fundamental difference. The child was not allowed to retrieve the object for the adult. S/he was held back by the parent, and not allowed to move freely once inside the house between each viewing of the video. The diameter of their pupil was measured at each stage.

Condition 3 was a 'third-person-help' condition. This was almost identical to condition 2, but as the child was held back from helping the adult, a second experimenter retrieved the object for them, and handed it back to the adult. As in conditions 1 and 2, a measure of their pupil was taken at each stage.

### Results

A one-way analysis of variance revealed that the size of the children's pupil dilation in condition 2 (no help) was larger than in conditions 1 and 3.

Discussion

The researchers conclude that this physiological measure, pupil dilation, offers support for the idea that helping behaviour in young children is motivated by genuine concern for others. The enlarged pupil dilation in the no-help condition indicates higher levels of sympathetic arousal than in conditions 1 and 3. In this condition, the adult has not been helped, either by the infant or someone else. Their eyes indicate continued concern for the adult. However, in conditions 1 and 3, the adult has been helped, either directly or indirectly. As such, concern wanes. It doesn't matter who helps, as long as someone does. The researchers suggest that 'young children are aroused when they see other people in need and are motivated to see them helped'.

However, this research focuses on a very specific indicator of helping behaviour: pupil dilation. Can we confidently conclude this physiological measure reflects a child's concern for an adult and a willingness to help? It is difficult to measure young children's concern for others, and their motivations to help. This study offers one solution, but are there others we might want to include?

To examine the consequences of guilt, social psychologists have induced people to transgress: to lie, to deliver shock, to knock over a table loaded with alphabetized cards, to break a machine, to cheat. Afterwards, the guilt-laden participants may be offered a way to relieve their guilt: by confessing, by disparaging the one harmed, or by doing a good deed to offset the bad one. The results are remarkably consistent: people will do whatever can be done to expunge the guilt, relieve their bad feelings and restore their self-image. The success of some religions could be explained by the offering of release from the guilt feeling. In the Catholic Church, confessing guilt has been institutionalized. The forgiveness of their sins makes people feel less blameworthy. The truth and reconciliation processes in South Africa had the same effect. Whites who blamed their brutality to Blacks on the apartheid system were forgiven and felt relieved.

> Prejudice in all forms (individual and group) is covered in Chapter 13 with intergroup relations and conflict.

Picture yourself as a participant in an experiment conducted with university students by David McMillen and James Austin (1971). You and another student, each seeking to earn credit towards a course requirement, arrive for the experiment. Soon after, a confederate enters, portraying himself as a previous participant looking for a lost book. He strikes up a conversation in which he mentions that the experiment involves taking a multiple-choice test, for which most of the correct answers are 'B'. After the accomplice departs, the experimenter arrives, explains the experiment, and then asks, 'Have either of you been in this experiment before or heard anything about it?'

Would you lie? The behaviour of those who have gone before you in this experiment – 100 per cent of whom told the little lie – suggests that you would. After you have taken the test (without receiving any feedback on it), the experimenter says: 'You are free to leave. However, if you have some spare time, I could use your help in scoring some questionnaires.' Assuming you have told the lie, do you think you would now be more willing to volunteer some time? Judging from the results, the answer again is yes. On average, those who had not been induced to lie volunteered only 2 minutes of time. Those who had lied were apparently eager to redeem their self-image; on average they offered a whopping 63 minutes. One moral of this experiment was well expressed by a 7-year-old girl, who, in one of our own experiments, wrote: 'Don't Lie or youl Live with gilt' (and you will feel a need to relieve it).

Guilt seems to go some way to explaining people's motives to volunteer to help others. Gil Clary and Mark Synder (1999) identify guilt as one of six motives behind volunteering behaviour. Giving one's time and energy to help others can alleviate feelings of guilt over being more fortunate than others or to simply escape from your own problems by focusing on somebody else's. Jackie Abell (2012) found that feeling guilty over what humankind has done to other animals, is important to volunteers in conservation organizations who work to protect those species humans have brought to the brink of extinction. A stain on our human identity can motivate helping behaviour and a positive volunteer identity.

Our eagerness to do good after doing bad reflects our need to reduce *private* guilt and restore a shaken self-image. It also reflects our desire to reclaim a positive *public* image. We are more likely to redeem ourselves with helpful behaviour when other people know about our misdeeds (Carlsmith & Gross, 1969).

All in all, guilt leads to much good. By motivating people to confess, apologize, help and avoid repeated harm, it boosts sensitivity and sustains close relationships.

*Exceptions to the Feel Bad–Do Good Scenario*

Among well-socialized adults, should we always expect to find the 'feel bad–do good' phenomenon? No. In Chapter 8 we saw that one negative mood, anger, produces anything but compassion. Another exception is profound grief. People who suffer the loss of a spouse or a child, whether through death or separation, often undergo a period of intense self-preoccupation, which restrains giving to others (Aderman & Berkowitz, 1983; Gibbons & Wicklund, 1982). There are, however, exceptions from this common reaction, especially if the person who suffers a loss is attending to the distress of others. Camille Roman (2006) tells of a person who helps her workmates deal with the death of a valued colleague while simultaneously struggling with her own personal feelings of loss.

In a powerful laboratory simulation of self-focused grief, William Thompson, Claudia Cowan and David Rosenhan (1980) had students listen privately to a taped description of a person (whom they were to imagine was their best friend of the other sex) dying of cancer. The experiment focused some students' attention on their own worry and grief:

> He (she) could die and you would lose him, never be able to talk to him again. Or worse, he could die slowly. You would know every minute could be your last time together. For months you would have to be cheerful for him while you were sad. You would have to watch him die in pieces, until the last piece finally went, and you would be alone.

For others, it focused their attention on the friend:

> He spends his time lying in bed, waiting those interminable hours, just waiting and hoping for something to happen. Anything. He tells you that it's not knowing that is the hardest.

The researchers report that regardless of which tape the participants heard, they were profoundly moved and sobered by the experience, yet not the least regretful of participating (although some participants who in a control condition listened to a boring tape were regretful). Did their moods affect their helpfulness? When immediately thereafter they were given a chance to help a graduate student with her research anonymously, 25 per cent of those whose attention had been self-focused helped. Of those whose attention was other-focused, 83 per cent helped. The two groups were equally touched, but only the other-focused participants found helping someone especially rewarding. In short, the feel bad–do good effect occurs with people whose attention is on others, people for whom altruism is therefore rewarding. Other-focused people help more than self-focused people. If they are not self-preoccupied by depression or grief, sad people are sensitive, helpful people.

### Feel Good, Do Good

Are happy people unhelpful? Quite the contrary. There are few more consistent findings in psychology: happy people are helpful people. This effect occurs with both children and adults, regardless of whether the good mood comes from a success, from thinking happy thoughts, or from any of several other positive experiences (Salovey et al., 1991). One woman recalled her experience after falling in love:

> At the office, I could hardly keep from shouting out how deliriously happy I felt. The work was easy; things that had annoyed me on previous occasions were taken in stride. And I had strong impulses to help others; I wanted to share my joy. When Mary's typewriter broke down, I virtually sprang to my feet to assist. Mary! My former 'enemy'!

(Tennov, 1979, p. 22)

Novels, drama and fictional literature often deal with the theme of how love and success make people generous and positive towards others. And the opposite: how misery and unfair treatment breed negative feelings and behaviour. In research on happiness and helpfulness this phenomenon is studied more systematically, with the aim of trying to explain what most people experience in their everyday life. Here is an example.

In Opole, Poland, Dariusz Dolinski and Richard Nawrat (1998) found that a positive mood of relief can dramatically boost helping. Imagine yourself as one of their unwitting subjects. After illegally parking your car for a few moments, you return to discover what looks like a ticket under your windshield wiper (where parking tickets are placed). Groaning inwardly, you pick up the apparent ticket, and then are much relieved to discover it is only an advertisement. Moments later, a university student approaches you and asks you to spend 15 minutes answering questions – to 'help me complete my MA thesis'. Would your positive, relieved mood make you more likely to help? Indeed, 62 per cent of people whose fear had just turned to relief agreed willingly. That was nearly double the number who did so when no ticket-like paper was left or when it was left on the car door (not the usual place for a ticket).

School child packing food donations for the needy. As children mature, they usually come to take pleasure in being helpful to others.

SOURCE: © McGraw-Hill Education/Eclipse Studios

If sad people are sometimes extra helpful, how can it be that happy people are also helpful? Experiments reveal that several factors are at work (Carlson et al., 1988). Helping softens a bad mood and sustains a good mood (Grant & Sonnentag, 2010). (Perhaps you can recall feeling good after giving someone assistance or support?) A positive mood is, in turn, conducive to positive thoughts and positive self-esteem, which predispose us to positive behaviour (Berkowitz, 1987; Cunningham et al., 1990; Isen et al., 1978). In a good mood – after being given a gift or while feeling the warm glow of success – people are more likely to have positive thoughts and associations with being helpful. Positive thinkers are likely to be positive actors.

### Helping Norms

Often we help others not because we have calculated consciously that such behaviour is in our self-interest but because of a subtler form of self-interest: because something tells us we *ought* to. We ought to help a new neighbour move in. We ought to return the wallet we found. We ought to take notes for a fellow student who is ill. Norms, the *oughts* of our lives, are the non-written rules for social behaviour. These norms are often unconscious. They are perceived as natural, or *habitus*; a set of acquired patterns of thought, behaviour and taste, which is said by the acclaimed French sociologist and writer Pierre Bourdieu (1977) to constitute the link between social structures and social action. There are also norms for helping behaviour, which inform us of what is expected of us if we experience somebody in need of help. But do these helping norms exist in urban cities, often characterized by selfish behaviour, individualistic goals, and the pursuit of materialistic goods? Yes, say Lilian Phenice, Robert Giffore and Kyungsook Lee (2010). In their observations of members of the public holding the door open for strangers in a busy shopping mall in Midwest America, they found that the majority of men and women observed did so. The researchers argue behavioural displays as small and apparently insignificant as opening the door for someone, can have positive consequences in producing a more civil and polite society. Norms of helping *prescribe* proper behaviour. They release more or less automatic behaviour. We think it is natural to act in the way the norms prescribe. We do not need any additional arguments. Researchers who study helping behaviour have classified two social norms that motivate altruism: the reciprocity norm and the social-responsibility norm.

### The Reciprocity Norm

**reciprocity norm** *an expectation that people will help, not hurt, those who have helped them*

Sociologist Alvin Gouldner (1960) contended that one universal moral code is a reciprocity norm: *to those who help us, we should return help, not harm.* Gouldner believed this norm is as universal as the incest taboo and starts at an early age. Young children seem to reciprocate prosocial behaviour spontaneously. Friends reciprocate gifts more frequently than non-friends, suggesting that friendship affects the amount of reciprocity expressed (Fujisawa et al., 2008). We 'invest' in others and expect dividends. Politicians know that the one who gives a favour can later expect a favour. Mail surveys and solicitations sometimes include a little gift of money or personalized address labels, assuming some people will reciprocate the favour. The reciprocity norm even applies in marriage. At times, one may give more than one receives, but in the long run the exchange should balance out. In all such interactions, to receive without giving in return violates the reciprocity norm. This reminds us of the social-exchange theory mentioned earlier: that the reciprocity norm is based on expected exchange and the social benefits of helping behaviour.

When people cannot reciprocate, they may feel threatened and demeaned by accepting aid. Thus, proud, high-self-esteem people are often reluctant to seek help (Nadler & Fisher, 1986). Receiving unsolicited help can take one's self-esteem down a notch (Schneider et al., 1996; Shell & Eisenberg, 1992). Generally, it is in many ways easier to give than to receive. The person receiving help may feel inferior and also obliged by the norm to give something in return (Shell & Eisenberg, 1992).

The reciprocity norm reminds us to balance giving and receiving in social relations. But reciprocity is not the only social norm influencing helping behaviour. I am sure you have experienced helping somebody who cannot give anything back. The social-reciprocity norm is not expected to be fulfilled, for instance, when offering charity for the homeless, or giving money to starving people on other continents. People in developed and wealthy countries often want to help those who are victims of natural disasters. Consider, for example, the wave of international aid following the tsunami disaster in December 2004, which killed hundreds of thousands of people in Asian countries. Those who helped the victims by giving money did not expect anything back. It was 'natural', a social responsibility, to help fellow-beings hit by an unforeseen catastrophe.

### The Social-responsibility Norm

With people who clearly are dependent and unable to reciprocate, such as children, the severely impoverished and those with disabilities, another social norm motivates our helping. The social-responsibility norm is the belief that people should help those who need help, without regard to future exchanges (Berkowitz, 1972; Schwartz, 1975). The norm motivates people to retrieve a dropped book for a person on crutches, for example. The social responsibility norm is fulfilled in different ways in different countries and cultures. In the welfare states in Europe, for instance in the Nordic countries, people pay higher taxes so everybody can have free health services. A redistribution of wealth and income is accepted because of the social responsibility norm. And the norm is nurtured by welfare politics. In India, a relatively collectivist culture, people support the social-responsibility norm more strongly than in the individualist West (Baron & Miller, 2000). They voice an obligation to help even when the need is not life-threatening or the needy person – perhaps a stranger needing a bone marrow transplant – is outside their family circle. In other collectivistic cultures, for instance in China, people take care of their family members and others close to them, but do not care to the same degree about people not belonging to their *guanxi*, or close social network. The Chinese philosopher Confucius (551–479 BC) is responsible for social norms focusing on the family and the obligation (the norm) for everybody to support their kin (see Chapter 7). Parents taking care of their offspring when their children need support can expect to be looked after by their children when they are in need of care. This illustrates that sometimes there is a combination of reciprocity and responsibility norms.

**social-responsibility norm** *an expectation that people will help those needing help*

Even when helpers in Western countries remain anonymous and have no expectation of any reward, they help needy people (Shotland & Stebbins, 1983). However, they usually apply the social-responsibility norm selectively to those whose need appears not to be due to their own negligence. Especially among political conservatives (Skitka & Tetlock, 1993), the norm seems to be: give people what they deserve. If they are victims of circumstance, such as natural disaster, then by all means be generous. If they seem to have created their own problems (by laziness, immorality or lack of foresight, for example), then, the norm suggests, they don't deserve help. Responses are thus closely tied to *attributions*. If we attribute the need to an uncontrollable predicament, we help. If we attribute the need to the person's choices, fairness does not require us to help; we say it's the person's own fault (Weiner, 1980).

The key, say Udo Rudolph and colleagues (2004) from their review of more than three dozen pertinent studies, is whether your attributions evoke sympathy, which in turn motivates helping (see Figure 10.1).

Imagine yourself as one of the students in a study by Richard Barnes, William Ickes and Robert Kidd (1979). You receive a call from 'Tony Freeman', who explains that he is in your introductory psychology class. He says that he needs help for the upcoming exam and that he got your name from the class roster. 'I don't know. I just don't seem to take good notes in there,' Tony explains. 'I know I can, but sometimes I just don't feel like it, so most of the notes I have aren't very good to study with.' How sympathetic would you feel towards Tony? How much of a sacrifice would you make to lend him your notes? If you are like the students in this experiment, you would probably be much less inclined to help than if Tony had explained that his troubles were beyond his control. Thus, the social-responsibility norm compels us to help those most in need and those most deserving. We also feel most responsible for, and have more sympathy with, people close to us.

As we will see later in this chapter, knowing the victim or regarding him or her as belonging to your ingroup matters. Tehila Kogut and Ilana Ritov (2007) at the Hebrew University in Israel reviewed research that shows people are more willing to help strangers when the victims are identified. In their own studies they found that only when the victims are perceived as belonging to their own ingroup, willingness to help a single identified individual is greater than willingness to help a group of individuals.

*Gender and Receiving Help*

If, indeed, perception of another's need strongly determines one's willingness to help, will women, if perceived as less competent and more dependent, receive more help than men? That is indeed the case, at least in Western societies. Alice Eagly and Maureen Crowley (1986) located 35 studies that compared help received by male or female victims. (Virtually all the studies involved short-term encounters with strangers in need – the very situations in which people expect males to be chivalrous, note Eagly and Crowley.)

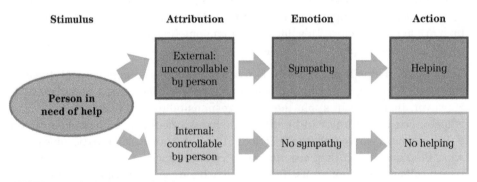

**FIGURE 10.1** Attributions and helping
In this model, proposed by German researcher Udo Rudolph and colleagues (2004), helping is mediated by people's explanations of the predicament and their resulting degree of sympathy.

Women offered help equally to males and females, whereas men offered more help when the persons in need were females. Several studies in the 1970s found that women with disabled cars (for example, with a flat tyre) got many more offers of help than men did (Penner et al., 1973; Pomazal & Clore, 1973; West et al., 1975). Similarly, solo female hitchhikers received far more offers of help than solo males or couples (Pomazal & Clore, 1973; Snyder et al., 1974). Since men dominate the crime statistics, with at least nine men for each woman in prison, most people are more afraid of helping a male than a female hitchhiker. Of course, men's chivalry towards lone women may be motivated by something other than pure altruism. As Pat Barclay (2010) suggests, appearing altruistic may make up for a less than attractive physical appearance in men. Women are more interested in good character than good looks. Unsurprisingly, men more frequently helped attractive than unattractive women (Mims et al., 1975; Stroufe et al., 1977; West & Brown, 1975).

Women not only receive more offers of help in certain situations but also seek more help (Addis & Mahalik, 2003). They are twice as likely to seek medical and psychiatric help. They are the majority of callers to radio counselling programmes and clients of college counselling centres. They more often welcome help from friends. Arie Nadler (1991), a Tel Aviv University expert on help seeking, attributes this to gender differences in independence versus interdependence. Most of the research about helping behaviour and gender is carried out in the West, in independent cultures with specific gender relationships. The results are not a consequence of biological sex differences. The gender differences are the consequence of ascribed sex-roles or gender differences related to norms for adequate male and female behaviour (Eagly & Crowley, 1986).

## EVOLUTIONARY EXPLANATIONS

Another explanation of helping behaviour comes from evolutionary psychology, presented and discussed in Chapters 1 and 14. As you may recall, evolutionary psychology contends that the essence of life is gene survival. Our genes drive us in adaptive ways that have maximized their chance of survival (Schmitt & Pilcher, 2004). When our ancestors died, their genes lived on, predisposing us to behave in ways that will spread them into the future.

But how do genes influence helping behaviour? We know that more than 90 per cent of the human's genes are similar in all individuals. We also have very similar genes to some animals, for instance monkeys and mice. Only a very small proportion of our genes are specific or unique to us, not shared with other people. And why should we be so interested to maximize the chance of survival for just these few specific genes and not the rest? It would in some way be more rational from a genetic point of view to secure the survival of most human genes by helping all humans.

How do we detect the people in which copies of our genes occur most abundantly? One clue lies in physical similarities. Some physical characteristics are gene dependent, for instance the colour of the eyes and the hair. If we are particularly interested in the survival of our individual genes then we would take more care of people with the same colour of hair to us. But this is not the case. We do not discriminate between who we help in this way. Our desire to help someone does not depend on our shared physical attributes but on our shared *social characteristics*.

Consider: if we did focus only on the genes in our own biological family, then parents should not treat adopted children in the same caring and helping way as they treat their biological children. But this is not the case. Adopted children are cared for and supported in the same way as biological children. The social norms for taking care of and protecting children and other vulnerable groups are more important in human societies than genetic or biological forces. The sociobiologist E. O. Wilson stated that kin selection was 'the enemy of civilization' (1978). If we only helped those we share genes with, human society would be in disarray.

As suggested by the title of Richard Dawkins' (1976) popular book *The Selfish Gene*, evolutionary psychology offers a humbling human image – one that psychologist Donald Campbell (1975a, 1975b) called a biological reaffirmation of a deep, self-serving 'original sin'.

When the *Titanic* sank, 70 per cent of the females and 20 per cent of the males survived. The chances of survival were 2.5 times better for a first than a third-class passenger. Yet, thanks to gender norms for altruism, the survival odds were better for third-class passengers who were women (47 per cent) than for first-class passengers who were men (31 per cent).

SOURCE: © Everett Collection Inc/Alamy Stock Photo

Genes that predispose individuals to self-sacrifice in the interests of strangers' welfare would not survive in the evolutionary competition. Genetic selfishness should, however, predispose us towards two specific types of selfless or even self-sacrificial helping: kin protection and reciprocity. But this is not often the reason why we support strangers in need of help. We are taught by social norms and attitudes in society, acquired during socialization in a culture to do so. As Samuel Bowles (2012) argues, it is perhaps the bloody and violent history that humans have endured, which has led to the evolution of altruistic norms.

### Kin Protection

According to some evolutionary psychologists our genes dispose us to care only for relatives. Thus, one form of self-sacrifice that *would* increase gene survival is devotion to one's biological children. Parents who put their children's welfare ahead of their own are more likely to pass their genes on than parents who neglect their biological children. As evolutionary psychologist David Barash (1979, p. 153) wrote, 'Genes help themselves by being nice to themselves, even if they are enclosed in different bodies'. Genetic egoism (at the biological level) fosters parental altruism (at the psychological level). Although evolution favours self-sacrifice for one's children, children have less at stake in the survival of their parents' genes. Thus, according to the theory, parents will generally be more devoted to their children than their children are to them.

And this is possibly the case in the modern Western, industrialized societies but not necessarily so in other cultures and societies. In traditional East Asian cultures with interdependent self-appraisal (Markus and Kitayama, 1991) and where the influence from Confucius is still prevalent, children both love and feel obliged to take care of their parents. *Filial piety* is a social norm bred for many centuries in these cultures. To help and support the parents when they are old is something natural in the same way as parents taking care of their adopted or biological children.

Some evolutionary psychologists note that kin selection predisposes ethnic ingroup favouritism – the root of countless historical and contemporary conflicts (Rushton, 1991). E. O. Wilson (1978) noted that kin selection is 'the enemy of civilization. If human beings are to a large extent guided ... to favour their own relatives and tribe, only a limited amount of global harmony is possible' (p. 167).

Yet in some cultures this family favouritism is considered to be a prerequisite for learning caring and helpful attitudes towards people outside of the family. This can aid a 'harmonious society' and global harmony.

## Reciprocity

Genetic self-interest, and self-interest in general, also predicts reciprocity. An organism helps another, biologist Robert Trivers argues, because it expects help in return (Binham, 1980). The giver expects later to be the getter, whereas failure to reciprocate gets punished. As we have already mentioned, Gouldner (1960) termed this the 'reciprocity norm' – which states that we should help those who help us.

Reciprocity among humans is stronger in rural villages than in big cities. Small schools, towns, sports clubs, work teams and dormitories are all conducive to a community spirit in which people care for one another. Compared with people in small-town or rural environments, those in big cities are less willing to relay a phone message, less likely to mail 'lost' letters, less co-operative with survey interviewers, less helpful to a lost child and less willing to do small favours (Hedge & Yousif, 1992; Steblay, 1987).

If individual self-interest inevitably wins in genetic competition, then why will we help strangers? Why will we help those whose limited resources or abilities preclude their reciprocating? And what causes soldiers to throw themselves on grenades? One answer, initially favoured by Darwin (then discounted by selfish-gene theorists, but now back again), is group selection: when groups are in competition, groups of mutually supportive altruists outlast groups of non-altruists (Krebs, 1998; McAndrew, 2002; Sober & Wilson, 1998).

Donald Campbell (1975a, 1975b) offered another basis for unreciprocated altruism: human societies evolved norms that serve as brakes on the biological bias towards self-interest. Commandments such as 'Love your neighbour as yourself' admonish us to balance self-concern with concern for the group, and so contribute to the survival of the group. Richard Dawkins (1976) offered a similar conclusion: 'Let us try to *teach* generosity and altruism, because we are born selfish. Let us understand what our selfish genes are up to, because we may then at least have the chance to upset their designs, something no other species has ever aspired to' (p. 3). This is what humans have been doing all the time, reflecting over their biological forces and tuning them to social norms and conscious behaviour.

## GENUINE ALTRUISM

Are life-saving heroes, everyday blood donors and Red Cross volunteers ever motivated by an ultimate goal of selfless concern for others? Or is their ultimate goal solely some form of self-benefit, such as gaining a reward, avoiding punishment and guilt or relieving distress?

Psychologist Daniel Batson (2001; Batson & Powell, 2003) theorizes that our willingness to help is influenced by both self-serving and selfless considerations

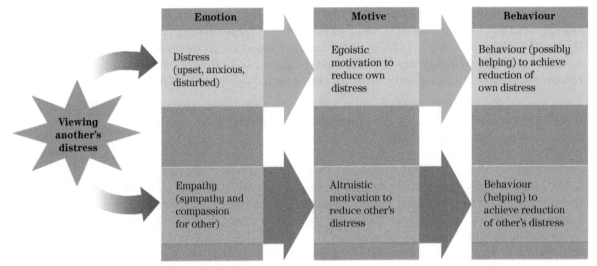

**FIGURE 10.2** Egoistic and altruistic routes to helping

Viewing another's distress can evoke a mixture of self-focused distress and other-focused empathy. Researchers agree that distress triggers egoistic motives. But they debate whether empathy can trigger a pure altruistic motive.

SOURCE: Adapted from Batson et al., 1987.

(Figure 10.2). **Distress over someone's suffering motivates us to relieve our upset, either by escaping the distressing situation (like the priest and the Levite) or by helping (like the Samaritan). But especially when we feel securely attached to someone, report both Batson and a team of attachment researchers led by Mario Mikulincer (2005), we also feel** empathy. **Loving parents suffer when their children suffer and rejoice over their children's joys – an empathy lacking in child abusers and other perpetrators of cruelty (Miller & Eisenberg, 1988). We also feel empathy for those with whom we identify. In September 1997 millions of people who never came within miles of England's Princess Diana (but who felt as if they knew her after hundreds of tabloid stories and magazine cover articles) wept for her and her motherless sons – but shed no tears for the nearly 1 million faceless Rwandans murdered or having died in squalid refugee camps since 1994. This illustrates how the mass media shapes or at least contributes to our empathy and reaction towards human suffering. The way human suffering is presented and how massive the information is has an impact on our feelings; to watch people becoming sad (e.g. in the wake of Princess Diana's death) may make me sad. Even if I did not know Diana personally, I take part in the grief since so many others do. We smile when others smile at us and we feel sad when others show sadness.**

empathy *the capacity of sharing or vicariously experiencing other people's feelings*

The degree of empathy we feel can vary depending on the situation and culture in which it is felt. Empathy can therefore also be seen to be a result of socialization or learned behaviour. The babies who cry when they hear another baby crying could be imitating the crying, but this does not mean that they are displaying empathy for the other baby. Caring may be a 'natural' trait, but for whom we care or feel empathy will depend on the social situation. Empathy can be developed by teaching infants to be helpful and interested in other people – to try to understand the other people's motives, emotions and their particular situation.

Often distress and empathy together motivate responses to a crisis. In 1983, people watched on television as an Australian bushfire wiped out hundreds of homes near Melbourne. Afterwards, Paul Amato (1986) studied donations of money and goods. He found that those who felt angry or indifferent gave less than those who felt either distressed (shocked and sickened) or empathic (sympathetic and worried for the victims).

To separate egoistic distress reduction from empathy-based altruism, Batson's research group conducted studies that aroused feelings of empathy. Then the researchers noted whether the aroused people would reduce their own distress by escaping the situation or whether they would go out of their way to aid the person. The results were consistent: with their empathy aroused, people usually helped.

In one of these experiments, Batson and his associates (1981) had female students observe a young woman suffering while she supposedly received electric shocks. During a pause in the experiment, the obviously upset victim explained to the experimenter that a childhood fall against an electric fence left her acutely sensitive to shocks. The experimenter suggested that perhaps the observer (the actual participant in this experiment) might trade places and take the remaining shocks for her. Previously, half of these actual participants had been led to believe the suffering person was a kindred spirit on matters of values and interests (thus arousing their empathy). Some also were led to believe that their part in the experiment was completed, so that in any case they were done observing the woman's suffering. Nevertheless, their empathy aroused, virtually all willingly offered to substitute for the victim.

Is this genuine altruism? Mark Schaller and Robert Cialdini (1988) doubted it. Feeling empathy for a sufferer makes one sad, they noted. In one of their experiments, they led people to believe that their sadness was going to be relieved by a different sort of mood-boosting experience – listening to a comedy tape. Under such conditions, people who felt empathy were not especially helpful. Schaller and Cialdini concluded that if we feel empathy but know that something else will make us feel better, we aren't so likely to help. Everyone agrees that some helpful acts are either obviously egoistic (done to gain external rewards or avoid punishment) or subtly egoistic (done to gain internal rewards or relieve inner distress). Is there a third type of helpfulness – a genuine altruism that aims simply to increase another's welfare (producing happiness for oneself merely as a by-product)? Is empathy-based helping a source of such altruism? Cialdini (1991) and his colleagues Mark Schaller and Jim Fultz have doubted it. They note that no study rules out all possible egoistic explanations for helpfulness.

But other findings suggest that genuine altruism does exist: with their empathy aroused, people will help even when they believe no one will know about their helping. Their concern continues until someone *has* been helped (Fultz et al., 1986). If their efforts to help are unsuccessful, they feel bad even if the failure is not their fault (Batson & Weeks, 1996). And people will sometimes persist in wanting to help a suffering person even when they believe their own distressed mood arises from a 'mood-fixing' drug (Schroeder et al., 1988).

'The measure of our character is what we would do if we were never found out.'
  Paraphrased from Thomas Macaulay

Might genuine altruism motivate an international health educator leading exercise with children in Uganda? Daniel Batson believes it might.

SOURCE: © RAJESH JANTILAL/Stringer

After 25 such studies testing egoism versus altruistic empathy in Western populations, Batson (2001) and others (Dovidio, 1991; Staub, 1991) believe that sometimes people do focus on others' welfare, not on their own. Batson, a former philosophy and theology student, had begun his research feeling 'excited to think that if we could ascertain whether people's concerned reactions were genuine, and not simply a subtle form of selfishness, then we could shed new light on a basic issue regarding human nature' (1999a). Two decades later he believes he has his answer. Genuine 'empathy-induced altruism is part of human nature' (1999b). In some ways all human behaviour is 'part of the human nature', but this 'nature' has to be bred and developed. Altruism is therefore nothing against nature, but it has to be stimulated in order to be practised. It will not automatically show itself in all circumstances. That empathy also is part of human nature, says Batson, raises the hope – confirmed by research – that inducing empathy might improve attitudes towards stigmatized people – people with AIDS, the homeless, the imprisoned and other minorities (see Focus On: The Benefit – and the Costs – of Empathy-induced Altruism). In collectivistic or interdependent cultures it is more common to focus on welfare of the family members since people do not separate themselves as individuals from their kin. They have other family members 'in their self' and they feel obliged to treat them in the same way as themselves.

## WHEN WILL WE HELP?

*What circumstances prompt people to help, or not to help? How and why is helping influenced by the number and behaviour of other bystanders? By the context? By mood states? By traits and values?*

On 13 March 1964, 28-year-old bar manager Kitty Genovese was set upon by a knife-wielding attacker as she returned from work to her Queens, New York, apartment house at 3 a.m. Her screams of terror and pleas for help – 'Oh my God, he stabbed me! Please help me! Please help me!' – aroused some of her neighbours (38 of them, according to an initial *New York Times* report, though the number was later disputed). Some came to their windows and caught fleeting glimpses of a couple quarrelling and also a woman lying in the street. Some saw the attacker leave the scene, but did not see him return. They therefore did not witness when Kitty was killed. According to the article in the *New York Times* none of the witnesses called the police. This has also been disputed and the police have been criticized for not taking the early phone calls seriously enough. Rachel Manning at University of the West of England, and Mark Levine and Alan Collins at Lancaster University argue that the Kitty Genovese case has became an iconic event in the history of helping research, and that the way it is presented in the literature is not supported by the available evidence. Using archive material, the authors show that there is no evidence for the presence of 38 witnesses, or that witnesses observed the murder, or that witnesses remained inactive (Manning et al., 2007). They also suggest that the story itself has become a modern parable, the telling of which has served to limit the scope of inquiry into emergency helping.

What is documented is that Kitty Genovese was murdered that night in New York and many neighbours heard her screaming. Irrespective of the details of what actually happened, the event initiated new theories in helping behaviour and paved the way for one of the most robust phenomena in social psychology – Bibb Latané and John Darley's (1970) bystander effect, the finding that individuals are more likely to help when alone than when in the company of others because of a diffusion of responsibility.

*bystander effect the finding that the presence of several bystanders makes it less likely that people will provide help. This tendency is often explained by disseminated responsibility and social comparison*

The questions raised by some social psychologists after the case was published on 27 March 1964 on page 1 of the *New York Times* were: why had Genovese's neighbours not come to her aid? Were they callous? Indifferent? Apathetic? If so, there are many people like them.

- ☐ 1965 in Brooklyn, 17-year-old Andrew Mormille was knifed in the stomach as he rode the subway home to Manhattan. After his attackers left the car, 11 other riders watched the young man bleed to death.

- ☐ On 7 September 2006 Eugene Obiora, a young man from Nigeria, visited a Social Office in Trondheim, Norway, to ask for money to celebrate his son's birthday. He had a discussion with the social officers and refused to leave until he was attended to. The social officers called the police. Obiora was handcuffed, kicked and dragged along the floor and the staircase. He died during the apprehension by the police using a fatal grip of the neck. Several people watched and listened to Obiora screaming and roaring: 'They kill me, they kill me.' Nobody intervened.

Bystander inaction. What influences our interpretations of a scene such as this, and our decisions to help or not to help?

SOURCE: © art-4-art/iStock

- ☐ Eleanor Bradley tripped and broke her leg while shopping. Dazed and in pain, she pleaded for help. For 40 minutes, the stream of pedestrians simply parted and flowed around her. Finally, a cab driver helped her to a doctor (Darley & Latané, 1968).

What is shocking is not that in these cases some people failed to help, but that in each of these groups (of 38, 11, hundreds and thousands) almost 100 per cent of those involved failed to respond. Why? In the same or similar situations, would you or I react as they did?

Social psychologists were curious and concerned about bystanders' lack of involvement during events such as Kitty Genovese's murder. So they undertook experiments to identify when people will help in an emergency. Then they broadened the question to: who is likely to help in non-emergencies – by such deeds as giving money, donating blood or contributing time? Let's examine these experiments by looking first at the *circumstances* that enhance helpfulness and then at the characteristics of the *people* who help.

## NUMBER OF BYSTANDERS

Bystander passivity during emergencies has prompted social commentators to lament people's 'alienation', 'apathy', 'indifference' and 'unconscious sadistic impulses'. By attributing the non-intervention to the bystanders' dispositions, we can reassure ourselves that, as caring people, we would have helped. But were the bystanders such inhuman characters?

Latané and Darley (1970) were unconvinced. They staged ingenious emergencies and found that a single situational factor – the presence of other bystanders – greatly decreased intervention. By 1980 they had conducted four dozen studies that compared help given by bystanders who perceived themselves to be either alone or with others. In about 90 per cent of those comparisons, involving nearly 6000 people, lone bystanders were more likely to help (Latané & Nida, 1981). In Internet communication, too, people are more likely to respond helpfully to a request (such as from someone seeking the link to the campus library) if they believe they alone (and not several others as well) have received it (Blair et al., 2005).

Sometimes the victim was actually less likely to get help when many people were around. When Latané, James Dabbs (1975) and 145 collaborators 'accidentally' dropped coins or pencils during 1497 elevator rides, they were helped 40 per cent of the time when one other person was on the elevator and less than 20 per cent of the time when there were six passengers.

Why do other bystanders sometimes inhibit helping? Latané and Darley surmised that as the number of bystanders increases, any given bystander is less likely to *notice* the incident, less likely to *interpret* the incident as a problem or an emergency, and less likely to *assume responsibility* for taking action (Figure 10.3).

### Noticing

Twenty minutes after Eleanor Bradley has fallen and broken her leg on a crowded city sidewalk, you come along. Your eyes are on the backs of the pedestrians in front of you (it is bad manners to stare at those you pass) and your private thoughts are on the day's events. Would you therefore be less likely to notice the injured woman than if the sidewalk were virtually deserted?

To find out, Latané and Darley (1968) had male students fill out a questionnaire in a room, either by themselves or with two strangers. While they were working (and being observed through a one-way mirror), there was a staged emergency: smoke poured into the room through a wall vent. Solitary students, who often glanced idly about the room while working, noticed the smoke almost immediately – usually in less than 5 seconds. Those in groups kept their eyes on their work. It typically took them about 20 seconds to notice the smoke.

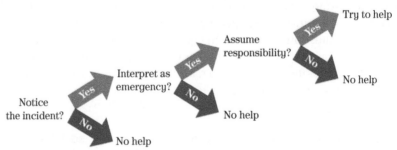

**FIGURE 10.3** Latané and Darley's decision tree
Only one path up the tree leads to helping. At each fork of the path, the presence of other bystanders may divert a person down a branch towards not helping.
SOURCE: Adapted from Darley & Latané, 1968.

Interpreting

Once we notice an ambiguous event, we must interpret it. Put yourself in the room filling with smoke. Though worried, you don't want to embarrass yourself by appearing flustered. You glance at the others. They look calm, indifferent. Assuming everything must be OK, you shrug it off and go back to work. Then one of the others notices the smoke and, noting your apparent unconcern, reacts similarly. This is yet another example of informational influence (Chapter 7). Each person uses others' behaviour as clues to reality. Such misinterpretations can contribute to a delayed response to actual fires in offices, restaurants and other multiple-occupancy settings (Canter et al., 1980).

The misinterpretations are fed by what Thomas Gilovich, Kenneth Savitsky and Victoria Husted Medvec (1998) call an *illusion of transparency* – a tendency to overestimate others' ability to 'read' our internal states. (See the Research Close-Up in Chapter 3.) In their studies, people facing an emergency presumed their concern was more visible than it was. More than we usually suppose, our concern or alarm is opaque. Keenly aware of our emotions, we presume they leak out and that others see right through us. Sometimes others do read our emotions, but often we keep our cool quite effectively. The result is what in Chapter 11 is called 'pluralistic ignorance' – ignorance that others are thinking and feeling what we are. In emergencies, each person may think, 'I'm very concerned', but perceive others as calm – 'so maybe it's not an emergency'.

So it happened in Latané and Darley's experiment. When those working alone noticed the smoke, they usually hesitated a moment, then got up, walked over to the vent, felt, sniffed and waved at the smoke, hesitated again, and then went to report it. In dramatic contrast, those in groups of three did not move. Among the 24 men in eight groups, only one person reported the smoke within the first four minutes (Figure 10.4). By the end of the 6-minute experiment, the smoke was so thick it was obscuring the men's vision and they were rubbing their eyes and coughing. Still, in only three of the eight groups did even a single person leave to report the problem.

Equally interesting, the group's passivity affected its members' interpretations. What caused the smoke? 'A leak in the air conditioning'. 'Chemistry labs in the building'. 'Steam pipes'. 'Truth gas'. Not one said, 'Fire'. The group members, by serving as non-responsive models, influenced one another's interpretation of the situation.

That experimental dilemma parallels real-life dilemmas we all face. Are the shrieks outside merely playful antics or the desperate screams of someone being assaulted? Is the boys' scuffling a friendly tussle or a vicious fight? Is the person slumped in the doorway sleeping, high on drugs or seriously ill, perhaps in a diabetic coma?

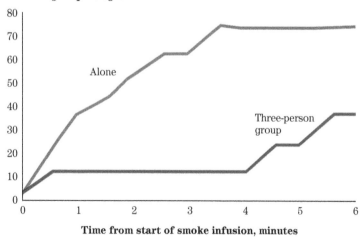

**Percentage reporting smoke**

**Time from start of smoke infusion, minutes**

**FIGURE 10.4** The smoke-filled-room experiment
Smoke pouring into the testing room was much more likely to be reported by individuals working alone than by three-person groups.

SOURCE: Data from Darley & Latané, 1968.

Unlike the smoke-filled-room experiment, these everyday situations involve another in desperate need. To see if the same *bystander effect* occurs in such situations, Latané and Judith Rodin (1969) staged an experiment around a woman in distress. A female researcher set male students to work on a questionnaire and then left through a curtained doorway to work in an adjacent office. Four minutes later she could be heard (from a tape recorder) climbing on a chair to reach some papers. This was followed by a scream and a loud crash as the chair collapsed and she fell to the floor. 'Oh, my God, my foot . . . I . . . I . . . can't move it,' she sobbed. 'Oh . . . my ankle . . . I . . . can't get this . . . thing . . . off me.' Only after 2 minutes of moaning did she manage to make it out of her office door.

Interpretations matter. Is this man locked out of his car or is he a burglar? Our answer affects how we respond.

Seventy per cent of those who were alone when they overheard the 'accident' came into the room or called out to offer help. Among pairs of strangers confronting the emergency, only 40 per cent of the time did either person offer help. Those who did nothing apparently interpreted the situation as a non-emergency. 'A mild sprain,' said some. 'I didn't want to embarrass her,' explained others. This again demonstrates the bystander effect. As the number of people known to be aware of an emergency increases, any given person becomes less likely to help. For the victim, there is no safety in numbers.

People's interpretations also affect their reactions to street crimes. In staging physical fights between a man and a woman, Lance Shotland and Margaret Straw (1976) found that bystanders intervened 65 per cent of the time when the woman shouted, 'Get away from me; I don't know you', but only 19 per cent of the time when she shouted, 'Get away from me; I don't know why I ever married you'. Assumed spouse abuse, it seems, just doesn't trigger as much intervention as stranger abuse.

### Assuming Responsibility

Failing to notice and misinterpretation are not the bystander effect's only causes. Sometimes an emergency is obvious. Those who saw and heard Kitty Genovese's pleas for help correctly interpreted what was happening. But the lights and silhouetted figures in neighbouring windows told them that others were also watching. That diffused the responsibility for action.

It is, however, not only the number of people that counts in assuming responsibility, but also the status and profession of those concerned. If those involved are expected to solve problems and give support then the bystanders are more reluctant to intervene even if there are not so many of them. That was the case when Eugene Obiora died under arrest. Nobody wanted to stop the police, and most people believed they knew how to handle a person without risking his life. The threshold for intervention is higher in a situation when you expect that the authorities will make the right decisions and handle people in the right way. People believe in experts and authority, and do not want to protest, but be in some way obedient (as we discussed in Chapter 7). To criticize the police for handling a person in a life-threatening manner is not what most people will do, especially if you can see no one else protesting.

Few of us have observed a murder, but all of us have at times been slower to react to a need when others were present. Passing a stranded motorist on a busy highway, we are less likely to offer help than on a country road. To explore bystander inaction in clear emergencies, Darley and Latané (1968) simulated the Genovese drama. They placed people in separate rooms from which the participants would hear a victim crying for help. To create that situation, Darley and Latané asked students to discuss their problems with university life over a laboratory intercom. The researchers told the students that to guarantee their anonymity, no one would be visible, nor would the experimenter eavesdrop. During the ensuing discussion, when the experimenter turned his microphone on, the participants heard one person lapse into a seizure. With increasing intensity and speech difficulty, he pleaded for someone to help.

Responsibility diffusion. The nine paparazzi photographers on the scene immediately after the Princess Diana car accident all had mobile phones. With one exception, none called for help. Their almost unanimous explanation was that they assumed 'someone else' had already called (Sancton, 1997).

SOURCE: © REUTERS/Alamy Stock Photo

Of those led to believe there were no other listeners, 85 per cent left their room to seek help. Of those who believed four others also overheard the victim, only 31 per cent went for help. Were those who didn't respond apathetic and indifferent? When the experimenter came in to end the experiment, most immediately expressed concern. Many had trembling hands and sweating palms. They believed an emergency had occurred but were undecided whether to act.

After the smoke-filled room, the woman-in-distress and the seizure experiments, Latané and Darley asked the participants whether the presence of others had influenced them. We know the others had a dramatic effect. Yet the participants almost invariably denied the influence. They typically replied, 'I was aware of the others, but I would have reacted just the same if they weren't there.' That response reinforces a familiar point: *we often do not know why we do what we do*.

Urban dwellers are seldom alone in public places, which helps account for why city people often are less helpful than country people. 'Compassion fatigue' and 'sensory overload' from encountering so many people in need further restrain helping in large cities across the world (Yousif & Korte, 1995). Fatigue and overload help explain what happened when Robert Levine and colleagues (1994) approached several thousand people in 36 US cities, dropping an unnoticed pen, asking for change, simulating a blind person needing help at a corner, and so forth. The bigger and more densely populated the city, the less likely people were to help. Levine (2001, 2003) found that willingness to help strangers also varies with culture and nationality (Figure 10.5). People in economically advanced countries tended to offer *less* help to strangers, and those in cultures marked by amiable and agreeable *simpat'a* (in Spanish) or *simpático* (in Portuguese) were *more* helpful. And many Europeans are more helpful than the US citizens of New York. So perhaps reduced helping is related to extreme individualism, with an increased focus on yourself and not on others.

Nations, too, have often been bystanders to catastrophes, even to genocide. As 800 000 people were murdered in Rwanda, most nations in the world stood by. And in this new century, we stood by again during the human slaughter in Sudan's Darfur region. 'With many potential actors, each feels less responsible,' notes Ervin

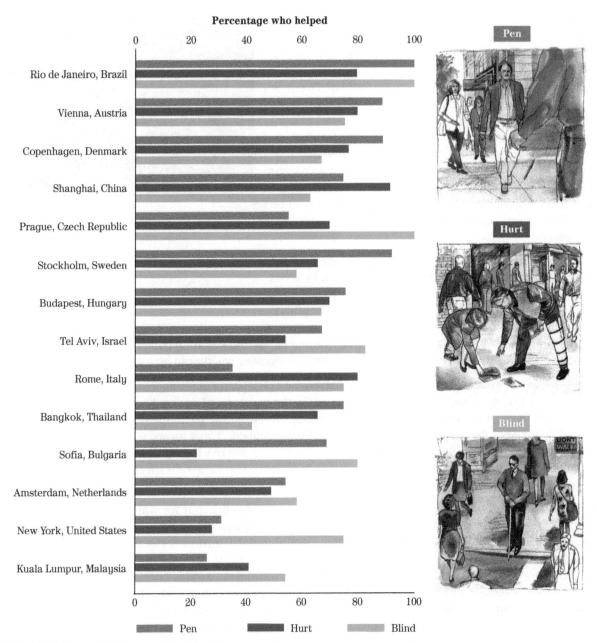

**Percentage who helped**

**FIGURE 10.5** A world of difference in helping strangers

To compare helping in different cities and cultures, Robert Levine and his collaborators would 'accidentally' drop a pen, drop magazines while limping with an apparently injured leg, or feign blindness when approaching a crossing as the light turned green. Those dropping a pen in Rio were, for example, four times more likely to be helped than those doing so in New York City or Kuala Lumpur. (This is a sample of data from 14 countries.)

SOURCE: Adapted from R. V. Levine (2003). The kindness of strangers. *American Scientist*, **91**, 226–233.

Staub (1997b). 'It's not our responsibility,' say the leaders of unaffected nations. However, this inaction by political regimes to intervene in humanitarian crises can prove to be more complex than simple diffusion of responsibility. Issues such as the financial cost, the ramifications in the political sphere of favouring one side over another and the increased risk of retaliation from other countries, for example, all play a part in this inaction, making it very different to the bystander effect. It should be noted that even when a country as a whole does nothing to intervene, its citizens may lobby the government for action, as witnessed on 15 February 2003, when over 600 cities worldwide marched in protest against the imminent war in Iraq.

## Revisiting Research Ethics

These studies raise again the issue of research ethics. Is it right to force unwitting people to overhear someone's apparent collapse? Were the researchers in the seizure experiment ethical when they forced people to decide whether to interrupt their discussion to report the problem? Would you object to being in such a study? Note that it would have been impossible to get your 'informed consent'; doing so would have destroyed the cover for the study.

The researchers were always careful to debrief the participants. After explaining the seizure experiment, probably the most stressful, the experimenter gave the participants a questionnaire. One hundred per cent said the deception was justified and that they would be willing to take part in similar studies in the future. None reported feeling angry at the experimenter. Other researchers confirm that the overwhelming majority of participants in such studies say that their participation was both instructive and ethically justified (Schwartz & Gottlieb, 1981). The positive feedback from the participants also tells us that people learn something valuable about themselves in these studies. Unaware of this tendency before, they were thankful of having the opportunity to correct themselves and to behave in a more prosocial way in the future.

But some social psychologists have deep reservations about the use of deception in research. Alan Elms and Diana Baumrind (2007) argued that deception is justified only when the benefits of research clearly outweigh the ethical costs of deception.

Remember that the social psychologist has a twofold ethical obligation: to protect the participants and to reveal hidden mechanisms explaining human behaviour. Such discoveries can alert us to unwanted influences and show us how we might exert positive influences. The ethical principle seems to be: after protecting participants' welfare, social psychologists fulfil their responsibility to society by doing such research.

## HELPING WHEN SOMEONE ELSE DOES

If observing aggressive models can heighten aggression (Chapter 8) and if unresponsive models can heighten non-responding, then will helpful models promote helping? Imagine hearing a crash followed by sobs and moans. If another bystander said, 'Uh-oh. This is an emergency! We've got to do something', would it stimulate others to help?

The evidence is clear: prosocial models do promote altruism. Kindness promotes kindness. Hostility breeds hostility. Here are some examples.

- Drivers were more likely to offer help to a female driver with a flat tyre if a quarter mile earlier they witnessed someone helping another woman change a tyre (Bryan & Test, 1967).

- In another experiment, Bryan and Test observed that Christmas shoppers were more likely to drop money in a Salvation Army collection tin if they had just seen someone else do the same.

419

☐ British adults were more willing to donate blood if they were approached after observing a confederate consent to donating (Rushton & Campbell, 1977).

☐ A glimpse of extraordinary human kindness and charity – such as in the examples of heroic altruism at this chapter's outset – often triggers what Jonathan Haidt (2003) calls *elevation*, 'a distinctive feeling in the chest of warmth and expansion' that may provoke chills, tears and throat clenching. Such elevation often inspires people to become more self-giving.

Models sometimes, however, contradict in practice what they preach. Parents may tell their children, 'Do as I say, not as I do'. Studies show that children learn moral judgements both from what they hear preached and from what they see practised (Rice & Grusec, 1975; Rushton, 1975). When exposed to hypocrites, they imitate: they say what the model says and do what the model does. But fortunately children are influenced by other means as well, not just sheer imitation of the wrongdoers.

### TIME PRESSURES

Darley and Batson (1973) discerned another determinant of helping in the Good Samaritan parable. The priest and the Levite were both busy, important people, probably hurrying to their duties. The lowly Samaritan surely was less pressed for time. To see whether people in a hurry would behave as the priest and the Levite did, Darley and Batson cleverly staged the situation described in the parable.

After collecting their thoughts before recording a brief extemporaneous talk (which, for half the participants, was actually on the Good Samaritan parable), Princeton Theological Seminary students were directed to a recording studio in an adjacent building. En route, they passed a man sitting slumped in a doorway, head down, coughing and groaning. Some of the students had been sent off nonchalantly: 'It will be a few minutes before they're ready for you, but you might as well head on over.' Of those, almost two-thirds stopped to offer help. Others were told, 'Oh, you're late. They were expecting you a few minutes ago … so you'd better hurry'. Of these, only 10 per cent offered help. Reflecting on these findings, Darley and Batson (1973) remarked:

> A person not in a hurry may stop and offer help to a person in distress. A person in a hurry is likely to keep going. Ironically, he is likely to keep going even if he is hurrying to speak on the parable of the Good Samaritan, thus inadvertently confirming the point of the parable. (Indeed, on several occasions, a seminary student going to give his talk on the parable of the Good Samaritan literally stepped over the victim as he hurried on his way!)

Are we being unfair to the seminary students, who were, after all, hurrying to *help* the experimenter? Perhaps they keenly felt the social-responsibility norm but found it pulling them two ways – towards the experimenter and towards the victim. In another enactment of the Good Samaritan situation, Batson and his associates (1978) directed 40 students to an experiment in another building. Half were told they were late, half that they had plenty of time. Half of each of these groups thought their participation was vitally important to the experimenter; half thought it was not essential. The results: those leisurely on their way to an unimportant appointment usually stopped to help. But people seldom stopped to help if they were late for a very important date.

Can we conclude that those who were rushed were callous? Did the seminarians notice the victim's distress and then consciously choose to ignore it? No. Harried, preoccupied, rushing to help the experimenter, they simply did not take time to tune in to the person in need. As social psychologists have so often observed, their behaviour was influenced more by context than by conviction.

## SIMILARITY

Because similarity is conducive to liking, and liking is conducive to helping, we are more empathic and helpful towards those *similar* to us (Miller et al., 2001). The similarity bias applies to both dress and beliefs and in general to those who share our social identity, our fellow ingroup members. But this rule is not without exception. Rich people do not donate money to other rich people. They donate, if they do at all, to the poor. Tim Emswiller and his fellow researchers (1971) arranged for confederates, dressed either conservatively or in counter-culture clothing, to approach 'conservative' and 'hip' university students seeking money for a phone call. Fewer than half of the students did the favour for those dressed differently from themselves. Two-thirds did so for those dressed similarly. Likewise, Scottish shoppers in a more homophobic era were less willing to give change to someone if the person wore a T-shirt with a pro-gay slogan (Gray et al., 1991). The tendency to help ingroup members was also revealed in the minimal group paradigm which we will discuss in Chapter 13. (See also Research Close-Up: Identity and Emergency Intervention.)

No face is more familiar than one's own. That explains why, when Lisa DeBruine (2002) made university students play an interactive game with a supposed other player, they were more trusting and generous when the other person's pictured face had some features of their own face morphed into it (Figure 10.6). In me I trust. Even just sharing a birthday, a first name or a fingerprint pattern leads people to respond more to a request for help (Burger et al., 2004). The question, however, is how big this effect actually is. Even if there are differences in helping behaviour depending on similarity and ingroup feeling this does not mean that

> Discussion of 'liking' in all forms can be found in Chapter 9, where we focus particularly on attraction and intimacy and how they come about.

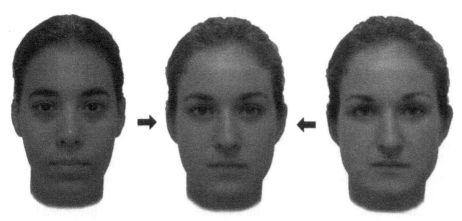

**FIGURE 10.6**  Similarity breeds co-operation.

we always help those more similar to ourselves or that we never help others. The situation and the context also play an important role in helping, and the complex and contextual real-life situation is something of a challenge to replicate in an experiment.

Lisa DeBruine (2002) morphed participants' faces (left) with strangers' faces (right) to make the composite centre face – towards whom the participants were more generous than towards the stranger.

### Cultural Context and Social Similarity

Darley and Latané's perspective and interpretation of Kitty's murder and how people reacted to it has recently been challenged by social psychologists in Europe and Canada. Sometimes a particular viewpoint or explanation of empirical facts dominates thinking. Few question the interpretation. The over-reliance upon Darley and Latané for many years as the only way to understand the lack of help given to Kitty inhibited other explanations, perspectives and interpretations. This happens in all sciences. People get accustomed to an obvious interpretation. This was the situation before Frances Cherry, a social psychologist at Carleton University in Canada and researchers at the Centre for Conflict and Social Solidarity in Lancaster, England, started to look at the Kitty Genovese case through new lenses. Mark Levine at the University of Exeter has argued that traditional explanations of Kitty's case are hampered by focusing on the physical presence of others rather than analysing the social meanings inherent in the (non) intervention (Levine, 1999).

When Frances Cherry wrote her book in the mid-1990s many social psychologists in Europe were interested in the social and historical context as something crucial to understanding bystander behaviour. Some were also becoming more critical towards the experimental method as a suitable method to reveal the complex impact from history and culture, from time and place (see also Chapters 1 and 2).

Frances Cherry wanted to focus on the social context surrounding Kitty's murder and the fact she was a black woman, raped and killed by a black man. She argued that Darley and Latané's interpretation stripped the case of vital aspects of the social and cultural context that help us to understand the bystanders' responses to it. She also argued that 'in 1964 we lived in a world that did not recognize . . . the widespread abuse of women' (Cherry, 1995).

The most important means of understanding the reaction to Kitty's murder, in terms of gender and sexual relations, has been removed from Darley and Latané's view and replaced by general, acultural and quantifiable variables such as the number of bystanders. The bystanders' responses are, however, according to Cherry, 'thoroughly suffused with societal assumptions, norms and values' (Burr, 2006).

This does not mean that experiments are unable to take into consideration sociocultural variables. There are actually experiments showing that gender relation is a vital factor in cases like Kitty's. Gerald Borofsky et al. (1971), using simulated attacks, found that men were less likely to intervene in an attack by a man on a woman, and Lance Shotland and Margaret Straw (1976) showed that intervention was less likely when the attacker and victim were perceived to be a couple.

Frances Cherry considers the lack of attention to matters of race and gender in bystander research probably has something to do with attitudes in the USA in the 1960s, towards women and black people. Cherry herself admits that she found the 'diffusion of responsibility' theory plausible as a student and that as she later developed her feminist awareness the alternative interpretation for what had happened in Kitty's case became possible for her. This tells us something about how scientific theories and explanations to some degree are products of their time and place, and seldom last 'for all time' (Burr, 2006).

### Perceived Social Similarity

Mark Levine, Amy Prosse, David Evans and Stephen Reicher represent another perspective on Kitty's murder and the bystander phenomenon. In line with the social identity approach (see Chapter 12 for an overview), these British social psychologists focus on the importance of ingroup similarity and self-categorization to understand the bystander phenomenon and helping behaviour more generally. That is, rather than pointing towards individual and interpersonal factors, these researchers emphasize the degree to which bystander and victim share a common identity. The categorization of others as members of the ingroup leads to perception of similarity, cohesion and an increased feeling of responsibility for the welfare of others. As a consequence – and as demonstrated by the experiments conducted by Levine and his colleagues reported in the Research Close-Up – a sense of 'we-ness' with the victim increases the likelihood of intervention (Dovidio et al., 1991). (See Research Close-Up: Identity and Emergency Intervention.)

We shouldn't, however, rule out the possibility that people may help those they consider to be different from themselves in some way. In experimental studies Esther van Leeuwen and Susanne Täuber (2011) have found that people who are members of low status groups (based upon poor performance in a general knowledge quiz) offer to help those in a high status group. Why? Well, the researchers suggest that by offering help the low status group can show that it does have something valuable to offer a higher status group. By doing so they increase their positive reputation in their own eyes and those of the outgroup.

The British bystander explanation represents an alternative theoretical explanation of why we do help and why we do not help others. Whether the person in need of help does or does not belong to 'my' group constitutes a crucial factor: I will be more willing to help a person if I perceive him or her as a member of my own group.

In sum, according to this perspective helping behaviour is based more on how I socially categorize myself and others than on my genetic make-up. In many ways the social identity approach to helping behaviour contrasts with the explanations given by evolutionary psychologists. It is not the genes that count, but whether I have something social in common with the people in need of help.

## HELPING ON THE INTERNET

As you will have recognized in this chapter, research on bystanders has often focused on real-life situations. The research tradition was inspired by a true dramatic incident. But what about virtual reality? Are we still inclined not to intervene in a situation if many others witness it in the virtual world? Patrick Markey (2000) studied online 'chat groups' to see if requests for help were met.

## research close-up

IDENTITY AND EMERGENCY INTERVENTION

*Source: Levine, M., Prosser, A., Evans, D., & Reicher, S. (2005). Identity and emergency intervention: How social group membership and inclusiveness of group boundaries shape helping behavior. Personality and Social Psychology Bulletin, 31(4), 443–453.*

### Introduction

Social psychologists have invested a lot of work into understanding when and why people offer help in times of an emergency. Likeness breeds liking, and liking elicits helping. So, do people offer more help to others who display similarities to themselves? And do they refuse help to those they do not like? To explore the similarity–helping relationship, Mark Levine, Amy Prosser and David Evans, England, joined with Stephen Reicher (2005) to study the behaviour of some Lancaster students who earlier had identified themselves as fans of the nearby Manchester United football team. Manchester United have dominated English football for many years. The success of this team has led to bitter rivalries between the fans of Manchester United and other football teams. One of the more notable rivalries is between supporters of Manchester United and those of Liverpool FC, a team that enjoyed huge success in the 1980s. Geographically close (just 30 miles apart), these teams have a long history of hostility towards one another. So, would a Manchester United supporter help a Liverpool fan if he was in trouble? Taking their cue from John Darley and Daniel Batson's (1973) famous Good Samaritan experiment, Levine and his colleagues decided to find out.

### Study 1

*Method*

Forty-five male Lancaster University students took part, aged between 18 and 21 years. Each participant was given two questionnaires. The first asked them about the football team they supported and why they did so. The second questionnaire required participants to answer on a 5-point scale, the extent to which they identified with fellow supporters of their team.

The researchers then directed each newly arrived participant to the laboratory in an adjacent building. Participants were told this was to watch a video about their team, supporters and crowd behaviour at football matches. En route, a confederate jogger – wearing a shirt from either Manchester United or rival Liverpool, or a plain shirt – seemingly slipped on a grass bank just in front of them, grasped his ankle, and groaned in apparent pain. This confederate did not ask for help, and did not make any eye contact with the participant. The participant was covertly observed.

A measure was taken of the degree of help (if any) the participant offered the confederate. The 5-point scale was taken from Darley and Batson's Good Samaritan experiment (1973).

A score of 1 was given to a participant who did not notice that the confederate needed help.

A score of 2 was given if the participant did notice help was required but failed to offer any.

A score of 3 was given if the participant asked the confederate if he needed help.

A score of 4 was given if the confederate asked the participant if he needed help and then offered some.

Finally, a score of 5 was awarded if the participant helped the confederate by remaining with him, and escorting him out of the experimental context.

## Results

Table 10.1 shows that more help was given to victims when they were in a Manchester United football shirt, than when in a plain or Liverpool shirt. A chi-square was conducted on this categorical data, to test if there was an association between type of shirt (Manchester United, Liverpool, Plain) and helping behaviour (No Help, Help). The result was statistically significant: $\chi^2$ (2, $N = 35$) = 12.07, $p = .0024$. There is an association between type of football shirt and helping behaviour.

**TABLE 10.1** Frequencies of helping by football shirt condition

| | Manchester United | Plain | Liverpool |
|---|---|---|---|
| No Help | 1 | 8 | 7 |
| Help | 12 | 4 | 3 |

As Figure 10.7 shows, the Manchester fans routinely paused to offer help to their fellow Manchester supporter but usually did not offer such help to a supposed Liverpool supporter.

## Study 2

### Method

The researchers wondered, what if we remind Manchester fans of the identity they share with Liverpool supporters – as football fans rather than as detractors who scorn football fans as violent hooligans? So they repeated the study with 32 male self-identified Manchester United football fans, but with one difference: before participants witnessed the jogger's fall, the researcher explained that the study concerned the positive aspects of being a football fan. Given that only a small minority of fans are troublemakers, this research aimed to explore what fans get out of their love for 'the beautiful game'. Now a jogger wearing a football club shirt, whether for Manchester or Liverpool, became one of 'us fans'. Would this make a difference to the results?

### Results

As Figure 10.8 shows, the grimacing jogger was helped regardless of which team he supported – and more so than if wearing a plain shirt.

Table 10.2 shows that more help was offered to both Manchester United and Liverpool football fans than to the victim wearing a plain shirt. A chi-square to test whether there is a significant association of football shirt (Manchester United, Plain, Liverpool) and helping behaviour (No Help, Help) was

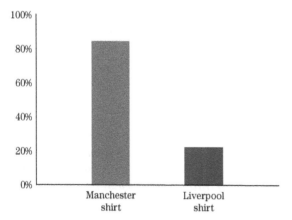

**FIGURE 10.7** Percentage of Manchester United fans who helped victim wearing Manchester or Liverpool shirt.

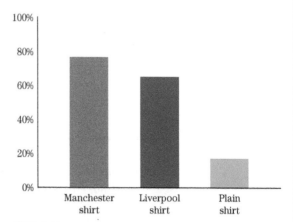

**FIGURE 10.8** Common fan identity condition: percentage of Manchester United fans who helped victim wearing Manchester, Liverpool or plain shirt.

significant: $\chi^2$ (2, $N = 29$) = 7.33, $p = .25$. Overall, type of shirt is associated with helping behaviour. Of particular interest is that more help was offered to Manchester United and Liverpool supporters, when participants were reminded of their common football supporter identity, than to plain-shirted supporters.

TABLE 10.2    Frequencies for helping by shirt condition

|  | Manchester United | Plain | Liverpool |
|---|---|---|---|
| No help | 2 | 7 | 3 |
| Help | 8 | 2 | 7 |

## Discussion

The principle in the two cases is the same, notes the research team: people are predisposed to help their fellow group members, whether those are defined more narrowly (as 'us Manchester fans') or more inclusively (as 'us football fans'). If even rival fans can be persuaded to help one another if they think about what unites them, then surely other antagonists can as well. One way to increase people's willingness to help others is to promote social identities that are inclusive rather than exclusive. By re-categorizing we create new allies belonging to our ingroup.

Of course we have to be somewhat cautious whenever we seek to apply findings from studies such as these to the wider population. Often the sample sizes are quite small, as in the current case. Moreover, as all the participants in these two studies were 18–21 and male, we do not know if there might be any age or gender differences in this study. Can we be confident that all participants were suitably fooled by the confederate? It is almost certainly impossible to design the perfect study, but work like this gives us some important insights into helping behaviour.

In particular Markey wanted to see if Latané and Darley's theoretical framework (the bystander effect) applied to these online situations. And indeed it did. Results showed that as the number of people in the chat group increased, it took longer for an individual to receive help. However, the bystander effect was virtually eliminated and help was received much more quickly when the person requiring help asked for a 'bystander's' name to help them – just as it is in the offline, real world. Marek Palasinski (2012) found that whether you thought you were being monitored also had an effect on the likelihood of offering help. In his study of cyberbystanders who witnessed a mock incident of sexual abuse against a minor in a chatroom, the likelihood of the participant intervening to help was reduced not only when more cyberbystanders were present, but also when they thought the chatroom was under surveillance.

## WHO WILL HELP?

*We have considered internal influences on the decision to help (such as guilt and mood) and external influences as well (such as social norms, number of bystanders, time pressures and similarity). We also need to consider the helpers' dispositions, including, for example, their personality traits, empathy and religious values.*

### PERSONALITY, GENDER AND AGE

Surely some traits must distinguish the Mother Teresa types. Faced with identical situations, some people will respond helpfully, others won't bother. Who are the likely helpers?

For many years social psychologists were unable to discover a single characteristic that predicted helping with anything close to the predictive power of the situation, guilt and mood factors. Modest relationships were found between helping and certain variables, such as a need for social approval. Also personal empathy has a strong influence on helping behaviour, as we've already seen. But, by and large, the personality tests were unable to identify the helpers. Studies of rescuers of Jews in Nazi Europe reveal a similar conclusion: although the social context clearly influenced willingness to help, there was no definable set of altruistic personality traits (Darley, 1995).

'There are ... reasons why personality should be rather unimportant in determining people's reactions to the emergency. For one thing, the situational forces affecting a person's decision are so strong.'
   Bibb Latané and John Darley (1970, p. 115)

If that has a familiar ring, it could be from a similar conclusion by conformity researchers (Chapter 7): conformity and obedience, too, seemed more influenced by the situation than by measurable personality traits. Perhaps, though, you recall from Chapter 3 that who we are does affect what we do.

Some people are, however, reliably more helpful. Those high in positive emotionality, empathy and self-efficacy are most likely to be concerned and helpful (Bierhoff et al., 1991; Eisenberg et al., 1991; Krueger et al., 2001). Perhaps you have the intuitive feeling that women are more helpful than men are. You are partly right in your conclusion. In their interviews with women home-based care volunteers, Thirusha Naidu and colleagues (2012) found that responsibility in caring for others had become 'feminized'. It seems being a 'mother' instills the necessary characteristics and aspirations of volunteering to look after people. The women's accounts included personal histories of looking after others and commitment to being of service. But this is not a rule without exception. Many studies have compared the helpfulness of male and female individuals. After analysing 172 studies with 50 000 respondents Alice Eagly and Maureen Crowley (1986) reported that when faced with potentially dangerous situations in which strangers need help (such as with a flat tyre or a fall in a subway), men more often help. In other situations, such as volunteering to help with an experiment or spend time with children with developmental disabilities, to volunteer with the Peace Corps and Doctors of the World (Becker & Eagly, 2004), women are slightly more likely to help. They also have been as likely as, or more likely than, men to risk death as Holocaust rescuers and to donate a kidney. Thus, the gender difference interacts with (depends on) the situation or the context.

Felix Warneken and Michael Tomasello studied how children as young as 18 months of age (pre-linguistic or just-linguistic) quite readily help others to achieve their goals even when the child self receives no immediate benefit and the person helped is a stranger. This behaviour requires both an understanding of others' goals and an altruistic motivation to help, and it seems that altruism can develop very early in humans (Warneken & Tomasello, 2006).

René Bekkers at Utrecht University made a random sample survey of altruistic behaviour in the Netherlands. Only 5.7 per cent donated the money they had received from taking part in the survey to a charity or an unknown person in need. Nearly 95 per cent of the respondents kept the money themselves (Bekkers,

2007). In line with other survey research on giving, generosity increased with age, education, income, trust and prosocial value orientation. Kristine Theurer and Andrew Wister (2010) suggest that altruism in older people, who may have retired from full-time employment, is based on having high social capital (feelings of belonging to, and engagement with, a community).

### RELIGIOUS FAITH

Confronted with a minor emergency, intrinsically religious people are only slightly more responsive than non-believers in Western countries (Trimble, 1993). In some Eastern countries like China and Japan most people do not have a religious faith in God and that does not mean that they help less than 'intrinsically' religious people in the West. This was demonstrated after the earthquake in Sichuan province in China on 12 May 2008. The whole country contributed to the welfare of the unknown, but Chinese, earthquake victims.

Yet in many countries worldwide with different faiths and belief systems there seems to be a correlation between helping behaviour and religiosity. Gallup polls conducted in more than 140 countries between 2006 and 2008 show that those whose responses identify them as highly religious are more likely than less religious respondents to report having donated money to a charity in that time and to say they've helped a stranger in the past month (see Figure 10.9).

These 'religion effects' are consistent across the world's largest faith traditions, including Christianity, Islam, Hinduism, Buddhism and Judaism. In each of these major religions, those who fall into the highly religious category are more likely than those who are less religious to say they've engaged in helping behaviours. We cannot, however, conclusively attribute the helping behaviours to the direct influence of religiosity, or claim that religion makes people more helpful.

Perhaps the differences occur because inherently helpful people are more attracted to religion. The World Gallup also reveals that poor people give more to those in need than wealthy people (Pelham & Crabtree, 2008). Among those highly religious respondents worldwide who reported their annual incomes, the average figure (converted into international dollars) was about $10 000. Among those *less* religious respondents who reported their incomes, the average was about $17 500.

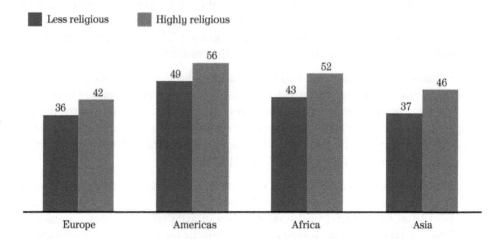

**FIGURE 10.9** Percentage of less religious and highly religious people reporting that they helped a stranger or someone they didn't know who needed help in the past month

Among Muslims it is common to support the poor with money collected during the Friday prayer in the Mosque, and many Muslims are much concerned about helping 'brothers' in need, that is, those having the same faith, even if they are not rich themselves.

But to have a religious faith is definitely not a guarantee of being a helpful or nice person. The fundamentalists, either Muslims, Christians or those of other beliefs, are sometimes willing to do a lot of harm in the name of God or Allah and their own religion. Some suicide bombers act in the name of Allah. The US President George W. Bush, the British ex-Prime Minister Tony Blair and the Norwegian Prime Minister Kjell Magne Bondevik (who is also a priest) are all sincere believers, but that did not stop them initiating and supporting wars. Under some historical circumstances religion has been far from promoting prosocial behaviour. The slogan 'Gott mit uns', or 'God with Us', has been used more than once in history to justify misdeed and evil. A religious belief does not guarantee prosociality. The function of religion also depends on the context.

## HOW CAN WE INCREASE HELPING?

*To increase individual helping, can we reverse the factors that inhibit helping? Or can we teach norms of helping and socialize people to see themselves as helpful?*

As social scientists, our goal is to understand human behaviour, thus also suggesting ways to improve it. So, how might we apply research-based understanding to increase helping? To make society more fair and equal, to redistribute wealth and income so the differences between the rich and poor diminish is one option. To establish a welfare state financed by taxes is, for instance, a measure that supports the poor without giving them the impression that they are inferior. At an individual level, one way to promote altruism is to reverse those factors that inhibit it. Given that hurried, preoccupied people focusing on themselves are less likely to help, can we think of ways to slow people down and turn their attention outwards, towards fellow human beings all over the world? If the presence of others diminishes each bystander's sense of responsibility, how can we enhance responsibility?

### REDUCE AMBIGUITY, INCREASE RESPONSIBILITY

If Latané and Darley's decision tree (see Figure 10.3) describes the dilemmas bystanders face, then prompting people to interpret an incident correctly and to assume responsibility should increase their involvement. Leonard Bickman and his colleague (Bickman, 1975, 1979; Bickman & Green, 1977) tested that presumption in a series of experiments on crime reporting. In each, they staged a shoplifting incident in a supermarket or bookstore. In some of the stores, they placed signs aimed at sensitizing bystanders to shoplifting and informing them how to report it. The researchers found that the signs had little effect. In other cases, witnesses heard a bystander interpret the incident: 'Say, look at her. She's shoplifting. She put that into her purse.' (The bystander then left to look for a lost child.) Still others heard this person add: 'We saw it. We should report it. It's our responsibility.' Both comments substantially boosted reporting of the crime.

The potency of personal influence is no longer in doubt. Robert Foss (1978) surveyed several hundred blood donors and found that neophyte donors, unlike veterans, were usually there at someone's personal invitation. Leonard Jason and his collaborators (1984) confirmed that personal appeals for blood donation are much more effective than posters and media announcements – if the personal appeals come from friends. Personalized non-verbal appeals can also be effective. Most AIDS volunteers got involved through someone's personal influence (Omoto & Snyder, 2002). A personal approach makes one feel less anonymous, more responsible.

Henry Solomon and Linda Solomon (1978; Solomon et al., 1981) explored ways to reduce anonymity. They found that bystanders who had identified themselves to one another – by name, age, and so forth – were more likely to offer aid to a sick person than were anonymous bystanders. Similarly, when a female experimenter caught the eye of another shopper and gave her a warm smile before stepping into an elevator, that shopper was far more likely than other shoppers to offer help when the experimenter later said, 'Damn. I've left my glasses. Can anyone tell me what floor the umbrellas are on?' Even a trivial momentary conversation with someone ('Excuse me, aren't you Suzie Spear's sister?' 'No, I'm not') dramatically increased the person's later helpfulness.

Helpfulness also increases when one expects to meet the victim and other witnesses again. Using a laboratory intercom system, Jody Gottlieb and Charles Carver (1980) led students to believe they were discussing problems of college living with other students. (Actually, the other discussants were tape-recorded.) When one of the supposed fellow discussants had a choking fit and cried out for help, she was helped most quickly by those who believed they would soon be meeting the discussants face to face. In short, anything that personalizes bystanders – a personal request, stating one's name, anticipation of interaction – increases willingness to help.

Personal treatment makes bystanders more self-aware and therefore more attuned to their own altruistic ideals. By contrast, 'deindividuated' people are less responsible. Thus, circumstances that promote self-awareness – name tags, being watched and evaluated, undisrupted quiet – should also increase helping. Shelley Duval, Virginia Duval and Robert Neely (1979) confirmed this. They showed some female students their own images on a television screen or had them complete biographical questionnaires just before giving them a chance to contribute time and money to people in need. Those made self-aware contributed more. Similarly, pedestrians who had just had their pictures taken by someone became more likely to help another pedestrian pick up dropped envelopes (Hoover et al., 1983). Self-aware people more often put their ideals into practice.

### GUILT AND CONCERN FOR SELF-IMAGE

Earlier we noted that people who feel guilty will act to reduce guilt and restore their self-worth. Can heightening people's awareness of their transgressions therefore increase desire to help? A Reed College research team led by Richard Katzev (1978) wondered. So when visitors to the Portland Art Museum disobeyed a 'Please do not touch' sign, experimenters reprimanded some of them: 'Please don't touch the objects. If everyone touches them, they will deteriorate.' Likewise, when visitors to the Portland Zoo fed unauthorized food to the bears, some of them were admonished with, 'Hey, don't feed unauthorized food to the animals. Don't you know it could hurt them?' In both cases, 58 per cent of the now guilt-laden individuals shortly thereafter offered help to another experimenter who had 'accidentally' dropped something. Of those not reprimanded, only one-third helped. Guilt-laden people are helpful people.

People also care about their public images. When Robert Cialdini and his colleagues (1975) asked university students to chaperone delinquent children on a zoo trip, only 32 per cent agreed to do so. With other students the questioner first made a very large request – that the students commit two years as volunteer counsellors to delinquent children. After getting the 'door in the face' in response to this request (all refused), the questioner then counter-offered with the chaperoning request, saying, in effect, 'OK, if you won't do that, would you do just this much?' With this door-in-the-face technique, nearly twice as many – 56 per cent – agreed to help.

*door-in-the-face technique manipulation technique for gaining concession in which after requesting something large (expecting that it will be turned down) the same requester counter-offers with a more reasonable request*

Cialdini and David Schroeder (1976) offer another practical way to trigger concern for self-image: ask for a contribution so small that it's hard to say no without feeling like a Scrooge. Cialdini (1995) discovered this when a United Way canvasser came to his door. As she solicited his contribution, he was mentally preparing his refusal – until she said magic words that demolished his financial excuse: 'Even a penny will help.' 'I had been neatly finessed into compliance,' recalled Cialdini. 'And there was another interesting feature of our exchange as well. When I stopped coughing (I really had choked on my attempted rejection), I gave her not the penny she had mentioned but the amount I usually allot to legitimate charity solicitors. At that, she thanked me, smiled innocently, and moved on.'

Was Cialdini's response atypical? To find out, he and Schroeder had a solicitor approach suburbanites. When the solicitor said, 'I'm collecting money for the American Cancer Society', 29 per cent contributed an average of $1.44 each. When the solicitor added, 'Even a penny will help', 50 per cent contributed an average of $1.54 each. When James Weyant (1984) repeated this experiment, he found similar results: The 'even a penny will help' boosted the number contributing from 39 to 57 per cent. And when 6000 people were solicited by mail for the American Cancer Society, those asked for small amounts were more likely to give – and gave no less on average – than those asked for larger amounts (Weyant & Smith, 1987). When previous donors are approached, bigger requests (within reason) do elicit bigger donations (Doob & McLaughlin, 1989). But with door-to-door solicitation, there is more success with requests for small contributions, which are difficult to turn down and still allow the person to maintain an altruistic self-image.

Labelling people as helpful can also strengthen a helpful self-image. After they had made charitable contributions, Robert Kraut (1973) told some Connecticut women, 'You are a generous person'. Two weeks later, these women were more willing than those not so labelled to contribute to a different charity.

## SOCIALIZING ALTRUISM

If we can learn altruism, then how might we socialize it? Here are five ways (Figure 10.10).

### Teaching Moral Inclusion

Rescuers of Jews in Nazi Europe, leaders of the American anti-slavery movement, Chinese peasants and medical missionaries shared at least one thing in common:

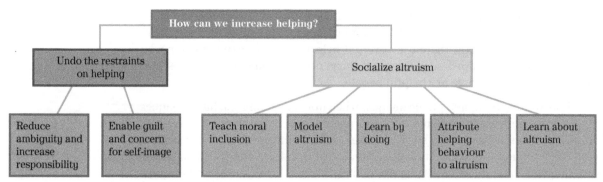

**FIGURE 10.10**   Practical ways to increase helping

moral exclusion *the perception of certain individuals or groups as outside the boundary within which one applies moral values and rules of fairness. Moral inclusion is regarding others as within one's circle of moral concern*

For further discussion of ingroup/outgroup behaviour and how this is created, see Chapter 13.

they included people who differed from themselves within the human circle to which their moral values and rules of justice applied.

Moral exclusion – omitting certain people (and animals) from one's circle of moral or social concern – has the opposite effect. It justifies all sorts of harm, from discrimination to genocide (Opotow, 1990; Staub, 2006; Tyler & Lind, 1990). Exploitation or cruelty becomes acceptable, even appropriate, towards those people we regard as undeserving or as non-persons (and also towards animals outside one's circle of concern). The Nazis excluded Jews, Gypsies, homosexuals, people with severe mental disorders and the mentally disabled from their moral community by killing them. Anyone who participates in enslavement, death squads or torture practises a similar exclusion. To a lesser extent, moral exclusion describes those of us who concentrate our concerns, favours and financial inheritance upon 'our people' (for example, our children) to the exclusion of others. This extreme social identity, caring only for those belonging to the ingroup, is therefore a dangerous strategy for everybody in the outgroups.

In Chapter 7 on conformity and obedience we reviewed how Stephen Reicher and his colleagues in Great Britain have re-examined the classical social psychological studies on 'banality of evil' and how perpetrators make a virtue out of evil (Staub, 1989). Genocides are perpetrated against others not because of what they have done but because of the groups they belong to. Creating a cohesive ingroup through shared social identification implies the exclusion of specific populations, regarding them as outgroups. By constituting the outgroup as a danger to the existence of the uniquely virtuous ingroup, the defence of the ingroup and the annihilation of the outgroup can be presented as a virtue to be celebrated (Reicher et al., 2008).

To focus on and favour 'our people' also implies restrictions in the public empathy for the human costs of war. Reported war deaths are typically 'our deaths'. Many Americans, for example, know that over 58 000 Americans died in the Vietnam War (their 58 248 names are inscribed on the Vietnam War Memorial). But few Americans know that the war also left some 2 million Vietnamese dead. During the recent Iraq war, news of American fatalities – 4300 by autumn 2009 – caused much more concern than the little-known number of Iraqi deaths, estimated to be between 600 000 and 1 million, mostly civilians. To perceive the enemy in a war as important as a human being as the soldier from your own country requires a recategorization and an extension of your social identity. There is nothing 'natural' in grieving only for the dead soldier from your own country and not showing the same sadness when the enemy dies. It depends on who we define as our ingroup.

A first step towards socializing altruism is therefore to counter the natural ingroup bias by broadening the range of people whose well-being concerns us. Daniel Batson (1983) claims that religious teachings do this by urging 'brotherly and sisterly' love towards all 'children of God' in the whole Christian 'family'. Inviting advantaged people to put themselves in others' shoes, to imagine how they feel, also helps (Batson and Powell, 2003). To 'do unto others as you would have them do unto you', one must take the others' perspective.

### Modelling Altruism

Earlier we noted that seeing unresponsive bystanders makes us less likely to help. People reared by extremely punitive parents, as were many delinquents and chronic criminals, also show much less of the empathy and principled caring that typifies altruists.

If we see or read about someone helping, we are more likely to offer assistance. It's better, find Robert Cialdini and his co-workers (2003), *not* to publicize rampant tax cheating, littering and teen drinking, and instead to emphasize – to define a norm of – people's widespread honesty, cleanliness and abstinence. In one experiment, they asked visitors not to remove petrified wood from along the paths of the Petrified Forest National Park. Some were also told that 'past visitors have removed the petrified wood'. Other people who were told that 'past visitors have left the petrified wood' to preserve the park were much less likely to pick up samples placed along a path.

Modelling effects were also apparent within the families who risked their lives to rescue Jews in the 1930s and 1940s, and of 1950s civil rights activists. In both cases these exceptional altruists said they had warm and close relationships with at least one parent who was, similarly, a strong 'moralist' or committed to humanitarian causes (Oliner & Oliner, 1988; Rosenhan, 1970). Their families and friends had taught them the norm of helping and caring for others. That 'prosocial value orientation' acquired during socialization led them to include people from other groups in their circle of moral concern and to feel responsible for others' welfare, noted altruism researcher Ervin Staub (1989, 1991, 1992).

Staub (1999) knows of what he speaks:

> As a young Jewish child in Budapest I survived the Holocaust, the destruction of most European Jews by Nazi Germany and its allies. My life was saved by a Christian woman who repeatedly endangered her life to help me and my family, and by Raoul Wallenberg, the Swede who came to Budapest and with courage, brilliance, and complete commitment saved the lives of tens of thousands of Jews destined for the gas chambers. These two heroes were not passive bystanders, and my work is one of the ways for me not to be one.

Do television's positive models promote helping, much as its aggressive portrayals promote aggression (see Chapter 8)? Prosocial television models have actually had even greater effects than antisocial models. Susan Hearold (1986) statistically combined 108 comparisons of prosocial programmes with neutral programmes or no programme. She found that, on average, 'If the viewer watched prosocial programmes instead of neutral programmes, s/he would [at least temporarily] be elevated from the 50th to the 74th per centile in prosocial behaviour – typically altruism'.

### Learning by Doing

Ervin Staub (2005a) has shown that just as immoral behaviour fuels immoral attitudes, so helping increases future helping. Children and adults learn by doing. In a series of studies with children near age 12, Staub and his students found that after children were induced to make toys for hospitalized children or for an art teacher, they became more helpful. So were children after teaching younger children to make puzzles or use first aid.

When children act helpfully, they develop helping-related values, beliefs and skills, notes Staub. Helping also helps satisfy their needs for a positive self-concept. On a larger scale, 'service learning' and volunteer programmes woven into a school curriculum have been shown to increase later citizen involvement, social responsibility, co-operation and leadership (Andersen, 1998; Putnam, 2000). Attitudes follow behaviour. Helpful actions therefore promote the self-perception that one is caring and helpful, which in turn promotes further helping.

### Attributing Helpful Behaviour to Altruistic Motives

Another clue to socializing altruism comes from research on what Chapter 4 called the *overjustification effect*: when the justification for an act is more than sufficient, the person may attribute the act to the extrinsic justification rather than to an inner motive. Rewarding people for doing what they would do anyway therefore undermines intrinsic motivation. We can state the principle positively: by providing people with just enough justification to prompt a good deed (weaning them from bribes and threats when possible), we may increase their pleasure in doing such deeds on their own.

Daniel Batson and his associates (1978, 1979) put the overjustification phenomenon to work. In several experiments, they found that students felt most altruistic after they agreed to help someone without payment or implied social pressure. When pay had been offered or social pressures were present, people felt less altruistic after helping.

In another experiment, the researchers led students to attribute a helpful act to compliance ('I guess we really don't have a choice') or to compassion ('The guy really needs help'). Later, when the students were asked to volunteer their time to a local service agency, 25 per cent of those who had been led to perceive their previous helpfulness as mere compliance now volunteered; of those led to see themselves as compassionate, 60 per cent volunteered. The moral? When people wonder, 'Why am I helping?' it's best if the circumstances enable them to answer, 'Because help was needed, and I am a caring, giving, helpful person'.

Although rewards undermine intrinsic motivation when they function as controlling bribes, an unanticipated compliment can make people feel competent and worthy. When Joel is coerced with 'If you quit being chicken and give blood, we'll win the fraternity prize for most donations', he isn't likely to attribute his donation to altruism. When Jocelyn is rewarded with 'That's terrific that you'd choose to take an hour out of such a busy week to give blood', she's more likely to walk away with an altruistic self-image – and thus to contribute again (Piliavin et al., 1982; Thomas & Batson, 1981; Thomas et al., 1981).

To predispose more people to help in situations where most don't, it can also pay to induce a tentative positive commitment, from which people may infer their own helpfulness. Delia Cioffi and Randy Garner (1998) observed that only about 5 per cent of students responded to a campus blood drive after receiving an e-mail announcement a week ahead. They asked other students to reply to the announcement with a yes 'if you think you probably will donate'. Of those, 29 per cent did reply and the actual donation rate was 8 per cent. They asked a third group to reply with a no if they did *not* anticipate donating. Now 71 per cent implied they might give (by not replying). Imagine yourself in this third group. Might you have decided not to say no because, after all, you *are* a caring person so there's a chance you might give? And might that thought have opened you to persuasion as you encountered campus posters and flyers during the ensuing week? That apparently is what happened, because 12 per cent of these students – more than twice the normal rate – showed up to offer their blood.

Inferring that one is a helpful person seems also to have happened when Dariusz Dolinski (2000) stopped pedestrians on the streets of Wroclaw, Poland, and asked them for directions to a non-existent 'Zubrzyckiego Street' or to an illegible address. Everyone tried unsuccessfully to help. After doing so, about two-thirds (twice the number of those not given the opportunity to try to help) agreed when asked by someone 100 metres farther down the road to watch their heavy bag or bicycle for 5 minutes.

### Learning about Altruism

Researchers have found another way to boost altruism, one that provides a happy conclusion to this chapter. Some social psychologists worry that as people become more aware of social psychology's findings, their behaviour may change, thus invalidating the findings (Gergen, 1994). Will learning about the factors that inhibit altruism reduce their influence? Sometimes, such 'enlightenment' is not our problem but one of our goals.

Arthur Beaman and his colleagues (1978) revealed that once people understand why the presence of bystanders inhibits helping, they become more likely to help in group situations. The researchers used a lecture to inform some students how bystander inaction can affect the interpretation of an emergency and feelings of responsibility. Other students heard either a different lecture or no lecture at all. Two weeks later, as part of a different experiment in a different location, the participants found themselves walking (with an unresponsive confederate) past someone slumped over or past a person sprawled beneath a bicycle. Of those who had not heard the helping lecture, a quarter paused to offer help; twice as many of those 'enlightened' did so.

Having read this chapter, perhaps you, too, have changed. As you come to understand what influences people's responses, will your attitudes and your behaviour be the same?

## focus on

THE BENEFITS – AND THE COSTS – OF EMPATHY-INDUCED ALTRUISM

People do most of what they do, including much of what they do for others, for their own benefit, acknowledge altruism researcher Daniel Batson and his colleagues (2004), in their summary of research on altruism among individuals in the West. It may be their results would have been different in other, more collectivistic cultures. But neither in individualistic nor in competitive cultures is egoism the whole story of helping. There is also a genuine altruism rooted in empathy, in feelings of sympathy and compassion for others' welfare. We are supremely social creatures. Consider the following.

**Empathy-induced altruism:**

☐ *produces sensitive helping.* Where there is empathy, it's not just the thought that counts, it's alleviating the other's suffering.

☐ *inhibits aggression.* Show Batson someone who feels empathy for a target of potential aggression and he'll show you someone who's unlikely to favour attack, someone who's as likely to forgive as to harbour anger. In general, women in the West report more empathic feelings than men, and they are less likely to support war and other forms of aggression (Jones, 2003). But women in political positions do not differ so much from men. The power of the situation is strong. Women also declare war when they are in the same positions as men. The British Prime Minister Margaret Thatcher's declaration of war against Argentina in 1982 serves as an example.

☐ *increases co-operation.* In laboratory experiments, Batson and Nadia Ahmad (2001) found that people in potential conflict are more trusting and co-operative when they feel empathy for the other. Personalizing an outgroup, by getting to know people in it, helps people understand their perspective.

☐ *improves attitudes towards stigmatized groups.* Take others' perspective, allow yourself to feel what they feel, and you may become more supportive of others like them (the homeless, those with AIDS, or even convicted criminals).

**But empathy-induced altruism comes with liabilities, notes the Batson group:**

☐ It can be harmful. People who risk their lives on behalf of others sometimes lose them. People who seek to do good can also do harm, sometimes by unintentionally humiliating or demotivating the recipient. Eagerness to help can also cause increased physical harm to victims. Consider the example of traffic accident victims where enthusiastic helpers may actually do more damage than good by moving them.

☐ It can't address all needs. It's easier to feel empathy for a needy individual than, say, for Mother Earth, whose environment is being stripped and warmed at the peril of our descendants.

☐ It burns out. Feeling others' pain is painful, which may cause us to avoid situations that evoke our empathy, or to experience 'burnout' or 'compassion fatigue'.

☐ It can feed favouritism, injustice and indifference to the larger common good. Empathy, being particular, produces partiality – towards a single child or family or pet. Moral principles, being universal, produce concern for unseen others as well.

Empathy-based estate planning bequeaths inheritances to particular loved ones, whereas morality-based estate planning is more inclusive. When their empathy for someone is aroused, people will violate their own standards of fairness and justice by giving that person favoured treatment (Batson et al., 1997b). Ironically, note Batson and his colleagues (1999a), empathy-induced altruism can therefore 'pose a powerful threat to the common good [by leading] me to narrow my focus of concern to those for whom I especially care – the needing friend – and in so doing to lose sight of the bleeding crowd'. No wonder charity so often stays close to home.

Consider suicide bombers. Could suicide bombing be looked upon as an altruistic act? The suicide bombers kill themselves because they believe they contribute to a better life for their ingroup and also their family. They sacrifice their life for the welfare of others. The question is not if they really contribute to a better world or not, but what the suicide bombers believe in and their motivation for killing themselves.

### QUESTIONS

**1** Do you think Batson's somewhat pessimistic conclusion correct? Is our motivation to help others primarily driven by a desire to benefit ourselves in some way?

**2** Can you think of a time when you were able to see a set of circumstances through the eyes of an outgroup? Did this change your perception of that group?

**3** Can you think of a time when empathizing with someone or a group was harmful either to you or the group or person concerned?

## SUMMING UP: HELPING

### WHY DO WE HELP?

☐ *The social-exchange theory* assumes that helping, like other social behaviours, is motivated by a desire to exchange rewards, to be fair and just, to give and receive. The rewards may be external, appreciated by others, or internal, improving personal self-esteem. Thus, after wrongdoing, people often become more willing to offer help. Sad people also tend to be helpful. Finally, there is a striking feel good–do good effect: happy people are helpful people.

☐ *The reciprocity norm* stimulates us to help those who have helped us.

☐ *The social-responsibility norm* beckons us to help needy people, even if they cannot reciprocate, so long as they are deserving. Women in crisis, partly because they may be seen as more needy, receive more offers of help than men, especially from men.

☐ *Evolutionary psychology* assumes two types of helping: devotion to kin and reciprocity. Some evolutionary psychologists, however, believe that the genes of selfish individuals are more likely to survive than the genes of self-sacrificing individuals. Thus, selfishness is our natural tendency and society must therefore teach helping.

☐ We can evaluate the theories according to the ways in which they characterize prosocial behaviour as based on tit-for-tat exchange and/or unconditional helpfulness. Each can be criticized for using speculative or after-the-fact reasoning, but they do provide a coherent scheme for summarizing observations of prosocial behaviour.

☐ In addition to helping that is motivated by external and internal rewards, and the evading of punishment or distress, there appears also to be a genuine, empathy-based altruism. With their empathy aroused, many people are motivated to assist others in need or distress, even when their helping is anonymous or their own mood will be unaffected.

## WHEN WILL WE HELP?

☐ Several situational influences work to inhibit or to encourage altruism. As the number of bystanders at an emergency increases, any given bystander is (1) less likely to notice the incident, (2) less likely to interpret it as an emergency, and (3) less likely to assume responsibility. Experiments on helping behaviour pose an ethical dilemma but fulfil the researcher's mandate to enhance human life by discovering important influences on behaviour.

☐ When are people most likely to help? One circumstance is when they have just observed someone else helping.

☐ Another circumstance that promotes helping is having at least a little spare time; those in a hurry are less likely to help. Personal influences such as mood also matter.

☐ We tend to help those whom we perceive as being close to us, our family or people we categorize as belonging to our ingroup. To help ingroup members strengthens our social identity and group cohesion, and boosts our self-image.

## WHO WILL HELP?

☐ In contrast to altruism's potent situational and mood determinants, personality test scores have served as only modest predictors of helping.

☐ Highly religious people donate more money to charity and help strangers more often than those not affiliated to a religion in societies where there are many believers.

☐ People in societies where few believe in a god help to the same degree as in other societies.

## HOW CAN WE INCREASE HELPING?

Research suggests that we can enhance helpfulness in three ways.

☐ First, we can reverse those factors that inhibit helping. We can take steps to reduce the ambiguity of an emergency to make a personal appeal, and to increase feelings of responsibility.

☐ Second, we can even use reprimands or the door-in-the-face technique to evoke guilt feelings or a concern for self-image.

☐ Third, we can teach altruism. Children who view helpful behaviour tend to act helpfully. If we want to promote altruistic behaviour, we should remember the overjustification effect: when we coerce good deeds, intrinsic love of the activity often diminishes. If we provide people with enough justification for them to decide to do good, but not much more, they will attribute their behaviour to their own altruistic motivation and henceforth be more willing to help. Learning about altruism, as you have just done, can also prepare people to perceive and respond to others' needs.

## CRITICAL QUESTIONS

**1** Would you expect the same motivation for helping in all cultures? Explain.

**2** Which arguments can be used in favour of and against genuine altruism?

**3** What kind of similarity enhances helping and how is it explained?

**4** What is the criticism against Darley and Latané's study of the bystander effect?

**5** Would you expect parents to care just as much for the adopted as for their biological children?

**6** In what way is empathy important for helping?

**7** How does mood influence helping?

## RECOMMENDED READINGS

### Classic Papers

Batson, D. C., Batson, J. G., Slingsby, J. K., Harrell, K. L., Peekna, H. M., & Todd, M. R. (1991). Empathic joy and the empathy-altruism hypothesis. *Journal of Personality & Social Psychology*, **61**(3), 413–426.

*Outlines the empathy explanation for altruistic behaviour in humans.*

Dawkins, R. (2006). *The Selfish Gene.* Oxford: Oxford University Press.

*Presents an evolutionary theoretical explanation for altruism in the natural world.*

Latané, B., & Darley, J. M. (1968). Bystander intervention in emergencies: Diffusion of responsibility. *Journal of Personality and Social Psychology*, **8**(4), 377–383.

*Original presentation of the bystander effect with an explanation for why it occurs.*

### Contemporary Papers

Fischer, P., Krueger, J. I., Greitemeyer, T., Vogrincic, C., Kästenmüller, A., Frey, D., Heene, M., Wicher, M., & Kainbacher, M. (2011). The bystander effect: A meta-analytic review on bystander intervention in dangerous and non-dangerous emergencies. *Psychological Bulletin*, **137**(4), 517–537.

*Presents a thorough review of classic and recent social psychological work on the bystander effect.*

Piliavin, J. A., & Charng, H. W. (1990). Altruism: A review of recent theory and research. *Annual Review of Sociology*, **16**, 27–65.

*Presents a review of social psychological literature on altruism. This includes work which argues altruism is a selfish act through to those who suggest pure altruism is possible in human beings.*

**11**

"*Never doubt that a small group of thoughtful, committed citizens can change the world.*"

*Anthropologist Margaret Mead*

# SMALL GROUP PROCESSES

In Chapter 7 we considered how people's actions and behaviour can be influenced to conform to, or obey, those around us. In this chapter we will examine how we are influenced when we are part of a small group. Can small and minority groups be just as influential as majority ones?

For the purposes of this chapter the term 'group', used throughout, is an inference to a 'social group' as opposed to a mere assemblage of persons or objects gathered or located together. At almost every turn, we are involved in small groups – couples having dinner, housemates hanging out, students in a seminar discussion group, workers for a company, soldiers plotting strategy. How do these groups influence individuals' behaviour, values, attitudes and beliefs?

Group interactions often have dramatic effects. Intellectual college students hang out with other intellectuals, and they strengthen one another's intellectual interests. Deviant youths may hang out with other deviant youths, amplifying one another's antisocial tendencies. But how do these groups affect the attitudes of the people in the group? And what influences lead groups to good and bad decisions?

Individuals influence their groups. As the 1957 classic film *12 Angry Men* opens, 12 wary murder trial jurors file into the jury room. It is a hot day. The tired jurors are close to agreement and eager for a quick verdict convicting a teenage boy of knifing his father. But one maverick, played by Henry Fonda, refuses to vote guilty. As the heated deliberation proceeds, the jurors one by one change their minds until they reach a unanimous verdict: 'Not guilty'. In real trials, a lone individual seldom sways the entire group. Yet history is made by minorities that sway majorities. What helps make a minority – or a leader – persuasive?

We will examine these intriguing phenomena of group influence one at a time. But first things first: what is a group and why do groups exist?

## WHAT IS A GROUP?

The answer to this question seems self-evident – until several people compare their definitions. Are jogging partners a group? Are airplane passengers a group? Is a group a set of people who identify with one another, who sense they belong together? Is a group those who share common goals and rely on one another? Does a group form when individuals become organized? Do their relationships with one another continue over time? These are among the social psychological definitions of a group (McGrath, 1984).

So does a collection of co-present individuals in a situation constitute a 'group'? Not according to group dynamics expert Marvin Shaw (1981), who argues that all groups have one thing in common: their members interact with one another. Therefore, he defines a group as two or more people who interact and influence one another. This would allow for online interactions between people to be thought of as 'groups'. Social psychologist John Turner (1987) argues that group members do not need to interact in order to feel being a 'group'. They don't need to be in one another's presence but group members simply have to identify as a group and perceive themselves as 'us' in contrast to 'them'. As such, an individual can act and think as a group member even when they're alone (see Chapters 12 and 13 for further discussion).

**group** *two or more people who interact with and influence one another and perceive one another as 'us'*

Groups may exist for a number of reasons – to meet a need to belong, to provide information, to supply rewards, to accomplish goals. Throughout this chapter we shall explore social psychological research that has started with varying understandings of what a 'group' is. At its simplest, people who are merely in one another's presence do sometimes influence one another. At a football game, they may perceive themselves as 'us' fans in contrast with 'them' who root for the other team. In this chapter we consider the structure and composition of groups, followed by three examples of collective influence: *social facilitation*, *social loafing* and *deindividuation*. These three phenomena can occur with minimal interaction (in what we call 'minimal group situations'). Then we consider three examples of social influence in interacting groups: *group polarization*, *groupthink* and *minority influence*.

In the 1957 film *12 Angry Men*, one lone juror goes against his fellow jurors and refuses to vote 'guilty'. Slowly but surely he influences the other 11 jurors to also conclude 'not guilty'. History tells of minorities who sway majorities into changing their minds.

SOURCE: © Getty Images

## THE STRUCTURE AND COMPOSITION OF GROUPS

### What Holds a Group Together?

Group cohesiveness is what holds a group together. A sense of team spirit and 'we-ness' rather than simply 'I'. Cohesion is about perceiving things in common with other group members. Social psychologists have understood group cohesiveness as being attraction to the group as a whole, rather than simply liking some individuals within it (Lott & Lott, 1965). The more cohesive the group, the more likely it is to remain together. Christina Badea and her colleagues (2012) observed that it also seems to be associated with success. When participants were presented with successful teams of fashion designers and architects, they regarded the groups as highly homogenous, and therefore highly cohesive. But can cohesiveness get in the way of performance? Michael Hogg and Sarah Hains (1998) found that very cohesive groups, built on strong identification and attraction to the group, tended to make poorer decisions than those groups based on friendship and interpersonal attraction. As we shall see later in the chapter, being too similar can be detrimental to the group.

So what is it that group members find so attractive? What are they conforming to? In Chapter 4, we examined how cultural and societal norms guide our perceptions, judgements and behaviour. Norms can be formal with legal recognition (e.g. do not commit murder), but can also be informal and implicit. Groups have their own sets of norms that differentiate them from others. These norms not only describe beliefs about the way the world is, but also regulate individual members' behaviour. You may remember in Chapter 7 we examined the formation of norms in Sherif's (1935, 1937) experiments on the autokinetic phenomenon. As the perceptual illusion made reality ambiguous, individuals turned to one another for the right answer about how far a pinpoint of light had moved in an otherwise dark room. These group judgements persisted even when individuals were asked to give a private judgement. We shall return to group norms in Chapter 12, but for now we can say that the more a member identifies with the group, the more likely they are to adhere to the group's norms (Livingstone et al., 2011). And violating a group norm may well result in that member being rejected by the rest of the group. The likelihood of being shunned by the group depends on that individual's role and status within the group.

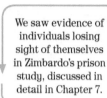

We saw evidence of individuals losing sight of themselves in Zimbardo's prison study, discussed in detail in Chapter 7.

While norms characterize the whole group, individuals occupy different roles in groups. These may be based on abilities and qualities, and/or their relationships with other members of the group. Whatever the role, they should improve the group in some way. The role one occupies in a group can offer a sense of identity and purpose, as well as a guide on what behaviour is expected of that person (see Chapters 3 and 13). Roles may be recognized formally (e.g. in the workplace) or informally (e.g. amongst a group of friends). Of course, conflict can arise as a consequence of these roles. Individuals with different roles may clash as they try to fulfil them (e.g. a headmaster and a teacher), or they may experience role conflict as they occupy different roles across different groups (e.g. a mother, teacher, wife). The danger of a role is that individuals may lose sight of themselves in acting it out.

But of course not all roles are equal, and people hold very different statuses within a group. Status can have consequences for how individuals identify and behave in relation to the group. Peter Fischer and colleagues (2007) found that low-status employees in a workplace displayed least cohesion to the group, had low identification with the group, and were most opposed to proposed changes to merge their workforce with another. Susanne Täuber and Esther van Leeuwen (2012) found that low-status members were more likely to offer help to outgroup members than high-status members. The leader of a group usually has the highest status as he or she is the most influential member, often with the power to change the structure and composition, and sometimes even the norms, of a group. Status is not a fixed entity but can change over time and space. We shall consider the role of leaders later in this chapter.

Formal and informal communication networks describe the paths along which individuals within a group interact. As people occupy different roles within a group, they will need to communicate to some individuals and not others. Communication networks have been most commonly examined in professional organizations where employers and employees recognize quite formal structures in their communications with each other. Within a small group, each individual member may be able to communicate directly with every other member, meaning a leader can discuss decisions with everyone. Leanne Boggs and her colleagues (2005) report research that shows 'all-channel communication' networks are typically associated with high levels of group morale and performance. 'Wheel' communication networks describe the leader as the central medium through which all group members interact. Prasad Balkundi and colleagues (2011) found that workplace leaders who interacted with lower-status group members were perceived as charismatic and enhanced group performance. However, in large groups such structures are not always sustainable. Those who make the decisions may not be able to discuss them with everyone. If you think of big organizations such as universities, it would become a very cumbersome experience if all ideas and decisions were discussed with every member of staff before they were carried out. As such, there will be patterns of communication, such as 'chains' of command, which dictate who communicates with who, and information is fed back to the decision-maker by means of a few select people rather than everyone. Of course this quest for efficiency and productivity can come at the cost of group satisfaction. The more input group members feel they've had over a decision the happier and more satisfied they are. So the roles we occupy will afford some people with the responsibility of making decisions on behalf of other members.

# SOCIAL FACILITATION: HOW ARE WE AFFECTED BY THE PRESENCE OF OTHERS?

Let's explore social psychology's most elementary question: are we affected by the mere presence of another person? 'Mere presence' means people are not competing, do not reward or punish, and in fact do nothing except be present as a passive audience or as co-actors. Would the mere presence of others affect a person's jogging, eating, typing or examination performance? The search for the answer is a scientific mystery story.

**co-actors**
*co-participants working individually on a non-competitive activity*

## THE MERE PRESENCE OF OTHERS

In Chapter 1 we considered one of social psychology's first experiments that took place more than a century ago. Norman Triplett (1898), a psychologist interested in bicycle racing, noticed that cyclists' times were faster when they raced together than when each one raced alone against the clock. Before he peddled his hunch (that others' presence boosts performance), Triplett asked children to wind string on a fishing reel as rapidly as possible. They wound faster when they worked with co-actors than when they worked alone.

Ensuing experiments found that others' presence improves the speed with which people do simple multiplication problems and cross out designated letters. It also improves the accuracy with which people perform simple motor tasks, such as keeping a metal stick in contact with a dime-sized disc on a moving turntable (Allport, 1920; Dashiell, 1930; Travis, 1925). This social facilitation effect also occurs with animals. In the presence of others of their species, ants excavate more sand, chickens eat more grain and sexually active rat pairs mate more often (Bayer, 1929; Chen, 1937; Larsson, 1956).

**social facilitation**
*(1) original meaning: the tendency of people to perform simple or well-learned tasks better when others are present (2) current meaning: the strengthening of dominant (prevalent, likely) responses in the presence of others*

## research close-up

### AN EXPERIMENT ON THE SOCIAL FACILITATION OF GAMBLING BEHAVIOUR

***Source***: *Rockloff, M. J., & Dyer, V. (2007). An experiment on the social facilitation of gambling behavior.* Journal of Gambling Studies, *23, 1–12.*

#### Introduction

Behaviours can be socially facilitated by the presence of others. Would gambling also be prone to social facilitation if it was done in the presence of other gamblers? Matthew Rockloff and Victoria Dyer wanted to know if gamblers gambled more frequently and intensively when surrounded by other gamblers. Does the desire to appear skilful to others, and the lights and bells signalling a 'win' on the machine, facilitate gambling behaviour? Or perhaps the presence of other gamblers might inhibit gambling behaviour if she or he fears appearing like an actual loser?

#### Method

Rockloff and Dyer recruited 116 participants (50 male, 66 female, aged 18–67) who were gamblers based in Queensland, Australia. They were all given $5 for agreeing to take part, and told they would be invited to gamble on an electronic gambling machine (EGM). They could, if they chose, use their

$5 participation fee as a stake, but any other money gambled would be their own. All participants agreed to this and their $5 was taken from them. All participants were led to a room on their own containing an EGM, where they took part. Players were informed it was possible to win up to $50 on a game. Their time ended when they either ran out of money or chose to quit. Unknown to the participants, half of them were given faked information via the sound of bells that a player in the room next to them had won, and half were not. Furthermore, half the participants witnessed flashing banners on their screen, which indicated a player in an adjacent room had won, and again half were not. Researchers were interested in the final payout each participant received from the EGM before they stopped playing (which would indicate how much they had lost), the number of games they played, the average amount they bet, and how quickly they played.

### Results

The researchers found that those participants who had received fake information through sound (bell) and sight (banner) gambled the most amount of money. They left the experiment with no money left. This was a significant difference from those participants who received either no fake information, or sound only, or sight only.

Bet-size did not differ between the participants regardless of which condition they were in.

Those participants subjected to both the sound of the bell and the flashing banner played more games than participants in either the bell only, the banner only, or no fake information conditions. The sound and sight participants also played more slowly than the other gamblers.

### Discussion

Rockloff and Dyer conclude that this experiment presents social facilitation effects on gambling behaviour when the presence of other 'winning' gamblers is implied. It increases gambling behaviour, the amount of money lost, and the speed of play. The researchers note the implications of their findings for gambling venues. The larger the venue and the more players there are, the greater the amount of gambling will be due to social facilitation effects.

However, this study only considers 'implied' presence of others. Nor does it examine why social facilitation effects occur. Rockloff and Dyer note that work now needs to be done in gambling venues to test the conclusions produced by their experiment.

But wait: other studies revealed that on some tasks the presence of others *hinders* performance. In the presence of others, cockroaches, parakeets and green finches learn mazes more slowly (Allee & Masure, 1936; Gates & Allee, 1933; Klopfer, 1958). This disruptive effect also occurs with people. Others' presence diminishes efficiency at learning nonsense syllables, completing a maze and performing complex multiplication problems (Dashiell, 1930; Pessin, 1933; Pessin & Husband, 1933). It can even interfere with passing your driving test, as Tova Rosenbloom and colleagues (2007) found when they compared learner drivers tested in pairs with those tested alone. It also seems that the presence of virtual others can hinder performance. Sung Park and Richard Catrambone (2007) found that while the presence of virtual humans facilitated their participants in achieving simple tasks, it hindered them in the accomplishment of complex tasks.

Saying that the presence of others sometimes facilitates performance and some-times hinders it is about as satisfying as the typical Scottish weather forecast – predicting that it might be sunny but then again it might rain. By 1940 research activity in this area had ground to a halt, and it lay dormant for 25 years until awakened by the touch of a new idea.

Social psychologist Robert Zajonc wondered whether these seemingly contradictory findings could be reconciled. As often happens at creative moments in science, Zajonc (1965) used one field of research to illuminate another. In this case the illumination came from a well-established principle in experimental psychology: arousal enhances whatever response tendency is dominant. Increased arousal enhances performance on easy tasks for which the most likely – 'dominant' – response is the correct one. People solve easy anagrams, such as *akec*, fastest when they are aroused. On complex tasks, for which the correct answer is not dominant, increased arousal promotes *incorrect* responding. On harder anagrams, such as *theloacco*, people do worse when anxious.

Could this principle solve the mystery of social facilitation? It seemed reasonable to assume that others' presence will arouse or energize people (Mullen et al., 1997); most of us can recall feeling tense or excited in front of an audience. If social arousal facilitates dominant responses, it should *boost performance on easy tasks* and *hurt performance on difficult tasks*.

With that explanation, the confusing results made sense. Winding fishing reels, doing simple multiplication problems, and eating were all easy tasks for which the responses were well learned or naturally dominant. Sure enough, having others around boosted performance. Learning new material, doing a maze and solving complex mathematics problems were more difficult tasks for which the correct responses were initially less probable. In these cases, the presence of others increased the number of *incorrect* responses on these tasks. The same general rule – *arousal facilitates dominant responses* – worked in both cases (see Figure 11.1). Suddenly, what had looked like contradictory results no longer seemed contradictory.

Zajonc's solution, so simple and elegant, left other social psychologists thinking what Thomas H. Huxley thought after first reading Darwin's *On the Origin of Species*: 'How extremely stupid not to have thought of that!' It seemed obvious – once Zajonc had pointed it out. Perhaps, however, the pieces fit so neatly only

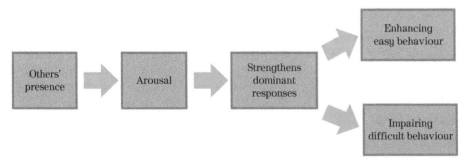

**FIGURE 11.1**  The effects of social arousal
Robert Zajonc reconciled apparently conflicting findings by proposing that arousal from others' presence strengthens dominant responses (the correct responses only on easy or well-learned tasks).

through the spectacles of hindsight. Would the solution survive direct experimental tests?

'Discovery consists of seeing what everybody has seen and thinking what nobody had thought.'

Albert von Szent-Györgyi, *The Scientist Speculates*, 1962

After 300 studies, conducted with the help of more than 25 000 volunteers, the solution has survived (Bond & Titus, 1983; Guerin, 1993, 1999). Social arousal facilitates dominant responses, whether right or wrong. For example, Peter Hunt and Joseph Hillery (1973) found that in others' presence, students took less time to learn a simple maze and more time to learn a complex one (just as the cockroaches do!). And James Michaels and his collaborators (1982) found that good pool players in a student union (who had made 71 per cent of their shots while being unobtrusively observed) did even better (80 per cent) when four observers came up to watch them play. Poor shooters (who had previously averaged 36 per cent) did even worse (25 per cent) when closely observed.

But what about people who are used to being in crowded contexts with lots of people around them? In the big cities and in collective cultures like India and China, we might wonder if they are influenced by the presence of others to the same degree as people in more sparsely populated areas and independent cultures. Presumably not. We get used to the presence of others as well as everything else in a culture. So crowding and the presence of others may not have similar impact in all cultures.

## WHY ARE WE AROUSED IN THE PRESENCE OF OTHERS?

What you do well, you will be energized to do best in front of others (unless you become hyper-aroused and self-conscious). What you find difficult may seem impossible in the same circumstances. What is it about other people that creates arousal? There is evidence to support at least three possible factors (Aiello & Douthitt, 2001): evaluation apprehension, distraction and mere presence.

### Evaluation Apprehension

**evaluation apprehension** *concern for how others are evaluating us*

Nickolas Cottrell surmised that observers make us apprehensive because we wonder how they are evaluating us. To test whether evaluation apprehension exists, Cottrell and his associates (1968) blindfolded observers, supposedly in preparation for a perception experiment. In contrast to the effect of the watching audience, the mere presence of these blindfolded people did *not* boost well-practised responses.

Other experiments confirmed Cottrell's conclusion: the enhancement of dominant responses is strongest when people think they are being evaluated. In one experiment, individuals running on a University of California at Santa Barbara jogging path sped up as they came upon a woman seated on the grass – *if* she was facing them rather than sitting with her back turned (Worringham & Messick, 1983).

Evaluation apprehension also helps explain:

☐ why people perform best when their co-actor is slightly superior (Seta, 1982)

☐ why arousal lessens when a high-status group is diluted by adding people whose opinions don't matter to us (Seta & Seta, 1992)

☐ why people who worry most about what others think are the ones most affected by their presence (Gastorf et al., 1980; Geen & Gange, 1983)

☐ why social facilitation effects are greatest when the others are unfamiliar and hard to keep an eye on (Guerin & Innes, 1982).

The self-consciousness we feel when being evaluated can also interfere with behaviours that we perform best automatically (Mullen & Baumeister, 1987). If self-conscious football players analyse their body movements while taking penalties, they are more likely to miss.

### Mere Presence

Zajonc, however, believes that the mere presence of others produces some arousal even without evaluation apprehension or arousing distraction. For example, most runners are energized when running with someone else, even one who neither competes nor evaluates.

This is a good time to remind ourselves that a good theory is a scientific shorthand: it simplifies and summarizes a variety of observations (see Chapter 2). Social facilitation theory does this well. It is a simple summary of many research findings. A good theory also offers clear predictions that (1) help confirm or modify the theory, (2) guide new exploration, and (3) suggest practical applications. Social facilitation theory has definitely generated the first two types of prediction: (1) the basics of the theory (that the presence of others is arousing and that this social arousal enhances dominant responses) have been confirmed, and (2) the theory has brought new life to a long-dormant field of research.

Are there (3) some practical applications? We can make some educated guesses. As Figure 11.2 shows, many new office buildings have replaced private offices with large, open areas divided by low partitions. Might the resulting awareness of others' presence help boost the performance of well-learned tasks but disrupt creative thinking on complex tasks? Can you think of other possible applications?

### Absent Friends

Of course, online groups do not involve the physical presence of others. People can be part of groups and communities without ever having physically met any of their fellow members. The rise in the use of Internet chat rooms, self-help groups and large forums such as Facebook, MySpace and Twitter has seen groups of people formed online, sharing stories, swapping experiences and motivating one another to achieve goals.

Patricia Beffa-Negrini and her colleagues (2002) point out that there are extra challenges in facilitating online groups. Without the physical presence of people who can show emotions such as empathy and offer immediate feedback, members of online groups can soon feel isolated and misunderstood. The challenge for online groups is to remain good-humoured, provide

FIGURE 11.2   In the 'open-office plan', people work in the presence of others. How might this affect worker efficiency?
SOURCE: © 06photo/iStock

each other with positive feedback and praise, and to encourage the expression of emotions.

Consider online teaching and learning. As teaching practices move more towards collaborative online environments to deliver information, this poses an interesting challenge to tutors and students. How can you facilitate and motivate a group you can't see? Elspeth McFadzean and Jane McKenzie (2001) suggest that tutors need to deliver information and encourage students to work collaboratively as a team. Marijke De Smet, Hilde Van Keer and Martin Valcke (2009) examined how tutors provide teaching and social support to students using online discussion groups. They found that, as time went on, tutor contributions decreased as students engaged more in peer tutoring. Students help each other to learn, teaching and motivating one another towards their common goal.

So where physical presence is not possible group members still require social facilitation but in a way that can be delivered online. As Beffa-Negrini et al. (2002) argue, this should be in the form of a sense of community, so each member can share their experiences, goals and aspirations.

## SOCIAL LOAFING: DO INDIVIDUALS EXERT LESS EFFORT IN A GROUP?

*In a team tug-of-war, will eight people on a side exert as much force as the sum of their best efforts in individual tugs-of-war? If not, why not? What level of individual effort can we expect from members of work groups?*

Social facilitation usually occurs when people work towards individual goals and when their efforts, whether winding fishing reels or solving maths problems, can be individually evaluated. These situations parallel some everyday work situations, but not those in which people pool their efforts towards a *common* goal and where individuals are *not* accountable for their efforts. A team tug-of-war provides one such example, so does a class group project on which all students get the same grade. On such 'additive tasks' – tasks where the group's achievement depends on the sum of the individual efforts – will team spirit boost productivity? Will bricklayers lay bricks faster when working as a team than when working alone? One way to attack such questions is with laboratory simulations.

### MANY HANDS MAKE LIGHT WORK

Nearly a century ago, French engineer Max Ringelmann (reported by Kravitz & Martin, 1986) found that the collective effort of tug-of-war teams was but half the sum of the individual efforts. That suggests, contrary to the presumption 'in unity there is strength', that group members may actually be *less* motivated when performing additive tasks. Maybe, though, poor performance stemmed from poor co-ordination – people pulling a rope in slightly different directions at slightly different times. A group of Massachusetts researchers led by Alan Ingham (1974) cleverly eliminated that problem by making individuals think others were pulling with them, when in fact they were pulling alone. Blindfolded participants were assigned the first position in the apparatus and told, 'Pull as hard as you can'. They pulled 18 per cent harder when they knew they were pulling alone than when they believed that behind them two to five people were also pulling.

Researchers Bibb Latané, Kipling Williams and Stephen Harkins (1979; Harkins et al., 1980) kept their ears open for other ways to investigate this phenomenon, which they labelled social loafing. They observed that the noise produced by six people shouting or clapping 'as loud as you can' was less than three times that produced by one person alone. Like the tug-of-war task, however, noise-making is vulnerable to group inefficiency. So Latané and his associates followed Ingham's example by leading their participants to believe others were shouting or clapping with them, when in fact they were doing so alone.

Their method was to blindfold six people, seat them in a semicircle and have them put on headphones, over which they were blasted with the sound of people shouting or clapping. People could not hear their own shouting or clapping, much less that of others. On various trials they were instructed to shout or clap either alone or along with the group. People who were told about this experiment guessed the participants would shout louder when with others, because they would be less inhibited (Harkins, 1981). The actual result? Social loafing: when the participants believed five others were also either shouting or clapping, they produced one-third less noise than when they thought themselves alone. Social loafing occurred even when the participants were high school cheerleaders who believed themselves to be cheering together rather than alone (Hardy & Latané, 1986).

Curiously, those who clapped both alone and in groups did not view themselves as loafing; they perceived themselves as clapping equally in both situations. This parallels what happens when students work on group projects for a shared grade. While they all agree loafing occurs – no one admits to doing the loafing.

Pascal Huguet and colleagues (1998, 1999) have found that individuals who see themselves as 'average' tend to be less likely to engage in social loafing than those who consider themselves to be of superior ability. This seems to be particularly the case when the collective task is an easy one. Evaluation apprehension also plays a role in the occurrence of social loafing. For example, Martha Arterberry and colleagues (2007) observed that when 5-year-old children were asked to complete an easy and a difficult puzzle with a partner, they displayed social loafing when they believed their individual input was left unevaluated compared to when they believed their efforts were being monitored. However, when asked to complete an easy puzzle with another child with their individual efforts being monitored, the children performed better than when they did the easy puzzle alone. The sense of having your efforts evaluated increases performance.

In this and 160 other studies (Karau & Williams, 1993, and Figure 11.3), we see a twist on one of the psychological forces that makes for social facilitation: evaluation apprehension. In the social loafing experiments, individuals believed they were

*social loafing the tendency for people to exert less effort when they pool their efforts towards a common goal than when they are individually accountable*

**Percentage of individual performance**

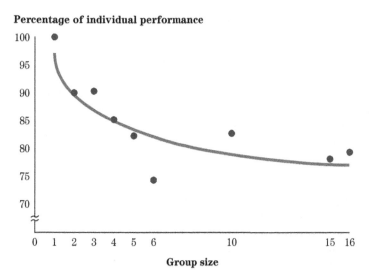

**FIGURE 11.3**  Effort decreases as group size increases

A statistical digest of 49 studies, involving more than 4000 participants, revealed that effort decreases (loafing increases) as the size of the group increases. Each dot represents the aggregate data from one of these studies.

SOURCE: from K. D. Williams et al., in *Social Dilemmas: Perspectives on Individuals and Groups*, edited by D. A. Schroeder. Copyright © 1992 by Praeger Publishers. Reprinted with permission of Greenwood Publishing Group, Inc., Westport, CT.

evaluated only when they acted alone. The group situation (rope pulling, shouting, and so forth) *decreased* evaluation apprehension. When people are not accountable and cannot evaluate their own efforts, responsibility is diffused across all group members (Harkins & Jackson, 1985; Kerr & Bruun, 1981). By contrast, the social facilitation experiments *increased* exposure to evaluation. When made the centre of attention, people self-consciously monitor their behaviour (Mullen & Baumeister, 1987). So, when being observed *increases* evaluation concerns, social facilitation occurs; when being lost in a crowd *decreases* evaluation concerns, social loafing occurs (Figure 11.4).

To motivate group members, one strategy is to make individual performance identifiable. Some football coaches do this by filming and evaluating each player individually. Whether in a group or not, people exert more effort when their outputs are individually identifiable: university swimming team members swim faster in intrasquad relay races when someone monitors and announces their individual times (Williams et al., 1989).

## SOCIAL LOAFING IN EVERYDAY LIFE

How widespread is social loafing? In the laboratory the phenomenon occurs not only among people who are pulling ropes, cycling, shouting and clapping, but also among those who are pumping water or air, evaluating poems or editorials, producing ideas, typing and detecting signals. Do these consistent results generalize to everyday worker productivity?

In one small experiment, assembly-line workers produced 16 per cent more product when their individual output was identified, even though they knew their pay would not be affected (Faulkner & Williams, 1996). And consider: a key job in a pickle factory is picking the right size dill pickle halves off the conveyor belt and stuffing them into jars. Unfortunately, workers are tempted to stuff any size pickle in, because their output is not identifiable (the jars go into a common hopper before reaching the quality-control section). Williams, Harkins and Latané (1981) note that research on social loafing suggests 'making individual production identifiable, and raises the question: "How many pickles could a pickle packer pack if pickle packers were only paid for properly packed pickles?" '

Some researchers have focused on perceptions of social loafing rather than its actual occurrence. Perceiving other members of a group as not contributing equally to a group goal can have implications for how that individual is treated by other group members. The tendency to perceive social loafing within a group has been shown to be related to how strongly an individual identifies with the group

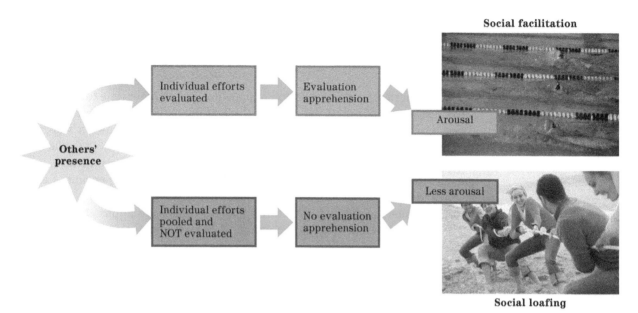

**FIGURE 11.4**  Social facilitation or social loafing?
When individuals cannot be evaluated or held accountable, loafing becomes more likely. An individual swimmer is evaluated on her ability to win the race. In tug-of-war, no single person on the team is held accountable, so any one member might relax or loaf.
SOURCE: (T) © Purestock/SuperStock; (B) © Thinkstock Images/Getty Images

and its purpose. For example, see Research Close-Up: The Relationship between Group Cohesion, Group Norms and Perceived Social Loafing in Soccer Teams.

In Rune Høigaard, Reidar Säfvenbom and Finn Egil Tønnessen's (2006) study of Norwegian football players, they found that those players who identified strongly with the team norm of competition and winning and regarded the group as cohesive, did not perceive their fellow team members as social loafers. However, those players who joined the team for social reasons rather than to win games, and did not regard the team as a cohesive unit, perceived high levels of social loafing among their fellow team members.

Researchers have also found evidence of social loafing in varied cultures, particularly by assessing agricultural output in formerly communist countries. On their collective farms under communism, Russian peasants worked one field one day, another field the next, with little direct responsibility for any given plot. For their own use, they were given small private plots. One analysis found that the private plots occupied 1 per cent of the agricultural land, yet produced 27 per cent of the Soviet farm output (H. Smith, 1976). In communist Hungary, private plots accounted for only 13 per cent of the farmland but produced one-third of the output (Spivak, 1979).

Latané and his co-researchers (Gabrenya et al., 1985) repeated their sound-production experiments in Japan, Thailand, Taiwan, India and Malaysia. They found that social loafing was evident in all those countries, too. Seventeen later studies in Asia reveal that people in collectivist cultures do, however, exhibit less social loafing than do people in individualist cultures (Karau & Williams, 1993; Kugihara, 1999). Loyalty to family and work groups runs strong in collectivist cultures. Christopher Earley (1989) has argued that those cultures which rest on collectivist beliefs rather than individualistic ones show less occurrence of social loafing. In his comparison of managerial trainees in the USA and China, he found that social loafing was much less prevalent among the Chinese workers. Likewise, women tend to be less individualistic than men – and to exhibit less social loafing.

In North America, workers who do not pay dues or volunteer time to their unions or professional associations nevertheless are usually happy to accept the benefits those organizations provide. So, too, are public television viewers who don't respond to their station's fund drives. This hints at another possible explanation of social loafing. When rewards are divided equally, regardless of how much one contributes to the group, any individual gets more reward per unit of effort by free-riding on the group. So people may be motivated to slack off when their efforts are not individually monitored and rewarded. Situations that welcome free-riders can therefore be, in the words of one commune member, a 'paradise for parasites'.

free-riders *people benefiting from the group but giving little in return*

But surely collective effort does not always lead to slacking off. Sometimes the goal is so compelling and maximum output from everyone is so essential that team spirit maintains or intensifies effort. In an Olympic crew race, will the individual rowers in an eight-person crew pull their oars with less effort than those in a one- or two-person crew?

The evidence assures us they will not. People in groups loaf less when the task is *challenging, appealing* or *involving* (Karau & Williams, 1993). On challenging tasks, people may perceive their efforts as indispensable (Harkins & Petty, 1982; Kerr, 1983; Kerr & Bruun, 1983). When people see others in their group as unreliable or as unable to contribute much, they work harder (Plaks & Higgins, 2000; Williams & Karau, 1991). Adding incentives or challenging a group to strive for certain standards also promotes collective effort (Harkins & Szymanski, 1989; Shepperd & Wright, 1989). Group members will work hard when convinced that high effort will bring rewards (Shepperd & Taylor, 1999).

Groups also loaf less when their members are *friends* or identified with their group, rather than strangers (Davis & Greenlees, 1992; Karau & Williams, 1997; Worchel et al., 1998). Even just expecting to interact with someone again serves to increase effort on team projects (Groenenboom et al., 2001). Collaborate on a class project with others whom you will be seeing often and you will probably feel more motivated than you would if you never expect to see them again. Leon notes that Israel's communal kibbutz farms have actually out-produced Israel's non-collective farms (Leon, 1969). Cohesiveness intensifies effort.

Some of these findings parallel those from studies of everyday work groups. When groups are given challenging objectives, when they are rewarded for group success and when there is a spirit of commitment to the 'team', group members work hard (Hackman, 1986). Miriam Erez and Anit Somech (1996) compared managers from an Israeli kibbutzim with those from urban Israel. They wondered how the presence or absence of specific goals, intragroup communication, group rewards and incentives, and cultural values would affect the chances of individuals engaging in social loafing. Erez and Somech make the point that many social psychological studies on social loafing involve groups where members do not know each other prior to the study so this may explain why we obtain high incidences of social loafing. There may also be no incentive or reward for taking part. It's also worth

## research close-up

### THE RELATIONSHIP BETWEEN GROUP COHESION, GROUP NORMS AND PERCEIVED SOCIAL LOAFING IN SOCCER TEAMS

*Source: Høigaard, R., Säfvenbom, R., & Tønnessen, F. E. (2006). The relationship between group cohesion, group norms, and perceived social loafing in soccer teams. Small Group Research, 37(3), 217–232.*

### Introduction

Social loafing suggests that when individuals work in a small group, the effort they put into the task is considerably reduced compared to the effort they would have put in had they worked on the task on their own. Høigaard, Säfvenbom and Tønnessen wondered why. Is this because everyone else in the group has actually reduced the amount of effort they're putting into the task, or just the perception that they have? As the researchers suggest, no-one wants to look like a sucker! Either way, the feeling that other group members are not pulling their weight can demotivate an individual's motivation to put in much effort to a small group task. Instead, they put in just enough effort to match what they think their fellow group members are putting in. Furthermore, Høigaard, Säfvenbom and Tønnessen wondered if group cohesion and norms would have an impact on social loafing. So does it matter if the group members are highly committed to the group and each other (i.e. cohesive), and if the group's norms about what's important affect whether social loafing will occur? The researchers decided to find out.

### Method

The participants were 118 junior male football players, aged between 15.5 and 19.6 years. They were asked to fill out a Perceived Social Loafing Questionnaire, containing five items, which assessed their perception of how much loafing goes on in their team. They were also given a Group Environmental Questionnaire (GEQ), containing 18 items, which measured how integrated into the team the player felt and how cohesive that team is. Finally, the participants were asked to complete the Team Sport Competition Norm Questionnaire (TSCNQ), containing nine items that measure the team's norms for competition, and whether there was a strong commitment to this norm in that team.

### Results

Correlating the scores from the three questionnaires, the researchers found some interesting results. First, they discovered a negative relationship between cohesiveness of the team (as measured by the GEQ) and perception of social loafing. So the less integrated a team player felt, the more likely he was to believe his fellow team members were engaging in social loafing. In addition, the norms of the group towards competition (as measured by the TSCNQ) also had an effect on social loafing. So if the desire to win in competitions was low in the group, then perceptions of social loafing amongst the team were prevalent. Put simply, a cohesive group with competitive norms inhibits the perception of social loafing.

### Discussion

Høigaard, Säfvenbom and Tønnessen conclude that group cohesion and norms have an impact on social loafing within a small group, such as a football team. The researchers state that more research is needed to see if perceived social loafing actually reflects real loafing. Further, while environmental factors seem to account for the occurrence (or perception) of social loafing within a small group, we should also consider whether personality factors explain differences in social loafing between individual members.

Social loafing occurs when people work in groups but without individual accountability – unless the task is challenging, appealing or involving and the group members are friends.

SOURCE: © Chris Ryan/age fotostock

remembering that those studies where evidence of social loafing is found have often taken place in individualistic cultures. Erez and Somech argue that the urban sector of Israel endorses the independent self, which is less affected by the presence of other group members. So for these group members in the absence of specific goals, rewards, incentives and communication, you will see social loafing. Their sense of self is not tied up with the group's performance. However, for those participants who are members of the Israeli kibbutzim where the interdependent self is upheld, their individual contribution to a group task enhances their sense of self. For these group members, even in the absence of specific goals, rewards and incentives, there is little evidence of social loafing. As Erez and Somech conclude, social loafing may actually be the exception rather than the rule.

## GROUP POLARIZATION: DO GROUPS INTENSIFY OUR OPINIONS?

*Many conflicts grow as people on both sides talk mostly with like-minded others. Does interaction with like-minded people amplify pre-existing attitudes? If so, why?*

Studies of people in small groups have produced a principle that helps explain both bad and good outcomes: group discussion often strengthens members' initial inclinations. The unfolding of this research on group polarization illustrates the process of enquiry – how an interesting discovery often leads researchers to hasty and erroneous conclusions, which ultimately are replaced with more accurate conclusions.

group polarization
*group-produced enhancement of members' pre-existing tendencies. When a rather homogenous group discusses a topic, the opinion of the group members often merges into a more extreme one, strengthening the members' average tendency*

### THE CASE OF THE 'RISKY SHIFT'

A research literature of more than 300 studies began with a surprising finding by James Stoner (1961), then an MIT graduate student. For his master's thesis in industrial management, Stoner tested the commonly held belief that groups are more cautious than individuals. He posed decision dilemmas in which the participant's task was to advise imagined characters how much risk to take. Put yourself in the participant's shoes: what advice would you give the character in this situation?

Helen is a writer who is said to have considerable creative talent but who so far has been earning a comfortable living by writing cheap westerns. Recently she has come up with an idea for a potentially significant novel. If it could be written and accepted, it might have considerable literary impact and be a big boost to her career. On the other hand, if she cannot work out her idea, or if the novel is a flop, she will have expended considerable time and energy without remuneration.

Imagine that you are advising Helen. Please check the *lowest* probability that you would consider acceptable for Helen to attempt to write the novel.

Helen should attempt to write the novel if the chances that the novel will be a success are at least:

___ 1 in 10

___ 2 in 10

___ 3 in 10

___ 4 in 10

___ 5 in 10

___ 6 in 10

___ 7 in 10

___ 8 in 10

___ 9 in 10

___ 10 in 10 (Place a check here if you think Helen should attempt the novel only if it is certain that the novel will be a success.)

After making your decision, guess what this book's average reader would advise. Having marked their advice on a dozen such items, five or so individuals would then discuss and reach agreement on each item. How do you think the group decisions compared with the average decision before the discussions? Would the groups be likely to take greater risks, be more cautious, or stay the same?

To everyone's amazement, the group decisions were usually riskier. Dubbed the 'risky shift phenomenon', this finding set off a wave of group risk-taking studies. These revealed that risky shift occurs not only when a group decides by consensus; after a brief discussion, individuals, too, will alter their decisions. What is more, researchers successfully repeated Stoner's finding with people of varying ages and occupations in a dozen nations.

During discussion, opinions converged. Curiously, however, the point towards which they converged was usually a lower (riskier) number than their initial average. Here was a delightful puzzle. The small risky shift effect was reliable, unexpected and without any immediately obvious explanation. What group influences produce such an effect? And how widespread is it? Do discussions in juries, business committees and military organizations also promote risk taking? Does this explain why teenage reckless driving, as measured by death rates, nearly doubles when a 16- or 17-year-old driver has two teenage passengers rather than none (Chen et al., 2000)?

However, the risky shift was not universal. There were decision dilemmas on which people became more *cautious* after discussion. One of these featured 'Roger', a young married man with two school-age children and a secure but low-paying job. Roger can afford life's necessities but few of its luxuries. He hears that the stock of a relatively unknown company may soon triple in value if its new product is favourably received or decline considerably if it does not sell. Roger has no savings. To invest in the company, he is considering selling his life insurance policy.

Can you see a general principle that predicts both the tendency to give riskier advice after discussing Helen's situation and more cautious advice after discussing Roger's? If you are like most people, you would advise Helen to take a greater risk than Roger, even before talking with others. It turns out there is a strong tendency for discussion to accentuate these initial leanings; groups discussing the 'Roger' dilemma became more risk-averse than they were before discussion.

So there seem to be other concerns that influence our risky or cautious decisions. Wayne Hensley (1977) has argued that one of the factors in making a risky decision is age. From his studies on the risky shift, he found that participants who were teenagers made riskier decisions than older participants. Dominic Abrams, Tim Hopthrow, Lorne Hulbert and Daniel Frings (2006) found that contrary to what you might think when people drink alcohol together as a group, they actually regulate each other's behaviour. So, sometimes, being part of a group may lead to safer decisions and behaviour rather than riskier ones. Phillip Finney (1978) observed that the desire to engage in risky behaviour may, to some extent, be understood by the culture the participant is from. He points out that many risky shift studies take place using North American participants, where the values of success, status and risk are held in high esteem. So to encourage someone to take further risks may reflect North American cultural values rather than just be a feature of small group decisions.

## DO GROUPS INTENSIFY OPINIONS?

Realizing that this group phenomenon was not a consistent shift towards increased risk, the phenomenon became reconceived as a tendency for group discussion to *enhance* group members' initial leanings. This idea led investigators to propose what Serge Moscovici and Marisa Zavalloni (1969) called group polarization: *discussion typically strengthens the average inclination of group members*.

### Group Polarization Experiments

This new view of the changes induced by group discussion prompted experimenters to have people discuss attitude statements that most of them favoured or most of them opposed. Would talking in groups enhance their shared initial inclinations as it did with the decision dilemmas? In groups, would risk takers take bigger risks, bigots become despisers, and givers become more philanthropic? That's what the group polarization hypothesis predicts (Figure 11.5).

Dozens of studies confirm group polarization.

Moscovici and Zavalloni (1969) observed that discussion enhanced French students' initially positive attitude towards their president and negative attitude towards Americans.

Markus Brauer and his co-workers (2001) found that French students' dislike for certain other people was exacerbated after discussing their shared negative impressions. Jerry Palmer and James Loveland (2008) observed that when interview panel members discussed interviewees post-interview it led to a polarized evaluation of candidates' performance as 'good' or 'bad', and individual pre-interview ratings became less accurate assessments.

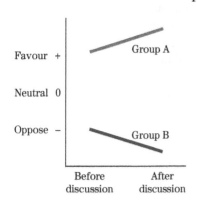

**FIGURE 11.5** Group polarization
The group polarization hypothesis predicts that discussion will strengthen an attitude shared by group members.

And Glen Whyte (1993) reported that groups exacerbate the 'too much invested to quit' phenomenon that has cost many businesses huge sums of money. Canadian business students imagined themselves having to decide whether to invest more money in the hope of preventing losses in various failing projects (for example, whether to make a high-risk loan to protect an earlier investment). They exhibited the typical effect: 72 per cent reinvested money they would probably not have invested if they were considering it as a new investment on its own merits. When making the same decision in groups, 94 per cent opted for reinvestment.

Another research strategy has been to pick issues on which opinions are divided and then isolate people who hold the same view. Does discussion with like-minded people strengthen shared views? Does it magnify the attitude gap that separates the two sides?

David Myers and George Bishop (1970) set up groups of relatively prejudiced and unprejudiced high school students and asked them to respond – before and after discussion – to issues involving racial attitudes, such as property rights versus open housing. They found that the discussions among like-minded students did indeed increase the initial gap between the two groups (Figure 11.6).

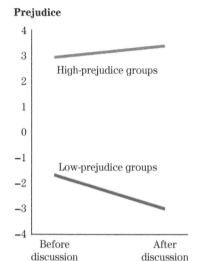

**FIGURE 11.6** Discussion increased polarization between homogeneous groups of high- and low-prejudice high school students. Talking over racial issues increased prejudice in a high-prejudice group and decreased it in a low-prejudice group.

SOURCE: Data from Myers & Bishop, 1970.

### Group Polarization in Everyday Life

In everyday life people associate mostly with others whose attitudes are similar to their own. (See Chapter 5, or just look at your own circle of friends.) Does everyday group interaction with like-minded friends intensify shared attitudes? Do nerds become nerdier?

It happens. The self-segregation of boys into all-male groups and of girls into all-female groups accentuates over time their initially modest gender differences, notes Eleanor Maccoby (2002). Boys with boys become gradually more competitive and action orientated in their play and fictional fare, and girls with girls become more relationally orientated, at least in those societies where these are considered to be the male and female roles respectively. However, this probably occurred even more before than after the women's liberation movements, where equality between the sexes has been a goal.

### Group Polarization in Schools

Another real-life parallel to the laboratory phenomenon is what education researchers have called the 'accentuation' effect: over time, initial differences among groups of college students become accentuated. If the first-year students at college X are initially more intellectual than the students at college Y, that gap is likely to increase by the time they graduate. Peter Kutnick, Peter Bletchford and Ed Baines (2005) have found that where children sit in the classroom can enhance or inhibit learning depending on the ability of the child and the task set. Who a child is grouped with determines with whom she or he interacts. The researchers suggest that while this may mean able students improve their learning by sharing knowledge on discussion tasks, less able students may voluntarily form a group, or be grouped together, and this can hinder their progress.

### Group Polarization in Communities

Polarization also occurs in communities, as people self-segregate. 'Crunchy places … attract crunchy types and become crunchier', observes David Brooks (2005). 'Conservative places … attract conservatives and become more so.' Neighbourhoods become echo chambers, with opinions ricocheting off kindred-spirited friends.

Animal gangs. The pack is more than the sum of the wolves.

SOURCE: © Shutterstock/karl umbriaco

In laboratory studies the competitive relationships and mistrust that individuals often display when playing games with one another often worsen when the players are groups (Winquist & Larson, 2004). During actual community conflicts, like-minded people associate increasingly with one another, amplifying their shared tendencies. Gang delinquency emerges from a process of mutual reinforcement within neighbourhood gangs, whose members share attributes and hostilities (Cartwright, 1975). If 'a second out-of-control 15-year-old moves in [on your block]', surmises David Lykken (1997), 'the mischief they get into as a team is likely to be more than merely double what the first would do on his own … A gang is more dangerous than the sum of its individual parts.' Indeed, 'unsupervised peer groups' are 'the strongest predictor' of a neighbourhood's crime victimization rate, report Bonita Veysey and Steven Messner (1999). Moreover, experimental interventions that take delinquent adolescents and group them with other delinquents actually – no surprise to any group polarization researcher – increase the rate of problem behaviour (Dishion et al., 1999). To the same degree missionaries who act together are more effective and able to convince heathens than when they are preaching alone. Both 'good' and 'evil' behaviour, deeds and misdeeds are fertilized by doing and being together.

### Group Polarization on the Internet

E-mail, blogs and electronic chat rooms offer a space for like-minded people to find one another and interact. At myspace.com, for example, there are tens of thousands of groups of kindred spirits discussing religion, politics, hobbies, cars, music, you name it. The Internet's countless virtual groups enable peacemakers and neo-Nazis, geeks and goths, conspiracy theorists and cancer survivors to chat with like-minded others and find support for their shared concerns, interests and suspicions. Without the non-verbal nuances of face-to-face contact, will such discussions produce group polarization? Choon-Ling Sia, Barnard Tan and Kwok-Kee Wei (2002) think so. Their experiments on the effects of computer-mediated communication (CMC) found that the lack of visual cues and the increase in anonymity led to raised group polarization. They suggest that people are more likely to generate novel arguments and engage in a game of one-upmanship when individuals' social presence is reduced. E-mail, Google and chat rooms 'make it much easier for small groups to rally like-minded people, crystallize diffuse hatreds and mobilize lethal force', observes Robert Wright (2003).

## EXPLAINING POLARIZATION

Why do groups adopt stances that are more exaggerated than that of their average individual member? Researchers hoped that solving the mystery of group polarization might provide some insights into group influence. Solving small puzzles sometimes provides clues for solving larger ones.

Among several proposed theories of group polarization, three are presented here. One deals with the arguments presented during a discussion, the second with how members of a group view themselves vis-à-vis the other members, and the third considers how a group's identity influences the decisions it makes. The first idea is an example of what Chapter 7 called *informational influence* (influence that results from accepting evidence about reality). The second is an example of *normative influence* (influence based on a person's desire to be accepted or admired by others). The third looks at *group identity* and takes a social identity and self-categorization theoretical approach.

Detailed discussion of social identity, self-categorization and group identity can be found in Chapters 12 and 13.

### Informational Influence

According to this explanation, group discussion elicits a pooling of ideas, most of which favour the dominant viewpoint. Some discussed ideas are common knowledge to group members (Gigone & Hastie, 1993; Larson et al., 1994; Stasser, 1991). Other ideas may include persuasive arguments that some group members had not previously considered. When discussing Helen the writer, someone may say, 'Helen should go for it, because she has little to lose. If her novel flops, she can always go back to writing cheap westerns.' Such statements often entangle information about the person's *arguments* with cues concerning the person's *position* on the issue. But when people hear relevant arguments without learning the specific stands other people assume, they still shift their positions (Burnstein & Vinokur, 1977; Hinsz et al., 1997). *Arguments*, in and of themselves, matter.

But there's more to attitude change than merely hearing someone else's arguments. *Active participation* in discussion produces more attitude change than does passive listening. Participants and observers hear the same ideas, but when participants express them in their own words, the verbal commitment magnifies the impact. The more group members repeat one another's ideas, the more they rehearse and validate them (Brauer et al., 1995). Just privately writing out one's ideas in preparation for an electronic discussion tends to polarize attitudes somewhat (Liu & Latané, 1998).

This illustrates a point made in Chapter 7. People's minds are not just blank tablets for persuaders to write upon. What people think in response to a message is crucial. Indeed, just thinking about an issue for a couple of minutes can strengthen opinions (Tesser et al., 1995). (Perhaps you can recall your feelings becoming polarized as you merely ruminated about someone you disliked, or liked.) Even just *expecting* to discuss an issue with an equally expert person holding an opposing view can motivate people to marshal their arguments and thus to adopt a more extreme position (Fitzpatrick & Eagly, 1981).

### Normative Influence

As we considered in Chapter 7, normative influence occurs when we conform to the expectations of others. We do what we 'ought' to do. Then norms of the group shape our behaviour. We allow ourselves to be led by the group for positive rewards such as social acceptance and approval. This process happens when we believe the group is monitoring our behaviour and has the power to punish or reward us (recall the explanation of Asch's line study in Chapter 7).

**social comparison**
*evaluating one's opinions and abilities by comparing oneself to others*

As Leon Festinger (1954) argued in his influential theory of social comparison, we humans want to evaluate our opinions and abilities, something we can do by comparing our views with others'. We are most persuaded by people in our 'reference groups' – groups we identify with (Abrams et al., 1986; Hogg et al., 1990). Moreover, wanting people to like us, we may express stronger opinions after discovering that others share our views.

**pluralistic ignorance**
*a false impression of what most other people are thinking or feeling, or how they are responding*

When we ask people to predict how others would respond to items such as the 'Helen' dilemma, they typically exhibit pluralistic ignorance (also see Chapter 12): they don't realize how strongly others support the socially preferred tendency (in this case, writing the novel). A typical person will advise writing the novel even if its chance of success is only 4 in 10, but will estimate that most other people would require 5 or 6 in 10. (This finding is reminiscent of the self-serving bias: people tend to view themselves as better-than-average embodiments of socially desirable traits and attitudes.) When the discussion begins, most people discover they are not outshining the others as they had supposed. In fact, some others are ahead of them, having taken an even stronger position in favour of writing the novel. No longer restrained by a misperceived group norm, they are liberated to voice their preferences more strongly.

Perhaps you can recall a time when you and someone else wanted to go out with each other but each of you feared making the first move, presuming the other probably did not have a reciprocal interest. Such pluralistic ignorance impedes the start-up of relationships (Vorauer & Ratner, 1996).

Or perhaps you can recall a time when you and others were guarded and reserved in a group, until someone broke the ice and said, 'Well, to be perfectly honest, I think . . .'. Soon you were all surprised to discover strong support for your shared views. Sometimes when a professor asks if anyone has any questions, no one will respond, leading each student to infer that he or she is the only one confused. All presume that fear of embarrassment explains their own silence but that everyone else's silence means they understand the material.

Dale Miller and Cathy McFarland (1987) bottled this familiar phenomenon in a laboratory experiment. They asked people to read an incomprehensible article and to seek help if they ran into 'any really serious problems in understanding the paper'. Although none of the individuals sought help, they presumed *other* people would not be similarly restrained by fear of embarrassment. Thus, they wrongly inferred that people who didn't seek help didn't need any. To overcome such pluralistic ignorance, someone must break the ice and enable others to reveal and reinforce their shared reactions.

This social comparison theory prompted experiments that exposed people to others' positions but not to their arguments. This is roughly the experience we have when reading the results of an opinion poll or of exit polling on election day. When people learn others' positions – without prior commitment and without discussion or sharing of arguments – will they adjust their responses to maintain a socially favourable position? As Figure 11.7 illustrates, they will. This comparison-based polarization is usually less than that produced by a lively discussion. Still, it's surprising that, instead of simply conforming to the group average, people often go one better.

Merely learning others' choices also contributes to the bandwagon effect that creates blockbuster songs, books and movies. Sociologist Matthew Salganik and his colleagues (2006) experimented with the phenomenon by engaging 14 341 Internet participants in listening to and, if they wished, downloading previously unknown songs. The researchers randomly assigned some participants to a condition that disclosed previous participants' download choices. Among those given that information, popular songs became more popular and unpopular songs became less popular.

Group polarization research illustrates the complexity of social psychological inquiry. Much as we like our explanations of a phenomenon to be simple, one explanation seldom accounts for all the data. Because people are complex, more than one factor frequently influences an outcome. In group discussions, persuasive arguments predominate on issues that have a factual element ('Is she guilty of the crime?'). Social comparison sways responses on value-laden judgements ('How long a sentence should she serve?') (Kaplan, 1989). On the many issues that have both factual and value-laden aspects, the two factors work together. Discovering that others share one's feelings (social comparison) unleashes arguments (informational influence) supporting what everyone secretly favours.

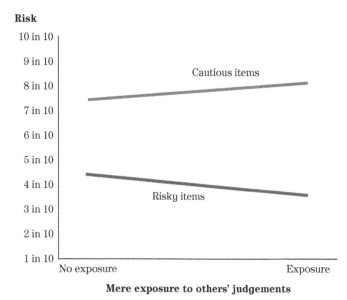

FIGURE 11.7   On 'risky' dilemma items (such as the case of Helen), mere exposure to others' judgements enhanced individuals' risk-prone tendencies. On 'cautious' dilemma items (such as the case of Roger), exposure to others' judgements enhanced their cautiousness.

SOURCE: Data from Myers, 1978.

### Group Identity

Some social psychologists, in particular social identity theorists (SITs) and self-categorization theorists (SCTs), have argued that the social groups to which we belong go some way to explaining why group polarization occurs (Turner, 1991; Turner et al., 1987). Recall John Turner's position about what constitutes a 'group' at the beginning of this chapter. A group does not necessarily have to constitute physically present individuals interacting with one another. Simply feeling and perceiving oneself to be a member of a group is sufficient to think and act as one. The groups to which we belong in society provide us with a 'social identity'. This identity means feeling psychologically attached to a group and having things in common with our fellow members (ingroup members), and thinking of ourselves as quite different from other social groups (outgroup members) in relevant ways. In distinguishing one group from another, group members may converge on a position in a debate that clearly marks them out from other groups. John Turner (1991) argues that they achieve consensus around the group's prototypical position, 'that best defines what the group has in common compared to other relevant outgroups' (pp. 76–77).

To illustrate what this means let's consider an experimental study by Michael Hogg, John Turner and Barbara Davidson (1990). They asked their participants to individually offer advice, choosing between a range of risky and cautious options, on a choice dilemma (as we've seen in the risky shift studies). Participants were then told they would be put in a group of people whose views on the dilemma best matched their own. They were shown photographs of their, supposed, ingroup engaged in debate, and listened to them using headphones. These discussions were of a group making a risky, a cautious or a neutral decision to a series of dilemmas. The participants were also given information about debates made by groups other than their own (outgroups). What Hogg and his colleagues wanted to know was what the effect of these group discussions would be on the participants' own decisions. What they found was that when participants believed they were members of a group that made risky decisions, when exposed to outgroups making cautious decisions the individual participant also made extremely risky choices. As social identity theory and self-categorization theory would predict, the participant was conforming to an ingroup norm (of risk) and exaggerating their decision to maximize the difference between their ingroup and the outgroup. Likewise, if a participant believed s/he belonged to a cautious group, when shown evidence of risky outgroups, the individual made very cautious decisions. As Hogg et al. suggest, 'an ingroup confronted by a risky outgroup will polarize towards caution, an ingroup confronted by a cautious outgroup will polarize towards risk' (1990, p. 77).

This explanation of behaviour in groups is something we will return to in Chapters 12 and 13 when we consider broader intergroup relations.

## GROUPTHINK: DO GROUPS HINDER OR ASSIST GOOD DECISIONS?

*When do group influences hinder good decisions? When do groups promote good decisions, and how can we lead groups to make optimal decisions?*

Do the social psychological phenomena we have been considering occur in sophisticated groups such as corporate boards or the president's cabinet? Is there likely to be self-justification, self-serving bias, a cohesive 'we feeling' promoting conformity and stifling dissent? Public commitment producing resistance to change? Group polarization? Social psychologist Irving Janis (1971, 1982) wondered whether such phenomena might help explain good and bad group decisions made by some twentieth-century American presidents and their advisers. To find out, he analysed the decision-making procedures that led to several major fiascos.

☐ *Pearl Harbor.* In the weeks preceding the December 1941 Pearl Harbor attack that put the USA into the Second World War, military commanders in Hawaii received a steady stream of information about Japan's preparations for an attack on the USA somewhere in the Pacific. Then military intelligence lost radio contact with Japanese aircraft carriers, which had begun moving straight for Hawaii. Air reconnaissance could have spotted the carriers or at least provided a few minutes' warning. But complacent commanders decided against such precautions. The result: no alert was sounded until the attack on a virtually defenceless base was under way. The loss: 18 ships, 170 planes and 2400 lives.

☐ *The Bay of Pigs invasion.* In 1961, US President John Kennedy and his advisers tried to overthrow Fidel Castro by invading Cuba with 1400 CIA-trained Cuban exiles. Nearly all the invaders were soon killed or captured, the USA was humiliated and Cuba allied itself more closely with the former USSR. After learning the outcome, Kennedy wondered aloud, 'How could we have been so stupid?'

☐ *The Vietnam War.* From 1964 to 1967, US President Lyndon Johnson and his 'Tuesday lunch group' of policy advisers escalated the war in Vietnam on the assumption that US aerial bombardment, defoliation and search-and-destroy missions would bring North Vietnam to the peace table with the appreciative support of the South Vietnamese populace. They continued the escalation despite warnings from government intelligence experts and nearly all US allies. The resulting disaster cost more than 58 000 American and 1 million Vietnamese lives, polarized Americans, drove the president from office and created huge budget deficits that helped fuel inflation in the 1970s.

Janis believed those blunders were bred by the tendency of decision-making groups to suppress dissent in the interests of group harmony, a phenomenon he called groupthink. In work groups, camaraderie boosts productivity (Mullen & Copper, 1994). It can also boost reputation. For example, Stefan Wuchty and his colleagues (2007) observed that team-work in academia seems to pay off. Science papers written by groups of authors were twice as likely to be read and cited by other authors than those papers written by individuals. Moreover, team spirit is good for morale. But when making decisions, close-knit groups may pay a price. Janis believed that the soil from which groupthink sprouts includes:

groupthink *'The mode of thinking that persons engage in when concurrence-seeking becomes so dominant in a cohesive in-group that it tends to override realistic appraisal of alternative courses of action'* (Irving Janis, 1971)

☐ an amiable, *cohesive* group

☐ relative *isolation* of the group from dissenting viewpoints

☐ a *directive leader* who signals what decision he or she favours.

When planning the ill-fated Bay of Pigs invasion, the newly elected President Kennedy and his advisers enjoyed a strong *esprit de corps*. Arguments critical of the plan were suppressed or excluded, and the president soon endorsed the invasion.

## SYMPTOMS OF GROUPTHINK

From historical records and the memoirs of participants and observers, Janis identified eight groupthink symptoms. These symptoms are a collective form of dissonance reduction that surface as group members try to maintain their positive group feeling when facing a threat (Turner et al., 1992).

The first two groupthink symptoms lead group members to *overestimate their group's might and right*.

☐ *An illusion of invulnerability.* The groups Janis studied all developed an excessive optimism that blinded them to warnings of danger. Told that his forces had lost radio contact with the Japanese carriers, Admiral Kimmel, the chief naval officer at Pearl Harbor, joked that maybe the Japanese were about to round Honolulu's Diamond Head. They actually were, but Kimmel's laughing at the idea dismissed the very possibility of its being true.

- *Unquestioned belief in the group's morality.* Group members assume the inherent morality of their group and ignore ethical and moral issues. The Kennedy group knew that adviser Arthur Schlesinger, Jr, and Senator J. William Fulbright had moral reservations about invading a small, neighbouring country. But the group never entertained or discussed those moral qualms.

Group members also become *closed minded*.

- *Rationalization.* The groups discount challenges by collectively justifying their decisions. President Johnson's Tuesday lunch group spent far more time rationalizing (explaining and justifying) than reflecting upon and rethinking prior decisions to escalate. Each initiative became an action to defend and justify.

- *Stereotyped view of opponent.* Participants in these groupthink tanks consider their enemies too evil to negotiate with or too weak and unintelligent to defend themselves against the planned initiative. The Kennedy group convinced itself that Castro's military was so weak and his popular support so shallow that a single brigade could easily overturn his regime.

Finally, the group suffers from pressures towards *uniformity*.

- *Conformity pressure.* Group members rebuffed those who raised doubts about the group's assumption and plans, at times not by argument but by personal sarcasm. Once, when President Johnson's assistant Bill Moyers arrived at a meeting, the president derided him with, 'Well, here comes Mr. Stop-the-Bombing'. Faced with such ridicule, most people fall into line.

- *Self-censorship.* Since disagreements were often uncomfortable and the groups seemed in consensus, members withheld or discounted their misgivings. In the months following the Bay of Pigs invasion, Arthur Schlesinger (1965, p. 255) reproached himself 'for having kept so silent during those crucial discussions in the Cabinet Room, though my feelings of guilt were tempered by the knowledge that a course of objection would have accomplished little save to gain me a name as a nuisance'.

- *Illusion of unanimity.* Self-censorship and pressure not to puncture the consensus create an illusion of unanimity. What is more, the apparent consensus confirms the group's decision. This appearance of consensus was evident in these three fiascos and in other fiascos before and since. Albert Speer (1971), an adviser to Adolf Hitler, described the atmosphere around Hitler as one where pressure to conform suppressed all deviation. The absence of dissent created an illusion of unanimity.

In normal circumstances people who turn their backs on reality are soon set straight by the mockery and criticism of those around them, which makes them aware they have lost credibility. In the Third Reich there were no such correctives, especially for those who belonged to the upper stratum. On the contrary, every self-deception was multiplied as in a hall of distorting mirrors, becoming a repeatedly confirmed picture of a fantastical dream world which no longer bore any relationship to the grim outside world. In those mirrors I could see nothing but my own face reproduced many times over. No external factors disturbed the uniformity of hundreds of unchanging faces, all mine. (p. 379)

'People "are never so likely to settle a question rightly as when they discuss it freely".'

John Stuart Mill, *On Liberty*, 1859

☐ *Mindguards.* Some members protect the group from information that would call into question the effectiveness or morality of its decisions. Before the Bay of Pigs invasion, Robert Kennedy took Schlesinger aside and told him, 'Don't push it any further'. Secretary of State Dean Rusk withheld diplomatic and intelligence experts' warnings against the invasion. They thus served as the president's 'mindguards', protecting him from disagreeable facts rather than physical harm.

Groupthink symptoms can produce a failure to seek and discuss contrary information and alternative possibilities (Figure 11.8). When a leader promotes an idea and when a group insulates itself from dissenting views, groupthink may produce defective decisions (McCauley, 1989). Some journalists, and political and financial commentators, have pondered the extent to which groupthink was a factor in the recent global economic crisis. Did banks and businesses fail to listen to critical voices from lone individuals and people outside of their institutions warning of a financial crisis if expansion and money-lending continued? According to a report published by the International Monetary Fund's Independent Evaluation Office, yes (IEO, 2011). The report found that despite concerns raised by board members and one staff member, who even wrote a paper detailing the path that the crisis would take, these apprehensions were not followed up on. Added to this, some of the IMF's staff felt that they could not voice their worries, for fear that it would negatively influence their career.

There is also some cross-cultural evidence for the occurrence of groupthink. Andrew Sai On Ko (2005) found that groupthink occurred in focus groups in Hong Kong when the group contained members who were recognized to be of high status. He suggests this reflects cultural rules about trusting those who are recognized as having high status.

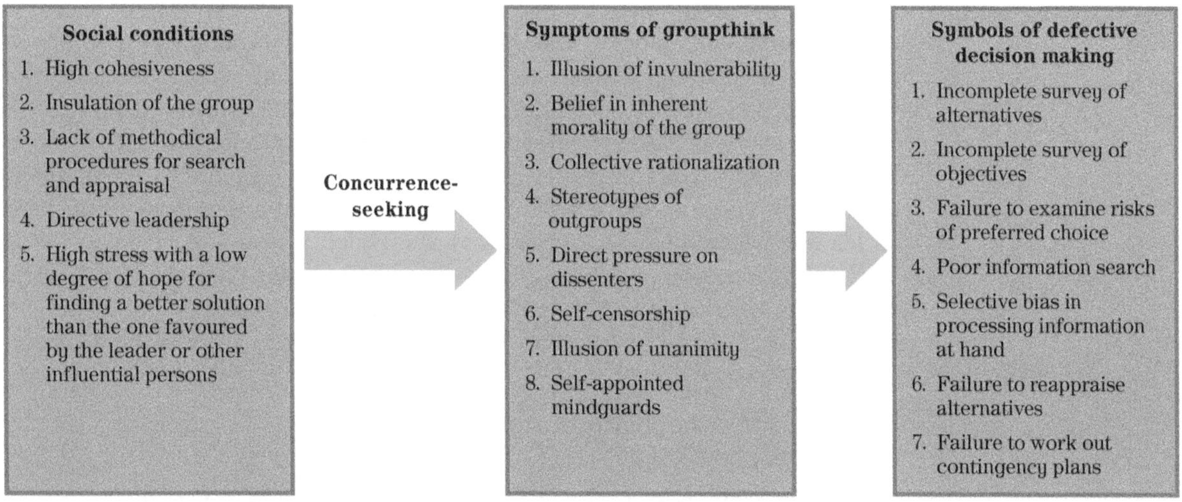

| Social conditions | | Symptoms of groupthink | | Symbols of defective decision making |
|---|---|---|---|---|
| 1. High cohesiveness | | 1. Illusion of invulnerability | | 1. Incomplete survey of alternatives |
| 2. Insulation of the group | | 2. Belief in inherent morality of the group | | 2. Incomplete survey of objectives |
| 3. Lack of methodical procedures for search and appraisal | Concurrence-seeking → | 3. Collective rationalization | → | 3. Failure to examine risks of preferred choice |
| 4. Directive leadership | | 4. Stereotypes of outgroups | | 4. Poor information search |
| 5. High stress with a low degree of hope for finding a better solution than the one favoured by the leader or other influential persons | | 5. Direct pressure on dissenters | | 5. Selective bias in processing information at hand |
| | | 6. Self-censorship | | 6. Failure to reappraise alternatives |
| | | 7. Illusion of unanimity | | 7. Failure to work out contingency plans |
| | | 8. Self-appointed mindguards | | |

**FIGURE 11.8** Theoretical analysis of groupthink

SOURCE: Janis & Mann, 1977, p. 132.

British psychologists Ben Newell and David Lagnado (2003) believe groupthink symptoms may have also contributed to the Iraq War. They and others contended that both Saddam Hussein and George W. Bush surrounded themselves with like-minded advisers and intimidated opposing voices into silence. Moreover, they each received filtered information that mostly supported their assumptions – Iraq's expressed assumption that the invading force could be resisted, and the USA's assumption that Iraq had weapons of mass destruction, that its people would welcome invading soldiers as liberators and that a short, peaceful occupation would soon lead to a thriving democracy.

CRITIQUING THE CONCEPT OF GROUPTHINK

Although Janis' ideas and observations have received enormous attention, some researchers are sceptical (Fuller & Aldag, 1998; Hart, 1998). The evidence was retrospective, so Janis could pick supporting cases. Follow-up experiments suggested that:

- directive leadership is indeed associated with poorer decisions, because subordinates sometimes feel too weak or insecure to speak up (Granstrom & Stiwne, 1998; McCauley, 2001)

- groups do prefer supporting over challenging information (Schulz-Hardt et al., 2000)

- when members look to a group for acceptance, approval and social identity, they may suppress disagreeable thoughts (Hogg & Hains, 1998; Turner & Pratkanis, 1997).

Yet friendships need not breed groupthink (Esser, 1998; Mullen et al., 1994). Secure, highly cohesive groups (say, a family) can provide members with freedom to disagree. Dominic Packer (2009) argues that we shouldn't assume individuals in groups are always reluctant to express private concerns. In fact those individuals who identify strongly with the group are willing to point out the flaws in a group's reasoning if s/he believes it will improve the group in some way. This seems to be enhanced when group members physically bump into one another all the time. The American entrepreneur Steve Jobs, founder of Apple Inc and Pixar Animation Studios, used this phenomenon to his advantage. Planning Pixar's headquarters, he ensured the building was structured in such a way that everyone who worked there would be forced into running into one another albeit working, going to the canteen, or even the bathroom (Lehrer, 2012). Jobs knew that accidental meetings with colleagues led to teamwork, resulting in creativity, debate and high-quality productivity. The norms of a cohesive group can favour either consensus, which can lead to groupthink, or critical analysis, which prevents it (Postmes et al., 2001). When academic colleagues in a close-knit department share their draft manuscripts with one another, they *want* critique: 'Do what you can to save me from my own mistakes.' In a free-spirited atmosphere, cohesion can enhance effective teamwork, too.

'Truth springs from argument amongst friends.'
  Philosopher David Hume, 1711–76

When Philip Tetlock and his colleagues (1992) looked at a broader sample of historical episodes, it became clear that even good group procedures sometimes yield ill-fated decisions. As US President Carter and his advisers plotted their humiliating attempt to rescue American hostages in Iran in 1980, they welcomed different views and realistically considered the perils. Had it not been for a helicopter problem, the rescue might have succeeded. (Carter later reflected that had he sent in one more helicopter, he would have been re-elected president.) To reword Mister Rogers, sometimes good groups do bad things.

Reflecting on the critiques of groupthink, Paul Paulus (1998) reminds us of Leon Festinger's observation that the only unchanging theory is an untestable one. 'If a theory is at all testable, it will not remain unchanged. It has to change. All theories are wrong.' Thus, said Festinger, we shouldn't ask whether a theory is right or wrong but, rather, 'how much of the empirical realm can it handle and how must it be modified'. Irving Janis, having tested and modified his own theory before his death in 1990, would surely have welcomed others continuing to reshape it. In science, that is how we grope our way towards truth, by testing our ideas against reality, revising them and then testing them some more.

## PREVENTING GROUPTHINK

Flawed group dynamics help explain many failed decisions; sometimes too many cooks spoil the broth. However, given open leadership, a cohesive team spirit can improve decisions. Sometimes two or more heads are better than one.

In search of conditions that breed good decisions, Janis also analysed two seemingly successful ventures: the Truman administration's formulation of the Marshall Plan for getting Europe back on its feet after the Second World War, and the Kennedy administration's handling of the former USSR's attempts to install missile bases in Cuba in 1962. Janis's (1982) recommendations for preventing groupthink incorporate many of the effective group procedures used in both cases.

- ☐ Be impartial – do not endorse any position.
- ☐ Encourage critical evaluation; assign a 'devil's advocate'. Better yet, welcome the input of a genuine dissenter, which does even more to stimulate original thinking and to open a group to opposing views, report Charlan Nemeth and her colleagues (2001a, 2001b).
- ☐ Occasionally subdivide the group, then reunite to air differences.
- ☐ Welcome critiques from outside experts and associates.
- ☐ Before implementing, call a 'second-chance' meeting to air any lingering doubts.

When such steps are taken, group decisions may take longer to make, yet ultimately prove less defective and more effective.

## GROUP PROBLEM SOLVING

Not every group decision is flawed by groupthink. As Noni Richardson Ahlfinger and James Esser (2001) have shown, when a group is led by someone who promotes their own solutions, they tend to fall into the trap of groupthink, making poor decisions. However, when their leader is a non-promotional one, ready to discuss a range of solutions, groupthink is much less likely to occur. Tom Postmes, Russell Spears and Sezgin Cihangir (2001) have made the point that it depends what norms a group is based on as to whether it will display groupthink. They observed that those groups whose norms mean that new information from outside the group is not valued, are much more likely to fall prey to groupthink than those whose norms permit the sharing of extra information.

So, under some conditions, two or more heads really are better than one. Patrick Laughlin and John Adamopoulos (1980; Laughlin, 1996; Laughlin et al., 2003) have shown this with various intellectual tasks. Consider one of their analogy problems:

Assertion is to disproved as action is to

a.  hindered

b.  opposed

c.  illegal

d.  precipitate

e.  thwarted.

Most college students miss this question when answering alone, but answer correctly (thwarted) after discussion. Moreover, Laughlin finds that if just two members of a six-person group are initially correct, two-thirds of the time they convince all the others. If only one person is correct, this 'minority of one' almost three-quarters of the time fails to convince the group. And when given tricky logic problems, three, four or five heads are better than two (Laughlin et al., 2006).

Dell Warnick and Glenn Sanders (1980) and Verlin Hinsz (1990) confirmed that several heads can be better than one when they studied the accuracy of eyewitness reports of a videotaped crime or job interview. Interacting groups of eyewitnesses gave accounts that were much more accurate than those provided by the average isolated individual. Several heads critiquing one another can also allow the group to avoid some forms of cognitive bias and produce some higher-quality ideas (McGlynn et al., 1995; Wright et al., 1990).

Brainstorming with computer communication allows creative ideas to flow freely (Gallupe et al., 1994). But contrary to the popular idea that face-to-face brainstorming generates more creative ideas than do the same people working alone, researchers agree it isn't so (Paulus et al., 1995, 1997, 1998, 2000; Stroebe & Diehl, 1994). And contrary to the popular idea that brainstorming is most productive when the brainstormers are admonished 'not to criticize', encouraging people to debate ideas appears to stimulate ideas and to extend creative thinking beyond the brainstorming session (Nemeth et al., 2004).

People *feel* more productive when generating ideas in groups (partly because people disproportionately credit themselves for the ideas that come out). But time and again researchers have found that people working alone usually will generate *more* good ideas than will the same people in a group (Rietzschel et al., 2006). Large brainstorming groups are especially inefficient. In accord with social loafing theory, large groups cause some individuals to free-ride on others' efforts. In accord with normative influence theory, they cause others to feel apprehensive about voicing oddball ideas. And they cause 'production blocking' – losing one's ideas while awaiting a turn to speak (Nijstad et al., 2003). As John Watson and Francis Crick demonstrated in discovering DNA, challenging two-person conversations can more effectively engage creative thinking. Watson later recalled that he and Crick benefited from *not* being the most brilliant people seeking to crack the genetic code. The most brilliant researcher 'was so intelligent that she rarely sought advice' (quoted by Cialdini, 2005). If you are (and regard yourself as) the most gifted person, why seek others' input? Like Watson and Crick, psychologists Daniel Kahneman and the late Amos Tversky similarly collaborated in their exploration of intuition and its influence on economic decision making. (See Chapter 4.)

However, Vincent Brown and Paul Paulus (2002) have identified three ways to enhance group brainstorming.

**1** *Combine group and solitary brainstorming.* Their data suggest using group brainstorming followed by solo brainstorming rather than the reverse order or either alone. With new categories primed by the group brainstorming, individuals' ideas can continue flowing without being impeded by the group context that allows only one person to speak at a time.

**2** *Have group members interact by writing.* Another way to take advantage of group priming, without being impeded by the one-at-a-time rule, is to have group members write and read, rather than speak and listen. Brown and Paulus describe this process of passing notes and adding ideas, which has everyone active at once, as 'brainwriting'.

**3** *Incorporate electronic brainstorming.* There is a potentially more efficient way to avoid the verbal traffic jams of traditional group brainstorming in larger groups: let individuals produce and read ideas on networked computers.

So, when group members freely combine their creative ideas and varied insights, the frequent result is not groupthink but group problem solving. The wisdom of groups is evident in everyday life as well as in the laboratory.

☐ *Game shows.* For a befuddled contestant on *Who Wants to Be a Millionaire?*, a valuable lifeline was to 'ask the audience', which usually offered wisdom superior to the contestant's intuition.

☐ *Google.* Google has become a dominant search engine by harnessing what James Surowiecki (2004) calls *The Wisdom of Crowds*. Google interprets a link to page X as a vote for page X, and weights most heavily links from pages that are themselves highly ranked. Harnessing the democratic character of the Web, Google often takes less than one-tenth of a second to lead you right to what you want.

Thus, we can conclude that when information from many, diverse people is combined, all of us together can become smarter than almost any of us alone. We're in some ways like a flock of geese, not one of which has a perfect navigational sense. Nevertheless, by staying close to one another, a group of geese can navigate accurately. The flock is smarter than the bird.

## HOW DO MINORITIES INFLUENCE THE GROUP?

*Groups influence individuals. But when – and how – do individuals and minority groups influence more powerful groups?*

Each chapter in this social influence unit concludes with a reminder of our power as individuals. We have seen that cultural situations mould us, but we also help create and choose these situations; pressures to conform sometimes overwhelm our better judgement, but blatant pressure motivates us to assert our individuality and freedom; persuasive forces are powerful, but we can resist persuasion by making public commitments and by anticipating persuasive appeals.

At the beginning of this chapter, we considered the film *12 Angry Men*, in which a lone juror eventually wins 11 others over to his view. Although that may be a rare occurrence in a jury room, in most social movements a small minority will sway, and then eventually become, the majority. 'All history', wrote Ralph Waldo Emerson, 'is a record of the power of minorities, and of minorities of one'. Think of Copernicus and Galileo, of Martin Luther King, Jr, of Nelson Mandela. The abolition of apartheid in South Africa and the move towards equality for Blacks and Whites is attributed to the influence of Nelson Mandela and those few who shared his vision for a peaceful transformation of the country. Indeed, if minority viewpoints never prevailed, history would be static and nothing would ever change.

What makes a minority persuasive? Experiments initiated by Serge Moscovici in Paris have identified several determinants of minority influence: *consistency*, *self-confidence* and *defection*. Throughout our discussion of minority influence, keep in mind that 'minority influence' refers to minority *opinions*, not to ethnic minorities.

### CONSISTENCY

More influential than a minority that wavers is a minority that sticks to its position. Moscovici developed his theory of social influence on the social psychological observation that people do not like inconsistency, conflict and disagreement. In fact, they are motivated to reduce it. When a minority tries to influence a majority they capitalize on this by creating uncertainty and anxiety among majority group members. As we know from the studies of social influence in Chapter 7, majority influence is based on preservation of dominant norms among the majority and the preservation of the status quo. But Moscovici argued that what distinguished minority influence was that it challenged these dominant norms, disrupted the status quo and could be revolutionary as it promoted social change. He claimed that many of the social psychological studies of majority influence were actually demonstrations of minority influence. Consider: Solomon Asch's line study displayed one true participant being influenced by a few stooges.

Moscovici argued that what was happening was a single participant was being influenced away from what everyone else would see in similar circumstances to what the stooges claimed to see. It was the power of consistency between minority members that caused a majority to rethink their ideas and be influenced. Moscovici and colleagues developed the blue–green studies (1969), which were a variation on Asch's earlier line studies. In the study four participants and two confederates of the experimenter were seated in a room and shown a series of slides. The slides were coloured blue. The participants were then asked to say out loud what colour they thought the slides were. In those trials where the two stooges consistently said 'green', the real participants became influenced. However, in those trials where the two stooges were inconsistent in their answers, influence did not occur. Moscovici concluded that minority influence occurs because it has particular effects on the majority: it creates doubt and offers a possible alternative way of looking at things. The only way to restore certainty and consistency is for the majority to shift to the viewpoint of the minority.

Experiments show – and experience confirms – that non-conformity, especially persistent non-conformity, is often painful, and that being a minority in a group can be unpleasant (Levine, 1989; Lücken & Simon, 2005). That helps explain a *minority slowness effect* – a tendency for people with minority views to express them less quickly than do people in the majority (Bassili, 2003). If you set out to be Emerson's minority of one, prepare yourself for ridicule – especially when you argue an issue that's personally relevant to the majority and when the group wants to settle an issue by reaching consensus (Kameda & Sugimori, 1993; Kruglanski & Webster, 1991; Trost et al., 1992). People may attribute your dissent to psychological peculiarities (Papastamou & Mugny, 1990). When Charlan Nemeth (1979) planted a minority of two within a simulated jury and had them oppose the majority's opinions, the duo was inevitably disliked.

Nevertheless, the majority acknowledged that the persistence of the two did more than anything else to make them rethink their positions. Indeed, a minority may stimulate creative thinking (Martin, 1996; Mucchi-Faina et al., 1991; Peterson & Nemeth, 1996). Jared Kenworthy, Miles Hewstone, John Levine and Hazel Willis (2008) found that participants placed in numerically minority groups generated more original arguments to strengthen their position on a debate than those placed within majority groups. Angelica Mucchi-Faina and Stefano Pagliaro (2008) have observed how the presence of a minority produces ambivalence among the majority, and under these circumstances the minority is likely to have influence. They suggest that the reason for this is that the state of ambivalence causes a state of cognitive dissonance (as we discussed in Chapter 4) and people are motivated to reduce the uncomfortable feelings this creates. Robin Martin, Miles Hewstone and Pearl Martin (2008) note that those arguments produced as a consequence of minority influence are much more resistant to counter-persuasion than those formed by a majority group. University students who have racially diverse friends, or who are exposed to racial diversity in discussion groups, display less simplistic thinking (Antonio et al., 2004). With dissent from within one's own group, people take in more information, think about it in new ways, and often make better decisions. Believing that one need not win friends to influence people, Nemeth quotes Oscar Wilde: 'We dislike arguments of any kind; they are always vulgar, and often convincing.'

Some successful companies have recognized the creativity and innovation sometimes stimulated by minority perspectives, which may contribute new ideas and stimulate colleagues to think in fresh ways. 3M, which has been famed for valuing 'respect for individual initiative', has welcomed employees spending time on wild ideas. The Post-it® notes adhesive was a failed attempt by Spencer Silver to develop a super-strong glue. Art Fry, after having trouble marking his church choir hymnal with pieces of paper, thought, 'What I need is a bookmark with Spencer's adhesive along the edge.' Even so, this was a minority view that eventually won over a sceptical marketing department (Nemeth, 1997).

## SELF-CONFIDENCE

Consistency and persistence convey self-confidence. Furthermore, Nemeth and Joel Wachtler (1974) reported that any behaviour by a minority that conveys self-confidence – for example, taking the head seat at the table – tends to raise self-doubts among the majority. By being firm and forceful, the minority's apparent self-assurance may prompt the majority to reconsider its position. This is especially so on matters of opinion rather than fact. Based on their research at Italy's University of Padova, Anne Maass and her colleagues (1996) report that minorities are less persuasive when answering a question of fact ('From which country does Italy import most of its raw oil?') than attitude ('From which country should Italy import most of its raw oil?').

## DEFECTIONS FROM THE MAJORITY

In 1904, Mark Twain wrote: 'Whenever you find yourself on the side of the majority, it's time to pause and reflect.' As we've seen, simply going along with the group may not always be the wisest thing to do. Alternative opinions are silenced, when in fact questioning the status quo may be worthwhile. A persistent minority punctures any illusion of unanimity. When a minority consistently doubts the majority wisdom, majority members become freer to express their own doubts and may even switch to the minority position. But what about a lone defector, someone who initially agreed with the majority but then reconsidered and dissented? In research with University of Pittsburgh students, John Levine (1989) found that a minority person who had defected from the majority was even more persuasive than a consistent minority voice. In her jury-simulation experiments, Nemeth found that – not unlike the *12 Angry Men* scenario – once defections begin, others often soon follow, initiating a snowball effect.

Are these factors that strengthen minority influence unique to minorities? Sharon Wolf and Bibb Latané (1985; Wolf, 1987) and Russell Clark (1995) believe not. They argue that the same social forces work for both majorities and minorities. Informational influence (via persuasive arguments) and normative influence (via social comparison) fuel both group polarization and minority influence. And if consistency, self-confidence and defections from the other side strengthen the minority, such variables also strengthen a majority. The social impact of any position, majority or minority, depends on the strength, immediacy and number of those who support it.

Anne Maass and Russell Clark (1984, 1986) agree with Moscovici, however, that minorities are more likely than majorities to convert people to *accepting* their views. And from their analyses of how groups evolve over time, John Levine and Richard Moreland (1985) conclude that new recruits to a group exert a different type of minority influence than do long-time members. Newcomers exert influence through the attention they receive and the group awareness they trigger in the old-timers. Established members feel freer to dissent and to exert leadership.

There is a delightful irony in this new emphasis on how individuals can influence the group. Until recently, the idea that the minority could sway the majority was itself a minority view in social psychology. Nevertheless, by arguing consistently and forcefully, Moscovici, Nemeth, Maass, Clark and others have convinced the majority of group influence researchers that minority influence is a phenomenon worthy of study. And the way that several of these minority influence researchers came by their interests should, perhaps, not surprise us. Anne Maass (1998) became interested in how minorities could effect social change after growing up in post-war Germany and hearing her grandmother's personal accounts of fascism. Charlan Nemeth (1999) developed her interest while she was a visiting professor in Europe 'working with Henri Tajfel and Serge Moscovici. The three of us were "outsiders" – I an American Roman Catholic female in Europe, they having survived World War II as Eastern European Jews. Sensitivity to the value and the struggles of the minority perspective came to dominate our work.'

Of course, the power of a minority over a majority may not always be positive. Roni Factor and colleagues (2011) argue that minority groups have a tendency to exhibit risky behaviours. This was certainly the case during the London riots of August 2011. The story of a 29-year-old man from Tottenham in London, who was killed by police officers led to widespread riots in the UK. Protest riots that began in the Tottenham area of London quickly spread to other parts of London and UK cities including Liverpool, Manchester and Birmingham. John Bohannon (2012) reports on the role of Twitter and other social media in spreading the news and opinions of what had happened to millions of people. Chaos ensued as incitements to riot were co-ordinated across social media. The riots evolved into large-scale protests against the economic downturn, a disaffected youth, and the State. People died as a result of the mayhem. Christina Salmivalli (2010) examined the influence of a minority on bullying behaviour in school. She observed how bullies who target victims become socially reinforced by the majority group. They come to be regarded as powerful, of high status, and the majority group accepts the behaviour. She argues that when we tackle bullying the focus should not simply be on the bully but on the influence exerted upon the whole group, which allows and encourages the behaviour. Being persuaded by a minority may not always be for the greater good.

> See Chapters 10 and 13 for further discussion on aggression and the influence on crowd behaviour.

## IS LEADERSHIP MINORITY INFLUENCE?

In 1910 the Norwegians and the English engaged in an epic race to the South Pole. The Norwegians, led effectively by Roald Amundsen, made it. The English, led ineptly by Robert Falcon Scott, did not; Scott and three team members died. Amundsen illustrated the power of leadership, the process by which individuals mobilize and guide groups. The presidency of George W. Bush illustrates 'the power of one', observes Michael Kinsley (2003). 'Before Bush brought it up [there was] no popular passion' for the idea 'that Saddam was a terrible threat and had to go … You could call this many things, but one of them is leadership. If real leadership means leading people where they don't want to go, George W. Bush has shown himself to be a leader.' Similarly in the UK, the decision of the then Prime Minister, Tony Blair, to support George Bush was taken against the wishes of many of the population and indeed his own political party. Was this true leadership?

**leadership** *the process by which certain group members motivate, guide and lead the group*

Some leaders are formally appointed or elected; others emerge informally as the group interacts. Theories of 'who' becomes the leader began with trying to identify the traits of leaders. Known as the trait approach, this tried to predict leaders on the basis of physical characteristics such as intelligence, height, extroversion, dominance and so on. This approach ground to a halt fairly quickly when it was recognized that not all leaders possess these traits and people with these traits did not necessarily become leaders.

**trait approach** *this approach to leadership regards certain physical characteristics, such as height and intelligence, as predictors of leadership*

What makes for good leadership often depends on the situation – the best person to lead the engineering team may not make the best leader of the sales force.

**task leadership**
*leadership that organizes work, sets standards and focuses on goals*

**social leadership**
*leadership that builds teamwork, mediates conflict and offers support*

Some people excel at task leadership – at organizing work, setting standards and focusing on goal attainment. Others excel at social leadership – at building teamwork, mediating conflicts and being supportive. Fred Fieldler's (1967) contingency approach proposes that 'who' is the leader, and what kind of leader they will be, is contingent upon the situation. The style of leadership adopted will depend on how much control s/he has in the environment. Where s/he has little control or their power is ambiguous, they may well adopt a more authoritative style of leadership. Similarly a leader may adapt a style to suit the requirements of their staff. If an employee is suffering a crisis in confidence a more supportive leadership style may be taken to try and address the problem.

*Task* leaders generally have a directive style – one that can work well if the leader is bright enough to give good orders (Fiedler, 1987). Being goal orientated, such leaders also keep the group's attention and effort focused on its mission. Experiments show that the combination of specific, challenging goals and periodic progress reports helps motivate high achievement (Locke & Latham, 1990).

*Social* leaders generally have a democratic style – one that delegates authority, welcomes input from team members and, as we have seen, helps prevent groupthink. Many experiments reveal that social leadership is good for morale. Group members usually feel more satisfied when they participate in making decisions (Spector, 1986; Vanderslice et al., 1987). Given control over their tasks, workers also become more motivated to achieve (Burger, 1987).

People tend to respond more positively to a decision if they are given a chance to voice their opinions during the decision-making process (van den Bos & Spruijt, 2002). People who value good group feeling and take pride in achievement therefore thrive under democratic leadership and participative management, a management style common in Sweden and Japan (Naylor, 1990; Sundstrom et al., 1990). Women more often than men exhibit a democratic leadership style (Eagly & Johnson, 1990).

British social psychologists Peter Smith and Monir Tayeb (1989) report that studies done in India, Taiwan and Iran have found that the most effective supervisors in coal mines, banks and government offices score high on tests of *both* task and social leadership. They are actively concerned with how work is progressing *and* sensitive to the needs of their subordinates.

Studies also reveal that many effective leaders of laboratory groups, work teams and large corporations exhibit the behaviours that help make a minority view persuasive. Such leaders engender trust by *consistently* sticking to their goals. And they often exude a *self-confident* charisma that kindles the allegiance of their followers (Bennis, 1984; House & Singh, 1987). Charismatic leaders typically have a compelling *vision* of some desired state of affairs, an ability to *communicate* that to others in clear and

Participative management, illustrated in this 'quality circle', requires democratic rather than autocratic leaders.

simple language, and enough optimism and faith in their group to *inspire* others to follow. They seem to have personal characteristics in common, including self-confidence, and have common appeal, which makes them attractive to their audience. However, rather than seeing charisma as an attribute of leaders, some theorists have suggested that it is the followers who read charisma into the behaviour of leaders by virtue of their role (Meindl, 1993).

So perhaps something more complex than simply matching leadership style to situation is going on. Victor Vroom and Arthur Jago (2007) warn that: 'viewing leadership in purely dispositional or purely situational terms is to miss a major proportion of the phenomenon … leadership is a process of motivating others to work together collaboratively to accomplish things' (p. 23). Without willing followers, there isn't a successful leader (also see Chapter 12 where we consider how identification with a group contributes to effective leadership). In one analysis of 50 Dutch companies, the highest morale was at firms with chief executives who most inspired their colleagues 'to transcend their own self-interests for the sake of the collective' (de Hoogh et al., 2004). Leadership of this kind – transformational leadership – motivates others to identify with and commit themselves to the group's mission. Transformational leaders – many of whom are charismatic, energetic, self-confident extraverts – articulate high standards, inspire people to share their vision and offer personal attention. In organizations, the frequent result of such leadership is a more engaged, trusting and effective workforce (Turner et al., 2002).

**transformational leadership** *leadership that, enabled by a leader's vision and inspiration, exerts significant influence*

To be sure, groups also influence their leaders. Sometimes those at the front of the herd have simply sensed where it is already heading. Political candidates know how to read the opinion polls. Someone who typifies the group's views is more likely to be selected as a leader; a leader who deviates too radically from the group's standards may be rejected (Hogg et al., 1998). Smart leaders usually remain with the majority and spend their influence prudently. In rare circumstances, the right traits matched with the right situation yield history-making greatness, notes Dean Keith Simonton (1994). To have a Winston Churchill or a Margaret Thatcher, a Nelson Mandela or a Karl Marx, a Napoleon or an Adolf Hitler, an Abraham Lincoln or a Martin Luther King, Jr, takes the right person in the right place at the right time. When an apt combination of intelligence, skill, determination, self-confidence and social charisma meets a rare opportunity, the result is sometimes a championship, a Nobel Prize, or a social revolution.

Charismatic leadership. The former leader of the African National Congress, ex-president of South Africa and anti-apartheid activist, Nelson Mandela.
SOURCE: © EdStock2/iStock

## focus on

### HAVE SMALL GROUP PROCESSES SUCH AS RISKY SHIFT AND GROUPTHINK CONTRIBUTED TO CYBER-BULLYING?

The invention of the Internet has changed our world. It has made information on most topics you can think of, readily available to us. The Internet has shaped the way we communicate with one another, and how we form friendships. The presence of forums such as Facebook, Twitter and MySpace has made us accessible to one another without too much effort. The invention is so good that many schools, colleges and universities integrate online learning with face-to-face learning, and study and support groups are set up online. However, has the invention of the Internet also led to increased opportunities for small groups (such as an online study group) to engage in bullying? The statistics for bullying suggest it has. Moreover, cyber-bullying tends to occur within social groups (Mishna et al., 2009, 2012). The i-SAFE Foundation (http://isafe.org/wp/) reports that over half of adolescents and teens have been subject to, or taken part in, cyber-bullying.

Remember the lessons from this chapter and also Chapters 7 and 8, that individuals often do things when they're in a group, which they wouldn't do on their own. Sometimes this is explained as a feature of anonymity and being lost in a crowd, but often online group members do know one another. They are not anonymous. In fact, it is precisely this knowing who somebody is that may explain why someone is singled out from a group and bullied online. Stacy Chaffin (2008) points out that adolescents and teenagers who are recognized as being outsiders to the group offline, may find those divisions reinforced online, as they become excluded from discussions, name-called, and therefore bullied. If the group is cohesive and maintains a norm of punishing those individuals it considers 'outsiders', some members may find themselves subject to harassment from the rest of the group. The small group processes of risky shift and groupthink can occur, such that risky decisions and negative forms of actions are collectively agreed on, and those members considered deviants find themselves severely harassed as a consequence. Chaffin observes that individuals desperate to 'fit in' with a group may engage in cyber-bullying to show themselves as true members and identify (and punish) those regarded as deviants and outsiders.

The occurrence of cyber-bullying is now taken so seriously that many agencies and websites have been set up to tackle the specific problem.

## QUESTIONS

**1** Are there any other reasons you can think of which might explain why cyber-bullying is on the increase?

**2** Do you think online learning groups are as effective as face-to-face ones?

# SUMMING UP: SMALL GROUP PROCESSES

## WHAT IS A GROUP?

☐ Social psychologists have differing definitions of a group, but what they agree on is that a group defines a collection of people who share a sense of 'we-ness'. They identify themselves as a group.

☐ But what holds groups together? Group cohesion is based on attraction to the group. The more cohesive the group, the greater the likelihood of its members sticking together as a group. Group cohesion is associated with group success but also failure.

☐ Groups are based on norms that describe their beliefs and regulate group members' behaviour.

☐ Individuals in groups occupy different roles that offer them a sense of identity and purpose. However, members may experience role clash or conflict.

☐ Different roles are associated with status, which has consequences for how much an individual identifies with the group and their behaviour within it. Group leaders have the highest status providing him or her with the means to change the group's norms, structure and composition if required.

☐ Communication networks are the formal and informal paths through which group members interact. The group's morale and productivity is often associated with the network that is in place. While direct access to the leader in order to influence decisions may be ideal, it is not always possible or desirable.

## SOCIAL FACILITATION: HOW ARE WE AFFECTED BY THE PRESENCE OF OTHERS?

☐ Social psychology's most elementary issue concerns the mere presence of others. Some early experiments on this question found that performance improved with observers or co-actors present. Others found that the presence of others can hurt performance. Robert Zajonc reconciled those findings by applying a well-known principle from experimental psychology: arousal facilitates dominant responses. Because the presence of others is arousing, the presence of observers or co-actors boosts performance on easy tasks (for which the correct response is dominant) and hinders performance on difficult tasks (for which incorrect responses are dominant).

☐ But why are we aroused by others' presence? Experiments suggest that the arousal stems partly from evaluation apprehension and partly from distraction – a conflict between paying attention to others and concentrating on the task. Other experiments suggest that the presence of others can be arousing even when we are not evaluated or distracted.

☐ In online groups, physical presence is not always possible. Instead social facilitation needs to be developed by other means, such as creating a sense of community through shared experiences, goals and aspirations.

## SOCIAL LOAFING: DO INDIVIDUALS EXERT LESS EFFORT IN A GROUP?

☐ Social facilitation researchers study people's performance on tasks where they can be evaluated individually. However, in many work situations, people pool their efforts and work towards a common goal without individual accountability.

☐ Group members often work less hard when performing such 'additive tasks'. This finding parallels everyday situations where diffused responsibility tempts individual group members to free-ride on the group's effort.

☐ People may, however, put forth even more effort in a group when the goal is important, rewards are significant, intragroup communication occurs and team spirit exists.

☐ Social loafing predominantly exists in cultures where an independent self is endorsed.

☐ Social loafing is much less prevalent in those cultures where an interdependent sense of self exists.

## GROUP POLARIZATION: DO GROUPS INTENSIFY OUR OPINIONS?

☐ Potentially positive and negative results arise from group discussion. While trying to understand the curious finding that group discussion enhanced risk taking, investigators discovered that discussion actually tends to strengthen whatever is the initially dominant point of view, whether risky or cautious.

☐ In everyday situations, too, group interaction tends to intensify opinions. This *group polarization* phenomenon provided a window through which researchers could observe group influence.

☐ Three explanations of group influence are: *informational*, *normative* and *group identity*.

## GROUPTHINK: DO GROUPS HINDER OR ASSIST GOOD DECISIONS?

☐ Analysis of several international fiascos indicates that group cohesion can override realistic appraisal of a situation. This is especially true when group members strongly desire unity, when they are isolated from opposing ideas, and when the leader signals what he or she wants from the group.

☐ Symptomatic of this overriding concern for harmony, labelled groupthink, are (1) an illusion of invulnerability, (2) rationalization, (3) unquestioned belief in the group's morality, (4) stereotyped views of the opposition, (5) pressure to conform, (6) self-censorship of misgivings, (7) an illusion of unanimity, and (8) 'mindguards' who protect the group from unpleasant information. Critics have noted that some aspects of Janis's groupthink model (such as directive leadership) seem more implicated in flawed decisions than others (such as cohesiveness).

☐ Both in experiments and in actual history, however, groups sometimes decide wisely. These cases suggest ways to prevent groupthink: upholding impartiality, encouraging 'devil's advocate' positions, subdividing and then reuniting to discuss a decision, seeking outside input, and having a 'second-chance' meeting before implementing a decision.

☐ Research on group problem solving suggests that groups can be more accurate than individuals; groups also generate more and better ideas if the group is small or if, in a large group, individual brainstorming follows the group session.

### HOW DO MINORITIES INFLUENCE THE GROUP?

☐ Although a majority opinion often prevails, sometimes a minority can influence and even overturn a majority position. Even if the majority does not adopt the minority's views, the minority's speaking up can increase the majority's self-doubts and prompt it to consider other alternatives, often leading to better, more creative decisions.

☐ In experiments, a minority is most influential when it is consistent and persistent in its views, when its actions convey self-confidence and after it begins to elicit some defections from the majority.

☐ Through their task and social leadership, formal and informal group leaders exert disproportionate influence. Those who consistently press towards their goals and exude a self-confident charisma often engender trust and inspire others to follow.

## CRITICAL QUESTIONS

1 What are some of the influences a small group can have on its members?

2 Under what conditions might social loafing occur in a group?

3 What explanations have been given for group polarization?

4 To what extent is the risky shift a cultural phenomenon?

5 How is minority influence different to majority influence?

## RECOMMENDED READINGS

Here are some recommended classic and contemporary readings on small group processes, covering some of the issues we've outlined in this chapter.

### Classic Papers

Fiedler, F. E. (1966). The effect of leadership and cultural heterogeneity on group performance: A test of the contingency model. *Journal of Experimental Social Psychology*, **2**(3), 237–264.

*Reports an experiment into how leadership style is contingent upon how much control a leader has in a situation. Cites evidence for Fiedler's contingency model of leadership.*

Janis, I. L. (1973). Groupthink and group dynamics: A social psychological analysis of defective policy decisions. *Policy Studies Journal,* **2**(1), 19–25.

*Outlines the groupthink phenomena and its affects upon small groups.*

Moscovici, S., Lage, E., & Naffrechoux, M. (1969). Influence of a consistent minority on the responses of a majority in a color perception task. *Sociometry,* **32**(4), 365–380.

*Presents the original blue-green slide experiment into the minority influence.*

Stoner, J. (1968). Risky and cautious shifts in group decisions: The influence of widely held values. *Journal of Experimental Social Psychology,* **4**, 442–459.

*Provides a comprehensive overview and original study of risky shift processes as identified by the author himself, which occur in small group decision-making tasks.*

Contemporary Papers

Abrams, D., Hopthrow, T., Hulbert, L., & Frings, D. (2006). 'Groupdrink'? The effect of alcohol on risk attraction among groups versus individuals. *Journal of Studies on Alcohol,* **67**(4), 628–636.

*A study into the effects of alcohol consumption in groups on risky decisions and behaviours. Concludes that while individuals make riskier decisions after drinking alcohol, groups do not as they collectively regulate their behaviour.*

Packer, D. J. (2009). Avoiding groupthink: Whereas weakly identified members remain silent, strongly identified members' dissent about collective problems. *Psychological Science,* **20**(5), 546–548.

*Presents research evidence that suggests small groups do not always descend into groupthink. Those individuals who identify most strongly with the group, avoid groupthink in an attempt to protect that group from making poor decisions.*

Vroom, V. H., & Jago, A. G. (2007). The role of the situation in leadership. *American Psychologist,* **62**(1), 17–24.

*Outlines classic approaches to leadership: trait, contingency model, and path-goal theory. This paper applies the contingency theory of leadership to contemporary professional contexts.*

**12**

"*Integrity simply means not violating one's own identity.*"
*Erich Fromm, sociologist and psychoanalyst*

# SOCIAL CATEGORIZATION AND SOCIAL IDENTITY

Human beings live in a complex social environment. Our social world is filled up with countless people. People we see when walking in the street or sitting on a train; people we interact with at work, or in a shop; people we see on television or read about in a newspaper. How do we navigate in this maze? How do we simplify, order and structure our social environment? How do we make sense of the people who cross our path in the multiplicity of social situations we are constantly involved in? What kind of strategies do we use in order to turn a potentially chaotic and unpredictable social reality into something that is understandable, manageable and predictable?

## A CATEGORIZED SOCIAL WORLD

social categorization *the cognitive partitioning of the social world into relatively discrete categories of individuals*

One of the main psychological tools that we use when trying to understand and make sense of people is social categorization (see Chapter 4 for a discussion of the various ways in which we make sense of social reality). I may not personally know the person who has just stepped into the bus where I am sitting, or the one who is checking my blood pressure in the hospital, or the one who is reading the morning news on the television channel I am watching. However, I can assign them to social categories. The person on the bus is 'elderly'; the one who is dealing with my blood pressure is a 'nurse'; the one who is reading the news is a 'journalist'. By putting these people into 'pigeonholes', I am able to interpret their behaviour and to respond to it appropriately.

Consider, however, that for social categorization to be really useful and to guide me through the social environment, the categories that I choose have to be relevant to the context I am dealing with. For instance, categorizing the person on the bus as elderly makes it possible for me to offer my seat to them. Categorizing him or her as a 'blue-eyed' person, or more generally as a 'man' or 'woman', would be irrelevant in that circumstance, and would prevent me from behaving in the most appropriate way. Consistent with this important caveat, the social psychologist Henri Tajfel defined the process of social categorization as 'the ordering of social environment in terms of groupings of persons in a manner which makes sense to the individual' (1978, p. 61). See 'Focus On: The Group in the Mind' at the end of the chapter.

### LEVEL OF CATEGORY INCLUSIVENESS

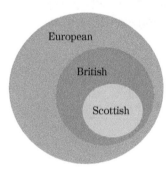

**FIGURE 12.1** The inclusiveness of social categories
Social categories vary in degree of inclusiveness. The category Scottish is included in that of British, which is included in the category European.

Social categories stand in hierarchical relationships, as they may have different levels of inclusiveness. For instance, the categories Tuscan and Sicilian are included in the category Italian, which in turn is included in the category European (Cantor & Mischel, 1979). Cognitive psychologists have found that, as far as non-social categories are concerned, basic-level categories tend to be used more often than either very inclusive or very exclusive categories (Figure 12.1). It is more common to identify an animal as a 'dog' (basic level) than as either a 'German shepherd' (lowest level) or as a 'mammal' (highest level). Eleanor Rosh and her colleagues (Rosh et al., 1976) argue that basic-level categories are the first to be learned, and the natural level at which objects are named. This, however, does not apply to social categories. As will become clearer later in the chapter, the categories we select to make sense of the social reality strongly depend on contextual, cultural and motivational factors.

## CATEGORY PROTOTYPES AND EXEMPLARS

On which basis are people assigned to categories? Do they have to possess a fixed number of characteristics in order to be seen as a category member? Social psychologists believe that this is not the case. Instead, people must possess some degree of resemblance to the category prototype. This is a category member that possesses a list of features that are seen as typical of the social category. Although the prototype may be represented by a specific and concrete individual, this is often not a true person but an abstraction, an ideal embodiment of the essence of the category (e.g. Cantor & Mischel, 1977; Rosh, 1978). Members of social categories differ in terms of how prototypical of the category they are seen to be. The closer one is to the prototype, the more prototypical he or she is considered to be. For instance, an Italian who is passionate, romantic and artistic minded will probably be seen as closer to the prototype of an Italian than one who is rather cold, controlled and technically minded.

*prototype a social category member who is believed to possess the typical features of the social category*

It is also possible to assign people to a social category on the basis of how similar they are to some category exemplar (Smith & Zárate, 1992). Instead of being abstractions, exemplars are category members that one has encountered. Madonna, Britney Spears and Beyoncé could be seen as exemplars of the category of 'pop singers'. As a consequence, if we see a person whose way of singing and performing is in some ways similar to one of these popular characters, we are likely to assign this person to the category of 'pop singers'.

## THE ACCENTUATION EFFECT

When we assign a person to a social category, not only do we rely on some fundamental similarities between the categorized person and either a prototype or a category exemplar, but we also take into account

Beyoncé: a worldwide famous exemplar of the category of 'pop singers'.
SOURCE: © EdStock/iStock

relevant differences between this person and those who belong to other categories. If we ascribe, say, John to the category of 'scientists', we are both establishing that John shares some characteristics in common with other scientists (a certain type of knowledge, an enquiring mind) and that he is different from 'lay people' or from 'artists'. The reason why social categorization is based on patterns of similarity and difference is that the best way to simplify and organize the social world is to make a clear distinction between those who belong and those who do not belong to a certain group.

However, category boundaries are not always clear-cut. Consider, for instance, the 'black' and 'white' people categories. While some individuals perfectly fit our notion of either a 'black' or a 'white' person, others fall somewhere between what we tend to recognize as 'black' and what we tend to see as 'white'. How, then, do we deal with this? How can a clear categorical distinction be created? If we act in a context where skin colour is not relevant at all, making clear distinctions in terms of the black–white dichotomy may simply not be necessary. However, when skin colour is important, as in some social and political contexts, our mind will tend

**accentuation effect** *a tendency to exaggerate similarities within categories and differences between categories*

to perceive those who lean slightly towards the black colour as more black than they really are, and those who lean towards white as whiter than they are. This phenomenon is known as the accentuation effect (Tajfel & Wilkes, 1963; Tajfel et al., 1964). Basically, both the differences between members of different categories and the similarities among members of the same categories are exaggerated. Through this cognitive accentuation, categories become unambiguous and the context becomes clear and intelligible. Obviously, accentuating the similarities among members of a category means to perceive all of them as more resemblant to the category prototype than we would normally do.

A classic demonstration of the accentuation effect was offered by Henri Tajfel and Alan Wilkes (1963). These researchers asked the participants in the experiment to judge the length of a set of individual lines from a continuous series. However, the four shorter lines were labelled as 'A' and the four longer ones as 'B'. They found that participants exaggerated the difference in length between lines belonging to the A type and lines pertaining to the B type (Figure 12.2).

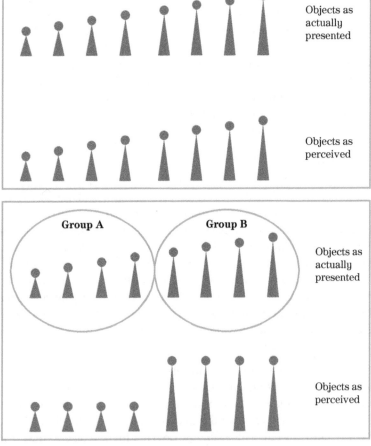

**FIGURE 12.2**   The accentuation effect

If a set of objects are not assigned to categories, people's perception of the objects' height will be correct. However, when objects are assigned to distinct categories, people will exaggerate differences between categories and similarities within categories, especially if categories are important to the perceivers. This effect applies not only to the physical world, but to the social world as well.

Clearly, this is only an indirect form of evidence for social categorization, as the stimuli used in the experiment are physical rather than social. However, social psychologists have provided plenty of evidence for the accentuation effect in the perception of people too. For instance, in an experiment run at the University of Geneva (Doise et al., 1978), a group of participants were asked to judge the members of three different social groups, by rating them in terms of characteristic traits. Some participants judged members of the three Swiss linguistic groups (Italian Swiss, French Swiss and German Swiss), while other participants judged members of two Swiss linguistic groups and members of a foreign national group (for instance, Italian Swiss, French Swiss and Germans). It was found that the members of the different Swiss linguistic groups were perceived as more similar to one another when judged in the context of a foreign group. Clearly, this is because in such a context the two Swiss groups were seen as part of an overall category, the Swiss, which was contrasted with the foreign group.

Because it is prone to the accentuation effect, social categorization is at the basis of a phenomenon that has been widely investigated by social psychologists: group homogeneity (Tajfel, 1978). This means that members of a group are seen as being 'all the same'. This is believed to be particularly true when one has to describe and judge groups that are in conflict with a group of which one is a member. This specific type of perception is defined as outgroup homogeneity.

*outgroup homogeneity a tendency to perceive and cognitively represent the members of an outgroup as very similar to one another, as being 'all the same'*

## SOCIAL CATEGORIES AND STEREOTYPES

Because social categorization exaggerates intra-category similarities, social psychologists see it as the basis of stereotype formation. A stereotype is a generalization about a social group, in the sense that similar characteristics are ascribed to virtually all group members (Allport, 1954). For example, in many societies 'women' are seen as emotional and volatile, 'Gypsies' are perceived as dirty and as inclined to theft, 'Germans' are considered inflexible and efficient, and 'pop stars' seem spoiled and capricious. Obvious variations among the members of a social category are often ignored.

Stereotypes tend to be culturally transmitted and are therefore widespread within society (Macrae et al., 1996; Tajfel & Forgas, 1981). According to Gordon Allport (1954), stereotypes obey the 'law of least effort'. They spare people from forming differentiated judgements about others by providing shortcuts for understanding others, in the form of sketchy representations and ready-to-use beliefs (Fiske, 1989b).

### The Selection of Social Categories

The social situations that we face often include people belonging to a variety of social categories. How do we decide which categories are relevant in each specific social situation?

Suppose I am attending a football match between Manchester United and Real Madrid (an English and a Spanish team respectively). Presumably, on the stands there will be individuals pertaining to all sorts of groups: 'men' and 'women', 'youngsters' and 'older' people, 'white' and 'black' people. Probably, there will also be 'taxi drivers', 'shop assistants', 'members of the Labour Party', and more or less numerous representatives of many other groups. Which categories will capture my attention? Which ones will I select and use? I will almost certainly focus my attention on 'Man. United supporters' and 'Real Madrid supporters'. I will look at the colour of the shirts and scarfs, and I will listen to the chants of the two groups of supporters. The reason why I will focus on these two categories and virtually ignore all others is obvious: these two are the categories that, in this situation, include the highest number of members and are more relevant and meaningful. That is, these are the categories that best 'fit' the situation (Bruner, 1957; Oakes et al., 1994).

Each individual in this picture can be seen as either a 'business person', or in terms of gender ('man' or 'woman'), or in racial terms ('white', 'black', 'Asian'). The social categories we focus upon will depend on how well these categories fit the situation and on how psychologically accessible they are.

SOURCE: © Yuri/iStock

But fit is not the only factor at play when selecting social categories. When we are involved in a social situation we don't come to it 'pure'. First, we bring with us our preconceptions and expectations. When I attend a psychology class at university, I am likely to see just many 'psychology students' and one 'lecturer' (students and lecturers being the categories that best fit the situation). This is because these are the categories that I expect to be represented during a university class. If there are some students' parents on the stands, I might overlook them simply because I do not expect them to be there. Second, we bring our desires, motivations and interests into a social situation, and these may also determine the social categories that I use. If I am interested in finding a romantic partner, I might subdivide the context into 'males' and 'females'. Or, if I was a person who is very sensitive to religious issues, I could immediately define the situation in terms of 'Christians' and 'Muslims'. This means that, when trying to make sense of a social situation, the social categories that have special relevance and importance to a person – or, as social psychologists tend to put it, the social categories that are more 'accessible' – are more likely to be employed.

It is important to note, however, that decisions about which categories are relevant actors within a given context, and which characteristics those categories have (i.e. their content, their prototypical members) are rarely made in isolation. In most situations we discuss, debate and argue over the nature of the social context and the social categories with other people through an incessant process of communication and negotiation (Billig, 1987). Our view of social categories, like our view of the social world in general, is inherently and inescapably social.

### The Fluidity of Social Categories and Stereotypes

The fact that social categories that are used to make sense of a social situation are selected on the basis of their fit with social context and their cognitive accessibility means that they are flexible and malleable psychological tools. If this was not the case, social categorization would not help people to represent an ever-changing, fluid and kaleidoscopic social reality. All aspects of social categories and social categorization are variable.

- ☐ Changes in the situation may shift the level of inclusiveness of the social categories we select. The experiment conducted by Doise and colleagues shows that in one context the Italian Swiss, the French Swiss and the German Swiss can be seen as three different social categories, but as soon as German Swiss are replaced by the social category of Germans, the Italian Swiss and the French Swiss are collapsed into a single, over-inclusive social category: that of Swiss people.

☐ The same social category may have different prototypes as the general frame changes. As a consequence, the stereotype content of a given social category will also change with the general frame (Ford & Stangor, 1992). Haslam et al. (1992) studied the way in which Australians represented Americans during the first Gulf War, in 1991. It was found that participants who were asked to judge both Americans and Russians perceived the Americans as more 'aggressive' than participants who judged Americans alone. Clearly, because Russians did not approve the American invasion of Iraq, bringing them into the context increased the perceived aggressiveness of Americans.

## THE SOCIAL CATEGORIZATION OF THE SELF

So far we have focused on the way we position other people into social categories. But the social world does not include just others. Importantly, the self tends to be part of the world we try to understand. In other words, in most circumstances we are part of the social context that we try to structure and make sense of. As a consequence, in those circumstances we assign ourselves to one of the social categories that are psychologically relevant; that is, we engage in self-categorization.

See Chapter 3 for a full treatment of how people think and feel about their own self, as well as how they go about understanding it.

'We live in a social environment which is in constant flux. Much of what happens to us is related to the activities of groups to which we do or do not belong.'
   Henri Tajfel, *Human Groups and Social Categories*, 1981

### Cognitive Aspects of Self-categories
From a cognitive perspective, self-categories are like other social categories.

☐ Self-categories have different degrees of inclusiveness. So, I can see myself as Flemish, a Belgian and a European.

☐ Self-categories have their prototypes and exemplars. If I am a Spanish socialist, I will have an idea of what the 'typical', 'true' socialist should be like (say, somebody with a strong belief in equality and solid anti-fascist values), and will consider Zapatero (the leader of the Spanish Socialist Workers' Party and current Prime Minister of Spain) as an exemplar of my category. Also, how typical of the socialist group I perceive myself to be will depend on how similar to the prototype of a socialist and to Zapatero I see myself.

☐ The similarities among the members of a self-category, including the self, and the differences between the members of a self-category and the members of another relevant category, are exaggerated. If I am a Roman Catholic and discuss religion with a Protestant, I may become acutely aware of the many similarities I have with other Roman Catholics, and of my differences from Protestants, as far as religious issues are concerned.

☐ The accentuation of similarities between myself and other members of my category will lead to self-stereotyping, that is, to self-perception in terms of some general features that are seen as applicable to virtually all members of my category.

### Contextual Variability in Self-categorization and Self-stereotyping
Self-categories are also similar to other social categories in terms of their contextual flexibility and variability. This means that the type of social categories

to which I ascribe myself, and the stereotypical content of these categories, shift from one context to another.

To start with, I can categorize myself as a member of totally unrelated categories depending on the situation. I will be a 'Buddhist' when I recite my mantras in the early morning, a 'student' when I attend a university class in the afternoon and a 'golf player' when I enjoy a golf match in the evening. Also, the self-categories I use in different contexts may have varying levels of inclusiveness. I can see myself as 'Scottish' during the six nations rugby tournament, as 'British' in the course of the Olympic Games, and as a 'European' when I am visiting the USA.

But the context does not only affect the type of self-category to which I ascribe, but also the way I perceive myself as a category member. For instance, suppose that I am a psychologist and I am discussing the importance of the scientific approach with a believer in magic. In this situation I may feel a highly prototypical member of the category of 'scientists'. However, if a physicist joins the debate, I may feel a bit less prototypical of the category. Even the content of the same self-category, that is my self-stereotype, may change depending on the comparative context. Nick Hopkins, Martin Regan and Jackie Abell (1997) investigated the way in which Scottish people stereotyped their own national group members in different contexts. When the participants in the study were asked to describe the Scottish and the Greeks, the Scottish were seen as aloof, hardworking, organized and not particularly warm. But when participants described the Scottish and the English, the Scottish were portrayed as warm and not so aloof. Fabio Sani, Mark Bennett, Sinéad Mullally and Jaime McPherson (2003; see also Sani & Bennett, 2001) found a similar phenomenon in an investigation of children's gender stereotypes. For instance, the study revealed that 5- to 7-year-old male children perceived themselves ('boys') as especially big, brave, strong and tough when judgements were made after judging the group of 'girls', but when the judgement was made after judging 'grown-up men' they saw themselves as mainly 'loud' and 'talkative'. In both studies mentioned above, the traits that are emphasized in the different contexts are those that maximize the differences between the self-category and the other category that is salient in the context.

### How do Social Categories Become Self-categories?

Although self-categories are more or less psychologically relevant depending on context, and their content and meaning are fluid and changeable, people do belong to a number of social categories in a stable fashion, and some of them may be particularly central to self and chronically salient. How do specific social categories become self-categories? Broadly speaking, there are two ways in which social categories are applied to self.

First, there are social categories we are socialized into from birth. For instance, apart from very rare cases, we are born as either a male or a female. Since cultures have strong expectations about appropriate male and female behaviours, attitudes and emotions, we very quickly learn that we are either male or female, and absorb the norms that apply to our category (see Chapter 14 for a fuller discussion of the social psychological implications of gender categories). Similarly, we grow up within specific families, social classes, ethnic groups and nations. These groups have their own beliefs, values, attitudes, mentalities and habits, which are transmitted to their members through a process of socialization and acculturation.

As with gender, we soon learn that we are members of specific families, social classes, ethnic and national groups, and we internalize the values and norms of those groups. Obviously, at some stage in life we may reject certain groups and decide we do not belong to them, but for most people these categories – or some of them at least – are the most important categories, and are therefore central to their sense of self.

Second, there are groups and categories that we choose to join at some point in life. We may join a social club, become supporters of a sports team, become members of a university, ascribe to a political party, join a band or affiliate to a religious organization. Some of these memberships may not be of special relevance to us, while others may become really important. Some football supporters, for instance, see their loyalty to the team as one of the most defining aspects of self (a phenomenon that is fairly common in Europe and South America). They travel all over the world to see their team play, avidly read all the news about their team, participate in Internet forums dedicated to their teams, and hang around in specific places to chat, conceive new songs and chants, and prepare banners and flags.

## SOCIAL IDENTITY

Although, from a purely cognitive perspective, self-categories are like other social categories, they are in many ways special. Self-categorization allows people to know where one stands in the social world, to distinguish between 'us' and 'them', to know who we are. Therefore, the social categorization of the self gives us an identity, more specifically a social identity. Social psychologists distinguish social (or group) identity from our personal (or individual) identity, which is to do with our unique, peculiar, idiosyncratic features, those aspects that are unrelated to membership of a group.

The notion of social identity is used in several disciplines, including sociology, anthropology, political science and, even, archaeology. However, in social psychology this concept is one of the pillars of social identity theory (Tajfel & Turner, 1986) and self-categorization theory (Turner et al., 1987), which have been conceived and systematized during the 1970s and 1980s.

Henri Tajfel defined social identity as 'that part of an individual's self-concept which derives from his knowledge of his membership of a social group (or groups) together with the value and emotional significance attached to that membership' (1978, p. 63). This definition makes it clear that being a member of a category is not sufficient to confer a social identity. For instance, the fact that I pay annual fees for membership of the association for the safeguarding of local monuments does not automatically imply that this membership is psychologically important to me. I may pay the fees out of habit, or simply because I feel some sort of civic or moral obligation to sustain the association, without necessarily feeling that membership of the association truly matters to the kind of person I am. To be identified with a category means to feel somehow attached to this category, to invest emotionally in this membership, to consider this category as important for my self-definition. If I feel attached to New Zealand and being a New Zealander matters to me, this means that this is part of my self-definition and that I am identified with New Zealand.

**social identity** *that part of our self-definition that derives from our membership of social groups*

**personal identity** *that part of our self-definition that derives from our unique, peculiar, idiosyncratic characteristics*

**social identity theory** *a theory accredited to Tajfel and Turner, which is based on the assumption that people belong to social groups and derive a social identity from these groups. According to the theory we derive much of our self-esteem from our social identity, and when social identity is not satisfactory we may pursue a number of strategies to improve it*

**self-categorization theory** *a theory about the ways in which people come to identify with groups and about the consequences of group (or social) identification, especially in terms of how people think and feel about their fellow ingroup members and the way people behave within the group*

As we anticipated above, the most important self-categories, and therefore the categories with which people tend to identify strongly, are often those we are born into, such as gender, family or ethnic self-categories. However, self-categories based on groups that we join later in life may also become important social identities. For instance, I may become involved in, or even be a funder of, a local bird-watching club, and devote many hours every week to the maintenance of the club and the promotion of its activities. This membership may become a crucial expression of what I like and what I do, and inform my sense of who I am. I may, that is, feel strongly identified with a local bird-watching club.

Social identity has very important implications for our relationships with other group members and for our relations with members of other groups too. In this chapter we will focus on the implications of social identity for processes within the group, leaving the discussion of social identity's consequences for processes between groups to the next chapter. First, we will discuss the implications of social identity for influence processes within groups.

In Chapter 7 we discussed how people facing a unanimous group may feel pressure to conform to the majority, even when the majority position is manifestly wrong. We saw that social psychologists have explained conformity as resulting from two types of influence. These are normative influence, based on people's need to avoid ridicule and isolation, and informational influence, derived from a need to be correct in tandem with an assumption that the unanimous majority must be correct. But does any majority influence people by virtue of being a majority, or does the influence depend largely on how the majority is perceived in relation to self?

### PEOPLE CONFORM TO MAJORITIES CATEGORIZED AS INGROUP

Available evidence suggests that the extent to which people conform to a majority depends on the relationship between the self and the majority. The majority position will lead to conformity only when the members of the majority are seen as sharing a social identity with the self (Balaam & Haslam, 1998). Therefore, a left-winger who gets involved in a discussion about the rights of immigrants with members of a neo-fascist group, will hardly be persuaded by the arguments put forward by the discussants, regardless of how united and unanimous they are. On the contrary, the same person might find the arguments that emerge from a discussion with other left-wingers to be very persuasive, even if he or she was initially a bit sceptical about those arguments. This phenomenon was demonstrated by Dominic Abrams and his colleagues (Abrams et al., 1986). They created a situation that was exactly like the one used by Asch in his classic studies of conformity. Basically, participants in the experiment had to judge which one of a set of three lines was similar to a standard line. However, only one participant produced spontaneous judgements, while, unknown to him/her, all the other participants had been instructed by the experimenter to make a wrong judgement. Results showed that the naive participant tended to conform to the unanimous (and wrong!) majority only when the members of such majority were designated as ingroup members (psychology students). Instead, when the confederates were presented as outgroup members (students of ancient history), the naive participant made independent, and correct, judgements.

For a detailed overview of the Asch conformity studies and their experimental situations, see Chapter 7.

We should keep in mind, however, that people may have different levels of identification with an ingroup, and that this has implications for the degree to which one is loyal to the group. Researchers have found that stronger levels of group identification enhance group members' willingness to comply with the group norms (Barreto & Ellemers, 2000).

## PEOPLE CONVERT TO MINORITIES SEEN AS INGROUP

The importance of shared social identity is not confined to conformity (i.e. situations in which a minority is influenced by a majority). As Barbara David and John Turner (1996, 1999) repeatedly demonstrated, as long as they are perceived as an ingroup source of information, a minority of people are perfectly capable of exerting influence on a majority up to the point of converting the majority members to the position of the minority. For instance, environmentalists exerted a very modest impact as long as they were seen as an outgroup made up of odd, bizarre and unconventional people. However, as it became obvious that they were speaking for 'us', and were therefore part of an ingroup, their campaigns were taken much more seriously and their ideas quickly absorbed by mainstream society.

## WHY ARE INGROUP MEMBERS ESPECIALLY INFLUENTIAL?

According to the self-categorization theory (Turner et al., 1987), the reason why members of an ingroup are especially influential is twofold. First, group members see one another as qualified to offer valid information about the correct beliefs and values (McGarty et al., 1993). Second, a collection of individuals sharing a social identity in common feel part of a social entity that transcends their own individual self, and that should maintain a level of cohesion and unity if it wants to exist as such. As a result, group members assume that there should be consensus on the group norms (values, beliefs, attitudes) (Haslam, 2004). After all, without some degree of consensus on group norms, a group could hardly be defined as a group at all.

In sum shared social identity (1) turns group members into reliable sources of information on the norms that should be consensually agreed, and (2) creates an expectation of agreement (Figure 12.3). This leads group members to give special consideration to each other's positions, and to be open to reciprocal influence, so that they gradually move towards an integrated and common position (Postmes, 2003). On the contrary, group members will expect to disagree with members of relevant outgroups. As a consequence, they will tend to distance themselves from the position of outgroup members, in order to emphasize and mark out the differences between the ingroup and the outgroup. (See Chapter 11 for the implications of these mechanisms for group polarization.)

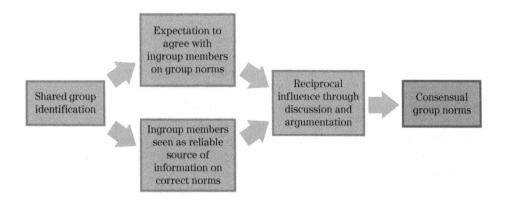

**FIGURE 12.3** From shared group identification to group consensus

Will members of this group be able to reach consensus? Their shared social identity will foster reciprocal trust and raise expectations of agreement, thereby facilitating the achievement of consensus.

SOURCE: © skynesher/iStock

This process was empirically demonstrated in an experiment conducted by Tom Postmes, Russell Spears and Martin Lea (2000). These researchers showed that when different groups of students were encouraged to communicate via e-mail, each group gradually converged towards both a common content (i.e. the type of humour they used) and a similar stylistic form (i.e. punctuation and capitalization) of their messages. This shows that once a collection of individuals share a common identification, reciprocal influence leads to the creation of consensual norms that distinguish the ingroup from the outgroups.

Note, however, that while shared social identity tends to *facilitate* the achievement of consensus, the content of social identity is not something that people accept automatically. People engage in an ongoing discussion in which the content of the group identity, the boundaries of the group, and the group prototype are argued over and negotiated, often through sophisticated linguistic and rhetorical strategies (Antaki & Widdicombe, 1998) (see Chapter 13 for more on the role played by language in the way we relate to the world). This implies that sometimes the process of communication that is meant to create consensus actually ends up in disagreement. As we will see later in this chapter, ingroup disagreement may, on occasions, give rise to factionalism and schism.

## research close-up

### LAUGHING: THE INFLUENCE OF THE INGROUP

*Source*: *Platow, M. J., Haslam, S. A., Both, A., Chew, I., Cuddon, M., Goharpey, N., Maurer, J., Rosini, S., Tsekouras, A., & Grace, D. (2005). It's not funny if they're laughing: Self-categorization, social influence, and responses to canned laughter.* Journal of Experimental Social Psychology, *41, 542–550.*

### Introduction

Some television programmes make use of pre-recorded (or 'canned') laughter in order to produce audience laughter, based on knowledge that people laugh and smile when seeing others doing so. Some researchers believe that laughing in response to others' laughter is an automatic response based on non-thinking conformity (Cialdini, 1993). However, rather than being entirely automatic, responses to canned laughter might be partly determined by *who* is laughing. Based on the self-categorization theory's assumption that social influence is largely a group process, and that people are more easily influenced by an ingroup rather than outgroup source, this study tests the hypothesis that canned laughter believed to originate from an ingroup will produce stronger laughter than canned laughter believed to come from an outgroup.

## Method

The experiment involved undergraduate students from La Trobe University in Australia. They sat individually at a desk facing a two-way mirror and listened to an audiotape of a man reciting a stand-up comedy routine, where various jokes were made. However, half of participants were told that the recording was made with a La Trobe University student audience (ingroup), while the other half were told that the recording was made with a One National Party audience (outgroup). Also, half of participants in either the ingroup or outgroup audience situation heard recorded laughter at the end of each joke, while half of participants did not hear any laughter. Therefore, this experiment included four conditions: ingroup audience laughing; ingroup audience not laughing; outgroup audience laughing; outgroup audience not laughing. After listening to the audiotape, participants were asked to rate the comedian in terms of how humorous and entertaining he was, using a 1 to 7-point scale (1 = not at all humorous/entertaining; 7 = extremely humorous/entertaining). In addition, the frequency with which participants smiled and laughed, as well as the total amount of time they spent laughing (calculated in seconds), were recorded by researchers placed behind the one-way mirror.

## Results

As one might expect, an audiotape including canned laughter prompted longer laughter than an audiotape without canned laughter. Concerning the nature of the audience (i.e., whether it was ingroup or outgroup), this had virtually no effects when the audiotape was without canned laughter, but had large and statistically significant effects when the audiotape included canned laughter. Specifically, participants rated the comedian as much more humorous and entertaining when the audience was believed to be made up of ingroup members than when it was believed to be formed by outgroup members. In addition, an ingroup audience led to three times as frequent smiling and laughing, and to four times longer laughter than an outgroup audience (see Figure 12.4).

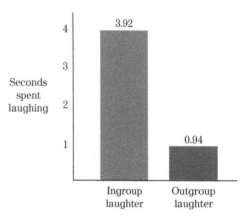

**FIGURE 12.4** Recorded average time laughing (in seconds) for participants hearing either an ingroup or an outgroup audience laughter

SOURCE: Based on Platow et al. (2005).

## Discussion

These results suggest that people find jokes particularly funny and laugh a lot when they hear fellow ingroup members laughing. Hearing outgroup members laughing produces much cooler reactions. This appears to confirm that ingroup members are the people we rely upon for information about the social world, and who therefore have the ability to influence us. It should be noted, however, that the outgroup used in this experiment (a political party that is known to be generally disliked by participants) was rather extreme. Future research should explore this process using different inter-group contexts. Also, studies should assess people's reaction when the group membership of a laughing audience is not known. In this case, it is possible that people's reaction is based on their guessed similarity with the audience.

## LEADERS AS 'ENTREPRENEURS OF SOCIAL IDENTITY'

What does it take to be a leader? In Chapter 11 we noted that the group has the capacity to shape the characteristics of its leader. Edwin Paul Hollander (1995), for instance, was very clear about the fact that a wanting-to-be group leader must take into consideration the needs and aspirations of the group members.

Researchers in the field of social identity have elaborated on this assumption, and have proposed that leadership is essentially a group phenomenon, and that the notion of social identity is central to a proper understanding of leadership (Hogg et al., 1998; Haslam et al., 2011). Social identity has two important implications for leadership.

**1** The ideal leader is expected to be a quintessential representation of the group identity. This means that the leader's ideas and behaviours are evaluated in terms of how closely they match the group prototype. A group member will be recognized as a true leader to the extent that he or she is seen as an incarnation of the group prototype. However, being recognized as the prototypical member of a social group, and therefore being accepted as group leader, doesn't just happen. Individuals who aspire to become leaders have to convince the group that they are true group prototypes.

**2** A highly prototypical leader will be able to exert a strong influence on the other group members. This is because this type of leader will be seen as especially qualified to indicate the correct group norms. A prototypical leader will therefore be in a position to define and shape the group identity (von Cranach, 1986). However, in order to transform and renew the group identity, a leader must persuade the group members that the new norms and values that he or she is proposing are consistent with the group identity.

In summary, either wanting-to-be leaders or actual leaders must use an array of linguistic and rhetorical strategies in order to construe (1) themselves as congruent with the group prototype, and (2) their proposed course of action as consistent with the group identity. Steve Reicher and Nick Hopkins (1996) – two British social psychologists who study the social construction of social categories and identities – have defined leaders as 'entrepreneurs of social identity'.

To illustrate the process of becoming prototypical of a social category, and of using prototypicality to shape social identity, we can reflect on the emergence of Silvio Berlusconi as political leader in Italy, in 1994. In the years preceding the 1994 Italian political elections, the old centrist political establishment had lost credibility because of the incrimination of several prominent politicians for corruption. As a consequence, the majority of Italians became political 'orphans' in search of a new referent. Berlusconi cleverly tried to fill this void by presenting himself as the incarnation of all the values that those Italians embraced, such as economic freedom and anti-communism. The fact that he was a very rich and successful businessman made his candidature credible. As a result, he was quickly recognized as the prototypical member of this social group. After becoming the leader of the centre-right political group, Berlusconi was able to turn his electorate against the judges who were investigating political corruption, because he himself was not on good terms with these judges. He presented them as rigid and authoritarian prosecutors, who were insensitive to the rights that people should be granted in democratic countries, and who aligned with the political adversaries of the centre-right, the 'communists'. In sum, before the elections Berlusconi modelled his programme and image on the expectations of the social group he aspired to represent, and once he was recognized as the group prototype he used his role to instil new beliefs in the group members, in accordance with his own agenda.

Silvio Berlusconi became the political leader of the centre-right in Italy by promoting the image of the prototypical entrepreneurial and anti-communist Italian. Once recognized as leader, Berlusconi was able to dictate the agenda of his political group.

SOURCE: © Markwaters/Dreamstime.com

Steve Reicher and Nick Hopkins' (1996) analysis of the speeches of two political leaders of the 1980s, Neil Kinnock (leader of the Labour Party) and Margaret Thatcher (leader of the Conservative Party), concerning the 1984–85 British miners' strike, constitutes another interesting example of how leaders try to shape identities (Figure 12.5). In their analysis, Reicher and Hopkins found that each leader described the context of the strike in terms of two social categories: a large and positively depicted social category, of which he or she was the prototypical representative, and a very small social category, which was identified as the enemy. As Reicher and Hopkins explain, 'Thatcher constructs a frame of "democracy against terrorism" wherein the inclusive category is British, is anti-strike, is represented by the Conservatives and the working miners and is defending itself against an exclusive category of the NUM [National Union of Mineworkers] executive. Kinnock constructs a frame of "Thatcherism against society" wherein the inclusive category is the people, is pro-strike, is represented by the Labour Party and the striking miners and is defending itself against an exclusive category of Margaret Thatcher' (1996, p. 369). In summary, Reicher and Hopkins show that, in this case, the aim of the speakers is to present themselves as the prototype of the national society, in order to back up either the aspiration to become the national leader (Kinnock) or the legitimization of an actual leadership (Thatcher).

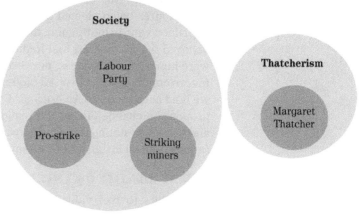

Categories constructed by Kinnock

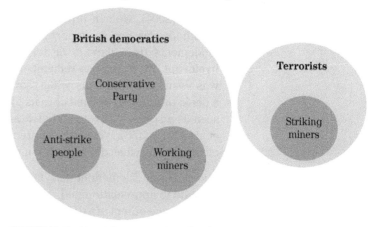

Categories constructed by Thatcher

FIGURE 12.5 Linguistic construction of social categories involved in the strike

Individuals who want to be seen as group prototypes may use ruthless and irresponsible strategies in order to achieve their aim. For instance, a leader who is struggling to be recognized as prototype, may use the 'us' versus 'them' rhetoric and show outgroup hostility in order to reinforce his or her position (Haslam, 2004). Such instances have been observed even in a controlled laboratory experiment, which showed that leaders whose position within their group was unstable were more inclined to promote intergroup conflict than leaders with a more secure position (Rabbie & Bekkers, 1978).

Clearly, wanting-to-be leaders may endorse change and renovation. This might seem to contradict the idea that, if they want to be accepted by their prospective followers, wanting-to-be leaders need to be seen as group prototypes. However, aspiring leaders who preach change and innovation do so in line with the 'group

Zeitgeist', and by arguing that change is needed to reinforce, strengthen or be faithful to the true group identity. Consider for instance Barack Obama's first speech after being elected as US president for the first time, in 2008. Here, he explained why, in his opinion, the American people had voted for him. He stated: 'I believed that Democrats and Republicans and Americans of every political stripe were hungry for new ideas, new leadership, and a new kind of politics – one that favors common sense over ideology; one that focuses on those values and ideals we hold in common as Americans.' Basically, Obama said that he won because he proposed a change that would realign the Americans with their own true values and beliefs. In stating this, Obama was presenting himself as a genuine incarnation (a prototypical instance) of the American identity.

## SOCIAL IDENTITY AND RESPECT

People like to feel valued and respected. Positive evaluation from others is normally welcome. But is our desire to feel wanted and liked unconditional? Do we welcome recognition and appreciation from anybody, indistinctively? Clearly this is not the case. As observed by Naomi Ellemers, Bertjan Doosje and Russell Spears (2004), we can probably remember situations in which the appreciation of others was not so important, as when we remained indifferent to positive judgements from parents or teachers because these judgements were simply irrelevant. We might also remember instances in which the appreciation of others was even unwelcome, as when 'someone we defined as less desirable (a nerd, a geek, or a no-no) latched onto us like a limpet, even worshipped us, but was just seen as a source of acute embarrassment in front of our "true" friends' (Ellemers et al., 2004, p. 155). When does appreciation and respect from others induce positive emotions, and when does it lead to indifference or even embarrassment and disgust?

According to Ellemers et al. (2004; see also Spears et al., 2005), the way people respond to appreciation and respect from others depends on how the self and the appreciative others are defined and categorized. As we have already pointed out, people seek validation of their beliefs from others who are categorized as ingroup members. As a consequence, appreciation and positive evaluation coming from an ingroup source is welcome, reassuring and flattering. On the contrary, people do not see outgroup members as a source of validation, and so their judgements have hardly any relevance to self. In fact, when differentiating between ingroup and outgroup is especially important, appreciation from outgroup members may be unwelcome, if not deeply embarrassing and displeasing. Ellemers and her colleagues offer the example of a male pop group that fashions itself as 'heavy-metal band from hell'. If it was discovered that the biggest fans of this band are teenyboppers and pensioners, the members of the band would probably be displeased.

To support their hypothesis, Ellemers et al. (2004) recruited some students from the University of Amsterdam for an experiment, and presented them with a vignette. Each participant had to imagine a situation in which he or she sits on a tram and, on seeing a young boy pushing an old lady away from the last available seat, comments that the old lady wanted to sit there. At this point, the participant had to imagine that a group of student bystanders respond favourably to the protagonist's behaviour and express their disapproval for the boy's behaviour. However, some participants in the experiment were told to imagine that the group of student bystanders are from the University of Amsterdam (the ingroup), while other participants were told to imagine that the bystanders are from the Free University (a rival university in Amsterdam, and therefore an outgroup). When, subsequently, participants were asked to rate how much collective self-esteem they would feel as members of the University of Amsterdam, those who had imagined that the bystanders were ingroup members produced higher collective self-esteem ratings than those who had imagined that the bystanders were outgroup members. These results are in line with a social identity approach to respect: positive feedback from an ingroup source will raise one's group-related self-regard more than appreciation from an outgroup source.

Positive judgements are especially appreciated when they come from ingroup members.

SOURCE: © track5/iStock

## SOCIAL IDENTITY AND HELP

In the Research Close-Up in Chapter 10 we discussed the experiment conducted by Mark Levine and his colleagues (2005), in which it was found that an injured stranger wearing an ingroup team shirt is more likely to receive help than when wearing a rival team shirt or an unbranded sports shirt. This is a clear demonstration that social identity may play a crucial part in helping behaviour and support; people will help to the extent that they share the same social identity with the person who needs help.

This assumption has been confirmed in other studies conducted by Levine and his colleagues. In one study, Mark Levine and Kirstien Thompson (2004) asked a sample of British students to specify the likelihood that they would offer financial help (money donations, giving old clothes) and political help (signing petitions, joining action groups) following a natural disaster in Europe. Results showed that students were more likely to help when their European identity was made psychologically salient (by displaying a large colour European Union flag on the cover of the questionnaire) than when the British identity was made salient (by displaying a colour reproduction of a large British Union flag). Intriguingly, these findings imply that identification with the whole world community might increase one's willingness to endorse global cooperation and policies aiming at increasing global public good. This found confirmation in a cross-national questionnaire study involving participants from United States, Italy, Russia, Argentina, South Africa and Iran, conducted by Buchan et al. (2011). Participants with higher scores on a scale measuring identification with 'the world as a whole' appeared to be more concerned with global issues such as global worming or the persistent gap between rich and poor people around the world.

There are cases, however, in which helping members of an outgroup may be a means to advance a group's interest. For instance, Nick Hopkins and his colleagues (2007) found that after being reminded of the English stereotype about Scottish people as 'mean', Scottish students were much more likely to give money to an outgroup (a Welsh charity organization) than when such a reminder did not take place. Importantly, whether they were reminded of their supposed meanness or not did not make any difference in terms of how much money they would donate to the ingroup (a Scottish charity organization). Clearly, these students were particularly concerned with denying a negative stereotype attached to the national ingroup, and used outgroup helping as a strategy to improve the image of the ingroup.

Perhaps this tendency to be particularly helpful to ingroup members is somehow related to a more general tendency to be especially self-involved in the emotional experiences of other members of an ingroup. For example, people show greater levels of arousal, empathy and attention when observing the pleasure and displeasure of others who belong to the same group as the self than when the observed others belong to an outgroup (Brown et al., 2006). Furthermore, people interpret facial expressions of emotions much more accurately when looking at ingroup members than when looking at members of an outgroup (Young & Hugenberg, 2010).

## GROUP IDENTITY NORMS, DEVIANCE AND SCHISM

Although shared group identification tends to accentuate the similarities among group members, and therefore their relative prototypicality, differences in prototypicality remain. While the more prototypical members are seen as core members, the less prototypical ones are considered as marginal and peripheral ones. These less prototypical members may be perceived as a serious threat to the integrity of the group. The values and beliefs held by group deviants deny social identity, because these values and beliefs undermine shared consensus and reciprocal validation within the group. So, how are marginal members treated by core members? How do mainstream members cope with threats to social identity coming from deviants?

### THE BLACK SHEEP EFFECT

A common reaction is to dislike ingroup deviants more than outsiders. After all, disagreement with outgroup members is not problematic and does not endanger the ingroup's worldviews. Outgroup members are different from 'us' by definition, and, as we have already seen, ingroup members do not expect nor want to be in agreement with them. Serious disagreement with ingroup members can, on the contrary, be profoundly destabilizing. How can we be sure that we are correct if even people who are meant to be like us contradict our position? In line with this, José Marques and Vincent Yzerbyt (1988) found that law students rated a good performance of another law student more favourably than an equally good performance of a philosophy student, but rated a poor performance by another law student less favourably than an equally poor performance by a philosophy student. Another study asked a sample of Belgian students to evaluate attractive and unattractive Belgian and North African students on a set of personality adjectives. It was found that while attractive Belgian students were evaluated more positively than attractive North African students, unattractive Belgian students were evaluated more negatively than unattractive North African students (Marques et al., 1988).

Unsurprisingly, deviants are often expelled from the group. The political and religious domains offer countless examples of members who are forced to leave the group because they are against the orthodoxy and are considered as traitors. However, getting rid of deviants is perhaps not the most important measure taken by the group establishment and majority. The existence of deviants may actually constitute an opportunity to reinforce the virtue of group identity. By harshly punishing deviant behaviour, the group establishment will be able to emphasize what is and is not normative and accepted behaviour within the group. As observed by Donelson Forsyth (2009), norms often appear as such only when they are violated and violation is sanctioned. Deviance can therefore help to define more precisely the normative criteria for group membership, and be seen as functional for social identity. The tendency to derogate ingroup deviant members in order to reinforce ingroup boundaries and stress normative and counter-normative behaviour is known as the black sheep effect (Figure 12.6) (Marques & Yzerbyt, 1988).

**black sheep effect** *the tendency to criticize and derogate more harshly than members of an outgroup the members of an ingroup who deviate from the group norms*

## WHEN DEVIANCE AND CRITICISM FROM THE INSIDE ARE ACCEPTED

Consider, however, that if group members who do not align completely with the group norms were systematically marginalized and rejected, all groups would be condemned to become very rigid entities that are unable to change and develop. However, this is not the case. In some cases group members who criticize the group do not prompt defensive and aggressive reactions from mainstream group members. Matthew Hornsey (2005) listed two circumstances in which criticism directed to the group coming from other group members is seen as legitimate and valuable. First, people will accept criticism coming from ingroup members when the critics are seen as genuinely aimed at improving the group. If those who criticize appear to be invested in the group and to care for it, then criticism will be seen as constructive and therefore legitimate (Hornsey et al., 2004). Second, internal criticism will be accepted when it is perceived as timely and as delivered in an appropriate manner.

There are also situations in which punishing deviants may simply not be a good idea from a strategic point of view. For instance, if the positions of a political party are unpopular with the voting public, stressing group norms may widen the gap between the party line and the voting public. Therefore, party members may strategically decide to give more support to deviants in order to enhance the group's chances of success. This has been demonstrated by Thomas Morton, Tom Postmes and Jolanda Jetten (2007). These researchers found that supporters of the Conservative Party in Britain gave more support to a potential leader who proposed to abandon ingroup norms and pursue radical change (i.e. a deviant

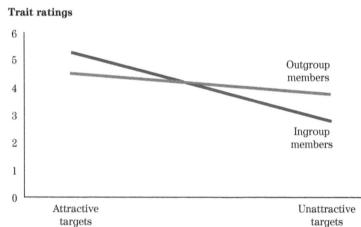

**Trait ratings**

FIGURE 12.6 The black sheep effect

When asked to rate target individuals by using trait adjectives, people give higher ratings to mainstream ingroup members than to mainstream outgroup members. However, concerning black sheep members (i.e. those members who do not conform to the group's normative expectations), people assign lower ratings to ingroup black sheep than to outgroup black sheep.

leader) when public support for the party was perceived to be decreasing than when it was perceived to be increasing.

The extent to which deviants are rejected may also vary depending on the group's cultural background. Groups endorsing a collectivistic ethos value relationships, harmony and the idea of 'sticking with the group' even when this implies a high personal cost. Because they are strongly concerned with group uniformity and oneness, these groups see deviance as a threat. On the contrary, individualistically orientated groups are socialized to value independence, autonomy and individual expressions. As a consequence, individualistic groups may see deviance as a manifestation of self-expression, and therefore they may accept it to a higher degree. This was demonstrated in an experiment about the attitude of collectivist and individualist people towards either deviant or mainstream members of the ingroup (Hornsey et al., 2006). Results showed that deviant opinions were evaluated less negatively when the group had an individualistic rather than collectivistic ethos. There is, however, a paradox here, in that valuing independence and an ability to stand out is in itself a norm to which members of groups with an individualistic ethos *conform* (Jetten et al., 2002). So, in some cases, people may conform to independence! See Research Close-Up: Evaluating Deviants in Individualistic and in Collectivistic Cultures.

## research close-up

### EVALUATING DEVIANTS IN INDIVIDUALISTIC AND IN COLLECTIVISTIC CULTURES

**Source**: *Hornsey, M. J., Jetten, J., McAuliffe, B. J., & Hogg, M. A. (2006). The impact of individualist and collectivist group norms on evaluations of dissenting group members.* Journal of Experimental Social Psychology, 42, 57–68.

### Introduction

Deviants are seen as a problem by mainstream group members. This is because those who challenge the group norms break the unity and cohesion of the group, and question the nature of the group identity. As a consequence, deviants tend to be disliked and sanctioned. But are deviants evaluated negatively in all types of groups? It is hypothesized that the extent to which deviants are disliked will depend on whether the group holds an individualistic or a collectivistic ethos. Groups that have an individualistic ethos place importance on independence, and value people who are able to elaborate and express their own opinions in spite of possible pressures from other group members. Therefore, as Jetten et al. (2002) showed, groups with an individualistic ethos have a norm that prescribes challenging the norms! On the other hand, groups holding a collectivistic ethos value group cohesion and harmony, as well as the pursuit of collective goals and objectives. As a consequence, these groups tend to value members who avoid conflict and criticism, and who make an effort to fit in.

### Method

This experiment was based on two conditions. In one condition, participants read a document emphasizing the collectivist orientation of students at the University of Queensland, while in the other condition participants read a document stressing the individualistic ethos of the students. At this point, the Australian government's proposal to introduce upfront fees was presented to all participants, who were subsequently told that the vast majority of University of Queensland students opposed this proposal. Finally, participants were asked to consider the opinion of an anonymous student about upfront fees, and evaluate this specific student by specifying how positively they saw him or her, on a scale ranging from 1 to 9, where the higher the rating the more positive the attitude. However, half of the participants were told that this anonymous student was against upfront fees (and was therefore 'concordant' with the group majority), while the other half were told that the anonymous student was in favour of upfront fees (and was therefore a 'deviant').

## Results

As shown in Figure 12.7, students who had been primed with an individualistic ethos evaluated the deviant more positively than students who believed that the group ethos was collectivistic (mean ratings were 4.62 and 3.14 respectively for each condition). This indicated clearly that the group holding an individualistic ethos accepted dissent and disagreement more than the group with a collectivistic ethos. Concerning the concordant student, participants in the collectivistic group gave slightly better evaluations than participants in the individualistic group, but differences were not statistically significant (means were 6.66 and 6.92 respectively).

## Discussion

This study demonstrates that group deviants are perceived and treated differently depending on the group cultural ethos. Individualistic groups will see deviants in a less negative light than collectivistic groups, due to the fact that individualistic cultures place greater emphasis on values such as independence and uniqueness. It should be noted, however, that the group ethos is not necessarily static. In fact, the group ethos may change at different stages of group development. For instance, Worchel (1998) suggested that collectivist norms are more commonly observed early in the life of a group, when the group needs clear, well-defined norms and goals, and that more individualistic norms may develop later in a group's life, once the group is well established.

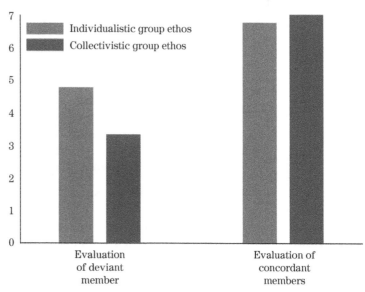

**Degree to which the evaluation is positive (higher values) or negative (lower values)**

FIGURE 12.7   Evaluation of deviant and concordant members in individualistic and collectivistic groups
Members of the University of Queensland student group who endorsed an individualistic group ethos evaluated ingroup members who deviated from the majority position more positively than members who endorsed a collectivistic group ethos. However, the favoured cultural ethos had no effects on the evaluations of concordant members.
SOURCE: Data from Hornsey et al., 2006.

## PERIPHERAL GROUP MEMBERS

Although, as discussed above, there may be group members who consciously decide to criticize the group and therefore accept to be seen, at least temporarily, as peripheral (non-prototypical) group members, there are also group members who are seen as peripheral against their will. These group members tend to feel more anxious and less confident than core (prototypical) group members (Louis, 1980; Moreland, 1985). What are the consequences of this emotionally aversive state? How do peripheral group members try to resolve this unpleasant situation? Researchers have investigated this issue, and found that peripheral group members employ a variety of strategies in order to feel, and to be seen by other ingroup members as, more prototypical. This is especially the case with members who value the group and strongly identify with it. Individuals for whom group membership is irrelevant will not be so concerned about their group prototypicality (Schmitt & Branscombe, 2002).

'Alienation from others is thus a deprivation of social being, for it is within our bonds that the self is forged and maintained.'
   Robert F. Murphy, *The Body Silent*, 1990

Increased Conformity to Ingroup Standards

One very common strategy adopted by marginal group members who invest psychologically in the group is to increase conformity to ingroup standards. This is exactly what Robert Wicklund and Ottmar Braun (1987) demonstrated in an experimental study: participants who were strongly committed to a social group but were not yet accomplished group members were more likely to describe themselves in terms of the group features than core members. In this study, it was also found that participants' conformity to the standards of a valued social group increased when their sense of accomplishment was threatened.

Increased Derogation of Non-prototypical Members and Praise of Prototypical Members

Threats to group prototypicality also affect how strongly a highly identified group member will use prototypical group features as a standard when judging other group members. Michael Schmitt and Nyla Branscombe (2002) argue that individuals whose prototypicality is questioned are induced to feel 'bad' group members, because they damage the distinctiveness of the group as well as its cohesion and homogeneity. As a consequence, these individuals will seek to be 'good' group members by vigorously endorsing and defending group identity. Schmitt and Branscombe suggest that a way of protecting group identity is evaluating group members in terms of their fit to the ingroup prototype. Consistent with this suggestion, these researchers found that men who highly identified with their gender group were much more derogatory towards non-prototypical men, and much more favourable towards prototypical men, when they were led to believe that they were non-prototypical compared to when they were told that they were highly prototypical. Intriguingly, these findings are nicely illustrated by a character from the 1999 Oscar-awarded movie *American Beauty*: the Colonel of the US Marine Corps, Frank Fitts, played by Chris Cooper. Fitts overtly hates homosexuals, and reacts violently to behaviours he dislikes. At one point in the movie, however, Fitts tries to kiss a neighbour who happens to be a male, thereby revealing the meaning of his constant effort to present himself in public as an uncompromised, quintessential 'man'.

Increased Derogation of Outgroup Members

High group identifiers who do not feel secure about their group prototypicality are also more prone to derogate members of relevant outgroups. Glynis Breakwell (1979) ran an experiment in which people were ostensibly tested in order to see if they could join a desirable 'good-anagram-solvers' group. However, some participants were given an opportunity to cheat on the scoring of an anagram test. Subsequently, these illegitimate members of the good-anagram-solvers groups displayed more extreme outgroup derogation than participants who felt legitimate members of the group. Breakwell, as well as other social psychologists (e.g. Tajfel, 1978), believe that group members who feel illegitimate derogate outgroups in order to justify their group membership to themselves, because no one else knows about their illegitimate membership. According to Jeffrey Noel, Daniel Wann and Nyla Branscombe (1995), however, illegitimate group members derogate the outgroup in order to present themselves as non-peripheral, legitimate group members to the eyes of other group members, so as to be accepted and improve their status and prototypicality within the group (Figure 12.8).

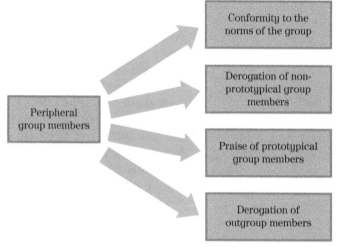

FIGURE 12.8   Strategies used by peripheral group members in order to enhance their position within the group

## CONTESTED IDENTITIES AND SCHISM

Who is a marginal and who is a core group member is not always consensually agreed within a group. In some cases, group members that are accused of denying and betraying the group identity may refute this accusation. They may claim that their beliefs and behaviours are consistent with the group identity, and that it is actually those who blame them who are the heretics. This is far from being unusual, and it is one of the possible consequences of shared social identity.

The group norms that define the group identity are not set in stone. On the contrary, the group members are involved in an ongoing process of negotiation about the nature of such norms. As a consequence, existing norms are constantly refined, adjusted, modified and, in some circumstances, dropped and replaced with entirely new norms. The aim of this process is to define the group identity in a clear and unambiguous way, thereby achieving consensus and unity. But sometimes consensus fails! Relatively homogeneous factions, each holding different views about what should and should not be the group identity, crystallize, which can result in conflict and tension within groups. This may eventually end up in a schism.

schism *the partition of a social group into separate factions and the ultimate secession of at least one faction from the group*

Fabio Sani and his colleagues have investigated the processes that underlie schisms in social groups in a series of studies involving real groups (see Sani, 2008, for a summary of research). The major study of this research programme concerned the schism within the Church of England over the issue of the ordination of women to the priesthood (Sani, 2005; Sani & Reicher, 1999, 2000; Sani & Todman, 2002).

In March 1994 the first 32 women were ordained priests at Bristol Cathedral. Over the following years a group formed by hundreds of clergymen and thousands of lay people left the Church of England because of women priesthood. Why did so many members of the Church of England leave their beloved church over this specific issue? Sani and colleagues studied this schism longitudinally using interviews and questionnaires completed by members of the Church of England who either accepted or rejected the new legislation. The data analysis revealed that for some members the Church of England's decision to ordain women to the priesthood signified a radical departure from its doctrine and creed, which implied a complete denial of its nature and identity. According to these members, the ordination of women was turning the Church of England into a different church, something that was completely different from what it used to be. As one interviewee declared, by ordaining women priests the Church of England had 'chucked up scripture, overcome authority, kicked tradition in the teeth, and decided it's a protestant sect' (Sani & Reicher, 1999). As a consequence of this position, many of these members seceded from the Church of England. Those members who supported the legislation had, however, a completely different view. In their opinion, the legislation was totally consistent with the history of the Church of England and its group identity. What is more, the supporters of women priesthood argued that the legislation allowed the Church to accomplish more fully its true identity. The then Archbishop of Canterbury put it plainly: 'We are not departing from a traditional concept of ministry, we are talking about an extension of the same ministry to include women . . . Christianity is all about God liberating, renewing and drawing out what has been there implicitly from the beginning.'

These analyses show that the schism resulted from a debate concerning the relationship between a specific norm (the legislation on women priests) and the group identity as a whole (the identity of the Church of England). Members perceived the norm either as fully consistent with the group identity, in which case they endorsed the norm and happily stayed in the group, or as overthrowing the group identity, in which case they strenuously opposed the norm and seriously considered joining a schism. Sani (2005) found that the main reasons why those who perceived group identity overthrowing developed schismatic intentions were that they experienced aversive emotions (especially dejection and agitation) and lost their identification with the group. Sani also found that the likelihood of unhappy members joining a schism depended ultimately on their perceived ability to voice their dissent within the group. The lower the perceived voice the higher the chances of leaving the group. Put differently, opponents wondered what might have happened to them in the future, as group members. If they foresaw ostracism, discrimination and isolation, they generally opted for a schism (Figure 12.9). On the other hand, if they believed that they would be respected and would retain an active role in the group, they were more inclined to stay.

Fabio Sani and Annarita Pugliese (2008) replicated these findings in a study of a schism that took place within an Italian right-wing political party, Alleanza Nazionale, in 2001. Alleanza Nazionale (AN) was founded in 1994, and constituted a renewed version of a party that was created after the end of the Second World War, which claimed the legitimacy of the fascist experience. Since the creation of Alleanza Nazionale the party secretary, Gianfranco Fini, had made it clear that the party

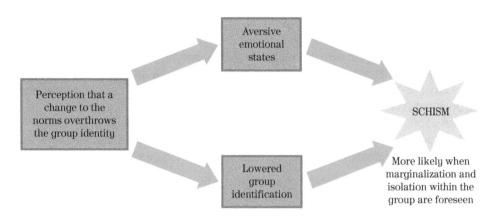

FIGURE 12.9 The schismatic process How a faction within a group may decide to join a schism and leave the group.

fully accepted democratic values. However, when in 2003 Fini visited Israel and there publicly defined fascism as the *male assoluto* ('ultimate evil') of the twentieth century, some party members who still had a sense of respect for Mussolini and felt nostalgia for the fascist regime rebelled. This group, led by Mussolini's niece, Alessandra Mussolini, decided to secede from AN and founded a new breakaway party. Sani and Pugliese found that those group members who left the party saw Fini's turn as a rupture with the historical continuity of the party, as a denial of the group identity, and also feared that they would end up being marginalized within the party. On the contrary, the majority that endorsed Fini's turn believed that the turn was a necessary development in line with the group identity.

## SOCIAL IDENTITY MOTIVES

Why do people identify with groups? Is social identification driven by some psychological motives? Obviously, there may be many motives, including instrumental and practical ones. However, social psychologists believe that some specific psychological motives are deeply ingrained in the human mind and are therefore widespread. Vivian Vignoles and his colleagues (2006) have demonstrated that social identities that satisfy important psychological motives are seen by people as more central to their self-definition. Below we briefly discuss five social identity motives that have been explored at length by social psychologists, some of which were also included in the list of motives studied by Vignoles et al.'s (2006) studies.

### THE SELF-ESTEEM MOTIVE

Social psychologists agree that a core motive for social identification is the one for self-esteem. As we discussed in Chapter 3, we strive for a positive evaluation of ourselves, and when our self-esteem is threatened we use a variety of strategies to restore or enhance self-esteem (Hoyle et al., 1999).

Being a member of a group may enhance two different, yet related types of self-esteem. First, a positively valued ingroup can be a source of collective self-esteem (Luhtanen & Crocker, 1992), that is, positive regard for the ingroup as a whole. Collective self-esteem is especially pursued in collectivistic cultures, which place

collective self-esteem *positive regard for a group of which one is a member* special emphasis on the importance of interconnectedness among individuals and on group goals and life. Researchers have found that collective self-esteem is higher among allocentric individuals – that is, people who have been socialized into collectivistic cultures – than among idiocentric individuals – that is, people who have been raised into individualistic cultures (Crocker et al., 1994). Second, a positively valued ingroup can be a source of personal self-esteem, that is positive regard for the individual self. Personal self-esteem is especially sought in individualistic societies, where people are socialized to focus their attention and invest their energies on the enhancement of the individual self.

Because highly regarded groups may satisfy both forms of self-esteem, people generally want to belong to groups that have high status and prestige (Tajfel & Turner, 1986). In order to assess the group status, group members compare the ingroup with relevant outgroups. This is a specific form of social comparison (a concept we have discussed in Chapter 3), in the sense that rather than comparing the individual self with other individuals, people compare their own group with other groups.

### THE DISTINCTIVENESS MOTIVE

Various social psychologists have observed that humans have a pervasive need for uniqueness and distinctiveness (Breakwell, 1986; Brewer, 1991). This is because highlighting the differences between self and others is an important aspect of self-definition, particularly in the West. How could a single individual know who he or she is without establishing the way in which he or she differs from others? Importantly, the need for distinctiveness does not apply exclusively to the personal self; it is just as much concerned with the collective self, that is social identity (Tajfel et al., 1971; Vignoles et al., 2000). As we have repeatedly observed, identifying with a social category implies recognition that we are similar to some people and different from others and the accentuation of these intra-group similarities and inter-group differences. This marks out the boundaries between 'us' and 'them', thereby providing group members with a sense of distinctiveness. Countless types of identity markers (e.g. flags, clothing, body painting, linguistic jargon, tastes) can be used to emphasize differences between groups and to maintain group distinctiveness (Sani & Thomson, 2001).

Jonah Berger and Chip Heath (2008) argue that members of a group may even abandon tastes and habits that have been adopted for a long time, if this allows distinction from an outgroup. These researchers found that a group of students stopped wearing a particular wristband after discovering that other students, from the 'geeky' academically focused dormitory next door, also began wearing that type of wristband.

### THE MOTIVE TO BELONG

See Chapter 9 on attraction and intimacy for a more extended discussion of the need to relate to others to become and remain a human being.

Another need that social psychologists believe to be fundamental and universal is the need to belong, or to relate to others, to become and remain a human being. Social identity provides a reassuring sense of inclusion, and therefore it constitutes a potent means for the satisfaction of the need to belong. Megan Knowles and Wendi Gardner (2008) conducted an experiment in which they asked a group of participants to think and write about a time in which they felt intensely rejected in some way, and another group to think and write about a time in which they felt very accepted in some way. Then, participants were asked to rate the perceived cohesiveness and importance of their ingroups. It was found that participants who thought about rejection saw their groups as much more cohesive and united than participants who thought about acceptance. Clearly, people primed with social rejection were motivated to be part of a meaningful and solid group. Interestingly, fear of rejection seems to have an effect on the size of groups that are sought out. Cynthia Pickett, Michael Silver and Marilynn Brewer (2002) have shown that if people's belongingness is threatened, as when they are told that they belong to a very rare personality category, they will seek out identification with larger and more inclusive groups.

## THE MOTIVE TO ACHIEVE SYMBOLIC IMMORTALITY

Through group identification people may become parts of collective entities that seem immune to the corrosion of time. The sense of belonging to something that transcends my mere individual existence may provide me with a sense of symbolic immortality; a sense that, while I may be physically mortal, a part of me (my values, beliefs and deeds) will survive through my group. This means that social identity protects people from the terror engendered by fear of death, which according to terror management theory (see Chapter 13 for more on this theory) is a fundamental, inescapable dimension of the human condition (Pyszczynski et al., 2000). Social psychologists have reasoned that, if it is true that social identification may protect against the terror prompted by the idea that we must ultimately die, then if people are reminded of their own mortality they should increase their identification with relevant groups. This proposition has been tested and confirmed by researchers. For instance, it has been found that after thinking and writing about the prospect of their own death, people exhibit an enhanced ingroup favouritism and identification (Castano et al., 2002), and endorse harsher punishment for group deviants (Rosenblatt et al., 1989). These findings have been confirmed by Fabio Sani, Marina Herrera and Mhairi Bowe (2009), who showed that fear of death enhances social identity to the extent that the values and beliefs of the group with which one identifies are perceived to endure through time.

*symbolic immortality a form of immortality that is not based on escaping physical death but on the symbolic continuation of the self across time (e.g. through offspring or the transmission of one's cultural values to the new generations)*

## THE MOTIVE FOR UNCERTAINTY REDUCTION

As many social psychologists have pointed out, people tend to have low tolerance for uncertainty about social reality and their own place in it (Festinger, 1950). According to Michael Hogg, Zachary Hohmann and Jason Rivera (2008), 'group membership is a very effective way to resolve epistemic uncertainty. This is because groups prescribe who we are and how we should behave. Groups also provide consensual validation for our perceptions, feelings, attitudes, and behaviors' (p. 1270). These social psychologists also state that groups that are perceived as having high entitativity – that is, groups that are seen as being very homogeneous and cohesive, thereby looking like single and bounded entities (Campbell, 1958; Hamilton & Sherman, 1996) – are better suited for uncertainty reduction.

*entitativity the extent to which a collection of individuals is perceived as forming a single, unified and cohesive entity*

This is because entitative groups provide people with clear norms and unambiguous social identities. To demonstrate this assumption, Michael Hogg and his colleagues (Hogg et al., 2007) asked members of either the Labor or the Liberal Party in Australia to rate the perceived entitativity of their own party. Then participants were instructed to think about those aspects of their life that made them feel uncertain about themselves, their life and their future. Finally, participants' identification with their political party was assessed. Results show that people whose self-uncertainty was primed identified more strongly with their political group when this was seen as high in entitativity.

It is important to note, however, that people will not be happy just with any version of what the group is like and where it comes from. The sense of being a cohesive entity with a clear trajectory and well-defined values and standards is important, but even more important is to claim for the group the desired history, values and standards. That means that 'who we are' and 'where we come from' are issues that are actively constructed by the members of a group – especially the group establishment and leaders – through language (Potter & Wetherell, 1987).

## SOCIAL IDENTITY AND HEALTH

Our social identity affects not only our social behaviours and thoughts, but also our health and the way we feel physically. There are three main ways in which social identity and health are connected.

1 Social identity influences our perception of, and response to, symptoms. For instance, concerning perception of symptoms, a soldier involved in a military campaign is likely to find a bone fracture less painful than an ordinary person, in line with values related to strength of character that are typical of a soldier identity. Regarding response to symptoms, refusal to see oneself as a 'cardio-vascular problem sufferer' might lead to downplaying early symptoms of a heart attack and failure to seek prompt medical attention.

2 Social identity has implications for health behaviour. Whether or not one engages in health-promoting behaviour may depend on the degree to which such behaviour is consistent with the norms of the social group with which one identifies. For example, identification with the group of 'athletes' is likely to restrain me from drinking; on the other hand, if I identify with the group of 'university students' I may indulge in binge drinking.

3 Social identity impacts upon our biology. When I identify with a group, I feel confident that ingroup members will offer help and support in case of difficulties. This is likely to increase my perceived ability to cope with tasks, thereby reducing the physiological stress I experience. For instance, if I identify strongly with my workplace I will tend to see my colleagues as reliable sources of support. This will enhance my perceived ability to cope with work-related tasks, and as a consequence will reduce stress and enhance well-being.

In this section we explore research on these three forms of interplay between social identity and health, in some details.

### SOCIAL IDENTITY AND SYMPTOM PERCEPTION

The relationship between the biological aspects of an illness and the perception of the relevant symptoms is not straightforward. For instance, the same injury can produce substantially different degrees of pain in different people, and even in the same person on different occasions (Melzack & Wall, 1988). That means that in many circumstances symptom perception may have more to do with psychology than biology. Social psychologists contend an important way in which our psychology affects symptom perception is through our social identity (St. Claire & Clucas, 2012). Researchers have found that social identity may impact upon symptom perception in at least two important ways.

First of all, social identity may influence the perceived severity of symptoms when one is ill. St. Claire and He (2009) asked older people about their levels of hearing after emphasizing either their membership in the 'group of older people' or their unique, individual characteristics. Participants who thought about themselves as older people reported more hearing-related problems than those who thought about themselves in terms of their individual traits. These results confirm that a person who suffers from an illness will likely identify with the group of people suffering from that specific illness and, as a consequence, will conform to symptoms that are believed to be normative of that illness group membership.

The second way in which social identity may impact upon symptom perception is by influencing how serious and distressing specific symptoms are perceived to be. For instance, symptoms may be perceived as especially serious when they constitute a threat to identity, as demonstrated by R. M. Levine (1999). This researcher primed a sample of female secretaries with either a 'secretary' or a 'female' identity, and then asked them to evaluate the seriousness of a number of different illnesses or injuries. Results revealed that judgements depended on the identity that had been primed. Participants who defined themselves in terms of their gender identity appeared to be especially worried by illnesses and injuries that threatened physical attractiveness (e.g., facial scar, a broken nose). On the other hand, those who saw themselves in terms of their professional identity (secretaries) emphasized the seriousness of illnesses and injuries that had negative implications for their work (e.g., painful hands, high fever).

## SOCIAL IDENTITY AND HEALTH BEHAVIOUR

In her opening to the 2002 World Health Report, the then director-general of the World Health Organization, Gro Harlem Brundtland, stated that 'too many of us are living dangerously – whether we are aware of that or not' (Brundtland, 2002, p. 3). This report intensified debate and research into health behaviour – broadly defined as behaviour that is somehow associated with one's health status, irrespective of current health or motivations (Morrison & Bennett, 2006). Why do people engage in risky behaviours, and how can we promote healthier behaviours?

The theory of reasoned action (TRA; Fishbein, 1979) and its extension, the theory of planned behaviour (TPB; Ajzen, 1985; Ajzen & Madden, 1986), have produced an ample volume of research on these themes (see Chapter 5 for a detailed description of these theories). Both theories assume that actual health behaviour is predicted by behavioural intention, which in turn is predicted by attitude toward the behaviour and by subjective norms. TPB also postulates the existence of a third predictor of behavioural intention: perceived behavioural control. In general, these theories are well supported by evidence. However, some studies have failed to produce convincing support for the role of subjective norms. For instance, Hunter, Gruenfeld and Ramirez (2003) found that subjective norms were not predictive of women's intention to see a doctor in relation to breast cancer symptoms. Social identity researchers argue that, rather than on subjective norms, we should focus on social identity-based norms. Consistent with that, Terry and Hogg (1996) found that, as long as a given health behaviour is relevant to an ingroup and that one has a relative level of identification with such ingroup, the ingroup norms will predict behavioural intentions. Specifically, these researchers found that identification with the group of 'friends and peers at university' positively influenced intentions to engage in regular exercise and in sun-protective behaviour among those who identified strongly with the group, as these behaviours were seen as normative of the group.

Similar results have emerged from other studies. Stewart-Knox et al. (2005) conducted a 3-year longitudinal interview study to investigate the reasons for taking up smoking among pre-adolescents from various economically deprived areas in Northern Ireland. Analysis of data revealed that the peer group influenced smoking uptake, but that this did not normally happen through direct persuasion, but rather because of children striving to conform to the normative behaviour of the peer group with which they identified. In a study involving a large sample of Danes aged 16–24 years, Verkooijen, de Vries and Nielsen (2007) found that risks of substance use were higher for participants who identified with pop, skate/hip-hop, techno and hippie groups than for participants who identified with sporty, quiet and religious groups. These effects were found to be positively mediated by the degree to which participants saw substance use as normative of the group. A study involving university students in the UK, for whom heavy drinking is normative, revealed that greater identification with the group of UK university students was associated with stronger drinking intentions (Livingstone et al., 2011).

The fact that different social contexts may prompt the salience of different social identities implies that one's normative attitudes toward health behaviour may shift across contexts. In other words, attitudes towards health behaviour may vary in accordance with the different social identities forming the basis for self-definition from situation to situation (Tarrant et al., 2012). Consistent with this principle, Tarrant and Butler (2011) found that university students expressed much lower intentions to engage in health-promoting behaviour when their student identity was made salient than when their national identity was emphasized.

Intriguingly, in some circumstances group identification and the consequent compliance with group norms may have positive implications not only for ingroup members but also for people coming into contact with them. In a study involving a sample of Swiss nurses, Falomir-Pichastor, Toscani, and Huyghues Despointes (2009) found that higher identification with the professional group of nurses was linked to higher likelihood to have received flu vaccination, a behaviour prescribed by the nurses' group norms. Because the vaccination of healthcare workers appears to be effective in reducing morbidity and mortality in residential care settings and long-term care hospitals (Carman et al., 2000), we can infer that the extent to which nurses identify with their professional group may have very important implications for patients' health.

## SOCIAL IDENTITY, POSITIVE PHYSIOLOGICAL PROCESSES AND HEALTH

Group identification has been found to promote positive physiological outcomes. Platow and his colleagues (2007) found that people undertaking a physically painful activity (i.e., immersing a hand into a bath of ice water) not only reported feeling less pain, but also had lower levels of physiological stress when they received support from an ingroup (i.e., a member of the same faculty) than when support was received from a member of an outgroup (i.e., a member of another faculty). Reicher and Haslam (2006) conducted a study where participants played the role of either prisoners or guards within a purpose-built environment. It was found that prisoners teamed up to challenge the guards, which increased group identification. In turn, this led to lower physiological stress (measured through levels of cortisol in saliva). On the contrary, because they felt uncomfortable with the exercise of power, guards failed to identify with their group. This produced increased levels of physiological stress (see Chapter 13 for a more detailed discussion of this study). Wegge, Schuh and van Dick (2012) conducted an experiment involving call centre agents, in which it was found that organizational identification functioned as a buffer against physiological stress – measured by assessing immunoglobulin A (IgA) concentration in participants' saliva – caused by unfriendly customers.

In line with the fact that group identification facilitates positive physiological processes, group identification has also been found to have positive effects on various dimensions of both physical and mental health. Shruti Tewari and her colleagues (2012) studied pilgrims' participation in a month-long Hindu religious festival. They found that, in spite of enduring hardship due to very low temperature, unsanitary conditions, severe cold and very high levels of noise, pilgrims' health and well-being increased during the festival. As the researchers explain, following their religious beliefs and enacting religious rituals allowed the pilgrims to affirm their social identity, which in turn benefited health. More specifically concerning mental health, a study of people with multiple sclerosis attending support groups revealed that patients who identified strongly with the support group had markedly lower levels of depression than patients who had lower identification with the support group (Wakefield et al., 2013). Latrofa, Vaes, Pastore and Cadinu (2009) studied a sample of Southern Italians, a group who suffers from a historical social stigma within Italy. Knowledge that they were the target of prejudice had a negative impact on the psychological well-being of participants in this study. However, increased identification with the group of Southern Italians had a positive impact on psychological well-being, thereby compensating for the detrimental effects of perceived prejudice.

A long duration mass gathering, such as the Indian pilgrimage event known as the Magh Mela, may attract millions of people. In spite of exposure to various health risks, as the event unfolds participants report improved levels of well-being, resulting from enactment of a valued social identity. (Tewari et al., 2012).

SOURCE: © Steve Reicher

Importantly, researchers have demonstrated that the positive impact of social identification on health is, at least in part, mediated by social support. In a study of theatre production teams during a production Haslam, Jetten and Waghorn (2009) found that higher team identification at the outset predicted lower likelihood to experience burnout during the most demanding phases of a production (i.e., dress rehearsal and performance), primarily because team identification facilitated reciprocal social support among team members. The interplay between social identity, mutual support and well-being has also been investigated by researchers of crowd behaviour in mass emergencies. John Drury (2012) argues that the experience of common threat that characterizes mass emergencies and disasters leads to a temporary breakdown in social class, ethnic group, and other hierarchical status distinctions among survivors, which in turn creates a sense of 'we-ness', a shared social identity. This enhances reciprocal helping, routine civility, and expectations of support, which in turn have positive consequences for well-being.

## THE DEVELOPMENT OF SOCIAL CATEGORIZATION AND SOCIAL IDENTITY

The tendency to structure the social world in terms of social categories, and to identify with certain categories, which is typical of adults, is not something people are born with. Developmental social psychologists have investigated which social categories are of paramount importance to children, when self-categorization emerges, and some central social identity processes (Barrett, 2007; Bennett & Sani, 2004, 2008).

### SOCIAL CATEGORIZATION IN CHILDREN

Developmental and social psychologists have assumed that gender and ethnicity are the two most important and psychologically consequential categories among

children. The ability to structure the social world in terms of gender and in terms of racial and ethnic categories emerges in early childhood (see Ruble et al., 2004, for an excellent review). Concerning gender, studies have revealed that many children start labelling the sexes shortly after their second birthdays, and that by 3 years of age all children can use gender as a criterion to sort photographs (Leinbach & Fagot, 1993). The ability to label people in accordance with their ethnicity emerges a bit later, after 3 years of age (Katz & Kofkin, 1997). However, awareness of ethnic categories develops rapidly after 4 years of age (Aboud & Amato, 2001).

By a very early age, children are able to categorize people in accordance with their ethnicity.

SOURCE: © ktaylorg/iStock

The features of category members upon which children appear to focus, change across the years (Sani et al., 2000). Prior to the age of 7–8 years, children seem to pay attention mainly to overt physical features and other external characteristics (skin colour, clothing, hairstyle), as well as traits and dispositions (nice, nasty). It is only later, at around 10 years of age, that children start conceiving of category members in terms of their shared beliefs and values.

### THE BEGINNINGS OF SELF-CATEGORIZATION

The development of self-categorization goes in parallel with that of social categorization. As children become able to order the environment in terms of relevant social categories, they also become able to assign the self to one category. In the second year of life children can allocate a picture of themselves to a set of pictures of other same-sex children (Ruble & Martin, 1998). With regard to race and ethnicity, Phyllis Katz and Jennifer Kofkin (1997) found that by 3 years of age, more than two-thirds of Euro-American children could attach ethnic labels to the self, but that only one-third of African-American children could do so. These findings show that the emergence of ethnic self-categorization may depend, in part at least, on the comparative value that society attaches to different ethnic groups. Children from disadvantaged and low-status groups find race self-labelling more problematic than children from higher-status groups.

What are the factors that facilitate the emergence of social categorization and self-categorization? According to Diane Ruble and her colleagues (Ruble et al., 2004) both cognitive and social factors are at play. From a cognitive point of view, the ability to see and partition the world in terms of social categories and the ability to categorize the self as a member of specific categories depends very much on children's appreciation of category constancy (Ruble et al., 2004). Children must be able to understand that certain social categories, such as gender and race, may have fixed properties, and that their members cannot switch from one category to another. As far as the role of society is concerned, it is obvious that which categories are known first and when depends largely on the cultural and societal background. For instance, in a very homogeneous cultural group, children may form an idea of ethnic categories later than in a multi-ethnic cultural group or a group characterized by inter-ethnic tension.

## FROM SELF-CATEGORIZATION TO SOCIAL IDENTITY

When does mere self-labelling ('I am French', 'I am a girl') turn into social identity? When does a child begin giving importance to being a member of a group rather than another? Quintana (1998) suggests that it is only at about 10 years of age that children start appreciating the relevance of social categories for society and for the self. At this age, self-categories become meaningful, central aspects of the self-concept, and a clear sense of being part of a group, a sense of 'we', accompanied by a clear sense of the value attached to the group, emerges.

However, other researchers contend that younger children may be more sophisticated than we imagine. In a year-long field study based on observation and interviews with children attending a multi-ethnic, inner-city primary school in England, Connolly (1998) found that children as young as 5 are perfectly capable of discussing and negotiating their gender, race and other group identities, in a fairly sophisticated fashion. In line with this, Diane Ruble and her colleagues (2004) suggest that incorporation of social category memberships into the self-concept may gradually take place during the school years, as this is the period when 'children's sense of self become more complex as they are exposed to a new social environment outside the family' (p. 34).

Fabio Sani and Mark Bennett (2009) have used an experimental approach to address the issue of the genesis of group identification in children aged 5 to 11. Following the self-categorization theory, they conceive group identification as the ability to perceive the self in terms of the stereotypes attached to the self-category. Consistent with such conceptualization of group identification, Sani and Bennett presented children with sets of cards identifying particular trait adjectives (e.g. nice, friendly, shy, loud) and asked them to rate the extent to which the traits applied to the self, the ingroup and the outgroup. After a distraction task, children were asked to remember for whom (self, ingroup or outgroup) each trait had been rated. Results showed that traits rated for the self were confused more frequently with traits rated for the ingroup than with traits rated for the outgroup. This was the case for all children, including the 5 year olds, and for all the ingroups that were considered, that is, the gender, age and family ingroup. Therefore, this study revealed that, at least from the age of 5 years, psychologically relevant ingroups become integral parts of children's self-system.

### SOCIAL IDENTITY AND DEROGATION OF INGROUP DEVIANTS

Recognizing that group norms deviance constitutes a departure from group norms, and that, therefore, deviant members may threaten social identity and its distinctiveness, is an important step into children's developing sense of 'we'. Dominic Abrams et al. (2003) argue that an understanding of the implications of atypicality and the importance of group loyalty imply a fairly sophisticated way of thinking, and therefore they appear later than group identification and group preference. Once children start appreciating the implications of group deviance, they engage in evaluative intra-group differentiation. That is, they compare ingroup members with one another and judge them on the basis of their adherence to the group norms. At this point, in line with the black sheep effect, children will dislike anti-normative ingroup members more than anti-normative outgroup members.

In a study involving children aged 6 and 11, Dominic Abrams et al. (2003) collected data confirming their prediction. Children who were participating in a summer school were presented with statements ostensibly made by other children – who were either attending the same summer school (ingroup members) or a different one (outgroup members) – concerning the comparative quality of the two summer schools. The 'typical' summer school attendants declared that their own summer school was better than the other (normative position), while 'deviants' stated that the two summer schools were equally enjoyable (anti-normative position). Results revealed that all children liked typical ingroup members more than typical outgroup members. However, in addition to this, the older children disliked ingroup deviants more than outgroup deviants.

## focus on

### THE GROUP IN THE MIND

Social psychologists studying group behaviour before the advent of the social identity approach tended to conceive a social group as a collection of individuals interacting and relating to one another merely in terms of their individual identities and characteristics. For instance, specifically concerning the nature of group cohesion, Lott and Lott (1961) argued that this emerges when interaction between different people allows achievement of goals or is rewarding in some other way. It did not occur to these researchers that – as contended by a social identity approach – group cohesion may actually result from an active effort to achieve unity made by people who have a sense of sharing the same group membership and identification.

The social identity approach to group processes started as a rebellion against the individualistic approach to group behaviour. According to a social identity perspective, people do not understand the social world merely as a collection of individuals interacting with one another *as individuals*. On the contrary, people see the social world as made of human aggregates standing in power and status relationships with one another, and see the self as being included in some of these categories and excluded from others. This, as we have seen in this chapter, has important consequences for our social conduct. To the extent that others are seen as members of an ingroup, we are more prone to be influenced by them, more willing to help them, and particularly flattered and pleased when they show admiration and respect towards us. Also, individuals who, despite their nominal membership in an ingroup, appear to deviate from the group norms, are especially disliked and derogated. In addition, identification with specific groups may affect our health in various ways. Last but not least, seeing others as members of an outgroup creates the preconditions for prejudice, bias, confrontation and aggression (as you will see in the next chapter).

The fact that *the group is in the mind*, is not important only for an understanding of how people relate to fellow ingroup members and to members of relevant outgroups. It is also crucial for making sense of social change. It is because people form representations of the social structure and their own place within it that they are able to conceive different structures and act upon the world in order to change the way things are. Had South African black people been unable to represent their social environment in terms of a hegemonic white group and an oppressed black group, they would have never conceived a different reality nor fought for the achievement of such alternative reality. Therefore, a social psychology that did not focus on people's representation of social reality in terms of ingroup and outgroup would be incapable of explaining the social psychological side of the radical changes that occurred in racial relations in South Africa over the last two decades.

In summary, individuals live in groups, but the groups are, in turn, in the mind of individuals. As John Turner and Penelope Oakes (1997) put it, *the mind is socially structured*; it has evolved to understand the world in terms of group relations, and to act upon the world in order to either maintain or change the nature of these relations. Appreciating this crucial assumption is a precondition for a full understanding of how people relate to one another.

## QUESTIONS

**1** Think about a social group (family, friends, sport team, etc.) to which you are strongly attached. Would you say that you relate to each single group member as an individual, independent from shared group membership, or that the fact of belonging to the same group adds a special flavour to the relationship with each group member?

**2** Can you think of any example from either past or contemporary history where awareness of sharing membership in a social group has led to important socio-political transformations?

## SUMMING UP: SOCIAL CATEGORIZATION AND SOCIAL IDENTITY

### A CATEGORIZED SOCIAL WORLD

☐ Social categories may be more or less inclusive. For instance, the social category 'European' is more inclusive than 'Italian', which in turn is more inclusive than 'Tuscan'.

☐ People are assigned to social categories on the basis of their resemblance to (1) the category prototype (an abstract idea representing the essence of the category), and (2) some category exemplar (a category member that one has encountered).

☐ The similarities among members of a social category are exaggerated in order to mark out differences between groups. This cognitive phenomenon is known as the 'accentuation effect'.

☐ The accentuation effect is the basis of stereotype formation. A stereotype is a generalization about a social group, in that similar characteristics are attributed to virtually all group members.

- [ ] The social categories that are used to make sense of a given situation are those that best 'fit' the situation and that are more 'accessible' to the perceiver.

- [ ] Social categories are flexible mental tools. The level of inclusiveness, the nature of prototype and exemplars, and the stereotypical content of a social category vary from situation to situation.

- [ ] The cognitive principles that characterize social categories also apply to self-categories, that is social categories to which one assigns oneself. This also implies that self-categories are contextually fluid, like any other social category.

- [ ] Social categories become self-categories either because we are socialized into them from birth, or from a very early stage in life (this is the case, for instance, with gender and ethnic categories), or because we intentionally join them at some point in life (this is, for instance, the case with social clubs and political parties).

## SOCIAL IDENTITY

- [ ] Social identity has important implications for social influence, in that (1) conformity to a majority is more likely when the majority is seen as sharing the same social identity with the target of influence, and (2) conversion to a minority is facilitated when the minority is seen as sharing the same social identity with the target of influence. Sources perceived as ingroup are more influential because they are seen as reliable and competent, and because people expect to agree with similar others.

- [ ] The group leader is expected to be as close as possible to the group prototype. At the same time, a leader that meets this requirement will exert a strong influence on group members and will therefore be able to define and shape the group identity. Group members wanting to be leaders will devise strategies to present themselves as group prototypes, and actual leaders will devise strategies to persuade followers about the necessity of given actions. Aspirant leaders and actual leaders can therefore be seen as 'entrepreneurs of identity'.

- [ ] People like to feel valued and respected, but their desire is not unconditional. Individuals seek respect from ingroup members, but tend to remain indifferent to, or even be annoyed and embarrassed by, respect coming from an outgroup source, because this may disconfirm and weaken their desire to incarnate ingroup values and norms, and to be different from the outgroup.

- [ ] People are more inclined to help others when they are categorized as ingroup, rather than outgroup. On occasion people may be particularly helpful to outgroup members in order to enhance the image of the ingroup.

## GROUP IDENTITY NORMS, DEVIANCE AND SCHISM

- [ ] Ingroup deviants are disliked and derogated more than outgroup members, because they threaten group unity and social identity. Sanctioning deviants is an opportunity for the majority to emphasize what is normative and what is counter-normative.

- [ ] Peripheral group members fear rejection and, as a consequence, employ strategies to increase their felt and perceived prototypicality. In particular, they may (1) increase conformity to ingroup standards, (2) vigorously derogate non-prototypical members and praise prototypical ones, and (3) publicly derogate outgroup members.

- [ ] The content of the group identity, as well as the degree of prototypicality of group members, is often debated and contested within a group. In some circumstances a minority may believe that the group as a whole has adopted norms that deny the group identity, and may not recognize the group leaders as truly prototypical. This may cause a schism, as the minority members may leave the group in order to join either a breakaway group or an already existing group.

## SOCIAL IDENTITY MOTIVES

☐ There are several motives that lead people to identify with social groups. One is a motive for individual and collective self-esteem. Valuing our group positively is a source of self-esteem.

☐ Social identity marks out the differences between 'us' and 'them', between ingroup and outgroup. This enhances the feeling of distinctiveness.

☐ The need to belong is widely considered as a necessity and characteristic of *Homo sapiens*. Social identity provides a source of affiliation and inclusion, thereby satisfying the need for belonging.

☐ Death is probably the major psychological threat in human experience. As a consequence, humans strive to achieve symbolic immortality. A way to achieve symbolic immortality is through social identity, because groups – especially kin, national and ethnic ones – tend to be perceived as longlasting and quasi-eternal entities.

☐ Groups prescribe people who they are and how they should behave. Groups also provide consensual validation for people's perceptions and beliefs. As such, they contribute to reduce uncertainty about self and social reality.

## SOCIAL IDENTITY AND HEALTH

☐ As well as affecting our social behaviour and thoughts, social identity may impact upon our mental and physical health.

☐ Social identity determines how severe a symptom is perceived to be. For instance, identifying with the group of 'older people' may increase one's sense of having hearing problems. Social identity may also influence the perceived seriousness of a symptom. A broken nose may raise greater worries among women identified with their gender group than among women identified with their professional group.

☐ Whether people engage or not in healthy behaviour will largely depend on group norms. If a given health behaviour is relevant to the norms of an ingroup (e.g., abstinence from drinking alcohol as a rule for members of a religious group), members of such ingroup are likely to comply with the behaviour. Compliance will be greater among members with strong levels of group identification.

☐ Group identification implies that social support received from a member of an ingroup is perceived as more genuine and disinterested, and produces more positive physiological outcomes, than support offered by a member of an outgroup. As a consequence, group identification may pave the way toward better mental and physical health.

## THE DEVELOPMENT OF SOCIAL CATEGORIZATION AND SOCIAL IDENTITY

☐ To date, research has shown that children can label people in terms of their gender by the age of 3, and in terms of their ethnic group by the age of 4. Also, the criteria for the assignment of individuals to social categories appears to change across development. Younger children focus exclusively on physical and other external characteristics, while older children are able to point to belief systems as well.

☐ The development of self-categorization goes in parallel with that of social categorization. However, ethnic self-categorization may appear later in children from minority groups than in children from majority groups. The emergence of self-categorization is based on both cognitive factors (e.g. the appreciation that social categories may be immutable) and social factors (e.g. ingroup status, relevance of a given category-system in society).

☐ The ability to identify with a social category, understood as stereotyping the self in terms of the group norms, probably emerges before the age of 5. From the age of 5 children also show an ability to discuss and negotiate gender, race and other identities. However, it is probably not until 10 years of age that children fully appreciate the deep meaning and the wider social implications of their social identities.

☐ Very soon after the beginnings of self-categorization and the first manifestations of social identification, children become sensitive to issues of group typicality and deviance. At approximately 8 years of age children already tend to derogate ingroup counter-normative behaviour, as a means to protect ingroup distinctiveness and identity.

## CRITICAL QUESTIONS

**1** Do you agree that in some circumstances we behave in terms of the norms of a relevant ingroup? Can you think of any example from your own experience?

**2** How important is it, in your opinion, that a wanting-to-be group leader present him/herself as a prototypical representative of the group?

**3** Why do mainstream group members see group deviants as a threat?

**4** Why is the 'accentuation effect' so important?

**5** Is any of the social identity motives discussed in this chapter more important than the others?

## RECOMMENDED READINGS

### Classic Studies

Tajfel, H. (1981). *Human Groups and Social Categories: Studies in Social Psychology*. Cambridge: Cambridge University Press.

*An extremely influential book where the development, core assumptions and applications of social identity theory are discussed in detail.*

Turner, J. C., Hogg, M. A., Oakes, P. J., Reicher, S. D., & Wetherell, M. S. (1987). *Rediscovering the Social Group: A Self-categorization Theory*. Oxford: Basil Blackwell.

*The first systematic exposition of self-categorization theory (the component of the social identity approach that is more strongly devoted to processes within groups) and its applications.*

### Contemporary Studies

Ellemers, N. (2012). The group self. *Science, 336*, 848–852.

*A short but very clear, thorough and updated review of the literature on group identity.*

Haslam, S. A. (2004). *Psychology in Organizations: The Social Identity Approach* (2nd edn). London: Sage.

*An excellent source about applications of the social identity approach to a range of organizational issues and processes.*

Haslam, S. A., O'Brien, A., Jetten, J., Vormedal, K., & Penna, S. (2005). Taking the strain: Social identity, social support, and the experience of stress. *British Journal of Social Psychology, 44*, 355–370.

*An influential paper demonstrating that shared group identification may reduce stress via the provision of social support.*

Leach, C. W., van Zomeren, M., Zebel, S., Vliek, M. L. W., Pennekamp, S. F., Doosje, B., & Spears, R. (2008). Group-level self-definition and self-investment: A hierarchical (multicomponent) model of in-group identification. *Journal of Personality & Social Psychology, **95**, 144–165.

*A very interesting paper about how the notion of group identification should be conceptualized and measured.*

**13**

"Why is it that people prefer to be addressed in groups, rather than individually?"

Soren Kierkegaard

# PREJUDICE, INTERGROUP RELATIONS AND CONFLICT

Following the annual Apprentice Boys' march in August 1969 a three-day riot broke out in Derry between both sides of the city's sectarian divide. The rioting spread to many areas across Northern Ireland where the escalating violence caused serious injury and deaths. Tensions between Catholic nationalists and Protestant loyalists continued until the peace process began in 1998 and an end to the Troubles was reached in 2007. In May 1985, the Heysel Stadium disaster saw 39 Juventus football fans crushed to death when a fence separating them from the Liverpool fans collapsed during a football game after fighting broke out between the rival club supporters. All English football clubs were banned from all European competitions for five years. In Oldham, a small town in the north-west of England, some of the worst racially motivated riots seen in recent times occurred between 26 and 28 May 2001. In a town with an Asian population of 11 per cent, underlying interracial tensions between Whites and Asian-Muslims in the area exploded into riots. This sparked race riots in other northern areas of England. In May 2008, newspapers reported attacks on Mozambique citizens in South Africa, which had caused them to flee the country.

**prejudice** *a preconceived negative judgement of a group and its individual members*

In our examples above, something they have in common is collective feelings of prejudice. Prejudice towards people of a different race or ethnicity. Prejudice towards people of a different religion. Prejudice towards people who support a different football team. Is what we're witnessing, then, simply a collection of highly prejudiced individuals who come together with malicious intent, or is there something about the relations between groups that shapes our behaviour in particular ways?

**intergroup relations** *when two or more groups interact*

The above are also examples of very negative intergroup relations. Intergroup relations are when two or more distinct groups interact. But of course relations between groups do not always involve violence and injury. We experience intergroup relations in our everyday lives. They include such things as political negotiations between parties, management and union talks, employer and employee relations, competitions between sports teams, international agreements between nations, and so on.

Social psychologists have a long-standing interest in intergroup relations as they affect our behaviour in profound ways. People often behave very differently when they're in a group than they would do on their own. You have probably experienced behaving differently when you're in an intergroup situation (e.g. a student protest) than you would do alone. So there seems to be something about intergroup relations that changes what we do and who we are. This chapter aims to explore the relationship between individuals, groups and prejudice, and explores social psychological suggestions for resolving intergroup conflict.

## UNDERSTANDING PREJUDICE

*Prejudice is one of the major topics of interest in social psychology. Key questions include: how do we define prejudice? When do intergroup relations and conflict result in acts of prejudice? Do some people have prejudiced personalities? Is it possible for people to be implicitly prejudiced? What social conditions foster prejudice? Is prejudice inevitable or can it be reduced? These are challenges social psychologists try to meet in understanding the causes of prejudice.*

## WHAT IS PREJUDICE?

To be prejudiced towards someone is to 'prejudge' them. Prejudice is an *attitude* about a group, or a member of a group based on their membership of it. In Chapter 5 on Attitudes and Behaviours we considered how an attitude is a distinct combination of feelings, inclinations to act, and beliefs. It can be easily remembered as the ABCs of attitudes: *a*ffect (feelings), *b*ehaviour tendency (inclination to act) and *c*ognition (beliefs). A prejudiced person may *dislike* those different from self and *behave* in a discriminatory manner, *believing* them ignorant and dangerous. Like many attitudes, prejudice is complex. For example, it may include a component of patronizing affection that serves to keep the victim disadvantaged.

Within social psychology the study of prejudice really came into being in the 1920s when the focus was on 'race' and 'racism'. In his classic book *The Nature of Prejudice*, Gordon Allport (1954) offered a famous definition of ethnic prejudice when he suggested it 'is ill thinking of others without sufficient warrant' (p. 6) and 'is an antipathy based on a faulty and inflexible generalization' (p. 9). Other groups face profound prejudice and discrimination too. When seeking love and employment, overweight people face slim prospects in modern Western societies. In correlational studies conducted in the West, overweight people marry less often, gain entry into less desirable jobs and make less money. In experiments where some people are made to appear overweight, they are perceived as less attractive, intelligent, happy, self-disciplined and successful (Gortmaker et al., 1993; Hebl & Heatherton, 1998; Pingitore et al., 1994). Weight discrimination seems to occur at every employment stage in Western and developed societies – hiring, placement, promotion, compensations, discipline and redundancy (Roehling, 2000).

Each of the situations just described involved a negative evaluation of some group. And that is the essence of prejudice: a preconceived negative judgement of a group and its individual members.

Let's distinguish prejudice from discrimination. While *prejudice* is a negative *attitude*, discrimination is negative *behaviour*. Discriminatory behaviour often has its source in prejudicial attitudes (Dovidio et al., 1996). As Chapter 5 emphasized, however, attitudes and behaviour are often loosely linked. Prejudiced attitudes need not breed hostile acts, nor does all oppression spring from prejudice. Racism and sexism are institutional practices that discriminate, sometimes even when there is no prejudicial intent. If word-of-mouth hiring practices in an all-White business have the effect of excluding potential non-White employees, the practice could be called racist – even if an employer intended no discrimination.

Prejudice pervades all areas of social life, but some people seem to express prejudice towards certain groups regardless of the situation. Their acts of prejudice are severe. Do some people have prejudiced personalities?

## THE PREJUDICED PERSONALITY

After the events of the Second World War social psychologists began to ask some searching questions about the nature of prejudice and 'who' was likely to be prejudiced. The kinds of questions asked were:

☐ Why are some people drawn to fascist ideologies and practices (and others are not)?

**discrimination**
*unjustified negative behaviour towards a group or its members*

**racism** *(1) an individual's prejudicial attitudes and discriminatory behaviour towards people of a given race, or (2) institutional practices (even if not motivated by prejudice) that subordinate people of a given race*

**sexism** *(1) an individual's prejudicial attitudes and discriminatory behaviour towards people of a given sex, or (2) institutional practices (even if not motivated by prejudice) that subordinate people of a given sex*

525

☐ Why are some people extremely prejudiced and racist?

☐ Why do some people obey and participate in unspeakable acts of racism and prejudice?

In the 1940s University of California, Berkeley, researchers – two of whom had fled Nazi Germany – set out on an urgent research mission: to uncover the psychological roots of anti-Semitism so poisonous that it caused the slaughter of millions of Jews and turned many millions of Europeans into indifferent spectators. Else Frenkel-Brunswik, Daniel Levinson and Nevitt Sanford were psychologists involved in personality research from a Freudian perspective. Theodor Adorno provided a political and sociological perspective to their most famous book, *The Authoritarian Personality* from 1950 (abridged version reprinted 1982). Although his name heads the alphabetical list of authors, Adorno made a relatively small contribution. His name is credited in only 5 of the 23 chapters in the book.

The Berkeley researchers discovered that hostility towards Jews often coexisted with hostility towards other minorities. In those who were strongly prejudiced, prejudice appeared to be not specific to one group but an entire way of thinking about those who are 'different'. Moreover, these judgemental, ethnocentric people shared certain tendencies: an intolerance for weakness, a punitive attitude and a submissive respect for their ingroup's authorities, as reflected in their agreement with such statements as 'Obedience and respect for authority are the most important virtues children should learn'. From those findings, Adorno and his colleagues (1950) theorized an authoritarian personality that is particularly prone to engage in prejudice and stereotyping.

ethnocentric *believing in the superiority of one's own ethnic and cultural group, and having a corresponding disdain for all other groups*

authoritarian personality *a personality that is disposed to favour obedience to authority and intolerance for outgroups and those of lower status*

They did not regard the cause of prejudice as a consequence of social conditions (e.g. conforming to a particular ideology), but instead argued that it was rooted within the individual's personality. A particular personality type was predisposed to prejudice. The authoritarian personality was characterized by the possession of particular traits including:

☐ high levels of prejudice towards minority groups

☐ the holding of positive sentiments about authority, and being submissive to those considered to be in authority to oneself

☐ very harsh behaviour towards those considered inferior to oneself

☐ a strong belief in power, dominance and discipline

☐ an obsession with rank and status

☐ an inability to tolerate ambiguity or uncertainty, and the need for a rigidly defined world

☐ have problems achieving intimacy, yet may have a preoccupation with sex

☐ tend to displace anger and resentment onto weaker others

☐ a high level of superstitious belief.

The original authoritarian personality research was based on what the authors hoped was as diverse a sample as possible of 2000 adult White Californians. They were all given questionnaires that measured their attitudes towards prejudice, anti-Semitism, ethnocentrism (racism), political preferences, economic conservatism and fascism. This became known as the F-Scale measuring anti-democratic personality. The hypothesis was that these factors on the questionnaire would correlate highly for those people who have a prejudiced personality. Or, in other words, people who are highly prejudiced are also politically right-wing or 'conventionalists' and highly authoritarian. The F-Scale contains 77 items in total. Here are a few examples.

- ☐ If people would talk less and work more, everybody would be better off.

- ☐ Some day it will probably be shown that astrology can explain a lot of things.

- ☐ Sex crimes, such as rape and attacks on children, deserve more than mere imprisonment; such criminals ought to be publicly whipped, or worse.

- ☐ Homosexuals are hardly better than criminals and ought to be severely punished.

- ☐ No insult to our honour should ever go unpunished.

- ☐ No matter how they act on the surface, men are interested in women for only one reason.

- ☐ Nobody ever learned anything really important except through suffering (taken from Adorno et al., 1982, pp. 184–186).

Adorno and his colleagues argued that people who agreed with the above items were displaying an authoritarian personality. But how did it arise?

To find out, they conducted clinical interviews with some of the participants to gain more factual material on their responses from the questionnaire, but also to allow freedom to express what they felt about their own situation and their relationships with other people. The schedule for these interviews included questions on their childhood, sex, politics, education and social relationships. One of the most cited findings of these interviews and questionnaires is consistently reported experiences of being dominated by excessively stern disciplinarian parents. Adopting a psychoanalytic stance, Adorno and his colleagues argued that while the child must repress his/her hostility towards their overpowering parents, they project it onto perceivably weaker others. The researchers proposed that these 'others' were typically ethnic minority groups often marginalized within society. These groups were perceived as dangerous elements within the world, which needed to be disciplined and controlled. An authoritarian personality seemed to be the result of this strict upbringing.

Although you might think recollections of childhood experiences with strict parents might be characterized by feelings of hatred, when individuals were interviewed about their upbringing they could offer glorified accounts of their parents; however, these tended to be based on their physical appearance rather than their personalities. Other patterns were apparent too. Highly prejudiced women gave stories of being victimized by their parents, being unjustly punished and picked on. Highly prejudiced men tended to display the highest levels of submission to parental authority and often magnified the status of their family.

Sigmund Freud's (1856–1939) work on psychoanalysis influenced Adorno's understanding of the nature of prejudice.

SOURCE: © Akademie/Alamy

Since this original study some distinct problems have been found with the F-Scale. The scale item wording is quite leading and it is scored in such a way that people's tendency to agree on items would produce artificial

**In what way are any or all of the following concepts interrelated?**

Buddhism, Capitalism, Catholicism, Christianity, Communism, Democracy, Fascism, Judaism, Protestantism, Socialism

**FIGURE 13.1** An example of one of the tests Rokeach devised to illustrate the relationship between cognitive style and prejudice. He suggested that a flexible thinker would notice that all the concepts are related as they define a set of beliefs or worldviews. A more rigid thinker might group the religions separately from the political beliefs.

correlations. Some social psychologists have raised the point that if researchers know what the experimental hypotheses are when they set out to do the research, they may well interpret the data in a way that supports them. In other words, they find what they set out to find. Also, as the authors themselves admit, while the sample is representative of 'non-Jewish, white, native-born, middle-class Americans' (Adorno et al., 1982, p. 23), it is difficult to generalize beyond that. In addition, how accurate are adults' recollections of their childhood?

Milton Rokeach (1960) agreed with the concept of a prejudiced personality, but wondered if it was more to do with a particular rigid style of thinking. Dogmatic and closed-minded thinking meant that such people were resistant to change their beliefs even in the light of new information. See Figure 13.1 for an example of one of Rokeach's tests for dogmatic and closed-minded thinking.

Despite these misgivings about the F-Scale many subsequent studies have shown that people who do have authoritarian sentiments also tend to have other things in common such as right-wing political ideas, idealization of parents, strong beliefs in strict parenting and a submissive acceptance of authority. The F-Scale has been subject to revisions in recent years and continues to be used in social psychology to measure levels of authoritarianism.

One major problem with these personality explanations of prejudice is that they tend to under-emphasize situational and cultural influences. The environment in which people live shapes their attitudes and behaviour and, as research has found, their prejudices.

> Groups tend to enhance the pre-existing tendencies of members. See more extensive treatment of group polarization in Chapter 11, with specific reference to its impact in and on groups.

For example, Siegel and Siegel (1957) conducted a field experiment on two groups of American students. While one group lived in housing that was positioned in a 'conservative' area, others resided in housing that was in an area characterized by more liberal attitudes. Levels of authoritarianism were recorded over 12 months using the F-Scale. Increases in levels of authoritarianism were observed in the group in the conservative housing over the 12 months, whereas those in the liberal housing decreased. Alberta Siegel and Sidney Siegel (1957) argue this demonstrates the impact our surroundings have on prejudiced attitudes. But an alternative explanation for these findings, however, might be that they reflect the phenomenon of 'group polarization'.

Clearly there's more to prejudice than just parental practices, so let's turn our attention to some explanations of prejudice that examine the influence of the situation and social environment or context.

## THE SOCIAL CONTEXT OF PREJUDICE

### Social Dominance Theory

Social dominance theory (SDT) assumes that some social groups are positioned higher in society than others, and as a result have access to more power and resources, and are valued more positively than those lower down. How people respond to this social hierarchy depends on their social dominance orientation.

Studies based on SDT, in cultures where equality is the norm, predict that those high in social dominance orientation will have a preoccupation with ensuring their own social group's high status and will seek to achieve high-status professional careers. Jim Sidanius, Felicia Pratto and their colleagues (Pratto et al., 1994) argue that this desire to be on top can result in prejudiced attitudes and behaviour as people at the top seek to maintain an unequal status quo, supporting practices that maintain the current ideological climate that keeps them there.

*social dominance orientation a motivation to have one's group dominate other social groups*

In some cultures, for instance East Asia, social hierarchies have a long tradition and are more accepted than in the West. Everybody has their place on the ladder, and it is regarded as natural that some people are leaders, holding dominant positions and obeyed by those occupying lower rungs of the ladder. Geert Hofstede (1980) characterized such societies as those with a large power distance. In most European societies and the USA, the power distance is much lower and the goal is for equal rights among its citizens.

Particularly striking are people high in social dominance orientation and authoritarian personality. For example, Christopher Stones (2006) found that anti-gay prejudice was predicted in men high in right-wing authoritarianism and social-dominance orientation. Jason Carter and colleagues (2006) observed that people who held authoritarian attitudes and were high in social dominance were much more likely to rely on stereotypical information about other social and cultural groups.

Although right-wing authoritarianism and social dominance seem to be important features in prejudice, identifying as belonging to a social group is also significant. For example, Angela Nickerson and Winnifred Louis (2008) reported that attitudes towards asylum seekers in Australia are predicted by right-wing authoritarianism, social dominance and social identification as Australian. Those who perceived themselves as Australian expressed much less welcoming attitudes to asylum seekers than those who self-identified as human.

### Terror Management Theory

Terror management theory (TMT) asserts that human beings are painfully aware of their own mortality, and this remains an anxiety throughout life. Human beings are the only species that know one day we will die. However, being a member of a culture serves as a buffer to such stress as it makes people feel valuable and meaningful contributors to a society, increasing their sense of positive self-esteem (also see Chapter 12 for further discussion of TMT). The work of A. Rosenblatt, Sheldon Solomon, Tom Pyszczynski and colleagues (1989) has proposed that cultures provide a sense of protection to individuals, giving them a sense of a 'just world' (recall Lerner's just world hypothesis from Chapter 4) and immortality as they contribute to a cultural community. Terror management theory claims that 'people will respond positively to those who bolster their cultural-anxiety-buffers and negatively to those who threaten their cultural-anxiety-buffers' (Rosenblatt et al., 1989, p. 682). For example, Greenberg and colleagues (1990) found that when participants' Christian religious background was made salient, they gave very positive evaluations of other Christians and negative evaluations of Jews. Perhaps this is unsurprising, but what they also found was very strong positive reactions to someone who praised their cultural worldview, and extremely negative reactions to those who opposed it. Interestingly, but perhaps not surprisingly, participants with high levels of authoritarianism were also very negative towards those whose attitudes were dissimilar to their own.

In study after study, thinking about your own mortality – by writing a short essay on dying and the emotions aroused by thinking about death – provokes enough insecurity to intensify ingroup favouritism and outgroup prejudice (Greenberg et al., 1990). One study found that, among Whites in the West, thinking about death can even promote liking for racists who argue for their group's superiority. With death on their minds, people exhibit terror management. They shield themselves from the threat of their own death by derogating those who further arouse their anxiety by challenging their worldviews. When people are already feeling vulnerable about their mortality, prejudice helps bolster a threatened belief system. Thinking about death can also, however, lead people to pursue communal feelings such as togetherness and altruism (McGregor et al., 2001).

Reminding people of their death can also affect support for important public policies. Before the 2004 US presidential election, giving people cues related to death – including asking them to recall their emotions related to the 9/11 attack or subliminally exposing them to 9/11-related pictures – increased support for President George W. Bush Jr and his anti-terrorism policies (Landau et al., 2004). In Iran, reminders of death increased college students' support for suicide attacks against the USA (Pyszczynski et al., 2006).

An Arizona State University research team argues that the nature of an outgroup threat influences perceptions of the outgroup (Cottrell & Neuberg, 2005; Maner et al., 2005). For example, when the safety of one's ingroup is threatened, people will be vigilant for signs of outgroup anger. When the researchers activated self-protection concerns (for example, by having participants view scary movie clips), they found that White people perceived greater anger in African American male and Arab faces.

Despised outgroups can also serve to strengthen the ingroup. The perception of a common enemy unites a group. School spirit is seldom so strong as when the game is with the arch-rival. The sense of comradeship among workers is often highest when they all feel a common antagonism towards management. When the need to belong is met, people become more accepting of outgroups, report Mario Mikulincer and Phillip Shaver (2001). They subliminally primed some Israeli students with words that fostered a sense of belonging (*love, support, hug*) and others with neutral words. The students then read an essay that was supposedly written by a fellow Jewish student and another by an Arab student. When primed with neutral words, the Israeli students evaluated the supposed Israeli student's essay as superior to the supposed Arab student's essay. When the participants were primed with a sense of belonging, that bias disappeared.

However, TMT tends to assume that all humans are motivated to avoid thinking about their own death. Thinking about death in this way tends to be more prevalent in independent and individualistic cultures with low population density than in interdependent and collectivistic cultures with high population density. In independent cultures each individual's focus is more on him/herself as someone unique and essential, whereas in interdependent and collectivistic cultures where people do not stand out but surrender to the group, the family, kin or

**terror management** *according to 'terror management theory', people are motivated to subdue the terror stemming from human awareness of mortality. Based on the notion that people would be restricted by the fear of their own death if they could not 'deal with this', the theory suggests that people adhere more strongly to their cultural worldviews and beliefs, and subscribe self-esteem from these, to suppress death-related thoughts*

nation, each individual accepts death to a greater extent in ensuring the survival of the group, or family. Furthermore, we cannot assume what 'cultural' values or norms an individual will identify with and conform to. For example, Donna Jessop and Jennifer Wade (2008) found that making binge and non-binge drinkers aware of the mortality risks of drinking actually increased binge-drinking in both samples! Participants drank more in order to bolster their self-esteem. They were conforming to cultural norms other than those desired by the researchers. Eva Jonas, Andy Martens, Daniela Kayser, Immo Fritsche, Daniel Sullivan and Jeff Greenberg (2008) note that cultures differ widely from one another, offering contradictory norms for behaviour. To understand how (or if) threats to mortality will influence behaviour we need to examine the cultural norms the group or individual is attending to at the time.

## Prejudice and Stereotyping

Chapter 12 discussed how stereotypes form as simplified representations of social groups. Many social psychologists have argued that these mental representations have a strong link to prejudice. The negative evaluations that mark prejudice are often supported by negative stereotypes. As we've already noted, to stereotype is to generalize. To simplify the world, we generalize: the British are reserved; Americans are outgoing; professors are absent-minded. Here are some widely shared stereotypes uncovered in recent research:

☐ During the 1980s, women who assumed the title of 'Ms' were seen as more assertive and ambitious than those who called themselves 'Miss' or 'Mrs' (Dion, 1987; Dion & Cota, 1991; Dion & Schuller, 1991). Now that 'Ms' is the standard female title, the stereotype has shifted. It's married women who keep their own surnames that are seen as assertive and ambitious (Crawford et al., 1998; Etaugh et al., 1999).

☐ Public opinion surveys reveal that Europeans have definite ideas about other Europeans. They see the Germans as relatively hard-working, the French as pleasure-loving, the British as cool and unexcitable, the Italians as amorous and the Dutch as reliable. (One expects these findings to be reliable, considering that they come from Willem Koomen and Michiel Bähler, 1996, at the University of Amsterdam.)

☐ Europeans also view southern Europeans as more emotional and less efficient than northern Europeans (Linssen & Hagendoorn, 1994). The stereotype of the southerner as more expressive even holds within countries: James Pennebaker and his colleagues (1996) report that across 20 northern hemisphere countries (but not in six southern hemisphere countries), southerners within a country are perceived as more expressive than northerners.

Familiar stereotypes:

'Heaven is a place with an American house, Chinese food, British police, a German car, and French art. Hell is a place with a Japanese house, Chinese police, British food, German art, and a French car.'
Anonymous, as reported by Yueh-Ting Lee (Bower, 1996)

Such generalizations can be more or less true (and are not always negative). Teachers' stereotypes of achievement differences in students from different gender, ethnic and class backgrounds tend to mirror reality (Madon et al.,

Basking in reflected glory. After Jamaican-Canadian sprinter Ben Johnson won the Olympic 100-metre race, Canadian media described this victory by a 'Canadian'. After Johnson's gold medal was taken away because of steroid use, Canadian media then emphasized his 'Jamaican' identity (Stelzl & Seligman, 2004).

SOURCE: © ROMEO GACAD/Stringer

1998). 'Stereotypes', note Lee Jussim, Clark McCauley and Yueh-Ting Lee (1995), 'may be positive or negative, accurate or inaccurate'. An accurate stereotype may even be desirable. We call it 'sensitivity to diversity' or 'cultural awareness in a multicultural world'. To stereotype the British as more concerned about punctuality than Mexicans is to understand what to expect and how to get along with others in each culture.

Mark Zanna (1993) suggests that prejudice arises as a consequence of holding negative stereotypes about a group, but also when we feel a group has blocked our own group's access to a valued goal or contradicts our 'norms' and 'values'; or it may be caused by having negative past experiences with members of a group, or arises as a consequence of having negative feelings towards a group. Patricia Devine (1989) argues that stereotyping is an inevitable consequence of cognition and directly linked to prejudice. She notes the example of White Americans, who have been exposed to a racist culture that denigrates African Americans. Through such conditioning white Americans hold negative stereotypes of African Americans.

Stereotyping of social groups has also been shown to affect how we 'see' them. Susan Fiske (1998) found that prejudice biases the way people perceive the facial appearance of outgroup members. In a study that examined how Moroccan faces were seen by participants in the Netherlands, she found that the negative stereotyped traits they held of Moroccans as being criminal were perceived as actually being visible in their faces.

Stereotypes do not just affect how we see outgroups but also how we perceive ourselves. Jacquie Vorauer et al. (1998; Vorauer & Sakamoto, 2008) found that White Canadians' perceptions of being negatively stereotyped by Aboriginal Canadians led to negative emotions about intergroup interaction and decreases in self-esteem. Moreover, highly prejudiced White Canadians felt stereotyped by Aboriginal Canadians even when they were not, and this affected their subsequent interactions with them.

Devine (1989) argues that only deliberate conscious acts to break the habit of prejudice will stop discrimination against this group. More specifically Bertram Gawronski, Roland Deutsch, Sawson Mbirkou, Beate Seibt and Fritz Strack (2008) have found that negative stereotypes can be inhibited if participants are given training in affirming positive counter-stereotypes of social groups. Interestingly, they found that if participants were given training in disconfirming negative stereotypes, this actually enhanced their activation.

### Social Identity Theory and Self-categorization Theory

In Chapter 12, we outlined the processes of categorization, identification with social groups, social comparison and stereotyping as fundamental features of SIT and SCT. Both theories point out that individuals are motivated to seek positive identity from their group memberships. Time after time, studies show that people promote their connection with someone who has been successful on the basis of sharing a common identity with him or her. More interesting is that this occurs when that person has had no involvement in their success. This phenomenon of basking in reflected glory (BIRG) has been most prominently investigated in relation to football fans and their association with the team they support. Filip Boen and colleagues (2002) showed that football supporters sought private contact

**basking in reflected glory (BIRG)** *to associate with a successful individual or group, despite having no direct involvement in their success*

with their team's players when the team had won. Robert Cialdini and his fellow researchers (1976) noted changes in students' language when their school football team won. Suddenly 'we' had won, rather than just the team! Furthermore, students wore more school-identifying clothes when the team had won as opposed to when it had lost. BIRGing isn't just limited to football support, but has been observed in friendships with popular young people. Jan Kornelis Dijkstra and a team of researchers (2010) found that those people who associated with popular peers, did so to achieve high status and popularity for themselves by basking in their reflected glory. The flipside of BIRGing, cutting off reflected failure (CORF) has also been identified as individuals try to distance themselves from unsuccessful individuals they would normally associate with. Filip Boen and his team found fans of unsuccessful teams did not seek out contact with team players when they lost a match. Chris Miller (2009) discovered that after a US presidential campaign, yard and window signs endorsing the successful Democrat candidate, Barack Obama, were displayed much longer than those supporting the Republican candidate, John McCain. So BIRGing and CORFing seem to be forms of impression management as we strive to maintain our positive identity. However, it seems self-esteem is also involved too, as those who are high in self-esteem seem to be less prone to CORFing than those with low self-esteem (Cialdini et al., 1976; Miller, 2009).

cutting off reflected failure (CORF) *to distance self from an individual or group you would usually identify with, when that individual or group fails*

Because of our social identifications, we conform to group norms (see Chapter 11). We sacrifice ourselves for team, family and even our nation. And the more important our social identity and the more strongly attached we feel to a group, the more we react prejudicially to threats from another group (Crocker & Luhtanen, 1990; Hinkle et al., 1996). Israeli historian and former Jerusalem deputy mayor Meron Benvenisti (1988) reported that among Jerusalem's Jews and Arabs, social identity has been so central to self-concept that it constantly reminds them of who they are not. Thus, on the integrated street where he lived, his own children – to his dismay – 'have not acquired a single Arab friend'.

However, this identification with a group and ingroup bias does not necessarily translate into prejudice against others. Rather it is about achieving positive intergroup differentiation rather than derogation of the outgroup. So positive feelings for our own groups need not be mirrored by equally strong negative feelings for outgroups. Where prejudice is possible is when intergroup comparison threatens the positive identity of the ingroup. When such threats are regarded as illegitimate acts on the part of low-status groups to challenge the position of a higher-status group, and group boundaries are perceived to be impermeable, intergroup prejudice is likely. For example, in Britain the migration of Polish workers into the British labour market has led to explicit and implicit prejudice aimed at the Polish outgroup. Such intergroup prejudice is based on perceptions of threat felt by some British workers in terms of their competence to carry out jobs given to Polish workers and the competition for work. To understand prejudice, we need some understanding of the concerns and the social context in which groups and the relationships between them are understood.

Prejudiced attitudes towards other groups not only influence how we behave towards them but also shape the way we judge their behaviour. An example of how we may attribute guilt based on stereotypes of social group membership is provided by John Dixon, Berenice Mahoney and Roger Cocks (2002). They found that White British participants thought a suspect was more likely to be guilty of

. a crime when he had a Birmingham accent (rather than standard pronunciation), was presented as Black (rather than White) and was accused of a blue-collar crime of armed robbery (rather than white-collar crime of cheque fraud). You can imagine how such prejudiced attitudes might have real-world consequences for the groups involved.

You may remember that in Chapter 4 we considered the fundamental attribution error: we attribute so much of other people's behaviour to their inner dispositions that we discount important situational forces. The error occurs partly because our attention focuses on the persons, not the situation. A person's ethnicity, race or sex gets vivid attention; the situational forces working upon that person are less visible. Until recently because gender-role constraints were hard to see, we attributed men and women's behaviour solely to their innate dispositions. Thomas Pettigrew's concept of the ultimate attribution error (UAE) (1979) proposes that groups account for their own behaviour in fundamentally different ways than they do the behaviour of other groups, especially when there is a history of conflict and tension between them. Positive behaviour by outgroup members is more often dismissed. It may be seen as a 'special case' ('He is certainly bright and hardworking – not at all like other ...'), as owing to luck or some special advantage ('She probably passed her driving test because the test centre needed to fill its quota of female drivers'), as demanded by the situation ('Under the circumstances the mean Scot had to pay the bill'), or as attributable to extra effort ('Asian students get better grades because they're so compulsive'). Disadvantaged groups and groups that stress modesty (such as the Chinese) exhibit less of this group-serving bias (Fletcher & Ward, 1989; Heine & Lehman, 1997; Jackson et al., 1993).

Such attributions often serve to warrant the stereotypes held about groups. A classic example comes from Donald Taylor and Vaishna Jaggi (1974), who found that Hindus in India explained the positive and negative behaviour of other Hindus and Muslims in ways predicted by the UAE.

The group-serving bias can subtly colour our language. A team of University of Padua (Italy) researchers led by Anne Maass (Maass, 1999; Maass et al., 1995) has found that positive behaviours by another ingroup member are often described as general dispositions (for example, 'Karen is helpful'). When performed by an outgroup member, the same behaviour is often described as a specific, isolated act ('Carmen opened the door for the man with the cane'). With negative behaviour, the specificity reverses: 'Eric shoved her' (an isolated act by an ingroup member) but 'Enrique was aggressive' (an outgroup member's general disposition). Maass calls this group-serving bias the *linguistic intergroup bias* (LIB). Furthermore, this effect is greater when a group is threatened by another, as Anne Maass and her colleagues (1996) discovered. Studying the opposed groups of hunters and environmentalists in northern Italy, they found that when hunters were presented with hostile messages about them from the environmentalists the LIB effect was stronger than when they received positive messages from this group. The same effect was found when environmentalists were presented with either negative or positive messages about themselves from the hunters. The LIB effect has also been associated with implicit prejudice. William von Hippel and his team (1997) reported those Caucasian participants who displayed implicit prejudice towards African-Americans by means of an IAT test reflected this bias in their linguistic

**group-serving bias**
*explaining away outgroup members' positive behaviours; also attributing negative behaviours to their dispositions (while excusing such behaviour by one's own group)*

reactions to the group. For bi- and multicultural individuals, it seems that they can reflect their identification with whichever culture is most salient to them at the time, by means of the LIB. Ling-Hui Hsu (2011) found that bicultural Asian American participants were able to switch their language to higher or lower abstraction towards ethnic Asians or European Americans, depending on which culture they were primed with and their identification with that group at the time. It seems that this ability to describe your talk about members of your own group in abstract positive ways, and dismiss ingroup members' negative incidents in isolated terms, is a marker of being a good group member (Assilaméhou and Testé, 2013).

However, intergroup attributions are not simply a matter of ingroup favouritism as suggested by Pettigrew, but tend to reflect wider societal norms and values. Miles Hewstone and Colleen Ward (1985) replicated Taylor and Jaggi's study in Malaysia and found that while Malay participants explained their own behaviour and that of the Chinese in ways predicted by the UAE, the Chinese participants also favoured the Malays, displaying outgroup favouritism. The researchers argue that this reflects the perceived legitimate lower social status of the Chinese in Malaysian society.

The important point is that prejudiced attitudes can affect group attributions. Peter Hegarty and Anne Golden (2008) found that participants who held prejudiced attitudes about stigmatized groups, such as gay men, lesbians and alcoholics, gave attributions for their behaviour that supported their prejudices and maintained their undesirable group position.

Prejudice and discrimination depend on the social climate and how acceptable it is to express prejudice within a society. It seems as if tolerance for derogatory utterances and discrimination is higher in some time periods than others. As such, some social psychologists have turned to look at how prejudice is produced in language, and what this tells us about the social context in which it occurs.

> IAT is covered later in this chapter with regard to prejudice and also in Chapter 5 with regard to attitudes; these sections help provide a more comprehensive overview of this measure.

## THE LANGUAGE OF PREJUDICE

### Discursive Psychology and Prejudice

Discursive psychologists have focused on prejudiced language. You may recall from Chapter 5 that discursive psychologists propose attitudes are evaluations made in discourse rather than underlying mental entities that drive behaviour. This has consequences for how they study prejudice. Not as an attitude, but as language.

### Categorization as a Discursive Process

SIT and SCT assume the cognitive process of categorization is crucial in explaining prejudice. Discursive psychologists challenge this, arguing instead that social groups, their meaning, membership and differences between them are produced in language. So instead of trying to uncover the inner cognitive motives that drive the expression of prejudice, discursive theorists treat its expression in language as the act of prejudice itself.

One of the forerunners of this model of prejudice is Michael Billig, based on his early work with Henri Tajfel. Billig (1985) points out that for us to categorize the social world, we must also be able to particularize it so that instances can be placed into a category. We must also be able to make judgements about which category, or social group, to use under a certain set of circumstances. So are we just bureaucrats doomed to an eternity of categorizing the world in the same way, forever filing papers into the same folders, or are we creative about how we organize our filing cabinet? Sometimes, we may not categorize at all. He argues that we are more creative than cognitive explanations of prejudice suggest. We often treat people as individuals rather than members of social groups, perhaps even arguing against their inclusion into a social group. This creativity, or flexibility in categorization and particularization, is a feature of language. We have available to us an infinite number of ways of describing the world. How we do it depends on what we're trying to do at a particular time. We have equal capacity to be prejudiced or tolerant in our language and in our thinking.

### The Ideology of Prejudice

ideology *a set of beliefs, ideas, aims and values, often proposed by a group or social class in society upon its members*

Billig notes that Tajfel never applied his own social identity theory to the event that concerned him the most – his experiences as a European Jew during the Holocaust. Perhaps Tajfel couldn't explain away the Holocaust as a simple process of categorization. Did Germans really murder Jews simply to enhance their ingroup self-esteem? Does depersonalization of people into a common outgroup really mean the same as their dehumanization? Tajfel recognized the role of ideology in how social groups were perceived, but little clue on how this might be analysed. There is clearly a difference between prejudice and bigotry. Stereotypes of Germans who reserve the sun-loungers with their beach towels are hardly comparable with Nazi German stereotypes of Jews deserving to be killed. Billig suggests we need to understand the ideological assumptions produced in the language of prejudice and hatred and the point at which prejudice becomes bigotry and murder.

Steve Reicher and Nick Hopkins (2001) call this the 'politics of category construction'. How social groups are understood discursively can justify discriminatory practices that disadvantage particular groups. For example, Danielle Every and Martha Augoustinos (2008) observe that asylum seekers in Australia are commonly referred to as 'illegal immigrants' by the media and government. This supports government policies that continue to marginalize and disadvantage asylum seekers in Australia by presenting them as deviant and criminal. In their study of interviews with White South Africans post-apartheid, Kevin Durrheim and John Dixon (2001) found they still portrayed Blacks as polluting the beaches with their uncivil behaviour. They have examined how this is reflected as Whites and Blacks continue to engage in racial segregation, populating different areas of the beach.

Ideology also influences the way we talk about sexuality. In Neill Korobov's (2004) interviews with heterosexual men, he found that they were often caught on the horns of an ideological dilemma. On the one hand, they do not want to appear homophobic or prejudiced, yet on the other, they wish to preserve traditional forms of masculinity that promote heterosexuality and debunk political correctness.

### The 'Taboo' of Prejudice

The studies we've just described use qualitative methods. Eduardo Bonilla-Silva and Tyrone Forman (2000) argue prejudiced views are captured in interviews and focus groups in ways that survey methods would miss. Ask someone directly if they are prejudiced or racist and they will probably tell you 'No'. Why? Participants are concerned with social desirability, wanting to appear tolerant and unprejudiced. So how much can we rely on questionnaires and surveys to find out about prejudice (see Chapter 2 for a discussion on methods)?

Martha Augoustinos and Danielle Every (2007a, 2007b) point to agreement across most social scientific disciplines that explicit forms of prejudice and 'old-fashioned racism' are taboo. But we should be wary of assuming this means people are now less prejudiced than they used to be. Martin Barker (1981) proposes that explicit forms of racism ('old racism') have been replaced with 'new racism'. Openly expressing racist or ethnocentric sentiments is taboo, but subtle prejudice or racism can work to present the speaker (or writer) as 'reasonable' while at the same time enabling him/her to engage in prejudice.

old racism *explicit, blatant forms and practices of racism*

new racism *implicit, subtle often disguised forms and practices of racism*

Of course, one strategy to avoid a charge of being prejudiced is to deny it. Teun van Dijk (1992, 1993) notes how people often use disclaimers such as: 'I'm not racist but . . .', and 'I'm not sexist but . . .'. This overt expression of cultural tolerance inoculates against the prejudiced remark which follows it.

Derek Edwards (2003) suggests people do prejudice by describing 'them' in ways that justify the negative views held of them. Consider the example below that comes from the work of Cristian Tileaga:

| 382 | Chris | To what extent do you think Romanies are to blame for these |
| 383 | | conflicts and violences? |
| 384 | Sandra | Cos' they don't (.) cos' they don't work (.) they <u>don't</u> |
| 385 | | like to work (.) They are not happy with (.) |
| 386 | Chris | How would you characterize them? |
| 387 | Sandra | Unadaptable (.) these ones are unadaptable (.) they cannot integrate |
| 388 | | in (.) in fact, even in the other countries (.) have their gypsies |
| 389 | | adapted? (.) No (.) Only that, it is the Romanians gypsies that |
| 390 | | Europe talks about, you have just these ones (.) it is only our |
| 391 | | gypsies that are the biggest thieves and bandits who strike (.) But |
| 392 | | Romanians have tried to integrate them, we made them schools (.) |
| 393 | | they have tv shows in the gypsy (.) language |

(taken from Tileaga, 2006, p. 27)

Sandra and Chris characterize 'the Romanies' behaviour in ways that are used to justify Romanian prejudice against them.

A common finding in discursive work is that people can justify racial prejudice towards other groups on non-racial grounds. Frank Reeves (1983) calls this deracialization. Martha Augoustinos and colleagues (1999) noted how racist comments directed at indigenous Australians were considered to be 'justifiable anger' on the basis that such groups received privileges from the government owing

deracialization *the justification of the racial marginalization of groups on the basis of non-racial features*

to their minority-group status. Lia Figgou and Susan Condor (2006) observed how Greek participants justified their prejudice against Albanian settlers into Greece on the basis of fear and risk to Greeks.

Minority groups can be presented in both positive and negative terms. Lynn and Lea (2003) examined media representations of asylum seekers in Britain as 'genuine' or 'bogus'. While 'we' will be hospitable to the 'genuine' ones, 'we' shall not be tolerant to the 'bogus' ones.

Jokes and humour disguise the seriousness of a prejudiced remark (Guerin, 2003). Michael Billig (2001) reports the use of jokes and humour to minimize the seriousness of extremely racist discourse on the Internet websites of the Ku Klux Klan.

But who determines what is racist? Derek Edwards (2003) warns that social psychologists should try to refrain from imposing their own judgements and instead listen to what their participants regard as prejudiced language. For example, Susan Condor and her team (2006) found that when people do recognize prejudice or racism in conversation, they may try to protect the 'face' of those who produced it. Consider an extract from her work:

1   Jack   [...] let's face it, it's not as if they're wanted here. We have enough low-
2          life here already without importing [other people's.
3   Hilda  [Jack! ((to Susan)) I'm sorry about
4          that. He's not xenophobic. It's it' not =
5   Jack   = it's not racist, no. We've never been racist, have we Hilda?
6   Hilda  No. We've got nothing against =
7   Jack   = nothing against the refugees. I have every sympathy for them. But
8          you'd be mad not to ask, why are they all coming *here*?

(taken from Condor et al., 2006, p. 452)

Language does not have to be blatantly racist for it to discriminate and oppress others.

## SUBTLE AND IMPLICIT PREJUDICE

Discursive theorists alert us to how prejudice might be communicated subtly through language. Aware of the social taboo of prejudice, people develop strategies for concealing prejudiced remarks. But are people sometimes simply unaware of their prejudices? How do we measure prejudice that people are unaware of, or in a way that doesn't cause participants to behave in a socially desirable manner? Social psychologists have developed methods for measuring subtle and implicit prejudice.

Let's look at some used to measure racial and ethnic prejudice.

### Racial and Ethnic Prejudice

In the context of the world, every race and ethnic group is a minority. Non-Hispanic Whites, for example, are only one-fifth of the world's people and will be one-eighth within another half-century. Thanks to mobility and migration over the past two centuries, the world's races and ethnic groups now intermingle, in relations that are sometimes hostile, sometimes amiable.

To a molecular biologist, skin colour is a trivial human characteristic, one controlled by a minuscule genetic difference. Moreover, nature doesn't cluster races in neatly defined categories. It is people, not nature, who sometimes label Tiger Woods 'African American' (his ancestry is 25 per cent African) or 'Asian American' (he is also 25 per cent Thai and 25 per cent Chinese) – or even as Native American or Dutch (he is one-eighth each).

Today blatant prejudice based on biological criteria has nearly disappeared. Previously such prejudice was upheld in the institutional practices of many societies. Until the 1970s many banks routinely denied mortgages to unmarried women and to minority applicants, with the result that most homeowners were White married couples. Films and television programmes have also reinforced prevailing cultural attitudes. The muddleheaded, wide-eyed African American butlers and maids in 1930s movies helped perpetuate the stereotypes they reflected. Today many people find such images offensive. We have seen the abolition of the regime of apartheid in South Africa, and the election of the USA's first Black president, Barack Obama. Considering what a thin slice of history is covered by the years since slavery was practised, the changes are dramatic.

Psychologists usually capitalize Black and White to emphasize that these are socially applied race labels, not literal colour labels for persons of African and European ancestry.

Shall we conclude, then, that racial and ethnic prejudice is extinct in the Western world? Not if we consider the 7649 perpetrators of reported hate crime incidents during 2004 in the USA (FBI, 2005), or the small proportion of Whites who, as Figure 13.2 shows, would not vote for a Black presidential candidate.

While the blatant expressions of prejudice may be on a sharp decline, and no longer receive the same kinds of institutional support they once did, more subtle forms of prejudice are still rife.

### Subtle Forms of Prejudice

So, prejudiced attitudes and discriminatory behaviour surface when they can hide behind the screen of some other motive. In Western countries blatant prejudice is being replaced by subtle prejudice (exaggerating ethnic differences, feeling less admiration and affection for immigrant minorities, rejecting them for supposedly non-racial reasons) (Pedersen & Walker, 1997; Tropp & Pettigrew, 2005a). Modern prejudice often appears subtly, in our preferences for what is familiar, similar and comfortable (Dovidio et al., 1992; Esses et al., 1993; Gaertner & Dovidio, 2005).

Modern prejudice even appears as a sensitivity that leads to exaggerated reactions to isolated minority persons – both over-praising their accomplishments and over-criticizing their mistakes (Fiske, 1989a; Hart & Morry, 1997; Hass et al., 1991). It also appears as patronization. For example, Kent Harber (1998) gave White students at Stanford University a poorly written essay to evaluate. When the students thought the writer was Black, they rated it *higher* than when they were led to think the author was White, and they rarely offered harsh criticisms. The evaluators, perhaps wanting to avoid the

Although prejudice dies last in socially intimate contacts, inter-racial marriage has increased in most countries (Pew, 2006).
SOURCE: © Jim Craigmyle/Getty Images

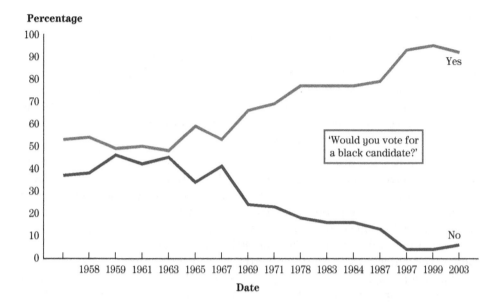

**FIGURE 13.2** Changing racial attitudes of White Americans from 1958 to 2003

SOURCE: Data from Gallup polls (gallup.com).

appearance of bias, patronized the essayists with lower standards. Such 'inflated praise and insufficient criticism' may hinder minority student achievement, Harber noted.

Irwin Katz and Glen Hass (1988) argue that people tend to not be against a group per se, but will have both positive and negative feelings towards them. This has been defined as ambivalent racism. Samuel Gaertner and John Dovidio (2000) distinguish the ambivalent racist from the aversive racist. The aversive racist will actively avoid interracial encounters because of the guilt they feel about their negative thoughts about Blacks. When such an encounter cannot be avoided, the aversive racist will promote egalitarian values, yet if their prejudice can be justified on non-racial grounds, they may then discriminate against them. See Table 13.1 for a summary.

**TABLE 13.1** Types of subtle racism

| Name | Primary citations | Description of main features |
|---|---|---|
| Symbolic racism | Henry & Sears (2002)<br>McConahay & Hough (1976)<br>Sears (1988) | Symbolic racists reject old-style racism but still express prejudice indirectly (e.g. as opposition to policies that help racial minorities) |
| Ambivalent racism | Katz (1981)<br>Katz & Hass (1988)<br>Katz et al. (1986) | Ambivalent racists experience an emotional conflict between positive and negative feelings towards stigmatized racial groups |
| Modern racism | McConahay (1986) | Modern racists see racism as wrong but view racial minorities as making unfair demands or receiving too many resources |
| Aversive racism | Gaertner & Dovidio (1986) | Aversive racists believe in egalitarian principles such as racial inequality but have a personal aversion towards racial minorities |

SOURCE: Scott Plous, 2008, Understanding Prejudice.

Implicit Prejudice

A raft of experiments (Banaji, 2004; Bargh & Chartrand, 1999; Devine, 1989, 2005; Fazio et al., 1995; Greenwald et al., 2000; Wittenbrink et al., 1997) suggest that prejudiced and stereotypic evaluations can occur outside people's awareness. We've considered the implicit association test (IAT) with respect to the measurement of attitudes (Chapter 5) and persuasion (Chapter 6). Implicit association tests measure reaction times to see how quickly people associate concepts, indicating their implicit attitudes. Some social psychological studies briefly flash words or faces that 'prime' (automatically activate) group stereotypes. Participants are unaware that their activated stereotypes may then bias their behaviour. For example, Ulrike Niens, Ed Cairns and Suzanne Bishop (2004) found that Northern Ireland students revealed more sectarian attitudes which favoured their Protestant (or Catholic) ingroup and were biased against the respective Catholic (or Protestant) outgroup, as compared to explicit measures of prejudice.

So, how widespread are automatic prejudiced reactions to African Americans? Experiments have used the IAT to show such reactions in varied contexts. For example, in experiments by Anthony Greenwald and his colleagues (1998, 2000), 9 in 10 White people took longer to identify pleasant words (such as *peace* and *paradise*) as 'good' when associated with Black rather than White faces. The participants consciously expressed little or no prejudice; their bias was unconscious and unintended. Moreover, report Kurt Hugenberg and Galen Bodenhausen (2003), the more strongly people exhibit such implicit prejudice, the readier they are to perceive anger in Black faces (Figure 13.3).

In separate experiments, Joshua Correll and co-workers (2002, 2006) and Anthony Greenwald and colleagues (2003b) invited people to press buttons quickly to 'shoot' or 'not shoot' men who suddenly appeared on-screen holding either a gun or a harmless object such as a flashlight or a bottle. The participants (both Blacks and Whites, in one of the studies) more often mistakenly shot harmless targets who were Black. In a related series of studies, Keith Payne (2001) and Charles Judd and colleagues (2004) found that when primed with a Black rather than a White face, people think guns: they more quickly recognize a gun and they more often mistake a tool, such as a wrench, for a gun. In a related study, Jennifer Eberhardt and her colleagues (2004) demonstrated that the reverse effect can occur. Exposing people to weapons makes them pay more attention to faces of African Americans and even makes police officers more likely to judge stereotypical-looking African Americans as criminals. These studies help explain why Amadou Diallo (a Black immigrant in New York City) was shot 41 times by police officers for removing his wallet from his pocket.

It also appears that different brain regions are involved in automatic and consciously controlled stereotyping (Correll et al., 2006; Cunningham et al., 2004; Eberhardt, 2005). Pictures of outgroups that elicit the most disgust (such as drug addicts and the homeless) elicit more amygdala than frontal cortex activity (Harris & Fiske, 2006). This suggests that automatic prejudices involve primitive regions of the brain associated with fear, such as the amygdala, whereas controlled processing is more closely associated with the frontal cortex, which enables conscious thinking.

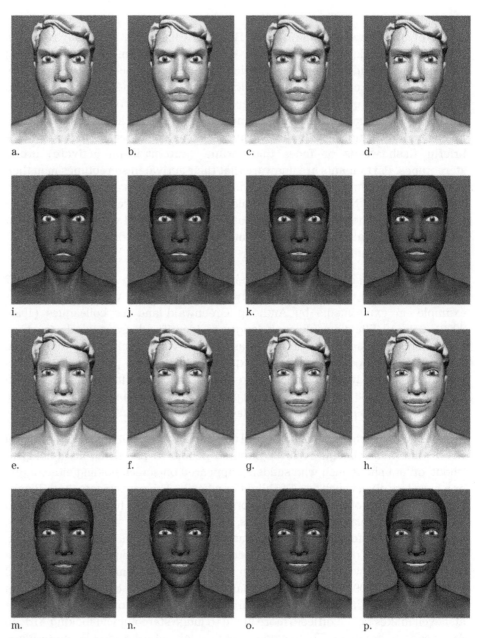

a.  b.  c.  d.

i.  j.  k.  l.

e.  f.  g.  h.

m.  n.  o.  p.

**FIGURE 13.3**  Facing prejudice
Where does the anger disappear? Kurt Hugenberg and Galen Bodenhausen showed university students a movie of faces morphing from angry to happy. Those who had scored as most prejudiced (on an implicit racial attitudes test) perceived anger lingering more in ambiguous Black than White faces.

Even the social scientists who study prejudice seem vulnerable to it, note Anthony Greenwald and Eric Schuh (1994). They analysed biases in authors' citations of social science articles by people with selected non-Jewish names (Erickson, McBride, etc.) and Jewish names (Goldstein, Siegel, etc.). Their analysis of nearly 30 000 citations, including 17 000 citations of prejudice research, found something remarkable: compared with Jewish authors, non-Jewish authors had 40 per cent higher odds of citing non-Jewish names. (Greenwald and Schuh could not determine whether Jewish authors were over-citing their Jewish colleagues or whether non-Jewish authors were over-citing their non-Jewish colleagues, or both.)

As we considered in Chapter 5, the use of IATs to measure implicit prejudice has not been without its critics. The creators of the IAT, Mahzarin Banaji and Anthony Greenwald, note that the findings of the IAT should be treated with caution, but it nevertheless measures implicit prejudice. Some social psychologists have contended that features of individual participants, such as their age, may be reflected in their performance on the IAT. For example, Brandon Stewart, William von Hippel and Gabriel Radvansky (2009) consider their finding that older White adults demonstrate more racial prejudice on the IAT than younger ones. Is it that older people are more prejudiced than younger ones? Stewart and his colleagues claim that what's being measured here is how much control participants have over suppressing prejudiced associations. With age, deficits occur in inhibitory ability.

Implicit prejudice. When Joshua Correll and his colleagues invited people to react quickly to people holding either a gun or a harmless object, race influenced perceptions and reactions.

SOURCE: © Ingram Publishing/Alamy

### Gender Prejudice

How pervasive is prejudice against women? In Israel the high court reconsidered a ruling on orthodox buses that segregate men from women. Previously women had been required to sit at the back of the bus so that they remain separated from men in public. The women challenging the bus system argued this was a form of gender prejudice. Here we consider gender stereotypes. Norms are prescriptive; stereotypes are descriptive.

### Gender Stereotypes

Two research conclusions are indisputable: strong gender stereotypes exist, and members of the stereotyped group accept the stereotypes. Men and women agree that you *can* judge the book by its sexual cover. In one survey, Mary Jackman and Mary Senter (1981) found that gender stereotypes were much stronger than racial stereotypes. For example, only 22 per cent of men thought the two sexes equally 'emotional'. Of the remaining 78 per cent, those who believed females were more emotional outnumbered those who thought males were by 15 to 1. And what did the women believe? To within 1 percentage point, their responses were identical.

**stereotype** *a generalized belief about the personal attributes of a group of people. Stereotypes are commonly widely held, oversimplified, inaccurate and resistant to new information*

Remember that stereotypes are generalizations about a group of people and may be true, false or overgeneralized from a kernel of truth. Sometimes stereotypes exaggerate differences. But not always, observed Janet Swim (1994). She found that Pennsylvania State University students' stereotypes of men's and women's restlessness, non-verbal sensitivity, aggressiveness, and so forth were reasonable approximations of actual gender differences. Moreover, such stereotypes have persisted across time and culture. Averaging data from 27 countries, John Williams and his colleagues (1999, 2000) found that people everywhere perceive women as more agreeable, men as more outgoing.

Stereotypes (beliefs) are not prejudices (attitudes). Stereotypes may support prejudice. One might believe, without prejudice, that men and women are 'different yet equal'. Let us see how researchers probe for gender prejudice.

### Sexism: Benevolent and Hostile

Alice Eagly and her associates (1991) and Geoffrey Haddock and Mark Zanna (1994) report that people don't respond to women with gut-level negative emotions as they do to certain other groups. Most people like women more than men. They perceive women as more understanding, kind and helpful. A *favourable* stereotype, which Eagly (1994) dubs the *women-are-wonderful effect*, results in a favourable attitude.

'Women are wonderful primarily because they are [perceived as] so nice. [Men are] perceived as superior to women in agentic [competitive, dominant] attributes that are viewed as equipping people for success in paid work, especially in male-dominated occupations.'
   Alice Eagly, 1994

But gender attitudes often are ambivalent, report Peter Glick and Susan Fiske (1996, 2001) and their colleagues (Glick et al., 2000) from their surveys of 15 000 people in 19 nations. They frequently mix a *benevolent sexism* ('Women have a superior moral sensibility') with *hostile sexism* ('Once a man commits, she puts him on a tight leash').

Stereotypes about men also come in contrasting pairs. Peter Glick and his colleagues (Glick et al., 2004) report ambivalent sexism towards men with *benevolent* attitudes of men as powerful and *hostile* attitudes that characterized men as immoral. People who endorse benevolent sexism towards women also tend to endorse benevolent sexism towards men. These complementary ambivalent sexist views of men and women may serve to justify the status quo in gender relations (Jost & Kay, 2005).

### Gender Discrimination

One heavily publicized finding of discrimination against women came from a 1968 study in which Philip Goldberg gave women students at Connecticut College several short articles and asked them to judge the value of each. Sometimes a given article was attributed to a male author (for example, John T. McKay) and sometimes to a female author (for example, Joan T. McKay). In general, the articles received lower ratings when attributed to a female. That's right: women discriminated against women.

David Myers obtained Goldberg's materials in 1980 and repeated the experiment with his own students. They (women and men) showed no such tendency to deprecate women's work. The most common result across 104 studies involving almost 20 000 people was *no difference*. On most comparisons, judgement of someone's work was unaffected by whether the work was attributed to a female or a male. Summarizing other studies of people's evaluations of women and men as leaders, professors, and so forth, Alice Eagly (1994) concluded, 'Experiments have *not* demonstrated any *overall* tendency to devalue women's work'.

Is gender bias fast becoming extinct in Western countries? Has the women's movement nearly completed its work? As with racial prejudice, both blatant gender prejudice and subtle remain present in society.

One such bias can be seen in analysis of birth announcements (Gonzalez & Koestner, 2005). Parents announce the birth of their baby boys with more pride than the birth of their baby girls. In contrast, they announce the birth of their baby girls with more happiness than the birth of their baby boys. It seems that even at birth, parents are already describing their boys in terms of status and their girls in terms of relationships.

In the world beyond democratic Western countries, gender discrimination looms even larger. Two-thirds of the world's unschooled children are girls (United Nations, 1991). Around the world, people tend to prefer having baby boys. In the USA in 1941, 38 per cent of expectant parents said they preferred a boy if they could have only one child; 24 per cent preferred a girl; and 23 per cent said they had no preference. In 2003 the answers were virtually unchanged, with 38 per cent still preferring a boy (Lyons, 2003; Simmons, 2000). With the widespread use of ultrasound to determine the sex of a foetus and the growing availability of abortion, these preferences are affecting the number of boys and girls. The net result is tens of millions of 'missing women'.

To conclude, overt prejudice against people of colour and against women is far less common today than it was in the mid-twentieth century. The same is true of prejudice against homosexual people. Nevertheless, techniques that are sensitive to subtle prejudice still detect widespread bias. And in parts of the world, gender prejudice makes for misery. Therefore, we need to look carefully and closely at the social, emotional and cognitive sources of prejudice.

## INTERGROUP CONFLICT

*People's identification with a social group can lead to conflict with other groups. The occurrence of intergroup conflict has been widely studied by social psychologists. Why does conflict between groups occur? Can social psychologists explain this conflict?*

Intergroup behaviour is behaviour based on the perception that individuals belong to distinct social groups.

Almost every nation claims concern not only for peace but, mistrusting other nations, arms itself in self-defence. The result is a world that has been spending in excess of $2 billion per day on arms and armies, while hundreds of millions die of malnutrition and untreated disease.

The elements of conflict are similar at many levels, whether we examine conflict between nations in an arms race, trying to control oil resources, religious factions

**intergroup conflict** *negative relations between social groups*

**intergroup behaviour** *behaviour that is based on the perception that individuals belong to distinct social groups*

**conflict** *a perceived incompatibility of actions, goals or values between two or more parties*

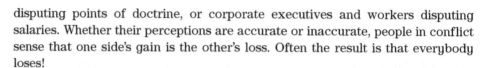

disputing points of doctrine, or corporate executives and workers disputing salaries. Whether their perceptions are accurate or inaccurate, people in conflict sense that one side's gain is the other's loss. Often the result is that everybody loses!

A relationship or an organization without conflict is possibly apathetic. Conflict signifies involvement, commitment and caring. If conflict is understood and recognized, it can end oppression and stimulate renewed and improved human relations. Without conflict, people seldom face and resolve their problems. Conflicts are necessary for development and change. Conflict in itself is not the evil. The problem is the means and weapons often used to solve or reduce that conflict.

Let's consider some social psychological explanations for intergroup conflict.

## REALISTIC CONFLICT THEORY

One explanation comes from Muzafer Sherif and Carolyn Sherif (1953, 1964; Sherif et al., 1961), who offer an environmental explanation for conflict between groups. Rather than conflict being the outcome of a dysfunction in individuals' psychological states, it is factors in the social situation that are thought to be to blame. Sherif and Sherif argue that it is competition for scarce resources that leads to intergroup conflict.

Sherif and Sherif thought the perceived differences in resources between groups became manifest as psychological states of the group members. This became the basis of their realistic conflict theory, illustrated in their series of boys' camp studies (see Research Close-Up).

Sherif and Sherif illustrated that conflict between groups is not simply down to the personalities of a few individuals, but a consequence of the environment, which can lead to displays of aggression, ingroup solidarity, stereotyping and prejudice.

Of course, not all intergroup conflict is characterized by competition over lack of scarce resources. Is simply feeling psychologically attached to a group sufficient to cause conflict and prejudice?

## CATEGORIZATION, STEREOTYPING AND SOCIAL GROUPS

Henri Tajfel was fascinated by the work of the Sherifs, but what had really caught his attention was the boys' identification with a group to which they had been randomly assigned. It seemed as though something psychological happened to people when they were put in a group (see Chapter 12).

In a group situation we stereotype ourselves and others on the basis of group membership. Walter Lippmann (1922) argued such mental shortcuts are mostly works of fiction. They are exaggerated generalizations that are partial, biased and contain evaluations, and in an intergroup situation used to perceive the outgroup as inferior and the ingroup as superior.

Tajfel wanted to see if people would favour their ingroup and be hostile to the outgroup even when there was no reward for doing so. In other words he wanted to know if the 'competition' between groups was simply about scarce resources, or if it was actually about being able to distinguish one's group favourably in comparison to another.

**realistic conflict theory** *negative relations between social groups are based on real competition for scarce resources*

**ingroup** *'us' – a group of people who share a sense of belonging, a feeling of common identity (often contrasted with* outgroup*)*

**outgroup** *'them' – a group that people perceive as distinctively different from or apart from their* ingroup

THE ROBBERS CAVE EXPERIMENT

*Source: Sherif, M. (1958). Superordinate goals in the reduction of intergroup conflict.* American Journal of Sociology, *63(4), 349–356.*

### Introduction

Muzafer Sherif noted that social scientists had not really effectively reduced intergroup conflict. Attempts to do so, which included contact between groups, appeals to fairness and morality, and addressing stereotypes, had in his opinion failed to understand and address intergroup conflict generally. Sherif began with the idea that it is conflict over resources that underlies prejudice between groups. To demonstrate this, a series of studies were conducted to show how intergroup conflict could be induced through competition over scarce resources. What Sherif wanted to know was, if competition was the basis for intergroup conflict, could it be reduced by bringing the groups together to work co-operatively for shared resources? To do this they conducted three boys' camp studies that ran in 1949, 1953 and 1954 at Robbers Cave State Park in Oklahoma.

### Method

The studies involved a two-week summer camp for 11- to 12-year-old white middle-class North American boys to engage in a series of activities during the summer holidays. Sherif notes that they were 'healthy, normal boys' and 'well adjusted in school and neighbourhood, and academically successful' with a mean IQ 'above average' (p. 353). Researchers, including Muzafer Sherif, acted as camp counsellors and activity leaders recording the behaviour of the boys throughout the two weeks. Across all three studies a pattern of stages in the experiment was implemented. The first was an initial milling period where the boys were free to form their own friendships. The second stage involved splitting the boys into two groups. Existing friendships that had formed in the initial milling period were split across the two groups. The two groups were kept separate from each other, and engaged in group-specific activities. During this time firm friendships formed within the groups as they developed a sense of group cohesion. In the third stage competitions were organized between the groups such that one group could only gain resources at the expense of the other group. In the later studies the researchers introduced a fourth stage that meant both groups had to work collaboratively in order to bring a positive reward for everyone. Collaborative activities included fixing the water supply for camp. These were goals that could not be achieved through the efforts of one group alone, but required both groups working together.

### Results

Sherif reports that across all of the studies, once competition between the two groups began, hostility arose. Negative stereotypes and attitudes were formed about members of the opposing group. They engaged in name-calling, cruel chanting, fights and raids of the other group's cabins. Furthermore, both groups expressed a desire to be as physically distant from one another as possible. However, ingroup solidarity and cooperation intensified, as the boys bonded within their groups more closely in the face of competition from the other group. Blatant bragging of their own group's superiority emerged. Sherif also witnessed rearrangements of power and status within each group, as the boys developed new norms and values to fit with the hostile situation they found themselves in.

As the groups were brought together through the introduction of superordinate goals, requiring they work together, Sherif observed that acts such as derogatory name-calling ceased. When asked to

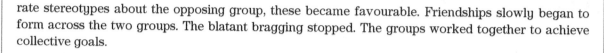

rate stereotypes about the opposing group, these became favourable. Friendships slowly began to form across the two groups. The blatant bragging stopped. The groups worked together to achieve collective goals.

## Discussion

Sherif concluded that this study showed that not only must groups communicate with one another in order to reduce conflict, but they should also work together to achieve goals that are beneficial for all concerned. So mere contact is insufficient on its own to dispel intergroup conflict. When pulling together for the good of everyone, groups learn about one another; negative stereotypes previously held about other groups are seen to be untrue. Sherif argued that this series of studies not only showed how conflict could be created between people and groups in terms of competing for scarce resources, but also shed light on how it could be resolved, by creating superordinate goals which required groups to work together in order to achieve them.

But is it the case that all intergroup conflict is based on competition over scarce or desired resources? Sherif seems to be able to explain some causes of conflict. Tensions can break out between groups when unemployment is high and available jobs and housing are scarce. But what about the conflict that exists between football fans, rival gangs, groups of children in the playground? Scarce resources are not the basis for all intergroup conflict.

Criticisms can also be levelled at Sherif's choice of sample and the artificial conditions under which the experiments were carried out. All of the sample were middle-class boys. The creation of the groups was artificial. How well does this reflect everyday intergroup conflict? Furthermore, if the groups had failed to achieve the superordinate goals, would the cross-group friendships have continued or would the original rivalry between the two groups have re-emerged?

Competition kindles conflict. Here, in one of Sherif's studies – the Robbers Cave experiment – one group of boys raids the bunkhouse of another group.

SOURCE: Courtesy of The Drs. Nicholas and Dorothy Cummings Center for the History of Psychology, The University of Akron

ingroup bias *the tendency to favour one's own group*

The experiment we discussed in Chapter 12, by Henri Tajfel and Michael Billig, demonstrated how little it takes to provoke favouritism towards 'us' and unfairness towards 'them'. The mere experience of being formed into groups may promote ingroup bias. Ask children, 'Which are the better, the children in your school or the children at [another school nearby]?' They will probably say their own school has better children. Dominic Abrams, Adam Rutland and Lindsey Cameron (2003) found that children as young as 5 years old display ingroup favouritism.

Tajfel suggested that these groups resulted in perceptual illusions, as individuals saw members of their own group and those of others, as more homogenous than they really are. As we discussed in Chapter 12, in an intergroup context, we experience accentuation effects.

### SOCIAL COMPARISON

But why do we engage in this ingroup favouritism? We evaluate ourselves partly by our group memberships. Having a sense of 'we-ness' strengthens our self-concepts. It *feels* good. We seek not only *respect* for ourselves but also *pride* in our groups (Smith & Tyler, 1997). Seeing our groups as superior helps us feel even better. It's as if we all think, 'I am an X [name your group]. X is good. Therefore, I am good.' As much of our lives is tied up with social group membership we are concerned with maintaining the positive image and evaluation of our group. One way of doing this is to compare your group with others in favourable terms. To do this, the group needs to compare itself with others on dimensions that are favourable for the ingroup.

Some social psychologists have argued that the motivation behind group comparisons isn't so much about self-esteem as about achieving optimal distinctiveness (Brewer, 1991) or reducing the uncertainty of social reality. Whatever the motivation, social psychologists who adopt a social identity theory (SIT) or self-categorization theory (SCT) perspective agree that the process of social comparison seems to be one that groups engage in to make their own group membership meaningful, and they strive to do so in ways that make their own group appear favourable.

Let's consider an example. Shereen Benjamin, Melanie Nind, Kathy Hall, Janet Collins and Kieron Sheehy (2003) conducted an ethnographic small-scale study of two English primary schools that promote educational inclusion, accepting children from a variety of backgrounds. However, they found that despite the spirit of inclusion the children understood each other as belonging to distinct social groups based on social class. To mark the boundaries between these groups, those children from middle-class backgrounds defined their 'success' based on their academic abilities, appearing superior to the working-class children. Those children from the working-class areas often sabotaged their academic abilities, instead preferring to define their 'success' on the basis of their street knowledge and extra-non-academic activities. So the dimension for social comparison moves so that the ingroup can regard itself as superior to the outgroup.

Thierry Devos, Lisa Silver, Diane Mackie and Eliot Smith (2002) note a wide range of emotions that can occur in various intergroup relations. A powerful outgroup can instil fear. One that threatens or blocks the goals of an ingroup can result in anger and frustration. In extreme cases, an outgroup whose moral standards don't quite match our own may evoke disgust. Colin Leach, Russell Spears, Nyla Branscombe and Bertjan Doojse (2003) investigated the feeling of 'schadenfreude' among Dutch football supporters. Schadenfreude is 'malicious pleasure' at the misfortune of someone else (also see Chapter 3). They found that Dutch football supporters experienced high levels of schadenfreude when the German football team lost to another international side in a football tournament.

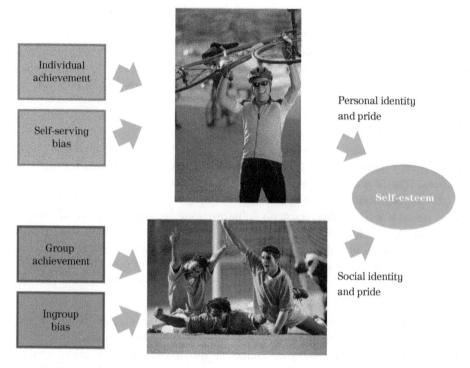

**FIGURE 13.4** Personal identity and social identity together feed self-esteem.
SOURCE: (T) © Terry Vine/ Blend Images LLC
(B) © Digital Vision/Punchstock

Lacking a positive personal identity, people may seek self-esteem by identifying with a group. Many disadvantaged youths find pride, power and identity in gang affiliations. Many superpatriots define themselves by their national identities (Staub, 1997a, 2005b). And many people at a loose end find identity in their associations with new religious movements, self-help groups or fraternal clubs (Figure 13.4).

'There is a tendency to define one's own group positively in order to evaluate oneself positively.'
    John C. Turner, 1984

## CROWDS

The early social explanations of aggressive behaviour in groups focused particularly on the crowd, and tried to answer the question why people behaved violently when surrounded by others.

### THE GROUP MIND

Gustave Le Bon (1841–1931) was one of the most influential writers on crowd behaviour (see Chapter 1). Writing during a time of political and social unrest in France he observed the revolutionary crowds in his country and tried to understand their behaviour. However, this was not really an objective exploration of the crowd. Le Bon, himself coming from a solidly bourgeois family, greatly mistrusted the uprising and revolutionary crowd, and was appalled by what he perceived as their savage behaviour. In his book *The Crowd* (1895) Le Bon argued that: 'By the mere fact that he forms part of an organised crowd, a man descends several rungs on the ladder of civilisation. Isolated he may be a cultivated individual; in a crowd he is a barbarian – that is a creature acting by instinct.' In Chapter 8 we briefly considered how Le Bon's ideas had been used to explain aggression. Le Bon thought that when individuals become immersed in a crowd they lose their conscious rationality and more primitive instincts take over, causing barbaric behaviour. Individuals lose control of their minds in a crowd. As the 'racial unconscious' takes over, crowds behave aggressively. Losing individual responsibility for their actions, crowd members feel invisible. Le Bon believed that aggressive impulses were transmitted to members of the crowd unconsciously by contagion. In this almost hypnotic state individuals follow others in acts that they would never usually do.

Sigmund Freud (1921) claimed that, within the crowd, the superego which contains society's norms and values that constrained primitive urges, was replaced by the primitive 'id', a bundle of uncontrolled and irrational impulses. These ideas clearly influenced Le Bon.

'Crowds are somewhat like the sphinx of ancient fable: It is necessary to arrive at a solution of the problems offered by their psychology or to resign ourselves to being devoured by them.'
Le Bon, 1908

Gustave Le Bon (1841–1931) was one of the most influential writers on crowd behaviour. He believed that people behaved like barbarians in crowds due to a loss of conscious rationality.
SOURCE: © Bettmann/Corbis

Le Bon's work was highly influential. It gave people a good excuse not to engage with the opinions and actions of the crowd. It also offered a way of controlling crowds at a time when people lived in fear of the collapse of the social order. Even the fascist dictator Mussolini noted his gratitude to Le Bon for such illumination on the matter. But subsequent social psychological theories have pointed out particular problems with Le Bon's theory:

1 Le Bon was describing the revolutionary crowds of France, yet they don't get a mention in his work. Are all crowds the same? Do they arise for the same reasons? What are they reacting against? The crowd is removed from the circumstances under which it arose.

2 It assumes crowds have a fixed set of behaviours that are released. But surely there is diversity within the crowd as well as between crowds.

3 It gives no indication of 'who' will be affected. By using the concepts of suggestion and contagion, surely everyone should join in. But this isn't the case. The police rarely join in with a rioting crowd. We might be a bit surprised if they did! So there must be some basis on which people identify with a crowd in order for them to join one.

4 It assumes crowd members are anonymous and irrational. Crowd members may be anonymous to those outside of the crowd, but they are often known to others within the crowd. So do they really lose their sense of self? What may seem irrational to an outsider may not be regarded as irrational to those within the crowd.

These concerns have been addressed in subsequent social psychological theories of the crowd. Let's begin by turning to one of Le Bon's claims which did inform a later theory on crowd behaviour: the idea that people become anonymous within the crowd.

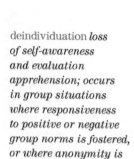

## DEINDIVIDUATION

deindividuation *loss of self-awareness and evaluation apprehension; occurs in group situations where responsiveness to positive or negative group norms is fostered, or where anonymity is increased*

Leon Festinger (Festinger et al., 1952) coined the term 'deindividuation' to explain what happens when people become anonymous within a crowd or group. Under these conditions, people's sense of individual identity and responsibility for their actions becomes lost as individuals become anonymous within the crowd. Studies that have tried to demonstrate the effects of deindividuation have tended not to focus on crowds, but on small and large groups. Remember that in Chapter 11 we saw how deindividuation led to social loafing, as people reduced their individual effort within the anonymity of the group.

Leon Festinger, Albert Pepitone and Theodore Newcomb (1952) found that when their group of participants were made unidentifiable by dressing in laboratory coats they were much more controversial, and some might say bold, in their discussions about their feelings towards their parents.

In one study that does examine crowds, Leon Mann (1981) observed baiting when a person threatened to commit suicide by jumping off a bridge or building. In his study of 21 cases, Mann found that in 10 of them the crowd started to bait and jeer at the person threatening to kill themselves. Mann suggests that deindividuation is partly responsible for this crowd behaviour, including the large size of the group, whether the attempt occurred at night-time and the physical distance between the crowd and victim. During the time of apartheid in South Africa, Andrew Colman (1991) reported how South African courts actually took deindividuation and the loss of responsibility into account when sentencing murderers. The Truth and Reconciliation Committees in South Africa maintain a defence that offences which took place during apartheid can be blamed on deindividuation within a political system, and as such the perpetrator can be forgiven on the basis s/he was serving that system. In one case, the court accepted extenuating circumstances for four out of eight railway worker defendants accused of murdering eight strike breakers. In another, the death sentences of five defendants for the 'necklace' killing of a young woman were reduced to 20 months' imprisonment. As Colman warns, such psychological explanations for crowd behaviour have practical and ethical implications for society.

The work of Philip Zimbardo has offered some of the most revealing work in the area. In a study reminiscent of Milgram's electric shock experiment, Zimbardo (1970) dressed some of his female participants in hoods and robes to deindividuate them. He paired them with a female confederate and asked the participant to assess how well the confederate did on a paired-associate learning task by administering electric shocks to them. He found that those dressed in hoods and robes gave much higher electric shocks than those participants who were not. Zimbardo argued that this had occurred because there had been a diffusion of responsibility across the hooded participants, causing a 'weakening of controls based on guilt, shame, fear and commitment'.

Zimbardo's Stanford Prison Experiment (1971) illustrated how people's behaviour is affected when they become deindividuated playing a particular role. In response to an advert for people to take part in a study based at Stanford University, 24 white middle-class male volunteers were randomly assigned on the toss of a coin to the role of 'prison guard' or 'prisoner'. They were then dressed in the appropriate uniform and lived in a mock-up of a prison camp based at the university. Although the study was planned to last two weeks, it was stopped after only six days. The participants quickly internalized their roles and began to behave accordingly. The guards became aggressive and brutal, subjecting their prisoners to inhumane conditions and acts of physical and verbal abuse. Those who had been assigned to the role of prisoner simply accepted the abuse. As the conditions of the prison deteriorated and the brutality of the guards escalated, the experiment was stopped. Was it the lack of self-awareness and feelings of deindividuation that led to such a shocking conclusion? In addition, the site presents a video on interracial marriage that explores the phenomenon of prejudice and its impact on its targets. As we shall see later in this chapter, Steve Reicher and Alex Haslam have challenged Zimbardo's conclusions.

Although a fascinating, if somewhat disturbing, insight into how deindividuation affects people's behaviour, it was Edward Diener (1980) who developed a model of crowd behaviour. He felt that when in a large group or crowd, individuals drifted towards an extreme lack of self-awareness. Under these conditions people do not self-monitor, are unable to retrieve standards and norms of behaviour from memory, do not plan action, become driven by immediate cues and feel little or no responsibility for their behaviour. Usual self-regulation of behaviour is blocked (see Figure 13.5).

Although proposed as a model of crowd behaviour, Diener's study remained at the level of small groups. With his colleagues, Diener's study of Halloween trick-or-treaters (Diener et al., 1976) explored whether being anonymous in a group would lead to the 'stealing' of sweets from those houses they had visited for Halloween. More stealing occurred when the children were anonymous and in a group. Diener also discovered that when one child was made the 'leader' of the group and told s/he was responsible for the actions of the group, but remained anonymous wearing a Halloween costume, if s/he stole then stealing by the other children in the group increased. Diener suggested that what was going on here was a modelling effect. The children copied their leader, especially when their leader was anonymous to those they stole from.

But does the crowd always behave aggressively? This seems to be a legacy that has come from Le Bon's particular political stance on the revolutionary crowds of France. Does deindividuation always result in negative behaviour? If so, why didn't the prisoners in the Zimbardo study also behave aggressively? It's the role of 'prisoner' or 'guard' that guides behaviour. Do people blindly accept the roles that are given to them and behave accordingly? Recent research suggests not. See Research Close-Up: The Psychology of Tyranny for a contemporary reinterpretation of Zimbardo's prison experiment, carried out by Steve Reicher and Alex Haslam.

## EMERGENT NORM THEORY

Ralph Turner and Lewis Killian (1972) say that the crowd is just an extreme form of a group. The only distinction between a crowd and a group is that groups usually have some history or tradition associated with them, whereas crowds are often spontaneous gatherings of people. Emergent norm theory was proposed to explain how this occurred. When potential crowd members first meet, an initial period of 'milling' occurs as members meet each other. Certain individuals become

emergent norms *those norms that 'emerge' within a group or crowd that influence the behaviour of those involved*

**I. Many or most everyday activities (not self-aware and not self-regulating)**

A. Habitual behavioural sequences
B. Scripted behaviours
C. Well-learned reactions to stimuli
D. Outward focus of attention
E. Well-planned sequences

**II. Self-awareness and self-regulation initiated by:**

A. Novel situations
B. Evaluation by others
C. Behaviour produces unexpected outcomes
D. Self-focusing stimuli
E. Behaviour clearly related to one's morals or standards

**III. Self-awareness and self-regulation:**

A. Self-monitoring
B. Retrieval of personal and social standards and comparison of own behaviour to standards
C. Self-reinforcement
D. Planning and foresight
E. Behaviour often inhibited by fear of punishment

**IV. Deindividuation caused by (self-awareness and individual self-conception blocked):**

A. Perceptual immersion in the group
B. Outcome attribution immersion
C. Action and other factors using conscious processing capacity
D. Outward focus of attention
E. Conceiving the group as a united whole

**V. Self-regulatory capacities lost when deindividuated:**

A. Can't easily monitor own behaviour or perceive products of own actions
B. Social and personal standards can't be retrieved and can't compare behaviour to own standards
C. Can't generate self-reinforcement
D. Can't use planning or foresight
E. Lack of ego inhibitions regarding future punishment
F. Person becomes more reactive to immediate cues, emotions and motivations

**FIGURE 13.5** Self-awareness and self-regulation versus deindividuation (Diener, 1980)
Individuals alternate between I, II and III all the time. When the self-regulatory feedback loop is blocked in stage IV (such as in a crowd), the individual enters stage V (deindividuation).

more prominent than others. Through 'keynoting activities' it is the behaviour of these prominent individuals that become characteristic of the crowd as a whole. So rather than individuals' identity being lost in a crowd it is maintained and becomes the basis for the formation of group norms. The crowd acts as one on the basis of norms which emerge during the initial milling process, and each individual being surveyed by other crowd members.

Some problems with this concept of crowd behaviour have been noted:

- ☐ How are these norms spread so rapidly across the group?

- ☐ Many crowds do have a history, so these norms do not always emerge spontaneously. So what is the difference between a group and a crowd?

- ☐ It seems as though the 'norms' of the group are actually determined by a few powerful individual personalities (keynoting activities), but why do other people follow them blindly?

- ☐ Is our behaviour in a group or crowd simply the result of being surveyed by others? Perhaps we behave in a particular way because we feel we should.

Emergent norm theory is an individualistic account of crowd behaviour reducing the explanation to a few individuals. Some social psychologists have argued that any theory of crowds needs to look at the individuals involved but also the crowd's norms which reflect a particular ideological understanding of the world and that group's place within it.

The theories we've considered so far try to explain a crowd in terms of what happens to the individuals who compose it. Put simply, what's missing so far is some consideration of the context in which crowds form. They don't just occur, but occur for a reason.

## SOCIAL IDENTITY THEORY AND CROWDS

Members of a crowd are usually bound together in a common cause. This might be in direct opposition to another crowd (as in a riot) or to make a collective statement about a political, religious or social cause, or even to raise awareness about a social problem.

Using a social identity theory (SIT) approach Steve Reicher (1984) focused on the riots that occurred in the St Paul's area of Bristol in England. On 2 April 1980, the police raided the Black and White café situated on Grosvenor Road in the St Paul's area. This was the start of a period of rioting where people were injured and arrested. Although the escalation of the riot was quick, those participating had a shared history and identity as the St Paul's community. Regarding the raid as another sign of being treated unfairly by the police, the residents reacted. Reicher observed the crowd behaving in a way that was consistent with the social identity of being 'St Paul's community'. Legitimate targets (the police) were distinguished from illegitimate targets (innocent bystanders). Twenty-one police vehicles were damaged and 22 police officers injured. Ordinary civilians were not attacked. Offices and shops that were regarded as representative of the 'establishment' were damaged (e.g. banks, post offices, Department of Health and Social Security buildings). There were also geographical limits to the crowd's behaviour. The police were chased out of the St Paul's area but not beyond its limits. This study raises some interesting challenges to the theories of crowd behaviour noted earlier. This is not an out-of-control crowd. Nor is there an absence of personal identity, but an increase in a shared social identity. This is the basis for a crowd that acts as one. Not everyone catches 'crowd fever'! Only those for whom 'St Paul's' is a meaningful identity, participate.

Similar studies have been conducted on football crowds, which emphasize the role of social identity in guiding behaviour. Clifford Stott and colleagues (2001)

 **research close-up**

THE PSYCHOLOGY OF TYRANNY

**Source**: *Haslam, S.A., & Reicher, S. (2012). When prisoners take over the prison: A social psychology of resistance.* Personality and Social Psychology Review, *16(2), 154–179.*

### Introduction

Phillip Zimbardo's classic Stanford Prison Experiment, conducted in 1971, had shown that simply asking people to fulfil a role (as a prisoner or guard) changed their thinking and their behaviour. Not only that, but this change could result in acts which that same individual would otherwise consider to be unacceptable and cruel. In December 2001, Steve Reicher and Alex Haslam partially replicated Zimbardo's classic Stanford Prison Experiment. Broadcast on the BBC for a period of eight days, 15 men put into the roles of prisoner or guard were watched by the researchers and the public. Would they observe the same results and reach the same conclusions in the UK as Zimbardo had 30 years earlier in the US?

### Method

Ensuring sample diversity across both roles, the researchers divided their participants into 5 guards and 10 prisoners. Those assigned to the role of guard were given uniforms and details of tasks the prisoners needed to do in order for the institution to run smoothly. Guards were given ways of enforcing their authority, including keys to lockable prison cells, 'treats' (such as sweets and cigarettes), and putting prisoners on a bread and water diet. The researchers carried out daily psychometric and physiological tests on the men, and the viewing public saw an edited hour of observational data as the men went about conducting their lives in accordance with the role they had been assigned to.

### Results

Reicher and Haslam found in their study that the guards did not take on their role easily. They reported being troubled with their authoritative role over the prisoners. Disagreeing on how to carry out their role, they failed to bond as a team.

The prisoners also failed to respond as a group, rejecting their low standard of living. They were given restricted living space, a poor diet and no privileges. The prisoners adopted their own strategies for dealing with this. Some accepted their lot while others tried to improve their conditions. But this all changed when a new prisoner, a trade union official, was included. This led to greater cohesion between the prisoners and by Day 4 they began to challenge the guards. Unlike what was experienced in Zimbardo's original study, here the prisoners mocked the guards, undermining their authority. On Day 6, some of the prisoners managed to break into and occupy the guards' area, and refused to leave.

The roles of prisoner and guard consequently collapsed and a new structure was developed creating greater equality between prisoners and guards. The prisoners were glad to have more access to resources and the guards were relieved to relinquish the power that had made them feel so uncomfortable. Indication of their relief is found in the increases in positive mental health at this time. The collapse of the prisoner–guard hierarchy led to a single self-governing commune. But those prisoners who had been very active in challenging the old regime sabotaged the new commune. Now feeling marginalized by the new 'equal' system, they tried to challenge it.

Some of the prisoners and guards decided to try and re-establish the original prisoner–guard structure. They would run the prison, and reinforce the parameters of prisoners (e.g. cramped living conditions, poor diet) and guards (good food, freedom). They met with researchers to request this structure, arguing for a structure of inequality for themselves. As the threat of tyranny loomed the programme was ended prematurely, in a move that mirrored the early end to Zimbardo's original study. While Zimbardo's study was ended when the original guards became too tyrannical, in Haslam and Reicher's experiment, it was brought to a close when some of the original guards and prisoners, dissatisfied with the commune that had emerged, eventually took on the identity of 'guard' and sought to impose a tyrannical regime.

## Discussion

Reicher and Haslam concluded that social identity is the basis for tyranny. People may behave in tyrannical ways when they accept a particular role or identity that seems to require it. In Zimbardo's original study, this is what had happened. The 'guards' had internalized their identity and acted accordingly, forcing the early close to the experiment. In Haslam and Reicher's study it was the failure to accept guard and prisoner identities that led to a shared social identity and the emergence of the commune. Tyranny was proposed when some of the prisoners and guards resisted this new shared social identity, and demanded a reinstatement of the old regime but under their control. It is the desire for an identity, or the wish to resist one, that can form the basis for tyranny.

Zimbardo has criticized Haslam and Reicher's study, noting that because it was televised, it wasn't a faithful replication of the prison conditions he had created at Stanford. However, as Haslam and Reicher point out, neither their study nor Zimbardo's could claim to replicate a true prison experience. People do not usually volunteer to go to prison, nor are they free to leave, as was the case for participants in both studies. Rather, the aim was to find out how people respond to roles given to them, their readiness to identify with them, and the behavioural consequences of living in an environment where inequality is initially established between them.

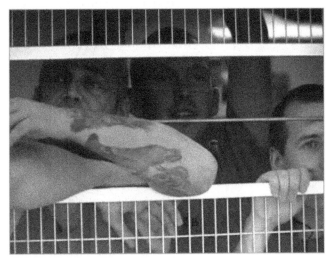

'Prisoners' in *The Experiment* on BBC.
SOURCE: © Haslam and Reicher/BBC

compared the experiences and actions of England and Scotland football hooligans. While the England fans have a historical tradition of aggressive behaviour, Scotland supporters do not. This has an impact on how they are perceived by other groups. During the France 1998 World Cup, Scotland fans were not expected to behave badly. The level of policing was minimal and the fans displayed a carnival atmosphere. In contrast the England fans, who were expected to behave aggressively, experienced extreme levels of policing. Stott makes the point that where this level of policing exceeds the potential threat posed by England fans, rioting behaviour is likely. From their observations and interviews conducted with supporters, they reported that England fans felt other groups treated them unfairly and often violently as they assumed that they would inevitably be met with hooliganism.

## INTERGROUP HARMONY

*So far we've focused on different types of intergroup conflict and prejudice, and examined them from a range of theoretical perspectives. But can we reduce intergroup conflict and prejudice? Let's consider some of the strategies social psychologists have proposed for improving intergroup relations.*

### CONTACT

Might putting two conflicting individuals or groups into close contact enable them to know and like each other?

A recent meta-analysis supports the argument that, in general, contact predicts tolerant attitudes. In a painstakingly complete analysis, Linda Tropp and Thomas Pettigrew (2005a; Pettigrew & Tropp, 2006) assembled data from 516 studies of 250 555 people in 38 nations. In 94 per cent of studies, *increased contact predicted decreased prejudice*. This is especially so for majority group attitudes towards minorities (Tropp & Pettigrew, 2005b).

Why? Gordon Allport is accredited with formulating the 'contact hypothesis'. This proposes that prejudice and conflict are often based on groups simply being ignorant of each other. As they lack knowledge of other groups' values and beliefs, they fear them and fail to notice when groups may have things in common with their own group. However, for Allport it wasn't simply that any contact would improve intergroup relations. Indeed, contact can fuel conflict and prejudice as negative expectations of outgroup members bias judgements of them and create self-fulfilling prophecies. Rather, contact should be done under a series of 'optimal conditions'. These are as follows:

**1** Contact is frequent and prolonged.

**2** Contact is with stereotypical members of the group.

**3** Contact is done with a genuine aspiration for improving relations.

**4** Contact occurs between individuals of equal status.

**5** Contact is free from competition.

**6** Contact is supported by formal structures (e.g. education, government policy).

**7** Contact is organized around the achievement of superordinate goals.

With such a long list you might wonder if contact under these conditions is really possible?

There is the further problem that it assumes prejudice is based on ignorance. The danger of course is that conflict is based on conflicts of interest. Such contact may only highlight the differences between groups rather than serve to dissolve them.

Contact, and Allport's 'contact hypothesis' in particular, have been used in social psychological studies that test improvement in intergroup relations. This has been researched in the area of ethnic conflict and prejudice towards minority groups seeking asylum in European countries. Another very prevalent area of research is that of racial conflict and prejudice.

### Does Desegregation Improve Racial Attitudes?

School desegregation has produced measurable benefits, such as leading more Blacks to attend and succeed in college (Stephan, 1988). On the surface this of course hits one of Allport's 'optimal conditions' for contact in terms of receiving institutional support. But does desegregation of schools, neighbourhoods and workplaces also produce favourable social results? The evidence is mixed.

On the one hand, many studies conducted during and shortly after mid-twentieth-century desegregation initiatives found Whites' attitudes towards Blacks improving markedly. Whether the people were department store clerks and customers, merchant marines, government workers, police officers, neighbours or students, racial contact led to diminished prejudice (Amir, 1969; Pettigrew, 1969). When Morton Deutsch and Mary Collins (1951) took advantage of a made-to-order natural experiment, they observed similar results. In accord with state law, New York City desegregated its public housing units; it assigned families to apartments without regard to race. In a similar development across the river in Newark, New Jersey, Blacks and Whites were assigned to separate buildings. When surveyed, White women in the desegregated development were far more likely to favour interracial housing and to say their attitudes towards Blacks had improved. Exaggerated stereotypes had wilted in the face of reality. As one woman put it, 'I've really come to like it. I see they're just as human as we are.'

Findings such as these have influenced broader policy decisions such as the desegregation of schools in the USA and South Africa. Yet studies of the effects of school desegregation have been less encouraging. After reviewing all the available studies, Walter Stephan (1986) concluded that racial attitudes had been little affected by desegregation. For Blacks, the noticeable consequence of desegregated schooling was less on Whites' attitudes than on their increased likelihood of attending integrated (or predominantly White) colleges, living in integrated neighbourhoods and working in integrated settings. Attitudes hadn't really changed.

Likewise, many student exchange programmes have had less-than-hoped-for positive effects on student attitudes towards their host countries. For example, when eager American students study in France, often living with other Americans as they do so, their stereotypes of the French tend not to improve (Stroebe et al., 1988). Contact also failed to allay the loathing of Rwandan Tutsis by their Hutu neighbours, or to eliminate the sexism of many men living and working in constant contact with women. People may more easily despise the homosexuals or immigrants whom they have never knowingly met, but they can also scorn people they see often.

Thus, we can see that sometimes desegregation improves racial attitudes; and sometimes – especially when there is anxiety or perceived threat (Pettigrew, 2004) – it doesn't. Such disagreements excite the scientist's detective spirit. What explains the difference? So far, we've been lumping all kinds of desegregation together. Actual desegregation occurs in many ways and under vastly different conditions.

### When Does Desegregation Improve Racial Attitudes?

Let's consider another of Allport's optimal conditions – frequent and prolonged contact. Might the frequency of interracial contact be a factor? Indeed it seems to be. Researchers have gone into dozens of desegregated schools and observed with whom children of a given race eat, talk and loiter. Race influences contact. Whites disproportionately associate with Whites, Blacks with Blacks (Schofield, 1982, 1986). In one study of Dartmouth University e-mail exchanges, Black students, though only 7 per cent of students, sent 44 per cent of their e-mails to other Black students (Sacerdote & Marmaros, 2005).

The same self-imposed segregation was evident in a South African desegregated beach, as John Dixon and Kevin Durrheim (2003) discovered when they recorded the location of Black, White and Indian beach-goers one midsummer (30 December) afternoon (Figure 13.6). Even in areas where segregation had never been a policy, desegregated neighbourhoods, cafeterias and restaurants, too, may fail to produce integrated interactions (Clack et al., 2005; Dixon et al., 2005a, 2005b).

Efforts to facilitate contact sometimes help, but sometimes fall flat. 'We had one day when some of the Protestant schools came over,' explained one Catholic youngster after a Northern Ireland school exchange (Cairns & Hewstone, 2002). 'It was supposed to be like … mixing, but there was very little mixing. It wasn't because we didn't want to; it was just really awkward.' The lack of mixing stems partly from 'pluralistic ignorance': many Whites and Blacks say they would like more contact but misperceive that the other does not reciprocate their feelings.

#### *Friendship*

In contrast, the more encouraging older studies of store clerks, soldiers and housing project neighbours involved considerable interracial contact, more than enough to reduce the anxiety that marks initial intergroup contact. Other studies involving prolonged, personal contact – between Black and White prison inmates, between Black and White girls in an interracial summer camp, between Black and White university room-mates, and between Black, Coloured and White South Africans – show similar benefits (Clore et al., 1978; Foley, 1976; Holtman et al., 2005; Van Laar et al., 2005). Among American students who have studied in Germany or in Britain, the greater their contact with host country people, the more positive their attitudes (Stangor et al., 1996). A range of studies suggest that those who form *friendships* with outgroup members develop more positive attitudes towards the outgroup (Pettigrew & Tropp, 2000; Wright & Bougie, 2007). For example, Elizabeth Page-Gould, Rodolfo Mendoza-Denton and Linda Tropp (2008) found that cross-group friendships between Latinos and Whites reduced intergroup anxiety and improved liking for the outgroup. Rhiannon Turner, Miles Hewstone and Alberto Voci (2007) reported similar findings for White

**FIGURE 13.6**   Desegregation needn't mean contact
After this Scottburgh, South Africa, beach became 'open' and desegregated in the new South Africa, Blacks (represented by red dots), Whites (blue dots) and Indians (yellow dots) tended to cluster with their own race.
SOURCE: Dixon & Durrheim, 2003.

school children who make friends who are South Asian. This isn't just reported in research on race but also in studies that consider prejudices on the basis of sexual orientation. For example, Christiana Vonofakou, Miles Hewstone and Alberto Voci (2007) noted how heterosexual men's attitudes towards gay men became much more positive when they made a gay friend. It's not just head knowledge of other people that matters; it's also the *emotional* ties that form with intimate friendships and that serve to reduce anxiety (Hewstone, 2003; Pettigrew & Tropp, 2000).

But 'group salience' also helps bridge divides between people. If you forever think of that friend solely as an individual, your affective ties may not generalize to other members of the friend's group (Miller, 2002). Ideally, then, we should form trusting friendships across group lines but also recognize that the friend represents those in another group – with whom we turn out to have much in common.

We will be most likely to befriend people who differ from us if their outgroup identity is initially minimized – if we see them as essentially like us rather than feeling threatened by their being different. If our liking for our new friends is to generalize to others, their group identity must at some point become salient. So, to reduce prejudice and conflict, we had best initially minimize group diversity, then acknowledge it, then transcend it.

Surveys of nearly 4000 Europeans reveal that friendship is a key to successful contact: if you have a minority group friend, you become much more likely to express sympathy and support for the friend's group, and even somewhat more support for immigration by that group. It's true of West Germans' attitudes towards Turks, French people's attitudes towards Asians and North Africans, Netherlanders' attitudes towards Surinamers and Turks, Britons' attitudes towards West Indians and Asians, and Northern Ireland Protestants' and Catholics' attitudes towards each other (Brown et al., 1999; Hamberger & Hewstone, 1997; Paolini et al., 2007; Pettigrew, 1997). Likewise, anti-gay feeling is lower among people who know gays personally (Herek, 1993; Kaiser Family Foundation, 2001). Additional studies of attitudes towards the elderly, the mentally ill, AIDS patients and those with disabilities confirm that contact and especially friendship often predicts positive attitudes (Hewstone, 2003).

### Equal-status Contact

Social psychologists who advocated desegregation never claimed that all contact would improve attitudes. They expected poor results when contacts were competitive, unsupported by authorities, and unequal (Pettigrew, 1988; Stephan, 1987). Before 1954 many prejudiced Whites had frequent contacts with Blacks – as shoeshine men and domestic workers. Such unequal contact can breed attitudes that merely justify the continuation of inequality. So it's important that the contact be equal-status contact, like that between the store clerks, the soldiers, the neighbours, the prisoners and the summer campers.

### Co-operation

Although equal-status contact can help, it is sometimes not enough. It didn't help when Muzafer Sherif stopped the competition at the summer camp and brought the two groups together for non-competitive activities such as watching films, eating and setting off fireworks. By that time the competition between the two groups was so strong that mere contact only provided opportunities for taunts

equal-status contact *the principle that to reduce prejudice between people these should have close contact, in a setting where equal status can be assured, while they work on shared goals requiring co-operation. In addition such initiatives should be supported and encouraged by a broader network*

Shared predicaments trigger co-operation, as these workers on strike in Germany demonstrate.

SOURCE: © ollo/iStock

and attacks. Desegregating the two groups promoted their social interaction. Another remedy had to be found. Co-operation was required to unite the two groups in working together to achieve a common goal. Think back to the successful and the unsuccessful desegregation efforts. The army's racial mixing of rifle companies not only brought Blacks and Whites into equal-status contact but also made them interdependent. Together, they were striving towards a shared goal.

So does competitive contact divide and *co-operative* contact unite? Consider what happens to people who together face a common predicament. In conflicts at all levels, from couples to rival teams to nations, shared threats and common goals breed unity.

### Common External Threats Build Cohesiveness

Together with others, have you ever been caught in a blizzard, punished by a teacher, or persecuted and ridiculed because of your social, ethnic, racial or religious identity? If so, you may recall feeling close to those with whom you shared the predicament. Perhaps previous social barriers were dropped as you helped one another dig out of the snow or struggled to cope with your common enemy.

Such friendliness is common among those who experience a shared threat. John Lanzetta (1955) observed this when he put four-man groups of naval Reserve Officers' Training Corps cadets to work on problem-solving tasks and then began informing them over a loudspeaker that their answers were wrong, their productivity inexcusably low, their thinking stupid. Other groups did not receive this harassment. Lanzetta observed that the group members under duress became friendlier to one another, more co-operative, less argumentative, less competitive. They were in it together. And the result was a cohesive spirit.

Having a common enemy unified the groups of competing boys in Sherif's camping experiments – and in many subsequent experiments (Dion, 1979). Times of interracial strife similarly heighten group pride. For Chinese university students in Toronto, facing discrimination has heightened a sense of kinship with other Chinese (Pak et al., 1991). Just being reminded of an outgroup (say, a rival school) heightens people's responsiveness to their own group (Wilder & Shapiro, 1984). When keenly conscious of who 'they' are, we also know who 'we' are.

Leaders may even create a threatening external enemy as a technique for building group cohesiveness. For the group, the nation, the world, having a common enemy is powerfully unifying. For example, Palestinian suicide bombers in Israel rallied partisan Jews behind the Prime Minister Ariel Sharon and his government, while the Israeli Defence Force killing of Palestines and the destruction of their property united Muslim factions in their animosity towards Sharon (Pettigrew, 2003). And, after the USA attacked Iraq, Pew Research Centre (2003) polls of Indonesian and Jordanian Muslims found rising anti-Americanism. The 53 per cent of Jordanians who expressed a positive view of Americans in the summer of 2002 plummeted to

18 per cent shortly after the war. 'Before the war, I would have said that if Osama [Bin Laden] was responsible for the two towers, we would not be proud of it,' said one Syrian 21-year-old Islamic law student. 'But if he did it now we would be proud of him' (Rubin, 2003).

### Superordinate Goals Foster Co-operation

Closely related to the unifying power of an external threat is the unifying power of superordinate goals, goals that unite all in a group and require co-operative effort. To promote harmony among his warring campers, Sherif introduced such goals. He created a problem with the camp water supply, necessitating both groups' co-operation to restore the water. Given an opportunity to rent a movie, one expensive enough to require the joint resources of the two groups, they again co-operated. When a truck 'broke down' on a camp excursion, a staff member casually left the tug-of-war rope nearby, prompting one boy to suggest that they all pull the truck to get it started. When it started, a backslapping celebration ensued over their victorious 'tug-of-war against the truck'.

*superordinate goal*
*a shared goal that necessitates co-operative effort; a goal that overrides people's differences from one another*

After working together to achieve such superordinate goals, the boys ate together and enjoyed themselves around a campfire. Friendships sprouted across group lines. Hostilities plummeted (Figure 13.7). On the last day, the boys decided to travel home together on one bus. During the trip they no longer sat by groups. As the bus approached Oklahoma City and home, they, as one, spontaneously sang 'Oklahoma' and then bade their friends farewell. With isolation and competition, Sherif made strangers into bitter enemies. With superordinate goals, he made enemies into friends.

Are Sherif's experiments mere child's play? Or can pulling together to achieve superordinate goals be similarly beneficial with adults in conflict? Robert Blake and Jane Mouton (1979) wondered. So in a series of two-week experiments involving more than 1000 executives in 150 different groups, they re-created the essential features of the situation experienced by the two boys groups in the summer camp. Each group first engaged in activities by itself, then competed with another group, and then co-operated with the other group in working towards jointly chosen superordinate goals. Their results provided 'unequivocal evidence that adult reactions parallel those of Sherif's younger subjects'.

The co-operative efforts by boys at Sherif's summer camp ended in success. Would the same harmony have emerged if the water had remained off, the movie unaffordable, the truck still stalled? Probably not. Stephen Worchel and his associates (1977, 1978; Worchel & Norvell, 1980) confirmed that *successful* co-operation between two groups boosts their attraction for each other. If previously conflicting groups *fail*

Group identity feeds, and is fed by, competition. *The Xenophobe's Guide to the Scots* makes the observation that Scots divide non-Scots 'into two main groups: (1) The English; (2) The Rest'. As rabid Chicago Cubs fans are happy if either the Cubs win or the White Sox lose, so rabid fans of Scottish soccer rejoice in either a Scotland victory or an England defeat. 'Phew! They Lost,' rejoiced one Scottish tabloid front-page headline after England's 1996 Euro Cup defeat – by Germany, no less.
SOURCE: © Michael Luhrenberg/iStock

**Ratings of outgroup, percentage totally unfavourable**

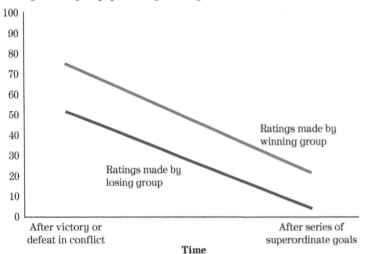

FIGURE 13.7  After competition, the groups of the Eagles and the Rattlers rated each other unfavourably. After they worked cooperatively to achieve superordinate goals, hostility dropped sharply.

SOURCE: Data from Sherif, 1966, p. 84.

in a co-operative effort, however, and if conditions allow them to attribute their failure to each other, the conflict may worsen. Sherif's groups were already feeling hostile to each other. Thus, failure to raise sufficient funds for the movie might have been attributed to one group's 'stinginess' and 'selfishness'. That would have exacerbated rather than alleviated their conflict.

Should we have 'known it all along'? Gordon Allport spoke for many social psychologists in predicting, 'Prejudice ... may be reduced by equal status contact between majority and minority groups in the pursuit of common goals' (1954, p. 281). Co-operative learning experiments confirmed Allport's insight, making Robert Slavin (1985) and his colleagues (Slavin et al., 2003) optimistic: 'Thirty years after Allport laid out the basic principles operationalized in cooperative learning methods, we finally have practical, proven methods for implementing contact theory in the desegregated classroom ... Research on cooperative learning is one of the greatest success stories in the history of educational research.'

So, co-operative, equal-status contacts exert a positive influence on boy campers, industrial executives, college students and schoolchildren. Does the principle extend to all levels of human relations? Are families unified by pulling together to farm the land, restore an old house or sail a sloop? Are communal identities forged by barn raisings, group singing or cheering on the football team? Is international understanding bred by international collaboration in science and space, by joint efforts to feed the world and conserve resources, by friendly personal contacts between people of different nations? Indications are that the answer to all those questions is yes (Brewer & Miller, 1988; Desforges et al., 1991, 1997; Deutsch, 1985, 1994). Thus, an important challenge facing our divided world is to identify and agree on our superordinate goals and to structure co-operative efforts to achieve them.

### Groups and Superordinate Identities

In everyday life, we often reconcile multiple identities (Gaertner et al., 2000, 2001; Hewstone & Greenland, 2000; Huo et al., 1996). We acknowledge our subgroup identity (as parent or child) and then transcend it (sensing our superordinate identity as a family). Blended families and corporate mergers leave us mindful of who we were, and who we are. Pride in our ethnic heritage can complement our larger communal or national identity. Being mindful of our *multiple* social identities, which

Promoting 'common ingroup identity'. The banning of gang colours and the common European practice of school uniform aim to change 'us' and 'them' to 'we'.

SOURCE: © Cultura/Image Source

we partially share with anyone else, enables social cohesion (Brewer & Pierce, 2005; Crisp & Hewstone, 1999, 2000). 'I am many things, some of which you are, too.'

'Most of us have overlapping identities which unite us with very different groups. We can love what we are, without hating what – and who – we are not. We can thrive in our own tradition, even as we learn from others, and come to respect their teachings.'

Kofi Annan, Nobel Peace Prize Lecture, 2001

But in ethnically diverse cultures, how do people balance their ethnic identities with their national identities? They may have what identity researcher Jean Phinney (1990) calls a 'bicultural' identity, one that identifies with both the ethnic culture and the larger culture. Ethnically conscious Asians living in England may also feel strongly British (Hutnik, 1985). French Canadians who identify with their ethnic roots may or may not also feel strongly Canadian (Driedger, 1975). Hispanic Americans who retain a strong sense of their 'Cubanness' (or of their Mexican or Puerto Rican heritage) may feel strongly American (Roger et al., 1991). As W. E. B. DuBois (1903, p. 17) explained in *The Souls of Black Folk*, 'The American Negro [longs] ... to be both a Negro and an American'.

Researchers have wondered whether pride in one's group competes with identification with the larger culture. We evaluate ourselves partly in terms of our group memberships. Seeing our own group (our school, our employer, our family, our race, our nation) as good helps us feel good about ourselves. A positive ethnic identity can therefore contribute to positive self-esteem; so can a positive mainstream culture identity. 'Marginal' people, who have neither a strong ethnic nor a strong mainstream cultural identity (Table 13.2), often have low self-esteem. Bicultural people, who affirm both identities, typically have a strongly positive self-concept (Phinney, 1990). Often, they alternate between their two cultures, adapting their language and behaviour to whichever group they are with (LaFromboise et al., 1993).

> Our own social identity is derived from the social groups we are members of and this feeds our self-esteem. Chapter 12 offers extensive coverage of social identity and how we evaluate ourselves in relation to this.

Debate continues over the ideals of multiculturalism, or pluralism (celebrating differences), versus assimilation (meshing one's values and habits with the prevailing culture). On one side are those who believe, as the Department of Canadian Heritage (2006) has declared, that 'multiculturalism ensures that all citizens can keep their identities, can take pride in their ancestry and have a sense of belonging. Acceptance gives Canadians a feeling of security and self-confidence, making them open to and accepting of diverse cultures.' On the other side are those who concur with Britain's Commission for Racial Equality chair, Trevor Phillips (2004), in worrying that multiculturalism separates people rather than encouraging common values, a view that inspired the Rwandan government to adopt the official view that 'there is no ethnicity here. We are all Rwandan.' In the aftermath of Rwanda's ethnic bloodbath, government documents and government-controlled radio and newspapers have ceased mentioning Hutu and Tutsi (Lacey, 2004). In the space between multiculturalism and assimilation lies 'diversity within unity', a perspective advocated by sociologist Amitai Etzioni (2005). 'It presumes that all members of a given society will fully respect and adhere to those basic values and institutions that are considered part of the basic shared framework of the society.

pluralism *respect for differences between cultures within a prevailing culture*

assimilation *meshing different cultural values and habits into the prevailing culture*

**TABLE 13.2** Ethnic and cultural identity

| Identification with majority group | Identification with ethnic group | |
|---|---|---|
| | Strong | Weak |
| Strong | Bicultural | Assimilated |
| Weak | Separated | Marginal |

At the same time, every group in society is free to maintain its distinct subculture – those policies, habits, and institutions that do not conflict with the shared core.'

By forging unifying ideals, immigrant countries such as the USA, Canada and Australia have avoided ethnic wars. In these countries, Irish and Italians, Swedes and Scots, Asians and Africans seldom kill in defence of their ethnic identities. Nevertheless, even the immigrant nations struggle between separation and wholeness, between people's pride in their distinct heritage and unity as one nation, between acknowledging the reality of diversity and questing for shared values.

de-categorization *where intergroup contact is facilitated by 'de-categorizing' group members through an emphasis on individual personal characteristics rather than group identity*

common ingroup identity model *when members of different social groups re-categorize themselves into one group*

How good relations between groups can be fostered has received much attention from SCT theorists. Norman Miller and Marilynn Brewer (1984) suggest that forms of intergroup contact can highlight group boundaries, so they propose a 'de-categorization' (or personalization) model where personal rather than group identity and contact is the focus. However, Samuel Gaertner suggests such avoidances of group boundaries are simply not possible in the real-world and offers the 'common ingroup identity model', where members of different groups are encouraged to 're-categorize' themselves as belonging to a common ingroup sharing a superordinate identity. Samuel Gaertner, John Dovidio and their collaborators (1993, 2000) report that working co-operatively leads people to define a new, inclusive group that dissolves their former subgroups. They define this as 're-categorization'. Old feelings of bias against another group diminish when members of the two groups sit alternately around a table (rather than on opposite sides), give their new group a single name, and then work together under conditions that foster a good mood. 'Us' and 'them' become 'we'. This has been demonstrated by Shui-fong Lam et al. (2006), who found that when Hong Kong adolescents were asked to read a newspaper article that suggested Hong Kong would be disadvantaged if China joined the World Trade Organization (WTO), they displayed negative attitudes towards Chinese mainlanders, especially when such judgements were made under time pressure. However, when they read a newspaper article that suggested the Chinese were facing an economic threat from Japan if China joined the WTO, they re-categorized themselves as Chinese and displayed negative evaluations of the Japanese.

re-categorization *where intergroup contact is facilitated by 're-categorizing' group members under an inclusive common ingroup focusing on a superordinate identity*

dual identities *where group individuals hold superordinate and subordinate identities*

More recently the idea of 'dual identities' has been proposed, which suggests that minority group members might adopt a strategy of holding both superordinate and subordinate identities, in order to fit into mainstream society. Demis Glasford and John Dovidio (2011) remark that a common ingroup identity can encourage positive intergroup attitudes and reduce tension. But, the values upon which this common identity is often based, 'favors advantaged groups'. So pure assimilation into the majority group may not be ideal for minority group members. In contrast, a dual identity not only promotes a common superordinate identity but also draws attention to, and respect for, distinct subordinate identities. Recognition of dual identities can help foster values that enable a multicultural society to respect both similarities and differences between groups. Where dual identity exists, minority group members are motivated to establish contact with the majority group to enhance greater intergroup harmony (Glasford and Dovidio, 2011). However, some researchers have argued that having a dual identity can be a double-edged sword. For it to work, the majority group must accept the superordinate identity claims of minority group members, and welcome the subordinate identity. Gülseli Baysu,

Karen Phalet and Rupert Brown (2011) looked at the high school experiences of Turkish Belgian young adults. They compared the different strategies that second-generation Turkish participants adopted to fit into high school in Belgium. They found that those who used a separated strategy, emphasizing their different ethnic Turkish identity, were very resilient in the face of discrimination and intergroup hostility. They performed well at school as they tried to overcome the negative stereotypes Belgians had of this group. Other students adopted an assimilation strategy, becoming acculturated into Belgian life and national identity. They upheld Belgian norms and values, and as such performed well when their own ethnic group was threatened. By distancing themselves from the Turkish ethnic group, they could affirm their commitment to the Belgian national group and display this through good academic performance.

A difficult balancing act. These ethnically conscious French Canadians – attending a rally during the Quebec referendum – may or may not also feel strongly Canadian. As countries become more ethnically diverse, people debate how we can build societies that are both plural and unified. SOURCE: © Brooks Kraft/Getty Images

Finally, those students who had adopted a dual identity approach, had a more difficult time. In Belgium, recognition and tolerance of other ethnic identities is poor. As such, those participants who adopted a dual identity found themselves unaccepted in terms of a common national (superordinate) Belgian identity, or an ethnic (Turkish) one. Baysu et al. (2011) point out that dual identity strategies do not seem to work in environments where a minority group is subject to high levels of threat. When the level of threat is low, and society is more accepting of diverse ethnic cultures, dual identifiers actually perform much better in school than those who adopt a separated or assimilated strategy.

## COMMUNICATION

To resolve a social dilemma, people must communicate. In the laboratory, as in real life, group communication sometimes degenerates into threats and name-calling (Deutsch & Krauss, 1960). More often, communication enables people to co-operate (Bornstein & Rapoport, 1988; Bornstein et al., 1989). Discussing the dilemma forges a group identity which enhances concern for everyone's welfare. It devises group norms and consensus expectations and puts pressure on members to follow them. Particularly when people are face to face it enables them to commit themselves to co-operation (Bouas & Komorita, 1996; Drolet & Morris, 2000; Kerr & Kaufman-Gilliland, 1994; Kerr et al., 1997; Pruitt, 1998).

Conflicting parties have other ways to resolve their differences. Andersen, Saribay and Thorpe (2008) note that how communication is done between groups can be extremely important for resolution of intergroup conflict. When we convey warmth, respect and co-operation, peace is more likely.

When husband and wife, or labour and management, or nation X and nation Y disagree, they can bargain with each other directly. They can ask a third party to mediate by making suggestions and facilitating their negotiations. Or they can

bargaining *seek resolution to a conflict through direct negotiation between parties*

mediate *an attempt by a neutral third party to resolve a conflict by facilitating communication and offering suggestions*

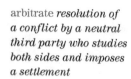

**arbitrate** *resolution of a conflict by a neutral third party who studies both sides and imposes a settlement*

arbitrate by submitting their disagreement to someone who will study the issues and impose a settlement.

### Bargaining

If you want to buy or sell a new car, are you better off adopting a tough bargaining stance – opening with an extreme offer so that splitting the difference will yield a favourable result? Or are you better off beginning with a sincere 'good-faith' offer?

Experiments suggest no simple answer. Tough bargaining may lower the other party's expectations, making the other side willing to settle for less (Yukl, 1974). But toughness can sometimes backfire. Being tough is a potential lose–lose scenario. If the other party responds with an equally tough stance, both may be locked into positions from which neither can back down without losing face. In the weeks before the 1991 Persian Gulf War, the first President Bush threatened, in the full glare of publicity, to 'kick Saddam's ass'. Saddam Hussein, no less macho, threatened to make 'infidel' Americans 'swim in their own blood'. After such belligerent statements, it was difficult for each side to evade war and save face.

### Mediation

A third-party mediator may offer suggestions that enable conflicting parties to make concessions and still save face (Pruitt, 1998). If my concession can be attributed to a mediator, who is gaining an equal concession from my antagonist, then neither of us will be viewed as weakly caving in to the other's demands.

#### *Turning Win–Lose into Win–Win*

Mediators also help resolve conflicts by facilitating constructive communication. Their first task is to help the parties rethink the conflict and gain information about others' interests (Thompson, 1998). Typically, people on both sides have a competitive 'win–lose' orientation: they are successful if their opponent is unhappy with the result, and unsuccessful if their opponent is pleased (Thompson et al., 1995). The mediator aims to replace this win–lose orientation with a co-operative 'win–win' orientation, by prodding both sides to set aside their conflicting demands and instead to think about each other's underlying needs, interests and goals. In experiments, Leigh Thompson (1990a, 1990b) found that, with experience, negotiators become better able to make mutually beneficial tradeoffs and thus to achieve win–win resolutions.

#### *Unravelling Misperceptions with Controlled Communications*

Communication often helps reduce self-fulfilling misperceptions. Perhaps you can recall experiences similar to that of this college student:

Often, after a prolonged period of little communication, I perceive Mary's silence as a sign of her dislike for me. She, in turn, thinks that my quietness is a result of my being mad at her. My silence induces her silence, which makes me even more silent . . . until this snowballing effect is broken by some occurrence that makes it necessary for us to interact. And the communication then unravels all the misinterpretations we had made about one another.

The outcome of such conflicts often depends on *how* people communicate their feelings to one another. Programmes train couples and children how to manage conflicts constructively (Horowitz and Boardman, 1994). If managed constructively, conflict provides opportunities for reconciliation and more genuine harmony. Psychologists Ian Gotlib and Catherine Colby (1988) offer advice on how to avoid destructive quarrels and how to have good quarrels.

Conflict researchers report that a key factor is *trust* (Ross & Ward, 1995). If you believe the other person is well intentioned, you are then more likely to divulge your needs and concerns. Lacking trust, you may fear that being open will give the other party information that might be used against you.

When the two parties mistrust each other and communicate unproductively, a third-party mediator – a marriage counsellor, a labour mediator, a diplomat – sometimes helps. Often the mediator is someone trusted by both sides. In the 1980s it took an Algerian Muslim to mediate the conflict between Iran and Iraq, and the Pope to resolve a geographical dispute between Argentina and Chile (Carnevale & Choi, 2000).

After coaxing the conflicting parties to rethink their perceived win–lose conflict, the mediator often has each party identify and rank its goals. When goals are compatible, the ranking procedure makes it easier for each to concede on less important goals so that both achieve their chief goals (Erickson et al., 1974; Schulz & Pruitt, 1978). South Africa achieved internal peace when Black and White South Africans granted each other's top priorities – replacing apartheid with majority rule and safeguarding the security, welfare and rights of Whites (Kelman, 1998).

The mediator will often structure the encounter to help each party understand and feel understood by the other. The mediator may ask the conflicting parties to restrict their arguments to statements of fact, including statements of how they feel and how they respond when the other acts in a given way. Also, the mediator may ask people to reverse roles and argue the other's position, or to imagine and explain what the other person is experiencing.

These peace-making principles – based partly on laboratory experiments, partly on practical experience – have helped mediate both international and industrial conflicts (Blake & Mouton, 1962, 1979; Fisher, 1994; Wehr, 1979). One small team of Arab and Jewish Americans, led by social psychologist Herbert Kelman (1997), has conducted workshops bringing together influential Arabs and Israelis. Another social psychologist team, led by Ervin Staub and Laurie Ann Pearlman (2005, 2006; Staub et al., 2005), worked in Rwanda between 1999 and 2003 training facilitators and journalists to understand and write about Rwanda's traumas in ways that promote healing and reconciliation. Using methods such as those we've considered, Kelman and colleagues counter misperceptions and have participants seek creative solutions for their common good. Isolated, the participants are free to speak directly to their adversaries without fear that their constituents are second-guessing what they are saying. The result? Those from both sides typically come to understand the other's perspective and how the other side responds to their own group's actions.

### Arbitration

Some conflicts are so intractable, the underlying interests so divergent, that a mutually satisfactory resolution is unattainable. In Bosnia and Kosovo, both Serbs and Muslims could not have jurisdiction over the same homeland. In this and many other cases, a third-party mediator may – or may not – help resolve the conflict.

If not, the parties may turn to *arbitration* by having the mediator or another third party *impose* a settlement. Disputants usually prefer to settle their differences without arbitration so that they retain control over the outcome. Neil McGillicuddy et al. (1987) observed this preference in an experiment involving disputants coming to a dispute settlement centre. When people knew they would face an arbitrated settlement if mediation failed, they tried harder to resolve the problem, exhibited less hostility and thus were more likely to reach agreement.

Typically, however, the final offer is not as reasonable as it would be if each party, free of self-serving bias, saw its own proposal through others' eyes. Negotiation researchers report that most disputants are made stubborn by 'optimistic overconfidence' (Kahneman & Tversky, 1995). Successful mediation is hindered when, as often happens, both parties believe they have a two-thirds chance of winning a final-offer arbitration (Bazerman, 1986, 1990).

### Conciliation

Sometimes tension and suspicion run so high that even communication, let alone resolution, becomes all but impossible. Each party may threaten, coerce or retaliate against the other. Unfortunately, such acts tend to be reciprocated, escalating the conflict. So, would a strategy of appeasing the other party by being unconditionally co-operative produce a satisfying result? Often not. In laboratory games, those who are 100 per cent co-operative often are exploited. Politically, a one-sided pacifism is usually out of the question.

Social psychologist Charles Osgood (1962, 1980) advocated a third option, one that is conciliatory yet strong enough to discourage exploitation. Osgood called it 'graduated and reciprocated initiatives in tension reduction'. He nicknamed it GRIT, a label that suggests the determination it requires. GRIT aims to reverse the 'conflict spiral' by triggering reciprocal de-escalation. To do so, it draws upon social psychological concepts, such as the norm of reciprocity and the attribution of motives.

GRIT *acronym for 'graduated and reciprocated initiatives in tension reduction' – a strategy designed to de-escalate international tensions*

GRIT requires one side to initiate a few small de-escalatory actions, after *announcing a conciliatory intent*. The initiator states its desire to reduce tension, declares each conciliatory act before making it and invites the adversary to reciprocate. Such announcements create a framework that helps the adversary correctly interpret what otherwise might be seen as weak or tricky actions. They also bring public pressure to bear on the adversary to follow the reciprocity norm.

Next, the initiator establishes credibility and genuineness by carrying out, exactly as announced, several verifiable *conciliatory acts*. This intensifies the pressure to reciprocate. Making conciliatory acts diverse – perhaps offering medical help, closing a military base and lifting a trade ban – keeps the initiator from making a significant sacrifice in any one area and leaves the adversary freer to choose its own means of reciprocation. If the adversary reciprocates voluntarily, its own conciliatory behaviour may soften its attitudes. Morton Deutsch (1993) captured the spirit of GRIT in advising negotiators to be '"firm, fair, and friendly"': *firm* in resisting intimidation, exploitation, and dirty tricks; *fair* in holding to one's moral principles and not reciprocating the other's immoral behaviour despite his or her provocations; and *friendly* in the sense that one is willing to initiate and reciprocate cooperation'.

Does GRIT really work? In laboratory dilemma games a successful strategy has proved to be simple 'tit-for-tat', which similarly begins with a co-operative opening play and thereafter matches the other party's last response (Axelrod & Dion, 1988; Parks & Rumble, 2001; Van Lange & Visser, 1999). Although it begins co-operatively, tit-for-tat immediately punishes non-co-operation and also immediately forgives hostile opponents as soon as they make a co-operative move. In a lengthy series of experiments Svenn Lindskold and his associates (1976 to 1988) found 'strong support for the various steps in the GRIT proposal'. In laboratory games, announcing co-operative intent *does* boost co-operation. Repeated conciliatory acts *do* breed greater trust (although self-serving biases often make one's own acts seem more conciliatory and less hostile than those of the adversary). Maintaining an equality of power *does* protect against exploitation.

Lindskold was not contending that the world of the laboratory experiment mirrors the more complex world of everyday life. Rather, experiments enable us to formulate and verify powerful theoretical principles, such as the reciprocity norm and the self-serving bias. As Lindskold (1981) noted, 'It is the theories, not the individual experiments that are used to interpret the world'.

## Real-world Applications

GRIT-like strategies have occasionally been tried outside the laboratory, with promising results. During the Berlin crisis of the early 1960s, US and Russian tanks faced each other barrel to barrel. The crisis was defused when the Americans pulled back their tanks step by step. At each step, the Russians reciprocated. Similarly, in the 1970s small concessions by Israel and Egypt (for example, Israel allowing Egypt to open up the Suez Canal, Egypt allowing ships bound for Israel to pass through) helped reduce tension to a point where the negotiations became possible (Rubin, 1981).

## focus on

### IS PREJUDICE ALL IN OUR HEADS?

Developments in the field of social neuroscience have influenced social psychologists interested in prejudice. As our ability to see neural processes in the brain increases with the advancement of brain-imaging techniques, does this mean we can observe neural reactions that might be responsible for our prejudices? Certainly there is evidence that some activity goes on in our brains which seems to be associated with racist attitudes. For example, Elizabeth Phelps and her colleagues (2000) found that when white participants saw African-American faces (black), there was greater amygdala activation than when they were shown European-American faces (white). But is it the brain causing the prejudice, or the prejudice causing the activity in the brain?

Remember our discussion of schemas in Chapter 4? There we considered work that noted how schemas help us to perceive the world around us. We are very quick to recognize what we 'expect' to see. Samuel Gaertner and John McLaughlin (1983), for example, found that participants were much quicker to recognize positive words when they were preceded by a white face than when preceded by a black face. Why? Well, that's because they fit our schemas, argue the researchers. So regardless of whether these participants think they are prejudiced or not, these racial stereotypes exist in their minds (Fiske & Taylor, 1991).

Alexander Todorov and his colleagues (2006) suggest that while we can see these processes in the brain, what they reflect is social and cultural learning, norms and values. They have been acquired in a particular social context, and tend to occur when we are asked to compare unfamiliar people on a salient group characteristic such as race. As social psychological work on categorization has emphasized, people are motivated to enhance their own group, and seek out information that maximizes differences between 'us' and 'them'. So when comparing black faces with white ones we see the neural processes associated with doing so.

Can we override this tendency to make negatively biased assumptions about another group? Yes, says Michael Inzlicht and his colleagues (2012). One way we can do this is to take the perspective of other group members. In Chapter 10, we considered how people are quick to help people they perceive to be fellow ingroup members. They feel empathy towards them. EEG studies back this up, showing that when white participants watch another white person perform an action, they 'mentally resonate' with them, exhibiting high levels of motor activity in their cortex (Gutsell & Inzlicht, 2012). However, when they see black people perform the same activity, this neural activity is absent. Inzlicht et al. (2012) propose that if racial prejudice is culturally learned, such that we do not 'mentally resonate' with other races, then it should be possible to override it, and reduce prejudice. In their study, some of their white participants were asked to mimic the actions of a black actor when he reached for a glass of water. When these participants were then measured for implicit racism, they showed reduced implicit racism unlike those white participants who had simply observed the black actor, but hadn't mimicked him. The researchers conclude that putting yourself in the shoes of a member of an outgroup can reduce prejudice, and kick-start those brain processes that underlie 'mentally resonating' with them.

## QUESTIONS

**1** Is it possible to 'unlearn' prejudice?

**2** To what extent do you think implicit measures of prejudice capture what is going on in our heads? Are they a faithful reflection of activity in the brain?

# SUMMING UP: PREJUDICE, INTERGROUP RELATIONS AND CONFLICT

## UNDERSTANDING PREJUDICE

☐ Social psychological explanations of prejudice have ranged from the study of personality characteristics, prejudiced attitudes, the demands of social cognition, its relationship to social context and its expression in language.

☐ Personality explanations have emphasized the role of authoritarianism, rigid thinking and political preferences in highly prejudiced individuals.

☐ Social cognition explanations have considered the role of categorization and the formation of stereotypes to ingroups and outgroups in prejudice.

☐ Some social psychologists have examined the social hierarchies of social groups within a society and considered how individuals' beliefs about the existence of inequalities are related to levels of prejudice.

☐ A threat to one's cultural worldview may cause even further faith in that worldview and prejudice towards those who challenge it.

☐ Discursive psychologists have investigated how prejudice is constructed in talk and text, producing and reproducing common-sense ways of understanding 'them' and 'us'.

☐ Prejudice exists in subtle and unconscious guises as well as overt, conscious forms. Researchers have devised subtle survey questions and indirect methods for assessing people's attitudes and behaviour to detect unconscious prejudice.

☐ Racial prejudice has become far less overtly prevalent, but it still exists in subtle forms.

☐ Similarly, prejudice against women has lessened in recent decades. Nevertheless, strong gender stereotypes and a fair amount of gender bias are still found. Though less obvious, prejudice lurks.

## INTERGROUP CONFLICT

☐ Intergroup conflict defines negative behaviour that occurs between distinct social groups on the basis of membership of that group. Social psychologists have been particularly concerned with the conditions under which conflict will occur.

☐ Realistic conflict theory suggests that conflict is likely between groups when there is a battle for scarce resources.

☐ Social identity theory and self-categorization theory argue that conflict will occur even in the absence of competition for scarce resources. Individuals identify with groups and stereotype the characteristics of their group and others in socially relevant and meaningful ways. Groups will engage in conflict when they perceive the existence of an outgroup group as a threat to the identity and values of the ingroup.

## CROWDS

☐ Social psychologists have examined the behaviour of crowds as visible demonstrations of negative intergroup relations.

☐ Some theorists have suggested that being in a crowd causes a psychological change within the individuals who constitute the crowd. Le Bon's 'group mind' emphasizes the irrationality of the crowd as individuals become submerged as the 'racial unconscious' takes over their usual psychological functioning.

☐ Deindividuation theorists have argued that people in crowds lose their sense of identity and responsibility. This decrease in self-monitoring leads to aggressive behaviour as individuals experience anonymity within the crowd.

☐ Emergent norm theorists have argued that, rather than losing identity, what happens in a crowd situation is that certain individuals engage in 'keynoting activities', which leads to the formation of emergent norms and values, collectively shared and expressed by the group as a whole.

☐ Social identity theorists have focused on the social context in which crowd behaviour occurs. The crowd distinguishes itself in meaningful ways from 'others', forming a social identity which guides appropriate and meaningful behaviour.

## INTERGROUP HARMONY

☐ *Contact, cooperation, communication* and *conciliation* can transform hostility into harmony; when contact encourages emotional ties with individuals identified with an outgroup and when it is structured to convey *equal status*, hostilities often lessen.

☐ Contacts are especially beneficial when people work together to overcome a common threat or to achieve a superordinate goal. Taking their cue from experiments on *co-operative contact*, several research teams have replaced competitive classroom learning situations with opportunities for co-operative learning, with heartening results.

☐ Conflicting parties often have difficulty communicating. A *third-party mediator* can promote communication by prodding the antagonists to replace their competitive win–lose view of their conflict with a more co-operative win–win orientation. Mediators can also structure communications that will peel away misperceptions and increase mutual understanding and trust. When a negotiated settlement is not reached, the conflicting parties may defer the outcome to an *arbitrator*, who either dictates a settlement or selects one of the two final offers.

☐ Sometimes tensions run so high that genuine communication is impossible. In such cases, small conciliatory gestures by one party may elicit reciprocal conciliatory acts by the other party. One such conciliatory strategy, GRIT (graduated and reciprocated initiatives in tension reduction), aims to alleviate tense international situations.

---

## CRITICAL QUESTIONS

**1** Is crowd behaviour irrational?

**2** What explanations have social psychologists offered for negative relations between groups?

**3** What are the possible limitations of a personality explanation of prejudice?

**4** How can the insights of social psychology be applied to tackling prejudice in the real world?

---

## RECOMMENDED READINGS

Listed below are some classic and contemporary readings in social psychology on intergroup relations, conflict and prejudice.

### Classic Sources

Adorno, T. W., Frenkel-Brunswik, E., Levenson, D. J., & Sanford, R. N. (1950). *The Authoritarian Personality*. New York: Harper and Row.

*The original study into an authoritarian personality explanation for prejudice.*

Allport, G. W. (1954). *The Nature of Prejudice*. Cambridge, MA: Perseus Books.

*An early text that regards prejudice as a group phenomenon, offering explanations and possible solutions.*

Reicher, S. D. (1984). The St Pauls' riot: An explanation of the limits of crowd action in terms of a social identity model. *European Journal of Social Psychology*, **14**, 1–21.

*Presents an empirical investigation of a social identity theoretical explanation for crowd behaviour.*

### Contemporary Sources

Condor, S., Abell, J., Figgou, L., Gibson, S., & Stevenson, C. (2006). 'They're not racist': Prejudice denial, mitigation and suppression in dialogue. *British Journal of Social Psychology*, **45**, 441–462.

*A qualitative study that investigates how people defend others against accusations of being racist.*

Durrheim, K., & Dixon, J. A. (2001). The role of place and metaphor in racial exclusion: South Africa's beaches as sites of shifting racialization. *Ethnic and Racial Studies*, **24**, 433–450.

*Examines South African newspaper articles that rhetorically construct certain public spaces (such as the beaches) as 'White' places, and under threat from Blacks.*

Glasford, D. E., & Dovidio, J. F. (2011). E pluribus unum: Dual identity and minority group members' motivation to engage in contact, as well as change. *Journal of Experimental Social Psychology*, **47**(5), 1021–1024.

*An empirical study into the effects that dual identity and common identity have on disadvantaged group members' willingness to engage in contact with advantaged group members.*

# 14

"By birth, the same; by custom, different."

Confucius, The Analects

# GENES, CULTURE AND GENDER

© Karl Lehmann/Getty Images

Throughout this book, we've considered some of the major topics social psychologists are interested in. As we noted in Chapter 1, social psychology is driven by the concerns of our social world. The topics we research are located within a particular time and space, as we seek to address issues that are of relevance to people at that time. In Chapter 2, we discussed how social psychologists have developed and used many different research methodologies to capture and analyse various aspects of our social world. These can include questionnaires, experiments, observations, recording conversations, interviews, and so on. As we've progressed through the book, you'll have seen how these different methods have been used to study each of the topics we've covered. Our excursion through the topics of social psychology has included the self (Chapter 3), social beliefs and judgements (Chapter 4), attitudes and behaviour (Chapter 5), persuasion (Chapter 6), conformity and obedience (Chapter 7), aggression (Chapter 8), attraction and intimacy (Chapter 9), helping (Chapter 10), small group processes (Chapter 11), social categorization and social identity (Chapter 12), and prejudice, intergroup relations and conflict (Chapter 13). These topics are familiar to us because social psychology is about our daily lives as well as large-scale social and cultural events.

Social psychological research helps illuminate the invisible strings by which our social worlds move us about. You may recall the five big ideas social psychology offers us, detailed in Chapter 1. Those ideas are based on the biological, social and cultural influences which shape our social lives. In this final chapter, we shall explore in more detail these influences, often referred to as the nature-nurture debate. As we shall see, the invisible strings that shape our behaviour cannot be illuminated easily with just a biological or cultural explanation. Rather it is a complex interaction of the two that drives our experiences. To explore the complexities of this relationship further, we shall draw on the example of gender; it will provide an illustration of the debate and the interplay of both culture and genes on our physiology and psychology. How do our biology and our culture shape our perceptions and experience as gendered beings? Can some things be attributed solely to one or the other? Gender can be considered an active example of how these two sides of the coin combine and work together with both choice and determinacy affecting our social nature.

Imagine just for a moment, approaching Earth from light-years away, alien scientists are assigned to study the species *Homo sapiens*. Their plan: to observe two randomly sampled humans. Their first subject, Jan, is a verbally combative trial lawyer who grew up in the northern English city of Manchester but moved south seeking the 'London lifestyle'. After an affair and a divorce, Jan is enjoying a second marriage. Friends describe Jan as an independent thinker who is self-confident, competitive and somewhat domineering.

Their second subject, Tomoko, lives with a spouse and their two children in a rural Japanese village, a walk from the homes of both their parents. Tomoko is proud of being a good child, a loyal spouse and a protective parent. Friends describe Tomoko as kind, gentle, respectful, sensitive and supportive of extended family.

From their small sample of two people of different genders and cultures, what might our alien scientists conclude about human nature? Would they wonder whether the two are from different subspecies? Or would they be struck by deeper similarities beneath the surface differences?

The questions faced by our alien scientists are those faced by today's earthbound scientists: how do we humans differ? How are we alike? Those questions are central to a world where social and cultural diversity has become obvious for everybody. In a world struggling with cultural differences, can we learn to accept our diversity, value our cultural identities and recognize the extent of our human kinship? Sure we can. To see why, let's consider the evolutionary, cultural and social roots of our humanity, and examine in what ways we are similar and how we are different. Then let's see how each might help us understand gender similarities and differences.

## HOW ARE WE INFLUENCED BY HUMAN NATURE AND CULTURAL DIVERSITY?

*Throughout its history, social psychology has grappled with nature and nurture explanations of human behaviour. Two perspectives dominate thinking about human similarities and differences, and what drives their behaviour: an evolutionary and biological perspective, emphasizing human kinship and physiology, and a cultural perspective, emphasizing human diversity and social ideologies.*

The relationship between genes and culture is complex but fascinating. In this chapter we consider this intriguing topic and ponder: how does the genetic outfit of a newborn baby prepare it for development to adulthood within a particular culture? How do genes and culture interact to create a mature person with mind, language and other psychological functions? There are no hard and fast answers. We cannot ignore the influence our genes have on human development and socialization. But neither can we explain away our attitudes, values, norms, motivation, cognitions, emotions and behaviour as simply a matter of genetics. Social psychologists need to take both elements into consideration.

Most people – and not least students of social psychology – have wondered how much of themselves stems from their parents and family, from their inherited genes, and how much is due to their upbringing, socialization and environment. Sometimes we recognize characteristics of our parents in our self and we see similarities in ways of talking, walking and even attitudes. Looking at our physical attributes we are definitely aware of inherited traits, for instance hair and eye colour, shape of face and length of legs. But what about psychological characteristics? Do we inherit from our parents how to think, feel and behave as well? Yes, most of us have to admit there are similarities. But are these psychological traits inherited in the same way as the physical marks? Are they something handed over from our ancestors through our genetic outfit, or is it a social and cultural heritage? Do we become similar to our family, parents and siblings because we learn to think, feel and behave like them through the socialization process? Questions like these have been topics in psychology for many years. Today most social psychologists agree that human biology and culture both contribute and in many ways influence each other. But *how* do they contribute and relate to each other?

Here we present a model for how our genes, instincts and inborn qualities interact with cultural influences and experiences. We will explore how higher psychological functions such as emotions, memory, motivation, attitudes and values develop in humans on the basis of inherited genes and elementary instinctive drives representing nature. But with the development of thinking and language in humans, we are not slaves to these instinctive drives. We can question, judge and rationalize our behaviour and that of others. We can create rules to facilitate a civil society, making some social acts and thoughts permissible and others prohibited. Our ways of perceiving, thinking and language are produced in a particular culture with its social rules, values and norms about what is desirable and what is not. To understand the development and creation of human psychology in this way makes it possible to explain why people are similar but also different.

**brain plasticity** *the changes that occur in the organization and structure of the brain as a result of experience and individual physical or psychological activity*

Most social psychologists today agree that we need to consider both the genetic outfit and the cultural impact to understand human beings: our genes and inborn qualities and instincts enable an adaptive and developing human brain – a cerebral structure that receives cultural impact due to its plasticity.

So what is the role of our body and brain in shaping our social behaviour and experiences of the world around us? Is our biological outfit independent of the cultural and social situation? Definitely not. Many body functions are dependent on the environment. Production of the hormones adrenalin and noradrenalin will be influenced by how stressful we regard a social situation to be. Other hormones and physiological processes also react to the environment. The brain adjusts to the social situation and our psychological reactions. It develops new capacity as a result of our physical and mental activity and how we cope with the situation. It stores what happens and creates new ways of thinking, feeling and behaving. Physical and mental activity produces structural changes in the brain due to the brain plasticity in humans (Kolb & Whishaw, 1998).

Two decades ago the brain was looked upon as anatomically hard-wired at birth. In the past two decades, however, an enormous amount of research has revealed that the brain never stops changing and adjusting. So it is not really legitimate any longer to regard the brain as a fixed collection of wired-up neurons like the hardware in a personal computer. The interconnections between neurons are changing all the time and brain structure is more like the software. This model explains the importance of social and cultural influences since experiences are internalized and stored both in mind and brain. Norman Doidge stated that neuroplasticity is 'one of the most extraordinary discoveries of the twentieth century' (Doidge, 2007).

### GENES, EVOLUTION AND BEHAVIOUR

The universal behaviours that define human nature arise from our biological similarity. We may say 'My ancestors came from Ireland' or 'My roots are in China' or 'I'm Italian', but anthropologists have told us that if we could trace our ancestors back 100 000 or more years, we would see that geographically we are all Africans (Shipman, 2003). But researchers studying human origins do not quite agree when and in what shape the hominids left Africa. According to the *Multiregional Continuity Model, Homo erectus* left Africa 2 mya (million years ago) to become *Homo sapiens* in different parts of the world. The *Out of Africa Model* claims that *Homo sapiens* evolved relatively recently in Africa and migrated into other parts of the world to replace other hominid species, including *Homo erectus* (Johanson, 2001). In response to climate change and the availability of food, those early hominids migrated across Africa into Asia, Europe, the Australian subcontinent and, eventually, the Americas. As they adapted to their new environments, early humans developed differences that, measured on anthropological scales, are relatively recent and superficial. For example, those who stayed in Africa had darker skin pigment – what Harvard psychologist Steven Pinker (2002) calls 'sunscreen for the tropics' – and those who went far north of the equator evolved lighter skins capable of synthesizing vitamin D in less direct sunlight.

We were Africans so recently that 'there has not been much time to accumulate many new versions of the genes', notes Steven Pinker (2002, p. 143). And, indeed, biologists who study our genes have found that we humans – even humans as seemingly different as Jan and Tomoko – are strikingly similar in their genes, like members of one tribe. We may be more numerous than chimpanzees, but chimps are more genetically varied. We also share the majority of our genes with other species – for instance, mice.

natural selection *the evolutionary process by which heritable traits that best enable organisms to survive and reproduce in particular environments are passed to ensuing generations*

To explain how *Homo sapiens*, and all species, developed, the British naturalist Charles Darwin (1859) and other contemporary scientists, proposed an evolutionary process. Darwin's idea, to which philosopher Daniel Dennett (2005) would give 'the gold medal for the best idea anybody ever had', was that natural selection enables evolution.

The idea behind natural selection, simplified, is as follows.

☐ Organisms have many and varied offspring (usually many more than humans).

☐ Those offspring compete for survival in their environment.

☐ Certain biological and behavioural variations increase their chances of reproduction and survival in that natural environment.

☐ Those offspring that do survive are more likely to pass their genes to ensuing generations.

☐ Thus, over time, population characteristics may change.

The exciting thing about evolution is not that our understanding is perfect or complete but that it is the foundation stone for the rest of biology.
   Donald Kennedy, Editor-in-Chief, *Science*, 2005

Natural selection implies that certain genes – those which predisposed traits that increased the odds of surviving long enough to reproduce and nurture descendants – became more abundant. In the snowy Arctic environment, for example, genes programming a thick coat of camouflaging white fur have won the genetic competition in polar bears. In hot, desert environments, genes programming estivation (the summer equivalent of hibernation) predominate in a number of species. So perhaps it is simply our selfish genes assuring their reproduction, which drive our behaviour and the way in which we experience the world around us.

Biologically speaking, one major purpose of life is to leave grandchildren. But biology does not have a conscious purpose. It does what it has to do without any intent. Different from other species, men and women can decide whether

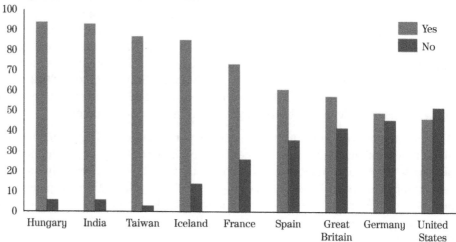

For you personally, do you think it is necessary to have a child at some point in your life in order to feel fulfilled?

FIGURE 14.1  Are children necessary? Culture counts.

SOURCE: Gallup Poll Global Study of Family Values (1997).

they want offspring or not. To produce children is, psychologically speaking, not always the purpose for humans, and there are huge variations between cultures or countries in the degree to which people consider children to be an important part of their lives (see Figure 14.1). In this way the biological evolutionary principle does not govern humans' behaviour in the same way as in other species. Due to its ability to reason, man's behaviour is not necessarily determined by the drives to leave offspring and continue to preserve its own genes for the future. When asked in a Gallup Poll Global Study of Family Values (1997), fewer than half of Germans and Americans thought it necessary to have a child in order to feel fulfilled. This is the exception, however: the majority of adults in most of the countries included in the survey (16 countries in Asia, Europe, North America and Latin America), say that having a child is necessary for them to feel personally fulfilled in life. About nine out of ten adults in India agree. The number is closer to six in ten in Europe. There are no gender differences. It is culture that seems to count.

The Gallup survey also revealed wide variations between countries in people's preferences for giving birth to a boy or girl. When asked to say which gender they would prefer if they could have just one child, there is a moderate preference around the world for boys. The preference for a male child is particularly strong in Thailand and India, where boys are favoured over girls by double-digit margins. In Great Britain 43 per cent of those surveyed had no preference, but among those who did, boys are favoured by a five-point margin, 31 per cent as opposed to 26 per cent who preferred to have a girl. Only in Spain is there a preference for girls (see Figure 14.2).

In the freezing temperatures of the Arctic, the polar bear has developed a thick white fur coat that not only maintains body heat, but also offers camouflage to aid hunting.

SOURCE: © Nik_niklz/Dreamstime

In some countries the sex of the offspring is so important that the unwanted sex embryo is removed by abortion. The mother can even be treated very badly if she is considered to be 'unable' to give birth to the preferred gender; rather ironic considering it's the father who determines the sex of a child!

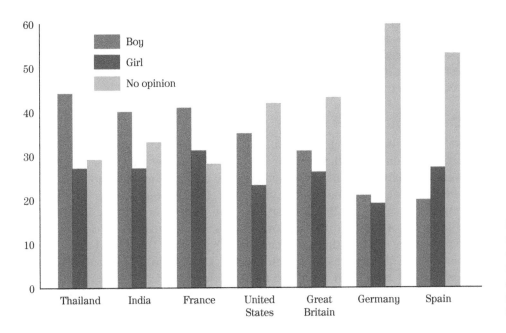

**FIGURE 14.2** Suppose you could only have one child. Would you prefer that it be a boy or a girl?
SOURCE: Gallup Poll Global Study of Family Values (1997).

Natural Selection and Evolutionary Psychology

Since Darwin wrote about evolution of the species more than 150 years ago, there have been competing explanations of how the selection process actually happens. Today we realize that the forces behind evolution are more complex than Darwin thought. Simply the survival of the fittest and natural selection does not fully explain how human beings develop and acquire their abilities and how they forward them to the next generation. Due to cultural impact, the way humans do this is different from how it is done in other animal species. For example, we've considered the impact that the forces of natural selection have on human behaviours relating to aggression (Chapter 8), attraction (Chapter 9), and helping (Chapter 10). In all of these cases, those forces do not simply drive the behaviour but function to a greater or lesser extent as part of a complex interaction with societal and cultural influences.

Natural selection, Darwin's principle for evolution of biological characteristics, has however gained popularity with some social psychologists. *Evolutionary psychology* studies how natural selection predisposes not just physical traits – polar bears' coats, bats' sonar, humans' colour vision – but psychological traits and social behaviours that enhance the preservation of one's genes (Buss, 2005). We humans are the way we are, say evolutionary psychologists, because nature selected those who had our physiological and psychological traits.

For an introduction to evolutionary psychology and its influence on social psychology, see Chapter 1.

According to evolutionary psychologists, this selection happened hundreds of thousands of years ago through innumerable generations and without any conscious contribution. It was nature that selected the traits, not humans. This understanding of human beings, as something without any consciousness, mind or will is very different from the human being social psychologists study today. To accept that humans do not exert an influence on their survival, fecundity and number of offspring, or that culture does not influence this to a greater extent than does nature, is not very realistic. Owing to their ability to think, to reason and the influence of their man-made culture, humans acquire a culturally distinctive stamp, which 'selects' what is appropriate rather than what the natural environment chooses. There are, of course, still human qualities that are independent of culture and similar for all individuals. But the task of the social psychologist is to study the 'cultural and social' human being.

## NEUROBIOLOGY AND CULTURE

We've considered research that has looked for a genetic explanation for social behaviours. Remember the 'warrior gene' from Chapter 8, thought to influence aggressive behaviour? The genes make up the structure and immediate function of the brain at birth. But the environment immediately begins to exert its heavy influence on the brain. Every day the newborn's brain is flooded with new information through the sensory organs. The neurons, or brain cells, are responsible for sending that information to the part of the brain best equipped to handle it. This requires that each neuron 'knows' the proper pathways. The genes have, at birth, laid down the mental road map neurons must follow and built its major 'highways' between the basic areas of the brain. Environmental influence plays the key role in forging a denser and more complex network of interconnections. These smaller avenues and side roads make the transfer of information between neurons more efficient and rich with situation-specific detail. At birth, each neuron has approximately 2500 synapses or connections. By the time we have reached 2–3 years of age, sensory stimulation and environmental experience have taken full advantage of the brain's plasticity; each neuron now boasts around 15 000 synapses (Gopnick et al., 1999). (For more details see http://www.memoryzine.com/neuroplasticity.htm.)

neurons *brain cells*

synapse *the connection between neurons*

Remember Jan and Tomoko at the start of this chapter? They are different and similar at the same time. As members of one great family, *Homo sapiens*, they share a common biology, behaviour tendencies, instincts and basic needs. Each of them sleeps and wakes, feels hunger and thirst, and develops language through identical mechanisms. As babies they both needed to be cared for by someone, and as they have developed from children to adults they have acquired from their specific culture (different) languages, norms and values, through identical mechanisms, and without even being aware of it. The cultural context in which we live influences our behaviour so we have to be sure to take this into account when studying social phenomena. Without it, differences which may be attributed largely to culture could be interpreted differently.

Everybody is therefore born into a specific, but dynamic culture that *cultivates* (the Latin word for culture) every human being. But what is actually culture? And in what way is culture different from a society or social forces?

*Culture* is a term that has been given many meanings. More than 50 years ago Alfred Kroeber and Clyde Kluckhohn (1952) presented in their article 'Culture: a critical review of concepts and definitions', no fewer than 164 definitions. In social psychology, culture is most commonly applied as the term for the patterns of knowledge, beliefs and behaviour, or the set of shared attitudes, norms, values, goals and practices that characterize a group. Language and culture have both emerged as means of using symbols to construct social identity. Children acquire language in the same way as they acquire basic cultural norms and values – through interaction with older members of their cultural group.

But not everybody agrees with this definition. Hubert Herman at Radboud University in the Netherlands, challenges the idea that a culture is an 'entity' or involves 'group membership'. He suggests that a culture emerges from patterns of meaning between people in dialogue with each other (Hermans, 2001; see also Adams & Markus, 2001).

There has been and probably still is some confusion between the concepts of 'society' and 'culture'. For most social psychologists, these are distinct concepts. Society usually refers to a clearly bounded group of people, whereas culture refers to permeable and plural human capacities and non-genetic human phenomena.

The Russian psychologist Lev Vygotsky founded the cultural-historical tradition in social psychology in the 1920s. According to Vygotsky, each individual's consciousness is built from outside through relations with others. When human beings participate in social interactions they develop, construct and create their psychological substance, ways of thinking, feeling, remembering, their sensation and perception. In this way culture becomes part of a person's nature. He distinguished between 'lower' or natural psychological functions and 'higher' or cultural functions (Van der Veer & Valsiner, 1991, 1994). The lower functions are biological mechanisms, such as blind reactions to stimuli as we would see in all animals. They do not involve conscious experience. Over time, these lower functions are transformed, and are controlled by higher 'cultural' functions. These higher psychological functions actually stimulate neuronal growth in particular directions and create their own biological mediations, restructuring the brain (Vygotsky, 1986; Wertsch, 2008).

This position does not leave out biological factors or disregard biological influences. According to cultural-historical psychology, biological phenomena provide the framework for mental phenomena rather than directly determining them. This leaves psychological activity as something to be built up from, rather than reduced to biology. To be human means that you have surpassed a level of functioning that your biological traits would otherwise dictate (Van der Veer and van Uzendoorn, 1985).

But if human psychology is socially and culturally determined, does this mean that the individual is reduced to an automaton that passively receives social influences? Quite the contrary: 'The child begins to see the external world not simply with his eye as a perceiving and conducting apparatus – the child sees with all of his previous experience' (Vygotsky & Luria, 1993, p. 148). Culture does not simply regulate natural processes; it supercedes lower elementary processes and forms the entire content of psychological phenomena (Ratner, 1991).

So, Jan and Tomoko – and all of us everywhere – are cultural and social creatures. We join groups, conform and recognize distinctions of social status. We return favours, punish offences and grieve a child's death. Confronted by those with dissimilar attitudes or attributes, perhaps belonging to 'outgroups', we react warily or negatively. Our alien scientists could drop in anywhere and find humans conversing and arguing, laughing and crying, feasting and dancing, singing and worshipping. Everywhere, humans prefer living with others – in families and communal groups – to living alone. Everywhere, the family dramas that entertain us – from Greek tragedies to Chinese fiction to Mexican soap operas – portray similar plots (Dutton, 2006). Similarly, adventure stories in which strong and courageous men, supported by wise old people, overcome evil to the delight of beautiful women or threatened children. Such commonalities define our shared human nature founded on our biological and genetic similarity.

## CULTURE AND BEHAVIOUR

Perhaps our most important similarity, the hallmark of our species, is our capacity to learn and use psychological tools like language. Evolution has prepared us to talk and acquire qualities and symbols from a culture and make them our own. Compared with bees, birds and bulldogs, nature has humans on a looser genetic leash. The natural genetic or instinctive driving forces are overruled by what is acquired during socialization. Ironically, it is our shared human biology that enables our cultural diversity. It enables those in one culture to value promptness, welcome frankness or accept premarital sex, whereas those in another culture do not. As social psychologist Roy Baumeister (2005b, p. 29) observes, 'Evolution made us for culture'. Biology and culture need to work together. Humans, more than any other animal, harness the power of culture to make life better. 'Culture is a better way of being social', Baumeister writes. We have culture to thank for our communication through language, our driving safely on one side of the road, our eating fruit in winter, and our use of money to pay for our cars and fruit. Culture facilitates our survival and reproduction, and nature has blessed us with a brain that, like no other, enables culture. Other animals show the rudiments of culture, thinking and language. Our biology, and especially our brain, developed through evolution and made thinking and language appropriation possible.

We humans have been selected not just for our big brains and biceps but also for our culture. We come prepared to learn language and to bond and cooperate with others in securing food, caring for young and protecting ourselves. Nature therefore predisposes us to learn, whatever culture we are born into (Fiske et al., 1998). The cultural perspective, while acknowledging that all behaviour requires our evolved genes, highlights human development and socialization. People's 'natures are alike', said Confucius; 'it is their habits that carry them far apart'. And far apart we are, note world culture researchers Ronald Inglehart and Christian Welzel (2005). Despite increasing education, 'we are not moving toward a uniform global culture: cultural convergence is not taking place. A society's cultural heritage is remarkably enduring' (p. 46).

But there are other social scientists who declare that 'the Age of Globalization' makes cultures and individuals more similar, and that we in the future will belong to the same 'World Culture'.

### Cultural Diversity

The diversity of our languages, customs and expressive behaviours confirms that much of our behaviour is socially programmed, not hard-wired. As sociologist Ian Robertson (1987) has noted:

> Americans eat oysters but not snails. The French eat snails but not locusts. The Zulus eat locusts but not fish. The Jews eat fish but not pork. The

Hindus eat pork but not beef. The Russians eat beef but not snakes. The Chinese eat snakes but not people. The Jalé of New Guinea find people delicious. (p. 67)

Increasingly, cultural diversity surrounds us and we become aware of different customs, lifestyles, ways of thinking and behaviour. Confronting another culture is sometimes a startling experience. A German student, accustomed to speaking to 'Herr Professor' only on rare occasions, considers it strange that at universities in other countries most faculty office doors are open and students stop by freely. An Iranian student on her first visit to a McDonald's restaurant fumbles around in her paper bag looking for the eating utensils until she sees the other customers eating their french fries with, of all things, their hands. In many areas of the globe, your best manners and mine are serious breaches of etiquette. Foreigners visiting Japan often struggle to master the rules of the social game – when to take their shoes off, how to pour the tea, when to give and open gifts, how to act towards someone higher or lower in the social hierarchy.

Migration and refugee evacuations are mixing cultures more than ever. 'East is East and West is West, and never the twain shall meet', wrote the nineteenth-century British author Rudyard Kipling. But today, East and West, and North and South, meet all the time. Italy is home to many Albanians, Germany to Turks, England to Pakistanis, and the result is both friendship and conflict.

Switzerland has the highest immigrant population of any European country with more than one and a half million residents, as 23 per cent of its 7.5 million residents are foreign-born. Countries in which immigrants form between 10 per cent and 20 per cent of the population include: Austria, Ireland, Germany, Sweden, Spain, France, the Netherlands, Denmark, Norway, Belgium, Greece, Portugal and the UK. In 2004 the number of people who became naturalized British citizens rose to a record 140 795 – a 12 per cent increase from the previous year, and a dramatic increase since 2000. Most new citizens came from Asia (40 per cent) or Africa (32 per cent).

As we work, play and live with people from diverse cultural backgrounds, it helps to understand how our cultures influence us and how our cultures differ. In a conflict-laden world, achieving peace requires a genuine appreciation for differences as well as similarities (see Chapter 13).

### Norms: Expected Behaviour

As etiquette rules illustrate, all cultures have their accepted ideas about appropriate behaviour. We often view these social expectations, or norms, as a negative force that imprisons people in a blind effort to perpetuate tradition. For example, in Chapter 7 on conformity and obedience we explored studies that illustrated how norms are established in a group, and discussed our tendency to follow group norms even when we personally dissociate ourselves from them. Cultural norms do restrain and control us – so successfully and so subtly that we hardly sense their existence. Like fish in the ocean, we are all so immersed in our cultures that we must leap out of them to understand their influence. 'When we see other Dutch people behaving in what foreigners would call a Dutch way', note Dutch psychologists Willem Koomen and Anton Dijker (1997), 'we often do not realize that the behaviour is typically Dutch'. We understand our motherland only by experience of a foreign country.

norms *standards for accepted, typical and expected behaviour. Norms* prescribe *'proper' behaviour. (In a different sense of the word, norms also describe what most others do – what is normal)*

Norms – unwritten rules for accepted and expected behaviour – vary by culture.

SOURCE: © Hofmeester/ Dreamstime.com

To many in the Western world, the Muslim woman's veil seems arbitrary and confining, but not to those Muslim cultures in which it is worn.

SOURCE: © Juanmonino/iStock

There is no better way to learn the norms of our culture than to visit or study another culture and see that its members do things *that* way, whereas we do them *this* way.

Social norms play an important role in all societies and groups. They make social relations more predictable and less perilous. Just as a stage play moves smoothly when the actors know their lines, so social behaviour occurs smoothly when people know what to expect. Norms grease the social machinery. In unfamiliar situations, when the norms may be unclear, we monitor others' behaviour and adjust our own accordingly.

Many people, social psychologists included, do not have any experience of East Asian cultures and few have read any scientific papers about Chinese social psychology. Sometimes the textbooks mention that the Chinese are more 'collectivistic' and less 'individualistic' than people in the West (see Chapter 3). But the Chinese, and the rest of people living in Asia, or Africa, were typically absent from social psychological textbooks. The focus was on the people living in the West, especially in North America. The Americans' and the Europeans' ways of thinking, feeling and behaving, and their psychological make-up were generalized to all people in the world (see also Chapter 1).

Today we know this is not correct. People in all cultures have certainly the same abilities and psychological make-up to some degree, but they are at the same time very different. The blend of components that make us a person differs from culture to culture, but the biological elements which make us a human being are the same. In all cultures there exists individualism and collectivism (Hofstede, 2001; Hofstede & Hofstede, 2005), and people acquire independent and interdependent ways of thinking in all cultures and societies. But the specific mixture of individualism and collectivism in a specific culture is unique (Kolstad & Horpestad, 2009).

Cultures vary in their norms for expressiveness, punctuality and personal space. To someone from a relatively formal northern European culture, a person whose roots are in an expressive Mediterranean culture may seem 'warm, charming, inefficient, and time-wasting'. To the Mediterranean person, the northern

European may seem 'efficient, cold, and overconcerned with time' (Triandis, 1981). Latin American business executives who arrive late for a dinner engagement may be mystified by how obsessed their North American counterparts are with punctuality. European and North American tourists in Japan may wonder about the lack of eye contact from passing pedestrians. (See Research Close-Up: Passing Encounters, East and West). People in the north of Norway, also called the 'Italians in Norway', are considered different from the more reserved and less emotional people in the south. And along the coastline of Scandinavia, where people are used to contact with foreigners, they seem to be more outgoing and talkative than the isolated farmers in the forests and mountains.

## CULTURAL SIMILARITY

Beneath the veneer of cultural differences, some cross-cultural psychologists look for 'an essential universality' (Lonner, 1980). As members of one species, we find that the processes that underlie our differing behaviours are much the same everywhere. At ages 4 to 5 children across the world begin to exhibit a 'theory of mind' that enables them to infer what others in their culture are thinking (Norenzayan & Heine, 2005). If they witness a toy being moved while another child isn't looking, they become able – no matter their culture – to infer that the other child will *think* it still is where it was.

### Universal Friendship Norms

People everywhere have some common norms for friendship. From studies conducted in Britain, Italy, Hong Kong and Japan, Michael Argyle and Monika Henderson (1985) noted several cultural variations in the norms that define the role of friend. For example, in Japan it's especially important not to embarrass a friend with public criticism. But there are also some apparently universal norms: respect the friend's privacy; don't divulge things said in confidence.

That said, some research has found differences in friendship between men and women. While communal characteristics including loyalty and trust are the hallmarks of friendship for both men and women, women consider their friendships to be a more important part of their lives than men do (Hall, 2011). And do you tend to think it's women who gossip? Well, research suggests that it is men! A study by David Watson (2012) found that gossip was a feature of good friendships for men, but not for women.

### Universal Social Belief Dimensions

Hong Kong social psychologists Kwok Leung and Michael Harris Bond (2004, 2009), state there are five universal dimensions of social beliefs. Leung and colleagues (2002) define social beliefs as a variety of social behaviours across contexts, actors, people and time periods. In short, they are statements about 'how the world functions' (Leung et al., 2002, p. 289). The Social Axioms Survey (SAS) is a measure of these beliefs. More than 40 national groups are studied and in each country people vary in the extent to which they endorse and apply these social understandings in their daily lives: cynicism, social complexity, reward for application, spirituality and fate control (Figure 14.5). People's adherence to these social beliefs appears to guide their living. Those who espouse cynicism express lower life satisfaction and favour assertive influence tactics and right-wing politics. Those who espouse reward for application are inclined to invest themselves in study, planning and competing (Bond et al., 2004).

Cultures mixing. As these schoolchildren illustrate, immigration and globalization are bringing once-distant cultures together.

SOURCE: © Caia Image/Glow Images

## RESEARCH CLOSE-UP

PASSING ENCOUNTERS, EAST AND WEST

*Source: Patterson, M. L., Iizuka, Y., Tubbs, M. E., Ansel, J., Tsutsumi, M., & Anson, J. (2007). Passing encounters East and West: Comparing Japanese and American pedestrian interactions.* Journal of Nonverbal Behaviour, *31, 155–166.*

### Introduction

This study was based on an observation by Erving Goffman. Goffman noticed that there are many interactions we have with strangers. These are often not verbal interactions but non-verbal ones. So as we pass a pedestrian on the street, we may glance in their direction to signal that we've seen them, but then quickly look away to show that we don't have any kind of relationship with that person nor do we want to invade their privacy. More specifically, it is once we are within 8 feet of the stranger that we avert our gaze at them. Goffman called interactions, such as these, 'civil inattention'. So far so good, but would the sex and behaviour of the stranger affect these kinds of interactions? And do different cultural norms also affect these kinds of interactions? An international team led by Miles Patterson and Yuichi Iizuka (2007) wanted to find out. They conducted a simple field study both in the USA and in Japan with the unwitting participation of 1037 American (437) and Japanese (600) pedestrians. The researchers proposed three experimental hypotheses. The first was that the culture of the pedestrian would have an effect upon their response to the confederate. Specifically, the Japanese pedestrians would respond with fewer smiles and glances than the USA confederates. The second was that regardless of culture, when a pedestrian is confronted with a glance and a smile from the passing confederate s/he will be more likely to glance and smile back. Finally, the team proposed that female confederates would be looked at more by pedestrians than would male confederates. Their procedure illustrates how social psychologists sometimes conduct unobtrusive research in natural settings.

### Method

Patterson and his colleagues set out to examine the effects of sex, culture and behaviour of a confederate on pedestrians as they passed each other on the pavement. So the independent variable (IV) was the sex (male or female), culture (USA or Japanese), and behaviour (avoid, look-only, look and smile) of the confederate, and the dependent variable (DV) was the reaction of the pedestrian. This gives an experimental design of 2 (sex of confederate) × 2 (culture) × 3 (condition: avoid, look-only, look and smile).

The unwitting USA and Japanese participants included 643 men and 380 women. They seemed to be between the ages of 18 and 40 years old. The experiment took place in three locations: the campus of Shimane University in Japan, the campus of University of Missouri-St Louis, and in downtown St Louis.

The confederates were 6 Japanese college students (3 men, 3 women) and 4 American college students (2 men, 2 women).

As Figure 14.3 depicts, a confederate (an accomplice of the experimenter) would initiate one of three behaviours when within about 12 feet of an approaching pedestrian on an uncrowded sidewalk:

(1) *avoidance* (looking straight ahead); (2) *glancing* at the person for less than a second; and (3) *looking* at the person and *smiling*. A trailing observer would then record the pedestrian's reaction. Did the pedestrian glance at the confederate? Smile? Nod? Verbally greet the confederate? (The order of the three conditions was randomized and unknown to the trailing observer, ensuring that the person recording the data was 'blind' to the experimental condition.)

## Results

The researchers used log-linear analysis to look for any relationships between the categorical variables of sex, culture and condition. What they discovered makes for some very interesting reading.

The team were able to support their first hypothesis. Pedestrians did give different responses to the confederate in accordance with the culture they were from. As Figure 14.4 shows, the culture differences were striking. As the research team expected, in view of Japan's greater respect for privacy and cultural reserve when interacting with outgroups, Americans were much more likely to smile at, nod to or greet the confederate.

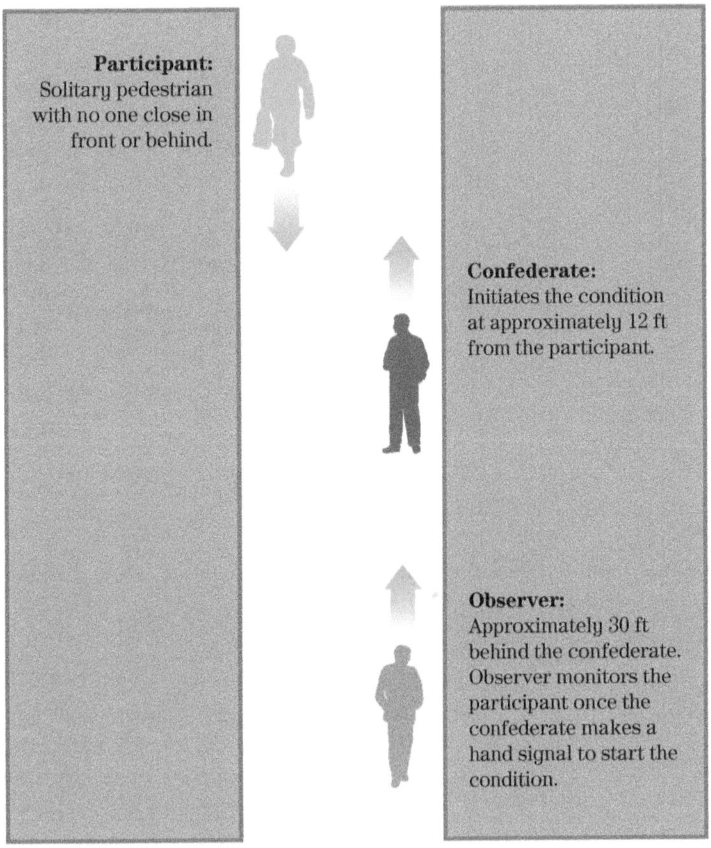

The researchers were also able to support their second and third experimental hypotheses. As you might expect, the pedestrians, regardless of culture, were much more likely to look back and nod and smile at someone who looked at them and smiled, especially when that someone was female rather than male. So the look-smile condition (condition 3) led to more responses of smiling, glancing and nodding, than avoid looking at a pedestrian (condition 1) or just glancing (condition 2). Furthermore, female confederates were responded to more than male confederates.

**Participant:** Solitary pedestrian with no one close in front or behind.

**Confederate:** Initiates the condition at approximately 12 ft from the participant.

**Observer:** Approximately 30 ft behind the confederate. Observer monitors the participant once the confederate makes a hand signal to start the condition.

**FIGURE 14.3** Illustration of passing encounter

SOURCE: Patterson et al., 2007.

## Discussion

The researchers concluded that cultural norms have an impact upon how we behave in 'civil inattentions'. They shape our interactions with strangers. In Japan, they conclude, 'there is little pressure to reciprocate the smile of the confederate because there is no relationship with the confederate and no obligation to respond'. By contrast, the Western norm is to reciprocate a friendly gesture.

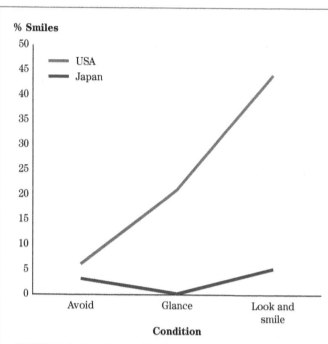

% Smiles

- USA
- Japan

Condition

Avoid    Glance    Look and smile

**FIGURE 14.4** American and Japanese pedestrian responses, by condition

SOURCE: Adapted from Patterson et al., 2007.

Interestingly though, sex differences were very similar in Japan and the USA. In both cultures, female confederates were glanced at more than male ones. The authors also add that male pedestrians tended to glance at confederates more than the female pedestrians did. Perhaps this tells us something about how gender is understood cross-culturally?

The researchers point out some limitations of their study. They note the geographical variations in each of the countries. To conclude that the findings here are true for the entire USA and Japan would be something of a leap. There may well be regional differences in how people behave in these kinds of encounters in the north and south, east and west of these countries. The researchers also note that the confederates and pedestrians were from majority ethnic groups in both countries. Might we have different findings if the confederates and/or the pedestrians were from ethnic minority groups?

While we must remain mindful of the limitations, what studies like this do offer us is a snapshot of how people behave in a real world setting.

Differences in the endorsement of social beliefs between religious groups have also been noted. A study conducted on 180 individuals who identified themselves as practising Muslims or Christians, living in three countries (Canada, the USA and the UK), found that Muslims scored higher on the subscales Social Cynicism, Fate Control and Religiosity (Safdar et al., 2008). Some social beliefs about the world seem to be useful defensive mechanisms, protecting people against anxieties about death. Higher levels of belief in fate control and lower levels of religiosity predicted greater death anxiety (Hui et al., 2007).

| The big five social beliefs | Sample questionnaire item |
| --- | --- |
| Cynicism | 'Powerful people tend to exploit others.' |
| Social complexity | 'One has to deal with matters according to the specific circumstances.' |
| Reward for application | 'One will succeed if he/she really tries.' |
| Spirituality | 'Religious faith contributes to good mental health.' |
| Fate control | 'Fate determines one's success and failures.' |

**FIGURE 14.5** Leung and Bond's universal social belief dimensions

### The Incest Taboo

The best-known universal norm is the taboo against incest: parents are not to have sexual relations with their children, nor siblings with one another. Although the taboo is apparently violated more often than psychologists once believed, the norm is still universal. Every society disapproves of incest. Given the biological penalties for inbreeding (through the emergence of disorders linked to recessive genes), we can easily understand why there is a norm against incest in all cultures.

Some norms are culture-specific, others are universal. The force of culture appears in varying norms, whereas it is largely our human nature – the characteristics of *Homo sapiens* – that accounts for the universality of some norms. Thus, we might think of nature as universal and nurture as culture-specific. We are born the same and become different.

So far in this chapter, we have affirmed our biological kinship as members of one human family. We have acknowledged our cultural diversity. And we have noted how norms vary within and across cultures. Remember that our quest in social psychology is not just to catalogue differences but also to identify universal principles and to explain why there are differences and similarities. Our aim is what cross-cultural psychologist Walter Lonner (1989) has called 'a universalistic psychology – a psychology that is as valid and meaningful in Omaha and Osaka as it is in Rome and Botswana'. And to explain the variations.

## HOW ARE GENDER SIMILARITIES AND DIFFERENCES EXPLAINED?

*Both evolutionary psychologists and psychologists working from a cultural perspective have sought to explain human similarity and variation. Before considering their views, let's look at some basic issues: how are we alike? How do we differ? And why?*

Let's consider a specific example, that of gender, to illustrate how these similarities and differences between us have been studied by social psychologists. The hunt for gender differences is probably the most explicit example of how biology and culture together influence and create human emotions, thinking, attitudes, self-appraisal and all the other psychological subjects social psychologists study.

**gender** *the characteristics, whether biological or socially influenced, by which people define male and female*

Sex and gender are not the same. Sex is used to refer to biological and reproductive characteristics. We are born a member of the male sex or the female sex. Gender is a pattern of behaviours recognized as 'feminine' or 'masculine', and as such gender roles are established. Gender is socially constructed and used to refer to those ways in which a culture elaborates upon the facts of nature.

**gender role** *the set of social expectations based on gender stereotypes of how a person should act, think and feel based on their actual or perceived sex*

There are many obvious dimensions of human diversity – height, weight, hair colour, to name just a few. But for people's self-concepts and social relationships, the dimension that matters most, and that people first attune to, is gender (Stangor et al., 1992). When you were born, the first thing people wanted to know about you was, 'Is it a boy or a girl?' When a hermaphrodite child is born with a combination of male and female sex organs, physicians and family have traditionally felt compelled to assign the child a gender and to diminish the ambiguity surgically. The simple message: everyone *must* be assigned a gender. Between day and night there is dusk. But between male and female there is, socially speaking, essentially nothing, at least not at birth. Later in life we accept that the strict either-or of the two genders may be oversimplistic. Individuals have used terms such as androgynous (the mixing of male and female characteristics), and the third gender or third sex (neither male nor female) are examples of the ways in which people describe themselves and challenge the male–female dichotomy.

*androgynous from andro (man) + gyn (woman) – thus mixing both masculine and feminine characteristics*

What behaviours are universally characteristic and expected of males? And of females?

'Of the 46 chromosomes in the human genome, 45 are unisex', notes Judith Rich Harris (1998). Females and males are therefore similar in many physical traits and developmental milestones, such as the age of sitting up, teething and walking. They are also alike in many psychological traits, such as overall vocabulary, creativity, intelligence, self-esteem and happiness. Indeed, notes Janet Shibley Hyde (2005) from her review of 46 meta-analyses (each a statistical digest of dozens of studies), the common result for most variables studied is *gender similarity*. Your 'opposite sex' is actually your nearly identical sex. Even in physical traits, individual differences among men and among women far exceed the average differences between the sexes.

Confirmation bias is discussed more extensively in Chapter 4 in relation to our social beliefs and judgements, and how we favour information that confirms our existing beliefs.

So shall we conclude that men and women are essentially the same, except for a few anatomical oddities that hardly matter apart from special occasions? Actually, there are some differences, and it is these differences, not the many similarities, that capture attention and make news. In both science and everyday life, differences excite interest. Take as an example Marie-France Marin and her colleagues' study (2012) that revealed women remember bad news better than men do. More disturbing though, was the declared finding that women were more stressed out by these news events. Interesting? Yes. Newsworthy? Yes, if we consider that this study was subsequently reported in online news forums. Accurate? Well, that's more tricky to answer. Its critics point to its small sample size (just 28 men and 28 women) and its calculation of the statistics (Willis, 2012). More recently, research has focused on debunking some of these stereotypic gender differences. For example, Swedish research has rebuked the commonly held notion that women are better at multi-tasking than men (Mäntylä, 2013). Similarly, work by Bobbi Carothers and Harry Reis (2012) refutes the view that men and women have distinctive traits. Contrary to popular belief, men can be empathic and women assertive. Previously, perhaps, there's been a tendency to publish those studies that reveal gender differences, and what we've been seeing is an example of confirmation bias, where we simply believe (and publish) what we expect to be the case. Contemporary research now questions many of these gendered assumptions.

The South African runner Caster Semenya was ordered to take a gender identity test when she blew everyone away in the women's 800-metre race at the World Championships in Berlin in September 2009. The tests revealed her to have three times the level of testosterone than expected in a woman. The case has sparked a debate about how to define 'men' and 'women' in international athletics.

SOURCE: © Grosremy/Dreamstime.com

In fact during the 1970s, many scholars worried that studies of gender differences might reinforce stereotypes and that differences were construed as women's deficits. Feminists have pointed the finger at social psychology's own culpability in reproducing stereotypes of differences between men and women. Until relatively recently, much social psychological research was conducted by (usually white, Western) male researchers on (usually white, Western) male participants, and the findings generalized to all people. Those who didn't conform to the norm were considered odd. When women were studied, differences found between their responses and those of their male counterparts were often attributed to them being deficient in some way. The feminist psychologist Sue Wilkinson quotes Naomi Weisstein's 1968 observation that in psychology women were regarded as 'inconsistent, emotionally unstable, lacking in a strong conscience … weaker … and if they are at all "normal" better suited to the home and family' (Wilkinson, 1997).

Of course the existence of these gender stereotypes influences gender roles and dictates to some degree the behaviours that are regarded as appropriate for men and women. Alice Eagly and Wendy Wood (1991) developed the *social role model* asserting that sex differences in social behaviour stem from perception of gender roles.

Let's compare men's and women's social connection, moral reasoning and dominance, and then consider how biology and culture might explain them. Do gender differences reflect biological differences or are they solely culturally constructed – a reflection of the roles that men and women often play and the situations in which they act? Or do genes and culture both play a role? Can we bend the genders?

## INDEPENDENCE VERSUS CONNECTEDNESS

Individual men display outlooks and behaviour that vary from fierce competitiveness to caring nurturance. So do individual women. Without denying that, researchers Nancy Chodorow (1978, 1989), Jean Baker Miller (1986), Carol Gilligan (1982) and her colleagues (1990), and Diane Felmlee and her team (2012) have contended that women more than men give priority to close, intimate relationships. Recall Weisstein's statement that social psychology had regarded differences between men and women as deficient in some way. The work of Lawrence Kohlberg (1958) on moral reasoning is a case in point. Testing his theory that there are six stages to moral development by asking male participants to resolve moral dilemmas involving male characters, he concluded that achieving stage six (universal ethical principles) was a reflection of superior moral development. When he tested his theory on women, using the same moral dilemmas, he found that they failed to achieve stage six. His conclusion was that women are unable to develop the same high levels of moral reasoning as men. Somewhat perturbed, Carol Gilligan (1982) focused on the moral outlook of American women and men. She had spotted that, in Kohlberg's analysis, high levels of moral reasoning were assumed to involve the implementation of abstract principles, whereas inferior levels were thought to include consideration of the local situation in which the dilemma had occurred. In her own study, Gilligan also found consistent differences between men and women in how they engaged in moral reasoning. When asked what it means to say something is morally right or wrong, men mentioned abstract ideals of duty, justice and individual freedom, while women raised the theme of helping others. This was not a case of inferior reasoning on the part of women, she argued, but simply reflected gender differences in how we do it. More recently Stacey Horn (2003) found that adolescent boys gave social regulatory and personal justifications for excluding someone from their peer group. Adolescent girls on the other hand, tended to give moral reasons such as breaking friendship norms (e.g. spreading gossip) within the group. Gilligan's work has met with some criticism. For example, Janet Sayers accuses her of presenting a more coherent view of women than might be the case. Women are more diverse in their psychological make-up than studies such as Gilligan's indicate (Sayers, 1986). Nithi Muthukrishna and Dhanasperi Govender (2011) found that South African children aged 6–8, regardless of their gender, tended to use a form of moral reasoning which emphasized care for others. This lacks the consistent gender differences in moral reasoning as identified by Gilligan. Eva Skoe and her colleagues (2002) at the Norwegian University of Science and Technology asked men and women to rate the importance of a range of moral dilemmas. They concluded that the observed differences between women and men were a function of gender-role identity rather than biological sex. Participants high in femininity showed more empathic concern for other people, and androgynous people reported more helpful behaviours than did all others. Such sex-role stereotypes have been established and are still prevalent in many cultures, reproduced in language for the next generation, impossible to escape being influenced by how your culture perceives gender characteristics.

As adults, women in the West describe themselves in more relational terms, welcome more help, experience more relationship-linked emotions, and are more attuned to others' relationships (Addis & Mahalik, 2003; Gabriel & Gardner, 1999; Tamres et al., 2002; Watkins et al., 1998, 2003). In conversation, men more often focus on tasks and on connections with large groups, women on personal relationships (Tannen, 1990). When in groups, women share more of their lives, and offer more support (Dindia & Allen, 1992; Eagly, 1987). Women's behaviour and perception in groups also depends on who is in the group. For example, Linda Carli found that when men and women rated the quality of the ideas they had contributed after either a mixed-sex or same-sex discussion, women evaluated their ideas as being of lower quality than men's in the mixed-sex context, but equally positively in the same-sex setting (Carli, 1989, reported in Carli, 1991).

In general women more than men give priority to helping others (Konrad et al., 2000). We discussed in Chapter 10 how these forms of helping had become feminized. Indeed, in most of the care-giving professions, such as social worker, teacher and nurse, women outnumber men. The reasons for this, however, are not obvious. Consider these two explanations: is it because women actually care more, or is it because women are fulfilling a stereotype that they *should* care more – and therefore find it easier to enter these professions more often than men do? Research by Ming Te Wang and colleagues (2013) found that although women perform just as well as men in science and maths subjects, they are much less likely to enter a STEM career. Why? The researchers hypothesize the answer may lie in the values they've been socialized into and their self-perceptions of what they're good at. If women are led to believe they are natural carers, and must balance work and family, then perhaps it is no surprise to see them in different careers to men.

Women's connections as mothers, daughters, sisters and grandmothers bind families (Rossi & Rossi, 1990). Women spend more time caring for both pre-schoolers and ageing parents than men do (Eagly & Crowley, 1986). Again this has to be explained by cultural expectations, gender roles and norms more than a result of something given by nature. In some Western cultures with public welfare and homes for the elderly, women do not care for their parents to the same degree as in traditional cultures, for instance in East Asia. Culture seems to have greater impact than biology.

Social psychologists still disagree as to why these gender differences occur. Research is ongoing but as yet no definitive conclusions can be drawn on this. Given the complexity of this area, it is likely that the results may show a combination of factors are behind these differences, but we still await research confirmation.

SOURCE: (L) © ArtisticCaptures/iStock; (R) © RichVintage/iStock

## SOCIAL DOMINANCE

Imagine two people. One is 'adventurous, autocratic, coarse, dominant, forceful, independent and strong'. The other is 'affectionate, dependent, dreamy, emotional, submissive and weak'. If the first person sounds more like a man to you and the second like a woman, you are not alone, report John Williams and Deborah Best (1990, p. 15). From Asia to Africa and Europe to Australia, people rate men as more dominant, driven and aggressive. Moreover, studies of nearly 80 000 people across 70 countries show that men more than women rate power and achievement as important (Schwartz & Rubel, 2005).

These perceptions and expectations correlate with reality. In essentially every society, men *are* socially dominant. In no known societies do women usually dominate men (Pratto, 1996). As we will see, gender differences vary greatly by culture, and gender differences are shrinking in many industrialized societies as women assume more managerial and leadership positions. Yet consider the following.

☐ In a survey of how many women occupied seats in 189 national Parliaments, they only accounted for 50 per cent or more in two countries: Rwanda (56 per cent) and Andorra (50 per cent). In 5 countries, women were not represented at all in their national Parliament (IPU, 2013).

☐ Men more than women are concerned with social dominance and are more likely to favour conservative political candidates and programmes that preserve group inequality (Eagly et al., 2004; Sidanius & Pratto, 1999). In 2005,

American men, by wide margins, were more supportive of capital punishment and the Iraq War (Gallup, 2005).

☐ Although women constitute 40 per cent of the world's workforce, they only hold 1 per cent of the world's wealth (World Bank, 2011).

☐ Despite more women now entering higher education in Europe, they are still more likely to be unemployed than men despite having the same level of qualifications (Eurostat, 2012).

Men's style of communicating undergirds their social power (see Research Close-Up: Gendered Wording in Job Advertisements Leads to Gender Inequality). In situations where roles aren't rigidly scripted, men tend to be more autocratic, women more democratic (Eagly & Johnson, 1990). We discussed leadership in Chapter 11. In leadership roles, men tend to excel as directive, task-focused leaders; women excel more often in the 'transformational' leadership that is favoured by more and more organizations, with inspirational and social skills that build team spirit (Eagly et al., 2003; van Engen & Willemsen, 2004). A Pew Global Survey in 2007 found cross-national mixed opinions about female political leaders. While nations in North America, Latin America and Western Europe rated women just as good at political leadership as men, Mali, Palestine, Kuwait, Pakistan, Bangladesh and Ethiopia thought men were better leaders. See Table 14.1.

Furthermore, it seems that men more than women place priority on winning, getting ahead and dominating others (Sidanius et al., 1994).

In writing, women tend to use more communal prepositions ('with'), fewer quantitative words and more present tense. One computer program, which taught itself to recognize gender differences in word usage and sentence structure, successfully identified the author's gender in 80 per cent of 920 British fiction and non-fiction works (Koppel et al., 2002).

Perhaps you have noticed that men and women not only talk about different topics but also use language and articulate words differently, at least in English? Peter Trudgill's work (1974) has been particularly helpful in revealing gender differences in spoken language. His studies conducted in many countries inside and outside Europe, found that when you control for factors such as social class, ethnicity and age, women consistently use prestigious forms of language. In other words, female speakers use linguistic forms that are considered to be more correct than those used by male speakers. Women and girls also become more flexible in their pronunciation. So informal forms of language are not just associated with working-class speech but with other aspects of working-class culture such as masculinity. This may lead men to adopt more non-standard linguistic forms than women. Men's and women's speech, as Trudgill (1974) has demonstrated, are not only different; women's speech is also (socially) better than men's speech.

In conversation, men's style reflects their concern for independence, women's for connectedness. Men are more likely to act as powerful people often do – talking assertively, interrupting intrusively, touching with the hand, staring more, smiling less (Anderson & Leaper, 1998; Carli, 1991; Ellyson et al., 1991). Stating the results from a female perspective, women's influence style tends to be more indirect – less interruptive, more sensitive, more polite, less cocky.

**TABLE 14.1**  Which sex generally make better political leaders?

| | Men % | Women % | Both equally % |
|---|---|---|---|
| U.S. | 16 | 6 | 75 |
| Canada | 10 | 8 | 80 |
| Chile | 26 | 5 | 66 |
| Argentina | 17 | 9 | 68 |
| Mexico | 12 | 9 | 76 |
| Venezuela | 11 | 6 | 82 |
| Brazil | 10 | 15 | 73 |
| Peru | 9 | 7 | 83 |
| Bolivia | 8 | 6 | 85 |
| France | 15 | 4 | 81 |
| Italy | 12 | 11 | 74 |
| Germany | 11 | 8 | 80 |
| Britain | 9 | 6 | 83 |
| Spain | 7 | 8 | 83 |
| Sweden | 3 | 6 | 90 |
| Russia | 40 | 7 | 44 |
| Ukraine | 34 | 7 | 52 |
| Bulgaria | 30 | 9 | 52 |
| Poland | 23 | 10 | 65 |
| Slovakia | 15 | 9 | 76 |
| Czech Rep. | 14 | 11 | 73 |
| Palest. ter. | 64 | 17 | 16 |
| Kuwait | 62 | 4 | 33 |
| Jordan | 49 | 6 | 42 |
| Egypt | 38 | 15 | 43 |
| Turkey | 34 | 10 | 51 |
| Lebanon | 34 | 11 | 53 |
| Israel | 30 | 14 | 53 |
| Morocco | 21 | 5 | 65 |
| Pakistan | 54 | 8 | 32 |
| Bangladesh | 52 | 8 | 41 |
| Indonesia | 43 | 3 | 52 |
| Malaysia | 43 | 4 | 52 |
| China | 28 | 4 | 64 |
| South Korea | 25 | 5 | 68 |
| India | 19 | 17 | 62 |
| Japan | 16 | 4 | 77 |
| Mali | 65 | 6 | 29 |
| Ethiopia | 51 | 3 | 45 |
| Nigeria | 48 | 6 | 45 |
| Ghana | 42 | 14 | 43 |
| Senegal | 36 | 15 | 48 |
| Ivory Coast | 31 | 9 | 60 |
| South Africa | 28 | 11 | 61 |
| Kenya | 27 | 10 | 62 |
| Uganda | 27 | 6 | 65 |
| Tanzania | 17 | 8 | 74 |

SOURCE: Pew Global Attitude Survey, 2007, which asked 47 countries whether men or women are better political leaders.

## research close-up

GENDERED WORDING IN JOB ADVERTISEMENTS LEADS TO GENDER INEQUALITY

*Source: Gaucher, D., Friesen, J., & Kay, A. C. (2011). Evidence that gendered wording in job advertisements exists and sustains gender inequality.* Journal of Personality and Social Psychology, *101(1), 109–128.*

### Introduction

Although we might believe we live in a world of gender equality, one look at the kinds of jobs where men and women are employed can dispel this notion. Danielle Gaucher and her colleagues note that women continue to be under-represented in stereotypically male-oriented jobs, such as engineering and business. The authors report that women themselves often justify this situation as the 'natural status quo' or 'the way things should be', and in doing so defend inequality. What the researchers of this paper were interested in, however, was not how women themselves justified this situation, but how employers might be putting women off applying for positions in traditionally male-dominated professions through the way that their advertisements are worded. Could it be the case that job adverts for male-dominated careers were using masculine type language (e.g. leader, competitive) and in doing so turning women off from applying? The research team decided to find out.

In total they conducted five studies, but we shall consider three of them here. Study 1 investigated if it was indeed the case that real job advertisements did use gendered wording. Study 2 examined how the wording of an advertisement affected potential applicants' perception of gender diversity within a workplace. Study 3 explored whether the wording of a job advertisement affected its appeal to women, and feelings of confidence in having the right skills and belongingness in that particular field.

### Study 1

*Method*

A random sample of 1493 online job advertisements of female-dominated and male-dominated careers were coded. Eleven occupations which are either very highly female-dominated or male-dominated were selected. This produced a final sample of 493 advertisements that fell into these 11 job types. The male-dominated job types were: plumber, electrician, mechanic, engineer, security guard and computer programmer. The female-dominated job types were: administrative assistant, early childhood educator, registered nurse, bookkeeper and HR professional. The authors chose to disregard any managerial positions as these were ambiguous in terms of their gender orientation.

The researchers then produced lists of masculine (e.g. competitive) and feminine (e.g. compassionate) trait words, based partly on Sandra Bem's Sex Role Inventory, and on other research that has identified these gendered words. Content-analysis was then applied to the 493 advertisements as they were coded for their masculine and feminine word content.

*Results*

A mixed 2 (occupation: male or female) × 2 (wording: male or female) ANOVA was conducted. This found that there was an overall effect of wording on the advertisements. There were more masculine words (M = .83%, SD = .70%) in all of the advertisements than feminine words (M = .63%, SD = .75%), $F(1, 491) = 3.02$, $p = .08$. Furthermore, masculine words were more likely to appear in male-dominated job advertisements (M = .97%, SD = .81%) than in advertisements for female-dominated jobs (M = .67%, SD = .73%), $t(491) = 4.35, p < .001, d = .40$. See Figure 14.6.

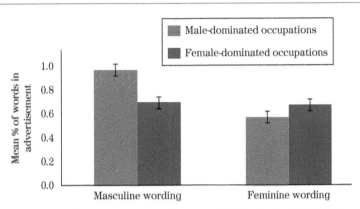

**FIGURE 14.6** Shows the mean percentage of gendered wording in each type of job advertisement

## Study 2

### Method

The participants for this study were 43 first-year Canadian students, of which 28 were women and 15 were men. Each participant was given six made-up job advertisements to read. Of these, two jobs were for a male-dominated post (engineer, plumber), two for a female-dominated post (registered nurse, administrative assistant), and two were gender-neutral (retail sales manager, real estate agent). The wording of these advertisements was also manipulated so that one of the male-dominated, female-dominated and gender-neutral adverts was written using masculine wording, and the other using feminine wording. The presentation of the advertisements was made online, and counterbalanced across all participants. After each advertisement was presented, the participants were asked to rate on a Likert scale (0–20) how many women they thought (a) worked for this company and (b) worked in the advertised position.

### Results

A mixed 3 (job type: male, female, neutral) × 2 (wording: male, female) × 2 (participant: male, female) ANOVA was conducted. The results showed that male-dominated jobs were perceived as having fewer women in them (M = 4.27, SD = 3.31) than neutral (M = 12.35, SD = 3.03), $t(80) = 16.12$, $p < .001$, $d = 2.62$ and female-dominated ones (M = 12.35, SD = 3.49), $t(80) = 16.50$, $p < .001$, $d = 2.13$. Furthermore, female participants thought that there would be more women in neutral jobs (M = 13.20, SD = 2.83) than male participants did (M = 10.64, SD = 2.73), $t(80) = 16.12$, $p < .001$, $d = 2.3$. Finally, all participants thought that those jobs advertised using masculine wording would have fewer women working in those positions (M = 9.06, SD = 4.80) than advertised jobs using feminine wording (M = 10.26, SD = 5.20) $F(92, 80) = 5.00$, $p < .05$.

## Study 3

### Method

One hundred and two first-year students took part, of which 63 were women and 33 men. As in Study 2, the participants were given six job advertisements to look at. These followed the same design as in Study 2. However, in Study 3, each participant was asked to rate on a 7-point Likert scale how appealing they thought the job was, and whether they felt they would belong in such an occupation (1 strongly agree, 7 strongly disagree).

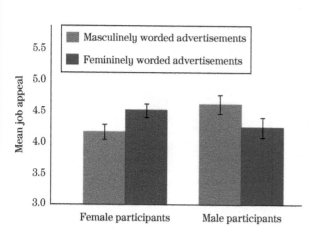

**FIGURE 14.7** Shows how appealing male and female participants considered the job advertisements to be, depending on how they were worded

### Results

A 3 (job type: male-dominated, female-dominated, neutral) × 2 (wording: feminine, masculine) × 2 (participant: male, female) mixed ANOVA was conducted on the responses to the items. The results showed that male-dominated advertisements were less appealing (M = 4.07, SD = 1.45) than female-dominated (M = 4.50, SD = 1.39) or neutral ones (M= 4.50, SD = 1.30), $t(188) = 2.71$, $p = .009$. Furthermore, women participants found occupations that were advertised using masculine wording much less appealing (M = 4.16, SD = 1.41) than those using feminine wording (M = 4.50, SD = 1.42), $F(1,62) = 6.74$, $p = .098$, regardless of the gender orientation of the job being advertised. Male participants found those job advertisements which used masculine wording (M = 4.61, SD = 1.34) slightly more appealing than those which used feminine wording (M = 4.22, SD = 1.29), $F(1, 32) = 3.58$, $p = .07$, regardless of the gender orientation of the advertised position. See Figure 14.7.

### Discussion

The researchers conclude that all of these studies demonstrate the effect wording has on job advertisements, their appeal, and whether individuals feel that there is gender diversity within that workplace. Using a Social Dominance theoretical perspective (see Chapter 13), the researchers argue that gendered wording in job recruitment reinforces gender inequalities in employment.

Study 1 shows that masculine wording is used more than feminine wording in all job advertisements, but especially in those jobs considered to be traditionally done by men. Study 2 illustrates people's perceptions of 'who' is likely to work in particular careers. How a job advertisement is worded has consequences for how much gender diversity we think there will be in the workplace. Finally, Study 3 reveals the impact the wording of a job advertisement has upon its appeal to men and women. Women, it seems, are turned off by advertisements that use masculine words. This may go some way to explaining why women are under-represented in certain job areas. Interestingly the researchers found that none of their participants observed that their perceptions of the advertised jobs had been affected by the wording of the advertisement. So we accept the status quo of inequality because we don't recognize how it occurs. We may be so entrenched in gender stereotypes, that we do not even notice linguistic styles that may be communicating and reinforcing them. In other words, we may be blind to institutional gender discrimination.

The researchers point out some limitations with their work. Laboratory studies such as these may not accurately reflect the real-world of job advertisements and job-seekers. In Studies 2 and 3, the researchers constructed their own advertisements. The participants were not genuine job-hunters but students. Would real adverts and job hunters produce the same results? The researchers also manipulated their gendered trait words in Studies 2 and 3. These may not reflect the language that is evident in real job advertisements. The researchers further reflect that we don't know what the effects of culture, race and ethnicity might have upon these results. The majority of their sample was White, and all were Canadians. Might a more heterogenous sample have given us different findings?

Much of the style we attribute to men is typical of people (men and women) in positions of status and power (Hall et al., 2006). For example, students nod more when speaking with professors than when speaking with peers, and women nod more than men (Helweg-Larsen et al., 2004). Men – and people in high-status roles – tend to talk more loudly and to interrupt more (Hall et al., 2005). Moreover, individuals vary; some men are characteristically hesitant and deferential, some women direct and assertive.

## EVOLUTION AND GENDER: DOING WHAT COMES NATURALLY?

*In explaining gender differences, inquiry has focused on two influences: evolution and culture.*

'What do you think is the main reason men and women have different personalities, interests, and abilities?' asked the Gallup Organization (1990) in a national survey in the USA. 'Is it mainly because of the way men and women are raised, or are the differences part of their biological makeup?' Among the 99 per cent who answered the question (apparently without questioning its assumptions), about the same percentage answered 'upbringing' as said 'biology'.

As we have already stated, there are, of course, certain salient biological sex differences. We also find them in most other species and the difference is important for many reasons. But do these natural distinctions in physical attributes, women with breasts and wide hips, men with more muscle mass and wide shoulders, also influence psychological characteristics and behaviour? To some extent. The biology, genes and hormones make psychological functions possible and they also can influence some different behaviour for the two sexes. For example, the fact that women give birth and can breastfeed their babies for months makes them necessarily related to their children, and they also feel more responsible for caring for their infants. Most cultures expect that women play this caring role more often than men do. Therefore we will find in most cultures that women take care of children. This fact is therefore partly a result of biology and partly a consequence of ascribed gender roles.

The male warrior hypothesis, developed by the evolutionary social psychologist Mark Van Vugt at the University of Amsterdam, the Netherlands, asserts that intergroup conflicts through history have affected the evolved psychologies of men and women differently (Van Vugt, 2009). Intergroup aggression has historically involved more men than women, and men respond more strongly than women to intergroup threats (Van Vugt et al., 2007). Studies also suggest that, compared with females, male psychology and behaviour is more strongly orientated towards intergroup conflict and competition, especially if there is a threat from an outgroup (Yuki & Yokota, 2009). This aspect of aggressive human psychology, characterizing the 'warriors', may therefore be more pronounced in men (also see Chapter 8 for a discussion on gender and aggression). To engage in such hostile activities will psychologically and genetically be costlier for women, according to Van Vugt. He also adds that socialization practices and cultural norms may exacerbate or undermine the evolutionary sex differences. Referring to the example of Israel, women are sometimes recruited as soldiers and participate in wars. Such practices may override any evolved psychological sex differences related to the male warrior hypothesis (Van Vugt, 2009).

## GENDER AND MATING PREFERENCES: THE EVOLUTIONARY APPROACH

Noting the worldwide persistence of gender differences in aggressiveness and dominance, evolutionary psychologist Douglas Kenrick (1987) suggested that 'we cannot change the evolutionary history of our species, and some of the differences between us are undoubtedly a function of that history'. Evolutionary psychology predicts no sex differences in all those domains in which the sexes faced similar adaptive challenges (Buss, 1995b), but does predict sex differences in behaviours relevant to dating, mating and reproduction. Evolutionary psychology suggests the physically dominant males were the ones who excelled in gaining access to females, which over generations enhanced male aggression and dominance as the less aggressive males had fewer chances to reproduce. Underlying the presumptions is a principle: *nature selects traits that help send one's genes into the future*. Little of this process is conscious. Few people in the throes of passion stop to think, 'I want to give my genes to posterity'. Rather, say evolutionary psychologists, our natural yearnings are our genes' way of making more genes.

'Humans are living fossils – collections of mechanisms produced by prior selections pressures,' says David Buss (1995a). And that, evolutionary psychologists believe, helps explain not only male aggression but also the differing sexual attitudes and behaviours of females and males. According to evolutionary psychology, sexual preferences are not something learned in a culture or a conscious approach; they are an unconscious necessity, forced by genetic fossils, note Buss (1994) and Alan Feingold (1992a).

According to evolutionary psychologists, men everywhere tend to feel attracted to women whose physical features, such as youthful faces and forms, suggest fertility. Moreover, the older the man, the greater the age difference he prefers when selecting a mate. In their twenties, men prefer, and marry, women only slightly younger. In their sixties, men prefer, and marry, women averaging about 10 years younger (Kenrick & Keefe, 1992). Women of all ages sometimes prefer men just slightly older than themselves and feel attracted to men whose wealth, power and ambition promise resources for protecting and nurturing offspring. Once again, say the evolutionary psychologists, we see that natural selection predisposes men to feel attracted to female features associated with fertility (Buss, 1989; also see Chapter 9). But as we saw in Figure 14.1 fewer than half of Germans and Americans think it is necessary to have a child in order to feel fulfilled, so why then should the majority of men look for a fertile women? These mate preferences in most (but not all) cultures also have a competing social explanation. Social norms regulate what is preferred and they can develop independent of any genetic selection. According to the values and norms in most cultures it would be something of a surprise if women were looking first and foremost for poor, stupid men who maltreat them, and if men wanted women who looked and behaved just the opposite of what the fashion, movie and entertainment industry told them was desirable and displayed status.

## REFLECTIONS ON EVOLUTIONARY PSYCHOLOGY

Without disputing natural selection – nature's process of selecting physical and behavioural traits that enhance gene survival – critics see a problem with evolutionary psychology. Evolutionary psychologists sometimes start with an effect (such as the male–female difference in mate preferences) and then work backwards to construct an explanation for it. That approach is reminiscent of functionalism, a dominant theory in psychology during the 1920s, whose logic went like this: 'Why does that behaviour occur? Because it serves such and such a function.' You may recognize both the evolutionary and the functionalist approaches as examples of hindsight reasoning. As biologists Paul Ehrlich and Marcus Feldman (2003) have pointed out, the evolutionary theorist can hardly lose when employing hindsight.

The way to overcome the hindsight bias is to imagine things turning out otherwise. Let's try it. Imagine that women were stronger and more physically aggressive than men. 'But of course!' someone might say, 'all the better for protecting their young'. And if human males were never known to have extramarital affairs, might we not see the evolutionary wisdom behind their fidelity? Because there is more to bringing offspring to maturity than merely depositing sperm, men and women both gain by investing jointly in their children. Males who are loyal to their mates and offspring are more apt to ensure that their young will survive to perpetuate their genes. Monogamy also increases men's certainty of paternity. (These are, in fact, evolutionary explanations – again based on hindsight – for why humans, and certain other species whose young require a heavy parental investment, tend to pair off and be monogamous.) But love and sex for pure pleasure and without the intention to produce offspring or any genetic payoff is also widespread in all cultures. There is more sexual intercourse due to plain pleasure and with contraception than with the purpose to continue genes, at least among humans.

So, our searching for a partner and for a love relationship is not simply a result of our genes' inclination to contribute to future generations. We are looking for somebody to love, and to make love with, for pleasure and because we prefer a partner who we immediately like and who is appreciated and has status in our culture.

## GENDER AND HORMONES

If genes predispose gender-related traits, they do so by their effect on our bodies. In male embryos, the genes direct the formation of testes, which begin to secrete testosterone, the male sex hormone that influences masculine appearance. Studies indicate that girls who were exposed to excess testosterone during foetal development tend to exhibit more tomboyish play behaviour than other girls (Hines, 2004). Other case studies have followed males who, having been born without penises, are reared as girls (Reiner & Gearhart, 2004). Despite their being put in dresses and treated as girls, most exhibit male-typical play and eventually – in most cases, not without emotional distress – come to have a male identity.

As people mature to middle age and beyond, a curious thing happens. Women become more assertive and self-confident, men more empathic and less domineering (Lowenthal et al., 1975; Pratt et al., 1990). Hormone changes are one possible explanation for the shrinking gender differences. Role demands are another. Some speculate that during courtship and early parenthood, social expectations lead both sexes to emphasize traits that enhance their roles. While courting, providing and protecting, men play up their macho sides and forgo their need for interdependence and nurturance (Gutmann, 1977). While courting and rearing young children, young women restrain their impulses to assert and be independent. As men and women graduate from these early adult roles, they supposedly express more of their restrained tendencies. Each becomes more *androgynous* – capable of both assertiveness and nurturance.

## CULTURE AND GENDER: DOING AS THE CULTURE SAYS?

*Culture's influence is vividly illustrated by differing gender roles across place and time.*

Culture, as we noted earlier, is what's shared by a large group and transmitted across generations – ideas, attitudes, behaviours and traditions. We can see the shaping power of culture in ideas about how men and women should behave – and in the disapproval they endure when they violate those expectations (Kite, 2001). In countries everywhere, research indicates girls spend more time helping with housework and childcare, and boys spend more time in unsupervised play (Edwards, 1991). Even in contemporary, dual-career marriages, men do most of the household repairs and women arrange the childcare (Bianchi et al., 2000; Biernat & Wortman, 1991).

John Dixon and Margaret Wetherell focused on the persistence of gender inequalities in domestic labour. In their study they found that despite their increasing participation in paid employment and the rise of egalitarian values, women in heterosexual relationships continue to bear more responsibility than their male partners for routine domestic tasks such as cleaning, cooking, shopping, laundry and nappy-changing. They bear more responsibility for tasks which have been variously described as 'mundane', 'repetitive', 'unrelenting' and 'nondiscretionary', and do more than double the housework that men do (Dixon & Wetherell, 2004). The researchers also found another paradox: when asked how in principle housework should be divided, most couples now endorse a principle of equality. In practice, however, the same couples also regard the unequal allocation of labour in their own homes as fair.

But are things changing in modern society? As gender equality becomes more embedded (and accepted?) within our cultural and social lives, is this reflected in domestic responsibilities such as caring for our children? In Denmark, the answer seems to be 'yes – to some extent'. Eva Silberschmidt Viala (2011) studied the lives of first-time parents resident in Denmark. Who would be caring for their children? What did they think the role of parent involved? The parents she interviewed noted joint parental responsibilities. A lack of experience meant a process of learning together in how to care for their child. Parenting was a challenge to be met equally by both parents. However, Viala found that participants also upheld traditional gender stereotypes to resolve parental care dilemmas. It was women who were expected to take leave from work to care for their children on the grounds that her job was less demanding than the father's. As Viala concludes, despite the visible appearance of equality within our societies, traditional gendered stereotypes still influence day-to-day parenting practices. Research by Sabra Katz-Wise and her team (2010) offers similar conclusions. They found that the onset of parenthood sparks traditional gender-role attitudes and behaviours in both parents, but especially women. As Dixon and Wetherell (2004) argued, these gender differences in domestic life may continue to be reified in a cultural language which regards these practices as fair. In trying to explain these paradoxes, researchers have recently looked at cognitions, attitudes and feelings that women may have. Instead Dixon and Wetherell seek to contribute to this move by drawing on recent developments in discursive psychology and argue that an adequate social psychology of domestic life requires attention to, and a perspective on, everyday language. Investigations of gender inequalities and negotiations over 'fair shares' can benefit from the new directions provided by social constructionism and the more complex views of subjectivity and social relations now emerging in psychology (Dixon & Wetherell, 2004).

## THE SOCIAL CONSTRUCTION OF GENDER

Social constructionists have been particularly interested in how gender roles, and therefore males and females, masculinity and femininity, are 'constructed' in a society, and 'assigned' certain traits and attributes. Gender roles and norms are the outcome of a socialization process based on the dominant values, norms and beliefs of society. Accordingly, gender differs between societies and across the social, ethnic and cultural groups within societies. Even for a single individual, gender behaviours change over time and within different social contexts. From birth onwards, both sexes are conditioned by parental and other adult responses to behave, think, act and interact in gender-specific role manifestations.

Simply living in our world exposes us to myriad images and ideas about desirable masculine and feminine identities. We receive messages from the day we are born about what is appropriate for a boy and girl, man and woman. Advertising, toys, clothing and popular media further disseminate notions of what is 'right' for girls and women; what is 'desirable' for men and boys. So our tendency to conform and to accept what seems 'natural' makes us easy targets for all marketing departments.

'At the United Nations, we have always understood that our work for development depends on building a successful partnership with the African farmer and her husband.'
   Secretary-General Kofi A. Annan, 2002

Some social psychologists have challenged gender difference research, questioning the extent to which researchers can use gender as an analytic category. To do so is to assume that gender is a fixed 'trait' that resides within individuals. It is based on a belief that all women share the same psychology of 'woman-ness'. The argument is that this kind of research simply reproduces the

A little girl playing in her toy kitchen.
SOURCE: © Photolyric/iStock

male–female dichotomy and results in an exaggeration of sex differences. If we go looking for gender differences, then we may surely find them. In her influential book *Gender Trouble* (1990), Judith Butler argues that the apparent coherence of the categories of sex, gender and sexuality (such as masculine heterosexual male) is culturally constructed and reinforced through the repetition of such behaviour publicly. These acts establish the appearance of an essential 'core' gender. But actually, gender is a social construct.

Some researchers have examined if and how people use 'gender' in their everyday interactions, and what they consider these gender identities to be and involve. Elizabeth Stokoe (2000, 2004) argues that the 'doing' of gender in a society is constituted in people's everyday communication. Focusing on these daily interactions can tell us a lot about how gender is culturally acquired and used. So rather than comparing what men and women say and do, we should look at when and how people themselves refer to their sex or gender in communication, and why. Let's illustrate with an example from Stokoe's work. Below is an extract taken from a discussion between a group of university students on how to complete a task that's been set them:

Ben     Is someone scribing, who's writing it?

Nick    Oh yeah

Mark    Well you can't read my writing [points to Kay] she wants to do it

Kay     Eh?

Nick    Well, secretary, female

Kay     Well, secretary female, eh heh heh heh, I'm wearing glasses, I must be the secretary

(Stokoe, 2004)

As we can see, the discussion immediately turns to the business of writing down an account of the decisions they make as a group. Stokoe directs us towards how the task of secretary is assigned to Kay by Nick on the basis of her gender. Here we can see how gender stereotypes are produced and reproduced in communication. Kay doesn't reject her assigned role, but she accepts it on the basis of her wearing glasses rather than being female. Qualitative research such as this, that focuses on when and how gender is mentioned by people, tells us something about how this identity is understood by people themselves, and what differences *they* construct between men and women (rather than the researcher).

## GENDER ROLES VARY WITH CULTURE

Despite gender role inequalities, the majority of the world's people would ideally like to see more parallel male and female roles. In 2003 a Pew Global Attitudes survey asked 38 000 people whether life was more satisfying when both spouses work and share childcare, or when women stay home and care for the children while the husband provides. A majority of respondents in 41 of 44 countries chose the first answer (see Figure 14.8).

However, there are big country-to-country differences. Egyptians disagreed with the world majority opinion by 2 to 1, whereas Vietnamese concurred by 11 to 1. A Global Gender Gap report (2008) from the World Economic Forum

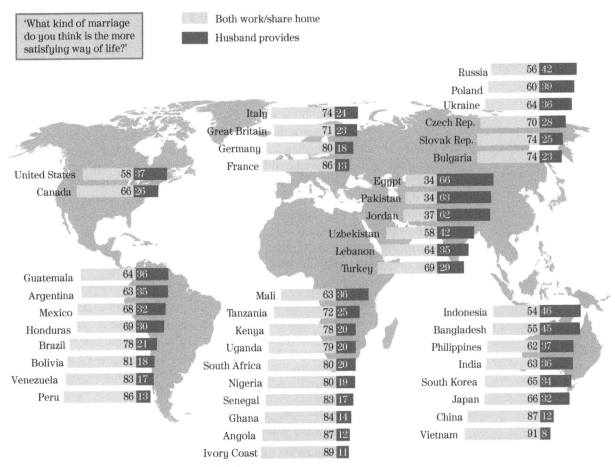

'What kind of marriage do you think is the more satisfying way of life?'

Both work/share home
Husband provides

| Country | Both work/share home | Husband provides |
|---|---|---|
| Russia | 56 | 42 |
| Poland | 60 | 39 |
| Ukraine | 64 | 36 |
| Czech Rep. | 70 | 28 |
| Slovak Rep. | 74 | 25 |
| Bulgaria | 74 | 23 |
| Italy | 74 | 24 |
| Great Britain | 71 | 23 |
| Germany | 80 | 18 |
| France | 86 | 13 |
| United States | 58 | 37 |
| Canada | 66 | 26 |
| Egypt | 34 | 66 |
| Pakistan | 34 | 63 |
| Jordan | 37 | 62 |
| Uzbekistan | 58 | 42 |
| Lebanon | 64 | 35 |
| Turkey | 69 | 29 |
| Guatemala | 64 | 36 |
| Argentina | 63 | 35 |
| Mexico | 68 | 32 |
| Honduras | 69 | 30 |
| Brazil | 78 | 21 |
| Bolivia | 81 | 18 |
| Venezuela | 83 | 17 |
| Peru | 86 | 13 |
| Mali | 63 | 36 |
| Tanzania | 72 | 25 |
| Kenya | 78 | 20 |
| Uganda | 79 | 20 |
| South Africa | 80 | 20 |
| Nigeria | 80 | 19 |
| Senegal | 83 | 17 |
| Ghana | 84 | 14 |
| Angola | 87 | 12 |
| Ivory Coast | 89 | 11 |
| Indonesia | 54 | 46 |
| Bangladesh | 55 | 45 |
| Philippines | 62 | 37 |
| India | 63 | 36 |
| South Korea | 65 | 34 |
| Japan | 66 | 32 |
| China | 87 | 12 |
| Vietnam | 91 | 8 |

**FIGURE 14.8** Approved gender roles vary with culture

SOURCE: Data from the 2003 Pew Global Attitudes survey.

(http://www3.weforum.org.docs/WEF_GenderGap_Report_2008.pdf) reported that Norway, Finland and Sweden have the greatest gender equality, and Saudi Arabia, Chad and Yemen the least. Even in industrialized societies, roles vary enormously. Women fill 1 in 10 managerial positions in Japan and Germany, and nearly 1 in 2 in Australia and the USA (ILO, 1997; Wallace, 2000). In North America most doctors and dentists are men; in Russia most doctors are women, as are most dentists in Denmark. What roles men and women perform in society are influenced by cultural norms and values.

## PEER-TRANSMITTED CULTURE

Cultures, like ice cream, come in many flavours. On Wall Street, men mostly wear suits and women often wear skirts and dresses; in Scotland, many men wear pleated skirts (kilts) as formal dress; in some equatorial cultures, men and women wear virtually nothing at all. How are such traditions preserved across generations?

The prevailing assumption is what Judith Rich Harris (1998) calls *the nurture assumption*: parental nurture, the way parents bring their children up, governs who their children become. On that much, Freudians and behaviourists – and

In Western countries, gender roles are becoming more flexible. No longer is firefighting necessarily men's work.

SOURCE: © WellfordT/iStock

your next-door neighbour – agree. Comparing the extremes of loved children and abused children suggests that parenting *does* matter. Moreover, children do acquire many of their values, including their political affiliation and religious faith, at home. But if children's personalities are moulded by parental example and nurture, then children who grow up in the same families should be noticeably alike, shouldn't they? Not necessarily. It depends on the ability and capacity measured. On some characteristics siblings are similar, in others they differ. Every individual has their own personal development and the impact from parents, siblings, family and culture is filtrated through the individuals' distinctiveness. The same social and cultural impact will result in different internal psychology and the differences increase with age. And since siblings are also influenced by each other they receive different impacts. This produces differences in their psychological make-up. Some research has indicated that firstborn and later-born siblings have different personalities. Firstborns are typically confident but conservative, while later-borns are flexible and innovative. These personality differences 'cannot be ascribed to genetics' (Gould, 1997). They are explainable only by their different experiences and parental treatment of firstborn and late-born children.

The family influence is of course important but there is also a significant *peer influence* (Harris, 1996). What older children and teens care most about is not what their parents think but what peers think. Children and youth learn their games, their musical tastes, their accents, even their dirty words, mostly from peers. In hindsight, that makes sense. It's their peers with whom they play and eventually will work and mate. Consider the following.

☐ Pre-schoolers will often refuse to try a certain food despite parents' urgings – until they are put at a table with a group of children who like it.

☐ Although children of smokers have an elevated smoking rate, the effect seems largely peer mediated. Such children more often have friends who model smoking, who suggest its pleasures, and who offer cigarettes.

☐ Young immigrant children whose families are transplanted into foreign cultures usually grow up preferring the language and norms of their new peer culture. They may switch to the customs of another culture ('code-switch') when they step back into their homes, but their hearts and minds are with their peer groups. Likewise, deaf children of hearing parents who attend schools for the deaf usually leave their parents' culture and assimilate into deaf culture.

Therefore, if we left a group of children with their same schools, neighbourhoods and peers but switched the parents around, says Harris (1996) in taking her argument to its limits, they 'would develop into the same sort of adults'. Parents have an important influence, but it's substantially indirect; parents help define the schools, neighbourhoods and peers that directly influence whether their children become delinquent, use drugs or get pregnant. Moreover, children often take their cues from slightly older children, who get their cues from older youth, who take theirs from young adults in the parents' generation.

Children learn many of their attitudes from their peers.
SOURCE: © kate_sept2004/iStock

# WHAT CAN WE CONCLUDE ABOUT GENES, CULTURE AND GENDER?

*Biology and culture play out in the context of each other. How, then, do biology and culture interact? And how do our individual personalities interact with our situations?*

## BIOLOGY *AND* CULTURE

We needn't think of evolution and culture as competitors. Cultural norms subtly but powerfully affect our attitudes and behaviour, but they don't do so independent of biology, as we described at the beginning of this chapter.

Advances in neurobiology and neuropsychology indicate how experience and activity change the brain and establish new connections between neurons (Quartz & Sejnowski, 2002). Our brain develops and increases its capacity due to its plasticity. Environmental stimuli can also produce new brain cells. Visual experience activates genes that develop the brain's visual area. Parental touch activates genes that help offspring cope with future stressful events. The brain is not hardware, a given structure, set in stone.

Alice Eagly and Wendy Wood (1999; Eagly, 1987) theorize how biological influences and childhood socialization predispose a sexual division of labour (Figure 14.9). In adult life the immediate causes of gender differences in social behaviour are the *roles* that reflect this sexual division of labour. Men, because of their biologically endowed strength and speed, tend to be found in roles demanding physical power. Women's capacity for childbearing and breastfeeding inclines them to more nurturant roles. Each sex, then, tends to exhibit the behaviours expected of those who fill such roles and to have their skills and beliefs shaped accordingly. Nature and nurture are a 'tangled web'. As role assignments become more equal, Eagly predicts that gender differences 'will gradually lessen'.

Indeed, note Eagly and Wendy Wood (1999), in cultures with greater equality of gender roles the gender difference in mate preferences (men seeking youth and domestic skill, women seeking status and earning potential) is less. Likewise, as women's employment in formerly male occupations has increased, the gender difference in self-reported masculinity/femininity has decreased (Twenge, 1997).

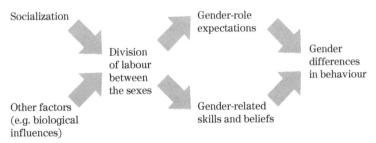

**FIGURE 14.9** A social-role theory of gender differences in social behaviour
Various influences, including childhood experiences and factors, bend males and females towards differing roles. It is the expectations and the skills and beliefs associated with these differing roles that affect men's and women's behaviour.
SOURCE: Adapted from Eagly, 1987, and Eagly & Wood, 1991.

As men and women enact more similar roles, their psychological differences shrink.

Although biology predisposes men to strength tasks and women to infant care, Wood and Eagly (2002) conclude that 'the behaviour of women and men is sufficiently malleable that individuals of both sexes are fully capable of effectively carrying out organizational roles at all levels'. For today's high-status and often high-technology work roles, male size and aggressiveness matter less and less. Moreover, lowered birth rates mean that women are less constrained by pregnancy and nursing. The end result, when combined with competitive pressures for employers to hire the best talent regardless of gender, is the inevitable rise in gender equality. This also illustrates that biology, and the biological differences between the sexes, loses its influence on psychological functions and behaviour. What happens in society and culture is more important than biology for gender roles and the relationships between men and women.

## THE POWER OF THE SITUATION *AND* THE PERSON

'There are trivial truths and great truths', declared the physicist Niels Bohr. 'The opposite of a trivial truth is plainly false. The opposite of a great truth is also true.' Social psychology teaches us a great truth: *the power of the situation*. This great truth about the power of external pressures would explain our behaviour if we were passive, like tumbleweeds. But, unlike tumbleweeds, we are not just blown here and there by the situations in which we find ourselves. We act; we react. We respond, and we get responses. We can resist the social situation and sometimes even change it. For that reason, we have chosen to conclude the 'social influence' chapters by calling attention to the opposite of the great truth: *the power of the person*.

Food for thought: if Bohr's statement is a great truth, what is its opposite?

Perhaps stressing the power of culture leaves you somewhat uncomfortable. Most of us resent any suggestion that external forces determine our behaviour; we see ourselves as free beings, as the originators of our actions (well, at least of our good actions). We worry that assuming cultural reasons for our actions might lead to what philosopher Jean-Paul Sartre called 'bad faith' – evading responsibility by blaming something or someone for one's fate.

Social situations do profoundly influence individuals. But individuals also influence social situations. The two *interact*. Every individual is not only influenced by culture – we also create and change culture by acting on it.

interaction *a relationship in which the effect of one factor (such as biology) depends on another factor (such as environment)*

The interaction occurs in at least three ways (Snyder & Ickes, 1985).

**1** *A given social situation often affects different people differently.* Because our minds do not see reality identically or objectively, we respond to a situation as we construe it. And some people (groups as well as individuals) are more sensitive and responsive to social situations than others (Snyder, 1983). The Japanese, for example, are more responsive to social expectations than the British (Argyle et al., 1978).

**2** *People often choose their situations* (Ickes et al., 1997). Given a choice, sociable people elect situations that evoke social interaction. When you chose your university or place to live, you were also choosing to expose yourself to a specific set of social influences.

**3** *People often create their situations.* Recall again that our preconceptions can be self-fulfilling: if we expect someone to be extraverted, hostile, intelligent or sexy, our actions towards the person may induce the very behaviour we expect.

The reciprocal causation between situations and persons allows us to see people as either *reacting to* or *acting upon* their environment. Each perspective is correct, for we are both the products and the architects of our culture and the social world.

Thus, power resides both in persons and in situations. We create and are created by our cultural worlds.

## focus on

### MIND THE GAP: FROM SEXED BRAINS TO GENDERED BEHAVIOUR

As we've seen in this chapter, there is a tendency for researchers to emphasize any differences between the genders. Arguably guilty of the confirmation bias, journals have been keen to publish those results that confirm what we believe about men and women. And what we often believe is that they are different. Socially, physiologically and psychologically. Books like John Gray's *Men Are from Mars, Women Are from Venus* have sold over 50 million copies. However, as we've also seen in this chapter, there is an increasing body of work that questions gender differences reported by earlier studies. One area that has been brought to task is that of neuroscience and its findings that men and women have different brains.

Cordelia Fine (2010) remarks that historically women have been thought to have smaller and lighter brains than men, and this was held responsible for their intellectual inferiority compared to men. Recent advances in neuroscience have meant that we can now see those differences. For example, one of the key differences neuroscientists claim to exist between men and women is that men use the left hemisphere for language and the right for visual processing. Women, on the other hand, use both for both types of processing. Biological differences such as these have been used to explain and perpetuate some gendered assumptions about the sexes. Men are better at visual processing and spatial awareness (and parking the car!) and women are better at language (and not at parking the car!). Men are better at science, because they focus on detail and can integrate information, and women are better at empathy. As Fine notes, the apparent 'facts' of neuroscience have become 'a springboard for scientifically unwarranted claims about men's and women's different psychological abilities'.

Fine points out that neuroscience results are often based on very small sample sizes (the technology is extremely expensive to use!), and the conclusions drawn are not always representative of what the neuroimaging shows. Researchers are keen to ignore similarities found between men and women and focus on any sex differences – no matter how small that difference may be. Furthermore, there is a tendency to leap to gender stereotypes to explain what those sex differences mean for our everyday lives (e.g. men are better at parking the car than women). And the impressive technology may mean we're keen to accord any results it produces with more credibility than we should. In short, researchers interested in gender might be guilty of what Fine calls 'neuro-realism'.

As we discussed earlier in this chapter, the brain is a piece of software, not hardware. Sex differences found in the brain might be a consequence of cultural impact rather than physiologically determined differences.

---

QUESTIONS

**1** How much weight should social psychologists give to the findings of neuroscience in explaining differences between men and women?

**2** Should we pursue neuroscientific techniques to better understand gender?

---

## SUMMING UP: GENES, CULTURE AND GENDER

### HOW ARE WE INFLUENCED BY HUMAN NATURE AND CULTURAL DIVERSITY?

☐ How are we humans alike, how do we differ – and why? Evolutionary psychologists study how natural selection favours behavioural traits that promote the perpetuation of one's genes. Although part of evolution's legacy is our human capacity to learn and adapt (and therefore to differ from one another), evolutionary psychologists highlight the kinship that results from our shared human nature and genetic selection.

☐ The *cultural perspective* highlights human diversity – the behaviours and ideas that define a group and that are transmitted across generations. The differences in attitudes and behaviours from one culture to another indicate the extent to which we are the products of cultural norms and roles. Yet cross-cultural psychologists also examine the 'essential universality' of all people. For example, despite their differences, cultures have a number of norms in common, such as disapproving of incest.

### HOW ARE GENDER SIMILARITIES AND DIFFERENCES EXPLAINED?

☐ Boys and girls, and men and women, are in many ways alike. Yet their differences attract more attention than their similarities.

☐ Social psychologists have explored gender differences in *independence* versus *connectedness*.

☐ Men and women also tend to exhibit differing social dominance. In every known culture on Earth, men tend to have more social power and this is reflected in their interactions.

☐ Some social psychologists have pointed to the constructed nature of gender, arguing that researchers should not go looking for gender differences, but should focus on how, when and why gender is invoked in everyday interaction.

### EVOLUTION AND GENDER: DOING WHAT COMES NATURALLY?

☐ Evolutionary psychologists theorize how evolution might have predisposed gender differences.

☐ Critics say that evolutionary explanations are sometimes after-the-fact conjectures that fail to account for the reality of cultural diversity.

☐ Although biology (for example, in the form of male and female hormones) plays an important role in sex differences, social roles are also a major influence in forming gender differences.

### CULTURE AND GENDER: DOING AS THE CULTURE SAYS?

☐ The most heavily researched of roles, gender roles, reflect some biological influence, but also illustrate culture's strong impact. The universal tendency has been for males, more than females, to occupy socially dominant roles.

☐ Gender roles show significant variation from culture to culture and from time to time. In Europe women's roles have become far more dominant and active since the mid-twentieth century.

□ Much of culture's influence is transmitted to children as they grow up not only by parents but also by peers.

□ Biological and cultural explanations need not be contradictory. Indeed, they interact. Biological factors operate within a cultural context, and culture builds on a biological foundation.

□ The great truth about the power of social influence is but half the truth if separated from its complementary truth: the power of the person. Persons and situations interact in at least three ways. First, individuals vary in how they interpret and react to a given situation. Second, people choose many of the situations that influence them. Third, people help create their social situations.

## CRITICAL QUESTIONS

**1** How is the interaction between biology and culture explained by Lev Vygotsky in the culture-historical theory?

**2** Explain the hindsight criticism of evolutionary psychology. Provide an example of this type of thinking in evolutionary psychology.

**3** What do we mean by 'plasticity of the brain' and why is it important for social psychological phenomena?

**4** Discuss cultural versus evolutionary explanations for gender differences.

**5** What is meant by androgynous and discuss if you will find androgynous people to the same degree in all cultures?

## RECOMMENDED READINGS

Here are some readings you might want to follow up to continue your exploration of the influence of biology and culture upon gender.

### Classic Readings

Darwin, C. (2009). *Origin of Species*. London: Penguin Classics.

*A revised version of Charles Darwin's classic 1859 book outlining his theory of evolution.*

Eagly, A. H. & Wood, W. (1999). The origins of sex differences in human behavior. *American Psychologist*, **54**(6), 408–423.

*Outlines two contrasting explanations for gender differences in behaviour: the evolutionary explanation and a social role explanation.*

Gilligan, C. (1982). *In A Different Voice: Psychological Theory and Women's Development*. Cambridge, MA: Harvard University Press.

*This is a classic book that argues for differences in moral reasoning between men and women. Gilligan asserts that these differences are not rooted in biology but in the socialization of boys and girls in the social world.*

**Contemporary Readings**

Butler, J. (2004). *Undoing Gender*. London: Routledge.

*This book challenges our taken-for-granted division of human beings into male and female, and argues that 'gender' (what it means to be male or female) is a product of culture and social norms.*

McDonald, M. M., Navarrete, C. D., & Van Vugt, M. (2011). Evolution and the psychology of intergroup conflict: the male warrior hypothesis. *Philosophical Transactions of the Royal Society*, **367**(1589), 670–679.

*An empirical examination of the 'male warrior hypothesis' that may underlie intergroup aggression, and which would explain the differing social behaviour of men and women.*

# References

## A

**Abbey, A.** (1987). Misperceptions of friendly behavior as sexual interest: A survey of naturally occurring incidents. *Psychology of Women Quarterly*, **11**, 173–194.

**Abbey, A.** (1991). Misperception as an antecedent of acquaintance rape: A consequence of ambiguity in communication between women and men. In A. Parrot (ed.), *Acquaintance rape*. New York: John Wiley.

**Abbey, A., McAuslan, P., & Ross, L. T.** (1998). Sexual assault perpetration by college men: The role of alcohol, misperception of sexual intent, and sexual beliefs and experiences. *Journal of Social and Clinical Psychology*, **17**, 167–195.

**ABC News** (2004, 28 December). Whistleblower revealed abuse at Abu Ghraib prison. ABCNEWS.go.com.

**Abell, J.** (2012). Volunteering to help conserve endangered species: An identity approach to human-animal relationships. *Journal of Community & Applied Social Psychology*, **23**, 157–170.

**Abell, J., & Stokoe, E. H.** (2001). Broadcasting the royal role: Constructing culturally situated identities in the Princess Diana Panorama interview. *British Journal of Social Psychology*, **40**, 417–435.

**Abelson, R. P.** (1972). Are attitudes necessary? In B. T. King & E. McGinnies (eds), *Attitudes, conflict and social change*. New York: Academic Press.

**Aboud, F. E., & Amato, M.** (2001). Developmental and socialization influences on intergroup bias. In R. Brown & S. Gaertner (eds), *Blackwell handbook of social psychology: Intergroup processes, Vol. 4*. Oxford: Blackwell.

**Abrams, D., Hopthrow, T., Hulbert, L. G., & Frings, D.** (2006). Groupdrink? The effect of alcohol on risk attraction among groups versus individuals. *Journal of Studies on Alcohol*, **67**(4), 628–636.

**Abrams, D., Rutland, A., & Cameron, L.** (2003). The development of subjective group dynamics: Children's judgements of normative and deviant in-group and out-group individuals. *Child Development*, **74**(6), 1840–1856.

**Abrams, D., Wetherell, M., Cochrane, S., Hogg, M. A., & Turner, J. C.** (1986). Knowing what to think by knowing who you are: Self-categorization and the nature of norm formation, conformity and group polarization. *British Journal of Social Psychology*, **29**, 97–119.

**Adams, G., & Markus, H. R.** (2001). Culture as patterns: An alternative approach to the problem of reification. *Culture & Psychology*, **7**(3), 283–296.

**Adams, J. M., & Jones, W. H.** (1997). The conceptualization of marital commitment: An integrative analysis. *Journal of Personality and Social Psychology*, **72**, 1177–1196.

**Addis, M. E., & Mahalik, J. R.** (2003). Men, masculinity, and the contexts of help seeking. *American Psychologist*, **58**, 5–4.

**Addison, S. J., & Thorpe, S. J.** (2004). Factors involved in the formation of attitudes towards those who are mentally ill. *Social Psychiatry and Psychiatric Epidemiology*, **39**, 228–234.

**Aderman, D., & Berkowitz, L.** (1983). Self-concern and the unwillingness to be helpful. *Social Psychology Quarterly*, **46**, 293–301.

**Adler, N. E., Boyce, T., Chesney, M. A., Cohen, S., Folkman, S., Kahn, R. L., & Syme, S. L.** (1993). Socioeconomic inequalities in health: No easy solution. *Journal of the American Medical Association*, **269**, 3140–3145.

**Adler, N. E., Boyce, T., Chesney, M. A., Cohen, S., Folkman, S., Kahn, R. L., & Syme, S. L.** (1994). Socioeconomic status and health: The challenge of the gradient. *American Psychologist*, **49**, 15–24.

**Adler, R. P., Lesser, G. S., Meringoff, L. K., Robertson, T. S., & Ward, S.** (1980). *The effects of television advertising on children*. Lexington, MA: Lexington Books.

**Adorno, T., Frenkel-Brunswik, E., Levinson, D., & Sanford, R. N.** (1950). *The authoritarian personality*. New York: Harper.

**Adorno, T. W., Frenkel-Brunswik, E., Levinson, D. J., & Sanford, R. N.** (1982). *The authoritarian personality*, abridged edn. London: Norton.

**Ahlfinger, N. R., & Esser, J. K.** (2001). Testing the groupthink model: Effects of promotional leadership and conformity predisposition. *Social Behavior and Personality*, **29**(1), 31–41.

**Aiello, J. R., & Douthitt, E. Z.** (2001). Social facilitation from Triplett to electronic performance monitoring. *Group Dynamics: Theory, Research, and Practice*, **5**, 163–180.

**Aikman, S. N., Min, K. E., & Graham, D.** (2006). Food attitudes, eating behaviour and the information underlying food attitudes. *Appetite*, **47**, 111–114.

**Ainsworth, M. D. S.** (1973). The development of infant-mother attachment. In B. Caldwell & H. Ricciuti (eds), *Review of child development research* (Vol. 3). Chicago: University of Chicago Press.

**Ainsworth, M. D. S.** (1979). Infant–mother attachment. *American Psychologist*, **34**, 932–937.

**Ajzen, I.** (1985). From intentions to actions: A theory of planned behaviour. In J. Kuhl & J. Beckmann (eds), *Action control: From cognition to behaviour* (pp. 11–39). Heidelberg: Springer Verlag.

**Ajzen, I., & Fishbein, M.** (1977). Attitude–behaviour relations: A theoretical analysis and review of empirical research. *Psychological Bulletin*, **84**, 888–918.

**Ajzen, I., & Fishbein, M.** (2005). The influence of attitudes on behavior. In D. Albarracin, B. T. Johnson & M. P. Zanna (eds), *The handbook of attitudes*. Mahwah, NJ: Erlbaum.

**Ajzen, I., & Madden, T. J.** (1986). Prediction of goal-directed behavior: Attitudes, intentions, and perceived behavioral control. *Journal of Experimental Social Psychology*, **22**, 453–474.

**Albarracin, D., Gillette, J. C., Ho, M-H., Earl, A. N., Glasman, L. R., & Durantini, M. R.** (2005). A test of major assumptions about behavior change: A comprehensive look at the effects of passive and active HIV-prevention interventions since the beginning of the epidemic. *Psychological Bulletin*, **131**, 856–897.

**Albarracin, D., McNatt, P. S., Klein, C. T. F., Ho, R. M., Mitchell, A. L., & Kumkale, G. T.** (2003). Persuasive communications to change actions: An analysis of behavioral and cognitive impact in HIV prevention. *Health Psychology*, **22**, 166–177.

**Allee, W. C., & Masure, R. M.** (1936). A comparison of maze behavior in paired and isolated shell-parakeets (*Melopsittacus undulatus Shaw*) in a two-alley problem box. *Journal of Comparative Psychology*, **22**, 131–155.

**Allemand, M., Amberg, I., Zimprich, D., & Fincham, F. D.** (2007). The role of trait forgiveness and relationship satisfaction in episodic forgiveness. *Journal of Social and Clinical Psychology*, **26**, 199–217.

**Allen, V. L., & Levine, J. M.** (1969). Consensus and conformity. *Journal of Experimental Social Psychology*, **5**, 389–399.

**Allison, S. T., Jordan, M. R., & Yeatts, C. E.** (1992). A cluster-analytic approach toward identifying the structure and content of human decision making. *Human Relations*, **45**, 49–72.

**Allison, S. T., Mackie, D. M., Muller, M. M., & Worth, L. T.** (1993). Sequential correspondence biases and perceptions of change: The Castro studies revisited.

*Personality and Social Psychology Bulletin*, **19**, 151–157.

Allport, F. (1920). The influence of the group upon association and thought. *Journal of Experimental Psychology*, **3**, 159–182.

Allport, F. (1924). *Social psychology*. Boston: Houghton Mifflin.

Allport, G. W. (1954). *The nature of prejudice*. Cambridge, MA: Perseus Books.

Altman, I., & Taylor, D. A. (1973). *Social penetration: The development of interpersonal relationships*. New York: Holt, Rinehart & Winston.

Amato, P. R. (1986). Emotional arousal and helping behavior in a real-life emergency. *Journal of Applied Social Psychology*, **16**, 633–641.

American Psychological Association (2002). *Ethical principles of psychologists and code of conduct 2002*. Washington, DC: APA (www.apa.org/ethics/code2002.html).

American Psychological Association Commission on Violence and Youth (1993). Violence and youth: Psychology's response. Washington, DC: Author.

Ames, D. R. (2004). Strategies for social inference: A similarity contingency model of projection and stereotyping in attitude prevalence estimates. *Journal of Personality and Social Psychology*, **87**, 573–585.

Amir, Y. (1969). Contact hypothesis in ethnic relations. *Psychological Bulletin*, **71**, 319–342.

Amodio, D. M., & Ratner, K. G. (2011). A memory systems model of implicit social cognition. *Current Directions in Psychological Science*, **20**, 143–148.

Andersen, S. M. (1998). *Service learning: a national strategy for youth development. A position paper issued by the Task Force on Education Policy*. Washington, DC: Institute for Communitarian Policy Studies, George Washington University.

Andersen, S. M., & Chen, S. (2002). The relational self: An interpersonal social-cognitive theory. *Psychological Review*, **109**, 619–645.

Andersen, S. M., Saribay, S. A., & Thorpe, J. S. (2008). Simple kindness can go a long way: Relationships, social identity and engagement. *Social Psychology*, **39**(1), 59–69.

Anderson, C., Keltner, D., & John, O. P. (2003). Emotional convergence between people over time. *Journal of Personality and Social Psychology*, **84**, 1054–1068.

Anderson, C. A. (1982). Inoculation and counter-explanation: Debiasing techniques in the perseverance of social theories. *Social Cognition*, **1**, 126–139.

Anderson, C. A. (1999). Attributional style, depression, and loneliness: A cross-cultural comparison of American and Chinese students. *Personality and Social Psychology Bulletin*, **25**, 482–499.

Anderson, C. A. (2003). Video games and aggressive behavior. In D. Ravitch and J. P. Viteritti (eds), *Kids stuff: Marking violence and vulgarity in the popular culture*. Baltimore, MD: Johns Hopkins University Press.

Anderson, C. A. (2004). An update on the effects of violent video games. *Journal of Adolescence*, **27**, 113–122.

Anderson, C. A., & Bushman, B. J. (1997). External validity of 'trivial' experiments: The case of laboratory aggression. *Review of General Psychology*, **1**, 19–41.

Anderson, C. A., & Sechler, E. (1986). Effects of explanation and counter-explanation on the development and use of social theories. *Journal of Personality and Social Psychology*, **50**, 24–34.

Anderson, C. A., Benjamin, A. J., Jr, & Bartholow, B. D. (1998). Does the gun pull the trigger? Automatic priming effects of weapon pictures and weapon names. *Psychological Science*, **9**, 308–314.

Anderson, C. A., Berkowitz, L., Donnerstein, E., Huesmann, L. R., Johnson, J. D., Linz, D., Malamuth, N. M., & Wartella, E. (2003). The influence of media violence on youth. *Psychological Science in the Public Interest*, **4**(3), 81–110.

Anderson, C. A., Carnagey, N. L., Flanagan, M., Benjamin, Jr, A. J., Eubanks, J., & Valentine, J. C. (2004). Violent video games: Specific effects of violent content on aggressive thoughts and behavior. *Advances in Experimental Social Psychology*, **36**, 199–249.

Anderson, C. A., Deuser, W. E., & DeNeve, K. M. (1995). Hot temperatures, hostile affect, hostile cognition, and arousal: Tests of a general model of affective aggression. *Personality and Social Psychology Bulletin*, **21**, 434–448.

Anderson, C. A., Horowitz, L. M., & French, R. D. (1983). Attributional style of lonely and depressed people. *Journal of Personality and Social Psychology*, **45**, 127–136.

Anderson, C. A., Lepper, M. R., & Ross, L. (1980). Perseverance of social theories: The role of explanation in the persistence of discredited information. *Journal of Personality and Social Psychology*, **39**, 1037–1049.

Anderson, C. A., Lindsay, J. J., & Bushman, B. J. (1999). Research in the psychological laboratory: Truth or triviality? *Current Directions in Psychological Science*, **8**, 3–9.

Anderson, K. J., & Leaper, C. (1998). Meta-analyses of gender effects on conversational interruption: Who, what, when, where, and how. *Sex Roles*, **39**, 225–252.

Andreas, J. B., & Watson, M. W. (2009). Moderating effects of family environment on the association between children's aggressive beliefs and their aggression trajectories from childhood to adolescence. *Development and Psychopathology*, **21**, 189–205.

Ang, R. P., & Goh, D. H. (2010). Cyberbullying among adolescents: the role of affective and cognitive empathy, and gender. *Child Psychiatry and Human Development*, **41**, 387–310.

Annan, K. A. (2002, 29 December) In Africa, AIDS has a woman's face. *The New York Times*. Available at: http://www.nytimes.com/2002/12/29/opinion/in-africa-aids-has-a-woman-s-face.html

Anseel, F., & Duyck, W. (2009). Implicit letter preferences in job choice: An experimental test of the role of cognitive load. *Journal of Psychology*, **143**, 207–224.

Antaki, C., & Widdicombe, S. (1998). *Identities in talk*. London: Sage.

Antonio, A. L., Chang, M. J., Hakuta, K., Kenny, D. A., Levin, S., & Milem, J. F. (2004). Effects of racial diversity on complex thinking in college students. *Psychological Science*, **15**, 507–510.

Archer, D., & Gartner, R. (1976). Violent acts and violent times: A comparative approach to postwar homicide rates. *American Sociological Review*, **41**, 937–963.

Archer, J. (1991). The influence of testosterone on human aggression. *British Journal of Psychology*, **82**, 1–28.

Archer, R. L., & Cook, C. E. (1986). Personalistic self-disclosure and attraction: Basis for relationship or scarce resource. *Social Psychology Quarterly*, **49**, 268–272.

Arendt, H. (1951). *The origins of totalitarianism*. New York: Harcourt Brace & Company.

Arendt, H. (1963/1994). *Eichmann in Jerusalem: A report on the banality of evil*. New York: Viking Press, Penguin.

Argyle, M., & Henderson, M. (1985). *The anatomy of relationships*. London: Heinemann.

Argyle, M., Shimoda, K., & Little, B. (1978). Variance due to persons and situations in England and Japan. *British Journal of Social and Clinical Psychology*, **17**, 335–337.

Arkes, H. R. (1990). Some practical judgment/decision making research. Paper presented at the American Psychological Association convention.

Arkin, R. M., & Burger, J. M. (1980). Effects of unit relation tendencies on interpersonal attraction. *Social Psychology Quarterly*, **43**, 380–391.

Arkin, R. M., Lake, E. A., & Baumgardner, A. H. (1986). Shyness and self-presentation. In W. H. Jones, J. M. Cheek & S. R. Briggs (eds), *Shyness: Perspectives on research and treatment*. New York: Plenum.

Armor, D. A., & Taylor, S. E. (1996). Situated optimism: Specific outcome expectancies and self-regulation. In M. P. Zanna (ed.), *Advances in experimental social psychology*, Vol. 30. San Diego: Academic Press.

Arms, R. L., Russell, G. W., & Sandilands, M. L. (1979). Effects on the hostility of spectators of viewing aggressive sports. *Social Psychology Quarterly*, **42**, 275–279.

Arnett, J. J. (2010). Oh, grow up! Generational grumbling and the new life stage of emerging adulthood – Commentary on Trzesniewski & Donnellan (2010). *Perspectives on Psychological Science*, **5**, 89–92.

Aron, A., & Aron, E. (1989). *The heart of social psychology*, 2nd edn. Lexington, MA: Lexington Books.

Aron, A., Dutton, D. G., Aron, E. N., & Iverson, A. (1989). Experiences of falling in love. *Journal of Social and Personal Relationships*, **6**, 243–257.

Aron, A., Fisher, H., Mashek, D. J., Strong, G., Li, H., & Brown, L. L. (2005). Reward, motivation, and emotion systems associated with early-stage intense romantic love. *Journal of Neurophysiology*, **94**, 327–337.

Aron, A., Melinat, E., Aron, E. N., Vallone, R. D., & Bator, R. J. (1997). The experimental generation of interpersonal closeness: A procedure and some preliminary findings. *Personality and Social Psychology Bulletin*, **23**, 363–377.

Aron, A., Norman, C. C., Aron, E. N., McKenna, C., & Heyman, R. E. (2000). Couples' shared participation in novel and arousing activities and experienced relationship quality. *Journal of Personality and Social Psychology*, **78**, 273–284.

Aron, E. N., & Aron, A. (1996). Love and expansion of the self: The state of the model. *Personal Relationships*, **3**(1), 45–58.

Aronson, E. (1980). *The social animal*. New York: Freeman.

Aronson, E. (1997). Bring the family address to American Psychological Society annual convention, reported in *APS Observer*, July/August, pp. 17, 34, 35.

Aronson, E., & Linder, D. (1965). Gain and loss of esteem as determinants of interpersonal attractiveness. *Journal of Experimental Social Psychology*, **1**, 156–171.

Aronson, E., & Mettee, D. R. (1974). Affective reactions to appraisal from others. *Foundations of interpersonal attraction*. New York: Academic Press.

Aronson, E., & Mills, J. (1959). The effect of severity of initiation on liking for a group. *Journal of Abnormal and Social Psychology*, **59**, 177–181.

Aronson, E., Turner, J. A., & Carlsmith, J. M. (1963). Communicator credibility and communicator discrepancy as determinants of opinion change. *Journal of Abnormal and Social Psychology*, **67**, 31–36.

Arora, R. (2005). China's 'Gen Y' bucks tradition. Gallup Poll, http://www.gallup.com/poll/15934/Chinas-Gen-Bucks-Tradition.aspx (accessed 27 August 2013).

Arterberry, M. E., Cain, K. M., & Chopko, S. A. (2007). Collaborative problem solving in five-year-old children: Evidence of social facilitation and social loafing. *Educational Psychology*, **27**(5), 577–596.

Asch, S. E. (1946). Forming impressions of personality. *Journal of Abnormal and Social Psychology*, **41**, 258–290.

Asch, S. E. (1952). *Social psychology*. Englewood-Cliffs, NJ: Prentice-Hall.

Asch, S. E. (1955, November). Opinions and social pressure. *Scientific American*, pp. 31–35.

Asch, S. E., & Zukier, H. (1984). Thinking about persons. *Journal of Personality and Social Psychology*, **46**, 1230–1240.

Asher, J. (1987, April). Born to be shy? *Psychology Today*, pp. 56–64.

Assiléméhou, Y., & Testé, B. (2013). How you describe a group shows how biased you are: Language abstraction and inferences about a speaker's communicative intentions and attitudes toward a group. *Journal of Language and Social Psychology*, **32**(2), 202–211.

Assouline, S. G., Colangelo, N., Ihrig, D., & Forstadt, L. (2006). Attributional choice for academic success and failure by intellectually gifted student. *Gifted Child Quarterly*, **50**(4), 283–294.

Astin, A. W. (1972). *Four critical years*. San Francisco: Jossey-Bass.

Augoustinos, M., & Every, D. (2007a). The language of 'race' and prejudice: A discourse of denial, reason, and liberal-practical politics. *Journal of Language and Social Psychology*, **26**(2), 123–141.

Augoustinos, M., & Every, D. (2007b). The language of contemporary racism. *Journal of Language and Social Psychology*, **26**(2), 123–141.

Augoustinos, M., Tuffin, K., & Sale, L. (1999). Race talk. *Australian Journal of Psychology*, **51**, 90–97.

Augoustinos, M., Walker, I., & Donaghue, N. (2006). *Social cognition: An integrated introduction*. London: Sage.

Averill, J. R. (1983). Studies on anger and aggression: Implications for theories of emotion. *American Psychologist*, **38**, 1145–1160.

Axelrod, R., & Dion, D. (1988). The further evolution of cooperation. *Science*, **242**, 1385–1390.

Axsom, D., Yates, S., & Chaiken, S. (1987). Audience response as a heuristic cue in persuasion. *Journal of Personality and Social Psychology*, **53**, 30–40.

Azrin, N. H. (1967, May). Pain and aggression. *Psychology Today*, pp. 27–33.

**B**

Baars, B. J., & McGovern, K. (1996). Cognitive views of consciousness: What are the facts? How can we explain them? In M. Velmans (ed.), *The science of consciousness: Psychological, neuropsychological, and clinical reviews*. London: Routledge.

Babad, E., Bernieri, F., & Rosenthal, R. (1991). Students as judges of teachers' verbal and nonverbal behavior. *American Educational Research Journal*, **28**, 211–234.

Back, M. D., Stopfer, J. M., Vazire, S., Gaddis, S., Schmukle, S. C., Egloff, B., & Gosling, S. D. (2010). Facebook profiles reflect actual personality, not self-idealization. *Psychological Science*, **21**, 372–374.

Badea, C., Brauer, M., & Rubin, M. (2012). The effects of winning and losing on perceived group variability. *Journal of Experimental Social Psychology*, **48**(5), 1094–1099.

Bailenson, J. N., & Yee, N. (2005). Digital chameleons: Automatic assimilation of nonverbal gestures in immersive virtual environments. *Psychological Science*, **16**, 814–819.

Balaam, B. J., & Haslam, S. A. (1998). A closer look at the role of social influence in the development of attitudes to eating. *Journal of Community & Applied Social Psychology*, **8**, 195–212.

Baldwin, M. W., Keelan, J. P. R., Fehr, B., Enns, V., & Koh-Rangarajoo, E. (1996). Social-cognitive conceptualization of attachment working models: Availability and accessibility effects. *Journal of Personality and Social Psychology*, **71**, 94–109.

Balkundi, P., Kilduff, M., & Harrison, D. A. (2011). Centrality and charisma: Comparing how leader networks and attributions affect team performance. *Journal of Applied Psychology*, **96**(6), 1209.

Banaji, M. R. (2004). The opposite of a great truth is also true: Homage of Koan #7. In J. T. Jost, M. R. Banaji & D. A. Prentice (eds), *Perspectivism in social psychology: The yin and yang of scientific progress*. Washington, DC: American Psychological Association.

Bandura, A. (1973). *Aggression: A social learning analysis*. Englewood Cliffs, NJ: Prentice-Hall.

Bandura, A. (1979). The social learning perspective: Mechanisms of aggression. In H. Toch (ed.), *Psychology of crime and criminal justice*.

New York: Holt, Rinehart & Winston.

**Bandura, A.** (1997). *Self-efficacy: The exercise of control.* New York: Freeman.

**Bandura, A.** (2000). Social cognitive theory: An agentic perspective. *Annual Review of Psychology,* **52**, 1–26.

**Bandura, A., & Walters, R. H.** (1959). *Adolescent aggression.* New York: Ronald Press.

**Bandura, A., & Walters, R. H.** (1963). *Social learning and personality development.* New York: Holt, Rinehart and Winston.

**Bandura, A., Pastorelli, C., Barbaranelli, C., & Caprara, G. V.** (1999). Self-efficacy pathways to childhood depression. *Journal of Personality and Social Psychology,* **76**, 258–269.

**Bandura, A., Ross, D., & Ross, S. A.** (1961). Transmission of aggression through imitation of aggressive models. *Journal of Abnormal and Social Psychology,* **63**, 575–582.

**Banks, S. M., Salovey, P., Greener, S., Rothman, A. J., Moyer, A., Beauvais, J., & Epel, E.** (1995). The effects of message framing on mammography utilization. *Health Psychology,* **14**, 178–184.

**Barash, D.** (1979). *The whisperings within.* New York: Harper & Row.

**Barber, B. M., & Odean, T.** (2001). Boys will be boys: Gender, overconfidence and common stock investment. *Quarterly Journal of Economics,* **116**, 261–292.

**Barclay, P.** (2010). Altruism as a courtship display: Some effects of third-party generosity on audience perceptions. *British Journal of Psychology,* **101**, 123–135.

**Barelds, D. P. H., & Barelds-Dijkstra, P.** (2007). Love at first sight or friends first? Ties among partner personality trait similarity, relationship onset, relationship quality, and love. *Journal of Social and Personal Relationships,* **24**(4), 479–496.

**Bargh, J. A., & Chartrand, T. L.** (1999). The unbearable automaticity of being. *American Psychologist,* **54**, 462–479.

**Bargh, J. A., & Ferguson, M. J.** (2000). Beyond behaviorism: On the automaticity of higher mental processes. *Psychological Bulletin,* **126**, 925–945.

**Bargh, J. A., Chen, M., & Burrows, L.** (1996a). Automaticity and social behavior: Direct effects of trait construct and stereotype activation, *Journal of Personality and Social Psychology,* **43**, 437–449.

**Bargh, J. A., Chen, M., & Burrows, L.** (1996b). Automaticity of social behavior: Direct effects of trait construct and stereotype activation on action. *Journal of Personality and Social Psychology,* **71**(2), 230–244.

**Bargh, J. A., McKenna, K. Y. A., & Fitzsimons, G. M.** (2002). Can you see the real me? Activation and expression of the 'true self ' on the Internet. *Journal of Social Issues,* **58**, 33–48.

**Barker, M.** (1981). *The new racism: Conservatives and the ideology of the tribe.* London: Junction Books.

**Barker, R., Dembo, T. & Lewin, K.** (1941). Frustration and aggression: An experiment with young children, *University of Iowa Studies in Child Welfare,* **18**, 1–314.

**Barnes, R. D., Ickes, W., & Kidd, R. F.** (1979). Effects of the perceived intentionality and stability of another's dependency on helping behavior. *Personality and Social Psychology Bulletin,* **5**, 367–372.

**Baron, J., & Miller, J. G.** (2000). Limiting the scope of moral obligations to help: A cross-cultural investigation. *Journal of Cross-Cultural Psychology,* **31**, 703–725.

**Baron, R. A.** (1977). *Human aggression.* New York: Plenum Press.

**Baron, R. A., & Byrne, D.** (2000). *Social psychology.* London: Prentice-Hall.

**Baron, R. S.** (2000). Arousal, capacity, and intense indoctrination. *Personality and Social Psychology Review,* **4**, 238–254.

**Baron, R. S., Kerr, N. L., & Miller, N.** (1992). *Group process, group decision, group action.* Pacific Grove, CA: Brooks/Cole.

**Barongan, C., & Hall, G. C. N.** (1995). The influence of misogynous rap music on sexual aggression against women. *Psychology of Women Quarterly,* **19**, 195–207.

**Barreto, M., & Ellemers, N.** (2000). The impact of respect versus neglect of self-identities on identification and group loyalty. *Personality & Social Psychology Bulletin,* **28**, 629–639.

**Barrett, M.** (ed.) (2007). *Children's knowledge, beliefs and feelings about nations and national groups.* New York: Psychology Press.

**Bartels, A., & Zeki, S.** (2000, 27 November). The neural basis of romantic love. *Neuroreport,* **11**, 3829–3834.

**Bartels, A., & Zeki, S.** (2004). The neural correlates of maternal and romantic love. *Neuroimage,* **21**, 1155–1166.

**Bartholomew, K., & Horowitz, L.** (1991). Attachment styles among young adults: A test of a four-category model. *Journal of Personality and Social Psychology,* **61**, 226–244.

**Bartholow, B. C., & Heinz, A.** (2006). Alcohol and aggression without consumption: Alcohol cues, aggressive thoughts, and hostile perception bias. *Psychological Science,* **17**, 30–37.

**Bartholow, B. C., Anderson, C. A., Carnagey, N. L., & Benjamin, Jr, A. J.** (2004). Interactive effects of life experience and situational cues on aggression: The weapons priming effect in hunters and nonhunters. *Journal of Experimental Social Psychology,* **41**, 48–60.

**Bartholow, B. D., Bushman, B. J., & Sestir, M. A.** (2006). Chronic violent video game exposure and desensitization: Behavioral and event-related brain potential data. *Journal of Experimental Social Psychology,* **42**(4), 532–539.

**Basch, C. E.** (1987). Focus group interview: An underutilized research technique for improving theory and practice in health education. *Health Education Quarterly,* **14**, 411–448.

**Bassili, J. N.** (2003). The minority slowness effect: Subtle inhibitions in the expression of views not shared by others. *Journal of Personality and Social Psychology,* **84**, 261–276.

**Bastian, B., & Haslam, N.** (2006). Psychological essentialism and stereotype endorsement. *Journal of Experimental Social Psychology,* **42**, 228–235.

**Bastounis, M., & Minibas-Poussard, J.** (2012). Causal attributions of work-place gender equality, just world belief, and the self/other distinction. *Social Behaviour and Personality,* **40**, 433–452.

**Batson, C. D.** (1983). Sociobiology and the role of religion in promoting prosocial behavior: An alternative view. *Journal of Personality and Social Psychology,* **45**, 1380–1385.

**Batson, C. D.** (1999a). Behind the scenes. In D. G. Myers, *Social psychology,* 6th edn. New York: McGraw-Hill.

**Batson, C. D.** (1999b). Addressing the altruism question experimentally. Paper presented at a Templeton Foundation/Fetzer Institute Symposium on Empathy, Altruism, and Agape, Cambridge, MA.

**Batson, C. D.** (2001). Addressing the altruism question experimentally. In S. G. Post, L. B. Underwood, J. P. Schloss & W. B. Hurlbut (eds), *Altruism and altruistic love: Science, philosophy, and religion in dialogue.* New York: Oxford University Press.

**Batson, C. D., & Ahmad, N.** (2001). Empathy-induced altruism in a prisoner's dilemma II: What if the target of empathy has defected? *European Journal of Social Psychology,* **31**(1), 25–36.

**Batson, C. D., & Powell, A. A.** (2003). Altruism and prosocial behavior. In T. Millon & M. J. Lerner (eds), *Handbook of psychology: Personality and social psychology,* vol. 5. Hoboken, NJ: Wiley.

**Batson, C. D., & Thompson, E. R.** (2001). Why don't moral people act morally? Motivational considerations. *Current Directions in Psychological Science,* **10**, 54–57.

**Batson, C. D., & Weeks, J. L.** (1996). Mood effects of unsuccessful helping: Another test of the empathy-altruism hypothesis. *Person-*

*ality and Social Psychology Bulletin*, **22**, 148–157.

Batson, C. D., Ahmad, N., & Stocks, E. L. (2004). Benefits and liabilities of empathy-induced altruism. In A. G. Miller (ed.), *The social psychology of good and evil*. New York: Guilford Publications.

Batson, C. D., Ahmad, N., Yin, J., Bedell, S. J., Johnson, J. W., Templin, C. M., & Whiteside, A. (1999a). Two threats to the common good: Self-interested egoism and empathy-induced altruism. *Personality and Social Psychology Bulletin*, **25**, 3–16.

Batson, C. D., Batson, J. G., Slingsby, J. K., Harrell, K. L., Peekna, H. M., & Todd, M. R. (1991). Empathic joy and the empathy-altruism hypothesis. *Journal of Personality and Social Psychology*, **61**(3), 413–426.

Batson, C. D., Coke, J. S., Jasnoski, M. L., & Hanson, M. (1978). Buying kindness: Effect of an extrinsic incentive for helping on perceived altruism. *Personality and Social Psychology Bulletin*, **4**, 86–91.

Batson, C. D., Duncan, B. D., Ackerman, P., Buckley, T., & Birch, K. (1981). Is empathic emotion a source of altruistic motivation? *Journal of Personality and Social Psychology*, **40**, 290–302.

Batson, C. D., Fultz, J., & Schoenrade, P. A. (1987). Distress and empathy: Two qualitatively distinct vicarious emotions with different motivational consequences. *Journal of Personality*, **55**, 19–40.

Batson, C. D., Harris, A. C., McCaul, K. D., Davis, M., & Schmidt, T. (1979). Compassion or compliance: Alternative dispositional attributions for one's helping behavior. *Social Psychology Quarterly*, **42**, 405–409.

Batson, C. D., Kobrynowicz, D., Dinnerstein, J. L., Kampf, H. C., & Wilson, A. D. (1997a). In a very different voice: Unmasking moral hypocrisy. *Journal of Personality and Social Psychology*, **72**, 1335–1348.

Batson, C. D., Sager, K., Garst, E., Kang, M., Rubchinsky, K., & Dawson, K. (1997b). Is empathy-induced helping due to self-other merging? *Journal of Personality and Social Psychology*, **73**, 495–509.

Batson, C. D., Thompson, E. R., & Chen, H. (2002). Moral hypocrisy: Addressing some alternatives. *Journal of Personality and Social Psychology*, **83**, 330–339.

Batson, C. D., Thompson, E. R., Seuferling, G., Whitney, H., & Strongman, J. A. (1999b). Moral hypocrisy: Appearing moral to oneself without being so. *Journal of Personality and Social Psychology*, **77**, 525–537.

Baumeister, R. F. (1996). Should schools try to boost self-esteem? Beware the dark side. *American Educator*, **20**, 14–19, 43.

Baumeister, R. F. (ed.) (1999). *The self in social psychology*. Philadelphia, PA: Psychology Press (Taylor & Francis).

Baumeister, R. F. (2005a). Rejected and alone. *The Psychologist*, **18**, 732–735.

Baumeister, R. F. (2005b). *The cultural animal: Human nature, meaning, and social life*. New York: Oxford University Press.

Baumeister, R. F., & Bratslavsky, E. (1999). Passion, intimacy, and time: Passionate love as a function of change in intimacy. *Personality and Social Psychology Review*, **3**, 49–67.

Baumeister, R. F., & Exline, J. J. (2000). Self-control, morality, and human strength. *Journal of Social and Clinical Psychology*, **19**, 29–42.

Baumeister, R. F., & Ilko, S. A. (1995). Shallow gratitude: Public and private acknowledgement of external help in accounts of success. *Basic and Applied Social Psychology*, **16**, 191–209.

Baumeister, R. F., & Leary, M. R. (1995). The need to belong: Desire for interpersonal attachment as a fundamental human motivation. *Psychological Bulletin*, **117**, 497–529.

Baumeister, R. F., & Scher, S. J. (1988). Self-defeating behavior patterns among normal individuals: Review and analysis of common self-destructive tendencies. *Psychological Bulletin*, **104**(1), 3–22.

Baumeister, R. F., Bratslavsky, E., Finkenauer, C., & Vohs, D. K. (2001). Bad is stronger than good. *Review of General Psychology*, **5**, 323–370.

Baumeister, R. F., Campbell, J. D., Krueger, J. I., & Vohs, K. D. (2003). Does high self-esteem cause better performance, interpersonal success, happiness, or healthier lifestyles? *Psychological Science in the Public Interest*, **4**(1), 1–44.

Baumeister, R. F., Muraven, M., & Tice, D. M. (2000). Ego depletion: A resource model of volition, self-regulation, and controlled processing. *Social Cognition*, **18**, 130–150.

Baumgardner, A. H., & Brownlee, E. A. (1987). Strategic failure in social interaction: Evidence for expectancy disconfirmation process. *Journal of Personality and Social Psychology*, **52**, 525–535.

Baumgardner, A. H., Kaufman, C. M., & Levy, P. E. (1989). Regulating affect interpersonally: When low esteem leads to greater enhancement. *Journal of Personality and Social Psychology*, **56**, 907–921.

Baxter, T. L., & Goldberg, L. R. (1987). Perceived behavioral consistency underlying trait attributions to oneself and another: An extension of the actor–observer effect. *Personality and Social Psychology Bulletin*, **13**, 437–447.

Bayer, E. (1929). Beitrage zur zeikomponenten theorie des hungers. *Zeitschrift fur Psychologie*, **112**, 1–54.

Baysu, G., Phalet, K., & Brown, R. (2011). Dual identity as a two-edged sword identity threat and minority school performance. *Social Psychology Quarterly*, **74**(2), 121–143.

Bazerman, M. H. (1986, June). Why negotiations go wrong. *Psychology Today*, pp. 54–58.

Bazerman, M. H. (1990). *Judgment in managerial decision making*, 2nd edn. New York: Wiley.

Beaman, A. L., & Klentz, B. (1983). The supposed physical attractiveness bias against supporters of the women's movement: A meta-analysis. *Personality and Social Psychology Bulletin*, **9**, 544–550.

Beaman, A. L., Barnes, P. J., Klentz, B., & McQuirk, B. (1978). Increasing helping rates through information dissemination: Teaching pays. *Personality and Social Psychology Bulletin*, **4**, 406–411.

Bearman, P. S., & Brückner, H. (2001). Promising the future: Virginity pledges and first intercourse. *American Journal of Sociology*, **106**, 859–912.

Becker, S. W., & Eagly, A. H. (2004). The heroism of women and men. *American Psychologist*, **59**, 163–178.

Beffa-Negrini, P. A., Cohen, N. L., & Miller, B. (2002). Strategies to motivate students in online learning environments. *Journal of Nutrition Education and Behavior*, **34**(6), 334–340.

Bekkers, R. (2007). Measuring altruistic behaviour in surveys: The all-or-nothing dictator. *Survey Research Methods*, **1**(3), 139–144.

Bekoff, M., & Bexell, S. M. (2010). Ignoring nature: Why we do it, the dire consequences, and the need for a paradigm shift to save animals, habitats and ourselves. *Human Ecology Forum*, **17**, 70–74.

Bell, P. A. (1980). Effects of heat, noise, and provocation on retaliatory evaluative behavior. *Journal of Social Psychology*, **110**, 97–100.

Bell, P. A. (2005). Reanalysis and perspective in the heataggression debate. *Journal of Personality and Social Psychology*, **89**, 71–73.

Belson, W. A. (1978). *Television violence and the adolescent boy*. Westmead: Saxon House, Teakfield Ltd.

Bem, D. J. (1972). Self-perception theory. In L. Berkowitz (ed.), *Advances in experimental social psychology*. Vol. 6. New York: Academic Press.

Bem, D. J. (2011). Feeling the future: Experimental evidence for anomalous retroactive influences on cognition and affect. *Journal of Personality and*

*Social Psychology*, **100**, 407–425.

**Bem, D. J., & McConnell, H. K.** (1970). Testing the self-perception explanation of dissonance phenomena: On the salience of premanipulation attitudes. *Journal of Personality and Social Psychology*, **14**, 23–31.

**Benjamin, S., Nind, M., Hall, K., Collins, J., & Sheehy, K.** (2003). Moments of inclusion and exclusion: Pupils negotiating classroom contexts. *British Journal of Sociology of Education*, **24**(5), 547–558.

**Bennett, M., & Sani, F.** (eds) (2004). *The development of the social self*. Hove: Psychology Press.

**Bennett, M., & Sani, F.** (2008). Children's subjective identification with social groups. In S. R. Levy & M. Killen (eds.), *Intergroup attitudes and relations in childhood through adulthood*. Oxford: Oxford University Press.

**Bennis, W.** (1984). Transformative power and leadership. In T. J. Sergiovani & J. E. Corbally (eds), *Leadership and organizational culture*. Urbana: University of Illinois Press.

**Bensley, L., & van Eenwyk, J.** (2001). Video games and real-life aggression: Review of the literature. *Journal of Adolescent Health*, **29**, 244–257.

**Benvenisti, M.** (1988, 16 October). Growing up in Jerusalem. *New York Times Magazine*, pp. 34–37.

**Berg, J. H.** (1984). Development of friendship between roommates. *Journal of Personality and Social Psychology*, **46**, 346–356.

**Berg, J. H.** (1987). Responsiveness and self-disclosure. In V. J. Derlega & J. H. Berg (eds), *Self-disclosure: Theory, research, and therapy*. New York: Plenum.

**Berg, J. H., & McQuinn, R. D.** (1986). Attraction and exchange in continuing and noncontinuing dating relationships. *Journal of Personality and Social Psychology*, **50**, 942–952.

**Berg, J. H., & Peplau, L. A.** (1982). Loneliness: The relationship of self-disclosure and androgyny. *Personality and Social Psychology Bulletin*, **8**, 624–630.

**Berger, J., & Heath, C.** (2008). Who drives divergence? Identity signaling, outgroup dissimilarity, and the abandonment of cultural tastes. *Journal of Personality and Social Psychology*, **95**, 593–607.

**Berglas, S., & Jones, E. E.** (1978). Drug choice as a self-handicapping strategy in response to noncontingent success. *Journal of Personality and Social Psychology*, **36**, 405–417.

**Berkowitz, L.** (1968, September). Impulse, aggression and the gun. *Psychology Today*, pp. 18–22.

**Berkowitz, L.** (1972). Social norms, feelings, and other factors affecting helping and altruism. In L. Berkowitz (ed.), *Advances in experimental social psychology* (Vol. 6). New York: Academic Press.

**Berkowitz, L.** (1978). Whatever happened to the frustration–aggression hypothesis? *American Behavioral Scientists*, **21**, 691–708.

**Berkowitz, L.** (1981, June). How guns control us. *Psychology Today*, pp. 11–12.

**Berkowitz, L.** (1983). Aversively stimulated aggression: Some parallels and differences in research with animals and humans. *American Psychologist*, **38**, 1135–1144.

**Berkowitz, L.** (1984). Some effects of thoughts on anti- and prosocial influences of media events: A cognitive-neoassociation analysis, *Psychological Bulletin*, **95**, 410–427.

**Berkowitz, L.** (1987). Mood, self-awareness, and willingness to help. *Journal of Personality and Social Psychology*, **52**, 721–729.

**Berkowitz, L.** (1989). Frustration–aggression hypothesis: Examination and reformulation. *Psychological Bulletin*, **106**, 59–73.

**Berkowitz, L.** (1995). A career on aggression. In G. G. Brannigan & M. R. Merrens (eds), *The social psychologists: Research adventures*. New York: McGraw-Hill.

**Berkowitz, L.** (1998). Affective aggression: The role of stress, pain, and negative affect. In R. G. Geen & E. Donnerstein (eds), *Human aggression: Theories, research, and implications for social policy*. San Diego: Academic Press.

**Berkowitz, L., & Geen, R. G.** (1966). Film violence and the cue properties of available targets. *Journal of Personality and Social Psychology*, **3**, 525–530.

**Berkowitz, L., & LePage, A.** (1967). Weapons as aggression-eliciting stimuli. *Journal of Personality and Social Psychology*, **7**, 202–207.

**Bernhardt, P. C., Dabbs, J. M., Jr, Fielden, J. A., & Lutter, C. D.** (1998). Testosterone changes during vicarious experiences of winning and losing among fans at sporting events. *Physiology and Behavior*, **65**, 59–62.

**Berntson, G. G., & Cacioppo. J. T.** (2000). Psychobiology and social psychology: Past present, and future. *Personality and Social Psychology Review*, **4**, 3–15.

**Berscheid, E.** (1981). An overview of the psychological effects of physical attractiveness and some comments upon the psychological effects of knowledge of the effects of physical attractiveness. In W. Lucker, K. Ribbens & J. A. McNamera (eds), *Logical aspects of facial form (craniofacial growth series)*. Ann Arbor: University of Michigan Press.

**Berscheid, E.** (1999). The greening of relationship science. *American Psychologist*, **54**, 260–266.

**Berscheid, E., Boye, D., & Walster (Hatfield), E.** (1968). Retaliation as a means of restoring equity. *Journal of Personality and Social Psychology*, **10**, 370–376.

**Berscheid, E., Dion, K., Walster (Hatfield), E., & Walster, G. W.** (1971). Physical attractiveness and dating choice: A test of the matching hypothesis. *Journal of Experimental Social Psychology*, **7**, 173–189.

**Berscheid, E., Graziano, W., Monson, T., & Dermer, M.** (1976). Outcome dependency: Attention, attribution, and attraction. *Journal of Personality and Social Psychology*, **34**, 978–989.

**Berscheid, E., Snyder, M., & Omoto, A. M.** (1989). Issues in studying close relationships: Conceptualizing and measuring closeness. In C. Hendrick (ed.), *Review of personality and social psychology*, Vol. 10. Newbury Park, CA: Sage.

**Berscheid, E., Walster, G. W., & Hatfield (was Walster), E.** (1969). Effects of accuracy and positivity of evaluation on liking for the evaluator. Unpublished manuscript. Summarized by E. Berscheid and E. Walster (Hatfield) (1978), *Interpersonal attraction*. Reading, MA: Addison-Wesley.

**Bertram, G., & Bodenhausen, G. V.** (2005). Accessibility effects on implicit social cognition: The role of knowledge activation and retrieval experiences. *Journal of Personality and Social Psychology*, **89**, 672–685.

**Besser, A., & Priel, B.** (2005). The apple does not fall far from the tree: Attachment styles and personality vulnerabilities to depression in three generations of women. *Personality and Social Psychology Bulletin*, **31**, 1052–1073.

**Bhatia, A.** (2008). Critical discourse analysis of political press conferences. *Discourse & Society*, **17**(2), 173–203.

**Bianchi, S. M., Milkie, M. A., Sayer, L. C., & Robinson, J. P.** (2000). Is anyone doing the housework? Trends in the gender division of household labor. *Social Forces*, **79**, 191–228.

**Bickman, L.** (1975). Bystander intervention in a crime: The effect of a mass-media campaign. *Journal of Applied Social Psychology*, **5**, 296–302.

**Bickman, L.** (1979). Interpersonal influence and the reporting of a crime. *Personality and Social Psychology Bulletin*, **5**, 32–35.

**Bickman, L., & Green, S. K.** (1977). Situational cues and crime reporting: Do signs make a difference? *Journal of Applied Social Psychology*, **7**, 1–18.

**Bierbrauer, G.** (1979). Why did he do it? Attribution of obedience and the phenomenon of dispositional bias. *European Journal of Social Psychology*, **9**, 67–84.

**Bierhoff, H. W., Klein, R., & Kramp, P.** (1991). Evidence for the altruistic personality from data on accident research. *Journal of Personality*, **59**, 263–280.

Biernat, M., & Wortman, C. B. (1991). Sharing of home responsibilities between professionally employed women and their husbands. *Journal of Personality and Social Psychology*, **60**, 844–860.

Biernat, M., Vescio, T. K., & Green, M. L. (1996). Selective self-stereotyping. *Journal of Personality and Social Psychology*, **71**, 1194–1209.

Billig, M. (1985). Prejudice, categorization and particularization: From a perceptual to a rhetorical approach. *European Journal of Social Psychology*, **15**, 79–103.

Billig, M. (1987). *Arguing and thinking: A rhetorical approach to social psychology*. Cambridge: Cambridge University Press.

Billig, M. (1989). The argumentative nature of holding strong views: A case study. *European Journal of Social Psychology*, **19**, 203–223.

Billig, M. (1996). *Arguing and thinking*. Cambridge: Cambridge University Press.

Billig, M. (2001). Humour and hatred: The racist jokes of the Ku Klux Klan. *Discourse & Society*, **12**(3), 267–289.

Biner, P. M. (1991). Effects of lighting-induced arousal on the magnitude of goal valence. *Personality and Social Psychology Bulletin*, **17**, 219–226.

Bingenheimer, J. B., Brennan, R. T., & Earls, F. J. (2005). Firearm violence exposure and serious violent behavior. *Science*, **308**, 1323–1326.

Binham, R. (1980, March–April). Trivers in Jamaica. *Science 80*, pp. 57–67.

Birger, M., Swartz, M., Cohen, D., Alesh, Y. A., Grishpan, C., & Kotelr, M. (2003). Aggression: the testosterone-serotonin link. *Israel Medical Association Journal*, **5**(9), 653–658.

Birnbaum, G. E., Weisberg, Y. W., & Jeffry A. Simpson, J. A. (2010). Desire under attack: Attachment orientations and the effects of relationship threat on sexual motivations. *Journal of Social and Personal Relationships*, **28**(4), 448–468.

Bivans, A. M. (1991). *Miss America: In pursuit of the crown*. New York: Mastermedia.

Bizman, A., & Yinon, Y. (2002). Social self-discrepancies and group-based emotional distress. In D. M. Mackie & E. R. Smith (eds), *From prejudice to intergroup emotions: Differentiated reactions to social groups*. New York & Hove: Psychology Press.

Bjorkqvist, K. (1994). Sex differences in physical, verbal and indirect aggression: A review of recent research. *Sex Roles*, **30**, 177–188.

Black, S., & Hausman, A. (2008). Adolescents' views of guns in a high-violence community. *Journal of Adolescent Research*, **23**(5), 592–610.

Blair, C. A., Thompson, L. F., & Wuensch, K. L. (2005). Electronic helping behavior: The virtual presence of others makes a difference. *Basic and Applied Social Psychology*, **27**, 171–178.

Blake, R. R., & Mouton, J. S. (1962). The intergroup dynamics of win–lose conflict and problem-solving collaboration in union-management relations. In M. Sherif (ed.), *Intergroup relations and leadership*. New York: Wiley.

Blake, R. R., & Mouton, J. S. (1979). Intergroup problem solving in organizations: From theory to practice. In W. G. Austin and S. Worchel (eds), *The social psychology of intergroup relations*. Monterey, CA: Brooks/Cole.

Blanchard, F. A., & Cook, S. W. (1976). Effects of helping a less competent member of a cooperating interracial group on the development of interpersonal attraction. *Journal of Personality and Social Psychology*, **34**, 1245–1255.

Blanchard-Fields, F., Hertzog, C., & Horhotta, M. (2012). Violate my beliefs? Then you're to blame! Belief content as an explanation for causal attribution biases. *Psychology and Aging*, **27**, 324–337.

Blank, H., Fischer, V., & Erdfelder, E. (2003). Hindsight bias in political elections. *Memory*, **11**, 491–504.

Blanton, H., Pelham, B. W., DeHart, T., & Carvallo, M.

(2001). Overconfidence as dissonance reduction. *Journal of Experimental Social Psychology*, **37**, 373–385.

Blass, T. (1990). Psychological approaches to the Holocaust: Review and evaluation. Paper presented to the American Psychological Association convention.

Blass, T. (1991). Understanding behavior in the Milgram obedience experiment: The role of personality, situations, and their interactions. *Journal of Personality and Social Psychology*, **60**, 398–413.

Blass, T. (1996). Stanley Milgram: A life of inventiveness and controversy. In G. A. Kimble, C. A. Boneau & M. Wertheimer (eds), *Portraits of pioneers in psychology*, Vol. II. Washington, DC: American Psychological Association.

Blass, T. (2000). The Milgram paradigm after 35 years: Some things we now know about obedience to authority. In T. Blass (ed.), *Obedience to authority: Current perspectives on the Milgram paradigm*. Mahwah, NJ: Erlbaum.

Blass, T. (2004). *The man who shocked the world: The life and legacy of Stanley Milgram*. New York: Basic Books.

Bleske-Rechek, A. L., & Buss, D. M. (2001). Opposite-sex friendship: Sex differences and similarities in initiation, selection and dissolution. *Personality and Social Psychology Bulletin*, **27**(10), 1310–1323.

Block J., & Funder, D. C. (1986). Social roles and social perception: Individual differences in attribution and error. *Journal of Personality and Social Psychology*, **51**, 1200–1207.

Bodenhausen, G. V. (1993). Emotions, arousal, and stereotypic judgments: A heuristic model of affect and stereotyping. In D. M. Mackie & D. L. Hamilton (eds), *Affect, cognition, and stereotyping: Interactive processes in group perception*. San Diego, CA: Academic Press.

Bodenhausen, G. V., Sheppard, L. A., & Kramer, G. F. (1994). Negative affect and social judgment: The dif-

ferential impact of anger and sadness. *European Journal of Social Psychology*, **24**, 45–62.

Boen, F., Vanbeselaere, N., & Feys, J. (2002). Behavioural consequences of fluctuating group success: An internet study of soccer-team fans. *The Journal of Social Psychology*, **142**(6), 769–781.

Bogardus, E. S. (1925). Measuring social distances. *Journal of Applied Sociology*, **9**, 299–308.

Boggiano, A. K., & Ruble, D. N. (1985). Children's responses to evaluative feedback. In R. Schwarzer (ed.), *Self-related cognitions in anxiety and motivation*. Hillsdale, NJ: Erlbaum.

Boggiano, A. K., Barrett, M., Weiher, A. W., McClelland, G. H., & Lusk, C. M. (1987). Use of the maximaloperant principle to motivate children's intrinsic interest. *Journal of Personality and Social Psychology*, **53**, 866–879.

Boggiano, A. K., Harackiewicz, J. M., Bessette, J. M., & Main, D. S. (1985). Increasing children's interest through performance-contingent reward. *Social Cognition*, **3**, 400–411.

Boggs, L., Carr, S. C., Fletcher, R. B., & Clarke, D. E. (2005). Pseudoparticipation in communication networks: The social psychology of broken promises. *The Journal of Social Psychology*, **145**(5), 621–624.

Bohannon, J. (2012). Tweeting the London riots. *Science*, **336**(18), 831.

Bohner, G., Bless, H., Schwarz, N., & Strack, F. (1988). What triggers causal attributions? The impact of valence and subjective probability. *European Journal of Social Psychology*, **18**, 335–345.

Bond, C. F., Jr, & Titus, L. J. (1983). Social facilitation: A meta-analysis of 241 studies. *Psychological Bulletin*, **94**, 265–292.

Bond, M. H., Leung, K., Au, A., et al. (2004). Culture-level dimensions of social axioms and their correlates across 41 cultures. *Journal of Cross-Cultural Psychology*, **35**(5), 548–570.

Bond, R., & Smith, P. B. (1996). Culture and conformity: A meta-analysis of studies using Asch's (1952b, 1956) line judgment task. *Psychological Bulletin*, **119**, 111–137.

Boniecki, K. A., & Brown, L. M. (1998). The influence of prejudice on stereotype formation: The justification hypothesis revisited. Paper presented at the American Psychological Association meeting, Washington, DC.

Bonilla-Silva, E., & Forman, T. (2000). I'm not a racist, but . . . : Mapping white college students' racial ideology in the USA. *Discourse & Society*, **11**(1), 50–85.

Boninger, D. S., Gleicher, F., & Strathman, A. (1994). Counterfactual thinking: From what might have been to what may be. *Journal of Personality and Social Psychology*, **67**, 297–307.

Borge, A. I. H., Rutter, M., Côté, S., & Tremblay, R. E. (2004). Early childcare and physical aggression: Differentiating social selection and social causation. *Journal of Child Psychology and Psychiatry*, **45**(2), 367–376.

Bornstein, G., & Rapoport, A. (1988). Intergroup competition for the provision of step-level public goods: Effects of preplay communication. *European Journal of Social Psychology*, **18**, 125–142.

Bornstein, G., Rapoport, A., Kerpel, L., & Katz, T. (1989). Within- and between-group communication in intergroup competition for public goods. *Journal of Experimental Social Psychology*, **25**, 422–436.

Bornstein, R. F. (1989). Exposure and affect: Overview and meta-analysis of research, 1968–1987. *Psychological Bulletin*, **106**, 265–289.

Bornstein, R. F. (1999). Source amnesia, misattribution, and the power of unconscious perceptions and memories. *Psychoanalytic Psychology*, **16**, 155–178.

Bornstein, R. F., & D'Agostino, P. R. (1992). Stimulus recognition and the mere exposure effect. *Journal of Personality and Social Psychology*, **63**, 545–552.

Bornstein, R. F., Galley, D. J., Leone, D. R., & Kale, A. R. (1991). The temporal stability of ratings of parents: Testretest reliability and influence of parental contact. *Journal of Social Behavior and Personality*, **6**, 641–649.

Borofsky, G. L., Stollak, G. E., & Messé, L. A. (1971). Sex differences in bystander reactions to physical assault. *Journal of Experimental Social Psychology*, **7**, 313–318.

Bossard, J. H. S. (1932). Residential propinquity as a factor in marriage selection. *American Journal of Sociology*, **38**, 219–224.

Botwin, M. D., Buss, D. M., & Shackelford, T. K. (1997). Personality and mate preferences: Five factors in mate selection and marital satisfaction. *Journal of Personality*, **65**, 107–136.

Bouas, K. S., & Komorita, S. S. (1996). Group discussion and cooperation in social dilemmas. *Personality and Social Psychology Bulletin*, **22**, 1144–1150.

Boulton, M. J., Smith, P. K., & Cowie, H. (2010). Short-term longitudinal relationships between children's peer victimization/bullying experiences and self-perceptions: Evidence for reciprocity. *School Psychology International*, **31**, 296–311.

Bourdieu, P. (1977). *Outline of a theory of practice*. Cambridge: Cambridge University Press.

Bower, B. (1996). Fighting stereotype stigma: Studies chart accuracy, usefulness of inferences about social groups. *Science News*, **149**(26), 408.

Bower, G. H. (1987). Commentary on mood and memory. *Behavioral Research and Therapy*, **25**, 443–455.

Bowlby, J. (1980). *Loss, sadness and depression. Vol. III of Attachment and loss*. London: Basic Books.

Bowlby, J. (1988). *A secure base: Parent–child attachment and healthy human development*. New York: Basic Books.

Bowlby, J. (1999). *Attachment. Vol. 1 Attachment and Loss*, 2nd edn. New York: Basic Books.

Bowles, S. (2012). Warriors, levelers, and the role of conflict in human social evolution. *Science*, **336**, 876–879.

Boyatzis, C. J., Matillo, G. M., & Nesbitt, K. M. (1995). Effects of the 'Mighty Morphin Power Rangers' on children's aggression with peers. *Child Study Journal*, **25**, 45–55.

Bozon, M., & Héran, F. (1989). Finding a spouse: A survey of how French couples meet, *Population, an English Selection*, **44**(1), 91–121.

Bradley, W., & Mannell, R. C. (1984). Sensitivity of intrinsic motivation to reward procedure instructions. *Personality and Social Psychology Bulletin*, **10**, 426–431.

Brand, R., Melzer, M., & Hagemann, N. (2011). Towards an implicit association test (IAT) for measuring doping attitudes in sports. Data-based recommendations developed from two recently published tests. *Psychology of Sport and Exercise*, **12**, 250–256.

Brauer, M., Judd, C. M., & Gliner, M. D. (1995). The effects of repeated expressions on attitude polarization during group discussions. *Journal of Personality and Social Psychology*, **68**, 1014–1029.

Brauer, M., Judd, C. M., & Jacquelin, V. (2001). The communication of social stereotypes: The effects of group discussion and information distribution on stereotypic appraisals. *Journal of Personality and Social Psychology*, **81**, 463–475.

Braverman, J. (2005). The effect of mood on detection of covariation. *Personality and Social Psychology Bulletin*, **31**, 1487–1497.

Breakwell, G. (1979). Illegitimate group membership and intergroup differentiation. *British Journal of Social and Clinical Psychology*, **18**, 141–149.

Breakwell, G. (1986). *Coping with threatened identities*. London: Methuen.

Brehm, J. W. (1956). Postdecision changes in desirability of alternatives. *Journal of Abnormal Social Psychology*, **52**, 384–389.

Brehm, S., & Brehm, J. W. (1981). *Psychological reactance: A theory of freedom and control*. New York: Academic Press.

Brewer, M. B. (1991). The social self: On being the same and different at the same time. *Personality and Social Psychology Bulletin*, **17**, 475–482.

Brewer, M. B., & Miller, N. (1988). Contact and cooperation: When do they work? In P. A. Katz & D. Taylor (eds), *Towards the elimination of racism: Profiles in controversy*. New York: Plenum.

Brewer, M. B., & Pierce, K. P. (2005). Social identity complexity and outgroup tolerance. *Personality and Social Psychology Bulletin*, **31**, 428–437.

Briggs, P., Burford, B., De Angeli, A., & Lynch, P. (2002). Trust in online advice. *Social Science Computer Review*, **20**(3), 321–332.

Brinol, P., & Petty, R. E. (2003). Overt head movements and persuasion: A self-validation analysis. *Journal of Personality and Social Psychology*, **84**(6), 1123–1139.

Briscoe, C., & Aboud, F. (2012). Behaviour change communication targeting four health behaviours in developing countries: A review of change techniques. *Social Science & Medicine*, **75**(4), 612–621.

British Psychological Society (2000). *Code of conduct, ethical principles and guidelines*. Leicester, UK: British Psychological Society (www.bps.org.uk/documents/Code.pdf).

Brock, T. C. (1965). Communicator–recipient similarity and decision change. *Journal of Personality and Social Psychology*, **1**, 650–654.

Brockner, J., & Hulton, A. J. B. (1978). How to reverse the vicious cycle of low self-esteem: The importance of attentional focus. *Journal of Experimental Social Psychology*, **14**, 564–578.

Brooks, D. (2004, 5 June). Circling the wagons. *New York Times* (www.nytimes.com).

Brooks, D. (2005, 10 August). All cultures are not equal. *New York Times*.

Brown, J. D. (1991). Accuracy and bias in self-knowledge: Can knowing the truth be hazardous to your health? In C. R. Snyder & D. F. Forsyth (eds), *Handbook of social and clinical psychology: The health perspective*. New York: Pergamon Press.

Brown, J. D., & Dutton, K. A. (1994). From the top down: Self-esteem and self-evaluation. Unpublished manuscript, University of Washington.

Brown, J. D., & Taylor, S. E. (1986). Affect and the processing of personal information: Evidence for mood-activated self-schemata. *Journal of Experimental Social Psychology*, **22**, 436–452.

Brown, L. M., Bradley, M. M., & Lang, P. J. (2006). Affective reactions to pictures of ingroup and outgroup members. *Biological Psychology*, **71**, 303–311.

Brown, R., Maras, P., Masser, B., Vivian, J., & Hewstone, M. (2001). Life on the ocean wave: Testing some intergroup hypotheses in a naturalistic setting. *Group Processes and Intergroup Relations*, **4**, 81–97.

Brown, R., Vivian, J., & Hewstone, M. (1999). Changing attitudes through intergroup contact: The effects of group membership salience. *European Journal of Social Psychology*, **29**, 741–764.

Brown, V. R., & Paulus, P. B. (2002). Making group brainstorming more effective: Recommendations from an associative memory perspective. *Current Directions in Psychological Science*, **11**, 208–212.

Brückner, H., & Bearman, P. (2005). After the promise: The STD consequences of adolescent virginity pledges. *Journal of Adolescent Health*, **36**, 271–278.

Brundtland, G. H. (2002). Message from the director-general. In: *The world health report 2002: Reducing risks, promoting healthy life*. Geneva: World Health Organization.

Bruner, J. S. (1957). On perceptual readiness. *Psychological Review*, **64**, 123–152.

Bruner, J. S. (1990). *Acts of meaning*. Cambridge, MA: Harvard University Press.

Bryan, J. H., & Test, M. A. (1967). Models and helping: Naturalistic studies in aiding behavior. *Journal of Personality and Social Psychology*, **6**, 400–407.

Bryman, A. (1988). *Quantity and quality in social research*. London: Routledge.

Buchan, N. R., Brewer, M. B., Grimalda, G., Wilson, R. K., Fatas, E., & Foddy, M. (2011). Global social identity and global cooperation. *Psychological Science*, **22**, 821–828.

Buehler, R., & Griffin, D. (2003). Planning, personality, and prediction: The role of future focus in optimistic time predictions. *Organizational Behavior and Human Decision Processes*, **92**, 80–90.

Buehler, R., Griffin, D., & Ross, M. (1994). Exploring the 'planning fallacy': When people underestimate their task completion times. *Journal of Personality and Social Psychology*, **67**, 366–381.

Buehler, R., Griffin, D., & Ross, M. (2002). Inside the planning fallacy: The causes and consequences of optimistic time predictions. In T. Gilovich, D. Griffin & D. Kahneman (eds), *Heuristics and biases: The psychology of intuitive judgment*. Cambridge: Cambridge University Press.

Buffardi, L. E., & Campbell, W. K. (2008). Narcissism and social networking websites. *Personality and Social Psychology Bulletin*, **34**, 1303–1314.

Bundy, T. (1989, 25 January). Interview with James Dobson. *Detroit Free Press*, 1A, 5A.

Bureau of the Census (1993, 4 May). Voting survey, reported by Associated Press.

Burger, J. M. (1987). Increased performance with increased personal control: A self-presentation interpretation. *Journal of Experimental Social Psychology*, **23**, 350–360.

Burger, J. M. (2009). Replicating Milgram: Would people still obey today? *American Psychologist*, **64**(1), 1–11.

Burger, J. M., & Caldwell, D. F. (2003). The effects of monetary incentives and labeling on the foot-in-the-door effect: Evidence for a self-perception process. *Basic and Applied Social Psychology*, **25**, 235–241.

Burger, J. M., & Pavelich, J. L. (1994). Attributions for presidential elections: The situational shift over time. *Basic and Applied Social Psychology*, **15**, 359–371.

Burger, J. M., Messian, N., Patel, S., del Prade, A., & Anderson, C. (2004). What a coincidence! The effects of incidental similarity on compliance. *Personality and Social Psychology Bulletin*, **30**, 35–43.

Burger, J. M., Soroka, S., Gonzago, K., Murphy, E., & Somervell, E. (2001). The effect of fleeting attraction on compliance to requests. *Personality and Social Psychology Bulletin*, **27**, 1578–1586.

Burke, R. D., & Sunley, R. (1998). Youth subcultures in contemporary Britain. In K. Hazelhurst and C. Hazlehurst (eds), *Gangs and youth subcultures: International explorations*. Edison, NJ: Transaction.

Burkholder, R. (2003, 14 February). Unwilling coalition? Majorities in Britain, Canada oppose military action in Iraq, *Gallup Poll Tuesday Briefing* (www.gallup.com/poll).

Burkitt, I. (1999). *Bodies of thought: Embodiment, identity and modernity*. London: Sage.

Burn, S. M. (1992). Locus of control, attributions, and helplessness in the homeless. *Journal of Applied Social Psychology*, **22**, 1161–1174.

Burnstein, E., & Vinokur, A. (1977). Persuasive argumentation and social comparison as determinants of attitude polarization. *Journal of Experimental Social Psychology*, **13**, 315–332.

Burnstein, E., & Worchel, P. (1962). Arbitrariness of frustration and its consequences for aggression in a social situation. *Journal of Personality*, **30**, 528–540.

Burr, V. (2006). Bystander intervention. In S. Taylor & D. Langdridge (eds), *Critical readings in social psychology*. Maidenhead: Open University Press.

Burr, W. R. (1973). *Theory construction and the sociology of the family*. New York: Wiley.

Burson, K. A., Larrick, R. P., & Klayman, J. (2006). Skilled or unskilled, but still unaware of it: How perceptions of difficulty drive miscalibration in relative comparisons. *Journal of Personality and Social Psychology*, **90**, 60–77.

Bushman, B. J. (1993). Human aggression while under the influence of alcohol and other drugs: An integrative research review. *Current Directions in Psychological Science*, **2**, 148–152.

Bushman, B. J. (1995). Moderating role of trait aggressiveness in the effects of violent media on aggression. *Journal of Personality and Social Psychology*, **69**, 950–960.

Bushman, B. J. (1998). Priming effects of media violence on the accessibility of aggressive constructs in memory. *Personality and Social Psychology Bulletin*, **24**, 537–545.

Bushman, B. J. (2002). Does venting anger feed or extinguish the flame? Catharsis, rumination, distraction, anger, and aggressive responding. *Personality and Social Psychology Bulletin*, **28**, 724–731.

Bushman, B. J. (2005). Violence and sex in television programs do not sell products in advertisements. *Psychological Science*, **16**, 702–708.

Bushman, B. J., & Anderson, C. A. (1998). Methodology in the study of aggression: Integrating experimental and nonexperimental findings. In R. Geen & E. Donnerstein (eds), *Human aggression: Theories, research and implications for policy*. San Diego: Academic Press.

Bushman, B. J., & Anderson, C. A. (2001). Media violence and the American public: Scientific facts versus media misinformation. *American Psychologist*, **56**, 477–489.

Bushman, B. J., & Anderson, C. A. (2002). Violent video

games and hostile expectations: A test of the general aggression model. *Personality and Social Psychology Bulletin*, **28**, 1679–1686.

Bushman, B. J., & Baumeister, R. (1998). Threatened egotism, narcissism, self-esteem, and direct and displaced aggression: Does self-love or self-hate lead to violence? *Journal of Personality and Social Psychology*, **75**, 219–229.

Bushman, B. J., & Bonacci, A. M. (2002). Violence and sex impair memory for television ads. *Journal of Applied Psychology*, **87**, 557–564.

Bushman, B. J., & Bonacci, A. M. (2004). You've got mail: Using e-mail to examine the effect of prejudiced attitudes on discrimination against Arabs. *Journal of Experimental Social Psychology*, **40**, 753–759.

Bushman, B. J., & Geen, R. G. (1990). Role of cognitiveemotional mediators and individual differences in the effects of media violence on aggression. *Journal of Personality and Social Psychology*, **58**, 156–163.

Bushman, B. J., Baumeister, R. F., & Phillips, C. M. (2001). Do people aggress to improve their mood? Catharsis beliefs, affect regulation opportunity, and aggressive responding. *Journal of Personality and Social Psychology*, **81**, 17–32.

Bushman, B. J., Baumeister, R. F., Thomaes, S., Ryu, E., Begeer, S., & West, S. G. (2009). Looking again, and harder, for a link between low self-esteem and aggression. *Journal of Personality*, **77**, 427–446.

Bushman, B. J., Bonacci, A. M., Pedersen, W. C., Vasquez, E. A., & Miller, N. (2005a). Chewing on it can chew you up: Effects of rumination on triggered displaced aggression. *Journal of Personality and Social Psychology*, **88**, 969–983.

Bushman, B. J., Wang, M. C., & Anderson, C. A. (2005b). Is the curve relating temperature to aggression linear or curvilinear? Assaults and temperature in Minneapolis reexamined. *Journal of Personality and Social Psychology*, **89**, 62–66.

Bushman, B. J., Wang, M. C., & Anderson, C. A. (2005c). Is the curve relating temperature to aggression linear or curvilinear? A response to Bell (2005) and to Cohn and Rotton (2005). *Journal of Personality and Social Psychology*, **89**, 74–77.

Buss, D. M. (1984). Toward a psychology of person-environment (PE) correlation: The role of spouse selection. *Journal of Personality and Social Psychology*, **47**, 361–377.

Buss, D. M. (1985). Human mate selection. *American Scientist*, **73**, 47–51.

Buss, D. M. (1989). Sex differences in human mate preferences: Evolutionary hypotheses tested in 37 cultures. *Behavioral and Brain Sciences*, **12**, 1–49.

Buss, D. M. (1994). *The evolution of desire: Strategies of human mating*. New York: Basic Books.

Buss, D. M. (1995a). Evolutionary psychology: A new paradigm for psychological science. *Psychological Inquiry*, **6**, 1–30.

Buss, D. M. (1995b). Psychological sex differences: Origins through sexual selection. *American Psychologist*, **50**, 164–168.

Buss, D. M. (ed.) (2005). *The handbook of evolutionary psychology*. New York: Wiley.

Buss, D. M., & Shackelford, T. K. (1997). Human aggression in evolutionary psychological perspective. *Clinical Psychology Review*, **17**, 605–619.

Buston, P. M., & Emlen, S. T. (2003). Cognitive processes underlying human mate choice: The relationship between self-perception and mate preference in Western society. *Proceedings of the National Academy of Sciences*, **100**, 8805–8810.

Butcher, S. H. (1951). *Aristotle's theory of poetry and fine art*. New York: Dover Publications.

Butler, J. (1990). *Gender trouble: Feminism and the subversion of identity*. New York: Routledge.

Butler, J. (2004). *Undoing gender*. London: Routledge.

Buunk, B. P., & Van Yperen, N. W. (1991). Referential comparisons, relational comparisons, and exchange orientation: Their relation to marital satisfaction. *Personality and Social Psychology Bulletin*, **17**, 709–717.

Byrne, D. (1971). *The attraction paradigm*. New York: Academic Press.

Byrne, D., & Clore, G. L. (1970). A reinforcement model of evaluative responses. *Personality: An International Journal*, **1**, 103–128.

Bytwerk, R. L. (1976). Julius Streicher and the impact of *Der Stürmer*. *Wiener Library Bulletin*, **29**, 41–46.

C

Cacioppo, J. T., & Berntson, G. G. (1992). Social psychological contributions to the decade of the brain: Doctrine of multilevel analysis. *American Psychologist*, **47**(8), 1019.

Cacioppo, J. T., & Decety, J. (2011). Social neuroscience: Challenges and opportunities in the study of complex behaviour. *Annals of the New York Academy of Sciences: The Year in Cognitive Neuroscience Issue*, 162–173.

Cacioppo, J. T., & Ortigue, S. (2011). Social neuroscience: How a multidisciplinary field is uncovering the biology of human interactions. *Cerebrum* 17. Published online 19 December.

Cacioppo, J. T., & Petty, R. E. (1981). Electromyograms as measures of extent and affectivity of information processing. *American Psychologist*, **36**, 441–456.

Cacioppo, J. T., & Petty, R. E. (1986). Social processes. In M. G. H. Coles, E. Donchin & S. W. Porges (eds), *Psychophysiology*. New York: Guilford Press.

Cacioppo, J. T., Crites, S. L., Gardner, W. L., & Berntson, G. G. (1994). Bioelectrical echoes from evaluative categorizations: I. A late positive brain potential that varies as a function of trait negativity and extremity. *Journal of Personality and Social Psychology*, **67**, 115–125.

Cacioppo, J. T., Petty, R. E., & Morris, K. J. (1983). Effects of need for cognition on message evaluation, recall, and persuasion. *Journal of Personality and Social Psychology*, **45**, 805–818.

Cacioppo, J. T., Petty, R. E., Feinstein, J. A., & Jarvis, W. B. G. (1996). Dispositional differences in cognitive motivation: The life and times of individuals varying in need for cognition. *Psychological Bulletin*, **119**, 197–253.

Cairns, E., & Hewstone, M. (2002). The impact of peacemaking in Northern Ireland on intergroup behavior. In S. Gabi & B. Nevo (eds), *Peace education: The concept, principles, and practices around the world*. Mahwah, NJ: Erlbaum.

Calvo-Merrino, B., Glaser, D. E., Grezes, J., Passingham, R. E., & Haggard, P. (2005). Action observation and acquired motor skills. *Cerebral Cortex*, **15**, 1243–1249.

Campbell, D. T. (1958). Common fate, similarity, and other indices of the status of aggregates of persons as social entities. *Behavioral Science*, **3**, 14–25.

Campbell, D. T. (1975a). The conflict between social and biological evolution and the concept of original sin. *Zygon*, **10**, 234–249.

Campbell, D. T. (1975b). On the conflicts between biological and social evolution and between psychology and oral tradition. *American Psychologist*, **30**, 1103–1126.

Campbell, J. D., & Fairey, P. J. (1989). Informational and normative routes to conformity: The effect of faction size as a function of norm extremity and attention to the stimulus. *Journal of Personality and Social Psychology*, **57**(3), 457.

Campbell, W. K., & Sedikides, C. (1999). Self-threat magnifies the self-serving bias: A meta-analytic integration. *Review of General Psychology*, **3**, 23–43.

Campbell, W. K., Rudich, E., & Sedikides, C. (2002). Narcissism, self-esteem, and the positivity of self-views: Two portraits of self-love. *Personality and Social Psychology Bulletin*, **28**, 358–368.

Canadian Psychological Association (2000). *Canadian code of ethics for psychologists*. Ottawa: Canadian

Psychological Association (www.cpa.ca/ethics2000.html).

Canter, D., Breaux, J., & Sime, J. (1980). Domestic, multiple occupancy, and hospital fires. In D. Canter (ed.), *Fires and human behavior*. Hoboken, NJ: Wiley.

Cantor, N. & Mischel, W. (1979). Prototypes in person perception. In L. Berkowitz (ed.), *Advances in experimental social psychology*, Vol. 12. New York: Academic Press.

Cantor, N., & Mischel, W. (1977). Traits as prototypes: Effects on recognition memory. *Journal of Personality & Social Psychology*, **35**, 38–48.

Caplan, N., & Nelson, S. D. (1973). On being useful: The nature and consequences of psychological research on social problems. *American Psychologist*, **28**, 199–211.

Caputo, D., & Dunning, D. (2005). What you don't know: The role played by errors of omission in imperfect self-assessments. *Journal of Experimental Social Psychology*, **41**, 488–505.

Carducci, B. J., Cosby, P. C., & Ward, D. D. (1978). Sexual arousal and interpersonal evaluations. *Journal of Experimental Social Psychology*, **14**, 449–457.

Carli, L. L. (1991). Gender, status, and influence. In E. J. Lawler, B. Markovsky, C. L. Ridgeway & H. Walker (eds), *Advances in group processes: Theory and research*, Vol. 8. Greenwich, CT: JAI Press.

Carlsmith, J. M., & Gross, A. E. (1969). Some effects of guilt on compliance. *Journal of Personality and Social Psychology*, **11**, 232–239.

Carlson, J., & Hatfield, E. (1992). *The psychology of emotion*. Fort Worth, TX: Holt, Rinehart & Winston.

Carlson, M., Charlin, V., & Miller, N. (1988). Positive mood and helping behavior: A test of six hypotheses. *Journal of Personality and Social Psychology*, **55**, 211–229.

Carlson, M., Marcus-Newhall, A., & Miller, N. (1990). Effects of situational aggression cues: A quantitative review. *Journal of*

*Personality and Social Psychology*, **58**, 622–633.

Carlson, N. R., Martin, G. N., & Buskist, W. (1989). *Psychology*. London: Pearson.

Carlston, D. E., & Shovar, N. (1983). Effects of performance attributions on others' perceptions of the attributor. *Journal of Personality and Social Psychology*, **44**, 515–525.

Carlston, D. E., & Skowronski, J. J. (2005). Linking versus thinking: Evidence for the different associative and attributional bases of spontaneous trait transference and spontaneous trait inference. *Journal of Personality and Social Psychology*, **89**, 884–898.

Carman, W. F., Elder, A. G., Wallace, L. A., McAulay, K., Walker, A., Murray, G., & Stott, D. J. (2000). Effects of influenza vaccination of health-care workers on mortality of elderly people in long-term care: A randomised controlled trial. *The Lancet*, **355**, 93–97.

Carnevale, P. J., & Choi, D.-W. (2000). Culture in the mediation of international disputes. *International Journal of Psychology*, **35**, 105–110.

Carothers, B. J., & Reis, H. T. (2012). Men and women are from Earth: Examining the latent structure of gender. *Journal of Personality and Social Psychology*, doi: 10.1037/a0030437

Carrasco, M., Barker, E. D., Tremblay, R. E., & Vitaro, F. (2006). Eysenck's personality dimensions as predictors of male adolescent trajectories of physical aggression, theft and vandalism. *Personality and Individual Differences*, **41**(7), 1309–1320.

Carroll, D., Davey Smith, G., & Bennett, P. (1994, March). Health and socioeconomic status. *The Psychologist*, 122–125.

Carter, J. D., Hall, J. A., Carney, D. R., & Rosip, J. C. (2006). Individual differences in the acceptance of stereotyping. *Journal of Research in Personality*, **40**, 1103–1118.

Carter, S., & Snow, C. (2004, May). Helping singles enter better marriages using

predictive models of marital success. Paper presented to the American Psychological Society convention.

Cartwright, D. S. (1975). The nature of gangs. In D. S. Cartwright, B. Tomson & H. Schwartz (eds), *Gang delinquency*. Monterey, CA: Brooks/Cole.

Carvallo, M., & Gabriel, S. (2006). No man is an island: The need to belong and dismissing avoidant attachment style. *Personality and Social Psychology Bulletin*, **32**, 697–709.

Carver, C. S., & Scheier, M. F. (1978). Self-focusing effects of dispositional self-consciousness, mirror presence, and audience presence. *Journal of Personality and Social Psychology*, **36**, 324–332.

Carver, C. S., & Scheier, M. F. (1981). *Attention and self-regulation*. New York: Springer-Verlag.

Caspi, A., & Herbener, E. S. (1990). Continuity and change: Assortative marriage and the consistency of personality in adulthood. *Journal of Personality and Social Psychology*, **58**, 250–258.

Caspi, A., McClay, J., Moffitt, T., Mill, J., Martin, J., Craig, I. W., Taylor, A., & Poulton, R. (2002). Role of genotype in the cycle of violence in maltreated children. *Science*, **297**, 851–854.

Cassidy, J. (2000). Adult romantic attachments: A developmental perspective on individual differences. *Review of General Psychology Special Issue: Adult attachment*, **4**, 111–131.

Castano, E., Yzerbyt, V., Paladino, M. P., & Sacchi, S. (2002). I belong, therefore, I exist: Ingroup identification, ingroup entitativity, and ingroup bias. *Personality and Social Psychology Bulletin*, **28**, 135–143.

Castelli, L., Macrae, N. C., Zogmaister, C., & Arcuri, L. (2004). A tale of two primes: Contextual limits on stereotype activation. *Social Cognition*, **22**(2), 233–247.

Cauberghe, V., De Pelsmacker, P., Janssens, W., & Dens, N. (2009). Fear, threat and efficacy in threat appeals: Message involvement as a key mediator to message acceptance.

*Accident Analysis and Prevention*, **41**(2), 276–285.

Cázares, A. (2010). Proficiency and attitudes toward information technologies' use in psychology undergraduates. *Computers in Human Behavior*, **26**(5), 1004–1008.

Cesarani, D. (2004). *Eichmann: His life and crimes*. London: Heinemann.

Cesario, J., & Higgins, E. T. (2008). Making message recipients 'feel right': How nonverbal cues can increase persuasion. *Psychological Science*, **19**(5), 415–420.

Cha, E. S., Kim, K. H., & Patrick, T. E. (2008). Predictors of intention to practice safer sex among Korean college students. *Archives of Sexual Behavior*, **37**, 641–651.

Chaffin, S. M. (2008). The new playground bullies of cyberspace: Online peer sexual harassment. *Howard Law Journal*, **51**(3), 773–818.

Chaiken, S. (1979). Communicator physical attractiveness and persuasion. *Journal of Personality and Social Psychology*, **37**, 1387–1397.

Chaiken, S. (1980). Heuristic versus systematic information processing and the use of source versus message cues in persuasion. *Journal of Personality and Social Psychology*, **39**, 752–766.

Chaiken, S., & Eagly, A. H. (1976). Communication modality as a determinant of message persuasiveness and message comprehensibility. *Journal of Personality and Social Psychology*, **34**, 605–614.

Chaiken, S., & Eagly, A. H. (1983). Communication modality as a determinant of persuasion: The role of communicator salience. *Journal of Personality and Social Psychology*, **45**, 241–256.

Chartrand, T. L., & Bargh, J. A. (1999). The chameleon effect: The perception–behavior link and social interaction. *Journal of Personality and Social Psychology*, **76**, 893–910.

Chase-Lansdale, P. L., Cherlin, A. J., & Kiernan, K. E. (1995). The long-term effects of parental divorce on the mental health of young adults: A developmental perspective. *Child Development*, **66**, 1614–1634.

Chassin, L., Presson, C. C., & Sherman, S. J. (1984). Cigarette smoking and adolescent psychosocial development. *Basic & Applied Social Psychology*, **5**(4), 295–315.

Check, J., & Malamuth, N. (1984). Can there be positive effects of participation in pornography experiments? *Journal of Sex Research*, **20**, 14–31.

Chen, F. F., & Kenrick, D. T. (2002). Repulsion or attraction? Group membership and assumed attitude similarity. *Journal of Personality and Social Psychology*, **83**, 111–125.

Chen, L.-H., Baker, S. P., Braver, E. R., & Li, G. (2000). Carrying passengers as a risk factor for crashes fatal to 16- and 17-year-old drivers. *Journal of the American Medical Association*, **283**, 1578–1582.

Chen, S. C. (1937). Social modification of the activity of ants in nest-building. *Physiological Zoology*, **10**, 420–436.

Chen, S., Lee-Chai, A. Y., & Bargh, J. A. (2001). Relationship orientation as moderator of the effects of social power. *Journal of Personality and Social Psychology*, **80**, 183–187.

Cheney, R. (2003, 16 March). Comments on Face the Nation, CBS News.

Cherry, F. (1995). *The stubborn particulars of social psychology*. London: Routledge.

Chodorow, N. J. (1978). *The reproduction of mother: Psychoanalysis and the sociology of gender*. Berkeley, CA: University of California Press.

Chodorow, N. J. (1989). *Feminism and psychoanalytic theory*. New Haven, CT: Yale University Press.

Choi, I., & Choi, Y. (2002). Culture and self-concept flexibility. *Personality and Social Psychology Bulletin*, **28**, 1508–1517.

Choi, I., Nisbett, R. E., & Norenzayan, A. (1999). Causal attribution across cultures: Variation and universality. *Psychological Bulletin*, **125**, 47–63.

Chua, H. F., Boland, J. E., & Nisbett, R. E. (2005a).

Cultural variation in eye movements during scene perception. *Proceedings of the National Academy of Sciences*, **102**, 12629–12633.

Chua, H. F., Leu, J., & Nisbett, R. E. (2005b). Culture and diverging views of social events. *Personality and Social Psychology Bulletin*, **31**, 925–934.

Chua-Eoan, H. (1997, 7 April). Imprisoned by his own passions. *Time*, pp. 40–42.

Cialdini, R. B. (1991). Altruism or egoism? That is (still) the question. *Psychological Inquiry*, **2**, 124–126.

Cialdini, R. B. (1993). *Social influence: Science and practice*, 3rd edn. New York: Harper & Collins.

Cialdini, R. B. (1995). A full-cycle approach to social psychology. In G. G. Brannigan & M. R. Merrens (eds), *The social psychologists: Research adventures*. New York: McGraw-Hill.

Cialdini, R. B. (2001). *Influence: Science and practice*, 4th edn. Boston: Allyn & Bacon.

Cialdini, R. B. (2005). Basic social influence is underestimated. *Psychological Inquiry*, **16**, 158–161.

Cialdini, R. B., & Goldstein, N. J. (2004). Social influence: Compliance and conformity. *Annual Review of Psychology*, **55**, 591–621.

Cialdini, R. B., & Schroeder, D. A. (1976). Increasing compliance by legitimizing paltry contributions: When even a penny helps. *Journal of Personality and Social Psychology*, **34**, 599–604.

Cialdini, R. B., Borden, R. J., Thorne, A., Walker, M. R., Freeman, S., & Sloan, L. R. (1976). Basking in reflected glory: Three (football) field studies. *Journal of Personality and Social Psychology*, **34**(3), 366.

Cialdini, R. B., Cacioppo, J. T., Bassett, R., & Miller, J. A. (1978). Lowball procedure for producing compliance: Commitment then cost. *Journal of Personality and Social Psychology*, **36**, 463–476.

Cialdini, R. B., Demaine, L. J., Barrett, D. W., Sagarin, B. J., & Rhoads, K. L. V. (2003). The poison parasite defense: A strategy for

sapping a stronger opponent's persuasive strength. Unpublished manuscript, Arizona State University.

Cialdini, R. B., Vincent, J. E., Lewis, S. K., Catalan, J., Wheeler, D., & Danby, B. L. (1975). Reciprocal concessions procedure for inducing compliance: The door-in-the-face technique. *Journal of Personality and Social Psychology*, **31**, 206–215.

Cialdini, R. B., Wosinska, W., Dabul, A. J., Whetstone-Dion, R., & Heszen, I. (1998). When social role salience leads to social role rejection: Modest self-presentation among women and men in two cultures. *Personality and Social Psychology Bulletin*, **24**, 473–481.

Cicerello, A., & Sheehan, E. P. (1995). Personal advertisements: A content analysis. *Journal of Social Behavior and Personality*, **10**, 751–756.

Cioffi, D., & Garner, R. (1998). The effect of response options on decisions and subsequent behavior: Sometimes inaction is better. *Personality and Social Psychology Bulletin*, **24**, 463–472.

Clack, B., Dixon, J., & Tredoux, C. (2005). Eating together apart: Patterns of segregation in a multi-ethnic cafeteria. *Journal of Community and Applied Social Psychology*, **15**, 1–16.

Clark, J. K., Wegener, D. T., Habashi, M. M., & Evans, A. T. (2012). Source expertise and persuasion: The effects of perceived opposition or support on message scrutiny. *Personality and Social Psychology Bulletin*, **38**(1), 90–100.

Clark, M. S. (1984). Record keeping in two types of relationships. *Journal of Personality and Social Psychology*, **47**, 549–557.

Clark, M. S. (1986). Evidence for the effectiveness of manipulations of desire for communal versus exchange relationships. *Personality and Social Psychology Bulletin*, **12**, 414–425.

Clark, M. S., & Bennett, M. E. (1992). Research on relationships: Implications for mental health. In D. Ruble & P. Costanzo (eds), *The social

psychology of mental health*. New York: Guilford Press.

Clark, M. S., & Mills, J. (1979). Interpersonal attraction in exchange and communal relationships. *Journal of Personality and Social Psychology*, **37**, 12–24.

Clark, M. S., & Mills, J. (1993). The difference between communal and exchange relationships: What it is and is not. *Personality and Social Psychology Bulletin*, **19**, 684–691.

Clark, M. S., Mills, J., & Corcoran, D. (1989). Keeping track of needs and inputs of friends and strangers. *Personality and Social Psychology Bulletin*, **15**, 533–542.

Clark, M. S., Mills, J., & Powell, M. C. (1986). Keeping track of needs in communal and exchange relationships. *Journal of Personality and Social Psychology*, **51**, 333–338.

Clark, R. D., III (1995). A few parallels between group polarization and minority influence. In S. Moscovici, H. Mucchi-Faina & A. Maass (eds), *Minority influence*. Chicago, IL: Nelson-Hall.

Clark, R. D., III, & Maass, S. A. (1988). The role of social categorization and perceived source credibility in minority influence. *European Journal of Social Psychology*, **18**, 381–394.

Clarke, A. C. (1952). An examination of the operation of residual propinquity as a factor in mate selection. *American Sociological Review*, **27**, 17–22.

Clary, G., & Snyder, M. (1999). The motivations to volunteer: Theoretical and practical considerations. *Current Directions in Psychological Science*, **8**, 156–159.

Cline, V. B., Croft, R. G., & Courrier, S. (1973). Desensitization of children to television violence. *Journal of Personality and Social Psychology*, **27**, 360–365.

Clore, G. L., Bray, R. M., Itkin, S. M., & Murphy, P. (1978). Interracial attitudes and behavior at a summer camp. *Journal of Personality and Social Psychology*, **36**, 107–116.

Clore, G. L., Wiggins, N. H., & Itkin, G. (1975). Gain and loss in attraction:

Attributions from nonverbal behavior. *Journal of Personality and Social Psychology*, **31**, 706–712.

Codol, J. P. (1975). On the so-called superior conformity of the self behavior: Twenty experimental investigations. *European Journal of Social Psychology*, **5**, 457–501.

Cohen, D. (1996). Law, social policy, and violence: The impact of regional cultures. *Journal of Personality and Social Psychology*, **70**, 961–978.

Cohen, D. (1998). Culture, social organization, and patterns of violence. *Journal of Personality and Social Psychology*, **75**, 408–419.

Cohn, E. G., & Rotton, J. (2005). The curve is still out there: A reply to Bushman, Wang, and Anderson's (2005) 'Is the curve relating temperature to aggression linear or curvilinear?'. *Journal of Personality and Social Psychology*, **89**, 67–70.

Coleman, L. M., Jussim, L., & Abraham, J. (1987). Students' reactions to teachers' evaluations: The unique impact of negative feedback. *Journal of Applied Social Psychology*, **17**, 1051–1070.

Collins, N. L., & Miller, L. C. (1994). Self-disclosure and liking: A meta-analytic review. *Psychological Bulletin*, **116**, 457–475.

Colman, A. (1991). Crowd psychology in South African murder trials. *American Psychologist*, **46**(10), 1071–1079.

Comstock, G., & Scharrer, E. (1999). *Television: What's on, who's watching and what it means*. San Diego: Academic Press.

Condor, S. (2006). Public prejudice as collaborative accomplishment: Towards a dialogic social psychology of racism. *Journal of Community and Applied Social Psychology*, **16**, 1–18.

Condor, S., Figgou, L., Abell, J., Gibson, S., & Stevenson, C. (2006). 'They're not racist . . .' Prejudice denial, mitigation and suppression in dialogue. *British Journal of Social Psychology*, **45**, 441–462.

Conger, R. D., Cui, M., Bryant, C. M., & Elder, G. H. (2000). Competence in early adult romantic relationships: A developmental perspective on family influences. *Journal of Personality and Social Psychology*, **79**, 224–237.

Connolly, P. (1998). *Racism, gender identities and young children: Social relations in a multi-ethnic, inner-city primary school*. New York: Routledge.

Conway, F., & Siegelman, J. (1979). *Snapping: America's epidemic of sudden personality change*. New York: Delta Books.

Conway, M., & Ross, M. (1986). Remembering one's own past: The construction of personal histories. In R. Sorrentino & E. T. Higgins (eds), *Handbook of motivation and cognition*. New York: Guilford Press.

Cook, T. D., & Flay, B. R. (1978). The persistence of experimentally induced attitude change. In L. Berkowitz (ed.), *Advances in experimental social psychology*, Vol. 11. New York: Academic Press.

Cooper, H. (1983). Teacher expectation effects. In L. Bickman (ed.), *Applied social psychology annual*, Vol. 4. Beverly Hills, CA: Sage.

Cooper, J. (1999). Unwanted consequences and the self: In search of the motivation for dissonance reduction. In E. Harmon-Jones & J. Mills (eds), *Cognitive dissonance: Progress on a pivotal theory in social psychology*. Washington, DC: American Psychological Association.

Cooper, J., & Mackie, D. (1986). Video games and aggression in children. *Journal of Applied Social Psychology*, **16**(8), 726–744.

Correia, I., Alves, H., Sutton, R., Ramos, M., Gouveia-Pereira, M., & Vala, J. (2012). When do people derogate or psychologically distance themselves from victims? Belief in a just world and ingroup identification. *Personality and Individual Differences*, **53**, 747–752.

Correll, J., Park, B., Judd, C. M., & Wittenbrink, B. (2002). The police officer's dilemma: Using ethnicity to disambiguate potentially threatening individuals. *Journal of Personality and Social Psychology*, **83**, 1314–1329.

Correll, J., Urland, G. R., & Ito, T. A. (2006). Event-related potentials and the decision to shoot: The role of threat perception and cognitive control. *Journal of Experimental Social Psychology*, **42**, 120–128.

Costanzo, M. (1998). *Just revenge*. New York: St Martin's.

Cota, A. A., & Dion, K. L. (1986). Salience of gender and sex composition of ad hoc groups: An experimental test of distinctiveness theory. *Journal of Personality and Social Psychology*, **50**, 770–776.

Cote, K. A., McCormick, C. M., Geniole, S. N., Renn, R. P., & MacAulay, S. D. (2013). Sleep deprivation lowers reactive aggression and testosterone in men. *Biological Psychology*, **92**, 249–256.

Cottrell, C. A., & Neuberg, S. L. (2005). Different emotional reactions to different groups: A sociofunctional threat-based approach to prejudice. *Journal of Personality and Social Psychology*, **88**, 770–789.

Cottrell, N. B., Wack, D. L., Sekerak, G. J., & Rittle, R. M. (1968). Social facilitation of dominant responses by the presence of an audience and the mere presence of others. *Journal of Personality and Social Psychology*, **9**, 245–250.

Coultas, J. C. (2004). When in Rome. . . An evolutionary perspective on conformity. *Group Processes and Intergroup Relations*, **7**(4), 317–331.

Coyne, S., & Archer, J. (2004). Indirect aggression in the media: A content analysis of British television programs. *Aggressive Behavior*, **30**, 254–271.

Crano, W. D., & Mellon, P. M. (1978). Causal influence of teachers' expectations on children's academic performance: A cross-legged panel analysis. *Journal of Educational Psychology*, **70**, 39–49.

Crawford, M., Stark, A. C., & Renner, C. H. (1998). The meaning of Ms.: Social assimilation of a gender concept. *Psychology of Women Quarterly*, **22**, 197–208.

Crawford, T. J. (1974). Sermons on racial tolerance and the parish neighborhood context. *Journal of Applied Social Psychology*, **4**, 1–23.

Crisp, R. J., & Hewstone, M. (1999). Differential evaluation of crossed category groups: Patterns, processes, and reducing intergroup bias. *Group Processes and Intergroup Relations*, **2**, 307–333.

Crisp, R. J., & Hewstone, M. (2000). Multiple categorization and social identity. In D. Capozza & R. Brown (eds), *Social identity theory: Trends in theory and research*. Beverly Hills, CA: Sage.

Crocker, J. (1981). Judgment of covariation by social perceivers. *Psychological Bulletin*, **90**, 272–292.

Crocker, J. (2002). The costs of seeking self-esteem. *Journal of Social Issues*, **58**, 597–615.

Crocker, J., & Knight, K. M. (2005). Contingencies of self-worth. *Current Directions in Psychological Science*, **14**, 200–203.

Crocker, J., & Luhtanen, R. (1990). Collective self-esteem and ingroup bias. *Journal of Personality and Social Psychology*, **58**, 60–67.

Crocker, J., & Luhtanen, R. (2003). Level of self-esteem and contingencies of self-worth: Unique effects on academic, social, and financial problems in college students. *Personality and Social Psychology Bulletin*, **29**, 701–712.

Crocker, J., & Park, L. E. (2004). The costly pursuit of self-esteem. *Psychological Bulletin*, **130**, 392–414.

Crocker, J., & Wolfe, C. (2001). Contingencies of self-worth. *Psychological Review*, **108**, 593–623.

Crocker, J., Luhtanen, R., Blaine, B., & Broadnax, S. (1994). Collective self-esteem and psychological wellbeing among white, black, and Asian college students. *Personality & Social Psychology Bulletin*, **20**, 503–513.

Croker. J., Hannah, D. B., & Weber, R. (1983). Person memory and causal attributions. *Journal of Personality and Social Psychology*, **44**, 55–66.

Croxton, J. S., Eddy, T., & Morrow, N. (1984). Memory biases in the reconstruction of interpersonal encounters. *Journal of Social and Clinical Psychology*, **2**, 348–354.

Croyle, R. T., & Cooper, J. (1983). Dissonance arousal: Physiological evidence. *Journal of Personality and Social Psychology*, **45**, 782–791.

Cuddy, A., Rock, M., & Norton, M. (2007). Aid in the aftermath of hurricane Katerina: Inferences of secondary emotions and intergroup helping. *Group Processes and Intergroup Relations*, **10**, 107–118.

Cunningham, J. D. (1981). Self-disclosure intimacy: Sex, sex-of-target, cross-national, and generational differences. *Personality and Social Psychology Bulletin*, **7**, 314–319.

Cunningham, M. R., Shaffer, D. R., Barbee, A. P., Wolff, P. L., & Kelley, D. J. (1990). Separate processes in the relation of elation and depression to helping: Social versus personal concerns. *Journal of Experimental Social Psychology*, **26**, 13–33.

Cunningham, W. A., Johnson, M. K., Raye, C. L., Gatenby, J. C., Gore, J. C., & Banaji, M. R. (2004). Separable neural components in the processing of black and white faces. *Psychological Science*, **15**, 806–813.

Custers, K., & Van den Bulck, J. (2013). The cultivation of fear of sexual violence in women processes and moderators of the relationship between television and fear. *Communication Research*, **40**(1), 96–124.

**D**

Dabbs, J. M., Jr, & Janis, I. L. (1965). Why does eating while reading facilitate opinion change? An experimental inquiry. *Journal of Experimental Social Psychology*, **1**, 133–144.

Dabbs, J. M., Jr, & Morris, R. (1990). Testosterone, social class, and antisocial behavior in a sample of 4,462 men. *Psychological Science*, **1**, 209–211.

Damon, W. (1995). *Greater expectations: Overcoming the culture of indulgence in America's homes and schools.* New York: Free Press.

D'Argenbeau, A., Collette, F., Van der Linden, M., Laureys, S., Del Fiore, G., Degueldre, C., Luxen, A., & Salmon, E. (2005). Self-referential reflective activity and its relationship with rest: A PET study. *Neuroimage*, **25**, 616–624.

Darley, J. M. (1995). Book review essay. *Political Psychology*.

Darley, J. M., & Batson, C. D. (1973). From Jerusalem to Jericho: A study of situational and dispositional variables in helping behavior. *Journal of Personality and Social Psychology*, **27**, 100–108.

Darley, J. M., & Berscheid, E. (1967). Increased liking as a result of the anticipation of personal contact. *Human Relations*, **20**, 29–40.

Darley, J. M., & Latané, B. (1968). Bystander intervention in emergencies: Diffusion of responsibility. *Journal of Personality and Social Psychology*, **8**, 377–383.

Darley, S., & Cooper, J. (1972). Cognitive consequences of forced noncompliance. *Journal of Personality and Social Psychology*, **24**, 321–326.

Darwin, C. (1859/1988). *The origin of species.* Vol. 15 of *The Works of Charles Darwin*, edited by P. H. Barrett & R. B. Freeman. New York: New York University Press.

Darwin, C. (2009). *On the origin of species.* London: Penguin Classics.

Das, E. H. H. J., de Wit, J. B. F., & Stroebe, W. (2003). Fear appeals motivate acceptance of action recommendations: Evidence for a positive bias in the processing of persuasive messages. *Personality and Social Psychology Bulletin*, **29**, 650–664.

Dashiell, J. F. (1930). An experimental analysis of some group effects. *Journal of Abnormal and Social Psychology*, **25**, 190–199.

David, B., & Turner, J. C. (1996). Studies in self-categorization and minority conversion: Is being a member of the out-group an advantage? *British Journal of Social Psychology*, **35**, 179–199.

David, B., & Turner, J. C. (1999). Studies in self-categorization and minority conversion: The in-group minority in intragroup and intergroup contexts. *British Journal of Social Psychology*, **38**, 115–134.

Davies, M. F. (1997). Belief persistence after evidential discrediting: The impact of generated versus provided explanations on the likelihood of discredited outcomes. *Journal of Experimental Social Psychology*, **33**, 561–578.

Davis, C. G., Lehman, D. R., Silver, R. C., Wortman, C. B., & Ellard, J. H. (1996). Self-blame following a traumatic event: The role of perceived avoidability. *Personality and Social Psychology Bulletin*, **22**, 557–567.

Davis, C. G., Lehman, D. R., Wortman, C. B., Silver, R. C., & Thompson, S. C. (1995). The undoing of traumatic life events. *Personality and Social Psychology Bulletin*, **21**, 109–124.

Davis, J. A. (2004). Did growing up in the 1960s leave a permanent mark on attitudes and values? Evidence from the GSS. *Public Opinion Quarterly*, **68**, 161–183.

Davis, J. H., Stasson, M. F., Parks, C. D., Hulbert, L., Kameda, T., Zimmerman, S. K., & Ono, K. (1993). Quantitative decisions by groups and individuals: Voting procedures and monetary awards by mock civil juries. *Journal of Experimental Social Psychology*, **29**, 326–346.

Davis, J. L., & Rusbult, C. E. (2001). Attitude alignment in close relationships. *Journal of Personality and Social Psychology*, **81**, 65–84.

Davis, K. E. (1985, February). Near and dear: Friendship and love compared. *Psychology Today*, 22–30.

Davis, K. E. (1995). *Reshaping the female body.* New York and London: Routledge.

Davis, K. E. (2002). A dubious equality: Men, women and cosmetic surgery. *Body Society*, **8**, 49–65.

Davis, K. E., & Jones, E. E. (1960). Changes in interpersonal perception as a means of reducing cognitive dissonance. *Journal of Abnormal and Social Psychology*, **61**, 402–410.

Davis, L., & Greenlees, C. (1992). Social loafing revisited: Factors that mitigate – and reverse – performance loss. Paper presented at the Southwestern Psychological Association convention.

Dawes, R. M. (1990). The potential nonfalsity of the false consensus effect. In R. M. Hogarth (ed.), *Insights in decision making: A tribute to Hillel J. Einhorn.* Chicago, IL: University of Chicago Press.

Dawes, R. M. (1994). *House of cards: Psychology and psychotherapy built on myth.* New York: Free Press.

Dawkins, R. (1976). *The selfish gene.* New York: Oxford University Press.

Day, R. D., Lewis, C., O'Brien, M., & Lamb, M. E. (2005). Fatherhood and father involvement: Emerging constructs and theoretical orientations. In V. L. Bengston, A. C. Acock, K. R. Allen, P. Dillworth-Anderson & D. M. Klein (eds), *Sourcebook of family theory and research.* Thousand Oaks, CA: Sage.

de Almeida, R. M., Ferrari, P. F., Parmigiani, S., & Miczek, K. A. (2005). Escalated aggressive behavior: dopamine, serotonin and GABA. *European Journal of Pharmacology*, **526**(1), 51–64.

De Bruijn, G. J., Kroeze, W., Oenema, A., & Brug, J. (2008). Saturated fat consumption and the theory of planned behaviour: Exploring additive and interactive effects of habit strength. *Appetite*, **51**, 318–323.

de Hoogh, A., den Hartog, D., Koopman, P., Thierry, H., van den Berg, P., van der Weide, J., & Wilderom, C. (2004). Charismatic leadership, environmental dynamism, and performance. *European Journal of Work and Organizational Psychology*, **13**(4), 447–471.

De Houwer, J. (2003). The extrinsic affective Simon task. *Experimental Psychology* (formerly *Zeitschrift Für Experimentelle Psychologie*), **50**(2), 77–85.

De Houwer, J., Thomas, S., & Baeyens, F. (2001). Associative learning of likes and dislikes: A review of 25 years of research on human evaluative conditioning. *Psychological Bulletin*, **127**, 853–869.

de Long, G. W. (1883). *The voyage of the Jeannette*. London: Kegan Paul, Trench.

De Smet, M., Keer, H. V., & Valcke, M. (2009). Cross-age peer tutors in asynchronous discussion groups: A study of the evaluation in tutor support. *Instrumental Science*, **37**, 87–105.

De Wit, J. B. F., Das, E., & Vet, R. (2008). What works best: Objective statistics or a personal testimonial? An assessment of the persuasive effects of different types of message evidence on risk perception. *Health Psychology*, **27**(1), 110–115.

DeBruine, L. M. (2002). Facial resemblance enhances trust. *Proceedings of the Royal Society of London*, **269**, 1307–1312.

DeBruine, L. M. (2004). Facial resemblance increases the attractiveness of same-sex faces more than other-sex faces. *Proceedings of the Royal Society of London, B*, **271**(1552), 2085–2090.

Decety, J., & Sommerville, J. A. (2003). Shared representations between self and other: a social cognitive neuroscience view. *Trends in Cognitive Science*, **7**, 527–533.

Deci, E. L., & Ryan, R. M. (1985). *Instrinsic motivation and self-determination in human behavior*. New York: Plenum.

Deci, E. L., & Ryan, R. M. (1987). The support of autonomy and the control of behavior. *Journal of Personality and Social Psychology*, **53**, 1024–1037.

Deci, E. L., & Ryan, R. M. (1991). A motivational approach to self: Integration in personality. In R. Dienstbier (ed.), *Perspectives on motivation*, Vol. 38. Lincoln, NE: University of Nebraska Press. Nebraska Symposium on Motivation.

Deci, E. L., & Ryan, R. M. (1997). Behaviorists in search of the null: Revisiting the undermining of intrinsic motivation by extrinsic rewards. Unpublished manuscript, University of Rochester.

Deci, E. L., La Guardia, J. G., Moller, A. C., Scheiner, M. J., & Ryan, R. M. (2006). On the benefits of giving as well as receiving autonomy support: Mutuality in close friendships. *Personality and Social Bulletin*, **32**, 313–327.

Delgado, J. (1973). In M. Pines, *The brain changers*. New York: Harcourt Brace Jovanovich.

della Cava, M. R. (2003, 2 April). Iraq gets sympathetic press around the world. *USA Today* (www.usatoday.com).

Dembroski, T. M., Lasater, T. M., & Ramirez, A. (1978). Communicator similarity, fear arousing communications, and compliance with health care recommendations. *Journal of Applied Social Psychology*, **8**, 254–269.

Dennett, D. (2005, 26 December). Spiegel interview with evolution philosopher Daniel Dennett: Darwinism completely refutes intelligent design. *Der Spiegel* (www.service.dspiegel.de).

Denson, T. F., DeWall, C. N., & Finkel, E. J. (2012). Self-control and aggression. *Current Directions in Psychological Science*, **21**(1), 20–25.

Denson, T. F., Ronay, R., von Hippel, W., & Schira, M. M. (2013). Endogenous testosterone and cortisol modulate neural responses during induced anger control. *Social Neuroscience*, **8**(2), 165–177.

Denson, T. F., von Hippel, W., Kemp, R., & Teo, L. S. (2010). Glucose consumption decreases impulsive aggression in response to provocation in aggressive individuals. *Journal of Experimental Social Psychology*, **46**(6), 1023–1028.

Department of Canadian Heritage (2006). What is multiculturalism? (www.pch.gc).

DePaulo, B. M., Charlton, K., Cooper, H., Lindsay, J. J., & Muhlenbruck, L. (1997). The accuracy–confidence correlation in the detection of deception. *Personality and Social Psychology Review*, **1**, 346–357.

Derlega, V., Metts, S., Petronio, S., & Margulis, S. T. (1993). *Self-disclosure*. Newbury Park, CA: Sage.

Dermer, M., & Pyszczynski, T. A. (1978). Effects of erotica upon men's loving and liking responses for women they love. *Journal of Personality and Social Psychology*, **36**, 1302–1309.

Desforges, D. M., Lord, C. G., Pugh, M. A., Sia, T. L., Scarberry, N. C., & Ratcliff, C. D. (1997). Role of group representativeness in the generalization part of the contact hypothesis. *Basic and Applied Social Psychology*, **19**, 183–204.

Desforges, D. M., Lord, C. G., Ramsey, S. L., Mason, J. A., Van Leeuwen, M. D., West, S. C., & Lepper, M. R. (1991). Effects of structured cooperative contact on changing negative attitudes toward stigmatized social groups. *Journal of Personality and Social Psychology*, **60**, 531–544.

Deutsch, M. (1985). *Distributive justice: A social psychological perspective*. New Haven: Yale University Press.

Deutsch, M. (1993). Educating for a peaceful world. *American Psychologist*, **48**, 510–517.

Deutsch, M. (1994). Constructive conflict resolution: Principles, training, and research. *Journal of Social Issues*, **50**, 13–32.

Deutsch, M., & Collins, M. E. (1951). *Interracial housing: A psychological evaluation of a social experiment*. Minneapolis: University of Minnesota Press.

Deutsch, M., & Gerard, H. B. (1955). A study of normative and informational social influence upon individual judgment. *Journal of Abnormal and Social Psychology*, **51**, 629–636.

Deutsch, M., & Krauss, R. M. (1960). The effect of threat upon interpersonal bargaining. *Journal of Abnormal and Social Psychology*, **61**, 181–189.

Devine, P. G. (1989). Stereotypes and prejudice: Their automatic and controlled components. *Journal of Personality and Social Psychology*, **56**, 5–18.

Devine, P. G. (2005). Breaking the prejudice habit: Allport's inner conflict revisited. In J. F. Dovidio, P. Glick & L. A. Rudman (eds), *On the nature of prejudice: Fifty years after Allport*. Malden, MA: Blackwell.

Devos, T., Silver, L. A., Mackie, D. M., & Smith, E. R. (2002). Experiencing intergroup emotions. In D. M. Mackie & E. R. Smith (eds), *From prejudice to intergroup emotions: Differentiated reactions to social groups*. Philadelphia, PA: Psychology Press.

Devos-Comby, L., & Salovey, P. (2002). Applying persuasion strategies to alter HIV-relevant thoughts and behavior. *Review of General Psychology*, **6**, 287–304.

DeWall, C. N., Baumeister, R. F., Stillman, T. F., & Gailliot, M. T. (2007). Violence restrained: Effects of self-regulation and its depletion on aggression. *Journal of Experimental Social Psychology*, **43**, 62–76.

DeWall, C. N., Pond, R. S., Jr, Campbell, W. K., & Twenge, J. M. (2011). Tuning in to psychological change: Linguistic markers of psychological traits and emotions over time in popular U.S. song lyrics. *Psychology of Aesthetics, Creativity, and the Arts*, **5**, 200–207.

Diamond, J. (1996, December). The best ways to sell sex. *Discover*, pp. 78–86.

DiDonato, T., Ullrich, J., & Krueger, J. I. (2011). Social perception as induction and inference: An integrative model of intergroup differentiation, ingroup favouritism, and differential accuracy. *Journal of Personality and Social Psychology*, **100**, 66–83.

Diekman, A. B., McDonald, M., & Gardner, W. L. (2000). Love means never having to be careful: The relationship between reading romance novels and safe sex behavior. *Psychology of Women Quarterly*, **24**, 179–188.

Diener, E. (1980). Deindividuation: The absence of self-awareness and self-regulation in group members. In P. B. Paulus (ed.), *The psychology of group influence*. Hillsdale, NJ: Erlbaum.

Diener, E., & Crandall, R. (1979). An evaluation of the Jamaican anticrime program. *Journal of Applied Social Psychology*, **9**, 135–146.

Diener, E., & Wallbom, M. (1976). Effects of self-awareness on antinormative behavior. *Journal of*

*Research in Personality*, **10**, 107–111.

Diener, E., Fraser, S. C., Beaman, A. L., & Kelem, R. T. (1976). Effects of deindividuation variables on stealing among Halloween trick-or-treaters. *Journal of Personality and Social Psychology*, **33**, 178–183.

Dienstbier, R. A., Roesch, S. C., Mizumoto, A., Hemenover, S. H., Lott, R. C., & Carlo, G. (1998). Effects of weapons on guilt judgments and sentencing recommendations for criminals. *Basic and Applied Social Psychology*, **20**, 93–102.

Dijksterhuis, A., Smith, P. K., van Baaren, R. B., & Wigboldus, D. H. J. (2005). The unconscious consumer: Effects of environment on consumer behavior. *Journal of Consumer Psychology*, **15**, 193–202.

Dijkstra, J. K., Cillessen, A. H., Lindenberg, S., & Veenstra, R. (2010). Basking in reflected glory and its limits: Why adolescents hang out with popular peers. *Journal of Research on Adolescence*, **20**(4), 942–958.

Dimberg, U., Thunberg, M., & Grunedal, S. (2002). Facial reactions to emotional stimuli: Automatically controlled emotional responses. *Cognition and Emotion*, **16**(4), 449–472.

Dindia, K., & Allen, M. (1992). Sex differences in self-disclosure: A meta-analysis. *Psychological Bulletin*, **112**, 106–124.

Dion, K. K., & Dion, K. L. (1985). Personality, gender, and the phenomenology of romantic love. In P. R. Shaver (ed.), *Review of personality and social psychology*, Vol. 6. Beverly Hills, CA: Sage.

Dion, K. K., & Dion, K. L. (1991). Psychological individualism and romantic love. *Journal of Social Behavior and Personality*, **6**, 17–33.

Dion, K. K., & Dion, K. L. (1996). Cultural perspectives on romantic love. *Personal Relationships*, **3**, 5–17.

Dion, K. K., & Stein, S. (1978). Physical attractiveness and interpersonal influence. *Journal of Experimental Social Psychology*, **14**, 97–109.

Dion, K. L. (1979). Intergroup conflict and intragroup cohesiveness. In W. G. Austin, & S. Worchel (eds), *The social psychology of intergroup relations*. Monterey, CA: Brooks/Cole.

Dion, K. L. (1987). What's in a title? The Ms. stereotype and images of women's titles of address. *Psychology of Women Quarterly*, **11**, 21–36.

Dion, K. L., & Cota, A. A. (1991). The Ms. stereotype: Its domain and the role of explicitness in title preference. *Psychology of Women Quarterly*, **15**, 403–410.

Dion, K. L., & Dion, K. K. (1988). Romantic love: Individual and cultural perspectives. In R. J. Sternberg & M. L. Barnes (eds), *The psychology of love*. New Haven, CT: Yale University Press.

Dion, K. L., & Schuller, R. A. (1991). The Ms. stereotype: Its generality and its relation to managerial and marital status stereotypes. *Canadian Journal of Behavioural Science*, **23**, 25–40.

Dion, K., Berscheid, E. & Walster, E. (1972). What is beautiful is good. *Journal of Personality and Social Psychology*, **24**, 285–290.

Dishion, T. J., McCord, J., & Poulin, F. (1999). When interventions harm: Peer groups and problem behavior. *American Psychologist*, **54**, 755–764.

Dixon, J., & Durrheim, K. (2003). Contact and the ecology of racial division: Some varieties of informal segregation. *British Journal of Social Psychology*, **42**, 1–23.

Dixon, J., & Wetherell, M. (2004). On discourse and dirty nappies: Gender, division of household labour and the social psychology of distributive justice. *Theory and Psychology*, **14**(2), 167–189.

Dixon, J., Durrheim, K., & Tredoux, C. (2005a). Beyond the optimal contact strategy: A reality check for the contact hypothesis. *American Psychologist*, **60**, 697–711.

Dixon, J., Mahoney, B., & Cocks, R. (2002). Accents of guilt? Effects of regional accent, race, and crime type on attributions of guilt. *Journal of Language and Social Psychology*, **21**(2), 162–168.

Dixon, J., Tredoux, C., & Clack, B. (2005b). On the microecology of racial division: A neglected dimension of segregation. *South African Journal of Psychology*, **35**, 395–411.

Dodge, M. (2006). Juvenile police informants: Friendship, persuasion, and pretense. *Youth Violence and Juvenile Justice*, **4**(3), 234–246.

Dogra, N., Omigbodum, O., Adedokun, T., Bella, T., Ronzoni, P., & Adesokan, A. (2012). Nigerian secondary school children's knowledge of and attitudes to mental health and illness. *Clinical Child Psychology and Psychiatry*, **17**(3), 336–353.

Doidge, N. (2007). *The brain that changes itself: Stories of personal triumph from the frontiers of brain science*. New York: Penguin Group.

Doise, W., Deschamps, J.-C., & Meyer, G. (1978). The accentuation of intra-category similarities. In H. Tajfel (ed.), *Differentiation between social groups*. London: Academic Press.

Dolinski, D. (2000). On inferring one's beliefs from one's attempt and consequences for subsequent compliance. *Journal of Personality and Social Psychology*, **78**(2), 260.

Dolinski, D., & Nawrat, R. (1998). 'Fear-then-relief' procedure for producing compliance: Beware when the danger is over. *Journal of Experimental Social Psychology*, **34**, 27–50.

Dollard, J., Doob, L., Miller, N., Mowrer, O. H., & Sears, R. R. (1939). *Frustration and aggression*. New Haven, CT: Yale University Press.

Dolnik, L., Case, T. I., & Williams, K. D. (2003). Stealing thunder as a courtroom tactic revisited: Processes and boundaries. *Law and Human Behavior*, **27**, 265–285.

Donnellan, M. B., Larsen-Rife, D., & Conger, R. D. (2005a). Personality, family history, and competence in early adult romantic relationships. *Journal of Personality and Social Psychology*, **88**, 562–576.

Donnellan, M. B., Trzesniewski, K. H., Robins, R. W., Moffitt, T. E., & Caspi, A. (2005b). Low self-esteem is related to aggression, antisocial behaviour, and delinquency. *Psychological Science*, **16**, 328–335.

Donnerstein, E. (1980). Aggressive erotica and violence against women. *Journal of Personality and Social Psychology*, **39**, 269–277.

Donnerstein, E. (1998). Why do we have those new ratings on television. Invited address to the National Institute on the Teaching of Psychology.

Donnerstein, E., Linz, D., & Penrod, S. (1987). *The question of pornography*. London: Free Press.

Doob, A. N., & McLaughlin, D. S. (1989). Ask and you shall be given: Request size and donations to a good cause. *Journal of Applied Social Psychology*, **19**(12), 1049–1056.

Doob, A. N., & Roberts, J. (1988). Public attitudes toward sentencing in Canada. In N. Walker & M. Hough (eds), *Sentencing and the public*. London: Gower.

Douglass, F. (1845/1960). *Narrative of the life of Frederick Douglass, an American slave: Written by himself*. (B. Quarles, ed.). Cambridge, MA: Harvard University Press.

Dovidio, J. F. (1991). The empathy-altruism hypothesis: Paradigm and promise. *Psychological Inquiry*, **2**, 126–128.

Dovidio, J. F., Brigham, J. C., Johnson, B. T., & Gaertner, S. L. (1996). Stereotyping, prejudice and discrimination: Another look. In C. N. Macrae, C. Stangor & M. Hewstone (eds), *Stereotypes and stereotyping*. New York: Guilford Press.

Dovidio, J. F., Gaertner, S. L., Anastasio, P. A., & Sanitioso, R. (1992). Cognitive and motivational bases of bias: Implications of aversive racism for attitudes toward Hispanics. In S. Knouse, P. Rosenfeld & A. Culbertson (eds), *Hispanics in the workplace*. Newbury Park, CA: Sage.

Dovidio, J. F., Piliavin, J. A., Gaertner, S. L., Schroeder, D. A., & Clark, R. D.,

(1991). The arousal: Cost-reward model and the process of intervention. In M. S. Clark (ed.), *Prosocial behavior*. Newbury Park, CA: Sage.

Drabman, R. S., & Thomas, M. H. (1974). Does media violence increase children's toleration of real-life aggression? *Developmental Psychology*, **10**, 418–421.

Drabman, R. S., & Thomas, M. H. (1975). Does TV violence breed indifference? *Journal of Communications*, **25**(4), 86–89.

Drabman, R. S., & Thomas, M. H. (1976). Does watching violence on television cause apathy? *Pediatrics*, **57**, 329–331.

Drewes, A. (2008). Bobo revisited: What the research says. *International Journal of Play Theory*, **17**(1), 52–65.

Driedger, L. (1975). In search of cultural identity factors: A comparison of ethnic students. *Canadian Review of Sociology and Anthropology*, **12**, 150–161.

Driskell, J. E., & Mullen, B. (1990). Status, expectations, and behaviour: A meta-analytic review and test of the theory. *Personality and Social Psychology Bulletin*, **16**(3), 541–553.

Drivdahl, S. B., Zaragoza, M. S., & Learned, D. M. (2009). The role of emotional elaboration in the creation of false memories. *Applied Cognitive Psychology*, **23**, 13–35.

Droba, D. D. (1932). Methods for measuring attitudes. *Psychological Bulletin*, **29**(5), 309–323.

Drolet, A. L., & Morris, M. W. (2000). Rapport in conflict resolution: Accounting for how face-to-face contact fosters mutual cooperation in mixed-motive conflicts. *Journal of Experimental Social Psychology*, **36**, 26–50.

Drury, J. (2012). Collective resilience in mass emergencies and disasters: A social identity model. In J. Jetten, C. Haslam & S. A. Haslam (eds), *The social cure: Identity, health and well-being*. Hove and New York: Psychology Press.

Drury, J., Stott, C., & Farsides, T. (2003). The role of police perceptions and practices in the development of

'public disorder'. *Journal of Applied Social Psychology*, **33**(7), 1480–1500.

DuBois, W. E. B. (1903/1961). *The souls of black folk*. Greenwich, CT: Fawcett Books.

Duffy, M. (2003, 9 June). Weapons of mass disappearance. *Time*, pp. 28–33.

Duffy, S. & Rusbult, C. E. (1986) Satisfaction and commitment in homosexual and heterosexual relationships. *Journal of Homosexuality*, **12**, 1–23.

Dufner, M., Rauthmann, J. F., Czarna, A. Z., and Denissen, J. J. A. (2013). Are narcissists sexy? Zeroing in on the effect of narcissism on short-term mate appeal. *Personality and Social Psychology Bulletin*, **39**, 870–882.

Dunlap, R. E. (2008) The new environmental paradigm scale: From marginality to worldwide use. *The Journal of Environmental Education*, **40**(1), 3–18.

Dunlap, R. E., & Van Liere, K. D. (1978). The 'new ecological paradigm': A proposed measuring instrument and preliminary results. *The Journal of Environmental Education*, **9**(4), 10–19.

Dunn, K. I., Mohr, P. B., Wilson, C. J., & Wittert, G. A. (2008). Beliefs about fast food in Australia: A qualitative analysis. *Appetite*, **51**, 331–334.

Dunning, D., & Hayes, A. F. (1996). Evidence for egocentric comparison in social judgment. *Journal of Personality and Social Psychology*, **71**, 213–229.

Dunning, D., Griffin, D. W., Milojkovic, J. D., & Ross, L. (1990). The overconfidence effect in social prediction. *Journal of Personality and Social Psychology*, **58**, 568–581.

Durrheim, K., & Dixon, J. (2001). Geographies of racial exclusion: Beaches as family spaces. *Ethnic and Racial Studies*, **24**, 333–350.

Dutton, D. (2006, 13 January). Hardwired to seek beauty. *The Australian* (www.theaustralian.news.com.au).

Dutton, D. G., & Aron, A. P. (1974). Some evidence for heightened sexual attraction under conditions of high anxiety. *Journal of Person-

ality and Social Psychology*, **30**, 510–517.

Duval, S., & Wicklund, R. A. (1972). *A theory of objective self-awareness*. New York: Academic Press.

Duval, S., Duval, V. H., & Neely, R. (1979). Self-focus, felt responsibility, and helping behavior. *Journal of Personality and Social Psychology*, **37**, 1769–1778.

**E**

Eagly, A. H. (1987). *Sex differences in social behavior: A social-role interpretation*. Hillsdale, NJ: Erlbaum.

Eagly, A. H. (1994). Are people prejudiced against women? Donald Campbell Award invited address, American Psychological Association convention.

Eagly, A. H., & Chaiken, S. (1993). *The psychology of attitudes*. San Diego: Harcourt Brace Jovanovich.

Eagly, A. H., & Chaiken, S. (1998). Attitude structure and function. In D. Gilbert, S. Fiske & G. Lindzey (eds), *The handbook of social psychology*, 4th edn. New York: McGraw-Hill.

Eagly, A. H., & Chaiken, S. (2005). Attitude research in the 21st century: The current state of knowledge. In D. Albarracín, B. T. Johnson, T. Blair & M. P. Zanna (eds), *The handbook of attitudes*. Mahwah, NJ: Lawrence Erlbaum.

Eagly, A. H., & Crowley, M. (1986). Gender and helping behavior: A meta-analytic review of the social psychological literature. *Psychological Bulletin*, **100**, 283–308.

Eagly, A. H., & Johnson, B. T. (1990). Gender and leadership style: A meta-analysis. *Psychological Bulletin*, **108**, 233–256.

Eagly, A. H., & Wood, W. (1991). Explaining sex differences in social behavior: A meta-analytic perspective. *Personality and Social Psychology Bulletin*, **17**, 306–315.

Eagly, A. H., & Wood, W. (1999). The origins of sex differences in human behavior: Evolved dispositions versus social roles. *American Psychologist*, **54**, 408–423.

Eagly, A. H., Ashmore, R. D., Makhijani, M. G., & Longo, L. C. (1991). What is

beautiful is good, but …: A metaanalytic review of research on the physical attractiveness stereotype. *Psychological Bulletin*, **110**, 109–128.

Eagly, A. H., Diekman, A. B., Johannesen-Schmidt, M. C., & Koenig, A. M. (2004). Gender gaps in sociopolitical attitudes: A social psychological analysis. *Journal of Personality and Social Psychology*, **87**, 796–816.

Eagly, A. H., Johannesen-Schmidt, M. C., & van Engen, M. L. (2003). Transformational, transactional, and laissez-faire leadership styles: A meta-analysis comparing women and men. *Psychological Bulletin*, **129**, 569–591.

Eagly, A. H., Wood, W., & Chaiken, S. (1978). Casual inferences about communicators and their effect on opinion change. *Journal of Personality and Social Psychology*, **36**, 424–435.

Earley, C. P. (1989). Social loafing and collectivism: A comparison of the United States and the People's Republic of China. *Administrative Science Quarterly*, **34**, 565–581.

Ebbesen, E. B., Duncan, B., & Konecni, V. J. (1975). Effects of content of verbal aggression on future verbal aggression: A field experiment. *Journal of Experimental Social Psychology*, **11**, 192–204.

Eberhardt, J. L. (2005). Imaging race. *American Psychologist*, **60**, 181–190.

Eberhardt, J. L., Purdie, V. J., Goff, P. A., & Davies, P. G. (2004). Seeing black: Race, crime, and visual processing. *Journal of Personality and Social Psychology*, **87**, 876–893.

Ebneter, D. S., Latner, J. D., & O'Brien, K. S. (2011). Just world beliefs, causal beliefs, and acquaintance: Associations with stigma toward eating disorders and obesity. *Personality and Individual Differences*, **51**, 618–622.

Edwards, C. P. (1991). Behavioral sex differences in children of diverse cultures: The case of nurturance to infants. In M. Pereira & L. Fairbanks (eds), *Juveniles: Comparative socioecology*.

Oxford: Oxford University Press.

Edwards, D. (1997). *Discourse and cognition*. London: Sage.

Edwards, D. (2003). Analysing racial discourse: The discursive psychology of mind-world relationships. In H. Van der Berg, M. Wetherell & H. Houtkoop-Seenstra (eds), *Analysing race talk: Multidisciplinary approaches to the interview*. Cambridge: Cambridge University Press.

Edwards, D., & Middleton, D. (1987). Conversation and remembering: Bartlett revisited. *Applied Cognitive Psychology*, **1**, 77–92.

Edwards, D., & Potter, J. (2005). Discursive psychology, mental states and descriptions. In H. te Molder & J. Potter (eds), *Conversation and cognition*. New York: Cambridge University Press.

Edwards, D. A., & Casto, K. V. (2013). Women's intercollegiate athletic competition: Cortisol, testosterone, and the dual hormone hypothesis as it relates to status among teammates. *Hormones and Behavior*, **64**(1), 153–160.

Ehrlich, P., & Feldman, M. (2003). Genes and cultures: What creates our behavioral phenome? *Current Anthropology*, **44**, 87–95.

Ehrlinger, J., Gilovich, T., & Ross, L. (2005). Peering into the bias blind spot: People's assessments of bias in themselves and others. *Personality and Social Psychology Bulletin*, **31**, 680–692.

Eibach, R. P., Libby, L. K., & Gilovich, T. D. (2003). When change in the self is mistaken for change in the world. *Journal of Personality and Social Psychology*, **84**, 917–931.

Eisenberg, N., Fabes, R. A., Schaller, M., Miller, P., Carlo, G., Poulin, R., Shea, C., & Shell, R. (1991). Personality and socialization correlates of vicarious emotional responding. *Journal of Personality and Social Psychology*, **61**, 459–470.

Eisenberger, R., & Rhoades, L. (2001). Incremental effects of reward on creativity. *Journal of Personality and Social Psychology*, **81**, 728–741.

Eisenberger, R., & Shanock, L. (2003). Rewards, intrinsic motivation, and creativity: A case study of conceptual and methodological isolation. *Creativity Research Journal*, **15**, 121–130.

Eisenberger, R., Rhoades, L., & Cameron, J. (1999). Does pay for performance increase or decrease perceived self-determination and intrinsic motivation? *Journal of Personality and Social Psychology*, **77**, 1026–1040.

Eiser, J. R., Sutton, S. R., & Wober, M. (1979). Smoking, seat-belts, and beliefs about health. *Addictive Behaviors*, **4**, 331–338.

Eldersveld, S. J., & Dodge, R. W. (1954). Personal contact or mail propaganda? An experiment in voting turnout and attitude change. In D. Katz, D. Cartwright, S. Eldersveld & A. M. Lee (eds), *Public opinion and propaganda*. New York: Dryden Press.

Ellemers, N. (2012). The group self. *Science, 336*, 848–852.

Ellemers, N., Doosje, B., & Spears, R. (2004). Sources of respect: The effects of being liked by ingroups and outgroups. *European Journal of Social Psychology*, **34**, 155–172.

Ellyson, S. L., Dovidio, J. F., & Brown, C. E. (1991). The look of power: Gender differences and similarities in visual dominance behavior. In C. Ridgeway (ed.), *Gender and interaction: The role of microstructures in inequality*. New York: Springer-Verlag.

Elms, A. C. (1995). Obedience in retrospect. *Journal of Social Issues*, **51**, 21–31.

Elms, A. C., & Baumrind, D. (2007). Issue 1: Is deception of human participants ethical? In J. A. Nier (ed.), *Taking sides: Clashing views in social psychology*, 2nd edn. New York: McGraw-Hill.

Emswiller, T., Deaux, K., & Willits, J. E. (1971). Similarity, sex, and requests for small favors. *Journal of Applied Social Psychology*, **1**, 284–291.

Engell, A.D., Haxby, J.V. & Todorov, A. (2007). Implicit trustworthiness decisions: Automatic coding of face properties in the human amygdala. *Journal of Cognitive Neuroscience*, **19**, 1508–1519.

Engemann, K. M., & Owyang, M. T. (2003, April). So much for that merit raise: The link between wages and appearance. *The Regional Economist* (www.stlouisfed.org).

English, D. J., Newton, R. R., Lewis, T. L., Thompson, R., Kotch, J. B., & Weisbart, C. (2009). At-risk and maltreated children exposed to intimate partner aggression/violence. *Child Maltreatment*, **14**(2), 157–171.

Ennis, B. J., & Verrilli, D. B., Jr (1989). Motion for leave to file brief amicus curiae and brief of Society for the Scientific Study of Religion, American Sociological Association, and others. US Supreme Court Case No. 88–1600, Holy Spirit Association for the Unification of World Christianity, et al., *v.* David Molko and Tracy Leal. On petition for write of certiorari to the Supreme Court of California. Washington, DC: Jenner & Block, 21 Dupont Circle NW.

Ennis, R., & Zanna, M. P. (1991). Hockey assault: Constitutive versus normative violations. Paper presented at the Canadian Psychological Association convention.

Epley, N., & Huff, C. (1998). Suspicion, affective response, and educational benefit as a result of deception in psychology research. *Personality and Social Psychology Bulletin*, **24**, 759–768.

Epley, N., Savitsky, K., & Kachelski, R. A. (1999, September/October). What every skeptic should know about subliminal persuasion. *Skeptical Inquirer*, pp. 40–45.

Epstein, S., & Feist, G. J. (1988). Relation between self and other-acceptance and its moderation by identification. *Journal of Personality and Social Psychology*, **54**, 309–315.

Erez, M., & Somech, A. (1996). Is group productivity loss the rule or the exception? Effects of cultural and groupbased motivation. *Academy of Management Journal*, **39**(6), 1513–1537.

Erickson, B., Holmes, J. G., Frey, R., Walker, L., & Thibaut, J. (1974). Functions of a third party in the resolution of conflict: The role of a judge in pretrial conferences. *Journal of Personality and Social Psychology*, **30**, 296–306.

Erickson, B., Lind, E. A., Johnson, B. C., & O'Barr, W. M. (1978). Speech style and impression formation in a court setting: The effects of powerful and powerless speech. *Journal of Experimental Social Psychology*, **14**, 266–279.

Erikson, E. H. (1963). *Childhood and society*. New York: Norton.

Eron, L. D. (1987). The development of aggressive behavior from the perspective of a developing behaviorism. *American Psychologist*, **42**, 425–442.

Eron, L. D., & Huesmann, L. R. (1980). Adolescent aggression and television. *Annals of the New York Academy of Sciences*, **347**, 319–331.

Eron, L. D., & Huesmann, L. R. (1984). The control of aggressive behavior by changes in attitudes, values, and the conditions of learning. In R. J. Blanchard & C. Blanchard (eds), *Advances in the study of aggression*, Vol. 1. Orlando, FL: Academic Press.

Eron, L. D., & Huesmann, L. R. (1985). The role of television in the development of prosocial and antisocial behavior. In D. Olweus, M. Radke-Yarrow & J. Block (eds), *Development of antisocial and prosocial behavior*. Orlando, FL: Academic Press.

Escobar-Chaves, S. L., Tortolero, S. R., Markham, C. M., Low, B. J., Eitel, P., & Thickstun, P. (2005). Impact of the media on adolescent sexual attitudes and behaviors. *Pediatrics*, **116**, 303–326.

Esser, J. K. (1998, February–March). Alive and well after 25 years. A review of groupthink research. *Organizational Behavior and Human Decision Processes*, **73**, 116–141.

Esses, V. M., Haddock, G., & Zanna, M. P. (1993). Values, stereotypes, and emotions as determinants of intergroup attitudes. In D. Mackie & D. Hamilton (eds), *Affect,* cognition and stereotyping: Interactive processes in intergroup perception. San Diego, CA: Academic Press.

**Etaugh, C. E., Bridges, J. S., Cummings-Hill, M., & Cohen, J.** (1999). 'Names can never hurt me': The effects of surname use on perceptions of married women. *Psychology of Women Quarterly*, **23**, 819–823.

**Etzioni, A.** (2005). *The diversity within unity platform*. Washington, DC: The Communitarian Network.

**Eurostat** (2012). *European Commission: Your key to European statistics*. Available at: http://epp.eurostat.ec.europa.eu/portal/page/portal/publications/regional_yearbook

**Every, D., & Augoustinos, M.** (2008). Constructions of Australia in pro- and anti-asylum seeker political discourse. *Nations and Nationalism*, **14**(3), 562–580.

**Ewert, A., Place, G., & Sibthorp, J.** (2005). Early-life outdoor experiences and an individual's environmental attitudes. *Leisure Sciences*, **27**, 225–239.

**Exline, J. J., & Lobel, M.** (1999). The perils of outperformance: Sensitivity about being the target of a threatening upward comparison. *Psychological Bulletin*, **125**, 307–337.

**F**

**Factor, R., Kawachi, I., and Williams, D. R.** (2011). Understanding high-risk behavior among non-dominant minorities: A social resistance framework. *Social Science & Medicine*, **73**, 1292–1301.

**Falomir-Pichastor, J. M., Toscani, L., & Huyghues Despointes, S.** (2009). Determinants of flu vaccination among nurses: The effects of group identification and professional responsibility. *Applied Psychology*, **58**, 42–58.

**Fanelli, D.** (2011). Negative results are disappearing from most disciplines and countries. *Scientometrics*, **90**, 891–904.

**Farquhar, J. W., Maccoby, N., Wood, P. D., Alexander, J. K., Breitrose, H., Brown, B. W., Jr, Haskell, W. L., McAlister, A. L.,**

**Meyer, A. J., Nash, J. D., & Stern, M. P.** (1977, 4 June). Community education for cardiovascular health. *Lancet*, **309**(8023), 1192–1195.

**Farr, R. M.** (1996). *The roots of modern social psychology*. Oxford: Blackwell.

**Farwell, L., & Weiner, B.** (2000). Bleeding hearts and the heartless: Popular perceptions of liberal and conservative ideologies. *Personality and Social Psychology Bulletin*, **26**, 845–852.

**Faulkner, S. L., & Williams, K. D.** (1996). A study of social loafing in industry. Paper presented to the Midwestern Psychological Association convention.

**Fazio, R.** (1987). Self-perception theory: A current perspective. In M. P. Zanna, J. M. Olson & C. P. Herman (eds), *Social influence: The Ontario symposium*, Vol. 5. Hillsdale, NJ: Erlbaum.

**Fazio, R. H., Jackson, J. R., Dunton, B. C., & Williams, C. J.** (1995). Variability in automatic activation as an unobtrusive measure of racial attitudes: A bona fide pipeline? *Journal of Personality and Social Psychology*, **69**, 1013–1027.

**Fazio, R. H., & Olson, M. A.** (2003). Implicit measures in social cognition research: Their meaning and use. *Annual Review of Psychology*, **54**(1), 297–327.

**Fazio, R. H., Zanna, M. P., & Cooper, J.** (1977). Dissonance versus self-perception: An integrative view of each theory's proper domain of application. *Journal of Experimental Social Psychology*, **13**, 464–479.

**Fazio, R. H., Zanna, M. P., & Cooper, J.** (1979). On the relationship of data to theory: A reply to Ronis and Greenwald. *Journal of Experimental Social Psychology*, **15**, 70–76.

**FBI** (2005). *Hate Crime Statistics, 2004* (www.fbi.gov/ucr/hc2004/section1/htm).

**Feeney, B. C., & Thrush, R. L.** (2010). Relationship in uences on exploration in adulthood: The characteristics and function of a secure base. *Journal of Personality and Social Psychology*, **98**, 57–76.

**Feeney, B. C., & Van Vleet M.** (2010). Growing through

attachment: The interplay of attachment and exploration in adulthood. *Journal of Personal and Social Relationships*, **27**(2), 226–234.

**Feeney, J. A.** (1996). Attachment, caregiving, and marital satisfaction. *Personal Relationships*, **3**, 401–416.

**Feeney, J. A., & Noller, P.** (1990). Attachment style as a predictor of adult romantic relationships. *Journal of Personality and Social Psychology*, **58**, 281–291.

**Feeney, J., Peterson, C., & Noller, P.** (1994). Equity and marital satisfaction over the family life cycle. *Personality Relationships*, **1**, 83–99.

**Feingold, A.** (1988). Matching for attractiveness in romantic partners and same-sex friends: A meta-analysis and theoretical critique. *Psychological Bulletin*, **104**, 226–235.

**Feingold, A.** (1990). Gender differences in effects of physical attractiveness on romantic attraction: A comparison across five research paradigms. *Journal of Personality and Social Psychology*, **59**, 981–993.

**Feingold, A.** (1992a). Gender differences in mate selection preferences: A test of the parental investment model. *Psychological Bulletin*, **112**, 125–139.

**Feingold, A.** (1992b). Good-looking people are not what we think. *Psychological Bulletin*, **111**, 304–341.

**Feldman, R. S., & Prohaska, T.** (1979). The student as Pygmalion: Effect of student expectation on the teacher. *Journal of Educational Psychology*, **71**, 485–493.

**Feldman, R. S., & Theiss, A. J.** (1982). The teacher and student as Pygmalions: Joint effects of teacher and student expectations. *Journal of Educational Psychology*, **74**, 217–223.

**Felmlee, D., Sweet, E., & Sinclair, H. C.** (2012). Gender rules: Same- and cross-gender friendships norms. *Sex Roles*, **66**(7-8), 518–529.

**Felson, R. B.** (1984). The effect of self-appraisals of ability on academic performance. *Journal of Personality and Social Psychology*, **47**, 944–952.

**Felton, B. J., Lehmann, S., Brown, P., & Liberatos, P.**

(1980). The coping function of sex-role attitudes during marital disruption. *Journal of Health and Social Behavior*, **21**(3), 240–248.

**Fenigstein, A., & Carver, C. S.** (1978). Self-focusing effects of heartbeat feedback. *Journal of Personality and Social Psychology*, **36**, 1241–1250.

**Fern, E. F., Monroe, K. B., & Avila, R. A.** (1986). Effectiveness of multiple request strategies: A synthesis of research results. *Journal of Marketing Research*, **23**, 144–152.

**Feshbach, N. D.** (1980). The child as 'psychologist' and 'economist': Two curricula. Paper presented at the American Psychological Association convention.

**Feshbach, S., & Singer, R. D.** (1971). *Television and aggression: An experimental field study*. San Francisco, CA: Jossey-Bass.

**Festinger, L.** (1950). Informal social communication. *Psychological Review*, **57**, 271–282.

**Festinger, L.** (1954). A theory of social comparison processes. *Human Relations*, **7**, 117–140.

**Festinger, L.** (1957). *A theory of cognitive dissonance*. Stanford, CA: Stanford University Press.

**Festinger, L.** (1964). *Conflict, decision, and dissonance*. Stanford, CA: Stanford University Press.

**Festinger, L., & Carlsmith, J. M.** (1959). Cognitive consequences of forced compliance. *Journal of Abnormal and Social Psychology*, **58**, 203–210.

**Festinger, L., & Maccoby, N.** (1964). On resistance to persuasive communications. *Journal of Abnormal and Social Psychology*, **68**, 359–366.

**Festinger, L., Pepitone, A., & Newcomb, T.** (1952). Some consequences of deindividuation in a group. *Journal of Abnormal and Social Psychology*, **47**, 382–389.

**Feynman, R.** (1967). *The character of physical law*. Cambridge, MA: MIT Press.

**Fiedler, F.** (1967). *A theory of leadership effectiveness*. New York: McGraw-Hill.

**Fiedler, F. E.** (1987, September). When to lead, when to

stand back. *Psychology Today*, 21(9), 26–27.

Fieldler, K., Schenck, W., Watling, M., & Menges, J. (2005). Priming trait inferences through pictures and moving pictures: The impact of open and closed mindsets. *Journal of Personality and Social Psychology*, 88, 229–244.

Figgou, L., & Condor, S. (2006). Irrational categorization, natural intolerance and reasonable discrimination: Lay representations of prejudice and racism. *British Journal of Social Psychology*, 45, 219–243.

Fincham, F. D., Jackson, H., & Beach, S. R. (2005). Transgression severity and forgiveness: Different moderators for objective and subjective severity. *Journal of Social and Clinical Psychology*, 24(6), 860–875.

Findley, M. J., & Cooper, H. M. (1983). Locus of control and academic achievement: A literature review. *Journal of Personality and Social Psychology*, 44, 419–427.

Fine, C. (2010). From scanner to sound bite: Issues in interpreting and reporting sex differences in the brain. *Current Directions in Psychological Science*, 19(5), 280–283.

Finkel, E. J., & Campbell, W. K. (2001). Self-control and accommodation in close relationships: An interdependence analysis. *Journal of Personality and Social Psychology*, 81, 263–277.

Finkel, E. J., Eastwick, P. W., Karney, B. R., Reis, H. T., & Sprecher, S. (2012). Online dating: A critical analysis from the perspective of psychological science. *Psychological Science in the Public Interest*, 13(1), 3–66.

Finney, P. (1978). Personality traits attributed to risky and conservative decision makers: Culture values more than risk. *Journal of Psychology: Interdisciplinary and Applied*, 99(2), 187–197.

Fischer, P., Greitemeyer, T., Omay, S. I., & Frey, D. (2007). Mergers and group status: the impact of high, low and equal group status on identification and satisfaction with a company merger, experienced controllability, group identity and group cohesion. *Journal of Community and Applied Social Psychology*, 17(3), 203–217.

Fischer, P., Krueger, J. I., Greitemeyer, T., Vogrincic, C., Kästenmüller, A., Frey, D., Heene, M., Wicher, M., & Kainbacher, M. (2011). The bystander effect: A meta-analytic review on bystander intervention in dangerous and non-dangerous emergencies. *Psychological Bulletin*, 137(4), 517–537.

Fischhoff, B. (1982). Debiasing. In D. Kahneman, P. Slovic & A. Tversky (eds), *Judgment under uncertainty: Heuristics and biases*. New York: Cambridge University Press.

Fischhoff, B., & Bar-Hillel, M. (1984). Diagnosticity and the base rate effect. *Memory and Cognition*, 12, 402–410.

Fisek, M. H., & Hysom, S. J. (2008). Status characteristics and reward expectations: A test of a theory of justice in two cultures. *Social Science Research*, 37(3), 769–786.

Fishbein, D., & Thelen, M. H. (1981a). Husband–wife similarity and marital satisfaction: A different approach. Paper presented at the Midwestern Psychological Association convention.

Fishbein, D., & Thelen, M. H. (1981b). Psychological factors in mate selection and marital satisfaction: A review (Ms. 2374). *Catalog of Selected Documents in Psychology*, 11, 84.

Fishbein, M. (1979). A theory of reasoned action: Some applications and implications. *Nebraska Symposium on Motivation*, 27, 65–116.

Fishbein, M., & Ajzen, I. (1974). Attitudes toward objects as predictive of single and multiple behavioral criteria. *Psychological Review*, 81, 59–74.

Fisher, H. (1994, April). The nature of romantic love. *Journal of NIH Research*, 6(4), 59–64.

Fisher, H. (2004). Dumped! *New Scientist*, 181, 2434–2441.

Fiske, A. P., Kitayama, S., Markus, H. R., & Nisbett, R. E. (1998). The cultural matrix of social psychology. In D. Gilbert, S. Fiske & G. Lindzey (eds), *The handbook of social psychology*, 4th edn. Hillsdale, NJ: Erlbaum.

Fiske, S. T. (1989a). Interdependence and stereotyping: From the laboratory to the Supreme Court (and back). Invited address, American Psychological Association convention.

Fiske, S. T. (1989b). Examining the role of intent: Toward understanding its role in stereotyping and prejudice. In J. S. Uleman & J. A. Bargh (eds), *Unintended thought*. New York: Guilford Press.

Fiske, S. T. (1998). Stereotypes, prejudice, and discrimination, In D. T. Gilbert, S. T. Fiske & G. Lindzey (eds), *Handbook of social psychology*, Vol. 2. New York: McGraw-Hill.

Fiske, S. T. (2004). *Social beings: A core motives approach to social psychology*. New York: Wiley.

Fiske, S. T., & Taylor, S. E. (1991). *Social cognition*, 2nd edn. London: McGraw-Hill.

Fiske, S. T., & Taylor, S. E. (2007). *Social cognition: From brains to culture*. London: McGraw-Hill.

Fiske, S. T., Harris, L. T., & Cuddy, A. J. C. (2004). Why ordinary people torture enemy prisoners. *Science*, 306, 1482–1483.

Fitzpatrick, A. R., & Eagly, A. H. (1981). Anticipatory belief polarization as a function of the expertise of a discussion partner. *Personality and Social Psychology Bulletin*, 1, 636–642.

Fletcher, A. C., Steinberg, L., & Williams-Wheeler, M. (2004a). Parental influences on adolescent problem behaviour: Revisiting Stattin and Kerr. *Child Development*, 75(3), 781–796.

Fletcher, G. J. O., & Ward, C. (1989). Attribution theory and processes: A cross-cultural perspective. In M. H. Bond (ed.), *The cross-cultural challenge to social psychology*. Newbury Park, CA: Sage.

Fletcher, G. J. O., Fincham, F. D., Cramer, L., & Heron, N. (1987). The role of attributions in the development of dating relationships. *Journal of Personality and Social Psychology*, 53, 481–489.

Fletcher, G. J. O., Simpson, J. A., Thomas, G., & Giles, L. (1999). Ideals in intimate relationships. *Journal of Personality and Social Psychology*, 76, 72–89.

Fletcher, G. J. O., Tither, J. M., O'Loughlin, C., Friesen, M., & Overall, N. (2004b). Warm and homely or cold and beautiful? Sex differences in trading off traits in mate selection. *Personality and Social Psychology Bulletin*, 30, 659–672.

Foa, U. G., & Foa, E. B. (1975). *Resource theory of social exchange*. Morristown, NJ: General Learning Press.

Foley, L. A. (1976). Personality and situational influences on changes in prejudice: A replication of Cook's railroad game in a prison setting. *Journal of Personality and Social Psychology*, 34, 846–856.

Fontaine, N., Carbonneau, R., Barker, E. D., Vitaro, F., Hébert, M., Côté, S. M., Nagin, D. S., Zoccolillo, M., & Tremblay, R. E. (2008). Girls' hyperactivity and physical aggression during childhood and adjustment problems in early adulthood. *Archives of General Psychiatry*, 65(3), 320–328.

Ford, T. E., & Stangor, C. (1992). The role of diagnosticity in stereotype formation: Perceiving group means and variances. *Journal of Personality and Social Psychology*, 63(3), 356.

Forgas, J. P. (1999). Behind the scenes. In D. G. Myers, *Social psychology*, 6th edn. New York: McGraw-Hill.

Forgas, J. P., & Moylan, S. (1987). After the movies: Transient mood and social judgments. *Personality and Social Psychology Bulletin*, 13, 467–477.

Forgas, J. P., Bower, G. H., & Krantz, S. E. (1984). The influence of mood on perceptions of social interactions. *Journal of Experimental Social Psychology*, 20, 497–513.

Forster, E. M. (1976). *Aspects of the novel* (Ed. O. Stallybrass). Harmondsworth: Penguin. (Original work published 1927.)

Forsyth, D. R. (2009). *Group dynamics*. Florence, KY: Wadsworth.

Foss, R. D. (1978). The role of social influence in blood donation. Paper presented at the American Psychological Association convention.

Foster, C. A., Witcher, B. S., Campbell, W. K., & Green, J. D. (1998). Arousal and attraction: Evidence for automatic and controlled processes. *Journal of Personality and Social Psychology, 74,* 86–101.

Frank, J. D. (1974). *Persuasion and healing: A comparative study of psychotherapy.* New York: Schocken.

Frank, J. D. (1982). Therapeutic components shared by all psychotherapies. In J. H. Harvey & M. M. Parks (eds), *The master lecture series: Vol. 1. Psychotherapy research and behavior change.* Washington, DC: American Psychological Association.

Frank, M. G., & Gilovich, T. (1989). Effect of memory perspective on retrospective causal attributions. *Journal of Personality and Social Psychology, 57,* 399–403.

Frank, R. (1999). *Luxury fever: Why money fails to satisfy in an era of excess.* New York: The Free Press.

Frankel, A., & Snyder, M. L. (1987). Egotism among the depressed: When self-protection becomes self-handicapping. Paper presented at the American Psychological Association convention.

Fraser, A. M., Padilla-Walker, L. M., Coyne, S. M., Nelson, L. J., & Stockdale, L. A. (2012). Associations between violent video gaming, empathic concern, and prosocial behavior toward strangers, friends, and family members. *Journal of Youth and Adolescence, 41*(5), 636–649.

Freedman, J. L., & Sears, D. O. (1965). Warning, distraction, and resistance to influence. *Journal of Personality and Social Psychology, 1,* 262–266.

Freedman, J. S. (1965). Long-term behavioral effects of cognitive dissonance. *Journal of Experimental Social Psychology, 1,* 145–155.

Freeman, M. A. (1997). Demographic correlates of individualism and collectivism: A study of social values in Sri Lanka. *Journal of Cross-Cultural Psychology, 28,* 321–341.

Friedman, H. S., Riggio, R. E., & Casella, D. F. (1988). Nonverbal skill, personal charisma, and initial attraction. *Personality and Social Psychology Bulletin, 14,* 203–211.

Friedman, T. L. (2003a, 9 April). Hold your applause. *New York Times* (www. nytimes. com).

Friedman, T. L. (2003b, 4 June). Because we could. *New York Times* (www. nytimes. com).

Frieze, I. H., Olson, J. E., & Russell, J. (1991). Attractiveness and income for men and women in management. *Journal of Applied Social Psychology, 21,* 1039–1057.

Froming, W. J., Walker, G. R., & Lopyan, K. J. (1982). Public and private self-awareness: When personal attitudes conflict with societal expectations. *Journal of Experimental Social Psychology, 18,* 476–487.

Fromm, E. (1973). *The anatomy of human destructiveness.* New York: Fawcett Crest Books.

Fujisawa, K. K., Kutsukake, N., & Hasegawa, T. (2008). Reciprocity of prosocial behavior in Japanese preschool children. *International Journal of Behavioral Development, 32*(2), 89–97.

Fuller, S. R., & Aldag, R. J. (1998). Organizational Tonypandy: Lessons from a quarter century of the groupthink phenomenon. *Organizational Behavior and Human Decision Processes, 73,* 163–185.

Fultz, J., Batson, C. D., Fortenbach, V. A., McCarthy, P. M., & Varney, L. L. (1986). Social evaluation and the empathy–altruism hypothesis. *Journal of Personality and Social Psychology, 50,* 761–769.

Furnham, A. (1982). Explanations for unemployment in Britain. *European Journal of Social Psychology, 12,* 335–352.

Furnham, A. (2003). Belief in a just world: Research progress over the past decade. *Personality and Individual Differences, 34,* 795–817.

**G**

Gabrenya, W. K., Jr, Wang, Y.-E., & Latané, B. (1985). Social loafing on an optimizing task: Cross-cultural differences among Chinese and Americans. *Journal of Cross-Cultural Psychology, 16,* 223–242.

Gabriel, S., & Gardner, W. L. (1999). Are there 'his' and 'hers' types of interdependence? The implications of gender differences in collective versus relational interdependence for affect, behavior, and cognition. *Journal of Personality and Social Psychology, 77,* 642–655.

Gaertner, L., Sedikides, C., & Graetz, K. (1999). In search of self-definition: Motivational primacy of the individual self-, motivational primacy of the collective self-, or contextual primacy? *Journal of Personality and Social Psychology, 76,* 5–18.

Gaertner, S. L., & Dovidio, J. F. (2000). *Reducing intergroup bias: The common ingroup identity model.* Philadelphia, PA: Psychology Press.

Gaertner, S. L., & Dovidio, J. F. (2005). Understanding and addressing contemporary racism: From aversive racism to the Common Ingroup Identity Model. *Journal of Social Issues, 61,* 615–639.

Gaertner, S. L., & McLaughlin, J. P. (1983). Racial stereotypes: Associations and ascriptions of positive and negative characteristics. *Social Psychology Quarterly, 46,* 23–40.

Gaertner, S. L., Dovidio, J. F., Anastasio, P. A., Bachman, B. A., & Rust, M. C. (1993). The Common Ingroup Identity Model: Recategorization and the reduction of intergroup bias. In W. Stroebe & M. Hewstone (eds), *European Review of Social Psychology,* Vol. 4. London: Wiley.

Gaertner, S. L., Dovidio, J. F., Nier, J. A., Banker, B. S., Ward, C. M., Houlette, M., & Loux, S. (2000). The common ingroup identity model for reducing intergroup bias: Progress and challenges. In D. Capozza & R. Brown (eds), *Social identity processes: Trends in theory and research.* London: Sage.

Gaertner, S. L., Mann, J., Murrell, A., & Dovidio, J. F. (2001). Reducing intergroup bias: The benefits of recategorization. In M. A. Hogg & D. Abrams (eds), *Intergroup relations: Essential readings.* Philadelphia, PA: Psychology Press.

Gailliot, M. T. (2008). Unlocking the energy dynamics of executive function: Linking executive functioning to brain glycogen. *Perspectives in Psychological Science, 3,* 245–263.

Gailliot, M. T., & Baumeister, R. F. (2007). Self-regulation and sexual restraint. Dispositionally and temporarily poor self-regulation abilities contribute to failures at restraining sexual behaviour. *Personality and Social Psychology Bulletin, 33,* 173–186.

Galak, J., LeBoeuf, R. L., Nelson, L. D., & Simmons, J. P. (2012). Correcting the past: Failures to replicate Psi. *Journal of Personality and Social Psychology, 103,* 933–948.

Galanter, M. (1989). *Cults: Faith, healing, and coercion.* New York: Oxford University Press.

Galanter, M. (1990). Cults and zealous self-help movements: A psychiatric perspective. *American Journal of Psychiatry, 147,* 543–551.

Galizio, M., & Hendrick, C. (1972). Effect of musical accompaniment on attitude: The guitar as a prop for persuasion. *Journal of Applied Social Psychology, 2,* 350–359.

Gallucci, M. (2002). I sell seashells by the seashore and my name is Jack: Comment on Pelham, Mirenberg, and Jones (2002). *Journal of Personality and Social Psychology, 85*(5), 789–799.

Gallup (2005). The gender gap (Iraq war survey, 29 April to 1 May; death penalty survey 2 May to 5 May). The Gallup Organization (www.gallup. com).

Gallup Organization (1990). 19–22 April survey reported in *American Enterprise,* September/October, p. 92.

Gallup Poll Global Study of Family Values (1997). Family values differ sharply around the world. Princeton, NJ, 7 November (http://www. hi-ho.ne.jp/taku77/refer/valu-poll.htm).

Gallupe, R. B., Cooper, W. H., Grise, M. L., & Bastianutti, L. M. (1994). Blocking electronic brainstorms. *Journal of Applied Psychology*, **79**, 77–86.

Gangestad, S. W., & Snyder, M. (2000). Self-monitoring: Appraisal and reappraisal. *Psychological Bulletin*, **126**, 530–555.

Gangestad, S. W., Simpson, J. A., & Cousins, A. J. (2004). Women's preferences for male behavioral displays change across the menstrual cycle. *Psychological Science*, **15**, 203–207.

Garcia-Marques, T., Mackie, D. M., Claypool, H. M., & Garcia-Marques, L. (2004). Positivity can cue familiarity. *Personality and Social Psychology Bulletin*, **30**, 585–593.

Gardner, M. (1997, July/August). Heaven's gate: The UFO cult of Bo and Peep. *Skeptical Inquirer*, 15–17.

Garner, D. M, Garfinkel, P. E., Schwartz, D., & Thompson, M. (1980). Cultural expectations of thinness in women. *Psychological Reports*, **47**, 183–191.

Garry, M., Manning, C. G., Loftus, E. F., & Sherman, S. J. (1996). Imagination inflation: Imagining a childhood event inflates confidence that it occurred. *Psychonomic Bulletin & Review*, **3**, 208–214.

Gastorf, J. W., Suls, J., & Sanders, G. S. (1980). Type A coronary-prone behavior pattern and social facilitation. *Journal of Personality and Social Psychology*, **8**, 773–780.

Gates, M. F., & Allee, W. C. (1933). Conditioned behavior of isolated and grouped cockroaches on a simple maze. *Journal of Comparative Psychology*, **15**, 331–358.

Gaucher, D., Friesen, J., & Kay, A. C. (2011). Evidence that gendered wording in job advertisements exists and sustains gender inequality. *Journal of Personality and Social Psychology*, **101**(1), 109–128.

Gavanski, I., & Hoffman, C. (1987). Awareness of influences on one's own judgments: The roles of covariation detection and attention to the judgment process. *Journal of Personality and Social Psychology*, **52**, 453–463.

Gawronski, B., Deutsch, R., Mbirkou, S., Seibt, B., & Strack, F. (2008). When 'just say no' is not enough: Affirmation versus negation training and the reduction of automatic stereotype activation. *Journal of Experimental Social Psychology*, **44**, 370–377.

Gazzaniga, M. S. (1985). *The social brain: Discovering the networks of the mind*. New York: Basic Books.

Geen, R. G., & Gange, J. J. (1983). Social facilitation: Drive theory and beyond. In H. H. Blumberg, A. P. Hare, V. Kent & M. Davies (eds), *Small groups and social interaction*, Vol. 1. London: Wiley.

Geen, R. G., & Quanty, M. B. (1977). The catharsis of aggression: An evaluation of a hypothesis. In L. Berkowitz (ed.), *Advances in experimental social psychology* (Vol. 10). New York: Academic Press.

Geen, R. G., & Thomas, S. L. (1986). The immediate effects of media violence on behavior. *Journal of Social Issues*, **42**(3), 7–28.

Geniole, S. N., Carré, J. M., & McCormick, C. M. (2011). State, not trait, neuroendocrine function predicts costly reactive aggression in men after social exclusion and inclusion. *Biological Psychology*, **87**(1), 137–145.

Gentile, D. A. (2004, 14 May). Quoted by K. Laurie in Violent games, *ScienCentral. com*.

Gentile, D. A., & Anderson, C. A. (2003). Violent video games: The newest media violence hazard. In D. A. Gentile (ed.), *Media violence and children*. Westport, CT: Ablex.

Gentile, D. A., Lynch, P. J., Linder, J. R., & Walsh, D. A. (2004). The effects of violent video game habits on adolescent hostility, aggressive behaviors, and school performance. *Journal of Adolescence*, **27**, 5–22.

Gerard, H. B. (1999). A social psychologist examines his past and looks to the future. In A. Rodrigues & R. Levine (eds), *Reflections on 100 years of experimental social psychology*. New York: Basic Books.

Gerard, H. B., & Mathewson, G. C. (1966). The effects of severity of initiation on liking for a group: A replication. *Journal of Experimental Social Psychology*, **2**, 278–287.

Gerard, H. B., Wilhelmy, R. A., & Conolley, E. S. (1968). Conformity and group size. *Journal of Personality and Social Psychology*, **8**, 79–82.

Gerbner, G. (1994). The politics of media violence: Some reflections. In C. Hamelink & O. Linne (eds), *Mass communication research: On problems and policies*. Norwood, NJ: Ablex.

Gerbner, G., Gross, L., Signorielli, N., Morgan, M., & Jackson-Beeck, M. (1979). The demonstration of power: Violence profile No. 10. *Journal of Communication*, **29**, 177–196.

Gergen, K. J. (1973). Social psychology as history. *Journal of Personality and Social Psychology*, **26**, 309–320.

Gergen, K. J. (1991). *The saturated self*. New York: Basic Books.

Gergen, K. J. (1994). *Toward transformation in social knowledge*, 2nd edn. London: Sage.

Gergen, K. J. (1999). *An invitation to social construction*. London: Sage.

Gerrig, R. J., & Prentice, D. A. (1991, September). The representation of fictional information. *Psychological Science*, **2**, 336–340.

Gibbons, A. (2004). American Association of Physical Anthropologists meeting: Tracking the evolutionary history of a 'warrior' gene. *Science*, **304**, 818–819.

Gibbons, F. X. (1978). Sexual standards and reactions to pornography: Enhancing behavioral consistency through self-focused attention. *Journal of Personality and Social Psychology*, **36**, 976–987.

Gibbons, F. X., & Wicklund, R. A. (1982). Self-focused attention and helping behavior. *Journal of Personality and Social Psychology*, **43**, 462–474.

Gibney, M., Howard-Hassman, R. E., Coicard, J., & Steiner, N. (2008). The age of apology: Facing up to the past. *International Journal of Transactional Justice*, **2**, 429–430.

Gibson, B., & Sachau, D. (2000). Sandbagging as a self-presentational strategy: Claiming to be less than you are. *Personality and Social Psychology Bulletin*, **26**, 56–70.

Gibson, B., & Sanbonmatsu, D. M. (2004). Optimism, pessimism, and gambling: The downside of optimism. *Personality and Social Psychology Bulletin*, **30**, 149–160.

Gigerenzer, G., & Goldstein, D. G. (1996). Mind as computer: Birth of a metaphor. *Creativity Research Journal*, **9**(2&3), 131–144.

Gigerenzer, G., & Todd, P. M. (1999). *Simple heuristics that make us smart*. New York: Oxford.

Gigone, D., & Hastie, R. (1993). The common knowledge effect: Information sharing and group judgment. *Journal of Personality and Social Psychology*, **65**, 959–974.

Gilbert, D. T., & Ebert, J. E. J. (2002). Decisions and revisions: The affective forecasting of changeable outcomes. *Journal of Personality and Social Psychology*, **82**, 503–514.

Gilbert, D. T., & Jones, E. E. (1986). Perceiver-induced constraint: Interpretations of self-generated reality. *Journal of Personality and Social Psychology*, **50**, 269–280.

Gilbert, D. T., & Wilson, T. D. (2000). Miswanting: Some problems in the forecasting of future affective states. In J. Forgas (ed.), *Feeling and thinking: The role of affect in social cognition*. Cambridge: Cambridge University Press.

Gilbert, D. T., Giesler, R. B., & Morris, K. A. (1995). When comparisons arise. *Journal of Personality and Social Psychology*, **69**, 227–236.

Gilbert, D. T., Krull, D. S., & Malone, P. S. (1990). Unbelieving the unbelievable: Some problems in the rejection of false information. *Journal of Personality and Social Psychology*, **59**, 601–613.

Gilbert, D. T., Pinel, E. C., Wilson, T. D., Blumberg, S.

J., & Wheatley, T. P. (1998). Immune neglect: A source of durability bias in affective forecasting. *Journal of Personality and Social Psychology*, **75**, 617–638.

Gilbert, D. T., Tafarodi, R. W., & Malone, P. S. (1993). You can't not believe everything you read. *Journal of Personality and Social Psychology*, **65**, 221–233.

Gilbert, G. N., & Mulkay, M. (1984). *Opening Pandora's box: A sociological analysis of scientists discourse*. Cambridge: Cambridge University Press.

Giles, M., McClenahan, C., Cairns, E., & Mallet, J. (2004). An application of the theory of planned behaviour to blood donation: The importance of self-efficacy. *Health Education Research*, **19**(4), 380–391.

Gilligan, C. (1982). *In a different voice: Psychological theory and women's development*. Cambridge, MA: Harvard University Press.

Gilligan, C., Lyons, N. P., & Hanmer, T. J. (eds) (1990). *Making connections: The relational worlds of adolescent girls at Emma Willard School*. Cambridge, MA: Harvard University Press.

Gilovich, T., & Douglas, C. (1986). Biased evaluations of randomly determined gambling outcomes. *Journal of Experimental Social Psychology*, **22**, 228–241.

Gilovich, T., & Medvec, V. H. (1994). The temporal pattern to the experience of regret. *Journal of Personality and Social Psychology*, **67**, 357–365.

Gilovich, T., Kerr, M., & Medvec, V. H. (1993). Effect of temporal perspective on subjective confidence. *Journal of Personality and Social Psychology*, **64**, 552–560.

Gilovich, T., Medvec, V. H., & Savitsky, K. (2000). The spotlight effect in social judgment: An egocentric bias in estimates of the salience of one's own actions and appearance. *Journal of Personality and Social Psychology*, **78**, 211–222.

Gilovich, T., Savitsky, K., & Medvec, V. H. (1998). The illusion of transparency: Biased assessments of others' ability to read one's

emotional states. *Journal of Personality and Social Psychology*, **75**, 332–346.

Glaser, B. G., & Strauss, A. L. (1965). *Awareness of dying*. Chicago: Aldine.

Glaser, B. G., & Strauss, A. L. (1967). *The discovery of grounded theory: Strategies for qualitative research*. New York: Aldine.

Glasford, D. E., & Dovidio, J. F. (2011). *E Pluribus Unum*: Dual identity and minority group members' motivation to engage in contact, as well as social change. *Journal of Experimental Social Psychology*, **47**, 1021–1024.

Glasford, D. E., Pratto, F., & Dovidio, J. F. (2008). Intragroup dissonance: Responses to ingroup violation of personal values. *Journal of Experimental Social Psychology*, **44**, 1057–1064.

Glass, D. C. (1964). Changes in liking as a means of reducing cognitive discrepancies between self-esteem and aggression. *Journal of Personality*, **32**, 531–549.

Glass, R. I. (2004). Perceived threats and real killers. *Science*, **304**, 927.

Gleason, M. E. J., Iida, M., Bolger, N., & Shrout, P. E. (2003). Daily supportive equity in close relationships. *Personality and Social Psychology Bulletin*, **29**, 1036–1045.

Glick, P. & others (2004). Bad but bold: Ambivalent attitudes toward men predict gender inequality in 16 nations. *Journal of Personality and Social Psychology*, **86**, 713–728.

Glick, P., & Fiske, S. T. (1996). The ambivalent sexism inventory: Differentiating hostile and benevolent sexism. *Journal of Personality and Social Psychology*, **70**, 491–512.

Glick, P., & Fiske, S. T. (2001). An ambivalent alliance: Hostile and benevolent sexism as complementary justifications for gender inequality. *American Psychologist*, **56**, 109–118.

Glick, P., Fiske, S. T. & 29 others (2000). Beyond prejudice as simple antipathy: Hostile and benevolent sexism across cultures. *Journal of Personality and Social Psychology*, **79**, 763–775.

Gobodo-Madikizela, P. (2003). *A human being died that night: A South African story of forgiveness*. Boston, MA: Houghton Mifflin.

Goethals, G. R., & Nelson, E. R. (1973). Similarity in the influence process: The belief–value distinction. *Journal of Personality and Social Psychology*, **25**, 117–122.

Goethals, G. R., Messick, D. M., & Allison, S. T. (1991). The uniqueness bias: Studies of constructive social comparison. In J. Suls & T. A. Wills (eds), *Social comparison: Contemporary theory and research*. Hillsdale, NJ: Erlbaum.

Goffman, E. (1959). *The presentation of self in everyday life*. New York: Anchor Books.

Goh, J. O., Chee, M. W., Tan, J. C., Venkatraman, V., Hebrank, A., Leshikar, E.D., Jenkins, L., Sutton, B. P., Gutchess, A. H., & Park, D. (2007). Age and culture modulate object processing and object-science binding in the ventral visual area. *Cognitive, Affective and Behavioral Neuroscience*, **7**, 44–52.

Goldhagen, D. J. (1996). *Hitler's willing executioners*. New York: Knopf.

Goldman, W., & Lewis, P. (1977). Beautiful is good: Evidence that the physically attractive are more socially skillful. *Journal of Experimental Social Psychology*, **13**, 125–130.

Goldsmith, C. (2003, 25 March). World media turn wary eye on US. *Wall Street Journal*, p. A12.

Goldstein, A. P., Glick, B., & Gibbs, J. C. (1998). *Aggression replacement training: A comprehensive intervention for aggressive youth*, rev. edn. Champaign, IL: Research Press.

Goldstein, D. G., & Gigerenzer, G. (2002). Models of ecological rationality: The recognition heuristic. *Psychological Review*, **109**(1), 75–90.

Goldstein, J. H., & Arms, R. L. (1971). Effects of observing athletic contests on hostility. *Sociometry*, **34**, 83–90.

Gonzalez, A. Q., & Koestner, R. (2005). Parental preference for sex of newborn as reflected in positive affect in

birth announcements. *Sex Roles*, **52**, 407–411.

Goodhart, D. E. (1986). The effects of positive and negative thinking on performance in an achievement situation. *Journal of Personality and Social Psychology*, **51**, 117–124.

Gopnik, A., Meltzoff, A., & Kuhl, P. (1999). *The scientist in the crib: Minds, brains, and how children learn*. New York: William Morrow.

Gordon, R. A. (1996). Impact of ingratiation on judgments and evaluations: A meta-analytic investigation. *Journal of Personality and Social Psychology*, **71**, 54–70.

Gortmaker, S. L., Must, A., Perrin, J. M., Sobol, A. M., & Dietz, W. H. (1993). Social and economic consequences of overweight in adolescence and young adulthood. *New England Journal of Medicine*, **329**, 1008–1012.

Gotlib, I. H., & Colby, C. A. (1988). How to have a good quarrel. In P. Marsh (ed.), *Eye to eye: How people interact*. Topsfield, MA: Salem House.

Gottlieb, J., & Carver, C. S. (1980). Anticipation of future interaction and the bystander effect. *Journal of Experimental Social Psychology*, **16**, 253–260.

Gottman, J. (with N. Silver) (1994). *Why marriages succeed or fail*. New York: Simon & Schuster.

Gottman, J. M. (1998). Psychology and the study of marital processes. *Annual Review of Psychology*, **49**, 169–197.

Gough, B., McFadden, M., & McDonald, M. (2013). *Critical social psychology: An introduction*, 2nd edn. London: Palgrave Macmillan.

Gough, S. (2003, 3 November). My journey so far (www. nakedwalk.alivewww.co.uk/about_me.htm).

Gould, M. S., & Shaffer, D. (1986). The impact of suicide in television movies: Evidence of imitation. *New England Journal of Medicine*, **315**, 690–694.

Gould, R., Brounstein, P. J., & Sigall, H. (1977). Attributing ability to an opponent: Public aggrandizement and private denigration. *Sociometry*, **40**, 254–261.

Gould, S. J. (1997). Dolly's fashion and Louis's passion. *Natural History*, **106**, 18–76.

Gouldner, A. W. (1960). The norm of reciprocity: A preliminary statement. *American Sociological Review*, **25**, 161–178.

Granstrom, K., & Stiwne, D. (1998). A bipolar model of groupthink: An expansion of Janis's concept. *Small Group Research*, **29**, 32–56.

Grant, A., & Sonnentag, S. (2010). Doing good buffers against feeling bad: Prosocial impact compensates for negative task and self-evaluations. *Organizational Behavior and Human Decision Processes*, **111**(1), 13–22.

Gray, C., Russell, P., & Blockley, S. (1991). The effects upon helping behaviour of wearing pro-gay identification. *British Journal of Social Psychology*, **30**, 171–178.

Graziano, W. G., Jensen-Campbell, L., & Finch, J. F. (1997). The self as a mediator between personality and adjustment. *Journal of Personality and Social Psychology*, **73**, 392–404.

Green, A. (2007). To know it is to love it? A psychological discussion of the mere exposure and satiation effects in music listening. *Psyke & Logos*, **28**(1), 210–227.

Green, M. C., Strange, J. J., & Brock, T. C. (eds) (2002). *Narrative impact: Social and cognitive foundations.* Mahwah, NJ: Erlbaum.

Greenberg, J., Pyszczynski, T., Solomon, S., Rosenblatt, A., Veeder, M., Kirkland, S., & Lyon, D. (1990). Evidence for terror management theory II: The effects of mortality salience on reactions to those who threaten or bolster the cultural worldview. *Journal of Personality and Social Psychology*, **58**, 308–318.

Greenberg, J., Solomon, S., & Pyszczynski, T. (1997). Terror management theory of self-esteem and cultural worldviews: Empirical assessments and conceptual refinements. *Advances in Experimental Social Psychology*, **29**, 61–142.

Greenwald, A. G. (1975). On the inconclusiveness of crucial cognitive tests of dissonance versus self-perception theories. *Journal of Experimental Social Psychology*, **11**, 490–499.

Greenwald, A. G. (1980). The totalitarian ego: Fabrication and revision of personal history. *American Psychologist*, **35**, 603–618.

Greenwald, A. G., & Banaji, M. R. (1995). Implicit social cognition: Attitudes, self-esteem, and stereotypes. *Psychological Review*, **102**, 4–27.

Greenwald, A. G., & Schuh, E. S. (1994). An ethnic bias in scientific citations. *European Journal of Social Psychology*, **24**, 623–639.

Greenwald, A. G., Abrams, R. L., Naccache, L., & Dehaene, S. (2003a). Long-term semantic memory versus contextual memory in unconscious number processing. *Journal of Experimental Psychology*, **29**(2), 235–247.

Greenwald, A. G., Banaji, M. R., Rudman, L. A., Farnham, S. D., Nosek, B. A., & Rosier, M. (2000). Prologue to a unified theory of attitudes, stereotypes, and self-concept. In J. P. Forgas (ed.), *Feeling and thinking: The role of affect in social cognition and behavior*. New York: Cambridge University Press.

Greenwald, A. G., McGhee, D. E., & Schwartz, J. L. K. (1998). Measuring individual differences in implicit cognition: The implicit association test. *Journal of Personality and Social Psychology*, **74**, 1464–1480.

Greenwald, A. G., Nosek, B. A., & Banaji, M. R. (2003b). Understanding and using the implicit association test: I. An improved scoring algorithm. *Journal of Personality and Social Psychology*, **85**, 197–216.

Greenwald, A. G., Poehlman, T. A., Uhlmann, E. L., & Banaji, M. R. (2009). Understanding and using the implicit association test: III. Meta-analysis of predictive validity. *Journal of Personality and Social Psychology*, **97**(1), 17–41.

Greifeneder, R., Scheibehenne, B., & Kleber, N. (2010). Less may be more when choosing is difficult: Choice complexity and too much choice. *Acta Psychologica*, **133**, 45–50.

Grewal, R., Mehta, R., & Kardes, F. R. (2000). The role of the social-identity function of attitudes in consumer innovativeness and opinion leadership. *Journal of Economic Psychology*, **21**, 233–252.

Griffiths, B., & Pedersen, A. (2009). Prejudice and the function of attitudes relating to Muslim Australians and indigenous Australians. *Australian Journal of Psychology*, **61**(4), 228–238.

Griffiths, M. D. (1994). The role of cognitive bias and skill in fruit machine gambling. *British Journal of Psychology*, **85**, 351–369.

Griffiths, M. D. (1997). Video games and aggression. *The Psychologist*, **10**(9), 397–401.

Griffitt, W. (1970). Environmental effects on interpersonal affective behavior. Ambient effective temperature and attraction. *Journal of Personality and Social Psychology*, **15**, 240–244.

Griffitt, W., & Veitch, R. (1971). Hot and crowded: Influences of population density and temperature on interpersonal affective behavior. *Journal of Personality and Social Psychology*, **17**, 92–98.

Groenenboom, A., Wilke, H. A. M., & Wit, A. P. (2001). Will we be working together again? The impact of future interdependence on group members' task motivation. *European Journal of Social Psychology*, **31**, 369–378.

Gross, A. E., & Crofton, C. (1977). What is good is beautiful. *Sociometry*, **40**, 85–90.

Grote, N. K., & Clark, M. S. (2001). Perceiving unfairness in the family: Cause or consequence of marital distress? *Journal of Personality and Social Psychology*, **80**, 281–293.

Grove, J. R., Hanrahan, S. J., & McInman, A. (1991). Success/failure bias in attributions across involvement categories in sport. *Personality and Social Psychology Bulletin*, **17**, 93–97.

Gruder, C. L. (1977). Choice of comparison persons in evaluating oneself. In J. M. Suls & R. L. Miller (eds), *Social comparison processes*. Washington: Hemisphere Publishing.

Gruder, C. L., Cook, T. D., Hennigan, K. M., Flay, B., Alessis, C., & Kalamaj, J. (1978). Empirical tests of the absolute sleeper effect predicted from the discounting cue hypothesis. *Journal of Personality and Social Psychology*, **36**, 1061–1074.

Grush, J. E. (1980). Impact of candidate expenditures, regionality, and prior outcomes on the 1976 Democratic presidential primaries. *Journal of Personality and Social Psychology*, **38**, 337–347.

Guadagno, R.E., Okdie, B. M., Kruse, S. A. (2011). Dating deception: Gender, online dating, and exaggerated self-presention. *Computers in Human Behavior.* **28**(2), 642–647

Guéguen, N., Martin, A., & Meineri, S. (2011). Mimicry and helping behavior: an evaluation of mimicry on explicit helping request. *The Journal of Social Psychology*, **151**(1), 1–4.

Guerin, B. (1993). *Social facilitation*. Paris: Cambridge University Press.

Guerin, B. (1999). Social behaviors as determined by different arrangements of social consequences: Social loafing, social facilitation, deindividuation, and a modified social loafing. *The Psychological Record*, **49**, 565–578.

Guerin, B. (2003). Combating prejudice and racism: New interventions from a functional analysis of racist language. *Journal of Community and Applied Social Psychology*, **13**, 29–45.

Guerin, B., & Innes, J. M. (1982). Social facilitation and social monitoring: A new look at Zajonc's mere presence hypothesis. *British Journal of Social Psychology*, **21**, 7–18.

Guffey, J. E., Larson, J. G., Zimmerman, L., & Shook, B. (2007). The development of a Thurstone scale for identifying desirable police officer traits. *Journal of Police and Criminal Psychology*, **22**(1), 1–9.

Guiness, O. (1993). *The American hour: A time of reckoning and the once and future role of faith*. New York: Free Press.

**Gundersen, E.** (2001, 1 August). MTV is a many splintered thing. *USA Today*, p. 1D.

**Gupta, U., & Singh, P.** (1982). Exploratory study of love and liking and type of marriages. *Indian Journal of Applied Psychology*, **19**, 92–97.

**Gurung, R., & Vespia, K.** (2007). Looking good, teaching well? Linking liking, looks, and learning. *Teaching of Psychology*, **34**(1), 5–10.

**Gutsell, J. N., & Inzlicht, M.** (2010). Empathy constrained: Prejudice predicts reduced mental stimulation of actions during observation of outgroups. *Journal of Experimental Social Psychology*, **46**, 841–845.

**Gutsell, J. N., & Inzlicht, M.** (2012). Intergroup differences in the sharing of emotive states: neural evidence of an empathy gap. *Social Cognitive and Affective Neuroscience*, **7**(5), 596–603.

**Gutmann, D.** (1977). The cross-cultural perspective: Notes toward a comparative psychology of aging. In J. E. Birren & K. Warner Schaie (eds), *Handbook of the psychology of aging*. New York: Van Nostrand Reinhold.

**H**

**Ha, T., van den Berg, J. E. M., Engels, R. C. M. E., & Lichtwarck-Aschoff, A.** (2011). Effects of attractiveness and status in dating desire in homosexual and heterosexual men and women. *Archives of Sexual Behaviour*, **41**, 673–682.

**Hackman, J. R.** (1986). The design of work teams. In J. Lorsch (ed.), *Handbook of organizational behavior*. Englewood Cliffs, NJ: Prentice-Hall.

**Haddock, G., & Zanna, M. P.** (1994). Preferring 'housewives' to 'feminists'. *Psychology of Women Quarterly*, **18**, 25–52.

**Hafner, H., & Schmidtke, A.** (1989). Do televised fictional suicide models produce suicides? In D. R. Pfeffer (ed.), *Suicide among youth: Perspectives on risk and prevention*. Washington, DC: American Psychiatric Press.

**Haidt, J.** (2003). The moral emotions. In R. J. Davidson (ed.), *Handbook of affective sciences*. Oxford: Oxford University Press.

**Haidt, J.** (2006). *The happiness hypothesis: Finding modern truth in ancient wisdom*. New York: Basic Books.

**Hall, J. A.** (2011). Sex differences in friendship expectations: A meta-analysis. *Journal of Social and Personal Relationships*, **28**(6), 723–747.

**Hall, J. A., Coats, E. J., & LeBeau, L. S.** (2005). Nonverbal behavior and the vertical dimension of social relations: A meta-analysis. *Psychological Bulletin*, **131**, 898–924.

**Hall, J. A., Rosip, J. C., LeBeau, L. S., Horgan, T. G., & Carter, J. D.** (2006). Attributing the sources of accuracy in unequal-power dyadic communication: Who is better and why? *Journal of Experimental Social Psychology*, **42**, 18–27.

**Hall, J., Whalley, H. C., McKirdy, J. W., Sprengelmeyer, R., Santos, I. M., Donaldson, D. I., McGonigle, D. J., Young, A. W., McIntosh, A. M., Johnstone, E. C., & Lawrie, S. M.** (2010). A common neural system mediating two different forms of social judgment. *Psychological Medicine*, **40**, 1183–1192.

**Hall, T.** (1985, 25 June). The unconverted: Smoking of cigarettes seems to be becoming a lower-class habit. *Wall Street Journal*, pp. 1, 25.

**Hamberger, J., & Hewstone, M.** (1997). Inter-ethnic contact as a predictor of blatant and subtle prejudice: Tests of a model in four West European nations. *British Journal of Social Psychology*, **36**, 173–190.

**Hamblin, R. L., Buckholdt, D., Bushell, D., Ellis, D., & Feritor, D.** (1969). Changing the game from get the teacher to learn. *Transaction*, January, pp. 20–25, 28–31.

**Hamilton, D. L., & Sherman, S. J.** (1996). Perceiving persons and groups. *Psychological Review*, **103**, 336–355.

**Han, S., & Northoff, G.** (2008). Culture-sensitive neural substrates of human cognition: A transcultural neuroimaging approach. *Nature Reviews Neuroscience*, **9**, 646–654.

**Haney, C., Banks, C., & Zimbardo, P.** (1973). A study of prisoners and guards in a simulated prison. In E. Aronson (ed.), *Readings about the social animal*, 3rd edn. San Francisco, CA: Freeman.

**Hannon, P. A., Rusbult, C. E., Finkel, E. J., & Kasashiro, M.** (2010). In the wake of betrayal: Amends, forgiveness, and the resolution of betrayal. *Personal Relationships*, **17**, 253–278.

**Hansen, J. & Wänke, M.** (2009). Liking what's familiar: The importance of unconscious familiarity in the mereexposure effect. *Social Cognition*, **27**(2), 161–182.

**Harber, K. D.** (1998). Feedback to minorities: Evidence of a positive bias. *Journal of Personality and Social Psychology*, **74**, 622–628.

**Hardy, C., & Latané, B.** (1986). Social loafing on a cheering task. *Social Science*, **71**, 165–172.

**Haritos-Fatouros, M.** (1988). The official torturer: A learning model for obedience to the authority of violence. *Journal of Applied Social Psychology*, **18**, 1107–1120.

**Haritos-Fatouros, M.** (2002). *The Psychological Origins of the Institutionalized Torture*. London: Routledge.

**Harkins, S. G.** (1981). Effects of task difficulty and task responsibility on social loafing. Presentation to the First International Conference on Social Processes in Small Groups, Kill Devil Hills, North Carolina.

**Harkins, S. G., & Jackson, J. M.** (1985). The role of evaluation in eliminating social loafing. *Personality and Social Psychology Bulletin*, **11**, 457–465.

**Harkins, S. G., & Petty, R. E.** (1981). Effects of source magnification of cognitive effort on attitudes: An information-processing view. *Journal of Personality and Social Psychology*, **40**, 401–413.

**Harkins, S. G., & Petty, R. E.** (1982). Effects of task difficulty and task uniqueness on social loafing. *Journal of Personality and Social Psychology*, **43**, 1214–1229.

**Harkins, S. G., & Petty, R. E.** (1987). Information utility and the multiple source effect. *Journal of Personality and Social Psychology*, **52**, 260–268.

**Harkins, S. G., & Szymanski, K.** (1989). Social loafing and group evaluation. *Journal of Personality and Social Psychology*, **56**, 934–941.

**Harkins, S. G., Latané, B., & Williams, K.** (1980). Social loafing: Allocating effort or taking it easy? *Journal of Experimental Social Psychology*, **16**, 457–465.

**Harmon-Jones, E., & Allen, J. J. B.** (2001). The role of affect in the mere exposure effect: Evidence from psychophysiological and individual differences approaches. *Personality and Social Psychology Bulletin*, **27**, 889–898.

**Harris, J. R.** (1996). Quoted from an article by Jerome Burne for the *Manchester Observer* (via Harris: 72073.1211@CompuServe.com).

**Harris, J. R.** (1998). *The nurture assumption*. New York: Free Press.

**Harris, L. T., & Fiske, S. T.** (2006). Dehumanizing the lowest of the low: Neuroimaging responses to extreme outgroups. *Psychological Science*, **17**(10), 847–853.

**Harris, M. B.** (1974). Mediators between frustration and aggression in a field experiment. *Journal of Experimental Social Psychology*, **10**, 561–571.

**Harris, M. J., & Rosenthal, R.** (1985). Mediation of interpersonal expectancy effects: 31 meta-analyses. *Psychological Bulletin*, **97**, 363–386.

**Harris, M. J., & Rosenthal, R.** (1986). Four factors in the mediation of teacher expectancy effects. In R. S. Feldman (ed.), *The social psychology of education*. New York: Cambridge University Press.

**Harrison, A. A.** (1977). Mere exposure. In L. Berkowitz (ed.), *Advances in experimental social psychology*, Vol. 10. New York: Academic Press.

**Hart, A. J., & Morry, M. M.** (1997). Trait inferences based on racial and behavioral cues. *Basic and Applied Social Psychology*, **19**, 33–48.

Hart, P. (1998). Preventing groupthink revisited: Evaluating and reforming groups in government. *Organizational Behavior and Human Decision Processes*, **73**, 306–326.

Haslam, N., Loughnan, S., & Sun, P. (2011). Beastly: What makes animal metaphors offensive? *Journal of Language and Social Psychology*, **30**, 311–325. doi: 10.1177/0261927X 11407168

Haslam, S. A. (2004). *Psychology in organizations: The social identity approach*, 2nd edn. London: Sage.

Haslam, S. A., Jetten, J., & Waghorn, C. (2009). Social identification, stress and citizenship in teams: A five-phase longitudinal study. *Stress and Health*, **25**, 21–30.

Haslam, S. A., O'Brien, A., Jetten, J., Vormedal, K., & Penna, S. (2005). Taking the strain: Social identity, social support, and the experience of stress. *British Journal of Social Psychology*, **44**, 355–370.

Haslam, S. A., Reicher, S. D., & Platow, M. J. (2011). *The new psychology of leadership: Identity, influence and power*. Hove and New York: Psychology Press.

Haslam, S. A., Turner, J. C., Oakes, P. J., McGarty, C., & Hayes, B. K. (1992). Context-dependent variation in social stereotyping 1: The effects of intergroup relations as mediated by social change and frame of reference. *European Journal of Social Psychology*, **22**, 3–20.

Hass, R. G., Katz, I., Rizzo, N., Bailey, J., & Eisenstadt, D. (1991). Cross-racial appraisal as related to attitude ambivalence and cognitive complexity. *Personality and Social Psychology Bulletin*, **17**, 83–92.

Hastorf, A. H., & Cantril, H. (1954). They saw a game: A case study. *Journal of Abnormal and Social Psychology*, **49**, 129–134.

Hatfield, E. (1988). Passionate and compassionate love. In R. J. Sternberg & M. L. Barnes (eds), *The psychology of love*. New Haven, CT: Yale University Press.

Hatfield, E., & Rapson, R. L. (1987). Passionate love: New directions in research. In W. H. Jones & D. Perlman (eds),

*Advances in personal relationships*, Vol. 1. Greenwich, CT: JAI Press.

Hatfield, E., & Rapson, R. (2006). Passionate love, sexual desire, and mate selection: Cross-cultural and historical perspectives. In P. Noller & J. A. Feeney (eds), *Close relationships: Functions, forms and processes*. Hove: Psychology Press/Taylor & Francis.

Hatfield, E., & Sprecher, S. (1986). *Mirror, mirror: The importance of looks in everyday life*. Albany, NY: SUNY Press.

Hatfield, E., Rapson, R. L., & Martel, L. D. (2007). Passionate love and sexual desire. In S. Kitayama & D. Cohen (eds), *Handbook of cultural psychology*. New York: Guilford Press.

Hatfield, E., Traupmann, J., Sprecher, S., Utne, M., & Hay, J. (1985). Equity and intimate relations: Recent research. In W. Ickes (ed.), *Compatible and incompatible relationships*. New York: Springer-Verlag.

Hatfield (was Walster), E., Walster, G. W., & Berscheid, E. (1978). *Equity: Theory and research*. Boston: Allyn and Bacon.

Haugtvedt, C. P., & Wegener, D. T. (1994). Message order effects in persuasion: An attitude strength perspective. *Journal of Consumer Research*, **21**, 205–218.

Hauser, D. (2005, 30 June). Five years of abstinence-only-until-marriage education: Assessing the impact. *Advocates for Youth* (www.advocatesforyouth.org).

Hayes, S. C., Rincover, A., & Volosin, D. (1980). Variables influencing the acquisition and maintenance of aggressive behavior: Modeling versus sensory reinforcement. *Journal of Abnormal Psychology*, **89**(2), 254–262.

Hazan, C., Gur-Yaish, N., & Campa, M. (2004). What does it mean to be attached? In W. S. Rholes and J. A. Simpson (eds), *Adult attachment: Theory, research, and clinical implications*. New York: Guilford Press.

Hearold, S. (1986). A synthesis of 1043 effects of television on social behavior. In G.

Comstock (ed.), *Public communication and behavior*, Vol. 1. Orlando, FL: Academic Press.

Heatherton, T. F., & Vohs, K. D. (2000). Interpersonal evaluations following threats to self: Role of self-esteem. *Journal of Personality and Social Psychology*, **78**, 725–736.

Heatherton, T. F., Macrae, C. N., & Kelley, W. M. (2004). What the social brain sciences can tell us about the self. *Current Directions in Psychological Science*, **13**, 190–193.

Hebl, M. R., & Heatherton, T. F. (1998). The stigma of obesity in women: The difference is black and white. *Personality and Social Psychology Bulletin*, **24**, 417–426.

Hedge, A., & Yousif, Y. H. (1992). Effects of urban size, urgency, and cost on helpfulness: A cross-cultural comparison between the United Kingdom and the Sudan. *Journal of Cross-Cultural Psychology*, **23**, 107–115.

Hegarty, P., & Golden, A. M. (2008). Attributional beliefs about the controllability of stigmatized traits: Antecedents or justifications of prejudice? *Journal of Applied Social Psychology*, **38**(4), 1023–1044.

Heider, F. (1958). *The psychology of interpersonal relations*. New York: Wiley.

Heine, S. J. (2005). Constructing good selves in Japan and North America. In R. Sorrentino, D. Cohen, J. M. Olson & M. P. Zanna (eds), *Culture and social behavior: The Ontario symposium*, **10**, 95–116. Hillsdale, NJ: Erlbaum.

Heine, S. J., & Lehman, D. R. (1997). The cultural construction of self-enhancement: An examination of groupserving biases. *Journal of Personality and Social Psychology*, **72**, 1268–1283.

Heine, S. J., Kitayama, S., Lehman, D. R., Takata, T., Ide, E., Leung, C., & Matsumoto, H. (2001). Divergent consequences of success and failure in Japan and North America: An investigation of self-improving motivations and malleable selves. *Journal of*

*Personality and Social Psychology*, **81**, 599–615.

Heine, S. J., Lehman, D. R., Markus, H. R., & Kitayama, S. (1999). Is there a universal need for positive self-regard? *Psychological Review*, **106**, 766–794.

Heisenberg, W. (1958). *Physics and philosophy: The revolution in modern science*. New York: Prometheus.

Helweg-Larsen, M., Cunningham, S. J., Carrico, A., & Pergram, A. M. (2004). To nod or not to nod: An observational study of nonverbal communication and status in female and male college students. *Psychology of Women Quarterly*, **28**, 358–361.

Hemsley, G. D., & Doob, A. N. (1978). The effect of looking behavior on perceptions of a communicator's credibility. *Journal of Applied Social Psychology*, **8**, 136–144.

Hendrick, C., & Hendrick, S. S. (2009). Love. In S. J. Lopez & C. R. Snyder (eds), *Oxford handbook of positive psychology*, 2nd edn. New York: Oxford University Press.

Hendrick, S. S., & Hendrick, C. (1995). Gender differences and similarities in sex and love. *Personal Relationships*, **2**, 55–65.

Hendrick, S. S., & Hendrick, C. (2008). Satisfaction, love, and respect in the initiation of romantic relationships. In S. Sprecher, A. Wenzel & J. Harvey (eds), *Handbook of relationship initiation*. New York: Psychology Press.

Hendrick, S. S., Hendrick, C., & Adler, N. L. (1988). Romantic relationships: Love, satisfaction, and staying together. *Journal of Personality and Social Psychology*, **54**, 980–988.

Hennigan, K. M., Del Rosario, M. L., Health, L., Cook, T. D., Wharton, J. D., & Calder, B. J. (1982). Impact of the introduction of television on crime in the United States: Empirical findings and theoretical implications. *Journal of Personality and Social Psychology*, **42**, 461–477.

Henry, P. J., & Sears, D. O. (2002). The symbolic racism 2000 scale. *Political Psychology*, **23**, 253–283.

Hensley, W. E. (1977). Probability, personality, age, and risk taking. *The Journal of Psychology*, **95**(1), 139–145.

Henslin, M. (1967). Craps and magic. *American Journal of Sociology*, **73**, 316–330.

Hepach, R., Vaish, A., & Tomasello, M. (2012). Young children are intrinsically motivated to see others helped. *Psychological Science*, **23**(9), 967–972.

Herek, G. M. (1987). Can functions be measured? A new perspective on the functional approach to attitudes. *Social Psychology Quarterly*, 285–303.

Herek, G. M. (1993). Interpersonal contact and heterosexuals' attitudes toward gay men: Results from a national survey. *Journal of Sex Research*, **30**, 239–244.

Hermans, H. J. M. (2001). The dialogical self: Toward a theory of personal and cultural positioning. *Culture & Psychology*, **7**(3), 243–281.

Herzlich, C. (1973). *Health and illness: A social psychological analysis*. Oxford: Academic Press.

Hewstone, M. (2003). Intergroup contact: Panacea for prejudice? *The Psychologist*, **16**, 352–355.

Hewstone, M., & Fincham, F. (1996). Attribution theory and research: Basic issues and applications. In M. Hewstone, W. Stroebe and G. M. Stephenson (eds), *Introduction to social psychology: A European perspective*. Oxford: Blackwell.

Hewstone, M., & Greenland, K. (2000). Intergroup conflict. Unpublished manuscript, Cardiff University.

Hewstone, M., & Ward, C. (1985). Ethnocentrism and causal attribution in Southeast Asia. *Journal of Personality and Social Psychology*, **48**, 614–623.

Higgins, E. T. (1987). Self-discrepancy: A theory relating self and affect. *Psychological Review*, **94**(3), 319–340.

Higgins, E. T., & Bargh, J. A. (1987). Social cognition and social perception. *Annual Review of Psychology*, **38**, 369–425.

Higgins, E. T., & McCann, C. D. (1984). Social encoding and subsequent attitudes, impressions and memory: 'Context-driven' and motiva-tional aspects of processing. *Journal of Personality and Social Psychology*, **47**, 26–39.

Higgins, E. T., & Rholes, W. S. (1978). Saying is believing: Effects of message modification on memory and liking for the person described. *Journal of Experimental Social Psychology*, **14**, 363–378.

Hilmert, C. J., Kulik, J. A., & Christenfeld, N. J. S. (2006). Positive and negative opinion modeling: The influence of another's similarity and dissimilarity. *Journal of Personality and Social Psychology*, **90**, 440–452.

Hilton, J. L., & von Hippel, W. (1990). The role of consistency in the judgment of stereotype-relevant behaviors. *Personality and Social Psychology Bulletin*, **16**, 430–448.

Hines, M. (2004). *Brain gender*. New York: Oxford University Press.

Hinkle, S., Fox-Cardamone, L., Haseleu, J. A., Brown, R., & Irwin, L. M. (1996). Grassroots political action as an intergroup phenomenon. *Journal of Social Issues*, **52**(1), 39–51.

Hinsz, V. B. (1990). Cognitive and consensus processes in group recognition memory performance. *Journal of Personality and Social Psychology*, **59**, 705–718.

Hinsz, V. B., Tindale, R. S., & Vollrath, D. A. (1997). The emerging conceptualization of groups as information processors. *Psychological Bulletin*, **121**, 43–64.

Hirt, E. R., & Markman, K. D. (1995). Multiple explanation: A consider-an-alternative strategy for debiasing judgments. *Journal of Personality and Social Psychology*, **69**, 1069–1088.

Hitsch, G. J., Hortaçsu, A., Ariely, D. (2010). What makes you click? Mate preferences in online dating. *Quantitative Marketing and Economics*, **8**(4), 393–427.

Hobden, K. L., & Olson, J. M. (1994). From jest to antipathy: Disparagement humor as a source of dissonance-motivated attitude change. *Basic and Applied Social Psychology*, **15**, 239–249.

Hodges, B. H., & Geyer, A. L. (2006). A nonconformist account of the Asch experiments: Values, pragmatics, and moral dilemmas. *Personality and Social Psychology Review*, **10**(1), 2–19.

Hofling, C. K., Brotzman, E., Dalrymple, S., Graves, N., & Pierce, C. M. (1966). An experimental study in nurse-physician relationships. *The Journal of Nervous and Mental Disease*, **143**(2), 171–180.

Hofmann, W., Gawronski, B., Gschwendner, T., Le, H., & Schmitt, M. (2005). A meta-analysis on the correlation between the implicit association test and explicit self-report measures. *Personality and Social Psychology Bulletin*, **31**, 1369–1385.

Hofstede, G. (1980). *Culture's consequences: International differences in work-related values*. Beverly Hills, CA: Sage.

Hofstede, G. (2001). *Culture's consequences, comparing values, behaviors, institutions, and organizations across nations*. Thousand Oaks, CA: Sage.

Hofstede, G., & Hofstede, G. J. (2005). *Cultures and organizations: software of the mind*. Revised and expanded 2nd edn. New York: McGraw-Hill.

Hogg, M. A., & Hains, S. C. (1998). Friendship and group identification: A new look at the role of cohesiveness in groupthink. *European Journal of Social Psychology*, **28**, 323–341.

Hogg, M. A., Hains, S. C., & Mason, I. (1998). Identification and leadership in small groups: Salience, frame of reference, and leader stereotypicality effects on leader evaluations. *Journal of Personality and Social Psychology*, **75**, 1248–1263.

Hogg, M. A., Hohman, Z. P., & Rivera, J. E. (2008). Why do people join groups? Three motivational accounts from social psychology. *Social and Personality Psychology Compass*, **2**, 1269–1280.

Hogg, M. A., Sherman, D. K., Dierselhuis, J., Maitner, A. T., & Moffitt, G. (2007). Uncertainty, entitativity, and group identification. *Journal of Experimental Social Psychology*, **43**, 135–142.

Hogg, M. A., Turner, J. C., & Davidson, B. (1990). Polar-ized norms and social frames of reference: A test of the self-categorization theory of group polarization. *Basic and Applied Social Psychology*, **11**, 77–100.

Hoigaard, R., Safvenbom, R., & Tonnessen, F. E. (2006). The relationship between group cohesion, group norms and perceived social loafing in soccer teams. *Small Group Research*, **37**(3), 217–232.

Holland, R. W., Hendriks, M., & Aarts, H. (2005). Smells like clean spirit: Nonconscious effect of scent on cognition and behavior. *Psychological Science*, **16**, 689–693.

Holland, R. W., Meertens, R. M., & Van Vugt, M. (2002). Dissonance on the road: Self-esteem as a moderator of internal and external self-justification strategies. *Personality and Social Psychology Bulletin*, **28**, 1712–1724.

Hollander, E. P. (1958). Conformity, status, and idiosyncrasy credit. *Psychological Review*, **65**, 117–127.

Hollander, E. P. (1995). Organizational leadership and followership. In P. Collett & A. Furnham (eds), *Social psychology at work: Essays in honour of Michael Argyle*. London: Routledge.

Holmberg, D., & Holmes, J. G. (1994). Reconstruction of relationship memories: A mental models approach. In N. Schwarz & S. Sudman (eds), *Autobiographical memory and the validity of retrospective reports*. New York: Springer-Verlag.

Holmes, J. G., & Rempel, J. K. (1989). Trust in close relationships. In C. Hendrick (ed.), *Review of personality and social psychology*, Vol. 10. Newbury Park, CA: Sage.

Holtgraves, T. (1997). Styles of language use: Individual and cultural variability in conversational indirectness. *Journal of Personality and Social Psychology*, **73**, 624–637.

Holtman, Z., Louw, J., Tredoux, C., & Carney, T. (2005). Prejudice and social contact in South Africa: A study of integrated schools ten years after apartheid. *South African Journal of Psychology*, **35**, 473–493.

Holtzworth, A., & Jacobson, N. S. (1988). An attributional approach to marital dysfunction and therapy. In J. E. Maddux, C. D. Stoltenberg & R. Rosenwein (eds), *Social processes in clinical and counseling psychology.* New York: Springer-Verlag.

Holtzworth-Munroe, A., & Jacobson, N. S. (1985). Causal attributions of married couples: When do they search for causes? What do they conclude when they do? *Journal of Personality and Social Psychology,* **48**, 1398–1412.

Hong, Y., Li, X., Mao, R., & Stanton, B. (2007). Internet use among Chinese college students: Implications for sex education and HIV prevention. *Cyber Psychology and Behavior,* **10**(2), 161–169.

Hood, K. B., & Shook, N. J. (2013). Conceptualizing women's attitudes toward condom use with the tripartite model. *Women and Health,* **53**(4), 349–368.

Hoorens, V., & Nuttin, J. M. (1993). Overvaluation of own attributes: Mere ownership or subjective frequency? *Social Cognition,* **11**, 177–200.

Hoorens, V., Nuttin, J. M., Herman, I. E., & Pavakanun, U. (1990). Mastery pleasure versus mere ownership: A quasi-experimental cross-cultural and cross-alphabetical test of the name letter effect. *European Journal of Social Psychology,* **20**, 181–205.

Hoover, C. W., Wood, E. E., & Knowles, E. S. (1983). Forms of social awareness and helping. *Journal of Experimental Social Psychology,* **19**, 577–590.

Hopkins, N., Regan, M., & Abell, J. (1997). On the context dependence of national stereotypes: Some Scottish data. *British Journal of Social Psychology,* **36**, 553–563.

Hopkins, N., Reicher, S., Harrison, K., Cassidy, C., Bull, R., & Levine, M. (2007). Helping to improve the group stereotype: On the strategic dimension of prosocial behavior. *Personality & Social Psychology Bulletin,* **33**, 776–788.

Hormuth, S. E. (1986). Lack of effort as a result of self-focused attention: An attributional ambiguity analysis. *European Journal of Social Psychology,* **16**, 181–192.

Horn, S. S. (2003). Adolescents' reasoning about exclusion from social groups. *Developmental Psychology,* **39**(1), 71.

Hornsey, M. J. (2005). Why being right is not enough: Predicting defensiveness in the face of group criticism. *European Review of Social Psychology,* **16**, 301–334.

Hornsey, M. J., Jetten, J., McAuliffe, B. J., & Hogg, M. A. (2006). The impact of individualist and collectivist group norms on evaluations of dissenting group members. *Journal of Experimental Social Psychology,* **42**, 57–68.

Hornsey, M. J., Trembath, M., & Gunthorpe, S. (2004). 'You can criticize because you care': Identity attachment, constructiveness, and the intergroup sensitivity effect. *European Journal of Social Psychology,* **34**, 499–518.

Hornstein, H. (1976). *Cruelty and kindness.* Englewood Cliffs, NJ: Prentice-Hall.

Horowitz, S. V., & Boardman, S. K. (1994). Managing conflict: Policy and research implications. *Journal of Social Issues,* **50**, 197–211.

Hoshino-Browne, E., Zanna, A. S., Spencer, S. J., & Zanna, M. P. (2004). Investigating attitudes cross-culturally: A case of cognitive dissonance among East Asians and North Americans. In G. Haddock & G. R. Maio (eds), *Contemporary perspectives on the psychology of attitudes.* New York: Psychology Press.

House, R. J., & Singh, J. V. (1987). Organizational behavior: Some new directions for I/O psychology. *Annual Review of Psychology,* **38**, 669–718.

Hovland, C. I., Janis, I. L., & Kelley, H. H. (1953). *Communication and persuasion.* New Haven, CT: Yale University Press.

Hovland, C. I., Lumsdaine, A. A., & Sheffield, F. D. (1949). *Experiments on mass communication. Studies in social psychology in World War II* (Vol. III).

Princeton, NJ: Princeton University Press.

Howard, D. J., & Kerin, R. A. (2011). The effects of name similarity on message processing and persuasion. *Journal of Experimental Social Psychology,* **47**(1), 63–71.

Hoyle, R. H. (1993). Interpersonal attraction in the absence of explicit attitudinal information. *Social Cognition,* **11**, 309–320.

Hoyle, R. H., Kernis, M. H., Baldwin, M. W., & Leary, M. R. (1999). *Selfhood: Identity, esteem, regulation.* Boulder, CO: Westview Press.

Hsee, C. K., & Hastie, R. (2006). Decision and experience: Why don't we choose what makes us happy? *Trends in Cognitive Sciences,* **10**, 31–37.

Hsu, L. H. (2011). Linguistic intergroup bias tells ingroup/outgroup orientation of bicultural Asian Americans. *International Journal of Intercultural Relations,* **35**(6), 853–866.

Huesmann, L. R., Lagerspetz, K., & Eron, L. D. (1984). Intervening variables in the TV violence–aggression relation: Evidence from two countries. *Developmental Psychology,* **20**, 746–775.

Huesmann, L. R., Moise-Titus, J., Podolski, C.-L., & Eron, L. D. (2003). Longitudinal relations between children's exposure to TV violence and their aggressive and violent behavior in young adulthood: 1977–1992. *Developmental Psychology,* **39**, 201–222.

Hugenberg, K., & Bodenhausen, G. V. (2003). Facing prejudice: Implicit prejudice and the perception of facial threat. *Psychological Science,* **14**, 640–643.

Huguet, P., Charbonnier, E., & Monteil, J.-M. (1999). Productivity loss in performance groups: people who see themselves as average do not engage in social loafing. *Group dynamics: Theory, research and practice,* **3**(2), 118–131.

Huguet, P., Latané, B., & Bourgeois, M. (1998). The emergence of a social representation of human rights via interpersonal communication: Empirical evidence

for the convergence of the two theories. *European Journal of Social Psychology,* **28**(5), 831–846.

Hui, C. H., & Tan, C. K. (1996). Employee motivation and attitudes in the Chinese workforce. In M. H. Bond (ed.), *The handbook of Chinese psychology.* New York: Oxford University Press.

Hui, V. K.-Y., Bond, M. H., & Ng, T. S. W. (2007). General beliefs about the world as defensive mechanisms against death anxiety. *Omega: Journal of Death and Dying,* **54**(3), 199–214.

Hume, D. (1739/1911). *A treatise on human nature,* 2 vols. London: Dent.

Hume, D. (1742; reprinted in 2006). *Essays: Moral, political and literary.* New York: Cosimo.

Hummert, M. L., Garstka, T. A., Greenwald, A. G., Mellott, D. S., & O'Brien, L. T. (2002). Using the implicit association test to measure age differences in implicit social cognitions. *Psychology and Aging,* **17**(3), 482–495.

Hunt, M. (1993). *The story of psychology.* New York: Doubleday.

Hunt, P. J., & Hillery, J. M. (1973). Social facilitation in a location setting: An examination of the effects over learning trials. *Journal of Experimental Social Psychology,* **9**, 563–571.

Hunter, J. D. (2002, 21–22 June). To change the world. Paper presented to the Board of Directors of the Trinity Forum, Denver, Colorado.

Hunter, M. S., Gruenfeld, E. A., & Ramirez, A. J. (2003). Help-seeking intentions for breast-cancer symptoms: A comparison of the self-regulation model and the theory of planned behaviour. *British Journal of Health Psychology,* **8**, 319–333.

Huo, Y. J., Smith, H. J., Tyler, T. R., & Lind, E. A. (1996). Superordinate identification, subgroup identification, and justice concerns: Is separatism the problem; is assimilation the answer? *Psychological Science,* **7**, 40–45.

Huston, A. C., Donnerstein, E., Fairchild, H.,

Feshbach, N. D., Katz, P. A., & Murray, J. P. (1992). *Big world, small screen: The role of television in American society.* Lincoln, NE: University of Nebraska Press.

Huston, T. L., & Chorost, A. F. (1994). Behavioral buffers on the effect of negativity on marital satisfaction: A longitudinal study. *Personal Relationships,* **1,** 223–239.

Huston, T. L., Niehuis, S., & Smith, S. E. (2001). The early marital roots of conjugal distress and divorce. *Current Directions in Psychological Science,* **10,** 116–119.

Hutnik, N. (1985). Aspects of identity in a multi-ethnic society. *New Community,* **12,** 298–309.

Hyde, J. S. (2005). The gender similarities hypothesis. *American Psychologist,* **60,** 581–592.

I

Ickes, B. (1980). On disconfirming our perceptions of others. Paper presented at the American Psychological Association convention.

Ickes, W., Patterson, M. L., Rajecki, D. W., & Tanford, S. (1982). Behavioral and cognitive consequences of reciprocal versus compensatory responses to preinteraction expectancies. *Social Cognition,* **1,** 160–190.

Ickes, W., Snyder, M., & Garcia, S. (1997). Personality influences on the choice of situations. In R. Hogan, J. Johnson & S. Briggs (eds), *Handbook of Personality Psychology.* San Diego: Academic Press.

IEO (Independent Evaluation Office) (2011). *IMF performance in the run-up to the financial and economic crisis: IMF surveillance in 2004–07.* Washington, DC: IMF Publications.

Ingham, A. G., Levinger, G., Graves, J., & Peckham, V. (1974). The Ringelmann effect: Studies of group size and group performance. *Journal of Experimental Social Psychology,* **10,** 371–384.

Inglehart, M. R., Markus, H., & Brown, D. R. (1989). The effects of possible selves on academic achieve-ment – a panel study. In J. P. Forgas & J. M. Innes (eds), *Recent advances in social psychology: An international perspective.* North-Holland: Elsevier Science Publishers.

Inglehart, R., & Welzel, C. (2005). *Modernization, cultural change, and democracy: The human development sequence.* New York: Cambridge University Press.

Insko, C. A., Nacoste, R. W., & Moe, J. L. (1983). Belief congruence and racial discrimination: Review of the evidence and critical evaluation. *European Journal of Social Psychology,* **13,** 153–174.

Insko, C. A., Schopler, J., Gaertner, L., Wildschut, T., Kozar, R., Pinter, B., …& Montoya, M.R. (2001). Interindividual–intergroup discontinuity reduction through the anticipation of future interaction. *Journal of Personality and Social Psychology,* **80**(1), 95.

International Labour Organization (ILO) (1997, 11 December). Women's progress in workforce improving worldwide, but occupational segregation still rife. Available at: http://www.ilo.org/global/about-the-ilo/newsroom/news/WCMS_008040/lang–en/index.htm

Inzlicht, M., Gutsell, J. N., & Legault, L. (2012). Mimicry reduces prejudice. *Journal of Experimental Social Psychology,* **48,** 361–365.

Ioannidis, J. P. A. (2005). Why most published research findings are false. *PLoS Medicine,* **2** (8): e124. doi:10.1371/journal.pmed.0020124.

IPU (Inter-Parliamentary Union) (2013). *Women in national parliaments: Situation as of 1st July 2013.* Available at: http://www.ipu.org/wmn-e/classif.htm

Ireland, T. O., & Smith, C. A. (2009). Living in partner-violent families: Developmental links to antisocial behavior and relationship violence. *Journal of Youth and Adolescence,* **38,** 323–339.

Isen, A. M., & Means, B. (1983). The influence of positive affect on decision-making strategy. *Social Cognition,* **2,** 28–31.

Isen, A. M., Shalker, T. E., Clark, M., & Karp, L. (1978). Affect, accessibility of material in memory, and behavior: A cognitive loop. *Journal of Personality and Social Psychology,* **36,** 1–12.

Ito, T. A., Miller, N., & Pollock, V. E. (1996). Alcohol and aggression: A meta-analysis on the moderating effects of inhibitory cues, triggering events, and self-focused attention. *Psychological Bulletin,* **120,** 60–82.

Iyengar, S. S., & Lepper, M. R. (2000). When choice is demotivating: Can one desire too much of a good thing? *Journal of Personality and Social Psychology,* **79,** 995–1006.

J

Jackman, M. R., & Senter, M. S. (1981). Beliefs about race, gender, and social class different, therefore unequal: Beliefs about trait differences between groups of unequal status. In D. J. Treiman & R. V. Robinson (eds), *Research in stratification and mobility,* Vol. 2. Greenwich, CT: JAI Press.

Jackson, J. W., Kirby, D., Barnes, L., & Shepard, L. (1993). Institutional racism and pluralistic ignorance: A cross-national comparison. In M. Wievorka (ed.), *Racisme et modernite.* Paris: Editions la Découverte.

Jackson, L. A., Hunter, J. E., & Hodge, C. N. (1995). Physical attractiveness and intellectual competence: A meta-analytic review. *Social Psychology Quarterly,* **58,** 108–123.

Jacobs, R. C., & Campbell, D. T. (1961). The perpetuation of an arbitrary tradition through several generations of a laboratory microculture. *Journal of Abnormal and Social Psychology,* **62,** 649–658.

Jaffe, Y., & Yinon, Y. (1983). Collective aggression: The group-individual paradigm in the study of collective antisocial behavior. In H. H. Blumberg, A. P. Hare, V. Kent & M. Davies (eds), *Small groups and social interaction,* Vol. 1. Cambridge: Wiley.

Jaffe, Y., Shapir, N., & Yinon, Y. (1981). Aggression and its escalation. *Journal of Cross-Cultural Psychology,* **12,** 21–36.

Jahoda, G. (2007). *A history of social psychology: From the eighteenth-century enlightenment to the Second World War.* Cambridge: Cambridge University Press.

James, W. (1890, reprinted 1950). *The principles of psychology,* Vol. 2. New York: Dover Publications.

Jamieson, D. W., Lydon, J. E., Stewart, G., & Zanna, M. P. (1987). Pygmalion revisited: New evidence for student expectancy effects in the classroom. *Journal of Educational Psychology,* **79,** 461–466.

Janes, L. M., & Olson, J. M. (2000). Jeer pressure: The behavioral effects of observing ridicule of others. *Personality and Social Psychology Bulletin,* **26,** 474–485.

Janis, I. L. (1971, November). Groupthink. *Psychology Today,* 43–46.

Janis, I. L. (1982). Counteracting the adverse effects of concurrence-seeking in policy-planning groups: Theory and research perspectives. In H. Brandstatter, J. H. Davis & G. Stocker-Kreichgauer (eds), *Group decision making.* New York: Academic Press.

Janis, I. L., & Mann, L. (1977). *Decision-making: A psychological analysis of conflict, choice and commitment.* New York: Free Press.

Janis, I. L., Kaye, D., & Kirschner, P. (1965). Facilitating effects of eating while reading on responsiveness to persuasive communications. *Journal of Personality and Social Psychology,* **1,** 181–186.

Janiszewski, C., & Uy, D. (2008). Precision of the anchor influences the amount of adjustment. *Psychological Science,* **19**(2), 121–127.

Jankowiak, W. R., & Fischer, E. F. (1992). A cross-cultural perspective on romantic love. *Ethnology,* **31,** 149–155.

Jaremka, L. M., Bunyan, D. P., Collins, N. L., & Sherman, D. K. (2011). Defensive distancing: Self-affirmation and risk regulation in response to relationship threats. *Journal of Experimental Social Psychology,* **47**(1), 264–268.

Jason, L. A., Rose, T., Ferrari, J. R., & Barone, R. (1984). Personal versus impersonal methods for recruiting blood donations. *Journal of Social Psychology*, **123**, 139–140.

Jelalian, E., & Miller, A. G. (1984). The perseverance of beliefs: Conceptual perspectives and research developments. *Journal of Social and Clinical Psychology*, **2**, 25–56.

Jellison, J. M., & Green, J. (1981). A self-presentation approach to the fundamental attribution error: The norm of internality. *Journal of Personality and Social Psychology*, **40**, 643–649.

Jennings, D. L., Amabile, T. M., & Ross, L. (1982). Informal covariation assessment: Data-based vs theory-based judgments. In D. Kahneman, P. Slovic & A. Tversky (eds), *Judgment under uncertainty: Heuristics and biases*. New York: Cambridge University Press.

Jervis, R. (1985). Perceiving and coping with threat: Psychological perspectives. In R. Jervis, R. N. Lebow & J. Stein (eds), *Psychology and deterrence*. Baltimore: Johns Hopkins University Press.

Jessop, D. C., & Wade, J. (2008). Fear appeals and binge drinking: A terror management theory perspective. *British Journal of Health Psychology*, **13**, 773–788.

Jetten, J., Hornsey, M. J., & Adarves-Yorno, I. (2006). When group members admit to being conformist: The role of relative intragroup status in conformity self-reports. *Personality and Social Psychology Bulletin*, **32**, 162–173.

Jetten, J., Postmes, T., & McAuliffe, B. J. (2002). We're *all* individuals: Group norms of individualism and collectivism, levels of identification and identity threat. *European Journal of Social Psychology*, **32**, 189–207.

Johanson, D. (2001). Origins of modern humas: Multiregional or Out of Africa? http://www. actionbioscience.org/evolution/johanson.html (accessed 26 November 2009).

Johnson, B. T., & Eagly, A. H. (1989). Effects of involvement on persuasion: A meta-analysis. *Psychological Bulletin*, **106**, 290–314.

Johnson, C. B., Stockdale, M. S., & Saal, F. E. (1991). Persistence of men's misperceptions of friendly cues across a variety of interpersonal encounters. *Psychology of Women Quarterly*, **15**, 463–475.

Johnson, D. J., & Rusbult, C. E. (1989). Resisting temptation: Devaluation of alternative partners as a means of maintaining commitment in close relationships. *Journal of Personality and Social Psychology*, **57**, 967–980.

Johnson, E. J., & Tversky, A. (1983). Affect, generalization, and the perception of risk. *Journal of Personality and Social Psychology*, **45**, 20–31.

Johnson, J. D., Jackson, L. A., & Gatto, L. (1995). Violent attitudes and deferred academic aspirations: Deleterious effects of exposure to rap music. *Basic and Applied Social Psychology*, **16**, 27–41.

Johnson, J. G., Cohen, P., Smailes, E. M., Kasen, S., & Brook, J. S. (2002). Television viewing and aggressive behavior during adolescence and adulthood. *Science*, **295**, 2468–2471.

Johnson, M. H., & Magaro, P. A. (1987). Effects of mood and severity on memory processes in depression and mania. *Psychological Bulletin*, **101**, 28–40.

Joiner, T. E., Jr (1999). The clustering and contagion of suicide. *Current Directions in Psychological Science*, **8**, 89–92.

Jonas, E., Martens, A., Kayser, D. N., Fritsche, I., Sullivan, D., & Greenberg, J. (2008). Focus theory of normative conduct and terror-management theory: The interactive impact of mortality salience and norm salience on social judgement. *Journal of Personality and Social Psychology*, **95**(6), 1239–1251.

Jonas, K. (1992). Modelling and suicide: A test of the Werther effect. *British Journal of Social Psychology*, **31**, 295–306.

Jones, E. E. (1964). *Ingratiation*. New York: Appleton-Century-Crofts.

Jones, E. E. (1976). How do people perceive the causes of behavior? *American Scientist*, **64**, 300–305.

Jones, E. E., & Davis, K. E. (1965). A theory of correspondent inferences: From acts to dispositions. *Advances in Experimental Social Psychology*, **2**, 219–266.

Jones, E. E., & Harris, V. A. (1967). The attribution of attitudes. *Journal of Experimental Social Psychology*, **3**, 2–24.

Jones, E. E., & Nisbett, R. E. (1971). *The actor and the observer: Divergent perceptions of the cases of behavior*. Morristown, NJ: General Learning Press.

Jones, E. E., Rock, L., Shaver, K. G., Goethals, G. R., & Ward, L. M. (1968). Pattern of performance and ability attribution: An unexpected primacy effect. *Journal of Personality and Social Psychology*, **10**, 317–340.

Jones, J. (2004). Whites are from Mars, OJ is from planet Hollywood: Blacks don't support OJ and Whites just don't get it. *Off White: Readings on power, privilege and resistance*. New York: Routledge. 89–97.

Jones, J. M. (1988). Racism in black and white: a bicultural model of reaction and evolution. In P. A. Katz and D. A. Taylor (eds), *Eliminating racism: Profiles in controversy*. New York: Plenum Press.

Jones, J. M. (2003). TRIOS: A psychological theory of the African legacy in American culture. *Journal of Social Issues*, **59**, 217–242.

Jones, J. T., & Cunningham, J. D. (1996). Attachment styles and other predictors of relationship satisfaction in dating couples. *Personal Relationships*, **3**, 387–399.

Jones, J. T., Pelham, B. W., & Mirenberg, M. C. (2002). Name letter preferences are not merely mere exposure: Implicit egotism as self-regulation. *Journal of Experimental Social Psychology*, **38**, 170–177.

Jones, J. T., Pelham, B. W., Carvallo, M., & Mirenberg, M. C. (2004). How do I love thee? Let me count the Js: Implicit egotism and interpersonal attraction. *Journal of Personality and Social Psychology*, **87**, 665–683.

Jones, R. A., & Brehm, J. W. (1970). Persuasiveness of one- and two-sided communications as a function of awareness there are two sides. *Journal of Experimental Social Psychology*, **6**, 47–56.

Jordan, C. H., Spencer, S. J., Zanna, M. P., Hoshino-Browne, E., & Correll, J. (2003). Secure and defensive high self-esteem. *Journal of Personality and Social Psychology*, **85**, 969–978.

Josephson, W. L. (1987). Television violence and children's aggression: Testing the priming, social script, and disinhibition predictions. *Journal of Personality and Social Psychology*, **53**, 882–890.

Jost, J. T., & Kay, A. C. (2005). Exposure to benevolent sexism and complementary gender stereotypes: Consequences for specific and diffuse forms of system justification. *Journal of Personality and Social Psychology*, **88**, 498–509.

Jourard, S. M. (1964). *The transparent self*. Princeton, NJ: Van Nostrand.

Judd, C. M., Blair, I. V., & Chapleau, K. M. (2004). Automatic stereotypes vs. automatic prejudice: Sorting out the possibilities in the Payne (2001) weapon paradigm. *Journal of Experimental Social Psychology*, **40**, 75–81.

Jussim, L. (1986). Self-fulfilling prophecies: A theoretical and integrative review. *Psychological Review*, **93**, 429–445.

Jussim, L. (2005). Accuracy in social perception: Criticisms, controversies, criteria, components and cognitive processes. *Advances in Experimental Social Psychology*, **37**, 1–93.

Jussim, L., & Harber, K. D. (2005). Teacher expectations and self-fulfilling prophecies: Knowns and unknowns, resolved and unresolved controversies. *Personality and Social Psychology Review*, **9**(2), 131–155.

Jussim, L., McCauley, C. R., & Lee, Y.-T. (1995). Introduction: Why study stereotype accuracy and inaccuracy? In Y. T. Lee, L. Jussim & C. R. McCauley (eds), *Stereotypes accuracy: Toward appreciating group differences*. Washington, DC: American Psychological Association.

## K

**Kagan, J.** (1989). Temperamental contributions to social behavior. *American Psychologist*, **44**, 668–674.

**Kahan, T. L., & Johnson, M. K.** (1992). Self effects in memory for person information. *Social Cognition*, **10**, 30–50.

**Kahle, L. R., & Berman, J.** (1979). Attitudes cause behaviors: A cross-lagged panel analysis. *Journal of Personality and Social Psychology*, **37**, 315–321.

**Kahneman, D., & Miller, D. T.** (1986). Norm theory: Comparing reality to its alternatives. *Psychological Review*, **93**, 75–88.

**Kahneman, D., & Snell, J.** (1992). Predicting a changing taste: Do people know what they will like? *Journal of Behavioral Decision Making*, **5**(3), 187–200.

**Kahneman, D., & Tversky, A.** (1979). Intuitive prediction: Biases and corrective procedures. *Management Science*, **12**, 313–327.

**Kahneman, D., & Tversky, A.** (1995). Conflict resolution: A cognitive perspective. In K. Arrow, R. Mnookin, L. Ross, A. Tversky & R. Wilson (eds), *Barriers to the negotiated resolution of conflict*. New York: Norton.

**Kaiser Family Foundation** (2001). National survey. Most gays and lesbians see greater acceptance. News release, 13 November, 2001, at www.kff.org.

**Kameda, T., & Sugimori, S.** (1993). Psychological entrapment in group decision making: An assigned decision rule and a groupthink phenomenon. *Journal of Personality and Social Psychology*, **65**, 282–292.

**Kammer, D.** (1982). Differences in trait ascriptions to self and friend: Unconfounding intensity from variability. *Psychological Reports*, **51**, 99–102.

**Kanagaretnam, K., Lobo, G. J., & Mohammad, E.** (2008). Determinants and consequences of large CEO pay. *International Journal of Accounting and Finance*, **1**, 61–82.

**Kanagawa, C., Cross, S. E., & Markus, H. R.** (2001). 'Who am I?' The cultural psychology of the conceptual self. *Personality and Social Psychology Bulletin*, **27**, 90–103.

**Kanazawa, S., & Kovar, J. L.** (2004). Why beautiful people are more intelligent. *Intelligence*, **32**, 227–243.

**Kandel, D. B.** (1978). Similarity in real-life adolescent friendship pairs. *Journal of Personality and Social Psychology*, **36**, 306–312.

**Kanekar, S., & Nazareth, A.** (1988). Attributed rape victim's fault as a function of her attractiveness, physical hurt, and emotional disturbance. *Social Behaviour*, **3**, 37–40.

**Kaplan, M. F.** (1989). Task, situational, and personal determinants of influence processes in group decision making. In E. J. Lawler (ed.), *Advances in group processes* (vol. 6). Greenwich, CT: JAI Press.

**Karau, S. J., & Williams, K. D.** (1993). Social loafing: A meta-analytic review and theoretical integration. *Journal of Personality and Social Psychology*, **65**, 681–706.

**Karau, S. J., & Williams, K. D.** (1997). The effects of group cohesiveness on social loafing and compensation. *Group Dynamics: Theory, Research, and Practice*, **1**, 156–168.

**Karney, B. R., & Bradbury, T. N.** (1995). The longitudinal course of marital quality and stability: A review of theory, method, and research. *Psychological Bulletin*, **118**, 3–34.

**Karney, B. R., & Bradbury, T. N.** (1997). Neuroticism, marital interaction, and the trajectory of marital satisfaction. *Journal of Personality and Social Psychology*, **72**, 1075–1092.

**Kashima, E. S., & Kashima, Y.** (1998). Culture and language: the case of cultural dimensions and personal pronoun use. *Journal of Cross-Cultural Psychology*, **29**, 461–486.

**Kashima, Y., & Kashima, E. S.** (2003). Individualism, GNP, climate, and pronoun drop: Is individualism determined by affluence and climate, or does language use play a role? *Journal of Cross-Cultural Psychology*, **34**, 125–134.

**Kassin, S. M., Goldstein, C. C., & Savitsky, K.** (2003). Behavioral confirmation in the interrogation room: On the dangers of presuming guilt. *Law and Human Behavior*, **27**, 187–203.

**Katz, D.** (1960). The functional approach to the study of attitudes. *Public Opinion Quarterly*, **6**, 248–268.

**Katz, E.** (1957). The two-step flow of communication: An up-to-date report on a hypothesis. *Public Opinion Quarterly*, **21**, 61–78.

**Katz, I.** (1981). *Stigma: A social psychological analysis*. Hillsdale, NJ: Erlbaum.

**Katz, I., & Hass, R. G.** (1988). Racial ambivalence and American value conflict: Correlational and priming studies of dual cognitive structures. *Journal of Personality and Social Psychology*, **55**, 893–905.

**Katz, I., Wackenhut, J., & Hass, R. G.** (1986). Racial ambivalence, value duality, and behavior. In J. Dovidio & S. L. Gaertner (eds), *Prejudice discrimination and racism: Theory and research*. New York: Academic Press.

**Katz, P. A., & Kofkin, J. A.** (1997). Race, gender, and young children. In S. S. Luthar, J. A. Burack, D. Cicchetti & J. Weisz (eds), *Developmental psychopathology: Perspectives on adjustment, risk, and disorder*. New York: Cambridge University Press.

**Katz-Wise, S. L., Priess, H. A., & Hyde, J. S.** (2010). Gender-role attitudes and behavior across the transition to parenthood. *Developmental Psychology*, **46**(1), 18.

**Katzev, R., & Wang, T.** (1994). Can commitment change behavior? A case study of environmental actions. *Journal of Social Behavior and Personality*, **9**, 13–26.

**Katzev, R., Edelsack, L., Steinmetz, G., & Walker, T.** (1978). The effect of reprimanding transgressions on subsequent helping behavior: Two field experiments. *Personality and Social Psychology Bulletin*, **4**, 126–129.

**Kazdin, A.** (2009). Psychological science's contribution to a sustainable environment.

**Keating, J. P., & Brock, T. C.** (1974). Acceptance of persuasion and the inhibition of counterargumentation under various distraction tasks. *Journal of Experimental Social Psychology*, **10**, 301–309.

**Keller, E. B., & Berry, B.** (2003). *The influentials: One American in ten tells the other nine how to vote, where to eat, and what to buy*. New York: Free Press.

**Kellerman, J., Lewis, J., & Laird, J. D.** (1989). Looking and loving: The effects of mutual gaze on feelings of romantic love. *Journal of Research in Personality*, **23**, 145–161.

**Kellermann, A. L.** (1997). Comment: Gunsmoke – changing public attitudes toward smoking and firearms. *American Journal of Public Health*, **87**, 910–912.

**Kellermann, A. L. & 9 others** (1993). Gun ownership as a risk factor for homicide in the home. *New England Journal of Medicine*, **329**, 1984–1991.

**Kelley, H. H.** (1973). The processes of causal attribution. *American Psychologist*, **28**(2), 107.

**Kelley, H. H., & Stahelski, A. J.** (1970). The social interaction basis of cooperators' and competitors' beliefs about others. *Journal of Personality and Social Psychology*, **16**, 66–91.

**Kelley, H. H., & Thibault, J. W.** (1978). *Interpersonal relationships: A theory of interdependence*. New York: John Wiley.

**Kelley, K., Dawson, L., & Musialowski, D. M.** (1989). Three faces of sexual explicitness: The good, the bad, and the useful. In D. Zillmann & J. Bryant (eds), *Pornography: Research advances and policy considerations*. Hillsdale, NJ: Erlbaum.

**Kellow, C. L., & Steeves, H. L.** (1998). The role of radio in the Rwandan genocide. *Journal of Communication*,

**48**, 107–128. doi: 10.1111/j. 1460-2466.1998.tb02762.x

Kelman, H. C. (1997). Group processes in the resolution of international conflicts: Experiences from the Israeli–Palestinian case. *American Psychologist*, **52**, 212–220.

Kelman, H. C. (1998). Building a sustainable peace: The limits of pragmatism in the Israeli–Palestinian negotiations. Address to the American Psychological Association convention.

Keltner, D., Gruenfeld, D. H., & Anderson, C. (2003). Power, approach, and inhibition. *Psychological Review*, **110**, 265–284.

Kenny, D. A. (1994). *Interpersonal perception: A social relations analysis*. Storrs, CT: Guilford Press.

Kenny, D. A., & Acitelli, L. K. (2001). Accuracy and bias in the perception of the partner in a close relationship. *Journal of Personality and Social Psychology*, **80**, 439–448.

Kenny, D. A., & Nasby, W. (1980). Splitting the reciprocity correlation. *Journal of Personality and Social Psychology*, **38**, 249–256.

Kenrick, D. T. (1987). Gender, genes, and the social environment: A biosocial interactionist perspective. In P. Shaver & C. Hendrick (eds), *Sex and gender: Review of personality and social psychology*, Vol. 7. Beverly Hills, CA: Sage.

Kenrick, D. T., & Keefe, R. C. (1992). Age preferences in mates reflect sex differences in reproductive strategies. *Behavioral and Brain Sciences*, **15**, 75–133.

Kenrick, D. T., & MacFarlane, S. W. (1986). Ambient temperature and horn-honking: A field study of the heat/aggression relationship. *Environment and Behavior*, **18**, 179–191.

Kenrick, D. T., & Trost, M. R. (1987). A biosocial theory of heterosexual relationships. In K. Kelly (ed.), *Females, males, and sexuality*. Albany: State University of New York Press.

Kenworthy, J. B., Hewstone, M., Levine, J. M., Martin, R., & Willis, H. (2008). The phenomenology of minority–majority status:

Effects on innovation in argument generation. *European Journal of Social Psychology*, **38**, 624–636.

Kernis, M. H. (2003). High self-esteem: A differentiated perspective. In E. C. Chang & L. J. Sanna (eds), *Virtue, vice, and personality: The complexity of behavior*. Washington, DC: APA Books.

Kerr, M., & Stattin, H. (2000). What parents know, how they know it, and several forms of adolescent adjustment: Further evidence for a reinterpretation of monitoring. *Developmental Psychology*, **36**, 366–380.

Kerr, N. L. (1983). Motivation losses in small groups: A social dilemma analysis. *Journal of Personality and Social Psychology*, **45**, 819–828.

Kerr, N. L., & Bruun, S. E. (1981). Ringelmann revisited: Alternative explanations for the social loafing effect. *Personality and Social Psychology Bulletin*, **7**, 224–231.

Kerr, N. L., & Bruun, S. E. (1983). Dispensability of member effort and group motivation losses: Free-rider effects. *Journal of Personality and Social Psychology*, **44**, 78–94.

Kerr, N. L., & Kaufman-Gilliland, C. M. (1994). Communication, commitment, and cooperation in social dilemma. *Journal of Personality and Social Psychology*, **66**(3), 513.

Kerr, N. L., Garst, J., Lewandowski, D. A., & Harris, S. E. (1997). That still, small voice: Commitment to cooperate as an internalized versus a social norm. *Personality and Social Psychology Bulletin*, **23**, 1300–1311.

Khan, S., & Pedersen, A. (2010). Black African immigrants to Australia: Prejudice and the function of attitudes. *Journal of Pacific Rim Psychology*, **4**(2), 116–129.

Kiesler, C. A. (1971). *The psychology of commitment: Experiments linking behavior to belief*. New York: Academic Press.

Kihlstrom, J. F., & Cantor, N. (1984). Mental representations of the self. In L. Berkowitz (ed.), *Advances*

*in experimental social psychology*, Vol. 17. New York: Academic Press.

Kim, H., & Cabeza, R. (2007). Trusting our memories: Dissociating the neural correlates of confidence in veridical versus illusory memories. *Journal of Neuroscience*, **27**(45), 12190–12197.

Kim, H., & Markus, H. R. (1999). Deviance of uniqueness, harmony or conformity? A cultural analysis. *Journal of Personality and Social Psychology*, **77**, 785–800.

Kim, J., & Hatfield, E. (2004). Love types and subjective well-being: A cross cultural study. *Social Behavior and Personality*, **32**(2), 173–182.

Kimmel, A. J. (1998). In defense of deception. *American Psychologist*, **53**, 803–805.

King, L. L. (1986, 6 February). Books of the times. *The New York Times*, available at: http://www.nytimes.com/1986/02/06/books/books-of-the-times-935886.html

Kinnier, R. T., & Metha, A. T. (1989). Regrets and priorities at three stages of life. *Counseling and Values*, **33**(3), 182–193.

Kinsley, M. (2003, 21 April). The power of one. *Time*, p. 86.

Kitayama, S. (1999). Behind the scenes. In D. G. Myers, *Social Psychology*, 6th edn. New York: McGraw-Hill.

Kitayama, S., & Karasawa, M. (1997). Implicit self-esteem in Japan: Name letters and birthday numbers. *Personality and Social Psychology Bulletin*, **23**, 736–742.

Kitayama, S., & Markus, H. R. (1995). Culture and self: Implications for internationalizing psychology. In N. R. Godlberger & J. B. Veroff (eds), *The culture and psychology reader*. New York: New York University Press.

Kitayama, S., & Markus, H. R. (2000). The pursuit of happiness and the realization of sympathy: Cultural patterns of self-, social relations, and well-being. In E. Diener & E. M. Suh (eds), *Subjective well-being across cultures*. Cambridge, MA: MIT Press.

Kite, M. E. (2001). Changing times, changing gender roles: Who do we want women and men to be? In R. K. Unger (ed.), *Handbook of the psychology of women and gender*. New York: Wiley.

Kjaer, T. W., Nowak, M., & Lou, H. C. (2002). Reflective self-awareness and conscious states: PET evidence for a common midline parietofrontal core. *Neuroimage*, **17**, 1080–1086.

Klaas, E. T. (1978). Psychological effects of immoral actions: The experimental evidence. *Psychological Bulletin*, **85**, 756–771.

Klein, I., & Snyder, M. (2003). Stereotypes and behavioral confirmation: From interpersonal to intergroup perspectives. *Advances in Experimental Social Psychology*, **35**, 153–235.

Klein, J. G. (1991). Negative effects in impression formation: A test in the political arena. *Personality and Social Psychology Bulletin*, **17**, 412–418.

Klein, O., Snyder, M., & Livingston, R. W. (2004). Prejudice on the stage: Self-monitoring and the public expression of group attitudes. *British Journal of Social Psychology*, **43**, 299–314.

Klein, W. M., & Kunda, Z. (1992). Motivated person perception: Constructing justifications for desired beliefs. *Journal of Experimental Social Psychology*, **28**, 145–168.

Kleinke, C. L. (1977). Compliance to requests made by gazing and touching experimenters in field settings. *Journal of Experimental Social Psychology*, **13**, 218–223.

Kleinke, C. L., Peterson, T. R., & Rutledge, R. R. (1998). Effects of self-generated facial expressions on mood. *Journal of Personality and Social Psychology*, **74**, 272–279.

Klentz, B., Beaman, A. L., Mapelli, S. D., & Ullrich, J. R. (1987). Perceived physical attractiveness of supporters and nonsupporters of the women's movement: An attitude-similarity-mediated error (AS-ME). *Personality and Social Psychology Bulletin*, **13**, 513–523.

Klinesmith, J., Kasser, T., & McAndrew, F. T. (2006). Guns, testosterone, and aggression. *Psychological Science*, 17(7), 568–571.

Klopfer, P. H. (1958). Influence of social interaction on learning rates in birds. *Science*, **128**, 903.

Knee, C. R., Lonsbary, C., Canevello, A., & Patrick, H. (2005). Self-determination and conflict in romantic relationships. *Journal of Personality and Social Psychology*, **89**(6), 997–1009.

Knight, J. A., & Vallacher, R. R. (1981). Interpersonal engagement in social perception: The consequences of getting into the action. *Journal of Personality and Social Psychology*, **40**, 990–999.

Knight, M. T. D., Wykes, T., & Hayward, P. (2003). 'People don't understand': An investigation of stigma in schizophrenia using interpretative phenomenological analysis (IPA). *Journal of Mental Health*, **12**(3), 209–222.

Knight, P. A., & Weiss, H. M. (1980). Benefits of suffering: Communicator suffering, benefitting, and influence. Paper presented at the American Psychological Association convention.

Knowles, E. D., & Peng, K. (2005). White selves: Conceptualizing and measuring a dominant-group identity. *Journal of Personality and Social Psychology*, **89**, 223–241.

Knowles, M. L., & Gardner, W. L. (2008). Benefits of membership: The activation and amplification of group identities in response to social rejection. *Personality and Social Psychology Bulletin*, **34**, 1200–1213.

Knox, R. E., & Inkster, J. A. (1968). Postdecision dissonance at post-time. *Journal of Personality and Social Psychology*, **8**, 319–323.

Ko, A. Sai On (2005). Organizational communications in Hong Kong: A cultural approach to groupthink. *Corporate Communications*, **10**(4), 351–357.

Koestner, R., & Wheeler, L. (1988). Self-presentation in personal advertisements: The influence of implicit notions of attraction and

role expectations. *Journal of Social and Personal Relationships*, **5**, 149–160.

Kogut, T., & Ritov, I. (2007). 'One of us': Outstanding willingness to help save a single identified compatriot. *Organizational Behavior and Human Decision Processes*, **104**(2), 150–157.

Kohlberg, L. (1958). The development of modes of thinking and choices in Years 10 to 16. PhD dissertation, University of Chicago.

Kolb, B., & Whishaw, I. Q. (1998). Brain plasticity and behaviour. *Annual Review of Psychology*, **49**, 43–64.

Kolstad, A., & Horpestad, S. (2009). Self-construal in Chile and Norway. Implications for cultural differences in individualism and collectivism. *Journal of Cross-Cultural Psychology*, **40**(2), 275–281.

Konrad, A. M., Ritchie, J. E., Jr, Lieb, P., & Corrigall, E. (2000). Sex differences and similarities in job attribute preferences: A meta-analysis. *Psychological Bulletin*, **126**, 593–641.

Koole, S. L., Dijksterhuis, A., & van Knippenberg, A. (2001). What's in a name? Implicit self-esteem and the automatic self. *Journal of Personality and Social Psychology*, **80**, 669–685.

Koomen, W., & Bahler, M. (1996). National stereotypes: Common representations and ingroup favouritism. *European Journal of Social Psychology*, **26**, 325–331.

Koomen, W., & Dijker, A. J. (1997). Ingroup and outgroup stereotypes and selective processing. *European Journal of Social Psychology*, **27**, 589–601.

Koonz, C. (2003). *The Nazi conscience*. Cambridge: Bellknap.

Koop, C. E. (1987). Report of the Surgeon General's workshop on pornography and public health. *American Psychologist*, **42**, 944–945.

Koppel, M., Argamon, S., & Shimoni, A. R. (2002). Automatically categorizing written texts by author gender. *Literary and Linguistic Computing*, **17**, 401–412.

Koriat, A., Lichtenstein, S., & Fischhoff, B. (1980). Reasons for confidence. *Journal of Experimental*

*Social Psychology: Human Learning and Memory*, **6**, 107–118.

Korn, J. H., & Nicks, S. D. (1993). The rise and decline of deception in social psychology. Poster presented at the American Psychological Society convention.

Korobov, N. (2004). Inoculating against prejudice: A discursive approach to homophobia and sexism in adolescent male talk. *Psychology of Men & Masculinity*, **5**(2), 178–189.

Koss, M. P., Heise, L., & Russo, N. F. (1994). The global health burden of rape. *Psychology of Women Quarterly*, **18**, 509–537.

Koval, P., Laham, S. M., Haslam, N., Bastian, B., & Whelan, J. A. (2012). Our flaws are more human than yours: Ingroup bias in humanising negative characteristics. *Personality and Social Psychology Bulletin*, **38**, 283–295. doi: 10.1177/0146167211423777

Krackow, A., & Blass, T. (1995). When nurses obey or defy inappropriate physician orders: Attributional differences. *Journal of Social Behavior and Personality*, **10**, 585–594.

Krahé, B. (1998). Sexual aggression among adolescents: Prevalence and predictors in a German sample. *Psychology of Women Quarterly*, **22**, 537–554.

Kraus, S. J. (1995). Attitudes and the prediction of behavior: A meta-analysis of the empirical literature. *Personality and Social Psychology Bulletin*, **21**, 58–75.

Kraut, R. E. (1973). Effects of social labeling on giving to charity. *Journal of Experimental Social Psychology*, **9**(6), 551–562.

Kraut, R. E., & Lewis, S. H. (1982). Person perception and self-awareness: Knowledge of influences on one's own judgments. *Journal of Personality and Social Psychology*, **42**, 448–460.

Kravitz, D. A., & Martin, B. (1986). Ringelmann rediscovered: The original article. *Journal of Personality and Social Psychology*, **50**, 936–941.

Krebs, D. L. (1970). Altruism – An examination of the concept and a review of the lit-

erature. *Psychological Bulletin*, **73**, 258–302.

Krebs, D. L. (1975). Empathy and altruism. *Journal of Personality and Social Psychology*, **32**, 1134–1146.

Krebs, D. L. (1998). The evolution of moral behaviors. In C. Crawford & D. L. Krebs (eds), *Handbook of evolutionary psychology: Ideas, issues and applications*. Mahwah, NJ: Lawrence Erlbaum.

Krebs, D. L., & Adinolfi, A. A. (1975). Physical attractiveness, social relations, and personality style. *Journal of Personality and Social Psychology*, **31**, 245–253.

Krisberg, K. (2004). Successful truth – antismoking campaign in funding jeopardy: New commission works to save campaign. *Medscape* (www.medscape.com).

Kroeber, A. L., & Kluckhohn, C. (1952). Culture: a critical review of concepts and definitions. Papers, Peabody Museum of Archaeology & Ethnology, Harvard University, **47**(1), viii, 223.

Krosnick, J. A., & Alwin, D. F. (1989). Aging and susceptibility to attitude change. *Journal of Personality and Social Psychology*, **57**(3), 416.

Krosnick, J. A. & Schuman, H. (1988). Attitude intensity, importance, and certainty and susceptibility to response effects. *Journal of Personality and Social Psychology*, **54**, 940–952.

Krueger, A. B., & Maleckova, J. (2003, 6 June). Seeking the roots of terrorism. *The Chronicle Review* (www.chronicle.com).

Krueger, J. (1996). Personal beliefs and cultural stereotypes about racial characteristics. *Journal of Personality and Social Psychology*, **71**, 536–548.

Krueger, J., & Clement, R. W. (1994). The truly false consensus effect: An ineradicable and egocentric bias in social perception. *Journal of Personality and Social Psychology*, **67**, 596–610.

Krueger, J. I., & Funder, D. C. (2004a). Towards a balanced social psychology: Causes, consequences and cures for the problem-seeking approach to social behavior and cognition. *Behavioral and Brain Sciences*, **27**(3), 313–327.

Krueger, J. I., & Funder, D. C. (2004b). Social psychology: A field in search of a center. *Behavioral and Brain Sciences*, **27**(3), 361–367.

Krueger, R. F., Hicks, B. M., & McGue, M. (2001). Altruism and antisocial behavior: Independent tendencies, unique personality correlates, distinct etiologies. *Psychological Science*, **12**, 397–402.

Kruger, J., & Dunning, D. (1999). Unskilled and unaware of it: How difficulties in recognizing one's own incompetence lead to inflated self-assessments. *Journal of Personality and Social Psychology*, **77**, 1121–1134.

Kruger, J., & Evans, M. (2004). If you don't want to be late, enumerate: Unpacking reduces the planning fallacy. *Journal of Experimental Social Psychology*, **40**, 586–598.

Kruger, J., Wirtz, D., & Miller, D. T. (2005). Counterfactual thinking and the first instinct fallacy. *Journal of Personality and Social Psychology*, **88**, 725–735.

Kruglanski, A. W., & Golec de Zavala, A. (2005). Individual motivations, the group process and organizational strategies in suicide terrorism. In Eva M. Meyersson Milgrom, (ed.), *Suicide missions and the market for martyrs: A multidisciplinary approach*, Princeton, NJ: Princeton University Press

Kruglanski, A. W., & Thompson, E. P. (1999). Persuasion by a single route: A view from the unimodel. *Psychological Inquiry*, **10**(2), 83–109.

Kruglanski, A. W., & Webster, D. M. (1991). Group members' reactions to opinion deviates and conformists at varying degrees of proximity to decision deadline and of environmental noise. *Journal of Personality and Social Psychology*, **61**, 212–225.

Krugman, P. (2003, 18 February). Behind the great divide. *New York Times* (www.nytimes.com).

Krull, D. S., Loy, M. H.-M., Lin, J., Wang, C.-F., Chen, S., & Zhao, X. (1999). The fundamental attribution error: Correspondence bias in individualist and collectivist cultures. *Personality and Social Psychology Bulletin*, **25**, 1208–1219.

Kubacka, K. E., Finkenauer, C., Rusbult, C. E., & Keijsers, L. (2011). Maintaining close relationships: Gratitude as a motivator and a detector of maintenance behavior. *Personality and Social Psychology Bulletin*, **37**(10), 1362–1375.

Kubany, E. S., Bauer, G. B., Pangilinan, M. E., Muroka, M. Y., & Enriquez, V. G. (1995). Impact of labeled anger and blame in intimate relationships. *Journal of Cross-Cultural Psychology*, **26**, 65–83.

Kubey, R., & Csikszentmihalyi, M. (2002, February). Television addiction is no mere metaphor. *Scientific American*, **286**, 74–82.

Kugihara, N. (1999). Gender and social loafing in Japan. *Journal of Social Psychology*, **139**, 516–526.

Kuhn, M., & McPartland, T. S. (1954). An empirical investigation of self-attitudes. *American Sociological Review*, **19**, 68–76.

Kuiper, N. A. (1981). Convergent evidence for the self as a prototype: The 'inverted-URT effect' for self and other judgments. *Personality and Social Psychology Bulletin*, **7**(3), 438–443.

Kuiper, N. A., & Rogers, T. B. (1979). Encoding of personal information: Self-other differences. *Journal of Personality and Social Psychology*, **37**, 499–514.

Kulik, J. A. (1983). Confirmatory attributions and the perpetuation of social beliefs. *Journal of Personality and Social Psychology*, **44**, 1171–1181.

Kumkale, G. T., & Albarracín, D. (2004). The sleeper effect in persuasion: A meta-analytic review. *Psychological Bulletin*, **130**(1), 143.

Kunkel, D., Cope-Farrar, K., Biely, E., Maynard-Farinola, W. J., & Donnerstein, E. (2001). *Sex on TV 2*. Menlo, CA: The Henry J. Kaiser Family Foundation.

Kunst-Wilson, W. R., & Zajonc, R. B. (1980). Affective discrimination of stimuli that cannot be recognized. *Science*, **207**, 557–558.

Kutnick, P., Blatchford, P., & Baines, E. (2005). Grouping of pupils in secondary school classrooms: Possible links between pedagogy and learning. *Social Psychology of Education*, **8**, 349–374.

**L**

La Rochefoucauld, F. (1665). *Maxims*.

Lacey, M. (2004, 9 April). A decade after massacres, Rwanda outlaws ethnicity. *New York Times* (www.nytimes.com).

LaFromboise, T., Coleman, H. L. K., & Gerton, J. (1993). Psychological impact of biculturalism: Evidence and theory. *Psychological Bulletin*, **114**, 395–412.

Lagerspetz, K. (1979). Modification of aggressiveness in mice. In S. Feshbach & A. Fraczek (eds), *Aggression and behavior change*. New York: Praeger.

Laird, J. D. (1974). Self-attribution of emotion: The effects of expressive behavior on the quality of emotional experience. *Journal of Personality and Social Psychology*, **29**, 475–486.

Laird, J. D. (1984). The real role of facial response in the experience of emotion: A reply to Tourangeau and Ellsworth, and others. *Journal of Personality and Social Psychology*, **47**, 909–917.

Lakin, J. L., & Chartrand, T. L. (2003). Using nonconscious behavioral mimicry to create affiliation and rapport. *Psychological Science*, **14**, 334–339.

Lalancette, M.-F., & Standing, L. (1990). Asch fails again. *Social Behavior and Personality*, **18**, 7–12.

Lalonde, R. N. (1992). The dynamics of group differentiation in the face of defeat. *Personality and Social Psychology Bulletin*, **18**, 336–342.

Lam, S., Chiu, C., Lau, I. Y., Chan, W., & Yim, P. (2006). Managing intergroup attitudes among Hong Kong adolescents: Effects of social category inclusiveness and time pressure. *Asian Journal of Social Psychology*, **9**, 1–11.

Lamal, P. A. (1979). College students' common beliefs about psychology. *Teaching of Psychology*, **6**(3), 155–158.

Lammers, J., & Stapel, D. A. (2011). Power increases dehumanization. *Group Processes and Intergroup Relations*, **14**(1), 113–126.

Lammers, J., Stapel, D. A., & Galinksy, A. D. (2010). Power increases hypocrisy: moralizing in reasoning, immorality in behaviour. *Psychological Science*, **21**(5), 737–744.

Lammers, J., Stoker, J. I., & Stapel, D. A. (2009). Differentiating social and personal power: Opposite effects on stereotyping, but parallel effects on behavioral approach tendencies. *Psychological Science*, **20**(12), 1543–1548.

Lampard, R. (2007). Couples' places of meeting in late 20th century Britain: Class, continuity and change. *European Sociological Review*, **23**, 357–371.

Landau, M. J., Meier, B. P., & Keefer, L. A. (2010). A metaphor-enriched social cognition. *Psychological Bulletin*, **136**, 1045–1067.

Landau, M. J., Solomon, S., Greenberg, J., Cohen, F., Pyszczynski, T., Arndt, J., Miller, C. H., Ogilvie, D. M., & Cook, A. (2004). Deliver us from evil: The effects of mortality salience and reminders of 9/11 on support for President George W. Bush. *Personality and Social Psychology Bulletin*, **30**, 1136–1150.

Landers, A. (1969, 8 April). Syndicated newspaper column. 8 April, 1969. Cited by L. Berkowitz in The case for bottling up rage. *Psychology Today*, September 1973, pp. 24–31.

Lane, E. R. (2000). *The loss of happiness in market democracies*. New Haven & London: Yale University Press.

Langbein, H. (1994). *Against all hope*. Saint Paul, MN: Paragon House.

Langdridge, D. (2007). *Phenomenological psychology: Theory, research and method*. Harlow: Pearson Education.

Langdridge, D. (2008). Phenomenology and

critical social psychology: Directions and debates in theory and research. *Social and Personality Psychology Compass*, **2**(3), 1126–1142.

Langer, E. J. (1977). The psychology of chance. *Journal for the Theory of Social Behavior*, 7, 185–208.

Langer, E. J., & Roth, J. (1975). Heads I win, tails it's chance: The illusion of control as a function of the sequence of outcomes in a purely chance task. *Journal of Personality and Social Psychology*, **32**, 951–955.

Langlois, J. H., Kalakanis, L., Rubenstein, A., Larson, A., Hallam, M., & Smoot, M. (1996). Maxims and myths of beauty: A meta-analytic and theoretical review. Paper presented to the American Psychological Society convention.

Langlois, J. H., Kalakanis, L., Rubenstein, A. J., Larson, A., Hallam, M., & Smoot, M. (2000). Maxims or myths of beauty? A meta-analytic and theoretical review. *Psychological Bulletin*, **126**, 390–423.

Lanzetta, J. T. (1955). Group behavior under stress. *Human Relations*, 8, 29–53.

LaPiere, R. T. (1934). Attitudes versus actions. *Social Forces*, **13**(2), 230–237.

Lapinski, M. K., & Boster, F. J. (2001). Modeling the ego-defensive function of attitudes. *Communication Monographs*, **68**(3), 314–324.

Larsen, K. S. (1974). Conformity in the Asch experiment. *Journal of Social Psychology*, **94**, 303–304.

Larsen, K. S. (1990). The Asch conformity experiment: Replication and transhistorical comparisons. *Journal of Social Behavior and Personality*, **5**(4), 163–168.

Larsen, R. J., & Diener, E. (1987). Affect intensity as an individual difference characteristic: A review. *Journal of Research in Personality*, **21**, 1–39.

Larson, J. R., Jr, Foster-Fishman, P. G., & Keys, C. B. (1994). Discussion of shared and unshared information in decision-making groups. *Journal of Personality and Social Psychology*, **67**, 446–461.

Larsson, K. (1956). *Conditioning and sexual behavior in the male albino rat*. Stockholm: Almqvist & Wiksell.

Lash, C. (1979). *The culture of narcissism: American life in an age of diminishing expectations*. New York: Norton & Company.

Lassiter, G. D., & Dudley, K. A. (1991). The a priori value of basic research: The case of videotaped confessions. *Journal of Social Behavior and Personality*, **6**, 7–16.

Lassiter, G. D., & Irvine, A. A. (1986). Videotaped confessions: The impact of camera point of view on judgements of coercion. *Journal of Applied Social Psychology*, **16**, 268–276.

Lassiter, G. D., Geers, A. L., Handley, I. M., Weiland, P. E., & Munhall, P. J. (2002). Videotaped interrogations and confessions: A simple change in camera perspective alters verdicts in simulated trials. *Journal of Applied Psychology*, **87**, 867–874.

Lassiter, G. D., Munhall, P. J., Berger, I. P., Weiland, P. E., Handley, I. M., & Geers, A. L. (2005). Attributional complexity and the camera perspective bias in videotaped confessions. *Basic and Applied Social Psychology*, **27**, 27–35.

Lasswell, H. D. (1948). The structure and function of communication in society. *The Communication of Ideas*, **37**, 215–228.

Latané, B. (1981). The psychology of social impact. *American Psychologist*, **36**(4), 343–356.

Latané, B., & Dabbs, J. M., Jr (1975). Sex, group size and helping in three cities. *Sociometry*, **38**, 180–194.

Latané, B., & Darley, J. M. (1968). Group inhibition of bystander intervention in emergencies. *Journal of Personality and Social Psychology*, **10**, 215–221.

Latané, B., & Darley, J. M. (1970). *The unresponsive bystander: Why doesn't he help?* New York: Appleton-Century-Crofts.

Latané, B., & Nida, S. (1981). Ten years of research on group size and helping. *Psychological Bulletin*, **89**, 308–324.

Latané, B., & Rodin, J. (1969). A lady in distress: Inhibiting effects of friends and strangers on bystander intervention. *Journal of Experimental Social Psychology*, **5**, 189–202.

Latané, B., Williams, K., & Harkins, S. (1979). Many hands make light the work: The causes and consequences of social loafing. *Journal of Personality and Social Psychology*, **37**, 822–832.

Latrofa, M., Vaes, J., Pastore, M., & Cadinu, M. (2009). 'United we stand, divided we fall'! The protective function of self-stereotyping for stigmatised members' psychological well-being. *Applied Psychology*, **58**, 84–104.

Laughlin, P. R. (1996). Group decision making and collective induction. In E. H. Witte & J. H. Davis (eds), *Understanding group behavior: Consensual action by small groups*. Mahwah, NJ: Erlbaum.

Laughlin, P. R., & Adamopoulos, J. (1980). Social combination processes and individual learning for six-person cooperative groups on an intellective task. *Journal of Personality and Social Psychology*, **38**, 941–947.

Laughlin, P. R., Hatch, E. C., Silver, J. S., & Boh, L. (2006). Groups perform better than the best individuals on letters-to-numbers problems: Effects of group size. *Journal of Personality and Social Psychology*, **90**, 644–651.

Laughlin, P. R., Zander, M. L., Knievel, E. M., & Tan, T. K. (2003). Groups perform better than the best individuals on letters-to-numbers problems: Informative equations and effective strategies. *Journal of Personality and Social Psychology*, **85**, 684–694.

Lazare, A. (2004). *On apology*. New York: Oxford University Press.

Le Bon, G. (1895). *Psychologie des foules*. Paris: University of France Press.

Le Bon, G. (1895/1995). *The crowd*. New Brunswick, NJ: Transaction.

Leach, C. W., & Spears, R. (2008). 'A vengefulness of the impotent': The pain of in-group inferiority and schadenfreude toward successful out-groups. *Journal of Personality and Social Psychology*, **95**, 1383–1396.

Leach, C. W., & Spears, R. (2009). Dejection at in-group defeat and schadenfreude toward second- and third-party out-groups. *Emotion*, **9**, 659–665.

Leach, C. W., Spears, R., Branscombe, N. R., & Doosje, B. (2003). Malicious pleasure: Schadenfreude at the suffering of another group. *Journal of Personality and Social Psychology*, **84**(5), 932–943.

Leach, C. W., van Zomeren, M., Zebel, S., Vliek, M. L. W., Pennekamp, S. F., Doosje, B., & Spears, R. (2008). Group-level self-definition and self-investment: A hierarchical (multicomponent) model of in-group identification. *Journal of Personality and Social Psychology*, **95**, 144–165.

Leary, M. R. (1998). The social and psychological importance of self-esteem. In R. M. Kowalski & M. R. Leary (eds), *The social psychology of emotional and behavioral problems*. Washington, DC: American Psychological Association.

Leary, M. R. (1999). The social and psychological importance of self-esteem. In R. M. Kowalski & M. R. Leary (eds), *The social psychology of emotional and behavioral problems*. Washington, DC: APA Books.

Leary, M. R. (2003). Interpersonal aspects of optimal self-esteem and the authentic self. *Psychological Inquiry*, **14**, 52–54.

Leary, M. R. (2004). *The curse of the self: Self-awareness, egotism, and the quality of human life*. New York: Oxford University Press.

Leary, M. R. (2007). Motivational and emotional aspects of the self. *Annual Review of Psychology*, **58**, 317–344.

Leary, M. R., Nezlek, J. B., Radford-Davenport, D., Martin, J., & McMullen, A. (1994). Self-presentation in everyday interactions: Effects of target familiarity and gender composition. *Journal of Personality and Social Psychology*, **67**, 664–673.

Lee, A. Y., & Aaker, J. L. (2004). Bringing the frame into focus: The influence of regulatory fit on processing fluency and persuasion. *Journal of Personality and Social Psychology*, **86**, 205–218.

Lee, F., Hallahan, M., & Herzog, T. (1996). Explaining real-life events: How culture and domain shape attributions. *Personality and Social Psychology Bulletin*, **22**, 732–741.

Lee, J. A. (1998). Ideologies of lovestyle and sexstyle. In V. C. de Munck (ed.), *Romantic love and sexual behavior: Perspectives from the social sciences*. Westport, CT: Praeger/Greenwood.

Lee, R. Y.-P., & Bond, M. H. (1996). How friendship develops out of personality and values: A study of interpersonal attraction in Chinese culture. Unpublished manuscript, Chinese University of Hong Kong.

Lee, Y-S., & Waite, L. (2005). Husband's and wife's time spent on housework: A comparison of measures. *Journal of Marriage and Family*, **67**, 328–336.

Leeuwen, E. V., & Täuber, S. (2011). Demonstrating knowledge: The effects of group status on outgroup helping. *Journal of Experimental Social Psychology*, **47**, 147–156.

Lefcourt, H. M. (1982). *Locus of control: Current trends in theory and research*. Hillsdale, NJ: Erlbaum.

Lehr, A. T., & Geher, G. (2006). Differential effects of reciprocity and attitude similarity across long- versus short-term mating contexts. *The Journal of Social Psychology*, **146**(4), 423–439.

Lehrer, J. (2012). *Imagine: How creativity works*. New York: Houghton Mifflin Harcourt.

Leinbach, M. D., & Fagot, B. I. (1993). Categorical habituation to male and female faces: Gender schematic processes in infancy. *Infant Behavior & Development*, **16**, 317–332.

Leippe, M. R., & Elkin, R. A. (1987). Dissonance reduction strategies and accountability to self and others: Ruminations and some initial research. Presentation to the Fifth International Conference on Affect, Motivation, and Cognition, Nags Head Conference Center.

LeMarquand, D. G., Pihl, R. O., Young, S. N., Tremblay, R. E., Seguin, J. R., Palmour, R. M., & Benkelfat, C. (1998). Tryptophan depletion, executive functions, and disinhibition in aggressive, adolescent males. *Neuropsychopharmacology*, **19**(4), 333–341.

Lennon, A., & Watson, B. (2011). 'Teaching them a lesson?' A qualitative exploration of underlying motivations for driver aggression. *Accident Analysis and Prevention*, **43**(6), 2200–2208.

Leon, D. (1969). *The Kibbutz: A new way of life*. London: Pergamon Press. Cited by B. Latané, K. Williams & S. Harkins (1979), Many hands make light the work: The causes and consequences of social loafing. *Journal of Personality and Social Psychology*, **37**, 822–832.

Lepper, M. R., & Greene, D. (eds) (1979). *The hidden costs of reward*. Hillsdale, NJ: Erlbaum.

Lerner, M. J. (1980). *The belief in a just world: A fundamental delusion*. New York: Plenum.

Lerner, M. J., & Miller, D.T. (1978). Just world research and the attribution process: Looking back and ahead. *Psychological Bulletin*, **85**, 1030–1051.

Lerouge, D., & Smeesters, D. (2008). Knowledge activation after information encoding: Implications of trait priming on person judgement. *Journal of Experimental Social Psychology*, **44**, 429–436.

Leung, K., & Bond, M. H. (2004). Social axioms: A model of social beliefs in multicultural perspective. *Advances in Experimental Social Psychology*, **36**, 119–197.

Leung, K., & Bond, M. H. (eds) (2009). *Psychological aspects of social axioms: Understanding global belief systems. International and cultural psychology series*, New York: Springer Science + Business Media.

Leung, K., Bond, M. H., Reimel de Carrasquel, S., Muñoz, C., Hernández, M., Murakami, F., Yamaguchi, S., Bierbrauer, G., & Singelis, T. M. (2002). Social axioms: The search for universal dimensions of general beliefs about how the world functions. *Journal of Cross-Cultural Psychology*, **33**, 286–302.

Leventhal, H. (1970). Findings and theory in the study of fear communications. In L. Berkowitz (ed.), *Advances in experimental social psychology*, Vol. 5. New York: Academic Press.

Levine, J. M. (1989). Reaction to opinion deviance in small groups. In P. Paulus (ed.), *Psychology of group influence: New perspectives*. Hillsdale, NJ: Erlbaum.

Levine, J. M., & Moreland, R. L. (1985). Innovation and socialization in small groups. In S. Moscovici, G. Mugny & E. Van Avermaet (eds), *Perspectives on minority influence*. Cambridge: Cambridge University Press.

Levine, M. (1999). Rethinking bystander non-intervention: Social categorization and the evidence of witnesses at the James Bulger Murder trial. *Human Relations*, **52**(9), 1133–1155.

Levine, M., & Thompson, K. (2004). Identity, place, and bystander intervention: social categories and helping after natural disasters. *Journal of Social Psychology*, **144**, 229–245.

Levine, M., Prosser, A., Evans, D., & Reicher, S. (2005). Identity and emergency intervention: How social group membership and inclusiveness of group boundaries shape helping behavior. *Personality and Social Psychology Bulletin*, **31**, 443–453.

Levine, R. M. (1999). Identity and illness: The effects of identity salience and frame of reference on evaluation of illness and injury. *British Journal of Health Psychology*, **4**, 63–80.

Levine, R. V. (2001). Cross-cultural differences in helping strangers. *Journal of Cross-Cultural Psychology*, **32**, 543–560.

Levine, R. V. (2003). The kindness of strangers. *American Scientist*, **91**, 226–233.

Levine, R. V., Martinez, T. S., Brase, G., & Sorenson, K. (1994). Helping in 36 US cities. *Journal of Personality and Social Psychology*, **67**, 69–82.

Levitan, L. C., & Visser, P. S. (2007). The impact of the social context on resistance to persuasion: Effortful versus effortless responses to counter-attitudinal information. *Journal of Experimental Social Psychology*, **44**, 640–649.

Levitt, M. (2013). Genes, environment and responsibility for violent behavior: 'Whatever genes one has it is preferable that you are prevented from going around stabbing people'. *New Genetics and Society*, **32**(1), 4–17.

Lewandowsky, S., Stritzke, W. G. K., Oberauer, K., & Morales, M. (2005). Memory for fact, fiction, and misinformation: The Iraq War 2003. *Psychological Science*, **16**, 190–195.

Lewin, K. (1936). *A dynamic theory of personality*. New York: McGraw-Hill.

Lewis, C., & Lamb, M. E. (2006). Father–child relationships and children's development: A key to durable solutions? In Rt Hon. Lord Justice Thorpe & R. Budden (eds), *Durable Solutions*. Bristol: Family Law/Jordans.

Lewis, C. S. (1952). *Mere Christianity*. New York: Macmillan.

Lewis, I., Watson, B., Tay, R., & White, K. M. (2007). The role of fear appeals in improving driver safety: A review of the effectiveness of fear-arousing (threat) appeals in road safety advertising. *International Journal of Behavioural Consultation and Therapy*, **3**(2), 203–222.

Lewis, R. S., Goto, S. G., & King, L. L. (2008). Culture and context: East Asian American and European American differences in P3 event-related potentials and self-construal. *Personality and Social Psychology Bulletin*, **34**, 623–634.

Leyens, J. P., Paladino, M. P., Rodriguez, R. T., Vaes, J., Demoulin, S., Rodriguez, A. P., & Gaunt, R. (2000). The emotional side of prejudice: The attribution of secondary emotions to ingroups and outgroups.

*Personality and Social Psychology Review*, **4**, 186–197.

Leyens, J.-P., Camino, L., Parke, R. D., & Berkowitz, L. (1975). Effects of movie violence on aggression in a field setting as a function of group dominance and cohesion. *Journal of Personality and Social Psychology*, **32**, 346–360.

Li, N. P., Bailey, J. M., Kenrick, D. T., & Linsenmeier, J. A. W. (2002). The necessities and luxuries of mate preferences: Testing the tradeoffs. *Journal of Personality and Social Psychology*, **82**, 947–955.

Liberman, A., & Chaiken, S. (1992). Defensive processing of personally relevant health messages. *Personality and Social Psychology Bulletin*, **18**, 669–679.

Lichtenstein, S., & Fischhoff, B. (1980). Training for calibration. *Organizational Behavior and Human Performance*, **26**, 149–171.

Lieberman, M. D. (2007). The X- and C-Systems: The neural basis of automatic and controlled social cognition. In E. Harmon-Jones & P. Winkielman (eds), *Social neuroscience: Integrating biological and psychological explanations of social behavior*. New York: Guilford Press.

Likert, R. (1932). A technique for the measurement of attitudes. *Archives of Psychology*, **140**, 1–55.

Linden-Andersen, S., Markiewicz, D., & Dole, A.-B. (2009). Perceived similarity among adolescent friends: The role of reciprocity, friendship quality, and gender. *The Journal of Early Adolescence*, **29**(5), 617–637.

Linder, J. R., & Gentile, D. A. (2009). Is the television rating system valid? Indirect, verbal, and physical aggression in programs viewed by fifth grade girls and associations with behavior. *Journal of Applied Developmental Psychology*, **30**, 286–297.

Lindsay, D. S., Hagen, L., Read, J. D., Wade, K. A., & Garry, M. (2004). True photographs and false memories. *Psychological Science*, **15**, 149–154.

Lindskold, S. (1978). Trust development, the GRIT proposal, and the effects of con-

ciliatory acts on conflict and cooperation. *Psychological Bulletin*, **85**, 772–793.

Lindskold, S. (1979a). Conciliation with simultaneous or sequential interaction: Variations in trustworthiness and vulnerability in the prisoner's dilemma. *Journal of Conflict Resolution*, **27**, 704–714.

Lindskold, S. (1979b). Managing conflict through announced conciliatory initiatives backed with retaliatory capability. In W. G. Austin & S. Worchel (eds), *The social psychology of intergroup relations*. Monterey, CA: Brooks/Cole.

Lindskold, S. (1981). The laboratory evaluation of GRIT: Trust, cooperation, aversion to using conciliation. Paper presented at the American Association for the Advancement of Science convention.

Lindskold, S. (1983). Cooperators, competitors, and response to GRIT. *Journal of Conflict Resolution*, **27**, 521–532.

Lindskold, S., & Aronoff, J. R. (1980). Conciliatory strategies and relative power. *Journal of Experimental Social Psychology*, **16**, 187–198.

Lindskold, S., & Collins, M. G. (1978). Inducing cooperation by groups and individuals. *Journal of Conflict Resolution*, **22**, 679–690.

Lindskold, S., & Finch, M. L. (1981). Styles of announcing conciliation. *Journal of Conflict Resolution*, **25**, 145–155.

Lindskold, S., & Han, G. (1988). GRIT as a foundation for integrative bargaining. *Personality and Social Psychology Bulletin*, **14**, 335–345.

Lindskold, S., Bennett, R., & Wagner, M. (1976). Retaliation level as a foundation for subsequent conciliation. *Behavioral Science*, **21**, 13–18.

Lindskold, S., Betz, B., & Walters, P. S. (1986a). Transforming competitive or cooperative climate. *Journal of Conflict Resolution*, **30**, 99–114.

Lindskold, S., Han, G., & Betz, B. (1986b). Repeated persuasion in interpersonal conflict. *Journal of Personality and Social Psychology*, **51**, 1183–1188.

Lindskold, S., Han, G., & Betz, B. (1986c). The essential elements of communication in the GRIT strategy. *Personality and Social Psychology Bulletin*, **12**, 179–186.

Lindskold, S., Walters, P. S., Koutsourais, H., & Shayo, R. (1981). Cooperators, competitors, and response to GRIT. Unpublished manuscript, Ohio University.

Lines, R. (2005). The structure and function of attitudes toward organizational change. *Human Resource Development Review*, **4**(1), 8–32.

Linssen, H., & Hagendoorn, L. (1994). Social and geographical factors in the explanation of the content of European nationality stereotypes. *British Journal of Social Psychology*, **33**, 165–182.

Lippa, R. A. (2007). The preferred traits of mates in a cross-national study of heterosexual and homosexual men and women: An examination of biological and cultural influences. *Archives of Sexual Behaviour*, **36**, 193–208.

Lippmann, W. (1922). *Public opinion*. Oxford: Harcourt and Brace.

Little, A. C., Jones, B. C., DeBruine, L. M., & Feinberg, D. R. (2008). Symmetry and sexual dimorphism in human faces: Interrelated preferences suggest both signal quality. *Behavioral Ecology*, **19**(4), 902–908.

Liu, J. H., & Latané, B. (1998). Extremitization of attitudes: Does thought- and discussion-induced polarization cumulate? *Basic and Applied Social Psychology*, **20**, 103–110.

Livingston, R. W. (2001). What you see is what you get: Systematic variability in perceptual-based social judgment. *Personality and Social Psychology Bulletin*, **27**, 1086–1096.

Livingstone, A. G., Young, H., & Manstead, A. S. R. (2011). 'We drink, therefore we are': The role of group identification and norms in sustaining and challenging heavy drinking 'culture'. *Group Processes and Intergroup Relations*, **14**, 637–649.

Locke, A., & Edwards, D. (2003). Bill and Monica: memory, emotion and normativity in Clinton's grand jury testimony. *British Journal of Social Psychology*, **42**, 239–256.

Locke, E. A., & Latham, G. P. (1990). Work motivation and satisfaction: Light at the end of the tunnel. *Psychological Science*, **1**, 240–246.

Locke, K. D., & Horowitz, L. M. (1990). Satisfaction in interpersonal interactions as a function of similarity in level of dysphoria. *Journal of Personality and Social Psychology*, **58**, 823–831.

Lockwood, P. (2002). Could it happen to you? Predicting the impact of downward comparisons on the self. *Journal of Personality and Social Psychology*, **87**, 343–358.

Lockwood, P., Dolderman, D., Sadler, P., & Gerchak, E. (2004). Feeling better about doing worse: Social comparisons within romantic relationships. *Journal of Personality and Social Psychology*, **87**, 80–95.

Lofland, J., & Stark, R. (1965). Becoming a worldsaver: A theory of conversion to a deviant perspective. *American Sociological Review*, **30**, 862–864.

Loftin, C., McDowall, D., Wiersema, B., & Cottey, T. J. (1991). Effects of restrictive licensing of handguns on homicide and suicide in the District of Columbia. *New England Journal of Medicine*, **325**, 1615–1620.

Loftus, E. F. (2003). Make-believe memories. *American Psychologist*, **58**, 867–873.

Loftus, E. F., & Bernstein, D. M. (2005). Rich false memories: The royal road to success. In A. F. Healy (ed.), *Experimental cognitive psychology and its applications*. Washington, DC: American Psychological Association.

Loftus, E. F., & Klinger, M. R. (1992). Is the unconscious smart or dumb? *American Psychologist*, **47**, 761–765.

Lombardo, J. P., Weiss, R. F., & Buchanan, W. (1972). Reinforcing and attracting functions of yielding. *Journal of Personality and Social Psychology*, **21**, 359–368.

Long, S., Mollen, D., & Smith, N. (2012). College women's attitudes towards sex workers. *Sex Roles*, **66**(1), 117–127.

Lonner, W. J. (1980). The search for psychological universals. In H. C. Triandis & W. W. Lambert (eds), *Handbook of cross-cultural psychology*, Vol. 1. Boston: Allyn and Bacon.

Lonner, W. J. (1989). The introductory psychology text and cross-cultural psychology: Beyond Ekman, Whorf, and biased I.Q. tests. In D. Keats, D. R. Munro & L. Mann (eds), *Heterogeneity in cross-cultural psychology*. Lisse, Netherlands: Swets & Zeitlinger.

Lord, C. G., Lepper, M. R., & Preston, E. (1984). Considering the opposite: A corrective strategy for social judgment. *Journal of Personality and Social Psychology*, **47**, 1231–1243.

Lord, C. G., Ross, L., & Lepper, M. (1979). Biased assimilation and attitude polarization: The effects of prior theories on subsequently considered evidence. *Journal of Personality and Social Psychology*, **37**, 2098–2109.

Losch, M. E., & Cacioppo, J. T. (1990). Cognitive dissonance may enhance sympathetic focus, but attitudes are changed to reduce negative affect rather than arousal. *Journal of Experimental Social Psychology*, **26**, 289–304.

Lott, A. J., & Lott, B. E. (1961). Group cohesiveness as interpersonal attraction: A review of relationships with antecedent and consequent variables. *Psychological Bulletin*, **64**, 259–309.

Lott, A. J., & Lott, B. E. (1965). Group cohesiveness as interpersonal attraction: A review of relationships with antecedent and consequent variables. *Psychological Bulletin*, **64**(4), 259.

Lott, A. J., & Lott, B. E. (1974). The role of reward in the formation of positive interpersonal attitudes. In T. Huston (ed.), *Foundations of interpersonal attraction*. New York: Academic Press.

Louis, M. R. (1980). Surprise and sense making: What newcomers experience in entering unfamiliar organizational settings. *Administrative Science Quarterly*, **25**, 226–251.

Lowenstein, D. (2000, 20 May). Interview. *The World Today* (www.cnn.com/TRANSCRIPTS/0005/20/stc.00.html).

Lowenthal, M. F., Thurnher, M., Chiriboga, D., Beefon, D., Gigy, L., Lurie, E., Pierce, R., Spence, D., & Weiss, L. (1975). *Four stages of life*. San Francisco: Jossey-Bass.

Loy, J. W., & Andrews, D. S. (1981). They also saw a game: A replication of a case study. *Replications in Social Psychology*, **1**(2), 45–59.

Lu, L. (2003). Defining the self-other relation: The emergence of a composite self. *Indigenous Psychological Research in Chinese Societies*, **20**, 139–207.

Lu, L., & Yang, K.-S. (2006). Emergence and composition of the traditional-modern bicultural self of people in contemporary Taiwanese societies. *Asian Journal of Social Psychology*, **9**(3), 167–175.

Lücken, M., & Simon, B. (2005). Cognitive and affective experiences of minority and majority members: The role of group size, status, and power. *Journal of Experimental Social Psychology*, **41**, 396–413.

Luhtanen, R., & Crocker, J. (1992). A collective self-esteem scale: Self-evaluation of one's social identity. *Personality & Social Psychology Bulletin*, **18**, 302–318.

Lumsdaine, A. A., & Janis, I. L. (1953). Resistance to 'counter-propaganda' produced by one-sided and two-sided 'propaganda' presentations. *Public Opinion Quarterly*, **17**, 311–318.

Lumsden, A., Zanna, M. P., & Darley, J. M. (1980). When a newscaster presents counter-additional information: Education or propaganda? Paper presented to the Canadian Psychological Association annual convention.

Luo, S., & Klohnen, E. C. (2005). Assortative mating and marital quality in newlyweds: A couple-centered approach. *Journal of Personality and Social Psychology*, **88**, 304–326.

Lydon, J., & Dunkel-Schetter, C. (1994). Seeing is committing: A longitudinal study of bolstering commitment in amniocentesis patients. *Personality and Social Psychology Bulletin*, **20**, 218–227.

Lykken, D. T. (1997). The American crime factory. *Psychological Inquiry*, **8**, 261–270.

Lykken, D. T., & Tellegen, A. (1993). Is human mating adventitious or the result of lawful choice? A twin study of mate selection. *Journal of Personality and Social Psychology*, **65**, 56–68.

Lynn, N., & Lea, S. J. (2003). A phantom menace and the new Apartheid: the social construction of asylum seekers in the United Kingdom. *Discourse and Society*, **14**(4), 425–452.

Lyons, L. (2003, 23 September). Oh, boy: Americans still prefer sons. *Gallup Poll Tuesday Briefing* (www.gallup.com).

## M

Ma, V., & Schoeneman, T. J. (1997). Individualism versus collectivism: A comparison of Kenyan and American self-concepts. *Basic and Applied Social Psychology*, **19**, 261–273.

Maass, A. (1998). Personal communication from Universita degli Studi di Padova.

Maass, A. (1999). Linguistic intergroup bias: Stereotype perpetuation through language. In M. P. Zanna (ed.), *Advances in Experimental Social Psychology*, **31**, 79–121.

Maass, A., & Clark, R. D., III. (1984). Hidden impact of minorities: Fifteen years of minority influence research. *Psychological Bulletin*, **95**, 428–450.

Maass, A., & Clark, R. D., III. (1986). Conversion theory and simultaneous majority/minority influence: Can reactance offer an alternative explanation? *European Journal of Social Psychology*, **16**, 305–309.

Maass, A., Milesi, A., Zabbini, S., & Stahlberg, D. (1995). Linguistic intergroup bias: Differential expectancies or in-group protection? *Journal of Personality and Social Psychology*, **68**, 116–126.

Maass, A., Volparo, C., & Mucchi-Faina, A. (1996). Social influence and the verifiability of the issue under discussion: Attitudinal versus objective items. *British Journal of Social Psychology*, **35**, 15–26.

Maccoby, E. E. (2002). Gender and group process: A developmental perspective. *Current Directions in Psychological Science*, **11**, 54–58.

Maccoby, E. E., & Jacklin, C. N. (1974). *The psychology of sex differences*. London: Oxford University Press.

Maccoby, N. (1980). Promoting positive health behaviors in adults. In L. A. Bond & J. C. Rosen (eds), *Competence and coping during adulthood*. Hanover, NH: University Press of New England.

Maccoby, N., & Alexander, J. (1980). Use of media in lifestyle programs. In P. O. Davidson & S. M. Davidson (eds). *Behavioral medicine: Changing health lifestyles*. New York: Brunner/Mazel.

MacDonald, G., Zanna, M. P., & Holmes, J. G. (2000). An experimental test of the role of alcohol in relationship conflict. *Journal of Experimental Social Psychology*, **36**, 182–193.

MacDonald, T. K., & Ross, M. (1997). Assessing the accuracy of predictions about dating relationships: How and why do lovers' predictions differ from those made by observers? Unpublished manuscript, University of Lethbridge.

Mack, D., & Rainey, D. (1990). Female applicants' grooming and personnel selection. *Journal of Social Behavior and Personality*, **5**, 399–407.

MacLeod, C., & Campbell, L. (1992). Memory accessibility and probability judgments: An experimental evaluation of the availability heuristic. *Journal of Personality and Social Psychology*, **63**, 890–902.

Macrae, C. N., & Bodenhausen, G. V. (2000). Social cognition: Thinking categorically about others. *Annual Review of Psychology*, **51**, 93–120.

Macrae, C. N., & Johnston, L. (1998). Help, I need somebody: Automatic action and inaction. *Social Cognition*, **16**, 400–417.

Macrae, C. N., & Martin, D. (2007). A boy primed Sue: feature-based processing and person construal. *European Journal of Social Psychology*, **37**, 793–805.

Macrae, C. N., Alnwick, M. A., Milne, A. B., & Schloerscheidt, A. M. (2002). Person perception across the menstrual cycle: Hormonal influences on social cognitive functioning. *Psychological Science*, **13**, 532–536.

Macrae, C. N., Stangor, C., & Hewstone, M. (1996). *Stereotypes and stereotyping*. London: Guilford Press.

Maddux, J. E., & Gosselin, J. T. (2003). Self-efficacy. In M. R. Leary, & J. P. Tangney (eds), *Handbook of self and identity*. New York: Guilford Press.

Maddux, J. E., & Rogers, R. W. (1983). Protection motivation and self-efficacy: A revised theory of fear appeals and attitude change. *Journal of Experimental Social Psychology*, **19**, 469–479.

Madon, S., Jussim, L., & Eccles, J. (1997). In search of the powerful self-fulfilling prophecy. *Journal of Personality and Social Psychology*, **72**, 791–809.

Madon, S., Jussim, L., Keiper, S., Eccles, J., Smith, A., & Palumbo, P. (1998). The accuracy and power of sex, social class, and ethnic stereotypes: A naturalistic study in person perception. *Personality and Social Psychology Bulletin*, **24**, 1304–1318.

Mae, L., Carlston, D. E., & Skowronski, J. J. (1999). Spontaneous trait transference to familiar communicators: Is a little knowledge a dangerous thing? *Journal of Personality and Social Psychology*, **77**(2), 233–246.

Mähöen, T. A., Jasinskaja-Lahti, I., & Liebkind, K. (2011). The impact of perceived social norms, gender, and intergroup anxiety on the relationship between intergroup contact and ethnic attitudes of adolescents. *Journal of Applied Social Psychology*, **41**(8), 1877–1899.

Malamuth, N. M. (1996). The confluence model of sexual aggression. In D. M. Buss & N. M. Malamuth (eds), *Sex, power, conflict: Evolutionary and feminist perspectives*. New York: Oxford University Press.

Malamuth, N. M. (2003). Criminal and noncriminal sexual aggressors: Integrating psychopathy in a hierarchicalmediational confluence model. In R. A. Prentky, E. Janus & M. Seto (eds), *Sexually coercive behavior: Understanding and management*. New York: Annals of the New York Academy of Sciences.

Malamuth, N. M., & Check, J. V. P. (1981). The effects of media exposure on acceptance of violence against women: A field experiment. *Journal of Research in Personality*, **15**, 436–446.

Malamuth, N. M., Haber, S., & Feshbach, S (1980). Testing hypotheses regarding rape: Exposure to sexual violence, sex differences and the 'normality' of rapists. *Journal of Research in Personality*, **14**, 121–137.

Malle, B. F. (2006). The actor–observer asymmetry in causal attribution: A (surprising) meta analysis. *Psychological Bulletin*, 132, 895–919.

Malle, B. F. & Holbrook, J. (2012). Is there a hierarchy of social inferences? The likelihood and speed of inferring intentionality, mind, and personality. *Journal of Personality and Social Psychology*, **102**, 661–684.

Manago, A. M., Graham, M. B., Greenfield, P. M., & Salimkhan, G. (2008). Self-presentation and gender on MySpace. *Journal of Applied Developmental Psychology*, **29**, 446–458.

Maner, J. K., Kenrick, D. T., Becker, V., Robertson, T. E., Hofer, B., Neuberg, S. L., Delton, A. W., Butner, J., & Schaller, M. (2005). Functional projection: How fundamental social motives can bias interpersonal perception. *Journal of Personality and Social Psychology*, **88**, 63–78.

Manis, M., Cornell, S. D., & Moore, J. C. (1974). Transmission of attitude-relevant information through a communication chain. *Journal of Personality and Social Psychology*, **30**, 81–94.

Mann, L. (1981). The baiting crowd in episodes of threatened suicide. *Journal of Personality and Social Psychology*, **41**(4), 703–709.

Manning, R., Levine, M., & Collins, A. (2007). The Kitty Genovese murder and the social psychology of helping: The parable of the 38 witnesses. *American Psychologist*, **62**(6), 555–562.

Mäntylä, T. (2013). Gender differences in multitasking reflect spatial ability. *Psychological Science*, **24**(4), 514–520.

Manuck, S. B., Flory, J. D., Ferrell, R. E., Muldoon, M. F. (2004). Socio-economic status covaries with central nervous system serotonergic responsivity as a function of allelic variation in the serotonin transporter gene-linked polymorphic region. *Psychoneuroendocrinology*, **21**(1), 20–25.

Marcus, S. (1974). Review of *Obedience to authority*. *New York Times Book Review*, 13 January, pp. 1–2.

Marcus-Newhall, A., Pedersen, W. C., Carlson, M., & Miller, N. (2000). Displaced aggression is alive and well: A meta-analytic review. *Journal of Personality and Social Psychology*, **78**, 670–689.

Margolin, G., Vickerman, K. A., Ramos, M. C., Duman Serrano, S., Gordis, E. B., Iturralde, E., Oliver, P. H., & Spies, L. A. (2009). Youth exposed to violence: Stability, co-occurrence and context. *Clinical Child and Family Psychology Review*, **12**, 39–54.

Marin, M. F., Morin-Major, J. K., Schramek, T. E., Beaupré, A., Perna, A., Juster, R. P., & Lupien, S. J. (2012). There is no news like bad news: Women are more remembering and stress reactive after reading real negative news than men. *PloS One*, **7**(10), e47189.

Markey, P. M. (2000). Bystander intervention in computer-mediated communication. *Computers in Human Behavior*, **16**(2), 183–188.

Markman, H. J., Floyd, F. J., Stanley, S. M., & Storaasli, R. D. (1988). Prevention of marital distress: A longitudinal investigation. *Journal of Consulting and Clinical Psychology*, **56**(2), 210–217.

Markman, K. D., & McMullen, M. N. (2003). A reflection and evaluation model of comparative thinking. *Personality and Social Psychology Review*, **7**, 244–267.

Marks, G., & Miller, N. (1987). Ten years of research on the false-consensus effect: An empirical and theoretical review. *Psychological Bulletin*, **102**, 72–90.

Markus, H. R. (2001, 7 October). Culture and the good life. Address to the Positive Psychology Summit conference, Washington, DC.

Markus, H. R. (2005). Telling less than we can know: The too tacit wisdom of social psychology. *Psychological Inquiry*, **16**(4), 180–184.

Markus, H. R., & Kitayama, S. (1991). Culture and the self: Implications for cognition, emotion, and motivation. *Psychological Review*, **98**, 224–253.

Markus, H. R., & Kitayama, S. (1994). A collective fear of the collective: Implications for selves and theories of selves. *Personality and Social Psychology Bulletin*, **20**, 568–579.

Markus, H. R., & Nurius, P. (1986). Possible selves. *American Psychologist*, **41**, 954–969.

Markus, H. R., & Wurf, E. (1987). The dynamic self-concept: A social psychological perspective. *Annual Review of Psychology*, **38**, 299–337.

Marques, J. M., & Yzerbyt, V. Y. (1988). The black sheep effect: Judgmental extremity towards ingroup members in inter- and intra-group situations. *European Journal of Social Psychology*, **18**, 287–292.

Marques, J. M., Yzerbyt, V. Y., & Leyens, J. P. (1988). The black sheep effect: Extremity of judgements towards in-group members as a function of group identification. *European Journal of Social Psychology*, **18**, 1–16.

Marsden, P., & Attia, S. (2005). A deadly contagion?

*The Psychologist, 18*, 152–155.

Marsh, H. W., & O'Mara, A. (2008). Reciprocal effects between academic self-concept, self-esteem, achievement, and attainment over seven adolescent years. Unidimensional and multidimensional perspectives of self-concept. *Personality and Social Psychology Bulletin, 34*, 542–552.

Marsh, H. W., & Young, A. S. (1997). Causal effects of academic self-concept on academic achievement: Structural equation models of longitudinal data. *Journal of Educational Psychology, 89*, 41–54.

Marsh, H. W., Kong, C.-K., & Hau, K.-T. (2000). Longitudinal multilevel models of the big-fish-little-pond effect on academic self-concept: Counterbalancing contrast and reflected-glory effects in Hong Kong schools. *Journal of Personality and Social Psychology, 78*, 337–349.

Marshall, R. (1997). Variances in levels of individualism across two cultures and three social classes. *Journal of Cross-Cultural Psychology, 28*, 490–495.

Martin, J., & Sugarman, J. (2009). Does interpretation in psychology differ from interpretation in natural science? *Journal for the Theory of Social Behaviour, 39*, 19–37.

Martin, L. L., & Erber, R. (2005). The wisdom of social psychology: Five commonalities and one concern. *Psychological Inquiry, 16*, 194–202.

Martin, R. (1996). Minority influence and argument generation. *British Journal of Social Psychology, 35*, 91–103.

Martin, R., Hewstone, M., & Martin, P. Y. (2008). Majority versus minority: The role of message processing in determining resistance to counter-persuasion. *European Journal of Social Psychology, 38*, 16–34.

Martino, S. C., Collins, R. L., Kanouse, D. E., Elliott, M., & Berry, S. H. (2005). Social cognitive processes mediating the relationship between exposure to television's sexual content and adolescents' sexual behav-ior. *Journal of Personality and Social Psychology, 89*, 914–924.

Maslow, A. H., & Mintz, N. L. (1956). Effects of esthetic surroundings: I. Initial effects of three esthetic conditions upon perceiving 'energy' and 'well-being' in faces. *Journal of Psychology, 41*, 247–254.

Masuda, T., & Kitayama, S. (2004). Perceiver-induced constraint and attitude attribution in Japan and the US: A case for the cultural dependence of the correspondence bias. *Journal of Experimental Social Psychology, 40*, 409–416.

Matheson, K., Cole, B., & Majka, K. (2003). Dissidence from within: Examining the effects of intergroup context on group members' reactions to attitudinal opposition. *Journal of Experimental Social Psychology, 39*, 161–169.

Maxwell, G. M. (1985). Behaviour of lovers: Measuring the closeness of relationships. *Journal of Personality and Social Psychology, 2*, 215–238.

Mayer, J. D., & Salovey, P. (1987). Personality moderates the interaction of mood and cognition. In K. Fiedler & J. Forgas (eds), *Affect, cognition, and social behavior*. Toronto: Hogrefe.

Mazur, A., & Booth, A. (1998). Testosterone and dominance in men. *Behavioral and Brain Sciences, 21*, 353–363.

Mazzuca, J. (2002, 20 August). Teens shrug off movie sex and violence. *Gallup Tuesday Briefing* (www.gallup.com).

McAlister, A., Perry, C., Killen, J., Slinkard, L. A., & Maccoby, N. (1980). Pilot study of smoking, alcohol and drug abuse prevention. *American Journal of Public Health, 70*, 719–721.

McAndrew, F. T. (1981). Pattern of performance and attributions of ability and gender. *Journal of Personality and Social Psychology, 7*, 583–587.

McAndrew, F. T. (2002). New evolutionary perspectives on altruism: Multilevel-selection and costly-signaling theories. *Current Directions in Psychological Science, 11*, 79–82.

McArthur, L. A. (1972). The how and what of why: Some determinants of consequences of causal attributions. *Journal of Personality and Social Psychology, 22*, 171–193.

McCann, C. D., & Hancock, R. D. (1983). Self-monitoring in communicative interactions: Social cognitive consequences of goal-directed message modification. *Journal of Experimental Social Psychology, 19*, 109–121.

McCarthy, J. F., & Kelly, B. R. (1978a). Aggression, performance variables, and anger self-report in ice hockey players. *Journal of Psychology, 99*, 97–101.

McCarthy, J. F., & Kelly, B. R. (1978b). Aggressive behavior and its effect on performance over time in ice hockey athletes: An archival study. *International Journal of Sport Psychology, 9*, 90–96.

McCauley, C. (1989). The nature of social influence in groupthink: Compliance and internalization. *Journal of Personality and Social Psychology, 57*, 250–260.

McCauley, C. D. (2001). Leader training and development. In S. J. Zaccaro & R. J. Klimoski (eds), *The nature of organizational leadership: Understanding the performance imperatives confronting today's leaders*. San Francisco: Jossey Bass.

McClure, J. (1998). Discounting causes of behavior: Are two reasons better than one? *Journal of Personality and Social Psychology, 74*, 7–20.

McConahay, J. B. (1986). Modern racism, ambivalence, and the modern racism scale. In J. F. Dovidio and S. L. Gaertner (eds), *Prejudice, discrimination and racism*. Orlando, FL: Academic Press.

McConahay, J. B., & Hough, J. C., Jr (1976). Symbolic racism. *Journal of Social Issues, 32*, 23–45.

McCullough, J. L., & Ostrom, T. M. (1974). Repetition of highly similar messages and attitude change. *Journal of Applied Psychology, 59*, 395–397.

McDermott, R., Tingley, D., Cowden, J., Frazzetto, G., & Johnson, D. D. (2009). Monoamine oxidase A gene (MAOA) predicts behavioral aggression following provocation. *Proceedings of the National Academy of Sciences, 106*(7), 2118–2123.

McDermott, T. (2005). *Perfect soldiers: The hijackers: Who they were, why they did it.* New York: HarperCollins.

McDonald, M. M., Navarrete, C. D. & Van Vugt, M. (2011). Evolution and the psychology of intergroup conflict: The male warrior hypothesis. *Philosophical Transactions of the Royal Society, 367*(1589), 670–679.

McDougall, W. (1908). *An introduction to social psychology.* London: Methuen.

McFadzean, E., & McKenzie, J. (2001). Facilitating virtual learning groups: A practical approach. *Journal of Management Development, 20*(6), 470–494.

McFarland, C., & Ross, M. (1985). The relation between current impressions and memories of self and dating partners. Unpublished manuscript, University of Waterloo.

McGarty, C., Turner, J. C., Oakes, P. J., & Haslam, S. A. (1993). The creation of uncertainty in the influence process: The roles of stimulus information and disagreement with similar others. *European Journal of Social Psychology, 23*, 17–38.

McGillicuddy, N. B., Welton, G. L., & Pruitt, D. G. (1987). Third-party intervention: A field experiment comparing three different models. *Journal of Personality and Social Psychology, 53*, 104–112.

McGinty, K., Knox, D., & Zusman, M. E. (2007). Friends with benefits: Women want 'friends,' men want 'benefits'. *College Student Journal, 41*(4), 1128–1131.

McGlone, M. S., & Tofighbakhsh, J. (2000). Birds of a feather flock conjointly (?): Rhyme as reason in aphorisms. *Psychological Science, 11*, 424–428.

McGlynn, R. P., Tubbs, D. D., & Holzhausen, K. G. (1995). Hypothesis generation in groups constrained by evidence. *Journal of Experimental Social Psychology, 31*, 64–81.

McGrath, J. E. (1984). *Groups: Interaction and*

*performance.* Englewood Cliffs, NJ: Prentice-Hall.

McGraw, A. P., Mellers, B. A., & Tetlock, P. E. (2005). Expectations and emotions of Olympic athletes. *Journal of Experimental Social Psychology*, **41**, 438–446.

McGregor, H. A., Lieberman, J. D., Greenberg, J., Solomon, S., Arndt, J., Simon, L., & Pyszczynski, T. (1998). Terror management and aggression: evidence that mortality salience motivates aggression against worldview-threatening others. *Journal of Personality and Social Psychology*, **74**(3), 590.

McGregor, I., Newby-Clark, I. R., & Zanna, M. P. (1998). Epistemic discomfort is moderated by simultaneous accessibility of inconsistent elements. In E. Harmon-Jones and J. Mills (eds), *Cognitive dissonance theory 40 years later: A revival with revisions and controversies.* Washington, DC: American Psychological Association.

McGregor, I., Zanna, M. P., Holmes, J. G., & Spencer, S. J. (2001). Conviction in the face of uncertainty: Going to extremes and being oneself. *Journal of Personality and Social Psychology*, **80**, 472–478.

McGuckin, C., & Lewis, C. A. (2003). A cross-national perspective on school bullying in Northern Ireland: A supplement to Smith et al. (1999). *Psychological Reports*, **93**, 279–287.

McGuckin, C., & Lewis, C. A. (2008). Management of bullying in Northern Ireland schools: A pre-legislative survey. *Educational Research*, **50**(1), 9–23.

McGuire, A. (2002, 19 August). Charity calls for debate on adverts aimed at children. *The Herald* (Scotland), p. 4.

McGuire, W. J. (1964). Inducing resistance to persuasion: Some contemporary approaches. In L. Berkowitz (ed.), *Advances in experimental social psychology*, Vol. 1. New York: Academic Press.

McGuire, W. J. (1985). Attitudes and attitude change. In G. Lindzey and E. Aronson (eds), *The handbook of social psychology*, Vol. 2. New York: Random House.

McGuire, W. J., & Padawer-Singer, A. (1978). Trait salience in the spontaneous self-concept. *Journal of Personality and Social Psychology*, **33**, 743–754.

McGuire, W. J., McGuire, C. V., & Winton, W. (1979). Effects of household sex composition on the salience of one's gender in the spontaneous self-concept. *Journal of Experimental Social Psychology*, **15**, 77–90.

McKay-Nesbitt, J., Manchanda, R. V., Smith, M. C., & Huhmann, B. A. (2011). Effects of age, need for cognition, and affective intensity on advertising effectiveness. *Journal of Business Research*, **64**(1), 12–17.

McKelvie, S. J. (1993). Vividness of visual imagery for faces as a predictor of facial recognition memory performance: A revised view. *Perceptual and Motor Skills*, **76**(3c), 1083.

McKelvie, S. J. (1995). Bias in the estimated frequency of names. *Perceptual and Motor Skills*, **81**, 1331–1338.

McKelvie, S. J. (1997). The availability heuristic: Effects of fame and gender on the estimated frequency of male and female names. *Journal of Social Psychology*, **137**, 63–78.

McKenna, K. Y. A., & Bargh, J. A. (2000). Plan 9 from cyberspace: The implications of the Internet for personality and social psychology. *Personality and Social Psychology Review*, **4**, 57–75.

McKenna, K. Y. A., Green, A. S., & Gleason, M. E. J. (2002). What's the big attraction? Relationship formation on the Internet. *Journal of Social Issues*, **58**, 9–31.

McKenzie-Mohr, D., & Zanna, M. P. (1990). Treating women as sexual objects: Look to the (gender schematic) male who has viewed pornography. *Personality and Social Psychology Bulletin*, **16**, 296–308.

McMillen, D. L., & Austin, J. B. (1971). Effect of positive feedback on compliance following transgression. *Psychonomic Science*, **24**, 59–61.

McPherson, M., Smith-Lovin, L., & Cook, J. M. (2001). Birds of a feather: Homophily in social networks. *Annual Review of Sociology*, **27**, 415–444.

Mead, G. H. (1934). *Mind, self, and society.* Chicago: University of Chicago Press.

Medvec, V. H., & Savitsky, K. (1997). When doing better means feeling worse: The effects of categorical cutoff points on counterfactual thinking and satisfaction. *Journal of Personality and Social Psychology*, **72**, 1284–1296.

Medvec, V. H., Madey, S. F., & Gilovich, T. (1995). When less is more: Counterfactual thinking and satisfaction among Olympic medalists. *Journal of Personality and Social Psychology*, **69**, 603–610.

Mehl, M. R., & Pennebaker, J. W. (2003). The sounds of social life: A psychometric analysis of students' daily social environments and natural conversations. *Journal of Personality and Social Psychology*, **84**, 857–870.

Meier, B. P., & Hinsz, V. B. (2004). A comparison of human aggression committed by groups and individuals: An interindividual–intergroup discontinuity. *Journal of Experimental Social Psychology*, **40**, 551–559.

Meindl, J. (1993). Reinventing leadership: a radical social psychological approach. In J. K. Murnigham (ed.), *Social psychology in organizations: Advances in theory and research.* Englewood Cliffs, NJ: Prentice-Hall.

Mellers, B., Hertwig, R., & Kahneman, D. (2001). Do frequency representations eliminate conjunction effects: An exercise in adversarial collaboration. *Psychological Science*, **12**, 269–275.

Melzack, R., & Wall, P. D. (1988). *The challenge of pain.* London: Penguin Books.

Merikle, P. M., Smilek, D., & Eastwood, J. D. (2001). Perception without awareness: Perspectives from cognitive psychology. *Cognition*, **79**, 115–134.

Merton, R. K. (1948). The self-fulfilling prophecy. *Antioch Review*, **8**, 193–210.

Mezulis, A. H., Abramson, L. Y., Hyde, J. S., & Hankin, B. L. (2004). Is there a universal positivity bias in attributions? A meta-analytic review of individual, developmental, and cultural differences in the self-serving attributional bias. *Psychological Bulletin*, **130**, 711–747.

Michaels, J. W., Blommel, J. M., Brocato, R. M., Linkous, R. A., & Rowe, J. S. (1982). Social facilitation and inhibition in a natural setting. *Replications in Social Psychology*, **2**, 21–24.

Michie, S., Lester, K., Pinto, J., & Marteau, T. M. (2005). Communicating risk information in genetic counseling: An observational study. *Health Education & Behavior*, **32**(5), 589–598.

Mickelson, K. D., Kessler, R. C., & Shaver, P. R. (1997). Adult attachment in a nationally representative sample. *Journal of Personality and Social Psychology*, **73**, 1092–1106.

Mikulincer, M., & Shaver, P. R. (2001). Attachment theory and intergroup bias: Evidence that priming the secure base schema attenuates negative reactions to out-groups. *Journal of Personality and Social Psychology*, **81**, 97–115.

Mikulincer, M., Florian, V., & Hirschberger, G. (2003). The existential function of close relationships: Introducing death into the science of love. *Personality and Social Psychology Review*, **7**, 20–40.

Mikulincer, M., Shaver, P. R., Gillath, O., & Nitzberg, R. A. (2005). Attachment, caregiving, and altruism: Boosting attachment security increases compassion and helping. *Journal of Personality and Social Psychology*, **89**, 817–839.

Milgram, A. (2000). My personal view of Stanley Milgram. In T. Blass (ed.), *Obedience to authority: Current perspectives on the Milgram paradigm.* Mahwah, NJ: Erlbaum.

Milgram, S. (1961, December). Nationality and conformity. *Scientific American*, 45–51.

Milgram, S. (1963). Behavioral study of obedience. *Journal of Abnormal and Social Psychology*, **67**, 371–378.

Milgram, S. (1965). Some conditions of obedience and disobedience to authority. *Human Relations*, **18**, 57–76.

Milgram, S. (1974). *Obedience to authority: An experimental view*. New York: Harper & Row.

Milgram, S., Bickman, L., & Berkowitz, L. (1969). Note on the drawing power of crowds of different size. *Journal of Personality and Social Psychology*, **13**, 79–82.

Millar, M. G., & Millar, K. U. (1996). Effects of message anxiety on disease detection and health promotion behaviors. *Basic and Applied Social Psychology*, **18**, 61–74.

Millar, M. G., & Tesser, A. (1992). The role of beliefs and feelings in guiding behavior: The mismatch model. In L. Martin & A. Tesser (eds), *The construction of social judgment*. Hillsdale, NJ: Erlbaum.

Miller, A. G. (2004). What can the Milgram obedience experiments tell us about the Holocaust? Generalizing from the social psychological laboratory. In A. G. Miller (ed.), *The social psychology of good and evil*. New York: Guilford Press.

Miller, A. G. (2006). Exonerating harmdoers: Some problematic implications of social-psychological explanations. Paper presented to the Society of Personality and Social Psychology convention.

Miller, A. G., Ashton, W., & Mishal, M. (1990). Beliefs concerning the features of constrained behavior: A basis for the fundamental attribution error. *Journal of Personality and Social Psychology*, **59**, 635–650.

Miller, A. G., Gillen, G., Schenker, C., & Radlove, S. (1973). Perception of obedience to authority. *Proceedings of the 81st annual convention of the American Psychological Association*, **8**, 127–128.

Miller, C. B. (2009). Yes we did! Basking in reflected glory and cutting off reflected failure in the 2008 Presidential Election. *Analyses of Social Issues and Public Policy*, **9**(1), 283–296.

Miller, C. E., & Anderson, P. D. (1979). Group decision rules and the rejection of deviates. *Social Psychology Quarterly*, **42**, 354–363.

Miller, D. T., & McFarland, C. (1987). Pluralistic igno-

rance: When similarity is interpreted as dissimilarity. *Journal of Personality and Social Psychology*, **53**, 298–305.

Miller, J. B. (1986 [1976]). *Toward a new psychology of women*. Boston, MA: Beacon Press.

Miller, K. I., & Monge, P. R. (1986). Participation, satisfaction, and productivity: A meta-analytic review. *Academy of Management Journal*, **29**, 727–753.

Miller, L. C. (1990). Intimacy and liking: Mutual influence and the role of unique relationships. *Journal of Personality and Social Psychology*, **59**, 50–60.

Miller, L. C., Berg, J. H., & Archer, R. L. (1983). Openers: Individuals who elicit intimate self-disclosure. *Journal of Personality and Social Psychology*, **44**, 1234–1244.

Miller, L. E., & Grush, J. E. (1986). Individual differences in attitudinal versus normative determination of behavior. *Journal of Experimental Social Psychology*, **22**, 190–202.

Miller, N. (2002). Personalization and the promise of contact theory. *Journal of Social Issues*, **58**, 387–410.

Miller, N. & Brewer, M. B. (eds) (1984). *Groups in contact: The psychology of desegregation*. New York: Academic Press.

Miller, N., & Campbell, D. T. (1959). Recency and primacy in persuasion as a function of the timing of speeches and measurements. *Journal of Abnormal and Social Psychology*, **59**, 1–9.

Miller, N., & Marks, G. (1982). Assumed similarity between self and other: Effect of expectation of future interaction with that other. *Social Psychology Quarterly*, **45**, 100–105.

Miller, N., Maruyama, G., Beaber, R. J., & Valone, K. (1976). Speed of speech and persuasion. *Journal of Personality and Social Psychology*, **34**, 615–624.

Miller, N., Pedersen, W. C., Earleywine, M., & Pollock, V. E. (2003). A theoretical model of triggered displaced aggression. *Personality and Social Psychology Review*, **7**, 75–97.

Miller, N. E. (1941). The frustration–aggression hypothesis. *Psychological Review*, **48**, 337–342.

Miller, P. A., & Eisenberg, N. (1988). The relation of empathy to aggressive and externalizing/antisocial behavior. *Psychological Bulletin*, **103**, 324–344.

Miller, P. A., Kozu, J., & Davis, A. C. (2001). Social influence, empathy, and prosocial behavior in cross-cultural perspective. In W. Wosinska, R. B. Cialdini, D. W. Barrett & J. Reykowski (eds), *The practice of social influence in multiple cultures*. Mahwah, NJ: Erlbaum.

Miller, P. J. E., & Rempel, J. K. (2004). Trust and partner enhancing attributions in close relationships. *Personality and Social Psychology Bulletin*, **30**, 695–705.

Miller, R. L., Brickman, P., & Bolen, D. (1975). Attribution versus persuasion as a means for modifying behavior. *Journal of Personality and Social Psychology*, **31**, 430–441.

Miller, R. S. (1997). Inattentive and contented: Relationship commitment and attention to alternatives. *Journal of Personality and Social Psychology*, **73**, 758–766.

Miller, R. S., & Schlenker, B. R. (1985). Egotism in group members: Public and private attributions of responsibility for group performance. *Social Psychology Quarterly*, **48**, 85–89.

Miller, R. S., & Simpson, J. A. (1990). Relationship satisfaction and attentiveness to alternatives. Paper presented at the American Psychological Association convention.

Millett, K. (1975). The shame is over. *Ms.*, January, 26–29.

Millon, T. (1996). *Disorders of personality: DSM-IV-TM and beyond*. New York: John Wiley & Sons.

Mims, P. R., Hartnett, J. J., & Nay, W. R. (1975). Interpersonal attraction and help volunteering as a function of physical attractiveness. *Journal of Psychology*, **89**, 125–131.

Mischel, W. (1968). *Personality and assessment*. New York: Wiley.

Mishna, F., Khoury-Kassabri, M., Gadalla, T.,

& Daciuk, J. (2012). Risk factors for involvement in cyber bullying: Victims, bullies and bully-victims. *Children and Youth Services*, **34**(1), 63–70.

Mishna, F., Saini, M., & Solomon, S. (2009). Ongoing and online: Children and youth's perceptions of cyber bullying. *Children and Youth Services Review*, **31**(12), 1222–1228.

Mita, T. H., Dermer, M., & Knight, J. (1977). Reversed facial images and the mere-exposure hypothesis. *Journal of Personality and Social Psychology*, **35**, 597–601.

Mitchell, T. L., Haw, R. M., Pfeifer, J. E., & Meissner, C. A. (2005). Racial bias in mock juror decision-making: A meta-analytic review of defendant treatment. *Law and Human Behavior*, **29**, 621–637.

Mitchell, T. R., & Thompson, L. (1994). A theory of temporal adjustments of the evaluation of events: Rosy prospection and rosy retrospection. In C. Stubbart, J. Porac & J. Meindl (eds), *Advances in managerial cognition and organizational information processing*. Greenwich, CT: JAI Press.

Mitchell, T. R., Thompson, L., Peterson, E., & Cronk, R. (1997). Temporal adjustments in the evaluation of events: The 'rosy view'. *Journal of Experimental Social Psychology*, **33**, 421–448.

Moeller, F. G., Dougherty, D. M., Swann, A. C., Collins, D., Davis, C. M., & Cherek, D. R. (1996). Tryptophan depletion and aggressive responding in healthy males. *Psychopharmacology*, **126**(2), 97–103.

Moffitt, T., Caspi, A., Sugden, K., Taylor, A., Craig, I. W., Harrington, H., McClay, J., Mill, J., Martin, J., Braithwaite, A., & Poulton, R. (2003). Influence of life stress on depression: Moderation by a polymorphism in the 5-HTT gene. *Science*, **301**, 386–389.

Monin, B., & Norton, M. I. (2003). Perceptions of a fluid consensus: Uniqueness bias, false consensus, false polarization, and pluralistic ignorance in a water conservation crisis. *Personality and Social Psychology*, **29**, 559–567.

Monson, T. C., Hesley, J. W., & Chernick, L. (1982). Specifying when personality traits can and cannot predict behavior: An alternative to abandoning the attempt to predict single-act criteria. *Journal of Personality and Social Psychology*, **43**, 385–399.

Montoya, R. M., & Horton, R. S. (2004). On the importance of cognitive evaluation as a determinant of interpersonal attraction. *Journal of Personality and Social Psychology*, **86**, 696–712.

Moody, M. K. (1983). *Children and food advertising: A selective bibliography* (No. 1285). Vance Bibliographies.

Moons, W. G., Mackie D. M., & Garcia-Marques, T. (2009). The impact of repetition-induced familiarity on agreement with weak and strong arguments. *Journal of Personality and Social Psychology*, **96**(1), 32–44.

Moore, D. W. (2003, 18 March). Public approves of Bush ultimatum by more than 2-to-1 margin. Gallup News Service (www.gallup.com).

Moore, D. W. (2004, 20 April). Ballot order: Who benefits? *Gallup Poll Tuesday Briefing* (www.gallup.com).

Moreland, R. L. (1985). Social categorization and the assimilation of 'new' group members. *Journal of Personality and Social Psychology*, **48**, 1173–1190.

Moreland, R. L., & Zajonc, R. B. (1977). Is stimulus recognition a necessary condition for the occurrence of exposure effects? *Journal of Personality and Social Psychology*, **35**, 191–199.

Morris, W. N., & Miller, R. S. (1975). The effects of consensus-breaking and consensus-preempting partners on reduction of conformity. *Journal of Experimental Social Psychology*, **11**, 215–223.

Morrison, V., & Bennett, P. (2006). *An introduction to health psychology*. London: Pearson-Prentice Hall.

Morrow, L. (1983, 1 August). All the hazards and threats of success. *Time*, 20–25.

Morton, T. A., Postmes, T., & Jetten, J. (2007). Playing the game: When group success is more important than downgrading deviants. *European Journal of Social Psychology*, **37**, 599–616.

Moscovici, S. (1985). Social influence and conformity. In G. Lindzey & E. Aronson (eds), *The handbook of social psychology*, 3rd edn. Hillsdale, NJ: Erlbaum.

Moscovici, S. (1988). Notes towards a description of social representations. *European Journal of Social Psychology*, **18**, 211–250.

Moscovici, S., & Zavalloni, M. (1969). The group as a polarizer of attitudes. *Journal of Personality and Social Psychology*, **12**, 124–135.

Moscovici, S., Lage, S., & Naffrechoux, M. (1969). Influence of a consistent minority on the responses of a majority in a color perception task. *Sociometry*, **32**(4), 365–380.

Mosquera, P. M. R., Manstead, A. S. R., & Fischer, A. H. (2002). The role of honour concerns in emotional reactions to offences. *Cognition and Emotion*, **16**(1), 143–163.

Motherhood Project (2001, 2 May). Watch out for children: A mothers' statement to advertisers. Institute for American Values (www.watchoutforchildren.org).

Mucchi-Faina, A., & Pagliaro, S. (2008). Minority influence: The role of ambivalence toward the source. *European Journal of Social Psychology*, **38**(4), 612–623.

Mucchi-Faina, A., Maass, A., & Volpato, C. (1991). Social influence: The role of originality. *European Journal of Social Psychology*, **21**, 183–197.

Muehlenhard, C. L. (1988). Misinterpreted dating behaviors and the risk of date rape. *Journal of Social and Clinical Psychology*, **6**, 20–37.

Mueller, C. W., Donnerstein, E., & Hallam, J. (1983). Violent films and prosocial behavior. *Personality and Social Psychology Bulletin*, **9**, 83–89.

Muthukrishna, N., & Govender, D. (2011). Moral reasoning in the early years: Age

and gender patterns amongst young children in South Africa. *Gender and Behaviour*, **9**(1).

Mullen, B., & Baumeister, R. F. (1987). Group effects on self-attention and performance: Social loafing, social facilitation, and social impairment. In C. Hendrick (ed.), *Group processes and intergroup relations: Review of personality and social psychology*, Vol. 9. Newbury Park, CA: Sage.

Mullen, B., & Copper, C. (1994). The relation between group cohesiveness and performance: An integration. *Psychological Bulletin*, **115**, 210–227.

Mullen, B., & Goethals, G. R. (1990). Social projection, actual consensus and valence. *British Journal of Social Psychology*, **29**, 279–282.

Mullen, B., & Riordan, C. A. (1988). Self-serving attributions for performance in naturalistic settings: A metaanalytic review. *Journal of Applied Social Psychology*, **18**, 3–22.

Mullen, B., Anthony, T., Salas, E., & Driskell, J. E. (1994). Group cohesiveness and quality of decision making: An integration of tests of the groupthink hypothesis. *Small Group Research*, **25**, 189–204.

Mullen, B., Bryant, B., & Driskell, J. E. (1997). Presence of others and arousal: An integration. *Group Dynamics: Theory, Research, and Practice*, **1**, 52–64.

Muller, S., & Johnson, B. T. (1990). Fear and persuasion: A linear relationship? Paper presented to the Eastern Psychological Association convention.

Mullin, C. R., & Linz, D. (1995). Desensitization and resensitization to violence against women: Effects of exposure to sexually violent films on judgments of domestic violence victims. *Journal of Personality and Social Psychology*, **69**, 449–459.

Muncer, S., Campbell, A., Jervis, V., & Lewis, R. (2001). Ladettes, social representations and aggression. *Sex Roles*, **44**, 33–44.

Muraven, M., Tice, D. M., & Baumeister, R. F. (1998). Self-control as a limited

resource: Regulatory depletion patterns. *Journal of Personality and Social Psychology*, **74**, 774–790.

Murphy, R. F. (1990). *The body silent*. New York: Norton.

Murray, J. P., & Kippax, S. (1979). From the early window to the late night show: International trends in the study of television's impact on children and adults. In L. Berkowitz (ed.), *Advances in experimental social psychology*, Vol. 12. New York: Academic Press.

Murray, S. L., & Holmes, J. G. (1997). A leap of faith? Positive illusions in romantic relationships. *Personality and Social Psychology Bulletin*, **23**, 586–604.

Murray, S. L., Gellavia, G. M., Rose, P., & Griffin, D. W. (2003). Once hurt, twice hurtful: How perceived regard regulates daily marital interactions. *Journal of Personality and Social Psychology*, **84**, 126–147.

Murray, S. L., Holmes, J. G., & Collins, N. J. (2006). Optimizing assurance: The risk regulation system in relationships. *Psychological Bulletin*, **5**, 641–666.

Murray, S. L., Holmes, J. G., & Griffin, D. W. (1996a). The self-fulfilling nature of positive illusions in romantic relationships: Love is not blind, but prescient. *Journal of Personality and Social Psychology*, **71**, 1155–1180.

Murray, S. L., Holmes, J. G., & Griffin, D. W. (1996b). The benefits of positive illusions: Idealization and the construction of satisfaction in close relationships. *Journal of Personality and Social Psychology*, **70**, 79–98.

Murray, S. L., Holmes, J. G., & Griffin, D. W. (2000). Self-esteem and the quest for felt security: How perceived regard regulates attachment processes. *Journal of Personality and Social Psychology*, **78**, 478–498.

Murray, S. L., Holmes, J. G., Gellavia, G., Griffin, D. W., & Dolderman, D. (2002). Kindred spirits? The benefits of egocentrism in close relationships. *Journal of Personality and Social Psychology*, **82**, 563–581.

Murstein, B. L. (1986). *Paths to marriage*. Newbury Park, CA: Sage.

Muson, G. (1978). Teenage violence and the telly. *Psychology Today*, March, 50–54.

Myers, D. G. (1978). Polarizing effects of social comparison. *Journal of Experimental Social Psychology*, **14**, 554–563.

Myers, D. G. (1993). *The pursuit of happiness*. New York: Avon.

Myers, D. G. (2000). *The American paradox: Spiritual hunger in an age of plenty*. New Haven, CT: Yale University Press.

Myers, D. G. (2004). The secret to happiness. *Yes!*, Summer, 13–16.

Myers, D. G., & Bishop, G. D. (1970). Discussion effects on racial attitudes. *Science*, **169**, 778–789.

Myers, D. G., & Scanzoni, L. D. (2005). *What God has joined together? A Christian case for gay marriage*. San Francisco: HarperSanFrancisco.

**N**

Nadler, A. (1991). Help-seeking behavior: Psychological costs and instrumental benefits. In M. S. Clark (ed.), *Prosocial behavior*. Newbury Park, CA: Sage.

Nadler, A., & Fisher, J. D. (1986). The role of threat to self-esteem and perceived control in recipient reaction to help: Theory development and empirical validation. In L. Berkowitz (ed.), *Advances in experimental social psychology*, Vol. 19. Orlando, FL: Academic Press.

Naidu, T., Sliep, Y., & Dageid, W. (2012). The social construction of identity in HIV/AIDS home-based care volunteers in rural KwaZulu-Natal, South Africa. *Journal of Social Aspects*, **9**(2), 113–126.

Naik, G. (2011, 2 December). Scientists' elusive goal: Reproducing study results. *The Wall Street Journal*.

Nail, P. R., MacDonald, G., & Levy, D. A. (2000). Proposal of a four-dimensional model of social response. *Psychological Bulletin*, **126**, 454–470.

National Research Council (2002). *Youth, pornography, and the Internet*. Washington, DC: National Academy Press.

National Television Violence Study (1997). National Television Violence Study (Vol.

2). Studio City, CA: Mediascope.

Naylor, T. H. (1990). Redefining corporate motivation, Swedish style. *Christian Century*, **107**, 566–570.

Neff, L. A., & Karney, B. R. (2005). To know you is to love you: the implications of global adoration and specific accuracy for marital relationships. *Journal of Personality and Social Psychology*, **88**, 480–497.

Nelson, L. D., & Morrison, E. L. (2005). The symptoms of resource scarcity: Judgments of food and finances influence preferences for potential partners. *Psychological Science*, **16**, 167–173.

Nemeth, C. (1979). The role of an active minority in intergroup relations. In W. G. Austin and S. Worchel (eds), *The social psychology of intergroup relations*. Monterey, CA: Brooks/Cole.

Nemeth, C. J. (1997). Managing innovation: When less is more. *California Management Review*, **40**, 59–74.

Nemeth, C. J. (1999). Behind the scenes. In D. G. Myers, *Social psychology*, 6th edn. New York: McGraw-Hill.

Nemeth, C. J., Brown, K., & Rogers, J. (2001a). Devil's advocate versus authentic dissent: Stimulating quantity and quality. *European Journal of Social Psychology*, **31**(6), 707–720.

Nemeth, C. J., & Chiles, C. (1988). Modelling courage: The role of dissent in fostering independence. *European Journal of Social Psychology*, **18**, 275–280.

Nemeth, C. J., Connell, J. B., Rogers, J. D., & Brown, K. S. (2001b). Improving decision making by means of dissent. *Journal of Applied Social Psychology*, **31**(1), 48–58.

Nemeth, C. J., Personnaz, B., Personnaz, M., & Goncalo, J. A. (2004). The liberating role of conflict in group creativity: A study in two countries. *European Journal of Social Psychology*, **34**, 365–374.

Nemeth, C. J., & Wachtler, J. (1974). Creating the perceptions of consistency and confidence: A necessary condition for minority influence. *Sociometry*, **37**, 529–540.

Neumann, R., & Strack, F. (2000). Approach and avoidance: The influence of proprioceptive and exteroceptive cues on encoding of affective information. *Journal of Personality and Social Psychology*, **79**, 39–48.

Newell, B., & Lagnado, D. (2003). Think-tanks, or think tanks. *The Psychologist*, **16**, 176.

Newell, B. R., & Shanks, D. R. (2007). Recognising what you like: Examining the relation between the mere-exposure effect and recognition. *European Journal of Cognitive Psychology*, **19**(1), 103–118.

Newman, H. M., & Langer, E. J. (1981). Post-divorce adaptation and the attribution of responsibility. *Sex Roles*, **7**, 223–231.

Newman, L. S. (1993). How individualists interpret behavior: Idiocentrism and spontaneous trait inference. *Social Cognition*, **11**, 243–269.

Newport, F., Moore, D. W., Jones, J. M., & Saad, L. (2003, 21 March). Special release: American opinion on the war. *Gallup Poll Tuesday Briefing* (www.gallup.com/poll/tb/goverpubli/s0030325.asp).

Nias, D. K. B. (1979). Marital choice: Matching or complementation? In M. Cook and G. Wilson (eds), *Love and attraction*. Oxford: Pergamon.

Nicholson, N., Cole, S. G., & Rocklin, T. (1985). Conformity in the Asch situation: A comparison between contemporary British and US university students. *British Journal of Social Psychology*, **24**, 59–63.

Nickerson, A. M., & Louis, W. R. (2008). Nationality versus humanity? Personality, identity, and norms in relation to attitudes toward asylum seekers. *Journal of Applied Social Psychology*, **38**(3), 796–817.

Nickerson, R. S. (1998). Confirmation bias: A ubiquitous phenomenon in many guises. *Review of General Psychology*, **2**, 175–220.

Niemi, R. G., Mueller, J., & Smith, T. W. (1989). *Trends in public opinion: A compendium of survey data*. New York: Greenwood Press.

Niens, U., Cairns, E., & Bishop, S. (2004). Prejudiced or not? Hidden sectarianism among students in Northern Ireland. *The Journal of Social Psychology*, **144**(2), 163–180.

Nigg, J. T. (2003). Response inhibition and disruptive behaviors. *Annals of the New York Academy of Sciences*, **1008**(1), 170–182.

Nijstad, B. A., Stroebe, W., & Lodewijkx, H. F. M. (2003). Production blocking and idea generation: Does blocking interfere with cognitive processes? *Journal of Experimental Social Psychology*, **39**, 531–548.

Nisbett, R. E. (1990). Evolutionary psychology, biology, and cultural evolution. *Motivation and Emotion*, **14**, 255–263.

Nisbett, R. E. (1993). Violence and US regional culture. *American Psychologist*, **48**, 441–449.

Nisbett, R. E. (2003). *The geography of thought: How Asians and Westerners think differently … and why*. New York: Free Press.

Nisbett, R. E., & Masuda, T. (2003). Culture and point of view. *Proceedings of the National Academy of Sciences*, **100**, 11163–11170.

Nisbett, R. E., & Ross, L. (1980). *Human inference: Strategies and shortcomings of social judgment*. Englewood Cliffs, NJ: Prentice-Hall.

Nisbett, R. E., & Schachter, S. (1966). Cognitive manipulation of pain. *Journal of Experimental Social Psychology*, **2**, 227–236.

Nisbett, R. E., Caputo, C., Legant, P., & Marecek, J. (1973). Behavior as seen by the actor and as seen by the observer. *Journal of Personality and Social Psychology*, **27**(2), 154–164.

Noel, J. G., Forsyth, D. R., & Kelley, K. N. (1987). Improving the performance of failing students by overcoming their self-serving attributional biases. *Basic and Applied Social Psychology*, **8**, 151–162.

Noel, J. G., Wann, D. L., & Branscombe, N. R. (1995). Peripheral ingroup membership status and public negativity toward outgroups. *Journal of Personality and*

*Social Psychology*, **68**, 127–137.

Nolan, S. A., Flynn, C., & Garber, J. (2003). Prospective relations between rejection and depression in young adolescents. *Journal of Personality and Social Psychology*, **85**, 745–755.

Noller, P., & Fitzpatrick, M. A. (1990). Marital communication in the eighties. *Journal of Marriage and the Family*, **52**, 832–843.

Norem, J. K. (2000). Defensive pessimism, optimism, and pessimism. In E. C. Chang (ed.), *Optimism and pessimism*. Washington, DC: APA Books.

Norem, J. K., & Cantor, N. (1986). Defensive pessimism: Harnessing anxiety as motivation. *Journal of Personality and Social Psychology*, **51**, 1208–1217.

Norenzayan, A., & Heine, S. J. (2005). Psychological universals: What are they and how can we know? *Psychological Bulletin*, **131**, 763–784.

North, A. C., Hargreaves, D. J., & McKendrick, J. (1997). In-store music affects product choice. *Nature*, **390**, 132.

Nosek, B. A., & Banaji, M. R. (2001). The go/no-go association task. *Social Cognition*, **19**(6), 625–666.

Nosek, B. A., Banaji, M. R., & Jost, J. T. (2009). The politics of intergroup attitudes. In J. T. Jost and A. C. Kay (eds), *Social and psychological bases of ideology and system justification*. New York: Oxford University Press.

Notarius, C., & Markman, H. J. (1993). *We can work it out*. New York: Putnam.

Nussbaum, D. (2012). The role of conceptual replication. *The Psychologist*, **25**, 350.

Nuttin, J. M., Jr (1987). Affective consequences of mere ownership: The name letter effect in twelve European languages. *European Journal of Social Psychology*, **17**, 318–402.

**O**

O'Connor, A. (2004, 14 May). Pressure to go along with abuse is strong, but some soldiers find strength to refuse. *New York Times* (www.nytimes.com).

O'Dea, T. F. (1968). Sects and cults. In D. L. Sills (ed.), *International encyclopedia of the social sciences*, Vol. 14. New York: Macmillan.

Oakes, J. P., Haslam, S. A., & Turner, J. C. (1994). *Stereotyping and social reality*. Oxford: Blackwell.

Oaten, M., & Cheng, K. (2006). Improved self-control: The benefits of a regular program of academic study. *Basic and Applied Social Psychology*, **28**, 1–16.

Oberholzer-Gee, F. (2007). The helping hand – a brief anatomy. Economics and psychology: A promising new cross-disciplinary field. In B. S. Frey & A. Stutzer (eds), *Economics and psychology: A promising new cross-disciplinary field. CESifo seminar series*. Cambridge, MA: MIT Press.

Ochsner, K. N., & Lieberman, M. D. (2001). The emergence of social cognitive neuroscience. *American Psychologist*, **56**, 717–734.

Ochsner, K. N., Beer, J. S., Robertson, E. R., Cooper, J. C., Gabrieli, J. D. E., Kihsltrom, J. F., & D'Esposito, M. (2005). The neural correlates of direct and reflected self-knowledge. *Neuroimage*, **28**, 797–814.

Oddone-Paolucci, E., Genuis, M., & Violato, C. (2000). A meta-analysis of the published research on the effects of pornography. In C. Violato (ed.), *The changing family and child development*. Aldershot: Ashgate.

Odgers, C. L., Moffitt, T. E., Tach, L. M., Simpson, R. J., Taylor, A., Matthews, C. L., & Caspi, A. (2009). The protective effects of neighborhood collective efficacy on British children growing up in deprivation: A developmental analysis. *Developmental Psychology*, **45**(4), 942–957.

O'Fallon, M. J., & Butterfield, K. D. (2012). The influence of unethical peer behaviour on observers' unethical behaviour: A social cognitive perspective. *Journal of Business Ethics*, **109**, 117–131.

Ohbuchi, K., & Kambara, T. (1985). Attacker's intent and awareness of outcome, impression management, and retaliation. *Journal of Experimental Social Psychology*, **21**, 321–330.

Oliner, S., and Oliner, P. (1988). *The altruistic personality: Rescuers of Jews in Nazi Europe*. New York: The Free Press.

Olson, I. R., & Marshuetz, C. (2005). Facial attractiveness is appraised in a glance. *Emotion*, **5**, 498–502.

Olson, J. M., & Cal, A. V. (1984). Source credibility, attitudes, and the recall of past behaviours. *European Journal of Social Psychology*, **14**, 203–210.

Olson, J. M., Roese, N. J., & Zanna, M. P. (1996). Expectancies. In E. T. Higgins & A. W. Kruglanski (eds), *Social psychology: Handbook of basic principles*. New York: Guilford Press.

Olson, M. A., & Fazio, R. H. (2001). Implicit attitude formation through classical conditioning. *Psychological Science*, **12**(5), 413–417.

Olweus, D. (1979). Stability of aggressive reaction patterns in males: A review. *Psychological Bulletin*, **86**, 852–875.

Olweus, D. (1993). *Bullying at school: What we know and what we can do*. Oxford: Blackwell.

Olweus, D., Mattsson, A., Schalling, D., & Low, H. (1988). Circulating testosterone levels and aggression in adolescent males: A causal analysis. *Psychosomatic Medicine*, **50**, 261–272.

Omoto, A. M., & Snyder, M. (2002). Considerations of community: The context and process of volunteerism. *American Behavioral Scientist*, **45**, 846–867.

ONS (Office for National Statistics) (2011). Smoking. In General Lifestyle Survey, http://www.ons.gov.uk/ons/rel/ghs/general-lifestyle-survey/2011/rpt-chapter-1.html.

Open Secrets (2005). 2004 election overview: Winning vs spending (www.opensecrets.org).

Opotow, S. (1990). Moral exclusion and injustice: An introduction. *Journal of Social Issues*, **46**, 1–20.

Orne, M. T. (1962). On the social psychology of the psychological experiment: With particular reference to demand characteristics and their implications. *American Psychologist*, **17**(11), 776–783.

Ornstein, R. (1991). *The evolution of conciousness: Of Darwin, Freud, and cranial fire: The origins of the way we think*. New York: Prentice-Hall.

Osberg, T. M., & Shrauger, J. S. (1986). Self-prediction: Exploring the parameters of accuracy. *Journal of Personality and Social Psychology*, **51**, 1044–1057.

Osberg, T. M., & Shrauger, J. S. (1990). The role of self-prediction in psychological assessment. In J. N. Butcher & C. D. Spielberger (eds), *Advances in Personality Assessment*, Vol. 8. Hillsdale, NJ: Erlbaum.

Osgood, C. E. (1962). *An alternative to war or surrender*. Urbana, IL: University of Illinois Press.

Osgood, C. E. (1980). GRIT: A strategy for survival in mankind's nuclear age? Paper presented at the Pugwash Conference on New Directions in Disarmament, Racine, WI.

Osofsky, M. J., Bandura, A., & Zimbardo, P. G. (2005). The role of moral disengagement in the execution process. *Law and Human Behavior*, **29**, 371–393.

Osterhouse, R. A., & Brock, T. C. (1970). Distraction increases yielding to propaganda by inhibiting counterarguing. *Journal of Personality and Social Psychology*, **15**, 344–358.

Ostrowsky, M. K. (2010). Are violent people more likely to have low self-esteem or high self-esteem? *Aggression and Violent Behavior*, **15**, 69–75.

Ouellette, J. A., & Wood, W. (1998). Habit and intention in everyday life: The multiple processes by which past behavior predicts future behavior. *Psychological Bulletin*, **124**, 54–74.

Owens, L., Shute, R., & Slee, P. (2000a). 'Guess what I just heard!': Indirect aggression among teenage girls in Australia. *Aggressive Behavior*, **26**, 67–83.

Owens, L., Slee, P., & Shute, R. (2000b). 'It hurts a hell of a lot …': The effects of indirect aggression on teenage girls. *School Psychology International*, **21**(4), 359–376.

Oyserman, D., Coon, H. M., & Kemmelmeier, M. (2002). Rethinking individualism and collectivism: Evaluation of theoretical assumptions and meta-analyses. *Psychological Bulletin*, **128**, 3–72.

Ozer, E. M., & Bandura, A. (1990). Mechanisms governing empowerment effects: A self-efficacy analysis. *Journal of Personality and Social Psychology*, **58**, 472–486.

**P**

Packer, D. J. (2009). Avoiding groupthink whereas weakly identified members remain silent, strongly identified members dissent about collective problems. *Psychological Science*, **20**(5), 546–548.

Page-Gould, E., Mendoza-Denton, R., & Tropp, L. R. (2008). With a little help from my cross-group friend: Reducing anxiety in intergroup contexts through crossgroup friendship. *Journal of Personality and Social Psychology*, **95**(5), 1080–1094.

Pak, A. W., Dion, K. L., & Dion, K. K. (1991). Social psychological correlates of experienced discrimination: Test of the double jeopardy hypothesis. *International Journal of Intercultural Relations*, **15**, 243–254.

Palasinski, M. (2012). The roles of monitoring and cyberbystanders in reducing sexual abuse. *Computers in Human Behavior*, **28**, 2014–2022.

Pallak, M. S., Mueller, M., Dollar, K., & Pallak, J. (1972). Effect of commitment on responsiveness to an extreme consonant communication. *Journal of Personality and Social Psychology*, **23**, 429–436.

Pallak, S. R., Murroni, E., & Koch, J. (1983). Communicator attractiveness and expertise, emotional versus rational appeals, and persuasion: A heuristic versus systematic processing interpretation. *Social Cognition*, **2**, 122–141.

Palmer, E. L., & Dorr, A. (eds) (1980). *Children and the faces of television: Teaching, violence, selling.* New York: Academic Press.

Palmer, J. K., & Loveland, J. M. (2008). The influence of group discussion on performance judgments: Rating accuracy, contrast effects, and halo. *Journal of Psychology: Interdisciplinary and Applied*, **142**(2), 117–130.

Paloutzian, R. (1979). Proecology behavior: Three field experiments on litter pickup. Paper presented at the Western Psychological Association convention.

Pandey, J., Sinha, Y., Prakash, A., & Tripathi, R. C. (1982). Right–left political ideologies and attribution of the causes of poverty. *European Journal of Social Psychology*, **12**, 327–331.

Paolini, S., Hewstone, M., & Cairns, E. (2007). Direct and indirect intergroup friendship effects: testing the moderating role of the affective-cognitive bases of prejudice. *PSPB*, **33**(10), 1406–1420.

Papastamou, S., & Mugny, G. (1990). Synchronic consistency and psychologization in minority influence. *European Journal of Social Psychology*, **20**, 85–98.

Park, S., & Catrambone, R. (2007). Social facilitation effects of virtual humans. *Human Factors*, **49**(6), 1054–1060.

Parke, J., Griffiths, M. D., & Parke, A. (2007). Positive thinking among slot machine gamblers: A case of maladaptive coping? *International Journal Mental Health Addiction*, **5**, 39–52.

Parke, R. D., Berkowitz, L., Leyens, J. P., West, S. G., & Sebastian, J. (1977). Some effects of violent and nonviolent movies on the behavior of juvenile delinquents. In L. Berkowitz (ed.), *Advances in experimental social psychology*, Vol. 10. New York: Academic Press.

Parker, I. (1989). *The crisis in modern social psychology, and how to end it.* London: Routledge.

Parker, I. (1992). *Discourse dynamics: Critical analysis for social and individual psychology.* London: Routledge.

Parker, I. (2002). *Critical discursive psychology.* London: Palgrave.

Parks, C. D., & Rumble, A. C. (2001). Elements of reciprocity and social value orientation. *Personality and Social Psychology Bulletin*, **27**(10), 1301–1309.

Pashupati, K. (2003). 'I know this brand, but did I like the ad?' An investigation of the familiarity-based sleeper effect. *Psychology & Marketing*, **20**(11), 1017–1043.

Patterson, D. (1996). *When learned men murder.* Bloomington, IN: Phi Delta Kappa Educational Foundation.

Patterson, G. R., Chamberlain, P., & Reid, J. B. (1982). A comparative evaluation of parent training procedures. *Behavior Therapy*, **13**, 638–650.

Patterson, G. R., Littman, R. A., & Bricker, W. (1967). Assertive behavior in children: A step toward a theory of aggression. *Monographs of the Society of Research in Child Development* (Serial No. 113), **32**, 5.

Patterson, M. L., Iizuka, Y., Tubbs, M. E., Ansel, J., & Anson, J. (2006). Passing encounters East and West: Comparing Japanese and American pedestrian interactions. Paper presented to the Society of Personality and Social Psychology convention.

Patterson, M. L., Iizuka, Y., Tubbs, M. E., Ansel, J., Tsutsumi, M., & Anson, J. (2007). Passing encounters East and West: Comparing Japanese and American pedestrian interactions. *Journal of Nonverbal Behaviour*, **31**, 155–166.

Patterson, T. E. (1980). The role of the mass media in presidential campaigns: The lessons of the 1976 election. *Items*, **34**, 25–30.

Paulhus, D. L., & Lim, D. T. K. (1994). Arousal and evaluative extremity in social judgments: A dynamic complexity model. *European Journal of Social Psychology*, **24**, 89–99.

Paulus, P. B. (1998). Developing consensus about groupthink after all these years. *Organizational Behavior and Human Decision Processes*, **73**, 362–375.

Paulus, P. B., Brown, V., & Ortega, A. H. (1997). Group creativity. In R. E. Purser and A. Montuori (eds), *Social creativity*, Vol. 2. Cresskill, NJ: Hampton Press.

Paulus, P. B., Larey, T. S., & Dzindolet, M. T. (1998). Creativity in groups and teams. In M. Turner (ed.), *Groups at work: Advances in theory and research.* Hillsdale, NJ: Erlbaum.

Paulus, P. B., Larey, T. S., & Dzindolet, M. T. (2000). Creativity in groups and teams. In M. Turner (ed.), *Groups at work: Advances in theory and research.* Hillsdale, NJ: Hampton.

Paulus, P. B., Larey, T. S., & Ortega, A. H. (1995). Performance and perceptions of brainstormers in an organizational setting. *Basic and Applied Social Psychology*, **17**, 249–265.

Paunonen, S. (2006). You are honest, therefore I like you and find you attractive. *Journal of Research in Personality*, **40**(3), 237–249.

Payne, B. K. (2001). Prejudice and perception: The role of automatic and controlled processes in misperceiving a weapon. *Journal of Personality and Social Psychology*, **81**, 181–192.

Pedersen, A., & Walker, I. (1997). Prejudice against Australian Aborigines: Old-fashioned and modern forms. *European Journal of Social Psychology*, **27**, 561–587.

Pedersen, E. R., LaBrie, J. W., & Lac, A. (2008). Assessment of perceived and actual alcohol norms in varying contexts: Exploring social impact theory among college students. *Addictive Behaviors*, **33**, 552–564.

Pedersen, W. C., Gonzales, C., & Miller, N. (2000). The moderating effect of trivial triggering provocation on displaced aggression. *Journal of Personality and Social Psychology*, **78**, 913–927.

Pegalis, L. J., Shaffer, D. R., Bazzini, D. G., & Greenier, K. (1994). On the ability to elicit self-disclosure: Are there gender-based and contextual limitations on the opener effect? *Personality and Social Psychology Bulletin*, **20**, 412–420.

Pelham, B., & Crabtree, S. (2008). Worldwide, highly religious more likely to help others. World Gallup, 8 October.

Pelham, B. W., Mirenberg, M. C., & Jones, J. T. (2002). Why Susie sells seashells by the seashore. Implicit egotism and major life decisions. *Journal of Personality and Social Psychology*, **82**(4), 469–487.

Pennebaker, J. W., Rimé, B., & Sproul, G. (1996). Stereotypes of emotional expressiveness of northerners and southerners: A cross-cultural test of Montesquieu's hypotheses. *Journal of Personality and Social Psychology*, **70**, 372–380.

Penner, L. A., Dertke, M. C., & Achenbach, C. J. (1973). The 'flash' system: A field study of altruism. *Journal of Applied Social Psychology*, **3**, 362–370.

*People* (2003, 1 September). Nipped, tucked, talking, pp. 102–111.

Peplau, L. A., & Gordon, S. L. (1985). Women and men in love: Gender differences in close heterosexual relationships. In V. E. O'Leary, R. K. Unger & B. S. Wallston (eds), *Women, gender, and social psychology*. Hillsdale, NJ: Erlbaum.

Perkins, A., Forehand, M., Greenwald, A., & Maison, D. (2008). Measuring the nonconscious: Implicit social cognition in consumer behaviour. In C. P. Haugtvedt, P. M. Herr and F. R. Kardes (eds), *Handbook of Consumer Psychology*. New York: Psychology Press.

Perls, F. S. (1973). *Ego, hunger and aggression: The beginning of Gestalt therapy*. Random House, 1969. Cited by Berkowitz in The case for bottling up rage. *Psychology Today*, July, pp. 24–30.

Perrin, S., & Spencer, C. (1981). Independence or conformity in the Asch experiment as a reflection of cultural or situational factors. *British Journal of Social Psychology*, **20**, 205–209.

Perrotta, C. (2006). Learning to be a psychologist: The construction of identity in an online forum. *Journal of Computer Assisted Learning*, **22**, 456–466.

Persico, N., Postlewaite, A., & Silverman, D. (2004). The effect of adolescent experience on labor market outcomes: The case of height. *Journal of Political Economy*, **112**, 1019–1053.

Persky, S., & Blascovich, J. (2005). Consequences of playing violent video games in immersive virtual environments. In A. Axelsson & R. Schroeder (eds), *Work and play in shared virtual environments*. New York: Springer.

Pessiglione, M., Petrovic, P., Daunizeau, J., Palminteri, S., Dolan, R. J., & Frith, C. D. (2008). Subliminal instrumental conditioning demonstrated in the human brain. *Neuron*, **59**(4), 561–567.

Pessin, J. (1933). The comparative effects of social and mechanical stimulation on memorizing. *American Journal of Psychology*, **45**, 263–270.

Pessin, J., & Husband, R. W. (1933). Effects of social stimulation on human maze learning. *Journal of Abnormal and Social Psychology*, **28**, 148–154.

Peterson, C. (1988). Explanatory style as a risk factor for illness. *Cognitive Therapy and Research*, **12**(2), 1573–2819.

Peterson, C., & Barrett, L. C. (1987). Explanatory style and academic performance among university freshmen. *Journal of Personality and Social Psychology*, **53**, 603–607.

Peterson, C., Schwartz, S. M., & Seligman, M. E. P. (1981). Self-blame and depression symptoms. *Journal of Personality and Social Psychology*, **41**, 253–259.

Peterson, R. S., & Nemeth, C. J. (1996). Focus versus flexibility: Majority and minority influence can both improve performance. *Personality and Social Psychology Bulletin*, **22**, 14–23.

Pettigrew, T. F. (1969). Racially separate or together? *Journal of Social Issues*, **2**, 43–69.

Pettigrew, T. F. (1979). The ultimate attribution error: Extending Allport's cognitive analysis of prejudice. *Personality and Social Psychology Bulletin*, **55**, 461–476.

Pettigrew, T. F. (1988). Advancing racial justice: Past lessons for future use. Paper for the University of Alabama Conference: Opening Doors: An Appraisal of Race Relations in America.

Pettigrew, T. F. (1997). Generalized intergroup contact effects on prejudice. *Personality and Social Psychology Bulletin*, **23**, 173–185.

Pettigrew, T. F. (2003). Peoples under threat: Americans, Arabs, and Israelis. *Peace and Conflict*, **9**, 69–90.

Pettigrew, T. F. (2004). Intergroup contact: Theory, research, and new perspectives. In J. A. Banks & C. A. McGee Banks (eds), *Handbook of research on multicultural education*. San Francisco: Jossey-Bass.

Pettigrew, T. F., & Tropp, L. R. (2000). Does intergroup contact reduce prejudice: Recent meta-analytic findings. In S. Oskamp (ed.), *Reducing prejudice and discrimination*. Mahwah, NJ: Lawrence Erlbaum.

Pettigrew, T. F., & Tropp, L. R. (2006). A meta-analytic test of intergroup contact theory. *Journal of Personality and Social Psychology*, **90**, 751–783.

Petty, R. E., & Cacioppo, J. T. (1979). Effects of forewarning of persuasive intent and involvement on cognitive response and persuasion. *Personality and Social Psychology Bulletin*, **5**, 173–176.

Petty, R. E., & Cacioppo, J. T. (1986). *Communication and persuasion: Central and peripheral routes to attitude change*. New York: Springer-Verlag.

Petty, R. E., & Krosnick, J. A. (eds). (1995). *Attitude strength: Antecedents and consequences*. Hillsdale, NJ: Erlbaum.

Petty, R. E., & Wegener, D. T. (1998). Attitude change: Multiple roles for persuasion variables. In D. Gilbert, S. Fiske & G. Lindzey (eds), *Handbook of social psychology*, 4th edn. New York: McGraw-Hill.

Petty, R. E., & Wegener, D. T. (1999). The elaboration likelihood model: Current status and controversies. In S. Chaiken & Y. Trope (eds), *Dual-process theories in social psychology*. New York: Guilford Press.

Petty, R. E., Briñol, P., & Tormala, Z. L. (2002). Thought confidence as a determinant of persuasion: The self-validation hypothesis. *Journal of Personality and Social Psychology*, **82**, 722–741.

Petty, R. E., Cacioppo, J. T., & Goldman, R. (1981). Personal involvement as a determinant of argument-based persuasion. *Journal of Personality and Social Psychology*, **41**, 847–855.

Petty, R. E., Haugtvedt, C. P., & Smith, S. M. (1995). Elaboration as a determinant of attitude strength: Creating attitudes that are persistent, resistant, and predictive of behavior. In R. E. Petty & J. A. Krosnick (eds), *Attitude strength: Antecedents and consequences. Ohio State University Series on Attitudes and Persuasion*, Vol. 4 (pp. 93–130). Hillsdale, NJ: Lawrence Erlbaum.

Petty, R. E., Schumann, D. W., Richman, S. A., & Strathman, A. J. (1993). Positive mood and persuasion: Different roles for affect under high and low elaboration conditions. *Journal of Personality and Social Psychology*, **64**, 5–20.

Pew (2003). Views of a changing world 2003. The Pew Global Attitudes Project. Washington, DC: Pew Research Center for the People and the Press (http://people-press.org/reports/pdf/185.pdf).

Pew (2006, 14 March). Guess who's coming to dinner. Pew Research Center (pewresearch.org).

Pew Global Attitudes Project (2007). Spring Survey. Available at: http://www.pewglobal.org/files/pdf/256topline.pdf

Phelps, E. A., O'Connor, K. J., Cunningham, W. A., Funayama, E. S., Gatenby, J. C., Gore, G. C., & Banaji, M. A. (2000). Performance on indirect measures of race evaluation predicts amygdala activation. *Journal of Cognitive Neuroscience*, **12**, 729–738.

Phenice, L., Griffore, R., & Lee, K. (2010). Altruism in public: Holding open doors for those who follow. *European Journal of Social Sciences*, **16**, 7–10.

Phillips, D. P. (1982). The impact of fictional television stories on U.S. adult fatalities: New evidence on the effect of the mass media on violence. *American Journal of Sociology*, **87**, 1340–1359.

Phillips, D. P. (1985). Natural experiments on the effects of mass media violence on fatal aggression: Strengths and weaknesses of a new approach. In L. Berkowitz (ed.), *Advances in experimental social psychology*, Vol. 19. Orlando, FL: Academic Press.

Phillips, D. P., Carstensen, L. L., & Paight, D. J. (1989). Effects of mass media news stories on suicide, with new evidence on the role of story content. In D. R. Pfeffer (ed.), *Suicide among youth: Perspectives on risk and prevention.* Washington, DC: American Psychiatric Press.

Phillips, T. (2004, 3 April). Quoted by T. Baldwin & D. Rozenberg in Britain must scrap multiculturalism. *The Times,* p. A1.

Phinney, J. S. (1990). Ethnic identity in adolescents and adults: Review of research. *Psychological Bulletin,* **108**, 499–514.

Pickett, C. L., Silver, M. D., & Brewer, M. B. (2002). The impact of assimilation and differentiation needs on perceived group importance and judgments of ingroup size. *Personality and Social Psychology Bulletin,* **28**, 546–558.

Pierce, J. P., & Gilpin, E. A. (1995). A historical analysis of tobacco marketing and the uptake of smoking by youth in the United States: 1890–1977. *Health Psychology,* **14**, 500–508.

Pierce, J. P., Lee, L., & Gilpin, E. A. (1994). Smoking initiation by adolescent girls, 1944 through 1988. *Journal of the American Medical Association,* **27**, 608–611.

Piliavin, J. A. (2003). Doing well by doing good: Benefits for the benefactor. In C. L. M. Keyes & J. Haidt (eds), *Flourishing: Positive psychology and the life well-lived.* Washington, DC: American Psychological Association.

Piliavin, J. A., & Charng, H. W. (1990). Altruism: A review of recent theory and research. *Annual Review of Sociology,* **16**, 27–65.

Piliavin, J. A., & Piliavin, I. M. (1973). The good Samaritan: Why *does* he help? Unpublished manuscript, University of Wisconsin.

Piliavin, J. A., Evans, D. E., & Callero, P. (1982). Learning to 'Give to unnamed strangers': The process of commitment to regular blood donation. In E. Staub, D. Bar-Tal, J. Karylowski & J. Reykawski (eds), *The development and maintenance of prosocial behavior: International perspectives.* New York: Plenum.

Pinel, E. C. (2002). Stigma consciousness in intergroup contexts: The power of conviction. *Journal of Experimental Social Psychology,* **38**, 178–185.

Pingitore, R., Dugoni, B. L., Tindale, R. S., & Spring, B. (1994). Bias against overweight job applicants in a simulated employment interview. *Journal of Applied Psychology,* **79**, 909–917.

Pinker, S. (2002). *The blank slate.* New York: Viking.

Pitner, R. O., Yu, M., & Brown, E. (2011). Exploring the dynamics of middle-aged and older adult residents' perceptions of neighborhood safety. *Journal of Gerontological Social Work,* **54**, 511–527.

Plaks, J. E., & Higgins, E. T. (2000). Pragmatic use of stereotyping in teamwork: Social loafing and compensation as a function of inferred partner–situation fit. *Journal of Personality and Social Psychology,* **79**, 962–974.

Platow, M. J., Haslam, S. A., Both, A., Chew, I., Cuddon, M., Goharpey, N., Mäurer, J., Rosini, S., Tsekouras, A., & Grace, D. M. (2005). It's not funny if *they're* laughing: Self-categorization, social influence, and responses to canned laughter. *Journal of Experimental Social Psychology,* **41**, 542–550.

Platow, M. J., Voudouris, N. J., Coulson, M., Gilford, N., Jamieson, R., Najdovski, L., Papaleo, N. Pollard, C., & Terry, L. (2007). In-group reassurance in a pain setting produces lower levels of physiological arousal: Direct support for a self-categorization analysis of social influence. *European Journal of Social Psychology,* **37**, 649–660.

Plous, S. (2008). The psychology of prejudice, stereotyping and discrimination: An overview (www.understandingPrejudice.org).

Pomazal, R. J., & Clore, G. L. (1973). Helping on the highway: The effects of dependency and sex. *Journal of Applied Social Psychology,* **3**, 150–164.

Pomerantz, A. (1978). Compliment responses. Notes on the cooperation of multiple constraints. In J. Schenkein (ed.), *Studies in the organisation of conversational interaction.* New York: Academic Press.

Poniewozik, J. (2003, 24 November). All the news that fits your reality. *Time,* 90.

Poobalan, A. S., Aucott, L. S., Clarke, A., Smith, W., & Cairns, S. (2012). Physical activity attitudes, intentions and behaviours among 18–25 year olds: A mixed methods study. *BMC Public Health,* **12**(1), 640–649.

Poortinga, W., Steg, L. & Vlek, C. (2004). Values, environmental concern, and environmental behaviour: A study into household energy use. *Environment and Behavior,* **36**(1), 70–93.

Popper, K. (1963). *Conjectures and refutations: The growth of scientific knowledge.* London: Routledge.

Postmes, T. (2003). A social identity approach to communication in organizations. In S. A. Haslam, D. van Knippenberg, M. J. Platow & N. Ellemers (eds), *Social identity at work: Developing theory for organizational practice.* Philadelphia, PA: Psychology Press.

Postmes, T., Spears, R., & Cihangir, S. (2001). Quality of decision making and group norms. *Journal of Personality and Social Psychology,* **80**, 918–930.

Postmes, T., Spears, R., & Lea, M. (2000). The formation of group norms in computer-mediated communication. *Human Communication Research,* **26**, 341–371.

Potter, J. (1996). *Representing reality: Discourse, rhetoric and social construction.* London: Sage.

Potter, J., & Wetherell, M. (1987). *Discourse and social psychology: Beyond attitudes and behaviour.* London: Sage.

Pratkanis, A. R., Greenwald, A. G., Leippe, M. R., & Baumgardner, M. H. (1988). In search of reliable persuasion effects: III. The sleeper effect is dead. Long live the sleeper effect. *Journal of Personality and Social Psychology,* **54**, 203–218.

Pratt, M. W., Pancer, M., Hunsberger, B., & Manchester, J. (1990). Reasoning about the self and relationships in maturity: An integrative complexity analysis of individual differences. *Journal of Personality and Social Psychology,* **59**, 575–581.

Pratto, F. (1996). Sexual politics: The gender gap in the bedroom, the cupboard, and the cabinet. In D. M. Buss & N. M. Malamuth (eds), *Sex, power, conflict: Evolutionary and feminist perspectives.* New York: Oxford University Press.

Pratto, F., Sidanius, J., Stallworth, L. M., & Malle, B. F. (1994). Social dominance orientation: A personality variable predicting social and political attitudes. *Journal of Personality and Social Psychology,* **67**, 741–763.

Praxmarer, S., & Rossiter, J. (2011). How does the presenter's physical attractiveness persuade? A test of alternative explanations. Working Paper, University of Wollongong.

Presson, P. K., & Benassi, V. A. (1996). Illusion of control: A meta-analytic review. *Journal of Social Behavior and Personality,* **11**, 493–510.

Price, G. H., Dabbs, J. M., Jr, Clower, B. J., & Resin, R. P. (1974). At first glance – Or, is physical attractiveness more than skin deep? Paper presented at the Eastern Psychological Association convention. Cited by K. L. Dion & K. K. Dion (1979). Personality and behavioral correlates of romantic love. In M. Cook & G. Wilson (eds), *Love and attraction.* Oxford: Pergamon.

Pritchard, I. L. (1998). The effects of rap music: On aggressive attitudes toward women. Master's thesis, Humboldt State University.

Pronin, E., Lin, D. Y., & Ross, L. (2002). The bias blind spot: Perceptions of bias in self versus others. *Personality and Social Psychology Bulletin*, **28**, 369–381.

Provine, R. R. (2005). Yawning. *American Scientist*, **93**, 532–539.

Pruitt, D. G. (1998). Social conflict. In D. Gilbert, S. T. Fiske & G. Lindzey (eds), *Handbook of social psychology*, 4th edn. New York: McGraw-Hill.

Pryor, J. B., DeSouza, E. R., Fitness, J., Hutz, C., Kumpf, M., Lubbert, K., Pesonen, O., & Erber, M. W. (1997). Gender differences in the interpretation of social-sexual behavior: A cross-cultural perspective on sexual harassment. *Journal of Cross-Cultural Psychology*, **28**, 509–534.

Puentes, J., Knox, D., & Zusman, M. E. (2008). Participants in 'friends with benefits' relationships. *College Student Journal*, **42**(1), 176–180.

Purvis, J. A., Dabbs, J. M., Jr, & Hopper, C. H. (1984). The 'opener': Skilled user of facial expression and speech pattern. *Personality and Social Psychology Bulletin*, **10**, 61–66.

Putnam, R. (2000). *Bowling alone: The collapse and revival of American community*. New York: Simon & Schuster.

Pyszczynski, T., & Greenberg, J. (1987). Self-regulatory perseveration and the depressive self-focusing style: A self-awareness theory of reactive depression. *Psychological Bulletin*, **102**, 122–138.

Pyszczynski, T., Abdollahi, A., Solomon, S., Greenberg, J., Cohen, F., & Weise, D. (2006). Mortality salience, martyrdom, and military might: The great Satan versus the axis of evil. *Personality and Social Psychology Bulletin*, **32**, 525–537.

Pyszczynski, T., Greenberg, J., & Solomon, S. (2000). Why do we need what we need? A terror management perspective on the roots of human social motivation. In E. T. Higgins & A. W. Kruglanski (eds), *Motivational science: Social and personality perspectives*. Philadelphia: Psychology Press.

## Q

Quadflieg, S., & Macrae, N. (2011). Stereotypes and stereotyping: What's the brain got to do with it? *European Review of Social Psychology*, **22**, 215–273.

Quartz, S. R., & Sejnowski, T. J. (2002). *Liars, lovers, and heroes: What the new brain science reveals about how we become who we are*. New York: Morrow.

Quintana, S. M. (1998). Development of children's understanding of ethnicity and race. *Applied & Preventive Psychology*, **7**, 27–45.

## R

Rabbie, J. M., & Bekkers, F. (1978). Threatened leadership and intergroup competition. *European Journal of Social Psychology*, **8**, 9–20.

Rajecki, D. W., Bledsoe, S. B., & Rasmussen, J. L. (1991). Successful personal ads: Gender differences and similarities in offers, stipulations, and outcomes. *Basic and Applied Social Psychology*, **12**, 457–469.

Ramirez, J. M., Bonniot-Cabanac, M.-C., & Cabanac, M. (2005). Can aggression provide pleasure? *European Psychologist*, **10**, 136–145.

Rank, S. G., & Jacobson, C. K. (1977). Hospital nurses' compliance with medication overdose orders: A failure to replicate. *Journal of Health and Social Behavior*, **18**, 188–193.

Ratner, C. (1991). *Vygotsky's sociohistorical psychology and its contemporary applications*. New York: Plenum Press.

Reeves, F. (1983). *British racial discourse*. Cambridge: Cambridge University Press.

Regan, D. T., & Cheng, J. B. (1973). Distraction and attitude change: A resolution. *Journal of Experimental Social Psychology*, **9**, 138–147.

Regan, D. & Morrison, T. G. (2011). Development and validation of a scale measuring attitudes toward nondrinkers. *Substance Use and Misuse*, **46**, 580–590.

Regan, P. C. (1998). What if you can't get what you want? Willingness to compromise ideal mate selection standards as a function of sex, mate value, and relationship context. *Personality and Social Psychology Bulletin*, **24**, 1294–1303.

Reicher, S. D. (1984). The St Pauls riot: An explanation of the limits of crowd action in terms of a social identity model. *European Journal of Social Psychology*, **14**, 1–21.

Reicher, S., & Haslam, S. A. (2006). Rethinking the psychology of tyranny: The BBC prison study. *British Journal of Social Psychology*, **45**, 1–40.

Reicher, S., & Hopkins, N. (1996). Self-category constructions in political rhetoric; an analysis of Thatcher's and Kinnock's speeches concerning the British miners' strike (1984–5). *European Journal of Social Psychology*, **26**, 353–371.

Reicher, S., & Hopkins, N. (2001). *Self and nation*. London: Sage.

Reicher, S., Haslam, S. A., & Platow, M. J. (2007). The new psychology of leadership. *Scientific American Mind*, **18**, 22–29.

Reicher, S. D., Haslam, S. A., & Rath, R. (2008). Making a virtue of evil: A five-step social identity model of the development of collective hate. *Social and Personality Psychology Compass*, **2**, 1313–1344.

Reicher, S. D., Haslam, S. A., & Smith, J. R. (2012). Working toward the experimenter: Reconceptualizing obedience within the Milgram paradigm as identification-based followership. *Perspectives on Psychological Science*, **7**, 315–324.

Reicher, S., Stott, C., Cronin, P., & Adang, O. (2004). An integrated approach to crowd psychology and public order policing. *Policing*, **27**(4), 558–572.

Reid, P., & Finchilescu, G. (1995). The disempowering effects of media violence against women on college women. *Psychology of Women Quarterly*, **19**, 397–411.

Reidy, D. E., Shelley-Tremblay, J. F., & Lilienfeld, S. O. (2011). Psychopathy, reactive aggression, and precarious proclamations: A review of behavioral, cognitive, and biological research. *Aggression and Violent Behavior*, **16**(6), 512–524.

Reidy, D. E., Shirk, S. D., Sloan, C. A., & Zeichner, A. (2009). Men who aggress against women: Effects of feminine gender role violation on physical aggression in hypermasculine men. *Psychology of Men & Masculinity*, **10**(1), 1–12.

Reiner, W. G., & Gearhart, J. P. (2004). Discordant sexual identity in some genetic males with cloacal exstrophy assigned to female sex at birth. *New England Journal of Medicine*, **350**, 333–341.

Reis, H. T., & Shaver, P. (1988). Intimacy as an interpersonal process. In S. Duck (ed.), *Handbook of personal relationships: Theory, relationships and interventions*. Chichester: Wiley.

Reis, H. T., Nezlek, J., & Wheeler, L. (1980). Physical attractiveness in social interaction. *Journal of Personality and Social Psychology*, **38**, 604–617.

Reis, H. T., Wheeler, L., Spiegel, N., Kernis, M. H., Nezlek, J., & Perri, M. (1982). Physical attractiveness in social interaction: II. Why does appearance affect social experience? *Journal of Personality and Social Psychology*, **43**, 979–996.

Reisenzein, R. (1983). The Schachter theory of emotion: Two decades later. *Psychological Bulletin*, **94**, 239–264.

Reynolds, J., & Wetherell, M. (2003). The discursive climate of singleness: The consequences for women's negotiation of a single identity. *Feminism and Psychology*, **13**(4), 489–510.

Rhine, R. J., & Severance, L. J. (1970). Ego-involvement, discrepancy, source credibility, and attitude change. *Journal of Personality and Social Psychology*, **16**, 175–190.

Rhodes, N., & Wood, W. (1992). Self-esteem and intelligence affect influenceability: The mediating role of message reception. *Psychological Bulletin*, **111**, 156–171.

Rhodewalt, F. (1987). Is self-handicapping an effective

self-protective attributional strategy? Paper presented at the American Psychological Association convention.

Rhodewalt, F., Saltzman, A. T., & Wittmer J. (1984). Self-handicapping among competitive athletes: The role of practice in self-esteem protection. *Basic and Applied Social Psychology*, **5**, 197–209.

Rholes, W. S., Newman, L. S., & Ruble, D. N. (1990). Understanding self and other: Developmental and motivational aspects of perceiving persons in terms of invariant dispositions. In E. T. Higgins & R. M. Sorrentino (eds), *Handbook of motivation and cognition: Foundations of social behavior*, Vol. 2. New York: Guilford.

Rice, M. E., & Grusec, J. E. (1975). Saying and doing: Effects on observer performance. *Journal of Personality and Social Psychology*, **32**, 584–593.

Rich, F. (2001, 20 May). Naked capitalists: There's no business like porn business. *New York Times* (www.nytimes.com).

Richardson, A., & Budd, T. (2003). *Home Office Research Study, 263: Alcohol, crime and disorder: A study of young adults*. London: Home Office.

Ridge, R. D., & Reber, J. S. (2002). 'I think she's attracted to me': The effect of men's beliefs on women's behavior in a job interview scenario. *Basic and Applied Social Psychology*, **24**, 1–14.

Ridley, M. (2003). *Nature via nurture*. London: HarperCollins.

Rietzschel, E. F., Nijstad, B. A., & Stroebe, W. (2006). Productivity is not enough: A comparison of interactive and nominal brainstorming groups on idea generation and selection. *Journal of Experimental Social Psychology*, **42**, 244–251.

Riggs, J. M. (1992). Self-handicapping and achievement. In A. K. Boggiano & T. S. Pittman (eds), *Achievement and motivation: A social-developmental perspective*. New York: Cambridge University Press.

Riordan, C. A. (1980). Effects of admission of influence on

attributions and attraction. Paper presented at the American Psychological Association convention.

Risen, J. L., & Gilovich, T. (2007). Target and observer differences in the acceptance of questionable apologies. *Journal of Personality and Social Psychology*, **92**(3), 418–433.

Risen, J. L., Gilovich, T., & Dunning, D. (2007). One-shot illusory correlations and stereotype formation. *Personality and Social Psychology Bulletin*, **33**(11), 1492–1502.

Ritchie, S. J., Wiseman, R., & French, C. C. (2012). Failing the future: Three unsuccessful replications of Bem's 'retroactive facilitation of recall' effect. *PLoS ONE*, **7** (3): e33423. doi:10.1371/journal.pone.0033423

Roach, M. (1998, December). Why men kill. *Discover*, 100–108.

Robberson, M. R., & Rogers, R. W. (1988). Beyond fear appeals: Negative and positive persuasive appeals to health and self-esteem. *Journal of Applied Social Psychology*, **18**, 277–287.

Roberts, B. W., Edmonds, G., & Grijalva, E. (2010). It is developmental me, not generation me: Developmental changes are more important than generational changes in narcissism – Commentary on Trzesniewski & Donnellan (2010). *Perspectives on Psychological Science*, **5**, 97–102.

Robertson, I. (1987). *Sociology*. New York: Worth Publishers.

Robins, R. W., Mendelsohn, G. A., Connell, J. B., & Kwan, V. S. Y. (2004). Do people agree about the causes of behavior? A social relations analysis of behavior ratings and causal attributions. *Journal of Personality and Social Psychology*, **86**, 334–344.

Robinson, M. D., & Ryff, C. D. (1999). The role of self-deception in perceptions of past, present, and future happiness. *Personality and Social Psychology Bulletin*, **25**, 595–606.

Robinson, T. N., Wilde, M. L., Navracruz, L. C., Haydel, F., & Varady, A. (2001). Effects of reducing

children's television and video game use on aggressive behavior. *Archives of Pediatric and Adolescent Medicine*, **155**, 17–23.

Rochat, F. (1993). How did they resist authority? Protecting refugees in Le Chambon during World War II. Paper presented at the American Psychological Association convention.

Rochat, F., & Modigliani, A. (1995). The ordinary quality of resistance: From Milgram's laboratory to the village of Le Chambon. *Journal of Social Issues*, **51**, 195–210.

Rockloff, M. J., & Dyer, V. (2007). An experiment on the social facilitation of gambling behavior. *Journal of Gambling Studies*, **23**, 1–12.

Roehling, M. V. (2000). Weight-based discrimination in employment: psychological and legal aspects. *Personnel Psychology*, **52**, 969–1016.

Roese, N. J. (1994). The functional basis of counterfactual thinking. *Journal of Personality and Social Psychology*, **66**, 805–818.

Roese, N. J. (1997). Counterfactual thinking. *Psychological Bulletin*, **121**(1), 133.

Roese, N. J., & Hur, T. (1997). Affective determinants of counterfactual thinking. *Social Cognition*, **15**, 274–290.

Roese, N. L., & Olson, J. M. (1994). Attitude importance as a function of repeated attitude expression. *Journal of Experimental Social Psychology*, **66**, 805–818.

Roger, L. H., Cortes, D. E., & Malgady, R. B. (1991). Acculturation and mental health status among Hispanics: Convergence and new directions for research. *American Psychologist*, **46**, 585–597.

Rogers, C. R. (1980). *A way of being*. Boston: Houghton Mifflin.

Rohrer, J. H., Baron, S. H., Hoffman, E. L., & Swander, D. V. (1954). The stability of autokinetic judgments. *The Journal of Abnormal and Social Psychology*, **49**, 595.

Rojahn, J., Komelasky, K. G., & Man, M. (2008). Opposite-sex peers with physical disabilities. *Journal of Developmental and Physical Disabilities*, **20**(4), 389–397.

Rokeach, M. (1960). *The open and closed mind: Investigations into the nature of belief systems and personality systems*. New York: Basic Books.

Rokeach, M. (1968). *Beliefs, attitudes, and values*. San Francisco: Jossey-Bass.

Roman, C. P. (2006). A worker's personal grief and its impact on processing a group's termination. *Social Work with Groups*, **29**(2–3), 235–242.

Rosch, E. (1975). Cognitive representations of semantic categories. *Journal of Experimental Psychology*, **104**(3), 192–233.

Rosenbaum, M. E. (1986). The repulsion hypothesis: On the nondevelopment of relationships. *Journal of Personality and Social Psychology*, **51**, 1156–1166.

Rosenberg, L. A. (1961). Group size, prior experience and conformity. *Journal of Abnormal and Social Psychology*, **63**, 436–437.

Rosenblatt, A., & Greenberg, J. (1988). Depression and interpersonal attraction: The role of perceived similarity. *Journal of Personality and Social Psychology*, **55**, 112–119.

Rosenblatt, A., & Greenberg, J. (1991). Examining the world of the depressed: Do depressed people prefer others who are depressed? *Journal of Personality and Social Psychology*, **60**, 620–629.

Rosenblatt, A., Greenberg, J., Solomon, S., Pyszczynski, T., & Lyon, D. L. (1989). Evidence for terror management theory: I. The effects of mortality salience on reactions to those who violate or uphold cultural values. *Journal of Personality and Social Psychology*, **57**(4), 681–690.

Rosenbloom, S. (2008, 3 January). Putting your best cyberface forward. *New York Times*, Style section.

Rosenbloom, T., Shahar, A., Perlman, A., Estreich, D., & Kirzner, E. (2007). Success on a practical driver's licence test with and without the presence of another testee. *Accident Analysis and Prevention*, **39**, 1296–1301.

Rosenfeld, D., Folger, R., & Adelman, H. F. (1980).

When rewards reflect competence: A qualification of the overjustification effect. *Journal of Personality and Social Psychology*, **39**, 368–376.

Rosenhan, D. L. (1970). The natural socialization of altruistic autonomy. In J. Macauley & L. Berkowitz (eds), *Altruism and helping behavior*. Orlando, FL: Academic Press.

Rosenthal, R. (1985). From unconscious experimenter bias to teacher expectancy effects. In J. B. Dusek, V. C. Hall & W. J. Meyer (eds), *Teacher expectancies*. Hillsdale, NJ: Erlbaum.

Rosenthal, R. (1991). Teacher expectancy effects: A brief update 25 years after the Pygmalion experiment. *Journal of Research in Education*, **1**, 3–12.

Rosenthal, R. (2002). Covert communication in classrooms, clinics, courtrooms, and cubicles. *American Psychologist*, **57**, 839–849.

Rosenthal, R. (2003). Covert communication in laboratories, classrooms, and the truly real world. *Current Directions in Psychological Science*, **12**, 151–154.

Rosenthal, R., & Jacobson, L. (1968). *Pygmalion in the classroom: Teacher expectation and pupils' intellectual development*. New York: Holt, Rinehart & Winston.

Rosh, E. (1978). Principles of categorization. In E. Rosh and B. B. Lloyd (eds), *Cognition and categorization*. Hillsdale, NJ: Erlbaum.

Rosh, E., Mervis, C. G., Gray, W. D., Johnson, D. M., & Bayes Braem, P. (1976). Basic objects in natural categories. *Cognitive Psychology*, **8**, 382–439.

Ross, E. A. (1908). *Social psychology*. New York: Macmillan.

Ross, L. (1977). The intuitive psychologist and his shortcomings: Distortions in the attribution process. In L. Berkowitz (ed.), *Advances in experimental social psychology*, Vol. 10. New York: Academic Press.

Ross, L. (1981). The 'intuitive scientist' formulation and its developmental implications. In J. H. Havell & L. Ross (eds), *Social cognitive development: Frontiers and possible futures*. Cambridge: Cambridge University Press.

Ross, L. (1988). Situationist perspectives on the obedience experiments. Review of A. G. Miller's *The obedience experiments. Contemporary Psychology*, **33**, 101–104.

Ross, L., & Anderson, C. A. (1982). Shortcomings in the attribution process: On the origins and maintenance of erroneous social assessments. In D. Kahneman, P. Slovic & A. Tversky (eds), *Judgment under uncertainty: Heuristics and biases*. New York: Cambridge University Press.

Ross, L., & Lepper, M. R. (1980). The perseverance of beliefs: Empirical and normative considerations. In R. A. Shweder (ed.), *New directions for methodology of behavioral science: Fallible judgment in behavioral research*. San Francisco: Jossey-Bass.

Ross, L., & Ward, A. (1995). Psychological barriers to dispute resolution. In M. P. Zanna (ed.), *Advances in experimental social psychology*, Vol. 27. San Diego: Academic Press.

Ross, L., Amabile, T. M., & Steinmetz, J. L. (1977). Social roles, social control, and biases in social-perception processes. *Journal of Personality and Social Psychology*, **35**, 485–494.

Ross, M., & Fletcher, G. J. O. (1985). Attribution and social perception. In G. Lindzey & E. Aronson (eds), *The handbook of social psychology*, 3rd edn. New York: Random House.

Ross, M., & Newby-Clark, I. R. (1998). Construing the past and future. *Social Cognition*, **16**, 133–150.

Ross, M., McFarland, C., & Fletcher, G. J. O. (1981). The effect of attitude on the recall of personal histories. *Journal of Personality and Social Psychology*, **40**, 627–634.

Rossi, A. S., & Rossi, P. H. (1990). *Of human bonding: Parent–child relations across the life course*. Hawthorne, NY: Aldine de Gruyter.

Roszell, P., Kennedy, D., & Grabb, E. (1990). Physical attractiveness and income attainment among Canadians. *Journal of Psychology*, **123**, 547–559.

Rotenberg, K. J., Gruman, J. A., & Ariganello, M. (2002). Behavioral confirmation of the loneliness stereotype. *Basic and Applied Social Psychology*, **24**, 81–89.

Rothbart, M., & Birrell, P. (1977). Attitude and perception of faces. *Journal of Research Personality*, **11**, 209–215.

Rothbart, M., & Taylor, M. (1992). Social categories and social reality. In G. R. Semin & K. Fielder (eds), *Language, interaction and social cognition*. London: Sage.

Rotter, J. (1973). Internal-external locus of control scale. In J. P. Robinson & R. P. Shaver (eds), *Measure of social psychological attitudes*. Ann Arbor: Institute for Social Research.

Rotton, J., & Frey, J. (1985). Air pollution, weather, and violent crimes: Concomitant time-series analysis of archival data. *Journal of Personality and Social Psychology*, **49**, 1207–1220.

Rowe, D. C., Almeida, D. M., & Jacobson, K. C. (1999). School context and genetic influences on aggression in adolescence. *Psychological Science*, **10**, 277–280.

Ruback, R. B., & Singh, P. (2007). Ingroup bias, intergroup contact and the attribution of blame for riots. *Psychology and Developing Societies*, **19**(2), 249–265.

Ruback, R. B., Carr, T. S., & Hoper, C. H. (1986). Perceived control in prison: Its relation to reported crowding, stress, and symptoms. *Journal of Applied Social Psychology*, **16**, 375–386.

Rubie-Davies, C. M. (2010). Teacher expectations and perceptions of student attributes: Is there a relationship? *British Journal of Educational Psychology*, **80**, 121–135.

Rubin, A. (2003, 16 April). War fans young Arabs' anger. *Los Angeles Times* (www.latimes.com).

Rubin, J. Z. (1986). Can we negotiate with terrorists: Some answers from psychology. Paper presented at the American Psychological Association convention.

Rubin, R. B. (1981). Ideal traits and terms of address for male and female college professors. *Journal of Personality and Social Psychology*, **41**, 966–974.

Rubin, Z. (1973). *Liking and loving: An invitation to social psychology*. New York: Holt, Rinehart & Winston.

Ruble, D. N., & Martin, C. L. (1998). Gender development. In D. W. Damon (ed.), *Handbook of child psychology*, Vol. 3, 5th edn. New York: Holt, Rinehart & Winston.

Ruble, D., Alvarez, J., Bachman, M., Cameron, J., Fuligni, A., Garcia Coll, C., & Rhee, E. (2004). The development of a sense of 'we': The emergence and implications of children's collective identity. In M. Bennett & F. Sani (eds), *The development of the social self*. Hove: Psychology Press.

Ruby, P., & Decety, J. (2004). How would you feel versus how do you think she would feel? A neuroimaging study of perspective-taking with social emotions. *Journal of Cognitive Neuroscience*, **16**, 988–999.

Rudman, L. A., & Glick, P. (2008). *The social psychology of gender: How power and intimacy shape gender relations*. New York: Guilford Press

Rudolph, U., Roesch, S. C., Greitenmeyer, T., & Weiner, B. (2004). A meta-analytic review of help giving and aggression from an attributional perspective: Contributions to a general theory of motivation. *Cognition and Emotion*, **18**, 815–848.

Ruiter, R. A. C., Abraham, C., & Kok, G. (2001). Scary warnings and rational precautions: A review of the psychology of fear appeals. *Psychology and Health*, **16**, 613–630.

Rule, B. G., Taylor, B. R., & Dobbs, A. R. (1987). Priming effects of heat on aggressive thoughts. *Social Cognition*, **5**, 131–143.

Rusbult, C. E., (1980). Commitment and satisfaction in romantic associations: A test of the investment model. *Journal of Experimental Social Psychology*, **16**, 172–186.

Rusbult, C. E., Johnson, D. J., & Morrow, G. D. (1986).

Impact of couple patterns of problem solving on distress and nondistress in dating relationships. *Journal of Personality and Social Psychology*, **50**, 744–753.

Rusbult, C. E., Martz, J. M., & Agnew, C. R. (1998). The investment model scale: Measuring commitment level, satisfaction level, quality of alternatives, and investment size. *Personal Relationships*, **5**, 357–391.

Rusbult, C. E., Morrow, G. D., & Johnson, D. J. (1987). Self-esteem and problem-solving behaviour in close relationships. *British Journal of Social Psychology*, **26**, 293–303.

Rusbult, C. E., Olsen, N., Davis, J. L., & Hannon, P. A. (2001). Commitment and relationship maintenance mechanisms. In J. Harvey & A. Wenzel (eds), *Close romantic relationships: Maintenance and enhancement*. Mahwah, NJ: Erlbaum.

Rushton, J. P. (1975). Generosity in children: Immediate and long-term effects of modeling, preaching, and moral judgment. *Journal of Personality and Social Psychology*, **31**, 459–466.

Rushton, J. P. (1991). Is altruism innate? *Psychological Inquiry*, **2**, 141–143.

Rushton, J. P., & Bons, T. A. (2005). Mate choice and friendship in twins. *Psychological Science*, **16**, 555–559.

Rushton, J. P., & Campbell, A. C. (1977). Modeling, vicarious reinforcement and extraversion on blood donating in adults: Immediate and long-term effects. *European Journal of Social Psychology*, **7**, 297–306.

Rushton, J. P., Fulker, D. W., Neale, M. C., Nias, D. K. B., & Eysenck, H. J. (1986). Altruism and aggression: The heritability of individual differences. *Journal of Personality and Social Psychology*, **50**, 1192–1198.

Russell, B. (1930/1980). *The conquest of happiness*. London: Unwin Paperbacks.

Russell, G. W. (1983). Psychological issues in sports aggression. In J. H. Goldstein (ed.), *Sports violence*. New York: Springer-Verlag.

Russell, N. J. C., & Gregory, R. J. (2005). Making the undoable doable: Milgram, the Holocaust, and modern government. *American Review of Public Administration*, **35**, 327–349.

Ruvolo, A., & Markus, H. (1992). Possible selves and performance: The power of self-relevant imagery. *Social Cognition*, **9**, 95–124.

Ryan, R. M., & Deci, E. L. (2000). Self-determination theory and the facilitation of intrinsic motivation, social development, and well-being. *American Psychologist*, **55**(1), 68.

Ryckman, R. M., Robbins, M. A., Kaczor, L. M., & Gold, J. A. (1989). Male and female raters' stereotyping of male and female physiques. *Personality and Social Psychology Bulletin*, **15**, 244–251.

**S**

Saad, L. (2002, 21 November). Most smokers wish they could quit. Gallup News Service (www.gallup.com/poll/releases/pr021121.asp).

Saal, F. E., Johnson, C. B., & Weber, N. (1989). Friendly or sexy? It may depend on whom you ask. *Psychology of Women Quarterly*, **13**, 263–276.

Sabini, J., & Silver, M. (1982). *Moralities of everyday life*. New York: Oxford University Press.

Sacerdote, B., & Marmaros, D. (2005). How do friendships form? NBER Working Paper No. 11530 (www.nber.org/papers/W11530).

Sacks, H. (1992). *Lectures on conversation*. 2 vols. Ed. G. Jefferson, with an introduction by E. A. Schegloff. Oxford: Blackwell.

Safdar, S., Lewis, J. R., Greenglass, E., & Daneshpour, M. (2008). An examination of proactive coping and social beliefs among Christians and Muslims. In K. Leung and M. H. Bond (eds), *Psychological aspects of social axioms: Understanding global belief systems*. New York: Springer.

Sagarin, B. J., Cialdini, R. B., Rice, W. E., & Serna, S. B. (2002). Dispelling the illusion of invulnerability: The motivations and mechanisms of resistance to persuasion. *Journal of Personality and Social Psychology*, **83**, 526–541.

Sales, S. M. (1972). Economic threat as a determinant of conversion rates in authoritarian and nonauthoritarian churches. *Journal of Personality and Social Psychology*, **23**, 420–428.

Salganik, M. J., Dodds, P. S., & Watts, D. J. (2006). Experimental study of inequality and unpredictability in an artificial cultural market. *Science*, **311**, 854–856.

Salmivalli, C. (2010). Bullying and the peer group: A review. *Aggression and Violent Behavior*, **15**, 112–120.

Salmivalli, C., Kaukiainen, A., Kaistaniemi, L., & Lagerspetz, K. M. J. (1999). Self-evaluated self-esteem, peer-evaluated self-esteem, and defensive egotism as predictors of adolescents' participation in bullying situations. *Personality and Social Psychology Bulletin*, **25**, 1268–1278.

Salovey, P., Mayer, J. D., & Rosenhan, D. L. (1991). Mood and healing: Mood as a motivator of helping and helping as a regulator of mood. In M. S. Clark (ed.), *Prosocial behavior*. Newbury Park, CA: Sage.

Saltzstein, H. D., & Sandberg, L. (1979). Indirect social influence: Change in judgmental processor anticipatory conformity. *Journal of Experimental Social Psychology*, **15**, 209–216.

Sancton, T. (1997, 13 October). The dossier on Diana's crash. *Time*, 50–56.

Sande, G. N., Goethals, G. R., & Radloff, C. E. (1988). Perceiving one's own traits and others': The multifaceted self. *Journal of Personality and Social Psychology*, **54**, 13–20.

Sanderson, C. A., & Cantor, N. (2001). The association of intimacy goals and marital satisfaction: A test of four mediational hypotheses. *Personality and Social Psychology Bulletin*, **27**, 1567–1577.

Sandfield, A., & Percy, C. (2003). Accounting for single status: Heterosexism and ageism in heterosexual women's talk about marriage. *Feminism & Psychology*, **13**(4), 475–488.

Sani, F. (2005). When subgroups secede: Extending and refining the social psychological model of schisms in groups. *Personality and Social Psychology Bulletin*, **31**, 1074–1086.

Sani, F. (2008). Schism in groups: A social psychological account. *Social & Personality Psychology Compass*, **2**, 718–732.

Sani, F., & Bennett, M. (2001). Contextual variability in young children's gender ingroup stereotype. *Social Development*, **10**, 221–229.

Sani, F., & Bennett, M. (2009). Children's inclusion of the group in the self: evidence from a self-ingroup confusion paradigm. *Developmental Psychology*, **45**, 503–510.

Sani, F., & Pugliese A. C. (2008). In the name of Mussolini: Explaining the schism in an Italian right-wing political party. *Group Dynamics: Theory, Research, and Practice*, **12**, 242–253.

Sani, F., & Reicher, S. (1999). Identity, argument and schism: two longitudinal studies of the split in the Church of England over the ordination of women to the priesthood. *Group Processes & Intergroup Relations*, **2**, 279–300.

Sani, F., & Reicher, S. (2000). Contested identities and schisms in groups: Opposing the ordination of women as priests in the Church of England. *British Journal of Social Psychology*, **39**, 95–112.

Sani, F., & Thomson, L. (2001). We are what we wear: The emergence of consensus in stereotypes of students and managers' dressing style. *Social Behaviour and Personality*, **29**, 695–700.

Sani, F., & Todman, J. (2002). Should we stay or should we go? A social psychological model of schisms within groups. *Personality and Social Psychology Bulletin*, **28**, 1647–1655.

Sani, F., & Todman, J. (2006). *Experimental design and statistics for psychology: A first course*. Malden: Blackwell.

Sani, F., Bennett, M., Agostini, L., Malucchi, L., &

**Ferguson, N.** (2000). Children's conception of characteristic features of category members. *Journal of Social Psychology*, **140**, 227–239.

**Sani, F., Bennett, M., Mullally, S., & McPherson, J.** (2003). On the assumption of fixity in children's stereotypes: A reappraisal. *British Journal of Developmental Psychology*, **21**, 113–124.

**Sani, F., Herrera, M., & Bowe, M.** (2009). Perceived collective continuity and ingroup identification as defence against death awareness. *Journal of Experimental Social Psychology*, **45**, 242–245.

**Sanna, L. J., Parks, C. D., Meier, S., Chang, E. C., Kassin, B. R., Lechter, J. L., Turley-Ames, K. J., & Miyake, T. M.** (2003). A game of inches: Spontaneous use of counterfactuals by broadcasters during major league baseball playoffs. *Journal of Applied Social Psychology*, **33**, 455–475.

**Sansone, C.** (1986). A question of competence: The effects of competence and task feedback on intrinsic interest. *Journal of Personality and Social Psychology*, **51**, 918–931.

**Sapolsky, B. S., & Tabarlet, J. O.** (1991). Sex in prime time television: 1979 versus 1989. *Journal of Broadcasting and Electronic Media*, **35**, 505(516).

**Sargent, J. D., Heatherton, T. F., & Ahrens, M. B.** (2002). Adolescent exposure to extremely violent movies. *Journal of Adolescent Health*, **31**, 449–454.

**Saucier, D. A., & Miller, C. T.** (2003). The persuasiveness of racial arguments as a subtle measure of racism. *Personality and Social Psychology Bulletin*, **29**, 1303–1315.

**Savitsky, K., & Gilovich, T.** (2003). The illusion of transparency and the alleviation of speech anxiety. *Journal of Experimental Social Psychology*, **39**, 618–625.

**Savitsky, K., Epley, N., & Gilovich, T.** (2001). Do others judge us as harshly as we think? Overestimating the impact of our failures, shortcomings, and mishaps.

*Journal of Personality and Social Psychology*, **81**, 44–56.

**Savitsky, K., Medvec, V. H., & Gilovich, T.** (1997). Remembering and regretting: The Zeigarnik effect and the cognitive availability of regrettable actions and inactions. *Personality and Social Psychology Bulletin*, **23**, 248–257.

**Sayers, J.** (1986). *Sexual contradictions*. New York: Routledge.

**Scanlon, L. J., & Kull, C. A.** (2009). Untangling the links between wildlife benefits and community-based conservation at Torra Conservancy, Namibia. *Development Southern Africa*, **26**(1), 75–93.

**Schachter, S.** (1951). Deviation, rejection and communication. *Journal of Abnormal and Social Psychology*, **46**, 190–207.

**Schachter, S.** (1959). *The psychology of affiliation*. Stanford, CA: Stanford University Press.

**Schachter, S.** (1964). The integration of cognitive and physiological determinants of emotional state. In L. Berkowitz (ed.), *Advances in experimental social psychology*, Vol 1. New York: Academic Press.

**Schachter, S., & Singer, J. E.** (1962). Cognitive, social and physiological determinants of emotional state. *Psychological Review*, **69**(5), 379–399.

**Schaffner, P. E.** (1985). Specious learning about reward and punishment. *Journal of Personality and Social Psychology*, **48**(6), 1377.

**Schaffner, P. E., Wandersman, A., & Stang, D.** (1981). Candidate name exposure and voting: Two field studies. *Basic and Applied Social Psychology*, **2**, 195–203.

**Schaller, M., & Cialdini, R. B.** (1988). The economics of empathic helping: Support for a mood management motive. *Journal of Experimental Social Psychology*, **24**, 163–181.

**Schimel, J., Arndt, J., Pyszczynski, T., & Greenberg, J.** (2001). Being accepted for who we are: Evidence that social validation of the intrinsic self reduces general defensiveness. *Journal of*

*Personality and Social Psychology*, **80**, 35–52.

**Schkade, D. A., & Kahneman, D.** (1998). Does living in California make people happy? A focusing illusion in judgments of life satisfaction. *Psychological Science*, **9**, 340–346.

**Schlenker, B. R.** (1976). Egocentric perceptions in cooperative groups: A conceptualization and research review. Final Report, Office of Naval Research Grant NR 170–797.

**Schlenker, B. R., & Miller, R. S.** (1977a). Group cohesiveness as a determinant of egocentric perceptions in cooperative groups. *Human Relations*, **30**, 1039–1055.

**Schlenker, B. R., & Miller, R. S.** (1977b). Egocentrism in groups: Self-serving biases or logical information processing? *Journal of Personality and Social Psychology*, **35**, 755–764.

**Schlenker, B. R., & Weigold, M. F.** (1992). Interpersonal processes involving impression regulation and management. *Annual Review of Psychology*, **43**, 133–168.

**Schlesinger, A. M., Jr** (1965). *A thousand days*. Boston: Houghton Mifflin. Cited by I. L. Janis (1972) in *Victims of groupthink*. Boston: Houghton Mifflin.

**Schlosser, E.** (2003, 10 March). Empire of the obscene. *New Yorker*, 61–71.

**Schmidt, K., & Nosek, B. A.** (2010). Implicit (and explicit) racial attitudes barely changed during Barack Obama's presidential campaign and early presidency. *Journal of Experimental Social Psychology*, **46**, 308–314.

**Schmitt, D. P., & Pilcher, J. J.** (2004). Evaluating evidence of psychological adaptation: How do we know one when we see one? *Psychological Science*, **15**, 643–649.

**Schmitt, D. P., Alcalay, L., Allensworth, M., Allik, J., Ault, L., Austers, I., ... & Kardum, I.** (2004). Patterns and universals of adult romantic attachment across 62 cultural regions are models of self and of other pancultural constructs? *Journal of Cross-Cultural Psychology*, **35**(4), 367–402.

**Schmitt, M. T., & Branscombe, N. R.** (2002). The meaning and consequences of perceived discrimination in disadvantaged and privileged social groups. *European Review of Social Psychology*, **12**, 167–199.

**Schnall, S., & Laird, J. D.** (2003). Keep smiling: Enduring effects of facial expressions and postures on emotional experience and memory. *Cognition and Emotion*, **17**, 787–797.

**Schneider, M. E., Major, B., Luhtanen, R., & Crocker, J.** (1996). Social stigma and the potential costs of assumptive help. *Personality and Social Psychology Bulletin*, **22**, 201–209.

**Schoeneman, T. J.** (1994). Individualism. In V. S. Ramachandran (ed.), *Encyclopedia of human behavior*. San Diego: Academic Press.

**Schofield, J.** (1982). *Black and white in school: Trust, tension, or tolerance?* New York: Praeger.

**Schofield, J. W.** (1986). Causes and consequences of the colorblind perspective. In J. F. Dovidio & S. L. Gaertner (eds), *Prejudice, discrimination, and racism*. Orlando, FL: Academic Press.

**Schroeder, D. A., Dovidio, J. F., Sibicky, M. E., Matthews, L. L., & Allen, J. L.** (1988). Empathic concern and helping behavior: Egoism or altruism? *Journal of Experimental Social Psychology*, **24**, 333–353.

**Schug, J., Yuki, M., Horikawa, H., & Takemura, K.** (2009). Similarity attraction and actually selecting similar others: How cross-societal differences in relational mobility affect interpersonal similarity in Japan and the USA. *Asian Journal of Social Psychology*, **12**(2), 95–103.

**Schulz, J. W., & Pruitt, D. G.** (1978). The effects of mutual concern on joint welfare. *Journal of Experimental Social Psychology*, **14**, 480–492.

**Schulz-Hardt, S., Frey, D., Luthgens, C., & Moscovici, S.** (2000). Biased information search in group decision making. *Journal of Personality and Social Psychology*, **78**, 655–669.

Schuman, H., & Kalton, G. (1985). Survey methods. In G. Lindzey & E. Aronson (eds), *Handbook of social psychology*, Vol. 1. Hillsdale, NJ: Erlbaum.

Schuman, H., & Scott, J. (1989). Generations and collective memories. *American Sociological Review*, **54**, 359–381.

Schumann, K. (2012). Does love mean never having to say you're sorry? Associations between relationship satisfaction, perceived apology sincerity, and forgiveness. *Journal of Social and Personal Relationships*, **29**(7), 997–1010.

Schutte, J. W., & Hosch, H. M. (1997). Gender differences in sexual assault verdicts: A meta-analysis. *Journal of Social Behavior & Personality*, **12**, 759–772.

Schwartz, B. (2000). Self-determination: The tyranny of freedom. *American Psychologist*, **55**, 79–88.

Schwartz, B. (2004). *The tyranny of choice*. New York: Ecco/HarperCollins.

Schwartz, C. E., Keyl, P. M., Marcum, J. P., & Bode, R. (2009). Helping others shows differential benefits on health and well-being for male and female teens. *Journal of Happiness Studies*, **10**(4), 431–448.

Schwartz, S. H. (1975). The justice of need and the activation of humanitarian norms. *Journal of Social Issues*, **31**(3), 111–136.

Schwartz, S. H., & Gottlieb, A. (1981). Participants' post-experimental reactions and the ethics of bystander research. *Journal of Experimental Social Psychology*, **17**, 396–407.

Schwartz, S. H., & Rubel, T. (2005). Sex differences in value priorities: Cross-cultural and multimethod studies. *Journal of Personality and Social Psychology*, **89**, 1010–1028.

Schwarz, N., & Clore, G. L. (1983). Mood, misattribution, and judgments of well-being: Informative and directive functions of affective states. *Journal of Personality and Social Psychology*, **45**, 513–523.

Schwarz, N., Bless, H., & Bohner, G. (1991). Mood and persuasion: Affective states influence the processing of persuasive communications. In M. Zanna (ed.), *Advances in experimental social psychology*, Vol. 24. New York: Academic Press.

Schwarz, N., Strack, F., Kommer, D., & Wagner, D. (1987). Soccer, rooms, and the quality of your life: Mood effects on judgments of satisfaction with life in general and with specific domains. *Journal of Applied Social Psychology*, **17**, 69–79.

Sears, D. O. (1979). Life stage effects upon attitude change, especially among the elderly. Manuscript prepared for Workshop on the Elderly of the Future, Committee on Aging, National Research Council, Annapolis, MD, 3–5 May.

Sears, D. O. (1986). College sophomores in the laboratory: Influences of a narrow data base on social psychology's view of human nature. *Journal of Personality and Social Psychology*, **51**, 515–530.

Sears, D. O. (1988). Symbolic racism. In P. A. Katz and D. A. Taylor (eds), *Eliminating racism: Profiles in controversy*. New York: Plenum.

Sedikides, C., Rudich, E. A., Gregg, A. P., Kumashiro, M., & Rusbult, C. (2004). Are normal narcissists psychologically healthy? Self-esteem matters. *Journal of Personality and Social Psychology*, **87**(3), 400–416.

Seidel, E-M., Eickhoff, S. B., Kellermann, T., Schneider, F., Gur, R. C., Habel, U., & Derntl, B. (2010). Who is to blame? Neural correlates of causal attribution in social situations. *Social Neuroscience*, **5**, 335–350.

Segerstrom, S. C. (2001). Optimism and attentional bias for negative and positive stimuli. *Personality and Social Psychology Bulletin*, **27**, 1334–1343.

Selfhout, M., Denissen, J., Branje, S., & Meeus, W. (2009). In the eye of the beholder: Perceived, actual, and peer-rated similarity in personality, communication, and friendship intensity during the acquaintanceship process. *Journal of Personality and Social Psychology*, **96**(6), 1152–1165.

Selfhout, M. H., Branje, S. J., & Meeus, W. H. (2007). Similarity in adolescent best friendships: The role of gender. *Netherlands Journal of Psychology*, **63**(2), 42–48.

Seligman, M. E. P. (1975). *Helplessness: On depression, development and death*. San Francisco: W. H. Freeman.

Seligman, M. E. P. (1991). *Learned optimism*. New York: Knopf.

Seligman, M. E. P. (1994). *What you can change and what you can't*. New York: Knopf.

Seligman, M. E. P. (2002). *Authentic happiness: Using the new positive psychology to realize your potential for lasting fulfillment*. New York: Free Press.

Sen, A. (2006). *Identity and violence: The illusion of destiny*. London: Penguin.

Seta, C. E., & Seta, J. J. (1992). Increments and decrements in mean arterial pressure levels as a function of audience composition: An averaging and summation analysis. *Personality and Social Psychology Bulletin*, **18**, 173–181.

Seta, J. J. (1982). The impact of comparison processes on coactors' task performance. *Journal of Personality and Social Psychology*, **42**, 281–291.

Shaffer, D. R., Pegalis, L. J., & Bazzini, D. G. (1996). When boy meets girls (revisited): Gender, gender-role orientation, and prospect of future interaction as determinants of self-disclosure among same- and opposite-sex acquaintances. *Personality and Social Psychology Bulletin*, **22**, 495–506.

Shane, J., & Heckhausen, J. (2013). University students' causal perceptions about social mobility: Diverging pathways for believers in personal merit and luck. *Journal of Vocational Behaviour*, **82**, 10–19.

Sharma, V., & Kaur, I. (1996). Interpersonal attraction in relation to the loss-gain hypothesis. *Journal of Social Psychology*, **136**(5), 635–638.

Shaver, P. R., & Hazan, C. (1993). Adult romantic attachment: Theory and evidence. In D. Perlman & W. Jones (eds), *Advances in personal relationships*, Vol. 4. Greenwich, CT: JAI.

Shaver, P. R., & Hazan, C. (1994). Attachment. In A. L. Weber & J. H. Harvey (eds), *Perspectives on close relationships*. Boston: Allyn & Bacon.

Shaver, P., Hazan, C., & Bradshaw, D. (1988). Love as attachment: The integration of three behavioral systems. In R. J. Sternberg & M. L. Barnes (eds), *The psychology of love*. New Haven: Yale University Press.

Shaw, M. E. (1981). *Group dynamics: The psychology of small group behavior*. New York: McGraw-Hill.

Sheese, B. E., & Graziano, W. G. (2005). Deciding to defect: The effects of videogame violence on cooperative behavior. *Psychological Science*, **16**, 354–357.

Shell, R. M., & Eisenberg, N. (1992). A developmental model of recipients' reactions to aid. *Psychological Bulletin*, **111**, 413–433.

Shepperd, J. A. (2003). Interpreting comparative risk judgments: Are people personally optimistic or interpersonally pessimistic? Unpublished manuscript, University of Florida.

Shepperd, J. A., & Arkin, R. M. (1991). Behavioral other-enhancement: Strategically obscuring the link between performance and evaluation. *Journal of Personality and Social Psychology*, **60**, 79–88.

Shepperd, J. A., & Taylor, K. M. (1999). Ascribing advantages to social comparison targets. *Basic and Applied Social Psychology*, **21**, 103–117.

Shepperd, J. A., & Wright, R. A. (1989). Individual contributions to a collective effort: An incentive analysis. *Personality and Social Psychology Bulletin*, **15**, 141–149.

Shepperd, J. A., Grace, J., Cole, L. J., & Klein, C. (2005). Anxiety and outcome predictions. *Personality and Social Psychology Bulletin*, **31**, 267–275.

Sherif, M. (1935). A study of some social factors in perception. *Archives of Psychology*, **187**.

Sherif, M. (1937). An experimental approach to the study of attitudes. *Sociometry*, **1**, 90–98.

Sherif, M. (1958). Superordinate goals in the reduction of intergroup conflict. *American Journal of Sociology*, **63**(4), 349–356.

Sherif, M. (1966). *In common predicament: Social psychology of intergroup conflict and cooperation*. Boston: Houghton Mifflin.

Sherif, M., & Sherif, C. W. (1953). *Groups in harmony and tension: An integration of studies in intergroup behavior*. New York: Harper & Row.

Sherif, M., & Sherif, C. W. (1964). *Reference groups*. New York: Harper & Row.

Sherif, M., & Sherif, C. W. (1969). *Social psychology*. New York: Harper & Row.

Sherif, M., Harvey, O. J., White, B. J., Hood, W., & Sherif, C. W. (1961). *Intergroup conflict and cooperation: The robbers cave experiment*. Norman, OK: University of Oklahoma Institute of Intergroup Relations.

Sherman, S. J., Cialdini, R. B., Schwartzman, D. F., & Reynolds, K. D. (1985). Imagining can heighten or lower the perceived likelihood of contracting a disease: The mediating effect of ease of imagery. *Personality and Social Psychology Bulletin*, **11**, 118–127.

Sherry, J. L. (2001). The effects of violent video games on aggression: A meta-analysis. *Human Communication Research*, **27**(3), 409–431.

Shipman, P. (2003). We are all Africans. *American Scientist*, **91**, 496–499.

Short, J. F., Jr (ed.) (1969). *Gang delinquency and delinquent subcultures*. New York: Harper & Row.

Shostak, M. (1981). *Nisa: The life and words of a !Kung woman*. Cambridge, MA: Harvard University Press.

Shotland, R. L. (1989). A model of the causes of date rape in developing and close relationships. In C. Hendrick (ed.), *Review of Personality and Social Psychology*, Vol. 10. Beverly Hills: Sage.

Shotland, R. L., & Stebbins, C. A. (1983). Emergency and cost as determinants of helping behavior and the slow accumulation of social psychological knowledge.

*Social Psychology Quarterly*, **46**, 36–46.

Shotland, R. L., & Straw, M. K. (1976). Bystander response to an assault: When a man attacks a woman. *Journal of Personality and Social Psychology*, **34**, 990–999.

Shotter, J. (1993). *The cultural politics of everyday life*. Buckingham: Open University Press.

Showers, C., & Ruben, C. (1987). Distinguishing pessimism from depression: Negative expectations and positive coping mechanisms. Paper presented at the American Psychological Association convention.

Shrauger, J. S. (1975). Responses to evaluation as a function of initial self-perceptions. *Psychological Bulletin*, **82**, 581–596.

Shrauger, J. S. (1983). The accuracy of self-prediction: How good are we and why? Paper presented at the Midwestern Psychological Association convention.

Sia, C. L., Tan, B. C. Y., & Wei, K. K. (2002). Group polarization and computer-mediated communication: Effects of communication cues, social presence, and anonymity. *Information Systems Research*, **13**(1), 70–90.

Sidanius, J., & Pratto, F. (1999). *Social dominance: An intergroup theory of social hierarchy and oppression*. New York: Cambridge University Press.

Sidanius, J., Pratto, F., & Bobo, L. (1994). Social dominance orientation and the political psychology of gender: A case of invariance? *Journal of Personality and Social Psychology*, **67**, 998–1011.

Sieff, E. M., Dawes, R. M., & Loewenstein, G. F. (1999). Anticipated versus actual responses to HIV test results. *American Journal of Psychology*, **112**, 297–311.

Siegel, A. E., & Siegel, S. (1957). Reference groups, membership groups and attitude change. *Journal of Abnormal and Social Psychology*, **55**, 360–364.

Siegel, E. F., Dougherty, M. R. & Huber, D. E. (2012). Manipulating the role of cognitive control while taking

the implicit association test. *Journal of Experimental Social Psychology*, **48**, 1057–1068.

Sigall, H. (1970). Effects of competence and consensual validation on a communicator's liking for the audience. *Journal of Personality and Social Psychology*, **16**, 252–258.

Sigall, H., & Page, R. (1971). Current stereotypes: A little fading, a little faking. *Journal of Personality and Social Psychology*, **18**, 247–255.

Sillience, E., Briggs, P., Harris, P., & Fishwick, L. (2007). Going online for health advice: Changes in usage and trust practices over the last five years. *Interacting With Computers*, **19**(3), 397–406.

Silver, M., & Geller, D. (1978). On the irrelevance of evil: The organization and individual action. *Journal of Social Issues*, **34**, 125–136.

Silvia, P. J. (2005). Deflecting reactance: The role of similarity in increasing compliance and reducing resistance. *Basic and Applied Social Psychology*, **27**, 277–284.

Silvia, P. J., & Duval, T. S. (2001). Objective self-awareness theory: Recent progress and enduring problems. *Personality and Social Psychology Review*, **5**, 230–241.

Simmons, J. P., Nelson, L. D., & Simonsohn, U. (2011). False-positive psychology undisclosed flexibility in data collection and analysis allows presenting anything as significant. *Psychological Science*, **22**, 1359–1366.

Simmons, W. W. (2000, December). When it comes to having children, Americans still prefer boys. *The Gallup Poll Monthly*, 63–64.

Simon, H. A. (1957). *Models of man: Social and rational*. New York: Wiley.

Simon, P. (1996, 17 April). American provincials. *Christian Century*, 421–422.

Simonton, D. K. (1994). *Greatness: Who makes history and why*. New York: Guilford.

Simpson, J. A., Gangestad, S. W., & Lerma, M. (1990). Perception of physical

attractiveness: Mechanisms involved in the maintenance of romantic relationships. *Journal of Personality and Social Psychology*, **59**, 1192–1201.

Simpson, J. A., Rholes, W. S., & Nelligan, J. S. (1992). Support seeking and support giving within couples in an anxiety-provoking situation: The role of attachment styles. *Journal of Personality and Social Psychology*, **62**, 434–446.

Simpson, J. A., Rholes, W. S., & Phillips, D. (1996). Conflict in close relationships: An attachment perspective. *Journal of Personality and Social Psychology*, **71**, 899–914.

Singer, M. (1979). Cults and cult members. Address to the American Psychological Association convention.

Singh, D. (1993). Adaptive significance of female physical attractiveness: Role of waist-to-hip ratio. *Journal of Personality and Social Psychology*, **65**, 293–307.

Singh, D., & Young, R. K. (1995). Body weight, waist-to-hip ratio, breasts, and hips: Role in judgments of female attractiveness and desirability for relationships. *Ethology and Sociobiology*, **16**, 483–507.

Singh, R., & Ho, S. J. (2000). Attitudes and attraction: A new test of the attraction, repulsion and similarity-dissimilarity asymmetry hypotheses. *British Journal of Social Psychology*, **39**, 197–211.

Singh, R., & Teoh, J. B. P. (1999). Attitudes and attraction: A test of two hypotheses for the similarity–dissimilarity asymmetry. *British Journal of Social Psychology*, **38**, 427–443.

Sivarajasingam, V., Moore, S., & Shepherd, J. P. (2005). Winning, losing, and violence. *Injury Prevention*, **11**, 69–70.

Skaalvik, E. M., & Hagtvet, K. A. (1990). Academic achievement and self-concept: An analysis of causal predominance in a developmental perspective. *Journal of Personality and Social Psychology*, **58**, 292–307.

Skinner, B. F. (1963). Operant behavior. *American Psychologist*, **18**, 503–515.

**Skinner, B. F.** (1971). *Beyond freedom and dignity*. New York: Knopf.

**Skitka, L. J.** (1999). Ideological and attributional boundaries on public compassion: Reactions to individuals and communities affected by a natural disaster. *Personality and Social Psychology Bulletin*, **25**, 793–808.

**Skitka, L. J., & Tetlock, P. E.** (1993). Providing public assistance: Cognitive and motivational processes underlying liberal and conservative policy preferences. *Journal of Personality and Social Psychology*, **65**, 1205–1223.

**Skitka, L. J., Bauman, C. W., & Sargis, E. G.** (2005). Moral conviction: Another contributor to attitude strength or something more? *Journal of Personality and Social Psychology*, **88**, 895–917.

**Skoe, E. E. A., Cumberland, A., Eisenberg, N., Hansen, K., & Perry, J.** (2002). The influences of sex and gender-role identity on moral cognition and prosocial personality traits. *Sex Roles*, **46**(9–10), 295–309.

**Skowronski, J., & Carlston, D.** (1987). Social judgment and social memory: The role of cue diagnosticity in negativity, positivity, and extremity biases. *Journal of Personality and Social Psychology*, **52**, 689–699.

**Skurnik, I., Yoon, C., Park, D. C., & Schwarz, N.** (2005). How warnings about false claims become recommendations. *Journal of Consumer Research*, **31**, 713–724.

**Slater, M., Antley, M., Davison, A., Swapp, D., Guger, C., Barker, C., Pistrang, N., & Sanchez-Vives, M. V.** (2006). A virtual reprise of the Stanley Milgram obedience experiments. *PLoS ONE*, **1**(1), e39. doi:10.1371/journal.pone.0000039 (open access).

**Slavin, R. E.** (1985). Cooperative learning: Applying contact theory in desegregated schools. *Journal of Social Issues*, **41**(3), 45–62.

**Slavin, R. E., Hurley, E. A., & Chamberlain, A.** (2003). Cooperative learning and achievement: Theory and research. In W. M. Reynolds

& G. E. Miller (eds), *Handbook of psychology: Educational psychology, Vol. 7*. New York: Wiley.

**Slovic, P.** (1972). From Shakespeare to Simon: Speculations – and some evidence – about man's ability to process information. *Oregon Research Institute Research Bulletin*, **12**(2).

**Slovic, P., & Fischoff, B.** (1977). On the psychology of experimental surprises. *Journal of Experimental Psychology: Human Perception and Performance*, **3**, 455–551.

**Smirles, K.** (2004). Attributions of responsibility in cases of sexual harassment: The person and the situation. *Journal of Applied Social Psychology*, **34**(2), 342–365.

**Smith, A.** (1759). *The theory of moral sentiments*. London: A. Millar.

**Smith, C. A., & Stillman, S.** (2002). What do women want? The effects of gender and sexual orientation on the desirability of physical attributes in the personal ads of women. *Sex Roles*, **46**, 337–341.

**Smith, D. E., Gier, J. A., & Willis, F. N.** (1982). Interpersonal touch and compliance with a marketing request. *Basic and Applied Social Psychology*, **3**, 35–38.

**Smith, E. R., & Zarate, M. A.** (1992). Exemplar-based model of social judgment. *Psychological Review*, **99**, 3–21.

**Smith, H.** (1976). *The Russians*. New York: Balantine Books. Cited by B. Latané, K. Williams, and S. Harkins in, Many hands make light the work. *Journal of Personality and Social Psychology*, 1979, **37**, 822–832.

**Smith, H. J., & Tyler, T. R.** (1997). Choosing the right pond: The impact of group membership on self-esteem and group-oriented behavior. *Journal of Experimental Social Psychology*, **33**, 146–170.

**Smith, J., Tran, G. Q., & Thompson, R. D.** (2008). Can the theory of planned behavior help explain men's psychological help-seeking? Evidence for a mediation effect and clinical implications. *Psychology of Men*

*and Masculinity*, **9**(3), 179–192.

**Smith, L., Gilhooly, K., & Walker, A.** (2003). Factors influencing prescribing decisions in the treatment of depression: A social judgement theory approach. *Applied Cognitive Psychology*, **17**, 51–63.

**Smith, M. B.** (1978). Psychology and values. *Journal of Social Issues*, **34**, 181–199.

**Smith, M. R., & Alpert, G. P.** (2007). Explaining police bias: A theory of social conditioning and illusory correlation. *Criminal Justice and Behavior*, **34**, 1262–1283.

**Smith, P. B.** (2005). Is there an indigenous European social psychology? *International Journal of Psychology*, **40**, 254–262.

**Smith, P. B., & Tayeb, M.** (1989). Organizational structure and processes. In M. Bond (ed.), *The cross-cultural challenge to social psychology*. Newbury Park, CA: Sage.

**Smith, R. H., Turner, T. J., Garonzik, R., Leach, C. W., Urch-Druskat, V., & Weston, C. M.** (1996). Envy and Schadenfreude. *Personality and Social Psychology Bulletin*, **22**, 158–168.

**Smith, S. W., Atkin, C. K., Martell, D., Allen, R., & Hembroff, L.** (2006). A social judgment theory approach to conducting formative research in a social norms campaign. *Communications Theory*, **16**, 141–152.

**Snyder, C. R.** (1980). The uniqueness mystique. *Psychology Today*, March, 86–90.

**Snyder, C. R., & Fromkin, H. L.** (1980). *Uniqueness: The human pursuit of difference*. New York: Plenum.

**Snyder, C. R., & Higgins, R. L.** (1988). Excuses: Their effective role in the negotiation of reality. *Psychological Bulletin*, **104**, 23–35.

**Snyder, M.** (1983). The influence of individuals on situations: Implications for understanding the links between personality and social behavior. *Journal of Personality*, **51**, 497–516.

**Snyder, M.** (1984). When belief creates reality. In L. Berkowitz (ed.), *Advances in experimental social psy-*

*chology*, Vol. 18. New York: Academic Press.

**Snyder, M.** (1987). *Public appearances/private realities: The psychology of self-monitoring*. New York: Freeman.

**Snyder, M., & Haugen, J. A.** (1994). Why does behavioral confirmation occur? A functional perspective on the role of the perceiver. *Journal of Experimental Social Psychology*, **30**, 218–246.

**Snyder, M., & Haugen, J. A.** (1995). Why does behavioral confirmation occur? A functional perspective on the role of the target. *Personality and Social Psychology Bulletin*, **21**, 963–974.

**Snyder, M., & Ickes, W.** (1985). Personality and social behavior. In G. Lindzey & E. Aronson (eds), *Handbook of social psychology*, 3rd edn. New York: Random House.

**Snyder, M., & Swann, W. B., Jr** (1976). When actions reflect attitudes: The politics of impression management. *Journal of Personality and Social Psychology*, **34**, 1034–1042.

**Snyder, M., Grether, J., & Keller, K.** (1974). Staring and compliance: A field experiment on hitch-hiking. *Journal of Applied Social Psychology*, **4**, 165–170.

**Snyder, M., Tanke, E. D., & Berscheid, E.** (1977). Social perception and interpersonal behavior: On the self-fulfilling nature of social stereotypes. *Journal of Personality and Social Psychology*, **35**, 656–666.

**Sober, E., & Wilson, D. S.** (1998). *Unto others: The evolution and psychology of unselfish behavior*. Cambridge, MA: Harvard University Press.

**Solano, C. H., Batten, P. G., & Parish, E. A.** (1982). Loneliness and patterns of self-disclosure. *Journal of Personality and Social Psychology*, **43**, 524–531.

**Solomon, H., & Solomon, L. Z.** (1978). Effects of anonymity on helping in emergency situations. Paper presented at the Eastern Psychological Association convention.

**Solomon, H., Solomon, L. Z., Arnone, M. M., Maur, B. J., Reda, R. M., & Rother,**

E. O. (1981). Anonymity and helping. *Journal of Social Psychology*, **113**, 37–43.

Spears, R., & Leach, C. W. (2004). Intergroup schadenfreude: Conditions and consequences. In L. Z. Tiedens & C. W. Leach (eds), *The social life of emotions: Studies in emotion and social interaction*. New York: Cambridge University Press.

Spears, R., Ellemers, N., & Doosje, B. (2005). Let me count the ways in which I respect thee: Does competence compensate or compromise lack of liking from the group? *European Journal of Social Psychology*, **35**, 263–279.

Spector, P. E. (1986). Perceived control by employees: A meta-analysis of studies concerning autonomy and participation at work. *Human Relations*, **39**, 1005–1016.

Speer, A. (1971). *Inside the Third Reich: Memoirs* (P. Winston & C. Winston. trans.). New York: Avon Books.

Spencer, S. M., & Norem, J. K. (1996). Reflection and distraction defensive pessimism, strategic optimism, and performance. *Personality and Social Psychology Bulletin*, 22, 354–365.

Spiegel, H. W. (1971). *The growth of economic thought*. Durham, NC: Duke University Press.

Spitz, H. H. (1999). Beleaguered *Pygmalion*: A history of the controversy over claims that teacher expectancy raises intelligence. *Intelligence*, **27**, 199–234.

Spivak, J. (1979, 6 June). Red shift. *Wall Street Journal*, 1–2.

Sprecher, S. (1987). The effects of self-disclosure given and received on affection for an intimate partner and stability of the relationship. *Journal of Personality and Social Psychology*, **4**, 115–127.

Sprecher, S. (1998). Insiders' perspective on reasons for attraction to a close other. *Social Psychology Quarterly*, **61**, 287–300.

Sprecher, S., & Toro-Morn, M. (2002). A study of men and women from different sides of Earth to determine if men are from Mars and women are from Venus in their beliefs about love and romantic relationships. *Sex Roles*, **46**, 131–147.

Sprecher, S., Aron, A., Hatfield, E., Cortese, A., Potapova, E., & Levitskaya, A. (1994a). Love: American style, Russian style, and Japanese style. *Personal Relationships*, **1**, 349–369.

Sprecher, S., Sullivan, Q., & Hatfield, E. (1994b). Mate selection preferences: Gender differences examined in a national sample. *Journal of Personality and Social Psychology*, **66**, 1074–1080.

Spunt, R. P., & Lieberman, M. D. (2013). The busy social brain: Evidence for automaticity and control in the neural systems supporting social cognition and action understanding. *Psychological Science*, **24**, 80–86.

St. Claire, L., & Clucas, C. (2012). In sickness and in health: Influences of social categorizations on health-related outcomes. In J. Jetten, C. Haslam & S. A. Haslam (eds), *The social cure: Identity, health and well-being*. Hove and New York: Psychology Press.

St. Claire, L., & He, Y. (2009). How do I know if I need a hearing aid? Further support for the self-categorisation approach to symptom perception. *Applied Psychology*, **58**, 24–41.

Stangor, C., Jonas, K., Stroebe, W., & Hewstone, M. (1996). Influence of student exchange on national stereotypes, attitudes and perceived group variability. *European Journal of Social Psychology*, **26**, 663–675.

Stangor, C., Lynch, L., Duan, C., & Glass, B. (1992). Categorization of individuals on the basis of multiple social features. *Journal of Personality and Social Psychology*, **62**, 207–218.

Staples, B. (2000, 26 June). Playing 'catch and grope' in the schoolyard. *New York Times* (www.nytimes.com).

Stark, R., & Bainbridge, W. S. (1980). Networks of faith: Interpersonal bonds and recruitment of cults and sects. *American Journal of Sociology*, **85**, 1376–1395.

Stasser, G. (1991). Pooling of unshared information during group discussion. In S. Worchel, W. Wood & J. Simpson (eds), *Group process and productivity*. Beverly Hills, CA: Sage.

Stattin, H., & Kerr, M. (2000). Parental monitoring: A reinterpretation. *Child Development*, **71**, 1070–1083.

Staub, E. (1989). *The roots of evil: The origins of genocide and other group violence*. Cambridge: Cambridge University Press.

Staub, E. (1991). Altruistic and moral motivations for helping and their translation into action. *Psychological Inquiry*, **2**, 150–153.

Staub, E. (1992). The origins of caring, helping and non-aggression: Parental socialization, the family system, schools, and cultural influence. In S. Oliner & P. Oliner (eds), *Embracing the other: Philosophical, psychological, and theological perspectives on altruism*. New York: New York University Press.

Staub, E. (1996). Altruism and aggression in children and youth: Origins and cures. In R. Feldman (ed.), *The psychology of adversity*. Amherst, MA: University of Massachusetts Press.

Staub, E. (1997a). Blind versus constructive patriotism: Moving from embeddedness in the group to critical loyalty and action. In D. Bar-Tal and E. Staub (eds), *Patriotism in the lives of individuals and nations*. Chicago: Nelson-Hall.

Staub, E. (1997b). Halting and preventing collective violence: The role of bystanders. Background paper for symposium organized by the Friends of Raoul Wallenberg, Stockholm, 13–16 June.

Staub, E. (1999). Behind the scenes. In D. G. Myers, *Social psychology*, 6th edn. New York: McGraw-Hill.

Staub, E. (2003). *The psychology of good and evil: Why children, adults, and groups help and harm others*. New York: Cambridge University Press.

Staub, E. (2005a). The origins and evolution of hate, with notes on prevention. In R. J. Sternberg (ed.), *The psychology of hate*. Washington, DC: American Psychological Association.

Staub, E. (2005b). The roots of goodness: The fulfillment of basic human needs and the development of caring, helping and nonaggression, inclusive caring, moral courage, active bystandership, and altruism born of suffering. In G. Carlo & C. P. Edwards (eds), *Moral motivation through the life span: Theory, research, applications. Nebraska Symposium on Motivation*, **51**. Lincoln, NE: University of Nebraska Press.

Staub, E. (2006). Reconciliation after genocide, mass killing, or intractable conflict: understanding the roots of violence, psychological recovery, and steps toward a general theory. *Political Psychology*, **27**(6), 867–894.

Staub, E., & Pearlman, L. A. (2005). Psychological recovery and reconciliation after the genocide in Rwanda and in other post-conflict settings. In R. Sternberg & L. Barbanel (eds), *Psychological interventions in times of crisis*. New York: Springer-Verlag.

Staub, E., & Pearlman, L. A. (2006). Advancing healing and reconciliation. In R. Sternberg & L. Barbanel (eds), *Psychological interventions in times of crisis*. New York: Springer.

Staub, E., Pearlman, L. A., Gubin, A., & Hagengimana, A. (2005). Healing, reconciliation, forgiving and the prevention of violence after genocide or mass killing: An intervention and its experimental evaluation in Rwanda. *Journal of Social and Clinical Psychology*, **24**, 297–334.

Steblay, N. M. (1987). Helping behavior in rural and urban environments: A meta-analysis. *Psychological Bulletin*, **102**, 346–356.

Steele, C. M. (1988). The psychology of self-affirmation: Sustaining the integrity of the self. In L. Berkowitz (ed.), *Advances in experimental social psychology*, Vol. 21. Orlando, FL: Academic Press.

Steele, C. M., & Southwick, L. (1985). Alcohol and social behavior I: The psychology of drunken excess. *Journal of Personality and Social Psychology*, **48**, 18–34.

Steele, C. M., Southwick, L. L., & Critchlow, B. (1981). Dissonance and alcohol: Drinking your troubles away. *Journal of Personality and Social Psychology*, 41, 831–846.

Steele, C. M., Spencer, S. J., & Lynch, M. (1993). Selfimage resilience and dissonance: The role of affirmational resources. *Journal of Personality and Social Psychology*, 64, 885–896.

Stelzl, M., & Seligman, C. (2004). The social identity strategy of MOATING: Further evidence. Paper presented at the Society of Personality and Social Psychology convention.

Stephan, W. G. (1986). The effects of school desegregation: An evaluation 30 years after *Brown*. In R. Kidd, L. Saxe & M. Saks (eds), *Advances in applied social psychology*. New York: Erlbaum.

Stephan, W. G. (1987). The contact hypothesis in intergroup relations. In C. Hendrick (ed.), *Group processes and intergroup relations*. Newbury Park, CA: Sage.

Stephan, W. G. (1988). School desegregation: Short-term and long-term effects. Paper presented at the national conference 'Opening doors: An appraisal of race relations in America', University of Alabama.

Stephan, W. G., Berscheid, E., & Walster, E. (1971). Sexual arousal and heterosexual perception. *Journal of Personality and Social Psychology*, 20, 93–101.

Sternberg, R. J. (1988). Triangulating love. In R. J. Sternberg & M. L. Barnes (eds), *The psychology of love*. New Haven: Yale University Press.

Sternberg, R. J. (1998). *Love is a story: A new theory of relationships*. New York: Oxford University Press.

Sternberg, R. J. (2004). A triangular theory of love. In H. T. Reis & C. E. Rusbult (eds), *Close relationships: Key readings*. Philadelphia, PA: Taylor & Francis.

Sternberg, R. J. (2006). A duplex theory of love. In R. J. Sternberg & K. Weis (eds), *The new psychology of love*. New Haven, CT: Yale University Press.

Sternberg, R. J., & Grajek, S. (1984). The nature of love. *Journal of Personality and Social Psychology*, 47, 312–329.

Stewart, B. D., von Hippel, W., & Radvansky, G. A. (2009). Age, race, and implicit prejudice: Using process dissociation to separate the underlying components. Research Report, *Psychological Science*, 20(2), 164–168.

Stewart-Knox, B. J., Sittlington, J., Rugkåsa, J., Harrisson, S., Treacy, M., & Abaunza, P. S. (2005). Smoking and peer groups: Results from a longitudinal qualitative study of young people in Northern Ireland. *British Journal of Social Psychology*, 44(3), 397–414.

Stocks, E. L., Lishner, D. A., & Decker, S. K. (2009). Altruism or psychological escape: Why does empathy promote prosocial behavior? *European Journal of Social Psychology*, 39(5), 649–665.

Stokoe, E. H. (2000). Toward a conversation analytic approach to gender and discourse. *Feminism Psychology*, 10, 552–563.

Stokoe, E. H. (2004). Gender and discourse, gender and categorization: Current developments in language and gender research. *Qualitative Research in Psychology*, 1(2), 107–129.

Stone, A. A., Hedges, S. M., Neale, J. M., & Satin, M. S. (1985). Prospective and cross-sectional mood reports offer no evidence of a 'blue Monday' phenomenon. *Journal of Personality and Social Psychology*, 49, 129–134.

Stone, A. L., & Glass, C. R. (1986). Cognitive distortion of social feedback in depression. *Journal of Social and Clinical Psychology*, 4, 179–188.

Stoner, J. A. F. (1961). A comparison of individual and group decisions involving risk. Unpublished master's thesis, Massachusetts Institute of Technology, 1961. Cited by D. G. Marquis in Individual responsibility and group decisions involving risk. *Industrial Management Review*, 3, 8–23.

Stones, C. R. (2006). Antigay prejudice among heterosexual males: right-wing authoritarianism as a stronger predictor than social-dominance orientation and heterosexual identity. *Social Behavior and Personality*, 34(9), 1137–1150.

Storms, M. D. (1973). Videotape and the attribution process: Reversing actors' and observers' points of view. *Journal of Personality and Social Psychology*, 27, 165–175.

Stott, C., Hutchison, P., & Drury, J. (2001). 'Hooligans abroad?': Inter-group dynamics, social identity and participation in collective 'disorder' at the 1998 World Cup finals. *British Journal of Social Psychology*, 40(3), 359–384.

Stotzer, R. L., & Hossellman, E. (2012). Hate crimes on campus racial/ethnic diversity and campus safety. *Journal of Interpersonal Violence*, 27(4), 644–661.

Strack, F., & Deutsch, R. (2004). Reflective and impulsive determinants of social behavior. *Personality and Social Psychology Review*, 8(3), 220–247.

Strack, F., Martin, L. L., & Stepper, S. (1988), Inhibiting and facilitating conditions of the human smiles: A nonobtrusive test of the facial feedback hypothesis. *Journal of Personality and Social Psychology*, 54, 768–776.

Strassberg, D. S., & Holty, S. (2003). An experimental study of women's Internet personal ads. *Archives of Sexual Behaviour*, 32(3), 253–260.

Straus, M. A., & Gelles, R. J. (1980). *Behind closed doors: Violence in the American family*. New York: Anchor, Doubleday.

Streeter, S. A., & McBurney, D. H. (2003). Waist–hip ratio and attractiveness: New evidence and a critique of 'a critical test'. *Evolution and Human Behavior*, 24, 88–98.

Stroebe, W., & Diehl, M. (1994). Productivity loss in ideagenerating groups. In W. Stroebe & M. Hewstone (eds), *European review of social psychology*, Vol. 5. Chichester: Wiley.

Stroebe, W., Insko, C. A., Thompson, V. D., & Layton, B. D. (1971). Effects of physical attractiveness, attitude similarity, and sex on various aspects of interpersonal attraction. *Journal of Personality and Social Psychology*, 18, 79–91.

Stroebe, W., Lenkert, A., & Jonas, K. (1988). Familiarity may breed contempt: The impact of student exchange on national stereotypes and attitudes. In W. Stroebe & A. W. Kruglanski (eds), *The social psychology of intergroup conflict*. New York: Springer-Verlag.

Strömwall, L. A., Alfredsson, H., & Landström, S. (2012). Rape victim and perpetrator blame and the just world hypothesis: The influence of victim gender and age. *Journal of Sexual Aggression*, 1–11.

Strong, S. R. (1978). Social psychological approach to psychotherapy research. In S. L. Garfield & A. E. Bergin (eds), *Handbook of psychotherapy and behavior change*, 2nd edn. New York: Wiley.

Stroufe, B., Chaikin, A., Cook, R., & Freeman, V. (1977). The effects of physical attractiveness on honesty: A socially desirable response. *Personality and Social Psychology*, 3, 59–62.

Stukas, A. A., Snyder, M., & Clary, E. G. (1999). The effects of 'mandatory volunteerism' on intentions to volunteer. *Psychological Science*, 10, 59–64.

Sui, J., & Liu, C. H. (2009). Can beauty be ignored? Effects of facial attractiveness on covert attention. *Psychonomic Bulletin & Review*, 16, 276–281.

Sullivan, A. (1999, 26 September). What's so bad about hate? *New York Times Magazine* (www.nytimes.com).

Suls, J., & Tesch, F. (1978). Students' preferences for information about their test performance: A social comparison study, *Journal of Applied Social Psychology*, 8, 189–197.

Suls, J., Wan, C. K., & Sanders, G. S. (1988). False consensus and false uniqueness in estimating the prevalence of health-protective behaviors. *Journal of Applied Social Psychology*, 18, 66–79.

Sundstrom, E., De Meuse, K. P., & Futrell, D. (1990). Work teams: Applications and effectiveness. *American Psychologist*, 45, 120–133.

Surowiecki, J. (2004). *The wisdom of crowds*. New York: Doubleday.

Swallow, S. R., & Kuiper, N. A. (1987). The effects of depression and cognitive vulnerability to depression on judgments of similarity between self and other. *Motivation and Emotion*, **11**(2), 157–167.

Swann, W. B., Jr, & Gill, M. J. (1997). Confidence and accuracy in person perception: Do we know what we think we know about our relationship partners? *Journal of Personality and Social Psychology*, **73**, 747–757.

Swann, W. B., Jr, & Predmore, S. C. (1985). Intimates as agents of social support: Sources of consolation or despair? *Journal of Personality and Social Psychology*, **49**, 1609–1617.

Swann, W. B., Jr, & Read, S. J. (1981). Acquiring self-knowledge: The search for feedback that fits. *Journal of Personality and Social Psychology*, **41**, 1119–1128.

Swann, W. B., Jr, Rentfrow, P. J., & Gosling, S. D. (2003). The precarious couple effect: Verbally inhibited men + critical, disinhibited women = bad chemistry. *Journal of Personality and Social Psychology*, **85**, 1095–1106.

Swann, W. B., Jr, Sellers, J. G., & McClarty, K. L. (2006). Tempting today, troubling tomorrow: The roots of the precarious couple effect. *Personality and Social Psychology Bulletin*, **32**, 93–103.

Swann, W. B., Jr, Stein-Seroussi, A., & Giesler, R. B. (1992a). Why people self-verify. *Journal of Personality and Social Psychology*, **62**, 392–401.

Swann, W. B., Jr, Stein-Seroussi, A., & McNulty, S. E. (1992b). Outcasts in a white lie society. The enigmatic worlds of people with negative self-conceptions. *Journal of Personality and Social Psychology*, **62**, 618–624.

Swann, W. B., Jr, Wenzlaff, R. M., Krull, D. S., & Pelham, B. W. (1991). Seeking truth, reaping despair: Depression, self-verification and selection of relationship partners. *Journal of Abnormal Psychology*, **101**, 293–306.

Swap, W. C. (1977). Interpersonal attraction and repeated exposure to rewarders and punishers. *Personality and Social Psychology Bulletin*, **3**(2), 248–251.

Swim, J. K. (1994). Perceived versus meta-analytic effect sizes: An assessment of the accuracy of gender stereotypes. *Journal of Personality and Social Psychology*, **66**, 21–36.

Symons, C. S., & Johnson, B. T. (1997). The self-reference effect in memory: A meta-analysis. *Psychological Bulletin*, **121**, 371–394.

## T

Tafarodi, R. W., & Vu, C. (1997). Two-dimensional self-esteem and reactions to success and failure. *Personality and Social Psychology Bulletin*, **23**, 626–635.

Tajfel, H. (1974). Social identity and intergroup behaviour. *Social Science Information*, **13**(2), 65–93.

Tajfel, H. (1978). *Differentiation between social groups*. London: Academic Press.

Tajfel, H. (1981). *Human groups and social categories: Studies in social psychology*. London: Cambridge University Press.

Tajfel, H., & Forgas, J. P. (1981). Social categorization: Cognitions, values, and groups. In J. P. Forgas (ed.), *Social cognition: Perspectives on everyday understanding*. London: Academic Press.

Tajfel, H., & Turner, J. C. (1986). The social identity theory of intergroup behaviour. In S. Worchel & W. G. Austin (eds), *Psychology of intergroup relations*, 2nd edn. Chicago: Nelson-Hall.

Tajfel, H., & Wilkes, A. L. (1963). Classification and quantitative judgment. *British Journal of Psychology*, **54**, 101–114.

Tajfel, H., Flament, C., Billig, M. G., & Bundy, R. F. (1971). Social categorization and intergroup behaviour. *European Journal of Social Psychology*, **1**, 149–177.

Tajfel, H., Sheikh, A. A., & Gardner, R. C. (1964). Content of stereotypes and the inference of similarity between members of stereotyped groups. *Acta Psychologica*, **22**, 191–201.

Talbert, B. (1997, 2 February). Bob Talbert's quote bag. *Detroit Free Press*, p. 5E, quoting *Allure* magazine.

Tamres, L. K., Janicki, D., & Helgeson, V. S. (2002). Sex differences in coping behavior: A meta-analytic review and an examination of relative coping. *Personality and Social Psychology Review*, **6**, 2–30.

Tang, S. H., & Hall, V. C. (1995). The overjustification effect: A meta-analysis. *Applied Cognitive Psychology*, **9**(5), 365–404.

Tannen, D. (1990). *You just don't understand: Women and men in conversation*. New York: Morrow.

Tarrant, M., & Butler, K. (2011). Effects of self-categorization on orientation towards health. *British Journal of Social Psychology*, **50**, 121–139.

Tarrant, M., Hagger, M. S., & Farrow, C. V. (2012). Promoting positive orientation towards health through social identity. In: J. Jetten, C. Haslam & S. A. Haslam (eds), *The social cure: Identity, health and well-being*. Hove and New York: Psychology Press.

Täuber, S., & van Leeuwen, E. (2012). When high group status becomes a burden. *Social Psychology*, **43**(2), 98–107.

Taubes, G. (1992). Violence epidemiologists tests of hazards of gun ownership. *Science*, **258**, 213–215.

Taylor, D. A., Gould, R. J., & Brounstein, P. J. (1981). Effects of personalistic self-disclosure. *Personality and Social Psychology Bulletin*, **7**, 487–492.

Taylor, D. M., & Jaggi, V. (1974). Ethnocentrism and causal attribution in a South Indian context. *Journal of Cross-Cultural Psychology*, **5**, 162–171.

Taylor, S. E. (1983). Adjusting to threatening events: A theory of cognitive adaptation. *American Psychologist*, **38**, 1161–1173.

Taylor, S. E. (1989). *Positive illusions: Creative self-deception and the healthy mind*. New York: Basic Books.

Taylor, S. E., & Brown, J. D. (1988). Illusion and well-being: A social psychological perspective on mental health. *Psychological Bulletin*, **103**(2), 193.

Taylor, S. E., Lerner, J. S., Sherman, D. K., Sage, R. M., & McDowell, N. K. (2003). Are self-enhancing cognitions associated with healthy or unhealthy biological profiles? *Journal of Personality and Social Psychology*, **85**, 605–615.

Taylor, S. P., & Chermack, S. T. (1993). Alcohol, drugs and human physical aggression. *Journal of Studies on Alcohol*, Supplement No. 11, 78–88.

Teigen, K. H. (1986). Old truths or fresh insights? A study of students' evaluations of proverbs. *British Journal of Social Psychology*, **25**, 43–50.

Teigen, K. H., Evensen, P. C., Samoilow, D. K., & Vatne, K. B. (1999). Good luck and bad luck: How to tell the difference. *European Journal of Social Psychology*, **29**, 981–1010.

Telch, M. J., Killen, J. D., McAlister, A. L., Perry, C. L., & Maccoby, N. (1981). Long-term follow-up of a pilot project on smoking prevention with adolescents. Paper presented at the American Psychological Association convention.

Tennov, D. (1979). *Love and limerence: The experience of being in love*. New York: Stein and Day.

Terry, D. J., & Hogg, M. A. (1996). Group norms and the attitude-behavior relationship: A role for group identification. *Personality and Social Psychology Bulletin*, **22**, 776–793.

Tesser, A. (1988). Toward a self-evaluation maintenance model of social behavior. In L. Berkowitz (ed.), *Advances in experimental social psychology*, Vol. 21. San Diego, CA: Academic Press.

Tesser, A., Martin, L., & Mendolia, M. (1995). The impact of thought on attitude extremity and attitude–behavior consistency. In R. E. Petty and J. A Krosnick (eds), *Attitude strength: Antecedents and consequences*. Hillsdale, NJ: Erlbaum.

Tesser, A., Rosen, S., & Conlee, M. C. (1972). News valence and available recipient as determinants of news transmission. *Sociometry*, **35**, 619–628.

Testa, M. (2002). The impact of men's alcohol consumption on perpetration of sexual aggression. *Clinical Psychology Review*, **22**, 1239–1263.

Tetlock, P. E. (1983). Accountability and complexity of thought. *Journal of Personality and Social Psychology*, **45**, 74–83.

Tetlock, P. E. (1998). Close-call counterfactuals and beliefsystem defenses: I was not almost wrong but I was almost right. *Journal of Personality and Social Psychology*, **75**, 639–652.

Tetlock, P. E. (1999). Theory-driven reasoning about plausible pasts and probable futures in world politics: Are we prisoners of our preconceptions? *American Journal of Political Science*, **43**, 335–366.

Tetlock, P. E., Peterson, R. S., McGuire, C., Chang, S., & Feld, P. (1992). Assessing political group dynamics: A test of the groupthink model. *Journal of Personality and Social Psychology*, **63**, 403–425.

Tewari, S., Khan, S., Hopkins, N., Srinivasan, N., & Reichers, S. (2012). Participation in mass gatherings can benefit well-being: Longitudinal and control data from a North Indian Hindu pilgrimage event. *PLoS One*, **7**, e47291.

Theurer, K., & Wister, A. (2010). Altruistic behaviour and social capital as predictors of well-being among older Canadians. *Ageing and Society*, **30**, 157–181.

Thi, M. D. A., Brickley, D. B., Vinh, D. T. N., Colby, D. J., Sohn, A. H., Trung, N. Q., Giang, L. T., & Mandel, J. S. (2008). A qualitative study of stigma and discrimination against people living with HIV in Ho Chi Minh City, Vietnam. *AIDS Behaviour*, **12**, 63–70.

Thomas, G. C., & Batson, C. D. (1981). Effect of helping under normative pressure on self-perceived altruism. *Social Psychology Quarterly*, **44**, 127–131.

Thomas, G. C., Batson, C. D., & Coke, J. S. (1981). Do Good Samaritans discourage helpfulness? Self-perceived

altruism after exposure to highly helpful others. *Journal of Personality and Social Psychology*, **40**, 194–200.

Thomas, L. (1981). The value of basic science. Rochester Review, University of Rochester, 1–7. Available at: http://www.lib.rochester.edu/IN/RBSCP/Databases/Attachments/Reviews/1981/43-4/1981_Summer.pdf.

Thompson, L. (1990a). An examination of naive and experienced negotiators. *Journal of Personality and Social Psychology*, **59**, 82–90.

Thompson, L. (1990b). The influence of experience on negotiation performance. *Journal of Experimental Social Psychology*, **26**, 528–544.

Thompson, L. (1998). *The mind and heart of the negotiator.* Upper Saddle River, NJ: Prentice-Hall.

Thompson, L., Valley, K. L., & Kramer, R. M. (1995). The bittersweet feeling of success: An examination of social perception in negotiation. *Journal of Experimental Social Psychology*, **31**, 467–492.

Thompson, S. C., Armstrong, W., & Thomas, C. (1998). Illusions of control, underestimations, and accuracy: A control heuristic explanation. *Psychological Bulletin*, **123**, 143–161.

Thompson, W. C., Cowan, C. L., & Rosenhan, D. L. (1980). Focus of attention mediates the impact of negative affect on altruism. *Journal of Personality and Social Psychology*, **38**, 291–300.

Thurstone, L. L. (1928a). Attitudes can be measured. *American Journal of Sociology*, **33**, 529–554.

Thurstone, L. L. (1928b). An experimental study of nationality preferences. *Journal of General Psychology*, **1**, 405–425.

Tice, D. M., Butler, J. L., Muraven, M. B., & Stillwell, A. M. (1995). When modesty prevails: Differential favorability of self-presentation to friends and strangers. *Journal of Personality and Social Psychology*, **69**, 1120–1138.

Tileaga, C. (2006). Representing the 'other': A discursive

analysis of prejudice and moral exclusion in talk about Romanies. *Journal of Community & Applied Social Psychology*, **16**, 19–41.

Timko, C., & Moos, R. H. (1989). Choice, control, and adaptation among elderly residents of sheltered care settings. *Journal of Applied Social Psychology*, **19**, 636–655.

Tinkler, P., & Jackson, C. (2007). 'Ladettes' and 'modern girls': 'Troublesome' young femininities. *The Sociological Review*, **55**(2), 251–272.

Todd, A. R., Molden, D. C., Ham, J., & Vonk, R. (2011). The automatic and co-occurring activation of multiple social inferences. *Journal of Experimental Social Psychology*, **47**, 37–49.

Todorov, A., Harris, L. T., & Fiske, S. T. (2006). Toward socially inspired social neuroscience. *Brain Research*, **1079**, 76–85.

Tomorrow, T. (2003, 30 April). Passive tense verbs deployed before large audience; stories remain unclear (www240.pair.com/tomtom/pages/ja/ja_fr.html).

Totterdell, P., Kellett, S., Teuchmann, K., & Briner, R. B. (1998). Evidence of mood linkage in work groups. *Journal of Personality and Social Psychology*, **74**(6), 1504.

Traut-Mattausch, E., Schulz-Hardt, S., Greitemeyer, T., & Frey, D. (2004). Expectancy confirmation in spite of disconfirming evidence: The case of price increases due to the introduction of the Euro. *European Journal of Social Psychology*, **34**, 739–760.

Trautwein, U., & Lüdtke, O. (2006). Self-esteem, academic self-concept, and achievement: How the learning environment moderates the dynamics of self-concept. *Journal of Personality and Social Psychology*, **90**, 334–349.

Travis, L. E. (1925). The effect of a small audience upon eye–hand coordination. *Journal of Abnormal and Social Psychology*, **20**, 142–146.

Trewin, D. (2001). *Australian social trends 2001.*

Canberra: Australian Bureau of Statistics.

Triandis, H. C. (1981). Some dimensions of intercultural variation and their implications for interpersonal behavior. Paper presented at the American Psychological Association convention.

Triandis, H. C. (1982). Incongruence between intentions and behavior: A review. Paper presented at the American Psychological Association convention.

Triandis, H. C. (1994). *Culture and social behavior.* New York: McGraw-Hill.

Triandis, H. C. (2000). Culture and conflict. *International Journal of Psychology*, **55**, 145–152.

Triandis, H. C., Bontempo, R., Villareal, M. J., Asai, M., & Lucca, N. (1988). Individualism and collectivism: Cross-cultural perspectives on self-ingroup relationships. *Journal of Personality and Social Psychology*, **54**, 323–338.

Trimble, D. E. (1993). Meta-analysis of altruism and intrinsic and extrinsic religiousness. Paper presented at the Eastern Psychological Association convention.

Triplett, N. (1898). The dynamogenic factors in pacemaking and competition. *American Journal of Psychology*, **9**, 507–533.

Trolier, T. K., & Hamilton, D. L. (1986). Variables influencing judgments of correlational relations. *Journal of Personality and Social Psychology*, **50**, 879–888.

Tropp, L. R., & Pettigrew, T. F. (2005a). Differential relationships between intergroup contact and affective and cognitive dimensions of prejudice. *Personality and Social Psychology Bulletin*, **31**, 1145–1158.

Tropp, L. R., & Pettigrew, T. F. (2005b). Relationships between intergroup contact and prejudice among minority and majority status groups. *Psychological Science*, **16**, 951–957.

Trost, M. R., Maass, A., & Kenrick, D. T. (1992). Minority influence: Personal relevance biases cognitive processes and reverses private acceptance. *Journal of Experimental Social Psychology*, **28**, 234–254.

**Trudgill, P.** (1974). *Sociolinguistics: An introduction to language and society.* London: Penguin Books.

**Trzesniewski, K., H., & Donnellan, M. B.** (2009). Reevaluating the evidence for increasingly positive self-views among high school students: More evidence for consistency across generations (1976–2006). *Psychological Science,* **20**, 920–922.

**Trzesniewski, K., H., & Donnellan, M. B.** (2010). Rethinking 'generation me': A study of cohort effects from 1976–2006. *Perspectives on Psychological Science,* **5**, 58–75.

**Tsai, C.-C., & Chang, C.-H.** (2007). The effect of physical attractiveness of models on advertising effectiveness for male and female adolescents. *Adolescence,* **42**, 827–836.

**Tsang, J.-A.** (2002). Moral rationalization and the integration of situational factors and psychological processes in immoral behavior. *Review of General Psychology,* **6**, 25–50.

**Turner, C. W., Hesse, B. W., & Peterson-Lewis, S.** (1986). Naturalistic studies of the long-term effects of television violence. *Journal of Social Issues,* **42**(3), 51–74.

**Turner, J. C.** (1984). Social identification and psychological group formation. In H. Tajfel (ed.), *The social dimensions: European developments in social psychology,* Vol. 2. London: Cambridge University Press.

**Turner, J. C.** (1987). *Rediscovering the social group: A self-categorization theory.* New York: Basil Blackwell.

**Turner, J. C.** (1991). *Social influence.* Pacific Grove, CA: Brooks/Cole.

**Turner, J. C., & Oakes, P. J.** (1997). The socially structured mind. In C. McGarty & S. A. Haslam (eds), *The message of social psychology.* Oxford: Blackwell.

**Turner, J. C., Hogg, M. A., Oakes, P. J., Reicher, S. D., & Wetherell, M.** (1987). *Rediscovering the social group: A self-categorisation theory.* Oxford and New York: Blackwell.

**Turner, M. E., & Pratkanis, A. R.** (1993). Effects of pref-erential and meritorious selection on performance: An examination of intuitive and self-handicapping perspectives. *Personality and Social Psychology Bulletin,* **19**, 47–58.

**Turner, M. E., & Pratkanis, A. R.** (1997). Mitigating groupthink by stimulating constructive conflict. In C. K. W. De Dreu & E. Van de Vliert (eds), *Using conflict in organizations.* London: Sage.

**Turner, M. E., Pratkanis, A. R., Probasco, P., & Leve, C.** (1992). Threat cohesion and group effectiveness: Testing a social identity maintenance perspective on groupthink. *Journal of Personality and Social Psychology,* **63**, 781–796.

**Turner, N., Barling, J., & Zacharatos, A.** (2002). Positive psychology at work. In C. R. Snyder & S. J. Lopez (eds), *The handbook of positive psychology.* New York: Oxford University Press.

**Turner, R. H., & Killian, L. M.** (1972). *Collective behaviour.* Englewood Cliffs, NJ: Prentice-Hall.

**Turner, R. N., Hewstone, M., & Voci, A.** (2007). Reducing explicit and implicit outgroup prejudice via direct and extended contact: The mediating role of self-disclosure and intergroup anxiety. *Journal of Personality and Social Psychology,* **93**(3), 369–388.

**Tversky, A., & Kahneman, D.** (1973). Availability: A neuristic for judging frequency and probability. *Cognitive Psychology,* **5**, 207–302.

**Tversky, A., & Kahneman, D.** (1974). Judgment under uncertainty: Heuristics and biases. *Science, New Series,* **185**(4157), 1124–1131.

**Tversky, A., & Kahneman, D.** (1983). Extensional versus intuitive reasoning: The conjunction fallacy in probability judgment. *Psychological Review,* **90**, 293–315.

**Twenge, J. M.** (1997). Changes in masculine and feminine traits over time: A meta-analysis. *Sex Roles,* **36**, 305–325.

**Twenge, J. M.** (2006). *Generation me.* New York: Free Press.

**Twenge, J. M., & Campbell, W. K.** (2009). *The narcissism epidemic: Living in an age of entitlement.* New York: Free Press.

**Twenge, J. M., & Campbell W. K.** (2010). Birth cohort differences in the monitoring the future dataset and elsewhere: Further evidence for generation me – Commentary on Trzesniewski & Donnellan (2010). *Perspectives on Psychological Science,* **5**, 81–88.

**Twenge, J. M., Catanese, K. R., & Baumeister, R. F.** (2003). Social exclusion and the deconstructed state: Time perception, meaninglessness, lethargy, lack of emotion, and self-awareness. *Journal of Personality and Social Psychology,* **85**, 409–423.

**Twenge, J. M., Konrath, S., Foster, J. D., Campbell, W. K., & Bushman, B. J.** (2008). Egos inflating over time: A cross-temporal meta-analysis of the Narcissistic Personality Inventory. *Journal of Personality,* **76**, 875–901.

**Tyler, T. R., & Lind, E. A.** (1990). Intrinsic versus community-based justice models: When does group membership matter? *Journal of Social Issues,* **46**, 83–94.

**U**

**Uleman, J. S.** (1989). A framework for thinking intentionally about unintended thoughts. In J. S. Uleman & J. A. Bargh (eds), *Unintended thought: The limits of awareness, intention, and control.* New York: Guilford Press.

**Unger, R. K.** (1979). Whom does helping help? Paper presented at the Eastern Psychological Association convention, April.

**Unger, R. K.** (1985). Epistemological consistency and its scientific implications. *American Psychologist,* **40**, 1413–1414.

**United Nations** (1991). *The world's women 1970–1990: Trends and statistics.* New York: United Nations.

**V**

**Vaillancourt, T.** (2012). Students aggress against professors in reaction to receiving poor grades: An effect moderated by student narcissism and self-esteem. *Aggressive Behavior,* **39**, 71–84.

**Vaillant, G. E.** (1977). *Adaptation to life.* Boston: Little, Brown.

**Vallone R. P., Griffin, D. W., Lin, S., & Ross, L.** (1990). Overconfident prediction of future actions and outcomes by self and others. *Journal of Personality and Social Psychology,* **58**(4), 582.

**Vallone, R. P., Ross, L., & Lepper, M. R.** (1985). The hostile media phenomenon: Biased perception and perceptions of media bias in coverage of the 'Beirut Massacre'. *Journal of Personality and Social Psychology,* **49**, 577–585.

**van Baaren, R. B., Holland, R. W., Karremans, R. W., & van Knippenberg, A.** (2003a). Mimicry and interpersonal closeness. Unpublished manuscript, University of Nijmegen.

**van Baaren, R. B., Holland, R. W., Kawakami, K., & van Knippenberg, A.** (2004). Mimicry and prosocial behavior. *Psychological Science,* **15**, 71–74.

**van Baaren, R. B., Holland, R. W., Steenaert, B., & van Knippenberg, A.** (2003b). Mimicry for money: Behavioral consequences of imitation. *Journal of Experimental Social Psychology,* **39**, 393–398.

**Van Boven, L., & Loewenstein, G.** (2003). Social projection of transient drive states. *Personality and Social Psychology Bulletin,* **29**, 1159–1168.

**van den Bos, K., & Spruijt, N.** (2002). Appropriateness of decisions as a moderator of the psychology of voice. *European Journal of Social Psychology,* **32**, 57–72.

**Van der Plight, J., Eise, J. R., & Spears, R.** (1987). Comparative judgments and preferences: The influence of the number of response alternatives. *British Journal of Social Psychology,* **26**, 269–280.

**Van der Veer, R., & Valsiner, J.** (1991). *Understanding Vygotsky: A quest for synthesis.* Oxford: Blackwell.

**Van der Veer, R., & Valsiner, J.** (1994). *The Vygotsky reader.* Oxford: Blackwell.

**Van der Veer, R., & van Uzendoorn, M. H.** (1985).

Vygotsky's theory of the higher psychological processes: some criticisms. *Human Development*, **28**, 1–9.

Van Dijk, T. A. (1992). Discourse and the denial of racism. *Discourse and Society*, **3**, 87–118.

Van Dijk, T. A. (1993). *Elite discourses and racism*. London: Sage.

van Engen, M. L., & Willemsen, T. M. (2004). Sex and leadership styles: A meta-analysis of research published in the 1990s. *Psychological Reports*, **94**, 3–18.

Van Goozen, S. H., Cohen-Kettenis, P. T., Gooren, L. J., Frijda, N. H., & Van De Poll, N. E. (1995). Gender differences in behaviour: Activating effects of cross-sex hormones. *Psychoneuroendocrinology*, **20**(4), 343–363.

Van Knippenberg, D., & Wilke, H. (1992). Prototypicality of arguments and conformity to ingroup norms. *European Journal of Social Psychology*, **22**, 141–155.

Van Laar, C., Levin, S., Sinclair, S., & Sidanius, J. (2005). The effect of university roommate contact on ethnic attitudes and behavior. *Journal of Experimental Social Psychology*, **41**, 329–345.

Van Lange, P. A., & Visser, K. (1999). Locomotion in social dilemmas: How people adapt to cooperative, tit-for-tat, and non-cooperative partners. *Journal of Personality and Social Psychology*, **77**(4), 762.

van Leeuwen, E., Taüber, S. (2011). Demonstrating knowledge: The effects of group status on outgroup helping. *Journal of Experimental Social Psychology*, **47**(1), 147–156.

Van Vugt, M. (2009). Sex differences in intergroup competition, aggression, and warfare. The male warrior hypothesis. *Annals of the New York Academy of Sciences*, **1167**, Issue values, empathy, and fairness across social barriers, 124–134.

Van Vugt, M., De Cremer, D., & Janssen, D. P. (2007). Gender differences in cooperation and competition: The

malewarrior hypothesis. *Psychological Science*, **18**(1), 19–23.

Van Yperen, N. W., & Buunk, B. P. (1990). A longitudinal study of equity and satisfaction in intimate relationships. *European Journal of Social Psychology*, **20**, 287–309.

Vandello, J. A., & Cohen, D. (2003). Male honor and female fidelity: Implicit cultural scripts that perpetuate domestic violence. *Journal of Personality and Social Psychology*, **84**(5), 997–1010.

Vanderslice, V. J., Rice, R. W., & Julian, J. W. (1987). The effects of participation in decision-making on worker satisfaction and productivity: An organizational simulation. *Journal of Applied Social Psychology*, **17**, 158–170.

Vazire, S., & Gosling, S. D. (2004). e-Perceptions: Personality impressions based on personal websites. *Journal of Personality and Social Psychology*, **87**, 123–132.

Verkooijen, K. T., de Vries, N. K., & Nielsen, G. A. (2007). Youth crowds and substance use: The impact of perceived group norm and multiple group identification. *Psychology of Addictive Behaviors*, **21**, 55–61.

Verplanken, B. (1991). Persuasive communication of risk information: A test of cue versus message processing effects in a field experiment. *Personality and Social Psychology Bulletin*, **17**, 188–193.

Veysey, B. M., & Messner, S. F. (1999). Further testing of social disorganization theory: An elaboration of Sampson and Groves's 'Community structure and crime'. *Journal of Research in Crime and Delinquency*, **36**, 156–174.

Viala, E. S. (2011). Contemporary family life: A joint venture with contradictions. *Nordic Psychology*, **63**(2), 68.

Vignoles, V. L., Chryssochoou, X., & Breakwell, G. M. (2000). The distinctiveness principle: Identity, meaning, and the bounds of cultural relativity. *Personality and Social Psychology Review*, **4**, 337–354.

Vignoles, V. L., Regalia, C., Manzi, C., Golledge, J., & Scabini, E. (2006). Beyond self-esteem: Influence of multiple motives on identity construction. *Journal of Personality and Social Psychology*, **90**, 308–333.

Vincent, W., Parrott, D. J., & Peterson, J. L. (2011). Combined effects of masculine gender–role stress and sexual prejudice on anger and aggression toward gay men. *Journal of Applied Social Psychology*, **41**(5), 1237–1257.

Visser, P. S., & Krosnick, J. A. (1998). Development of attitude strength over the life cycle: Surge and decline. *Journal of Personality and Social Psychology*, **75**, 1389–1410.

Visser, P. S., & Mirabile, R. R. (2004). Attitudes in the social context: The impact of social network composition on individual-level attitude strength. *Journal of Personality and Social Psychology*, **87**, 779–795.

Vitelli, R. (1988). The crisis issue assessed: An empirical analysis. *Basic and Applied Social Psychology*, **9**, 301–309.

Vollum, S., & Buffington-Vollum, J. (2010). An examination of social-psychological factors and support for the death penalty: Attribution, moral disengagement, and the value-expressive function of attitudes. *American Journal of Criminal Justice*, **35**, 15–36.

von Arnim, E. (1922). *The Enchanted April*. London: Macmillan.

von Cranach, M. (1986). Leadership as a function of group action. In C. F. Graumann & S. Moscovici (eds), *Changing conceptions of leadership*. New York: Springer-Verlag.

von Hippel, W., Sekaquaptewa, D., & Vargas, P. (1997). The linguistic intergroup bias as an implicit indicator of prejudice. *The Journal of Experimental and Social Psychology*, **33**, 490–509.

Vonk, R. (1998). The slime effect: suspicion and dislike of likeable behaviour toward superiors. *Journal of Personality and Social Psychology*, **74**(4), 849–864.

Vonofakou, C., Hewstone, M., & Voci, A. (2007). Contact with out-group friends as a predictor of meta-attitudinal strength and accessibility of attitudes towards gay men. *The Journal of Personality and Social Psychology*, **92**(5), 804–820.

Vorauer, J. D., Main, K. J., & O'Connell, G. B. (1998). How do individuals expect to be viewed by members of lower status groups? Content and implications of meta-stereotypes. *Journal of Personality and Social Psychology*, **75**(4), 917.

Vorauer, J. D., & Ratner, R. K. (1996). Who's going to make the first move? Pluralistic ignorance as an impediment to relationship formation. *Journal of Social and Personal Relationships*, **13**, 483–506.

Vorauer, J. D., & Sakamoto, Y. (2008). Who cares what the outgroup thinks? Testing an information search model of the importance individuals accord to an outgroup member's view of them during intergroup interaction. *Journal of Personality and Social Psychology*, **95**, 1467–1480.

Vroom, V. H., & Jago, A. G. (2007). The role of the situation in leadership. *American Psychologist*, **62**(1), 17–24.

Vygotsky, L. S. (1986). *Thought and language*. Cambridge, MA: MIT Press.

Vygotsky, L., & Luria, A. (1993). *Studies on the history of behavior. Ape, primitive, and child*. Hillsdale, NJ: Erlbaum. (Original work published 1930.)

## W

Wagenaar, W. A. (1988). *Paradoxes of gambling behaviour*. London: Lawrence Erlbaum.

Wagstaff, G. F. (1983). Attitudes to poverty, the Protestant ethic, and political affiliation: A preliminary investigation. *Social Behavior and Personality*, **11**, 45–47.

Wakefield, J. R. H., Bickley, S., & Sani, F. (2013). The effects of identification with a support group on the mental health of people with multiple sclerosis. *Journal of Psychosomatic Research*, **74**, 420–426.

**Walker, R.** (2004, 5 December). The hidden (in plain sight) persuaders. *New York Times Magazine* (www. nytimes.com).

**Wall, B.** (2002, 24–25 August). Profit matures along with baby boomers. *International Herald Tribune*, p. 13.

**Wallace, M.** (1969), *New York Times*, 25 November.

**Wallace, M.** (2000). Workplace training initiatives: implications for women in the Australian workforce. *Journal of European Industrial Training*, **24**(5), 268–274.

**Waller, J.** (2002). *Becoming evil: How ordinary people commit genocide and mass killing*. New York: Oxford.

**Walster (Hatfield), E.** (1965). The effect of self-esteem on romantic liking. *Journal of Experimental Social Psychology*, **1**, 184–197.

**Walster (Hatfield), E., & Festinger, L.** (1962). The effectiveness of 'overheard' persuasive communications. *Journal of Abnormal and Social Psychology*, **65**, 395–402.

**Walster (Hatfield), E., Aronson, V., Abrahams, D., & Rottman, L.** (1966). Importance of physical attractiveness in dating behavior. *Journal of Personality and Social Psychology*, **4**, 508–516.

**Walther, J. B., Van Der Heide, B., Kim, S-Y., Westerman, D., & Tong, S. T.** (2008). The role of friends' appearance and behaviour on evaluations of individuals on Facebook: Are we known by the company we keep? *Human Communication Research*, **34**, 28–49.

**Wang, M. T., Eccles, J. S., & Kenny, S.** (2013). Not lack of ability but more choice individual and gender differences in choice of careers in science, technology, engineering, and mathematics. *Psychological Science*, **24**(5), 770–775.

**Ward, W. C., & Jenkins, H. M.** (1965). The display of information and the judgment of contingency. *Canadian Journal of Psychology*, **19**, 231–241.

**Warneken, F., & Tomasello, M.** (2006). Altruistic helping in human infants and young chimpanzees. *Science*, **311**, 1301–1303.

**Warneken, F., & Tomasello, M.** (2008). Extrinsic rewards undermine altruistic tendencies in 20-month-olds. *Developmental Psychology*, **44**(6), 1785–1788.

**Warnick, D. H., & Sanders, G. S.** (1980). The effects of group discussion on eyewitness accuracy. *Journal of Applied Social Psychology*, **10**, 249–259.

**Warren, N. C.** (2005, 4 March). Personal correspondence from founder of eHarmony. com.

**Wason, P. C.** (1960). On the failure to eliminate hypotheses in a conceptual task. *Quarterly Journal of Experimental Psychology*, **12**, 129–140.

**Waterman, A. S.** (1984). *The psychology of individualism*. New York: Praeger.

**Watkins, D., Akande, A., & Fleming, J.** (1998). Cultural dimensions, gender, and the nature of self-concept: A fourteen-country study? *International Journal of Psychology*, **33**, 17–31.

**Watkins, D., Cheng, C., Mpofu, E., Olowu, S., Singh-Sengupta, S., & Regmi, M.** (2003). Gender differences in self-construal: How generalizable are Western findings? *Journal of Social Psychology*, **143**, 501–519.

**Watson, D.** (1982, November). The actor and the observer: How are their perceptions of causality divergent? *Psychological Bulletin*, **92**, 682–700.

**Watson, D. C.** (2012). Gender differences in gossip and friendship. *Sex Roles*, **67**(9–10), 494–502.

**Weary, G., & Edwards, J. A.** (1994). Social cognition and clinical psychology: Anxiety, depression, and the processing of social information. In R. Wyer & T. Srull (eds), *Handbook of social cognition*, Vol. 2. Hillsdale, NJ: Lawrence Erlbaum.

**Webb, T. L., & Sheeran, P.** (2006). Does changing behavioral intentions engender behavior change? A meta-analysis of the experimental evidence. *Psychological Bulletin*, **132**, 249–268.

**Weber, A. L., & Harvey, J. H.** (eds) (1994). *Perspective on close relationships*. Boston: Allyn & Bacon.

**Wegge, J., Schuh, S. C., & van Dick, R.** (2012). 'I feel bad', 'we feel good'? Emotions as a driver for personal and organizational identity and organizational identification as a resource for serving unfriendly customers. *Stress and Health*, **28**, 123–136.

**Wegner, D. M.** (2002). *The illusion of conscious will*. Cambridge, MA: MIT Press.

**Wegner, D. M., Sparrow, B., & Winerman, L.** (2004). Vicarious agency: Experiencing control over the movements of others. *Journal of Personality and Social Psychology*, **86**, 838–848.

**Wehr, P.** (1979). *Conflict regulation*. Boulder, CO: Westview Press.

**Weiner, B.** (1980). A cognitive (attribution)-emotion-action model of motivated behavior: An analysis of judgments of help-giving. *Journal of Personality and Social Psychology*, **39**, 186–200.

**Weiner, B.** (1981). The emotional consequences of causal ascriptions. Unpublished manuscript, UCLA.

**Weiner, B.** (1985). 'Spontaneous' causal thinking. *Psychological Bulletin*, **97**, 74–84.

**Weiner, B.** (1986). *An attribution theory of motivation and emotion*. New York: Springer.

**Weiner, B.** (1995). *Judgments of responsibility: A foundation for a theory of social conduct*. New York: Guilford Press.

**Weinstein, N. D.** (1980). Unrealistic optimism about future life events. *Journal of Personality and Social Psychology*, **39**, 806–820.

**Weinstein, N. D.** (1982). Unrealistic optimism about susceptibility to health problems. *Journal of Behavioral Medicine*, **5**, 441–460.

**Weiss, J., & Brown, P.** (1976). Self-insight error in the explanation of mood. Unpublished manuscript, Harvard University.

**Wells, G. L., & Petty, R. E.** (1980). The effects of overt head movements on persuasion: Compatibility and incompatibility of responses. *Basic and Applied Social Psychology*, **1**, 219–230.

**Wener, R., Frazier, W., & Farbstein, J.** (1987, June). Building better jails. *Psychology Today*, 40–49.

**Wenzlaff, R. M., & Prohaska, M. L.** (1989). When misery prefers company: Depression, attributions, and responses to others' moods. *Journal of Experimental Social Psychology*, **25**, 220–233.

**Werner, C. M., Stoll, R., Birch, P., & White, P. H.** (2002). Clinical validation and cognitive elaboration: Signs that encourage sustained recycling. *Basic and Applied Social Psychology*, **24**, 185–203.

**Wertsch, J. W.** (2008). From social interaction to higher psychological processes. *Human Development*, **51**, 66–79.

**West, S. G., & Brown, T. J.** (1975). Physical attractiveness, the severity of the emergency and helping: A field experiment and interpersonal simulation. *Journal of Experimental Social Psychology*, **11**, 531–538.

**West, S. G., Whitney, G., & Schnedler, R.** (1975). Helping a motorist in distress: The effects of sex, race, and neighborhood. *Journal of Personality and Social Psychology*, **31**, 691–698.

**Wetherell, M. & Potter, J.** (1992). *Mapping the language of racism: Discourse and the legitimation of exploitation*. Hemel Hempstead: Harvester Wheatsheaf.

**Wetherell, M., & Maybin, J.** (1996). The distributed self: A social costructionist perspective. In R. Stevens (ed.), *Understanding the self* (1). London: Sage.

**Weyant, J. M.** (1984). Applying social psychology to induce charitable donations. *Journal of Applied Social Psychology*, **14**, 441–447.

**Weyant, J. M., & Smith, S. L.** (1987). Getting more by asking for less: The effects of request size on donations of charity. *Journal of Applied Social Psychology*, **17**, 392–400.

**Wheeler, L., Koestner, R., & Driver, R. E.** (1982). Related attributes in the choice of comparison others: It's there, but it isn't all there is. *Journal of Experimental Social Psychology*, **18**, 489–500.

White, G. L. (1980). Physical attractiveness and courtship progress. *Journal of Personality and Social Psychology*, **39**, 660–668.

White, G. L., & Kight, T. D. (1984). Misattribution of arousal and attraction: Effects of salience of explanations for arousal. *Journal of Experimental Social Psychology*, **20**, 55–64.

White, J. W., & Kowalski, R. M. (1994). Deconstructing the myth of the nonaggressive woman: a feminist analysis. *Psychology of Women Quarterly*, **18**, 487–508.

White, K., & Lehman, D. R. (2005). Culture and social comparison seeking: The role of self-motives. *Personality and Social Psychology Bulletin*, **31**, 232–242.

White, L., & Edwards, J. (1990). Emptying the nest and parental well-being: An analysis of national panel data. *American Sociological Review*, **55**, 235–242.

Whittaker, J. O., & Meade, R. D. (1967). Social pressure in the modification and distortion of judgment: A cross-cultural study. *International Journal of Psychology*, **2**, 109–113.

Whitty, M. T. (2008). Revealing the 'real' me, searching for the 'actual' you: Presentations of self on an Internet dating site. *Computers in Human Behavior*, **24**, 1707–1723.

Whyte, G. (1993). Escalating commitment in individual and group decision making: A prospect theory approach. *Organizational Behavior and Human Decision Processes*, **54**, 430–455.

Wicker, A. W. (1969). Attitudes versus actions: The relationship of verbal and overt behavioral responses to attitude objects. *Journal of Social Issues*, **25**, 41–78.

Wicklund, R. A., & Braun, O. L. (1987). Incompetence and the concern with human categories. *Journal of Personality & Social Psychology*, **53**, 373–382.

Wiebe, D. J. (2003). Homicide and suicide risks associated with firearms in the home: A national case-control study. *Annals of Emergency Medicine*, **41**, 771–782.

Wiegman, O. (1985). Two politicians in a realistic experiment: Attraction, discrepancy, intensity of delivery, and attitude change. *Journal of Applied Social Psychology*, **15**, 673–686.

Wieselquist, J., Rusbult, C. E., Foster, C. A., & Agnew, C. R. (1999). Commitment, pro-relationship behavior, and trust in close relationships. *Journal of Personality and Social Psychology*, **77**, 942–966.

Wiggins, S., Potter, J., & Wildsmith, A. (2001). Eating your words: Discursive psychology and the reconstruction of eating practices. *Journal of Health Psychology*, **6**(1), 5–15.

Wilder, D. A. (1990). Some determinants of the persuasive power of in-groups and out-groups: Organization of information and attribution of independence. *Journal of Personality and Social Psychology*, **59**, 1202–1213.

Wilder, D. A., & Shapiro, P. N. (1984). Role of out-group cues in determining social identity. *Journal of Personality and Social Psychology*, **47**, 342–348.

Wiley, M., Crittenden, K., & Birg, L. (1979). Why a rejection? Causal attribution of a career achievement effect. *Social Psychology Quarterly*, **42**(3), 214–222.

Wilkinson, S. (1997). Feminist psychology. In D. Fox & I. Prilleltensky (eds), *Critical psychology: An introduction*. Thousand Oaks, CA: Sage.

Williams, D. K., Bourgeois, M. J., & Croyle, R. T. (1993). The effects of stealing thunder in criminal and civil trials. *Law and Human Behavior*, **17**, 597–609.

Williams, J. E., & Best, D. L. (1990). *Measuring sex stereotypes: A multination study*. Newbury Park, CA: Sage.

Williams, J. E., Satterwhite, R. C., & Best, D. L. (1999). Pancultural gender stereotypes revisited: The Five Factor model. *Sex Roles*, **40**, 513–525.

Williams, J. E., Satterwhite, R. C., & Best, D. L. (2000). Five-factor gender stereotypes in 27 countries. Paper presented at the XV Congress of the International Association for Cross-Cultural Psychology, Pultusk, Poland.

Williams, K. D., & Karau, S. J. (1991). Social loafing and social compensation: The effects of expectations of coworker performance. *Journal of Personality and Social Psychology*, **61**, 570–581.

Williams, K. D., Harkins, S., & Latané, B. (1981). Identifiability as a deterrent to social loafing: Two cheering experiments. *Journal of Personality and Social Psychology*, **40**, 303–311.

Williams, K. D., Jackson, J. M., & Karau, S. J. (1992). Collective hedonism: A social loafing analysis of social dilemmas. In D. A. Schroeder (ed.), *Social dilemmas: Social psychological perspectives*. New York: Praeger.

Williams, K. D., Nida, S. A., Baca, L. D., & Latané, B. (1989). Social loafing and swimming: Effects of identifiability on individual and relay performance of intercollegiate swimmers. *Basic and Applied Social Psychology*, **10**, 73–81.

Williams, T. M. (ed.) (1986). *The impact of television: A natural experiment in three communities*. Orlando, FL: Academic Press.

Willis, F. N., & Hamm, H. K. (1980). The use of interpersonal touch in securing compliance. *Journal of Nonverbal Behavior*, **5**, 49–55.

Willis, M. (2012, 15 October). Forgettable study sparks sexist headlines about women remembering. *The Conversation*. Available at: http://theconversation.com/forgettable-study-sparks-sexist-headlines-about-women-remembering-10112

Wilson, E. O. (1978). *On human nature*. Cambridge, MA: Harvard University Press.

Wilson, J. Q., & Kelling, G. L. (1982). Broken windows. *Atlantic Monthly*, **249**(3), 29–38.

Wilson, R. C., Gaft, J. G., Dienst, E. R., Wood, L., & Bavry, J. L. (1975). *College professors and their impact on students*. New York: Wiley.

Wilson, R. S., & Matheny, A. P., Jr (1986). Behavior genetics research in infant temperament: The Louisville twin study. In R. Plomin & J. Dunn (eds), *The study of temperament: Changes, continuities, and challenges*. Hillsdale, NJ: Erlbaum.

Wilson, S. and MacLean, R. (2011). *Research methods and data analysis for psychology*. London: McGraw-Hill.

Wilson, T. D. (1985). Strangers to ourselves: The origins and accuracy of beliefs about one's own mental states. In J. H. Harvey & G. Weary (eds), *Attribution in contemporary psychology*. New York: Academic Press.

Wilson, T. D. (2002). *Strangers to ourselves: Discovering the adaptive unconscious*. Cambridge, MA: Harvard University Press.

Wilson, T. D., & Gilbert, D. T. (2005). Affective forecasting: Knowing what to want. *Current Directions in Psychological Science*, **14**, 131–134.

Wilson, T. D., Dunn, D. S., Kraft, D., & Lisle, D. J. (1989). Introspection, attitude change, and attitude–behavior consistency: The disruptive effects of explaining why we feel the way we do. In L. Berkowitz (eds), *Advances in experimental social psychology*, Vol. 22. San Diego, CA: Academic Press.

Wilson, T. D., Laser, P. S., & Stone, J. I. (1982). Judging the predictors of one's mood: Accuracy and the use of shared theories. *Journal of Experimental Social Psychology*, **18**, 537–556.

Wilson, W. R. (1979). Feeling more than we can know: Exposure effects without learning. *Journal of Personality and Social Psychology*, **37**, 811–821.

Winch, R. F. (1958). *Mate selection: A study of complementary needs*. New York: Harper & Row.

Wines, M. (2005, 23 September). Crime in South Africa grows more vicious. *New York Times* (www.nytimes.com).

Winquist, J. R., & Larson, J. R., Jr (2004). Sources of the discontinuity effect: Playing against a group versus being in a group. *Journal of Experimental Social Psychology*, **40**, 675–682.

Winter, F. W. (1973). A laboratory experiment of individual attitude response to advertising exposure. *Journal of Marketing Research*, **10**, 130–140.

Wisman, A., & Koole, S. L. (2003). Hiding in the crowd: Can mortality salience promote affiliation with others who oppose one's worldviews? *Journal of Personality and Social Psychology*, **84**, 511–526.

Wittenbrink, B., Judd, C. M., & Park, B. (1997). Evidence for racial prejudice at the implicit level and its relationship with questionnaire measures. *Journal of Personality and Social Psychology*, **72**, 262–274.

Wixon, D. R., & Laird, J. D. (1976). Awareness and attitude change in the forced-compliance paradigm: The importance of when. *Journal of Personality and Social Psychology*, **34**, 376–384.

Wodak, R. (2009). *The discourse of politics in action: Politics as usual*. Basingstoke: Palgrave Macmillan.

Wodak, R., & Meyer, M. (2009). *Methods for critical discourse analysis*. London: Sage.

Wohl, M. J. A., & Enzle, M. E. (2002). The deployment of personal luck: Sympathetic magic and illusory control in games of pure chance. *Personality and Social Psychology Bulletin*, **28**, 1388–1397.

Wojciszke, B., Bazinska, R., & Jaworski, M. (1998). On the dominance of moral categories in impression formation. *Personality and Social Psychology Bulletin*, **24**, 1251–1263.

Wolf, S. (1987). Majority and minority influence: A social impact analysis. In M. P. Zanna, J. M. Olson & C. P. Herman (eds), *Social influence: The Ontario symposium on personality and social psychology*, Vol. 5. Hillsdale, NJ: Erlbaum.

Wolf, S., & Latané, B. (1985). Conformity, innovation and the psycho-social law. In S. Moscovici, G. Mugny & E. Van Avermaet (eds), *Perspectives on minority influence*. Cambridge: Cambridge University Press.

Wolfradt, U. & Dalbert, C. (2003). Personality, values and belief in a just world. *Personality and Individual Differences*, **35**, 1911–1918.

Wong, C. L., Harris, J. A., & Gallate, J. E. (2012). Evidence for a social function of the anterior temporal lobes: Low-frequency rTMS reduces implicit gender stereotypes. *Social Neuroscience*, **7**, 90–104.

Wood, J. V., Heimpel, S. A., & Michela, J. L. (2003). Savoring versus dampening: Self-esteem differences in regulating positive affect. *Journal of Personality and Social Psychology*, **85**, 566–580.

Wood, R. T. A., & Griffiths, M. D. (2004). Adolescent lottery and scratchcard players: Do their attitudes influence their gambling behaviour? *Journal of Adolescence*, **27**, 467–475.

Wood, W., & Eagly, A. H. (2002). A cross-cultural analysis of the behavior of women and men: Implications for the origins of sex differences. *Psychological Bulletin*, **128**, 699–727.

Woodzicka, J. A., & LaFrance, M. (2001). Real versus imagined gender harassment. *Journal of Social Issues*, **57**(1), 15–30.

Worchel, S. (1998). A developmental view of the search for group identity. In S. Worchel, J. F. Morales, D. Páez & J.-C. Deschamps (eds), *Social identity: International perspectives*. London: Sage.

Worchel, S., & Norvell, N. (1980). Effect of perceived environmental conditions during cooperation on intergroup attraction. *Journal of Personality and Social Psychology*, **38**, 764–772.

Worchel, S., Andreoli, V. A., & Folger, R. (1977). Intergroup cooperation and intergroup attraction: The effect of previous interaction and outcome of combined effort. *Journal of Experimental Social Psychology*, **13**, 131–140.

Worchel, S., Axsom, D., Ferris, F., Samah, G., & Schweitzer, S. (1978). Deterrents of the effect of intergroup cooperation on intergroup attraction. *Journal of Conflict Resolution*, **22**, 429–439.

Worchel, S., Rothgerber, H., Day, E. A., Hart, D., & Butemeyer, J. (1998). Social identity and individual productivity within groups. *British Journal of Social Psychology*, **37**, 389–413.

Workman, E. A., & Williams, R. L. (1980). Effects of extrinsic rewards on intrinsic motivation in the classroom. *Journal of School Psychology*, **18**, 141–147.

Workman, M. (2010). A behaviourist perspective on corporate harassment online: Validation of a theoretical model of psychological motives. *Computers & Security*, **29**, 831–839.

World Bank (2011). *World Development Report 2011: Conflict, security, and development*. Washington DC: World Bank.

World Health Organization (2005). *The World Health Report*. New York: World Health Organization.

Worringham, C. J., & Messick, D. M. (1983). Social facilitation of running: An unobtrusive study. *Journal of Social Psychology*, **121**, 23–29.

Wright, E. F., Lüüs, C. A., & Christie, S. D. (1990). Does group discussion facilitate the use of consensus information in making causal attributions? *Journal of Personality and Social Psychology*, **59**, 261–269.

Wright, R. (2003, 29 June). Quoted by Thomas L. Friedman, 'Is Google God?' *New York Times* (www.nytimes.com).

Wright, S. C., & Bougie, E. (2007). Intergroup contact and minority-language education: Reducing language-based discrimination and its negative impact. *Journal of Language and Social Psychology*, **26**(2), 157–181.

Wuchty, S., Jones, B. F., & Uzzi, B. (2007). The increasing dominance of teams in production of knowledge. *Science*, **316**, 1036–1039.

Wundt, W. (1916). *Elements of folk psychology: Outlines of a psychological history of the development of mankind*. London: Allen & Unwin (German original 1912).

**Y**

Yong, E. (2012). Bad copy. *Nature*, **485**, 298–300.

Yoon, K., Kim, C. H., & Kim, M. S. (1998). A cross-cultural comparison of the effects of source credibility on attitudes and behavioral intentions. *Mass Communication and Society*, **1**(3&4), 153–173.

Young, R., Sweeting, H., & West, P. (2007). A longitudinal study of alcohol use and antisocial behaviour in young people. *Alcohol and Alcoholism*, 30 October, 1–11. doi:10.1093/alcalc/agm147

Young, S. G., & Hugenberg, K. (2010). Mere social categorization modulates identification of facial expressions of emotion. *Journal of Personality and Social Psychology*, **99**, 964–977.

Young, W. R. (1977, February). There's a girl on the tracks! *Reader's Digest*, pp. 91–95.

Yousif, Y., & Korte, C. (1995). Urbanization, culture, and helpfulness. *Journal of Cross-Cultural Psychology*, **26**, 474–489.

Yovetich, N. A., & Rusbult, C. E. (1994). Accommodative behavior in close relationships: Exploring transformation of motivation. *Journal of Experimental Social Psychology*, **30**, 138–164.

Yuchtman (Yaar), E. (1976). Effects of social-psychological factors on subjective economic welfare. In B. Strumpel (ed.), *Economic means for human needs*. Ann Arbor: Institute for Social Research, University of Michigan.

Yuki, M., & Yokota, K. (2009). The primal warrior: Outgroup threat priming enhances intergroup discrimination in men but not women. *Journal of Experimental Social Psychology*, **45**(1), 271–274.

Yukl, G. (1974). Effects of the opponent's initial offer, concession magnitude, and concession frequency on bargaining behavior. *Journal of Personality and Social Psychology*, **30**, 323–335.

Yzerbyt, V. Y., & Leyens, J.-P. (1991). Requesting information to form an impression: The influence of valence and confirmatory status. *Journal of Experimental Social Psychology*, **27**, 337–356.

Yzerbyt, V., Schadron, G., Leyens, J.-P., & Rocher, S. (1994). Social judgeability: The impact of meta-informational cues on the use of stereotypes. *Journal of Personality and Social Psychology*, **66**, 48–55.

**Z**

Zajonc, R. B. (1965). Social facilitation. *Science*, **149**, 269–274.

Zajonc, R. B. (1968). Attitudinal effects of mere exposure. *Journal of Personality and Social Psychology*, **9**, Monograph Suppl. No. 2, part 2.

Zajonc, R. B. (1970, February). Brainwash: Familiarity breeds comfort. *Psychology Today*, 32–35, 60–62.

Zajonc, R. B. (1980). Feeling and thinking: Preferences need no inferences. *American Psychologist*, **35**, 151–175.

Zajonc, R. B. (1998). Emotions. In D. Gilbert, S. T. Fiske & G. Lindzey (eds), *Handbook of social psychology*, 4th edn. New York: McGraw-Hill.

Zajonc, R. B. (2000). Massacres: Mass murders in the name of moral imperatives. Unpublished manuscript, Stanford University.

Zajonc, R. B. (2004). Exposure effects: An unmediated phenomenon. In A. S. R. Manstead, N. Frijda & A. Fischer (eds), *Feelings and emotions: The Amsterdam symposium. Studies in emotion and social interaction*. New York: Cambridge University Press.

Zajonc, R. B., Reimer, D. J., & Hausser, D. (1973).

Imprinting and the development of object preference in chicks by mere repeated exposure. *Journal of Comparative and Physiological Psychology*, **83**, 434–440.

Zanna, M. P. (1993). Message receptivity: A new look at the old problem of open- vs closed-mindedness. In A. Mitchell (ed.), *Advertising: Exposure, memory and choice*. Hillsdale, NJ: Erlbaum.

Zanna, M. P., & Olson, J. M. (1982). Individual differences in attitudinal relations. In M. P. Zanna, E. T. Higgins, & C. P. Herman, *Consistency in social behavior: The Ontario symposium*, Vol. 2. Hillsdale, NJ: Erlbaum.

Zanna, M. P., & Rempel, J. K. (1988). Attitudes: A new look at an old concept. In D. Bar-Tal and A. Kruglanski (eds), *The Social Psychology of Knowledge*. New York: Cambridge University Press.

Zebrowitz, L. A., & Montepare, J. A. (2008). Social psychological face perception: Why appearance matters. *Social and Personality Psychology Compass*, **2**(3), 1497–1517.

Zebrowitz, L. A., Collins, M. A., & Dutta, R. (1998). The relationship between appearance and personality across the life span. *Personality and Social Psychology Bulletin*, **24**, 736–749.

Zebrowitz, L. A., Olson, K., & Hoffman, K. (1993). Stability of babyfaceness and

attractiveness across the life span. *Journal of Personality and Social Psychology*, **64**, 453–466.

Zebrowitz, L., White, B., & Wieneke, K. (2008). Mere exposure and racial prejudice: Exposure to other-race faces increases liking for strangers of that race. *Social Cognition*, **26**(3), 259–275.

Zebrowitz-McArthur, L. (1988). Person perception in cross-cultural perspective. In M. H. Bond (ed.), *The cross-cultural challenge to social psychology*. Newbury Park, CA: Sage.

Zillman, D. (1979). *Hostility and aggression*. Hillsdale, NJ: Erlbaum.

Zillmann, D. (1988). Cognition–excitation interdependences in aggressive behavior. *Aggressive Behavior*, **14**(1), 51–64.

Zillmann, D. (1989a). Aggression and sex: Independent and joint operations. In H. L. Wagner & A. S. R. Manstead (eds), *Handbook of psychophysiology: Emotion and social behavior*. Chichester: John Wiley.

Zillmann, D. (1989b). Effects of prolonged consumption of pornography. In D. Zillmann & J. Bryant (eds), *Pornography: Research advances and policy considerations*. Hillsdale, NJ: Erlbaum.

Zillmann, D., & Weaver, J. B., III (1999). Effects of prolonged exposure to gratuitous media violence on

provoked and unprovoked hostile behavior. *Journal of Applied Social Psychology*, **29**, 145–165.

Zillmer, E. A., Harrower, M., Ritzler, B., & Archer, R. P. (1995). *The Quest for the Nazi Personality: A Psychological Investigation of Nazi War Criminals*. Hillsdale, NJ: Erlbaum.

Zimbardo, P. G. (1970). The human choice: Individuation, reason, and order versus deindividuation, impulse, and chaos. In W. J. Arnold & D. Levine (eds), *Nebraska symposium on motivation, 1969*. Lincoln: University of Nebraska Press.

Zimbardo, P. G. (2007). *The Lucifer effect: Understanding how good people turn evil*. Random House: New York.

Zimmer, C. (2005, November). The neurobiology of the self. *Scientific American*, 93–101.

Zucker, G. S., & Weiner, B. (1993). Conservatism and perceptions of poverty: An attributional analysis. *Journal of Applied Social Psychology*, **23**, 925–943.

Zuckerman, E. W., & Jost, J. T. (2001). What makes you think you're so popular? Self-evaluation maintenance and the subjective side of the 'friendship paradox'. *Social Psychology Quarterly*, **64**, 207–223.

# Name Index

# Subject Index